HANDBOOK
of
PARTY POLITICS

HANDBOOK
of
PARTY POLITICS

WITHDRAWN

Edited by
RICHARD S. KATZ
AND
WILLIAM CROTTY

SSAGE Publications

London ● Thousand Oaks ● New Delhi

SAGE Publications Ltd
1 Oliver's Yard
55 City Road
London EC1Y 1SP

SAGE Publications Inc.
2455 Teller Road
Thousand Oaks, California 91320

SAGE Publications India Pvt Ltd
B-42, Panchsheel Enclave
Post Box 4109
New Delhi 110 017

British Library Cataloguing in Publication data

A catalogue record for this book is available from the British Library

ISBN 0 7619 4314 5

Library of Congress Control Number 2005928697

Typeset by C&M Digitals (P) Ltd, Chennai, India
Printed on paper from sustainable resources
Printed in Great Britain by Cromwell Press Ltd, Trowbridge, Wiltshire

CONTENTS

CONTENTS   vii

ACKNOWLEDGEMENTS

The editors would like to thank Lucy Robinson and David Mainwaring of Sage Publications, London, who sponsored this project, and who have attended with dispatch and good humor to the numerous organizational problems inherent in any book with so many contributors.

Richard S. Katz would like to thank the staff of the Political Science Department at Johns Hopkins, and would especially like to thank Judith Katz for her editorial assistance and enormous patience.

William Crotty would like to recognize the work of Ben Lampe, Amy Richey, Jenniter Hackbush and Alisa Houghton in particular, of the Center for the Study of Democracy at Northeastern University for their assistance in developing this book.

Most of all, the editors are indebted to the authors for their efforts toward what we feel is an important contribution to the understanding of institutions that have served democratic ends extraordinarily well.

Richard S. Katz
William Crotty

LIST OF CONTRIBUTORS

Brian J. Brox is Assistant Professor of Political Science, Department of Political Science, Tulane University, USA.

Ian Budge is Research Professor at the Department of Government, University of Essex, UK.

Kris Deschouwer is Professor of Political Science at the Vrije Universiteit Brussel, Belgium.

Lieven De Winter is Professor and Director of the Centre de Politique Comparée at the Université Catholique de Louvain, Belgium.

David A. Dulio is Assistant Professor of Political Science, Department of Political Science, Oakland University, USA.

Patrick Dumont is Researcher at the Université du Luxembourg, Luxembourg and a member of the Centre de Politique Comparée at the Université Catholique de Louvain, Belgium.

James W. Endersby is Associate Professor of Political Science, Department of Political Science, University of Missouri, USA.

Zsolt Enyedi is Associate Professor of Political Science at the Department of Political Science, Central European University, Hungary.

David M. Farrell is Professor and Head of Government, International Politics and Philosophy at the University of Manchester, UK.

John C. Green is Distinguished Professor of Political Science and Director of the Ray C. Bliss Institute of Applied Politics at the University of Akron, USA.

Reuven Y. Hazan is Senior lecturer in the Department of Political Science at The Hebrew University of Jerusalem, Israel.

Knut Heidar is Professor of Political Science, Department of Political Science, University of Oslo, Norway.

Marjorie Randon Hershey is Professor of Political Science at the Department of Political Science, Indiana University, Bloomington, USA.

Jonathan Hopkin is Lecturer in Comparative Politics, Department of Government, London School of Economics and Political Science, UK.

James Johnson is Associate Professor in the Department of Political Science, University of Rochester, USA.

Hans Keman is Professor of Comparative Political Science at the Vrije Universiteit Amsterdam, the Netherlands, and Visiting Professor at the European University Institute, Florence, Italy.

Herbert Kitschelt is George V. Allen Professor of International Relations in the Political Science Department at Duke University, USA.

Robin Kolodny is Associate Professor at the Department of Political Science, Temple University, USA.

André Krouwel is Lecturer in Comparative Politics at the Department of Political Science, Vrije Universiteit Amsterdam, the Netherlands.

Robert Ladrech is Senior Lecturer in Politics at the School of Politics, International Relations and the Environment, Keele University, UK.

Kay Lawson is Professor Emerita at San Francisco State University, USA.

Paul G. Lewis is Professor of European Politics in the Faculty of Social Sciences, Open University, UK.

Daniel H. Lowenstein is Professor of Law at the University of California, Los Angeles, USA.

Scott Mainwaring is Director of the Helen Kellogg Institute for International Studies and Eugene and Helen Conley Chair in Political Science, University of Notre Dame, USA.

Peter Mair is Professor of Comparative Politics at the European University Institute, Florence, Italy, and at Leiden University, the Netherlands.

Helen Margetts is Professor of Society and the Internet in the Oxford Internet Institute, University of Oxford, UK.

Shaheen Mozaffar is Professor of Political Science in the Department of Political Science, Bridgewater State College, USA.

Wolfgang C. Müller is Professor of Comparative Government at the University of Mannheim and currently Director of the Mannheim Centre of European Social Research (MZES), Germany.

Karl-Heinz Nassmacher is Professor of Political Science at the Institute of Political Science, Carl von Ossietzky Universität Oldenburg, Germany.

Pippa Norris is the McGuire Lecturer in Comparative Politics at the John F. Kennedy School of Government and the Government Department, Harvard University, USA.

John R. Petrocik is Professor of Political Science and Chair of the Department, University of Missouri-Columbia, USA.

Thomas Poguntke is Professor of Political Science and Director of the Institute for German Studies, University of Birmingham, UK.

Nicol C. Rae is Professor of Political Science at Florida International University, Miami, USA.

Gideon Rahat is Lecturer in the Department of Political Science at The Hebrew University of Jerusalem, Israel.

Vicky Randall is Professor in the Department of Government, University of Essex, UK.

Susan E. Scarrow is Associate Professor of Political Science, Department of Political Science, University of Houston, USA.

Holli A. Semetko is Vice Provost for International Affairs, Director of the Claus M. Halle Institute for Global Learning and Professor of Political Science at Emory University in Atlanta, USA.

Daron R. Shaw is Associate Professor of Government at the University of Texas at Austin, USA.

Peter M. Siavelis is Associate Professor of Political Science at Wake Forest University, USA.

Ulrich Sieberer is Lecturer in Political Science, Department of Social Sciences, University of Mannheim, Germany.

Mariano Torcal is Professor and Chair of the Department of Political and Social Sciences of the Pompeu Fabra University, Barcelona, Spain.

Eric M. Uslaner is Professor of Government and Politics at the University of Maryland, College Park, USA.

Francesca Vassallo is Assistant Professor of Political Science, Department of Political Science, University of Southern Maine, USA.

Alan Ware is Professor and Tutor in Politics, Worcester College, Oxford University, UK.

Paul Webb is Professor of Politics, School of Social Sciences and Cultural Studies, University of Sussex, UK.

John Kenneth White is Professor of Politics at the Catholic University of America, Washington, DC, USA.

Clyde Wilcox is Professor of Government at Georgetown University, Washington, DC, USA.

Steven B. Wolinetz is Professor of Political Science at Memorial University of Newfoundland, Canada.

INTRODUCTION

Richard S. Katz
William Crotty

Political parties have repeatedly been acknowledged as the critical link to democratic governance. An open, participant-oriented, viable, and representative system of parties operating within free and fair electoral procedures performs duties that make democratic government possible; without such parties, a democracy can hardly be said to exist.

Political commentators, both within and outside of the academy, have for a long time sought to describe and explain how parties are structured and mobilized, as well as the nature of their programmatic appeals to meet the demands of effective governance. A number of early studies deserve special mention. Among these are Lipset and Rokkan (1967); Epstein (1967); LaPalombara and Weiner (1966); Duverger (1954); and Neumann (1956). In more recent decades, there have been Powell (1982); Harmel and Janda (1982); Lawson and Merkl (1988); Klingemann *et al.* (1994); Dalton *et al.* (1984); and Lijphart (1999). The field is rich in its explorations, and these represent but a sample of the major studies undertaken.

As these works, and innumerable others, show, parties differ in regard to their operations in parliament, in electoral campaigns, in organizing and mobilizing a democratic citizenry in support of policy positions, and in developing and expressing in real-world political terms systematic ideologies of governance. Whatever their differences, however, democratic political parties have much in common in how they approach their functional roles in a society and in their broad impact in shaping the character of the democratic experience.

PARTIES AND CHANGE

Parties have always been in a process of change. In part, this is because they have had to adapt to developments in their societies, and in the context in which they operate more broadly. Particularly in recent decades, these changes – including the globalization of trade, finance, and markets; the collective and multinational creation of regional political alignments such as the European Union and NATO; the communications revolution brought on by the electronic media, the Internet, cell phones, and the resulting high-speed access to news; transportation, technological, and democratizing developments that threaten the traditional and familiar – have cumulated, and their impacts have compounded. While they may not be different in kind from changes to which parties have had to adapt in the past, and their depth and breadth may prove to be no greater, as with much in the contemporary world the pace with which they confront the parties and the speed with which parties must react if they are to be successful are without precedent.

At the same time, however, one must recognize that many of these changes in the environment in which parties operate are not exogenous to the parties, but rather are the consequences of the policies that the parties have chosen to put into place, or have chosen to allow to come about unopposed. Thus, parties are changing partly because they have created the circumstances that facilitate those changes. Even if parties did not create religious beliefs or class or regional differences, they (or their leaders or founders) chose to politicize some and not to politicize others. While parties did not invent radio or television or the Internet (misrepresentations of Al Gore's claims to have facilitated the development of the latter notwithstanding), as governors they largely set the rules that determine their relevance. Even from this perspective, however, the pace of change has increased.

A different kind of change has come about as a result of the dramatic spread of democratic government that Huntington (1991) has identified as the 'third wave' of democratization. Not only has the number of democratic parties and party systems increased, but also this increase has occurred under significantly different circumstances than was the case with earlier 'waves'. Aside from the circumstances already suggested as affecting the established parties, these 'third wave' cases have benefited (or suffered) from unprecedented levels of international scrutiny and involvement, in particular through a variety of democracy promotion agencies such as International IDEA, IFES, and the United Nations.

MODELS OF PARTY

A great variety of models of party are either implicit or explicit in the chapters of this *Handbook*. Abstractions from two of them have, however, been particularly influential in shaping both theories and research agendas, and can serve to suggest some of the most important parameters of change. These are derived particularly from Epstein's (1967) analysis of European and American parties, one of the foundational studies for an appreciation of comparative parties in an earlier era.

Epstein compares the loosely federated American party coalitions, or what he refers to as a 'pluralist' party system, with a 'programmatic' party approach more generally associated with Europe. There is a divide of consequence here, and Epstein's claim is that the pluralist system, compared with the programmatic, mass-based dominant European parties, may better serve national policy and democratic ends, and is more cohesive, policy-oriented, and better mobilized than its cousin on the Continent. Other scholars have come to quite different evaluative judgments. There is agreement, however, that operations of the parties in such areas as campaigning, policy formulation and implementation, staffing and organization, resource base, and sources of funding are characteristically different.

As time has evolved, the American parties have increasingly come to fit conceptions of a free market competitive, candidate-centered, electorally focused party system. There are signs that the European parties – at different rates of change in various countries and among individual parties – have begun to move in this direction. Such a transition represents an enormous functional and organizational shift in emphasis and conception for the Continental parties, more so than for the loosely structured, campaign-oriented parties in the United States. The changes under way are clearly significant for both types of party systems. They raise fundamental questions as to the continuing role of parties and the extent of their social relevance and interaction within the society. In particular, campaign-only organizations of the American type, given their dependence on extensive non-party funding, their failure to engage in activities not directly related to campaigning for public office, the fragmentation of political coalitions and the increasing independence of electorates that follow, and the fragmentation and subservience (to candidates) of the party organization, tend to ignore many of the functions regarded as central to parties in the European mold.

Epstein (1967: 357) argues that the non-programmatic nature of the looser American associational model allows

> a leadership capable of responding to diverse electoral considerations, and a transactional or brokerage view of political activity. A party may still be associated with particular policies and interests, presumably in accord with habitual voting patterns of large portions of the electorate, but it preserves, in theory as in practice, a loose and accommodating character. Such a party, while having had patronage seeking memberships in the past, does not usually have large numbers of program-committed members. The brokerage party … is unattractive to members of this kind … it does not have the need of a majoritarian party to legitimize, through mass-membership participation, any program or policies. For electoral purposes which are of prime importance, a cadre organization suffices.

This approach contrasts with the 'class consciousness' that he presumes to define the most significant electoral cleavages in the European model, and the mass-mobilized, highly organizationally articulated, and (at least in some cases) highly patronage-oriented parties of European nations.

These dimensions highlight the fundamental distinctions in form and operations of categories of comparative party systems and serve as a starting point in tracing the broad changes that have taken place in recent decades. A side issue of related importance, and of greater significance than the actual forms the parties take, is which type of party best serves broader ends of social integration, political mobilization, policy representation, and democratic governance, the ultimate criteria by which all party systems are judged.

It is Epstein's (1967: 357) contention

> that the looser American-style parties better serve the democratic purpose as it is conceived in pluralist terms. The pluralist democrat rejects the validity or legitimacy, and even the regularized existence, of a majority electorate united over the wide range of complex issues in a modern nation. Separate majorities on separate issues, or perhaps on sets of issues, there may be, but that is very different from believing in a single majority for almost all issues … the pluralist cannot recognize the claims of a programmatic party, with or without a membership organization, to represent a coherent majority for all of its policies. Behind this denial of majoritarian-party claims lies the pluralist's disbelief in a majority-class interest, the simplest theoretical support for the strong-party school.

These assertions can be debated, and have been extensively. There is wide agreement, however, that the basic objective of serving societal needs and the related questions as to the extent to which parties in different societies can be engineered to serve public interests in what is perceived to be a more efficient and productive manner are centrally important. As a result, understanding the degree to which the political environment predicts the parties' character and role, and defines the boundaries for consciously designed change, becomes significant. To the extent that those boundaries are highly restrictive, arguments over preferred party roles and models may well have little ultimate effect on the quality of their political representation.

These types of questions have engaged party analysts for generations. However, while the basic concern with democratic performance remains, more recent research, as indicated by the chapters in this volume, is evidencing the impact of forces on party behavior that have tended to separate parties of both original types from their societal roots. The American parties have moved towards the pure electoral campaign- and candidate-oriented model. The European mass parties, while significantly more cohesive and more programmatic in general, are beginning to evidence similar trends. The legislative parties in both types of systems have developed a degree of distance from the electoral parties. Should such trends continue,

which is likely, what then can be said about the quality and comprehensiveness of the parties' contribution to the operations of democratic government? These are among the fundamental issues forcing contemporary party research and, as indicated, are addressed in varying contexts in the analysis in this volume.

A HANDBOOK OF PARTY POLITICS

The widely acknowledged centrality of parties, coupled with the obvious scope and pace of party change, makes political parties both an important and an exciting field for research. As with any rapidly developing and substantively broad field, the parties literature is itself both broad and rapidly developing – and, moreover, in many respects quite fragmented. In this context, we had two objectives in inviting many of the world's leading scholars in the field of political parties to contribute to this *Handbook*.

The first objective is to provide a reliable and thorough summary of the major theories and approaches that have been, and continue to be, prominent in the development of the field. The chapters that follow aim to provide a concise 'road map' to the core literatures in the various subfields of party-related research. While no single volume can hope to summarize – or, indeed, even to cite – all of the authors who have made significant contributions to our current understanding of parties, each chapter aims to summarize where we are and how we have arrived at that point for its own topic area.

The other, and complementary, objective is to identify the theories, approaches, and research efforts that define the current 'cutting edge' of the field. What do these scholars understand to be the most important questions that need to be addressed and what do they see as the most promising avenues for addressing them?

In general, the chapters are broadly comparative, defined by a substantive question rather than by geography. As in many other areas of political research, however, the literature on political parties has had to confront the question of 'American exceptionalism', and that is reflected in the organization of this *Handbook*. In some subfields, it is reasonable to include the United States as simply one more case, or perhaps even as the precursor of developments that may be expected to spread more broadly. In others, however, the United States – whether for reasons of history, or culture, or political institutions – is too different to be comfortably included with the rest of the world. For these subfields, we have included separate chapters on the United States. Other areas also have their own peculiarities, addressed in separate chapters as well.

Given the complexity of the subject, there is no unproblematic way to organize the literature on parties, and hence no straightforward way to organize and order the chapters that follow. Rather, we have simply grouped them under a few broad headings. The first is concerned with a range of questions of definition: What is a party, where did parties come from, and how were they integrated into theoretical understandings of politics? How do political parties fit into theories of democracy? How can we classify differing party types and differing types of party systems? The second broad heading concerns the functions of parties. What do parties do, and how do they do it? Third, how do parties organize, and how are party organizations changing? Fourth, how do political parties relate to society more broadly? Fifth, how do parties relate to the state, and how does the state relate to and regulate the parties? Finally, what can we say about trends that are of relatively recent origin (parties in the media and cyber age, parties in the European Union) and about their future?

The subjects of these broad sections obviously overlap. In many cases, rather than addressing different subjects, they address the same subject from different perspectives. In doing so, they reflect the richness and complexity of the field of party research.

REFERENCES

Dalton, Russell, Flanagan, Scott and Beck, Paul Allen (eds) (1984) *Electoral Change in Advanced Industrial Democracies*. Princeton, NJ: Princeton University Press.

Duverger, Maurice (1954) *Political Parties*. New York: Wiley.

Epstein, Leon (1967) *Political Parties in Western Democracies*. New York: Praeger.

Harmel, Robert and Janda, Kenneth (1982) *Parties and Their Environments*. New York: Longman.

Huntington, Samuel P. (1991) *The Third Wave: Democratization in the Late Twentieth Century*. Norman: University of Oklahoma Press.

Klingemann, Hans-Dieter, Hofferbert, Richard and Budge, Ian (1994) *Parties, Policies and Democracy*. Boulder, CO: Westview Press.

LaPalombara, Joseph and Weiner, Myron (eds) (1966) *Political Parties and Political Development*. Princeton, NJ: Princeton University Press.

Lawson, Kay and Merkl, Peter (eds) (1988) *When Parties Fail: Emerging Alternative Organizations*. Princeton, NJ: Princeton University Press.

Lijphart, Arend (1999) *Patterns of Democracy*. New Haven, CT: Yale University Press.

Lipset, Seymour Martin and Rokkan, Stein (eds) (1967) *Party Systems and Voter Alignments*. New York: Free Press.

Neumann, Sigmund (ed.) (1956) *Modern Political Parties*. Chicago: University of Chicago Press.

Powell, G. Bingham, Jr. (1982) *Contemporary Democracies*. Cambridge, MA: Harvard University Press.

PART I

DEFINITION OF PARTY

1

WHAT IS A POLITICAL PARTY?

John Kenneth White

'But who do you say that I am?' – Jesus Christ to his disciples, Matthew 16: 15

Defining political parties is a task that at first glance appears to be relatively simple. In 1984, political scientist Robert Huckshorn provided 'a pragmatic definition' of parties in his textbook *Political Parties in America*: '[A] political party is an autonomous group of citizens having the purpose of making nominations and contesting elections in hope of gaining control over governmental power through the capture of public offices and the organization of the government'.[1] For Huckshorn, the *raison d'état* for having political parties was simple: they were the means necessary to win elections and provide direction to government.

But is that really so? As students of political parties are well aware, many legitimate political parties exist for reasons that have little to do with winning elections. How else would one explain the proliferation of third parties in recent years? For example, while the Beer-Lovers' Party in Poland began as a prank, over time it developed a serious platform for which the humorously stated goals of the party – lively political discussion in pubs serving excellent beer – became associated with the values of freedom of association and expression, intellectual tolerance, and a higher standard of living. In 1991, it captured 16 seats in the Sejm, the lower house of the Polish parliament. Thus, while the Beer-Lovers' Party had

satirical origins, it became a force in Polish politics due to its ideas – not because it was formed with the stated purpose of winning elections. Much the same could be said of the Green Party in the United States. As the party's website states, Greens are 'committed to environmentalism, non-violence, social justice, and grassroots organizing'. The Greens are especially supportive of a campaign finance reform law that would renew democracy 'without the support of corporate donors'.[2] Like the Beer-Lovers' Party, the Greens have almost no hope of winning most US elections – including the most important one of all, the presidency. The 2000 Green Party presidential nominee, Ralph Nader, though he cost Democrat Al Gore the presidency in 2000, won a mere 2.7 percent of the popular vote cast.[3]

Yet political scientists would unanimously classify most third parties (including the Beer-Lovers' party and the Greens, along with many others) as legitimate parties. But concomitant with such legitimacy come numerous assumptions made by academics as to what political parties *are* and *are not* – and, even more frequently, what they *should be*. If parties are to act as 'mediating institutions' between the governors and the governed, then what tasks should they be performing? Should they be election facilitators who provide candidates with ballot access? Or do they exist to promote ideas no matter how controversial? Just as political scientists make assumptions about party behavior, they also make many presuppositions about *partisan* behavior. For example, do voters behave in an entirely rational manner, thus making parties objects of political utility? Or do voters eschew parties altogether and bring other considerations – if any – into the making of their ballot selections?

Thus, defining what a political party is and what functions it should assume is hardly an objective task. Rather, it is a normative one, and the answers given by political scientists have varied over time. Below are several oft-cited responses to the question 'What is a political party?':

- Edmund Burke (1770): '[A] party is a body of men united, for promoting by their joint endeavours the national interest, upon some particular principle in which they are all agreed.'[4]
- Anthony Downs (1957): 'In the broadest sense, a political party is a coalition of men seeking to control the governing apparatus by legal means. By *coalition*, we mean a group of individuals who have certain ends in common and cooperate with each other to achieve them. By *governing apparatus*, we mean the physical, legal, and institutional equipment which the government uses to carry out its specialized role in the division of labor. By *legal means*, we mean either duly constituted or legitimate influence.'[5]
- V.O. Key, Jr (1964): 'A political party, at least on the American scene, tends to be a "group" of a peculiar sort. ... Within the body of voters as a whole, groups are formed of persons who regard themselves as party members. ... In another sense the term "party" may refer to the group of more or less professional workers. ... At times party denotes groups within the government. ... Often it refers to an entity which rolls into one the party-in-the-electorate, the professional political group, the party-in-the-legislature, and the party-in-the-government ... In truth, this all-encompassing usage has its legitimate application, for all the types of groups called party interact more or less closely and at times may be as one. Yet both analytically and operationally the term 'party' most of the time must refer to several types of group; and it is useful to keep relatively clear the meaning in which the term is used.'[6]
- William Nisbet Chambers (1967): '[A] political party in the modern sense may be thought of as a relatively durable social formation which seeks offices or power in government, exhibits a structure or organization which links leaders at the centers

of government to a significant popular following in the political arena and its local enclaves, and generates in-group perspectives or at least symbols of identification or loyalty.'[7]
- Leon D. Epstein (1980): '[What] is meant by a political party [is] any group, however loosely organized, seeking to elect government officeholders under a given label.'[8]
- Ronald Reagan (1984): 'A political party isn't a fraternity. It isn't something like the old school tie you wear. You band together in a political party because of certain beliefs of what government should be.'[9]
- Joseph Schlesinger (1991): 'A political party is a group organized to gain control of government in the name of the group by winning election to public office.'[10]
- John Aldrich (1995): 'Political parties can be seen as coalitions of elites to capture and use political office. [But] a political party is more than a coalition. A political party is an institutionalized coalition, one that has adopted rules, norms, and procedures.'[11]

While these definitions vary and many have persisted throughout the ages, they remain controversial. Should parties emphasize their ideological roots, as Burke and Reagan prefer? Or are parties merely tools for gaining access to governmental office, as Epstein, Schlesinger, and Aldrich indicate? Or are they important mediating instruments designed to organize and simplify voter choices in order to influence the actions of government, as Downs, Key, and Chambers imply? Even Downs thought his original definition was misguided, since the governing party did not conform to his idea of 'a single, rational, decision-making entity controlling government policy'. Thus, Downs redefined parties as follows: 'A political party is a team of men seeking to control the governing apparatus by gaining office in a duly constituted election. By *team*, we mean a coalition whose members agree on all their goals instead of on just part of them.'[12]

Such hedging – along with the widespread lack of consensus within the political science community as to what political parties exactly are or should be – calls to mind the various responses Jesus Christ received when he queried his disciples, asking them 'Who do people say that the Son of Man is?'. They replied: 'Some say John the Baptist, others Elijah, still others Jeremiah or one of the prophets.' Jesus persisted, asking his disciples 'But who do you say that I am?' One of them, Simon Peter, responded: 'You are the Messiah, the Son of the Living God.'[13] If only, in a more secular fashion, there could be such a definitive definition as to what parties are and what they ought to do.

Because neither citizens nor scholars have ever satisfactorily answered these normative questions, the attempt to define what a political party is – and what tasks should be entrusted to it – has often produced more confusion than explanation. In the United States, the confusion dates back to the inception of the modern American polity. In *The Federalist*, James Madison likened parties to interest groups which he derisively labeled as 'factions'. Yet Madison's discussion of 'faction' is rather vague, with a primary emphasis on controlling the 'mischiefs' of the propertied interests.[14] One reason for the framers' lack of intellectual coherence was their distrust of those repositories of political power. To the Federalists, the word 'power' had such negative connotations that Alexander Hamilton substituted the word 'energy' for it.[15] One Democratic-Republican party opponent spoke out against the Federalist energizers in 1802, saying, 'I would as soon give my vote to a wolf to be a shepherd, as to a man, who is always contending for the *energy of government*'.[16]

Not surprisingly, the framers were reluctant to sharpen their thinking about political parties. Instead, they often made a virtue out of political stalemate, which essentially guaranteed querulous parties arguing over limited objectives. Alexis de Tocqueville wrote in *Democracy in America* that 'parties are an evil inherent in free governments'.[17] The beneficent effect of parties, said Tocqueville, was that the governmental competition ensured by the US Constitution made them small-minded: 'They glow with a fractious zeal; their language is violent, but their progress is timid and uncertain. The means they employ are as disreputable as the aim sought.'[18] The result, Tocqueville claimed, was that 'public opinion is broken up ad infinitum about questions of detail'.[19]

With the passage of time, scholars have sought to redefine political parties and distinguish them from 'factions' – i.e., interest groups – often assigning more noble tasks to the former than the latter. In 1942, V. O. Key, Jr. suggested that interest groups 'promote their interests by attempting to influence the government rather than by nominating candidates and seeking the responsibility for the management of government [as political parties do]'.[20] Other scholars disagree, noting that in an age of weakened political parties, interest groups frequently influence nominations, are instrumental in electing favorite candidates, and help manage the government by influencing

both the appointment of officials and the actual decision-making process itself.

THE PARTY CONSENSUS

Even though there exists a rather profound disagreement among political scientists as to *how* political parties ought to operate, there has emerged a passionate consensus behind many of the normative arguments made on their behalf. Beginning with the publication of *The American Commonwealth* in 1888, James Bryce began a tradition that consisted of scholarly investigation and laudatory treatment: 'Parties are inevitable. No free country has been without them. No one has shown how representative government could be worked without them. They bring order out of chaos to a multitude of voters'.[21] Nearly six decades later, E.E. Schattschneider echoed Bryce, writing in his masterful book, *Party Government*, that 'modern democracy is unthinkable save in terms of the parties'.[22] Schattschneider's passion for parties remained undimmed. Shortly before his death, he said: 'I suppose the most important thing I have done in my field is that I have talked longer and harder and more persistently and enthusiastically about political parties than anyone else alive'.[23] His enthusiasm has been echoed by political scientists in the generations since. For example, Giovanni Sartori claimed parties were '*the* central intermediate structures between society and government'.[24] Clinton Rossiter applied the following tautology to the American context: 'No America without democracy, no democracy without politics, and no politics without parties'.[25]

Rossiter's axiom has been applied by other political scientists to their home governments around the globe. For example, in the once communist-controlled 'Captive Nations' of eastern Europe, the emergence of party competition (including Poland's Beer-Lovers' Party) is used to measure the varying progress of these countries toward democracy. Likewise, in the former Soviet Union, signs of a fledgling party system win accolades from the vast majority of scholars. In the western hemisphere, the march toward democracy in South America is celebrated, as one country after another has discarded dictatorship in favor of democratic party rule. Thus, political scientists measure the march toward democracy in such diverse nations as Iraq, Haiti, Bosnia, and the former Soviet Union in terms of those countries' capacities to develop strong party organizations that are the foundations for free, democratic elections. The US-based Committee for Party Renewal summarized the prevailing consensus about the role parties should play – and the discipline's passion for them – in a 1996 amicus curiae brief filed with the US Supreme Court:

> Political parties play a unique and crucial role in our democratic system of government. Parties enable citizens to participate coherently in a system of government allowing for a substantial number of popularly elected offices. They bring fractured and diverse groups together as a unified force, provide a necessary link between the distinct branches and levels of government, and provide continuity that lasts beyond terms of office. Parties also play an important role in encouraging active participation in politics, holding politicians accountable for their actions, and encouraging debate and discussion of important issues.[26]

The equating of successful parties to efficiently productive government structures is largely a twentieth-century phenomenon. In 1949, political scientist Hugh McDowall Clokie observed: 'Party government is without doubt the distinctive feature of modern politics. … [Parties are] fully accepted today as essential organizations for government in the modern state, recognized under varying conditions as entitled to give direction to the course of politics, and endowed either by law or usage with a special status and function in the constitutional system in which they operate.'[27] One underlying reason for Clokie's contention that party and government are as one is the increased attention given to defining what a political party is as a matter of state law. For example, Missouri state law defines an 'established political party' as 'a political party which, at either of the last two general elections, polled for its candidate for any statewide office, more than two percent of the entire vote cast for the office'.[28] New York's statute is similar: an 'officially recognized party' is one that polled 50,000 or more votes for governor in the previous statewide election.[29] In 1986, Leon D. Epstein usefully compared political parties to quasi-governmental agencies that were akin to regulated public utilities, noting that state governments frequently defined political parties and regulated their functions.[30]

THE VIEW FROM THE TRIPOD

In ancient Greece, when the priestess of Apollo at Delphi made ready to deliver a prophesy,

she positioned herself on a special seat supported by three legs, the tripod. The tripod gave the priestess a clear view of the past, present, and future.[31] By linking parties so closely with government, political scientists – most prominently, V.O. Key, Jr. – devised the tripod of party-in-the-electorate (PIE), party organizations (PO), and party-in-government (PIG), as a means of teaching what parties were and what they were meant to accomplish.[32] The tripod became a convenient teaching tool, as well as a means of assessing party performance. Frank J. Sorauf, whose 1968 textbook has been used to educate three generations of students in American political parties courses, described parties as 'tripartite systems of interactions'.[33] Everett Carll Ladd, Jr. maintained that the PIE–PO–PIG tripod could be used as a means of measuring social change and the institutional party response to it:

1. *Party as Organization.* There is the formal machinery of party ranging from local committees (precinct, ward, or town) up to state central committees, and the people who man and direct there. The party is 'the organization' or 'the machine.'
2. *Party as the Mass of Supporters.* For some, this identification is strong, and they consistently back candidates running under the party label. For others, the attachment is relatively weak and casual. Here, party exists in the eyes of its beholder; it is a bundle of electoral loyalties.
3. *Party as a Body of Notables.* Most political leaders in government and outside it are identified by a party label. *Party* is sometimes used to refer to that collectivity of notables who accept the party label, and party policy then becomes the *prevailing policy tendencies* among this collectivity.[34]

But while parties have been inextricably linked to government's performance, many reject the PIE–PO–PIG model. Rather than being passionate about parties, ambivalence is often a more common emotion on both the part of the public and elected officials. As George Washington once observed, 'In a Government of a Monarchical cast, Patriotism may look with indulgence, if not with favor, upon the spirit of the party. But in those of popular character, in Governments purely elective, it is a spirit not to be encouraged.'[35] Washington's distrust of parties was shared by his peers. Prior to the end of the Revolutionary War, John Adams bemoaned the drift of the country's elites toward party politics: 'There is nothing I dread so much as a division of the Republic

suspicio re-parties in CEE

into two great parties, each arranged under its leader and converting measures in opposition to each other.'[36] His spouse, Abigail Adams, agreed: 'Party spirit is blind, malevolent, uncandid, ungenerous, unjust, and unforgiving.'[37] Thomas Jefferson declared in 1789 that if he 'could not go to heaven but with a party', he 'would not go there at all'.[38] Alexander Hamilton associated parties with 'ambition, avarice, personal animosity'.[39] And James Madison famously wrote that it was necessary to devise a republic that would 'break and control the violence of faction'.[40]

The public disdain for parties continues to persist – especially in the United States. In 1940, Pendleton Herring wrote that American political parties could not adhere to an ideology: 'At best,' Herring wrote, 'all a party can hope to maintain is an attitude, an approach.'[41] But with the passing decades public hostility toward parties has grown, as Americans prefer to eschew them as unreliable advocates and unfaithful governors. In 1982, 40 percent of Massachusetts residents told one pollster: 'Instead of being the servants of the people, elected officials in Massachusetts are really *the enemy of the people*'.[42] A decade later, when ten registered voters from across the nation were asked what political parties meant to them, two shouted 'Corruption!'. Others used words like 'rich', 'self-serving', 'good-old-boy networks', 'special interests', 'bunch of lost causes', 'lost sheep', 'immorality,' 'going whatever way is on top', and 'liars'[43]. Campaigning for the presidency in 2000, George W. Bush mentioned the Republican Party just twice in accepting the nomination – once in order to scold his fellow partisans to 'end the politics of fear and save Social Security', and once to tout his bipartisan success: 'I've worked with Republicans and Democrats to get things done.'[44] Democratic candidate Al Gore never mentioned his party in his acceptance speech.[45] A poll taken in December 2001 found public skepticism toward the two major parties continued to be high: 56 percent believed the Democrats were 'taking advantage of the current mood to push the interests of their special interests supporters'; 60% thought the Republicans were guilty of doing the same thing.[46]

As they have on so many other occasions, Californians have become trend-setters by taking their scorn for political parties to new heights. In 1998, they were allowed to vote for candidates from different parties in what is called a blanket primary. Party affiliation did not matter, as Democrats, Republicans, and even independents could support the candidates of their choice whatever their party listing. According to one exit poll, 58% liked this new method of choosing party candidates; only 9% found it confusing.[47] But the result has been to make party membership so casual that it has virtually no relevance. In 2003, Californians voted to recall an unpopular Democratic governor, Gray Davis. While the recall portion of the ballot required a simple 'yes' or 'no' vote, the second ballot contained a list of 135 possible replacements. Such is the state of California politics when political parties are insufficiently vested with the power to organize voter choices, as the vast majority of academicians would prefer.

PARTY PARADIGMS

One reason why academics believe that political parties are essential to governing is the rather 'perverse and unorthodox' belief, as political scientist V.O. Key, Jr. expressed it in 1966, that 'voters are not fools'.[48] This rather novel idea has guided two especially important party paradigms that emerged in the twentieth century: *the rational-efficient model* and *the responsible parties* model.

The rational-efficient model

First advocated by Anthony Downs, the rational-efficient model emphasizes the parties' electoral activities at the expense of virtually all other party functions. As Downs stated in his 1957 book, *An Economic Theory of Democracy*:

> Our model is based on the assumption that every government seeks to maximize political support. We further assume that the government exists in a democratic society where periodic elections are held, that its primary goal is reelection, and that election is the goal of those parties out of power. At each election, the party which receives the most votes (though not necessarily a majority) controls the entire government until the next election, with no intermediate votes either by the people as a whole or by a parliament. The governing party thus has unlimited freedom of action, within the bounds of the constitution.[49]

Thus, the rational-choice model envisions the winning of elections not as a welcome outcome but as the only outcome worth having. As a victorious Richard Nixon told cheering supporters upon finally winning the presidency in 1968: 'Winning's a lot more fun.'[50] From the rational-efficient perspective, parties exist to win elections and all party-related projects are designed to make that happen. Incentives to participate in the process come from the patronage jobs that are to be had once victory is ensured.

From the voters' perspective, the party-in-the-electorate behaves rationally – i.e., using the information provided by the party candidates to make rational selections that will benefit them personally. This view of the electorate's voting considerations is far from universal. Some believe that parties are the emotional ties that bind – thus, while voters may rationalize their selections to pollsters there is an emotive quality to their vote. As with sports, it is hard to know with certainty why fans root for particular teams. Others see the electorate as lacking any rationality whatsoever. Walter Lippmann, for one, wrote in 1925 that there was hardly any intelligence behind the balloting:

> We call an election an expression of the popular will. But is it? We go into a polling booth and mark a cross on a piece of paper for one of two, or perhaps three or four names. Have we expressed our thoughts on the public policy of the United States? Presumably we have a number of thoughts on this and that with many buts and ifs and ors. Surely the cross on a piece of paper does not express them.[51]

The organizational structure of rational-efficient parties consists of a cadre of political entrepreneurs. There is a large degree of centralization and no formal party membership. The organizational style is professional where workers, leaders, and candidates are often recruited from outside the organization or are self-recruited. Efficiency is stressed above all else. There is little, if any, organizational continuity after the election.

In the rational-efficient model, elected officials are allowed to do as they wish once elected, as long as their activities help to win the next election. As political parties wane in influence, Downs's rational-choice model has become the one most often used by political scientists to explain voter behavior. According to the Social Sciences Citation Index, since the 1980s citations from Downs's *Economic Theory of Democracy* have steadily risen.[52] In a 1965 foreword to the paperback edition of *An Economic Theory of Democracy*, Stanley Kelley wrote that years from now he would 'be surprised if Downs's work is not recognized as the starting point of a highly important development in the study of politics'.[53]

The responsible parties model

While the framers of the US Constitution viewed political parties with a jaundiced eye, by the 1830s those in government came to see the utility of having effective parties. Martin Van Buren, for one, believed parties rendered an important public service when they were organized around issues of principle:

> Doubtless excesses frequently attend [parties] and produce many evils, but not so many as are prevented by the maintenance of their organization and vigilance. The disposition to abuse power, so deeply planted in the human heart, can by no other means be more effectually checked; and it has always therefore struck me as more honorable and manly and more in harmony with the character of our people and of our institutions to deal with the subject of political parties in a sincerer and wiser spirit – to recognize their necessity, to prove and to elevate the principles and objects to our own [party] and to support it faithfully.[54]

Van Buren's notion of a principle-based party system formed the genesis for the 'responsible party' school that became popular in the mid-twentieth century. The idea for the responsible parties model formed the basis for a report issued by the American Political Science Association's Committee on Political Parties in 1950: 'An effective party system requires, first, that the parties are able to bring forth programs to which they commit themselves and, second, that the parties possess sufficient internal cohesion to carry out these programs.'[55] Achieving party unity around a coherent set of ideas matters because (1) it gives voters a clear choice in election campaigns; (2) it gives the winning political party a mandate for governing; and (3) it ensures the party as the likely instrument whereby voters can make a legal revolution.

While the responsible parties model gives priority to the enunciation of the majority party's platform, it also envisions a vibrant role for the opposition: 'The fundamental requirement of accountability is a two-party system in which the opposition party acts as the critic of the party in power, developing, defining and presenting the policy alternatives which are necessary for a true choice in reaching public decisions.'[56] No wonder that the Committee on Political Parties began its work on the following premise: 'Throughout this report political parties are treated as indispensable instruments of government.'[57]

The committee's passion for parties became endemic throughout the academy. Fifty years after its publication, _Toward a More Responsible Two-Party System_ remains required reading. Evron Kirkpatrick praised the report as 'a landmark in the history of political science as policy science'.[58] Theodore J. Lowi ranked the report as 'second only to the 1937 President's Committee on Administrative Management as a contribution by academics to public discourse on the fundamentals of American democracy'.[59] William Crotty claimed that publication of _Toward a More Responsible Two-Party System_ 'may have been the most significant influence on the debate over the operation of political parties that occurred between the Progressive period and the party reform movement of the 1970s'.[60]

Yet the responsible party argument is not without its critics. The most prominent of these, ironically, was Evron M. Kirkpatrick, a member of the Committee on Political Parties.[61] In 1970, Kirkpatrick renounced the report as 'irrelevant and disturbing', explaining it was 'disturbing to any political scientist who believes that the discipline can provide knowledge applicable to the solution of human problems and the achievement of human goals'.[62] Others saw a tension in the report between those who advocated intra-party debate and those who preferred inter-party conflict. Austin Ranney wondered if it is 'possible for twenty-seven million Democrats to "participate" in the close supervision of their government any more than it is for one-hundred-fifty-million Americans to do so'.[63] Clearly, the Committee envisioned an enlightened issue activism, with the rank-and-file guiding the party's direction and emboldening it with purpose. But the Committee also envisioned a party council – an elitist, national body that suggested party responsibility was something that flowed from the top down. Murray S. Stedman, Jr. and Herbert Sonthoff thought the party council was another illustration of the 'increasingly administrative or even quasi-military approach to the study of political problems'[64]. Julius Turner worried that such placement of power in the hands of party elites would result in control by unrepresentative factions.[65]

The responsible party advocates' contention that political parties are vital to successful governing appears to be so self-evident that it is often forgotten that it was a contentious subject in the early years of political science. At the turn of the twentieth century, some scholars wondered whether any polity could (or should) be characterized by a commitment to _collective_ (meaning party) responsibility or to _individual_ responsibility. M.I. Ostrogorski criticized the discipline's infatuation with collective responsibility: 'This theory appeared alluring enough to be adopted by some writers of prominence, and expanded in certain cases, with brilliancy of literary style. It has, however, one defect: it is not borne out by the facts.'[66] William Graham Sumner agreed. A believer in individual responsibility, Sumner wrote in 1914: 'I cannot trust a party; I can trust a man. I cannot hold a party responsible; I can hold a man responsible. I cannot get an expression of opinion which is single and simple from a party; I can get that only from a man.'[67] Herbert Croly maintained that party government was undesirable because it 'interfered with genuine popular government both by a mischievous, artificial and irresponsible [i.e. parochial and localistic] method of representation, and by an enfeeblement of the administration in the interest of partisan subsistence'.[68]

Others disagreed. In 1900, Frank A. Goodnow made the case for collective party responsibility: 'The individual candidate must be sunk to a large extent in the party. Individual responsibility must give place to party responsibility.'[69] Perhaps no scholar better demonstrates the movement of the political science community toward party responsibility (and the inherent conflicts contained therein) than Woodrow Wilson. At first, Wilson maintained that party responsibility was more fiction than fact. Addressing the Virginia Bar Association in 1897, he declared:

> I, for my part, when I vote at a critical election, should like to be able to vote for a definite line of policy with regard to the great questions of the day – not for platforms, which Heaven knows, mean little enough – but for _men_ known and tried in public service; with records open to be scrutinized with reference to these very matters; and pledged to do this or that particular thing; to take a definite course of action. As it is, I vote for nobody I can depend upon to do anything – no, not if I were to vote for myself.[70]

Later, Wilson saw collective responsibility as not only desirable but also necessary. In a 1908 book, _Constitutional Government in the United States_, Wilson wrote: 'There is a sense in which our parties may be said to have been our real body politic. Not the authority of Congress, not the leadership of the President, but the discipline and zest of parties has held us together, has made it possible for us to form and to carry out national programs.' He added: 'We must think less of checks and balances and more of coordinated power, less of separation of functions and more of the synthesis of action.'[71]

There is a creative tension in Wilson's scholarship. He believes that collective responsibility is essential, but couples it with a plea for individual responsibility by emphasizing the president's role as party leader. In an article about Grover Cleveland's cabinet, Wilson observes: 'What we need is harmonious, consistent, responsible party government, instead of a wide dispersion of function and responsibility; and we can get it only by connecting the President as closely as may be with his party in Congress.'[72] In subsequent editions of *Congressional Government*, Wilson goes further in placing the president at the apex of responsible party government:

> If there be one principle clearer than another, it is this: that in any business, whether of government or of mere merchandising, *somebody must be trusted*, in order that when things go wrong it may be quite plain who should be punished ... *Power and strict accountability for its use* are the essential constituents of good government. A sense of highest responsibility, a dignifying and elevating sense of being trusted, together with a consciousness of being in an official station so conspicuous that no faithful discharge of duty can go unacknowledged and unrewarded, and no breach of trust undiscovered and unpunished – these are the influences, the only influences, which foster practical, energetic, and trustworthy statesmanship.[73]

Wilson's predilection for individual (read presidential) responsibility was not universally accepted by subsequent generations of political scientists. As the Committee on Political Parties warned in its 1950 report: 'When the president's program actually is the sole program, either his party becomes a flock of sheep or the party falls apart.'[74] In 1955, former Committee on Political Parties member V.O. Key, Jr. introduced the concept of 'critical elections', with political parties acting as catalysts in electoral realignments.[75]

By 1950, collective party responsibility had become political science's First Commandment and digressions from it were often considered heretical. One reason for the espousal of collective party responsibility was the desire of many political scientists to limit conflict. In *The Semi-Sovereign People*, E.E. Schattschneider wrote: 'The best point at which to manage conflict is before it starts.'[76] His argument reflected one made by social scientist Lewis Coser. In Coser's *The Functions of Social Conflict*, Schattschneider heavily underlined this passage: 'One unites in order to fight, and one fights under the mutually recognized control of

norms and rules.'[77] Parties, therefore, became a sort of 'thought police' in the establishment and maintenance of order.

THE DECLINE OF MEDIATING INSTITUTIONS

In the Information Age, many scholars argue that political parties 'aren't what they used to be'. Voters may not pay as much attention to party labels as before, though some believe that increased ideological polarization and greater organizational skills are helping to bring parties back to life.[78] There exists a lively academic debate between those who say parties are in an irreversible decline and those who see a party revival.[79] Many of the arguments center around the ideas presented in this chapter – i.e., what are the normative functions that should properly be ascribed to political parties? The differing answers only add more intensity to the passions on both sides.

But the twenty-first-century phenomenon that will cause political parties to either adapt or wither away is the decline of mediating institutions. Robert Putnam believes we are in an era where citizens are more likely than ever before to be 'bowling alone'.[80] In Putnam's view, social capital is slowly eroding as more citizens than ever before refuse to join either bowling leagues or other civic-minded institutions – including political parties. The Internet is contributing to this development, as citizens sit alone at a computer without the social and community interactions so favored by the political parties of the nineteenth and twentieth centuries. Thus, the 'quality' of political participation is quite different and less interactive. Citizens may be able, for example, to select a party's nominees by voting on their computer without any guidance from the party organizations. At once, the Internet has leveled the playing field, as information becomes available to party producers and consumers alike. In short, political parties no longer provide a filter for information. Instead, they are just one provider – among many – of several different types of information that are available on the World Wide Web. As political parties adapt to these new conditions, new definitions of parties – replete with new normative assumptions about their functions – are likely to shape the ongoing debate about political parties in the twenty-first century.

NOTES

1. Robert Huckshorn, *Political Parties in America* (Monterey, CA: Brooks/Cole, 1984), p. 10.
2. See Green Party of the United States website, http://www.gp.org (accessed October 13, 2003).
3. In Florida, Nader received more than 97,000 votes, the vast majority of which would have either supported Al Gore or stayed home. If Gore had won Florida, he would have received at least 292 electoral votes, 22 more than the 270 majority required to win in the Electoral College.
4. *Thoughts on the Cause of the Present Discontents* (1770), in Paul Langford, ed., *The Writings and Speeches of Edmund Burke* (Oxford: Clarendon Press, 1981), p. 317.
5. Anthony Downs, *An Economic Theory of Democracy* (New York: Harper, 1957), pp. 24–5.
6. V.O. Key, Jr., *Politics, Parties, and Pressure Groups* (New York: Crowell, 1964), pp. 163–5. First edition published in 1942.
7. William Nisbet Chambers, 'Party Development and the American Mainstream'. in Chambers and Walter Dean Burnham (eds), *The American Party Systems* (New York: Oxford University Press, 1967), p. 5.
8. Leon D. Epstein, *Political Parties in Western Democracies* (New Brunswick, NJ: Transaction Books, 1980), p. 9.
9. Hugh Sidey, 'A Conversation with Reagan', *Time*, September 3, 1984.
10. Joseph A. Schlesinger, *Political Parties and the Winning of Office* (Ann Arbor: University of Michigan Press, 1991).
11. John H. Aldrich, *Why Parties?* (Chicago: University of Chicago Press, 1995), p. 19
12. Downs, *An Economic Theory of Democracy*, p. 25.
13. Matthew 16: 13–16.
14. James Madison, *Federalist #10*, Clinton Rossiter ed., (New York: New American Library, 1961)
15. In *The Federalist*, Hamilton wrote: 'Energy in the executive is the leading character in the definition of good government.' See Alexander Hamilton, 'Federalist #70', in Alexander Hamilton, James Madison, and John Jay, *The Federalist Papers*, ed. Clinton Rossiter, (New York: New American Library, 1961), p. 423.
16. Quoted in Ronald P. Formisano, *The Transformation of Political Culture: Massachusetts Parties, 1790s–1840s* (New York: Oxford University Press, 1983), p. 8.
17. Alexis de Tocqueville, *Democracy in America*, ed. J. P. Mayer (Garden City, NY: Doubleday, 1969), p. 174.
18. Ibid., p. 175.
19. Ibid., p. 176. Tocqueville added that the demise of great parties in the United States had resulted in a 'great gain in happiness, but not in morality' (p. 176).
20. Key, *Politics, Parties, and Pressure Groups*, p. 18.
21. Quoted in Leon D. Epstein, *Political Parties in the American Mold* (Madison: University of Wisconsin Press, 1986), p. 18.
22. E.E. Schattschneider, *Party Government in the United States* (New York: Rinehart, 1942), p. 1.
23. Quoted in Epstein, *Political Parties in the American Mold*, p. 32.
24. Giovanni Sartori, *Parties and Party System: A Framework for Analysis* (Cambridge, MA: Harvard University Press, 1976), p. ix.
25. Clinton Rossiter, *Parties and Politics in America* (Ithaca, NY: Cornell University Press, 1960), p. 1.
26. Amicus curiae brief filed by the Committee for Party Renewal in *Colorado Republican Federal Campaign Committee v. Federal Election Commission* (February 1996), p. 3.
27. Hugh McDowall Clokie, 'The modern party state', in Norman L. Zucker (ed.), *The American Party Process: Readings and Comments* (New York: Dodd, Mead and Company, 1968), pp. 5, 7.
28. Cited in Frank J. Sorauf and Paul Allen Beck, *Party Politics in America* (Glenview, IL: Scott, Foresman and Company, 1988), p. 9.
29. See Howard A. Scarrow, *Parties, Elections, and Representation in the State of New York* (New York: New York University Press, 1983), p. 2.
30. Leon D. Epstein, *Political Parties in the American Mold*, pp. 155–199. During the 1980s, the Committee for Party Renewal, a multi-partisan group of US political scientists sought to 'deregulate' political parties by challenging the state laws in the courts. Most notably, the committee succeeded in the landmark US Supreme Court decision *Eu v. San Francisco Democratic Central Committee*, 489 US 214 (1989).
31. See Everett Carll Ladd with Charles D. Hadley, *Transformations of the American Party System* (New York: W.W. Norton, 1975), p. 1.
32. See Key, *Politics, Parties, and Pressure Groups*, p. 164. The person who invented the PIE–PO–PIG analogy was Ralph M. Goldman. See Ralph M. Goldman, 'Party chairmen and party factions, 1789–1900'. Unpublished Ph.D. dissertation, University of Chicago, 1951, ch. 17. Paul S. Herrnson subsequently introduced a fourth component, the party-in-the-campaign. See Paul S. Herrnson, *Party Campaigning in the 1980s* (Cambridge, MA: Harvard University Press, 1988).
33. See Frank J. Sorauf, *Party Politics in America* (Boston: Little, Brown and Co., 1972 edition), p. 9.

34. Everett Carll Ladd, Jr., *American Political Parties: Social Change and Political Response* (New York: W.W. Norton, 1970), p. 8.

35. Quoted in A. James Reichley, *The Life of the Parties* (Lanham, MD: Rowman and Littlefield, 2000), p. 17.

36. Quoted in David McCullough, *John Adams* (New York: Simon and Schuster, 2001), p. 422.

37. Quoted in Reichley, *The Life of the Parties*, p. 26.

38. Ibid., p. 17.

39. Ibid.

40. Madison, 'Federalist 10', in Clinton Rossiter, ed., (New York: New American Library, 1961), p. 77.

41. Pendleton Herring, *The Politics of Democracy: American Parties in Action* (New York: W.W. Norton, 1940).

42. Emphasis added: See John Kenneth White, *The Fractured Electorate* (Hanover, NH: University Press of New England, 1983), p. 103

43. See Richard Morin and E.J. Dionne, Jr., 'Majority of voters say parties have lost touch', *Washington Post* (July 8, 1992), p. A-1.

44. George W. Bush, Acceptance Speech, Republican National Convention, Philadelphia (August 3, 2000).

45. See Al Gore, Acceptance Speech, Democratic National Convention, Los Angeles (August 17, 2000).

46. Greenberg, Quinlan, Rosner survey (December 2–4, 2001).

47. CNN exit poll (June 2, 1998).

48. V.O. Key, Jr., *The Responsible Electorate: Rationality in Presidential Voting, 1936–1960* (Cambridge, MA: Harvard University Press, 1966), p. 7.

49. Downs, *An Economic Theory of Democracy*, pp. 11–12.

50. See Stephen C. Shadegg, *Winning's a Lot More Fun* (New York: Macmillan, 1969).

51. Walter Lippmann, *The Phantom Public* (New York: Harcourt, Brace, 1925), pp. 56–7.

52. See Martin P. Wattenberg, *The Rise of Candidate-Centered Politics* (Cambridge, MA: Harvard University Press, 1991), p. 18.

53. Ibid., pp. 18–19.

54. Ibid., 100.

55. Committee on Political Parties, *Toward a More Responsible Two-Party System* (New York: Rinehart, 1950), p. 1.

56. Ibid., pp. 1–2.

57. Ibid., p. 15.

58. Evron M. Kirkpatrick, 'Toward a more responsible party system: political science, policy science, or pseudo science?' Paper presented at the Sixty-Sixth Annual Meeting of the American Political Science Association, Los Angeles, September 8–12, 1970. This paper was subsequently published in *American Political Science Review*, 65 (December 1971), 965–990.

59. Theodore J. Lowi, *The Personal President: Power Invested, Promise Unfulfilled* (Ithaca, NY: Cornell University Press, 1985), p. 68.

60. William J. Crotty, 'The philosophies of party reform', in Gerald M. Pomper (ed.), *Party Renewal in America* (New York: Praeger, 1980), p. 35.

61. One reason why the report may have been subjected to so much criticism is that its recommendations appeared to have the imprimatur of the American Political Science Association. The report was first published as a supplement to the *American Political Science Review*. But the APSA took no position as to the recommendations made in the report and, in fact, the *Review* provided a forum for critics including Julius Turner's 'Responsible Parties: Dissent from the Floor', *American Political Science Review* (March 1951), 143–52.

62. Kirkpatrick, 'Toward a more responsible party system'.

63. Austin Ranney, *The Doctrine of Responsible Party Government: Its Origins and Present State* (Urbana: University of Illinois Press, 1954), p. 491.

64. Murray S. Stedman, Jr. and Herbert Sonthoff, 'Party responsibility – a critical inquiry', *Western Political Quarterly*, IV(3)(1951), 460.

65. Turner, 'Responsible parties', p. 151.

66. Moisei Iakovlevitch Ostrogorski, *Democracy and the Party System in the United States* (New York: Macmillan 1910), p. 380. Quoted in Ranney, *The Doctrine of Responsible Party Government*, p. 116.

67. See A.G. Keller (ed.), *The Challenge of Facts and Other Essays*, (New Haven: Yale University Press, 1914), p. 367. Quoted in Ranney, *The Doctrine of Responsible Party Government*, p. 14.

68. Quoted in David E. Price, *Bringing Back the Parties* (Washington, DC: Congressional Quarterly Press, 1984), p. 102.

69. Quoted in Ranney, *The Doctrine of Responsible Party Government*, p. 96.

70. Woodrow Wilson, 'Leaderless government', an address before the Virginia Bar Association (August 4, 1897), in *Public Papers* I, pp. 336–59. Quoted in Ranney, *The Doctrine of Responsible Party Government*, p. 33.

71. Quoted in Price, *Bringing Back the Parties*, p. 103.

72. Woodrow Wilson, 'Mr. Cleveland's Cabinet', in *Public Papers*, I, pp. 221–2. Quoted in Ranney, *The Doctrine of Responsible Party Government*, p. 30.

73. The emphasis is Wilson's. Quoted in Ranney, *The Doctrine of Responsible Party Government*, p. 29.

74. Committee on Political Parties, *Toward a More Responsible Two-Party System*, p. 14.

75. V.O. Key Jr., 'A theory of critical elections', *Journal of Politics*, 17 (February 1955), 3–18.

76. E.E. Schattschneider, *The Semi-Sovereign People: A Realist's View of Democracy in America* (Hinsdale, IL: Dryden Press, reprint 1975), p. 15.

77. Lewis Coser, *The Functions of Social Conflict* (Glencoe, IL: Free Press, 1956), p. 121. I am grateful to Professor Morton Tenzer of the University of Connecticut for providing Schattschneider's marked copy of Coser's book.

78. See Xandra Kayden and Eddie Mahe, Jr., *The Party Goes On: The Persistence of the Two-Party System in the United States* (New York: Basic Books, 1985) and Larry J. Sabato, *The Party's Just Begun* (Glenview, IL: Scott, Foresman/ Little Brown, 1988).

79. For an illustration of the decline arguments see David S. Broder, *The Party's Over* (New York: Harper & Row, 1982).

80. Robert D. Putnam, *Bowling Alone: The Collapse and Revival of American Community* (New York: Simon and Schuster, 2000).

2

THE NINETEENTH-CENTURY ORIGINS OF MODERN POLITICAL PARTIES: THE UNWANTED EMERGENCE OF PARTY-BASED POLITICS

Susan E. Scarrow

Party-based politics was one of the transforming inventions of the 19th century. Of course, parties were not unknown before this time, but it was not until the 19th century that they emerged as central organizing features in many countries' politics. Before this, parties were loose groupings at best, linked by support for a particular leader or political idea. Often they were equated with 'factions', unwanted divisions that endangered the national order. Yet despite these widespread and deep-rooted anti-party biases, during the 19th century parties took on a well-defined shape both inside and outside of the legislatures in many countries.

These changes in political parties coincided with, and stimulated, a much wider transformation of politics. Across Europe and North America the 19th century witnessed a broad movement towards mass electoral politics. As the electorate grew, so too did the seeming inevitability of party-organized electoral competition. Because of this, the presence of multiple, competing, political parties gradually came to be considered one of the hallmarks of a democratic regime: as E. E. Schattschneider (1942: 1) would put it in the middle of the 20th century, 'political parties created democracy, and modern democracy is unthinkable save in terms of the parties'. Along with this shift came new definitions that highlighted electoral aspirations as the most important feature which distinguished political parties from other groups seeking to influence public policy. In the succinct words of Anthony Downs (1957: 25), a party is 'a team seeking to control the

governing apparatus by gaining office in a duly constituted election'. Though electoral competition came to be seen as a core activity for parties, in more elaborate functionalist descriptions parties did much more than this. They performed multiple tasks, including, according to one list, selecting official personnel, formulating public policies, conducting and criticizing government, providing political education, and intermediating between individuals and government (Merriam, 1923: 391). All this was a far cry from Edmund Burke's late 18th century definition, in which a party was 'a body of men united, for promoting by their joint endeavours the national interest, upon some particular principle in which they are all agreed' (Burke, 1889: 530).

The best way to understand how this transformation occurred, and how party-based politics came to be a central feature of modern democratic practice, is to look to political developments in the 19th century.

THE CONCEPTUAL HERITAGE: ARE ALL PARTIES FACTIONS?

As suggested above, political parties as we know them today have their roots in distinctly inhospitable intellectual soil. Versions of the word 'party', derived from the Latin *partir* (to divide), were in use in all the major European languages by the 18th century. At this stage the term was most usually applied in a negative sense, interchangeably with the term 'faction', to describe divisions around ideas or personal interests which threatened peaceful government. The label 'party' was not confined to the realm of secular politics: it also was applied to rival religious factions, whether within the Catholic Church or as a designation for protestant sects (Sartori, 1976: 5–12; Beyme, 1978: 677–701). This broad usage of the party label lingered, particularly in continental Europe.

The slow emergence of a secular and non-pejorative definition of parties is evident in political practice as well as theory. Through the 18th century and well into the 19th century, most of those involved in what we would now describe as political parties themselves rejected the label: in fact, many claimed the moral high ground of pursuing the best path for the nation, while deriding their opponents for being 'partisan'. Such a reaction was seen perhaps most strongly in the French Revolution. Influenced by Rousseau's ideal of the General Will, and his attack on associations that rallied only a part of the nation, rival groups staked claims to speak for all the people. Ironically, though the Revolutionary groupings claimed to be above party, later French commentators who rejected the Revolution viewed these groups as prime exemplars of partisan excesses, so that in France one of the enduring legacies of the Revolution was an anti-party bias across the political spectrum (Ignazi, 1996: 282–6).

Though this strand of French thought was perhaps extreme in its anti-partisanship, much of the 19th century's intellectual anti-party heritage was rooted in the long-standing equation of parties with factions, that is, with groups pursuing private ends at the cost of the broader public welfare. Factions were by definition immoderate and self-serving, and factional rivalry threatened public order. Thus, Lord Bolingbroke, an English politician and writer, warned in 1738 against the dangers of parties, arguing that they were qualitatively little different from factions, because all pursued particular ends instead of the good of the whole state: 'party is a political evil, and faction is the worst of all parties' (Bolingbroke, 1881: 219). A few years later, in 1742, David Hume gave a somewhat more sympathetic account of political parties, but he nonetheless compared them with dangerous weeds that are difficult to extirpate (see Hume, 1953: 77–84). Fifty years later, in 1796, Burke went further than Hume's cautious defense of parties, but his willingness to see some types of parties as compatible with public welfare was by no means the norm for this period. More typical of the lingering suspicion

of parties were the sentiments expressed in the new American republic, where luminaries such as President Washington warned in 1796 against the 'baneful effects of the spirit of party' (see Washington, 1896: 218).

Such prejudices notwithstanding, political parties developed rapidly in the new American republic (Aldrich, 1995: 68–96). And here as elsewhere, anti-party attitudes gradually changed as experience with political parties grew. By the middle of the 19th century political life in many countries had begun to be defined in terms of partisan struggles. Reflecting this shift, 19th-century writing about political parties shows a similar move away from questions about whether countries were better off without parties at all, towards a discussion of party types and party features. As this sequence suggests, views of parties tended to be reactive, shaped by experiences with parties rather than pointing the way towards changes in political practice. Thus, to understand the development of party scholarship, we need some understanding of when and why parties themselves began to assume the characteristics of modern parties.

WHY PARTIES?

The newfound prominence of political parties in much of 19th-century Europe seems clearly linked to two distinct but interrelated developments: the transfer of political power to legislatures, and the expansion of the electorate. Many authors have emphasized the temporal and causal priority of parliamentarization in this process: 'First there is the creation of parliamentary groups, then the appearance of electoral committees, and finally the establishment of a permanent connection between these two elements' (Duverger, 1954: xxiv). Sartori described a similar sequence: legislatures became more responsible, then parties became more important, then party competition led parties to try to gain an electoral edge by enfranchising new, and presumably grateful, voters. Finally, the need to mobilize a larger electorate stimulated the parties to develop more formal organizations (Sartori, 1976: 23). The sequential models proposed by Duverger and Sartori apply well to Britain, but they seem less useful for understanding countries such as Denmark, where large expansions of the franchise *preceded* the emergence of legislative parties. Their model also ignores the extent to which parties in some countries were

Table 2.1   Steps toward institutional democratization in western Europe

	Parliamentarization[a]	Suffrage for lower house exceeds 10% of population over 19 years old[b]	Universal manhood suffrage[a]
Austria	1919	1873	1907
Belgium	1831	1894	1894/1919
Denmark	1901	1849	1849
Finland	1917	1907	1907
France	1875	1848	1919
Germany	1919	1871	1871
Italy	1861	1882	1913/1919
Netherlands	1868	1888	1918
Sweden	1917	1875	1911
Switzerland	1848	1848	1848
United Kingdom	1832–35	1869	1918

Sources: [a]Kohl, 1983: 396; [b]Bartolini, 2000: 582–5

important in winning more responsibility for the legislature – in some instances, parliamentarization was as much a product as a cause of party growth (Svåsand, 1980). These gaps may be the reason others have emphasized the causal priority of the expanding franchise in stimulating the emergence of parties in the modern, that is, electoral, sense of the word. As Epstein (1980: 23) put it most concisely, 'the enlargement of the suffrage accounts for the development of modern parties'.

In any case, it is unlikely that a single model can explain why parties emerged when they did, because, as Table 2.1 illustrates for some countries in western Europe, the sequence of changes in the legislative and electoral realms varied broadly. Countries can be roughly divided into three categories: those where the shift of decision-making to legislatures ('parliamentarization') preceded the creation of a large electorate, those where legislative sovereignty increased only after the creation of a large electorate, and those where the two changes occurred more or less simultaneously. These patterns are clearly key to any model that hopes to explain why recognizably modern, electorally-oriented, political parties emerged where and when they did. Unfortunately, it is much more difficult to pinpoint the year when modern parties began to play a role in each country's political life. Though Duverger (1954: xxxix) writes figuratively about 'the birth certificate of a party', in many cases these birthdates are hard to establish, particularly for the earliest parties. The lack of such firm dates is one reason why it is difficult definitively to link these two institutional changes with the timing of party emergence. Still, it seems evident that differences in institutional change affected both the timing and the particulars of party development. They also affected perceptions about the need for parties.

For instance, in the United States, both representative government and a broad franchise were present at the country's independence, and national political parties developed in the wake of both. In contrast, in Britain the superiority of the elected chamber of Parliament was established by 1832, and soon thereafter parties began organizing daily activity within the House of Commons (Cox, 1987). However, it was not until the election of 1885 that more than half of British adult males had the right to vote (Williams and Ramsden, 1990: 285). Thus, in Britain parties emerged as established parliamentary groupings before they became organized forces to contest elections (McKenzie, 1955). But contra Duverger and Sartori, a sequence like that in Britain did not inevitably lead to electorally-oriented parties with extra-parliamentary organization. This was amply illustrated by experiences in Italy. In this newly created country the parliament had constitutionally-guaranteed dominance from the time of the country's independence in 1860 (indeed, this supremacy stretched back to 1848 in Piedmont, the constitutional monarchy which became the nucleus of the new Italian state). Yet the franchise remained limited in Italy, and parties had little incentive to build up extra-parliamentary electoral organizations. Politicians also felt little incentive to form binding ties within the legislature, and they valued independence from party as an honorable course (Carstairs, 1980: 149–50). In the three countries named above, 'parliamentarization' occurred comparatively early, but the development of parties differed greatly.

Outside Switzerland, most continental European powers retained strong monarchies and weak legislatures well into the middle of the 19th century. These systems were shaken by the revolutions of 1848, but, with the exception of Piedmont, the democratic constitutions of 1848–49 were quickly replaced by more autocratic ones which discouraged popular political activity. Because of this, for much of the 19th century political observers in these countries might describe national political disputes in partisan terms, but there was no need for these 'partisans' to form strong associational links: legislators seldom voted, and governments did not get their mandate from legislative coalitions. As a result, late parliamentarization may have affected not only the nature of the parties which developed (legislative links were more loosely organized), but also their number (in countries where parties did not form governments, there were fewer incentives to work together).

In many places, democratization of the suffrage outpaced the transfer of responsibility to the legislature, so that countries like Germany and France had manhood suffrage long before their elected bodies received a full mandate to govern. In Germany and Austria this sequence led to the development of active extra-parliamentary organizing even before the representative assemblies gained complete authority. However, the same did not happen in Second Empire France, where broad suffrage elections preceded parliamentarization, but where partisan organizing was almost entirely prohibited. This brings up a third, and often overlooked, set of institutional constraints that were important determinants of the timing of political party emergence: laws governing the right to free assembly, free association, and free speech.

WHY NOT PARTIES?

When trying to explain why parties emerged when and where they did, it is as important to consider the institutional obstacles to party building as to look at the institutional incentives for organized competition. These obstacles can easily be overlooked by those who study party emergence in the Anglo-American realms, because they played such a minor role in these countries. Yet one of the things which made the United States and Great Britain unusual in the first half of the 19th century was the extent to which their citizens enjoyed the right to form political organizations and to express opposition to government policies. Press freedom and the right to free assembly were enshrined in the US Constitution, though even here press freedom (freedom from prior censorship) initially was viewed as being compatible with public action against those deemed to be disseminating views which threatened public order (Levy, 1985). This interpretation reflected the prevailing view in British Common Law. British censorship laws were abolished at the end of the 17th century, but well into the mid-19th century strict libel laws hampered the publication of remarks which might be construed as attacks on the government or on those who governed (Harling, 2001). But British laws did allow groups to organize to petition Parliament to present their grievances. Thus, for instance, while the violence associated with the Chartist protests of the 1830s was illegal, the petition itself was legitimate and was voted on by the Parliament (though soundly rejected). At a time when the electorate was very small, the Chartist protests did not lead to the foundation of a political party, but this episode demonstrates the comparatively wide scope of freedom of political association that Britons enjoyed by the first part of the 19th century.

The case was sharply different on much of the European continent. Here, many countries maintained laws throughout the 19th century that were designed to inhibit the development of organized political groupings and to stifle views hostile to those of the government. In central Europe, the brief period of relative freedom after Napoleon's defeat was ended by the 1819 promulgation of the Karlsbad Decrees, which committed all states in the German Federation to establish political censorship and other restrictions on political activities. In 1831 these common measures were extended to forbid all political gatherings, and in 1832 it became illegal to form a political organization (Beyme, 1978: 707). These laws severely limited political opposition, but they did not entirely prevent the articulation of liberal and nationalist positions. Such ideas found their place in books (very long documents were exempt from censorship), in private associations, and, to a lesser extent, in the legislatures of some of the German states (Blackbourn, 1997: 125). In much of Germany direct press censorship was ended by 1850, but even after this governments continued using other legal tools to harass publishers of unsympathetic newspapers (Ruud, 1979: 525). The combined result of these restrictions was that schools of 'partisan' thought emerged within these countries well in advance of the appearance of organized parties.

Across continental Europe, prohibitions against political organizing were briefly lifted after the revolutions of 1848–49, but they were quickly reimposed once these revolutions failed. Such strictures gradually relaxed, but in many countries their remnants lingered well into the 20th century. For instance, until 1899 German laws prevented all cross-regional links between party associations, and until 1908 local political associations in most German states had to notify local authorities whenever they held public meetings: women and minors were legally excluded from all such gatherings. Germany also had another type of legal obstacle to party development: laws intended to thwart the development of specific parties. Most notably, from 1878 to 1890, Germany's anti-socialist laws banned socialist or communist publications, and prohibited public meetings to promote socialist and communist aims, though they did allow Social Democratic candidates to compete in Reichstag elections and to take their seats if they won (Fairbairn, 1996; Turk, 1990; Ruud, 1979: 525).

Legal measures in France also inhibited party formation for most of the 19th century. Laws that limited the right to freedom of assembly and freedom of association were legacies of the reaction to the first French Revolution. These laws were carried forward into the 19th century, becoming progressively more restrictive. For instance, at the beginning of the 19th century political gatherings of fewer than 20 people were allowed to assemble without a permit, and some political organizers tried to create networks based on small cells. But even this type of organizational effort was thwarted after 1834, when laws against political gatherings were extended to cover groups of all sizes (Huard, 1996: 77). Many restrictions against political organization continued for some years after the regime democratized in 1871, although they were no longer so strictly enforced. They were not entirely abolished until 1901, when a new law of association gave parties the same standing as other organizations (Huard, 1996: Ch. 11). In addition, through the end of the Second Empire governments continued to use post-publication legal procedures to harass or shut down newspapers expressing views hostile to the government. Restrictions on press freedom were not lifted until 1881 (Ruud, 1979: 524). The combination of these restrictions did not entirely stifle partisan organization in the Second Empire and the early Third Republic, but they certainly discouraged efforts to build permanent structures for mobilizing political support.

This brief review makes clear that the emergence of modern parties was not just a function of changing organizational incentives. It also was influenced by the strength of organizational *disincentives*: in many places party development was retarded by laws deliberately designed to stifle political opinions and political organizations, particularly those that might threaten the status quo.

WHY THESE PARTICULAR PARTIES?

In addition to trying to explain the overall emergence of modern parties, party scholars also have been interested in explaining why certain *types* of parties developed when and where they did. Klaus von Beyme gives one of the best brief overviews of the development of different 'party families', and he offers considerations about the interaction between the development of various party types, noting for example that 'Radical parties emerged mainly in those countries in which the Socialist movement developed into a powerful factor rather late' (1985: 43), and that Conservative parties have usually been 'the second party to develop, the organizational response to the challenge of Liberalism and Radicalism' (1985: 46). But as intriguing as his observations are, they beg the question of why the earliest parties emerged. One type of answer looks to sociological factors to explain why and when certain party types appeared. From this perspective, parties are entrepreneurs which try to exploit existing social divisions, transforming social identities into political ones. Thus, in Seymour Lipset's and Stein Rokkan's (1967) oft-cited account of cleavage-based party formation, different types of parties were the products of successive social revolutions that brought new conflicts to the fore.

More recent investigations of the development of particular party families have been less concerned with general explanations and more concerned with the reasons why similar social conditions did not always produce similar party formations. For instance, in separate studies Stathis Kalyvas (1996) and Carolyn Warner (2000) have sought to explain why Christian Democrats flourished in countries such as Belgium and Italy but not in France. Stefano Bartolini (2000) has examined the factors in addition to the industrialization of the labor force which explain the varying timing and success of left parties. These accounts do not reject the importance of societal pre-conditions, but they have tended to stress the importance of decisions by individual politicians, and of institutional settings which made it more or less easy for new parties to compete. They reject (as did Lipset and Rokkan) a simple mechanical model whereby cleavages are automatically translated into parties, and focus instead on the process by which political entrepreneurs more or less successfully mobilized these cleavages and created new political identities.

POLITICAL PARTIES AS OBJECTS OF ANALYSIS

The study of political parties developed much more slowly than the emergence of parties themselves. Reviews of the American and European party literature of the 19th century clearly show how little is written about political parties until after the first third of the century (see Scarrow, 2003). This doubtless reflects the limited experiences with political parties up to that time, but it also reflects the very slow recognition of parties as a legitimate part of the governing process. Thus, in the United States, where recognizably modern parties developed comparatively early, prior to the 1840s few analysts paid much attention to parties as institutions (though particular parties figured more prominently in political polemics). Alexis de Tocqueville, the perceptive French observer of Jacksonian America, was one of the earliest commentators to devote an extended reflection to the role of the parties in American political life. He saw American parties through the lens of French anti-party prejudices, and hence argued that the American parties founded on selfish and even petty interests were more conducive to public welfare than parties based on high principles, because the latter are less willing to compromise (Tocqueville, 1839: Ch. 10).

Tocqueville's comments on the desirability of different types of parties were typical of one of the most prominent strands of writing about parties prior to the 1840s. Around this time, however, the emphasis in the literature started to shift, particularly in countries which were beginning to acquire more experience with party politics.

In Britain, for instance, changes in political practice in the wake of the Reform Act of 1832 prompted some sharp debates about the new-found prominence of parties in parliamentary life. Some observers were profoundly disturbed by the growing expectation of party loyalty within governing cabinets, and of party-line voting within Parliament, viewing these changes as an unwise retreat from the Burkean ideal of parties as uncoerced coalitions united by shared principles. One such critic was Lord Brougham, a politician who served as a Whig minister during the 1830s, but who split with his colleagues because he prized his political independence. Brougham (1839: 300) denounced the increasingly partisan politics of the 1830s as 'this most anomalous state of things, – this arrangement of political affairs which systematically excludes at least one-half of the great men of each age from their country's service, and devotes both classes infinitely more to maintaining a conflict with one another than to furthering the general good'. Although other British analysts shared Brougham's regret over the disappearing role for the independent legislator, by mid-century most Anglo-Saxon commentators tended to accept party discipline as a necessary cost of parliamentary government. One of the most prominent advocates of this view was Henry George, Earl Grey, the son of a prime minister and himself a member of several cabinets. In a treatise that was quickly translated into several languages he argued that 'Parliamentary Government is essentially a government by party', and that cohesive parties led to better government even if some of this cohesion was 'purchased' by the favors which ministers could offer to their supporters (Grey, 1858). A few years later, Walter Bagehot (1867) amplified on this theme of the centrality of cohesive parties in parliamentary government.

Even in continental Europe, where parties and legislatures were much less developed than their Anglo-American counterparts, there is also evidence of an increased awareness of party politics by the second third of the 19th century. Some of their earliest concerns were taxonomical efforts to categorize parties conceived of as schools of political thought. One of the earliest and most elaborate of these taxonomies was developed by Friedrich Roehmer (1844), whose observation of Swiss politics led him to develop a very elaborate classification based on the four ages of man. Roehmer's categories were not widely adopted – they were in fact painstakingly dismissed in articles like that published a few years later in the *Staatslexicon* (Abt, 1848) – but many agreed with Roehmer's central premise that there were cross-national similarities in the varieties of available political alternatives.

Britain's comparatively early experience with party-based parliamentary government was on the minds of many across the continent who sought to establish more constitutional forms of government. Some saw Britain as a model worth emulating, such as the Austrian translator of Earl Grey's treatise on parliamentary government (Grey, 1863) and the German legal scholar Robert von Mohl (1872). Yet defenders of more autocratic systems tended to disparage party-based government and the party discipline this seemed to demand. For instance, in 1871, a few months after the formation of the new German empire, the influential German historian Heinrich von Treitschke pointedly rejected the British example, arguing that Germany benefited from having a constitutional monarch who was 'above the parties' (Treitschke, 1903). Four decades later, on the eve of World War I, German authors continued to debate the desirability of party participation in public life. While the liberal theorist Friedrich Naumann still found it necessary to defend parties as being a necessary form of contemporary political life, with educational and creative value (see Naumann, 1964: 214), others voiced concern about the partiality of parties, and repeated Treitschke's argument that constitutional monarchy was a good form of government precisely because monarchy transcended partisan divisions (Hasbach, 1912: 586).

American observers also responded to British accounts of party-based parliamentary life. Perhaps most famously, the young Woodrow Wilson (1885) was inspired by his studies of British politics to argue that American government could be improved by the advent of 'real party government', under which there would be a more secure link between Congress and the Executive. Others emphasized the special role of parties in the ethnically diverse and politically divided American federation, stressing parties' beneficial role as a 'nationalizing influence' (Ford, 1898). These responses to the British experience were the origins of what would become a long-running debate among US academics about the feasibility, and desirability, of responsible party government in the United States (see Ranney, 1954).

The 1890s saw the emergence of another concern that would form the basis for much subsequent party scholarship: writings on parties as extra-legislative organizations. A great deal of this commentary was fuelled by the perception that party organizations were becoming too powerful and well organized, with the prime example of this being the 'machines' that dominated politics in many American cities at the time. One of the most enduring of these works was Moisei Ostrogorski's (1902) comparison of party organizations in Britain and the United States. Ostrogorksi was a French-educated Russian whose suspicion of the benefits of organized political parties was shared by other French scholars of the period (Quagliariello, 1996). Others also shared his interest in parties' organizational activities. For instance in Germany, where Social Democratic organization had inspired other parties to strengthen their own extra-parliamentary associations, Robert Michels and Max Weber were soon to write their now classic comments on the relations between parties' professional organizers and their rank-and-file supporters (Michels, 1959; Weber, 1982). But it was observers of US politics who wrote the most on this subject, undoubtedly because at the beginning of the 20th century the US parties had the strongest organizations.

The roots of the strong American party organizations extended back to the Jacksonian era, when the Democratic Party dominated national politics for much of the 1830s. This party shocked many contemporary observers by its unabashed use of public resources for party ends, but patronage politics quickly emerged as the new norm. From the Jacksonian era through the end of the 19th century and beyond, American parties often treated electoral victory as a license to distribute government jobs and other public assets to their supporters. Reactions against such intermingling of public and private interest became an increasingly prominent strain in 19th-century American political debates.

These attacks came to the fore in the final decade of the century, when 'good government' reformers and Populists became ever more strident in denouncing the evils of existing political parties and in promoting institutional innovations like referendums that would enable 'the people' to bypass the parties. Academic observers also were troubled by party corruption, but they were less willing to attack the existence of parties. By this time many saw parties as essential to the functioning of the US political system (Beard, 1910; Macy, 1904). Though very few defended the party machines, some did argue that the spoils of office might be a necessary price to pay for having parties which were strong enough to coordinate politics within the institutionally and geographically fragmented United States (Goodnow, 1900; see also Ford, 1898).

CONCLUSION

This chapter has tried to show how the roots of modern parties, and of modern party scholarship, are to be found in the 19th century. The emergence of party-organized politics was an unanticipated, and even unwanted, side-effect of the liberalization and democratization of politics in that century. Although countries took varied routes to the modern party era, by the beginning of the 20th century recognizably modern parties had begun to play an important role in many places, structuring electoral choices, coordinating legislative and executive action, mobilizing the electorate, and recruiting candidates. The study of political parties developed largely in the wake of these changes. The attitude towards parties changed as well. For much of the 19th century, many who wrote about political parties approvingly quoted Burke's late-18th-century definition, according to which parties were groups united in pursuit of the *national* interest. By the end of the 19th century, however, some analysts had begun to question Burke's emphasis on parties' pursuit of the national interest, arguing that competing parties served the national welfare precisely because they pursued *particular* (as opposed to national) interests: as the American Anson Morse (1896: 80) put it, 'the true end of party ... is, in ordinary times, to promote not the general interest, but the interest of a class, a section or some one of the many groups of citizens which are to be found in every state'. This kind of emerging acceptance of the inevitability and necessity of party competition laid the groundwork for a view of parties that was to become dominant in much of the 20th century, a pluralist view that saw parties as beneficial mediators of individual and group demands. It is only by appreciating the views of parties that preceded this pluralist conception that we can understand how big a shift this new vision of politics represented.

REFERENCES

Abt, Gottlieb Christian (1848) 'Parteien', in Carl von Rotteck and Carl Welcker (eds), *Staats-Lexicon: Enzyclopädie der sämmtlichen Staatswissenschaften.* Altona: Verlag von Johann Friedrich Hammerlich.
Aldrich, John (1995) *Why Parties? The Origin and Transformation of Political Parties in America.* Chicago: University of Chicago Press.
Bagehot, Walter (1867) *The English Constitution.* London: Chapman & Hall.

Bartolini, Stefano (2000) *The Political Mobilization of the European Left, 1860–1980.* Cambridge: Cambridge University Press.
Beard, Charles (1910) *American Government and Politics.* New York: Macmillan.
Beyme, Klaus von (1978) 'Partei, Faktion', in Otto Brunner, Werner Conze, and Reinhart Koselleck (eds), *Geschichtliche Grundbegriffe*, Vol. 4. Stuttgart: Klett-Cotta, pp. 677–735.
Beyme, Klaus von (1985) *Political Parties in Western Democracies*, trans. Eileen Martin. Aldershot: Gower.
Blackbourn, David (1997) *The Long Nineteenth Century.* Oxford: Oxford University Press.
Bolingbroke, Henry Saint-John, Viscount (1881). 'On the idea of a patriot king', in *Letters on the Study and Use of History, etc.* London: Ward, Lock & Co.
Brougham, Henry Lord (1839) *Historical Sketches of Statesmen who Flourished in the Time of George III.* London: Charles Knight & Co.
Burke, Edmund (1889) 'Thoughts on the present discontents', in *The Works of the Right Honorable Edmund Burke*, vol. 1, 9th edn. Boston: Little, Brown and Co., pp. 433–551
Carstairs, Andrew (1980) *A Short History of Electoral Systems in Western Europe.* London: George Allen & Unwin.
Cox, Gary (1987) *The Efficient Secret.* Cambridge: Cambridge University Press.
Downs, Anthony (1957) *An Economic Theory of Democracy.* New York: Harper.
Duverger, Maurice (1954) *Political Parties: Their Organization and Activity in the Modern State*, trans. Barbara and Robert North. New York: Wiley.
Epstein, Leon (1980) *Political Parties in Western Democracies*, 2nd edn. New Brunswick, NJ: Transaction.
Fairbairn, Brett (1996) 'Political mobilization', in Roger Chickering (ed.), *Imperial Germany: A Historiographical Companion.* Westport, CT: Greenwood Press, pp. 303–42.
Ford, Henry Jones (1898) *The Rise and Growth of American Politics.* New York: Macmillan.
Goodnow, Frank (1900) *Politics and Administration.* London: Macmillan.
Grey, Henry George, Earl (1858) *Parliamentary Government Considered with a Reference to a Reform of Parliament.* London: Richard Bentley.
Grey, Henry George, Earl (1863) *Die Parlamentarische Regierungsform*, trans. Graf Leopold von Thun-Hohenstein. Prague: Verlag Friedrich Tempsky.
Harling, Philip (2001) 'The law of libel and the limits of repression, 1790–1832', *Historical Journal*, 44: 107–34.
Hasbach, Wilhelm (1912) *Die moderne Demokratie.* Jena: Gustav Fischer Verlag.
Huard, Raymond (1996) *La Naissance du parti politique en France.* Paris: Presses de la Fondation Nationale des Sciences Politiques.

Hume, David (1953) 'Of parties in general', in *Political Essays*. Indianapolis, IN: Liberal Arts Press.

Ignazi, Piero. (1996) 'The intellectual basis of right-wing anti-partyism', *European Journal of Political Research*, 29: 279–96.

Kalyvas, Stathis (1996) *The Rise of Christian Democracy in Europe*. Ithaca, NY: Cornell University Press.

Kohl, Jürgen (1983) 'Zur langfristigen Entwicklung der politischen Partizipation', in Otto Büsch and Peter Steinbach (eds), *Vergleichende europäische Wahlgeschichte*. Berlin: Colloquium Verlag, pp. 377–411.

Levy, Leonard (1985) *The Emergence of a Free Press*. Oxford: Oxford University Press.

Lipset, Seymour M. and Rokkan, Stein (1967) 'Cleavage structures, party systems, and voter alignments', in Seymour M. Lipset and Stein Rokkan (eds), *Party Systems and Voter Alignments*. New York: Free Press, pp. 1–64.

Macy, Jesse (1904) *Party Organization and Machinery*. New York: Century.

McKenzie, Robert (1955) *British Political Parties*. Melbourne: William Heinemann.

Merriam, Charles (1923) *The American Party System*. New York: Macmillan.

Michels, Robert (1959) *Political Parties*, trans. Eden Paul and Cedar Paul. New York: Dover Publications.

Mohl, Robert von (1872) *Enzyclopädie der Staatswissenschaft*, 2nd edn. Frieburg i B: J.C.B. Mohr.

Morse, Anson (1896) 'What is a party?', *Political Science Quarterly*, 11: 68–81.

Naumann, Friedrich (1964) 'Schriften zum Parteiwesen und zum Mitteleuropaproblem', in *Werke*, Vol. 4. Cologne: Westdeutscher Verlag.

Ostrogorski, Moisei (1902) *Democracy and the Organization of Political Parties*, 2 vols, trans. Frederick Clarke. New York: Macmillan.

Quagliariello, Gaetano (1996) *Politics without Parties*, Aldershot: Avebury.

Ranney, Austin (1954) *The Doctrine of Responsible Party Government*. Urbana: University of Illinois Press.

Roehmer, Friedrich (1844) *Die vier Parteien*. Zurich: Ch. Beyel.

Ruud, Charles (1979) 'Limits on the "freed" press of 18th- and 19th-century Europe', *Journalism Quarterly*, 56: 521–30.

Sartori, Giovanni (1976) *Parties and Party Systems*. Cambridge: Cambridge University Press.

Scarrow, Susan (2003) *Perspectives on Political Parties: Classic Readings*. New York: Palgrave.

Schattschneider, E.E. (1942) *Party Government*. New York: Holt, Rinehart & Winston.

Svåsand, Lars (1980) 'Democratization and party formation in Scandinavia', in Otto Büsch (ed.), *Wählerbewegung in der Europäischen Geschichte*. Berlin: Colloquium Verlag, pp. 398–419.

Tocqueville, Alexis de (1839) *Democracy in America*, trans. Henry Reeve. New York: George Adelard.

Treitschke, Heinrich von (1903) 'Parteien und Fractionen', in *Freiheit und Königthum*. Vol. 3 of *Historische und Politische Aufsätze*, 6th edn. Leipzig: G. Hirzel Verlag, pp. 565–627.

Turk, Eleanor (1990) 'German liberals and the genesis of the Association Law of 1908', in Konrad Jarausch and Larry Eugene Jones (eds), *In Search of a Liberal Germany*. New York: Berg. pp. 237–60.

Warner, Carolyn (2000) *Confessions of an Interest Group*. Princeton, NJ: Princeton University Press.

Washington, George (1896) 'Farewell address', in James D. Richardson (ed.), *A Compilation of the Messages and Papers of the Presidents 1789–1897*, Vol. 1. Washington, DC: Government Printing Office, pp. 213–24.

Weber, Max (1982) *Politik als Beruf*, 7th edn. Berlin: Duncker & Humblot.

Williams, Glyn and Ramsden, John (1990) *Ruling Britannia: A Political History of Britain, 1688–1988*. London: Longmans.

Wilson, Woodrow (1885) *Congressional Government: A Study in American Politics*. Boston: Houghton, Mifflin and Co.

3

PARTY ORIGINS AND EVOLUTION IN THE UNITED STATES

William Crotty

INTRODUCTION

Political parties evolved in America quite simply because the new nation could not function without them. Democratic representation depended on a new and unique system linking voters to political office-holders and holding those in power accountable to the mass electorate.

The relationship between theory and practice, with the theory usually preceding, and making the case for, the institutional development to follow, was not the case with political parties. A need to align forces to develop coalitions of interest to elect representatives, including the president, resulted in the uncertain evolution of the party system.

In the United States the parties were not welcome, and to a large degree and despite their utility they remain objects of suspicion and distrust. They are extra-constitutional structures not envisioned by the framers of the Constitution. From the earliest beginnings, they have been objects of criticism. In *The Federalist*, which was meant to rally support for the new Constitution of 1787, James Madison (1961) warned against 'factions' that would divide the new nation and emphasize the economic, regional, and state divisions. The new Constitution had been agreed to in an effort to provide the foundation for a nation and a new system of governance, one that united the colonies and provided a basis for a national accommodation and unity. The parties threatened to undo what had been accomplished.

The parties initially grew out of need. The theoretical justification of the parties followed later. The argument that evolved in time was that political parties are indispensable to a democracy. They fulfill functions that no other organization, then or now, could. These include: representing the interests of the mass of voters; mobilizing them to support candidates and parties; presenting issue alternatives relevant to the problems facing the nation and enacting them once in office; recruiting candidates to run for public office and supporting them in campaigns; and providing the unity and cohesion to make a fragmented governing system perform adequately.

These are not easily achievable objectives. Yet they are crucial to democratic governance. Political parties provided the critical linkage in any society whose ultimate power rests on elections.

A final general point is that the parties are agents of democratization in another regard. In the competitive battle for additional sources of support for winning elections and exercising power, the parties pushed the bounds of the electorate to greater inclusiveness (Keyssar, 2000). The parties extended the reach of the franchise, from a select few in the colonial period, to a mass-based male electorate, to the inclusion of women (denied the vote until 1920), minorities (effectively disfranchised until the Civil Rights and Voting Right Acts of the 1960s), and younger members of the society (the 18-year-old vote in the 26th Amendment to the Constitution).

PARTIES AND THE DEMOCRATIC STATE

The lineage of parties in America and elsewhere is directly tied to democratizing forces within society. Political parties are agents of democracy, critical to any system intending to represent and institutionalize the rule of the mass.

There are a number of ways of making this point. Henry Jones Ford wrote in 1898:

> The bane of the Whig ideal of government was party spirit. It introduced principles of association inconsistent with the constitutional scheme. Because of party spirit gentlemen betrayed the interests of their order and menaced the peace of society by demagogic appeals to the common people. Instead of the concert of action which should exist between the departments of government as the result of a patriotic purpose common to all, devotion to party was substituted, and the constitutional depositaries of power were converted into the fortifications of party interest. (Ford, 1967: 90)

Everett Carll Ladd, Jr. (1970: 16–17) puts the matter somewhat differently:

> Political parties are children of egalitarianism. They have no place in pre-egalitarian societies, and their presence in some form which denotes the basic commonality of function cannot be avoided in any egalitarian system. … We can … understand the egalitarian revolution and the manner in which it produced the social base for new political institutions like parties by noting its enemy – what it was directed against. It was an attack on *ascriptive class societies*, societies in which social position was determined by birth. These are commonly called *aristocratic* since *aristocracy* is a generic name for the hereditary ruling class of an ascriptive class society. The aristocracy, a small fraction of the population, typically possessed a monopoly of all or nearly all the components of high social position, such as wealth, prestige, and power, and occupied a position of legally defined privilege. Most people in aristocratic societies were blanks, having no say in the social, economic, and political decisions of the system, and were permanently fixed in a distinctly subordinate position.

Changes of such a radical nature towards egalitarianism and an emphasis on the individual's self-definition of interests in society were revolutionary, undermining the old order and replacing it with a new and uncertain social and political structure. For those who held power by reason of birth or wealth, it was a development fraught with fears as to the dissolution of the state and the destruction of society, its norms and value commitments as they then existed. Such fears proved to be well founded.

A second point in this regard: Political parties evolved (they were not planned and, as indicated, were believed to be disruptive and corruptive of a sound order). They were created out of need, instituted as a practical and effective mechanism (whatever their faults) for mobilizing and representing the mass of people. The party systems gave meaning to the Constitution; they incorporated millions of newcomers into the politics of the society; and they made the promise of democratic participation in self-government a universal reality.

THE AMERICAN EXPERIENCE

The Constitution of the United States does not mention political parties. How the society should mobilize a mass electorate was unknown; the implicit expectation was that individual voters would inform and motivate themselves and decide the public interest. The government would be based on a unified nation and rule in its best interest. It was to be a poor reading of human nature, although one familiar in early theorizing on democracy. It also evidenced a large degree of naiveté concerning the functioning of the new system:

> In the process of party building, American founders confronted and effectively solved a long series of political problems. Some were foreseen and some unforeseen, some were at hand from the outset and some emerged only in the course of the work. It was throughout an endeavor of pragmatic adaptation and inventiveness under necessity, guided at the beginning by immediate purposes or a general desire to prove the republican experiment, informed only later by a conception of party as a goal. The problem of establishing the republic and of establishing party overlapped, and in a sense they all involved the practical fulfillment of the nation and democratic promise of the Declaration of Independence. (Chambers, 1963: 10–11).

Parties provided a link between ruled and ruler, and a vehicle to channel representative need upwards. Democratic politics is grounded in conflict. It pits groups, regions, ethnic affiliations, religious denominations, races and even such things as lifestyle commitments against each other. The role of the parties is to allow peaceful resolution of differences and to compromise and accommodate the conflicting interests. The parties help provide a sense of national identification and participation in policy-making necessary to the functioning and adaptability of a democratic system.

The initial impetus for the American party system developed out of just such struggles. The competition was over nothing less than the nature and operation of the constitutional Republic. In many respects it is a curious story, one that combines institutional and systemic needs with values that forcefully disparage the form of an agency that could fill those needs.

There was no model of a party system that the founders could adapt to the American situation. It had to be created in response to the pressures for representation and governance. It was to be experimental. Those involved in its creation intended it as temporary.

The Federalist, in promoting the new national Constitution, warned of the necessity of curbing the evils of faction. It was a position shared by James Madison and Alexander Hamilton, principal authors of the appeal for a unified nation in *The Federalist*, and, in short order, among the primary architects of the evolving party system.

George Washington, in his 'Farewell Address', warned against 'the baneful effects of the Spirit of Party; a conflict that would divide and potentially destroy the new nation' (Washington, 1896: 218). John Adams, who followed Washington in the presidency, wrote that 'a division of the republic into two great parties … is to be dreaded as the greatest political evil under our Constitution' (quoted in White and Shea (2000: 15); on the same subject see McCulloch (2001)). Such warnings came at the precise time the new party system was in its formative stages. Thomas Jefferson was to be the founding force (along with Madison) of the earliest of the mass-based political parties (the Democratic-Republicans or Jeffersonian Republicans, or, more simply, the Jeffersonians, which became the base for the later Democratic party). This party was to compete with the elitist Federalists (then dominant under George Washington and his successor John Adams) and was intended to oppose Adams, Hamilton and their policies by organizing an opposition force of interests and, in 1800, electing Jefferson to the presidency.

The elitist Federalists had little motivation, or belief for that matter, in extending the scope of decision-making and no desire to create any type of permanent party system (as neither did Jefferson nor Madison). The new parties were

considered temporary expedients to meet an immediate national emergency. Parties were looked upon as 'sores on the body politic' (Chambers, 1963: 68; Hofstadter, 1969).

The divisions that led to the efforts to expand the conflict to a public beyond the bounds of political office-holders and to solidify support for policies enacted, or to be enacted, began at the very birth of the nation. Hamilton, for example, initiated support at the Constitutional Convention for his conception of a strong federal government with financial, budgetary, and economic powers sufficient to stabilize the trade and international dealings of the new country.

There was, of course, opposition. Many believed the farm-oriented, rural nature of the country should predominate in federal policy-making. They also favored a system recognizing the preeminent role of the states in the Union (rather than a centralized federal government). In their minds, and largely consistent with the history of constitutional development in the new nation, a state-centered political system expressed the reality of the American experience. It was the basis upon which the Revolution had been fought. For such advocates, a strong presidency with extensive powers over the states and the nation's economic and monetary policy sowed the seeds for a return to the monarchy from which they had just freed themselves. Jefferson was to emerge as the champion of this political faction and in 1800 he and his new party (built on a coalition of southern states allied in the North with Governor George Clinton of New York) contested Adams and the Federalists for the presidency and won.

The precipitating issues, in addition to economic favoritism for mercantile trade and financial institutions, were the Alien and Sedition Acts of 1798. Both these acts (especially the latter) severely compromised the rights of citizens, including the right to criticize in speech or through the press the government, its leaders, or its policies.

The opposing sides, Federalists and Jeffersonian Democrats, did not consider themselves to be parties in the contemporary sense of offering electors alternative voting choices and as representing group coalitions intended to dominate governance, although of course this is what they did. The divide was far more serious and involved nothing less than what the United States should become as a nation: what the text of the Constitution actually meant in practice; the distribution of powers within the federal system; the rights to be guaranteed to individuals; the manner in which political power was to be exercised; and the economic and political sectors that should, by right, be favored by the government.

There was little give on either side, limited room for compromise, and a belief in the total acceptance of one set of values over the other:

> The Federalists and Republicans [Jeffersonian Democratic-Republicans] did not think of each other as alternating parties in a two-party system. Each hoped instead to eliminate party conflict by persuading and absorbing the more acceptable and 'innocent' members of the other; each side hoped to attack the stigma of foreign allegiance [England for the Federalists; France for the Jeffersonians] and disloyalty to the intractable leaders of the other, and to put them out of business as a party. (Hofstadter, 1969: 8)

The Federalists were a party without a broad mass base. After their defeat in the presidential election of 1800, they soon disappeared, leaving a period of one-party dominance by the Jeffersonians. As an indicator of the totality of the divide between parties, the Jeffersonians believed they had established the nature, limits, and purpose of the new nation: 'The one-party power that came with the withering away of Federalism was seen by the Republicans [Jeffersonians] not as anomalous or temporary, much less as an undesirable eventuality, but as evidence of the correctness of their view and of the success of the American system' (Chambers, 1963).

It would take decades, if not generations, before the full conception of competing ideological and policy-making agendas, both representing legitimately contrasting strains of representation, intended to be resolved by the parties' election outcomes, was to be accepted. Pragmatic tolerance of an opposition, operating within the bounds of constitutionally-validated institutional structure, evolved over time, but its roots were embryonic in the organizations mobilized in the 1790s.

One other point is significant: the party system itself actively and rapidly evolved (more quickly than its popular acceptance). Essentially created (in an uncertain manner) at the birth of the nation and following a period of one-partyism that ended with the election of Andrew Jackson in 1828, it took forms that have come down to us in the contemporary period. Its initial development and permanence in American politics provide testimony to its crucial contributions to a functioning democratic system.

FACTORS INFLUENCING THE DEVELOPMENT OF PARTIES IN THE UNITED STATES

The American party system has a number of distinguishing characteristics, which have influenced its evolution and served to define its special character, its structures, and its operations.

Federalism

The American parties had to adapt to a federal structure of government. This ensured a loose structure, a party system sensitive to state and local concerns while attempting to put together coalitions for national office. The parties thus were weakly structured organizations appealing to a variety of interests and attempting to unite political forces within a national entity sufficiently to compete effectively for the presidency. The result was not only that they managed to do this, but their coalitional nature has come to be recognized as a superior mobilizing device, as opposed to single-issue or one-group (religious, ethnic, religious class, regional) parties (however large their membership). The coalitional party helps to promote a more tolerant, compromising, and inclusive democratic electorate.

Another somewhat surprising development, given the basic nature, loose structure, weak incentive and reward systems, and inability to discipline party activists or office-holders (conditions that are the direct opposite of the mass parties of Europe), has been the major parties' ability, consistently over time, to represent broadly antagonistic and competing coalitions for power. The Democrats, evolving from the days of Jefferson, have generally been more sensitive to the needs of the less well-off in society, the Republicans more representative of wealth, corporate, and financial power.

The United States does not have a true class-based political structure, although the New Deal coalition came close. Still, while emphasizing cross-cutting cleavages, there has been a broad economic and class dimension to the two parties' coalitions that has been consistent throughout America's electoral history.

The electoral system

The United States employs a single member district electoral system with a first-past-the-post decision rule in elections. This is not the most accurate gauge of a populace's views or its vote (proportional representation systems do this far better). It has been argued that it does contribute to a more decisive electoral outcome and therefore greater stability in governance. It is also a force in pushing for combining into two broad party coalitions.

The Electoral College was meant to break the impasse at the Constitutional Convention among big and small states, national and state-oriented forces and those favoring popular democratic election. The compromise solution was that a form of filter on the public will and indirect decision-making by a group of elders or more politically astute electors was included in the Constitution. With the possible exception of George Washington, preordained as the first president, it has never worked well and has been a constant object of proposals for reform, amendment, or replacement by direct election. It does serve to reemphasize the winner-takes-all nature of single member districts in electing presidents, and therefore pressures voting blocs into one party or the other. It serves to reemphasize the coalitional nature of party politics and that an election in the United States can be won only by one of the two major voting blocs. In the process, third, minor, and splinter parties have little or no chance of success.

Third parties

In any given election of consequence, there will be a number of third or minor party candidates on the ballot. More recently, minor candidacies have made a practice of competing in presidential and state party primaries as a means of promoting their views and gaining support for their positions (abortion, limits on taxation, animal rights, environmental concerns, anti-vivisectionism, fundamentalist religion, and family values being some of the causes promoted). These are basically ideological and policy-driven, single-issue groups who use the elections to further public awareness of their positions. V.O. Key, Jr. (1964) has labeled them 'ideological interest groups'. They are not serious threats to unseat or replace the dominant parties. In addition, the major parties' electoral superiority has been reemphasized by state and local regulation as to registration requirements and ballot access provisions. These work to minimize or eliminate minor party candidacies and, not by accident, decisively favor the principal parties.

There has, of course, been limited evidence of third party success. Abraham Lincoln and the new Republican Party managed to win the presidency within 6 years of the party's founding. It is a feat that proves an exception to one of the most enduring rules in the political landscape. It is constantly cited by any serious alternative party that challenges the major parties. A three-way split in 1912, brought on by Theodore Roosevelt's Bull Moose party, led to the election of Democrat Woodrow Wilson in an era of Republican dominance. The breakaway of liberals (the Progressive party of Henry Wallace) and of states-rights, anti-civil-rights Dixiecrats (under Governor Strom Thurmond of South Carolina) from the Democratic party in 1948 was predicted to derail the reelection of Harry S. Truman. Truman won a close race. Alabama Governor George Wallace ran a similar (to Thurmond) race-based law-and-order campaign focused primarily in one region (the South) in 1968 and 1972 that developed some national support. Ross Perot in 1992 and 1996 financed his own Reform Party that attracted (for a third party) an impressive share of the vote (18.9 percent in 1992; 8.4 percent in 1996).

Others have run as small party candidates with little success: Ralph Nader's candidacy in 2000 did affect the election's outcome by drawing enough support to give the pivotal Florida popular vote, and with it the Electoral College, to George W. Bush. Lyndon LaRouche, a perennial candidate with an authoritarian streak, has contested a number of elections and party primaries. John Anderson was a liberal Republican who contested the election of Ronald Reagan in 1980. A number of other minor candidates, such as Gary Bauer, Alan Keyes, and the Reverend Al Sharpton, have run in the primaries of one party or the other.

Primary nominations

The most radical democratic initiative was opening the parties' nominating process to mass-based influence through the primaries. The primary largely replaced caucuses (the first system used) and conventions. The national convention remains as the official party vehicle for deciding presidential nominees, but its function in the contemporary period is to legitimize decisions already made in the primaries. Caucuses and conventions are still used in the states on a limited basis. The primaries include all party activists (and in some states, any elector who chooses to vote in the prenomination phase) and the decision of these party activists is binding on delegates to the national conventions.

One consequence is to include more voters in the most important of party decisions, the selection of its nominees for public office. It replaces a mixed nominating system composed of conventions, caucuses, and largely advisory ('beauty contest') primaries. The final decision in the older system was mostly influenced by party regulars, their leaders, and the major interest group representatives important to the party in its campaign for office. Opening the nomination system has significantly reinforced the broad and flexible nature of party coalitions while further lessening the structural and institutional coherence of the party itself. Curiously, perhaps, it has not diluted the partisan differences in policies or ideology that separate the core identifiers of the two parties (Miller, 1988; Miller and Jennings, 1986). In addition, it has indirectly weakened the need or capacity of third parties to contest elections. A variety of choices on a range of issues, one left-leaning in the American political mainstream, the other right-leaning, are offered to primary participants.

Regionalism

This was once the primary force in shaping party agendas and coalitions and the issues and groups to which the parties directed their appeals. Regionalism faded in the 1920s, although it has still had some relevance (the South in its Republican vote being the most prominent example) in recent generations. The New Deal led to more nationalized and class-based politics and the issue-driven campaigns of recent generations, and regionalism has fallen to a decidedly second-level influence.

Party loyalty

There is no clear indicator of an individual's party allegiance. In the American context, aggregate party loyalty is a fuzzy concept based on registration figures (often inadequate and outdated), the division of the vote in any given election, or people's statements as to which party they support. There is no such thing as a mass-based, dues-paying loyal party membership. Party 'members' are free to affiliate with and support the candidates of their choice (in or between parties). The system allows a significant degree of cross-party votes in elections, often one predictor of the likely winner.

The most accepted and analytically useful indicator of party support has been the concept of party identifications developed in *The*

American Voter (Campbell *et al.*, 1960). As explained in *The New American Voter* (Miller and Shanks, 1996: 120), an update of the original study:

> Party identification is a concept derived from reference and small group theory positing that one's sense of self may include a feeling of personal identity with a secondary group such as a political party. In the United States, the feeling is usually expressed as 'I am a Democrat' or 'I am a Republican.' This sense of individual attachment to party need not reflect a formal membership in or active connection with a party organization. Moreover, one's sense of party identification does not necessarily connote a particular voting record, although the influence of party allegiance on electoral behavior is strong, and there is evidence of a reciprocal relationship in which voting behavior helps establish, and solidify or strengthen, one's sense of party allegiance. The tie between individual and party is psychological – an extension of one's ego to include feeling a part of a group. Party identification can persist without legal recognition or formal evidence of its existence; it can even persist without resting on or producing a consistent record of party support either in one's attitudes or one's actions.

It is a measure of an individual's psychological identification with one party or the other. It has proven remarkably consistent in identifying the intensity and voting loyalties of various categories of identifiers and, if not the major force in voter decision-making, it rivals issue positions and candidate perceptions in importance. Its role is central as an explanatory variable in explaining both voting outcomes and party ties: 'personal identifications with the Republican or Democratic party are more stable than any other variable and play a major role in shaping most other political attitudes as well as vote choice' (Miller and Shanks, 1996: 18).

STAGES OF PARTY DEVELOPMENT

Five broad stages of party development can be identified. Each phase served historically different needs for the nation and evidenced different patterns of party support.

The *first stage* involved the creation of the political parties. It extended from the 1790s to what could be called the reinvention, or revitalization, of the party system after the collapse of the Federalists and the one-party era of Jefferson and Madison's Republican-Democrats (the early Democratic party) up to 1828. In this era, the 'parties and the party system appear to have served particularly significant integrative functions in the period of nation-building' (Chambers and Burnham, 1975: 7).

The *second stage*, begun with the Jacksonian presidency and continued to the Civil War, witnessed the development of the party structures, from state and national nominating conventions to party institutions and campaign operations and approaches. These initial institutional forms have come down to the contemporary period (with the addition of the direct primary in the early years of the twentieth century and the opening of party operations in the late 1960s and early 1970s) in forms recognizable since their adoption. It is during this period that parties set their competitive patterns as well as the institutional forms that have endured.

The Democratic party fragmented in the 1840s and 1850s over questions of slavery, the role of the states in the Union, interpretations as to the divisions of constitutional powers, and expansionist issues the political system had been attempting to deal with since the nation's founding. The era also witnessed the failure of the Whigs, a party with a policy agenda and roots broadly similar to the early Federalists. This left the initiative to the new Republican party, and its 1860 presidential candidate Abraham Lincoln, to unify and mobilize sentiment in the North to resolve the cleavages over the states' place in the national system and, during the Civil War, to end slavery, an issue that had divided the nation since its birth, and one the Constitution did little to resolve permanently.

The most significant development, from a party and representative standpoint, of the second period may well have been the establishment of an enduring mass base to the party system, the national government, and policymaking (Chambers and Burnham, 1975: 11). The ends of an inclusive, representative democracy came to fruition during the years 1828–60. To these could be added 'those of egalitarianism', symbolized by the election of Andrew Jackson in 1828, in contrast to the elitist oligarchies of Massachusetts and Virginia that had held power to this point.

The *third stage* of party development encompassed the years 1865–1932 and is referred to as 'a derivative stage', that is, a period of 'adjustment rather than creativity' (Chambers and Burnham, 1975: 14). It was also a period that saw the nationalization of American problems and the incorporation of vast numbers of immigrants into the nation's politics, parties,

and democratic value structures. In these regards, it was a dynamic period of expansion and economic development for the country, one the party system both adapted itself to and encouraged.

The institutional developments did see the advent of the urban boss and the political machines. They also saw a level of corruption in all phases and all forms of government activities not experienced before or since.

The period was characterized by a one-party Republican dominance outside the South, and by competitive two-party elections nationwide with the Republicans normally victorious. The presidential election of 1876 (Hayes–Tilden), decided by the Congress, ended efforts (until the 1950s and 1960s) to integrate the races in the South and established the primacy of Democrats in the region. It would turn out to be a mixed blessing in that, while critical to the Democratic Party's success in national elections, this rise of Southern Democrats added a conservative and often racist component to what was the nation's more liberal party.

The election of 1896 (McKinley–Bryan) pitted a populist (Bryan) against a conservative, expansionist, and pro-corporate interest Republican. The Republican Party won overwhelmingly and cemented its position as the nation's dominant party up to the New Deal and the candidacy of Franklin Delano Roosevelt. The Republican control of the presidency after 1896 was broken by Woodrow Wilson's two terms (1912–20), brought on by a split among Republicans (between Teddy's Roosevelt's Bull Moose party and the Republican Party 'regulars' as represented by incumbent William Howard Taft).

The *fourth stage* of party development was the New Deal era symbolized by Franklin D. Roosevelt's victory in 1932 and to a large extent a product of the Great Depression. The New Deal party system was built on a class division, the less well-off voting Democrat, the better-off economically voting Republican. This division had been present throughout American political history, but the New Deal gave it a voice and meaning previously not apparent.

Among the consequences were the creation of the social welfare state, the regulation in the public interest of financial and corporate activities, and an expansion of the federal government and its powers. The New Deal permanently established Washington as the centerpiece of American politics.

The *fifth stage* of political development is basically the post-New Deal era with the full incorporation of African-Americans into politics and American society, and an end to the expansion of the welfare state. It led to a Republican ascendancy from 1968 on (broken by the presidencies of two southern centrist Democrats, Jimmy Carter (1977–1981) and Bill Clinton (1993–2001).

Dominant in this stage of development, beginning with the Nixon presidency and developed most determinedly in the Ronald Reagan administration and pursued by the presidency of George W. Bush (2001–09), has been an effort to curtail social programs and spending, revise the tax code to redistribute wealth upwards (a contrast with the policies of the New Deal era), run budgetary deficits of historic proportions, a greater militarization, and, in the second Bush's term in office, the necessity of dealing with global terrorism.

The new era has seen a weakening of party bonds, a seismic increase in the cost of politics, a polarization of the electorate, the growth of an independent vote, a rise in the importance of issue voting, and candidate-centered (as against party-centered) campaigns. The political party in this era remains a symbolic attachment for most Americans but its actual influence over voters and office-holders has declined:

> the modern mass party retained a virtual monopoly over one key component – access to office for ambitious politicians – and with that political careers remained party centered. It was this virtual monopoly that disappeared in the critical era of the 1960s, and with its disappearance, the modern mass party also disappeared as an institutional form. It was a casualty of social, political, and technological changes and its own weakening institutions; but it was above all the loss of its virtual monopoly control over campaigns as candidates were able to develop an alternative to the party-centered campaign – the candidate-centered campaign organization – that made the modern mass party collapse … With that the century and a half of party-centered elections ended and the contemporary era of candidate-centered elections began. (Aldrich, 1995: 269)

The contemporary era has seen a refocusing of party efforts and a decrease in the party's powers to influence elections, manage and finance campaigns, and choose through nomination processes its preferred candidates. The trade-off has been an increased role in party decision-making by the party's base and a freedom to organize campaigns and seek elective office by respective candidates. Such changes

in the political environment have not been universally acclaimed. They may be inevitable and unquestionably establish more demanding barriers for the parties to surmount.

CONCLUSION

The party system was created out of necessity. Its development mirrors the expansion and increasing democratization of the nation. It has never been a welcome addition to American politics, although the services it provides a democratic society are invaluable. The system began in the efforts of the 1790s to mobilize support for the competing conceptions of government and to answer the policy demands of opposing constituencies. The two parties' coalitions and policy agendas when in office continue to respond to the same dynamics.

The parties of the contemporary era reflect their births and the pressure for representation and national development within a society in constant change. The weakening of party ties and institutional structure in the modern period introduces a new period of adaptive and political stress to institutions that have served the nation well.

REFERENCES

Aldrich, John R. (1995) *Why Parties?* Chicago: University of Chicago Press.

Campbell, Angus, Converse, Phillip E., Miller, Warren E. and Stokes, Donald E. (1960) *The American Voter*. New York: John Wiley and Sons.

Chambers, William Nesbit (1963) *Political Parties in a New Nation: The American Experience 1776–1809*. New York: Oxford University Press.

Chambers, William Nesbit and Burnham, Walter Dean (eds) (1975) *The American Party Systems: Stages of Political Development*. New York: Oxford University Press.

Ford, Henry Jones (1967) *The Rise and Growth of American Politics: A Sketch of Constitutional Development*. New York: De Capo Press.

Hofstadter, Richard (1969) *The Idea of a Party System*. Berkeley: University of California Press.

Key, V.O., Jr. (1964) *Politics, Parties and Pressure Groups*. New York: Cromwell.

Keyssar, Alexander (2000) *The Right to Vote: The Contested History of Democracy in the United States*. New York: Basic Books.

Ladd Jr., Everett Carll (1970) *American Political Parties: Social Change and Political Response.* New York: W.W. Norton.

Madison, James (1961) 'The Federalist No. 10' in Alexander Hamilton, James Madison, and John Jay, *The Federalist Papers*, Clinton Rossiter (ed.). New York: New American Library.

McCulloch, David (2001) *John Adams*. New York: Touchstone.

Miller, Warren E. (1988) *Without Consent: Mass-Party Linkages in Presidential Politics.* Lexington, KY: University of Kentucky Press.

Miller, Warren E. and Jennings, M. Kent (1986) *Parties in Transition: A Longitudinal Study of Party Elites and Party Supporters*. New York: Russell Sage Foundation.

Miller, Warren E. and Shanks, J. Merrill (1996) *The New American Voter*. Cambridge, MA: Harvard University Press.

Washington, George (1896) 'Farwell address', in James D. Richardson (ed.), *A Compilation of the Messages and Papers of the Presidents 1789–1897*, Vol. 1. Washington, DC: Government Printing Office, pp. 213–24.

White, John Kenneth and Shea, Daniel M. (2000) *New Party Politics: From Jefferson and Hamilton to the Information Age*. Boston: Bedford/St. Martin's.

4

PARTY IN DEMOCRATIC THEORY

Richard S. Katz

Notwithstanding that the democracy of Athens clearly predated the invention of political parties in the modern sense of formal organizations that promote candidates for office under a common identifying label, and notwithstanding the persistence of a few small democracies in which parties have not taken root (Anckar and Anckar, 2000) and the somewhat more common phenomenon of non-partisan local governments within systems that have parties at the national level, it is widely accepted 'that the political parties created democracy and that modern democracy is unthinkable save in terms of the parties' (Schattschneider, 1942: 1). Behind this apparent consensus, however, there is a wide range of views about what democracy means, and correspondingly about the proper nature and functions of political parties and party systems in a democracy.

Despite the great divergence of views, however, they can be organized around a relatively short list of interrelated questions. Three clusters of these questions bear directly on the definition of democracy:

1. Is democracy primarily about the discovery and implementation of the 'popular will', or is it primarily about popular imposition and enforcement of limits on government power? If democracy is about the implementation of the 'popular will', how is that defined and identified? And if democracy is about the limitation of government, can this be reconciled with majority rule, or does it require that minority groups that might be victimized by an arbitrary majority be able to impose a veto?

2. Is democracy primarily about outcomes or is it primarily about process, and if democracy is primarily about outcomes, is the meaning of 'outcomes' restricted to choices of policy or personnel, or does it extend to consequences for the moral or psychological development of citizens?

3. Is democracy to be understood as a macro or a micro phenomenon – as Sartori (1965: 124) might ask, is 'democracy on a large scale … the sum of many little democracies'? Sartori's answer was no.).

Others bear more directly on the nature of parties or party systems:

4. Are parties properly considered as autonomous actors in the political process among which voters are called upon to choose or are they channels through which citizens themselves act politically?

5. Ought parties to be distinctive and exclusive with regard to their policies and support bases, or ought they to be convergent and overlapping?

PARTIES IN POPULAR SOVEREIGNTY THEORIES OF DEMOCRACY

The simplest, and – at least through the 1970s – the dominant normative and (except with regard to the United States) empirical answers to these questions in Anglo-American political science begin with the 'responsible two-party government' model (Ranney, 1962; American Political Science Association Committee on Political Parties, 1950; with regard to party government more generally, see Rose, 1974; Castles and Wildenmann, 1986; Katz, 1987). In its essence similar to Lijphart's (1999) model of majoritarian democracy, which focuses heavily on political parties, but also to Riker's (1982) model of populism in which parties are at most implicit, this model identifies democracy with the majority choice between two distinctive alternatives. These alternatives are embodied in political parties of which one, because there are exactly two, must win a majority at any election. That party then assumes control over the government until the next election, and because that control is undivided, the governing party can be held unequivocally responsible for its stewardship at the next election. Clearly this collective responsibility is contingent upon the cohesion of the party in power – and by extension to prospective voting, upon the cohesion of the opposition party as well.

Beyond this, however, the cohesion of the responsible two-party government model itself breaks down along a number of dimensions. The first concerns the basis of party cohesion. Is it cohesive support for a particular leader or team of leaders as in Beer's model of Tory democracy (1982: 91–8), or for a particular line of policy, as in his model of Socialist democracy (1982: 79–86)? Alternatively, is electoral politics about finding the popular will by allowing the people to put 'predominant political control in the possession of those who are by descent, by character, by education, and by experience best fitted to exercise it' (Hearnshaw, 1933: 293–4) in a society where social classes are hierarchically ordered but not divided by fundamental interest (Tory democracy), or is electoral politics a peaceful alternative to warfare between classes whose interests are fundamentally opposed (Socialist democracy)?

Beer describes these models as 'collectivist', but particularly the Socialist (policy-oriented) model has individualist equivalents in what I have described as binary and Downsian models of popular sovereignty (Katz, 1997). In the first, issues are assumed to form two clusters – the generalization of Duverger's (1959: 215) claim 'that political choice usually takes the form of a choice between two alternatives' – so that the two parties, each representing one of these clusters, take distinctly different policy stands. In the second, issue positions are assumed to be the equivalent of points on a policy line, with the parties remaining cohesive with respect to policy but tending to converge on the first preference of the median voter. The Downsian model of democracy also

differs from binary democracy (and indeed from all of the other popular sovereignty models) in its assumptions (in the case of Downsian democracy explicit; in the cases of the other models implicit) concerning the relationship between the goals of policy-seeking and office-seeking (Strøm, 1990). In the Downsian model, parties formulate policy proposals in order to win elections; in the other models, parties try to win elections (seek office) in order to be able to formulate public policy.

The second dimension concerns the social basis of parties, in particular whether party is understood to be the political arm of a coherent social group or class in a fundamentally segmented society (e.g., the party of the working class or of farmers or of the religious) or alternatively as an alliance or representative of citizens who share common, but potentially mutable, views on issues. The former, which corresponds to the 'i' (ideological oppositions) end of the functional dimension developed by Lipset and Rokkan (1967: 10) from Parsons' (1959) scheme of functional subsystems in society, is associated with the mass party of integration, and a political strategy of mobilization and encapsulation; the latter corresponds to the 'a' (interest-specific oppositions) end of the dimension, and to the catch-all (Kirchheimer, 1966), or electoral-professional (Panebianco, 1988: 262–7) models of party, and to a strategy of compromise and conversion.

The third, and related, dimension concerns what Ranney (1962: 156) described as 'the little civil war about "internal democracy"' On one side, early 20th-century scholars like Frank Goodnow (1900), the mid-20th century Committee on Political Parties of the American Political Science Association, advocates of the 'Socialist democracy' model of party government, and the parties of the 'new left' (although, as small parties, not advocates of the two-party model) see internal democracy as necessary for various combinations of three reasons. Particularly from the perspective of 'Socialist democracy,' internal party democracy is essential in order for the party to be able to speak as the authentic voice of the social segment it represents, and this in turn both legitimizes the dominance of the party on the ground over the party in public office (Katz and Mair, 1993) and privileges the party manifesto over the individual judgement or consciences of elected officials. Particularly from the perspective of the new left, internal democracy allows ordinary party members to become actively involved as participants in policy-making for the party, and thus in true self-governance as citizens (see below). Finally, all advocates of internal party democracy see it as essential as a way to hold party leaders accountable, or, in the terms of principal-agent models, internal democracy is seen as a way of enforcing the control of party members as the principals over both party officials and public officials elected under the party's banner as their agents.

On the other side, the principal argument is that internal democracy is incompatible with external cohesion (Ford, 1900, 1909; Downs, 1957: 25), or simply that democracy is about what happens between parties, not within them (Schattschneider, 1942). Moreover, if one assumes that the Downsian assumptions that lead to the expectation of party convergence on the first preference of the median voter would be translated to intraparty politics as well, then even if the parties could each present a coherent face to the electorate the result of intraparty democracy would be to fix each of the parties at the median of its own supporters, obviating the virtues of two-party competition. In principal-agent terms, the complaint is that public officials should be the agents of the electorate as a whole, and that the conflict of interest entailed in expecting them also to be the agents of their party membership organizations will allow, or even force, them to shirk this primary responsibility. Often in the American case this is supplemented by the claim that the entire enterprise – which in the absence of true membership organizations generally equates the party's membership with its electoral supporters or at least its registrants or primary election voters (e.g., V.O. Key's (1964: 163–5) category of 'the party in the electorate') – is fundamentally misguided: parties, in this view, are alliances of leaders between which voters choose, and not organizations of the citizens themselves (Schattschneider, 1942: 59).

The assumptions that there is a common interest that is identifiable by an elite who will be recognized by ordinary voters (Tory democracy), or that there are only two cohesive social groups competing for political power (Socialist democracy[1]), or that even if there are two sides to every issue, they are the same two sides across all issues (binary democracy), or that an entire program of policy proposals can be reduced to a single point on a single dimension (Downsian democracy), each in its own way justifies a two-party system as both adequate and, given the presumed importance of having a stable majority outcome, desirable. Each is, however, also highly questionable.

Given its privileging of 'strong and stable government first' (Amery, 1947: 19), there really is no Tory-like alternative to two-party government, and hence no way of dealing with the implausibility of its underlying assumptions about the nature of society and of the common interest or popular will. Each of the other models, however, can be adapted to a multi-party version that does not depend on such highly restrictive premises.

The easiest to adapt institutionally is Socialist democracy; if one replaces the Marxian assumption that there is an all-subsuming division between the proletarian and bourgeois classes with a more general cleavage-based view of society, then the Socialist prescription of two cohesive parties can be generalized to a prescription of a one-to-one correspondence between fundamental social segments and integrative parties. The problem is to get from this multi-party system of group representation to a decision process that can be assumed to result in the popular will, particularly in light of the well-known 'paradox of voting' (Brams, 1976; Condorcet, 1975 [1785]; Arrow, 1963).

The same problem arises with individualist theories of popular sovereignty as soon as the binary or unidimensional assumptions are violated. One of the classic statements of the problem in the first case comes from Moisei Ostrogorski's (1902: II, 618–19) study of late 19th-century politics in the United States:

> what was pompously called the national verdict was, as a rule, tainted with ambiguity and uncertainty … after 'the voice of the country had spoken', people did not know exactly what it had said; … for, however paramount a particular question may have been in the public mind, considerations foreign to it constantly entered into the 'popular verdict'.

The problem in the second case has been extensively explored in the rational choice literature; simply, if preferences are not single-peaked (i.e., if there is not a single underlying dimension), then there is no stable equilibrium or Condorcet choice except under unbelievably restrictive conditions (Plott, 1967; for a full discussion of this literature in empirical as well as theoretical terms, see the chapter by Budge in this volume).

Ostrogorski's solution was to replace permanent and all-encompassing parties with what would amount to a series of two-party systems (what he called 'single issue parties' (1902: II, 658–63), each of which would address one issue, resolve it, and then be replaced by a new pair of parties taking the two sides of a new issue.[2] If issues are understood as continua rather than dichotomies, then one might imagine the same idea applied one dimension at a time instead of

Table 4.1   *Summary of popular sovereignty theories of democracy and competitive party systems*

Theory of democracy	Ideal number of parties	Should the parties be durable over time and comprehensive with respect to issues?	Should parties be primarily office-seeking or policy-seeking?	Should party coalitions cut across social divisions?
Binary	2	yes	policy	yes
Downsian	2	yes	office	yes
Ostrogorskian	2 (at any one time)	no	policy	yes
Legislative	As many as there are distinct combinations of policy preferences	yes	policy	yes
Tory	2	yes	policy	yes
Socialist	2	yes	policy	no

one issue at a time. Aside from the question of whether problems can be solved one-at-a-time and once-and-for-all, the obvious danger here is that if a succession of transient amateur administrations does not lead to chaos, it will lead to the dominance of the administrative officials as the sole possessors of the networks and expertise required for the government of a complex state (Ranney, 1962: 129).

The alternative is a multi-party system in which the parties are identified with unique combinations of policy positions rather than with social categories, and the problem of arriving at particular decisions on particular questions is transferred from the electoral arena to the legislature, leading to a model of democracy that might be called 'legislative popular sovereignty'. This opens the possibility of coalition formation through the trading of votes, and if not the likelihood of a Condorcet outcome, then at least the plausible argument that parties, as the representatives of groups of people who are in fundamental agreement across issues, and provided that their representation in the legislature is proportional to the size of those groups among the citizens, will reach the same outcome that the citizens would have reached themselves had direct democracy been possible.[3]

The implications of each of these six models of popular sovereignty democracy for the proper nature of political parties are summarized in Table 4.1.

PARTIES IN LIBERAL THEORIES OF DEMOCRACY

The six models of democracy suggested in the previous section all identify democracy with

the discovery and implementation of the popular will. The major alternative family of democratic theories is concerned primarily with the liberal value of popular self-protection. This shift in value priorities implies a shift in attitude toward the relationship between government and citizens as well: for the popular sovereignty theories, government is a tool of the people, and therefore in a sense a part of them, whereas for the liberal theories the government is a potential danger to the people, and therefore necessarily separate. In principal-agent terms, while many, but by no means all, popular sovereignty theories recognize agency slack (with the individual parties or office-holders as the agents) as a potential problem, for liberal theories agency slack (with the government as the agent) is one of the two principal problems that must be addressed in institutionalizing democratic government.

All democratic theories must be concerned with the problem of the unchecked rule of a minority over the majority. That is, of course, the reason for the concern with majority formation in popular sovereignty theories. Liberal theories also rely on popular elections to control this danger. But where the converse problem of the unchecked rule of a minority *by* the majority is at most of secondary concern for popular sovereignty theories (which define democracy as the implementation of the will of the majority), it is the other principal problem for liberal democratic theories.[4]

That said, liberal theories of democracy can be classified into four types, defined by the intersection of their assumptions about the nature of conflicting interests in society and therefore about the way in which what might be called majority tyranny can be avoided, on the one hand, and their assumptions about the relative commitments to liberal values of elites and of ordinary citizens, and therefore about the centrality of agency slack, on the other.[5] As with the popular sovereignty theories, each set of assumptions has implications concerning the proper nature and role of political parties and party systems.

The first pair of liberal theories may be identified as 'pluralist'. The defining assumption is that the cleavages among interests are fluid and cross-cutting, rather than fixed and mutually reinforcing. As a result, institutions – including political parties – can be structured so as to make it difficult for any enduring majority to form while at the same time moderating the temptation of any majority of the moment to abuse its position.

Like the responsible two-party government models, these theories generally call for a two-party system, albeit primarily because this will allow the majority to evict a government – what Pinto-Duschinsky (1997, 1999) has called 'removal van democracy' – rather than to ensure either stable government or popular endorsement of the policies to be pursued by government. They differ most centrally from the responsible two-parties models, and indeed in the American debate over responsible two-party government these pluralist liberal models represent the other side of the debate, in that they call for parties that are not cohesive with regard to policy, and especially not cohesive with regard to their social basis. Rather, the claim is that if each party depends at least in part on the support of groups that also support the other party, then neither party will be able to participate in the unreasonable exploitation of any group without itself suffering significant loss of support from that group.

This emphasis on weak and incoherent parties, coupled with confidence in the ability of ordinary voters armed simply with the right of frequent elections to prevent leaders from intruding on their rights, is particularly evident in pre-20th-century versions of majoritarian or pluralist liberal theory. Prominent examples include Jeremy Bentham's call for annual elections to allow voters to '[divest] of their power all unfit representatives, before they had time to produce any lasting mischief' (1962: III, 561) coupled with his hostility to political organizations, as exemplified by the weak cohesion of his own Radical Party, or the antipathy for political parties expressed in *The Federalist* coupled with the call for biennial elections of the House of Representatives.

Particularly after the collapse of democratic governments in Europe in the inter-war years, and in response to survey research that showed

elites to be more committed to liberal values than were ordinary citizens, the focus shifted to place greater emphasis on the self-restraint of leaders, on the sociological preconditions of cross-cutting cleavages and dispersed and variegated access to politically relevant resources, and on regular competition among elites. Prominent examples of theorists of this genre include Schumpeter (1962), Sartori (1965), and Dahl (1956, 1966, 1971) – for a critique, see Bachrach (1967). As in the Downsian model of popular sovereignty, parties are understood to be teams of leaders rather than organizations of citizens, but unlike the Downsian assumption of prospective policy-oriented competition, the pluralist liberal ideal is retrospective result-oriented judgement by voters whose vocabulary is necessarily limited to 'yes' or 'no' (Schattschneider, 1942: 52). Moreover, because ordinary citizens are not only illiberal but also incompetent – 'the typical citizen drops down to a lower level of mental performance as soon as he enters the political field' (Schumpeter, 1962: 262) – leaders ought not to be restrained (e.g., by intraparty democracy) from presenting the people with 'results they never thought of and would not have approved of in advance' (Schumpeter, 1962: 278).

If cross-cutting cleavages are a prerequisite for stable liberal democracy, as the pluralists argue, then such a regime ought not to exist in countries where cleavages are deep and mutually reinforcing. Yet, as Lijphart (1968) observed, the Netherlands (divided by religion), Belgium (divided by language), and Switzerland (divided by both religion and language) appeared to defy this rule. In response, he advanced the model of consociational democracy, based on his observation of democracy in the Netherlands. In many respects, this was a modern version of Calhoun's (1943) model of 'concurrent majorities', taking account of the fact that the fundamental social segments might not be coterminous with the geographic subdivisions of a federal state, and, as with the more recent versions of pluralist liberal theory, assuming that greater elite autonomy is both necessary and desirable. Together, they exemplify theories that can be identified as 'veto-group liberalism'.

As the name implies, these theories solve the problem of majority exploitation by abandoning the majority principle altogether, and replacing it with a system of mutual vetoes. In Calhoun's version of this model, the central government would be relatively limited in scope, and the vetoes would be exercised by

Table 4.2 *Summary of liberal theories of democracy and competitive party systems*

Theory of democracy	Ideal number of parties	Cohesiveness of parties	Should party coalitions cut across social divisions?	What level of constraints should the party impose on its leaders?
Benthamite or Madisonian	2	low	yes	strong
Schumpeterian or polyarchal	2	low	yes	weak
Concurrent majorities	At least one for each social segment	high	no	strong
Consociational	One for each social segment	high	no	weak

the subnational governments. There is nothing directly said about the nature of the political parties operating within each subnational system, although given the tenor of his argument, it would appear that subnational governments are meant to operate under some version of responsible party government. One may infer, however, from Calhoun's (1943: 34) disdain for separation of powers as an adequate guarantor against the majority faction, that coherent national parties are incompatible with his vision of democracy.

The basic claim of the consociational model is that 'overarching cooperation at the elite level can be a substitute for crosscutting affiliations at the mass level' (Lijphart, 1968: 200). It is a government by elite cartel[6] characterized by four conditions: 'government by a grand coalition of the political leaders of all significant segments of a plural society'; operation of a system of mutual vetoes by the leaders of all significant segments of society; proportionality as the standard for allocation of all or most political 'goods'; and a high degree of internal autonomy for each group (Lijphart, 1968: 25). This system is supported by an electoral system of closed-list proportional representation with a single national district, all of which implies cohesive national political parties dominated by their leaders. Further, while the implication of Calhoun's argument is that there would be a separate party system within each of the significant social segments (subnational units), in the ideal consociational system, there would be a one-to-one correspondence between parties and social groupings.[7] Finally, in contrast to the pluralist vision of continuous, if moderated, interparty conflict between elections, the veto group liberal model assumes that electoral conflict will be replaced by inter-elite cooperation that is made

necessary precisely by the mutual hostility of the social groupings' members. This means that the parties' leaders, whether initially chosen 'democratically' or not, must have the autonomy to override the unwillingness of their followers to compromise.

Table 4.2 summarizes the prescriptions for political parties of these liberal models of democracy.

CONSENSUS DEMOCRACY

As indicated above, the responsible two-party government model corresponds quite closely to Lijphart's model of majoritarian democracy. While the alternative, consensus democracy, has much in common with consociational democracy, from which it might be understood to be derived, it is also different in three important respects that bear on the role of political parties in democracy.

Consociational democracy explicitly rests on a system of mutual vetoes. In consensus democracy, the emphasis is instead on negotiation, and indeed Lijphart (1999: 2) indicates that Kaiser's (1997: 434) term 'negotiation democracy' might be adopted as a synonym. With regard to the majority principle, which veto group liberalism overtly rejects as inadequate, consensus democracy takes a more ambiguous position. While oversized majorities clearly are preferred to minimum winning coalitions, this is still less than demanding a grand coalition. On the other side, minority governments are also preferred to minimum winning coalitions, because this implies constantly shifting majorities supporting particular issues in place of one stable majority. Nonetheless, the ultimate decision *rule* remains the majority principle. At the same time, however, the simple distinction between 'the majority', which can be held accountable for all of the government's decisions, and 'the minority', which might replace it if enough voters change their preferences, is obscured.

The second respect in which consensus democracy differs from consociational democracy concerns the basis of the divisions among parties. In the consociational model, parties clearly are reflections of deep social cleavages. While the consensus model recognizes sociological dimensions of party competition, the very use of the dimensional metaphor, not to mention consideration of both a socioeconomic and a post-materialist dimension, implies a continuous multi-dimensional policy space in which parties choose positions, rather than a categoric 'menu' of parties directly corresponding to social structure.

The third difference concerns what I have called the 'partyness of government' (Katz, 1986: 40–6). While one might argue about which 'aspect' of a segment's identity (party, church, press, union) is dominant in any particular arena, the fundamental point for the consociational model is that the leadership cadre of each segment forms a kind of 'interlocking directorate' (Lijphart, 1968: 59–70), so that party is intimately connected to the full range of governmental activity, and indeed the full range of political activity more widely understood. Among the defining characteristics of consensus democracy, on the other hand, is the explicit exclusion of party from the judiciary and central bank coupled with limitation of party influence through strong corporatist institutions (which are understood to be competitors for party dominance), territorial division of power, and presidentialism.

The conjunction of these three differences implies a model that is different both from popular sovereignty, which is about finding the popular will, and from liberalism, which is about the containment of conflict. Instead, consensus democracy appears to be about equitable management in the pursuit of objectives that have been defined *a priori* to be good. One of these 'goods' is demographic representativeness. Having cut party free from social cleavage, and in any event including gender – which has never been taken to define a social cleavage analogous to race or language group, or economic sector – among the traits that ought to be mirrored in a representative body, one must presume that parties individually are to be demographically representative, either of the population as a whole or of their individual

but heterogeneous electorates. Another 'good' is economic prudence; presumably parties should both advocate economically prudent policies and advance leaders who will be competent in their pursuit. In other words, consensus democracy appears to limit not only the role of parties in societal governance, but also the scope for politics within the parties. Indeed, in its tendency to judge outcomes by technocratic standards, one might ask whether it also limits the scope for citizens to engage in politics, and in this sense ask whether it is an alternative form of democracy, or rather a lesser democracy.[8]

DEMOCRACY AS A WAY OF LIFE

Both popular sovereignty and liberal theories define democracy in terms of what the government does (or does not do). While they often make prescriptions concerning process, these are justified by their impact on, or necessity for, the valued policy outputs. Other theories, however, identify democracy with its impact on those who participate in it, which they attribute to the process itself. In contrast to Schumpeter's (1962: 242) definition of democracy as a 'type of institutional arrangement for arriving at political – legislative and administrative – decisions', these theories in their fullest form see democracy as a way of life. As John Dewey (1927: 143) put it, 'The idea of democracy is a wider and fuller idea than can be exemplified in the state even at its best. To be realized it must affect all modes of human association, the family, the school, industry, religion.'

Even if attention is limited to the narrowly political sphere, in which political parties may be expected to be relevant, these theories are concerned with the development of citizens in the sense of being efficacious people who have fully developed their individual capacities and have achieved self-mastery (Bachrach, 1967: 4; Mill, 1962: 49–52; Lane, 1962: 161 (quoting Margaret Mead)) and of understanding themselves to be members of a community who can and do make civil judgements and evaluate goods in public terms (Mill, 1962: 71–3; Barber, 1984: 158), rather than merely being citizens in the juridical sense. Clearly simply going into a voting booth every few years and making a private choice (both in the sense of being motivated by private passions and in the sense of neither being revealed nor justified in public) among parties or candidates will be inadequate to further these objectives.[9] But what is the role of parties in this process of democratic development?

One answer has already been indicated with regard to the attitudes of new left parties to

mandators, or the delegates over the delegators. Who says organization says oligarchy'. The precise implication for the relationship between parties and democracy is open to debate. Most commonly, the iron law is taken to imply that large-scale democracy is impossible, and that if political parties are essential

institutions of large-scale democracy, then they are part of the problem. If democracy is a state to be achieved, then this reading clearly is correct. If, however, democracy is a state to be approached to a greater or lesser degree, then Michels himself suggests an alternative interpretation. Within only a few pages of the iron law itself, Michels (1962: 366, 369) observes that only the 'blind and fanatical' could fail 'to see that the democratic current daily makes undeniable advance'. Moreover, '[s]ometimes … the democratic principle carries with it, if not a cure, at least a palliative, for the disease of oligarchy'. A democratic movement (or society), 'in virtue of the theoretical postulates it proclaims, is apt to bring into existence (in opposition to the will of the leaders) a certain number of free spirits who … desire to revise the base upon which authority is established'. If all this is true, then although party as organization may contribute to the problem, party as the carrier of the democratic ideology may be a palliative.

In the American context, Herbert Croly (1909, 1914) also argued that political parties, whatever their virtues in the original transition from colonial rule, were an impediment to democracy. The reason was twofold. On one hand, parties imply 'a separation of actual political power from official political responsibility … The leader or leaders of the [electoral] machine are the rulers of the community, even though they occupy no offices and cannot be held in any way publicly responsible' (Croly, 1909: 125). On the other hand, parties demand of citizens 'that they think and act in politics not under the influence of their natural class or personal convictions, but according to the necessities of an artificial partisan classification' (Croly, 1914: 341). Democracy, however, requires direct rather than mediated public decision: initiative, referendum, and recall, rather than periodic partisan election (Croly, 1914: 324). It also requires citizens to think and act as members of a community, habits which party, precisely because it is 'part', destroys. His conclusion was that democracy was, at least when he was writing, impossible at the national level in the United States, where representative government, which could never be truly democratic in part because it requires parties, would have to do. At the state level, however, institutions could be devised that would allow what he identified as direct democracy.[11] Democracy could thus be advanced by shifting the locus of power to smaller units, which would make parties unnecessary.

This prescription, that power be shifted to more local units, is a recurring theme among democratic theorists who are more concerned with the impact of democracy on the human development of citizens than with the policy outputs of government (Pateman, 1970; Barber, 1984; Mansbridge, 1980). A second recurring theme is the importance of applying the democratic virtues of equality and collective self-rule beyond the narrowly governmental, in particular to include workplace democracy. What is conspicuous by its marginality, and often by its complete absence, is any mention of political parties.

PARTIES AND REPRESENTATION

No discussion of contemporary democracy can ignore the fact that modern democracy necessarily is representative democracy. And since parties are intimately involved in the process of representation, this means that consideration of the place of parties in democratic theory must address the place of parties in the theory of representation.

Analysis of representation involves three questions: Who are the represented? Who is the representative? What is it that the representative does in representing the represented?

Beginning with the last of these questions, the literature suggests five basic answers. The first mode of representation is the descriptive mirroring of demographic characteristics. With the second mode of representation, it is the distribution of opinions rather than of personal characteristics that is to be mirrored. With these two modes, representation means *standing for* the represented. The other three modes understand representation as *acting for* the represented. The third and fourth modes relate to the classic distinction between the representative as delegate and the representative as trustee (see, for example, Wahlke *et al.*, 1962). The delegate serves as the direct agent of his or her constituents, doing what the represented want him or her to do, serving as a conduit for their opinions, following their direct instructions. The trustee, on the other hand, acts for the represented by using his or her own judgement to advance their interests, but not necessarily in accordance with their currently expressed opinions. The fifth mode of representation is to act for the represented in the role of ombudsman, or more generally of provider of constituency service.

While party is implicated as the representative in all five of these modes of representation, whether it is the individual but partisan official, the constituency party, the national party, or the parliament as a whole (with the individual parties contributing to its composition) that should be understood as the primary representative varies from one mode of representation to another, and among alternative conceptions of democracy. Similarly, whether the represented should be understood primarily as the citizenry as a whole, the citizens of particular areas or groups, the citizens who are voters of the party (again either as a whole or in particular areas or groups), the individual citizens, or indeed the party membership organization itself also varies depending on the particular sense of representation and the general conception of democracy being considered.

In its original implications, the distinction between trustee and delegate roles refers not just to the decision process underlying the representative's vote (do what one's constituents want or do what they would want if they were as wise as the representative), but to the nature of the democratic process as well. The delegate orientation only makes sense if one regards democracy primarily to be about the aggregation of interests or opinions; since the citizens cannot all be present to express their views or defend their interests, they 'hire' a representative to speak for them. If, however, democracy is about deliberation, then one naturally asks, as Edmund Burke asked in his 1774 address to the electors of Bristol, 'what sort of reason is that, in which the determination precedes the discussion; in which one set of men deliberate, and another decide; and where those who form the conclusion are perhaps three hundred miles distant from those who hear the arguments?' and thus arrives at a trusteeship model of representation. Parties contribute to this kind of representation as the members of parliament, but it is a form of representation in which the real representative is the parliament as a whole representing the people as a whole. This is very much an 18th-century view of representation based on an assumption of nascent and weak parties, but it is also reflected in the model of consensus democracy, with its emphasis on parliamentary (as opposed to cabinet) power, and Tory democracy, with its emphasis on independent leadership pursuing a singular national interest.

The conjunction of the idea of parliament as the representative and the idea that deliberation is essential to democracy also underlies many of the claims for representation in the sense of mirroring. The claim that the demographic characteristics of the citizens should be mirrored by the representatives has three primary justifications: that inclusion of minority or otherwise disadvantaged groups signifies their status as full citizens; that people in different social positions bring different experiences to bear on deliberations; and that differing groups have interests that are sufficiently at variance that a member of one group cannot represent the interests of another (see Kymlicka, 1993: 67, and the works cited there). The claim for the mirroring of opinions, on the other hand, has two justifications. The first is instrumental, and has already been elaborated in the discussion of legislative democracy: since there are too many possible combinations of policies across diverse issues for any one combination to receive majority support in the electorate in competition with all of the others, and since it is impossible to anticipate all of the questions that might arise between elections, parliament can only be expected to make the decisions that the people would have made themselves if it reflects the full diversity of their views. While this is true even if decision-making is simply the serial taking of votes on isolated issues, it is especially true if one takes into account alternative possibilities for vote trading or compromise and accommodation, both of which could be understood as equivalent to deliberation. The other justification for the mirroring of opinions is expressive: those who hold unpopular views deserve to have those views expressed in parliament, regardless of outcome, and moreover are more likely peacefully to accept their defeat if they have, at least, had their say.

The equality of citizens is a vital value to any theory of democracy. To say that demographic mirroring is important for its symbolic attestation of equality, however, is to imply that it is representation that would not happen otherwise. It thus suggests that parties should take affirmative steps, such as the implementation of ethnic or gender quotas both for positions within their own organizations and in the selection of candidates for public office. On the other hand, precisely because this form of representation is symbolic, it has also been associated with what might be called 'sham democracies'; the high demographic representativeness of the parliaments of Soviet bloc countries was indicative of the powerlessness of those bodies – and correspondingly of the impotence of political parties as well.

The idea of demographic mirroring, or at least the direct representation of members of traditionally disadvantaged groups, has recently been recast in terms of a 'politics of presence' (Phillips, 1995). While retaining some of the symbolic argument (it is harder to treat a group unfairly when some of its members are in the room), this is supplemented by the claim that the lived experience of members of these groups gives them a perspective that cannot be represented adequately by a mere sympathizer. This has two important implications for parties and representation. First, it clearly implies a deliberative assembly and therefore a trusteeship model of representation. Second, if parties are to be significant at all, then it calls for descriptive representation not only in parliament as a whole, but within each party, and within the executive, as well. (See the chapter by Paul Lewis in this volume.)

Obviously representation as mirroring can only be effected by a collective representative, but should the individual parties be representative (either of their own electorates or memberships, or each representative of the population as whole), or is it only the parliament that must be representative (which would naturally result from the aggregation of individually representative parties, but might also occur even if the individual parties were unrepresentative) – or must not only the parliament but also the cabinet be demographically representative? While these questions have been raised in the literature primarily with respect to judging electoral systems, they also have implications for parties. On one hand, mirroring by the parliament as a whole may have little practical value if the true locus of deliberation and decision is the majority party caucus or the cabinet room. On the other hand, the more parties are constrained to look and think like the population as a whole, the less substantive choice is left to the voters.

The emphasis on deliberation that is implicit in representation as demographic mirroring, and indeed in representation as opinion mirroring, raises another tension in the theory of representative democracy. Are elections primarily about the choice of representatives, or are they primarily about the choice of government (Milnor, 1969)? In part, to address this question is simply to revisit the question of the appropriateness of two-party versus multiparty systems raised with regard to popular sovereignty and liberal models of democracy. In part, it revisits the question of whether the venue in which representation primarily takes place and should be assessed is the parliament as a whole (choice of representatives) or the decision-making venue of the governing party or coalition (choice of government). It also raises the question of delegation or trusteeship, since the negotiators of post-election coalition agreements cannot in any strong sense be other than trustees of the voters who supported their parties, and, indeed, even with the greater possibility of consultation during the negotiating process, must largely operate as trustees of their party organizations as well.

CONCLUSION

This overview of the question of parties in democratic theory has necessarily been incomplete. As the careful reader will have noted, it has also left a number of loose ends. Some of these are tied up (or at least tied off) in other chapters of this *Handbook,* but many are not. The careful reader also will have noted sections with few or no references to 'the literature'. Both the loose ends and the scarce references reflect the facts that although the literature of democratic theory is immense, it has developed largely without reference to the richness and complexity of empirical studies of political parties, and that although scholars of parties often make introductory reference to their centrality to modern democracy, they rarely go beyond this to consider the distinctions among varieties of normative democratic theories. When parties scholars consider varieties of democracy, they usually refer to the distinctions between presidential and parliamentary systems, or between bipolar and fragmented patterns of competition. When democratic theorists think about parties, it is generally to ask whether they need be democratic in their own organizations, or indeed whether parties are a precondition or an impediment to democracy.

Work that took seriously both the empirical study of parties and the normative complexity of democracy tended to appear in the period between about 1880 and 1920, as the transition from *régimes censitaires* to mass suffrage democracy was taking place, with the attendant transformation from cadre to mass parties, and again in the period between 1945 and 1960, in response to the problems of reestablishing democracy in Germany and Italy and attempting to establish democracy in the former colonies of the British and French empires. With the collapse of communist regimes in eastern and central Europe, it would appear that the stage is set for a third wave of analyses connecting parties and democracy.

NOTES

1. Strictly speaking, the socialist assumption is that there is one naturally or properly cohesive social group, the working class, in opposition to another group or groups, the cohesion of which is assumed only in the sense that they are the opponents of the working class.
2. In his own terms, it would be more accurate to describe Ostrogorski's prescription as anti-party, because he assumed parties must be like those he saw in Britain and the United States: permanent; 'imposing' positions over a range of unrelated issues on their supporters and office-holders; and dominated by self-interested politicians rather than public-spirited citizens.
3. This raises the question of vote trading, its efficiency or inefficiency, and its relation to the paradox of voting. For a brief summary of this literature and its implications for legislative democracy, see Katz (1997: 42–3).
4. The secondary importance of minority tyranny in liberal democratic theories follows from the ready assumption that this problem has been 'solved' by the electoral principle, coupled with relative indifference as between alternative majorities.
5. In the original version of this typology (Katz, 1997: Ch. 4), I identified six variants of liberal theory. In this chapter, I have collapsed what I there identified as 'majoritarian' theories into the 'pluralist' category.
6. Indeed, in the Dutch-language version, Lijphart (1982) identified the model as 'kartel demokratie'.
7. In the Dutch case, the secular 'pillar' represented a partial exception, with both a liberal (i.e., bourgeois) party (the Vereniging voor Vrijheid en Democratie) and a Socialist Party (the Partij van de Arbeid).
8. This latter interpretation is furthered by Lijphart's inclusion of the European Union, which is generally considered to suffer from a severe 'democratic deficit', as one of the exemplars of consensus democracy.
9. I use the word 'further' rather than 'achieve' because these theories understand democracy always to be a 'work in progress'.
10. All this ignores the possibility that far from being authentically democractic, the 'participatory' model may simply empower the most stubborn – those who are prepared to wait everyone else out at meetings.
11. Clearly, the ideal of direct democracy is the Athenian Assembly, the Swiss *Landesgemeinde*, or the New England town meeting, in which citizens meet together both to debate and to decide. A recurring point of contention is whether institutions like referendum and initiative, which involve direct popular decision, but not involvement in debate, are more or less democratic than partisan elections with their opportunities, many of which are provided by the parties themselves, for popular participation in discussion.

REFERENCES

American Political Science Association Committee on Political Parties (1950) *Toward a More Responsible Two-Party System*. New York: Rinehart.

Amery, L.S. (1947) *Thoughts on the Constitution* (Oxford: Oxford Univesity Press).

Anckar, D. and Anckar, C. (2000) 'Democracies without Parties', *Comparative Political Studies*, 33: 225–47.

Arrow, Kenneth (1963) *Social Choice and Individual Values*. New York: Wiley.

Bachrach, Peter (1967) *The Theory of Democratic Elitism: A Critique*. Boston: Little, Brown and Co.

Barber, Benjamin R. (1984) *Strong Democracy: Participatory Politics for a New Age*. Berkeley: University of California Press.

Beer, Samuel H. (1982) *Modern British Politics*. New York: W. W. Norton.

Bentham, Jeremy (1962) *The Works of Jeremy Bentham*. New York: Russell and Russell.

Brams, Steven J. (1976) *Paradoxes in Politics: An Introduction to the Nonobvious in Political Science*. New York: Free Press.

Calhoun, John C. (1943) *Disquisition on Government*. New York: Peter Smith.

Castles, Francis G. and Wildenmann, Rudolf (eds) (1986) *Visions and Realities of Party Government*. Berlin: de Gruyter.

Condorcet, M. de (1975 [1785]) *Essai sur l'Application de l'Analyse à la Probabilité des Decisions Rendues à la Pluralité des Voix*. Paris: Imprimerie Royale.

Croly, Herbert (1909) *The Promise of American Life*. New York: Macmillan.

Croly, Herbert (1914) *Progressive Democracy*. New York: Macmillan.

Dahl, Robert A. (1956) *A Preface to Democratic Theory*. Chicago: University of Chicago Press.

Dahl, Robert A. (1966) *Political Oppositions in Western Democracies*. New Haven, CT: Yale University Press.

Dahl, Robert A. (1971) *Polyarchy*. New Haven, CT: Yale University Press.

Dewey, John (1927) *The Public and Its Problems*. New York: Henry Holt.

Downs, Anthony (1957) *An Economic Theory of Democracy*. New York: Harper and Row.

Duverger, Maurice (1959) *Political Parties*. New York: John Wiley.

Ford, Henry Jones (1900) Review of Frank Goodnow's *Politics and Administration*, *Annals of the American Academy of Political and Social Science*, 15: 145–59.

Ford, Henry Jones (1909) 'The direct primary', *North American Review*, 90: 1–14.

Goodnow, Frank. (1900) *Politics and Administration*. New York: Macmillan.

Hearnshaw, F.J.C. (1933) *Conservatism in England*. London: Macmillan.

Kaiser, André (1997) 'Types of democracy: From classical to new institutionalism', *Journal of Theoretical Politics*, 9(October): 419–44.

Katz, Richard S. (1986) 'Party government: A rationalistic conception', in Francis G. Castles and Rudolf Wildenmann (eds), *Visions and Realities of Party Government*. Berlin: de Gruyter, pp. 31–71.

Katz, Richard S. (ed.) (1987) *Party Governments: European and American Experiences*. Berlin: de Gruyter.

Katz, Richard S. (1997) *Democracy and Elections*. New York: Oxford University Press.

Katz, Richard S. and Mair, Peter (1993) 'The evolution of party organizations in Europe: The three faces of party organization', *American Review of Politics*, 14: 593–618.

Key, V.O., Jr. (1964) *Politics, Parties, and Pressure Groups*. New York: Thomas Crowell.

Kirchheimer, Otto (1966) 'The transformation of West European party systems', in Joseph LaPalombara and Myron Weiner (eds), *Political Parties and Political Development*. Princeton, NJ: Princeton University Press, pp. 199–200.

Kitschelt, Herbert (1982) *The Logics of Party Formation: Ecological Politics in Belgium and West Germany*. Ithaca, NY: Cornell University Press.

Kymlicka, Will (1993) 'Group representation in Canadian politics', in F. Leslie Seidle (ed.), *Equity and Community: The Charter, Interest Advocacy and Representation*. Montreal: Institute for Research on Public Policy, pp. 61–90.

Lane, Robert (1962) *Political Ideology*. Glencoe, IL: Free Press.

Lijphart, Arend (1968) *Politics of Accommodation*. Berkeley: University of California Press.

Lijphart, Arend (1982) *Verzuiling, pacificatie en kentering in de Nederlandse politiek*. Amsterdam: J.H. de Bussy.

Lijphart, Arend (1999) *Patterns of Democracy: Government Forms and Performance in Thirty-Six Countries*. New Haven, CT: Yale University Press.

Lipset, Seymour Martin and Rokkan, Stein (1967) 'Cleavage structures, party systems, and voter alignments: An introduction', in Seymour Martin Lipset and Stein Rokkan (eds), *Party Systems and Voter Alignments: Cross-National Perspectives*. New York: Free Press.

Mansbridge, Jane J. (1980) *Beyond Adversary Democracy*. New York: Basic Books.

Michels, Robert (1962) *Political Parties: A Sociological Study of the Oligarchical Tendencies of Modern Democracy*. New York: Free Press.

Mill, John Stuart (1962) *Considerations on Representative Government*. Chicago: Henry Regnery.

Milnor, A.J. (1969) *Elections and Political Stability*. Boston: Little, Brown and Co.

Ostrogorski, Moisei (1902) *Democracy and the Organization of Political Parties*, 2 vols. New York: Macmillan.

Panebianco, Angelo (1988) *Political Parties: Organization and Power*. Cambridge: Cambridge University Press.

Parsons, Talcott (1959) 'General theory in sociology', in Robert K. Merton, Leonard Broom and Leonard S. Cottrell, Jr. (eds), *Sociology Today*. New York: Basic Books.

Pateman, Carole (1970) *Participation and Democratic Theory*. Cambridge: Cambridge University Press.

Phillips, Anne (1995) *The Politics of Presence*. Oxford: Clarendon Press.

Pinto-Duschinsky, Michael (1997) 'Britain's removal van democracy', *The Times*, September 25: 20.

Pinto-Duschinsky, Michael (1999) 'A reply to the critics', *Representation*, 36(2): 148–55.

Plott, Charles A. (1967) 'A nation of equilibrium and its possibility under majority Rule', *American Economic Review*, 57: 767–806.

Ranney, Austin (1962) *The Doctrine of Responsible Party Government: Its Origins and Present State*. Urbana: University of Illinois Press.

Riker, William H. (1988) *Liberalism against Populism*. Prospect Heights, IL: Waveland Press.

Rose, Richard (1974) *The Problem of Party Government*. London: Macmillan.

Sartori, Giovanni (1965) *Democratic Theory*. New York: Praeger.

Schattschneider, Elmer E. (1942) *Party Government*. New York: Holt, Rinehart, and Winston.

Schumpeter, Joseph (1962) *Capitalism, Socialism and Democracy*. New York: Harper and Row.

Strøm, Kaare (1990). 'A behavioral theory of competitive political Parties', *American Journal of Political Science*, 34(2): 565–98.

Wahlke, John C., Eulau, Heinz, Buchanan, William and Ferguson, LeRoy C. (1962) *The Legislative System: Explorations in Legislative Behavior*. New York: Wiley.

5

POLITICAL PARTIES AND DELIBERATIVE DEMOCRACY?

James Johnson

The study of political parties is related to the study of democratic theory in complex, ongoing ways (see Chapter 4, this volume). Over the past two decades democratic theorists have devoted considerable attention to what is called 'deliberative democracy' (Bohman, 1998; Freeman, 2000). This literature largely neglects the topic of political parties. Empirical and analytical research on political parties has reciprocated and passes over the topic of deliberation largely without comment. In this essay, then, I will not review a large body of research. That is not possible since such a literature does not exist. Instead, I first suggest that the neglect of parties by advocates of deliberation is somewhat surprising. I then identify the source of that neglect. Finally, I sketch one way that we might reconnect the study of democratic deliberation and political parties.

DEMOCRACY AND DELIBERATION

Democracy is among the institutional arrangements that people have adopted to address what can be called the 'circumstances of politics' (Waldron, 1999; Weale, 1999). For any population these circumstances are constituted by inescapable diversity across multiple, overlapping dimensions, including material interests, moral commitments, and cultural attachments. Such diversity means, in turn, that disagreement is an unavoidable condition of politics. This is, in part, because the individuals and groups who constitute some relevant population have interests, commitments, and attachments

that are not only diverse, but irreducibly so. There simply is no neutral metric that will accommodate competing demands without remainder. But the inevitability of disagreement also partly reflects the fact that, precisely as members of a relevant population, those individuals and groups are, as it were, stuck with one another. In short, their lives are highly, irrevocably interdependent. Thus, despite their diversity and the disagreement to which it gives rise, they require some means of coordinating their ongoing social and economic interaction.

At the most general level, democracy means 'rule by the people'. More specifically, democracy consists in an institutional arrangement for making binding political decisions in ways that are responsive to the views of the public. Any such arrangement will include formal or official decision-making forums, even if it additionally requires such features as a sustaining set of civil and political rights, supporting institutions (such as schools), and an extensive environment of political organizations and secondary associations. It perhaps is easiest to see where political parties fit into this definition, namely as political organizations that connect citizens to government by coordinating citizens for electoral purposes. Beyond that, however, the analytical and empirical literature on parties is divided regarding the more precise roles that parties play in democratic politics. Indeed, even the fundamental question of whether parties make government more or less responsive to the views of the electorate remains unsettled (Stokes, 1999).

Advocates of deliberation insist that political argument or debate conducted under conditions of freedom and equality is a crucial component of any democratic decision-making process. They commonly insist that, so understood, deliberation aims at the formation of political judgements or preferences. In this sense it stands in contrast to voting, which seeks solely to aggregate pre-existing preferences. Deliberation thus is best seen as part of a process of forming majorities which is a crucial aspect of democratic politics (Spitz, 1984). In this respect it would seem that advocates of democratic deliberation might find political parties a natural focus of inquiry. Unfortunately they rarely so much as mention parties.

This state of affairs is somewhat surprising. Historically, theorists such as Edmund Burke or John Stuart Mill 'who stress the role of deliberation … in politics' also 'justify the existence of parties' (Manin, 1987: 368). What is more striking is that two of the now classic essays in the contemporary literature explicitly accord political parties a central role in democratic deliberation. Cohen (1989: 31–2) insists that independent, publicly funded political parties could contribute to democratic deliberation in two ways. First, because parties provide organizational resources, they might help offset the material inequalities that render the outcomes of deliberative processes suspect. Second, because parties, unlike interest groups, need to address a broad range of issues, they could help keep the focus of political debate on matters of general concern rather than on local or issue-specific matters. Manin (1987: 356–7) insists that political parties are an important means of overcoming the necessarily 'bounded' nature of deliberative processes. Since not all possibilities can be examined, parties operate to focus discussion and debate on some subset of the possible ways to resolve any political disagreement. After this apparently promising start, however, the subsequent literature on deliberative democracy has almost nothing to say about political parties. One exception is Christiano (1996: 222–4, 244–8) who argues, like Cohen, that parties work to focus on general issues and away from candidate-centered politics and, like Manin, that they operate to focus attention on particular sorts of response to political problems. And he stresses that parties play a useful role in the political division of labor by structuring discussion of public issues in ways that are accessible to non-specialist voters. He depicts political parties as actors in electoral campaigns which he interprets, in turn, as a 'process of competitive debate' aimed at persuading voters. But among recent advocates of deliberation Christiano is a clear exception.

WHY THE NEGLECT OF PARTIES?

One might conjecture that the reason why theorists of deliberative democracy neglect parties is that their concerns are primarily normative while the literature on parties is primarily empirical. But recent surveys make clear that analysis of parties is suffused with normative concerns (Pomper, 1992; Stokes, 1999). Conversely, theories of democratic deliberation raise sets of analytical and empirical problems that cannot plausibly be set aside to concentrate solely on normative concerns (Johnson, 1998). One might, alternatively, argue that the neglect of parties reflects the abstract level at which treatments of deliberation are pitched. But this suggestion, too, is unpersuasive. Even briefs for democratic deliberation that focus on problems of institutions (Ferejohn, 2000; Guttmann and Thompson, 2004) or that purportedly analyse 'actual deliberation in non-ideal conditions', do not treat parties in any sustained way (Guttmann and Thompson, 1996: 39; 2004; Macedo, 1999).

The source of neglect resides more plausibly in the way advocates of deliberation frame their enterprise and specifically in the fact that they consistently defend the relative normative attractiveness of 'deliberative' practices and institutions by setting them in opposition to 'aggregative' ones. Thus, in an early essay Cohen (1989: 29) insists that his 'deliberative conception' of democracy 'construes politics as aiming in part at the formation of preferences and convictions, not just at their articulation and aggregation'. And much more recently, two prominent theorists ask rhetorically 'Why is deliberative democracy better than aggregative democracy?' (Guttmann and Thompson, 2004: 13). The problem should be clear. Political parties typically are understood as ways of coordinating citizens for electoral purposes (Pomper, 1992). They thus fall on the aggregative side of this divide and so beyond what most advocates of deliberation take as their purview. Unsurprisingly, the few advocates of deliberation who do discuss political parties in a serious manner resist the aggregation–deliberation dichotomy (Christiano, 1996).

Framing the discussion of democratic politics in this way – in terms of deliberative versus aggregative conceptions – is doubly unhelpful. First, it distorts the history of political thought in which defenses of representative government standardly insist that it both relies on elections to select government officials and demands that binding political decisions must survive prior public discussion and debate (Manin, 1997). In short, modern democratic institutions do not break down easily along the deliberative–aggregative divide. Second, the deliberative–aggregative dichotomy distracts attention from theoretical reasons we have for suspecting that neither mechanism alone affords a sufficient basis for arriving at political decisions within a democratic framework. Advocates of deliberation offer no reason to suspect that, given the circumstances of politics as I describe them above, political discussion, debate or argument will generate substantive consensus on even minor policy matters. Nor have they offered any reason to think that such substantive agreement is uniformly desirable in a complex, pluralist society (Knight and Johnson, 1994). Conversely, social choice theorists notoriously argue that any voting mechanism that meets even a relatively minimal set of normative criteria can generate cyclical or unstable collective choices.

RECONNECTING DELIBERATION AND PARTIES

Consider an alternative approach. Instead of setting deliberation and aggregation in opposition to one another, we might examine the way they interact in democratic politics. The first step here would be to recall that if the preference rankings of individual voters are structured in particular ways then voting mechanisms need not generate the collective instability that social choice theorists identify. The most regularly discussed of these preference structures is 'single-peakedness', but there are several others that are sufficient to avoid collective irrationality (Sen, 1966). If voters have single-peaked preferences they essentially share a common understanding of the issue space that sets the parameters on any substantive political disagreement they might have. Put otherwise, while they might continue to disagree substantively, voters with single-peaked preferences agree in a second-order way. The second step would be to recognize that political debate and argument can induce just such a shared understanding. This point was intimated by prominent social choice theorists (Arrow, 1963: 85; Riker, 1988: 122, 128), was spelled out explicitly in relatively early discussions of the relationship between deliberation and aggregation (Miller,

1992; Knight and Johnson, 1994), and has been revived even more recently in the same context (Dryzek and List, 2003).

The payoff that advocates of deliberation might derive from these insights is considerable. First, there is some empirical evidence that deliberative practices do indeed help to structure preferences in just this way (List *et al.*, 2000). Thus the approach just sketched will afford them an empirically plausible mechanism for explaining how deliberation 'works' (Johnson, 1998). Second, the claim that deliberation establishes second-order agreement deflates the complaints of postmodern critics who presume that deliberation necessarily aims at unwarranted consensus (Mouffe, 2000). The reason is simple. This view does not require that deliberation induces consensus. In the first place, a shared understanding about the dimensions of conflict does not eliminate substantive disagreement over how best to resolve the conflict. What is common to members of the relevant population is the structure of their preference orderings, not the content of their preferences. But, perhaps more importantly, even second-order agreement regarding what is at stake in a given conflict need not be unanimous. Indeed, aggregation mechanisms can generate collectively rational outcomes if as few as 70–75 percent of the relevant population have single-peaked preferences (Niemi, 1969). There is, in other words, room for considerable disagreement among the population over both substantive matters and second-order understandings. It is, therefore, perhaps more appropriate to claim that deliberation structures disagreement rather than to insist that it induces agreement. Finally, since advocates of deliberation are not committed to direct democracy (Cohen, 1989), the focus on the interaction of deliberation and aggregation locates their work more firmly in the tradition of democratic theorists as various as James Madison, John Stuart Mill, and John Dewey, all of whom defended representative government as including both aggregative and deliberative aspects.

Here we return to the question that motivates this entry. Where do political parties enter into all this? In a rare discussion of deliberation from the perspective of one who studies political parties, Ian Budge (2000: 206) sees party competition as imposing a left–right dimension on electoral issues and hence as an *alternative* to deliberation. In so doing Budge, tacitly at least, embraces the aggregation–deliberation dichotomy that frames most briefs for deliberative democracy. Moreover, his view of the effects of party activity is not universally accepted (Stokes, 1999). Yet here we might well elaborate on Christiano – who in turn follows Mill (1991: 315), for whom public debate fulfills the 'function of antagonism' in politics – and interpret party competition as a vehicle for rather than an alternative to public persuasion and debate. Then, if we understand the primary effect of deliberation as establishing second-order agreement on the dimensions of conflict, a clear confluence emerges between the case for deliberative democracy and the analysis of political parties. This is a proposition that bears scrutiny.

REFERENCES

Arrow, Kenneth (1963) *Social Choice and Individual Values,* 2nd edn. New Haven, CT: Yale University Press.

Bohman, James (1998) 'The coming of age of deliberative democracy', *Journal of Political Philosophy,* 6: 400–25.

Budge, Ian (2000) 'Deliberative democracy versus direct democracy – plus political parties!', in Michael Saward (ed.), *Democratic Innovation.* London: Routledge.

Christiano, Thomas (1996) *The Rule of the Many.* Boulder, CO: Westview Press.

Cohen, Joshua (1989) 'Deliberation and democratic legitimacy', in A. Hamlin and P. Pettit (eds), *The Good Polity.* Oxford: Basil Blackwell.

Dryzek, John and List, Christian (2003) 'Social choice theory and deliberative democracy', *British Journal of Political Science,* 33: 1–28.

Ferejohn, John (2000) 'Instituting deliberative democracy', in Ian Shapiro and Stephen Macedo (eds), *Designing Democratic Institutions – NOMOS XLII.* New York: New York University Press.

Freeman, Samuel (2000) 'Deliberative democracy: A sympathetic comment', *Philosophy & Public Affairs,* 29: 371–418.

Guttmann, Amy and Thompson, Dennis (1996) *Democracy and Disagreement.* Cambridge, MA: Harvard University Press.

Guttmann, Amy and Thompson, Dennis (2004) *Why Deliberative Democracy?* Princeton, NJ: Princeton University Press.

Johnson, James (1998) 'Arguing for deliberation', in Jon Elster (ed.), *Deliberative Democracy.* Cambridge: Cambridge University Press.

Knight, Jack and Johnson, James (1994) 'Aggregation and deliberation', *Political Theory,* 22: 277–98.

List, Christian, Fishkin, James, Luskin, Robert and McLean, Iain (2000) 'Can deliberation induce greater preference structuration?' Paper presented at the Annual Meetings of the American Political Science Association, Washington, DC.

Macedo, Stephen (ed.) (1999) *Deliberative Politics.* New York: Oxford University Press.

Manin, Bernard (1987) 'On legitimacy and democratic deliberation', *Political Theory,* 15: 338–68.

Manin, Bernard (1997) *Principles of Representative Government.* Cambridge: Cambridge University Press.

Mill, John Stuart (1991) 'Considerations of representative government', in *On Liberty and Other Essays.* Oxford: Oxford University Press.

Miller, David (1992) 'Deliberative democracy and social choice', *Political Studies,* XL: 45–67.

Mouffe, Chantal (2000) *The Democratic Paradox.* London: Verso.

Niemi, Richard (1969) 'Majority decision-making with partial unidimensionality', *American Political Science Review,* 63: 488–97.

Pomper, Gerald (1992) 'Concepts of political parties', *Journal of Theoretical Politics,* 4: 143–59.

Riker, William (1988 [1982]) *Liberalism against Populism.* Prospect Heights, IL: Waveland Press.

Sen, Amartya (1966) 'A possibility theorem on majority decisions', *Econometrica,* 34: 491–9.

Spitz, Elaine (1984) *Majority Rule.* Chatham, NJ: Chatham House.

Stokes, Susan (1999) 'Political parties and democracy', *Annual Review of Political Science,* 2: 243–67.

Waldron, Jeremy (1999) *Law and Disagreement.* New York: Oxford University Press.

Weale, Albert (1999) *Democracy.* Basingstoke: Palgrave/Macmillan.

6

PARTY SYSTEMS AND PARTY SYSTEM TYPES

Steven B. Wolinetz

166

Political parties competing with each other for elective office and control of government form a party system. Party systems have been a key factor in the study of political parties and more broadly in comparative analysis. Reasons for this are not difficult to fathom: the number of parties contesting elections shapes the menu of choices which voters face when they cast ballots. The number of parties winning seats in legislative elections affects the ease with which governments can be formed in parliamentary systems and the ease with which political executives can find support in presidential systems. Because party systems are so closely linked to democratic control and government formation, political scientists have sought not only to characterize them, but also to understand their causes and consequences, particularly their sources in electoral laws and cleavage structures and their effects on cabinet and system stability, and more broadly, the quality of democracy.

Research on party systems falls into different streams or literatures. We can distinguish an American and a comparative literature. The former is concerned primarily with the American two-party system and the ways in which it has changed over time, as well as ways in which state party systems have differed from each other and from the larger national party system. A portion of the American literature focuses on partisan realignment and the extent to which the two national parties reflect or blur different lines of cleavage. Changes in cleavage structures and partisan balance over time have been central concerns, and the term 'party system' is used to denote periods of time, often a generation or more in length, exhibiting different cleavage structures and patterns of party strength

(Key, 1964; Burnham, 1970; Sundquist, 1983). A separate literature considers the extent to which state party systems reflect national patterns. Particularly in the long period in which the South was solidly Democratic, students of politics such as Key (1949) documented variation in state party systems, particularly patterns of factional competition in the dominant party. A third stream has focused on the quality of democracy within the American party system, particularly the perceived need for 'a more responsible two-party system' (American Political Science Association, 1950; Schattschneider, 1960).

The comparative literature has moved in different directions. Here the primary concern has been variation among national party systems, particularly differences in numbers of political parties, patterns of competition, and what difference they make. Initially, the central distinctions were either between two-party and multiparty systems, or among one-party, two-party, and multiparty systems. However, scholars such as Holcombe (1933) and Almond (1956) argued that one-party systems were qualitatively different, while Neumann (1956) argued that one-party systems were a 'a contradiction in terms'. Insisting that the term 'party' implied parts of a larger whole and that systems had to be made up of regularly interacting parts, Sartori (1976) made the point even more strongly: although he had no difficulty conceiving of a party-state system in which one party monopolized political life, parties were, by definition, parts of a larger whole. A party system (see below) had to be made up of more than one party.

Thinking about party systems has paralleled the development of comparative analysis. Initially, political scientists focused on a limited range of countries: the United States and Britain with two-party systems, and countries such as France or Germany, with multiparty competition. Distinctions between two-party and multiparty systems were attributed to electoral systems, and multipartyism was associated with – and in the view of authors such as Hermens (1941) and Duverger (1954) caused by – proportional representation. Two-party systems were typically associated with strong, effective, and decisive government, multiparty competition with cabinet and system instability (cf. Hermens, 1941). Almond (1956) found it necessary to distinguish between continental multiparty systems, more typically clogged and unstable, and 'working multiparty systems' (see also Almond and Coleman, 1960; Almond and Powell, 1978). Earlier assumptions were revised in the 1960s and 1970s. Political scientists began to take account of a broader range of liberal democracies. When the scope of comparative politics broadened in the 1960s, political scientists developed more complex typologies distinguishing party systems according to patterns of opposition (Dahl, 1966), the relative size and strength of parties (Blondel, 1968; Rokkan, 1970), or, in the case of Sartori (1966, 1976), the number of parties and the degree of ideological polarization among them (see Mair, 1996, 2002; and Ware, 1996). Sartori's work provided a way to separate cases of polarized pluralism, wracked by centrifugal tendencies and cabinet instability, from moderate pluralism, in which the direction of competition was centripetal and stable multiparty competition was the norm.[1]

The focus of the literature has changed over time. The initial preoccupation with cabinet and system stability reflected the tumult of the interwar experience, and the fact that countries with extreme multiparty systems, such as Weimar Germany (1919–33) or Second Republic Spain (1931–36) had seen the collapse of liberal democracy. As the interwar period faded, emphases shifted. Taking as gospel Lipset and Rokkan's (1967) observation that the party systems of the 1960s reflected those of the 1920s, students of party systems focused on continuity and change. Initially, the emphasis was on continuity; more recently it has been on change. In addition, transitions to democracy have sparked interest in how party systems become entrenched or institutionalized.

This chapter explores thinking about party systems and the ways in which they have developed over time. We begin by examining the definition of a party system, then consider efforts to order complexity and discover patterns of interaction, as well as their causes and consequences.

THE SYSTEMIC DIMENSION: PARTY SYSTEM PROPERTIES

A party system consists of regular and recurring interactions among its component parties. Although the term 'party system' came into use well before he wrote (see, for example, Holcombe, 1933), one of the first 'systemic' uses of the term can be found in Duverger's *Political Parties*. Duverger (1954: 203) argues that:

> With the exception of the single-party states, several parties co-exist in each country: the forms and modes of their coexistence define the 'party system' of the particular country being considered.

In addition to characteristics of the parties, these include

> new elements that do not exist for each party community considered in isolation: numbers, respective sizes, alliances, geographical localization, political distribution and so on. A party system is defined by a particular relationship amongst all these characteristics. (Duverger, 1954: 203)

Although the definition of party system is not separate from the characteristics of the parties themselves, Duverger's reference to 'forms and modes of their coexistence' and 'characteristics that do not exist for each party community considered in isolation' indicates the importance of interaction.

Sartori (1976: 44) argues:

> Parties make for a 'system' only when they are parts (in the plural); and a party system is precisely the *system of interactions* resulting from interparty competition. That is, the system in question bears on the relatedness of parties to each other, on how each party is a function (in a mathematical sense) of the other parties and reacts, competitively or otherwise, to the other parties.

As such, a party system is distinct and different from the parties forming the system.

Sartori's insistence on the systemic properties not only enables him to separate party-state systems monopolized by a single party from party systems in which there is competition for government, but also provides a basis for examining their most important features. These are relational and arise both from their competition for elective office and interaction in between elections in both the formation and support of governments and the legislative process. Parties compete for a share of the vote and, in doing so, try both to shore up their own support and pry votes from their competitors. The strategy and tactics which they employ are influenced by what other parties have done in the past and expectations about what they will do in the future. The ability of parties to cooperate with each other after elections will depend not only on their size and relative strength, but also on their distance from each other on key issues and the ways in which they present themselves during elections. Equally, parties may discover that choices made in political office – e.g. decisions to participate in or remain aloof from coalitions, as well as policies pursued in government or opposition – can affect their ability to win electoral support.

Party systems have a number of distinct features which arise from electoral competition and parties' relation to each other. These include the number of parties contesting elections and winning legislative seats, their relative size and strength, the number of dimensions on which they compete, the distance which separates them on key issues, and their willingness to work with each other in government formation and the process of governing. Party systems can vary on any or all of these. Voters, politicians, and political analysts often think of parties divided along a left–right spectrum, but it is not unusual for party systems, at least in their origins, to reflect multiple dimensions of conflict. European party systems, for example, often reflect not only economic or distributional issues, but also religion and religiosity and, in certain instances, urban–rural cleavages (Lijphart, 1982). Party systems can be more or less polarized on any or all of these dimensions. Other features on which party systems may differ include the degree to which their competition for government is open to all parties or closed – restricted only to certain parties or combinations of parties (Mair, 1996, 2002) – and the degree to which the party system itself is institutionalized or entrenched (Mainwaring and Scully, 1995). However, this latter facet reflects not so the much the ways in which parties relate to each other, as the degree to which parties, taken together, are able to enlist durable support and structure the electorate.

Because party systems can vary on any or all of these features, students of political parties often try to simplify the world around them by grouping them into distinct types. The most common classifications usually differentiate party systems according to the number of parties winning seats and one or more relational features, such as size and relative strength or the ability of parties to work with each other. The most obvious distinctions are between two-party systems and multiparty systems, but

two-party systems may be more or less polarized, and not all multiparty systems are necessarily the same: there is considerable difference between a party system with three or four parties and one with six or seven or eight. Even so, this depends on how parties are counted and what weights are assigned to different sizes of parties. Typically, classifications count major parties, but, as Sartori (1976) has pointed out, clear rules are needed to determine which parties should be counted and which should be excluded. Once this is done, other questions remain: whether the number of parties is a sufficient criterion, or whether relative sizes and strengths of parties and mechanics (or direction of competition) should be taken into account as well. Efforts to do so have given rise to distinct typologies, as well as continuous measures, such as Laakso and Taagepera's (1979) effective number of political parties, which weights parties according to their size.

Counting parties

The oldest distinctions are among one-party, two-party and multiparty systems; almost all classifications of party systems make distinctions on the basis of number. However, decisions have to be made about whether to consider all parties contesting elections, only those winning seats in the legislature, or only those involved in government formation. Although continuous measures such as Rae's fractionalization index (Rae, 1967; Rae and Taylor, 1970) or Laakso and Taagepera's (1979) effective number of political parties can be used to measure the number of parties contesting elections, counts of political parties are usually based on the number of parties winning seats in parliament. As Table 6.1 demonstrates, in the 2005 British general election, a total of 14 parties, one local list and one nonpartisan group ran candidates for parliament. Of these, 12 won seats in parliament and the overwhelming share of the vote was won by three national parties. Except for the anti-war coalition, Respect, which won one seat, all other parties winning seats were regionally based: the Scottish National Party, Plaid Cymru (Welsh Nationalists), and three Northern Irish parties. The Social Democratic and Labour Party and one local list also won seats. However, no one would term the British party system a 12-party system, and in view of the regional concentration of the vote for smaller parties, few would characterize it as a ten-party system. More problematic is whether the

Table 6.1   *The British General Election of 2005*

	percentage of the vote	number of seats
Labour Party	35.2	356
Conservative Party	32.3	197
Liberal Democrats	22.0	62
United Kingdom Independence Party	2.3	–
Scottish National Party	1.5	6
Green Party of England and Wales	1.0	–
Democratic Unionist Party	0.9	9
British National Party	0.7	–
Plaid Cymru/Party of Wales	0.6	3
Sinn Fein	0.6	5
Ulster Unionist Party	0.5	1
Social Democratic and Labour Party	0.5	3
Respect	0.2	1
Scottish Socialist Party	0.2	–
Kidderminster Hospital and Health Concern	0.1	1
Non-partisan	0.1	1
Vacant		1
Total	100.0	646

Source: BBC as cited by http://www.electionworld.org/unitedkingdom.htm

Liberal Democrats' 22% of the vote makes Britain a three-party system rather than a two-party system.

Once a decision has been made to focus on parties winning seats in the national parliament, further decisions must be made about which parties to count. This can be done in several ways: All parties can be counted (although in the British case this would lead to results which are counter-intuitive) or some can be excluded on the basis of either size or standards of relevance. Many characterizations of the number of political parties focus implicitly only on major political parties. However, this presumes some kind of criterion. Alan Ware (1996) excludes all parties with less than 3% of the vote. In contrast, Sartori (1976), argues that relevance should be assessed according to coalition potential and blackmail potential. Smaller parties are counted only if their seats in parliament are needed to form coalitions, or alternatively if they have sufficient seats to block the formation of coalitions. If we follow Ware, we would call Britain a three party system. If we follow Sartori, Britain remains a two party system because, despite winning almost 20% in most elections since 1974, the Liberal Democrats have rarely been able to affect government formation. Only in the late 1970s were their seats in parliament needed to keep a Labour government in office. Nevertheless, we could argue that three way competition in individual districts makes

them electorally relevant; both Labour and Conservatives need to worry about third party candidates depriving them of seats they might otherwise win.

In other political systems, parties with considerably less than the British Liberals' 22% are counted, typically because proportional representation gives them a similar percentage of seats in parliament. In Germany, Free Democratic Party (FDP) support has ranged from a high of 12–13% of the vote and seats in parliament to a low of 6–7%. In contrast to the British Liberals, the FDP has been particularly relevant: through 1998, it could often determine whether the Federal Republic of Germany would have a center-left or center-right government. The presence of the FDP ensured that the Federal Republic after 1957 would be considered a three-party or in some instances a two-and-a-half-party system (see below). After 1983, a fourth party, the Greens, leapt the 5% threshold, winning 5.6–8.6% of the vote and seats in the Bundestag. If we were to follow Ware's criteria, we would consider Germany a four-party system after 1983, and with the entry of the Party of Democratic Socialism (PDS) in 1990 a five-party system, because the PDS had more than 3% of the vote. In contrast, Sartori would argue that the Greens only became relevant when they began joining provincial and later federal coalitions in the 1990s. The PDS would not be considered relevant because their votes have not been needed to form coalitions, they have not been able to block the formation of coalitions, and their presence has not altered the direction of competition.

Weighted or disaggregated measures provide an alternative to simple counting, with or without explicit cutoffs for smaller or irrelevant parties. Two have been used in the parties literature: Rae's fractionalization index (for electoral fractionalization or for legislative fractionalization) and Laakso and Taagepera's effective number of political parties. Fractionalization does not measure the number of political parties directly, but estimates the probability that any two randomly chosen voters or legislators will be of the same party (Rae, 1967). The effective number of parties is measured by dividing 1 by the sum of the squares of proportions of votes (effective number of electoral parties, ENEP) or seats won by each party (effective number of parliamentary parties, ENPP). This results in a number which is typically smaller than the actual number of parties contesting elections or represented in parliament. Squaring the decimal shares of votes or seats won gives additional weight to larger political parties. Smaller parties which would be excluded under Sartori's decision rules are counted, but they do not count for very much: a party like Plaid Cymru, with 0.6% of the vote only adds to 0.000036 to the denominator of the measure.

Measures like the effective number of political parties finesse the problem of exclusion or inclusion and provide a continuous measure which can be used in correlation and regression. This has been particularly useful in assessing the effects of electoral systems and can be used to examine changes in the number of parties over time. Compressing the actual numbers of political parties, measurement of the effective number of electoral or legislative parties produces a series of decimals ranging from 1.8 or 1.9 for systems with two parties to 5 or more for systems with eight or more parties in parliament. On the other hand, Dunleavy and Boucek (2003) argue not only that Laakso and Taagepera's index and related measures obscure variations in relative size and strengths of parties, but also that the index behaves quirkily rather than continuously for certain values.

PARTY SYSTEM TYPES

Students of party systems have moved beyond number and attempted to construct typologies which capture relationships and interactions. This can be done in different ways: combining numbers of parties with information about their relative size and strength, as Jean Blondel (1968) and Alan Siaroff (2000) have done, or looking at patterns of government formation and party interaction, as Rokkan (1970) and Dahl (1966) and more recently Peter Mair (1996, 2002) do, or, in the case of Sartori (1966, 1976), considering polarization and internal dynamics as well as the number of parties.

Classification on the basis of relative strength and size of parties

Jean Blondel (1968) was one of the first to move beyond simple counting and consider the relative size or strengths of political parties. Blondel used the share of the vote won by political parties in elections from 1945 through 1966 to construct a fourfold typology. He distinguishes two-party systems, two-and-a-half-party systems, multiparty systems with a predominant party and multiparty systems without a predominant party. His typology is derived by looking at the average share of the vote won by the largest two parties and then considering the ratio of the first party's share to the second and third parties. In the five two-party systems (the United States, New Zealand, Australia, the United Kingdom, and Austria), the two-party share was greater than 89% and closely balanced between the two parties. In the next cluster, the two party share ranged from 75% to 80% of the vote cast but there was a wider average difference (10.5%) between the first and second parties. Although these could be considered three-party systems, Blondel categorizes them as two-and-a-half-party systems to take account of the imbalance in parties' share of the vote. These include Canada, the Federal Republic of Germany, and Ireland. Blondel then distinguishes among party systems with four or more major parties: those with one larger party winning 40% or more of the vote and typically twice as much as the second party in the system are multiparty systems with a predominant party (e.g. Sweden, Norway, Denmark, Italy, and Iceland) or, if this is not the case, multiparty systems without a predominant party (Netherlands, Switzerland, France, Finland).

Blondel's typology is useful both because it permits us to distinguish among different types of multiparty systems and brings out differences and similarities among pure two-party systems and systems like the Federal

Republic of Germany, with two larger parties and a relatively smaller party sometimes able to play a balancing role between them. Although a refinement over simple counting, the scheme is problematic. As Mair (1996, 2002) points out, Blondel's scheme disaggregates the multiparty category, but his categories bring together party systems whose dynamics are not necessarily the same. Multiparty systems with a dominant party include both Norway and Sweden, with predominant social democratic parties, and the much more polarized pre-1993 Italian party system. Multiparty systems without a dominant party include consociational democracies such as the Netherlands and Switzerland, in which elite cooperation is said to outweigh centrifugal tendencies, and more polarized party systems such as France and Finland.

The designation of two-and-a-half-party systems captures differences between pure two-party systems, on one hand, and moderate multiparty systems, on the other. However, the two-and-a-half-party category brings together party systems in which the role of the smaller party differs considerably. As Siaroff (2003) notes, the role of the 'half party' varies from hinge parties, located between two larger parties, such as the German Free Democrats, influential because their votes were needed to make parliamentary majorities, and 'wing parties' such as the Canadian New Democratic Party, less influential because their votes are rarely needed either to form coalitions or ensure that legislation is passed. In the first instance, the hinge party determines who governs; in the second, the wing party's influence is at best confined to agenda setting and proposing policies which may be taken over by larger parties. There is also a question of why smaller 'half parties' should be highlighted in what otherwise would be three-party systems but not in multiparty systems with a larger number of parties.

Patterns of government formation

Looking at the relative size and strength of parties is only one way to refine classifications based on number. Patterns of government formation and party interaction can also be considered. Examining patterns of opposition in Western democracies, Dahl (1966) uses parties' behavior in electoral and legislative arenas to develop a fourfold scheme. Patterns of opposition can be strictly competitive (Britain), cooperative and competitive (the USA, France and Italy), coalescent and competitive (Austria

and wartime Britain), or strictly coalescent (Colombia). Where necessary, each of these types can be further broken down into two-party and multiparty categories. Dahl's scheme is not a classification of party systems, *per se*, but of patterns of opposition. The scheme demonstrates that two-party and multiparty systems need not be as different as either simple counting or standard typologies assume. Both the competitive and coalescent and competitive categories bring together party systems which might otherwise be categorized as two-party and multiparty systems.

Rokkan (1970) uses patterns of government formation to classify the party systems of smaller democracies. Rokkan distinguishes among party systems, such as Austria and Ireland, which display a 1 vs. 1 + 1 format, akin to a British and German pattern, Scandinavian 1 vs. 3–4 pattern (Norway, Sweden, Denmark), and 'even multiparty systems' which display a one vs. one vs. two-three (1 vs. 1 vs. 1+2–3) pattern of competition. Like Blondel's scheme, this is an attempt to disaggregate the multiparty category (Mair, 1996, 2002), but the organizing principle is patterns of government and opposition rather than relative size.

Sartori's typology: moderate versus polarized pluralism

Sartori argues that the standard distinction among one-party, two-party, and multiparty competition is too crude to explain very real differences among party systems. After separating out party-state systems, he proceeds to establish rules which tell practitioners which parties to count and which to exclude. The next steps are to select cutoff points, establish classes, and take account of special cases like segmented societies. Classes are then distilled into distinct types. Sartori ends up with a typology based on numbers (properly counted), whose principal distinction is not number as such, but rather the degree of polarization and whether party competition, and thus the mechanics of the system, are centripetal or centrifugal.

Sartori begins by establishing explicit counting rules. He argues that the criterion by which parties, large or small, should be counted is their effect on party competition. Smaller parties are relevant when they have either *coalition potential* or *blackmail potential*. Coalition potential depends on parties having sufficient seats to make coalitions feasible and is measured by their having participated in or made cabinet coalitions possible; parties whose seats are never needed are deemed irrelevant. The second criterion is their impact on the direction of party competition: parties, large or small, are relevant when their existence alters the direction of party competition leftward or rightward, changing the direction of competition from centripetal to centrifugal.

Sartori's next step is to establish classes of party systems. He begins by breaking down what he describes as the one party and multiparty 'lumps'. The first consists of a mixed bag of one-party and hegemonic party political systems, not properly competitive and predominant party systems in which one party that regularly wins 50% of the seats in parliament predominates over a number of smaller parties; no other party can govern because of the predominant position of the first. Multiparty systems are grouped into two classes: limited pluralism, with three, four, or five relevant parties, and extreme pluralism, with six, seven, or eight. Finally, Sartori adds a residual category, atomized party systems, which are so fragmented that the addition of one more party makes no difference to the pattern of competition. These party systems are insufficiently structured or consolidated to be considered.

Sartori then refines the multiparty categories. Here no party has or is likely to obtain an absolute majority. Sartori argues power structures (relations among the parties) are important and then proceeds to differentiate party systems according to their mechanical predisposition, or, more specifically, relations among the parties. Doing so enables him to establish criteria for moderate and polarized pluralism. The crucial factors are the direction and character of competition: competition under moderate pluralism resembles competition in two-party systems. The system is bipolar and competition is centripetal: parties on either side of the spectrum compete for votes in the center. Polarized pluralism is different. Although the center is occupied, the dynamics of the system are centrifugal rather than centripetal. Anti-system parties at the extremes compete with parties in the center, pulling parties and voters toward them. Because bilateral oppositions located 'two poles apart' cannot coalesce, parties in the center govern without the benefit of an alternative government which can replace them. As such, the system is characterized by ideological divisions, centrifugal drives, 'irresponsible oppositions' and a politics of 'outbidding or over-promising'.

The initial criterion for distinguishing between moderate and polarized pluralism is the number of political parties, but the cutoff point, five or more, is in Sartori's view an artifact. Segmented systems characterized by elite accommodation are cases of moderate pluralism because the mechanics of the system are centripetal rather than centrifugal. The mechanics of competition and particularly the extent of polarization are more important than the number of relevant parties. Sartori ends up with a fourfold typology: predominant party systems, two-party systems, moderate pluralism, and polarized pluralism.

More recent schemata

Since the typologies which we have been considering were developed and refined in the 1960s and 1970s, transitions to democracy in different parts of the world have given us a larger range of political systems to take into account, and party spectra in older liberal democracies have become increasingly crowded by the addition of green and new politics parties, and by the entry and growth of new right and neo-populist parties. Nevertheless, few of the latter can be characterized as fundamentally opposed to liberal democracy. Instead, as Mair (1996, 2002) has observed, Sartori's polarized pluralism has emptied out, while moderate pluralism has become increasingly crowded. Included are not only the German, Austrian and Scandinavian party systems, as well as the Dutch and Belgian, but also the French and the post-1993 Italian party system. Like its predecessor, the post-1993 Italian party system contains a large number of relevant political parties, but it lacks anti-system parties at its extremes.[2] There are also fewer two-party systems: following a change in its electoral law in 1994, New Zealand changed from a pure two-party system to a multiparty system. Dominated by a single party from 1979 to 1997, Britain in the Thatcher–Major era should be classified as a predominant party system (Mair, 1996, 2002).

Students of party systems have yet to come to grips with the changed situation, let alone refine moderate pluralism. Building on Dahl and Rokkan, Peter Mair (1996, 2002) has suggested using competition for government as a device for distinguishing among party systems. In party systems in which competition for government is closed, there is either wholesale alternation between parties or groups of parties, governing formulae are familiar rather than novel or innovative, and access to government is typically restricted to only a few parties. In contrast, in systems in which the structure of competition is open, there is partial alternation: some parties rotate in and out of government, while others remain, and as new parties appear, there is frequent recourse to innovate governing formulas. Closed structures of competition were typical of the United Kingdom, Japan, pre-1994 New Zealand, and Ireland over the period 1948–89. Open patterns of competition characterize both the Netherlands and Denmark, as well as newly emerging party systems: in the Netherlands, new parties have been incorporated into governing coalitions; in Denmark, novel coalitions and new forms of minority governments were used to accommodate changes in the number of parties (Mair, 1996, 2002).

Mair argues that focusing on structures of competition not only directs attention to key relationships among political parties, but also allows the party system to function as an independent variable to which parties and voters may respond. He illustrates his point by demonstrating the ways in which changes in Irish coalition patterns – the willingness of Fianna Fáil to enlist coalition partners after refusing to do so since the 1940s – paved the way for shifts in voting alignments and further shifts in coalition patterns (Mair, 1996, 2002). Using open or closed competition for government is novel, but its full potential has not yet been explored.

An alternative approach is to sort moderate pluralism according to the size and relative strength of parties. Alan Siaroff (2000) does this by refining and building on Blondel's earlier typology. Siaroff uses multiple measures to tap the relative size and strength of political parties winning more than 3% of the seats. He ends up with an eightfold classification, distinguishing: (1) pure two-party systems, with a mean two party share of 95%; (2) moderate multiparty systems with three to five parties above 3% (which he argues are in fact two-and-a-half-party systems); (3) moderate multiparty systems with one dominant party; (4) moderate multiparty systems with two main parties, (5) moderate multiparty systems with a balance among parties; (6) extreme multiparty systems with one dominant party; (7) extreme multiparty systems with two main parties; and (8) extreme multiparty systems with a balance among parties. The resulting scheme categorizes party systems according to the number of parties (two-party systems, moderate multiparty systems with three to five parties, and extreme multiparty systems with six to eight) and the relative balance among parties (one dominant party among

Table 6.2 *Siaroff's classificiation of party systems*

System	ENPP
Two-party	1.92
Two-and-a-half-party	2.56
Moderate multiparty with one dominant party	2.95
Moderate multiparty with two main parties	3.17
Moderate multiparty with balance among main parties	3.69
Extreme multiparty with one dominant party	3.96
Extreme multiparty with two main parties	4.41
Extreme multiparty with balance among the parties	5.56

Source: Siaroff, 2000

others, two main parties, or an even or nearly even balance among them), which can then be related to electoral systems, length of cabinet formation, type of cabinet (e.g., minimum winning or not), as well as duration of governments. As Table 6.2 demonstrates, Siaroff's categories tap variations in the effective number of parliamentary parties.

If the aim is to disaggregate moderate pluralism, then Siaroff has succeeded. In place of a single overloaded category, we now have a more refined scheme with several categories. The large number of categories also permits Siaroff to analyze changes over time. However, some 'party systems' last no longer than a single election period. This is difficult to accept if, following Sartori, we believe that party systems consist of recurring rather than one-off relationships. Siaroff is in fact referring not to party systems but to patterns of party strengths which have resulted from particular election outcomes. This difficulty can be overcome either by changing the terminology, so that we are referring to patterns of party competition, some more permanent than others, rather than party systems, or by averaging results over two or more elections to tap more durable features. More problematic is the complexity of the scheme. With eight categories more or less arrayed on two dimensions, Siaroff's scheme lacks simplicity or parsimony. Whether it will gain acceptance remains to be seen.

NEW DIRECTIONS

One of the more surprising features of this exercise is the absence of new typologies.[3] Little has occurred since Sartori (1976). In some respects, this is a testament to his success. More than its predecessors, Sartori's typology sorted the available cases, and it did so in a meaningful way. Nevertheless, its utility is increasingly problematic. We now have almost no cases of polarized pluralism, save for the now historical instances for which it was developed, and moderate pluralism is increasingly overcrowded (Mair, 1996, 2002). The party systems of most stable liberal democracies fall within its reach. If we believe that there are no significant differences among these party systems, there is no cause for concern. If not, then we need to emulate Sartori and consider how relevant cases can be sorted.

The number of parties does matter. There is considerable difference between countries with two, three, or perhaps four parties, and those with six or eight or more. Voters in the former face simpler choices than voters in the latter. Similarly, politicians – assuming that we are talking about a parliamentary system – find the task of forming governments easier when there are fewer parties. However, this depends not only on the number of parties, but also on the degree of polarization and the extent to which parties cluster together, forming durable coalitions and alliances. How can we distinguish such systems?

One strategy is to use Laakso and Taagepera's index. Both ENEP, the effective number of legislative parties, and ENPP, the effective number of parliamentary parties, have been used to great advantage in analyses of the effects of different types of electoral laws (Lijphart, 1994; Taagepera and Shugart, 1989; Cox, 1997). However, despite their advantage for correlation and regression, ENEP and ENPP blur distinctions and tell us little about relationships among parties or the dynamics of different types of party systems. One advantage of simple counting, with or without explicit cutoffs for smaller parties, is that it produces outcomes which are readily (if not always correctly) understood.

Space does not permit development of a new typology, but it is possible to suggest features which one should display. Typologies work when they sort the available cases into types which are mutually exclusive and can be understood easily (Lange and Meadwell, 1991). Siaroff's scheme, a by-product of a larger effort at data collection, falls short because it has too many categories, and does not explain why the relationships which it captures are relevant. The most important features of party systems are those on which Sartori and successive scholars have focused: numbers of parties and relationships among them. The greater the number of parties, the more complex their interrelations are likely to be. Equally important is the degree of polarization: parties in most party systems may no longer be two poles apart, but some party systems are more polarized than others. There is a considerable difference between the more polarized pre- and post-1993 Italian party systems, and the Dutch party system, which continues to have a large number of parties in parliament, but is rarely so polarized that parties are unable to work with each other.

Relative size may also be important (Blondel, 1968; Rokkan, 1970; Siaroff, 2000), but the relative size or strength of parties is a tertiary characteristic less likely, in and of itself, to shape relationships among parties. In addition, in a period of pronounced electoral volatility, in which fewer and fewer parties can count on automatic support from loyal electorates, the size and strength of parties may be too variable to reflect the durable systemic relationships at the core of the study of party systems. More important in systems with six or more parties competing are relationships among parties: for example, do parties compete around the center, the mode of competition at the core of Sartori's category of moderate pluralism, or is competition more centrifugal, centering around two poles, even if not as thoroughly polarized as the Weimar Republic or First Republic Italy, as Sartori understood it? Equally important, do parties compete as independent entities or cluster into semi-permanent alliances, as parties in Fifth Republic France, Israel, or Italy after 1993 have done? Clustering is important because it mitigates some, but not all, of the effects of multipartyism. In systems like Fifth Republic France or Italy after 1993, parties still face competition on their flanks, and voters are still presented with a wide array of choices. However, when parties cluster into distinct blocs – left and right in France, Olive Tree and the House of Liberty in Italy – voters receive additional information about how parties are likely to behave after elections. The number of alternatives is reduced, simplifying some choices, while making others more complex. Clustering into distinct blocs also structures and sometimes simplifies post-election processes of government formation.

A new typology, refining Sartori's moderate pluralism, should consider the number of parties, their interrelationships, and the presence or absence of clustering, as well as centripetal versus centrifugal drives. Clear, neutral labels are needed. Like Siaroff (2000), students of party systems frequently distinguish moderate and extreme multipartyism. Moderate multipartyism – typically three to five parties, centripetal drives and competition around the center – is clear enough, but extreme multipartyism is more problematic. We typically mean multiparty competition with more than three to five parties. However, 'extreme' conjures up other implications: multiparty competition with extremist or anti-system parties and, of course, polarized pluralism. In an era in which there are fewer and fewer viable or presentable alternatives to liberal democracy, few (if any) of the left libertarian or neo-populist parties which have crowded political spectra since the 1970s are opposed to liberal democracy. These parties, to be sure, oppose some of the policies and practices of older and more established parties, but not the system itself (Abedi, 2002; Zaslove, 2003a, 2003b). Their appearance and relative success have made a difference – new right populist parties have strained the boundaries of political correctness and forced other parties to take up some of their claims – but this has been done working within the boundaries of liberal democracy. If we are going to use labels like extreme multipartyism, then we must neuter the term, stripping it of its earlier connotations. If not, then we should substitute more neutral terms, such as extended rather than extreme multipartyism.

Finally, new typologies should be based on parties and their interrelationships, rather than on properties of the parties themselves. This is difficult because properties of party systems can never be entirely separate from the parties which populate them. Relationships depend on numbers. Examining the ways in which Scott Mainwaring (1999; see also Mainwaring and Scully, 1995) has approached party systems in transitional democracies illustrates the problem. He has developed measures to compare the degree to which Latin American party systems are institutionalized or entrenched in their societies. These include the age of parties – how long individual parties as distinct organizations have been around – as well as aggregate electoral volatility as a measure of the collective ability of parties in a party system to maintain stable bases of support. Using these measures, he is able to show considerable difference between more institutionalized party systems, such as Argentina, Mexico, and Venezuela, and less institutionalized systems such as Peru, Bolivia, Ecuador, or Brazil. Similar comparisons can be made between the increasingly institutionalized systems of newer central European

democracies such as Hungary, the Czech Republic, and more recently Poland, and inchoate party systems, like that of Russia or other parts of the former Soviet Union. Measuring the average age of party alternatives says something about the degree to which party systems are entrenched.

Using electoral volatility as an index of party system institutionalization is questionable. Electoral volatility measures the ability of parties to build loyal followings and collectively structure the electorate. These are properties of parties, individually and collectively, rather than aspects of the party system – that is, parties and the ways in which they relate to each other. Rates of electoral volatility have increased in well-established party systems, such as the Netherlands and Austria, in part because older lines of cleavage have weakened and established parties have had less loyal electorates than in the past. This is a new development, which may reflect changes in the media and the ways in which parties approach voters. However, the diminishing ability of parties to hold voters does not necessarily mean that the party system is becoming less entrenched or institutionalized: even if they have lost support for a time, older parties retain resources, which enable them to continue and often recover in subsequent elections. We still have few examples where established parties have disappeared or have in large measure been replaced. Most are found in Italy, where most parties in the pre-1993 party system have been supplanted. However, the Italian case remains an exception rather than the rule.

Thus far, Mainwaring's set of measures are the only ones brought forth. They are useful in that they link to measures already in use in the parties literature, but problematic because of the presumptions made about the degree to which voters should – or in the future are likely to – have stable party preferences in a world dominated by rapid electronic media. Nevertheless, Mainwaring's measures provide a starting point from which comparisons can be drawn. Clearly, we need ways to take account of variation in party systems. At issue are not only the number of parties and the ways in which they compete, but also, in a period in which multilevel governance is increasingly prominent, ways of describing and categorizing links among party systems at local, regional, national, and transnational levels of governance. Also important is the impact of institutions – whether the system is presidential, semi-presidential or parliamentary – on parties and party systems. Clearly, new research is needed, if not new categories.

NOTES

1   Sartori's contribution was reinforced by inclusion of smaller democracies in the comparative literature. Consociationalism also helped to explain cooperation despite fragmentation (Dahl, 1966; Lijphart, 1968, 1975, 1977; Daalder, 1966).

2   This of course depends on how we define anti-system parties. Capoccia (2002) argues that the concept has been stretched considerably. In order to retain it, he suggests distinguishing between *relational anti-system parties*, which advance an ideology different than other parties, and polarize in the way that Sartori argues anti-system parties do, and *ideological anti-system parties*, which oppose liberal democracy or, in some instances, the predominant ideology advanced by those who control the system.

3   One test is to consider broader comparative analyses. Concerned primarily with party system performance, G. Bingham Powell (1982) distinguishes between strong party systems, typically two-party, with broad, aggregative parties, and those which are more fragmented and less aggregative. However, some of the indicators he uses to measure party system performance – such as party links to social groups and volatility of electoral support – are characteristics of parties and their ability to mobilize support rather than characteristics of the party system (e.g. parties and the ways in which they interact). No new classification is advanced. Using a factor analysis, Lane and Errson (1987) argue that West European party systems can be differentiated on five dimensions which constitute their properties. These include fractionalization, functional orientation (defined as variation between 'traditional bourgeois' and 'religious and ethnic' parties), polarization, radical orientation (the strength of leftist parties), and volatility. However, they make no effort to define a new typology, relying instead on counting relevant parties. Lijphart (1984, 1999) argues that party systems are a key dimension differentiating democracies, but is content to differentiate them into two-party systems, which are generally adversarial, and multiparty systems which are more likely to be consensual.

REFERENCES

Abedi, Amir (2002) 'Challenges to established parties: The effects of party system features on the electoral fortunes of anti-political-establishment parties', *European Journal of Political Research*, 41: 551–83.

Almond, Gabriel A. (1956) 'Comparative political systems', *Journal of Politics*, 28: 391–401.

Almond, Gabriel and Coleman, James S. (1960) *The Politics of the Developing Areas*. Princeton, NJ: Princeton University Press.

Almond, Gabriel A. and Powell, G. Bingham (1978) *Comparative Politics: System, Process, and Policy*. Boston: Little, Brown.

American Political Science Association, Committee on Political Parties (1950) *Toward a More Responsible Two Party System: A Report*. New York: Rinehart.

Blondel, Jean (1968) 'Party systems and patterns of government in Western democracies', *Canadian Journal of Political Science*, 1: 180–203.

Burnham, Walter Dean (1970) *Critical Elections and the Mainsprings of American Politics*. New York: Norton.

Capoccia, Giovanni (2002) 'Defending democracy: Reactions to political extremism in inter-war Europe', *European Journal for Political Research*, 39: 431–60.

Cox, Gary W. (1997) *Making Votes Count: Strategic Coordination in the World's Electoral Systems*. Cambridge: Cambridge University Press.

Daalder, Hans (1966) 'The Netherlands: Opposition in a segmented society', in Robert A. Dahl (ed.), *Political Oppositions in Western Democracies*. New Haven, CT: Yale University Press.

Dahl, Robert A. (1966) 'Patterns of opposition', in Dahl (ed.), *Political Oppositions in Western Democracies*. New Haven, CT: Yale University Press, pp. 332–47.

Dunleavy, Patrick, and Françoise Boucek (2003) 'Constructing the number of parties', *Party Politics*, 9: 291–315.

Duverger, Maurice (1954) *Political Parties: Their Organization and Activity in the Modern State*, trans. Barbara and Robert North. New York: Wiley.

Hermens, F.A. (1941) *Democracy or Anarchy: A Study in Proportional Representation*. Notre Dame, IN: The *Review of Politics*, University of Notre Dame.

Holcombe, Arthur (1933) 'Parties, political', in Edwin R.A. Seligman (ed.), *Encyclopaedia of the Social Sciences*. New York: Macmillan Vol. 11, pp. 590–4.

Key, V.O., Jr. (1949) *Southern Politics in State and Nation*. New York: Albert A. Knopf.

Key, V.O., Jr. (1964) *Politics, Parties, and Pressure Groups*, 5th edn. New York: Crowell.

Laakso, M. and Taagepera, R. (1979) 'Effective number of parties: A measure with appplication to West Europe', *Comparative Political Studies*, 12: 3–27.

Lane, Jan-Erik and Errson, Svante O. (1987) *Politics and Society in Western Europe*. London: Sage.

Lange, Peter and Meadwell, Hudson (1991) 'Typologies of democratic systems: From political inputs to political economy', in Howard Wiarda (ed.), *New Directions in Comparative Politics* Boulder, CO: Westview, pp. 59–81.

Lijphart, Arend (1968) 'Typologies of political systems', *Comparative Political Studies*, 1: 3–44.

Lijphart, Arend (1975) *The Politics of Accommodation: Pluralism and Democracy in the Netherlands*, 2nd edn, revised. Berkeley: University of California Press.

Lijphart, Arend (1977) *Democracy in Plural Societies*. New Haven, CT: Yale University Press.

Lijphart, Arend (1982) 'The relative salience of the socio-economic and religious issue dimensions: Coalition formation in ten western democracies, 1919–1979', *European Journal of Political Research*, 10: 201–11.

Lijphart, Arend (1984) *Democracies: Patterns of Majoritarian and Consensus Government in Twenty-One Countries*. New Haven, CT: Yale University Press.

Lijphart, Arend (1994) *Electoral Systems and Party Systems: A Study of Twenty-Seven Democracies, 1945–1990*. Oxford: Oxford University Press.

Lijphart, Arend (1999) *Patterns of Democracy: Government Forms and Performance in Thirty-Six Countries*. New Haven, CT: Yale University Press.

Lipset, Seymour Martin and Rokkan, Stein (1967) 'Cleavage structures, party systems and voter alignments: An introduction', in S.M. Lipset and S. Rokkan (eds), *Party Systems and Voter Alignments*. New York: Free Press, pp. 1–64.

Mainwaring, Scott P. (1999) *Rethinking Party Systems in the Third Wave of Democratization*. Stanford, CA: Stanford University Press.

Mainwaring, Scott and Scully, Timothy R. (eds) (1995) *Building Democratic Institutions: Party Systems in Latin America*. Stanford, CA: Stanford University Press.

Mair, Peter (1996) 'Party systems and structures of competition', in Lawrence LeDuc, Richard G. Niemi and Pippa Norris (eds), *Comparing Democracies: Elections and Voting in Global Perspective*. Thousand Oaks, CA: Sage, pp. 49–82.

Mair, Peter (2002) 'Comparing party systems', in Lawrence LeDuc, Richard G. Niemi, Pippa Norris (eds), *Comparing Democracies 2: New Challenges in the Study of Elections and Voting*. London: Sage, pp. 88–107.

Neumann, Sigmund (ed.) (1956) *Modern Political Parties: Approaches to Comparative Politics*. Chicago: University of Chicago Press.

Powell, G. Bingham (1982) *Contemporary Democracies: Participation, Stability and Violence*. Cambridge, MA: Harvard University Press.

Rae, Douglas (1967) *The Political Consequences of Electoral Laws*. New Haven, CT: Yale University Press.

Rae, Douglas and Taylor, Michael (1970) *The Analysis of Political Cleavages*. New Haven, CT: Yale University Press.

Rokkan, Stein (1970) *Citizens, Elections, Parties: Approaches to the Comparative Study of Political Development*. Oslo: Universitetsforlaget.

Sartori, Giovanni (1966) 'European political parties: The case of polarized pluralism', in Joseph LaPalombara and Myron Weiner (eds), *Political Parties and Political Development*. Princeton, NJ: Princeton University Press, pp. 137–76.

Sartori, Giovanni (1976) *Parties and Party Systems: A Framework for Analysis*. Cambridge and New York: Cambridge University Press.

Schattschneider, E.E. (1960) *The Semi-Sovereign People: A Realist's View of Democracy in America*. New York: Holt, Rinehart, and Winston.

Siaroff, Alan (2000) *Comparative European Party systems: An Analysis of Parliamentary Elections since 1945*. New York: Garland Publishing.

Siaroff, Alan (2003) 'Two-and-a-half-party systems and the comparative role of the "half"', *Party Politics*, 9: 267–90.

Sundquist, James, L. (1983) *Dynamics of the Party Systems: Alignment and Realignment of Political Parties in the United States*, rev. edn. Washington, DC: Brookings Institution.

Taagepera, Rein and Shugart, Matthew Soberg (1989) *Seats and Votes: The Effects and Determinants of Electoral Systems*. New Haven, CT: Yale University Press.

Ware, Alan (1996) *Political Parties and Party Systems*. Oxford: Oxford University Press.

Zaslove, Andrej (2003a) 'Is fascism still relevant? The radical right and the search for a definition'. Paper presented to the Annual Meeting, Canadian Political Science Association, Halifax, Nova Scotia.

Zaslove, Andrej (2003b) 'The politics of radical right populism: Post-Fordism, the crisis of the welfare state, and the Lega Nord'. Ph.D. thesis. York University, Toronto.

7

PARTY SYSTEM CHANGE

Peter Mair

INTRODUCTION: PARTY SYSTEM CHANGE AND THE CLASSIFICATION OF PARTY SYSTEMS

The key problem with the phenomenon of party system change is that it is seen as either happening all the time or as scarcely happening at all. This is not a reflection on the state of the world, and it is not intended to suggest that the frequency of cases of party system change echoes the proverbial complaint about London buses: you wait for ages for one to come along, and suddenly three arrive together. Rather, it is a reflection on the approaches to the classification of party systems that are currently to be found in the literature, and that have already been discussed by Steven Wolinetz in Chapter 6 of this volume.

There are two approaches to classifying party systems that are relevant here, in the sense that both have quite distinct implications for how party system change is treated. On the one hand, there is the traditional comparative approach developed by scholars such as Duverger, Blondel, and Sartori, which aims to categorize party systems into distinct classes or types, such as two-party systems, systems of moderate pluralism, multiparty systems, or whatever. Following this approach, party systems scarcely change at all, in that a change of party system necessarily involves the case in question moving from one category to another – from the two-party to the multiparty category, or from moderate pluralism to polarized pluralism, and so on – and the conditions that allow for such a reclassification are usually so demanding that it rarely occurs in practice. Some years ago, for example, I sketched an

analytic history of the Irish party system in which, by using Sartori's categories, I tried to show that there had been a shift from polarized pluralism to moderate pluralism, and then to a predominant-party system over a period of some 20 years (Mair, 1979). In a similar vein, Arian and Shamir (2001: 705) have recently pointed to what they see as evidence of 'tremendous change' in the Israeli party system since 1948: the transition from a stable dominant-party system to a competitive two-bloc system and then to the contemporary situation in which the configuration is highly unstable. These sorts of shift seem quite exceptional, however. More typical is the British case, which, over a much longer period, disallowing short-term flux and wartime peculiarities, scarcely deviated from its well-entrenched two-partyism. To see party systems in terms of discrete categories is therefore to bias one's analysis in favour of the absence of change.

The other approach to classifying party systems effectively avoids the issue of classification entirely, and instead employs continuous numeric variables to 'summarize' or 'define' the party system, usually for the purposes of cross-national inquiry. These continuous variables are almost always based on a calculation of the number and relative size – whether electoral or parliamentary – of the parties present in the system. In the earlier literature, the preferred version was Rae's (1968) index of fractionalization (see Shamir, 1984), whereas the more recent literature tends to prefer the version of this index that is modified as 'the effective number of parties' (Laakso and Taagepera, 1979; see also Wolinetz, Chapter 6, this volume). Following this approach, differences between party systems are treated as a matter of degree rather than of kind, and hence party system change is a continuous phenomenon. It is also a confusing phenomenon, since these particular summary measures conflate changes in the number of parties with changes in their relative weights, thereby leaving the observer in the dark as to what sort of change was actually involved (see Pedersen, 1980). For example, the British party system could be said to have 'changed' when the effective number of parties fell from 3.45 following the election of 1983, to 3.33 following the election of 1987 (see the figures in Webb, 2004: 22), even though most observers, and, indeed, most British citizens, would have been very hard pressed to identify what precisely had happened to account for this shift. To see party systems in terms of these continuous variables is therefore to record constant and confusing change, and to bias one's analysis against the identification of stability.

Over the past three decades or so, the literature on party systems has tended to move away from the discussion of discrete categories and to rely more heavily on continuous variables. In part, this is because there has been very little new thinking on how to classify systems since the seminal work of Sartori (1976; see also Wolinetz, Chapter 6, this volume). In part, it is because of a drift away from case-sensitive and thickly descriptive comparative case studies towards the analysis of more broad-ranging cross-national research questions. Categorical classifications of party systems do not easily lend themselves to quantitative research; or at least they are not likely to result in attractive correlation coefficients. Lijphart's influential study of alternative models of democracy is a very good case in point here. Coming from the older comparative politics tradition, in which he has also been one of the leading figures, Lijphart (1999: 62–9) begins his discussion of the relevance of party systems to his models of democracy by highlighting the categorical distinction between two-party systems and multiparty systems, and by linking the former type to the majoritarian model of democracy and the latter to the consensus model. As his analysis progresses, however, and as he begins to apply his framework, this categorical distinction becomes translated into a continuous measurement of the effective number of parties, eventually leading to the calculation of a distinct numerical score for each of the 36 polities that concern him.[1] This is the approach that has now come to dominate quantitative cross-national research. By affording room for measuring endless variation between party systems, however,

and by failing to establish plausible thresholds that could be used to identify the emergence of a new or a different party system, it implicitly renders meaningless any notion of party system change.

AGAINST NUMBERS

It also renders meaningless any notion of party systems. These summary variables count the number of parties in a polity and take account of their relative size, but, in itself, this tells us little of importance about the system as such, or about system change. Indeed, with the exception of the limiting case of polities that have only two more or less equally sized parties, and hence that maintain a pure two-party system, numbers as such have little systematic relevance.[2] We speak of Britain, or the USA, or Greece, or especially Malta, as having two-party systems, but, as Wolinetz reminds us, this is not always because there are only two parties in each of these polities (see also Mair, 2002b: 93–4). Indeed, there were 12 parties that actually won representation in the British House of Commons in 2005 – some of them, to be sure, could have travelled there in the back of a taxi – as did one independent candidate. In Malta, however, which has the purest and most fully mobilized two-party system in Europe, the Democratic Alternative – which was a Green party and the third party of the system – won only 0.7 per cent of the vote on a 96 per cent turnout in 2003, and thereby scarcely rocked the established two-party balance. In any case, the more general rule is that two-party systems are two-party systems not because there are only two parties as such, but because we judge that there are only two parties which are involved in, or are relevant to, government formation. It then also follows that multiparty systems are multiparty because more than two parties are involved in government formation. But beyond possibly providing this information, knowledge of how many parties exist in the polity can tell us next to nothing in itself about how the party system works. For that, we need to know how the various parties can and do act.[3]

This stricture also applies to the classic Sartori typology, despite Sartori's own best efforts to rescue party numbers as a key variable. For Sartori (1976: 128), the number of parties matters, in that the format of the system has 'mechanical predispositions' – that is, knowing how many parties exist gives the observer a good indication of how these parties are likely to interact. But even within Sartori's own framework, this is true only to a certain limited extent. Numbers as such cannot allow us to distinguish the different mechanisms that operate within the many and varied cases of moderate pluralism, for example, in that they cannot tell us whether such a system is likely to be characterized by competing coalitions and wholesale alternation in government, or by overlapping coalitions and partial alternation. Moreover, while numbers can be important in marking the crucial difference between moderate and polarized pluralism, this is not always the case, particularly when the fragmentation in question has been induced by a multiplicity of domains of identification rather than by a stretching of the dimension of competition, that is, by polarization (Sani and Sartori, 1983: 335–7). Numbers alone can also give us no indication about whether we are dealing with a predominant-party system.

Since numbers alone have little meaningful systemic relevance, numerical change cannot be considered to be the same as system change. Hence, the fact that the number of parties has grown significantly through the postwar years in the advanced industrial democracies (Dalton *et al.*, 2000: 40–3; Mair, 2002a: 133–5) does not necessarily indicate that the party systems in these democracies have been transformed. Denmark offers one of the most telling examples in this regard. Until the end of the 1960s, in the context of what had become 'one of the most dull countries to deal with for an empirically oriented student of voting behaviour' (Pedersen, 1968: 253),[4] the party system had contained some five parties of varying electoral strengths. In 1973, this number suddenly doubled as the result of a so-called 'earthquake' election, and since then there have always been at least eight parties represented in the parliament (Bille, 1989; Bille and Pedersen, 2004). In terms of the functioning of the system itself, however, and in terms of the way parties interact with one another, it can be argued that even post-earthquake Denmark reflects more evidence of persistence than of change (Mair, 2002b: 101–2). In this sense, if somewhat ironically, we see that numbers do not always count.

Reverting to the older classifications of comparative politics also offers little guidance in the identification and interpretation of party system change, however. The most traditional classification, that which distinguishes two-party and multiparty systems, is simply too crude for most scholarly purposes. There are not enough two-party systems in the world to allow this to function as a balanced classification, and the multiparty category is itself too overcrowded and undifferentiated. To limit instances of party system change to shifts across this particular boundary would be to impoverish our understanding. The same holds true when looking at Sartori's typology which, however insightful, is also proving less and less appropriate to the task of identifying distinctions within the contemporary world. Indeed, the demise of the traditional anti-system party (see also below) effectively brings the range of Sartori's types back to the two-*versus* multiparty distinction, although in his more nuanced version this distinction translates as that between two-party systems and systems of moderate pluralism.

UNDERSTANDING PARTY SYSTEM CHANGE

In order to understand and identify the phenomenon of party system change, we therefore need to adopt an alternative perspective, one that is neither overly constrained by the traditional classifications, on the one hand, nor too easily dissolved into crude quantitative indicators, on the other. This alternative perspective also needs to address the essence of the party system; that is, it needs to address the principal modes of interaction between the parties and the way in which they compete with one another (see Smith, 1989a, 1989b). Party system change at the margins, even if this could be specified, is of little interest. What matters is change at the core.

Let us be clear on the terms of reference here. First, the core of any party system *qua* system is constituted by the structure of competition for control of the executive. Despite the differing perspectives advanced by the various classifications to be found in the literature, ranging from those of Duverger, Dahl and Rokkan, to those of Blondel and Sartori, this remains a point of more or less widespread agreement: defining a party system begins with an understanding of how governmental power is contested. It is here that the core of the party system is to be found, and hence the parties which count are those that are involved in or have an impact on that competition.

Second, it then follows that a party system changes when there is a change in the structure of competition. And this, in turn, may be broken down into three related components. The first of these identifies change in the structure of competition as taking place when there is a change in the prevailing pattern of alternation in government, such that, for example, there is a shift from a prevailing pattern of wholesale alternation to one of partial alternation, or vice versa, or there is a shift from a prevailing pattern of non-alternation to one of partial or wholesale alternation. The second component refers to the extent to which the governing alternatives in the system prove stable or consistent over time, or whether they involve innovative formulae. The important change in the structure of competition that is identified here occurs when a period of consistency in the make-up of government is then succeeded by a new and innovative alternative. The third component refers to the question of who governs, and to the extent to which access to government is either open to a wide range of diverse parties or limited to a smaller subset of established governing parties. Seen in this light, change in the structure of competition is perhaps most easily observed when it involves a new party arriving in office; by definition, this will also involve the adoption of an innovative governing formula.[5]

This also allows us to classify party systems as such, of course, for by combining information about the patterns of alternation, the degree of innovation, and the access of new parties to government we can begin to distinguish between *closed* and *open* structures of competition, and hence between different party systems. At the same time, we can also gain a sense of the degree of *systemness* of any individual party system. The two limiting cases here are, on the one hand, those party systems in which competition is wholly closed, and in which the pattern of alternation is entirely predictable, the competing protagonists are wholly familiar, and no new party or alliance has any real hope of gaining government; and, on the other hand, those in which competition is wholly open, in which there is little that is predictable or familiar in either the patterns of competition or the make-up of the competing forces, and in which new parties and alliances need place no limit on their expectations. The one case reflects an exceptionally high level of systemness and constitutes a very strong party system, while the other reflects a very low level of systemness and a very weak party system. Indeed, at the latter limit, we see what is scarcely a party system at all, since there is so little here that is clearly patterned: the parties themselves are very fluid, and their interactions relatively shapeless. In their application of a similar approach to the party systems of Latin America, Mainwaring and Scully (1995a) adopt the useful terms 'institutionalized' systems and 'inchoate' systems to refer to this distinction; strictly speaking, however, an inchoate system, or a system with a wholly open structure of competition, is not really a system at all. Systemness implies institutionalization.

More importantly for present purposes, however, these three elements afford a practical set of guidelines for identifying when and how party systems change. As specified above, a party system changes when there is a change in the prevailing structure of competition. That is, a party system changes when there is a change in the pattern of government alternation, when a new governing alternative emerges, and/or when a new party or alliance of parties gains access to office for the first time. It follows that for any such change to occur and be noted, there must have already existed a prior and well-established pattern of competition, and the importance or weight of any change will depend on how stable and well established that prior pattern proved to be.

This last may seem an obvious point, but it is worth spelling out more fully: under normal circumstances, we cannot identify a new mode of alternation in government except by contrast to an already existing pattern, and we cannot speak of an innovative governing formula except by reference to other formulae that are already established. In other words, we cannot speak of a change of party system unless a more or less robust system was already in place. There is one important exception to this rule, of course, and that is when an otherwise 'inchoate' system is replaced by a more patterned system, as happens when newly democratized systems become established for the first time (Holmes, 1998; see also Sartori, 1994: 37). In this case there is obviously no older established pattern that is being displaced, but instead, as has recently been the case in the Czech Republic, for example (Kopecký, 2005), a formerly incoherent set of interactions begins to take shape and acquires structure. But although this is, formally speaking, a process of party system change, it might be better and more informative to treat it as a case of party system institutionalization. At the other extreme, we can also conceive of cases of party system deinstitutionalization – that is, when a prevailing structure of competition breaks up or collapses, and is succeeded by a unformed, inchoate set of interactions. In this case, an existing party system loses shape and becomes destructured without any alternative system emerging in its place. These extremes notwithstanding, the majority of cases of party system change involve the replacement of one type by another. That is, a prevailing structure of competition is broken, and is replaced by a new structure of competition. Just such a change appears now to be the case in contemporary Germany, for example, in that a new pattern of bipolar competition – pitting a centre-left coalition of Social Democrats and Greens against a centre-right coalition of Christian Democrats and Liberals – seems set to replace the older pattern of overlapping opposition, whereby Christian Democrats and Social Democrats sought to gain office with the help of the once pivotal Liberal party. A similar shift towards bipolarism appears to be occurring in Austria. In Italy, the long-standing postwar party system, most aptly characterized in Sartori's terms as a system of polarized pluralism, in which government was always formed from the centre, has also moved towards bipolarism, with the emergence of two more or less coherent and quite distinct electoral alliances that now dominate national competition (Bartolini *et al.*, 2004). All of these shifts are easily identified by reference to the changing patterns of alternation in government, and to the ways in which executive office is being contested. More importantly, perhaps, they have also all involved a break with what had been a persistent and long-standing pattern of competition, even though it may take some time before we can be sure that a new stable structure has been established in place of what went before. Indeed, as Müller and Fallend (2004: n. 6) note, verifying that this sort of change has taken place needs patience.

This is far from being a uniform or standardized process, however, and any application of these guidelines requires sensitivity to the peculiarities of the case. This may also preclude an easy application within cross-national quantitative research. Not all cases of new governing alternatives or even of new parties arriving in government will constitute cases of party system change, for example, and the impact of such changes will clearly differ from one polity to the next. In other words, while the factors identified above offer a useful set of common guidelines, their weight will always remain context-specific. In one context, the structure of competition might be normally very open and flexible, and we might only be able to speak of the emergence of something new at the point when the system closes down. In another, regular access of new parties into government might constitute one key feature of the party system, such as it is, and we might only begin to talk of change when this pattern

ceases to apply. In other words, adding a new party to the ranks of the governors will not make for a new party system if the provision of access to new parties has always been a normal part of the political process.

The contrasting cases of Finland and Ireland offer useful reference points in this regard. Across the past half-century of democratic politics, Finland experienced more than 30 changes in the partisan composition of government, almost all of which resulted from instances of partial alternation – that is, from a reshuffling of existing coalitions and/or from the incorporation of additional parties into pre-existing alliances. For more than two-thirds of this period, Finland was governed by innovative governments, that is, by parties or combinations of parties that had never previously held office using the same governing formula (Mair, forthcoming). The result was a remarkably unstructured and unpredictable pattern of competition, and hence a remarkably open and poorly defined party system, such that the factors that would be seen to constitute a case of party system change in a more closed system proved much less relevant in the Finnish case. In Ireland, by contrast, these sorts of changes were anything but marginal or routine, and when the newly formed Progressive Democrats took office in 1989 as the junior coalition partner of the long-dominant Fianna Fáil party, it marked a major change in the system. For the first time in its long and successful history, Fianna Fáil took part in a coalition government, and for the first time since at least 1948 competition no longer revolved around the opposition between Fianna Fáil on its own, on one side, and a coalition of more or less all remaining parliamentary parties, on the other. In the Irish case, in other words, a very long-standing and familiar pattern was broken open by the sort of innovative coalition that would have proved quite commonplace in Finland.

The Irish case is also a useful illustration of how party systems stabilize around particular assumptions, and how they can suddenly be broken open when those assumptions are challenged.[6] The simple question of time is obviously important here, in that the cumulating daily practice of politics may lead both voters and party leaders to become used to thinking within a particular, and hence institutionalized, set of terms of reference. If the range of governing alternatives has been limited in the past, then this is likely to encourage both observers and participants to believe that they may also be limited in the present. If, to cite this Irish example, previous governments have been formed only by either Fianna Fáil on its own, on the one hand, or a coalition of more or less all other parties, on the other hand, then it is unlikely that voters will be easily persuaded to think in terms of any alternative constellations. It is in this sense that a system becomes predictable and familiar: the alternatives appear to be constrained by particular options being ruled out as unthinkable. Constraining the alternatives will also be the result of elite choices and elite political culture, with the leaders of the established parties being keen to promote the maintenance of the patterns that have served to guarantee them success in the past (see Schattschneider, 1960: 60–74). Conversely, party systems may change when new leaders or new parties begin to explore and then act upon new alternatives.

The nature of the wider institutional structure within which the party system is located can also serve to limit the scope for party system change. In the first place, this wider institutional context will help to define and hence to limit the potential alternatives which are seen to be available. As noted above, bipolarity in the party system of the Fifth French Republic was clearly helped by the institution of the presidency, for example, and by the way in which the parties learned to compete within the presidential arena (see Bartolini, 1984). In Switzerland, the maintenance of the 'magic formula' has been facilitated by the depoliticization of government and the displacement of ultimate decision-making authority to the popular referendum. In the United States, the survival of a stable two-party system in the context of quite flexible and changeable political parties owes a great deal to the restrictive practices in electoral registration and ballot access. In the United Kingdom, two-partyism is helped by the combination of a plurality system of elections to the House of Commons and pronounced party discipline in Westminster. In other words, the institutions of politics provide us with the means and the language for thinking about political alternatives, and this also holds true for the party system, as well as for those institutions which work through the party system. They help to impart a language of politics which, when learned, is likely to become taken for granted and to resist change.

In addition, party system change will also be limited by the sheer stability of the wider institutional order within which it is nested. A party system, as Jepperson (1991: 151) notes of any given institution, 'is less likely to be vulnerable to intervention if it is more embedded in a framework of [other] institutions'. And if these other institutions are themselves relatively stable, then it follows that the party system is more likely to remain intact. Conversely, a change in the institutional setting can provoke quite significant party system change. The case of Italy is the most obvious example here, in that the shift to the largely plurality voting formula in 1993 was one of the key factors that promoted the emergence of the new bipolar competition.

In sum, by focusing on the structure of competition for government, and by adopting a series of guidelines that indicate how that competition can change, we gain a perspective on party system change and stability that is not limited by the traditional categories that are found in the older literature, and that is more meaningful than the perspective offered by simple numerical summaries. There are four key advantages to this approach.

First, it enables us to make the crucial distinction between party system change, on the one hand, and party change, on the other, or between what Lipset and Rokkan (1967) famously referred to as the 'freezing' (and 'unfreezing') of party systems and the 'freezing' (and 'unfreezing') of individual parties. These are obviously two different processes, and can be applied quite independently of one another. As indicated above, parties may change quite substantially, and prove quite flexible and adaptable, and yet the party system can remain intact. Indeed, as I have suggested elsewhere (Mair, 1997: 16), party systems often manage to survive precisely because the parties refuse to be pinned down. At the same time, the parties can remain more or less the same, but because of a short-term change in elite preferences, or even because of a small change in voting patterns, their strategies can suddenly shift, and what had been a long-standing pattern of competition can suddenly be broken open. Britain, which has perhaps one of the most stable party systems in the world, came close to such a break in the lead-up to the 1997 election, when Labour considered a possible coalition with the Liberal Democrats (Webb, 2004: 26).

The second advantage of this approach is that it draws the emphasis away from the numerical criterion. When seen in very simplistic terms, party system change can be taken to be the same as numerical change – the system is different because the number of parties is different. This is very misleading, however, since, as argued above, numbers often fail to count in systemic terms, and they appear to count less and less as more and more parties join in electoral competition and win representation in parliament. In other words, while party systems have become more fragmented in recent years, this does not necessarily imply that the systems themselves have changed.

Third, and following from this, party system change conceived in these terms has the advantage of focusing on change at the core rather than at the margins. The stronger a party system is, the more easily we can see that it revolves around a core opposition – that it is 'about' something (Mair, 1997: 13–14). In Britain, the party system is about the conflict between Labour and Conservative; in France, it is about 'left' against 'right', often without a particular party specification; in Sweden, it is about the Social Democrats against the more loosely determined bourgeois bloc, and so on. In other words, the structure of competition, once established, becomes dominated by a particular choice, and other considerations become secondary. Conversely, to the extent that no single conflict manages to become established, the party system is likely to remain inchoate and ill defined. By tracing patterns in the competition for government, this distinction can easily be brought to light.

Finally, once we deal with party system change in these terms, it becomes relatively easy to pin down more or less precise moments in which prevailing patterns are suddenly broken – as was the case in Ireland in July 1989, in Italy in May 1994, in Germany in October 1998, and in Austria in February 2000. In other words, although it may take time before a new party system develops, and before a new structure of competition becomes established, a breakdown in the old pattern can be seen to have occurred quite suddenly and abruptly. And this, in turn, can open up the possibility of going on to treat party system change as an independent rather than just a dependent variable. It is one thing to identify the factors that lead to party system change, be these social, organizational or institutional, and allowing for the different conceptions of party system change that are used in the literature, this is a well-covered theme. It is quite another to trace the effects of party system change – whether on the component parties themselves, or on the voters – and this is something which, at least as yet, is a relatively neglected research question.

PARTY SYSTEM CHANGE: FUTURE TRENDS

There are two important developments that have recently impacted on parties and on party systems and that are likely to shape the direction of party system change in the coming years. The first of these is what has been called 'the victory of democracy': the ending of the cold war, the collapse of the former Soviet Union, and the success of liberalism (or neo-liberalism) in establishing itself as a more or less universal source of governing principles. This is obviously a new and unprecedented situation, in which, as Perry Anderson (2000: 17) puts it, 'there are no longer any significant oppositions – that is, systematic rival outlooks – within the thought-world of the West; and scarcely any on a world scale either'. The victory of democracy also makes for an enormous change in the context within which party systems operate, although its impact is sometimes difficult to appreciate. Given that the party systems in the long-established democracies grew up and became consolidated in an international context in which democracy was daily contested by non-democratic alternatives, and given that this international battle was often translated by competing political parties into a form of domestic opposition, the sudden ending of this conflict has had effects that reach into the heart of contemporary politics. One such effect has been the effective disappearance of any possible challenge to democracy at the domestic level – as Juan Linz (1997: 404) has noted, we are all democrats now, and 'no anti-democratic ideology appeals to politicians, intellectuals, religious leaders … as an alternative to political democracy' – and hence the disappearance of the traditional anti-system party (see also Capoccia, 2002). With the demise or transformation of the former communist parties, and the effective disappearance of the traditional fascist alternative, there are no longer any important pariah parties in competition. In contemporary politics, in other words, and probably for the first time in democratic history, almost all parties have become *salonfähig*.

This obviously also now holds true even for the parties of the new radical right (see Bale, 2003; see also Mudde, 2001). These parties differ from the mainstream, sometimes dramatically so, in terms of policy, and often also in style, but they rarely differ in terms of any ultimate commitment to the maintenance of democratic procedures. As such, however unpalatable it sometimes seems, both domestically and internationally, mainstream parties do find it possible to forge compromises with these new parties and to bring them into government. Indeed, in recent years, this has become almost commonplace in Western Europe (see Heinisch, 2003), with the Freedom Party in Austria, the Lega Nord in Italy, and the Pim Fortuyn List in the Netherlands becoming full-fledged parties of government, and with recent centre-right minority governments in Denmark and Norway relying on support from Danish People's Party and Progress Party, respectively. The lesson here is evident: policy differences, however sharp, are always negotiable. The degree to which anti-systemness has now become a thing of the past was also made evident when the right-wing nationalist party Sinn Féin became part of the extraordinary coalition running the newly devolved government in Northern Ireland, even though its associated military wing, the Irish Republican Army, a terrorist organization, had not yet surrendered or decommissioned all of its weapons (Tonge, 2000).

The second important change that is likely to have an impact on the future direction of party system change has been the decline of parties as membership organizations, and the ascendancy of the party in public office within the party writ large (Katz and Mair, 1995, 2002). This general shift, which may be observed in traditional mainstream parties in almost all long-established democracies, and which, in its end state, is also often characteristic of emerging parties in both new and old democracies, has obviously many implications for how the individual parties behave and for how they communicate with and relate to the wider society (see Krouwel, Chapter 21, in this volume; see also van Biezen, 2003). This also has implications for party systems, however, the most important of which is that it helps to bring the parties closer to one another, This is especially true when judged from the perspective of the shared ambitions of comparable office-holding and office-seeking elites, and it is something that helps to push the parties further along the road towards becoming the sort of top-heavy campaigning organizations that are exemplars of the Schumpeterian or Downsian version of electoral politics: that is, teams of leaders who compete for the favour of the people's vote (see Beyme, 1996; Farrell and Webb, 2000).

The combination of both of these factors suggests that the party systems of the future are more and more likely to reflect the type of bipolar competition that has long been characteristic of the French Fifth Republic, and that is now also clearly evident in Italy. This same pattern may also be emerging in Austria and Germany, and is already beginning to be established – whether in two-party or two-bloc form – in many of the newer democracies in southern and post-communist Europe, as well as in Latin

America (Bale, 2003; Mainwaring and Scully, 1995b). This trajectory is likely for two related reasons. First, precisely because the substantive differences between mainstream parties are less pronounced,[7] and because these parties can no longer function primarily as representatives in an ideological or purposive sense, elections will inevitably come to revolve more closely around the choice of persons rather than that of policies (see also Mair, 2003). Second, in order to help facilitate a choice of persons, and in order to ensure at least some degree of popular accountability and legitimacy, the parties will almost inevitably find themselves being driven towards bipolar competition, and hence towards an electoral process that affords voters a choice among alternative governments, and among alternative teams of leaders. Parties that govern have a clearer need for immediate electoral accountability than do parties that also represent, and unless accountability is promoted by the provision of clear alternatives in the electoral process, the parties themselves are likely to be seen as less legitimate. In this sense, we can see a version of the so-called Americanization of party systems – a downgrading of the role of policy in competition, and an enhancement of the role of personality, leading to the provision of clear choices between opposing candidates or teams of candidates. This is certainly the direction in which many party systems are now travelling.[8]

It is therefore interesting that when we look across the contemporary advanced democracies, we see only a handful of polities that still appear to maintain a traditional pattern of overlapping coalitions with a more or less extended post-election negotiating period: Belgium, Luxembourg, the Netherlands and Finland. These countries, together with the special case of Switzerland, now constitute the only set of democracies where voters are effectively denied a direct say in the formation of the government. This is, in all likelihood, a dying tradition. Once parties present themselves to the public primarily as governors rather than as representatives, as is more and more often the case, then they will come under increasing pressure to cede to that public the choice of who will actually win office. In some cases, especially in the old consociational democracies, this may well require a major restructuring of the party system as a whole.

Two other changes may well go hand in hand with such a general shift in direction. First, a move towards bipolarity may well serve to facilitate party and party system renewal. If we assume continuing multipartyism, and hence also relatively permissive electoral systems, then bipolarity will almost certainly have to follow the pattern set by France or Italy rather than that of Britain or the USA. That is, it will involve competition between more or less flexible and malleable blocs of parties, or electoral alliances, rather than single parties or tight coalitions. Other things being equal, these blocs will be seen as being of the centre-left and centre-right, even though in practice there may be little in policy terms to choose between them. As in France and Italy, this will be what the party system is about – this will be the core. The result is that *within* each bloc it is likely that there will be less and less privileging of particular party organizations or labels, and more room for the free competition for influence and control. It is here that renewal will be found. The broad *tendances* will remain stable while the various parties reshuffle within them. Core coalitional continuity will coexist with an unsettled range of partisan or semi-partisan components.

Second, as elections increasingly come to revolve around personalities or teams of personalities, it is likely that the policy-making process will become ever more depoliticized. In other words, leaders who are chosen primarily because of their simple electoral appeal or celebrity status are more likely to seek to delegate decisions to non-political agencies.[9] They are also more likely to be encouraged to do so by those around them. This process of delegation is already well advanced in most democratic polities, and was accelerated very substantially in the wake of the victory of democracy and the ending of the cold war. In practice, it means more decision-making power being ceded to so-called non-majoritarian institutions, a greater role for judges and other expert arbiters, and even more influence being accumulated by bodies such as the European Union, the World Trade Organization and the International Monetary Fund. Elections lead to office, but not necessarily to authority, and almost certainly not to expertise. As Schumpeter (1947: 288) once put it, 'selection by means of success at the polls may work against people who would be successes at the head of affairs. And even if the products of this selection prove successes in office these successes may well be failures for the nation.'[10] Hence the perceived need for delegation.

In sum, the future trend for party systems may well be in the direction of a world that was already sketched by Schumpeter more than half a century ago: a world in which parties are teams of leaders, who compete for majority support in party systems that are increasingly bipolar, and who then rely on a host of expert agencies and international organizations to deal with their decision-making problems. Party systems may well become more competitive, and hence elections may well become decisive, but they also risk becoming less meaningful. Even if choice becomes more apparent, it may yet count for less.

NOTES

1. Only two of these 36 cases – Portugal and Sweden – end up with identical mean scores (Lijphart, 1999: 76–7, Table 5.2), suggesting that there is a unique solution, and hence a unique party system, for each polity, and, once we move away from mean values, for each individual election.
2. The other limiting case is that in which there are so many parties, and in which the system is so highly fragmented, that it is not possible to discern any stable or patterned interactions. The case of Poland in the early 1990s comes close to this extreme, in that 29 parties won representation in the 1991 Sejm, with the biggest single party commanding just 13.5 per cent of the seats (Szczerbiak, 2001: 15–18).
3. This is also the conclusion that is reached by Bogaards (2004) in a recent evaluation of classifications of party systems in sub-Saharan Africa.
4. Pedersen went on to note that 'the Danish political system lacks most of those characteristics that form the point of departure for many modern research workers, i.e. conflicts, cleavages, and instabilities'.
5. For a more extended account of this approach, see Mair (2001a, 2002b: 94–7).
6. See Mair (2001b), from which some of the following is drawn.
7. Policy differences between the mainstream and the new radical right remain quite pronounced, of course, even though incorporation in public office does appear to have a taming effect on the latter (see Heinisch, 2003; Minkenberg, 2001).
8. But not at the European Union level, which may well explain much of the scepticism and lack of interest with which many European voters approach elections to the European Parliament: no government is being elected, and no real alternatives are on offer – and yet the parties that mainly contest these elections seem no longer in a position to provide effective representation. The result is that they have little to offer the voters, and little to encourage their engagement.
9. See also Strøm *et al.* (2003), who deal with this issue extensively.

10. A similar conclusion was later reached by March and Olsen (1995: 136): 'It is not self-evident that electoral political competition will necessarily produce leaders who represent the interests of the people well or who are competent to govern ... Nor is it self-evident that the capabilities needed to succeed in political competition are the same as the capabilities needed to govern.'

REFERENCES

Anderson, Perry (2000) 'Editorial: Renewals,' *New Left Review II*, 1: 5–24.

Arian, Asher and Shamir, Michal (2001) 'Candidates, parties and blocs: Israel in the 1990s', *Party Politics*, 7: 689–710.

Bale, Tim (2003) 'Cinderella and her ugly sisters: The mainstream and extreme right in Europe's bipolarising party systems', *West European Politics*, 26(3): 67–90.

Bartolini, Stefano (1984) 'Institutional constraints and party competition in the French party system', *West European Politics*, 7(4): 103–27.

Bartolini, Stefano, Chiaramonte, Alessandro and D'Alimonte, Roberto (2004) 'The Italian party system between parties and coalitions', *West European Politics*, 27(1): 1–19.

Beyme, Klaus von (1996) 'Party leadership and change in party systems: Towards a postmodern party state?', *Government and Opposition*, 31(2): 135–59.

Bille, Lars (1989) 'Denmark: The oscillating party system', *West European Politics*, 12(4): 42–58.

Bille, Lars and Pedersen, Karina (2004) 'Electoral fortunes and responses of the Social Democratic Party and Liberal Party in Denmark: Ups and downs', in Peter Mair, Wolfgang C. Müller and Fritz Plasser (eds), *Political Parties and Electoral Change: Party Responses to Electoral Markets*. London: Sage, pp. 207–33.

Bogaards, Matthijs (2004) 'Counting parties and identifying dominant party systems in Africa', *European Journal of Political Research*, 43(2): 173–97.

Capoccia, Giovanni (2002) 'Anti-system parties: A conceptual reassessment', *Journal of Theoretical Politics*, 14(1): 9–35.

Dalton, Russell J., McAllister, Ian and Wattenberg, Martin P. (2000) 'The consequences of partisan dealignment', in Russell J. Dalton and Martin Wattenberg (eds), *Parties without Partisans*. Oxford: Oxford University Press, pp. 37–63.

Farrell, David M. and Webb, Paul (2000) 'Political parties as campaign organizations', in Russell J. Dalton and Martin Wattenberg (eds), *Parties without Partisans*. Oxford: Oxford University Press, pp. 102–28.

Heinisch, Reinhard (2003) 'Success in opposition – failure in government: Explaining the performance of right-wing populist parties in public office', *West European Politics*, 26(3): 91–130.

Holmes, Leslie (1998) 'Towards a stabilisation of party systems in post-communist countries?', *European Review*, 6(2): 233–48.

Jepperson, Ronald L. (1991) 'Institutions, institutional effects, and institutionalism', in Walter W. Powell and Paul J. DiMaggio (eds), *The New Institutionalism in Organizational Analysis*. Chicago: University of Chicago Press, pp. 143–163.

Katz, Richard S. and Mair, Peter (1995) 'Changing models of party organization and party democracy: The emergence of the cartel party', *Party Politics*, 1(1): 5–28.

Katz, Richard S. and Mair, Peter (2002) 'The ascendancy of the party in public office: Party organizational change in twentieth-century democracies', in Richard Gunther, José Ramón Montero and Juan J. Linz (eds), *Political Parties. Old Concepts and New Challenges*. Oxford: Oxford University Press, pp. 113–135.

Kopecký, Petr (2005) 'Building party government: Political parties in the Czech and Slovak republics', in Paul Webb, Stephen White and David Stansfield (eds), *Political Parties in Transitional Democracies*. Oxford: Oxford University Press, forthcoming.

Laakso, Markku and Taagepera, Rein (1979) 'Effective number of parties: A measure with application to West Europe', *Comparative Political Studies*, 12(1): 3–27.

Lijphart, Arend (1999) *Patterns of Democracy: Government Forms and Performance in Thirty-Six Countries*. New Haven, CT: Yale University Press.

Linz, Juan J. (1997) 'Some thoughts on the victory and future of democracy', in Axel Hadenius (ed.), *Democracy's Victory and Crisis: Nobel Symposium No. 93*. Cambridge: Cambridge University Press, pp. 404–26.

Lipset, Seymour Martin and Rokkan, Stein (1967) 'Cleavage structures, party systems and voter alignments: An introduction', in Seymour Martin Lipset and Stein Rokkan (eds), *Party Systems and Voter Alignments*. New York: Free Press, pp. 1–64.

Mainwaring, Scott and Scully, Timothy R. (1995a) 'Introduction: Party systems in Latin America', in Scott Mainwaring and Timothy R. Scully (eds), *Building Democratic Institutions: Party Systems in Latin America*. Stanford, CA: Stanford University Press, pp. 1–34.

Mainwaring, Scott and Scully, Timothy R. (eds) (1995b) *Building Democratic Institutions: Party Systems in Latin America*. Stanford, CA: Stanford University Press.

Mair, Peter (1979) 'The autonomy of the political: The development of the Irish party system', *Comparative Politics*, 11(4): 445–65.

Mair, Peter (1997) *Party System Change: Approaches and Interpretations*. Oxford: Oxford University Press.

Mair, Peter (2001a) 'Party systems', in Neil J. Smelser and Paul B. Baltes (eds), *International Encyclopedia of the Social & Behavioral Sciences*, Vol. 16. Amsterdam: Elsevier, pp. 11,106–8.

Mair, Peter (2001b) 'The freezing hypothesis: An evaluation', in Lauri Karvonen and Stein Kuhnle (eds), *Party Systems and Voter Alignments Revisited*. London: Routledge, pp. 27–44.

Mair, Peter (2002a) 'In the aggregate: Mass electoral behaviour in Western Europe, 1950–2000', in Hans Keman (ed.), *Comparative Democratic Politics*. London: Sage, pp. 122–40.

Mair, Peter (2002b) 'Comparing party systems', in Lawrence LeDuc, Richard G. Niemi and Pippa Norris (eds), *Comparing Democracies 2: New Challenges in the Study of Elections and Voting*. London: Sage, pp. 88–107.

Mair, Peter (2003) 'Political parties and democracy: What sort of future?', *Central European Political Science Review*, 4(13): 6–20.

Mair, Peter (forthcoming) 'Alternation in government', in Luciano Bardi (ed.), *Partiti e sistemi di partito tra i due secoli. Il cartel party e oltre*. Bologna: Il Mulino.

March, James G. and Olsen, Johan P. (1995) *Democratic Governance*. New York: Free Press.

Minkenberg, Michael (2001) 'The radical right in public office: Agenda-setting and policy effects', *West European Politics*, 24(4): 1–21.

Mudde, Cas (2001) 'The paradox of the anti-party party: Insights from the extreme right', *Party Politics*, 2: 265–76.

Müller, Wolfgang C. and Fallend, Franz (2004) 'Changing patterns of party competition in Austria: From multipolar to bipolar system', *West European Politics*, 27(5): 801–35.

Pedersen, Mogens N. (1968) 'Current electoral research in Denmark', *Scandinavian Political Studies*, 3: 253–6.

Pedersen, Mogens N. (1980) 'On measuring party system change: A methodological critique and a suggestion', *Comparative Political Studies*, 12(4): 387–403.

Rae, Douglas W. (1968) 'A note on the fractionalisation of European party systems', *Comparative Political Studies*, 1(4): 413–18.

Sani, Giacomo and Sartori, Giovanni (1983) 'Polarization, fragmentation and competition in Western democracies', in Hans Daalder and Peter Mair (eds), *Western European Party Systems: Continuity and Change*. London: Sage, pp. 307–40.

Sartori, Giovanni (1976) *Parties and Party Systems: A Framework for Analysis*. Cambridge: Cambridge University Press.

Sartori, Giovanni (1994) *Comparative Constitutional Engineering: An Inquiry into Structures, Incentives and Outcomes*. Basingstoke: Macmillan.

Schattschneider, E.E. (1960) *The Semi-Sovereign People*. New York: Holt, Rinehart and Winston.

Schumpeter, Joseph A. (1947) *Capitalism, Socialism, and Democracy* (2nd edn). New York: Harper.

Shamir, Michal (1984) 'Are Western European party systems "frozen"?', *Comparative Political Studies*, 17(1): 35–79.

Smith, Gordon (1989a) 'A system perspective on party system change', *Journal of Theoretical Politics*, 1(3): 349–64.

Smith, Gordon (1989b) 'Core persistence: System change and the "People's Party"', *West European Politics*, 12(4): 157–68.

Strøm, Kaare, Müller, Wolfgang C. and Bergman, Torbjörn (2003) 'Challenges to parliamentary democracy', in Kaare Strøm, Wolfgang C. Müller and Torbjörn Bergman (eds), *Delegation and Accountability in Parliamentary Democracies*. Oxford: Oxford University Press, pp. 707–50.

Szczerbiak, Aleks (2001) *Poles Together? Emergence and Development of Political Parties in Post-communist Poland*. Budapest: Central European University Press.

Tonge, Jonathan (2000) 'The formation of the Northern Ireland Executive', *Irish Political Studies*, 15: 153–61.

van Biezen, Ingrid (2003) *Political Parties in New Democracies: Party Organization in Southern and East-Central Europe*. Basingstoke: Palgrave.

Webb, Paul (2004) 'Party responses to the changing electoral market in Britain', in Peter Mair, Wolfgang C. Müller and Fritz Plasser (eds), *Political Parties and Electoral Change: Party Responses to Electoral Markets*. London: Sage, pp. 20–48.

PART II

FUNCTIONS OF PARTY

8

POLITICAL PARTIES AS MECHANISMS OF SOCIAL CHOICE*

Marjorie Randon Hershey

INTRODUCTION: RATIONALITY APPROACHES AND THE STUDY OF POLITICAL PARTIES

If the use of rational choice theory in the study of political parties were a political candidate, it would be considered a front-runner with high negatives. Approaches that emphasize rationality have produced a large theoretical and empirical literature and a number of fruitful and provocative findings and have also generated intense criticism. The aim of this chapter is to set out the central tendencies of these approaches to the study of political parties, summarize some of their main applications in the field, discuss ways in which they have added to our understanding of party politics, and evaluate some of the main critiques of their use.

Rationality approaches, the general class to which social choice analysis belongs, begin with the premise that people behave purposefully.[1] Individuals are goal-directed actors. These approaches do not attempt to explain why people hold particular goals; rather, taking the goals as given, they assume that individuals will try to achieve their goals through instrumental, efficient means. In practice, the use of efficient means can be understood as the effort by individuals to increase the benefits they expect to receive from their actions relative to the costs they expect to pay.[2]

This purposeful behavior takes place in an environment whose characteristics affect the individual's ability to achieve his or her goals. Any environment will have a given level of information, a set of institutional rules, and a historical context.[3] Political environments have some unique qualities that affect individuals' choices. For one, governments are responsible for *public goods* – those shared by all members of the society, whose provision cannot be limited to some members and withheld from others. Although individuals may vary in their ability to take advantage of such goods as improved air quality or stronger national defense, for example, they cannot be delivered to only those people who pay taxes to fund them while excluding those who do not.

One of the most intriguing insights of the rationality approaches is that to create these public goods – to clean the air and defend the nation – requires collective action, but collective action is vulnerable to specific and serious problems. In particular, the actions that would be required to achieve a public good may not be in the individual interest of any of the actors. Why should a member of Congress choose to spend her valuable time negotiating the content of bills and making appropriations to cut air pollution – a policy that will benefit all her congressional colleagues and all their constituents – while her colleagues are then freed to spend their own time pursuing pork barrel projects, casework, and other activities that will help ensure their own re-election? And if it is in nobody's individual interest to devote their personal resources to pursuing collective goals, then how can those goals, which are in everyone's interest, be achieved?

Analysts have shown that when a number of legislators or other individuals make choices on policies based on their own preferences, acting independently of one another, they can produce an outcome that all of them would consider worse than outcomes they could gain by organizing, even though each is behaving in ways that are entirely rational.[4] Consider, for example, the chief executives of two cellulose plants located on the same lake. Because they are in competition, each plant chooses independently to reduce its costs by dumping chemical wastes into the lake. To recycle wastes would increase the expenses of the plant that did it and weaken its competitive position in the market. But dumping the wastes causes water quality to deteriorate. As a result, both plants, which need a relatively unpolluted source of water in order to produce their product, suffer long-term costs. In the short run it is rational for each plant to find ways to cut its costs. But the longer-range result is to increase the costs paid by each plant and by the larger community, which is clearly a suboptimal outcome.[5]

These problems of collective action can be solved in a variety of ways. Collections of individuals or legislators can agree to act cooperatively in making their decisions. They can create sets of rules and expectations to structure their joint activity: these decision rules are termed 'processes of social choice'. Stable sets of rules and expectations become organizations and institutions. These institutions can deal with collective action problems by creating inducements for individuals to act so as to further the interests of the collectivity or community as a whole.

A political party is one of these institutions: a means by which people can agree to behave cooperatively over the long term so as to secure benefits that they would not have been able to gain as individuals. A party could provide the mechanism for solving several kinds of social choice and collective action problems. Within a legislature, parties can make it possible to create lasting majorities for policies on important issues. In campaigns, parties can help candidates coordinate their behavior (their fund-raising, for example) in order to achieve mutual gain. They can make organized efforts to register and turn out voters so as to reduce the individual campaigns' costs.

In elections, affiliating with a party lets a candidate offer potential supporters a means of reducing their information costs; knowing that a candidate is a Republican or a Democrat permits the citizen to infer a series of conclusions about the candidate's policy stands and general approach to public life. Lower information costs increase the likelihood that the citizen will vote.[6] For these and other reasons, practitioners of rationality approaches argue, it is instructive to conceptualize parties as institutions designed to solve problems of collective choice.[7]

RATIONALITY APPROACHES TO THE STUDY OF PARTIES

Every functioning democracy has political parties. Nascent parties were created in the United States within the first decade after the signing of the Constitution. Interestingly, they were created by political leaders who had expressed strong anti-party sentiments, who had denounced the idea of parties as self-serving, dissension-provoking, and likely to be harmful to the new republic. Why did some political leaders choose to create parties at this time? What is the evidence that parties were created as a vehicle to solve problems of collective action? And why did these politicians form parties rather than some other kind of political organization?

One of the most insightful accounts of the rise of parties in the United States that explicitly adopts the rational choice perspective is that of John Aldrich in *Why Parties?* For Aldrich, the provocation for the formation of parties was a dilemma of social choice. Members of the infant federal government faced a large number of decisions on vital issues, ranging from the nature of government involvement in the economy to the location of the capital. The choice situation at this time, however, was fluid and unstable.[8] Members of Congress and other federal notables were pulled and tugged on several dimensions simultaneously: their ideological beliefs about the scope and power of the federal government, their attitudes toward other issues, sectional concerns, and inter-state and intra-state rivalries. Majorities were fleeting and unstable; vote-trading deals were made and then unraveled. In short, the Congress was in the grip of a social choice problem.

One of those most concerned with the fluidity of this situation was Alexander Hamilton.

Hamilton had initially enjoyed majority support in Congress for his vision of a strong central government. But he was having trouble holding that support; Hamilton's chief antagonist, James Madison, won some key debates by prospecting for votes among Hamilton supporters on an issue-by-issue basis. If Hamilton hoped to win consistent majorities for the principle of a federal government with expanded power and to establish a clear precedent for future action consistent with this principle, then he needed a means of keeping his supporters together over a range of votes.

As Aldrich shows, Hamilton succeeded by laying the groundwork for a legislative party. As Secretary of the Treasury, he was able to set the congressional agenda by submitting a plan for dealing with the public debt. He worked with allies in the House to coordinate which bills were offered and to enlist his supporters to vote for them. In these ways, Hamilton was able to ensure that those in Congress who shared his views about the role of the federal government could overcome the problem of fleeting and unstable majorities and translate their preference into government action. In social choice terms, a form of institutional structure was created to reduce the number of competing bases for choice, to bring equilibrium instead of disequilibrium, and thus to produce an answer to the fundamental question that faced the new government.[9]

Once Hamilton's legislative 'party' had come into existence, as the majority, it was able to win on any votes where it organized. The opposing group, headed by Madison and Thomas Jefferson, then had no alternative but to try to alter the status quo by changing the membership of Congress in the next congressional elections. They set up a number of 'committees of correspondence' to encourage the election of other Jeffersonians and succeeded in winning control of the House in 1792. By that time, voting behavior in the House and Senate had moved from 'widely dispersed scatters' to 'two clear and quite separate blocs … not just polarized but also very strongly related to partisan affiliations,'[10] consistent with Aldrich's expectation.

A second major dilemma of collective action, Aldrich argues, can be seen in relation to the formation of the first true mass-based American party, the Democrats, in the late 1820s.[11] Recall that a central issue in collective action is that even though something might be in the collective interest of a large number of people, no individual may see it in his or her personal interest to contribute to that goal. The

collective interest in this case was the election of a president. As will be shown later, individuals will be tempted to abstain from voting because even the small costs of gathering information and going to the polls are likely to outweigh the minimal benefits the individual expects to get from the outcome. But mass abstention can be a big problem for politicians, because they need votes in order to fulfill their ambitions.

In the relatively fluid politics of the 1820s, a number of ambitious politicians, notably Martin Van Buren and Andrew Jackson, came together to create an institutional structure – a mass party – that would enable them to attract more votes and thus benefit from control of government. This form of political party used mass rallies, parades, and other means to provide citizens with information about the election. By doing so, the mass party reduced citizens' information costs and, by working to mobilize citizens, helped bring more prospective voters into the polling booths.

But to help solve the collective action problem for prospective voters, those who wanted to organize a mass party faced a collective action problem of their own: organizing a mass party is a costly enterprise for individuals, given that the benefits will be shared. Aldrich posits that the party's midwives would have tried to reduce these costs by building on the organizations in states where there was already the start of a party infrastructure. Once these new forms of party were developed, they would focus their efforts at voter mobilization in those states and in elections that were expected to be close, because those are the races in which a party's effort would be most likely to make a difference.

Consistent with his hypotheses, Aldrich finds major increases in turnout in the New England and 'middle' states (New Jersey and Delaware), where there was high competitiveness and where the Democratic Party had successfully organized. Because these existing local organizations were more likely to join the mass party if they were able to maintain a substantial amount of independence (a selective incentive), this choice by the founders of the mass party laid the groundwork for a degree of local party autonomy in American politics that has long been unusual among the world's democratic party systems.[12]

Aldrich's third main contribution is to use rationality assumptions to explain the major recent change in the American parties: the movement from the mass party to the 'party in service', which developed around the 1960s.

This development was caused by several long-term changes in the parties' environment, which altered the structure of rewards and opportunities. Changes in the electorate, such as increasing educational levels and the assimilation of immigrant populations, reduced the number of people who needed the help provided by the older mass parties at the local level. Changes in national policy, especially expansion of the New Deal entitlement programs, further reduced the need for the local party's assistance. The steady inroads of Progressive and Populist reforms and of ticket splitting restricted the party organization's ability to control access to office and to control office-holders once they were elected.

In addition, the rise of national media enabled individual candidates to reach voters, contributors, and issue- and candidate-oriented campaign activists without needing to work through a party organization. The size of the new voting population and the changes in communications media meant that campaigns would have to be directed by experts in these new media and other technologies: professionals rather than volunteers. In the mass party of earlier years, candidates were generally subordinate to the party organization in campaigns. But by the 1960s, ambitious candidates could (and usually had to) win office without the party's direction. Candidates, not parties, became dominant. The parties, adapting as they have throughout their long lives in American politics, thus had to gear up to become 'parties in service' to provide services and expertise in order to retain at least an active role, if no longer a dominant one, in candidates' campaigns.[13]

Do we need the logic of social choice to explain why parties formed and why they changed during the last half of the 20th century? Probably not. It might be possible, alternatively, to argue that people's affiliative needs lead them to identify with and become active in parties and that the rise and fall of partisan behavior over time reflects changes in the available alternatives for affiliation. Some might respond that the need for affiliation itself could be interpreted as a rational process; but if so, then it is fair to ask whether rational choice is a falsifiable system of analysis.

Whether or not it is the only defensible explanation, does the rationality approach give us new insight into these vital periods of party change? Clearly it does. In the case of the parties' founding, for instance, the approach calls attention to the fact that it was not enough for most members of Congress to agree that the

new national government should assume the debts incurred by the states before the Republic was formed. Most members did agree, yet they were unable to act initially on that agreement. Institutional arrangements had to be created to produce incentives for the members of that majority to vote on the basis of their felt need for a strong national government rather than on other possible bases. As an approach, then, it has considerable power to stimulate insights about the behavior of political parties.

MOBILIZING FOR COLLECTIVE ACTION

If we accept Aldrich's premise that a party is a means to an end, created and shaped by office-holders because they find it to be in their personal interest, then we are led to ask a variety of questions about the relationship between institutional structure and the ambition of candidates and public officials. Analysts in the rational choice school have examined this relationship in three major areas. The first is voter choice; as in the case of Van Buren and Jackson, candidates need to get voters to support them in elections and to mobilize activists on their behalf. Second, elected officials need to resolve conflicts over leadership recruitment and succession: who will have the opportunity to run for which office at a given time. Finally, office-holders continue to deal with the challenges that the early Congresses faced: what alternatives to public policy problems will be considered, in what order, and who will get what, when, and how from government?

In a democracy, citizens must have some role in choosing important government personnel. Writers and activists may differ on the thresholds they would prefer, but it is fair to assume that at least some minority of officials with significant decision-making authority must be elected by citizens. Yet with even a minimal definition of 'democratic', we quickly run into a major problem of collective action. Although governments in modern industrial democracies make decisions about virtually every aspect of their citizens' lives, citizens' awareness of that impact may be slight. The effects of many government decisions are complex and long-range. People's immediate needs for food, shelter, and entertainment dominate their thinking and their time; developing an interest and a desire to become informed about an entity that seems to be faceless and remote is not common. Yet without at least some minimal citizen participation, a democratic government lacks legitimacy. So how is it possible to get citizens to go to the polls to choose elected officials if they would rather watch football, if their interest in politics and information levels are low, and if they feel confident that government will continue functioning without their input?

When a democracy begins to expand, nascent party organizations have a straightforward incentive to selectively stimulate citizen participation. The more voters they are able to mobilize, the greater their likelihood of electing their candidates. The early Democratic Republicans (Jeffersonians) clearly followed that path in reaching out to citizens in the localities; party leaders further had an incentive to expand the right to vote in order to gain power using the votes of these newly enfranchised groups. Although the Federalists may also have seen the logic of enlisting new voters, they were less well suited to do so because the policies that animated the Federalist Party had much greater appeal to merchants, bankers, and other elites – who already had the right to vote and who were limited in numbers – than to the immigrants and frontiersmen who initially lacked that right.

As a democracy matures and the franchise expands to approach its natural limits, the challenge then becomes the need to motivate qualified voters to go to the polls. Parties can serve this need in several ways. For Anthony Downs, the use of a party ideology can be a 'rational habit' for voters. When an individual has carefully informed herself about the parties and policy stands in preceding elections and has always come to the same decision, she could reasonably conclude that the probability of changing that decision is too small to warrant investing time and energy in gathering information about the current election. As long as conditions remain the same, this habitual decision helps to reduce the citizen's costs and thus to increase the probability that she will vote. If conditions change beyond a certain threshold, she should see the need to gather information again.[14]

Others also view the existence of parties in the electorate, or party identification, as a means of simplifying voters' choices and therefore making it easier for them to choose to vote. For Morris Fiorina, for example, citizens can use the device of retrospective analysis to reduce their costs. Although politics is confusing, Fiorina writes, voters 'typically have one comparatively hard bit of data: they know what life has been like during the incumbent's administration'.[15] Presuming that the parties are reasonably consistent in their policies over time, this retrospective judgment asks less of citizens than does an approach that expects considerable data-gathering; information about the past is cheaper to obtain than information about the future. Retrospective voting could refer only to a particular administration but it could also be extended to a standing assessment of the administration's party.

In any of several ways, then, citizens can use party as a means of drawing inferences about the candidates' characteristics and policy stands. It is a form of stereotyping that can be used to shortcut the process of gathering information about the choices in an election. It can summarize the likely impact of each candidate or party or simply reduce the voter's choices to a manageable number. Through whatever means, the party symbol's function as a stereotype or heuristic is a means of getting a lot of useful information cheaply, and that, in turn, increases the likelihood that a citizen will vote.[16]

In addition to these two means by which party can solve this collective action problem – as a symbol by conveying a fairly cheap package of useful information and as an organization by reaching out to citizens who might not otherwise vote – party can also cut citizens' costs of involvement in government by linking them to their representatives. Some evidence suggests that party identifiers are more likely to contact and request services from a US House representative if he or she shares the identifier's party affiliation.[17]

RECRUITING LEADERS AND REGULATING ACCESS TO POLITICAL OFFICE

Democracies need to recruit leaders as well as voters. Political leadership is a public good so, as we have seen, problems of collective choice arise in its selection. Collective action problems should be mitigated in the *recruitment* of leaders by the fact that those who win office get selective benefits – power, importance, and other perquisites of holding office, at least at higher levels. These benefits can be offset, however, by the many challenges that face elected officials in the form of public cynicism, media criticism, and the larger salaries and bigger perks that are available in comparable positions in the private sector.

Why would parties serve as useful devices for leadership recruitment rather than, say, non-profit groups like the United Way or for-profit organizations? A new party would have the motivation to do so as a means of securing power for itself. Federalists in the new American government sought like-minded allies to establish Hamilton's proposals as the blueprint for the new central government. Then the Federalists' opponents saw the need to serve as an alternative channel of candidate recruitment. By encouraging both the spread of local party organizing among leaders who held the same general sentiment and the connections among these local parties in this recruitment process, the Democratic Republicans helped to further their own ambitions as well as to strengthen the existence of the federal system.[18]

As this party competition becomes more established, a party hoping to maintain (or obtain) dominance in government should not only seek like-minded individuals to run for office under the party's label but also offer help in the form of campaign expertise, money, and other resources to increase their chances of winning. This seems to be an almost universal activity of party organizations, though the extent of its provision varies over time. The locus of parties' provision of resources varies as well; as many local party organizations struggled to deal with changes in society and in communications media during the 1960s and 1970s, organizations of the party in government such as the congressional campaign committees (and currently state legislative campaign committees as well) began to collect resources to aid party candidates in their campaigns.[19]

Parties have never been able to monopolize the provision of resources to candidates in American society; the rise of new types of organized interests and methods of communication has made this point more obvious in recent decades. But the major parties have found a way to compensate for this weakness. They have used their dominance of the legislative and judicial branches to pass rafts of laws giving easy access to the ballot to candidates running as Democrats or Republicans and seriously disadvantaging those who want to run as independents or under a minor party label. These ballot access rules and a range of other laws and court decisions have protected the two major parties' status as the main channel through which all but a very few resource-rich candidates must run for office.[20]

The parties' institutional rules for selecting candidates also offer a means of solving problems of collective choice. Larry Bartels has examined the ways in which the individual preferences of voters in presidential primaries are combined into a single collective choice. Bartels notes that the nominating process differs from a classic public choice situation in that it is dynamic; it consists of a series of primaries on successive dates over a five-month period. The set of competing candidates can change from primary to primary, the electorate clearly changes, and voters in each primary contest can learn from the primaries that took place before. So learning and momentum characterize the process. These characteristics help to produce 'a genuine majority for a single alternative', as opposed to a situation in which no candidate can muster a real majority.[21]

MAKING DECISIONS AND ALLOCATING RESOURCES IN GOVERNMENT

Finally, governments must make decisions as to what will be done and in what order. How are these decisions to be made? If majority rule is the chosen mechanism, as is commonly the case in a democracy, then how will a majority be created? In particular, how can the possibility of continually cycling majorities, the social choice problem described by Arrow,[22] be resolved?

Creating and sustaining parties within government is one such means. As we have seen, partisanship can provide a tool with which groups of decision-makers who have common goals can build relationships of trust and predictable patterns of agreement. It can also simplify deliberation and act to sanction trust-breakers in order to protect that predictability.

Much of the rational choice work on governmental decision-making, like most other analyses of national political institutions, focuses on Congress. The work of the national legislature is more public and produces more usable data than do bureaucratic agencies and federal courts. Within Congress, analysts usually focus on roll call voting, the final step in House and Senate action on a bill. Rationality approaches to committee and subcommittee markup and the work of conference committees, which are just as vital to the legislative process, are limited by the problems all congressional researchers face in getting access to these aspects of congressional behavior.

What is the nature of the legislative parties in the rational choice perspective? Let us begin, as many students of congressional behavior do, with David Mayhew's analysis of Congress members as single-minded seekers of re-election. Mayhew shows how this single goal can explain a series of important institutional features of Congress. Members of Congress, in order to get re-elected, have designed an institution that enables them to meet their needs for three important activities: advertising themselves favorably, claiming credit for desirable behavior (such as casework), and taking positions on bills and other issues. One aspect of this institutional design, Mayhew writes, is that the congressional parties were organized to allow each member to take positions that benefit his or her re-election. Party leaders, then, were inclined to tell their members to vote their constituency's interests rather than to risk losing an election by supporting a party position that is unpopular in their district.[23]

In Mayhew's Congress, in short, the congressional parties and their leaders have very limited power; the primacy of individual members' re-election needs does not leave room for party leaders to demand obedience to a 'party line'. Yet since Mayhew's analysis was published in 1974, other researchers in the rational choice tradition have described congressional parties that are considerably stronger. Gary W. Cox and Mathew D. McCubbins, for example, begin with the same assumption as does Mayhew: that legislators are guided by a desire for re-election. But for Cox and McCubbins, members' re-election depends not just on their own personal qualities and votes but also on public perceptions of their party's record, as can be seen in such collective phenomena as electoral tides. Somebody, then, needs to marshal the forces for creating and protecting that record.[24]

Who has the motivation and the ability to do so? The legislative party leaders, in Cox and McCubbins's view, are a means of dealing with the collective action problem of getting someone to do what members of the party in Congress all want done but do not want to spend the time and resources doing. Some in the mainstream of their legislative party will find it attractive to take on these legislative tasks – to monitor the situation and use selective incentives to encourage other legislators to act on the party's preferences – in return for the rewards of holding leadership positions, and particularly because the successful completion of these tasks could increase their party's chance of becoming (or remaining) the majority.

Because they are in their party's preference mainstream and usually from safe districts, these party leaders are not likely to suffer in their own re-elections from acting on their party colleagues' preferences. So they internalize the party's collective interests; they structure the legislative process so as to keep members of the majority from 'cheating' on deals and unraveling the majority coalition.

Using statistical evidence, Cox and McCubbins show that party leadership does structure the legislative process. They demonstrate that the legislative party finds a variety of ways of controlling the legislative agenda in the interests of its members. They show that members are more likely to receive desirable committee assignments if they demonstrate more loyalty to the party leadership.[25] More generally, they confirm that members of Congress behave so as to support the partisan structures that can constrain their self-interested activities. The result, they argue, is that the legislative parties in the House, and especially the majority party, have become 'legislative cartels' in that they have taken the power to make the rules that guide the movement of legislation.

That leaves us with an interesting puzzle. Two sets of researchers, each working within the rationality tradition, have reached different conclusions as to the strength of party in the legislative process. How can these differences be explained? David Rohde has developed and John Aldrich has added to a theory they call *conditional* party government. In brief, they contend that the party's members in Congress will grant their leaders greater power under certain conditions. In particular, the amount of power the party leaders will hold, and thus the degree to which the party is able to affect the voting behavior of its members, depends on two factors: the extent of internal agreement within each legislative party (preference homogeneity) and the distance between the two parties on important issues (preference conflict).[26]

Rohde and Aldrich argue that these two factors have electoral roots. As the parties outside of Congress – voters and activists – have become more homogeneous internally and more polarized relative to one another, they have elected representatives who are closer to the center of their party's caucus than was the case in earlier years. In particular, the shifting partisanship of conservative Southerners, from their traditional Democratic identification to Republican affiliation, has 'purified' the ideological composition of the two parties in the House; as a result, members of each House party caucus have become more inclined to delegate power to their party leaders. Others suggest that the members' own beliefs are probably central to this change as well. It could be that the decisions of ambitious candidates have played an independent role in reorienting the party preferences of conservative Southerners and other partisans.[27]

It is clearly true, as we will see, that House members have voted with the majority of their party colleagues to a much greater extent since the 1980s than was the case when Mayhew wrote *Congress: The Electoral Connection*. But not everyone agrees that this demonstrates the increasing power of the legislative parties as a means of rationalizing decision-making. Keith Krehbiel has argued that party power in Congress is an illusion; instead, what we term 'party' is simply a surrogate for individual preferences. When members' preferences on issues (as measured by interest group ratings, which are based in turn on roll call votes) are controlled, Krehbiel writes, the effects of party and partisanship are rare. Rather, he argues, members of Congress vote with fellow members simply because they agree on the policy in question. To Krehbiel, then, what Rohde regards as the conditions for strong legislative parties are nothing more than a change in Congress members' preferences, which Rohde has misla-beled as 'party'.[28]

Krehbiel's argument is a major challenge to the view that parties structure the legislative process. But it has been critiqued from a number of perspectives. One is his reliance on a measure based on roll call voting; any such empirical test does not rule out the possibility that parties act at other points in the legislative process, for example, in helping to shape the drafting of bills, their markup in committee, and their placement on the legislative calendar. Another is the observation that the legislative parties do have incentives to offer their members in return for party support and that recent changes in the organization of the congressional parties have increased the ability and the willingness of party leaders to use these incentives to pressure their members.

The incentives available to House party leaders were expanded by the Democratic caucus beginning in the early 1970s.[29] Reforms that reduced the autonomy of committee chairs increased the power of both the caucus and the party's legislative leadership. Then, after the 1994 Republican takeover of the House and Senate, the Republican House party restricted the committee chairs' independence further,

term-limiting the chairs and freeing the party leadership from seniority rules in selecting the chairs. More recently, after the Republican victories in 2002, which left the Republican House delegation even more uniformly conservative than before, the party's leaders in the House gained greater power. The new reforms elimi-nated the term limit adopted in 1995 for the Speaker, weakened the seniority system again so as to permit the House Republican leader-ship to award subcommittee chairs on the powerful Appropriations committee to their loyal allies (and thus increase leadership con-trol over bills dealing with federal spending), and cracked down on Republican members who opposed the leadership.[30] In addition, the Republican leadership restricted Democratic participation on conference committees and resolved more of the details of legislation at the leadership level rather than in committee and on the floor.[31]

The stated aim of the 2002 reforms was to help the leadership push the Bush economic and social agenda through the contentious House and thus move the inevitable compromise with the Senate more toward the House's stance: in other words, to create rules that would offer an incentive for party legislators to accept the disci-pline necessary to pass the president's program. A key House Republican pointed out: 'By aban-doning the seniority system, the leadership was able to ensure that it had its team on the com-mittees. It reinforced the idea that chairmen are not autonomous. They owe their allegiance to the leadership.'[32] This certainly seems to suggest that the legislative parties have provided inducements to members to vote with their party, which goes beyond a story of the simple expression of shared policy goals.[33]

Several researchers also demonstrate that the increased voting cohesion of the congres-sional parties goes beyond what we would expect from similarity of preferences alone. Cox and Poole, for example, measure the dif-ference between votes on policy and votes on procedure. The latter, they argue, would be more likely to elicit pressure from congres-sional party leaders. In fact, they find that members are more likely to vote with their party on procedure, suggesting that the differ-ence is caused by pressure from the leaders.[34] Snyder and Groseclose write that when we measure Congress members' votes on what are assumed to be 'free votes' – issues on which one party is overwhelmingly likely to prevail, and thus members are probably free to vote their own and/or their constituency's preference – and then take into account the party's stance, there is consistent evidence of party influence affecting the individual legislator's 'true' preference.[35]

Some ingenious quasi-experimental studies provide further evidence that party makes a difference independent of members' preferences on issues. Wright and Schaffner, for example, compare the organization and the coalition formation in the non-partisan Nebraska state legislature with that of the partisan Kansas legislature 'next door'. They find that although candidates for the Nebraska legislature do identify as Democrats and Republicans and show evidence of party polarization in their views on issues, the roll call voting of the elected representatives in Nebraska, where the legislature is not organized by party, does not show any clear pattern. Roll call voting in the Kansas Senate, on the other hand, shows clear partisan divisions. 'Party', they conclude, 'lends order to conflict',[36] just as a rationality approach would predict.

There is persuasive support, then, for the idea that the American legislative parties developed not just as an expression of members' shared preferences but also as means of stabilizing and controlling the congressional agenda and of regularizing and satisfying members' institutional ambitions. Governing parties formulate policies in order to further the interests – policy, re-election, or other – of the individual office-holders and office-seekers who comprise them. These sets of positions on issues have the effect of structuring conflict on policies, and thus structuring the approach of a legislature to its environment.

THE VALUE AND LIMITS OF RATIONALITY APPROACHES

How much value do we gain from the use of rationality approaches to study political parties? The author of a recent article in the *American Political Science Review* described rational choice theory as 'arguably the most popular and fastest-growing theoretical orientation in contemporary political science.'[37] It has substantially changed the way political scientists study political parties, he wrote. In fact, because rationality approaches could be considered a universal theory of political and social behavior, these approaches can be the means of helping social scientists integrate the study of parties with that of other institutions.

Many would agree with this assessment. The use of social choice analysis has been central to the institutional approaches that have undergone a renaissance in political science.[38] One of the most valuable contributions of these approaches is the reminder they provide that democratic institutions are not self-generating. The simple and powerful fact that the collective interest is not sufficient in itself as a motivator for any one individual's behavior, without some specific benefit to the individual making the decision, demands the effort of political scientists to explain why democratic rules develop, how they are maintained, and what undermines them.

These approaches have generated a great deal of criticism, however, some of it intense. In one of the best-known critiques, Donald Green and Ian Shapiro charge that rationality approaches, including the social choice approach to the study of political parties, practice 'post hoc theory development': theorists, they argue, first look at empirical evidence and then design a model that fits it, rather than making falsifiable predictions, testing them, and then adapting the model.[39] In a later defense of their critique, they suggest that 'Rather than ask "What causes X?" [a rational choice model] begins with the question "How might my preferred theoretical or methodological approach account for X?"'[40] If this is so, then the approach might produce an interpretation of a series of events, and perhaps a most interesting interpretation, but not a prediction that can be falsified. To prove useful, a theoretical approach has to go beyond simply relabeling existing findings or showing that results are consistent with expectations that may, of course, have been influenced by prior knowledge of the results.

Aldrich avoids this trap in his analysis of parties; he posits that actors will seek solutions to the collective and social choice challenges that he spells out, but does not assume that these solutions will necessarily take the form of political parties. Not all rationality approaches are as careful. In the effort to explain why citizens vote, for instance, it has been generally accepted that the main determinants are the costs of voting and registration and the benefits to the individual: the likelihood that his or her vote will make a difference in the election outcome and the extent to which the citizen expects the election of one party to bring greater benefits to him or her than the election of the other party. The problem is that in many if not most cases, even the relatively small costs of voting are likely to overwhelm the benefits an individual can expect to derive from going to the polls. Thus one empirical study suggests that voters' perception of a narrowing gap between the policy stands of the major British parties helps to explain the recent decline in British voter turnout.[41] In the same sense, most people will not find much reason to try to inform themselves about the issues and the candidates. Why, then, does anybody vote?

This problem can be handled. Some posit, for example, that parties or candidates use resources to mobilize voters in close races and thus overcome the collective action problem without having to claim that voters gain much benefit from going to the polls.[42] In many cases, however, analysts have resorted instead to putting a figurative thumb on the 'benefits' side of the scale by adding an unspecified 'sense of citizen duty' or support for democracy, even in the absence of careful empirical data about these costs and benefits.[43] Others simply posit that individuals can have a 'taste for participation' in social acts and for improving the lot of other people because they have group interests as well as individual goals.[44] In the worst cases, this can amount to saying that people vote because they value voting, which does not carry us very far toward an understanding of voting behavior.[45]

Another criticism raised by Green and Shapiro is that the body of work using rationality approaches in political science is empirically challenged. There has been an emphasis on developing theory and formal analysis but the effort to engage in systematic empirical testing has been given short shrift. This criticism, while widespread, is not entirely fair. There are notable examples of extensive empirical research in the rational choice tradition, such as Elinor Ostrom's work on institutional development.[46]

Nevertheless, the use of formal analysis can limit the approach's ability to guide empirical research. The benefits of formal analysis are greatest when the model is elegant, when the number of variables can be reduced to the bare minimum and represented in mathematical form. But elegance of presentation – a great strength – is also a great weakness in that it prevents us from exploring the complexity of situations, which is, for many analysts, what makes politics interesting. Some practitioners suggest that this is not a reasonable criticism, in that when we consider the various models as pieces of one puzzle, then we might represent the complexity that is necessary to an understanding of political life. But it is fair to say that the practitioners have the burden of

pulling these models together if they are to argue that the enterprise has value, rather than putting the onus on the reader.

The primary question in evaluating these approaches is whether the social choice framework gives us greater purchase on such questions as why parties form and why they delegate greater or lesser power to party leaders than would an explanation that did not make use of social choice tools. What are the alternatives to rationality approaches? Many political psychologists would contend that at least some behaviors are expressive, in the sense that individuals choose these behaviors for their own sake, rather than for the goals to which they lead. Others would offer cultural explanations for behavior: that people behave according to social norms or attachments – because the group indicates that the behavior is appropriate – rather than because the individual calculates that it will bring her closer to a particular goal.[47] Dennis Chong writes: 'In the political realm, it also appears that social norms, principled commitments, and expressive or symbolic benefits are often needed to motivate participation in collective action. Whether these so-called extrarational incentives stretch the rational choice model or break it is the source of much controversy in the field.'[48]

Still others have shown that outcomes are not the only important motivating forces. Psychologist Tom Tyler has demonstrated that individuals are more concerned with the fairness of a decision process, as they perceive it, than with the benefit that it produces for themselves.[49] Political scientists John Hibbing and John Alford show that the value people place on outcomes depends more on what they see others as receiving than with the simple value of the outcome to themselves. Individuals are more inclined to value payoffs from decisionmakers who do not seem to be taking too big a share for themselves and who seem reluctant to hold the power to make the decisions, presumably indicating that they are not greedy for more. Hibbing and Alford interpret their findings as evidence for the existence, even the prevalence, of non-maximizing behavior.[50]

Proponents of rationality approaches would argue that many of these explanations can be subsumed under rational choice – in the case of expressive behaviors, for instance, by positing that the expressiveness itself is a goal, for which the particular behavior is chosen. But this must be done with care. It is straightforward to interpret material rewards for behavior. Classifying 'civic duty' and 'affiliative needs' as benefits can make it difficult to explain why anyone *would not* vote or participate.

The vehemence of this debate, which can be seen in mentions of the 'pathologies' of rationality approaches, or, on the other side, references to the 'Luddite' version of an interpretation,[51] makes its resolution unlikely. As Michael Taylor points out, the gulf between practitioners of rationality approaches and others is wide enough to include disputes ranging from philosophy to methods.[52] One survey found that a plurality of members of the American Political Science Association rejected the fundamental rational choice assumption that 'individuals are rational utility-maximizers', and only a third agreed with it, but that 78 percent of public choice scholars (largely economists) accepted the assumption.[53] And a number of political scientists find the methodological tools of many social choice studies (formal modeling in particular) impenetrable.

The debate has even developed partisan overtones. Some scholars have claimed that the public choice perspective reflects an individualist philosophy with a normative slant toward tax-cutting, privatizing,[54] and, in a word, conservatism, or even Republicanism. In fact, a survey of public choice scholars showed that most agreed with the statements that government does more to create and protect monopoly power than it does to prevent it (64 percent) and that when transaction costs are low, the market achieves the efficient allocation of resources regardless of how property rights are assigned (70 percent).[55] But as Bernard Grofman observes, whether or not many proponents of rational choice analysis are themselves politically conservative, the form of analysis itself has no necessary partisan or ideological slant.[56]

WHERE CAN WE GO FROM HERE?

It would be a fatal weakness to find that a body of propositions that purports to be a general theory does not have universal application. But it is nevertheless plausible to suggest that a particular theoretical approach does a better job of explaining some aspects of politics than others. In the case of social choice approaches, their application to the behavior of political activists and leaders would seem to be more productive than their application to those who are closer to the periphery of political life.

As Joseph Schlesinger suggests, rationality approaches work best in well-defined institutional settings where the benefits are clear and observable and the costs are easy to calculate.[57] A legislature is one such setting. The choices repeat more frequently in legislative voting and committee action than they do in a voter's occasional forays into the polling place. That facilitates the calculation of costs and benefits. More generally, people who are involved in some active political role are likely to be in choice situations that are salient to them and characterized by fairly clear expectations and observable consequences. Activists, candidates, and public officials probably hold better-defined goals for their political activity than do those who play less active political roles as well as greater ability to determine whether or not these goals have been met. As Fiorina writes, 'rational choice models are most useful where stakes are high and numbers low, in recognition that it is not rational to go to the trouble to maximize if the consequences are trivial and/or your actions make no difference'.[58]

If we were to array individuals along a continuum from higher-level political actors to those who are relatively uninvolved with politics, then, the balance between instrumental and purely expressive behaviors probably shifts toward the instrumental the closer we come to the higher-level political actors. The less engaging the behavior, the more room there will be for expressive behaviors, for symbolic concerns rather than self-interest to prompt decisions.[59] How else can we explain the importance of such issues as gay marriage in guiding the behavior of prospective voters, given that the level of self-interest for most Americans is nil? (Candidates and other political leaders, of course, can derive individual benefits from persuading voters that the issue affects them.)

We have seen that rationality approaches have been fruitfully applied to elements of the party in government and to Congress in particular. Applications to the study of party organization could be just as useful. There has been a resurgence of interest in party organization in the last two decades[60] and in party activists more recently.[61] Joseph Schlesinger has made several important contributions to this enterprise. He notes, for instance, the important implications of the fact that parties compensate their participants indirectly rather than directly, and that the party organization maintains itself through market exchange, offering candidates and policies in return for votes with which to win office. Because winning office is so vital to parties, those who occupy the offices – the candidates and office-holders – inevitably hold positions of strength within the party.[62]

Further work in this tradition could benefit us even more. It might be especially fruitful to draw on the insights generated by rational choice analysis of interest groups, which bear some interesting similarities to and differences from parties. For instance, consider Mancur Olson's formulation of the 'free rider' problem with regard to interest groups, and especially large interest groups.[63] Several analysts have focused on the role of selective incentives – individual benefits that they do not need to share – in explaining why individuals do in fact join large groups that are designed to achieve a collective goal, and on the possibility that some individuals overestimate their impact on such a group to the point where they believe that they are capable of making a difference in the group's outcome even if, objectively, they ought to free-ride.[64]

Jack Walker has offered a different explanation: that patrons and sponsors such as private foundations helped to reduce the costs of collective action for many organized interests.[65] Does this happen in the case of parties? Surely it does in some third parties, as in the case of Ross Perot and the Reform Party. The Supreme Court's recent ruling on the McCain–Feingold campaign finance reforms indicated that patrons can continue to donate unlimited amounts to newly-organizing parties.[66] Major parties have sponsors too, including the corporate patrons who underwrite their national nominating conventions. Clearly, there are important differences between parties and organized interests. Yet the similarities are significant enough to raise questions about whether some of the insights into interest groups as mechanisms of social choice could be applied more fully to parties.

As the front-runner with high negatives, the social choice approach to studying political parties faces as big a challenge as do political candidates in the same position. If political scientists are to gain greater understanding of parties and their impact on politics and policy, it would benefit us to take insights from wherever we can get them. If the social choice proponents accept that challenge, then, like Aldrich, they need to lay aside their equations on occasion and speak directly to those who see parties in cultural, expressive, or other non-maximizing terms. And scholars on all sides need to recognize that a gentling of the rhetoric in continuing this dialog can go a long way toward reducing the high negatives and increasing our ability to learn from one another.

NOTES

*   I am most grateful to Michael D. McGinnis for his help.
1. See Morris P. Fiorina, 'Rational choice, empirical contributions, and the scientific enterprise', *Critical Review*, 9 (Winter–Spring 1995), p. 87.
2. See, for example, Dennis Mueller, *Public Choice II* (Cambridge: Cambridge University Press, 1989).
3. See Elinor Ostrom, *Governing the Commons* (Cambridge: Cambridge University Press, 1990).
4. Gary W. Cox and Mathew D. McCubbins, *Legislative Leviathan* (Berkeley: University of California Press, 1993), pp. 83–4.
5. This is an example of a problem termed the 'tragedy of the commons' by Garrett Hardin. See his 'The tragedy of the commons', *Science*, 162 (1968), pp. 1243–8. Note, however, that Elinor Ostrom argues in *Governing the Commons* that the incidence of commons problems is smaller than previously assumed because many of the users of common-pool resources find ways to organize, make rules, and enforce them on one another.
6. John H. Aldrich, *Why Parties?* (Chicago: University of Chicago Press, 1995), pp. 48–50. See also Raymond E. Wolfinger and Steven J. Rosenstone, *Who Votes?* (New Haven, CT: Yale University Press, 1980), pp. 18–22.
7. See, for example, Joseph A. Schlesinger, 'On the theory of party organization', *Journal of Politics*, 46(1984): 369–400.
8. See Aldrich, *Why Parties?*, Chapter 3.
9. Ibid., p. 93.
10. Ibid., pp. 75–6.
11. This account relies on ibid., Chapter 4.
12. Ibid., p. 124.
13. Ibid., pp. 266–74.
14. Anthony Downs, *An Economic Theory of Democracy* (New York: Harper & Row, 1957), pp. 85–6.
15. Morris P. Fiorina, *Retrospective Voting in American National Elections* (New Haven, CT: Yale University Press, 1981), p. 5.
16. See Wendy M. Rahn, 'The role of partisan stereotypes in information processing about political candidates', *American Journal of Political Science*, 37(1993): 472–96, and Richard R. Lau and D.P. Redlawsk, 'Advantages and disadvantages of cognitive heuristics in political decision-making', *American Journal of Political Science*, 45(2001): 951–71.
17. Michael W. Wagner, 'Representation in the U.S. House: Does the opposing constituency participate?' Paper presented at the 2003 Annual Meeting of the Midwest Political Science Association, Chicago, April.
18. Theodore J. Lowi, 'Toward a more responsible three-party system: Deregulating American democracy', in John C. Green and Rick Farmer

(eds), *The State of the Parties*, 4th edn (Lanham, MD: Rowman & Littlefield, 2003), pp. 357–8.

19. See Marjorie Randon Hershey, *Party Politics in America*, 11th edn (New York: Longman, 2005), Chapters 3 and 4.

20. See Marjorie Randon Hershey, 'Third parties: The power of electoral laws and institutions', in Matthew J. Streb (ed.), *Law and Election Politics: The Rules of the Game* (Boulder, CO: Lynne Rienner Publishers, 2005, pp. 23–42). See also John F. Bibby and L. Sandy Maisel, *Two Parties – Or More?*, 2nd edn (Boulder, CO: Westview, 2003) and Joseph A. Schlesinger, *Political Parties and the Winning of Office* (Chicago: University of Chicago Press, 1991).

21. Larry M. Bartels, *Presidential Primaries and the Dynamics of Public Choice* (Princeton, NJ: Princeton University Press, 1988), especially Chapter 12. The quotation is from p. 307.

22. Kenneth J. Arrow, *Social Choice and Individual Values* (New York: Wiley, 1951).

23. David R. Mayhew, *Congress: The Electoral Connection* (New Haven, CT: Yale University Press, 1974), pp. 99–100.

24. Cox and McCubbins, *Legislative Leviathan*, Part Two.

25. Ibid., Chapter 8.

26. David W. Rohde and John H. Aldrich, 'The logic of conditional party government: revisiting the electoral connection', in Lawrence C. Dodd and Bruce I. Oppenheimer (eds), *Congress Reconsidered*, 7th edn (Washington, DC: CQ Press, 2001), Chapter 12. See also David W. Rohde, *Parties and Leaders in the Postreform House* (Chicago: University of Chicago Press, 1991). Note that Rohde and Aldrich differ from Mayhew in that they assume members of Congress are not exclusively concerned with re-election but have policy goals as well.

27. Stephen Ansolabehere, James M. Snyder, Jr., and Charles Stewart, III, find in 'Candidate positioning in U.S. House elections', *American Journal of Political Science*, 45(2001): 136–59 that candidates diverge on policy positions over time and that voters then choose the candidate closer to them.

28. Keith Krehbiel, 'Where's the party?', *British Journal of Political Science*, 23(1997): 235–66. See also Krehbiel, 'Party discipline and measures of partisanship', *American Journal of Political Science*, 44(2000): 212–27.

29. See Leroy N. Rieselbach, *Congressional Reform* (Washington, DC: CQ Press, 1986) and Bruce I. Oppenheimer, 'The Rules Committee: New arm of leadership in a decentralized House', in Lawrence C. Dodd and Bruce I. Oppenheimer (eds), *Congress Reconsidered* (New York: Praeger, 1977), pp. 96–116.

30. Jim VandeHei and Juliet Eilperin, 'GOP leaders tighten hold in the House', *Washington Post* (January 13, 2003), p. A1. See also R. Jeffrey Smith, 'GOP's pressing question on Medicare vote', *Washington Post* (December 23, 2003), p. Al.

31. Jonathan Allen and John Cochran, 'The might of the right', *CQ Weekly* (November 8, 2003), p. 2761.

32. VandeHei and Eilperin, 'GOP leaders tighten hold'.

33. Aldrich, *Why Parties?*, Chapter 7.

34. Gary Cox and Keith Poole, 'On measuring partisanship in roll-call voting: The U.S. House of Representatives 1877–1999', *American Journal of Political Science*, 46(2002): 477–89.

35. James M. Snyder, Jr., and Tim Groseclose, 'Estimating party influence in congressional roll-call voting', *American Journal of Political Science*, 44(2000): 193–211.

36. Gerald C. Wright and Brian F. Schaffner, 'The influence of party: Evidence from the state legislatures', *American Political Science Review*, 96(2002): 367.

37. Paul K. MacDonald, 'Useful fiction or miracle maker: The competing epistemological foundations of rational choice theory', *American Political Science Review*, 97(2003): 551.

38. See James G. March and Johan P. Olsen, 'The new institutionalism: Organizational factors in political life', *American Political Science Review*, 78(1984): 734–49. See also Kenneth A. Shepsle, 'Institutional arrangements and equilibrium in multidimensional voting models', *American Journal of Political Science*, 23(1979): 27–59.

39. Donald P. Green and Ian Shapiro, *Pathologies of Rational Choice Theory* (New Haven, CT: Yale University Press, 1984), pp. 34–5.

40. Donald P. Green and Ian Shapiro, 'Pathologies revisited: Reflections on our critics', *Critical Review* 9 (Winter–Spring 1995), p. 238.

41. Paul Webb, 'Political parties in Britain', in Paul Webb, David M. Farrell, and Ian Holliday, *Political Parties in Advanced Industrial Democracies* (Oxford: Oxford University Press, 2002), pp. 21 and 35.

42. See, for example, John H. Aldrich, 'Rational choice and turnout', *American Journal of Political Science*, 37 (1993): 246–78. See also John H. Aldrich and Michael D. McGinnis, 'A model of party constraints on optimal candidate positions', *Mathematical and Computer Modeling*, 12(1989): 437–50.

43. See William H. Riker and Peter C. Ordeshook, 'A theory of the calculus of voting', *American Political Science Review*, 62(1968): 25–43.

44. See, for example, Howard Margolis, *Selfishness, Altruism, and Rationality* (Cambridge: Cambridge University Press, 1982), p. 21 and Chapter 3.

45. See Brian Barry, *Sociologists, Economists, and Democracy* (London: Collier-Macmillan, 1970).

46. Ostrom, *Governing the Commons*.

47. Robert P. Abelson, 'The secret existence of expressive behavior', *Critical Review*, 9(1995), pp. 25–36.

48. Dennis Chong, 'Rational choice theory's mysterious rivals', *Critical Review*, 9(1995), p. 40.

49. Tom R. Tyler, 'The psychology of public dissatisfaction with government', in John R. Hibbing and Elizabeth Theiss-Morse (eds), *What Is It about Government that Americans Dislike?* (Cambridge: Cambridge University Press, 2001), pp. 227–42.

50. John R. Hibbing and John R. Alford, 'Accepting authoritative decisions: Humans as wary cooperators', *American Journal of Political Science*, 48(2004): 62–76.

51. For the latter, see Robert W. Jackman, 'Rationality and political participation', *American Journal of Political Science*, 37(1993): 279.

52. Michael Taylor, 'Battering RAMs', *Critical Review*, 9(1995), p. 223.

53. Jac C. Heckelman and Robert Whaples, 'Are public choice scholars different?', *PS*, 36(2003): 798–99.

54. Lionel Orchard and Hugh Stretton, 'Public choice', *Cambridge Journal of Economics*, 21(1997): 409–30.

55. Heckelman and Whaples, 'Are public choice scholars different?', pp. 797–9.

56. Bernard Grofman, 'On the gentle art of rational choice bashing', in Bernard Grofman (ed.), *Information, Participation, and Choice: An Economic Theory of Democracy in Perspective* (Ann Arbor: University of Michigan Press, 1993), pp. 239–42.

57. Schlesinger, 'On the theory of party organization', p. 386.

58. Fiorina, 'Rational Choice, Empirical Contributions, and the Scientific Enterprise', p. 88.

59. See, for example, David O. Sears, Richard R. Lau, Tom R. Tyler, and Harris M. Allen, Jr., 'Self-interest vs. symbolic politics in policy attitudes and presidential voting', *American Political Science Review*, 74(1980): 670–84. For a different view, see Jackman, 'Rationality and Political Participation', pp. 279–90.

60. See, for example, Malcolm E. Jewell and Sarah M. Morehouse, *Political Parties and Elections in American States*, 4th edn (Washington, DC: CQ Press, 2001); Cornelius P. Cotter, James L. Gibson, John F. Bibby, and Robert J. Huckshorn, *Party Organizations in American Politics* (New York: Praeger, 1984); and John Frendreis and Alan R. Gitelson, 'Local parties in the 1990s', in John C. Green and Daniel M. Shea (eds), *The State of the Parties*, 3rd edn (Lanham, MD: Rowman & Littlefield, 1999), pp. 135–53.

61. For example, Sidney Verba, Kay Lehman Schlozman, and Henry E. Brady, *Voice and Equality* (Cambridge, MA: Harvard University Press, 1995); John C. Green, John S. Jackson, and Nancy L. Clayton, 'Issue networks and party elites in 1996', in Green and Shea, *The State of the Parties*; and Henry E. Brady, Kay Lehman Schlozman, and Sidney Verba, 'Prospecting for participants', *American Political Science Review*, 93(1999): 153–68.

62. Schlesinger, 'On the Theory of Party Organization', p. 390.

63. Mancur Olson, Jr., *The Logic of Collective Action* (Cambridge, MA: Harvard University Press, 1965).

64. Terry M. Moe, *The Organization of Interests* (Chicago: University of Chicago Press, 1980). On the importance of subjective considerations in motivating participation, see Allan J. Cigler, 'Interest groups: A subfield in search of an identity', in William Crotty (ed.), *Political Science: Looking to the Future*, Vol. 4 (Evanston, IL: Northwestern University Press, 1991), pp. 108–9.

65. Jack L. Walker, Jr., 'The origins and maintenance of interest groups', *American Political Science Review*, 77(1983): 390–406.

66. The Supreme Court's majority in *McConnell v. Federal Election Commission* (2003) stated that although no one can give more than $25,000 to the national committee of a political party per year, this provision applies only to organizations that have been granted official status as 'national committees' by the FEC. The Reform Party did not have that status in 1995 or 1996, and the designation is typically not made by the FEC until a party has run candidates in a presidential and several congressional elections. See Richard Winger, 'Supreme Court Rules Against Parties', *Ballot Access News*, 19 (January 1, 2004), p. 2.

9

RECRUITMENT

Pippa Norris

One classic function of political parties concerns their gatekeeping role in nominating candidates for office at all levels of government. Political recruitment is not just a matter of nominating elected representatives at local, regional, national, and subnational levels, the core focus of this chapter, but also of filling a wide range of patronage appointments to public office. This is exemplified by party nominations to the proliferation of non-governmental organizations in Britain, the thousands of positions in various government branches and federal agencies allocated by the patronage of the incoming American president, and the depth of patron–client relations in Brazil. The process of recruitment to elected and appointed office is widely regarded as one of the most important residual functions for parties, with potential consequences for the degree of intra-party conflict, the composition of parliaments and governments, and the accountability of elected members.[1]

The opening section considers 'Who is eligible?' by outlining an analytical model of candidate selection, identifying the key steps in this process, and considering the 'certification' stage of recruitment. The second section considers 'Who nominates?' The core issue surrounds identifying the location and scope of decision-making by different party agencies and organizational bodies, and whether many established democracies have gradually decentralized the nomination process by shifting power from a small group of local party activists toward the grassroots membership. The third section examines 'Who is nominated?', in particular, whether parties have adapted in recent decades to pressures to diversify the candidacy pool and the composition of parliamentary elites, through the use of positive action strategies designed to include more women and ethnic minorities, and whether these strategies have succeeded. The final section considers the consequences of recruitment, particularly how party nomination processes interact with the electoral system in generating the chain of democratic accountability linking citizens and elected representatives.

WHO IS ELIGIBLE?

The schematic model illustrated in Figure 9.1 identifies the main factors influencing the candidate recruitment process. This model suggests that three successive stages operate in this process: *certification,* involving electoral law, party rules, and informal social norms defining the criteria for eligible candidacy; *nomination,* involving the supply of eligibles seeking office and the demand from selectors when deciding who is nominated; and *election,* the final step determining which nominees win legislative office. Each of these stages can be seen as a progressive game of 'musical chairs': many are eligible, few are nominated, and even fewer succeed.

The certification process, defining who is eligible to pursue candidacies for elected office, is shaped by a number of factors. The most comprehensive and detailed analysis of the formal legal requirements for candidacy has been carried out based on constitutional documents and

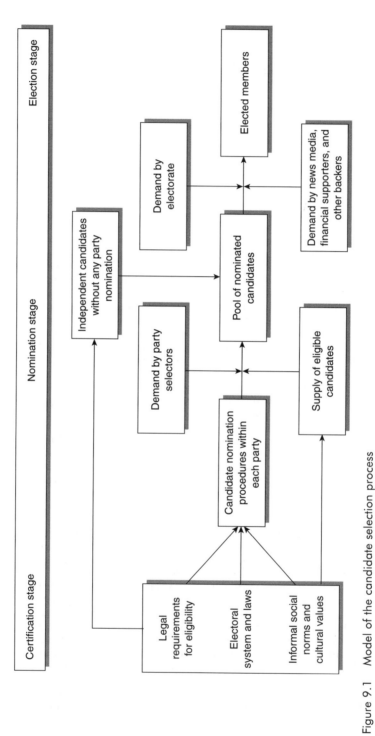

Figure 9.1   Model of the candidate selection process

electoral laws in 63 democracies by Massicotte, Blais and Yoshinaka.[2] Some legal restrictions on eligibility prove fairly universal and uncontroversial, such as age and citizenship requirements, while others are more exceptional, such as educational or literacy qualification. The main legal regulations include those relating to age, citizenship, residence, incompatibilities, monetary deposits, and the need to gather supporting signatures.

The minimum age for candidates is sometimes the same as that established to qualify for the voting franchise, but slightly higher age requirements are also used for legislative bodies, on the basis that a certain level of maturity and experience is desirable for public leaders. All the countries under comparison demanded citizenship for presidential elections and almost all followed similar requirements for legislative office. The more restrictive systems require citizenship by birth, for example in Brazil and the Philippines, although others allow naturalized citizens also to run for office. The majority of democracies do not impose any local district residency requirements for nomination, so that candidates can fight any seat, on the grounds that it is desirable that elected members should represent national as well as local interests. But nine countries, including Chile, Panama, and Taiwan, impose some conditions of residency in the electoral district, to prevent 'carpet-baggers' with weak constituency ties or knowledge of the local area. The main category of incompatibility concerns holding public office, such as civil servants, judges, and holders of elected office at other local or regional levels, since these are thought to create a conflict of interest. There are also legal restrictions associated with holding a criminal record, convicted felons, and bankrupts. But many democracies also require a financial deposit designed to screen out frivolous candidacies, with most refundable depending upon winning a minimum share of the vote. Another less common screening device includes requiring a certain number of signatures to be collected. In short, all countries impose some minimal legal restrictions on who is qualified to run for legislative office but most are not very stringent, and the majority of citizens would qualify according to these conditions.

In addition to the legal requirements, other certification requirements are set by parties through their internal rules, constitutions, and by-laws. Most commonly these stipulate that party membership is required for a specified period prior to candidacy, to ensure party loyalty and familiarity with party policies. Some are more restrictive. For example, in earlier decades eligible nominees had to meet a range of criteria in the Belgian Socialist party: '(1) have been a member at least five years prior to the primary; (2) have made annual minimum purchases from the Socialist co-op; (3) have been a regular subscriber to the party's newspaper; (4) have sent his children to state rather than Catholic schools; and (5) have his wife and children enrolled in the appropriate women's and youth organizations'.[3] The certification process is also influenced more generally by the informal social norms and cultural values in each country shaping perceptions of appropriate nominees, such as what sort of experience and background is most suitable for legislative careers. For example, people are more likely to consider running for parliament if they have professional legal training, experience of policy-oriented think-tanks, or careers in journalism and local government, all occupational channels providing skills and experiences valuable for higher office, reflecting the current typical composition of legislative elites. Although informal eligibility perceptions are most difficult to establish with any systematic evidence, they probably shape who comes forward, and who is deterred, from pursuit of a legislative career.

Independent candidates who meet the certification requirements are entitled to stand for elected office without any party backing. Independents can succeed in countries with exceptionally weak party organizations and with some single-member districts; for example, non-partisans have formed at times about one-quarter of the Ukrainian parliament and one-sixth of the Russian Duma. In a few countries such as Uganda party labels are legally banned and members are either elected from single-member districts or from special interest groups such as trade unions, the army, and young people. But in most democracies independents usually have a minimal realistic chance of electoral success at national level without the official endorsement, financial assistance, and organizational resources that parties provide. The US House of Representatives, for example, currently contains only one independent (Bernie Sanders, Vermont). As discussed below, political parties play the central role in nominating legislative candidates and they also shape the recruitment 'supply' of potential candidates by providing social networks, training, civic skills, and organizational experiences that are valuable in the pursuit of elected office.

Once nominated, as discussed in the conclusion, the role of the electoral system becomes critical in determining the final stage of entry into parliament. The electoral success of candidates is also shaped by non-partisan gate-keepers, including the type of coverage, publicity and endorsement provided by the news media, the financial backing of any donor organizations, and campaign support such as volunteers and office facilities provided by affiliated trade union, business, professional and community groups. These forms of support are particularly important in contexts where parties provide weak organizational structures and minimal institutional resources, exemplified by primary elections in the United States.

WHO NOMINATES?

Despite the acknowledged importance of the candidate nomination process, and although there are many descriptive case studies of the candidate recruitment process within specific parties, and some documentation of the formal party rules, relatively little is known about the structure and dynamics of the process in practice, or how and why this varies among parties and countries.[4] For those interested primarily in the internal life of parties as organizations, the nomination process is regarded as the dependent variable which serves as a prism for understanding the distribution of intra-party power among different organs and factions.[5] In Schattschneider's words: 'The nominating process has become the crucial process of the party. He who can make the nominations is the owner of the party.'[6] In a few countries certain aspects of the nomination process are governed by law; for example, in Germany and Finland there are broad requirements for parties to adopt democratic processes in candidate selection. In most, however, parties are entitled to decide their own processes and internal regulations. The key question is 'who decides?' The key dimensions of internal party democracy here are: (i) the degree of *centralization*, namely how far nominations are either determined mainly by the national party leadership or devolved downward to regional, district or local bodies; (ii) the breadth of *participation*, a related but distinct matter concerning whether just a few selectors pick candidates or whether many people are involved in this process; and (iii) the *scope* of decision-making, concerning whether there is a choice of one, a few, or multiple contenders vying for nomination.

In centralized organizations, exemplified by the Liberal Democratic Party in Japan, PASOK in Greece, or the Christian Democrats in the Netherlands, party leaders have considerable powers of patronage, enabling them to place 'their' chosen candidates into electorally favorable districts, seats, ridings, or constituencies, or in high-ranked positions on party lists. Most European parties, however, have greater internal democracy, so that although national leaders can sometimes exercise a veto, the key decisions determining who is nominated are made by officials, delegates, and activists at regional or local levels. In the most decentralized processes, nomination decisions in each local area rest in the hands of all grassroots party members who cast votes in closed primaries, or even the mass public in open primaries.

The locus of decision-making has been studied most commonly by classifying the legal regulations, party constitutions; and formal party rules which govern selection; for example, studies have developed typologies based on the Western European data set collected by Katz and Mair.[7] Based on this source, a recent comparison of nomination rules in Western Europe by Lars Bille classified the final level of decision-making regarding candidate selection into six categories ranging from the most centralized (national organs control completely) to the most localized (using ballots among all party members). As shown in Table 9.1, the most common process (in eight out of ten European parties) is one where subnational party organs either decide subject to leadership approval, or else they control the process completely.

Much of the debate in the literature has sought to determine whether parties have been actively democratizing the selection process, transferring decisions downwards from local office-holders and local activists to ordinary grassroots party members, and, if so, what consequences this process might have for the balance of power within the party. Table 9.1 compares the level of decision-making in the nomination process according to the formal rules in 1960 and 1989.[8] Bille concluded on this basis that most parties had experienced little change in the levels of decision-making in the candidate selection process during this era. Nevertheless some democratization had occurred involving a modest shift from decision-making by local officials and activists within subnational bodies down towards the engagement of all party members through the use of individual membership ballots, often by post.

Table 9.1   *The degree of centralization of the nomination process*

	1960		1989	
	No.	%	No.	%
National leadership controls completely	2	4	3	4
National leadership nominates from list provided by subnational organs	5	9	10	14
Subnational organs nominate from list provided by national leadership	3	5	1	1
Subnational organs nominate subject to approval by national leadership	22	39	23	32
Subnational organs control completely	25	44	34	48
Ballot applied to all party members	9	16	16	23
Total	57	100%	71	100%

Note: The 'final' level of decision-making in party nomination processes for candidacies for the lower house of the national legislature in 11 Western European countries.

Source: summarized from Table 1 in Lars Bille (2001) 'Democratizing a democratic procedure: Myth or reality? Candidate selection in Western European parties, 1960–1990; *Party Politics*, 7: 363–80.

Other studies also report that political parties have democratized their candidate selection processes during the post-war period, thereby widening participation among the selectorate.[9] During recent decades these changes are evident in the British Labour party, the ÖVP and SPÖ in Austria, the CDU and SPD in Germany, and by Fine Gael in Ireland. The main reason for this trend, commentators suggest, is an attempt to attract new members, or at least to staunch membership losses, by offering engagement in the candidate nomination process as a selective benefit. Nevertheless Scarrow, Webb and Farrell point out that despite these patterns, there have not been parallel moves to weaken or even eliminate the vetoes over this process held by central party elites, ensuring that the leadership retains the ability to exclude unwanted nominees.[10] Why should the location of nomination decision-making vary from one party to another? Krister Lundell sought to explain the degree of centralization of nomination decision-making in parties in 21 established democracies.[11] The study concluded that the nomination process was usually more decentralized in smaller parties (defined by their share of the vote), in far right and far left parties, and among parties within the Nordic region, compared with Mediterranean Europe. Many other common assumptions about the primary drivers in this process did not prove important, however, including the territorial organization of parties, their age and the mean district magnitude.

Yet the attempt to determine the 'main' location of decision-making in the nomination process typically encounters a number of limitations, so we need to be cautious about these conclusions. As with any study of written constitutions, there are often significant differences between the *de jure* and *de facto* decision-making bodies, especially in poorly institutionalized parties where democratic rulebooks and procedures exist on paper but are widely flouted in practice. The nomination process often involves a complex sequence of steps from the initial decision to consider running for office through a winnowing process with veto points that operates at multiple national, regional, local, or factional levels until the formal nomination or adoption meeting. In the British Conservative party, for example, there are a series of at least eight distinct stages from the submission of the formal application form to Central Office, an interview with party officials, a 'weekend' selection board, entry into the national list of approved candidates, application to particular constituencies, the short-listing and interview process by local constituency parties, and the final nomination meeting among party members. Some steps may prove to be mere rubber-stamp formalities. Others may involve competition among hundreds of applicants, uncertain outcomes, and heated internal battles, especially for 'safe' party seats where the incumbent is retiring.[12] Classifications of the degree of centralization or participation which attempt to reduce all this complicated multi-stage process with multiple actors into a single 'final decision' or 'cut-off' point may prove arbitrary and unreliable.[13]

Moreover, just like the studies of community power in the 1960s, any focus on 'who nominates' inevitably neglects the prior question of what Bacharatz and Baratz termed 'non-decisions', for example if certain groups such as ethnic minorities are discouraged by the formal or informal rules of the game and never even come forward to pursue elected office.[14] The focus on 'who nominates' also neglects the logically prior question 'what choices are available?'. Even with the same formal rules, some contexts present selectors with a wide range of choices among multiple contenders facing selectors, while in others, such as where an incumbent is automatically returned, there is none. For example, if we compare the way the presidential primary process worked in the United States during the 2004 contest, Democrats involved in the Iowa caucus and the subsequent New Hampshire primary in mid-to-late January faced a broad range of contenders, and caucus and primary participants played a decisive role in winnowing this field down. Once the Democratic race had been decided in favor of John Kerry in mid-March, however, subsequent primaries were merely a ritual endorsement of the outcome. In the Republican camp, President Bush faced no challengers so there was no contest. Therefore although grassroots Democrats and Republicans had the formal power to become engaged in the search for their presidential nominee through state caucuses and primary elections, in practice the real power of participants was determined by the electoral timetable. In the broader context, the range of choices facing selectors varies substantially in legislative seats where there is already an unchallenged incumbent, one or two rivals, or a multiple set of contenders. Any analysis of decision-making processes according to the formal rules ideally needs to be supplemented by a labor-intensive program mixing participant observation, qualitative interviews, and/or survey-based studies of the informal social norms among eligible candidates and party selectors that determine the outcome of this process. Detailed multi-method case studies remain relatively uncommon and, moreover, it becomes difficult to generalize across parties within and between nations on this basis[15].

We can conclude that the evidence suggests that a slight democratization of the nomination process has occurred within European parties, with the circle of decision-making widened slightly from local activists and office-holders downward to grassroots party members using ballots. Nevertheless, although the potential number of participants has increased slightly, at the same time the choice of nominees has been more greatly constrained by the adoption of rules designed to generate more inclusive legislatures. The most important of these concerns positive action strategies for women which have been implemented through reserved seats, statutory gender quotas and voluntary gender quotas. How do these affect both the process and the outcome?

WHO IS NOMINATED?

Rather than focusing upon the internal life of parties, other scholars of legislative elites, gender and racial politics are often more interested primarily in understanding the *outcome* of the nomination process. In this perspective, these processes are regarded as the independent variable which, in turn, can throw light upon who enters legislative elites and what consequences this has for the broader political system. The nomination process is the central mechanism for electing delegates to parliament and for holding them accountable. This perspective emphasizes that the type of candidate nominated by parties has the capacity to influence the quality of the members of the legislature, and ultimately the composition of government as well. For example, it is likely to have consequences for the legislative, policy-making, and scrutiny capacity of parliaments if parties decide to select professional lawyers or local constituency activists, minor celebrities or ambitious political entrepreneurs, seasoned party officials or inexperienced opportunists. The sociological study of political elites has long been concerned to document the composition of parliaments, the gradual transformation of legislative elites in terms of their occupational class, age, education, gender, and ethnic background, and the consequences for representative democracy that flow from these patterns[16]. Building upon this older tradition, in recent decades an extensive body of literature has sought to understand the barriers facing women and ethnic minority candidates, and which structural reforms prove most effective in widening opportunities for underrepresented groups.

During the last decade many policy initiatives have attempted to increase the number of women in elected and appointed office. As shown in Figure 9.2, the most common strategies fall into three main categories.

The issue of the basic *electoral system* has moved up the agenda in many established democracies, as exemplified by major electoral reforms introduced during the last decade in New Zealand, Italy, and Britain. The establishment of the basic electoral system is also obviously a critical issue that needs to be determined in transitional and consolidating democracies, such as Afghanistan and Iraq. This issue affects the nomination process since it is now widely understood that more women usually are elected under proportional than majoritarian electoral systems. This thesis has been

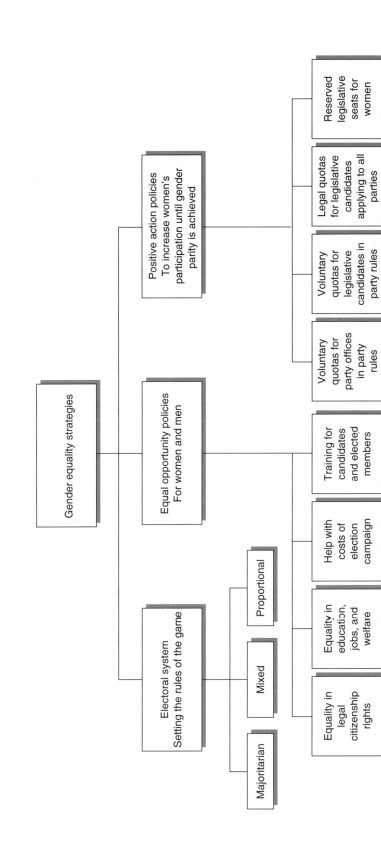

Figure 9.2   Gender equality strategies

confirmed in a series of studies since the mid-1980s, based on research comparing both established democracies and also a broader range of developing societies worldwide[17]. Within proportional electoral systems, district magnitude has commonly been regarded as a particularly important factor, with more women usually elected from large multimember constituencies. A worldwide comparison of the proportion of women in parliament confirms how women are far more successful under proportional representation (PR) list systems. As a simple rule, women proved almost twice as likely to be elected under proportional than under majoritarian electoral systems[18]. Accordingly where women are mobilized around the debates about electoral reform they have often fought to achieve PR systems.

Equal opportunity policies are designed to provide a level playing field so that women can pursue political careers on the same basis as men. Common examples include programs of financial aid to assist with electoral expenses, candidate training in the skills of communication, public speaking, networking, campaigning, and news management, and the provision of crèches and childcare facilities within legislative assemblies. Equal opportunity strategies can be gender-neutral in design, for example opportunities for training can be offered to both female and male parliamentary candidates, and childcare can be used by both parents, although their effects may be beneficial primarily to women. Equal opportunity policies are valuable in the long term, especially when used in conjunction with other strategies, but, by themselves, they often prove to have little impact in boosting women's representation.

Positive action strategies, by contrast, are explicitly designed to benefit women as a temporary stage until such time as gender parity is achieved in legislative and elected bodies. Positive action includes three main strategies:

* the use of *reserved seats* for women established in electoral law;
* *statutory gender quotas* controlling the composition of candidate lists for all parties in each country;
* *voluntary gender quotas* used in the regulations and rules governing the candidate selection procedures within particular parties.

Positive action has become increasingly popular in recent decades, as one of the most effective policy options for achieving short-term

change, although the use of these policies remains a matter of controversy within and outside of the women's movement.

By electoral law, some countries have stipulated a certain number of reserved seats that are only open to women or ethnic minority candidates. This policy has been adopted to boost women's representation under majoritarian electoral systems in developing nations in Africa and South Asia, particularly those with a Muslim culture (see Table 9.2). Reserved seats have been used for the lower house in Morocco (elected from a national list of 30 women members out of 325 representatives), Bangladesh (30/300), Pakistan (60/357), Botswana (2 women appointed by the president out of 44 members), Taiwan (elected), Lesotho (3 women appointed out of 80 seats), and Tanzania (37 women out of 274 members, distributed according to parties' share of seats in the House of Representatives)[19]. This mechanism guarantees a minimum number of women in elected office, although some have argued that it may be a way to appease, and ultimately sideline, women. Being elected does not necessarily mean that women are given substantive decision-making power, especially given the weakness of many of these legislative bodies. An important distinction needs to be drawn between those filled by direct election and those filled by appointment. Where women have an electoral base they can be more independent of the party leadership and they gain legitimacy derived from the democratic process. In India, for example, reserved seats have also been used at local level with considerable success. One-third of the seats on local municipal elections are reserved for directly elected women, empowering thousands of women[20]. By contrast, where appointed by the president or another body, if lacking an independent electoral or organizational base, women may be marginalized from any real decision-making responsibility, and their appointment can reinforce control of parliament by the majority party. In Uganda, for example, 53 parliamentary seats out of 292 are reserved for women (18%), who are indirectly elected, along with seats set aside for representatives drawn from groups such as the army, youth, the disabled, and trade unions, despite a ban on opposition parties standing for election.[21] Reserved seats based on regional, linguistic, ethnic, or religious ethnopolitical cleavages have also been used, for example for the Maoris in New Zealand, although their effects depend upon the size and spatial concentration of minority populations.

Table 9.2   *Reserved seats for women used by the lower house of parliament worldwide*

	Election	Selection method	Total number of MPs in the lower house	Number of seats reserved for women	% of seats reserved for women
Appointed by another body					
Tanzania	2000	Appointed	295	48	16.2
Zimbabwe	2000	Appointed	274	37	13.5
Botswana	1999	Appointed	44	2	4.5
Jordan	2003	Appointed	120	6	5.5
Lesotho	1998	Appointed	80	3	3.8
Bangladesh	2001	Appointed	300	30	10.0
Uganda	2001	Appointed	292	56	19.1
Direct election					
Pakistan	2002	FPTP[a]	357	60	16.8
Sudan	2000	FPTP[a]	360	35	9.7
Morocco	2002	FPTP[a]	325	30	9.2
Taiwan	1996	Combined-independent (SNTV and closed PR list)[b]	334	Varies	Varies
Djibouti	2003	Party Block[c]	65	7	10.7

Notes: Reserved seats in the lower house of the national parliament are defined as those seats that by law can only be filled by women, either by appointment, indirect election, or direct election.

[a]FPTP First-past-the-post (with single-member districts and plurality election).

[b]The combined-independent electoral system uses both single non-transferable vote and PR party list in parallel. This policy is currently being considered for elections in Afghanistan and Iraq.

[c]The party block electoral system uses plurality elections in multimember districts.

Sources: The Electoral Institute of Southern Africa (www.eisa.org.za); *Elections around the World* (www.electionworld.org); International IDEA (www.IDEA.int); Pippa Norris (2004) *Electoral Engineering* (Cambridge: Cambridge University Press).

Legal gender quotas

Positive action strategies also include gender quotas applied by law to all political parties, specifying that women must constitute a minimal proportion of parliamentary candidates or elected representatives within each party. Quotas represent an instrument that introduces specific formal selection criteria, in the form of minimal or maximal thresholds for a given group, into selections procedures, whether for elected or appointed office in the public sphere or for personnel recruitment in the private sector, such as for trade union office. There is an important distinction drawn between *statutory* gender quotas introduced by law, and thereby applying to all parties within a country, and *voluntary* gender quotas implemented by internal regulations and rule books within each party. Quotas can be specified for women and men, or for other relevant selection criteria, such as ethnicity, language, social sector, or religion. Statutory gender quota laws have been applied to elections in Belgium, France, and Italy, to many nations in Latin America (see Table 9.3), as well as to appointments to public bodies and consultative committees in many countries such as Finland and Norway.[22]

As shown by the last column in Table 9.3, in some countries and in some elections, legal gender quotas appear to have worked far more effectively than in other cases. Hence the substantial rise in women in parliament found in Argentina, the modest growth in Peru and Belgium, but minimal progress evident in France, Mexico, or Brazil. Why is this? The effective implementation of legal gender quotas depends upon multiple factors, including most importantly how the statutory mechanisms are put into practice, the level of the gender quota specified by law, whether the rules for party lists regulate the rank order of female and male candidates, whether party lists are open or

Table 9.3 Statutory gender quotas in use worldwide

Country	Date of law	Gender quota %	Legislative Body	Electoral system	List open or closed	% Women MPs before law (i)	% Women MPs after law (ii)	Change(i)–(ii)
✦ Argentina	1991	30	Lower house	Proportional	Closed	6	27	+21
Armenia	1999	5	Lower house	Combined	Closed		3.1	
✦ Belgium	1994	33	Lower house	Proportional	Open	18	23	+5
Bolivia	1997	30	Lower house	Combined	Closed	11	12	+1
Bolivia	1997	30	Senate	Combined	Closed	4	4	0
Bosnia & Herzegovina	2001	33	Lower house	Proportional	Open		14.3	
Brazil	1997	30	Lower house	Proportional	Open	7	6	–1
✦ Costa Rica	1997	40	Unicameral	Proportional	Closed	14	19	+5
Dominican Republic	1997	25	Lower house	Proportional	Closed	12	16	+4
Ecuador	1997	20	Unicameral	Combined	Open	4	15	+11
✦ France	1999	50	Lower house	Majoritarian	–	11	12	+1
Indonesia	2003	30	Lower house	Proportional	Open	9	N/A	N/A
Korea, North	–	20	Lower house	Majoritarian	–		20.1	
Macedonia	2001	30	Lower house	Combined	Closed		17.5	
Mexico	1996	30	Senate	Combined	Closed	15	16	+1
Mexico	1996	30	Lower house	Combined	Closed	17	16	–1
Nepal	1990	5	Lower house	Majoritarian	–		5.9	
Panama	1997	30	Unicameral	Combined	Closed	8	10	+2
Paraguay	1996	20	Senate	Proportional	Closed	11	18	+7
Paraguay	1996	20	Lower house	Proportional	Closed	3	3	0
Peru	1997	30	Unicameral	Proportional	Open	11	18	+7
Philippines	1995	20	Lower house	Combined	Closed		17.8	
Serbia	2002	30	Lower house	Proportional	Open	7.5	N/A	N/A
Venezuela	1998	30	Lower house	Combined	Closed	6	13	+7
Venezuela	1998	30	Senate	Combined	Closed	8	9	+2
Average		30				10	14	+4

Note: *Legal gender quotas for the lower house of national parliaments are defined as laws which specify that each party must include a minimum proportion of women on party lists of candidates. Change is estimated based on the percentage of women MPs in the parliamentary election held immediately before and after implementation of the gender quota law.*

Sources: Mala Htun (2001) 'Electoral rules, parties, and the election of women in Latin America,' paper for the Annual Meeting of the American Political Science Association, San Francisco; Mala Htun and Mark Jones (2002) 'Engendering the Right to Participate in Decision-making: Electoral quotas and women's leadership in Latin America', in Nikki Craske and Maxine Molyneux (eds), *Gender and the Politics of Rights and Democracy in Latin America* (London: Palgrave); International IDEA, *Global Database of Quotas for Women* (www.idea.int).

closed, and also the penalties associated with any failure to comply with the law. Positive action policies alter the balance of incentives for the party selectorate. Where these laws are implemented, then selectors need to weigh the potential penalties and benefits if they do or do not comply. Selectors may still prefer the default option of nominating a male candidate under certain circumstances, for example if the laws are designed as symbolic window-dressing more than as *de facto* regulations; if the regulation specifies that a certain proportion of women have to be selected for party lists but fails to specify their rank order so that female candidates cluster in unwinnable positions at the bottom of the list; or if the sanctions for non-compliance are weak or non-existent. As in many attempts to alter the incentive structure, the devil lies in the details, so apparently similar legislative policies turn out to have different consequences in different nations.

In *Belgium* the Electoral Act of 24 May 1994 specified that no more than two-thirds of the candidates on any party electoral list may be of the same sex. The minimum representation requirement is thus exactly the same for men and women. It applies to the Chamber of Representatives and the Senate, and also to regional, community, provincial and municipal councils, as well as elections to the European Parliament. If this requirement is not respected, the list candidacies that would otherwise have been held by women have to be left blank or the whole list is declared invalid.[23] The Act was first fully enforced in the 1999 European elections that saw the proportion of Belgian women MEPs rise from 18.5% to 23.3%. However, the power of incumbency means that it will take many successive elections under the new rules before women become a third or more of Belgian parliamentarians.

In 1999 *France* passed the parity law, a constitutional amendment requiring parties to include 50% representation of women in their party lists for election, with financial penalties attached for failure to do so. The gender parity law passed in June 2000 specified that for elections to the National Assembly between 48% and 52% of all candidates presented nation-wide by any given political party must be women. If this percentage is higher or lower, the state will cut its financial contribution. The results of the first elections held in March 2001 under the new rules indicate a substantial impact at municipal level, almost doubling the number of women in local office from 25% to 47%. Nevertheless in the first elections to the French National Assembly held under the parity rules,

in June 2002, the proportion of elected women rose by only 1.4 percentage points, from 10.9% to 12.3%. Only eight more women entered the Assembly, dashing the hopes of the reformers. The main reasons were that the parity law failed to specify the selection of women for particular types of single-member seats, so that women nominees could be concentrated in unwinnable constituencies. Moreover, the major parties decided to favor incumbents and largely ignored the financial penalty of reduced party funding associated with imbalanced party lists.[24] The sanction is a reduction in the public funding received for each party's campaign on a sliding scale of 5% for a gender difference of 10% on party lists of candidates, 30% for a difference of 60%, and a maximum 50% for a difference of 100%. Hence an all-male list would still get half the public funding. Despite the parity law, the proportion of women in the Chamber of Deputies means that France is ranked 61st worldwide after reform, compared with 59th before parity was introduced.

Another parallel European case concerns *Italy*, where a quota system was introduced in 1993 into the legislation governing municipal, provincial, and national elections[25]. These laws asserted that a minimum of 30% of both sexes had to be present in electoral lists. In 1995, however, the Italian Constitutional Tribunal repealed these regulations, considering that they were contrary to the principle of equality. Some parties have introduced voluntary gender quotas into their party rules, set at 50% for Verdi, 40% for DS, 40% for the PRC, and 20% for the PPI. Yet in the 2001 election women accounted for only 9.8% of the Italian Chamber of Deputies, ranking Italy 77th worldwide. In *Armenia*, the 1999 Electoral Code states that the voting lists of the parties involved in the proportional parliamentary electoral system should contain not less than 5% female candidates, but the low level and poor implementation meant that women in the June 1999 elections were only 3.1% of the national parliament.

During the early 1990s, with the expansion of democracy, the popularity of statutory gender quotas spread rapidly in Latin America. The first and most effective law (the Ley de Cupos) was passed in *Argentina* in 1991, introducing an obligatory quota system for all parties contesting national elections to the Chamber of Deputies – '*lists must have, as a minimum, 30% of women candidates and in proportions with possibilities of being elected. Any list not complying with these requisites shall not be approved*'. Most importantly, the law stipulates that women must be ranked throughout party lists, not consigned to the end where they face no realistic chance of election. Party lists failing to comply with the law are rejected. If a rejected list is not corrected so as to bring it into compliance with the law, the party in question cannot compete in that district's congressional election. The provincial branches of the political parties create the closed party lists from which the Argentine deputies are elected, although at times the national party intervenes to impose a list. Following the implementation of the law, in the 1993 Chamber election, 21.3% (27 of 127) of the deputies elected were women, compared to only 4.6% (6 of 130) in the election of 1991. A decade after passage, the proportion of women in the Chamber of Deputies had risen to 30.7% (79 out of 257), ranking Argentina ninth from the top worldwide in the representation of women. In total 11, Latin American countries have now adopted national laws establishing a minimum percentage for women's participation as candidates in national elections and a twelfth – *Colombia* – had approved a quota of 30% for women in senior positions in the executive branch[26]. Although their impact has been varied, in these countries a comparison of the elections held immediately before and after passage of these laws suggests that legislative quotas generated on average an eight percentage point gain in women's election to congress. Variation in the effectiveness of the quotas can be explained by whether the PR list is open or closed (with the latter most effective), the existence of placement mandates (requiring parties to rank women candidates in high positions on closed party lists), district magnitude (the higher the number of candidates in a district, the more likely quotas are to work), and good-faith party compliance.

Statutory gender quotas have also been applied to local, municipal, and regional contests. In *South Africa* the Municipal Structures Act states that political parties must seek to ensure that women comprise 50% of lists submitted for election at the local level. Following the municipal elections in 2000, 28.2% of local councilors were women. In the *Namibian* local authority elections in 1992 and 1998, the law required political parties to include at least 30% women on their party candidate lists.

The comparison of legal gender quotas suggests grounds for caution for those who hope that these strategies will automatically produce an immediate short-term rise in women legislators. The French case, in particular, illustrates the way the detailed aspects of how such quotas are implemented, and the sanctions for non-compliance, can generate very different results even for municipal and national elections within the same country. The variations in the results across Latin America confirm these observations.

Voluntary gender quotas in party rules

Most commonly, however, voluntary gender quotas have been introduced within specific parties, particularly those of the left, rather than being implemented by electoral law[27]. Rules, constitutions, and internal regulations determined within each party are distinct from electoral statutes enforceable by the courts. Parties in Scandinavia, Western Europe, and Latin America often have used voluntary gender quotas, and Communist parties in Central and Eastern Europe employed them in the past. It is difficult to provide systematic and comprehensive analysis of party rules worldwide, but in spring 2003 International IDEA's *Global Database of Quotas for Women* estimated that 181 parties in 58 countries used gender quotas for electoral candidates for national parliaments[28]. The effects of these measures can be analyzed by focusing on their use within the European Union, since this allows us to compare a range of representative democracies at similar levels of socioeconomic development. Table 9.4 compares the use of gender quotas for the candidate selection process in national elections in the 15 EU member states. By 2000, among 76 relevant European parties (with at least ten members in the lower house), almost half (35 parties) used gender quotas, and two dozen of these had achieved levels of female representation in the lower house of parliament over 24%[29]. Among the European parties using gender quotas, on average one-third (33%) of their elected representatives were women. By contrast, in the European parties without gender quotas, only 18% of their members of parliament were women. Of course it might be misleading to assume any simple 'cause' and 'effect' at work here, since parties more sympathetic towards women in public office are also more likely to introduce gender quotas. European parties of the left commonly introduced voluntary gender quotas during the 1980s, including Social Democratic, Labour, Communist, Socialist and Green parties, before the practice eventually spread to other parties. Nevertheless the 'before'

Table 9.4   *Voluntary gender quotas in party rules, used in the EU-15, 1996–2000*

	Party	Country	Election year	Total number of party MPs	% Women	Gender quota
1.	VIHR	Finland	1999	11	81.8	✓
2.	PDS	Germany	1998	36	58.3	✓
3.	B90/Grüne	Germany	1998	47	57.4	✓
4.	Centerpartiet	Sweden	1998	18	55.6	✗
5.	GroenLinks	Netherlands	1998	11	54.5	✓
6.	Miljöpartiet de Grona	Sweden	1998	16	50.0	✓ ↓
7.	Social Democrats	Sweden	1998	131	49.6	✓
8.	PvdA	Netherlands	1998	45	48.9	✓
9.	Ecolo	Belgium	1999	11	45.5	✓
10.	SDP	Finland	1999	51	43.1	✓
11.	D'66	Netherlands	1998	14	42.9	✗
12.	Vänsterpartiet	Sweden	1998	43	41.9	✓
13.	Christian Democrats	Sweden	1998	42	40.5	✓
14.	SKL	Finland	1999	10	40.0	✓
15.	Socialistisk Folkeparti	Denmark	1998	13	38.5	✗
16.	Venstre Liberale Parti	Denmark	1998	42	38.1	✗
17.	KOK	Finland	1999	46	37.0	✓
18.	Social Democrats	Denmark	1998	63	36.5	✗
19.	SPÖ	Austria	1999	65	35.5	✓
20.	Folkpartiet Liberelna	Sweden	1998	17	35.3	✓
21.	Social Democrats	Germany	1998	298	35.2	✓
22.	IU	Spain	1996	21	33.3	✓
23.	KF	Denmark	1998	16	31.3	✗
24.	Christian Democrats	Netherlands	1998	29	31.0	✓
25.	Dansk Folkeparti	Denmark	1998	13	30.8	✗
26.	Moderata Samlings	Sweden	1998	82	30.5	✗
27.	VAS	Finland	1999	20	30.0	✓
28.	PCP	Portugal	1999	17	29.4	✗
29.	ÖVP	Austria	1999	52	28.4	✓
30.	PSOE	Spain	1996	141	27.7	✓
31.	KESK	Finland	1999	48	27.1	✗
32.	VVD	Netherlands	1998	39	25.6	✓
33.	SFP/RKP	Finland	1999	12	25.0	✓
34.	Rifond. Communista	Italy	1996	32	25.0	✓
35.	C.I.U	Spain	1996	16	25.0	?
36.	**Labour**	**UK**	**1997**	**418**	**24.2**	✓
37.	POSL/LSAP	Luxembourg	1999	13	23.1	✓
38.	PRL-FDF	Belgium	1999	18	22.2	✗
39.	FDP	Germany	1998	43	20.9	✗
40.	Socialist Party	Portugal	1999	115	20.0	✓
41.	PD	Luxembourg	1999	15	20.0	✗
42.	CDU	Germany	1998	200	19.5	✓
43.	PDS	Italy	1996	156	19.2	✗
44.	CVP	Belgium	1999	22	18.2	✓
45.	KKE	Greece	2000	11	18.2	?
46.	VLD	Belgium	1999	23	17.4	✗
47.	FPÖ	Austria	1999	52	17.3	✗
48.	**Partie Socialiste**	**France**	**1997**	**251**	**16.7**	✓
49.	PCS/CSV	Luxembourg	1999	19	15.8	✓
50.	Popular Party	Spain	1996	156	14.1	?
51.	PSD	Portugal	1999	81	13.6	✗
52.	CSU	Germany	1998	45	13.3	✗
53.	Labour	Ireland	1997	17	11.8	✓

(Continued)

Table 9.4   *(Continued)*

	Party	Country	Election year	Total number of party MPs	% Women	Gender quota
54.	PCF	France	1997	36	11.1	✓
55.	Fine Gael	Ireland	1997	54	11.1	?
56.	PASOK	Greece	2000	158	10.8	✓
57.	Socialist Party	Belgium	1999	19	10.5	✗
58.	Fianna Fáil	Ireland	1997	77	10.4	?
59.	Lega Nord	Italy	1996	59	10.2	✗
60.	PSC	Belgium	1999	10	10.0	✗
61.	Verdi (Greens)	Italy	1996	21	9.5	✗
62.	Forza Italia	Italy	1996	123	8.1	✗
63.	New Democrats	Greece	2000	125	8.0	✓
64.	**Conservative**	**UK**	**1997**	**165**	**7.9**	✗
65.	P-S-P-U-P	Italy	1996	67	7.5	✗
66.	CDS-PP	Portugal	1999	15	6.7	?
67.	Vlaams Blok	Belgium	1999	15	6.7	✗
68.	**Liberal Democrats**	**UK**	**1997**	**45**	**6.5**	✗
69.	RCV	France	1997	33	6.1	?
70.	UDF	France	1997	113	5.3	✗
71.	Alleanza Nazionale	Italy	1996	93	4.3	✗
72.	Lista Dini	Italy	1996	25	4.0	✗
73.	**RPR**	**France**	**1997**	**140**	**3.6**	✗
74.	CCD-CDU	Italy	1996	30	3.3	✗
75.	**UUP**	**UK**	**1997**	**10**	**0.0**	✗
76.	SP	Belgium	1999	14	0.0	✗

Notes: Voluntary gender quotas are defined as internal party rules, regulations, or constitutions specifying that the party should include a minimum proportion of women as candidates for elected office. The table only includes relevant parties (i.e. those with at least ten seats in the lower house of the national parliament). The data, derived originally from the Council of Europe database, has some important limitations. It should be noted that the definition and meaning of 'quota' can differ among parties, and some may use this only for internal organizational posts rather than for candidate nomination. Parties without a formal quota may instead apply a 'gender target', adhered to more or less rigidly in candidate selection. Parties in **bold** are in countries using majoritarian electoral systems.

✓   Gender quota is currently used by this party for parliamentary nominations.
✗   Gender quota is not currently used by this party for parliamentary nominations.
?   Information on gender quotas is not available from this source.

Source: Pippa Norris (2004) *Electoral Engineering* (New York: Cambridge University Press).

and 'after' test, exemplified by cases such as their deployment by parties in Scandinavia, in Germany, and in the British Labour party, suggests that the effect of voluntary gender quotas within parties also varies substantially.

Many of the parties ranking at or near the top of the proportion of women MPs in Table 9.4 are in Scandinavia. The Norwegian Labor Party was the first in this region to implement a 40% gender quota for all elections in 1983, although this did not specify the location of women candidates within their lists. Other Norwegian parties followed suit, including the Social Left, the Center Party, and the Christian Democrats[30]. This was followed by Denmark

where the Social Democratic Party introduced a 50% quota for elections in 1988[31]. Because the rank position of candidates on the party list is critical to their success in being elected, in 1994 the Swedish Social Democratic Party introduced the principle of including a woman as every second name on the list – the 'zipper' or 'zebra' principle. In Sweden, since the general election in 1994, the largest political party, the Social Democrats, and later the Greens and the Christian Democrats, have systematically alternated women's and men's names in their lists of the constituency candidates for parliamentary, local, regional, and the EU Parliament elections. If we compare the Swedish parties ranked high in Table 9.4, it is apparent that gender quotas are used by some such as the Social Democrats and the Vänsterpartiet, although not all the credit should go to the use of positive action, as other Swedish parties including the Centerpartiet, also have a substantial number of female members of parliament despite not using any gender quotas.

Elsewhere in Western Europe, as shown in Table 9.4, formal practices vary among countries and parties. In Germany, for example, three of the five major political parties have a 40–50% quota system in their party rules. In 1980, when the Greens turned from a social movement into a political party, they instilled gender balance by including a strict 50% quota combined with a zipper system in their statutes. Except for the very top positions in government, the Greens have been more or less able to meet their requirements. In 1988 the Social Democrats followed suit by stipulating in party rules that in all internal party elections at least one third of candidates must be female. Since 1994, 40% of all party positions must be held by women. For election lists, parliamentary mandates, and public office a transition period with lower percentages was agreed. It started with one-quarter in 1988, required one-third in 1994, and reached 40% in 1998. The SPD met the targets within the party but fell slightly short for seats in parliaments and in governments. In 1996 the Christian Democratic Party (CDU) introduced the so-called 'quorum' requiring 30% female representation in both party functions and election lists, but so far these targets have not been met. After German unification the Partei des Demokratischen Sozialismus (PDS, former East German Communist party) introduced a strict 50% quota in combination with a zipper system. In many elections the PDS has outperformed its own targets. Currently only the Christlich-Soziale Union (CSU, the Bavarian sister party of the CDU) and the Liberals (Freie Demokratische Partei, FDP) refuse to introduce voluntary gender quotas.

It is often easier to implement positive action in proportional elections using party lists, but these strategies can also be used under majoritarian rules. In Britain, the Labour party first agreed the principle of quotas to promote women's representation in internal party positions in the late 1980s.[32] In 1988 a minimalist measure was agreed for candidate selection for Westminster, so that if a local branch proposed a woman, at least one woman should be included on the constituency shortlist. In 1993, following an electoral defeat where the party failed to attract sufficient support amongst women voters, it was decided that more radical measures were necessary. Consequently the Labour party's annual conference agreed that in half the seats where Labour MPs were retiring, and in half the Party's key target marginal seats, local party members would be required to select their parliamentary candidate from an all-women shortlist. Other seats would be open to both women and men. Although this policy was subsequently dropped under legal challenge, it still proved highly effective, contributing to a doubling of the number of women in the UK House of Commons between 1992 and 1997[33]. Despite abandoning the original policy, low levels of incumbency turnover maintained most of these gains in the subsequent general election in 2001. For the first elections to the new Scottish Parliament, Welsh Assembly and Greater London Assembly, Labour adopted a 'twinning' policy. The system 'twinned' neighboring seats, taking into account their 'winnability', so that each pair would select one man and one woman. This opportunity was uniquely available, given that there were no incumbent members. Under this system, local party selectors in the two constituencies would come together to pick candidates, and each would have two votes – one for a woman and one for a man.

Gender quotas are by no means limited to established democracies. In South Africa, for example, in 1994 the African National Congress introduced a 33.3% gender quota, while in Mozambique in 1999 the Frelimo Party introduced a 30% quota on electoral lists. This policy has been particularly common among parties of the left, and Socialist International Women lists 57 socialist parties using gender quotas in April 2002, ranging from 20% to 50%, including the Israeli Meretz (40%), the Mali Adema-Pasj (30%), the Nicaraguan FSLN (30%), and the Turkish CHP (25%)[34]. Gathering systematic and reliable data on the use of such strategies worldwide is difficult, but a global review of practices by the Inter-Parliamentary Union in 1993 found that 22 parties employed gender quotas for legislative elections, while 51 parties used them for elections to internal party posts[35]. By contrast, in the first democratic elections following the fall of the Berlin Wall, parties within Central and Eastern Europe often moved in the opposite direction, abandoning gender quotas for parliament and local government that were regarded as part of the old Communist state[36], although occasionally later reinstating this practice, as in the case of the Czech SDP (25%), the Bosnian SDP (30%) and the Lithuanian SDP (30%).

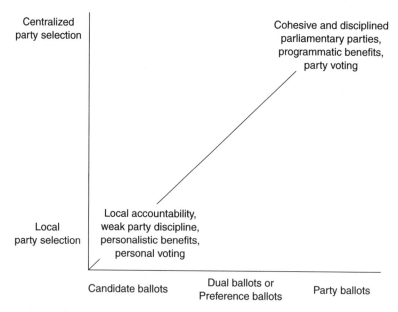

Figure 9.3   The interaction of selection rules and ballot structures

WHAT ARE THE CONSEQUENCES FOR DEMOCRATIC ACCOUNTABILITY?

What are the consequences of party recruitment processes for power and decision-making within political parties, for the inclusiveness of legislative bodies, and for the chain of accountability in representative democracies? Underlying studies of both the process and the outcome of candidate nomination are a set of broader normative values about how recruitment should work ideally in any representative democracy[37]. Most commonly, evaluations of the process are framed against the standards of internal party democracy, as well as in terms of its procedural 'fairness', 'simplicity', and/or 'transparency'. The outcome is usually judged by the inclusiveness of all major social sectors in the electorate, and also by the ways in which the process is thought to influence the role of elected members.

Figure 9.3 illustrates schematically how the chain of accountability linking citizens and elected representatives is thought to work. The vertical axis distinguishes the location of the decisions about candidate nomination, whether centralized among the party leadership or alternatively devolved downwards to grass-roots level in each area. Ballot structures can be classified into the following categories based on the choices facing electors when they enter the voting booth:

- *Candidate ballots.* In single-member districts, citizens in each constituency cast a single ballot for an individual candidate. The candidate winning either a plurality or majority of votes in each district is elected. Through casting a ballot, electors indirectly express support for parties, but they have to vote directly for a particular candidate. In this context, politicians have a strong incentive to offer particularistic benefits, exemplified by casework helping individual constituents and by the delivery of local services ('pork'), designed to strengthen their personal support within local communities. This inducement is particularly powerful in marginal seats where a handful of additional votes may make all the difference between victory and defeat.
- *Preference ballots.* In open-list multimember districts electors cast a ballot for a party, but they can express their preference for a particular candidate or candidates within a party list. Where citizens exercise a preference vote, this strengthens the chances that particular candidates from the list will be elected and therefore changes their rank. Under these rules, politicians have a moderately strong incentive to offer particularistic benefits, to stand out from rivals within their own

party. In most nations the choice of exercising one or more preferential votes is optional, and the practical effect of preference ballots is contingent upon how many citizens choose to 'vote the party ticket' without expressing a preferential vote. If most people decide to vote for the party list, then the effects are similar to party ballots, whereas if most choose to exercise a preferential vote for an individual on the list, then the effects are similar to candidate ballots.

Preference ballots are employed in party list PR used in 27 electoral systems worldwide, including Belgium and the Czech Republic, as well as in single transferable vote elections in Ireland. This ballot is also used in plurality and majoritarian electoral systems, such as in the single non-transferable vote that has been used in the Republic of Korea, Japan and Taiwan[38]. The majoritarian block vote, used in Bermuda, the Philippines and Mauritius, also allows citizens to vote for individual candidates in multimember districts with party lists of candidates. There are some variants to these rules. In Finland, people must vote for individual candidates, and the number of votes won by candidates determines their party's share of seats. The *panachage* system used in Luxembourg and Switzerland gives each elector as many votes as there are seats to be filled, and electors can distribute them either within or across different party lists.

- *Dual ballots.* In 'combined' (or 'mixed') electoral systems voters can cast separate ballots in both single-member and multimember districts, as exemplified by elections in Italy, Germany and New Zealand. This category can be divided into either combined-independent (where the votes in both types of seats determine the results independently of each other) or combined-proportional where the share of the vote cast for the party list determines the final allocation of seats). Where combined systems operate, most use closed-list multimember districts, so that citizens can cast a ballot for a candidate in their single-member districts as well as for a party in their multimember districts. The effects of dual ballot elections depend upon what proportion of seats are allocated through single-member or multimember districts: where most seats are single-member then the effects will be closer to candidate ballots, and where most are multimember then the effects will be closer to party ballots.
- *Party ballots.* In closed-list multimember districts, citizens cast a single ballot for a

party. Each party ranks the order of the candidates to be elected within their list, based on the decisions of the party selectorate, and the public cannot express a preference for any particular candidate within each list. Closed-list multimember districts, where voters can only 'vote the ticket' rather than supporting a particular candidate, are expected to encourage politicians to offer programmatic benefits, focused on the collective record and program of their party, and to strengthen cohesive and disciplined parliamentary parties.

This system is used in party list PR in 35 electoral systems worldwide, such as Norway and Romania. It also operates in the party block vote system, where electors can cast a ballot for the party list, and the party with a simple plurality of votes in each district is duly elected, as in Singapore, Ecuador and Senegal.

While there are many reasons to believe that the ballot structure is important for the chain of accountability from legislators to voters and parties, nevertheless it is only one factor at work here. A related arrangement is the mean district magnitude (referring to the number of seats per district). Extremely large multimember districts are likely to weaken the incentive to cultivate a personal vote in preference ballot elections, as it will be difficult for any individual candidate to stand out from the throng; alternatively, they may encourage candidates to develop local bailiwicks, effectively dividing the large district into personal 'subdistricts'. Moderate or small multimember districts, on the other hand, are expected to have the opposite tendency, for example where four or five candidates are rivals in STV seats in Ireland.

The nomination process within parties is therefore expected to interact with the electoral system, determining the final stage of recruitment. Members are expected to be most accountable to both local parties and local citizens in systems where the powers of nomination rest in the hands of the local party selectorate, such as grassroots members in each seat, and where the electoral system uses candidate ballots, typified by single-member districts. Such a context is thought to encourage members to focus on delivering particularistic benefits to their district, exemplified by constituency casework and the provision of pork. By contrast, a combination of centralized party selection and the use of party ballots is thought to generate cohesive and disciplined parliamentary parties, with members focused on the

provision of collective programmatic benefits[39].
Rather than a 'one size fits all' approach, the
most suitable nomination processes therefore
depend upon their interaction with the ballot
structures, and whether it is thought to be more
important in any political system to prioritize
local accountability or cohesive and disciplined
parliamentary parties.

There are also certain non-congruent cases.
Although it is often assumed that party nomination rules will tend to reflect the structure of
the electoral system, in fact, as Lundell observed,
the degree of centralization of the candidate
nomination process is quite complex and diverse
among parties, depending upon their structure
and organization[40]. In mass-branch parties with
a tradition of internal democracy, for example
many Scandinavian parties, we have already
seen that candidate selection decisions are
localized even within party ballot elections. At
the same time, the party leadership can play an
important role in internal party decisions about
nominations, for example vetoing unacceptable nominees, even in candidate ballot elections[41]. In non-congruent cases, it remains to be
seen whether elected representatives regard
themselves as more accountable to the party
selectorate or to the electorate.

CONCLUSIONS

Overall the evidence therefore suggests that
grassroots members in many European parties
have gradually been given greater opportunities
to nominate candidates. At the same time selectors are operating within a more constrained
scope of decision-making, due to the simultaneous adoption of rules implementing positive
action strategies. A wider number of members
are therefore able to engage in selection decisions, but they face a more restricted range of
choices. We can conclude that the recruitment
process to elected office may appear to be one of
the more hidden and technical aspects of party
politics, but this process has many consequences
for the division of power within party organizations, the barriers and opportunities facing
women and ethnic minority candidates, and also
for the accountability of elected representatives.

NOTES

1. For reviews of the earlier literature on this topic
   see Moshe M. Czudnowski (1975) 'Political
   recruitment', in Fred Greenstein and Nelson
   W. Polsby (eds), *Handbook of Political Science,
   Vol. 2: Micropolitical Theory* (Reading, MA:
   Addison-Wesley); Donald R. Matthews (1985)
   'Legislative recruitment and legislative careers',
   in Gerhard Loewenberg, Samuel C. Patterson
   and Malcolm E. Jewell (eds), *Handbook of
   Legislative Research* (Cambridge, MA: Harvard
   University Press); Gerhard Loewenberg and
   Samuel C. Patterson (1979) *Comparing
   Legislatures* (Boston: Little, Brown); Austin
   Ranney (1981) 'Candidate selection', in David
   Butler, Howard Penniman and Austin Ranney
   (eds), *Democracy at the Polls* (Washington, DC:
   AEI). Comparative studies can be found in
   Michael Gallagher and Michael Marsh (eds)
   (1988) *Candidate Selection in Comparative
   Perspective* (London: Sage) and Pippa Norris (ed.)
   (1998) *Passages to Power* (Cambridge: Cambridge
   University Press).

2. Louis Massicotte, André Blais and Antoine
   Yoshinaka (2004) *Establishing the Rules of the Game*
   (Toronto: University of Toronto Press), Chapter 2.
   See also details of the legal qualifications to
   become a candidate in legislative elections pro-
   vided by the Election Process Information
   Collection (EPIC) project (http://epic.at.org/
   EPIC/multi).

3. Quoted from Jeffrey Obler in Gideon Rahat and
   Reuven Y. Hazan (2001) 'Candidate selection
   methods – An analytical framework', *Party
   Politics*, 7: 297–322.

4. See Czudnowski, 'Political recruitment'.

5. Angelo Panebianco (1988) *Political Parties:
   Organisation and Power* (Cambridge: Cambridge
   University Press); Richard S. Katz (2001) 'The
   problem of candidate selection and models of
   party democracy', *Party Politics*, 7: 277–96.

6. E.E. Schatterschneider (1942) *Party Government*
   (New York: Holt, Rinehart and Winston), p. 101.

7. Richard S. Katz and Peter Mair (1992) *Party
   Organisations: A Data Handbook on Party Organi-
   zations in Western Democracies, 1960–90* (London:
   Sage).

8. Lars Bille (2001) 'Democratizing a democratic
   procedure: Myth or reality? Candidate selection
   in Western European parties, 1960–1990', *Party
   Politics*, 7: 363–80.

9. See Rahat and Hazan, 'Candidate selection
   methods'; Reuven Y. Hazan (2002) 'Candidate
   selection', in Lawrence LeDuc, Richard Neimi
   and Pippa Norris (eds), *Comparing Democracies 2*
   (London: Sage). For similar conclusions, see also
   Susan Scarrow, Paul Webb and David M. Farrell
   (2000) 'From social integration to electoral contestation', in Russell J. Dalton and Martin P.
   Wattenberg (eds), *Parties without Partisans:
   Political Change in Advanced Industrial Democracies*
   (Oxford: Oxford University Press); J. Hopkin

(2001) 'Bringing the members back in? Democratizing candidate selection in Britain and Spain', *Party Politics*, 7: 343–61; J. Hopkin (2003) 'Political decentralization, electoral change and party organizational adaptation – A framework for analysis', *European Urban and Regional Studies*, 10: 227–237.

10. Scarrow, Webb and Farrell, 'From social integration to electoral contestation'.

11. Krister Lundell (2004) 'Determinants of candidate selection – The degree of centralization in comparative perspective', *Party Politics*, 10: 25–47.

12. See, for example, Pippa Norris and Joni Lovenduski (1995) *Political Recruitment: Gender, Race and Class in the British Parliament* (Cambridge: Cambridge University Press).

13. For a discussion see Rahat and Hazan, 'Candidate selection methods'; Alan Ware (1987) *Political Parties: Electoral Change and Party Response* (Oxford: Oxford University Press).

14. Peter Bacharatz and M.S. Baratz (1963) 'Decisions and non-decisions: an analytical framework', *American Political Science Review*, 57: 632–42.

15. See, however, Hanne Marthe Narud, Morgens N. Pedersen and Henry Valen (2002) *Party Sovereignty and Citizen Control* (Odense: University Press of Southern Denmark).

16. For the most extensive research project collecting systematic data in this area, see Heinrich Best and Maurizio Cotta (eds) (2000) *Parliamentary Representatives in Europe, 1848–2000* (Oxford: Oxford University Press).

17. Pippa Norris (1985) 'Women in European legislative elites', *West European Politics*, 8(4): 90–101; Wilma Rule and Joseph Zimmerman (1992) *Electoral Systems in Comparative Perspective: Their Impact on Women and Minorities*. Westport, CT: Greenwood Press; Arend Lijphart (1994) *Electoral Systems and Party Systems: A Study of Twenty-Seven Democracies, 1945–1990*. Oxford: Oxford University Press; Richard Matland (1998) 'Women's representation in national legislatures: Developed and developing countries', *Legislative Studies Quarterly*, 23(1): 109–25; Andrew Reynolds (1999) 'Women in the legislatures and executives of the world: knocking at the highest glass ceiling', *World Politics* 51: 547–72; Lane Kenworthy and Melissa Malami (1999) 'Gender inequality in political representation: A worldwide comparative analysis', *Social Forces* 78(1): 235–69; Alan Siaroff (2000) 'Women's representation in legislatures and cabinets in industrial democracies', *International Political Science Review*, 21: 197–215. For the argument that these patterns do not hold in post-Communist states, however, see Robert G. Moser (2001) 'The effects of electoral systems on women's representation in post-communist states', *Electoral Studies*. 20: 353–69.

18. Pippa Norris (2004) *Electoral Engineering* (New York and Cambridge: Cambridge University Press), Chapter 8.

19. It should be noted that reserved seats for women have also been used previously in Eritrea but that parliament is currently suspended in this country. Their use is currently being considered for the new Afghanistan and Iraqi electoral laws.

20. Cathryn Hoskins and Shirin Rai (1998) 'Gender, class and representation: India and the European Union', *European Journal of Women's Studies*, 5: 345–55.

21. D. Pankhurst (2002) 'Women and politics in Africa: The case of Uganda', *Parliamentary Affairs*, 55(1): 119–25.

22. Council of Europe (2000) *Positive Action in the Field of Equality between Women and Men: Final Report of the Group of Specialists on Positive Action in the Field of Equality between Women and Men*, EG-S-PA (Strasbourg: Council of Europe); Anne Peters, Robert Seidman and Ann Seidman. (1999) *Women, Quotas, and Constitutions: A Comparative Study of Affirmative Action for Women under American, German and European Community and International Law* (The Hague: Kluwer Law International).

23. Petra Meie (2000) 'The evidence of being present: Guarantees of representation and the example of the Belgian case', *Acta Politica* 35(1): 64–85; A. Carton (2001) 'The general elections in Belgium in June 1999: A real breakthrough for women politicians', *European Journal of Women's Studies*, 8(1): 127–35.

24. Karen Bird (2002) 'Who are the women? Where are the women? And what difference can they make? The effects of gender parity in French municipal elections', paper presented at the Annual Meeting of the American Political Science Association, Boston; Janine Mossuz-Lavau (1998) *Femmes/hommes. Pour la parité.* (Paris: Presses de Sciences Po); Mariette Sineau (2002) 'La parité in politics: From a radical idea to a consensual reform', in Isabelle de Courtivron (ed.), *Beyond French Feminisms: Debates on Women, Politics and Culture in France, 1980–2001* (New York: Palgrave).

25. The Italian articles included law 277\93 for elections to the House of Representatives, law 81\93 for local elections, and law 43\95 regional elections. For details see *Women in Decision-making: European database* (www.db-decision.de).

26. Mark Jones (1996) 'Increasing women's representation via gender quotas: The Argentine Ley de Cupos', *Women & Politics*, 16(4): 75–98; Mark Jones (1998) 'Gender quotas, electoral laws, and the election of women – Lessons from the Argentine provinces', *Comparative Political*

Studies, 31(1): 3–21; Mark Jones (1999) 'Assessing the effectiveness of gender quotas in open-list proportional representation electoral systems', *Social Science Quarterly*, 80: 341–55; Mala Htun and Mark Jones (2002) 'Engendering the right to participate in decision-making: Electoral quotas and women's leadership in Latin America', in Nikki Craske and Maxine Molyneux (eds), *Gender and the Politics of Rights and Democracy in Latin America* (London: Palgrave); Mala Htun (2002) 'Women and political power in Latin America', in *Women in Parliament. Beyond Numbers*, Latin America edition (Stockholm: International IDEA).

27. Joni Lovenduski and Pippa Norris (1993) *Gender and Party Politics* (London: Sage); Norris, *Passages to Power*; Drude Dahlerup (1998) 'Using quotas to increase women's political representation', in Azza Karam (ed.), *IDEA: Women in Politics Beyond Numbers* (Stockholm: IDEA); Council of Europe, *Positive Action in the Field of Equality between Women and Men*.

28. International IDEA (2003) *Global Database of Quotas for Women* (http://www.idea.int/quota/index.cfm).

29. Meg Russell (2000) *Women's Representation in UK Politics: What Can Be Done within the Law?* (Constitution Unit Report, University College London). See also Meg Russell (2001) *The Women's Representation Bill: Making it Happen* (Constitution Unit Report, University College London).

30. Richard E. Matland (1993) 'Institutional variables affecting female representation in national legislatures: The case of Norway', *Journal of Politics*, 55: 737–55.

31. Lauri Karvonen and Per Selle (eds) (1995) *Women in Nordic Politics* (Aldershot: Dartmouth).

32. Joni Lovenduski and Pippa Norris (1994) 'Women's quotas in the Labour Party', in David Broughton *et al.* (eds), *British Parties and Elections Yearbook, 1994* (London: Frank Cass), pp. 167–81; Maria Eagle and Joni Lovenduski (1998) *High Time or High Tide for Labour Women?* (London: Fabian Society).

33. Joni Lovenduski (2001) 'Women and Politics: Minority representation or critical mass?', in Pippa Norris (ed.), *Britain Votes 2001* (Oxford: Oxford University Press); Sarah Perrigo (1996) 'Women and change in the Labour Party 1979–1995', in Joni Lovenduski and Pippa Norris (eds), *Women in Politics* (Oxford: Oxford University Press); Pippa Norris (2001) 'Breaking the barriers: British Labour Party quotas for women', in Jyette Klausen and Charles S. Maier (eds), *Has Liberalism Failed Women? Assuring Equal Representation in Europe and the United States* (New York: Palgrave), pp. 89–110.

34. Socialist International Women (2002) www.socintwomen.org.uk/Quota.

35. Inter-Parliamentary Union (1992) *Women and Political Power* (Geneva: Inter-Parliamentary Union). For a more recent discussion, see Dahlerup, 'Using quotas to increase women's political representation'.

36. Carol Nechemias (1994) 'Democratization and women's access to legislative seats – The Soviet case, 1989–1991', *Women & Politics*, 14(3): 1–18; Robert G. Moser (2001) 'The effects of electoral systems on women's representation in post-communist states', *Electoral Studies*, 20: 353–369.

37. Heinz Eulau and Jon C. Wahlke (1978) *The Politics of Representation* (London: Sage).

38. See, for example, Bernard Grofman, Sung-Chull Lee, Edwin A. Winckler and Brian Woodall (eds) (1997) *Elections in Japan, Korea and Taiwan under the Single Non-Transferable Vote: The Comparative Study of an Embedded Institution* (Ann Arbor: University of Michigan Press).

39. Some empirical support for this proposition has been found by Simon Hix (2001) 'How electoral institutions shape legislative behavior: Explaining voting defection in the European parliament', EPRG Working Paper 10 (http://www.lse.ac.uk/Depts/eprg/).

40. Lundell, 'Determinants of candidate selection'.

41. Pippa Norris (1996) 'Candidate recruitment', in Lawrence LeDuc, Richard Niemi and Pippa Norris (eds), *Comparing Democracies* (Thousand Oaks, CA: Sage).

10

CANDIDATE SELECTION:
METHODS AND CONSEQUENCES

Reuven Y. Hazan and Gideon Rahat*

Whatever the electoral formula used in elections, candidate selection is one of the first things that political parties must do before they take place. Those who are eventually elected to office will be the successful candidates that the parties previously selected, and they are the ones who will determine much of how the party looks and what it does. That is, the results of the candidate selection process will affect the party a long time after the election itself is over.

Candidate selection is, according to Ranney (1981: 75), the 'process by which a political party decides which of the persons legally eligible to hold an elective office will be designated on the ballot and in election communications as its recommended and supported candidate or list of candidates'. Candidate selection is, therefore, not the same as legislative recruitment; the latter is more comprehensive and actually includes the former. Legislative recruitment involves such aspects of the political system as the legal, electoral and party frameworks (Norris, 1996, 1997, see also Chapter 9 this volume). Candidate selection may, indeed, be described as a 'key stage' in the recruitment process (Gallagher, 1988a: 2), or even as 'the most important stage' (Czudnowski, 1975: 219).

Candidate selection takes place almost entirely *within* particular parties. There are very few countries – e.g., Germany, Finland and Norway – where the legal system specifies criteria for candidate selection. Only in the United States does the legal system extensively regulate the process of candidate selection. In most countries, the parties themselves are allowed to determine the rules of the game

for their selection of candidates. Candidate selection should, therefore, be seen as a particular and important aspect of legislative recruitment that takes place *inside* the party arena and is predominantly *extralegal*.

The following sections in this chapter elaborate why it is important for students of party politics to understand the mechanisms and dynamics of candidate selection; what the main factors are that delineate candidate selection methods; and how different candidate selection methods have significant consequences for central aspects of democracy, such as participation, representation, competition, and responsiveness.

WHY STUDY CANDIDATE SELECTION?

Until recently, candidate selection received relatively little attention. This dearth of scholarly literature has raised a formidable obstacle in the path of researchers who wish to undertake cross-national analyses of the subject. A few pioneering ventures, however, did take place, with initial attempts to produce a theory or a framework for analysis, but they remain few and far between (Duverger, 1959; Czudnowski, 1975; Epstein, 1980; Ranney, 1981; Gallagher and Marsh, 1988; Hazan and Pennings, 2001; Narud *et al.*, 2002). This is partially due to the objective difficulties and obstacles one encounters in any attempt to conduct research on candidate selection – namely, the lack and inaccessibility of empirical data. It is not by chance that Gallagher and Marsh's (1988) work on

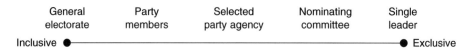

Figure 10.1   Party selectorates (updated from Rahat and Hazan, 2001)

candidate selection calls it the 'secret garden' of politics. However, the more recent research into this subfield, particularly in the last decade, eschews many of the earlier assumptions, penetrates new grounds of empirical research, and shows that candidate selection has wide-ranging and significant implications for political parties, party members, leaders, and democratic governance.

Beyond being a significant stage in the recruitment process (Norris, this volume), candidate selection is also an important arena for internal party power struggles. Schattschneider's (1942: 64) argument concerning this issue is worth citing in full:

> Unless the party makes authoritative and effective nominations, it cannot stay in business, for dual or multiple party candidacies mean certain defeat. As far as elections are concerned, the united front of the party, the party concentration of numbers, can be brought about only by a binding nomination. The nominating process thus has become the crucial process of the party. The nature of the nominating process determines the nature of the party; he who can make the nominations is the owner of the party. This is therefore one of the best points at which to observe the distribution of power within the party.

Ranney (1981: 103) endorses this statement.

> It is therefore not surprising that the most vital and hotly contested factional disputes in any party are the struggles that take place over the choice of its candidates; for what is at stake in such a struggle, as the opposing sides well know, is nothing less than control of the core of what the party stands for and does.

Gallagher (1988a: 3) takes it a step further, stating that 'the contest over candidate selection is generally even more intense than the struggle over the party manifesto'. Indeed, after an election, what largely remains as the functioning core of almost any party is its office-holders – its successful candidates.

Thus, the importance of candidate selection methods for understanding party politics can be explained by a combination of the three elements elaborated above: First, candidate selection

reflects and defines the character of a party and its internal power struggle. Second, it is relatively easy for parties to alter their candidate selection methods. Third, a change in candidate selection methods will affect party politics.

AN ANALYTICAL FRAMEWORK FOR STUDYING CANDIDATE SELECTION

In any analysis of candidate selection methods, the unit of analysis is a single party in a particular country at a specific time. Only in those cases where several parties in a particular country use similar methods (usually due to legal requirements), or where a single party uses a similar candidate selection method over time, can one begin to make generalizations about the candidate selection process.

The procedure for classifying candidate selection methods elaborated here is based on four criteria: the selectorate; candidacy; decentralization; and voting versus appointment (Rahat and Hazan, 2001).

Selectorate

The selectorate is the body that selects the candidates. It is, as Best and Cotta (2000: 11) argue, 'an important intermediary actor in the process of recruitment'. The selectorate can be composed of one person or many people – up to the entire electorate of a given nation. On the inclusiveness to exclusiveness continuum, as presented in Figure 10.1, at one extreme the selectorate is the most inclusive, i.e., the entire electorate that has the right to vote in the general elections. At the other extreme, the selectorate – or rather the selector – is the most exclusive, i.e., a nominating entity of one leader.

Between these two extremes, the selectorate of each single party is classified according to its degree of inclusiveness. For example, American *non-partisan* primaries, in which every registered voter can vote for candidates from any party, are located near the inclusive end of

Figure 10.2   Candidacy (updated from Rahat and Hazan, 2001)

the continuum (Ranney, 1981). American *closed* primaries, on the other hand, which demand voters' registration according to their party affiliation before the day of the primaries, are located slightly away from the inclusive end. The exact location of American primaries will, therefore, depend on the restrictions that are defined by the different state laws (Kolodny and Katz, 1992).

The inclusive end of the continuum also includes examples from Iceland and Spain. According to Kristjánsson (1998), from 1971 on, several parties in Iceland adopted open primaries, where every citizen in a particular electoral district could participate. The Spanish Catalan Party opened its candidate selection to 'registered "sympathizers"' – non-members who can register as party supporters without paying any membership fee (Hopkin, 2001).

Party primaries, in which the selectors are party members, would be located closer to the middle of the selectorate continuum (Gallagher, 1988a). More and more Western democracies allot their party members a significant role in candidate selection (Bille, 2001). The purest type of party primary is where the party members' vote alone decides the composition and rank of the candidates. Less pure types allow the party members to select the party candidates from a short-list determined either by party agencies or by a nominating committee, and/or allow the party headquarters to veto certain candidates.

When the selectorate is an agency of the party, we find ourselves in the middle of the continuum. Inside the party, the relative size of each agency is a sign of its inclusiveness: conventions are usually larger than central committees, which in turn are usually larger than executive bodies, such as bureaus. As the size of the particular party agency gets smaller, we move further toward the exclusive pole of the continuum.

An extremely inclusive selectorate is, for example, a special nomination committee that is composed of a few leaders or their aficionados, and whose composition is ratified *en bloc*. The extreme end of the exclusive pole is defined by a selectorate comprised of a single individual. Israel's ultra-orthodox religious

parties serve as an example of such an extremely exclusive selectorate. In one party, a single rabbi was authorized to decide the composition and order of the party list (Rahat and Sher-Hadar, 1999).

Candidacy

Candidacy addresses the question of who can present himself or herself as the candidate of a particular party. Again we can posit an inclusiveness to exclusiveness continuum (Figure 10.2). At one end, the inclusive pole, every voter is eligible to stand as a party's candidate. Some US states are close to this pole. At the exclusive pole, we encounter a series of restrictive conditions. Consider Obler's (1974: 180) account of the requirements that applied to potential candidates in the Belgian Socialist Party.

> While the exact requirements vary from one constituency to another, they generally stipulate that to be placed on the primary ballot aspirants must (1) have been a member of the Socialist party, trade union, co-operative and insurance association for at least five years prior to the primary; (2) have made annual minimum purchases from the Socialist co-op; (3) have been a regular subscriber to the party's newspaper; (4) have sent his children to state rather than Catholic schools; and (5) have his wife and children enrolled in the appropriate women's and youth organizations. These conditions, in effect, require that a candidate serve as a member of an activist subculture before he becomes eligible to run for Parliament. They involve a form of enforced socialization during which it is assumed (or hoped) that the aspirant will absorb the appropriate values and attitudes as well as a keen commitment to the party.

More common requirements are less demanding, such as a minimal length of membership prior to the presentation of candidacy and pledges of loyalty to the party. At times, parties will ignore their own candidacy regulations, largely due to electoral considerations. For example, even the exclusive Italian Communist Party included non-members as candidates (Wertman, 1988).

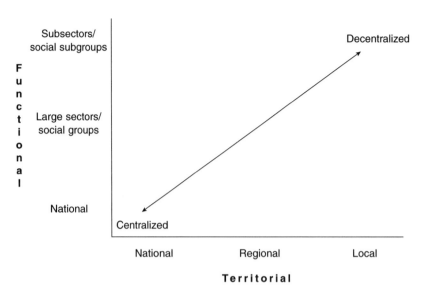

Figure 10.3   Centralization and decentralization (Rahat and Hazan, 2001)

Decentralization

A common error in studies that address candidate selection methods is that of considering decentralization and inclusiveness (and centralization and exclusiveness) as conceptually similar, or at least as describing the same dimension of candidate selection methods (Bowler *et al.*, 1999; Shugart, 2001). Analytically, though, they are different. Decentralization could mean only that control over candidate selection has passed from the national oligarchy to a local oligarchy. For example, if the selectorate is decentralized from a national party conference of several thousand participants to ten local committees each consisting of a few dozen activists and leaders, the overall selectorate has been decentralized, but has not become more inclusive – and has actually become more exclusive.

Party selection methods may be seen as decentralized in two senses (see Figure 10.3), which are parallel to the concepts Lijphart (1984) proposed when he dealt with the division of power in federal and unitary democratic regimes. Decentralization can be *territorial*, i.e., when local party selectorates nominate party candidates – such as a local leader, a party branch committee, or all party members or voters in an electoral district. Decentralization of the selection method can also be *functional*, i.e., ensuring representation for representatives of such groups as trade unions, women, or minorities.

Decentralization based on territorial mechanisms, in order to ensure regional and local representation, is rather straightforward. In many European cases, the selectorate at the district level plays the crucial role in candidate selection. The Norwegian case falls close to the territorial decentralization pole. National party agencies cannot veto a candidacy that is determined at the district level, and territorial representation is taken into account *inside* each district (Valen, 1988; Valen *et al.*, 2002).

More complex mechanisms are required for ensuring functional representation via decentralization. There are two mechanisms commonly used. The first is the reserved place mechanism, which guarantees a minimal number of positions on the list (or minimal number of safe seats in the case of single-member districts) for candidates belonging to a distinct sector or social group. This mechanism implies the decentralization of candidacy alone. Candidates who are eligible for reserved places compete for their place on the list against all of the candidates and are selected by the same selectorate, and the reserved representation mechanism is implemented only if the candidates do not attain the reserved position or a higher one. Establishing quotas for women, a practice adopted by many parties, is one example.

The second mechanism used to ensure functional representation is the sectarian or social group district, where the candidates and the selectors are members of the same sector or social group. This mechanism decentralizes both candidacy and the selectorate. Belgium supplies us with examples of both of the functional representation mechanisms, which were used at the district level. In the Belgian Christian Social Party in 1961, the reserved place mechanism was used when it was decided that in some of the Brussels districts, Flemish and Francophone candidates would get every other seat on the party list. In 1965, separate intra-party subdistricts were actually established when Francophone and Flemish party members in these districts selected, separately, Francophone and Flemish candidates for parliament (Obler, 1974).

Voting versus appointment

It is usually the case that in smaller and more exclusive selectorates, candidates are appointed, while larger selectorates usually vote in order to choose their candidates. However, a voting system can, theoretically, be used in a selectorate of two or more people, and appointments can take place in bodies that include several dozens of people. When the selection process includes a procedure by which votes determine whether someone is named as the party's candidate in an election, and/or his or her position on the list, we are dealing with a *voting procedure*. It should be noted that while a voting procedure can be used by an appointment body of two people or more, it is not considered a voting system unless two conditions are filled: first, each candidacy must be determined exclusively by votes, and not, for example, by an agreed-upon list or an allocation that is ratified by a unanimous or majority vote; and second, the voting results must be presented officially to justify and legitimize the candidacy. When candidacy is determined without fulfilling these conditions, we refer to this as an *appointment system*. In a pure appointment system, candidates are appointed with no need for approval by any party agency except the nominating organ itself. In a pure voting system, all candidates are selected through a voting procedure, and no other selectorate can change the composition of the list.

Cases located between these extremes are called appointment–voting systems. Such is the *en bloc* ratification vote that was used in Belgium. In many constituencies, party members were asked either to vote for a 'model list' – a list of candidates determined by

a local party agency – or to express their preferences regarding the candidates. Only if more than 50% of party members did not ratify the model list were the other votes counted, and thus they did not carry much weight (Obler, 1974; de Winter, 1988). In Norway, appointments were more open to change in the ratification process. Lists that were recommended by a nominating committee were then ratified by a majority of a selected party agency, position by position (Valen, 1988).

Voting systems can be further distinguished on the basis of two elements. One is the position allocation formula, i.e., proportional representation (PR), semi-PR, semi-majoritarian, and majoritarian systems. The distinction among these four kinds of voting system is based on their potential level of proportionality. Proportional voting systems in this context will usually be personalized. For example, three of the four largest Irish parties in the 1980s – Fianna Fáil was the exception – used the single transferable vote (STV) system that was also used in general elections to determine the composition of their candidate lists. Semi-proportional systems are those in which the number of votes each selector has is *smaller* than the number of safe seats being contested. This is the intra-party version of a limited-vote electoral system. In a majoritarian system, the number of votes and safe seats/positions is *equal*. In many cases, every position is contested separately, making the system almost parallel to single-member district elections. Semi-majoritarian systems are defined as systems where the number of votes that each selector receives is *higher* than the number of safe seats contested. While such a system is majoritarian – as a majority block can be organized and can take over all of the safe positions[1] – it is 'semi' in the sense that incentives for organizing a plurality or majority bloc vote are weaker than in the pure majoritarian case.[2]

The second parameter distinguishes between single-round and multi-round selection methods. In the former, all safe positions are selected at one and the same time, whereas in the latter, the safe positions are filled gradually. The importance of this distinction lies in the opportunities to control and/or balance the composition of the lists that a gradual selection process gives the parties.

There is a connection between the voting system used in the final stage of the candidate selection process and the national electoral system. Where national elections are conducted in single-member districts, the voting system used in the candidate selection process must be majoritarian, in order to produce a single candidate. For example, the exhaustive ballot was used by the British Conservative and Labour parties in the final stage of their selection process,[3] while the Liberals used the majoritarian method of the alternative vote (Denver, 1988). On the other hand, when general elections take place in multi-member districts, the voting system does not need to be majoritarian. For example, in Ireland the exhaustive ballot was used by Fianna Fáil in order to determine its candidate list, position by position, while the next three largest parties used a one-round STV method.

There is also a connection between the selectorate size and the use of either single-round or gradual selection. In smaller selectorates, it is possible to adopt either method. However, when the selectorate is larger – especially in those cases where it includes all party members or the entire electorate – logistics makes the use of a single round almost a must.[4]

THE POLITICAL CONSEQUENCES OF CANDIDATE SELECTION METHODS

As elaborated above, the classification of candidate selection methods can be based on four major dimensions: selectorate; candidacy; decentralization; and voting versus appointment. The different methods used along these dimensions produce different political consequences. For example, when it comes to the decentralization dimension, territorial decentralization of the candidate selection method could lead to increased responsiveness of members of parliament to the demands and grievances of their (newly created) constituency (Hazan, 1999) – similar to an electoral system founded on small districts. On the voting dimension, parties that use more proportional voting methods, or parties that use appointment methods, could control intra-party conflicts by balancing representation better than parties that use centralized methods and majoritarian voting systems. Concerning candidacy rules, parties could influence the composition of the parliamentary party group by adopting term limits or setting additional criteria for incumbents. Conversely, parties could make the life of incumbents easier by adopting an almost automatic reselection procedure.

The selectorate, however, determines the most significant and far-reaching consequences (Scarrow, 2000; Best and Cotta, 2000). Therefore, this section focuses on the political consequences of the *inclusiveness of the selectorate*. The impact of this foremost dimension will be assessed according to four important aspects of democracy: participation, representation, competition, and responsiveness.

Participation

When we talk about political participation, we must distinguish between the quantity of participants and the quality of their participation. It is obvious that in terms of quantity, the more inclusive selectorates are the more participatory ones. Indeed, political participation is at its lowest when a few party leaders, or their aficionados, produce the list of candidates. A selectorate that is composed of hundreds, or even thousands, of delegates (a party agency, such as a central committee or a convention) comes closer to the democratic ideal, especially since the party members usually select these delegates. A selectorate that includes tens, and even hundreds, of thousands of party members can be seen, from the quantitative perspective, as an open arena for political participation.

When looking beyond the numbers, in an attempt to analyze the quality of membership and its meaning, the picture becomes quite obscure. Citizens positively perceive the attempts of parties to enhance participation by adopting a more inclusive selectorate in their candidate selection processes. However, most of them do not even bother to join the parties in order to enjoy the now empowered benefits of membership. Numerous country studies, such as Britain (Webb, 2002), Germany (Scarrow, 2002), France (Knapp, 2002), the Scandinavian countries (Sundberg, 2002) and Ireland (Murphy and Farrell, 2002), show that parties try to meet the challenge of declining party membership by empowering party members, yet these efforts have failed to enlarge the number of party members significantly.

Furthermore, many of those who join the parties do not satisfy even the minimum expectations of party members – to be loyal party voters and to be affiliated with the party for more than a short period. Research on Israeli party primaries found that many of the new party members joined the party (or rather were recruited) with the sole purpose of supporting a certain candidate. Approximately one-third of those who joined the party were not even aware of the fact that they were party members. One-tenth were actually members of more than one party. Moreover, many party members voted for other parties in the general elections

(Rahat and Hazan, forthcoming). Studies of candidate selection in Canada show that most of those who joined the parties in order to participate in the candidate selection process were 'instant members'. These members joined the party solely in order to select a leader, or a candidate for parliament, and left the party as soon as the selection was over (Carty and Blake, 1999; Carty, 2002; Malloy, 2003). It appears that the parties, for their part, prefer to 'improve membership statistics' (Scarrow, 1994: 46) as a demonstration of their public 'credibility', rather than to embark on a search for measures to improve the quality of membership alongside its expansion.

The rate of turnout in party primaries is another interesting indicator of the (lack of) quality of a more inclusive selectorate. Kuitunen (2002: 74–5, 77) reports that turnout in primaries in Finland ranged from 20% to 63%. De Winter (1988: 26) reports a decline in the participation by Belgian party members from 51% in 1958 to 25% in 1985. According to Rahat and Hazan (forthcoming), turnout in primaries in Israel during the 1990s ranged from 51% to 75%, while Gallagher (1988b: 246) reports that in the Austrian People's Party (ÖVP) in 1975 it was 63%. These statistics indicate two things: first, turnout in the party primaries is lower than in the general elections; and second, on average, about one-half of the dues-paying, empowered party members do not bother to collect the 'merchandise' that they paid for, and do not participate in their party's candidate selection process.

A more inclusive policy is also likely to erode, in the long run, the loyal core of party activists. Enhanced, and equivalent, political participation in candidate selection damages the differential structure of rewards (or 'selective incentives') in parties when the privileges of long-time loyal activists are made equal to those of new, temporary and unfaithful registrants. This may be the actual aim of those who employ this policy (Katz, 2001), or may be an unintended consequence of it (Hazan, 2002).

Representation

Among the many notions of representation, two distinct concepts can be used to illustrate the influence of candidate selection. The first is the representation of *ideas*, as described by Pitkin (1976), which implies that the representatives reflect the political beliefs of their voters. The second is representation as *presence*, which relates to the descriptive characteristics of the representatives – whether their identity is similar to those whom they represent or not (Phillips, 1995). Both kinds of representation are relevant to candidate selection because parties – in their attempt to address the electorate, and to control intra-party conflicts – are likely to try to balance their list of candidates in terms of both notions of representation.

Smaller, exclusive selectorates will be more capable of balancing representation in both senses. When selection can be controlled by a party oligarchy that appoints candidates – and to a lesser extent, when voting takes place in a party agency and can be coordinated – there are more chances that different ideological and social groups (women, minorities, etc.) within the party will be allocated safe positions on the party list, or safe constituency seats. The parties themselves, according to their behavior, appear to validate this claim. The process of democratization of the candidate selection methods in western Europe (Hazan and Pennings, 2001) took place parallel to the increase in the use of representation correction mechanisms (Caul, 1999). Parties increasingly tend to restrict the choices of their more inclusive selectorates in order to ensure representation as presence, particularly that of women (Norris, this volume).

Competition

The candidate selection process pits against each other numerous candidates who aspire to be among those few that will compete in safe seats, or in safe list positions, during an election. There are various ways to measure and compare the level of competition in candidate selection. For example, one can calculate the average number of candidates who compete per safe seat or list position; alternatively, in cases where voting takes place, one can analyze the spread of the votes among the competing candidates. Incumbency, or the level of turnover, could serve as an indicator for the level of competition. For example, higher turnover could signify higher levels of competition.

While incumbency is an advantage in every kind of candidate selection method, as it is in every type of electoral system (Somit *et al.*, 1994), the differences in the inclusiveness of the selectorate are likely to create variations in the extent of this advantage. Smaller selectorates allow aspiring candidates a chance to be known and to personally contact their selectors. When the selectorate is inclusive, i.e., composed of party members at large, support cannot be based on personal affiliations and incumbency is thus likely to offer a larger advantage. This is mainly because, as public officials, incumbents enjoy publicity and the ability to demonstrate responsiveness to the demands of the selectorate, interest groups, financial supporters, etc. The American experience supplies clear evidence of the advantage of incumbents in primaries (a very inclusive selectorate). Between 1978 and 1992, in only 47 cases out of 3166 (1.5%) were incumbents seeking re-election to the House of Representatives defeated in the primaries, and in only 13 cases out of 236 (5.5%) were incumbents seeking re-election to the Senate defeated in the primaries (Jackson, 1994). As Maisel and Stone (2001: 43) point out, 'It is clear that primary elections do not serve to stimulate more competition, and to the extent that competition is an essential ingredient of democracy, it is not clear they accomplish their intended purpose of enhancing U.S. democracy'.

If we accept the argument that party agencies are more competitive than primaries because of the shorter 'distance' between the candidates and selectors, then nomination committees (a very exclusive selectorate) can be expected to be even more competitive. This is because it is easier for each candidate to be in personal contact with each member of the committee than would be the case in a more inclusive selectorate. However, this prediction misses an important part of the picture. The nomination committee suffers – because of its small size and informal, non-transparent working procedures – from a lack of popular democratic legitimacy, i.e., a democratic deficit. The best strategy for the nomination committee to legitimize its decisions in the eyes of the party members, the party agencies and even the general public is to present a list that is largely composed of incumbents – i.e., a list that reflects the existing balance of power and will thus not encounter much antagonism. There will be changes, to demonstrate that something was changed and that the nomination committee is not a rubber stamp, but they will be minimal. The result is that party agencies, located in the middle of the inclusive–exclusive selectorate dimension, are likely to be the most competitive selectorates. The more exclusive selectorates, such as nominating committees, are likely to be the least competitive, while the most inclusive selectorates, such as primaries, are likely to be moderately competitive (Rahat and Hazan, 2005). More data and more empirical analysis are needed in order to validate and strengthen this assessment, because to date there are few studies of competition in the candidate selection process outside the inclusive American arena.

Responsiveness

Since a central motivation, and constraint, for the behavior of members of parliament (the successful candidates) is their wish to be reselected, they will pay special attention to the grievances and demands of their selectorate. The composition of the selectorate is thus likely to influence the behavioral patterns of parliamentarians and of their parent organization, the political party. Bowler (2000), for example, argues that the best explanation for the collective action of legislators is the nomination procedures in general, and who nominates in particular.

One approach claims that there are negative relationships between inclusiveness and party cohesion because the role of non-party actors in candidate selection rises with an increase in the inclusiveness of the selectorate, and also their importance as an object of responsiveness. Legislators who were selected by small nominating committees owe their positions to the party leadership, and are therefore likely to be first and foremost party players. Legislators who were selected by party agencies are likely to be party players at most times, but nevertheless will be somewhat differentiated in their efforts to promote the demands and interests of the groups within the party that serve as their power base. Legislators who were selected in primaries need the help of non-party actors in order to reach their massive, fluid, and somewhat apathetic audience. In the more inclusive selectorates, candidates need political 'mediators' who can supply the resources needed to address the large number of party members: capital holders who can supply the necessary finances to address a huge selectorate; interest group leaders who command the votes of hundreds, and even thousands, of members; and the mass media. All of these mediators have narrower – and sometimes different – interests and perceptions than the party as a whole. Facing the plurality of pressures that characterize the more inclusive selectorates, the cohesion of the parties is likely to decrease, as parliamentarians behave more like individuals than team players.

Comparing the level of party cohesion in the US Congress to levels of party cohesion in other Western democracies illustrates this point: the relatively low cohesion of US parties can be explained by their adherence to extremely inclusive candidate selection methods. Candidates select their party label with little to no say on the part of the party institutions. In most other cases, where cohesion is much higher, the parties as such have a say in candidate selection. First of all, party institutions often take part in candidate selection: filtering candidacies, validating their selection and sometimes playing the central role in their selection (Bille, 2001). Even when a growing number of parties allow their members a crucial role in candidate selection, membership, as such, is far more exclusive than in the USA (Epstein, 1980). As Gallagher (1988b: 271) argued, 'It may not matter much, in this sense [level of party cohesion], *which* party agency selects candidates, but it does matter that *some* party agency selects them'. Second, Western European parties still put some formal and informal limits on candidacy. Third, US parties have lost most of their control over candidate selection. The most they can do – and even in this they are limited – is to endorse a certain candidate competing in the party primaries for the use of the party label (Jewell and Morehouse, 2001). Another case in point is that of the democratization of candidate selection methods in Israel, Iceland, and Taiwan. In all three countries, the adoption of a more inclusive selectorate led to a decrease in party cohesion (Rahat and Hazan, 2001; Kristjánsson, 1998; Baum and Robinson, 1999).

A second approach, based on the logic of the cartel party model (Mair, 1994, 1997; Katz and Mair, 1995; Katz, 2001) and on the Canadian experience (Carty, 2004), claims that inclusive selectorates actually increase the power of party elites and help preserve party cohesion. An increase in nominal power at the base of the party is achieved at the expense of the middle-level activists, as they are the ones who might be able to coordinate an effective challenge to the autonomy of the party leaders. The rationale behind this approach is that the less intense (atomistic, unorganized, unstable) audience of party members is more likely to take cues from the highly visible party leadership. Empirical support for this approach comes from the Canadian case of inclusive selectorates and high party cohesion, and from other cases in which the opening up of candidate selection did not lead to a decrease in cohesion. However, as in the case of competition, the study of the impact of candidate selection methods on responsiveness, and in

particular on party cohesion, is still in an embryonic phase. More data and empirical analysis, such as Hix (2004), are needed to assess its ramifications comprehensively.

Intra-party democracy

The political consequences of the selectorate dimension in candidate selection reveal that more democracy in one dimension does not necessarily lead to more democracy in other dimensions. For example, parties that use small nomination committees can ensure representation, but are problematic in the participatory sense. On the other hand, parties that select their candidates through primaries enjoy high levels of participation, but can hardly balance representation. This indicates that in order to be considered truly 'more' democratic, parties should look for a candidate selection method that could optimally balance different democratic dimensions, such as participation, representation, competition, and responsiveness. It is the challenge of future research to clarify the relationship between these dimensions, based on the much needed empirical research, so that the study of candidate selection can supply a solid base for improved theoretical and political understanding of democracy in general and democracy within parties in particular.

CHALLENGES FOR FUTURE RESEARCH

The major challenge for the study of candidate selection methods is to bring it closer to the state that the study of electoral system was in approximately 40 years ago, when Rae's (1967) seminal work *The Political Consequences of Electoral Laws* was published. That is, we need cross-party and cross-national empirical studies of the political consequences of candidate selection methods.

Achieving this is by no means easy. Existing theoretical frameworks, particularly those concerning party politics, provide substantial propositions for the study of candidate selection. The lack of cross-national empirical studies is, nonetheless, the Achilles heel of any attempt to make further progress. The problem with a cross-national empirical study is that it requires familiarity with local politics and accessibility (in terms of language, as well as in other more basic terms) to intra-party data.

Candidate selection methods not only affect party politics, they can also reflect party politics. There is, therefore, a need to analyze candidate selection methods both as a dependent and as an independent variable. Prominent examples of treating candidate selection as a dependent variable, in the rather exceptional case of the United States, range from Key (1949) to Ware (2002). The possible links between candidate selection and such variables as the structure of government, the electoral system, the political culture, and the nature of the party were already suggested long ago (Gallagher and Marsh, 1988), but were only recently put to a cross-national empirical test (Lundell, 2004). There is a dire need for additional data, before any conclusive findings can be reached.

An additional path is the study of the politics of reform of candidate selection methods – why, when, and in what circumstances parties change (or preserve) their candidate selection methods. Several studies have suggested various explanations for such changes, for example, the democratization of candidate selection methods (Katz, 2001; Scarrow, 1999; Hazan and Pennings, 2001). Yet there remains a need for a more integrative look at the phenomenon, one that would account not only for overall trends but also for the differences among parties and among nations that may result from interactions at the inter- and intra-party levels.

Sailing the uncharted waters of candidate selection could help us better understand the nature of party membership, the kind of candidates selected, the dynamics exhibited within the party, the power and performance of the party in parliament, and our overall ability to evaluate party politics. Behind closed party doors, this 'secret garden' of politics is still largely unexplored.

NOTES

*   This chapter is largely based on published and unpublished research by the authors, *inter alia* Rahat and Hazan (2001, 2005, forthcoming), Hazan (2002), and Hazan and Rahat (2002a, 2002b, 2005).

1   The concept of *safe* positions on the candidate list, or safe seats when dealing with majoritarian systems, is used quite freely in the research literature. Here we define it according to the following criteria. Although the size of the party's legislative representation is not known in advance – intra-party selection is made before the general election – parties and politicians tend to relate to their party's *actual* representation as the one that distinguishes 'safe' list positions from 'unsafe' positions. As for new parties that did not compete previously, and thus cannot relate to any existing size, we are forced to estimate according to their *projected* size, using opinion polls.

2   When the number of votes is equal to the list size (ratio = 1), a majority bloc can take over all of the safe list positions. When the ratio is lower – or 'limited' in electoral studies terminology – even in the case of bloc voting, more than one bloc can win 'safe' seats. When the ratio is higher than one, a bloc equal to the size of the legislative list can be formed. Such a bloc can try to manipulate the results by asking voters to vote for it and spread the rest of their votes among many different candidates, thereby wasting the surplus votes. However, to organize such a vote under competitive conditions requires very high levels of mutual political trust and excellent coordination – conditions that are rare – and even the attempt might create an effective counter-reaction by other blocs.

3   The exhaustive ballot is a selection method according to which a series of ballots takes place, with the bottom candidate being eliminated after each round, until a candidate wins an absolute majority of the vote.

4   The tools offered in this section can be easily used when analysing a simple, one-stage, uniform candidate selection method. Empirically, however, we often encounter complex candidate selection methods. For solutions to classification problems, see Rahat and Hazan (2001).

REFERENCES

Baum, Julian and Robinson, James A. (1999) *Party Primaries in Taiwan: Trends, Conditions, and Projections in Candidate selection.* Occasional Papers/Reprints Series in Contemporary Asian Studies, No. 155. Baltimore: University of Maryland Law School.

Best, Heinrich and Cotta, Maurizio (2000) 'Elite transformation and modes of representation since the mid-nineteenth century: Some theoretical considerations', in Heinrich Best and Maurizio Cotta (eds), *Parliamentary Representatives in Europe 1848–2000.* Oxford: Oxford University Press.

Bille, Lars (2001) 'Democratizing a democratic procedure: Myth or reality? Candidate selection in

Western European parties 1960–90', *Party Politics*, 7: 363–80.

Bowler, Shaun (2000) 'Parties in legislatures: Two competing explanations', in Russell J. Dalton and Martin P. Wattenberg (eds), *Parties Without Partisans*. Oxford: Oxford University Press.

Bowler, Shaun, Farrell, David and Katz, Richard S. (1999) 'Party cohesion, party discipline, and parliaments', in Shaun Bowler, David Farrell and Richard S. Katz (eds), *Party Discipline and Parliamentary Government*. Columbus: Ohio State University Press.

Carty, Kenneth R. (2002) 'Canada's nineteenth-century cadre parties at the millennium', in Paul Webb, David Farrell and Ian Holliday (eds), *Political Parties in Advanced Democracies*. Oxford: Oxford University Press.

Carty, Kenneth R. (2004) 'Parties as franchise systems: The stratarchical organizational imperative', *Party Politics*, 10: 5–24.

Carty, Kenneth R. and Blake, Donald E. (1999) 'The adoption of membership votes for choosing party leaders', *Party Politics*, 5: 211–24.

Caul, Miki (1999) 'Women's representation in parliament: The role of political parties', *Party Politics*, 5: 79–98.

Czudnowski, Moshe M. (1975) 'Political recruitment' in F.I. Greenstein and N.W. Polsby (eds), *Handbook of Political Science*, Vol. 2. Reading, MA: Addison-Wesley.

De Winter, Lieven (1988) 'Belgium: democracy or oligarchy?', in Michael Gallagher and Michael Marsh (eds), *Candidate Selection in Comparative Perspective*. London: Sage.

Denver, David (1988) 'Britain: Centralized parties with decentralized selection', in Michael Gallagher and Michael Marsh (eds), *Candidate Selection in Comparative Perspective*. London: Sage.

Duverger, Maurice (1959) *Political Parties: Their Organization and Activity in the Modern State*. New York: John Wiley and Sons.

Epstein, Leon D. (1980) *Political Parties in Western Democracies*. New Brunswick, NJ: Transaction Books.

Gallagher, Michael (1988a) 'Introduction', in Michael Gallagher and Michael Marsh (eds), *Candidate Selection in Comparative Perspective*. London: Sage.

Gallagher, Michael (1988b) 'Conclusion', in Michael Gallagher and Michael Marsh (eds), *Candidate Selection in Comparative Perspective*. London: Sage.

Gallagher, Michael and Michael Marsh (eds) (1988) *Candidate Selection in Comparative Perspective: The Secret Garden of Politics*. London: Sage.

Hazan, Reuven Y. (1999) 'Constituency interests without constituencies: The geographical impact of candidate selection on party organization and legislative behavior in the 14th Israeli Knesset, 1996–99', *Political Geography*, 18: 791–811.

Hazan, Reuven Y. (2002) 'Candidate selection', in Lawrence LeDuc, Richard G. Niemi and Pippa Norris (eds), *Comparing Democracies*. London: Sage.

Hazan, Reuven Y. and Pennings, Paul (eds) (2001) 'Democratizing candidate selection: Causes and consequences', special issue of *Party Politics*, 7(3).

Hazan, Reuven Y. and Rahat, Gideon (2002a) 'The impact of candidate selection methods on legislative politics: Theoretical propositions and preliminary findings'. Presented at the Workshop on A Renewal of Parliaments in Europe? MPs' Behavior and Action Constraints, European Consortium for Political Research 30th Joint Session of Workshops, University of Turin, Italy.

Hazan, Reuven Y. and Rahat, Gideon (2002b) 'The political consequences of candidate selection for parties, parliaments and governance'. Presented at the International Conference on Political Parties, Parliamentary Committees, Parliamentary Leadership and Governance, Research Committee of Legislative Specialists, International Political Science Association, Bilgi University, Istanbul, Turkey.

Hazan, Reuven Y. and Rahat, Gideon (2005) 'A new instrument for evaluating, comparing and classifying legislatures? Candidate selection methods'. Presented at the Workshop on Evaluating, Comparing and Classifying Legislatures, European Consortium for Political Research 33rd Joint Session of Workshops, University of Granada, Spain.

Hix, Simon (2004) 'Electoral institutions and legislative behavior: Explaining voting defection in the European Parliament', *World Politics*, 56: 194–223.

Hopkin, Jonathan (2001) 'Bringing the members back in? Democratising candidate selection in Britain and Spain', *Party Politics*, 7: 343–61.

Jackson, John S. (1994) 'Incumbency in the United States', in Albert Somit, Rudolf Wildenmann, Bernhard Boll and Andrea Römmele (eds), *The Victorious Incumbent*. Aldershot: Dartmouth.

Jewell, Malcolm E. and Morehouse, Sarah M. (2001) *Political Parties and Elections in the American States*. Washington, DC: CQ Press.

Katz, Richard S. (2001) 'The problem of candidate selection and models of party democracy', *Party Politics*, 7: 277–96.

Katz, Richard S. and Mair, Peter (1995) 'Changing models of party organization and party democracy: The emergence of the cartel party', *Party Politics*, 1: 5–28.

Key, V.O., Jr. (1949) *Southern Politics*. New York: Alfred A. Knopf.

Knapp, Andrew (2002) 'France: Never a golden age', in Paul Webb, David Farrell and Ian Holliday (eds), *Political Parties in Advanced Democracies*. Oxford: Oxford University Press.

Kolodny, Robin, and Katz, Richard S. (1992) 'The United States', in Richard S. Katz and Peter Mair (eds), *Party Organizations: A Data Handbook on Party Organizations in Western Democracies, 1960–90*. London: Sage.

Kristjánsson, Svanur (1998) 'Electoral politics and governance: Transformation of the party system in Iceland 1970–1996', in Paul Pennings and Jan-Erik Lane (eds), *Comparing Party System Change*. London: Routledge.

Kuitunen, Soile (2002) 'Finland: Formalized procedures with member predominance', in Hanne Marthe Narud, Mogens N. Pedersen and Henry Valen (eds), *Party Sovereignty and Citizen Control*. Odense: University Press of Southern Denmark.

Lijphart, Arend (1984) *Democracies: Patterns of Majoritarian and Consensus Government in Twenty-one Countries*. New Haven, CT: Yale University Press.

Lundell, Krister (2004) 'Determinants of candidate selection: The degree of centralization in comparative perspective', *Party Politics*, 10: 25–47.

Mair, Peter (1994) 'Party organizations: From civil society to the state', in Richard S. Katz and Peter Mair (eds), *How Parties Organize: Change and Adaptation in Party Organizations in Western Democracies*. London: Sage.

Mair, Peter (1997) *Party System Change: Approaches and Interpretations*. Oxford: Oxford University Press.

Maisel, L. Sandy and Stone, Walter J. (2001) 'Primary elections as a deterrence to candidacy for the U.S. House of Representatives', in Peter F. Galderisi, Marni Ezra, and Michael Lyons (eds), *Congressional Primaries and the Politics of Representation*. New York: Rowman and Littlefield.

Malloy, Jonathan (2003) 'High discipline, low cohesion? The uncertain patterns of Canadian parliamentary party groups', *Journal of Legislative Studies*, 9(4): 116–29.

Murphy, R.J. and Farrell, David (2002) 'Party politics in Ireland: Regularizing a volatile system', in Paul Webb, David Farrell and Ian Holliday (eds), *Political Parties in Advanced Democracies*. Oxford: Oxford University Press.

Narud, Hanne Marthe, Pedersen, Mogens N. and Valen, Henry (eds) (2002) *Party Sovereignty and Citizen Control: Selecting Candidates for Parliamentary Elections in Denmark, Finland, Iceland and Norway*. Odense: University Press of Southern Denmark.

Norris, Pippa (1996) 'Legislative recruitment', in Lawrence LeDuc, Richard G. Niemi and Pippa Norris (eds), *Comparing Democracies*. Thousand Oaks, CA: Sage.

Norris, Pippa (ed.) (1997) *Passages to Power: Legislative Recruitment in Advanced Democracies*. Cambridge: Cambridge University Press.

Obler, Jeffrey (1974) 'Intraparty democracy and the selection of parliamentary candidates: The Belgian case', *British Journal of Political Science*, 4(2): 163–85.

Phillips, Anne (1995) *The Politics of Presence*. Oxford: Clarendon.

Pitkin, Hanna (1976) *The Concept of Representation*. Berkeley: University of California Press.

Rae, Douglas W. (1967) *The Political Consequences of Electoral Laws*. New Haven, CT: Yale University Press.

Rahat, Gideon, and Hazan, Reuven Y. (2001) 'Candidate selection methods: An analytical framework', *Party Politics*, 7: 297–322.

Rahat, Gideon, and Hazan, Reuven Y. (2005) 'On the difference between democracy within parties and democracy within states: The uneasy relationship between participation, competition and representation'. Presented at the Workshop on Parties and Democracy, European Consortium for Political Research 33rd Joint Session of Workshops, University of Granada, Spain.

Rahat, Gideon and Hazan, Reuven Y. (forthcoming) 'Political participation in party primaries: increase in quantity, decrease in quality?', in Thomas Zittel and Dieter Fuchs (eds), *Participatory Democracy and Political Participation*. London: Routledge.

Rahat, Gideon and Sher-Hadar, Neta (1999) *Intra-party Selection of Candidates for the Knesset List and for Prime-Ministerial Candidacy 1995–1997*. Jerusalem: Israel Democracy Institute (in Hebrew).

Ranney, Austin (1981) 'Candidate selection', in David Butler, Howard R. Penniman and Austin Ranney (eds), *Democracy at the Polls*. Washington, DC: American Enterprise Institute.

Scarrow, Susan E. (1994) 'The "paradox of enrollment": Assessing the costs and benefits of party membership', *European Journal of Political Research*, 25: 41–60.

Scarrow, Susan E. (1999) 'Parties and the expansion of direct democracy: Who benefits?', *Party Politics*, 5: 341–62.

Scarrow, Susan E. (2000) 'Parties without members?', in Russell J. Dalton and Martin P. Wattenberg (eds), *Parties Without Partisans*. Oxford: Oxford University Press.

Scarrow, Susan E. (2002) 'Party decline in the parties state? The changing environment of German politics', in Paul Webb, David Farrell and Ian Holliday (eds), *Political Parties in Advanced Democracies*. Oxford: Oxford University Press.

Schattschneider, E.E. (1942) *Party Government*. New York: Farrar and Rinehart.

Shugart, Matthew S. (2001) 'Extreme electoral systems and the appeal of the mixed-member alternative', in Matthew S. Shugart and Martin P. Wattenberg (eds), *Mixed-Member Electoral Systems*. Oxford: Oxford University Press.

Somit, Albert, Wildenmann, Rudolf, Boll, Bernhard and Römmele, Andrea (eds) (1994) *The Victorious Incumbent: A Threat to Democracy?* Aldershot: Dartmouth.

Sundberg, Jan (2002) 'The Scandinavian party model at the crossroads', in Paul Webb, David Farrell and

Ian Holliday (eds), *Political Parties in Advanced Democracies*. Oxford: Oxford University Press.

Valen, Henry (1988) 'Norway: Decentralization and group representation', in Michael Gallagher and Michael Marsh (eds), *Candidate Selection in Comparative Perspective*. London: Sage.

Valen, Henry, Narud, Hanne Marthe and Skare, Audun (2002) 'Norway: party dominance and decentralized decision-making', in Hanne Marthe Narud, Mogens N. Pedersen and Henry Valen (eds), *Party Sovereignty and Citizen Control*. Odense: University Press of Southern Denmark.

Ware, Alan (2002) *The American Direct Primary*. Cambridge: Cambridge University Press.

Webb, Paul (2002) 'Political parties in Britain: Secular decline or adaptive resilience?', in Paul Webb, David Farrell and Ian Holliday (eds), *Political Parties in Advanced Democracies*. Oxford: Oxford University Press.

Wertman, Douglas A. (1988) 'Italy: Local involvement, central control', in Michael Gallagher and Michael Marsh (eds), *Candidate Selection in Comparative Perspective*. London: Sage.

11

POLITICAL PARTIES IN A CHANGING CAMPAIGN ENVIRONMENT

David M. Farrell

Election campaigns are a central feature in the life of political parties, and certainly since the onset of representative democracy, a party's principal *raison d'être*.[1] Therefore, in a context in which election campaign styles have been changing,[2] it is important to get some perspective on what implications this has for political parties.[3] This chapter is arranged in four sections. We start with an overview of the campaign literature, where it interfaces with the party politics literature, and the arguments about the nature and causes of campaign change. The next two sections explore the principal features of campaign change and their impact on political parties. The chapter concludes by proposing areas for further study.

THE STUDY OF CAMPAIGNS

In the last two decades of the 20th century the study of campaigning came into its own as a significant field of research in the political science community. Two principal factors help to explain this change in emphasis: one relating to the parties literature, and another more closely associated with the electoral behavior literature. In the first case, the party literature has undergone something of a paradigm shift (Mair, 1990). The classic party studies (e.g. Duverger, 1954; Sartori, 1976) tended, on the whole, to feature a pre-eminent concern with the study of party systems. From about the 1980s onwards there was a distinct shift in focus: political scientists started looking inside the 'black box' of parties as entities in their own right; new studies appeared examining,

in some detail, features of party organizations and their evolution or demise (e.g. Janda, 1980; Katz and Mair, 1992; Panebianco, 1986); and election campaigning emerged as a field of inquiry (e.g. Bowler and Farrell, 1992; Butler and Ranney, 1992). It is obvious that the classic party literature would have had a systemic focus at a time when the party systems themselves were unchanging, making it worthwhile to explore dimensions of variation across different systems (Duverger, 1954; Sartori, 1976), and explanations for their stability (Lipset and Rokkan, 1967). With the arrival of party system de-alignment and electoral volatility, not only was there no longer much point in trying to assess (ever-changing) systems, it was also far more interesting to start examining the parties themselves, not only in terms of their reaction to the change, but also in terms of how, by their organizational evolution and new campaign styles, they may, in part, have been behind some of these developments (Mair, 1983).

First tastes of this new emphasis in the literature were provided in the 1960s by scholars such as Kirchheimer (1966) and Epstein (1967), and a lot of their ideas were further developed and elaborated in the 1980s and 1990s, for instance, in the work of Panebianco (1986) and Katz and Mair (1995). The focus of much of the discussion was on the demise of the mass party and its replacement by new models of organization, showing a shift in focus by the parties away from inward concerns with party members and activists towards more outward concerns with voters. A crucial feature to all of this was the growing attention being given by parties to campaign goals.

A second factor behind the rise of campaign research related to studies in an electoral behavior tradition: there was a growing realization, by politicians and political scientists, that election campaigns 'matter' (Farrell and Schmitt-Beck, 2002). In an age of electoral stability, in which voters voted on the basis of their social class locations and political predispositions, there seemed little point in trying to assess the influence of campaigns, because patently they could only have minor influence on the vote. And even if political scientists had wanted to assess election campaigns, they were constrained by the lack of appropriate research tools to deal with campaign influences on the vote. The standard methods of studying voting behavior at the time were single-shot, cross-section surveys, which were incapable of examining campaign effects.

The research agenda started changing from the 1980s onwards, with far more attention being devoted to the (national) campaigns of the parties. Obviously, one reason for this was the arrival of voter de-alignment, suggesting that, perhaps, campaigns could, indeed, matter. Concomitantly, the nature of campaigning itself changed, becoming more professionally organized, and this attracted growing academic interest. And, of course, the political scientists began to deploy research methods more appropriate for the type of analysis required to measure campaign effects, such as panels, rolling cross-sectional surveys, qualitative methods, and content analysis.

In and among all of this has been a steadily growing body of research on the national campaign itself (i.e. as opposed to its effects), which has tended to come in three main forms. First, there are the historical/descriptive studies of individual campaigns, as best embodied in Britain by the Nuffield series dating back to the 1950s (e.g. Butler and Kavanagh, 1997). Also to be included here are the journalistic studies which mushroomed after Theodore White's classic studies of US elections in the 1960s and 1970s (e.g. White, 1961). By their nature, these are inevitably single-country studies and therefore provide little scope for the cross-national study of parties and elections.

Second, there is the increasingly popular 'political marketing' tradition, in which, in essence, scholars have taken the logical step of applying sophisticated marketing frameworks to the study of election campaigns that themselves are becoming ever more like marketing exercises.[4] This political marketing subdiscipline appears to be gathering steam, as witnessed, among other things, by studies that seek to apply political marketing frameworks to recent election campaigns (e.g. Foglio, 1999; Newman, 1999b); the publication of special issues of journals,[5] and even the recent launch of a dedicated journal, *The Journal of Political Marketing*.

Like the historical/descriptive studies, to date the bulk of the political marketing literature has also tended to be country-based; what has been lacking is sustained cross-national research in a political marketing tradition.[6] Furthermore, notwithstanding grandiloquent claims about the contribution of political marketing to our understanding of election campaign dynamics (e.g. Lees-Marshment, 2003), a question must be asked over the heuristic value of this approach: indeed, often the impression is given that it is more useful for assessing the strength of the marketing framework than it is for providing new insights into how elections, and the parties' role in them, are changing (for sustained critique, see Cornelissen, 2002).

The third approach to studying campaigns, and the one deployed in this chapter, is centered more on a party literature tradition: the principal concern here is with trying to explore the role of parties in the new campaign process, as well as the role of the new campaign process in affecting the parties. The general starting point tends to be with trends in the United States. From Epstein (1967) onwards, there has been a concern with the extent to which the USA might be blazing a trail which other countries have, to varying degrees, been following. This is not the place to scrutinize US campaign styles and how they have been changing (see Chapter 13 in this volume for more detail) – nevertheless, the principal characteristics can be summarized as follows: an emphasis on the candidate and the candidate's personal campaign organization; the prominent role of professional campaign consultants; and the need for plenty of campaign funds. Most scholars are in agreement that the changing dynamics of campaigning in the USA have contributed to the steady decline of US parties (e.g. Wattenberg, 1998), thereby begging an obvious question over whether similar campaign changes in other countries (assuming these can be shown) may have similar effects on parties.

Proponents of the view that we are witnessing a process of 'Americanization' in how election campaigns are fought include Mancini and Swanson (1996: 4), who suggest that 'campaigning in democracies around the world is becoming more and more Americanized as candidates, political parties, and news media take cues from their counterparts in the United States'. They are, however, careful to point out that they use the term quite loosely, seeing it in large part as a surrogate for 'modernization'. In similar fashion, Margaret Scammell (1997: 4) suggests that Americanization is 'useful as a shorthand description of global trends ... the U.S. is a leading exporter and role model of campaigning'. From this perspective, therefore, Americanization is seen as helping in the assessment of developments in the campaign process, not as an indicator of fundamental shifts in political practice.[7]

It is certainly apparent that US campaign practices have had some influence on the campaign activities of parties in other countries. The overriding, and hardly controversial, assumption is that the flow of influence is predominantly from the USA: campaigners in other countries are copying (willy nilly, or in some adapted form) the latest techniques and practices of their US counterparts.[8] But actually demonstrating this has proven quite difficult. For a long time the principal problem was a shortage of cases, leading to a certain Western European bias in much of the comparative analysis of parties and elections (e.g. Bowler and Farrell, 1992); however, given the recent burgeoning of new democracies across Latin America, parts of Africa, Eastern and Central Europe, and the former Soviet Union, the comparative scholar now has a number of new clues with which to provide a rather more informed answer. Any consideration of comparative trends, therefore, needs to take account of what has been happening in the newer democracies; however, given the wealth of material on the Western European case it is useful to begin here.

Viewed through Western European lenses, there are two possible answers to the question of whether the tendencies in the US electoral process are unique: (i) yes; (ii) maybe once, but Europe is catching up. The 'yes' perspective is based on an appreciation of the fundamental differences between the two continents, in terms of history, culture and institutions. In particular, Western European countries have well-developed, highly cohesive political parties, based on strong ideological cleavages which formed the original party systems at the time of mass enfranchisement in the early decades of the 20th century (Lipset and Rokkan, 1967). The traditional organizational structure common to most Western European parties is the 'mass' party, characterized by a large and active membership, a well-resourced organizational bureaucracy, and a stress on internal democracy (Duverger, 1954). By contrast, the US party model is far more fluid: the ideological differences between Democrats and Republicans are less distinct. There is not much organizational structure, apart from the roles played by the various semi-autonomous congressional

campaign committees. American parties are best described as 'empty vessels' (Katz and Kolodny, 1994). From this perspective, therefore, there is good reason to expect significant differences in the styles of campaigning.

The second answer – that Europe has been catching up with US campaign practices – accepts the basic picture just presented, but adds an important temporal dimension, in recognition of the evident fact that the parties and party systems of Western Europe underwent significant transformation in the final quarter of the 20th century. In this respect, one could argue that, until relatively recently, Western European parties have felt somewhat constrained. Given that most of them originated (or at least passed through a phase) as 'mass' parties, with all the attendant features of that form, it is perhaps no surprise to find some delay in switching over to new US styles of campaigning. However, it is evident that political parties in the newly emerging democracies have not experienced the same mass party phase. This raises an intriguing question as to whether Western Europe (and the other older democracies outside the USA) might be seen as the 'exceptional' region in terms of party change and styles of campaigning. The last decade or so has seen the rise of a plethora of new democracies across Latin America, Eastern and Central Europe, the former Soviet Union and parts of Africa. The nature of party organization which has emerged in many of these new democracies is characterized by a far looser organization, with little emphasis on a mass membership, less attention to long-term organizational goals, and more focus on the immediacy of the election campaign (Kopecký, 1995; Lewis, 1996; Mainwaring and Scully, 1995; Mair, 1997). The fact is that the process of campaign modernization in the newer democracies has kept pace with trends in the more established democracies, and in many respects the newer democracies may be developing US-style techniques faster than in Western Europe (for more discussion, see Farrell, 1996; Farrell et al., 2001).

It is now time to become more specific about what is meant by campaign change, about how campaigns have evolved and, in particular, how this has affected political parties. In recent years, there has been a veritable growth industry in the study of campaigns and their modernization (Bowler and Farrell, 1992; Butler and Ranney, 1992; Gunther and Mughan, 2000; Swanson and Mancini, 1996). Studies have shown how electioneering by parties and (especially in the USA) candidates has changed in terms of the three 'Ts' of technology, technicians and techniques. By the turn of the millennium the talk was of how electioneering had entered a new phase of modernization, referred to variously as the 'telecommunications revolution' (Farrell, 1996), the 'digital age' (Farrell, 2002), 'post-Fordist' (Denver and Hands, 2002), or even 'post-modern' (Norris, 2000). The implication is that the parties and candidates have moved to a stage beyond the 'TV age' of centralized, standardized, one-size-fits-all national campaigns; they are embracing the new media technologies – especially those centered around the World Wide Web and the Internet – and running campaigns which differ in some quite fundamental ways from those of a mere ten or twenty years before.[9]

The three stages in the evolution of the campaign process are summarized in Table 11.1, which (following Farrell and Webb, 2000) avoids labeling them, for to call the third stage 'post-modern' raises wider epistemological connotations as well as questions over what we might label any future stage, while to give it a title such as the 'telecommunications revolution' or 'the digital age' would provoke obvious criticisms of being technologically deterministic. Given that the focus of this chapter is primarily on the interface between campaigns and parties, we will not spend too much time detailing the precise ways in which campaigns have been changing (for that, see, *inter alia*, Farrell, 1996; Norris, 2000); instead, we shall be assessing the ways in which campaign change has affected parties, and we shall arrange the discussion in terms of two main features, 'organizational dynamics' and 'communications strategy', starting with the first of these features in the next section.

THE ORGANIZATIONAL DYNAMICS OF CHANGES IN CAMPAIGN STYLES

As indicated by the first part of Table 11.1, the period of campaign preparations has been extending, to the extent that it is now reaching a point in which a good campaign is seen as one that is in a state of perpetual readiness – the 'permanent campaign' of Sydney Blumenthal (1982). The concomitant is a more centrally coordinated campaign process and an emphasis on recruiting professional staff. These developments have affected parties in at least four main respects. First, there have been moves to establish appropriately staffed, full-time campaign units, dedicated to preparing for

and managing the campaign process. Some indications of this are provided in the first column of Table 11.2, which shows how, without exception, the political parties in the Katz–Mair data set all saw expansions in their headquarters staff, an expansion which, with one exception (Italy, in large part due to its Tangentopoli scandal) continued through to the close of the 20th century (Webb, 2002: 443). The importance attached to creating effective campaign units has even, in some prominent cases, extended to relocating them outside party headquarters (as in the case of the British Labour Party in 1997, a move likely to be emulated by its Conservative Party counterpart in the 2005 election; and the German SPD's *Kampa* in 1998).

Second, campaign specialists and agencies have been playing an ever more prominent role in election campaigns. For a long time, this trend was reined in and/or disguised in the Western European mass parties by subtle changes in their staffing policy, thereby making it possible until relatively recently (and, in many cases, still to this day) to maintain the distinction between a US 'consultant' and a European 'party employee' specializing in campaign strategy; they may well share certain commonalities in terms of their specialisms but their status and loyalties were always seen as different. Now such a distinction is increasingly difficult to maintain (as Western European campaigns have 'caught up' with their counterparts in newer democracies which have not been constrained by mass party traditions; see Farrell *et al.*, 2001): more and more parties are inclined to call in external consulting expertise to supplement the work of their traditional staff (e.g. the Irish Fianna Fáil's use of a prominent US consulting firm; or the 'war of the US campaign consultants' in the 1999 Israeli election[10]); more and more parties are inclined to put campaign specialists on their payroll (perhaps on temporary contracts); in an increasing number of cases, party leaders are inclined to deploy their own personal staff specifically to promote their personal campaign image (e.g. recent French presidential campaigns; Berlusconi in Italy; Blair in Britain; Schröder in Germany; Barak in Israel) (more generally, see Farrell *et al.*, 2001).[11] In a growing number of countries, this has culminated in the emergence of an indigenous 'campaign industry', providing strong competition to US consultants in the overseas markets (Plasser and Plasser, 2002).

Third, across western Europe (to say nothing, for instance, of the presidential political systems

Table 11.1 The evolution of the campaign process

	Stage I	Stage II	Stage III
Organizational dynamics			
Preparations	Short-term, ad hoc	Long campaign	Permanent campaign
Finance	Income: membership dues; local sources Expenditure: decentralized Costs: low budget	Income: membership dues; state funding Expenditure: centralized Costs: moderate	Income: state funding; external fundraising; Expenditure: targeted Costs: high
Staffing and coordination	Decentralized Staffing: party/local candidate-based, voluntary	Nationalization, centralization Staffing: party-based, salaried professional; growth of central HQ	Nationally coordinated but decentralized operations; Staffing: party/leadership-based, professional, contract work; use of campaign HQ
Leader's role	Party > leader	Party = leader	Party < leader
Agencies, consultants	Minimal use; 'generalist' role	Growing prominence of 'specialist' consultants	Consultants as campaign personalities
Communications strategy			
Targeting of voters	Social class support base Maintain vote of specific social categories	Catch-all Trying to mobilize voters across all categories	Market segmentation Targeting of specific categories of voters
Feedback	Local canvassing and party meetings	Occasional opinion polls	Regular opinion polls plus focus groups and interactive websites
Campaign events	Local public meetings, whistle-stop tours	News management, daily press conferences, controlled photo opportunities	Extension of news management to routine politics and government
Media	Partisan press, local posters and pamphlets; focus on newspaper and radio coverage	Television broadcasts through main evening news	Targeted use of broadcast media, direct mail, targeted ads
Orientation	Propaganda orientation aimed at mobilization	Selling orientation aimed at persuasion	Marketing orientation aimed at 'product placement'

Sources: adapted from Farrell, 1996; Farrell and Webb, 2000; Norris, 2000

Table 11.2   *Campaign resource developments in Western European parties in the closing decades of the 20th century*

	Percentage increase/decrease in		
	Central party staff	Central party income	Central party campaign expenditure
Austria	+36	+192	+14
Britain	+18	+42	+25
Denmark	+33	+66	+22
Finland	+91	−13	+13
West Germany	+8.6	−22	n.a.
Ireland	+216	+91	+162
Netherlands	+61	+90	+39
Norway	+59	−16	+6
Sweden	+39	−17	+18

Notes: The change refers to the difference between the position in the late 1960s or early 1970s and that in the late 1980s or early 1990s; only those parties are included where it proved possible to make a direct comparison over time. The financial data have been standardized using cost of living deflators (base year of 1987).

Sources: Farrell and Webb, 2000; Katz and Mair, 1992; International Financial Statistics Yearbook 1979; World Bank, World Tables 1992

of Latin America) there has been a distinct shift in campaign focus, with much greater attention focused on the party leader (Bowler and Farrell, 1992; Farrell, 1996; Swanson and Mancini, 1996). To a large degree this process has been fueled by television and its requirements (see the second column of Table 11.3); it is also consistent with efforts to concentrate party resources at the center, particularly around the party leadership. This trend reflects a power shift within political parties, but it also is suggestive of a change in the nature of campaign discourse, with image and style increasingly pushing policies and substance aside. Clearly, there may be a number of factors determining whether the party leader is not a dominant, but rather a major theme, not least the issue of his or her personal popularity and/or tendency to tread on banana skins. The relevant distinction for our purposes is whether the leader is merely a minor theme. Today, it is very hard to find any examples among the main parties of a national election campaign where the party leader is consigned to a minor role. In short, there is little disputing the fact that campaigns have become 'presidentialized' (Mughan, 2000; Donsbach and Jandura, 2003).

The fourth major impact of recent campaign changes on the parties' organizational dynamics is, inevitably, financial. As Tables 11.2 and 11.3 suggest, this has several features. In the first instance, in Table 11.2 (final column), we see how the amount that parties claim to spend on their campaigns rose in the last quarter of the 20th century. Gathering accurate information on parties' campaign expenditure is

notoriously difficult; the data used in Table 11.2 were accumulated as part of the Katz–Mair project. Based on subsequent information provided by national experts, it is possible to sketch a rough picture of how party campaign expenditure trends developed through to the end of the millennium (Farrell and Webb, 2000). Countries where campaign expenditure continued to rise included Britain, Canada, Germany, Sweden, and the USA. For the most part, these increases reflect the growing expense of the modern campaign. But in at least some cases the increase was simply due to state finance laws which have built-in inflators to take account of cost of living increases or population growth (Bowler et al., 2004).[12] By contrast, there are a number of countries where campaign expenditure appears to have either stabilized (Australia, France, Ireland) or decreased (Belgium, Finland, Italy). The Australian and Irish trends reflect a period of retrenchment by overstretched party organizations, and also a degree of more targeted spending (e.g., Irish parties have shifted away from expensive newspaper advertising toward greater use of outdoor billboard advertising). French campaigns costs have plateaued since the 1980s when legislation was passed restricting the use of new campaign technology. In Finland, an economic crisis forced the parties to cut back on their campaign expenditures. In Italy the retrenchment was forced on the parties by reductions in access to state funding. Similarly, in Belgium (which, like Italy, went through its own party funding scandal) the expenditure reductions were the direct result of

Table 11.3 *The campaign 'environment' in OECD countries*

	TV spots	Leaders' 'debates'	Restrictions on TV access	Other campaign restrictions	Campaign finance
Australia	Yes*	Yes	Proportionate		Yes*
Austria	Yes*	Yes*	Proportionate		Yes
Belgium	No	Yes	Proportionate	Limits on expend.	No
Canada	Yes	Yes	No	Limits on expend.; 48-hour ban on polls	Yes
Denmark	No	Yes	Equal		No
Finland	Yes*	Yes	Equal		No
France	No*	Yes	Equal	Limits on expend.; 7-day ban on polls	Yes*
Germany	Yes*	Yes	Proportionate		Yes
Ireland	No	Yes*	Proportionate	Limits on expend.*	Yes*
Italy	Yes*	No	No	7-day ban on polls	Yes*
Japan	Yes*	Yes	Proportionate	Limits on expend.; candidate restrictions**	No
Netherlands	Yes*	Yes	No		No
New Zealand	Yes	Yes*	Proportionate	Limits on expend.	No
Norway	No	Yes	No		No
Sweden	Yes*	Yes	Equal		No
Switzerland	No	No	Proportionate		No
UK	No	No	Proportionate	Limits on expend.*	No
USA	Yes	Yes	No	Limits on Pres. expend.	Yes (for Pres.)

*Indicates a change since the early 1980s.
**Most of the restrictions are focused on candidates (not parties), among them: ban on campaigning until final 15 days; no doorstep canvassing; restrictions on speech-making and on distribution of written materials.

*Sources:*Bowler *et al.*, 2004; Farrell and Webb, 2000

new legislation designed to force the parties to spend less. Indeed, there appears to be a trend developing in terms of efforts to limit the amount parties can spend on their campaigns (Table 11.3, column 4).

For all the efforts of the state to limit campaign expenditure, election campaigns are still very expensive enterprises; and the indications are that the parties have been able to swell their bank balance to cover the increasing costs. As Table 11.2 (second column) shows, in Western European parties, central party income rose in most cases in the final quarter of the 20th century, and the evidence for a wider subset of OECD countries indicates that, with the exception of Italy, party income continued to rise through to the turn of the century (Webb, 2002: 443). To an extent – and consistent with the cartel party thesis – this is facilitated by access to state funding of campaigns (Table 11.3, final column) and party organizations (Bowler *et al.*, 2004), but it also reflects growing attention by the parties to professional external fundraising operations.

CHANGES IN CAMPAIGN COMMUNICATIONS STRATEGY

Earlier we referred to how campaigns have been changing in terms of the three 'Ts' of technology, technicians and techniques. A fourth 'T' that should be added to this is terrain or campaign environment. As Table 11.3 shows (more generally, see Bowler *et al.*, 2004), the campaign environment has altered quite dramatically in recent years, and nowhere is this more apparent than with regard to the role of the other two main sets of actors in the electoral process, the voters and the media – with significant implications for the campaign communications strategies of political parties (Schmitt-Beck and Farrell, 2002). In the first instance, as levels of partisan attachment and electoral turnout have declined (Dalton, 2000; Wattenberg, 2002), parties have to strive harder to chase elusive votes – in Norris's (2000: 171) words, they 'have to run up the down escalator simply to stay in place'. This is one significant factor behind an apparent shift in the nature of campaign communications, which is usefully encapsulated by the political marketing literature as a move from 'selling' to 'marketing'. As the means of accumulating feedback have become more sophisticated, and the desire to test opinion more ever-present, there has been a perceptible shift in the politician's psyche from treating politics as an art to treating it instead as a science (Rose, 1967). The initial standpoint

used to be one of setting the product (usually based on some predetermined ideology) and seeking to steer public opinion in this direction. Saliency theory (Budge and Farlie, 1983) argued that certain types of parties 'owned' certain types of policies (e.g., defense for the right, and health policy for the left) around which they centered their campaigns. Today, political strategy increasingly appears to center on finding out what the public wants to hear – deploying all the latest methods of gathering information on voter attitudes – and marketing the product accordingly. In the context of centralized party resources that facilitate carefully coordinated campaigns, this enhances the strategic autonomy and flexibility of leaderships. Such policy movements may improve the responsiveness of parties to popular demands, but they may also render enduring policy reputations harder to identify; in the UK, for instance, the New Labour party of Tony Blair (which seems to exemplify the marketing approach) leapfrogged the Liberal Democrats in order to dominate the ideological center-ground (Budge, 1999: 5–6); similar tendencies were noted in Germany before its 1998 election. This trend seems destined to continue as the traditional party hierarchies are replaced by brash new professionals whose primary loyalty is to the leader rather than to an ideology or a party tradition.

Nevertheless, while the shift from selling to marketing may seem persuasive, and while there may be plenty of anecdotal evidence, and in some cases first-rate qualitative research (Scammell, 1995), of such tendencies in recent elections, actually trying to demonstrate this quantitatively has so far proven rather elusive. For instance, Caul and Gray (2000) employ cross-national manifesto data to examine the extent to which parties have been adopting less stable issue positions in recent years, but produce quite mixed results.

It is not only shifts in the nature of voter (non-)behavior that may explain recent changes in the nature of parties' campaign communication strategies, as suggested above; also of relevance here are recent changes in the nature of media coverage of elections – from a predominant interest in policy issues, through a phase of focusing on strategy and the campaign 'game', and on to a more contemporary interest in what Esser *et al.* (2001: 17) refer to as 'metacoverage' – 'self-referential reflections on the nature of the interplay between political public relations and political journalism'. As a consequence, the parties have to pay more attention to how they promote themselves in the media. This has resulted in two important developments in how parties seek to communicate with voters. First, every effort is made to maximize positive coverage in the main media outlets, both through the more effective use of news management (and here, consistent with the move toward permanent campaigning, this is no longer tied solely to the 'campaign period' itself) and, in the case of the broadcasting media, by seeking to usurp news executives' intentions by using alternative means of making contact with voters (such as by appearing on early afternoon chat shows).

Second, the contemporary campaign makes much more use of direct means of targeted voter contact, via 'paid media' such as TV spots (see Table 11.3, column 1), and of course the increasingly ubiquitous Internet, which is becoming the major campaign tool. A quick glance at the Parties on the Web site (http://www.electionworld.org/parties.htm; see also Norris, 2001) shows how virtually all parties today have their own websites, but we have yet to see the kind of use being made of them during election campaigns that has been evident in the USA (and particularly so in the 2004 presidential campaign of Howard Dean). This can only be a matter of time. On the basis of their review of the British evidence, Gibson and Ward (1998: 33) speculate that '[g]iven the speed of developments during the last five years, … it is not unreasonable to assume that over the next decade party communication and campaigning on the Internet will have moved from the fringe toward the mainstream'.[13]

Needless to say, the internet is by no means the only new campaign tool in the armory of contemporary campaigners. Focus groups abound, direct mail and telephone canvassing are becoming the norm in a range of different campaign contexts. Clintonesque 'rapid rebuttals' and 'war rooms' have also featured prominently (for British, German and Austrian examples, see respectively Butler and Kavanagh, 1997; Bergmann and Wickert, 1999; Holtz-Bacha, 2002; Strugl et al., 1999). Similarly, much like Clinton's 'new Democrats', recent campaigns of Social Democratic parties in Britain, Germany and Israel all placed heavy emphasis on the image, and in two of the cases also the prefix, of 'new' – as in 'New Labour', 'new Center' (in Germany), and 'One Israel'.

NEW CAMPAIGNS STYLES AND THE STATE OF PARTIES

As was suggested above, the fact that the new campaign styles have required political parties to adapt their organizational dynamics as well as their communication strategies does not of itself imply that the parties are somehow weaker as a consequence, but what certainly cannot be disputed is that they have been forced to adapt; standing still was never an option. This chapter has reviewed the main ways in which the parties have adapted, but in a number of respects we have barely started to scratch the surface. With the exceptions of case studies of campaigns (e.g. the Nuffield series) or the groundbreaking survey work on campaign consultants by Plasser and Plasser (2002; see also Bowler and Farrell, 2000), the political science community has had very little direct access to what actually goes on behind closed doors; in many respects (and *pace* Gallagher and Marsh, 1988), this area of the discipline remains one of the most secret of 'gardens'. Much more data gathering and analysis is needed, in particular in the following four areas:

- changes in the nature of party staffing (locations, types and permanence of staff; party line management structures) and the role of external consultants and agencies;
- sources and means of campaign fundraising and campaign expenditure;
- the decision-making process in campaign organizations;
- the emphasis placed by parties on leader image, on candidate-centered dynamics, and the implications for internal power structures.

NOTES

1 By this, it is not meant to imply that all parties are vote maximizers; whatever its objectives, the campaign is undoubtedly an important event in the life of a party.

2 Some might say 'professionalizing' – but, see Lilleker and Negrine (2002).

3 Needless to say, while it is recognized that the parties are not passive actors in this regard – i.e. they have a central role in explaining why and how campaigns have been changing (Gibson and Römmele, 2001) – the perspective of this chapter is to assess the specific implications for parties of the new campaign styles.

4 It should be noted that political marketing studies are not only focused on the campaign process. There has also been an interest in developing all-encompassing models of parties as marketing organizations (e.g. Butler and Collins, 1999).

5 Such as the special issues of the *European Journal of Marketing* in 1996 (vol. 30, no. 10/11) and 2001 (vol. 35, no. 9/10).

6   For some exceptions, see Farrell and Wortmann (1987) and Newman (1999a).

7   Negrine and Papathanassopoulos (1996) argue for a more complex and considered view of how the term 'Americanization' may account for far more significant shifts in the nature and practice of politics globally.

8   Two possibilities present themselves: there has been a selective or partial adoption of US campaign techniques, contributing to an overall professionalization of campaign practice, but with minimal influence on the nature of electoral politics; or there has been a large-scale adoption of techniques and styles, producing a transformation of the nature of party politics. The first of these possibilities can be characterized as a 'shopping model', the second as an 'adoption model' (Plasser et al., 1999: 104–5; Farrell, 2002). Needless to say, of course, there is some two-way traffic: there are well-known instances of US campaign consultants having copied techniques used in other countries. In the case of developing democracies, there are also instances of diffusion of campaign practice from other regional contexts, notably by European campaign consultants (Bowler and Farrell, 2000; Plasser and Plasser, 2002).

9   Some scholars have suggested that these characterizations exaggerate the true extent of campaign change; indeed, some even go so far as to suggest that perhaps there never was a premodern campaign Golden Age (Bartels, 1992; Dionne, 1976). However, historical analysis has demonstrated that campaigns have evolved through three stages (e.g. Farrell, 2004; Norris, 2000; Wring, 1996). These stages roughly coincide with the evolution of party types (see Chapter 21 in this volume) as mass (stage I), catch-all (stage II), and cartel (stage III).

10   In that campaign the two main Israeli parties tried to out-macho each other by boasting of the number of US campaign consultants they had in their employ (private interviews by the author with Israeli campaign strategists).

11   On the Forza Italia phenomenon, see Mellone (2002). Needless to say, there are always instances of where parties eschew the use of specialist campaign consultants, preferring instead to rely on more traditional tried and trusted techniques (e.g. Nord, 2001).

12   The German case is interesting here because a recent reform of the state funding laws has linked state funding to the numbers of paid-up members. This change has hurt the Green Party in particular, given its fluid organizational structure.

13   More generally, see Margolis and Resnick (2000) and the special issue in Party Politics on 'Party politics on the Net' (vol. 9, no. 1, 2003).

REFERENCES

Bartels, Larry M. (1992) The impact of electioneering in the United States', in David Butler and Austin Ranney (eds), Electioneering: A Comparative Study of Continuity and Change. Oxford: Clarendon.

Bergmann, Knut and Wickert, Wolfram (1999) 'Selected aspects of communication in German election campaigns', in Bruce Newman (ed.), Handbook of Political Marketing. London: Sage.

Blumenthal, Sydney (1982) The Permanent Campaign. New York: Simon and Schuster.

Bowler, Shaun and Farrell, David (eds) (1992) Electoral Strategies and Political Marketing, Basingstoke: Macmillan.

Bowler, Shaun and Farrell, David (2000) 'The internationalization of campaign consultancy', in James Thurber and Candice Nelson (eds), Campaign Warriors: Political Consultants in Elections. Washington, DC: Brookings Institution Press.

Bowler, Shaun, Carter, Elisabeth and Farrell, David (2004) 'Changing party access to elections', in Bruce Cain, Russell Dalton and Susan Scarrow (eds), Democracy Transformed? Oxford: Oxford University Press.

Budge, Ian (1999) 'Party policy and ideology: Reversing the 1950s?', in Geoffrey Evans and Pippa Norris (eds), Critical Elections: British Parties and Voters in Long-Term Perspective. London: Sage.

Budge, Ian and Farlie, Dennis J. (1983) Explaining and Predicting Elections: Issue Effects and Party Strategies in Twenty-Three Democracies. London: George Allen & Unwin.

Butler, David and Kavanagh, Dennis (1997) The British General Election of 1997. Basingstoke: Macmillan.

Butler, David and Ranney, Austin (eds) (1992) Electioneering. Oxford: Clarendon.

Butler, Patrick and Collins, Neil (1999) 'A conceptual framework for political marketing', in Bruce Newman (ed.), Handbook of Political Marketing. London: Sage.

Caul, Miki and Gray, Mark (2000) 'From platform declarations to policy outcomes: Changing party profiles and partisan influence over policy', in Russell Dalton and Martin Wattenberg (eds), Parties without Partisans: Political Change in Advanced Industrial Democracies. Oxford: Oxford University Press.

Cornelissen, Joep (2002) 'Metaphorical reasoning and knowledge generation: The case of political marketing', Journal of Political Marketing, 1(1): 193–208.

Dalton, Russell (2000) 'The decline of party identifications', in Russell Dalton and Martin Wattenberg (eds), Parties without Partisans: Political Change in Advanced Industrial Democracies. Oxford: Oxford University Press.

Denver, David and Hands, Gordon (2002) 'Post-Fordism in the constituencies? The Continuing development of constituency campaigning in Britain', in David Farrell and Rüdiger Schmitt-Beck (eds), *Do Political Campaigns Matter?* London: Routledge.

Dionne, E.J. (1976) 'What technology has not changed: Continuity and localism in British politics', in Louis Maisel (ed.), *Changing Campaign Techniques: Elections and Values in Contemporary Democracies.* Beverly Hills, CA: Sage.

Donsbach, Wolfgang and Jandura, Olaf (2003) 'Chances and effects of authenticity: Candidates of the German federal election in TV news', *Press/Politics*, 8(1): 49–65.

Duverger. Maurice (1954) *Political Parties.* London: Methuen.

Epstein, Leon (1967) *Political Parties in Western Democracies.* New York: Praeger.

Esser, Frank, Reinemann, Carsten and Fan, David (2001) 'Spin doctors in the United States, Great Britain, and Germany: Metacommunication about media manipulation', *Press/Politics*, 6(1): 16–45.

Farrell, David (1996) 'Campaign strategies and tactics', in L. LeDuc, R. Niemi and P. Norris (eds), *Comparing Democracies.* Thousand Oaks, CA: Sage.

Farrell, David (2002) 'Campaign modernization and the West European party', in Richard Luther and Ferdinand Müller-Rommel (eds), *Political Parties in the New Europe: Political and Analytical Challenges.* Oxford: Oxford University Press.

Farrell, David (2004) 'Before campaigns were "modern": Irish electioneering in times past', in Tom Garvin, Maurice Manning and Richard Sinnott (eds), *Government, Elections and Political Communication: A Festschrift in Honour of Brian Farrell.* Dublin: University College Dublin Press.

Farrell, David and Schmitt-Beck, Rüdiger (eds) (2002) *Do Political Campaigns Matter?* London: Routledge.

Farrell, David and Webb, Paul (2000) 'Political parties as campaign organizations', in Russell Dalton and Martin Wattenberg (eds), *Parties without Partisans: Political Change in Advanced Industrial Democracies.* Oxford: Oxford University Press.

Farrell, David and Wortmann, Martin (1987) 'Party strategies in the electoral market: Political marketing in West Germany, Britain and Ireland', *European Journal of Political Research*, 15: 297–318.

Farrell, David, Kolodny, Robin and Medvic, Stephen (2001) 'Parties and campaign professionals in a digital age: Political consultants in the United States and their counterparts overseas', *Press/Politics*, 6(4): 11–30.

Foglio, Antonio (1999) *Il Marketing Politico ed Elettorale.* Milan: Franco Angeli.

Gallagher, Michael and Marsh, Michael (eds) (1988) *Candidate Selection in Comparative Perspective.* London: Sage.

Gibson, Rachel and Römmele, Andrea (2001) 'A party-centered theory of professionalized campaigning', *Press/Politics*, 6(4): 31–43.

Gibson, Rachel and Ward, Stephen (1998) 'U.K. political parties and the Internet: "Politics as usual" in the new media?', *Press/Politics*, 3: 14–38.

Gunther, Richard and Mughan, Anthony (eds) (2000) *Democracy and the Media: A Comparative Perspective.* Cambridge: Cambridge University Press.

Holtz-Bacha, Christina (2002) 'Professionalization of political communication: The case of the 1998 SPD campaign', *Journal of Political Marketing*, 1(4): 23–37.

Janda, Kenneth (1980) *Political Parties: A Cross-National Survey.* New York: Free Press.

Katz, Richard S. and Kolodny, Robin (1994) 'Party organization as an empty vessel: Parties in American politics', in R.S. Katz and P. Mair (eds), *How Parties Organize.* London: Sage.

Katz, Richard S. and Mair, Peter (eds) (1992) *Party Organizations: A Data Handbook.* London: Sage.

Katz, Richard S. and Mair, Peter (1995) 'Changing models of party organization and party democracy: The emergence of the cartel party', *Party Politics*, 1: 5–28.

Kirchheimer, Otto (1966) 'The transformation of West European party systems', in Joseph LaPalombara and Myron Weiner (eds), *Political Parties and Political Development.* Princeton, NJ: Princeton University Press.

Kopecký, Petr (1995) 'Developing party organizations in East-Central Europe', *Party Politics*, 1: 515–34.

Lees-Marshment, Jennifer (2003) 'Political marketing: How to reach that pot of Gold', *Journal of Political Marketing*, 2(1): 1–32.

Lewis, Paul (1996) *Party Structure and Organization in East-Central Europe.* Cheltenham: Edward Elgar.

Lilleker, Darren G. and Negrine, Ralph (2002) 'Professionalization: Of what? Since when? By whom?', *Press/Politics*, 7(4): 98–103.

Lipset, Seymour Martin and Rokkan, Stein (1967) 'Cleavage structures, party systems and voter alignments', in Seymour Matin Lipset and Stein Rokkan (eds), *Party Systems and Voter Alignments.* New York: Free Press.

Mainwaring, Scott and Scully, Timothy (1995) *Building Democratic Institutions: Party Systems in Latin America.* Stanford, CA: Stanford University Press.

Mair, Peter (1983) 'Adaptation and control: Towards an understanding of party and party system change', in Hans Daalder and Peter Mair (eds), *Western European Party Systems: Continuity and Change.* London: Sage.

Mair, Peter (ed.) (1990) *The West European Party System.* Oxford: Oxford University Press.

Mair, Peter (1997) *Party System Change: Approaches and Interpretations.* Oxford: Clarendon.

Mancini, Paolo and Swanson, David (1996) 'Politics, media, and modern democracy: Introduction', in David Swanson and Paolo Mancini (eds), *Politics, Media, and Modern Democracy*. Westport, CT: Praeger.

Margolis, Michael and Resnick, David (2000) *Politics as Usual: The Cyberspace 'Revolution'*. Thousand Oaks, CA: Sage.

Mellone, Angelo (2002) 'La campagna permanente di Forza Italia', in Angelo Mellone (ed.), *Il Circuito Politico-Mediale*. Rome: Rubbettino.

Mughan, Anthony (2000) *Media and the Presidentialization of Parliamentary Elections*. Basingstoke: Palgrave Macmillan.

Negrine, Ralph and Papathanassopoulos, S. (1996) 'The "Americanization" of Political Communication: A Critique', *Press/Politics*, 1: 45–62.

Newman, Bruce (ed.) (1999a) *Handbook of Political Marketing*. London: Sage.

Newman, Bruce (1999b) *The Mass Marketing of Politics: Democracy in an Age of Manufactured Images*. Thousand Oaks, CA.: Sage.

Nord, Lars (2001) 'Americanization v. the Middle Way: New trends in Swedish political communication', *Press/Politics*, 6(1): 113–19.

Norris, Pippa (2000). *A Virtuous Circle: Political Communications in Postindustrial Societies*. Cambridge: Cambridge University Press.

Norris, Pippa (2001) *Digital Divide*. Cambridge: Cambridge University Press.

Panebianco, A. (1986) *Political Parties*. Cambridge: Cambridge University Press.

Plasser, Fritz with Plasser, Gunda (2002) *Global Political Campaigning: A Worldwide Analysis of Campaign Professionals and their Practices*. Westport, CT: Praeger.

Plasser, Fritz, Scheucher, Christian and Senft, Christian (1999) 'Is there a European style of political marketing? A survey of political managers and consultants', in Bruce Newman (ed.), *Handbook of Political Marketing*. London: Sage.

Rose, Richard (1967) *Influencing Voters: A Study of Campaign Rationality*. New York: St Martin's.

Sartori, Giovanni (1976) *Parties and Party Systems: A Framework for Analysis*. Cambridge: Cambridge University Press.

Scammell, Margaret (1995) *Designer Politics: How Elections are Won*. Basingstoke: Macmillan.

Scammell, Margaret (1997) 'The wisdom of the war room: US campaigning and Americanization', *Shorenstein Center Research Paper* R-17.

Schmitt-Beck, Rüdiger and Farrell, David (2002) 'Studying political campaigns and their effects', in David Farrell and Rüdiger Schmitt-Beck (eds), *Do Political Campaigns Matter?* London: Routledge.

Strugl, Michael, Lugmayr, Hans and Weissmann, Klaus (1999) 'The impact of Dr. Joe's strategic positioning: A case study of a successful marketing-based election campaign in Upper Austria', in Bruce Newman (eds), *Handbook of Political Marketing*. London: Sage.

Swanson, David and Mancini, Paolo (eds) (1996) *Politics, Media, and Modern Democracy*. Westport, CT: Praeger.

Wattenberg, Martin (1998) *The Decline of American Political Parties, 1952–1996*. Cambridge, MA: Harvard University Press.

Wattenberg, Martin (2002) *Where Have all the Voters Gone?* Cambridge, MA: Harvard University Press.

Webb, Paul (2002) 'Conclusion: Political parties and democratic control in advanced industrial societies', in Paul Webb, David Farrell and Ian Holliday (eds), *Political Parties in Advanced Industrial Democracies*. Oxford: Oxford University Press.

White, Theodore (1961) *The Making of the President 1960*. New York: Atheneum.

Wring, Dominic (1996) 'From mass propaganda to political marketing', in C. Rallings, D. Farrell, D. Denver and D. Broughton (eds), *British Elections and Parties Yearbook 1995*. London: Cass.

12

ON THE CUSP OF CHANGE: PARTY FINANCE IN THE UNITED STATES

John C. Green

As the 21st century begins, American politics is experiencing another period of campaign finance reform, with a special focus on the major political parties (on the history of reform, see Corrado, 1997). After a decade of rapid innovation in party finance, the Bipartisan Campaign Reform Act of 2002 (BCRA, also known as 'McCain–Feingold' after its Senate co-sponsors) was enacted by Congress and signed by President Bush (Corrado, 2003). As with past reforms, this legislation prompted an immediate court challenge, and a little more than a year later, the US Supreme Court affirmed most of its provisions in *McConnell v. Federal Election Commission* (24 S. Ct. 619 [2003]).

BCRA prohibited the raising and spending of 'soft money' by national party committees, a major innovation of the 1990s, and included other changes designed to bolster this prohibition. From the perspective of the 2000 election, BCRA represented a major change in party finance. But from a slightly longer perspective, BCRA largely returned the campaign finance regime to the situation before soft money, which was based on the Federal Election Campaign Act (FECA) of 1971 as amended by Congress and interpreted by the courts (Corrado *et al.*, 1997). The fundamental issue in BCRA was the *size and source* of campaign funds raised by national parties.

Of course, the more interesting timeframe is the future: how will the major parties and their allies adapt to BCRA? What follows is a brief discussion of American party finance on the eve of BCRA, the changes brought about by the new law, and a sketch of possible adaptations.

PARTIES AND MARSHALLING RESOURCES

Chief among the activities of party organizations is marshalling resources – collecting, organizing, and deploying people and things useful in seeking control of the personnel of government. Money is only one such resource, but an especially valuable one in an advanced industrial society. And marshalling money is of particular importance in the United States, where the 'two-party' system is nearly comprehensive but organizationally fragmented (Green, 2002). Even at the national level, separation of powers produces three separate organizations for the Democrats and Republicans – the national (or presidential), senatorial, and congressional committees. Meanwhile, federalism generates 50 state committees (typically linked to governors and other elected executives), not to mention legislative campaign committees (tied to the chambers of the state legislatures), and thousands of local party organizations (principally county and city committees). As if this fragmentation were not enough, nomination via the direct primary has encouraged a 'candidate-centered' politics with thousands of separate candidate committees. Finally, a wide variety of interest groups adds several thousand political action committees (PACs) and other organizations to the mix.

Scholars have long noted the usefulness of American parties in bringing cohesion to this fragmentation. Although more honored in the breach than in the observance (Sorauf, 2002), party organizations have from time to time played a significant role in marshalling money from these fragmented sources. The exact nature of these arrangements depended on the incentives and circumstances of the moment, including the relevant laws governing party finance. In the last thirty years, the advent of capital-intensive electioneering has provided new incentives for the parties to marshal money (Herrnson, 1988), reinforced by the increased competitiveness of federal and state elections in the 1990s (Green and Farmer, 2003). In response, the major parties and their allies found ways to greatly expand fundraising under FECA. These innovations were so successful that they substantially undermined the existing rules and inspired the passage of BCRA.

THE PRE-BCRA FINANCE REGIME[1]

The 2000 campaign is a useful benchmark for assessing the situation BCRA sought to correct. Two parallel systems of party finance had developed, one involving 'federal' or 'hard money' (funds regulated under FECA) and the other 'non-federal' or 'soft money' (funds not regulated by FECA). Tables 12.1 and 12.2 summarize the legal dimension of the two systems from the perspective of party fundraising (these tables also identify the changes created by BCRA, which we will discuss presently).

Federal (hard money) receipts

The federal or hard money system began with the 1974 amendment to FECA, which included a set of contribution limits upheld by the US Supreme Court in *Buckley v. Valeo* (424 U.S. 1 [1976]). With regard to parties, FECA set a maximum that any one individual or political committee could donate to each of the three major national party organizations (Biersack and Haskell, 1999). For example, individuals could give a maximum of $20,000 per year (or $40,000 per two-year election cycle) to any national committee. PACs ('multicandidate committees') could give a maximum of $15,000 per year (or $30,000 per election cycle). There were also limits on contributions to PACs and candidate campaign committees.[2]

Formally non-political organizations were prohibited from donating directly to party committees (or any federal campaign), including business corporations, labor unions, trade associations, and non-profit groups. With just a few exceptions (such as non-profit corporations organized for explicitly political

purposes), any such organization had to form a PAC and participate in the hard money system.

Individuals, PACs, and candidate committees were limited to a maximum of $5000 per year (or $10,000 per election cycle) to state and local party committees for federal elections (treated in most instances as a unit). Non-political organizations were also prohibited from making donations to state/local parties for federal elections, but were often allowed to donate to parties under state laws for state elections (an important matter to which we will return below).

Some additional limitations also affected federal party finance: individual donors were limited to an aggregate of $25,000 to all federal committees per year (or $50,000 per election cycle) and full disclosure was required of individual donations over $200 and of all organizational contributions. Interestingly, none of these contribution limits were indexed for inflation, so that as time passed, the value of legal contributions declined steadily. For example, the $20,000 maximum national party donation was worth about $7600 by 2000. One area left unregulated was transfers among national, state, and local party committees, allowing for unlimited transfers between party committees and from candidate campaign committees to party committees (Bedlington and Malbin, 2003: 136).

Federal (hard money) expenditures

FECA also set limits on contributions from party committees to PAC and candidate committees (Biersack and Haskell, 1999): national and state/local committees could each give a maximum of $5000 per year to a PAC, $5000 per election to a congressional candidate, a combined total of $17,500 per election to senatorial candidates, and nothing to presidential candidates who accepted public financing (also initiated by FECA in 1974 and 1976). FECA also allowed party committees to engage in limited 'coordinated expenditures' on behalf of their nominees. Based on a per eligible voter formula, coordinated expenditures were much higher than the direct contribution. Furthermore, coordinated expenditures were adjusted for inflation, but contributions were not.

The initial interpretation of the FECA contribution and coordinated expenditure limits in the 1976 campaign eliminated much traditional grassroots party activity, such as voter registration drives and get-out-the-vote (GOTV) efforts.

Table 12.1   *Political parties and the federal (hard money) system, before and after BCRA*

	Before BCRA	**After BCRA**
Receipts		
National committees[a]		
Individuals[b]	$20,000 per year[e]	$25,000 per year[f]
PACs	$15,000 per year[e]	No change
Non-political organizations	Prohibited	No change
Party committees	Unlimited transfers	No change
State/local committees[c]		
Individuals[b]	$5,000 per year[e]	$10,000 per year[f]
PACs	$5,000 per year[e]	No change
Non-political organizations	Prohibited	No change
Party committees	Unlimited transfers	No change
Expenditures		
National, state/local committees		
Direct donations:[d]		
Senate candidates	$17,500 per election[e]	$35,000 per election[e]
House candidates	$5,000 per election[e]	No change
PACs	$5,000 per year[e]	No change
Coordinated expenditures	Formula varied by office[f]	No change[g]
Grassroots party activities	Unlimited	No change
Independent expenditures	Unlimited	No change[g]
Transfers:		
Party committees	Unlimited	No change
Non-political organizations	Unlimited	No change

Notes:
[a]Includes the national, senatorial, and congressional committees, the limits applied to each committee.
[b]Before BCRA, individuals were subject to an overall limit of $25,000 per year in hard money donations; after BCRA, $97,500 per two-year period, with no more than $57,500 to all party committees combined.
[c]Before BCRA state/local committees treated together; limits applied to all state/local committees in a given year. After BCRA, the limit applies to state and local committees separately, within the overall limit.
[d]If presidential candidate accepts public financing of the general election, no direct contributions are allowed; national/state party senatorial limit combined.
[e]Disclosure required, not indexed for inflation; jointly shared limit between national and state parties under FECA; jointly shared between national and senate committee under BCRA.
[f]Disclosure required, indexed for inflation. Coordinated expenditures based on eligible voters formula and indexed for inflation. In 2000, presidential $13.7 million; for House candidates $33,780 from both national and state committees; for Senate candidates ranged from $67,560 to $1,636,438 depending on the state.
[g]US Supreme Court struck down BCRA provision requiring parties to choose between coordinated or independent expenditures in a given race.

In response, Congress amended FECA in 1979 to exempt such traditional grassroots activities from the hard money limits. In an earlier decision, the Federal Election Commission (FEC) allowed state/local parties to pay for such activities with funds raised under state law (Corrado, 2000: 20–1, 3). These changes gave national party committees access to non-federal funds for grassroots activities (a matter whose relevance we will consider momentarily).

In *Buckley v. Valeo*, the US Supreme Court struck down limits on campaign expenditures by candidates and other political actors on First Amendment grounds (see Banks and Green, 2001: Chapters 3, 4). The High Court recognized, however, that at some point expenditures can become a method for circumventing the very contribution limits it also found constitutional. The resulting attempt to balance these competing values spawned two additional kinds of expenditures available to party committees: independent expenditures and issue advocacy.

An 'independent expenditure' is a campaign expenditure concerning a candidate that is not coordinated with candidate's campaign (in the absence of such independence, such an expenditure would be an 'in-kind' contribution and

Table 12.2 *Political parties and the non-federal (soft money) system, before and after BCRA*

	Before BCRA	After BCRA
Receipts		
National committees[a]		
All sources (including non-political organizations)	Unlimited	Prohibited in all contexts
State committees		
All sources	Varied with state law	Prohibited in federal elections
Local committees		
All sources	Varied with state law	Up to $10,000 for voter programs (Levin committee rules)[b]
Expenditures		
National committees		
Direct expenditures:	Unlimited, Formula for soft money[c]	Unlimited, 100% hard money
Transfers:		
State/local party committee	Unlimited	Prohibited
Non-political organizations	Unlimited	Prohibited
State committees	Unlimited, Formula for soft money[c]	Unlimited, 100% hard money
Local committees	Unlimited, Formula for soft money[c]	Unlimited, (Levin committee rules)[b]
Transfers:		
National party committees	Unlimited	Prohibited

Notes:

[a] Includes the national, senatorial, and congressional committees, the limits applied to each committee.

[b] See text on Levin committees.

[c] For national party committees, 65% hard money in presidential years; 60% in non-presidential years. For state/local committees, hard money reflected ratio of state and federal offices on the ballot. Typically, state formulae allowed for more soft money.

subject to limitation). The case law defining 'independence' eventually expanded to include party committees. Independent expenditures are unlimited in size, but have to be paid for with hard money donations and disclosed (Corrado, 2000: 15–19).

A second kind of expenditure arose from a distinction between 'express advocacy' (directly advocating the election or defeat of a candidate) and 'issue advocacy' (advocating on behalf of an issue) in *Buckley v. Valeo*. Contribution and coordinated expenditure limits were express advocacy and thus could be regulated (with independent expenditures representing a special case). However, issue advocacy could not be regulated because it did not apply to federal elections. The Court drew a 'bright line' distinction between express and issue advocacy by identifying particular words and phrases, such as 'vote for' and 'vote against' a specific candidate (Corrado, 2000: 24–5). In essence, this distinction defined expenditures outside the

hard money system which could nevertheless influence election outcomes (an issue we will discuss momentarily).

Overall, the hard money system was problematic for the major parties, setting strict limits on past sources of party money, limiting party expenditures to and for party candidates, and giving candidate committees and PACs an enhanced role (Sorauf, 2002). However, the parties quickly adapted to the hard money system (Herrnson, 1988). Freed from the need to finance presidential campaigns (due to public financing), the national committees responded by broadening the financial base of individual contributors. Party committees turned to mass solicitation of small donations via direct mail and telemarketing, and developed cadres of solicitors to raise larger donations from many people. The parties also became adept at organizing donations from PACs and their own candidates. Despite the high costs of such fundraising efforts, the national parties developed extensive financial resources; many state and even local parties followed a similar path (Bibby, 1999). Republicans did a bit better in raising hard money, creating incentives for Democrats to push the boundaries of the system.

These robust party organizations turned increasingly from contributions to expenditures, including services to candidates, coordinated spending, grassroots activities in cooperation with state/local parties, and eventually independent and issue advocacy advertising. These practices led to the creation of a parallel non-federal or soft money system.

Non-federal (soft money) receipts

At the heart of the soft money system was the fact that party committees participate in both federal and non-federal elections. The hard money system applied only to the former and not the latter (nor, in fact, to non-electoral activities). Thus, parties could raise funds unregulated by FECA for purposes other than explicitly influencing federal elections.

The non-federal or 'soft money' system began around 1980, as the parties sought to raise non-federal funds for grassroots activities exempted from the hard money limits. Closely linked with presidential campaigns, the national parties and their state affiliates began to raise funds that would otherwise be illegal under FECA due to size (many donations were much larger than the hard dollar limits), source (such as corporate and union treasuries), and lack of disclosure. The Dukakis presidential campaign in 1988 was especially effective at raising this 'soft money', a pattern quickly copied by the Republicans. By 1991, soft money had become sufficiently large that the Federal Election Commission required the national parties to disclose their non-federal accounts, albeit in a less rigorous fashion than the hard money system (state parties disclosed a portion of the funds under state law, which varied enormously) (Corrado, 2000: 23–4).

From a fundraising perspective, the chief benefit of soft money was its relative efficiency: the costs of soliciting wealthy people, corporations, and unions were low and the amounts raised large (often greater than $100,000).[3] Because the national parties could raise and spend such funds across the country, soft money was effectively unlimited. Indeed, a complex system developed to navigate the web of state rules so as to maximize soft money collections and disbursements (see for example, Barber, 2003: 19–21). Federal officeholders became central to soliciting soft money, with President Clinton's well-known fundraising at the White House just the best-known example of a practice common in both parties.

What made soft money especially valuable, however, was the ways in which it could be spent. Initially, soft money was used largely for grassroots party activities. In an attempt to set some limit on these expenditures, the FEC mandated a mix of hard and soft money for 'joint activities' undertaken under federal and state law in 1991. If national parties engaged in such expenditures directly in a presidential year, 65% had to be hard money and 35% could be soft money (in a non-presidential year the relevant percentages were 60 and 40%, respectively). State party expenditures were subject to a different formula based on the ratio of state to federal candidates on the ballot. In many cases, this formula allowed for the proportion of soft money to be higher, and as a result the national parties began to make larger transfers of hard and soft money to the state committees to maximize expenditures (Corrado, 2000: 78–80).

By 1996 a new outlet for soft money expenditures had become common: issue advocacy. Recall that court rulings excluded issue advocacy expenditures from hard money regulations. Led by President Clinton, the Democratic National Committee began running broadcast advertisements in support of and opposition to candidates, carefully avoiding the language of expressed advocacy. The GOP quickly followed suit in support of its nominee, Bob Dole. However, analysis of the issue advocacy ads revealed that they differed little from express advocacy ads run by candidates' own campaigns (Herrnson and Dwyre, 1999). Using the mechanism of transfers to state parties, party committees were able to engage in a very high level of campaign advertising, reaching saturation levels in competitive states and districts by 2000 (Dwyre and Kolodny, 2002).

The party committees were not alone in pursuing issue advocacy. By the mid-1990s, labor unions, business corporations, and a host of non-profit groups were using funds outside the hard money system to pay for advertisements and other campaign activities. Some of these efforts were organized as tax-exempt entities under sections 501c(3), 501c(4), and 527 of the Internal Revenue Code. The law did not require disclosure of receipts or expenditures by these groups. The various 501c committees

Table 12.3   *Major party receipts in 2000 election cycle (in $millions)*

	Republicans	Democrats
Federal (hard money):		
National committees:[a]		
Individuals:		
Under $200	167.9	56.7
$200–$500	40.9	12.2
$501–$1,000	21.4	11.2
$1,001–$5,000	23.3	25.3
$5,001–$10,000	16.3	22.7
$10,001–$19,999	11.4	9.5
$20,000	13.4	13.9
Other committees	25.7	19.6
National subtotal	**320.3**	**171.1**
State/local committees:[b]		
Individuals		
Under $200	55.3	16.4
$200–$500	25.2	9.7
$501–$1,000	12.0	7.5
$1,001–$4,999	4.0	4.7
$5,000	4.0	5.0
Other committees	3.2	12.0
State/local subtotal	**103.7**	**55.3**
Hard money total	**424.0**	**226.4**
Non-federal (soft money):[c]		
National committees	249.9	245.2
State committees	98.1	116.2
Soft money total	**348.0**	**361.4**
Grand Total	**772.0**	**587.8**

Notes:

[a]Includes the national, senatorial, and congressional committees. Figures include only 1999–2000 receipts from individuals, candidate committees and PACs. Party transfers, cash on hand and other sources of funds excluded. Figures derived from Federal Election Commission.

[b]Includes all state and local committees reporting federal activity. Figures include only 1999–2000 receipts from individuals, candidate committees and PACs. Party transfers, cash on hand and other sources of funds excluded. Figures derived from Federal Election Commission.

[c]National soft money figures come from Federal Election Commission. State figures from Barber (2003) and exclude transfers from national committees.

carried legal restrictions on the type and level of political activity, but the 527 committees had no such limitations (and were dubbed 'stealth PACs' by critics). In response to the proliferation of 527 committees, the Congress enacted disclosure requirements in 2000, but set no other limits on their activities (Cigler, 2002).

Table 12.3 reports the major sources of party receipts in the 2000 election cycle, revealing the dimensions of the hard and soft money systems – see Magleby (2003) and Corrado (2001) for good overviews of 2000 finances. These figures exclude other sources of party money, such as transfers, cash on hand, and loans.[4]

Federal or hard money was still a significant source of receipts in 2000, accounting for 57 percent of the total of national party receipts. Non-federal or soft money accounted for the rest. However, if state-level 'soft money' is included, hard money falls to just 48 percent of the total. These state-level funds must be viewed with some caution, since some might well have met hard money requirements and a large proportion was used in state-level campaigns (Morehouse and Jewell, 2003). However, these funds were potentially available to the parties in the 2000 campaign and thus represent the furthest extent of the soft money system.

An important partisan difference appears in these figures. For the Republicans, hard money receipts accounted for nearly 55 percent of the total, but for the Democrats, soft money made up 61 percent. The principal reason for this pattern was the Republican ability to raise contributions under $200 in hard money. In 2000, the GOP national committees raised $167.9 million in this category and the state affiliates raised another $55.3 million. In contrast, the Democrats raised only about one-third as much, $56.7 and $16.4 million, respectively. In fact, the Republican advantage extended to individual donations of $1000 or less. The Democrats performed roughly as well and sometimes better among donations of over $1000, especially at the maximum levels.

The substantial Republican hard dollar advantage was not new in 2000, having existed since the origins of FECA. But the essential parity between the major parties in soft money represented an important change. At the national level, the Republicans had only a very tiny advantage in soft money, and if state-level funds are included, the Democrats were modestly ahead. In essence, soft money allowed the Democrats to make up for some of the deficit in hard money. Near parity in the funding of each party's federal candidates also helped offset the GOP hard money advantage (Herrnson and Patterson, 2002).

PACs and candidate committees accounted for only a small portion of party hard money in 2000. When the receipts of federal and state/local committees were combined, the parties were nearly even (although such donations were twice as important in relative terms for the Democrats, 14 to 7 percent). Here it is worth mentioning the importance of candidate contributions, especially from members of Congress. In 2000, Republican members provided some $14.7 million to their national committees by one means or another and the Democrats $7.8 million (Bedlington and Malbin, 2003: 134).

Direct campaign spending by interest groups allied with the major parties is not included in Table 12.3, but was clearly important in the 2000 campaign. PACs spent at least $38.9 million in hard money in the form of independent expenditures and internal communications with their members (Cigler, 2002: 174–5). Issue advocacy was very difficult to assess due to the lack of disclosure, but one study found $91 million in non-party issue advocacy television ads during the 2000 general election campaign (Annenberg Public Policy Center, 2001: 6–7). There are no good estimates for non-broadcast expenditures on

such things as direct mail, voter registration, and GOTV efforts by 501c(3), 501c(4) and 527 committees, but such expenditures could easily have equaled the hard money campaign expenditures of PACs (Magleby, 2000). All told, such 'outside spending' may have equaled about one-third of the soft money raised by the national parties.

THE NEW BCRA REGIME[5]

How did BCRA and its validation in *McConnell v. FEC* change the campaign finance regime? By far the most important change is a direct assault on soft money: national party committees are prohibited from raising or spending soft money in any form or for any purpose (Table 12.2). In addition, state and local party committees are prohibited from using soft money for most 'federal election activity', including voter registration activities within 120 days of an election, GOTV activity of any kind in connection with a federal election, and communications that promote or attack a named federal candidate.

BCRA did include a modest exception to the soft money ban at the subnational level, the so-called 'Levin committees' (Table 12.2). Up to $10,000 in soft money per year from any source legal under state law may be raised by a local party committee for the purpose of voter registration and GOTV activities. Such funds must meet special criteria: (i) the soft money must be matched with hard money as per FEC allocation rules; (ii) federal office-holders, candidates, national parties, their affiliates or agents may not raise such funds; (iii) the funds may not be used for federal candidate-specific or generic advertising; (iv) party committees may not jointly raise these funds; (v) such funds may not be transferred between party committees and may not be raised for use in other states; and (vi) all receipts and expenditures must be disclosed under federal law.

These extensive limitations were placed on the Levin committees in the hope that they would not become a means of reconstituting a version of the soft money system. In addition, BCRA contained additional prohibitions to achieve this purpose. For example, federal office-holders, candidates, national party committees, their affiliates or agents may not solicit, receive, direct, transfer, or spend any soft money in connection with a federal election (including Levin committees). National party committees are prohibited from soliciting or transferring soft money to 527 committees as well.

Here, too, BCRA includes modest exceptions. Federal officie-holders and candidates may solicit funds without limit for the general treasury of a 501c tax-exempt organization if the principal purpose of the organization is not to conduct federal election activity. Such fundraising is limited to hard money if the funds are earmarked for voter registration and GOTV programs. Also, federal office-holders may attend state/local fundraising events as long as they do not participate in soft money fundraising for federal purposes.

By far the most controversial provision of BCRA was a limit on issue advocacy expenditures by formally non-political organizations. The act bans corporations (of all types, not just businesses) and labor unions from directly or indirectly making or financing 'electioneering communication' with soft money. 'Electioneering communication' is defined as a broadcast, cable or satellite communication that identifies a specific federal candidate within 60 days of a general election or 30 days of a primary, and that is 'targeted' (received by 50,000 or more persons in a district or state where the election is held).

Any entity not engaged in electioneering communication, or which is funded by sources other than corporate or union treasury funds, is not subject to the BCRA restrictions. However, the act did require disclosure of electioneering communications by individuals or organization entities within 24 hours once an aggregate of $10,000 was spent and thereafter after each time $10,000 was spent. These provisions cover 527 committees and other tax-exempt groups.

BCRA also sought to tighten the meaning of 'coordination' between candidates and expenditures by individuals or organizations. 'Coordination' was defined as payment made in cooperation with, at the request or suggestion of, a candidate, a candidate's agent, campaign, or party. Neither explicit agreement nor formal collaboration between actors was needed to establish coordination. All such coordinated expenditures count as in-kind contributions to a candidate under the hard money limits.

One of the few provisions of BCRA struck down by the High Court was a requirement that party committees choose between coordinated and independent expenditures on behalf of their nominees. FEC regulations allowing parties to engage in coordinated expenditures before a candidate was formally nominated were also allowed to stand pending further litigation. So,

hard money independent expenditures are still legal for party committees as long as the new standard of coordination is not violated.

Finally, BCRA increased some hard money contribution limits to parties (Table 12.1). Individual contributions to each national party committee were increased to $25,000 and contributions to state *or* local party committees were increased to $10,000 (that could be spent in conjunction with Levin committee funds). Indeed, the recognition of local committees as separate hard money fundraisers is a potentially important change. Maximum individual contributions to candidates were also increased from $1000 to $2000. The aggregate limits for an individual's contributions were altered as well. Individuals were allowed to give up to $97,500 per two-year election cycle consistent with the following sublimits: (i) a maximum of $37,500 to federal candidates; (ii) a maximum of $57,500 to all party committees and PACs combined, with no more than $37,500 to all PACs (if no PAC donations are made, a maximum of $57,500 could be contributed to all party committees combined). These increases do not completely restore the loss due to inflation of the original 1974 hard money limits. But BCRA did index the new limits in the same fashion as party coordinated expenditures.

BCRA AND THE PARTY FINANCES

The most immediate effect of BCRA will be to substantially reduce the funds available to national party committees. If the 2000 numbers are any guide, it will cost the national parties approximately $250 million dollars in soft money (and if state non-federal funds are counted, the loss will be roughly $350 million). Such a decline in funds can only hurt party campaign efforts, and it is likely to hurt the Democrats more than the Republicans. The long-standing hard money disparity between the parties may well remain in 2004, a forecast supported by the fundraising reports in 2003 (Edsall, 2004a). A clearer effect is the likely decentralization of party decision-making: in the absence of the soft money, national party leaders may be less able to secure the cooperation of their state and local counterparts (Dwyre and Kolodny, 2003; La Raja, 2003).

Although the parties will still have substantial hard money resources with which to influence federal elections, they will face strong incentives to replace the lost soft money (see

Green and Farmer, 2003: Chapters 6–8). BCRA suggests three major avenues for replacing these funds: an increase in hard money, an expansion of fundraising by state and local party committees, and a shift of funds to tax-exempt groups, such as 527 and 501c committees. No single avenue is likely to replace the lost soft money in the short run, but, taken together, each might contribute to the goal.

An increase in hard money is the easiest avenue to follow (Dwyre and Kolodny, 2003), and here the best opportunity lies with the increased individual contribution limits to the national parties. If all of the roughly 700 maximum donors in 2000 gave the full aggregate amount of $57,500, it would generate an additional $26 million for each party. If the parties could double the number of maximum givers from among their soft money donors (another 700 people), $40 million more would be available. The sum of these figures, $66 million, is about one-quarter of the soft money raised by the national parties in 2000 (see Fred, 2004, for early evidence on this point).[6]

The major parties will have strong incentives to maximize their smaller donations as well. If Howard Dean's 2003 success at raising internet donors could be duplicated by the national party committees, then tens of millions of dollars could be added (see Farhi, 2004). Such an innovation might be especially valuable for the Democrats, who could reduce the small-donor gap with the GOP. Likewise, if George W. Bush's success at high-dollar networking with 'Pioneers' and 'Rangers' could be emulated, each party could expand its base of larger donors (see Campaign Finance Institute, 2004, on the 2004 primary fundraising).

Yet another possibility is for each party to further tap their candidates for funds. After all, the maximum individual donation doubled from $1000 to $2000, making it easier for candidates to raise funds and pass them on to the party committees. In this regard, presidential politics might be a source of new funds as well. For reasons largely unrelated to BCRA, the major presidential candidates in 2004 opted out of the public financing system in the primaries and could raise large amounts of money (Green and Corrado, 2003). If such circumstances persisted in the future, the presidential candidates might be able to provide their national party committees with a large sum of money on the eve of the general election. Indeed, the unprecedented primary fundraising by presidential candidates George W. Bush and John Kerry (more than $200 and $180 million, respectively) revealed the value of candidate fundraising under the BCRA regime. Thanks to Kerry's efforts, the Democratic National Committee laid ambitious plans to fund a $100 million independent expenditure campaign in the 2004 campaign based on resoliciting Kerry donors for the national party; the Republican National Committee may well follow suit (Edsall, 2004d). It is unclear what proportion of the presidential primary donors might provide new funds to the national parties, but $50 million in additional funds would represent a significant achievement.

It would surely be counted a great success if all these sources of hard money generated $110 million in new money for each party – a little more than two-fifths of the 2000 soft money at the national level. Initial indications from 2003 are encouraging on this score (Ornstein and Corrado, 2003).

Another promising avenue for additional funds is at the state and local level (La Raja, 2003). Some portion of the state-level soft money could be converted into hard money so it could be spent in support for federal elections. It is unclear how much money this would involve, but judging from the 2000 numbers it could be substantial. In addition, BCRA allows state committees to double the maximum individual contributions from $5000 to $10,000. And local committees are allowed to operate independently of state committees in the hard money system, creating a new forum for raising funds. Local parties can also set up Levin committees, tapping soft money directly, albeit in just $10,000 amounts. Suppose, for instance, that 500 local committees in each major party raised $50,000 in hard money and $50,000 in soft money. Such figures may seem daunting in the short run, but none are especially unrealistic. After all, 500 committees is less than one-sixth of the counties in the United States. Under these assumptions, the Levin committees would raise $50 million – or about one-fifth of the 2000 national soft money in each party.

A third alternative lies with tax-exempt groups and the possibility of shifting large amounts of soft money into such entities. In 2003, labor unions, liberal and Democratic activists organized half a dozen 527 committees for exactly this purpose (dubbed the 'shadow Democratic Party' – see Meyerson, 2003; Edsall, 2004b; Drinkard, 2004). The most prominent of these groups was Americans Coming Together (ACT), which received a $12 million pledge from financier George Soros to finance GOTV programs in key states. All together these groups projected raising a little over $300 million for grassroots activities and campaign advertising. If successful, this goal would roughly equal the national soft money and allied group issue advocacy in 2000. This goal is certainly ambitious: in 2003 these Democratic 'shadow' committees raised $22 million; all similar groups raised $72 million (including ideological groups such as moveon.org); and the universe of 527 committees (more than 300) raised a combined total of $102 million (see Center for Responsive Politics, 2004, for early evidence).[7]

Republican activists had a similar idea, but met with less success. Indeed, one of these committees, Americans for a Better Country, asked and received an advisory opinion from the FEC in early 2004, aimed at restricting the Democratic 'shadow' committees. In essence, the FEC advisory opinion would apply BCRA to 527 committees, treating them as PACs if their activities 'promote, support, attack or oppose one or more clearly identified candidates'. This rule would have severely restricted the ability of such committees to raise soft money (Theimer, 2004), but it was put on hold until after the 2004 election (Edsall, 2004c). Earlier, the Internal Revenue Service applied the BCRA standard to the political activities of 501c tax-exempt committees (Chappie, 2004). So, at this writing, the legal status of shifting soft money into 'shadow' party committees is unclear.

However, if each party's allied tax-exempt groups were able to raise $100 million in new funds, it would account for about two-fifths of the soft money raised by the national parties in 2000. (On the broader question of how interest groups will respond to BCRA apart from party finance, see Boatright et al., 2003.)

Thus, if all three avenues were exploited simultaneously, the major parties might be able to replace the soft money lost to BCRA, and perhaps even exceed it. And in the longer term, one or another of these avenues might prove especially fruitful for party finance. But to be successful, all of these options require extensive engagement of the parties in marshalling money. Here BCRA creates some major stumbling blocks: national parties, elected officials and their agents cannot be directly involved in the mechanics of such innovations. This fact does not mean, however, that such innovations cannot take place within the limits of the law.

Post-BCRA fundraising of these sorts will surely require a new cadre of fundraisers. Local party leaders, wealthy contributors, interest group leaders, and/or political consultants are likely candidates to fill this role. The organizing of these fundraisers would also require a new set of intermediaries apart from the national parties or public officials. In addition, the requirements of BCRA may well require stark divisions of labor. For instance, much fundraising may need to operate at arm's length from campaigns and candidates, strategists and operatives. Also, different funding streams may need to be dedicated to particular tasks. For instance, grassroots activities may be undertaken by some organizations (local committees and allied 501c groups), issue advertising by others (PACs and 527 committees), and formal campaigns by yet others (national party committees and the candidates). None of these features are unprecedented in American party politics.

Such specialization would give the component organizations strong incentives to cooperate with one another. Indeed, under such a system, the various specialties would need each other in order to finance winning campaigns. Cohesion would also be fostered by extensive information about politics and campaigns, information that is becoming widely available anyway, especially via the Internet. In addition, common interests and ideology could weld together such a decentralized system, a prospect enhanced by the recent polarization of American politics. Indeed, if one thinks of political parties less as the hired staffs of national bureaucracies and more as collections of 'like-minded men' (and women) on the hustings, then such a system is quite plausible – and the very thing American parties have been about historically.

Of course, if these kinds of innovations were to occur, American party finance would change in important ways, much as it changed after the 1974 amendments to FECA. BCRA might not limit the aggregate level of party finance, but could profoundly alter the way money is raised and spent. It would be ironic indeed if the financial demands of capital-intensive, media-driven politics produced a highly decentralized and ideological fundraising structure. In any event, American party finance stands on the cusp of major changes.

NOTES

1. This section relies heavily on Corrado (2000), the best short summary of the pre-BCRA party finance.
2. 'Non-multicandidate' committees, principally candidate campaign committees, faced the same

limits as individuals and party organizations. Individuals were limited to a maximum contribution of $1000 and PACs to $5000 per election to candidate committees.

3. For a full account of soft money donors, see the Center for Responsive Politics website (www.opensecrets.org).

4. The source of the hard money and national figures is reports by the FEC. However, Table 12.3 only reports receipts and not transfers, loans, cash on hand, or soft money transferred to the national committees to pay the non-federal share of joint activities with state/local parties. If all of these figures were included, the total receipts of the Republican committees would be $465 million and for the Democrats $275 million. The author wishes to thank Robert Biersack of the FEC for his invaluable help in assembling these data. The state-level soft money comes from Barber (2003).

5. This section was written before the completion of the 2004 campaign. For the final result consult the Campaign Finance Institute (www.cfinist.org). This section relies heavily on Malbin (2003). Additional information came from the Campaign Legal Center (www.campaignlegalcenter.org). For an excellent summary of the issues and perspective behind *McConnell v. FEC*, see Corrado *et al.* (2003). For a summary of BCRA from the perspective of the FEC, see 'BCRA Campaign Guide Supplement', *Federal Election Commission Record*, 29(1), 2003.

6. These estimates exclude the handful of individuals who gave the maximum of $20,000 in both 1999 and 2000.

7. The $72 million figure comes from the Center for Responsive Politics (www.opensecrets.org) and the $102 million figure from Political Money Line (www.politicalmoneyline.com).

REFERENCES

Annenberg Public Policy Center (2001) *Issue Advertising in the 1999–2000 Election Cycle.* Philadelphia: Annenberg Public Policy Center (www.appcpenn.org).

Banks, Christopher and Green, John C. (eds) (2001) *Superintending Democracy: The Courts and the Political Process.* Akron, OH: University of Akron Press.

Barber, Denise (2003) *Life before BCRA.* Institute on Money in State Politics (www.followthemoney.org).

Bedlington, Anne H. and Malbin, Michael J. (2003) 'The party as an extended network: Members giving to each other and their parties', in Michael J. Malbin (ed.), *Life after Reform.* Lanham, MD: Rowman & Littlefield, pp. 121–40.

Bibby, John F. (1999) 'Party networks: National-state integration, allied groups, and issue activists', in John C. Green and Daniel M. Shea (eds), *The State of the Parties*, 3rd edn. Lanham, MD: Rowman & Littlefield, pp. 69–85.

Biersack, Robert, and Haskell, Melanie (1999) 'Spitting on the umpire: Political parties, the Federal Election Campaign Act, and 1996 campaigns', in John C. Green (ed.), *Financing the 1996 Elections.* Armonk, NY: M.E. Sharpe.

Boatright, Robert G., Malbin, Michael J., Rozell, Mark J., Skinner, Richard M. and Wilcox, Clyde (2003) 'BCRA's impact on interest groups and advocacy organizations', in Michael J. Malbin (ed.), *Life after reform.* Lanham, MD: Rowman & Littlefield, pp. 43–60.

Campaign Finance Institute (2004) 'Democrats harvested ten times as much in under-$200 donations as in 2000; Bush's small donors quadrupled', Press Release, July 23 (www.cfinst.org).

Center for Responsive Politics (2004) '527s not filling soft money gap; Hard money giving tops $1 billion', Press Release, June 25.

Chappie, Damon (2004) 'New IRS guidance may open loophole', *Roll Call*, January 26.

Cigler, Allan J. (2002) 'Interest groups and financing the 2000 elections', in David B. Magleby (ed.), *Financing the 2000 Elections.* Washington, DC: Brookings Institution, pp. 163–87.

Corrado, Anthony (1997) 'Money and politics: A history of federal campaign finance law', in Anthony Corrado *et al.*, *Campaign Finance Reform: A Sourcebook.* Washington, DC: Brookings Institution, pp. 25–60.

Corrado, Anthony (2000) *Campaign Finance Reform.* New York: Century Foundation.

Corrado, Anthony (2001) 'Financing the 2000 elections', in Gerald M. Pomper (ed.), *The Elections of 2000.* New York: Chatham House.

Corrado, Anthony (2003) 'The Legislative odyssey of BCRA', in Michael J. Malbin (ed.), *Life after Reform.* Lanham, MD: Rowman & Littlefield, pp. 21–42.

Corrado, Anthony, Mann, Thomas E., Ortiz, Daniel R., Potter, Trevor, Sorauf, Frank J. *et al.* (1997) *Campaign Finance Reform: A Sourcebook.* Washington, DC: Brookings Institution.

Corrado, Anthony, Mann, Thomas E. and Potter, Trevor (2003) *Inside the Campaign Finance Battle.* Washington, DC: Brookings Institution.

Drinkard, Jim (2004) '"Outside" political groups full of party insiders', *USA Today*, June 28, 7A.

Dwyre, Diana and Kolodny, Robin (2002) 'Throwing out the rule book: Party financing of the 2000 elections', in David B. Magleby (ed.), *Financing the 2000 Elections.* Washington, DC: Brookings Institution, pp. 133–62.

Dwyre, Diana and Kolodny, Robin (2003) 'National parties after BCRA', in Michael J. Malbin (ed.), *Life after Reform.* Lanham, MD: Rowman & Littlefield, pp. 83–100.

Edsall, Thomas B. (2004a) 'McCain-Feingold helps GOP', *Washington Post*, February 7.

Edsall, Thomas B. (2004b) 'FEC chairman backs organization's use of "soft money"', *Washington Post*, February 16.

Edsall, Thomas B. (2004c) 'In boost for democrats, FEC rejects proposed limits on small donors', *Washington Post* May 14: A9.

Edsall, Thomas B. (2004d) 'Party's strategy an "independent" spending blitz: Democrats to use novel approach to finance advertising', *Washington Post*, July 30: A1.

Farhi, Paul (2004) 'Small donors grow into big political force: Both parties see number of contributors soaring', *Washington Post*, May 3: A6.

Fred, Sheryl (2004) 'Party time: Prohibited from collecting six- and seven-figure contributions, party committees vie for $25,000 donors', Center for Responsive Politics, press release, March 11.

Green, John C. (2002) 'Still functional after all these years: Parties in the United States, 1960–2000', in Paul Webb, David Farrell, and Ian Holliday (eds), *Political Parties in Advanced Industrial Democracies.* Oxford: Oxford University Press, pp. 310–44.

Green, John C. and Corrado, Anthony (2003) 'The impact of BCRA on presidential campaign finance', in Michael J. Malbin (ed.), *Life after Reform.* Lanham, MD: Rowman & Littlefield, pp. 175–98.

Green, John C. and Farmer, Rick (2003) 'The state of the parties in an evenly divided nation', in John C. Green and Rick Farmer (eds), *The State of Parties*, 4th edn, Lanham, MD: Rowman & Littlefield, pp. 1–18.

Herrnson, Paul S. (1988) *Party Campaigning in the 1980s.* Cambridge, MA: Harvard University Press.

Herrnson, Paul S. and Dwyre, Diana (1999) 'Party issue advocacy in congressional election campaigns', in John C. Green and Daniel M. Shea (eds), *The State of the Parties*, 3rd edn. Lanham, MD: Rowman & Littlefield, pp. 86–104.

Herrnson, Paul S. and Patterson, Kelly D. (2002) 'Financing the 2000 congressional election', in David B. Magleby (ed.), *Financing the 2000 Elections.* Washington, DC: Brookings Institution, pp. 106–32.

La Raja, Raymond J. (2003) 'State parties after BCRA', in Michael J. Malbin (ed.), *Life after Reform.* Lanham, MD: Rowman & Littlefield, pp. 101–20.

Magleby, David B. (ed.) (2000) *Election Advocacy: Soft Money and Issue Advocacy in the 2000 Congressional Elections.* Brigham Young University, Center for the Study of Elections and Democracy.

Magleby, David B. (ed.) (2003) *Financing the 2000 Election.* Washington, DC: Brookings Institution.

Malbin, Michael J. (2003) 'Thinking about reform', in Michael J. Malbin (ed.), *Life after Reform.* Lanham, MD: Rowman & Littlefield, pp. 3–20.

Meyerson, Harold (2003) 'Judging Terry', *American Prospect*, November, 17.

Morehouse, Sarah M. and Jewell, Malcolm E. (2003) 'State parties: Independent partners in the money relationship', in John C. Green and Rick Farmer (eds), *The State of Parties*, 4th edn. Lanham, MD: Rowman & Littlefield, pp. 151–70.

Ornstein, Norman and Corrado, Anthony (2003) ' "Hard money" is easy to come by', *New York Times*, September 5.

Sorauf, Frank J. (2002) 'Power, money, and responsibility in the major American parties', in John C. Green and Paul S. Herrnson (eds), *Responsible Partisanship?* Lawrence: University Press of Kansas.

Theimer, Sharon (2004) 'FEC issues new limits on big donations', *Associated Press*, February 18.

13

POLITICAL PARTIES, AMERICAN CAMPAIGNS, AND EFFECTS ON OUTCOMES

Brian J. Brox and Daron R. Shaw

INTRODUCTION

For almost 150 years, two facts about American elections seemed incontrovertible. First, campaigns were an integral part of elections. It is the campaign that conveys information to voters who, in turn, use it to reach individual and collective judgments about the relative merits of candidates. The apparent rationality of election outcomes in the United States – candidates presiding over failing economies or unpopular wars lose, while candidates presiding over economic growth and popular wars win – strongly suggested that political information was reaching the public. Furthermore, it validated the perception that campaigns, as the most obvious conduit of this information, were important institutions.

Second, the role of parties in democratic processes was no less critical. The parties developed the capacity to contact individual voters, to advertise through partisan newspapers and pamphlets, to publicize and carry out events such as picnics, carnivals, parades, and rallies, and to print and distribute ballots. These capacities cannot be overemphasized. Candidates were recruited and controlled by parties. It is true, of course, that certain popular individuals had a greater say in how the party handled their candidacy and campaign. But it is equally true that parties dominated the relationship.

The perceived importance of campaigns and parties was largely unchallenged by practitioners, pundits, and scholars well into the 20th century. Three developments, however, called the conventional wisdom into question. First,

as scholars collected data from surveys in the 1940s and 1950s, they began to realize that the American public was not nearly as informed about or interested in politics as they had assumed. This finding shook the broader assumption of voters as attentive observers of the day-to-day events and policy pronouncements of the election campaign.

Second, the development of broadcast technologies – especially the emergence and proliferation of television – fundamentally changed the way in which information is disseminated. In particular, by the 1960s television had allowed individuals to communicate and to develop personal connections with an audience without the human resources necessitated by face-to-face contact. This, obviously, had the potential to empower candidates at the expense of political parties.

Third, in the late 1960s and early 1970s, the American parties reformed their internal nomination processes to increase democratic input. The direct result was an almost complete reliance on primary elections to determine candidates. The indirect result was a forfeiture of party control over nominating processes. In the words of Alan Ehrenhalt (1991), candidates were asked to 'nominate themselves'. Furthermore, as candidates began to contest primary elections, they developed campaign organizations and expertise independent of the political party. These candidates not only were *not* beholden to the party when they won the nomination, but also often had personal campaign organizations and did not need help from the party as they turned their attention to the general election contest.

Together, these three developments led scholars to suggest that by the late 1960s we had entered a period of 'candidate-centered politics' in the USA (Wattenberg, 1991). The central idea is that candidates drove electoral and electioneering processes during this era. A corollary idea is that as candidates have been ascendant, parties have scrambled to remain relevant. Indeed, much of the recent literature on the American parties has emphasized the attempts of parties to recraft their functional and theoretical roles in light of more 'personalized' and candidate-driven politics.

At the same time, these developments have also prompted a number of interesting studies analyzing the effects of these candidate campaigns on voters and elections. More specifically, the persistent finding that voters do not know very much about politics and do not pay much attention to politics (or campaigns) has led scholars to look at the impact of other factors on elections. Indeed, the success of voting models that rely on factors such as incumbency, presidential approval, and economic performance has produced a sizable group of political scientists who view campaigns skeptically.

In this chapter, we review the classic literature on campaigns, elections, and voting behavior. This review, however, consciously attempts to recognize subtle and complex arguments on campaign effects. We will then discuss the sources of renewed interest in (1) campaign effects and (2) the role of parties in campaigns, before moving on to a delineation of the most recent findings produced by this renaissance. We close the chapter by discussing the prospects for continued party involvement with election campaigns. Our focus throughout is on presidential elections, although we comment from time to time on US congressional races.

WHAT CLASSIC STUDIES TELL US ABOUT CAMPAIGN EFFECTS

A functioning democracy presumes voters have enough information to reward successful office-holders or to punish unsuccessful ones (e.g., Key, 1966; Fiorina, 1981). The initial empirical work of political scientists casts doubt on even this low-level rationality, and the empirical findings underpinning this doubt became the focus of subsequent scholarship. The finding that voters may not have the requisite information to hold public officials accountable for performance in office creates a profound disconnect: if people are so ignorant,

why are presidents who preside over economic recessions or unpopular wars or political scandals thrown out of office? Why does the system appear to function rationally in the aggregate if there is, in fact, no individual-level rationality?

Voting, written by Bernard Berelson, Paul Lazarsfeld, and William McPhee, was published in 1954. It employed a panel study to examine the political opinions, attitudes, and candidate preferences of residents of Elmira, New York, during the 1948 presidential election campaign. The broad argument – that voters tend to get their preferences from contact with 'opinion leaders' within their social groups – is familiar to any college student who has taken a course on public opinion and voting behavior. What is less well known is that the authors explicitly acknowledge the fact that political campaigns can have an effect on both individual voters and aggregate outcomes.

For example, the authors estimate that 16% of their sample 'wavered' between the parties during the campaign, while an additional 13% 'wavered' between a party and neutrality. The shifts were particularly evident amongst Elmira's small Democratic population, with 36% of these voters wavering between the parties and another 14% wavering between the Democrats and neutrality (Berelson *et al.*, 1954: 16–18). More to the point, the whole of Chapter 12 of *Voting* analyzes the trend towards Truman that took place late in the 1948 campaign, arguing that the Democratic rally was due to previously disaffected Democrats (and Democratic-leaning groups) responding to the class issues emphasized by Truman's 'Fair Deal' campaign. A decade later, survey researchers in Ann Arbor also acknowledged the potential for campaign effects. The reliance of *The American Voter* on party identification as an explanation for vote choice has led many to conclude that the Michigan scholarship did not consider presidential campaigns as significant. But this is to ignore the actual argument of the text. In Chapter 19 of *The American Voter*, the authors pointedly contend that party identification is one of *several* factors that determine vote choice. The specific argument is that attitudes towards the candidates, domestic issues, foreign policy issues, parties as managers of government, and group-related attitudes drive votes, with party therefore serving as a critical but non-omnipotent conditioning variable (Campbell *et al.*, 1960: 531). This position should come as no surprise given that the elections serving as the backdrop for this analysis saw the minority party candidate wallop the majority party candidate. The potential significance of campaigns is even apparent in the funnel of causality, in which party identification screens the acquisition and acceptance of political information. In their schematic, Campbell *et al.* place factors other than party identification, including issues and candidate perceptions, closer to the bottom of the funnel, indicating that political context is a critical variable for understanding voting.

In 'The nature of belief systems in mass publics', Philip Converse (1964) describes the American public as largely uninformed and unengaged, and uses this as the basis for arguing that persuasive information – a category into which campaign messages most certainly fall – faces significant partisan resistance (at the level of the ideologue) or falls on deaf ears (at most other levels of sophistication). Zaller's *The Nature and Origins of Mass Opinion* (1992) demonstrates, however, that a sophisticated reading of Converse does not necessarily lead to a minimal effects perspective. Zaller, in fact, uses Senate election data to suggest that voters with 'middle level' awareness may be quite susceptible to information flows. So while Zaller himself is agnostic as to whether there are significant persuasive campaign effects in presidential elections (at least in this study), it is certainly a possibility given his understanding of Converse's theoretical construct.

WHAT CONTEMPORARY STUDIES TELL US ABOUT CAMPAIGN EFFECTS

Despite scholarly fascination with non-campaign factors during the past sixty years, there have been significant studies of presidential candidate activities (e.g., Kelley, 1983) and media influence (Iyengar, 1991; Iyengar and Kinder, 1987). But because the Columbia and Michigan schools estimate that only 10–15% of voters are persuadable; with net effects thus constrained to only a few points, political scientists have looked for subtle, less direct campaign effects, as well as for other causal explanations for variance in voting behavior.

Of course, alternative explanations were readily identified. The activation of party identification was developed as a dynamic explanation for aggregate- and individual-level movement over the course of a presidential campaign. Gelman and King (1993) observe that shifts in the fortunes of candidates over the campaign largely involve uneven sequences of partisan activation. Persuasion is confined to independents

and some weaker identifiers, and tends to be driven by conditional and objective circumstances, such as the state of the economy and presidential job approval. Party identification thus determines the base vote a candidate can expect, with genuine (but limited) potential existing for significant improvement (Iyengar and Petrocik, 2000).

Aside from party identification, the role of economic variables in shaping candidate preferences has been a consistent theme in the voting literature. In the 1970s, political economists began modeling presidential elections as a function of macroeconomic factors such as economic growth and unemployment rates (see Fair, 1978; Tufte, 1978). During the 2000 election there were at least seven distinct presidential forecasting models.[1] What is interesting is that the forecasting models do not universally posit that campaigns do not affect presidential voting behavior. Most of them, for example, offer presidential job approval as a predictor of the vote, and approval rates could clearly be affected by the campaign. Moreover, a few models rely on past vote totals to predict the upcoming race, leaving open the possibility that past campaigns might affect current elections. Even forecast models with no endogenous (or lagged endogenous) variables frequently admit that campaigns are necessary to educate voters about the external reality upon which their predictions are based. Furthermore, some modelers have even suggested that campaigns are *not* equally skilled at accomplishing this.

Besides party identification and economic variables, political scientists have continued to develop the sociological framework established by the Columbia school. Specifically, political communication scholarship has explored the interpersonal networks through which people acquire their political information. The key findings from this literature are that (1) opinion leaders exist and are critical to informing the less aware members of a group, (2) communication differences between and among groups appear to be a function of the distribution of political awareness throughout a particular group, and (3) interpersonal communication remains vital, even as television has come to dominate the broader dissemination of information (Huckfeldt and Sprague, 1995; Johnson and Huckfeldt, 2001; see also Putnam, 2000).

The upshot of these studies is that understanding elections and voting does not require an understanding of campaigns. Though not irrelevant, presidential campaigns are epiphenomenal. The minimal effects perspective is therefore not a direct attack on campaigns. Rather, it is an inferred perspective; an attributed position based on its emphasis of non-campaign factors in studies of voting and elections. There have been almost no serious scholarly analyses suggesting that campaigning does not influence voters in congressional or local elections. In fact, the ability to raise and spend funds is a large part of the explanation for incumbency advantages in the US House and Senate (Jacobson, 1983; Mayhew, 1974). The minimal effects inference is confined to research on presidential voting. This, of course, makes sense. There are particular circumstances surrounding the presidential election that make it especially unlikely that a campaign will be decisive.[2]

More specifically, the minimal effects scholarship does not contend that no one is persuaded by the presidential campaign, but rather that the net effect is typically incidental to the election outcome. The broader theoretical point of the minimal effects perspective should not be misconstrued, however. Most scholars writing from this point of view seem to believe that campaigns *are* important. First, presidential campaigns serve as exemplars for citizen responsibility and control over political power. Second, and perhaps more pragmatically, they mobilize support for the two major party candidates. Indeed, this mobilization process might *not* occur without prompting by the parties. In addition, the way in which campaigns mobilize voters (the particular appeals, the commitments made, the understanding of their own coalition) could be a critical factor for understanding subsequent governance and public policy decisions. Still, scholars who emphasize non-campaign factors typically argue that differential mobilization effects between the parties are unlikely, and this severely limits the chance that campaigns will determine who wins the presidency.

Despite its reasonableness and scholarly foundations, political pundits and casual observers of politics – both of whom tend to see presidential campaigns as decisive – show disdain for this view. Perhaps more interestingly, political communication scholars are somewhat perplexed by this because a slightly different minimal effects debate has already been resolved in their field.

As with the initial empirical studies of election campaigns, early analyses of news media had a difficult time finding effects. In their watershed article on agenda setting, McCombs and Shaw (1972) point out that voluminous research up to that time revealed precious little correlation between the tone and content of reporting on a given subject and the attendant nature of public opinion. In fact, research up until the early 1970s showed that citizens were quite capable of reading newspapers and watching television without much effect on their opinions and attitudes.

The suspicion that news media effects exist persisted, however, and led political communication scholars to posit and investigate more subtle influences. McCombs and Shaw (1972) presented persuasive evidence that the media's influence is not in telling people what to think, but rather what to think about. The idea that media effects occur primarily through 'agenda setting' turned the minimal effects perspective upside down and paved the way for other, more subtle understandings of impact. Iyengar and Kinder (1987) used extensive empirical evidence of public opinion and news media coverage surrounding the Iran-Contra affair to contend that the media 'prime' citizens to use certain criteria when evaluating a particular figure or issue.[3] Iyengar (1991) also explored the possibility that the 'frame' used by the news media to present a given story can create politically significant connections in voters' minds. This research tends to be dominated by experiments, which allow greater control over (and isolation of) stimuli and effects. It has unquestionably transformed the nature of the debate on media effects and leaves many political communication scholars wondering what all the fuss is about when it comes to campaign effects. Surely the debates among campaign scholars could be resolved by a more sophisticated conceptualization of effects and greater flexibility and subtlety in research design.

NEW PERSPECTIVES ON CAMPAIGN EFFECTS

Given the array of studies questioning the significance of campaigns in US elections, is there any reason to cling to a more traditional perspective? We argue that there is. Recent research provides evidence that campaigns may, in fact, be more influential than heretofore believed. In particular, we point to four areas in which clear gains in our understanding of campaigns have been made: (1) estimating the net effects of campaigns, (2) measuring information effects from campaigns, (3) gauging the effects of specific campaign activities, and (4) identifying how candidates and campaigns approach the campaign. This section considers each of these in turn.

Estimations of the net effects of campaigns

Over the past fifteen years, there have been several estimates of the overall magnitude of presidential campaign effects. Moreover, these have tended to be fairly conservative. Steven Finkel (1993) uses the Major Panel Survey of 1980 to analyze individual-level movement in presidential preferences. He finds that while many respondents change their preferences, the net movement is 2–3 points at most. At the aggregate level, Gelman and King (1993) demonstrate that there is significant volatility in pre-election survey estimations of presidential preferences, but that net campaign effects are almost zero because the vote tends to converge on a predictable point on or around election day.[4] Erikson and Wlezien (2001) use time series estimation techniques to calculate an aggregate preferences shift of about 5 points in recent presidential campaigns. Unlike Gelman and King, however, they attribute the considerable preference volatility over the election cycle to campaign factors.

In addition to studies of preference shifts, some have suggested that general campaign effects can be understood as the residual variance from multivariate models of the presidential vote, presuming that those models contain only exogenous variables. Bartels (1993) uses this logic to estimate that presidential campaign effects are typically on the order of 2–3 points. The forecasting models discussed earlier can be viewed in this light, with the mean error estimates – which generally run between 1 and 4 points – serving as estimates of campaign effects.

Campaigns as information sources

Despite the continued prominence of articles and books on the presidential campaign's influence on votes, some scholars have argued that the focus on vote choice is an overly narrow way to consider campaign effects. In particular, a number of analyses focusing on how campaigns affect voters' information have been produced since 1990. In addition to the information processing models proposed by Zaller (1990) and Lodge et al. (1995), several scholars trace the path of campaign information. Building on studies of Alvarez (1997), Lupia and McCubbins (1998), and Popkin (1991), William Bianco (1998) finds that voters in Senate elections can fulfill the expectations of both rational choice scholars and political psychologists by using information readily provided in the early stages of political campaigns. Kahn and Kenney (1997: 1173)

go one step further; after examining the impact of intensity in 97 Senate races between 1988 and 1992, they contend that:

> Intense campaigns encourage individuals to rely more heavily on both sophisticated criteria and simple decision rules when forming impressions of candidates. As campaigns become more hard-fought, people are more likely to consider policy and ideology as well as partisanship and retrospective evaluations of the president and the economy. While the campaign setting clearly affects citizens' decision-making processes, different types of people react differently to the intensity of the campaign. As races become more competitive, novices begin to rely more heavily on issues, sociotropic assessments, party identification, and presidential approval, whereas political experts are less affected by changes in the campaign environment.[5]

Based on these studies of how campaigns affect the information levels of voters, political scientists have recently taken to estimating the 'informed preferences' of voters to determine if a fully informed electorate would elect the same candidates as the actual electorate. In his study of information effects in presidential elections, Larry Bartels (1996: 194) contends that:

> At the individual level, the average deviation of actual vote probabilities from hypothetical 'fully informed' vote probabilities is about ten percentage points. In the electorate as a whole, these deviations are significantly diluted by aggregation, but by no means eliminated: incumbent presidents did almost five percentage points better, and Democratic candidates did almost two percentage points better, than they would have if voters had in fact been 'fully informed.'

Scott Althaus (2001) expands Bartels' analysis by including non-voters in his study of how full information affects congressional vote preferences. Like Bartels, he finds differences between informed and uninformed voters, although Althaus does not find the same systematic party differences at the congressional level that Bartels finds at the presidential.

In addition to these innovative designs, there have also been a few experimental studies investigating the *kinds* of information that voters want to access about candidates and how that information affects the vote decision. Richard Lau and David Redlawsk (1997) conducted a series of computer-based experiments investigating these questions during the mid-1990s. They found that voters favor biographical information over hard issue information, and that information containing an affective component tends to be more influential than issue-based information. This corroborates other recent analyses arguing that emotion plays a considerable role in the presidential voting decision (e.g., Marcus and MacKuen, 1993).

Specific campaign effects

While analyses of political information and campaigns have helped us understand what presidential campaigns do, analyses of specific types of campaign activity have sharpened our understanding of *how* (and how much) campaigns influence voters. This trend toward disaggregating the specific manifestations of presidential campaigning has been matched by a tendency toward more innovative data and research designs. Consider the following aspects of electioneering that have received substantive empirical treatment over the past ten years.

Phones and direct mail

The most notable works in this area have been the 'field experiments' conducted by Alan Gerber and Donald Green (2000, 2001). During the 1998 elections in Oregon, Gerber and Green randomly selected voters from statewide voter lists, assigning them to control and treatment groups. The treatment groups received either (1) campaign mail from a candidate but no phone calls, (2) campaign phone calls but no direct mail, or (3) direct mail and phone calls. The control group received no campaign contacts. The authors took pains to ensure that their mail and phone calls were as realistic as possible, using genuine campaign consultants to design the materials. Controlling for a host of factors, Gerber and Green found that direct mail increased the candidate's vote share 10% beyond what would otherwise be expected, but that phone calls actually had a negative impact on aggregate vote share. They also tested the effects of face-to-face contacting, which they found had a highly significant and positive impact on vote share.

Mobilization

Rosenstone and Hansen (1993) offer one of the most ambitious claims of all the recent campaign analyses when they contend that the decline in party mobilization efforts is a significant cause of the decline in aggregate turnout in the USA. This result is corroborated by Brady *et al.* (1995), who argue that party and candidate mobilization efforts can substantially reduce the costs of voting and make it easier

for people with limited social capital to overcome the impediments to voting. More recently, Endersby and Petrocik (2001) argue that mobilization is perhaps the critical component to contemporary presidential election campaigns. They use National Election Study and exit polling data to build a compelling empirical case that while persuasion is minimal in presidential elections, the mobilization efforts of parties and candidates are critical to activating partisan predispositions.

Television advertising

This is where the renewed interest in campaign effects has been most evident. One of the first of the 'modern' works was Darrell West's study of the nature and effects of television advertising in federal elections. West (1983) essentially upheld the conventional wisdom that TV advertisements elicit minimal effects, but he also observed that campaigns do not expect these advertisements to persuade a large proportion of voters. Narrow, targeted effects are what campaigns seek and, West admits, we have little relevant evidence on their effectiveness. But it was Ansolabehere and Iyengar (1995) who revolutionized the study of campaign and political advertising with their experiments on TV advertisement effects in California during the 1990 and 1992 elections. They directly confronted the conventional wisdom of minimal effects by demonstrating that campaign advertisements significantly correlate with changes in candidate appraisals as well as the likelihood of turning out to vote. In particular, they argue that negative advertising mobilizes partisans but depresses turnout among independents.

The Ansolabehere and Iyengar experiments have prompted a slew of challenges. For example, Finkel and Geer (1998) take issue with Ansolabehere and Iyengar on the question of campaign tone and turnout. Using aggregate turnout rates and evaluations of campaign tone, they contend that negative campaigns tend to be coincident with relatively higher turnout. Wattenberg and Brians (1999) examine individual-level survey data and ultimately side with Finkel and Geer's claim that negative advertisements increase turnout. Interestingly, although there is debate concerning the effects of negativity, all of these studies find effects.

Candidate appearances

Several studies have updated the influential work of Stanley Kelley (1983) on the effects of candidates' visits on local preferences. For example, Bartels (1985) estimated the pattern and impact of Jimmy Carter's travel in the 1976 election. He argues that effects are not substantial, but that this is understandable because appearances are motivated by multiple factors, some of which are unconcerned with improving the candidate's trial ballot standing. Shaw (1999a, 1999b) has examined both the pattern and effect of presidential candidate appearances from 1988 to 1996. He argues that three extra visits to a state are worth approximately one point in the polls. Two current projects, one by Thomas Holbrook and the other by Scott Althaus, Peter Nardulli, and Daron Shaw, are recreating candidate travel from presidential elections going back to 1948. The availability of more reliable data on candidate schedules and public opinion from the libraries of presidential candidates may allow us to calculate precise estimates of appearance effects.

In 2000, the scope of inquiry expanded to include appearance effects in primary elections. Using data from the New Hampshire primaries, Vavreck et al. (2002) demonstrate that personal contact with the candidate can do more than mobilize; it can actually persuade people to support a candidate. Voters who had met a particular candidate were significantly more likely to support the candidate. The authors argue that the effect holds even controlling for the fact that one is more likely to meet a candidate for whom one is predisposed to vote.

Campaign events

Thomas Holbrook (1994, 1996) finds that conventions and presidential debates are the proverbial 800-pound gorillas of campaign events; both clearly influence voters' preferences. This contention is backed by specific studies of campaign events by Campbell et al. (1992), Geer (1988), Lanoue (1991), and Shelley and Hwang (1991). Holbrook's estimates of the effects of other events are much more ambiguous, suggesting that other campaign event effects are inconsistent and contextually dependent.

Holbrook's research is consistent with Shaw's (1999a) work on the matter, with a few addenda.[6] First, Shaw finds that gaffes or mistakes are strongly correlated with changes in candidate preference. Second, Shaw finds that scandals are not especially significant for vote change (for a contrary view, see Fackler and Lin, 1995). Third, Shaw finds that messages (or

policy initiatives) tend to be uncorrelated with contemporaneous shifts in candidate preference. Fourth and finally, Shaw's research indicates that not all event effects persist; some efforts are durable over a period of ten days while others fade and still others grow. Put another way, the functional form of campaign effects depends on the nature of the event.

Media effects

Several studies show that media exposure, while not influencing candidate preferences per se, influences a range of other political attitudes and impressions (Freedman and Goldstein, 1999; Brians and Wattenberg, 1996). Collectively, these analyses suggest that (1) we have been looking at the wrong variable when considering campaign effects, and (2) news media coverage matters because it affects impressions of candidates and issues and these, in turn, influence vote choice.

We should add, somewhat belatedly, that while there is no consensus that the news media have an ideological slant (but for a contrary view see Goldberg, 2003), a plethora of recent studies have empirically considered this possibility. Most notably, several studies of the 1992 presidential election show a significant anti-Bush tone to coverage (see, for instance, Sabato, 1993; Kerbel, 1995; Lichter and Noyes, 1995). More specifically, they show that economic coverage was far more negative than the objective condition of the economy and that this was the primary frame used to portray Bush and his administration (Hetherington, 1999; Lichter and Noyes, 1995). It is also the case that Bush received unfavorable coverage even when he was ahead in the polls (up until late June 1992), so it is difficult to blame the horserace for the tone of media coverage. Clinton, on the other side of the ledger, received positive coverage but only after he took the lead in the presidential preference polls just before the Democratic Convention. No such slant was discernible in 1996, at least not after controlling for Clinton's large and persistent advantage over Dole in the race. Internal studies of broadcast and print media conducted by the Bush campaign indicate that coverage of the 2000 race was mixed, essentially following the polls. All of these suggest news media coverage is influenced by professional biases (see Robinson and Sheehan, 1983; Sigal, 1973), and these tend to produce favorable coverage for frontrunners and unfavorable coverage for underdogs. These biases, however, have not been connected to support shifts among voters.

Candidate and campaign approaches

In addition to these advances in the study of specific manifestations of the presidential campaign, there have been changes in the way we view both candidates and voters, and how they interact. These new conceptualizations, in turn, have affected our view of what campaigns are about.

Arguably, the most intriguing conceptual advance in the past decade's studies of presidential elections is John Petrocik's notion of 'issue ownership'. Petrocik (1996) posits that candidates use election campaigns to convince voters that their issues are more important than the opposition's issues. Campaigns do not compete for the median voter along some summary left–right issue dimension; rather, they fight to set the agenda, knowing that Democratic and Republican candidates have different credibilities on different issues. Democrats, for instance, want to make elections about health care and the environment, while Republicans want to make them about taxes and defense. This comports with common sense, but it is quite different from how political scientists have traditionally conceived of electoral competition and (consequently) campaigns.

Another intriguing area of research focuses on the role of gender and ethnicity in how candidates are perceived and how voters react to candidates and campaigns. Two studies in this area merit particular attention, the first because of its impact on subsequent research and the second because of its innovative research design. The first study is Kahn's (1993) analysis of gender differences in campaign messages and voters' reactions. She finds that gender does indeed matter to both candidates and voters. Female candidates are more likely than males to emphasize 'nurturing' issues such as health care and education. Moreover, voters perceive female candidates as more credible and empathetic on these issues, irrespective of the actual positions or personalities.

The second study focuses on the effects of racial priming in news media coverage of issues such as crime. Nicholas Valentino (2001) uses experiments in which issues and images are altered slightly to determine if racial cues are being primed by the local news media's presentation of certain issues. More importantly for this study, he extends the analysis to

claim that such priming can affect candidate evaluations (presumably to the detriment of Democratic candidates) by raising the salience of racially charged subjects. While the evidence for Clinton evaluations in 1996 is weak, the connection posited by Valentino is interesting, particularly in light of the corroborative work by Tali Mendelberg (2001), who contends that racial priming has been a (successful) feature of Republican candidate advertising in recent elections.[7]

NEW PERSPECTIVES ON THE ROLE OF PARTIES IN CAMPAIGNS

It is clear that parties today are stronger than they have been in the last thirty years, though by no means as strong as they were during their machine-politics heyday. Yet parties have adapted to remain relevant to elections by working with candidates and voters alike. While it is unlikely that, short of a serious upheaval in the political system, parties will deviate from their current status as service organizations, it seems probable that they will seek to exert greater influence over elections. Based on current trends in party electoral activity, we see three areas in which the academic understanding of parties needs to focus: (1) the developing role of parties in campaign finance, (2) advances in service provision, and (3) efforts to influence nomination politics.

Developments in party financing of campaigns

Several scholars have already begun to explore new avenues for party fundraising, avenues that will certainly expand under the Bipartisan Campaign Reform Act (BCRA) of 2002. Herrnson (2000) notes the rise in 'party connected contributions', or campaign contributions that occur from members, former members, or leadership political action committees (PACs) established by current members of Congress. Leadership PACs, in particular, have become an increasingly important way for parties to influence campaigns. In the 1999–2000 election cycle, contributions from leadership PACs of both parties were ten times the amount contributed in the 1983–84 election cycle and two and a half times the amount contributed in 1995–96 (Potoski et al., 2003). As Potoski et al. note, the implications of the BCRA suggest that leadership PACs may play an even greater role in the future, given that PACs can contribute $5000 per campaign (whereas individual contributions are limited to $2000 per campaign), and members can control multiple leadership PACs.

Of particular interest will be research into the use of new and existing committees by parties seeking creative means to cope with the implementation of the BCRA. Members of Congress and the parties have already established new 'shadow' committees designed to get around BCRA restrictions by accepting the 'soft' money that once went to national party committees (Edsall, 2002). In addition, Senate candidates in 2000 began creating 'victory committees' – joint fundraising committees that were operated by the candidate and the party. These victory committees would raise both hard and soft money, the latter being transferred to the national party which would send it on to various state and local parties – though frequently these funds would be transferred back to the state of the candidate involved in the joint effort (Dwyre and Kolodny, 2002). The role of the Hill committees will also be important.[8] Existing studies suggest that the Hill committees are quite active, raising and spending both hard and soft money (Dwyre and Kolodny, 2002) and channeling resources with the goal of maximizing seats rather than encouraging party support in Congress (Damore and Hansford, 1999).[9] With BCRA's soft money ban, researchers will have to reassess the role of Hill committees as the latter reinvent themselves to work only with hard money.

State parties stand to win in the wake of the BCRA, as soft money finds its way to state party organizations, especially the parties in the 14 states that do not impose limits on corporate contributions and those in the 19 states that do not impose limits on contributions from labor unions (Dunbar, 2002). The role of state parties in financing state legislative campaigns varies greatly by state (Gierzynski and Breaux, 1998). State parties do play an important (if not overwhelming) role in financing some federal campaigns; in the case of campaigns for the US Senate in 2000, the Democratic Party even entrusted the responsibility for making coordinated expenditures to the state parties (Brox, 2004). State legislative committees, similar to the Hill committees, are also emerging as a force in campaign finance (Gierzynski and Breaux, 1998).

Advances in party service provision

Research into the service role of parties has expanded as parties have become more active

and more valuable to the candidates they serve. And though television advertising is likely to remain the dominant form of party campaigning in the near future, parties are expressing renewed interest in applying the shoe-leather techniques of an earlier era, enhanced with advances in technology (Balz and Allen, 2003; Nagourney, 2002). For example, the Bush campaign and the Republican National Committee are using the Internet to recruit volunteers, and they are creating mobilization strategies that incorporate early voting programs and a '72 Hour' plan for election day get-out-the-vote drives (Balz and Allen, 2003). In addition, both the Republicans and the Democrats are implementing technology in their search for voters; in 2004 the parties will be using advanced software to target likely voters. This software incorporates extremely large – 160 million records – voter lists augmented with political, demographic, consumer, and personal data to help the parties coordinate email, phone, and direct mail efforts for both fundraising and mobilization (Theimer, 2003).

The literature on parties is only beginning to assess the impact of these efforts. Gerber and Green (2000, 2001) have cleared a path for a number of innovative studies (many using natural experiments) to gauge the effectiveness of these mobilization strategies. Their latest work suggests that face-to-face efforts are effective at stimulating turnout in local elections (Green et al., 2003). The vanguard of this work seeks to discover the effects of these mobilization efforts on particular demographic groups. Elizabeth Bennion (2003) finds that personal contact using a non-partisan get-out-the-vote message was (somewhat) effective at mobilizing young voters in South Bend, Indiana, during the 2002 campaign. Melissa Michelson also explores the effectiveness of personal contact mobilization, focusing on a Latino population in California. She finds that face-to-face canvassing was effective at mobilizing Latino voters for a school board election in 2001 (Michelson, 2002), though that canvassing effort did not translate to increased turnout in 2002 among those subjected to the mobilization treatment in 2001 (Michelson, 2003). And Wong (2003) finds modest effects of telephone and mail mobilization efforts on Asian-Americans in Los Angeles County, California, with the effects varying by ethnic group. Future research will continue to tease out how party mobilization efforts vary based on the groups targeted, the type of appeals offered (partisan vs. non-partisan) and the mode of contact (face-to-face, telephone, mail, internet).

Another unique feature of parties that is being developed in the literature is an understanding of parties as brokers of services (Herrnson, 1986b), or as liaisons between candidates, consultants, and PACs. Herrnson (2002) reports that parties help candidates by facilitating contact between candidates and consultants and by guiding candidates toward PACs for contributions. From the point of view of the PAC, parties provide election information, guidance regarding which candidates to support, and opportunities to meet and greet candidates and elected officials. And consultants also use the parties as brokers; during election years, they benefit from the contacts with candidates that the parties make possible, and during non-election years parties often hire consultants to assist with long-range planning (Herrnson, 1988, 2002; Kolodny, 2000; Sabato, 1988).

The ability of parties to perform their service role has been enhanced over the last decade by continued institutionalization and nationalization of the Democratic and Republican parties. In terms of institutionalization, national party organizations have more money, more staff and better infrastructure, and they are more involved with PACs and with state and local party organizations (Herrnson, 2002). As parties become more institutionalized, their role in elections becomes more relevant. Large amounts of hard and soft money have allowed national party organizations to have greater (though by no means complete) control over the content and strategy of their candidates' campaigns (La Raja, 2002). Further, parties have nationalized, with national party organizations using their financial resources to influence the activities of state and local party organizations (Bibby, 1998), effectively making the latter into branches of the former (La Raja, 2002).

Renewed efforts at influencing nominations

Earlier we noted that the parties have generally lost the ability to control which politicians get to run for office. Yet new research suggests that parties are attempting to regain some of their previous power with respect to candidate selection. Maisel et al. (2002) find that party officials are playing an increasingly important role in candidate recruitment through contacting potential candidates. Buchler and La Raja (2002) find that party activity and incentives (such as primary endorsements) increase not only the likelihood of recruiting a candidate for

the US House, but also the quality of that candidate – but only for Republican state parties.

Though they are not as important as they once were (Jewell and Morehouse, 2000), endorsements also help parties play a role in candidate selection. Cohen et al. (2001) find that presidential candidates who are broadly endorsed by party elites are more likely to win the nomination. Dominguez (2003) also looks at the impact of endorsements by party elites; she finds that 'party loyal' donors react to elite endorsements when making contributions during the primaries.

DISCUSSION

We believe the pendulum is swinging back on the campaign effects argument, and part of this is driven by the increasing relevance of parties. Having settled into their roles as service organizations, they have proceeded to expand their influence in elections through innovative use of campaign funds and the implementation of unique technologies that enhance the value of the services they provide.

Looking to the future, we see two points that ought to be kept in mind. First, parties are probably going to remain relevant for the foreseeable future. Despite recent efforts at campaign finance reform that seek to limit issue advocacy and eliminate soft money, parties will continue to be a stable conduit for the large sums of money that will inevitably find their way into politics. State parties appear to be in a prime position to take up much of the slack resulting from the BCRA's soft money ban at the national level. Leadership PACs run by members of the party in government are also likely winners if the reforms are kept in place. Parties will continue to provide services to their candidates and will continue to be vital to the identification, registration, and mobilization of voters.

Second, campaigns and parties throughout the world are going to look increasingly like those in the United States – if not ideologically, then structurally and in terms of their strategies and outreach. We have already seen political consultants from the United States going abroad, using their expertise to help devise strategy for campaigns in Israel, the former Soviet Union, Europe, and Latin America (Arterton, 2000; Harman, 1999; Beamish, 1994). In addition, both major American parties send staff members abroad to help developing democracies establish party systems (Holley, 2003; Dobbs, 2001). Campaigns are ultimately about helping candidates talk to voters. Parties help candidates undertake that communication effort, and they help make sure voters hear the message. It is likely that the trends and developments taking place in the United States will spread to other parts of the world; as a result, the United States is no longer 'exceptional', it is at the vanguard.

NOTES

1. This list includes Holbrook, Erikson and Wlezien, Lewis-Beck and Tien, Campbell, Fair, Abramowitz, and Norpoth.
2. To be more precise, there are at least four reasons why presidential elections are relatively impervious to campaign effects. First, federal election law imposes spending limits on the candidates' campaigns in exchange for public funding. Second, the proliferation of polling and focus group technologies makes it unlikely that either campaign will achieve an advantage with respect to strategic information. Third, both candidates are likely to bring an equal amount of expertise to the table in a given election. Fourth and finally, presidential campaigns tend to involve 'tit-for-tat' spending patterns. That is, campaigns probably buy television time where their opponents are on the air and at about the same level of intensity. Similarly, candidates stalk each other around the country, in effect canceling out whatever bounce occurs when one of them visits a particular city.
3. McCombs and Evatt (1995) consider 'priming' an instance of what they call 'second-level agenda setting'.
4. It is not clear why election day seems to have this magical, 'enlightening' quality.
5. But see Dalager (1996) for a dissenting view on Senate races.
6. While Holbrook uses three categories to classify campaign events (conventions, debates, and other events), Shaw uses eleven. These findings are thus properly viewed as 'further explorations' rather than challenges to Holbrook's work.
7. On the subject of race/ethnicity and voting, there is also the work of Bobo and Gilliam (1990) on the positive effects of black candidates on black turnout, as well as the work of Shaw *et al.* (2000) on the positive effects of 'in-group' contacting (Latino groups contacting Latino registrants) on Latino turnout.
8. The Hill committees are the National Republican Senatorial Committee, the Democratic Senatorial Campaign Committee, the Democratic Congressional Campaign Committee, and the National Republican Campaign Committee.

9. Buchler (2003), however, argues that despite the appearance of strategic contributions, the Hill committees have become less efficient in their campaign contributions as a result of being 'captured' by safe incumbents.

REFERENCES

Althaus, Scott (2001) 'Who's voted in when the people tune out? Information effects in congressional elections', in Roderick P. Hart and Daron R. Shaw (eds), *Communication in U.S. Elections: New Agendas*. Lanham, MD: Rowman and Littlefield Publishers.

Alvarez, R. Michael (1997) *Information and Elections*. Ann Arbor: University of Michigan Press.

Ansolabehere, Stephen D. and Iyengar, Shanto (1995) *Going Negative: How Attack Ads Shrink and Polarize the Electorate*. New York: Free Press.

Arterton, Chris (2000) '20/20 Vision', *Campaigns & Elections*, April.

Balz, Dan and Allen, Mike (2003) '2004 is now for Bush's campaign', *Washington Post* (November 30), p. A01.

Bartels, Larry (1985) 'Resource allocation in a presidential campaign', *Journal of Politics*, 47: 928–36.

Bartels, Larry (1993) 'Messages received: The political impact of media exposure', *American Political Science Review*, 87: 267–85.

Bartels, Larry (1996) 'Uninformed votes: Information effects in presidential elections', *American Journal of Political Science*, 40: 194–230.

Beamish, Rita (1994) 'Ex-Soviets learn campaign techniques from American experts', AP Newswire (April 4).

Bennion, Elizabeth A. (2003) 'Message, context, and turnout: A voter mobilization field experiment', Presented at the annual meeting of the Midwest Political Science Association, Chicago (April 3–6).

Berelson, Bernard, Lazarsfeld, Paul F. and McPhee, William (1954) *Voting*. Chicago: University of Chicago Press.

Bianco, William (1998) 'Different paths to the same result: Rational choice, political psychology, and impression formation in campaigns', *American Journal of Political Science*, 42: 1061–81.

Bibby, John F. (1998) 'State party organizations: Coping and adapting to candidate-centered politics and nationalization', in L. Sandy Maisel (ed.), *The Parties Respond: Changes in American Parties and Campaigns*, 3rd edition. Boulder, CO: Westview Press.

Bobo, Lawrence and Gilliam, Franklin D., Jr. (1990) 'Race, sociopolitical participation, and black empowerment', *American Political Science Review*, 84: 377–93.

Brady, Henry E., Verba, Sidney and Schlozman, Kay Lehman (1995) 'Beyond SES: A resource model of participation', *American Political Science Review*, 89: 271–94.

Brians, Craig L. and Wattenberg, Martin P. (1996) 'Campaign issue knowledge and salience: Comparing reception from TV commercials, TV news, and newspapers', *American Journal of Political Science*, 40: 172–93.

Brox, Brian J. (2004) 'State parties in the 2000 Senate elections', *Social Science Quarterly*, 85: 107–20.

Buchler, Justin (2003) 'Incumbent protection and the declining efficiency of contributions from the congressional campaign committees'. Presented at the annual meeting of the American Political Science Association, Philadelphia (August 28–31).

Buchler, Justin and La Raja, Raymond J. (2002) 'Do party organizations matter? The electoral consequences of party resurgence'. Presented at the annual meeting of the Midwest Political Science Association, Chicago (April 25–28).

Campbell, Angus, Converse, Philip E., Miller, Warren E. and Stokes, Donald E. (1960) *The American Voter*. New York: John Wiley.

Campbell, James E., Cherry, Lynne and Wink, Kenneth (1992) 'The convention bump', *American Politics Quarterly*, 20: 287–307.

Cohen, Marty, Karol, David, Noel, Hans and Zaller, John R. (2001) 'Beating reform: The resurgence of parties in presidential nominations, 1980–2000'. Presented at the annual meeting of the American Political Science Association, San Francisco (August 30–September 2).

Converse, Philip E. (1964) 'The nature of belief systems in mass publics', in David E. Apter (ed.), *Ideology and Discontent*. New York: Free Press.

Dalager, John K. (1996) 'Voters, issues, and elections: Are the candidates' messages getting through?', *Journal of Politics*, 58: 486–515.

Damore, David F. and Hansford, Thomas G. (1999) 'The allocation of party controlled campaign resources in the House of Representatives, 1989–1996', *Political Research Quarterly*, 52: 371–85.

Dobbs, Michael (2001) 'Investment in freedom is flush with peril', *Washington Post* (January 25), A1.

Dominguez, Casey B.K. (2003) 'Not all primaries are created equal: The effects of primary election environments on candidates and party elites.' Presented at the annual meeting of the Midwest Political Science Association, Chicago (April 3–6).

Dunbar, John (2002) 'Shays-Meehan shifts soft money focus to the states: An investigative report of the Center for Public Integrity'. http://www.public integrity.org/report.aspx?aid=203&sid=200.

Dwyre, Diana and Kolodny, Robin (2002) 'Throwing out the rule book: Party financing of the 2000 elections', in David B. Magleby (ed.), *Financing the 2000 Election*. Washington, DC: Brookings Institution Press.

Edsall, Thomas B. (2002) 'Campaign money finds new conduits as law takes effect', *Washington Post* (November 5), A2.

Ehrenhalt, Alan (1991) *The United States of Ambition: Politicians, Power, and the Pursuit of Office*. New York: Times Books.

Endersby, James W. and Petrocik, John R. (2001) 'Campaign spending influence on turnout: Mobilization versus agenda-setting'. Presented at the annual meeting of the Southwestern Social Science Association, Fort Worth, TX (March 16–18).

Erikson, Robert S. and Wlezien, Christopher (2001) 'After the election: Our forecast in retrospect', *American Politics Research*, 29: 320–8.

Fackler, Tim and Lin, Tse-min (1995) 'Political corruption and presidential elections, 1929–1992', *Journal of Politics*, 57: 971–93.

Fair, Ray C. (1978) 'The effect of economic events on votes for president', *Review of Economics and Statistics*, 60: 159–73.

Finkel, Steven (1993) 'Reexamining the "Minimal Effects" model in recent presidential campaigns', *Journal of Politics*, 55: 1–21.

Finkel, Steven and Geer, John G. (1998) 'A spot check: Casting doubt on the demobilizing effect of attack advertising', *American Journal of Political Science*, 42: 573–95.

Fiorina, Morris (1981) *Retrospective Voting in American National Elections*. New Haven, CT: Yale University Press.

Freedman, Paul and Goldstein, Kenneth M. (1999) 'Measuring media exposure and the effects of negative campaign ads', *American Journal of Political Science*, 43: 1189–1208.

Geer, John G. (1988) 'The effects of presidential debates on the electorate's preferences for candidates', *American Politics Quarterly*, 16: 486–501.

Gelman, Andrew and King, Gary (1993) 'Why are American presidential election polls so variable when votes are so predictable?', *British Journal of Political Science*, 23: 409–51.

Gerber, Alan S. and Green, Donald P. (2000) 'The effects of canvassing, telephone calls, and direct mail on voter turnout: A field experiment', *American Political Science Review*, 94: 653–63.

Gerber, Alan S. and Green, Donald P. (2001) 'Do phone calls increase voter turnout? A field experiment', *Public Opinion Quarterly*, 65: 75–85.

Gierzynski, Anthony and Breaux, David (1998) 'The financing role of parties', in Joel Thompson and Gary Moncrief (eds), *Campaign Finance in State Legislative Elections*. Washington, DC: Congressional Quarterly Press.

Goldberg, Bernard (2003) *Bias: A CBS Insider Exposes How the Media Distort the News*. New York: Perennial.

Green, Donald P., Gerber, Alan S. and Nickerson, David W. (2003) 'Getting out the vote in local elections: Results from six door-to-door canvassing experiments', *Journal of Politics*, 65: 1083–96.

Harman, Danna (1999) 'Carville: This game is over, and I am outta here', *Jerusalem Post* (May 20).

Herrnson, Paul S. (1986a) 'Do parties make a difference? The role of party organizations in congressional elections', *Journal of Politics*, 48: 589–615.

Herrnson, Paul S. (1986b) 'Political party organizations and congressional campaigning'. Presented at the annual meeting of the Midwest Political Science Association, Chicago (April 27–30).

Herrnson, Paul S. (1988) *Party Campaigning in the 1980s*. Cambridge, MA: Harvard University Press.

Herrnson, Paul S. (2000) *Congressional Elections: Campaigning at Home and in Washington*, 3rd edition. Washington, DC: Congressional Quarterly Press.

Herrnson, Paul S. (2002) 'National party organizations at the dawn of the 21st century', in L. Sandy Maisel (ed.), *The Parties Respond: Changes in American Parties and Campaigns*, 4th edition. Boulder, CO: Westview Press.

Hetherington, Marc J. (1999) 'The effect of political trust on the presidential vote, 1968–96', *American Political Science Review*, 93: 311–26.

Holbrook, Thomas M. (1994) 'Campaigns, national campaigns, and U.S. presidential elections', *American Journal of Political Science*, 38: 973–98.

Holbrook, Thomas M. (1996) *Do Campaigns Matter?* Thousand Oaks, CA: Sage.

Holley, David (2003) 'Voters doubt fairness of Georgian election', *Los Angeles Times* (November 3).

Huckfeldt, Robert and Sprague, John (1995) *Citizens, Politics, and Social Communication: Information and Influence in an Election Campaign*. New York: Cambridge University Press.

Iyengar, Shanto (1991) *Is Anyone Responsible?: How Television Frames Political Issues*. Chicago: University of Chicago Press.

Iyengar, Shanto and Kinder, Donald (1987) *News that Matters. Television and American Opinion*. Chicago: University of Chicago Press.

Iyengar, Shanto and Petrocik, John R. (2000) '"Basic rule" voting: The impact of campaigns on party and approval-based voting', in James Thurber, Candice J. Nelson and David A. Dulio (eds), *Crowded Airwaves: Campaign Political Advertising in Elections*. Washington, DC: Brookings Institution Press.

Jacobson, Gary C. (1983) *The Politics of Congressional Elections*. Boston: Little, Brown and Company.

Jewell, Malcolm E. and Morehouse, Sarah M. (2000) *Political Parties and Elections in American States*, 4th edition. Washington, DC: Congressional Quarterly Press.

Johnson, Paul E. and Huckfeldt, Robert (2001) 'Persuasion and political heterogeneity within networks of political communication: Agent-based explanations for the survival of disagreement'. Presented at the annual meeting of the American Political Science Association, San Francisco (August 30–September 2).

Kahn, Kim Fridkin (1993) 'Gender differences in campaign messages: The political advertisements of men and women candidates for U.S. Senate', *Political Research Quarterly*, 46: 481–502.

Kahn, Kim Fridkin and Kenney, Patrick J. (1997) 'A model of candidate evaluations in Senate elections: The impact of campaign intensity', *Journal of Politics*, 59: 1173–1205.

Kelley, Stanley, Jr. (1983) *Interpreting Elections*. Princeton, NJ: Princeton University Press.

Kerbel, Matthew (1995) *Remote Controlled: Media Politics in a Cynical Age*. Boulder, CO: Westview.

Key, V.O., Jr. (1966) *The Responsible Electorate: Rationality in Presidential Voting, 1936–1960*. Cambridge, MA: Harvard University Press.

Kolodny, Robin (2000) 'Electoral partnerships: Political consultants and political parties', in James A. Thurber and Candace J. Nelson (eds), *Campaign Warriors: Political Consultants in Elections*. Washington, DC: Brookings Institution Press.

Lanoue, David J. (1991) 'The "turning point": Viewers' reactions to the second 1988 presidential debate', *American Politics Quarterly*, 19: 80–95.

La Raja, Ray (2002) 'Political parties in the era of soft money', in L. Sandy Maisel (ed.), *The Parties Respond: Changes in American Parties and Campaigns*, 4th edition. Boulder, CO: Westview Press.

Lau, Richard R. and Redlawsk, David P. (1997) 'Voting correctly', *American Political Science Review*, 91: 585–99.

Lichter, S. Robert and Noyes, Richard E. (1995) *Good Intentions Make Bad News: Why Americans Hate Campaign Journalism*. Lanham, MD: Rowman and Littlefield.

Lodge, Milton, Steenbergen, Marco and Brau, Shawn (1995) 'The responsive voter: Campaign information and the dynamics of candidate evaluation', *American Political Science Review*, 89: 309–26.

Lupia, Arthur and McCubbins, Mathew D. (1998) *The Democratic Dilemma: Can Citizens Learn What They Need to Know?* New York: Cambridge University Press.

Maisel, L. Sandy, Maestas, Cherie and Stone, Walter J. (2002) 'The party role in congressional competition', in L. Sandy Maisel (ed.), *The Parties Respond: Changes in American Parties and Campaigns*, 4th edition. Boulder, CO: Westview Press.

Marcus, George E. and MacKuen, Michael B. (1993) 'Anxiety, enthusiasm, and the vote: The emotional underpinnings of learning and involvement during presidential campaigns', *American Political Science Review*, 87: 672–85.

Mayhew, David (1974) *Congress: The Electoral Connection*. New Haven, CT: Yale University Press.

McCombs, Maxwell E. and Evatt, Dixie (1995) 'Los temas y los aspectos: Explorando una nueva dimensión de la agenda setting', *Comunicación y Sociedad*, 8: 7–32.

McCombs, Maxwell E. and Shaw, Donald L. (1972) 'The agenda-setting function of mass media', *Public Opinion Quarterly*, 36: 176–87.

Mendelberg, Tali (2001) *The Race Card: Campaign Strategy, Implicit Messages, and the Norm of Equality*. Princeton NJ: Princeton University Press.

Michelson, Melissa R. (2002) 'Turning out Latino voters'. Presented at the annual meeting of the American Political Science Association, Boston (August 29–September 1).

Michelson, Melissa R. (2003) 'Dos Palos revisited: Testing the lasting effects of voter mobilization'. Presented at the annual meeting of the Midwest Political Science Association, Chicago (April 3–6).

Nagourney, Adam (2002) 'TV's tight grip on campaigns is weakening', *New York Times* (September 5), A1.

Petrocik, John R. (1996) 'Issue ownership in presidential elections, with a 1980 case study', *American Journal of Political Science*, 40: 825–50.

Popkin, Samuel L. (1991) *The Reasoning Voter: Communication and Persuasion in Presidential Campaigns*. Chicago: University of Chicago Press.

Potoski, Matthew, Lowry, Robert C. and Talbert, Jeffery (2003) 'Leadership PACs, campaign finance and congressional elections'. Presented at the annual meeting of the American Political Science Association, Philadelphia (August 28–31).

Putnam, Robert (2000) *Bowling Alone: The Collapse and Revival of American Community*. New York: Simon and Schuster.

Robinson, Michael J. and Sheehan, Margaret (1983) *Over the Wire and on T.V.: CBS and UPI in Campaign '80*. New York: Russell Sage Foundation.

Rosenstone, Steven and Hansen, Mark (1993) *Mobilization, Participation, and Democracy in America*. New York: Macmillan.

Sabato, Larry J. (1988) *The Party's Just Begun: Shaping Political Parties for America's Future*. Glenview, IL: Scott, Foresman.

Sabato, Larry J. (1993) *Feeding Frenzy: How Attack Journalism Has Transformed American Politics*. New York: Free Press.

Shaw, Daron R. (1999a) 'A study of presidential campaign event effects from 1952 to 1992', *Journal of Politics*, 61: 387–422.

Shaw, Daron R. (1999b) 'The effect of TV ads and candidate appearances on statewide presidential votes, 1988–96', *American Political Science Review*, 93: 345–61.

Shaw, Daron R., de la Garza, Rodolfo O. and Lee, Jongho (2000) 'Examining Latino turnout in 1996: A three-state, validated survey approach', *American Journal of Political Science*, 44: 338–46.

Shelley, Mack C., II and Hwang, Hwang-Du (1991) 'The mass media and public opinion polls in the 1988 presidential election', *American Politics Quarterly*, 19: 59–79.

Sigal, Leon (1973) *Reporters and Officials: The Organization and Politics of Newsmaking*. Lexington, MA: D.C. Heath.

Theimer, Sharon (2003) 'Parties study data to target voters', Associated Press wire report (October 20).

Tufte, Edward R. (1978) *Political Control of the Economy*. Princeton, NJ: Princeton University Press.

Valentino, Nicholas A. (2001) 'Group priming in American elections', in Roderick P. Hart and Daron R. Shaw (eds), *Communication in U.S. Elections: New Agendas*. Lanham, MD: Rowman and Littlefield.

Vavreck, Lynn, Spiliotes, Constantine J. and Fowler, Linda L. (2002) 'The effects of retail politics in the New Hampshire primary', *American Journal of Political Science*, 46: 595–610.

Wattenberg, Martin P. (1991) *The Rise of Candidate Centered Politics*. Cambridge, MA: Harvard University Press.

Wattenberg, Martin P. and Brians, Craig L. (1999) 'Negative campaign advertising: Demobilizer or mobilizer?', *American Political Science Review*, 93: 891–9.

West, Darrell (1983) 'Constituencies and travel allocations in the 1980 presidential campaign', *American Journal of Political Science*, 27: 515–29.

Wong, Janelle (2003) 'Getting out the vote among Asian Americans: A field experiment'. Presented at the annual meeting of the American Political Science Association, Philadelphia (August 28–31).

Zaller, John R. (1990) 'Political awareness, elite opinion leadership and mass survey response', *Social Cognition*, 8: 125–53.

Zaller, John R. (1992) *The Nature and Origins of Mass Opinion*. New York: Cambridge University Press.

14

PARTIES AND GOVERNMENT: FEATURES OF GOVERNING IN REPRESENTATIVE DEMOCRACIES

Hans Keman

INTRODUCTION

Government, properly instituted, is a major impetus to economic growth, political development, and collective goods. Government, badly instituted, is a major font of poor economic performance, elitist privilege, and social waste. (Levi, 2002: 54–5)

Governing society is one of the foremost topics for any student of representative democracy, for it concerns directly the complexities of the politics–polity–policy triad (see Keman, 1997, Ch. 1). This approach implies that *party government* is the irreducible core of any representative democracy because the political executive is constitutionally empowered to run the 'affairs of the state' based on a system of 'checks and balances' between the executive and legislature. This relationship differs across democratic polities, but at the end of the day it binds government in its capacities to act. In other words, the formal rules of the democratic game define the 'room for maneuver' of government and thus of the crucial actors making up government in all representative democracies: *political parties.*[1]

The institutional context of government has been conducive to the development of informal rules, or conventions, to play the game in reality. These 'rules of the game' have emerged over time and define the parties' actual scope for action. It is the interaction between parties that molds the pursuit of their main goals: *policy*-seeking and *office*-seeking. The former goal represents parties' efforts to make government do what is in their interest and reflects their ideas about how society ought to be directed by means of public goods (e.g. socioeconomic policy-making, conducting foreign policy, etc.). The latter goal is to gain access to the decision-making arena (parliament and government) by competing with other parties. There is no policy-seeking behavior possible without being in office (seats in parliament or ministers in government). This type of behavior of parties and the resulting interaction between the executive and legislature is typical of parliamentary democracies (Strøm, 1990; Lijphart, 1999).

The core *actors* within systems of representative democracy, then, are political *parties*, i.e. the elected representatives having a 'mandate' to make policy choices and the 'assignment' to control government. *Party government* is the executive body responsible for policy-making and representing the top level within the polity. Hence, if one wishes to understand the working of the policy-making capacities of parliamentary party government, it is useful to introduce two concepts that indicate the 'good governance' of parliaments and governments (as expressed in the quote from Margaret Levi): whether or not government and parliament are sufficiently *responsive* to societal and political issues;[2] and whether or not the policy choices made are indeed carried through (by parties) and effectively carried out (by government). This is what we call *accountability*. Both concepts allow for scrutinizing the procedural quality and material performance of representative government (Klingemann *et al.*, 1994; Budge *et al.*, 2002; Keman, 2002b).

In this contribution I shall elaborate on the act of governing by means of party government. Before scrutinizing this in more detail, in the next section I will introduce the debate on the position and role of party government that has dominated much of the literature on politics and government since the 1960s. From this debate a number of propositions have been derived which will be employed to dig deeper into the present 'state of the art' as regards party government. I shall first discuss the 'history' of this debate in qualitative and quantitative terms (see, for instance, Hibbs, 1992; Schmidt, 1996). This lays the foundation for the remainder of this chapter in which the various aspects of party government will be discussed.

DOES POLITICS MATTER – AND DO PARTIES IN PARTICULAR?

As early as the 1960s, studies appeared explaining variations in public expenditure, either across nations or over time (Pryor, 1968; Wilensky, 1975). On the one hand, it was claimed that ideological differences mattered in this respect, and on the other, it was stated that sociocultural and economic factors were decisive (for an overview, see Castles, 1981; Keman, 1993). This debate is still relevant for two reasons: First, if politics is not relevant for studying government, why bother about the role of parties in parliament and government? Second, if parties are not essential, why bother about the accountability and responsiveness of party government?

In retrospect this has been an important clash of views. For, if it can be demonstrated that electoral change between parties and a change in the party composition of government is related to changes in policy programs, then politics becomes an important factor not only in explaining policies, but also because this would imply that democratic governance makes a difference. An additional point of importance that made this debate relevant is that it implied a shift in focus within political science.

This debate made clear that the so-called 'output' (or public policy-making) ought to be taken into account. The debate on whether politics matters therefore had an important side effect: it made it clear that political science was not only about the relationships *within* the

political system, but also about what party government produced *for society* (Lane and Ersson, 2000). The main attention of the participants in the debate has been on explaining the growth of 'big government' in the latter half of the 20th century (Wilensky, 1975; Castles, 1982; Hicks and Swank, 1992; Keman, 2002b). Those who claimed that 'politics does *not* matter' argued along three different lines, that state intervention is the result of: economic development and growth; structural social change; path-dependent and incremental trajectories. The counterarguments of political scientists were that, although economic resources and affluence are required to undertake public action, social needs and ideological preferences do shape the character and urgency of political demands. Yet, before one could seriously move on to explain how, to what extent and, in particular, why the patterns of public policy-making were also the result of politics and deliberate policy choices, these counterarguments had to be investigated. This has been conducive to a host of analyses that show that the 'politics does *not* matter' school cannot uphold its claim, nor is it empirically feasible to claim that parties and governments do not matter (for an overview, see Hibbs, 1992; Castles, 1998). Let us therefore turn now to the issue of how it is that parties matter.

Parties do matter: but how?

Three different analytical clusters as regards the relationship between electoral representation of the citizen and the eventual pattern of governing represent the evolution of the debate: the impact of parties, in particular in relation to their policy-seeking behavior; the composition (type and color) of party government; and the form and organization of party government. Below we shall present the core elements of these three by means of the main theoretical propositions that represent the core of the 'do politics and parties matter?' literature.

The 'partisan theory of policy-making'

Party democracy is characterized by the idea that the political process enhances the transformation of citizens' preferences by means of party mediation (i.e. responsiveness) into policy choices and related governmental action (i.e. accountability). From this rather abstract point of departure one can infer a series of assumptions that allow for examining this process empirically.

First, the electorate has certain social and cultural characteristics that are conducive to having different preferences that will affect the direction and level of policy choices represented in party platforms (or manifestoes; for an empirical example, see Budge *et al.*, 2001). This assumption has been elaborated by means of two propositions:

1. The *left versus right* distribution of political parties across party systems influences policy choices (like the degree of state intervention in shaping society).
2. The existence of *organized class interests* will influence the development of welfare state related policy choices (like the 'butter versus guns' discussion).

Second, the role of parties is in part driven by their social constituency, and in part by their multi-functional organization: they are (and must be) policy-seeking *and* office-seeking (Strøm, 1990; Katz and Mair, 2002). The following propositions can be derived from this assumption:

3. *Differences between parties* matter according to their size and representation in parliament as well as in government (this is the 'office-seeking' argument; see Laver and Schofield, 1990; Müller and Strøm, 1999).
4. *Parties in government* pursue policies that are by and large compatible with their social constituency and policy program, i.e. the color of party government (this concerns the 'policy-seeking' argument; see Budge and Keman, 1990; Pennings, 1997).

Third, the capacity for policy-making of parties in government is dependent on the composition of government and the degree of executive dominance. This idea is reflected in two propositions:

5. The *type of government* matters with respect to policy choices – it matters, for instance, whether there is a 'single-party government', a 'coalition government', or a 'minority government' (Gallagher *et al.*, 2006; Woldendorp *et al.*, 2000).
6. The development of policy formation depends on how *government works*. Both the organizational make-up and the form of a party government will influence its viability and activities (van Roozendaal, 1997; Laver and Shepsle, 1996).

These assumptions and propositions of the 'partisan theory' are thus all characterized by the fact that *actors*, parties and governments, are considered to be *crucial* for explaining variations in governing and types of state intervention. This approach to the question of whether or not party politics matters has dominated the debate since the 1970s. Most analyses within the debate shared two characteristics. On the one hand, the dominant mode of analysis was of a *comparative* nature (and confined to the OECD world; see for instance, Castles, 1982). On the other hand, many studies tended to emphasize the policy *performance* of party government (e.g. Hibbs, 1992). Although this is a perfectly acceptable and viable research strategy, the danger is that 'party government' as such and the role of political parties in particular will disappear from the analysis. Keeping this caveat in mind, we shall now turn to empirical results of the debate on whether parties matter and then elaborate on the hypotheses central to this debate.

The empirical investigation of the impact of parties

The early empirical analyses almost always focused on the comparative influence of *non-political* factors (such as economic growth, age of the population, rates of unemployment and inflation: see Wilensky, 1975; Cameron, 1978; Alt, 1985), on the one hand, and on political parties (in government or not) and the role of trade unions (Hibbs, 1977; Korpi, 1983; Esping-Andersen, 1985; Armingeon, 2002) on the other hand. In this type of comparison, political parties appeared less determinative than social and economic factors. However, the *unexplained* variation remained considerable (Keman, 2002b). Hence, there was still ample room for further analysis regarding parties' influence on making policy choices. Subsequent research therefore focused on more ideological differences between parties and the impact of organized interests. These analyses revealed that the differences in terms of left versus right and a strong representation of, in particular, trade unions did indeed matter in making policy choices (Cameron, 1984; Laver and Budge, 1992; Huber *et al.*, 1993; Cusack, 1997). Hence, parties and interest groups appear to matter and could account for the cross-national and cross-time variation in, for example, the development of the welfare state or the size of the public economy (see Castles, 1998).

More importantly, what came out of this empirically driven debate was the following:

1. The presence of *parties in government* is more important than a party's vote share or representation in parliament; hence incumbency seems to matter.
2. The strength of the *non-left parties in government* is more relevant than the impact of – for example – social democrats as the main party of the left.
3. The *type and color of party government* matter considerably as regards the actual policy outcomes for society.

In sum, the debate has led to the conclusion (*ceteris paribus*) that party government appears to be the pivot for studying partisan influence on policy-making. Yet one must consider in more detail the type, color and composition to assess why and how this is the case.

PARTY GOVERNMENT: TYPE, COLOR AND COMPOSITION

The type and color of party government

After elections the distribution of parliamentary seats among the parties in competition is known and a government must be formed. The result of the formation leads to both the *type and color* of party government. These are by and large the result of a negotiation process (unless one party forms the government) – this will be examined in the next subsection. First we focus on *types* of government, using classifications derived from the composition of parliament.

The first distinction concerns the number of parties in government (one or more) and the second concerns a party having a majority or minority in parliament. In the past many political scientists argued that single-party majority government would be more efficient and effective in governing, for, so the argument goes, government is coherent (one party) and unified with respect to its policy program (see Duverger, 1968). This argument must be qualified, however, because it assumes that parties are unitary actors and governing only means (mechanically) executing policy priorities that are derived from party programs. As we know from empirical experience, this is not true: parties in government are not always unified in action, nor making policies consistent with their programs (an example of the former is the Liberal Democratic Party in Japan; examples of the latter are the Italian Democrazia Cristiana until the early 1990s and the French Gaullists).

A similar argument was made with respect to 'minority' government. First of all, such a government would hardly be capable of governing because it lacks sufficient parliamentary support. Second, due to lack of support this type of government would not last long. Yet, as for example Woldendorp *et al.* (2000: 86) found, 22% of all parliamentary governments in 48 democracies were 'minority' governments, lasting on average 440 days. Hence minority party government is not an exceptional phenomenon and its duration appears sufficient for effective governing. As Strøm (1984) has demonstrated (but see also Laver and Schofield, 1990; Warwick, 1994), minority governments do make policy. However, in contrast to other types of party government, minority governments obviously are dismissed more often due to conflict with the parliamentary majority. Hence, the distinction between the minority and majority type of government seems to be overdone and is less relevant than the distinction between 'single-party' and 'multi-party' government. The latter type is evidently always the product of *coalition formation* (see below).

A related distinction that turns out to be relevant for understanding the impact of parties is the color of government. This idea was introduced in the late 1980s (see Budge and Keman, 1990), and attempts to capture a more qualitative element. The variable reflects the presence of parties of the left, the center and the right according to their parliamentary strength and number of ministers in government. Hence, the color of party government indicates *both* the ideological tendency (i.e. centrality) of a government and the numerical weight (dominance) of the participating parties (see Laver and Shepsle, 1996; van Roozendaal, 1997). The idea behind this classification of governments has been to demonstrate not merely that parties do matter, but that the composition of government matters even more (van Roozendaal, 1992; De Winter, 2002). And, as we observed earlier, party differences do matter as regards *policy-seeking behavior*. We argue therefore that for the understanding of governing by parties in representative democracies, the type and color of government are indispensable features to take into account (see Table 14.1 below).

The formation of party government

Apart from single-party government, the formation of governments is a complex process which in some cases (e.g. Belgium and the Netherlands) can take 3–6 months (Keman,

2002a). This is understandable. As we discussed above, it is not merely a matter of gaining governmental power (i.e. office-seeking), but of doing so in such a way that the collective choices as regards policy-making are as close as possible to the parties' interests (i.e. policy-seeking).[3]

Much theory on government formation has been developed over time, and a large number of overviews have been published (see Lijphart, 1984; Budge and Keman, 1990; Laver and Schofield, 1990; Müller and Strøm, 1999). The basic idea of most of these theories is that mutual collaboration between parties in government depends on necessity (to form a majority) and familiarity (to be able to cooperate). In addition, one can distinguish two 'schools' of thought that explain the eventual outcome of the negotiation process between parties. On the one hand, there is the office-seeking school that assumes that self-interested behavior drives all actors. On the other hand, there is the policy-seeking school where coalescence and cooperation emanate from (more and less) shared values and policy choices.

The office-seeking approach argues that numerical conditions predominate and determine the outcome, in particular that the number of parties in government is never more than is necessary for a parliamentary majority. This is called 'minimal winning coalition government'.[4] Obviously this approach disregards ideological party differences as well as other types of social and political animosities that do exist in reality (e.g. cleavages in consociational democracies or class ideology in Scandinavia). Empirically, however, many coalitions formed are not minimal winning (Woldendorp et al., 2000).

The policy-seeking 'school' attempts to account for this lack of 'reality' and introduces the feature of party distances (in terms of left versus right or shared policy aims), which are based on divisions within party systems. The bigger the ideological gap between parties, the less likely these parties will form a government together. This assumption has induced new types of government: minimal winning (but) connected coalitions, minimal range coalitions, and policy viable coalitions. Yet this is basically an extension of the minimal winning coalition approach: the assumption remains that the smaller the number of parties, the happier the coalition will be. The genuine policy-seeking approach, however, leaves behind the numerical dimension and even, to some extent, the majority principle as a prerequisite for forming a viable party government. The formation process can then lead to types of party government that are 'broad' (cf. Lijphart, 1984) or 'oversized' (cf. Budge and Keman, 1990): there are more parties in government than strictly necessary (thus violating the minimum winning principle). In addition, this 'school' claims to explain the formation of durable minority governments. The argument is that the other parties in parliament have in common that they dislike each other more than the party (or parties) in government. As a result they are prepared to accept a minority government until they find a suitable alternative combination (Strøm, 1984). A final consideration within this approach is that particular circumstances (a 'crisis') or institutions (e.g. needing a qualified majority) may well be conducive to the formation and maintenance of a government that cannot be explained by policy- or office-seeking motives alone (e.g. in Belgium in the process of developing towards a federal polity, or in Switzerland to consolidate unity at the federal level).

More recently, government formation theory has tended to focus more on the process of formation and its ramifications for government *composition*. In addition to the color of party government, more attention is paid to the conditions under which parties negotiate (Laver and Budge, 1992; Müller and Strøm, 1999). An important feature of this process is 'government agreement', on the one hand, and negotiating 'portfolio distribution' among coalition parties, on the other (Budge and Keman, 1990; Laver and Shepsle, 1994; De Winter, 2002). Government agreements concern the policy program the parties will pursue in government and the distribution of ministerial portfolios. In some cases these agreements are quite specific (and lengthy, for instance in the Benelux countries: Keman, 2002a). The agreement serves the purpose of binding all parties in government so as to preserve its policy viability. Often this implies a rather *monistic* relationship with parliament, which tends to become a powerless institution. Portfolio distribution is often characterized by the rule of proportionality: the relative size of the governing parties in parliament correlates highly with the number of ministries acquired (see Budge and Keman, 1990; Woldendorp et al., 2000). Hence, the portfolio distribution reflects the color of government by distributing the ministries mainly according to the policy preferences of participating parties (Laver and Budge, 1992; Müller and Strøm, 1999).

There are many theoretical explanations with respect to the formation of party government.

Table 14.1 *Features of government in representative democracies (averages by country, 1946–98)*

Country	Number	Duration	Type	Color	Support (%)
Australia	28	660.8	1.8	2.5	58.7
Austria	20	917.2	2	3.3	76.7
Belgium	36	510.9	2.5	2.4	63.2
Canada	20	946.6	2.1	1	55.2
Czech Rep.	5	739.4	2	1.6	56.7
Denmark	28	637.6	4.1	3.2	40.6
Finland	45	404.3	3.6	2.6	52.8
France V	56	335.6	3.2	2.1	62.7
Germany	25	660	2.7	1.9	55.1
Greece	52	303.3	3	2.9	54.4
Hungary	2	757	3	2	59.4
Iceland	21	880	2.2	2.5	56.8
Ireland	20	900.1	2.8	1.5	50.9
Israel	42	409.5	3.1	3.2	61
Italy	55	330.8	3.7	1.6	53.5
Japan	40	460.8	2.1	1.2	54.4
Luxembourg	16	1135.8	2.1	2.3	70.8
Netherlands	20	879.1	3.3	2	61.8
New Zealand	24	793.8	1.4	2.5	56
Norway	24	774.5	3.2	3.6	47.1
Poland	6	251.2	3.8	2.7	47.9
Portugal	12	586.4	2.3	2.4	52.7
Slovakia	5	180.2	2.4	2.4	53.6
Slovenia	4	502.3	2.3	2.7	60
South Africa	3	501	2.3	0	73.3
Spain	7	982.9	3.1	3.1	49.8
Sweden	24	752	3.3	4.1	47.4
Switzerland	52	365.1	2.9	1.9	80.6
Turkey	37	465	2.3	2.9	65.2
UK	19	995.4	1.2	2.5	54.5
USA	10	1924	1	2.5	0
Mean	25	633.95			57.76
Std.dev		336.10			13.36

Number = no. of governments formed (total N = 758); Duration = no. of days; Type = type of government (1 = single party, ..., 5 = Minority); Color = color of government (1 = rightwing; 3 = centrist; 5 = leftwing); Support = percentage of seats of governing parties in parliament.

Source: Woldendorp *et al.*, 2000: 79

Yet at the end of the day it is a process that is mainly directed by the organization and working of the party system with respect to party competition and programmatic differences. In addition, special features such as government agreements and conventions play their part. These features differ considerably across representative democracies. The cross-national variation of party government's features discussed here is illustrated in Table 14.1.

The average duration of party government is below 2 years (Luxembourg, Spain, and the UK are on top, Greece, France and Italy are quite below the average). This means that party governments of whatever type are less

durable than many think[5]. The types of government resulting from the formation process do vary, but most polities score between 2 and 3.5. This means that in many representative democracies the tendency is to form a minimal winning coalition or a surplus or oversized party government. The exceptions are the polities belonging to the Westminster type of democracy (see: Lijphart, 1984): Australia, Canada, New Zealand, and the United Kingdom. On the other hand there are those polities where a tendency towards minority government can be observed: Denmark, Finland, Italy and Poland. This is also reflected in their average support of government in parliament, which is below 50% (also in Norway and Sweden where minority and minimal winning coalition governments alternate). Finally, the color of government, the proxy for the policy-seeking tendency of a party government, varies considerably: in a number of countries the average value is below 2.0 (i.e. rightwing or center right), but only in Sweden can the opposite be noticed (4.1). Yet, most noteworthy is the fact that more than one-quarter of all governments can be considered as centrist. Hence, type and color of party government do vary across and within nations and seem to matter in terms of government formation. Parties are apparently concerned about which parties they share power with (in a coalition) and how this may work out with respect to governing. This is also dependent on the 'form' of cabinet government.

Forms of cabinet government: Hierarchy and collegiality

Governing in a parliamentary system depends very much on the balance between prime minister and ministers. How the executive is organized often implies a tension between collegiality and hierarchy, between a pre-eminent chief minister and a ministerial college of political equals.

Presently, it appears that the office of prime minister is acquiring more weight in the cabinet, even in quite egalitarian cabinet systems. It is argued that the increasing role of the media and thus of the prime minister as spokesman for government as a whole as well as the increasing importance of international meetings of government leaders have caused this. This development can be observed in particular in Western Europe due to the process of political integration of the European Union. Increasingly the final decision-making of the EU takes place via transnational bodies involving the national heads of government. At the same time there is an increased need for concertation and coordination of domestic policy formation. Nevertheless, the prime minister remains a 'first among equals' in a *collegial cabinet government*, since the principle of collegial decision-making is (still) predominant.

This recent development also implies a change with respect to the role of chairmen or leaders of parties in some countries. Especially in fragile coalition situations, these persons were often not included in government but remained in parliament, in part because they functioned as a 'chief whip'. Yet, in contrast to their Anglo-Saxon counterparts, these continental party leaders to a large extent control *both* the parliamentary party and their ministers in government (this has been the case in many consociational democracies: see Daalder, 1987). More recently, 'other' parties have tried to exclude dominant politicians from the coalition (for instance, in Austria and Italy). Finally, it ought to be pointed out that ministers, especially in ministerially organized cabinets, do not always honor their party mandate. Of course, this type of behavior can jeopardize the stability of government (Blondel and Thiébault, 1991).

The principle of 'collegiality' involves not only equality in rank-and-file within government, but also the idea that all decisions are made *collectively*. A minister who has been outvoted has no right to go public and to distance him or herself, but rather must share collective responsibility with the whole cabinet *vis-à-vis* parliament. If not, then the minister is expected to resign. This convention is becoming rare, however, since in most systems nowadays, dissent more often than not means that the cabinet government as a whole resigns (De Winter, 2002). With a *coalition* government this is virtually a fixed, if informal, rule. The reason is that the parties in government will not allow the upset of the delicate inter-party balance established, and reflected in the portfolio distribution among the participating parties. This type of organization of government is almost exclusively Western European and is typical of the slow process of democratization in the 19th and 20th centuries, especially in constitutional monarchies. Two other types of cabinet government have evolved over time, however: prime ministerial cabinets, on the one hand, and ministerial governance, on the other.

Prime ministerial cabinets have developed in most Anglo-Saxon countries, where, due to the 'first-past-the-post' electoral system, there is (almost) always a majority party in parliament. Hence, this party forms the government and the leader is in a position to appoint and dismiss ministers. The United Kingdom and Canada are typical examples of this type of *single-party government*. Prime ministerial government also exists, however, in some parliamentary systems where a coalition is necessary to govern. Here the prime minister derives his or her dominant position from the *formal* relations between the executive and legislature: the prime minister is often less vulnerable because of the 'constructive vote of no confidence', meaning that such a motion is only allowed if and when there is an alternative prime minister *with* a parliamentary majority (this principle exists, for example, in Germany and Spain). In this type of cabinet government it is the 'chancellor' who deals with parliament and with the individual ministers. In a sense, the chancellor is the 'conductor' and supervisor with respect to policy coordination. Although the role of the prime minister appears to be quite dominant, it must be noted that the stability of this type of cabinet government depends on the unity and homogeneity of the governing party. If there are strong rival factions, internal conflict may well lead to the replacement of the prime minister or of dominant ministers (this happens more often than not in Japan, but also occurs in the United Kingdom – Thatcher in 1990 – and Germany – Brandt in 1974). Hence prime ministerial party governments are more hierarchically organized than collegial coalition government but not always more homogeneous.

Finally, there is the *ministerial cabinet government*. In this case the institutions are not in place to induce collegial behavior between the ministers, nor has the prime minister sufficient powers to act as a 'supremo'. Each and every minister is responsible for his or her policy area and, consequently, there is less policy coordination. In fact, the prime minister is basically a power broker who is involved in two arenas: *within* government and *vis-à-vis* parliament. This form of party government can be found in Belgium and Italy (De Winter, 2002; Laver and Shepsle, 1996). It should not come as a surprise that ministerial cabinet governments are less enduring than others and are considered to be less efficient in decision-making compared with other government types.

The division of responsibilities is also a major feature of the organization of what I will call *dual cabinet government* (Weaver and Rockman, 1993). This type of government, inspired by the phenomenon of 'semi-presidentialism', is based on a division of responsibilities, but here between the head of government and the head of state. In organizational terms it means that the decision-making powers are shared, while the implementation of policies as well as accountability *vis-à-vis* parliament rest solely with the cabinet. Hence, the relationship within government is neither hierarchical nor exactly collegial in nature. In particular, the prime minister is in a delicate position: dependent on the president for a number of matters (often foreign affairs and defense) and responsible to parliament. It goes almost without saying that this form of government can be rather problematic, or at least is restricted in its actions. Dual cabinet government is further

complicated by the fact that many of these are coalition governments or, to make things worse, the president is confronted with a hostile parliamentary majority (i.e. 'cohabitation' and 'divided government'). This can be conducive to deadlock in decision-making and gridlock in policy implementation. Typical cases are France, and until recently Finland and Portugal. Yet, despite these drawbacks it can be noted that this type of organization of governing has been a model for many of the recently democratized countries in Central and Eastern Europe (Elgie, 1999). Table 14.2 reports some of the features discussed in this section.

Obviously the *collegial* form of government is the most prevalent type. This is quite understandable given the high number of parliamentary regimes in our universe of analysis. Nevertheless the more hierarchically organized forms together outnumber the collegial type. What also should be noted is that four out of the seven polities with prime ministerial organization are those of the established democracies that have experienced an autocratic regime in the 20th century. Another institutional legacy is the 'constructive vote of confidence' that is required in Germany and Spain to dismiss government. The other hierarchical cases are Anglo-Saxon, having inherited the Westminster type of political system (apart from Canada, where the central government has a distinctive role within its federal constitution: Braun *et al.*, 2002).

The dual form of cabinet government goes, of course, together with variations of semi-presidentialism. Israel is the outlier in this respect, but belonged to this category due to the rule that the prime minister was directly elected. Hence both the head of government and the head of state are more or less independent of parliamentary intervention. This is also the case in South Africa, albeit that one person is head of both state and government.[6] Dualist party governments thus have in common that heads of state and of government share political responsibilities. This makes this form different from the pure prime ministerial form.

The most prevalent form of party government in representative democracies is thus collegial cabinet government. It occurs in almost one-third of all countries under review here. What they have in common is that these countries are characterized by a multi-party system and thus by coalition government. The collegial principle can be considered as an institutional guarantee for the participating parties: on the one hand, it implies veto power for all

Table 14.2   *Form and fabric of party government*

Country	PM dominant	Collective DM	Confidence	Gov->Parl	FormCabinet
Australia	3	3	1	1.5	1
Austria	3	1	1	1	1
Belgium	1	3	1	1.5	4
Canada	3	3	1	1.5	2
Czech Rep.	1	2	1	1	3
Denmark	1	3	1	1.5	3
Finland	2	2	0	1.5	2
France V	2	2	0	1	2
Germany	3	1	1*	1.5	1
Greece	2	3	1	1.5	3
Hungary	2	3	1	0	3
Iceland	1	3	1	1.5	3
Ireland	2	2	1	1.5	1
Israel	2*	2	1	1	2
Italy	1	2	1	0.5	4
Japan	3	2	1	1.5	1
Luxembourg	1	3	1	1	3
Netherlands	1	3	1	0.5	3
New Zealand	2	2	0	1	3
Norway	1	3	1	1	3
Poland	2	3	1	1	2
Portugal	2	2	1	1	2
Slovakia	2	2	1	0	4
Slovenia	2	3	1	1	3
South Africa	2	3	1	1	2
Spain	3	2	1*	1.5	1
Sweden	1	3	1	2	3
Switzerland	NA	2	0	1	4
Turkey	3	1	1	1	2
UK	3	3	0	1.5	1
USA	NA	1	0	1	NA

PM dominant: 3 = strong supremo; 2 = weak supremo; 1 = *primus inter pares* (* PM directly elected).

Collective DM: 1 = PM & ministers individually responsible; 2 = government as a whole is responsible; 3 = Both situations apply.

Confidence: vote of confidence is required; 1 = government must resign; 0 = can be ignored (* constructive vote required).

Gov -> Parl: degree of dominance of government over parliament – high values = more dominant.

FormCabinet: 1 = prime ministerial; 2 = dualistic; 3 = collegial; 4 = ministerial cabinet.

NA = not applicable.

Source: Woldendorp *et al.*, 2000: 56–7, 68–9

involved: on the other hand, it is conducive to this type of government that the parties act as unitary actors (De Winter, 2002). Another feature is that in most of these cases the dominance of government over parliament is limited. Hence, parties in government and in opposition tend to seek cooperation rather than conflict (Tsebelis, 1990; Keman, 1997; Lijphart, 1999).

The final category with respect to the fabric of party government concerns those cases where this unifying behavior is seemingly absent – for example, Belgium, Italy, Slovakia and Switzerland. For historical and special reasons it appears that cabinet government is better off without the restrictions of collegial behavior in these countries. In Switzerland central government can be considered as an executive committee held together by means of its 'magic formula'.[7] Belgium established this practice to enable coalitions across the language-cum-territorial divide (Keman, 2002a), whereas Italy developed it to allow for minority government as well as to exclude the Communist party (during the Cold War). Finally, in Slovakia no party government could otherwise have been formed due to the deep-seated divisions within parliament.

In conclusion, the organization of party government is quite diverse. Four types have been distinguished here: collegial, prime ministerial, ministerial, and dual cabinet government. It is obvious that collegial cabinet government is the least hierarchical of the four parliamentary forms of government. The prime ministerial and dual forms are more or less of a hybrid nature, whereas the ministerial form is most typical for a government dominated by parliamentary parties (De Winter, 2002). This section on the fabric of party government in representative democracies shows, *inter alia*, that its organization is in part shaped by formal rules and related conventions. And yet students of party government more often than not overlook precisely the role of formal *and* informal institutions.

POLITICAL INSTITUTIONS MATTER FOR GOVERNING – BUT IN WHAT WAY?

Governing is not just about settling conflicting demands and opposed ideologies between parties. Politics is embedded in institutional arrangements that have been devised to process citizens' preferences and collective demands and to manage these conflicting demands. This requires a certain consensus among political parties for further cooperation by avoiding enduring stalemate. Institutions are seen to modify and regulate the behavior of the political actors (Tsebelis, 1990; Shepsle, 1995; Scharpf, 1998; Keman, 1999). Institutional arrangements differ considerably across nations and in their degree of formality. They may be simply established practices to tackle problems (e.g. deadlock and stalemate situations) or they may be derived from constitutions and related basic laws that direct the process of decision-making (Weaver and Rockman, 1993; Colomer, 2002). Surprisingly enough, this feature of representative democracy is often overlooked or taken for granted in the literature on the 'partisan theory of policy-making'. This points to a bias which should be avoided: actors alone are not sufficient to explain the organization and working of party government. Hence, we argue that the set of institutions and practices of a polity may well influence the room to maneuver of party government. It would be wrong therefore *not* to include the institutional configuration of representative democracies if one studies the

question of whether or not party government matters with respect to the crucial purpose of governing: solving the problem of collective action by means of public authority. And this is dependent on the institutional arrangement within which a party government operates. In the literature one finds many different strands of thought that discuss this approach. We confine ourselves here to the latest book of Arend Lijphart, *Patterns of Democracy*, in which he has made a seminal contribution to the study of the relation between the institutions and public action of party government.

Lijphart (1999) focuses on the institutional constraints that can be derived from basic laws. In addition, the focus is on the institutionalized practices that have developed as consequences of formal requirements (see also Weaver and Rockman, 1993; Czada *et al.*, 1998; Lane and Ersson, 2000; Colomer, 2002). The study of institutions is then considered as crucial to understanding the public actions of party government. The point of departure is the proposition that the institutional *configuration* of the decision-making process in relation to political actors and organized interests in representative democracies drives this process.

Lijphart (1984) developed a dichotomy with respect to the working of liberal democracies: *consensus democracy versus majoritarian democracy*. In *Patterns of Democracy* he developed both types further, and related these types to the way each performs in terms of governing the realm. Lijphart claims that consensual types of democracy perform better (even if they are necessarily not 'kinder and gentler') in the sense that they are more *responsive* in translating citizens' preferences into governmental action by providing higher levels of public welfare. Why is this?

The first point is that when a democratic polity is forced to make decisions under circumstances of divided social constituencies then the institutional context must be organized in such a way that veto players tend to comply and cooperate. This would solve the so-called 'collective action' problem (Keman, 1997; Scharpf, 1998). Therefore parties (and organized interests) ought to be allowed to have access to the decision-making arena, on the one hand, and must all be in position to gain from the eventual results, on the other. Of course, this requires that the alternative option of maximizing a single party's own gains is precluded. This is precisely what often occurs (sooner or later) within party democracy where conflicting demands prevail, and where the institutional context allows for stalemates (see also Tsebelis, 1990; Lane and Ersson, 2000). According to Lijphart, the principal requirements of a consensus democracy are:[8]

1. *broad coalition government* (i.e. the oversized type of government 'Type' category 3 in Table 14.1) which induces power sharing and may well be conducive to *optimal* policy choices by parties *in* government;
2. relative *dominance of government* over parliament (i.e. category 'Gov→Parl' in Table 14.2) which allows for *discrete* policy choices on the basis of 'government agreements' enabling policy *viable* coalitions;
3. *proportional representation*, allowing for all 'minorities' to be represented in parliament which may more or less diminish the use of *veto* play.

In short, consensual democracy is an institutional configuration allowing for political compromise and viable governing by party government. At the end of the day – according to Lijphart – this type of representative democracy will perform better. This is less likely to occur in a majoritarian type of democracy where confrontation and the principle of 'winner takes all' prevail.

The second line of thought regarding the impact of institutions concerns the way societal interests are represented with respect to the *scope* of political decision-making. In political science[9] the idea of interest representation – parallel to that of parties – and, in particular interest intermediation is often called *corporatism* (see Schmitter and Lehmbruch, 1979; Crépaz, 1992; Woldendorp, 1997). Corporatism is the emergence and eventual institutionalization of consensual relations between organizations representing labor, capital (or business), and government. According to students of corporatism this institutional mechanism has been a key feature of concerted policy-making, particularly in many Western European democracies, in the post-war era (Armingeon, 2002). The basic idea is that it is possible to transform conflicting societal interests from a zero-sum to a positive-sum game. Most students of corporatism have pointed to the beneficial influence of this institutionalized pattern of interest intermediation. However, a requirement is that party government be composed in such a way that the corporatist forms of interest intermediation are recognized (Keman, 1999; Armingeon, 1999). In other words, corporatism can be seen as an institutional configuration devised to promote policy *concertation* and to foster political *co-operation* between

societal interests and party. It will be clear that corporatist institutions will only bear fruit if and when party government is able to develop policies that foster stable policy outcomes.

Both institutional arrangements, 'consensus democracy' and 'corporatist intermediation', are considered as important assets to create consensus rather than conflict in representative democracies. Institutions are considered as constraints on party behavior in government, but also as an opportunity structure for parties to further their own interests (Shepsle, 1995; Scharpf, 1998). Comparative research has demonstrated that these institutional arrangements shape the room for maneuver of party government (Katzenstein, 1985; Scharpf, 1987; Laver and Shepsle, 1996; Woldendorp, 1997; Lane and Ersson, 2000). Interestingly, the results are interpreted differently. A number of studies conclude, like Lijphart, that institutional configuration favoring consensual behavior of parties and organized interests is better for party government and society as a whole. Conversely, other studies do not deny the impact of institutions and related behavior of party governments, but rather question whether or not this itself enhances the democratic *quality* of governance. In this view, political parties, organized interests and the rules of the game within a democratic polity not only shape the room to maneuver, but also define the quality of governing by party government in a representative democracy. That quality depends on the degree of 'responsiveness' of parties and on the 'accountability' of party government.

PARTY GOVERNMENT: RESPONSIVENESS AND ACCOUNTABILITY

Responsiveness and accountability are two important aspects of the process of democratic decision-making and therefore central features for assessing the quality of any party government. *Responsiveness* – the extent to which parties in and out of government do indeed translate citizens' preferences into public policy choices – is reflected in the relationship between ideological position and policy stance of parties. *Accountability* is the extent to which parties in government do indeed carry through their policy promises made during election campaigns. This Schumpeterian view of democratic quality still remains a valuable idea in assessing whether or not representative government works well (Klingemann *et al.*, 1994; Budge *et al.*, 2002).

In this section we will focus on the responsiveness and accountability of parties and government, an argument that is strongly linked to the *mandate theory*. This theory assumes that voters expect parties to fulfill their promises once they are in office, i.e. participate in party government. According to the mandate theory, the way parties govern depends not only on their ideological or programmatic stance, but also on the type and form of party government. This implies that the 'mandate' will not and often cannot be carried out as originally was thought. Government agreements, unstable coalitions or minority government and changing (external) circumstances often stand in the way. Yet, a number of students of government have attempted to establish how responsive parties are, in particular when they are in government, and to what extent party governments are accountable for their governing.[10]

An empirical approach to testing mandate theory has been developed by the Manifesto Research Group (Budge *et al.*, 2001). On the basis of a comparative contents analysis of party programs in OECD countries, it was possible to describe which political parties emphasized what salient issues in terms of policy priorities. Hence, the degree of responsiveness could be established in two ways: first, by comparing issues with programs; and second, by comparing how parties responded in terms of *policy choices* (see Laver and Budge, 1992; Pennings *et al.*, 2005).

From the analysis it became clear that parties in general do respond to changing situations – for instance, through international crises and in the domestic economy (Keman, 1993; Pennings, 1997). Surprisingly perhaps, the response is not very different among parties. Yet it becomes different if and when parties are *in* government. Although parties do react to external stimuli, such as political issues and socioeconomic problems, party government actions appear to depend on its *type and color* (see Laver and Shepsle, 1996; Keman, 2002b): the more leftwing a coalition is, for instance, the more active policy-making will be if levels of unemployment rise. Conversely, the more rightwing a coalition is, the less generous the welfare state tends to become (Castles, 1998). It also makes a difference whether a government is 'single-party' or an 'oversized coalition': one-party governments tend to make drastic policy changes, whereas (broad) coalitions appear to go for 'piecemeal engineering' (Gallagher *et al.*, 2005; Royed, 1996).

All in all, one may well conclude that parties are responsive to what goes on in society and can be held accountable for how they react if and when in government. At the same time, however, it is also clear that it depends on the type and color of government, and that its form also matters.

CONCLUSION: PARTY GOVERNMENT MATTERS!

Party government – making policy choices, allocating fiscal means, and producing rules – is one of the most discussed items in the media. The general public assumes that policy-making by government is by and large a response to their demands and related preferences. In a representative democracy, party government is held responsible for managing and solving *collective action problems* within a society. Not only symbolic responsiveness counts, but also the material output that is produced. Government, and in particular the parties participating in it, are held accountable. This implies that the academic debate revolving around the question of whether or not 'parties matter' has wider implications. Answers to this question also imply an assessment of the working of representative democracy and whether or not political parties are functioning in an adequate fashion (Dahl, 2000; Schmidt, 2000; Keman, 2002c).

Our analysis has revealed that, generally speaking, party government influences the type and direction of policy choices made in a representative democracy. This conclusion holds notwithstanding the fact that other factors – economic circumstances, demographic development and path-dependent trajectories – are relevant as well. Hence, it can be argued that the 'partisan theory of policy-making' is a viable approach to understanding party government. However, one must bear in mind that the *formation* of a government and the resulting *form* are complex features of party government that influence its room to maneuver. Equally obvious is that the institutional make-up of the government and concomitant mechanisms that allow for more or less consensus, co-operation, and viable coalitions are also conducive to good governance. Precisely for this reason, it makes sense to investigate the quality of this process in terms of responsiveness and accountability in a representative democracy.

The overall conclusion is therefore that the institutional organization of representative democracy is a determinant of the capabilities of parties in government with respect to collective action problems that vary according to the extent to which consensus and integrative mechanisms exist and do work. The 'proof of the pudding' of this lies – so we argue – in the extent to which party governments are 'responsive' and 'accountable', on the one hand, and in the way political parties are able to function properly as viable and credible agents between politics and society, on the other hand.

NOTES

1. Of course, other organized interests also have access to the decision-making arena that is controlled by government. However, it is not our aim to analyze the decision-making process, nor public policy formation.
2. In particular, parties are expected to play this role; they are considered to be the mediating actors between politics and society, especially within representative or indirect democracies (see Budge, 1996).
3. This process of government formation by parties is often discussed under the rabric of 'coalition theory'. This is, however, misleading: the term 'coalition' refers to any type of collaboration between at least two actors under circumstances where one cannot achieve his/her goals individually (i.e. the collective action problem). The term 'government formation theory' would therefore appear to be preferable.
4. Variations on this theme are *minimum size* (i.e. the smallest number of seats required to have a majority in parliament) and *bargaining* (i.e. the smallest possible number of parties in government); see Lijphart (1999: 91–6).
5. This observation is reinforced if the USA is taken out – here the administration cannot be dismissed, as it can in most other countries listed in Table 14.1.
6. This implies that if the prime minister loses parliamentary confidence the president is in fact also dismissed.
7. The 'magic formula' implies a fixed distribution of the seven seats in the federal government among the four main parties in the federal parliament. This convention has been in place ever since 1956 (see Steiner, 1974).
8. In addition to this there is a second dimension which Lijphart calls 'unitary/federal' and is operationalized in terms of a (de)centralized state or not, bicameralism or not, and a flexible constitution. This dimension does not concern us here.
9. One ought to note: in European political science in particular. Corporatism as an approach has mainly been developed in Europe and can be seen as an alternative to 'pluralism' as regards explaining policy choice (see Armingeon, 2002).
10. It should be understood that this is not the same as the so-called 'political business cycle'. This approach is used to explain why incumbent parties suffer or benefit from governing or not at elections in relation to economic cycles (Hibbs, 1977; Whiteley, 1980; Budge and Keman, 1990).

REFERENCES

Alt, J. (1985) 'Political parties, world demand and unemployment: Domestic and international sources of economic activity', *American Political Science Review*, 79: 1016–40.

Armingeon, K. (1999) 'Consociationalism and economic performance in Switzerland 1968–1998', in: T. Ertman (ed.), *The Fate of Consociationalism.* London: Oxford University Press.

Armingeon, K. (2002) 'Interest intermediation: The cases of consociational democracy and corporatism', in H. Keman (ed.), *Comparative Democratic Politics. A Guide to Present Theory and Research.* London: Sage.

Blondel, J. and Thiébault, J.-L. (eds) (1991) *The Profession of Government Minister in Western Europe,* London: Macmillan.

Braun, D., Bullinger, A-B. and Walti, S. (2002) 'The influence of federalism on fiscal policy-making', *European Journal of Political Research,* 41(1): 115–46.

Budge, I. (1996) *The New Challenge of Direct Democracy.* Cambridge: Polity Press.

Budge, I. and Keman, H. (1990) *Parties and Democracies. Coalition Formation and Government Functioning in 20 States.* Oxford: Oxford University Press.

Budge, I., Klingemann, H.D., Volkens, A., Bara, J. and Tanenbaum, E. (2001) *Mapping Policy Preferences: Parties, Governments, Electors 1945–1998.* Oxford: Oxford University Press.

Budge, I., Hofferbert, R., Keman, H., McDonald, M. and Pennings, P. (2002) 'Comparative government and democracy', in: H. Keman (ed.), *Comparative Democratic Politics. A Guide to Present Theory and Research.* London: Sage.

Cameron, D.R. (1978) 'The expansion of the public economy: A comparative analysis', *American Political Science Review*, 72: 1243–61.

Cameron, D.R. (1984) 'Social democracy, corporatism, labour quiescence and the representation of economic interest in advanced capitalist society', in J.H. Goldthorpe (ed.), *Order and Conflict in Contemporary Capitalism.* Oxford: Clarendon Press.

Castles, F.G. (1981) 'How does politics matter? Structure or agency in the determination of public policy outcomes', *European Journal of Political Research*, 9: 119–32.

Castles, F.G. (ed.) (1982) *The Impact of Parties: Politics and Policies in Democratic Capitalist States*. London: Sage.

Castles, F.G. (1998) *Comparative Public Policy: Patterns of Postwar Transformation*, Cheltenham: Edward Elgar.

Colomer, J. (ed.) (2002) *Political Institutions in Europe*, 2nd edn. London: Routledge.

Crépaz, M.M.L. (1992) 'Corporatism in decline? An empirical analysis of the impact of corporatism on macroeconomic performance and industrial disputes in 18 industrialized democracies', *Comparative Political Studies*, 25(2): 139–68.

Cusack, T.R. (1997) 'Partisan politics and public finance: Changes in public spending in the industrialized democracies, 1955–1989', *Public Choice*, 91: 375–95.

Czada, R.M., Héritier, A. and Keman, H. (1998) *Institutions and Political Choice. On the Limits of Rationality*. Amsterdam: VU University Press.

Daalder, H. (ed.) (1987) *Party Systems in Denmark, Austria, Switzerland, The Netherlands and Belgium*. London: Frances Pinter.

Dahl, R.A. (2000) *On Democracy*. New Haven, CT, and London: Yale University Press.

De Winter, L. (2002) 'Parties and government formation, portfolio allocation and policy definition', in K.R. Luther and F. Müller-Rommel (eds), *Political Parties in the New Europe. Political and Analytical Challenges*. Oxford: Oxford University Press.

Duverger, M. (1968) *The Study of Politics*. London: Routledge.

Elgie, R. (1999) *Divided Government in Comparative Perspective*. Oxford: Oxford University Press.

Esping-Andersen, G. (1985). *Politics against Markets. The Social Democratic Road to Power*. Princeton, NJ: Princeton University Press.

Gallagher, M., Laver, M. and Mair, P. (2006) *Representative Government in Western Europe*, 4th edn. New York: McGraw-Hill.

Hibbs, D.A., Jr. (1977) 'Political parties and macroeconomic policy', *American Political Science Review*, 71: 1467–87.

Hibbs, D.A., Jr. (1992). 'Partisan theory after fifteen years', *European Journal of Political Economy*, 8: 361–73.

Hicks, A.M. and Swank, D.H. (1992) 'Politics, institutions, and welfare spending in industrialized democracies, 1960–82', *American Political Science Review*, 86, 658–74.

Huber, E., Ragin, C. and Stephens, J.D. (1993) 'Social democracy, Christian Democracy, constitutional structure, and the welfare state', *American Journal of Sociology*, 99: 711–49.

Katz, R.S. and Mair, P. (2002) 'The ascendancy of party in public office: Party organizational change in twentieth century democracies', in R. Gunther, J. Montero and J.J. Linz (eds), *Political Parties: Old Concepts and New Challenges*. Oxford: Oxford University Press.

Katzenstein, P.J. (1985) *Small States in World Markets. Industrial Policy in Europe*. Ithaca, NY, and London: Cornell University Press.

Keman, H. (1993) 'The politics of managing the mixed economy', in H. Keman (ed.), *Comparative Politics. New Directions in Theory and Method*. Amsterdam: VU University Press.

Keman. H. (ed.) (1997) *The Politics of Problem-Solving in Postwar Democracies*. Basingstoke: Macmillan.

Keman, H. (1999) 'Political stability in divided societies: A rational-institutional explanation', *Australian Journal of Political Science*, 34: 249–68.

Keman, H. (2002a) 'The Low Countries. Confrontation and coalition in segmented societies', in J. Colomer (ed.), *Political Institutions in Europe*, 2nd edn. London: Routledge.

Keman, H. (2002b) 'Policy-making capacities of European party government', in K.R. Luther and F. Müller-Rommel (eds), *Political Parties in the New Europe. Political and Analytical Challenges*. Oxford: Oxford University Press.

Keman, H. (2002c) 'Democratic institutions, governance and political performance', in H. Keman (ed.), *Comparative Democratic Politics. A Guide to Present Theory and Research*. London: Sage.

Klingemann, H.-D., Hofferbert, R.I., Budge, I. *et al.*, (1994) *Parties, Policies and Democracy*. Boulder, CO: Westview Press.

Korpi, W. (1983) *The Democratic Class Struggle*. London: Routledge & Kegan Paul.

Lane, J.E. and Ersson, S.O. (2000) *The New Institutional Politics. Performances and Outcomes*. London: Routledge.

Laver, M. and Budge, I. (1992) *Party Policy and Government Coalitions*. Basingstoke: Macmillan.

Laver, M. and Schofield, N. (1990) *Multiparty Government. The Politics of Coalition in Europe*. Oxford: Oxford University Press.

Laver, M. and Shepsle, K.E. (eds) (1994) *Cabinet Ministers and Parliamentary Government*. Cambridge: Cambridge University Press.

Laver, M. and Shepsle, K.E. (1996) *Making and Breaking Governments*. Cambridge: Cambridge University Press.

Levi, M. (2002) 'The state of the study of the state', in I. Katznelson and H.V. Milner (eds), *Political Science – State of the Discipline*. New York: W.W. Norton.

Lijphart, A.(1984) *Democracies. Patterns of Majoritarian and Consensus Government in 21 Countries*. New Haven, CT, and London: Yale University Press.

Lijphart, A. (1999) *Patterns of Democracy. Government Forms and Performance in 36 Countries*. New Haven, CT, and London: Yale University Press.

Müller, W.C. and Strøm, K. (eds) (1999) *Coalition Governments in Western Europe.* Oxford: Oxford University Press.

Pennings, P. (1997) 'Socioeconomic problem-solving between conflict and consensus', in H. Keman (ed.), *The Politics of Problem-Solving in Postwar Democracies.* Basingstoke: Macmillan.

Pennings, P. and Lane, J.-E. (eds) (1998) *Comparing Party System Change.* London: Routledge.

Pennings, P., Keman, H. and Kleinnijenhuis, J. (2005) *Doing Research in Political Science,* 2nd edn. London: Sage.

Pryor, F.L. (1968) *Public Expenditures in Communist and Capitalist Nations.* London: Allen & Unwin.

Royed, T.J. (1996) 'Testing the mandate model in Britain and the United States: Evidence from the Reagan and Thatcher eras', *British Journal of Political Science,* 26(1): 45–60.

Scharpf, F.W. (1987) 'A game-theoretical interpretation of inflation and unemployment in Western Europe', *Journal of Public Policy,* 7: 227–57.

Scharpf, F.W. (1998) 'Political institutions, decision styles and policy choices', in R.M. Czada, A. Héritier and H. Keman (eds), *Institutions and Political Choice. On the Limits of Rationality.* Amsterdam: VU University Press.

Schmidt, M.G. (1996) 'When parties matter: A review of the possibilities and limits of partisan influence on public policy', *European Journal of Political Research,* 30: 155–83.

Schmidt, M.G. (2000). *Demokratietheorien,* 3rd edn. Opladen: Leske + Budrich.

Schmitter, P.C. and Lehmbruch, G. (eds) (1979) *Trends towards Corporatist Intermediation.* London: Sage.

Shepsle, K.A. (1995) 'Studying institutions: some lessons from the rational choice approach', in J. Farr, J.S. Dryzek and S.T. Leonard (eds), *Political Science in History.* Cambridge: Cambridge University Press.

Steiner, J.A. (1974) *Amicable Agreement versus Majority Rule: Conflict Resolution in Switzerland.* Chapel Hill: University of North Carolina Press.

Strøm, K. (1984) *Minority Government and Majority Rule.* Cambridge: Cambridge University Press.

Strøm, K. (1990) 'A behavioral theory of competitive political parties', *American Journal of Political Science,* 34: 565–98.

Tsebelis, G. (1990) *Nested Games: Rational Choice in Comparative Politics.* Berkeley: University of California Press.

Van Roozendaal, P. (1992) 'The effect of dominant and central parties on cabinet composition and durability', *Legislative Studies Quarterly,* 17: 5–36.

Van Roozendaal, P. (1997) 'Formation and termination of cabinets in West European multi-party systems', in H. Keman (ed.), *The Politics of Problem- Solving in Postwar Democracies.* Basingstoke: Macmillan.

Warwick, P.V. (1994) *Government Survival in Parliamentary Democracies.* Cambridge: Cambridge University Press.

Weaver, R.K. and Rockman, B.A. (1993) *Do Institutions Matter?* Washington, DC: Brookings Institution.

Whiteley, P. (ed.) (1980) *Models of Political Economy.* London: Sage.

Wilensky, H.L. (1975) *The Welfare State and Equality: Structural and Ideological Roots of Public Expenditures.* Berkeley: University of California Press.

Woldendorp, J.J.W. (1997) 'Neo-corporatism and macroeconomic performance in 8 small West-European countries (1970-1990)', *Acta Politica,* 32(1): 49–79.

Woldendorp, J.J., Keman, H. and Budge, I. (2000) *Party Government in 48 Democracies (1945–1998). Composition-Duration-Personnel.* Dordrecht: Kluwer Academic.

15

PARTIES INTO GOVERNMENT: STILL MANY PUZZLES

Lieven De Winter and Patrick Dumont

INTRODUCTION

The process of government formation constitutes a crucial phase and arena in democratic governance: it concerns the translation of electoral and parliamentary power into executive power, and the possibility of implementing policies that have been democratically endorsed and legitimated by the electorate. As an increasing number of Western European governments are based on a coalition of political parties,[1] studying the process of coalition formation has never been as relevant for the understanding of parliamentary democracies.

This chapter focuses on the executive office- and policy-seeking behavior of parties and on the institutional mechanisms and contexts that make possible or impede responsible party government, especially in the case of government coalitions. The following questions will be addressed:

1. Which parties get into government, and how is coalition composition decided?
2. How are portfolios allocated between and within parties?
3. How are governmental policies defined during government formation?

COALITION COMPOSITION

The most substantive research question studied in recent decades concerning parties and governments has undoubtedly been 'Which parties get in?'. This is most relevant in 'minority situations', that is, when election outcomes do not fully decide this question by awarding one party a majority of seats in parliament. With the increasing fragmentation of European party systems (Lane and Ersson, 1999: 142), minority situations and executive power sharing are more and more the normal outcome of elections. Hence, the process of bargaining over who will share power, and under what terms and with what policy content, is a core moment of European politics, and in many countries central to defining public policies.

Given this substantive importance, the theoretical literature on government coalition formation is one of the most active areas of research in the discipline, and, as a result, the literature is now replete with theories, hypotheses, and empirical tests regarding why some coalitions form while others do not, produced by scholars from different disciplines using ever more sophisticated statistical methods and increasingly rich data sets. However, this high level of scientific endeavor has hardly resulted in significant comprehensive progress in explaining and predicting real-world government compositions.

Office and policy

The first school of coalition theory was strongly inspired by game theory (Von Neumann and Morgenstern, 1953; Riker, 1962) and spatial theories of party and electoral competition (Downs, 1957; Black, 1958). Political parties and their leaders are conceived as rational actors, searching to maximize their utility by gaining office.

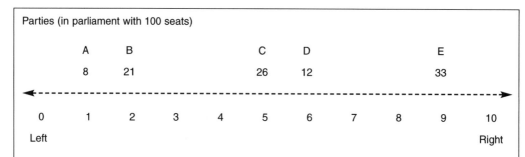

Figure 15.1   Cabinet coalitions predicted by unidimensional coalition theories for a hypothetical distribution of seats (adapted from Lijphart, 1999: 93)

The 'size school' (also referred to as office-seeking or policy-blind theories) has formulated several 'classic' propositions or rules:

1   The 'winning' proposition stipulates that only majority governments will form, as the core feature of parliamentary government is that a government can only survive if it is supported by a majority in parliament. A minority cabinet reaping all the benefits of office would not be tolerated by a majority opposition consisting of pure office-seeking actors.

2   The 'minimal winning coalition' (Von Neumann and Morgenstern, 1953; Riker, 1962) proposition stipulates that coalitions should not contain any 'surplus' members (i.e., parties whose omission would not make the coalition lose its parliamentary majority). As the pay-offs (the number of ministerial offices) of coalition are fixed, the inclusion of a surplus party would force coalition partners to share 'unnecessarily' the spoils of office with the surplus member(s) in such a constant-sum game.

These two propositions predicted an often high number of equiprobable 'rational' outcomes (see Figure 15.1), and at the same time

were rather unsuccessful in predicting coalitions formed in the real world.[2] Theoretical refinements of the size principle aimed at increasing its predictive efficiency by reducing the number of rational outcomes:

3   The 'minimum seats' proposition states that in the case of different minimal winning solutions, the minimal winning coalition that controls the minimum number of seats will form (Riker, 1962). If in forming a minimal winning coalition a party can choose between a larger or smaller partner, it will opt for the smaller, assuming that each partner will receive ministerial offices in proportional to its weight in terms of parliamentary seats in the coalition (Gamson, 1961).

4   The 'minimum parties' proposition – also called the 'bargaining proposition' (Leiserson, 1966) – stipulates that when different minimal winning solutions exist, the minimal winning coalition that includes the smallest number of parties will form. Here, the argument is not based on the size of the rewards, but on 'bargaining facility'. The smaller the number of partners at the negotiation table, the more smoothly the bargaining is supposed to go, the easier it is to reach an agreement, the more rapidly office

rewards can be reaped, and the more durable these rewards will be (increasing the number of partners would raise the probability of conflicts between cabinet parties and would thus endanger the coalition's stability).

Although these propositions greatly reduced the set of rational outcomes, they often still allowed for multiple predictions. Moreover, the reduction of the prediction set was accompanied by a decrease of the success rate in predicting the actual governments (Browne, 1973: 28). In order to improve the predictive power of rational office-seeking theories, policy proximity was introduced as an additional constraint on the 'size and number'-based propositions:

5 The 'minimal range' proposition (Leiserson, 1966) stipulates that parties wish to be part of a minimal winning coalition with minimal ideological diversity. Hence, of the minimal winning coalitions, the coalition with the smallest ideological range, defined as the distance (on the main dimension of competition) between the two most extreme members, will be formed.

6 The 'minimal connected winning' proposition (Axelrod, 1970) also concerns policy proximity, stipulating that, amongst the minimal winning coalitions, a coalition whose members are ideologically 'adjacent' will form. Removing any of the partners would render the coalition either non-connected or non-winning. Hence, contrary to the previous proposition, no 'gaps' are permitted in the ordinal scaling of coalition parties on the main policy dimension of party competition, which sometimes necessitates the inclusion of a small surplus party ideologically situated between two otherwise unconnected partners.

While both scholars only added policy as an additional concern of office-seeking political parties, De Swaan (1973) shifted the emphasis towards policy, arguing that parties first try to maximize 'policy coherence' (expressed in terms of a minimal distance between coalition policies and the party's own most preferred policy). Hence, he formulated:

7 The 'minimal policy distance' proposition, predicting that of the winning coalitions a coalition for which the member parties expect that the coalition will adopt a policy that is as close as possible to their own most preferred policy will be formed.

Some extreme versions of the policy-seeking approach have abandoned office motivations altogether.

8 The 'median legislator' proposition is drawn from majority-rule spatial voting models. The median legislator is the member of parliament who occupies the median position on the relevant policy dimension. Formal theory shows that when parties compete along a single policy dimension, the party controlling the median legislator can act as a 'policy dictator', as it cannot be defeated by a majority of parties on its left or on its right and one can therefore predict that this policy dictator party will always get into the government (Laver and Schofield, 1990: 111).[3] While this theory does not predict full coalition composition outcomes, it does theoretically help to solve another of the main real-world paradoxes of the game-theoretic approach, namely the frequent occurrence of minority governments that obviously violate the basic 'winning' proposition.

Laver and Schofield (1990: 88) argued that minority governments may occur because of policy divisions amongst opposition parties, so that they cannot combine and agree on a viable policy alternative. Minority governments exploit these divisions by forming majorities on an issue-by-issue basis. Strøm (1990) devised the following testable proposition:

9 The 'division of the opposition' proposition: the more ideologically divided an opposition controlling a majority of parliamentary seats, the higher the chances that a minority cabinet will form. For an ideologically extreme party, sustaining a minority solution can represent a good solution, as participating in a coalition could cause electoral damage due to the policy compromises it would trigger, while bringing down a minority government could result in the subsequent formation of a majority coalition ideologically more distant from the extreme party than is the current minority government.[4]

Generally, adding policy to the propositions has improved the predictive value of the early pure office-seeking theories.[5] Still, the empirical results remain modest.[6] While obviously richer in theoretical terms, policy-driven coalition theories require parties to be placed in an ideological space (which can be one- or multidimensional) before they can be tested empirically.

Whatever the placement method chosen (manifesto content analysis, survey analysis of electorates' or elites' policy positions, expert surveys), measuring party positions remains a difficult exercise. It is all the more so for multi-dimensional models of coalition formation, to which we now turn.

Most early policy-driven theories were uni-dimensional, although the policy space in some of the countries on which the theories were tested were recognized to be multicleavage polities (Lipset and Rokkan, 1967; Lijphart, 1984: 130). Hence, by only focusing on the left-right dimension, researchers may miss an important part of the real-world picture of party policy competition. Especially in multi-dimensional fragmented party systems, there is a wide range of smaller parties that may seek to realize their policy preferences elsewhere than on the left-right divide (centre-periphery, postmaterialism, etc.). Hence, including such parties may produce a coalition that appears to be unconnected, simply because one is looking at the wrong policy dimension, while the coalition may be perfectly connected on other policy dimensions more relevant to those parties. Hence, a single-minded focus on the left-right divide may well obscure rational policy-seeking behavior on other dimensions. The incorporation of multiple dimensions is increasingly warranted, given the emergence of new cleavages, the shift from social-structural voting to issue voting (Dalton, 1996) and increasing party system fragmentation.

A large number of multidimensional coalition formation theories have been formulated[7]. They all share the assumption that parties want to be members of a winning coalition that is as close as possible to their own ideal position in the multidimensional space. The theories differ strongly, however, in their definitions of which coalition produces the highest utility, that is, satisfies best the smallest distance assumption (De Vries, 1999: 16–17).

Multidimensional models also share several theoretical and practical problems. First, most of them generally do not predict a single or limited number of outcomes unless rather unlikely conditions are fulfilled. Second, most spatial theories are not designed to predict coalitions but to search for an 'undominated policy point' in the space. Additional inferences are thus needed to identify which parties stand a better chance of being included in the coalition. Third, they require metric data on party positions on the relevant dimensions. Because dimensions other than left-right are dealt with in party manifestoes, most authors use the Manifesto Research Group data. However, these data were collected to measure the salience of issues and not parties' policy positions. It may thus require a heroic leap to infer party positions from such a data set. On the other hand, expert surveys are only snap-shots and may be subject to other sources of errors such as the contamination of experts' placement of parties by their knowledge of prior coalition government experiences. Most often, different data sets produce different party positions (De Vries, 1999: 240), and the need for measurement on multiple dimensions increases the risks of such discrepancies, which in turn generate different predictions for the same models. Although multidimensional models aim to be more realistic, they are quite unstable, and empirical results are unimpressive.[8] Finally, multidimensional models assume that party leaders are aware of their exact policy positions, and those of all the other parties represented in parliament, on a number of relevant dimensions of competition, and are, moreover, sophisticated enough to carry out quite complicated calculations to determine the coalition that will be closest to their preferred policy positions.

The role of institutions in coalition formation

New institutionalism emerged in the early 1980s as a major alternative to the traditional institution-free approaches by emphasizing the role of different types of institutions in structuring the outcomes of the coalition formation process. The new institutionalist approaches do not reject office- and policy-seeking rationales, but add constraints imposed by institutional rules. Institutions are defined as any restriction on the set of feasible cabinet coalitions that is beyond the short-term control of the players (Strøm et al., 1994). Hence, differences in coalition outcomes (especially relevant for cross-country comparisons) are predicted on the basis of institutional differences with regard to coalition bargaining rules and norms that allocate power differently between (party) actors in the bargaining process.

One can distinguish neo-institutional theories based on the rules and norms governing the process of government formation itself, from the (more recent) theories that focus on the rules that structure cabinet decision-making and inter-party bargaining in the post-formation phase.

Institutions structuring the formation bargaining process

The first group of institutions (for inventories, see Strøm et al., 1994; Laver and Schofield, 1990; Mershon, 1994) includes the following:

1 'Recognition rules' that stipulate which party or parties will be asked to form a government, and in what order. This recognition may be enshrined in formal and even constitutional rules, or invested in other actors such as the head of state (Bogdanor, 1984). Recognition invests a formateur (and his party) with the power to propose the coalition alternatives over which bargaining will take place. Potential partners must accept or reject the proposals brought forward by this formateur before bargaining over other proposals can proceed. Hence, a formateur party should be able to guarantee its own entry into the government as well as to propose and have accepted coalitions composed of parties that it finds to be most compatible with its own policy preferences. As formal recognition rules are quite rare, in the real world the largest party generally tends to become the formateur party (Diermeier and Merlo, 2004), while according to Morelli (1999) it is the median party in systems where the head of state has discretionary power over the selection of formateurs.

2 The power to control the timing of the bargaining over a new cabinet, especially by incumbent prime ministers. Strøm et al. (1994) argue that an incumbent cabinet that manages to stay in office during the (usually post-electoral) formation bargaining over its successor, enjoys an advantage in the coalition negotiations, as it constitutes the fall-back or 'reversion outcome' if bargaining goes on endlessly or breaks down. Thus, parties whose most preferred outcome coincides with this reversion outcome enjoy a particular advantage, as they have an interest in boycotting or sabotaging any other alternative coalition formation attempt to which they are invited.[9]

3 Investiture rules stipulating whether a new government must pass a formal vote in the legislature, and with what kind of majority. Theoretically and empirically, minority governments are more likely to form in the absence of an investiture rule, since their general policy program need not be subjected to a formal parliamentary go-ahead at the cabinet's initiation. In countries with such 'negative investiture' rules, minority governments can avoid instant 'political death sentences' expressed by a motion of defiance from majority opposition by skillfully manipulating the legislative agenda and building ad hoc majorities on each separate issue the government submits to a vote in the legislature (Bergman, 1995).

4 Rules constraining the party composition of a government (such as the Belgian constitutional rule that requires an equal number of French- and Dutch-speaking ministers) or the size of a 'winning' majority, which has for too long been narrowed down to controlling a simple majority. In certain systems, controlling a majority of seats in the parliament is just not enough to implement an 'ordinary' policy agenda. First, there are policies that require constitutional reform, for which in many countries a special threshold (of two-thirds or more) has to be attained, sometimes spanning two legislatures (Lijphart, 1999: 217–23). Also, in many countries particular policy sectors require special majorities (Müller, 2000: 91). Recently, scholars set out to explore the consequences of bicameralism for government formation. Parties seem to anticipate the potential instability induced by the presence of a second legislative chamber and decide to form larger coalitions in the lower house (Diermeier et al., 2002, forthcoming) or, minority coalitions if they rely on a majority in the upper house (Druckman et al., forthcoming).[10]

Some behavioral rules, not enshrined in formal institutions, also affect the bargaining process and outcome. The most prominent is the respect of pre-electoral commitments between parties to form the next government, election results permitting. This can either take the form of a positive statement that commits a party to form a government with another party (thereby implicitly excluding other parties that did not sign the pact), or negatively, as an 'anti-pact' in which parties declare that they will not coalesce, for instance by ruling out either any coalition that includes a particular 'pariah party', or the party's participation in a specific coalition or any coalition. Given the general moral principle of pacta sunt servanda and credibility as a central ingredient for successful coalition building, public pre-formation commitments to rule or not to rule with some other parties constitute very powerful real-world constraints on coalition bargaining (Martin and Stevenson, 2001; Golder, 2004).

Most existing theories are 'history blind' in another way, by assuming that the formation of a particular government will not be influenced by the formation of preceding governments. Some authors introduced parties' past histories in the form of mutual satisfaction based on past gains. In particular, 'familiarity' between parties that governed together in the past enhances the probability of governing together in the future, thereby showing that governments are not formed *ab nihilo* (Franklin and Mackie, 1983).

Institutions structuring post-formation government decision-making

Other recent theories explore the constraints on coalition composition of rules that structure government decision-making once a new government is in place, thus effectively ruling out certain combinations and making others more likely by anticipation. These include cabinet operational rules (e.g., the balance between collective cabinet and individual ministerial policy jurisdiction (Laver & Shepsle, 1996; for a critique, see Dunleavy and Bastow, 2001), the prime minister's power to reshuffle or deselect ministers (Strøm, 1998), political responsibility and resignation rules); parliamentary rules (decision rules such as qualified majority votes, the right to turn any vote on a specific issue into a vote of confidence (Huber, 1996)); rules for dissolving the legislature and for calling early elections (Strøm and Swindle, 2002); electoral system rules; rules granting power to external veto players (head of state, domestic pressure groups), etc. Strøm *et al.* (1994) demonstrated on a small sample that the institutional constraints model manages to predict the cabinets actually formed better than simple size- and policy-driven models, but verification of the full institutional model on a large number of cases is still lacking.

Bargaining theories and actor-oriented theories

In some theories, parties' chances of being included in government depend on their strategic position in legislative bargaining games. Hence, they focus on the existence and properties of such special 'powerful' or 'dominant' players,[11] and the probability of these parties getting into government, rather than the probability of particular coalition formulae.

The most basic and best-known version of this approach is the median legislator theory mentioned above. Another actor-oriented bargaining approach developed voting power indices, of which the Shapley-Shubik (1954) index and the Banzhaf (1965) index are the most renowned. The voting power of a player, which is calculated by listing all the coalitions in which it makes the coalition win or lose (the number of pivots or swings), is compared to the voting power of other parliamentary parties. The voting power of individual parties may differ starkly from their weight in seats: a rather small party may be as powerful (and, depending on the index used, may be even more powerful) than a much bigger one within a given distribution of seats. Although hitherto rarely employed,[12] the inclusion of the power indices instead of the party weights, and their combination with the assumptions on policy distance and institutional constraints used in formal theories, could well be one of the most promising new avenues for formal as well as descriptive research on coalition formation in terms of composition, portfolio allocation, policy formulation and process. Notice also that following Warwick's (1996) analysis of factors affecting individual parties' odds of becoming government formateur or coalition partner, some scholars looked more specifically at parties' results in the elections preceding the formation of a government (Mattila and Raunio, 2004; Isaksson, 2005).

Discussion

After four decades of comparative research on the party composition of cabinets, this research field has become highly mature, in terms of the diversity of theoretical approaches and paradigms that are competing, their degree of formalization, the variety and sophistication of methods applied, and the scope and richness of the data sets used for testing hypotheses.

However, there are still major shortcomings. First, existing theories do not predict and therefore sufficiently explain a significant proportion of cabinet compositions formed in the real world. Whereas the latest comprehensive model of Martin and Stevenson does predict correctly an impressive number (about half) of real-world coalitions, this is done by lumping together two dozen variables drawn from three main schools, and the model therefore lacks parsimony and internal consistency. Still, a systematic comparative testing of theories and families of theories against each other, in combination with each other,[13] as well as against randomly generated solutions seems a promising path in evaluating the predictive capacity of coalition theories (De Vries, 1999; Martin and Stevenson, 2001). Studies that concentrate on parties getting into government as the unit of analysis rather than the full cabinet composition have better prediction rates, but they clearly explain less. More generally, focusing on predictions is only one part of a causal explanation, which needs both an account of causal effects of independent variables and a verification of the real-world presence of the causal mechanisms posited by a theory. This goal may be achieved by combining quantitative tests of existing theories with a qualitative treatment of cases that confirm and cases that disconfirm the theory, by tracing the process and the variables that caused the observed outcome (Bäck and Dumont, 2004).

Second, in order to test existing spatial theories, especially multidimensional models, one needs more reliable data on party policy positions. Also many formal models theorize variables that in practice are hard to operationalize, especially for cabinets in the more distant past (such as actors' electoral expectations or satisfaction with former experiences with partners in government). It comes as no surprise that the authors who formulate such abstract models at best give one or two examples that seem to fit their model. The insertion of institutional variables into formal models, albeit generally easy to collect and boosting the prediction rate, tends to lead to unacceptable simplifications of reality and/or to unmanageable mathematical complexities (De Vries, 1999).

Finally, although most scholars acknowledge that during government formation a lot of bargaining goes on *within* parties (Luebbert, 1986; Laver and Schofield, 1990; Müller and Strøm, 1999), for the sake of model simplicity as well as data collection problems on internal party divisions, almost all theories treat parties as unitary actors (for exceptions, see Robertson, 1976; Budge and Farlie, 1983; Maor, 1995). One operational indicator of internal divisions could be voting behavior during party investitures (De Winter *et al.*, 2000: 345). The support expressed for the upcoming coalition within intra-party arenas may serve as a more valid proxy for party cohesion than parliamentary group cohesion in investiture votes.

PORTFOLIO ALLOCATION

The question 'Who gets what in coalition government?' is even older than the question of 'Who gets in?'. The basic finding of the first analyses inspired by rational choice, that is, the existence of an 'iron law' of proportionality

(Gamson, 1961), has generally been confirmed by subsequent research (Browne and Franklin, 1973; Browne and Feste, 1975; Budge and Keman, 1990). While this proportionality norm may seem trivial, it actually is not, especially seen from a bargaining perspective. Hence, interest in the question of portfolio allocation has revived in recent years in order to provide a more solid theoretical grounding for this empirical law, to explain marginal but significant deviations from the rule, and to produce weights and data (through expert surveys) for different types of ministerial portfolios (prime minister, senior ministers, ordinary and junior ministers).

The iron law of proportionality

The starting point for the proportionality rule is the assumption that players have a specific weight, usually assumed to be proportional to the number of seats in parliament. Gamson (1962: 158) postulates that 'any participant will expect others to demand from a coalition a share of the payoff proportional to the amount of resources which they contribute to a coalition'. Still, a minor player should be capable of increasing its office share if it were necessary to keep a third player out of the coalition (Gamson, 1961). As all players consider proportionality as their bottom-line demand and concede that the other players take proportionality as their minimum expectation, proportionality becomes the only allocation principle on which all can agree.

Empirical analyses confirm the proportionality thesis (over 90% of the variance explained), sometimes with smaller parties getting bonus portfolios, probably in order to avoid their potential defection to another coalition that would offer a better payoff or simply because their small size would not have allowed them to receive any portfolio under pure proportionality.[14]

Still, this very strong relationship between seat weight and portfolio allocation is puzzling from a bargaining perspective: if bargaining is the predominant logic behind coalition formation, and if a party's bargaining power is dependent on its strategic position rather than on its size alone, what in practice prevents parties with great bargaining power from claiming a disproportionate share of the portfolios?[15]

Qualitative portfolio allocation

Apart from the quantitative questions of portfolio allocation, there is the question of which party, intra-party faction, and individual gets which type of portfolio (in terms of policy domain, prestige, spending power, etc.). Until the 1990s, few empirical theories on qualitative portfolio allocations were tested (Budge and Keman 1990). Laver and Shepsle's (1996) assumption of ministerial portfolio dictatorship, coupled with the hypothesis that the median party on the relevant policy dimension will get the specific portfolio, has drawn new attention to the qualitative aspect of portfolio allocation.

A first qualitative distinction between portfolios is policy domain. Some link was found between parties' ideological profile and their control of a particular domain of ministries. Browne and Feste (1975) explain this party–portfolio link by the 'possible reinforcement of the loyalty of each party clientele's group'. A basic problem of the empirical testing of this nexus is the a priori assumption of the static nature of party families' portfolio preferences, which are assumed constant over time and between countries (Budge and Keman, 1990). The empirical findings are therefore rather weak. Budge and Keman (1990: 98–102) also focused on the prime ministerial portfolio, predicting that the premiership goes to the major party (which actually occurs in 80% of the post-war European coalition governments). Again, under the proportionality rule, one can expect that the largest party can claim the largest spoils, and therefore can choose the biggest prize. The few deviations can be explained by presidential nomination power, by a rough equality of size between the main coalition parties, and by intra-party dissensus impeding the largest party from nominating a candidate for this office.

This points to a wider question of party unity in seeking portfolios. Case studies on factionalized parties – such as Christian Democrats in Latin countries (Blondel and Cotta, 1996; Mershon, 2001) – highlight the role of factions in distributing ministerial portfolios within parties. In addition, even in unitary parties, party leaders have to take into account a series of equilibria, in terms of the territorial background of ministers, constituency party support, gender, distribution between first and second chamber, etc. Hence, intra-party decision-making rules and constraints, and the old question of party cohesion, have entered the most recent research (Laver and Shepsle, 2000; Pennings, 2000).

Discussion

By linking the coalition formation process to the portfolio allocation process, some recent formal theories have tried to overcome the limits of the first generations of quantitative and qualitative portfolio allocation theories. This linkage is made by assuming that portfolios are all about policy, and that obtaining 'policy portfolios' rather than 'offices and their perks' is the core of the coalition bargaining process (Austen-Smith and Banks, 1990; Schofield, 1993; Laver and Shepsle, 1990, 1996). Although these theories have been empirically tested on only a few selected cases, these formal theories also introduce a variety of institutional conditions under which the policy portfolio bargaining is supposed to occur, and thus, unlike their predecessors, are not institution-blind. They include rules concerning the nomination discretion of the prime minister and the head of state, the power of the finance minister, the role of party leaders, etc. Yet, rather than equating portfolio bargaining to policy bargaining, one should keep these goals analytically separate, as parties may differ in the emphasis they put on maximizing policy, office or vote (Strøm and Müller, 1999). These disparities allow for tradeoffs between the different payoffs, which in principle should facilitate coalition formation. For instance, office-seeking parties may want to trade policy concessions to the policy-seeking parties in return for a disproportionate share of portfolios.

Moreover, a number of questions remain unanswered regarding the dependent and independent variables, the process that links them and the potential effects on coalition governance and outputs in this type of research. As far as the dependent variables are concerned, the study of the full range of relevant offices has only very recently started. Junior ministerships are often used as spare change to round off or fine-tune portfolio deals but sometimes also are considered to be policy-relevant (Mershon, 2001; Thies, 2001; Manow and Zorn, 2004). In some countries, the 'offices cake' should be extended to include the Speaker in parliament or the European Commissioner.

Although important efforts have recently been made to weight a wide range of portfolios (Druckman and Warwick, 2005), we still know little about how parties in practice weigh portfolios and which criteria they use to do so: policy relevance (Dumont, 1998), interests of traditional or new clienteles, patronage opportunities, prestige, visibility, distributive versus redistributive policy departments, goodness of fit with the qualifications of the *ministrables* available in the party, the appetite of *incontournable ministrables*, etc.). In several countries, parties or the head of state allot certain portfolios to non-partisan technocrats (De Winter, 1991; Strøm, 2000; Amorim Neto and Strøm, 2004), a practice that certainly contradicts the office-seeking drive on which most portfolio theories are based.

With regard to the policy impact of portfolio bargaining, it is also important to know when portfolio bargaining actually starts: at the end of the policy negotiations (as most research seems to suggest), or before. This question is linked to decision-making within parties. Are *ministrables* members of the negotiating teams that draft the policy agreement and bargain over portfolios? Do they help themselves to a portfolio of their liking? Does such interlocking of principal and agent, when party leaders bargain over portfolios that they themselves would like to occupy (Andeweg, 2000), allow ministers to become unaccountable policy dictators (Laver and Shepsle, 1996), in spite of the formal existence of a collective coalition agreement? To date, most empirical analyses suggest that only the allocation between parties matters with regard to policy outputs (Laver and Shepsle, 1994; Klingemann *et al.*, 1994).

POLICY FORMULATION

There are two contrasting views concerning the policy relevance of coalition negotiations (Timmermans, 2003): the 'positive' version considers the formulation of coalition agreements as a genuine opportunity for parties to influence the future government's policy agenda (Peterson *et al.*, 1983; Peterson and De Ridder, 1986); the 'sceptics' consider coalition negotiations as 'policy irrelevant', being either just a 'ritual' carried out to ease the transition from election campaign competition to inter-party governmental co-operation (Luebbert, 1986), or because the link is only conditionally relevant, that is, it is relevant only if policy proposals supported in the coalition agreement are supported by the party that receives the relevant ministerial portfolio (Laver and Shepsle, 1996: 42).

Empirical studies tend to support the positive view. In most countries, policy bargaining is the main subject of the formation negotiation process. This can be inferred from numerous indicators. First, there is a growing tendency in West-European governments to draft a government policy agreement (Müller and Strøm, forthcoming). Policy bargaining consumes most time in the bargaining process (often weeks or months), while the allocation of portfolios is settled in a few hours or days

(De Winter and Dumont, forthcoming). Apart from Italy, portfolio allocation follows the conclusion of a general agreement on policy between the parties that will constitute the next government (Budge and Laver, 1992: 415), and most formation attempts break down on policy, not on the allocation of portfolios. Coalition agreements tend to grow in length and detail, and they mostly cover substantive policy areas (Müller and Strøm, 2000). Second, coalition agreements contain issues that are salient to the member parties and for which they have formulated policy pledges, even when they disagree on the solution of such issues (Thomson, 1999). They do not focus only on non-divisive issues (Klingemann *et al.*, 1994), and when divisive ones are not mentioned in the agreement, mechanisms to deal with these during the life of the cabinet are often specified (Timmermans, 2003). But overall, during the negotiations the pledges most salient to each party tend to receive explicit attention.

Regarding their potential policy impact, although coalition agreements are never legally binding, in practice they often do bind partners strongly. In fact, these agreements usually are endorsed by the parties' main decisional body (e.g., the party congress, parliamentary party or party executive), and, as such, this endorsement legitimately binds all the other sections of the party, from the rank-and-file members to constituency party organizations, individual members of parliament and ministers, the party executive, and the party leader. The party investiture is therefore a crucial moment for making agreements stick, not only between parties but also, more importantly, within parties (De Winter *et al.*, 2000).

In most countries these coalition agreements are widely available to the general public, which expands their utility for scrutinizing government performance by party bodies, as well as by other actors, such as interest groups, the media, and retrospective voters. Coalition cabinets and parties have, in addition, set up a variety of mechanisms and rules to facilitate the smooth implementation of these agreements, to solve conflicts over the way they should be interpreted, to formulate an answer to issues not anticipated by or included in the agreement, and to amend these agreements without jeopardizing the coalition's survival.

Recent empirical research (Müller and Strøm, forthcoming) suggests that in most countries coalition agreements are central instruments for coalition policy-making. They also have an important theoretical role in the process of governance once a cabinet has been formed:

they are vital devices that make coalition government possible and help tackle some of the severe and complex bargaining problems and inherent weaknesses of coalitions, such as limited information, non-simultaneity of exchange, cyclical voting, formal ministerial discretion over departmental policy agendas, their implementation and coordination, problems of interdepartmental interdependency, shared competencies, changes in external context, etc. (Lupia and Strøm, forthcoming).

Hence, from an empirical and theoretical point of view, coalition agreements emerge as one of the main institutions that make collective coalition cabinets viable. Still the practical working of 'governing by contract' remains to a large extent a black box.[17]

CONCLUSION

The formation of a government is a crucial aspect of democratic politics, because it deals with the conquest of power and the possibility of implementing policies that have been democratically endorsed and legitimated by the voters. This field of party studies is, together with voting, probably the most mature field in party research, in terms of the variety of competing theoretical frameworks produced by scholars from different disciplines, the sophistication of statistical techniques, and the richness of available data sets. However, this high level of scientific activity has in the last decade scarcely resulted in significant comprehensive progress in explaining and predicting real-world government compositions. Models aggregating current knowledge still do not manage to predict correctly more than half of the coalitions actually formed in the real world.

The field still has several shortcomings. First, the inclusion or exclusion of explanatory variables in formal models is often determined by difficulties of operationalization rather than by theoretical coherence. Also, some crucial variables are often poorly operationalized, leading to unreliable and unstable conclusions, especially in the field of party ideological positions. There is also the problem of selection bias as the prediction success rate of composition and portfolio allocation theories differs between countries (and to a lesser extent between time periods). The goodness of fit of theories is thus conditional on the countries and time frames selected.

Furthermore, some essential components of coalition formation are traditionally neglected,

like the frequently occurring formation failures (Müller and Strøm, 2000: 570). Also we know very little about the operation of the formation process, in terms of negotiators, their autonomy *vis-à-vis* their party principals, their tactics and games, their criteria for evaluating alternative policy and portfolio proposals, the benefits of a retreat into opposition, etc. Also, political parties figure as the main actors in explaining coalition outcomes in almost all theories, while in certain systems the head of state, pressure groups, or foreign powers sometimes have a significant formal or informal veto power.

Many of the real-world formations remain theoretical puzzles, of which vital explanatory pieces are lacking (De Winter *et al.*, forthcoming). Government formation, like all politics, is conducted by human actors, but unlike studies of most other political activity (e.g., voting, political participation, legislative behavior), coalition formation theory does not pay much attention to the accounts and explanations of the human actors involved in government formations themselves. This imbalance can be redressed by 'thick' descriptions of government formations, preferably using information from participants obtained through elite interviewing, analyses of memoirs, etc. Only in this way can we try to reconstruct actors' preferences, motivations, strategies, evaluation of past experiences, anticipation of future developments, perception of the credibility of other negotiators, capacity to commit their party, and the perceived impact of formal and informal institutional constraints and veto players. However, the ultimate aim of such an inductive approach should not be the writing of a thriller reconstructing dramatic deviant formations, but to feed new explanations – discovered by thick descriptions – back into theory formulation. As such, inductive research should serve as a complement, not as an alternative, to existing formal theories that have considerably contributed to our current state of understanding of government formation.

NOTES

1. In 17 countries of post-war Europe (1945–99), more than 80% of the majority governments formed were coalition governments (Strøm *et al.*, forthcoming).
2. In the vast majority of comparative studies conducted since the early 1970s, of governments formed one third or more were minority cabinets and at most 40% were minimal winning.

3. In the 1945–99 period, roughly 80% of Western European parliamentary governments included the median legislator party on the first dimension (Strøm *et al.*, forthcoming), while two-thirds of the minority governments formed in 13 countries of post-war western Europe contained the median party on the first dimension (Müller and Strøm, 2000: 561, 564).

4. Amongst the other incentives facilitating minority governments, Strøm (1990) added legislatures with a strong committee system that allows opposition parties to have a say in legislation without carrying the electoral burden of incumbency, Kalandrakis (2004) added the (low) share of central government in total public spending, while Indridason (2004) added the lack of government opportunities for clientelism (which render parties less office-seeking).

5. While in most of the composition models discussed up until now, parties are predominantly office- and/or policy-seekers, some authors explicitly refer to their vote-seeking motivations (Strøm, 1990; Warwick, 2000, 2005; Austen-Smith and Banks, 1988; Baron, 1993; Baron and Diermeier, 2001; and especially Strøm and Müller, 1999). Although taken up by a number of scholars, the office cum policy cum voting framework has not yet been systematically tested in a quantitative, comparative way but relies on formal models or thick descriptions of a number of instances in which parties had to make particularly difficult choices between the three objectives.

6. In the 1945–99 period, of parliamentary governments in 17 western European countries (excluding cases of single-party majority governments) slightly more than one third were connected, but less than one-fifth were minimal connected winning (Strøm *et al.*, forthcoming). Martin and Stevenson (2001: 47) show that coalitions that have, according to traditional size and policy variables, the highest chances of forming actually form in the real world only 11% of the time!

7. See Grofman's (1982) protocoalition formation model, Schofield's (1993, 1995) model of the political heart, De Swaan's (1973) policy distance theory, Laver and Shepsle's (1990, 1996) winset theory on credibility proposals, etc.

8. Testing Grofman's model of protocoalition formation, a highly disaggregated 20-dimensional representation triggered better predictive rates than unidimensional models in less than half of the countries covered in Laver and Budge's (1992: 413) volume, and a two-dimensional representation was better than a unidimensional one in only one of the 11 countries studied!

9. For empirical testing, see Diermeier and Merlo (2004), Warwick (1996), and Martin and Stevenson (2001).

10. Downs (1998) also investigated whether the composition of coalitions formed at a subnational level has an effect on the formation of national-level governments.

11. Peleg (1980) introduced the concept of the 'dominant player', while Van Deemen (1991) introduced the concept of the 'central player'.

12. Van Deemen (1997) combined power indices with an actor-oriented theory when he introduced power indices in the 'power-excess' theory. Different chapters in Strøm *et al.* (forthcoming) use Banzhaf power indices and the measure of fragmentation of individual parties' shares of power to reflect bargaining complexity in coalition formation, duration, and termination.

13. Martin and Stevenson (2001) compared the predictions generated from different families of coalition theories with the coalitions that actually formed in 14 countries in roughly the 1945–85 period. They conclude that nine size- and ideology-based variables predict actually formed government compositions only 11% of the time, that adding eight pre-formation institutional factors increases the prediction success rate to 40%, while adding four post-formation variables drawn from the portfolio allocation approach predicts the correct government approximately half the time.

14. The proportionality norm is also respected when one takes the relative saliency of different ministerial portfolios into account (Warwick and Druckman, 2001, 2004; Druckman and Warwick, 2005).

15. On this debate see Warwick and Druckman (2004) and Ansolabehere *et al.* (2005).

16. On the implementation of coalition contracts, see Klingemann *et al.*, 1994; Thomson, 1999; Timmermans, 2003; Moury, 2005.

REFERENCES

Amorim Neto, Otavio and Strøm, Kaare (2004) 'Presidents, voters and non-partisan cabinet members in European parliamentary democracies', presented at the Annual Meeting of American Political Science Association, Chicago, September 2–5, 2004.

Andeweg, Rudy (2000) 'Ministers as double agents? The delegation process between cabinet and ministers', *European Journal of Political Research*, 3: 377–95.

Ansolabehere, Stephen, Snyder Jr., James M., Strauss, Aaron B. and Ting, Michael M. (2005) 'Voting weights and formateur advantages in the formation of coalition governments', *American Journal of Political Science*, 49(3): 550–63.

Austen-Smith, David, and Banks, Jeffrey S. (1988), 'Elections, coalitions and legislative outcomes', *American Political Science Review*, 82: 405–22.

Austen-Smith, David and Banks, Jeffrey S. (1990) 'Stable governments and the allocation of portfolios', *American Political Science Review*, 84: 891–906.

Axelrod, Robert (1970) *Conflict of Interest*. Chicago: Markham.

Bäck, Hanna and Dumont, Patrick (2004) 'A Combination of methods. The way forward in coalition research', presented at the Annual Meeting of American Political Science Association, Chicago, September 2–5, 2004.

Banzhaf John (1965) 'Weighted voting doesn't work: A mathematical analysis', *Rutgers Law Review*, 19: 317–43.

Baron, David P. (1993) 'Government formation and endogenous parties', *American Political Science Review*, 88: 33–47.

Baron, David and Diermeier, Daniel (2001) 'Elections, governments and parliaments in proportional representation systems', *The Quarterly Journal of Economics*, 116(3): 933–67.

Bergman, Torbjörn (1995) *Constitutional Rules and Party Goals in Coalition Formation*. Umeå: Umeå University Press.

Black, Duncan (1958) *The Theory of Committees and Elections*. Cambridge: Cambridge University Press.

Blondel, Jean and Cotta, Maurizio (1996) *Party and Government. An Inquiry into the Relationship between Governments and Supporting Parties in Liberal Democracies*. London: Macmillan.

Bogdanor, Vernon (1984) 'The government formation process in the constitutional monarchies of northwest Europe', in David Kavanagh and Gillian Peele (eds), *Comparative Government and Politics. Essays in the Honour of S.E. Finer*. London: Heinemann, pp. 49–72.

Browne, Eric C. (1973) *Coalition Theories: a Logical and Empirical Technique*. London: Sage.

Browne, Eric C. and Feste, Karen (1975) 'Qualitative dimensions of coalition payoffs', *American Behavioral Scientist*, 18: 530–56.

Browne, Eric C. and Franklin, Mark (1973) 'Aspects of coalition payoffs in European parliamentary democracies', *American Journal of Political Science*, 67: 453–69.

Budge, Ian and Farlie, Dennis (1983) *Voting and Party Competition*. London: Wiley.

Budge, Ian and Keman, Hans (1990) *Parties and Democracy. Coalition Formation and Government Functioning in Twenty States*. Oxford: Oxford University Press.

Budge, Ian and Laver, Michael (1992) 'The relationship between party and coalition policy in Europe: An empirical synthesis', in Michael Laver and Ian Budge, *Party Policy and Government Coalitions*. London: Macmillan.

Dalton, Russell (1996) 'Political cleavages, issues and electoral change' in Lawrence LeDuc, Richard Niemi and Pippa Norris (eds), *Comparing Democracies. Elections and Voting in Global Perspective*, Thousand Oaks, CA: Sage.

De Swaan, Abram (1973) *Coalition Theories and Cabinet Formation*. Amsterdam: Elsevier.

De Vries, Miranda (1999) 'Governing with your closest neighbour: An assessment of spatial coalition formation theories', PhD dissertation, University of Nijmegen.

De Winter, Lieven (1991) 'Parliamentary and party pathways to the cabinet', in Jean Blondel and Jean-Louis Thiébault, *The Profession of Government Minister in Western Europe*. London: Macmillan, pp. 44–69.

De Winter, Lieven and Dumont, Patrick (forthcoming) 'Bargaining Complexity, Formation Duration, and Bargaining Rounds' in Kaare Strøm, Wolfgang C. Müller and Torbjörn Bergman (eds), *Cabinet Governance: Bargaining and the Cycle of Democratic Politics*. Oxford: Oxford University Press.

De Winter, Lieven, Andeweg, Rudy B. and Dumont, Patrick (eds) (forthcoming) *Puzzles of Government Formation*. London: Routledge.

De Winter, Lieven, Timmermans, Arco and Dumont, Patrick (2000) 'Coalition formation and governance in Belgium: Of government gospels, evangelists, followers and traitors', in Kaare Strøm and Wolfgang Müller (eds), *Coalition Governments in Western Europe*. Oxford: Oxford University Press, pp. 300–55.

Diermeier, Daniel and Merlo, Antonio (2004) 'An empirical investigation of coalitional bargaining procedures', *Journal of Public Economics*, 88(3–4): 783–97.

Diermeier, Daniel, Eraslan, Hülya and Merlo, Antonio (2002) 'Coalition governments and comparative constitutional design', *European Economic Review*, 46: 893–907.

Diermeier, Daniel, Eraslan, Hülya and Merlo, Antonio (forthcoming) 'The effects of constitutions on coalition governments in parliamentary democracies', in Roger Congleton (ed.), *Constitutional Political Economy*. Cambridge: Cambridge University Press.

Downs, Anthony (1957) *An Economic Theory of Democracy*. New York: Harper & Row.

Downs, William (1998) *Coalition Government Subnational Style: Multiparty Politics in Europe's Regional Parliaments*. Columbus: Ohio State University Press.

Druckman, James N. and Warwick, Paul V. (2005) 'The missing piece: measuring portfolio salience in Western European parliamentary democracies', *European Journal of Political Research*, 44: 17–41.

Druckman, James, Martin, Lanny and Thies, Michael (forthcoming) 'Influence without confidence: upper chambers and government formation', *Legislative Studies Quarterly*.

Dumont, Patrick (1998) 'Keys for the analysis of the relation between parties' programmatic preferences and portfolio allocation in government formation', presented at the Joint Sessions of Workshops of the European Consortium for Political Research, Warwick, 23–28 March, 1998.

Dunleavy, Patrick and Bastow, Simon (2001) 'Modelling coalitions that cannot coalesce: a critique of the Laver-Shepsle approach', *West European Politics*, 24(1): 1–26.

Franklin, Mark and Mackie, Thomas (1983) 'Familiarity and inertia in the formation of governing coalitions in parliamentary democracies', *British Journal of Political Science*, 13: 275–98.

Gamson, William (1961) 'A Theory of Coalition Formation', *American Sociological Review*, 26: 373–82.

Gamson, William (1962) 'Coalition formation at presidential nominating conventions', *American Journal of Sociology*, 2: 157–71.

Golder, Sona (2004) 'The effect of electoral coalitions on government formation', presented at the Annual Meeting of American Political Science Association, Chicago, September 2–5, 2004.

Grofman, Bernard (1982) 'A dynamic model of protocoalition formation in ideological *n*-space', *Behavioral Science*, 27: 77–90.

Huber, John D. (1996) 'The vote of confidence in parliamentary democracies', *American Political Science Review*, 90: 269–82.

Indridason, Indridi (2004) 'Coalitions and clientelism: explaining cross-national variation in patterns of coalition formation', manuscript available at <http://www.hi.is/~ihi>, September 30, 2004.

Isaksson, Guy-Erik (2005) 'From election to government: principal rules and deviant cases', *Government and Opposition*, 40(3): 329–57.

Kalandrakis, Tasos (2004) 'Genericity of minority governments: the role of policy and office', Wallis Working Papers WP39, University of Rochester, Wallis Institute of Political Economy.

Klingemann, Hans-Dieter, Hofferbert, Richard and Budge, Ian (eds) (1994) *Parties, Policies, and Democracy*. Boulder, CO: Westview.

Lane, Jan-Erik and Ersson, Svente (1999) *Politics and Society in Western Europe*. London: Sage

Laver, Michael and Budge, Ian (1992) *Party Policy and Government Coalitions*. London: Macmillan.

Laver, Michael and Shepsle, Kenneth (1990) 'Coalitions and cabinet governance', *American Political Science Review*, 84: 873–90.

Laver, Michael and Shepsle, Kenneth (eds) (1994) *Cabinet Ministers and Parliamentary Government*. Cambridge: Cambridge University Press.

Laver, Michael and Shepsle, Kenneth (1996) *Making and Breaking Governments*. Cambridge: Cambridge University Press.

Laver, Michael and Shepsle, Kenneth (2000) 'Ministrables and government formation: Munchkins, players and big beasts in the jungle', *Journal of Theoretical Politics*, 12: 113–24.

Laver, Michael and Schofield, Norman (1990) *Multiparty Government. The Politics of Coalition in Europe*. Oxford: Oxford University Press.

Leiserson, Michael (1966) 'Coalitions in politics. A theoretical and empirical study', PhD thesis, Yale University.

Lijphart, Arend (1984) *Democracies*. New Haven, CT: Yale University Press.

Lijphart, Arend (1999) *Patterns of Democracy*. New Haven, CT: Yale University Press.

Lipset, Seymour Martin and Rokkan, Stein (1967) 'Cleavage structures, party systems, and voter alignments: an introduction', in Martin Lipset and Stein Rokkan (eds), *Party Systems and Voter Alignments. Cross-national Perspectives*. New York: Free Press.

Luebbert, Gregory (1986) *Comparative Democracy: policymaking and governing coalitions in Europe and Israel*. New York: Columbia University Press.

Lupia, Arthur and Strøm, Kaare (forthcoming) 'A theory of cabinet governance: bargaining, electoral connections, and the shadow of the future', in Kaare Strøm, Wolfgang C. Müller and Torbjörn Bergman (eds), *Cabinet Governance: Bargaining and the Cycle of Democratic Politics*. Oxford: Oxford University Press.

Manow, Philip and Zorn, Hendrik (2004) 'Office versus policy motives in portfolio allocations: the case of junior ministers', *MPLFG Discussion Paper* 04/9, available at http://www.mpi-fg-koeln.mpg.de/pu/mpifg_dp/dp04-9.pdf

Maor, Moshe (1995) 'Intra-party determinants of coalition bargaining', *Journal of Theoretical Politics*, 7: 65–91.

Martin, Lanny and Stevenson, Randolph (2001) 'Cabinet formation in parliamentary democracies', *American Journal of Political Science*, 45: 33–50.

Mattila, Mikko and Raunio, Tapio (2004) 'Does winning pay? Electoral success and government formation in 15 West European countries', *European Journal of Political Research*, 43: 263–85.

Mershon, Carol (1994) 'Expectations and informal rules in coalition formation', *Comparative Political Studies*, 27: 40–79.

Mershon, Carol (2001) 'Contending models of portfolio allocation and office payoffs to party factions: Italy, 1963–79', *American Journal of Political Science*, 45(2): 277–93.

Morelli, Massimo (1999) 'Demand competition and policy compromise in legislative bargaining', *American Political Science Review*, 93(4): 809–20.

Moury, Catherine (2005) *Coalition Government and Party's Mandate: Is the Government Bounded by the Coalition Agreement?* Dissertation, CirCap, University of Siena.

Müller, Wolfgang (2000) 'Austria: Tight coalitions and stable government', in Wolfgang Müller and Kaare Strøm (eds), *Coalition Governments in Western Europe*. Oxford: Oxford University Press.

Müller, Wolfgang and Strøm, Kaare (eds) (1999) *Policy, Office, or Votes?* Cambridge: Cambridge University Press.

Müller, Wolfgang C. and Strøm, Kaare (2000) 'Conclusion: cabinet governance in Western Europe', in Wolfgang C. Müller and Kaare Strøm (eds), *Coalition Governments in Western Europe.* Oxford: Oxford University Press, pp. 559–592.

Müller, Wolfgang C. and Strøm, Kaare (forthcoming) 'Types of coalition contracts', in Kaare Strøm, Wolfgang C. Müller and Torbjörn Bergman (eds), *Cabinet Governance: Bargaining and the Cycle of Democratic Politics.* Oxford: Oxford University Press.

Peleg, Bezalel (1980) 'A theory of coalition formation in committees', *Journal of Mathematical Economics,* 7: 115–34.

Pennings, Paul (2000) 'The consequences of ministerial recruitment for the functioning of cabinets in Western Europe', *Acta Politica,* 35: 86–103.

Peterson, Robert and De Ridder, Martine (1986) 'Government formation as a policy making arena', *Legislative Studies Quarterly,* 11: 565–81.

Peterson, Robert, De Ridder, Martine, Hobbs, John and McClellan, E.F. (1983) 'Government formation and policy formulation: Patterns in Belgium and the Netherlands', *Res Publica,* 25: 49–82.

Riker, William (1962) *The Theory of Political Coalitions.* New Haven, CT: Yale University Press.

Robertson, David (1976) *A Theory of Party Competition.* London: John Wiley & Sons.

Schofield, Norman (1993) 'Political competition and multiparty coalition governments', *European Journal of Political Research,* 23: 1–33.

Schofield, Norman (1995) 'Coalition politics: A formal model and empirical analysis', *Journal of Theoretical Politics,* 7: 245–81.

Shapley, Lloyd S. and Shubik, Martin (1954) 'A method for evaluating the distribution of power in a committee system', *American Politics Science Review,* 48: 787–92.

Strøm, Kaare (1990) *Minority Government and Majority Rule.* Cambridge: Cambridge University Press.

Strøm, Kaare (1998) 'Making and breaking governments', *Legislative Studies Quarterly,* 1: 127–43.

Strøm, Kaare (2000) 'Parties at the core of government', in Russell J. Dalton and Martin P. Wattenberg (eds), *Parties without Partisans: Political Change in Advanced Industrial Democracies.* Oxford: Oxford University Press, pp. 180–207.

Strøm, Kaare and Müller, Wolfgang (1999) 'The keys to togetherness: Coalition agreements in parliamentary democracies', *Journal of Legislative Studies,* 5: 255–82.

Strøm, Kaare and Swindle, Stephen M. (2002) 'Strategic parliamentary dissolution', *American Political Science Review,* 96: 575–91.

Strøm, Kaare, Budge, Ian and Laver, Michael (1994) 'Constraints on cabinet formation in parliamentary democracies', *American Journal of Political Science,* 38: 303–35.

Strøm, Kaare, Müller, Wolfgang C., and Bergman Torbjörn (eds) (forthcoming) *Cabinet Governance: Bargaining and the Cycle of Democratic Politics.* Oxford: Oxford University Press.

Thies, Michael F. (2001) 'Keeping tabs on partners: the logic of delegation in coalition governments', *American Journal of Political Science,* 45: 580–98.

Thomson, Robert (1999) *The Party Mandate. Election Pledges and Government Actions in the Netherlands, 1986–1998.* Thela Thesis Publishers.

Timmermans, Arco (2003) *High Politics in the Low Countries: An Empirical Study of Coalition Agreements in Belgium and the Netherlands.* Aldershot: Ashgate.

Van Deemen, Ad (1991) 'Coalition formation in centralized policy games', *Journal of Theoretical Politics,* 3: 139–61.

Van Deemen, Ad (1997) *Coalition Formation and Social Choice.* Amsterdam: Kluwer.

Von Neumann, John and Morgenstern, Oskar (1953) *Theory of Games and Economic Behavior.* Princeton, NJ: Princeton University Press.

Warwick, Paul (1996) 'Coalition government membership in West European Parliamentary democracies', *British Journal of Political Science,* 26: 471–99.

Warwick, Paul (2000) 'Policy horizons in West European parliamentary systems', *European Journal of Political Research,* 38: 37–61.

Warwick, Paul (2005) 'Do policy horizons structure the formation of parliamentary governments?: The evidence from an expert survey', *American Journal of Political Science,* 49(2): 373–87.

Warwick, Paul and Druckman, James (2001) 'Portfolio salience and the proportionality of pay-offs in coalition governments', *British Journal of Political Science,* 31: 627–49.

Warwick, Paul and Druckman, James (2004) 'The portfolio allocation paradox: an investigation into the nature of a very strong but puzzling relationship', presented at the Annual Meeting of American Political Science Association, Chicago, September 2–5, 2004.

16

PARTY PATRONAGE AND PARTY COLONIZATION OF THE STATE

Wolfgang C. Müller

INTRODUCTION

Party patronage is the use of public resources in *particularistic* and *direct* exchanges between clients and party politicians or party functionaries. Directness means that, in contrast to programmatic linkages, the parties are able to identify their clients individually and engage in a contract-like exchange relationship in which politicians provide goods and services in exchange for some kind of support. Typically, party patronage is disguised for official purposes as norm application and, indeed, many patronage acts do not violate legal norms. Yet, clients who receive public goods and services understand that their party connection has been critical for that purpose. A party connection may be essential because the bureaucracy is inefficient and unresponsive and/or because it helps to use administrative discretion to the benefit of the client, indeed, up to the point of bending the law.

A judgemental classification of some Western democracies, worked out by the author in cooperation with Herbert Kitschelt, distinguishes four categories of countries:

- No or virtually no party patronage: Denmark, Finland, Norway, and Sweden.
- Low level of party patronage: the Netherlands, Switzerland, and the UK.
- Medium level of party patronage: France, Germany, Iceland, Ireland, Luxembourg, Portugal, Spain and the USA.
- High level of party patronage: Austria, Belgium, Greece, and Italy.

Although there are relevant differences between the countries within each group, this ordering is alphabetical and not an attempt to assign rank order.

THE BENEFITS OF CLIENTS

A number of client benefits have been identified in the international literature on party patronage. They can be located on a continuum between incentive and compulsion. In the first case, the client receives something of value to him, in the latter case the client is protected from some negative event. Often, the patron not only is able to prevent negative events but also can make them more likely to occur in the case of disobedience. The following discussion moves from the least coercive to the most coercive of these exchanges.

There are non-material and material patronage goods. Among the first ones is *know-how*, especially for dealing with authorities. If the bureaucratic requirements for claiming public services are highly formalized, complicated, and tedious, and therefore difficult for the 'ordinary' citizen to cope with, the intermediary role of delegates and party functionaries may consist solely of putting through their rightful claims. It is also possible, however, for these professional intermediaries, backed up by the power of a party, to expand illicitly the interpretation of the conditions for allocating services. In this case, the patronage resource is no longer know-how concerning access to government services, but the services themselves.

Non-material status improvements (such as titles or knighthoods) are another benefit often exchanged in patronage relations (Blondel and Cotta, 1996, 2000).

Material patronage goods cover a wide range. Until the late 1950s, packets of macaroni were still distributed in Italian election campaigns to 'persuade' the recipients (Zuckerman, 1979). Most material patronage resources are, however, rather more subtle (Mühlmann and Llayora, 1968: 32; Chubb, 1982: 11ff). *Public money* is used directly in various ways: *grants, subsidies, government contracts, tax reliefs,* and *sponsored credits.* Handing out the money can take different forms, from administrative decisions to tailor-made pork barrel legislation. Another resource is *licences,* e.g. for practising certain professions or businesses. Such a licence grants entry to some partly protected sector of the economy and hence provides the holder with a relatively safe income. In many countries *public housing* is a classic patronage resource (Higgins, 1982: 172–3; Chubb, l982: 172–3; Müller, 1989). Yet, the most important patronage resource may be *jobs* in the public sector. Two forms of 'job patronage' can be distinguished: service patronage and power patronage (Eschenburg, 1961). *Service patronage* refers to employment or promotion in exchange for the client's loyalty outside his or her job. *Power patronage* refers to the allocation of important positions. The decisive question in selecting personnel is what the client, once appointed, will be able and willing to do for the party.

The above suggests that the greater the public sector, the greater is the potential for patronage. This is true. However, shrinking the public sector leads to enormous increases in patronage resources in the short term. If privatization is carried out according to considerations of patronage rather than efficiency, the parties in charge of making these decisions have greater patronage resources than their predecessors, in effect being able to use the 'capital' of the public sector for patronage, where their predecessors, in maintaining the public sector, could only use 'the interest'. Industrial privatization in the former Soviet Union and Eastern Europe often seems to have followed that logic and the political relations of potential buyers of public sector property seem to have been important in Western European countries, as well (Feigenbaum *et al.*, 1998). Such deals have the potential of generating enormous kickbacks for the parties in charge of making the decisions. At the same time privatization can also undermine existing patronage relations

(e.g. those between public sector employees and their parties). This is not an inconsistency in party strategy, as the parties carrying out privatizations typically are different from the ones that hold party sector strongholds.

Finally, patronage can also be used for the purpose of *waiving administrative penalties.* Opportunities for imposing such penalties nearly always exist. By having patronage a client can get around them. Government parties abuse public authority not for bribing firms to contribute to their resources, but forcing them to do so. Firms that do not contribute run the risk of being *excluded* from all kinds of government contracts. Rather than providing 'preferential treatment' for party donors, non-donors are punished, e.g. for not observing environmental standards or safety regulations, and thorough inspections by the tax authorities (see Chubb, 1982). Italy and France come close to the coercion solution (Ruggiero, 1996; Nelken, 1996). The business contributions to party finance, as revealed, for instance, in the *Tangentopoli* scandal, have more resemblance to a tax imposed on the firms than to voluntary bargains.

BENEFITS OF THE PARTIES

Political parties, party factions, and individual politicians expect the following pay-offs from patronage: votes, labour, money, strategic flexibility, and policy-making capacity.

Votes

The simplest expectation in patronage relations is that the clients vote for the party that has provided the goods or services. Provided the electoral institutions allow, votes can be more narrowly targeted to factions or individual politicians (Golden, 2003). Note, however, that policing the deal is difficult for the party (Warner, 1997). This problem can be solved if the party manages to make their patronage relations a social exchange that creates the feeling of belonging (Eisenstadt and Roniger, 1984; Guterbock, 1980). Alternatively, the party can use proxies for the electoral loyalty of its clients, such as their participation in elections (provided that there are not suitable alternatives) or use institutional remedies (Müller, 2006), though this is not always possible. Political parties may therefore be better off concentrating on other potential benefits of patronage relations.

Labour and money

Political parties can tend to confine their patronage to party members and hence provide incentives for enrolment. Dues-paying members, in turn, provide the party with financial resources. Some members become activists who also devote labour to the party. Many parties critically depend on the work of activists for maintaining their mass organization and conducting campaigns. Yet, from the point of view of the party, labour and money, to some extent, can serve as substitutes for one another (Strøm, 1990). Therefore, party patronage never was confined to the masses of the lower social strata. While patronage for businesses is unlikely to tie great numbers of voters to the party or fill its ranks of activists, monetary returns can be used for buying professional services such as opinion polls, political consulting, and television spots on the market which, in turn, are designed to help boosting the party's electoral performance (Wolfinger, 1972: 393).

Strategic flexibility

Party activists typically have some influence on the course of their party, either via intra-party democracy or via the law of anticipated reaction, i.e. their capacity to withhold vital resources such as their financial and labour contributions. How much activists are likely to indeed exercise their power, however, varies and partly depends on the types of compensation they receive for their work. Party activists who are mainly motivated by their ideological commitments and their policy expectations typically will insist on the party taking these positions (Schlesinger, 1984). Party leadership initiatives that are not in agreement with these views will meet with their resistance and will often be watered down or delayed. Party activists who are primarily socially motivated, in turn, are likely to resist organizational reforms that upset their 'club life'. In contrast, activists who are primarily patronage-motivated will impose fewer constraints on the party's flexibility in terms of policy and organizational innovation as long as their compensation is not in jeopardy. Yet, exclusively patronage-motivated activists are likely to be less reliable in hard times for the party, when rewards are not around the next corner.

Policy-making capacity

As already indicated, political parties can increase their policy-making capacity by exercising patronage. Although money can buy all kinds of know-how, real-world parties use their funds mostly for the expertise required for running their organization and electoral campaigns. The bulk of expertise required for policy-making, however, comes from people on the public payroll. In spoils systems such as the USA, political parties can temporarily fill a thick layer of positions with policy-making capacity with their adherents. In such cases party patronage is overt and part of the system's normal working. Yet, administrative systems built almost exclusively on a professional civil service with a merit system are not necessarily free from patronage. In many Western European systems (Austria, Belgium, and Italy traditionally stand out) political parties have used every opportunity to fill the ranks of the civil service with their adherents. By planting their trustees in the administration and the public sector more generally, political parties can make their policies better informed and smooth their implementation, a strategy labelled power patronage above.

Power patronage, of course, violates the idea of bureaucratic neutrality, but it is in tune with an extensive interpretation of the idea of party government (Katz, 1986). However, these appointments may turn out to be an obstacle to party government if they are permanent and government power passes from one party or coalition to another. Partisan civil servants are not only important as faithful implementers when their party is in office. When it is out of office they may act as party spies, keeping their political masters informed about the inner life of government. They may also try to use their influence to block, delay, or water down what are, from their party's point of view, particularly undesirable policies. Finally, in a system that claims to be based on merit and recruits top administrators out of the lower civil servant ranks, it is important for political parties that come to office to have some of their adherents waiting in the wings so that they have suitable candidates when top positions become vacant.

In recent years the classic merit system has been augmented by new public management (NPM) methods. Under the NPM model, administrators have fixed goals in terms of outputs or outcomes. As goal achievement is the criterion for the evaluation of their performance (Lane, 2000; Peters and Pierre, 2001), there should be little room for patronage. Yet, the goals cannot always be stated so clearly that performance evaluation becomes mechanical. If the performance of the administrators is subject to interpretation by the incumbent politicians, patronage rather than efficiency may be the result. Rather than making appointments more rational from a system perspective, NPM techniques may ease making them according to party needs. NPM civil servants with short-term contracts may generally be more willing to help in raising patronage resources than the members of an old-fashioned merit bureaucracy with permanent appointments.

While party patronage is openly recognized under the US spoils system, appointments under the other systems can be made in a partisan manner but disguised as merit or technocratic. A qualitative assessment of Western European parliamentary democracies suggests that partisanship has no relevance for making civil service appointments in only five countries (Denmark, Finland, Ireland, the Netherlands, and Norway) while in Sweden and the UK it affects the appointment of top officials only (Strøm et al., 2003). In the remaining countries political parties have entrenched themselves in the bureaucracy more broadly. In the most clientelist systems – Austria, Belgium, and Italy – relevant civil service appointments are routinely made with a strong partisan bias.

With regard to the judicial branch of government, party patronage seems to be less widespread and less consequential, if the silence of the literature can be taken as a valid indicator. There is, however, considerable party patronage in appointing judges who have to settle political disputes in some systems. Thus, constitutional judges in France, Austria, and Germany, and Supreme Court judges in the USA are typically selected on the basis of their party adherence. Parties certainly hope that their appointees will help their cause in the case of conflicting interpretations of the constitution. Yet, this is not always the case as the design of the appointment procedure may favour candidates who are acceptable to other parties and the judges themselves tend to be concerned about their professional reputation.

Maintaining the patronage system

While public sector jobs are an important patronage resource themselves, it is also important to consider the indirect effects of making patronage appointments to these jobs. Bureaucrats and public sector managers control a wealth of other resources that can be used in party patronage. Having party comrades appointed to relevant positions, parties will often find it easy to get civil servants to do them a 'favour' and to provide resources required for patronage. Using public resources for party or personal purposes should be easiest under the spoils model. After all, politicians and officials share the bonds of co-partisanship, and if patronage has the intended effects it will help to keep both of them in office. The more the merit system de facto has been turned into a party patronage system, the more we can expect civil servants to apply political criteria in their decisions (Della Porta and Vannucci, 1996: 357–62).

SYSTEMIC CONSEQUENCES OF PATRONAGE

Finally, what are the system effects of party patronage? Without claiming completeness, the following effects can be identified.

Political and social integration

Beginning with Merton (1968: 127–9), functional perspectives have identified potentially beneficial effects of party patronage. Accordingly, parties that exercise patronage 'fulfill existing needs somewhat more effectively' than the official structure. 'In our prevailing impersonal society' a patronage party, the machine, 'fulfills the important social function of humanizing and personalizing all manner of assistance to those in need' and provides help for the 'deprived classes'. It also provides alternative channels of social mobility. In that vein patronage has been characterized as a way of integrating split societies (cf. Scott, 1972). In this sense, the proportional patronage of the immediate post-war period in Austria is a case in point. It undoubtedly contributed to the integration of the 1934 civil war opponents and the reintegration of the former Nazis in the political system. Although party patronage violated the classical concept of a 'neutral' or 'nonpartisan' bureaucracy, it led to a civil service and an army which for the first time in modern Austrian history incorporated both major political subcultures and were thus fully acceptable to both major subcultures (Secher, 1958: 807). Yet, patronage systems have the inherent tendency to develop towards less desirable consequences (Piattoni, 2001). It is often argued in the literature that patronage undermines horizontal social relations. Instead of class and status solidarity, the vertical patron–client relationship dominates and clients see other people merely as rivals for patronage benefits (see Banfield, 1958; Belloni *et al.*, 1979: 272; Graziano, 1973: 5; Higgins, 1982: 133; Mühlmann and Llayora, 1968: 33). This characterization is most accurate for the classic patron–client relationship (e.g. landlord–peasant). Yet, it is also of relevance for 'democratized' patronage through political parties, as 'democratization' always needs to remain incomplete in a patronage system. Maintaining the effectiveness of the patronage system means that the parties must refrain from levelling social dependencies and inequalities (Belloni *et al.*, 1979: 268).

Economic inefficiency

Once parties subscribe to a patronage strategy, it tends to develop a strong dynamic of its own, constantly drawing in new areas until a patronage system exists (cf. Eschenburg, 1961: 24). There is wide consensus in the literature that party patronage is expensive and economically inefficient. Where state activity is determined by patronage this tends to result in a bloated civil service. Patronage also inflates demands and hence, in order to keep its effects constant, its costs increase over time (Belloni *et al.*, 1979; Caciagli and Belloni, 1981). Patronage leads to overinvestment in those goods that are required as a means in patronage exchanges (Weingast *et al.*, 1981; Brosio, 1988; Golden, 2002). Positions created or allocated on the basis of patronage are often superfluous and the relevant appointments suboptimal; public funds distributed (primarily) on patronage criteria are often of only very limited value in achieving the nominal goal (cf. Scott, 1969).

Systemic corruption

Party patronage violates the ideal of bureaucratic rationality and undermines central constitutional principles such as equality before the law (cf. Eschenburg, 1961; Armin, 1980).[1]

Populist backlash

Unjustified preferential treatment of individuals and firms, economic inefficiency, a bloated public sector, and the resulting consequences of high taxation and/or increasing public debt are likely to outrage citizens. Of course, those citizens who bear the costs of a patronage system but have no advantage have every reason to turn against it. Yet, even recipients of party patronage are likely to join the protest, provided that they have received their share, and new patronage to other clients is likely to diminish the relative value of the goods they have received (e.g., additional licences make new competitors, public housing given to immigrants devalues their housing rights). Hence, patronage systems include the germ of populist protest. Indeed, the western European countries with the highest levels of party patronage have the strongest populist parties, the rise of which owes much to their targeting of party patronage and corruption (Kitschelt, 2000). What is less clear, however, is whether these parties are more interested in abolishing the system or getting their share.

THE FUTURE OF PARTY PATRONAGE

As time passes, party patronage changes both in scope and form. The literature on mass patronage in Western democracies generally suggests that it has been in decline in recent decades (Theobald, 1983). For one thing, mass patronage comes under pressure from the resource side. Mass patronage is expensive and inflationary. Yet, today's decision-makers are increasingly confronted with budget constraints and forced to look for economically efficient solutions. Likewise, privatization removes a great number of jobs and other patronage resources from the public sector. On the demand side we see that the market increasingly offers substitutes to the goods traded by political actors in mass patronage deals and that an increasing proportion of the citizens are able to purchase these goods there and hence no longer depend on patronage exchange.

With the decline of party identification (Dalton, 2004), it has become much more difficult to construct patronage deals as *social exchange*. Anecdotal evidence such as the apparently increasing number of party finance scandals (Ridley and Doig, 1995; Della Porta and Mény, 1997; Della Porta and Pizzorno, 1996; Rhodes, 1997; Ruggiero, 1996; de Sousa, 2001) suggests that a shift from mass patronage to deals with business entrepreneurs is occurring in Western democracies (e.g. Moss, 1995). This shift is causally related not only to the changes affecting patronage deals but also to changes in political organization and campaigning. Money has turned out to be the most valuable resource in (the permanent) campaign, given the large markets of voters without any party attachment. As a consequence patronage may place itself more clearly under the label of political corruption than traditionally was the case.

NOTE

1 Note that the countries placed in the same patronage category in this chapter show considerable variation in terms of perceived corruption according to the Corruption Perception Index (CPI) of Transparency International. Likewise, countries with similar levels of perceived corruption are classified as displaying quite different levels of corruption. Given the CPI's heavy reliance on the images of corruption in various countries as held by international businessmen, it is not a good proxy for mass patronage.

REFERENCES

Armin, Hans Herbert von (1980) *Ämterpatronage durch politische Parteien.* Wiesbaden: Karl-Bräuer-Institut des Bundes der Steuerzahler.

Banfield, Edward C. (1958) *The Moral Basis of a Backward Society.* New York: Free Press.

Belloni, Frank, Caciagli, Mario, and Liborio, Mattina (1979) 'The Mass Clientelism Party: The Christian, Democratic Party in Catania and in Southern Italy', *European Journal of Political Research,* 7: 235–75.

Blondel, Jean and Cotta, Maurizio (eds) (1996) *Party and Government.* Basingstoke: Macmillan.

Blondel, Jean and Cotta, Maurizio (eds) (2000) *The Nature of Party Government.* Basingstoke: Macmillan.

Brosio, Giorgio (1988) 'Patronage and bureaucratic efficiency', *European Journal of Political Economy,* 4(extra issue): 95–104.

Caciagli, Mario and Belloni, Frank P. (1981) 'The new clientelism in southern Italy: The Christian Democratic Party in Catania', in S.N. Eisenstadt and René Lemarchand (eds), *Political Clientelism, Patronage and Development.* Beverly Hills, CA: Sage.

Chubb, Judith (1982) *Patronage, Power and Poverty in Southern Italy.* Cambridge: Cambridge University Press.

Dalton, Russell J. (2004) *Democratic Challenges, Democratic Choices. The Erosion of Political Support in Advanced Industrial Democracies.* Oxford: Oxford University Press.

De Sousa, Luís (2001) 'Political parties and corruption in Portugal', *West European Politics,* 24(1): 157–80.

Della Porta, Donatella and Mény, Yves (eds) (1997) *Democracy and Corruption in Europe.* London: Pinter.

Della Porta, Donatella and Pizzorno, Alessandro (1996) 'The business politicians: reflections from a study of political corruption', *Journal of Law and Society,* 23: 113–31.

Della Porta, Donatella and Vannucci, Alberto (1996) 'Controlling political corruption in Italy: What did not work, what can be done', *Res Publica,* 38: 352–68.

Derlien, Hans-Ulrich (1991) 'Regierungswechsel, Regimewechsel und Zusammensetzung der politisch-administrativen Elite', *Leviathan,* Sonderheft 12: 253–70.

Eisenstadt, S.N. and Roniger, L. (1984) *Patrons, Clients and Friends,* Cambridge: Cambridge University Press.

Eschenburg, Theodor (1961) *Ämterpatronage.* Stuttgart: Curt E. Schwab.

Feigenbaum, Harvey, Henig, Jeffrey, and Hamnett, Chris (1998) *Shrinking the State. The Political Underpinnings of Privatization.* Cambridge: Cambridge University Press.

Golden, Miriam A. (2002) 'Does globalization reduce corruption? Some political consequences of economic integration', Prepared for the conference on Globalization and Egalitarian Redistribution, Santa Fe Institute, May 17–19.

Golden, Miriam A. (2003) 'Electoral connections: The effects of the personal vote on political patronage, bureaucracy and legislation in postwar Italy', *British Journal of Political Science,* 33: 189–212.

Graziano, Luigi (1973) 'Patron–client relationships in Southern Italy', *European Journal of Political Research,* 1: 3–34.

Guterbock, Thomas M. (1980) *Machine Politics in Transition.* Chicago: University of Chicago Press.

Higgins, Michael D. (1982) 'The limits of clientelism', in Christopher Clapham (ed.), *Private Patronage and Public Policy.* London: Croom Helm.

Katz, Richard S. (1986) 'Party government: A rationalistic conception', in Francis G. Castles and Rudolf Wildenmann (eds), *Visions and Realities of Party Government.* Berlin: de Gruyter.

Kitschelt, Herbert (2000) 'Citizens, politicians, and party cartellization: Political representation and state failure in post-industrial democracies', *European Journal of Political Research,* 37: 149–79.

Lane, Jan-Erik (2000) *New Public Management.* London: Routledge.

Merton, Robert K. (1968) *Social Theory and Social Structure.* New York: Free Press.

Moss, David (1995) 'Patronage revisited: The dynamics of information and reputation', *Journal of Modern Italian Studies,* 1: 58–93.

Mühlmann, W.E. and Llayora, R.J. (1968). *Klientschaft, Klientel und Klientelsystem in einer sizilianischen Agro-Stadt.* Tübingen: Mohr.

Müller, Wolfgang C. (1989) 'Party patronage in Austria', in Anton Pelinka and Fritz Plasser (eds), *The Austrian Party System.* Boulder, CO: Westview.

Müller, Wolfgang C. (2006) 'Political institutions and linkage strategies', in Herbert Kitschelt and Steven I. Wilkinson (eds), *Patrons or Policies? Citizen–Politician Linkages in Democratic Politics*. Cambridge: Cambridge University Press.

Nelken, David (1996) 'A legal revolution?', in S. Gundle and S. Parker (eds), *The New Italian Republic*. London: Routledge.

Peters, B. Guy and Pierre, Jon (eds) (2001) *Politicians, Bureaucrats, and Administrative Reform*. London: Routledge.

Piattoni, Simona (ed.) (2001) *Clientelism, Interests, and Democratic Representation*. Cambridge: Cambridge University Press.

Rhodes, Martin (1997) 'Financing party politics in Italy: A case of systemic corruption', *West European Politics*, 20(1): 54–80.

Ridley, F.F. and Doig, Alan (eds) (1995) *Sleaze*. Oxford: Oxford University Press.

Ruggiero, Vincenzo (1996) 'France: Corruption as resentment', *Journal of Law and Society*, 23: 113–31.

Schlesinger, Joseph A. (1984) 'On the theory of party organization', *Journal of Politics*, 46: 369–400.

Scott, James C. (1969) 'Corruption, machine politics and political change', *American Political Science Review*, 63: 1142–58.

Scott, James C. (1972) *Comparative Political Corruption*. Englewood Cliffs, NJ: Prentice Hall.

Secher, Herbert P. (1958) 'Coalition government: The case of the Second Republic', *American Political Science Review*, 52: 791–809.

Strøm, Kaare (1990) 'A behavioral theory of competitive political parties'. *American Journal of Political Science*, 34: 565–98.

Strøm, Kaare, Müller, Wolfgang C. and Bergman, Torbjörn (eds) (2003) *Delegation and Accountability in Parliamentary Democracies*. Oxford: Oxford University Press.

Theobald, Robin (1983) 'The decline of patron–client relations in developed societies', *Archives Européennes de Sociologie*, 24: 136–47.

Warner, Carol M. (1997) 'Political parties and the opportunity costs of patronage', *Party Politics*, 3: 533–48.

Weingast, Barry R., Shepsle, Kenneth A. and Johnsen, Christopher (1981) 'The political economy of benefits and costs: A neoclassical approach to distributive politics', *Journal of Political Economy*, 89: 642–64.

Wolfinger, Raymond E. (1972) 'Why political machines have not withered away and other revisionist thoughts', *Journal of Politics*, 34: 365–98.

Zuckerman, Alan (1979). *The Politics of Faction*. New Haven, CT: Yale University Press.

17

EXCEPTIONALISM IN THE UNITED STATES

Nicol C. Rae

In advanced democracies party government is the norm. A party or a coalition of parties in the legislature forms a cabinet responsible to the lower house. Legislators from the governing party (or parties) in turn have incentives in terms of reelection, career and policy goals to sustain the government in office. At election time the government is held accountable as voters vote for or against the candidates of the governing party (or parties). This in a nutshell is the theory of 'responsible party government' (Ranney, 1982). Organized and disciplined mass party organizations provide the policies and the personnel for the executive, sustain the government in the legislature, and structure the vote at election time, thereby allowing the public to hold the government to account.

Party government has been elusive in the United States, however. This is partly due to the American 'presidential' system of separation of executive and legislative powers that makes party government difficult or even impossible. The organizational weakness of American parties also impairs their role as electoral vehicles for democratic accountability. This weakness, moreover, is due to a deep-rooted hostility to political parties in American political culture. This attitude, combined with the peculiar circumstances of America's socio-economic development in the 19th century, explains the failure of European style 'mass parties' (Duverger, 1964) to develop in the United States.

Each of these factors will now be discussed in order to account for the relative absence of party as a governing institution in America.

A SEPARATED SYSTEM OF GOVERNMENT

Party government requires that governmental power be concentrated so that it can be totally controlled by a party or coalition and that party or coalition be held accountable in its entirety to the legislature and ultimately to the voters. Thus in the parliamentary systems that predominate in most modern democracies, the legislative and executive branches are joined by the device of an executive cabinet of ministers chosen from and accountable to the legislature.

Wary of the potential for the 'tyranny of the majority' on the part of the democratically elected House of Representatives or an authoritarian president, the framers of the American constitution took some pains to ensure that the legislative and executive branches were elected separately rather than the one being effectively chosen by the other. These constitutionally separated institutions, moreover, shared most of the significant governmental powers in an elaborate system of checks and balances that also provided for a second chamber or Senate with special powers over foreign policy and presidential appointments, and a Supreme Court with the power of judicial review.

The framers of the US constitution did not think highly of 'parties', which they equated with 'factions' or interest groups rather than governing institutions (Madison, Federalist 51: see Hamilton *et al.*, 1961), and the governmental system they devised effectively precludes the kind of party government outlined above. The president, Senate and House of

Representatives are separately elected and at different times. Federalism, with important powers reserved to the state governments, sets another barrier against concentrated party government in the USA.

Although the American presidential system thus makes party government difficult, the political parties are the only American political institutions that can bridge the separation of powers, no matter how imperfectly. And despite the framers' disdain, political parties formed as early as the 1790s: the Federalists led by John Adams and Alexander Hamilton, and the Jeffersonians led by Jefferson and Madison (Goodman, 1975). This rudimentary party system proved to be short-lived, but as the franchise was extended to cover most adult white males – the world's first mass electorate – by the mid-1820s, so more permanent political parties arrived on the scene to structure mass electoral choice.

The archetypal American parties formed around presidential elections and the candidacy of General Andrew Jackson, frontiersman, military hero, and spokesman for a mass constituency of farmers, laborers, and artisans that distrusted the commercially oriented federal government. After being robbed of the presidency in the electoral college in 1824, Jackson and his supporters (principally campaign manager Martin Van Buren, the father of American political parties) decided to short-circuit the electoral college (where it was intended that citizens vote for electors from their state worthy to choose a president) by putting forward 'slates' of electors committed to vote for Jackson, and creating a national political organization to rally Jackson's voters behind those slates on election day (Ceaser, 1979). This national political organization became the Democratic Party, and the formation of the American two-party system was completed when Jackson's opponents coalesced to form the Whig party by 1840.

THE RISE OF THE AMERICAN PARTY SYSTEM

During the mid- to late 19th century it often appeared that American political parties had overcome the constitutional barriers and achieved party government. On closer inspection the 19th-century American parties were fundamentally less concerned with governing than with using government at all levels to reward their supporters and keep themselves in being organizationally. Yet voters undoubtedly identified with these parties and came to the polls to support them at levels astonishing by today's standards (Silbey, 1994).

The Jacksonian era party system established a framework for American national parties that in many aspects persists to this day. The Democrat and Whig parties were alliances of pro- or anti-Jackson state organizations and they remained highly decentralized organizationally. This was hardly surprising since the level of government that was most significant to most 19th-century Americans was state and local government. This is also where most of the patronage that kept the party machines in business was available. The sole manifestation of a national party was the quadrennial national party convention (pioneered by the obscure Anti-Masonic Party in 1828) composed of state delegations selected by state party leaders to nominate presidential and vice-presidential candidates.

Although the Democrats and Whigs reflected genuine regional, socioeconomic, ethnic, and policy differences, they were hardly ideological parties. When the Jacksonian Democrats took power they thought it legitimate to divide the 'spoils' of victory among their followers who had hitherto felt excluded from the American political system. The Whigs adopted a similar attitude. Both political parties constructed formidable local and state party machines on the basis of jobs and political favors for the machines' supporters in exchange for votes (Silbey, 1994). By necessity these organizations were well organized and disciplined, even if the national parties as a whole were highly decentralized. With livelihoods at stake, the voters' motivation to become involved with parties and campaigns was greatly enhanced.

The political upheaval and national trauma of the Civil War era did not disrupt the pattern, except for the disintegration of the Whig Party and its eventual replacement by the more clearly anti-slavery Republican Party: the last time a third party supplanted a major party in the USA. Yet third parties, although invariably quickly suppressed by the cruel electoral logic of the plurality voting system, have played a critical role in American political history by channeling political protest into the electoral arena and acting as harbingers of change in the electoral/political order (Sundquist, 1983).

The American party system reached its zenith in the post-civil war period (1865–96). The two national parties – Democrats and Republicans – were remarkably evenly matched, with presidential elections being decided by very narrow margins in both the electoral and popular vote. Election turnouts reached their highest levels in American history, and the US federal government came close to genuine party government. Yet these 'governments' were not led from the presidency (which remained in a generally weakened position during the period) but from the House of Representatives under the rigid party discipline imposed by Speakers Thomas B. Reed (1889–91 and 1895–99) and Joseph G. Cannon (1903–11). Indeed Woodrow Wilson, the most prominent congressional scholar of the time, envisaged the strong speakership evolving into a 'Westminster-style' parliamentary system (Wilson, 1981).

State and local level party machines continued to dominate as the spoils system reached new heights in the era of *laissez-faire*, rapid industrialization and urbanization (Ostrogorski, 1982). The onset of mass immigration also provided a new source of electoral support for machine politics. The continued weakness of the presidency was more or less guaranteed by the bosses' control of the national party conventions, where their criteria for the selection of a nominee – offend no significant section of the party, deliver federal patronage if elected, and on no account challenge the basis of the patronage system – guaranteed a succession of mediocre and ineffectual occupants of the White House.

As in the Jacksonian system, party differences were grounded in regionalism, religion, and ethnicity – North/South, immigrants/WASPs, Protestant/Catholic – rather than doctrine. As national entities the American parties still possessed only an ephemeral existence in presidential election years. Despite powerful machines at the state and local levels and occasional strong party leadership in Congress, these parties little resembled the great mass ideological organizations budding contemporaneously in Europe. And this failure of the mass organized political party and its founding ideology – socialism – to take root remains key to understanding American exceptionalism in party development.

THE ANTI-PARTY CENTURY: 1900–2000

A backlash against strong political parties and party machines arose in the first decade of the 20th century that effectively locked American

political parties into a totally divergent pattern of political development from their European counterparts.

Anti-partisan sentiments aroused by short-term factors during the Progressive era (1900–20) resonated with deeply-rooted themes in US political culture. Suspicion of parties or any large concentration of political power had always been intrinsic to the American political tradition. The Lockean liberalism that inspired the American revolution focused on the rights of individuals as opposed to collective organizations. Classical Republican themes in the framers' writings, moreover, equated parties with factions: selfish interests that would seek to control government for their own ends and thus were a threat to Republican virtue (Madison, Federalist 10). The evolution of the framers' aristocratic republic into a mass democracy (Wood, 1992) necessitated the development of political parties to structure mass electoral preferences, inform and organize the mass electorate, and provide electoral accountability. The evolution of these parties into alliances of blatantly corrupt and self-interested state and local political machines, however, made the framers' warning relevant again – particularly to the educated, professional, middle-class that constituted the core of the Progressive movement (Hofstadter, 1955).

The social fallout from rapid industrialization – overcrowded cities, disease, monopoly capitalism, exploitation of farmers and laborers – engendered a multifaceted reform movement that sought a greater role for government in regulation of the economy and social reform. America's emergence as a world power also made reform of an inefficient and outdated governmental system even more imminent. Modern industrial society demanded a more extensive and professional government manned by educated bureaucrats with qualifications rather than the placemen of the party machines (Hofstadter, 1955). Starting with the 1883 Pendleton Act, reforms of the civil service at federal, state, and local levels gradually removed from political appointments thousands of patronage jobs that constituted the lifeblood of the political machines. The ending of mass immigration in 1924 also dried up the constant supply of poor immigrants on whom the machines had relied for electoral support. The advent of government welfare benefits superseded the minimal welfare functions that the machines had performed for some of their loyal supporters.

Aside from these long-term factors, the parties also came under direct assault from progressive reformers who saw them, correctly, as the principal vehicle by which corruption, voter intimidation, and electoral fraud entered into American politics. In their zeal to extirpate these malign influences, reformers at the state and local levels fought for the adoption of a state-provided, secret electoral ballot, and official voter registration to eliminate fraud. At the state level they introduced the initiative, referendum, and recall to circumvent machine-dominated state government and even prohibited party labels from appearing on local government ballots altogether in many areas (Hofstadter, 1955).

The most significant of the Progressive reforms, however, was the introduction of the direct primary election, a peculiarly American political device that removes from the party organization even the ability to select its own candidates. Of course that was the whole point of the reform: to take control over party nominations away from the corrupt state and local party leaders and instead have the voters choose party nominees for office in a formal election either among all voters voting in the primary of their choice or limited to those voters who indicated a particular partisan preference on registration. The primary had the additional benefit of providing some electoral choice in the many areas of the USA where one party overwhelmingly predominated.

The primary soon became almost universal at all electoral levels below the presidential. Party bosses were still sufficiently powerful in the major states to control national convention delegations and they controlled presidential selection for at least another half-century. In most states the machines were also sufficiently powerful to organize themselves for a primary election, and the difference in party control of American politics was not immediately apparent.

The long term effect of the primary however would be to undermine traditional party organizations, as the reformers intended. Walter Dean Burnham (1982) has demonstrated that a long-term decline in electoral turnout and participation in the USA began during the progressive era and has continued to the present interrupted only by a temporary revival following the New Deal. During the 20th century the great state and local party machines gradually eroded as their lifeblood, governmental patronage, evaporated due to civil service reform, and their underprivileged electoral constituencies moved up the socioeconomic scale or found other means of subsistence. The last of the great party bosses, Mayor Richard J. Daley

of Chicago, died in 1976, and his formidable Democratic political organization did not survive him.

The University of Michigan surveys of the American electorate in the 1950s (Campbell *et al.*, 1960) found that levels of voter identification with the parties were still high and that most Americans approached politics through the prism of a partisan identity, and voted straight party tickets. By the early 1970s, however, levels of party identification had dropped precipitously, with an increasing number of voters becoming independents, a drop in the intensity of identification among identifiers, and an increasing voter propensity to split their party tickets (Nie *et al.*, 1979).

The electoral consequence was divided partisan control of the national government. In the half century between 1950 and 2000 Washington experienced 32 years of divided partisan control between Congress and the presidency and only 18 years of single-party control. In part this was due to the breakdown in partisan affiliations in the electorate mentioned above. The nature of the presidency and the membership of Congress, however, also evolved in a less partisan direction over the course of the 20th century.

The growth in the scope and extent of presidential power paralleled the slow decline of the major political parties. The decentralized nature of the traditional American parties and the key role played by state and local party bosses militated against strong national leadership in the presidency, as demonstrated by the nondescript presidents the bosses nominated during the late 19th-century heyday of American political parties. By the early 20th century the expectations of the office had changed as a result of America's emergence as a world power and the new demands for strong national leadership for social and political reform and to regulate business. The tumult of the Progressive era produced two remarkably assertive presidents – Theodore Roosevelt and Woodrow Wilson – whose political strength came less from their partisan affiliation than from a direct popular appeal made possible by the new mass political media engendered by the telegraph, and advances in literacy and printing technology (Tulis, 1987).

While the bosses still controlled the presidential nominating process, they could no longer afford to select presidents who did not appear to possess the basic competence to perform a much expanded governmental role at home and abroad. The incompatibility of the modern presidency and the traditional party system was made glaringly apparent by the

New Deal. Franklin Roosevelt originally hoped that he could use the Democratic Party as his vehicle to expand the role of the federal government in economic and social policy. As the New Deal became more radical, however, FDR encountered resistance from conservative southern Democrats and some urban machine bosses. The failure of FDR's attempt to 'purge' dissident Democrats in 1938 by campaigning openly to defeat them in the 1938 primaries convinced him that he would have to rely on the office of the presidency alone as his governing instrument. Thus Roosevelt and his successors increasingly disregarded the apparently outmoded parties and utilized the Executive Office of the Presidency (established in 1940) to govern directly from the White House, and relied on the new mass media of radio and later television to rally popular support (Milkis, 1993).

Presidential nominating politics was also changing. Increasingly presidential candidates were mounting pre-convention media campaigns such as that behind the unknown Wendell Willkie for the Republican nomination in 1940. Presidential aspirants also competed increasingly in primary elections to generate favorable press coverage and momentum for their candidacy, and pre-convention opinion polls became increasingly important. The Democratic convention in 1952 was the last to require a second ballot for the presidential nomination, as the nominating process began to move outside the convention hall.

FDR accomplished an electoral realignment during the 1930s but the top-heavy Democratic coalition was now too broad to be useful to him, encompassing groups as diverse as northern blacks, Jews, union members, and southern segregationist conservatives. In Congress the latter increasingly sided with the Republicans and in the period from 1938 to 1975 both houses, while under nominal Democratic control most of the time, were effectively controlled by a conservative coalition of Republicans and southern Democrats. In 1910 an alliance of progressive Republicans and Democrats had stripped Speaker Joseph Cannon of most of his powers and replaced strong party leadership with a congressional power structure based on specialized committees in both chambers, with the committee leadership determined by seniority (Schickler, 2001). The impact of the primary and the slow decline of traditional state and local party organizations also led to the emergence of a new type of member of Congress, largely self-selected and financed and less beholden to the party in getting to Washington and less likely to adhere to a party line once elected. At mid-century party government seemed increasingly remote on Capitol Hill as well as the White House, and committee chairs and cross-party coalitions were the norm in passing major legislation.

The death-knell for the traditional parties finally arrived during the 1960s and 1970s. In 1964 – with most of its traditional party machines having disappeared – the Republican Party nominated Barry Goldwater, a conservative ideologue, for president. The Goldwater nomination campaign was based on the candidate's personality and conservative issue positions rather than the traditional party criterion of general election strength and/or ability to unite the party. Conservative and other single-issue groups supplied the activists and hundreds of thousands of small conservative donors financed the campaign. Although Goldwater was overwhelmingly defeated in the general election, the style of the Goldwater campaign was the wave of the future in presidential politics (Brennan, 1995).

The Democratic Party's machines lasted longer due to the party's grip on power since the New Deal, but in 1968 they suffered a serious assault from the anti-Vietnam War forces of Senator Eugene McCarthy. With a political style and organizational make-up very similar to the 1964 Goldwater Republicans, the McCarthy campaign drove incumbent President Lyndon Johnson from office, and undermined the legitimacy of the eventual nominee, old New Dealer and Cold Warrior, Vice President Hubert Humphrey and the Chicago convention (dominated by Mayor Daley) that nominated him. With violence outside and mayhem inside the convention hall, Humphrey was forced to concede a commission to study possible reforms in the nominating process. When Humphrey lost in the fall, control of the reform commission – chaired initially by the party's eventual 1972 presidential nominee, Senator George McGovern – fell into the hands of the reformers who adopted a series of reforms to ensure that convention delegates were selected by open participatory processes involving rank-and-file Democrats rather than by state and local party leaders (Shafer, 1983). These rules were enforced by the national committee on the state parties and most conformed over the next eight years by moving towards primary elections for choosing national convention delegates. Despite McGovern's landslide 1972 general election defeat, by 1976 over three-quarters of the delegates in each party (the Republicans followed suit because of state electoral laws and because they had no reason not to) would be chosen in primaries.

Thus control over presidential nominations moved away from the national convention and into a series of state primary elections with self-selected candidates building their own campaign organizations and financing. This completed the elimination of the traditional political party as a significant institution in American politics. As a governing institution, at least at the federal level, it had only been intermittently useful due to the formidable barriers of the separation of powers and federalism. Its peculiar 20th-century evolution towards greater organizational weakness (by contrast with the rise of mass parties and party government in most other advanced democracies) made the governing functions of American parties appear even less relevant. By the last quarter of the 20th-century the American parties seemed to have become little more than the instruments of candidates or interest groups that captured the party label, reduced to little more than their basic 'vote-structuring' function in US elections (Ranney, 1978).

THE ABSENCE OF MASS PARTIES IN THE USA

The fundamental reason why America does not have party government is the absence of mass parties. Maurice Duverger (1964), building on the earlier work of Robert Michels (1962), devised the concept of the mass party: the dues-paying, organized, disciplined, hierarchical, and ideological political organizations that had arisen following industrialization in Europe to represent the claims of the emergent industrial working class, hitherto excluded from political participation. Duverger saw the mass party as the archetypal modern political form since it provided the only effective means for the newly enfranchised masses to participate in politics. Mass parties started on the political left since working-class power depended on tight organization (financed by mass membership dues) to capitalize on the sole political advantage of the disadvantaged – their numbers.

Once the mass party had proved its electoral success through the dramatic growth in electoral support for socialism in most European nations by the time of the First World War, those opposed to socialism on the center and right of the political spectrum were compelled to imitate the mass party's organizational form and political style in a process that Duverger (1964) termed 'contagion from the left'.

The absence of the mass party in America is thus linked to the absence of socialism as a major political force. Since Werner Sombart (1976) first raised the issue in 1906, America's individualistic political culture, mass immigration, a divided American working class and labor movement, and political repression have all been offered as sole or partial explanations (Lipset and Marks, 2000). Perhaps the most plausible explanation is that offered by Leon Epstein (1980). He argues that America had a mass electorate by 1830, prior to the social ravages of industrialization. Thus when the American 'proletariat' finally emerged after the Civil War it did not have to fight for voting and other basic political rights to the same extent as its European counterparts. In Europe industrialization occurred prior to or contemporaneously with political enfranchisement and the potential for radical ideologies to mobilize the working class was therefore much greater. In short, because America never experienced feudalism or absolutism, it also lacks the mass socialism that almost inevitably occurs when a feudal or absolutist regime has to deal with the social consequences of industrialization.

Epstein also argued against Duverger's tendency to regard American parties as retarded forms of political development. In fact, argues Epstein, these parties make excellent sense in the American political context, which is much more culturally resistant to large concentrations of political power. This, combined with the association of America's traditional major political parties with corruption, has led to what Epstein (1980) describes as the American tendency to treat parties as 'public utilities', subjecting them to a great deal of governmental regulation to the point of severely debilitating them organizationally. In a sense Americans have recognized that the vote-structuring function of the parties is so intrinsic to democracy that they have to be severely regulated against the danger of corrupting or misrepresenting the popular will or threatening individual rights. However, one price of such regulation is the virtual impossibility of a third party being able to organize nationally and meet the ballot requirements and various regulations on parties in all 50 states, and thus the Democrat–Republican duopoly is preserved at the possible expense of more radical alternatives.

SIGNS OF REVIVAL

Since the nadir of the mid-1970s there have been signs of revival of the American parties in almost all aspects.

The political upheaval of the civil rights revolution finally ended the conservative coalition and allowed more ideologically coherent national parties to develop. In Congress this led to a rise in the power of the party leadership and party voting in both chambers. The seniority rule has also been superseded by partisan considerations and the committees are no longer fiefdoms independent of the party leadership (Sinclair, 1995).

The national party committees have also become more important, and play a greater role than ever these days in promoting party positions and messages, recruiting candidates at all levels of the party, and raising funds and participating directly and indirectly in campaigns on behalf of party candidates. State parties have also revived as fundraising and campaigning organizations (Reichley, 1992).

At the mass level there are indications that the decline in party identities bottomed out in the 1970s and that these have stabilized and even revived somewhat. Levels of split-ticket voting have also declined from their 1970s peaks (Jacobson, 2000; Green et al., 2002). There has been no great revival in electoral participation, but ironically this has probably enhanced the role of parties and encouraged political polarization by making mobilization of each party's voter base more important in election campaigns (Schier, 2000).

In presidential politics, at least since the election of Ronald Reagan in 1980, American presidents have relied more on their parties as a base of support in Congress, and a source of direction and ideas for their administrations. Both conservative and liberal think-tanks have sprouted in close association with the parties since each has become more coherently liberal or conservative in ideology, and these have supplied much of the policy and personnel for Democratic and Republican administrations.

Yet mass party development or party government in the USA remains highly unlikely to occur. Much of the apparent revival of parties and partisanship in the USA is a consequence of the 'capture' of both parties by coalitions of single-issue and ideological interests who use the party labels as instruments to achieve their ends. Low-turnout primary and general elections enhance the control of these groups over party nominations, and campaign finance legislation has made candidates of both parties more heavily dependent on these groups than they are on the party (Schier, 2000). The separation of powers still militates against party government, since even if one party controls all three branches of the federal government the

shortness of the election cycle – 2 years – entails that the long-term control necessary for party government is hard to achieve. Moreover, given the nature of the separated system, prolonged single-party control of the three branches of the federal government would likely lead to a weakening of party control on Capitol Hill (as occurred in 1910 and after the New Deal realignment) to preserve the constitutional prerogatives and institutional power of the House and Senate against the encroachments of the executive.

Parties fulfill essential functions in American democracy in terms of structuring electoral choices for which no effective substitute has been devised, and they also play a crucial role in organizing the legislature. Party government in the USA, however, is likely to remain an elusive and ephemeral phenomenon due to the constitutional system, American political culture, and the extreme unlikelihood of anything resembling European-style mass parties emerging in the United States.

REFERENCES

Brennan, Mary C. (1995) *Turning Right in the Sixties: The Conservative Capture of the GOP*. Chapel Hill: University of North Carolina Press.

Burnham, Walter Dean (1982) *The Current Crisis in American Politics*. New York: Oxford University Press.

Campbell, Angus, Converse, Philip E., Miller, Warren E. and Stokes, Donald E. (1960) *The American Voter*. New York: Wiley.

Ceaser, James W. (1979) *Presidential Selection: Theory and Development*. Princeton, NJ: Princeton University Press.

Duverger, Maurice (1964) *Political Parties: Their Organization and Activity in the Modern State*. London: Methuen.

Epstein, Leon (1980) *Political Parties in Western Democracies*. New Brunswick, NJ: Transaction Publishers.

Goodman, Paul (1975) 'The first American party system', in William Nisbet Chambers and Walter Dean Burnham (eds), *The American Party Systems: Stages of Political Development*. New York: Oxford University Press, pp. 56–89.

Green, Donald, Palmquist, Bradley and Schickler, Eric (2002) *Partisan Hearts and Minds: Political Parties and the Social Identities of Voters*. New Haven, CT: Yale University Press.

Hamilton, Alexander, Madison, James and Jay, John (1961) *The Federalist Papers*. New York: Mentor.

Hofstadter, Richard (1955) *The Age of Reform: From Bryan to FDR*. New York: Knopf.

Jacobson, Gary C. (2000) 'Party polarization in national politics: The electoral connection', in Jon R. Bond and Richard Fleisher (eds), *Polarized Politics: Congress and the President in a Partisan Era*. Washington, DC: CQ Press.

Lipset, Seymour Martin, and Marks, Gary (2000) *It Didn't Happen Here: Why Socialism Failed in the United States*. New York: Norton.

Michels, Robert (1962) *Political Parties: A Sociological Study of the Oligarchical Tendencies of Modern Democracy*. New York: Free Press.

Milkis, Sidney M. (1993) *The President and the Parties: The Transformation of the American Party System since the New Deal*. New York: Oxford University Press.

Nie, Norman H., Verba, Sidney and Petrocik, John R. (1979) *The Changing American Voter*, enlarged edn. Cambridge, MA: Harvard University Press.

Ostrogorski, Moisei (1982) *Democracy and the Organization of Political Parties, Volume II: The United States*. New Brunswick, NJ: Transaction Publishers.

Ranney, Austin (1978) 'The political parties: Reform and decline', in Anthony King (ed.), *The New American Political System*. Washington, DC: American Enterprise Institute.

Ranney, Austin (1982) *The Doctrine of Responsible Party Government, Its Origins and Present State*. Westport, CT: Greenwood Press.

Reichley, A. James (1992) *The Life of the Parties: A History of American Political Parties*. New York: Free Press.

Schickler, Eric (2001) *Disjointed Pluralism: Institutional Innovation and the Development of the US Congress*. Princeton, NJ: Princeton University Press.

Schier, Steven E. (2000) *By Invitation Only: The Rise of Exclusive Politics in the United States*. Pittsburgh: University of Pittsburgh Press.

Shafer, Byron E. (1983) *Quiet Revolution: The Struggle for the Democratic Party and the Shaping of Post-Reform Politics*. New York: Russell Sage Foundation.

Silbey, Joel (1994) *The American Political Nation: 1838–1893*. Stanford, CA: Stanford University Press.

Sinclair, Barbara (1995) *Legislators, Leaders, and Lawmaking: the US House of Representatives in the Postreform Era*. Baltimore, MD: Johns Hopkins University Press.

Sombart, Werner (1976) *Why Is There No Socialism in the United States?* White Plains, NY: International Arts and Sciences Press.

Sundquist, James L. (1983) *Dynamics of the Party System*, revised edn. Washington, DC: Brookings Institution.

Tulis, Jeffrey (1987) *The Rhetorical Presidency*. Princeton, NJ: Princeton University Press.

Wilson, Woodrow (1981) *Congressional Government: A Study in American Politics*. Baltimore, MD: Johns Hopkins University Press.

Wood, Gordon S. (1992) *The Radicalism of the American Revolution*. New York: Knopf.

18

PARTY SYSTEM INSTITUTIONALIZATION AND PARTY SYSTEM THEORY AFTER THE THIRD WAVE OF DEMOCRATIZATION*

Scott Mainwaring and Mariano Torcal

The main argument of this chapter is that the level of institutionalization is a critical dimension for understanding party systems. Until the mid-1990s, the literature on parties and party systems neglected this fact, as most work on these subjects implicitly assumed a high level of institutionalization of the party system. Yet without focusing on institutionalization, it is impossible to account for important characteristics of party systems in most post-1978 democracies and semi-democracies. Voters, parties, and party systems in most post-1978 competitive regimes are qualitatively different from those of the advanced industrial democracies.

We focus on the first two dimensions of party system institutionalization that Mainwaring and Scully (1995) and Mainwaring (1999: 22–39) developed: the stability of interparty competition and the depth of party roots (or anchoring) in society. In these two dimensions, there are persistent and large differences in institutionalization between most post-1978 democracies and semi-democracies and the advanced industrial democracies. Most of the advanced industrial democracies exhibit far greater stability in interparty competition than most post-1978 democracies.

In addition, party roots in society are far stronger in most of the advanced industrial democracies than in most post-1978 democracies and semi-democracies. Much of the literature assumes strong party roots in society. In fact, party roots in society range from strong in most of the advanced industrial to weak in most post-1978 competitive regimes. We analyze two empirical manifestations of the variable strength of party roots in society. First, considerable theoretical and comparative literature presupposes that programmatic or ideological linkages are at the root of stable linkages between voters and parties. In these theories, voters choose a party or candidate on the basis of their ideological or programmatic preferences. In most post-1978 democracies and semi-democracies, however, programmatic or ideological linkages between voters and parties are weak. Weak programmatic and ideological linkages between voters and parties are a key part of weaker party roots in society.

The other empirical manifestation of weak party roots in society that we address is that linkages between voters and candidates are more personalistic in most post-1978 competitive regimes than in the advanced industrial democracies. Outside the advanced democracies, more voters choose candidates on the basis of their personal characteristics without regard to party, ideology, or programmatic issues. The high degree of personalism reflects weak party roots in society and runs counter to what one would expect on the basis of most of the theoretical literature on voters and party systems. Personalism taps an important criterion for assessing the institutionalization of political parties: the depersonalization of parties and party competition (Mény, 1990: 67).

In the conclusion, we argue that weak institutionalization has negative consequences for electoral accountability. Weakly institutionalized party systems are more vulnerable to allowing anti-party politicians to come to power. Many such anti-party politicians (e.g., President Alberto Fujimori in Peru, 1990–2000; President Hugo Chávez in Venezuela, 1998–present) have had adverse effects on democracy. We also argue that weak institutionalization hampers electoral accountability, which is a key underpinning of democracy.

Until the 1980s, the theoretical literature on parties and party systems focused on or implicitly assumed well-institutionalized systems. There were few democracies and semi-democracies with weakly institutionalized party systems. Since the beginning of the third wave of democratization (Huntington, 1991), however, weakly institutionalized party systems have become commonplace in competitive political regimes. These systems have different characteristics and dynamics than well-institutionalized systems. Social scientists need to modify the dominant theoretical literature to understand these less institutionalized party systems.

This chapter builds on Mainwaring and Scully (1995) and Mainwaring (1999: 22–39), which spawned most of the contemporary work on party system institutionalization. We add to these earlier works in four ways. First, we provide more systematic empirical evidence by using cross-national surveys to demonstrate some of the earlier propositions about party system institutionalization. Based on survey data, we also develop new indicators to assess the strength of parties' programmatic roots in society. Second, we analyze a broader range of countries than these earlier works and other previous work on this subject. Third, we analyze some new aspects of party system theory that these previous works did not address in detail; in particular, we question the assumption of programmatic/ideological linkages that permeates some of the literature. Finally, we present more rigorous tests of some empirical propositions while dropping some earlier and harder-to-test claims about consequences of low institutionalization. The second half of the chapter, while building conceptually and theoretically on Mainwaring and Scully (1995) and Mainwaring (1999), presents new arguments and evidence.

Unlike Mainwaring and Scully, we do not compare party systems on all four dimensions of party system institutionalization. Given spatial constraints and because of the difficulties of obtaining comparable valid empirical information for all four dimensions for a wide range of countries, we preferred to develop some points in greater depth and for a wider range of countries rather than provide a superficial discussion of all four dimensions. Our analysis is limited exclusively to democracies and semi-democracies;[1] parties that function in authoritarian regimes fall outside our purview.

COMPARING PARTY SYSTEMS: THE LEVEL OF INSTITUTIONALIZATION

A party system is the set of parties that interact in patterned ways. This definition implies three boundaries between systems and non-systems. First, as Sartori (1976) pointed out, a system must have at least two constituent elements; therefore a party system must have at least two parties. Second, the notion of patterned interactions suggests that there are some regularities in the distribution of electoral support by parties over time even if some parties rise and others decline. Third, the idea of a system implies some continuity in the components that form the system. Therefore, 'party system' implies some continuity in the parties that form the system – that is, the institutionalization of political parties.

Party systems vary on many dimensions, but social scientists strive to identify the most important among them to facilitate categorization and comparison. How, then, should social scientists compare and classify party systems? Sartori's (1976) seminal book identified two dimensions of party systems as particularly important: the number of relevant parties and the degree of ideological polarization. However, he inadequately conceptualized an equally important property of party systems: their level of institutionalization.

In his discussion of the difference between consolidated party systems and non-systems, Sartori (1976: 244–8) was prescient in recognizing the importance of party system institutionalization (which he called 'consolidation'). However, we disagree with three aspects of his conceptualization of institutionalization. First, he posited a dichotomy between consolidated systems and non-systems, whereas we find it much more useful to conceive of institutionalization as a continuum. Nothing in the definition of 'system' justifies a rigid dichotomous demarcation between a system and a non-system provided that there is some pattern in interparty competition and some continuity in the main parties of the system. These two criteria are easy to meet in a minimal way. Sartori's dichotomous categories ignore important variance within each of those categories. Moreover, a dichotomy requires a precise and inevitably arbitrary cut point: a case must be categorized as consolidated or as a non-system.

Second, Sartori set an excessively high threshold for what constitutes a party system. For example, he claimed that Colombia did not have a party system in the 1970s when in fact it had one of the oldest party systems in the world. The Liberals and Conservatives had been the main electoral contenders for decades whenever elections were relatively free and fair, and both parties had strong roots in society.

Third, because he treated non-systems as falling outside the framework of his main theorizing and did not examine variance in institutionalization among party systems or among what he regarded as non-systems, Sartori relegated institutionalization to a secondary position. For example, considerations of institutionalization are entirely absent from his classification of party systems. We believe that the institutionalization of party systems requires center stage. Some of the most important differences among party systems revolve around differences in institutionalization.

A classification of party systems based on the number of parties and the level of polarization overlooks substantial differences in the level of institutionalization, and hence in how party competition functions in less institutionalized contexts. In comparing and classifying party systems beyond the advanced industrial democracies, political scientists who work on Latin America (Bendel, 1993; Coppedge, 1998: 559–61; Kitschelt, 2003; Mainwaring, 1999; Mainwaring and Scully, 1995; Molina and Pérez, 2004; Payne et al., 2002: 127–54; Schedler, 1995; Van Cott, 2000), Africa (Kuenzi and Lambright, 2001), Asia (Johnson, 2002; Stockton, 2001), and the postcommunist regions (Bielasiak, 2002; Grzymala-Busse, 2002; Mair, 1997: 175–98; Markowski, 2000; Moser, 1999, 2001; Rose and Munro, 2003; Stoner Weiss, 2001; Tavits, 2005; Tóka, 1997) have increasingly recognized the need to pay attention to the level of institutionalization in addition to Sartori's two dimensions.[2] Institutionalized party systems structure the political process to a high degree. In fluid systems, parties are important actors in some ways, but they do not have the same structuring effect.

Institutionalization refers to a process by which a practice or organization becomes well established and widely known, if not universally accepted. Actors develop expectations, orientations, and behavior based on the premise that this practice or organization will prevail into the foreseeable future. In politics, institutionalization means that political actors have clear and stable expectations about the behavior of other actors. In Huntington's (1968: 12) words, 'Institutionalization is the process by which organizations and procedures acquire value and stability'. An institutionalized party system, then, is one in which actors develop expectations and behavior based on the premise that the fundamental contours and rules of party competition and behavior will prevail into the foreseeable future. In an institutionalized party system, there is stability in who the main parties are and how they behave. The notion of institutionalization should not be teleological, nor is the process linear; there is no necessary progression from weak to greater institutionalization. Party systems can deinstitutionalize, as the Italian, Peruvian, and Venezuelan cases in the 1990s show.

Following Mainwaring (1999: 22–39) and Mainwaring and Scully (1995), we conceptualize four dimensions of party system institutionalization. First, more institutionalized systems manifest considerable stability in patterns of party competition (Przeworski, 1975). This is the easiest dimension of institutionalization to measure, and perhaps the most important because institutionalization is conceptually very closely linked to stability.

Second, in more institutionalized systems, parties have strong roots in society and most voters, conversely, have strong attachments to parties. Most voters identify with a party and vote for it most of the time, and some interest associations are closely linked to parties. Strong party roots in society help provide the regularity in electoral competition that institutionalization entails. Party roots in society and the stability of interparty competition, while analytically separable, are intertwined because strong party roots in society stabilize electoral competition. If most citizens support the same party from one election to the next, there are fewer floating voters, hence less likelihood of massive electoral shifts that are reflected in high volatility. Conversely, where parties have weak roots in society, more voters are likely to shift electoral allegiances from one election to the next, thus bringing about greater potential for high electoral volatility.

Third, in more institutionalized systems, political actors accord legitimacy to parties. They see parties as a necessary part of democratic politics even if they are critical of specific parties and express skepticism about parties in general (Torcal et al., 2002). Legitimacy helps stabilize party systems and hence is a meaningful attitudinal dimension of institutionalization.

Finally, in more institutionalized systems, party organizations are not subordinated to the interests of a few ambitious leaders; they acquire an independent status and value of their own (Huntington, 1968: 12–24).[3] The institutionalization of political parties is limited as long as a party is the personal instrument of a leader or a small coterie (Janda, 1980). When the electorally successful parties are personalistic vehicles, system-level institutionalization is low on this fourth dimension. Solid organizations reflect and reinforce parties' penetration in society.

Although we diverge from Sartori in thinking of institutionalization as a continuum rather than a dichotomy, he deserves great credit for recognizing that there are profound differences in party systems according to the level of institutionalization. After Sartori's classic work, this issue was completely neglected until Bendel (1993) and Mainwaring and Scully (1995).

Party systems characterized by a low degree of institutionalization can be called fluid or weakly institutionalized. Institutionalization is a continuous variable that goes from institutionalized to fluid party systems. Compared to more institutionalized party systems, fluid systems are characterized by less regularity in patterns of party competition; weaker party roots in society; less legitimacy accorded to parties; and weaker party organizations, often dominated by personalistic leaders.

THE STABILITY OF INTERPARTY COMPETITION: ELECTORAL VOLATILITY

To develop the argument that contemporary competitive party systems differ in important ways that cannot be captured by Sartori's typology, we compare 39 countries according to the first dimension of institutionalization: that patterns of party competition manifest regularity. It is the easiest of the four dimensions of institutionalization to measure systematically, specifically by comparing electoral volatility. Electoral volatility refers to the aggregate turnover from one party to others, from one election to the next (Pedersen, 1983; Przeworski, 1975; Roberts and Wibbels, 1999). It is computed by adding the net change in percentage of votes gained or lost by each party from one election to the next, then dividing by 2.[4]

Table 18.1 shows electoral volatility for lower chamber elections of the post-1978 period for 39 democracies and semi-democracies. We limited the case selection to countries that as of 2003

had experienced at least three consecutive lower chamber elections when the country's Freedom House combined score was 10 or less.[5] Countries with a mean combined score of 11 or more had authoritarian regimes and are classified by Freedom House as 'not free'. Parties have different functions in authoritarian regimes compared to democracies and semi-democracies. Authoritarian regimes do not allow free and fair elections. Their control of elections favors the governing party and tends to limit electoral volatility, so it is usually misleading to compare electoral volatility between the two kinds of regimes. Only the most recent democratic period is counted in countries where there was a democratic breakdown. We use only post-1978 elections.[6]

Table 18.1 includes countries from the 1995–97 wave of World Values Survey (WVS) and the Comparative Study of Electoral Systems.[7] Among the WVS countries that met the Freedom House criterion for at least three consecutive elections, we included all those with a population of at least 10 million. Table 18.1 also includes seven countries (Denmark, Norway, Portugal, Sweden, Switzerland, Latvia, and Lithuania) that had under 10 million inhabitants so as to analyze some smaller countries, and Bolivia and Ecuador so as to reduce the underrepresentation of poor countries.

Party systems range from very stable (the USA, Australia, etc.) to extremely volatile (Ukraine, Latvia, Romania, Peru, Russia, Poland, and Estonia). Electoral change is on average far greater in the developing democracies and semi-democracies than in the advanced industrial democracies, even if, as Dalton et al. (2000) argue, volatility has increased in recent decades in the advanced industrial democracies. In the USA the results of the previous lower chamber election serve as an excellent predictor of subsequent election results by party, erring on average by only 3.2%. In contrast, in Ukraine the identical procedure offers little predictive capacity with an average error of 59.2% (18 times greater than in the USA). Lipset and Rokkan (1967) characterized the Western European party systems as 'frozen'. In contrast, many contemporary party systems in competitive political regimes are highly fluid.

The volatility scores underline the advantage of conceptualizing institutionalization as a continuous variable. Any attempt to establish a dichotomous cut point would be arbitrary. The same observation also applies to the other indicators developed later in this chapter.

Table 18.1   *Electoral volatility, Human Development Index, per capita GDP, and Freedom House scores, 39 countries*

	Mean electoral volatility, lower chamber	Elections included for volatility	Human Development Index (HDI) 2001	Per Capita GDP (PPP US$) 2001	Combined Freedom House scores, 2001–2
United States	3.2	1978–2002	0.937	34,320	2,F
Australia	6.4	1980–2001	0.939	25,370	2,F
Greece	6.9	1981–2000	0.892	17,440	4,F
United Kingdom	8.2	1979–2001	0.930	24,160	3,F
Germany	8.7	1980–2002	0.921	25,350	–
Switzerland	9.4	1979–2003	0.932	28,100	2,F
Belgium	11.5	1978–2003	0.937	25,520	3,F
Denmark	12.2	1979–2001	0.930	29,000	2,F
Sweden	13.5	1979–2002	0.941	24,180	2,F
Norway	14.1	1981–2001	0.944	29,620	2,F
Portugal	14.1	1979–2002	0.896	18,150	2,F
Spain	16.5	1979–2000	0.918	20,150	3,F
Netherlands	16.6	1981–2003	0.938	27,190	2,F
Chile	16.7	1989–2001	0.831	9,190	4,F
France	17.5	1978–2002	0.925	23,990	3,F
Japan	18.6	1979–2000	0.932	25,130	3,F
Taiwan	18.7	1996–2001	–	–	3,F
Italy	22.1	1979–2001	0.916	24,670	3,F
Colombia	22.1	1978–2002	0.779	7,040	8,PF
Mexico	22.7	1988–2000	0.800	8,430	5,F
Brazil	24.1	1986–2002	0.777	7,360	6,PF
South Korea	24.6	1988–2000	0.879	15,090	4,F
Argentina	24.9	1983–2001	0.849	11,320	6,PF
India	25.0	1980–1999	0.590	2,840	5,F
Hungary	25.1	1990–2002	0.837	12,340	3,F
Czech Republic	25.7	1990–2002	0.861	14,720	3,F
Venezuela	31.3	1978–2001	0.775	5,670	8,PF
Ecuador	36.4	1979–1998	0.731	3,280	6,PF
Bulgaria	36.8	1990–2001	0.795	6,890	4,F
Slovenia	38.2	1992–2000	0.881	17,130	3,F
Bolivia	39.8	1980–2002	0.672	2,300	4,F
Estonia	42.4	1992–2003	0.833	10,170	3,F
Poland	46.6	1991–2001	0.841	9,450	3,F
Lithuania	49.2	1992–2000	0.824	8,470	3,F
Russia	50.0	1993–1999	0.779	7,100	10,PF
Peru	51.9	1980–2001	0.752	4,570	4,F
Romania	53.0	1990–2000	0.773	5,830	4,F
Latvia	58.2	1993–2002	0.811	7,730	3,F
Ukraine	59.2	1994–2002	0.766	4,350	8,PF

Sources: HDI and GDP values in 2001 are from United Nations Development Programme, 2003. Freedom House scores found at http://polisci.la.psu.edu/faculty/Casper/FHratings.pdf; F=Free; PF=Partly Free

Table 18.1 also presents the 2001 Human Development Index (HDI) for these 39 countries – as reported in the *Human Development Report* (United Nations Development Programme, 2003) – and their 2003 Freedom House scores. In general, wealthier countries have lower electoral volatility. In an ordinary least squares (OLS) regression with countries' mean volatility as the dependent variable and their HDI in 2001 as the only independent variable, the HDI variable was highly significant ($p < 0.0005$) and had a strong substantive impact; every increase of 0.100 in the HDI led to an expected decrease of 12.5% in electoral volatility. The HDI accounted for 46.3% of the variance in volatility scores. In a second OLS regression with only one independent variable, gross domestic product (GDP) per capita was an even more powerful predictor of volatility, accounting for 60.6% of variance in volatility scores. The per capita GDP variable was highly significant ($p < 0.0005$), and it had a strong substantive impact; a $1000 increase in per capita GDP produces an expected decrease of 1.29% in electoral volatility. These results show that the advanced industrial democracies have much more stable party systems than the less developed democracies and semi-democracies. The correlation between countries' per capita income and their mean electoral volatility was an impressive –0.78, significant at $p < 0.0005$, two-tailed. The 16 countries with the highest HDIs (HDI ≥ 0.892) are among the 18 countries with the lowest electoral volatility.

The causes of the powerful correlation between a higher level of development and lower electoral volatility require further research beyond what is possible here; we offer only some brief reflections. The fact that most western European party systems stabilized before World War II (Bartolini and Mair, 1990; Lipset and Rokkan, 1967), when those countries had much lower standards of living than they currently enjoy, indicates that the main explanation is not a modernization argument by which a higher level of development causes lower electoral volatility. In most of what are now the advanced industrial democracies, parties were vehicles of social and political integration of masses of new citizens (Chalmers, 1964; Pizzorno, 1981). They pushed for the extension of the franchise and thereby created new citizens. They built encompassing organizations and solidified strong loyalties. In most late democratizing countries, parties were less central in the struggle to expand citizenship, and they never had the far-reaching social functions or fostered the strong identities that they did in the early democratizers (Gunther and Diamond, 2003). These differences in historical patterns (i.e., path dependence) help account for the high correlations between a higher level of development and a more stable party system. Poor economic performance in many less developed countries has also contributed to high electoral volatility (Remmer, 1991; Roberts and Wibbels, 1999). A final contributing factor to high electoral volatility in many less developed countries has been frequent supply-side changes, as political elites shift from one party to another (Rose and Munro, 2003).

Converse (1969) argued that party systems would become more stable over time as voters came to identify with certain parties.[8] Some recent research, however, has indicated that most voters learn fairly quickly to locate parties' positions (Kitschelt *et al.*, 1999), and that party systems in less developed countries do not on average tend to become more stable over time (Bielasiak, 2002). Our data on electoral volatility seem to support this argument. For the 19 countries in Table 18.1 with HDI less than 0.850, for the first electoral period included, electoral volatility averaged 38.2%. In subsequent electoral periods, volatility for these countries averaged 33.1% ($n=19$), 34.8% ($n=16$), 35.0% ($n=10$), and 27.9% ($n=7$). None of the volatility averages after the first electoral period differs statistically ($p < 0.10$, two–tailed) from the 39.6% average for the first period, so there is no statistically significant tendency toward diminishing volatility over time. The data on volatility thus indicate that institutionalization is not linear or teleological. Rose and Munro (2003) refer to this phenomenon of extended time without institutionalization as 'competition without institutionalization'. Weak institutionalization (and high volatility) could go on for an extended period.

During the post-1980 period, most countries have not experienced huge shifts in electoral volatility from one election to the next. The correlation between countries' scores in the first electoral period used in Table 18.1 and the second is 0.68 ($n=39$; $p < 0.0005$); between the second and third periods it is 0.83 ($n=34$; $p < 0.0005$), between the third and fourth periods it is 0.73 ($n=27$; $p < 0.0005$), and between the fourth and fifth periods it is 0.69 ($n=23$; $p < 0.0005$). Even over an extended period, the correlations hold up at moderately strong levels. For example, the correlation between volatility in the first and the fifth periods is 0.54 ($p = 0.008$) and between the second and fifth it is 0.69 ($p < 0.0005$). A few countries exhibit marked declines in volatility over time (e.g., Brazil after 1994), while a few manifest notable increases over time (e.g., Italy after 1993, Venezuela after 1988), but volatility is fairly stable in most countries.

PARTY ROOTS IN SOCIETY: IDEOLOGICAL VOTING

The second dimension of party system institutionalization is party anchoring in society. In more institutionalized party systems, parties develop strong and stable roots in society. Where parties have strong roots in society, most voters feel connected to a party and regularly vote for its candidates.

Most theories about why individuals develop strong allegiances to parties – or, stated conversely, why parties develop strong roots in society – focus on ideological or programmatic linkages between voters and parties. According to such theories, voters choose a party because it represents their ideological or programmatic preferences. The assumption of strong programmatic or ideological linkages characterizes proximity and directional spatial models of voting, the literature on the left–right schema (Fuchs and Klingemann, 1990), social cleavage approaches to party systems (Lipset and Rokkan, 1967), and some prominent theories on party realignments in the advanced industrial democracies (Inglehart, 1984, 1990; Kitschelt, 1994). We agree that programmatic or ideological linkages are an important means of stabilizing electoral competition (though clientelistic and traditional/affective linkages can have this effect); we disagree that such linkages are strong in most party systems and instead show that there is wide variance in the strength of ideological linkages.

Spatial models of voting are one of the most important approaches to understanding how individuals develop attachments to specific parties and why parties develop deep roots in society. The proximity spatial model of voting is associated with Budge (1994), Cox (1990), Downs (1957), Enelow and Hinich (1984), Hinich and Munger (1994), and Westholm (1997), among others. Hinich and Munger (1994) developed a particularly sophisticated proximity spatial model. They argue that spatial competition does not necessarily occur along a left–right economic dimension,[9] but they still assume that voters choose a party or candidate on the basis of ideology. In this theory, individuals develop attachments to parties because they believe that those parties best advance their interests. Their argument about why large numbers of individuals become attached to parties revolves around the ideological congruence between voters and their preferred parties. Voters choose a candidate or party on the basis of a decision about which one best advances their programmatic interests. Ideology serves as a shortcut for this electoral decision.

Directional spatial models agree that voters choose a candidate or party based on ideological position, but they differ from proximity spatial models in one key respect. In directional theories, citizens vote not according to which party is closest to them on the left–right scale,

but rather according to the parties' ideological orientation on a few issues about which the voter has an intense preference (Rabinowitz and MacDonald, 1989; Rabinowitz et al., 1991). The directional approach shares with the proximity models the view that ideological position determines voters' preferences for candidates or parties and is responsible for creating party roots in society.[10]

Other major bodies of literature about parties and voters implicitly assume that voting is programmatic or ideological.[11] Lipset and Rokkan's (1967) social cleavage theory of party systems assumes that voters identify their interests on the basis of their sociological position in society – class, religion, ethnicity or nationality, and urban/rural residence. Implicitly in their argument, some parties programmatically or ideologically advance the interests of different sectors of society, and individuals form their party preference on the basis of the programmatic/ideological interests that result from these sociological positions (see also Bartolini and Mair, 1990; Scully, 1992; Valenzuela, 1997).

Another important scholarly tradition sees the left–right schema, which synthesizes ideological orientations, as a stabilizing psychological anchor that influences the vote. According to this literature, individuals determine their party preferences on the basis of their ideological orientation (Inglehart and Klingemann, 1976; Klingemann, 1979; Inglehart, 1979; Laponce, 1981; Fuchs and Klingemann, 1990; Fleury and Lewis-Beck, 1993; Knutsen, 1997).

In sum, three important scholarly traditions assume that the linkages between voters and parties are programmatic or ideological. In contrast, we show that there is great variance in the extent to which party competition in different countries is programmatic or ideological. Ideological voting as measured by the traditional left–right schema varies enormously.[12]

The final column of Table 18.2 provides a measure of the cross-national variance in ideological voting based on the results of a logistic regression analysis (Columns 2 through 4). In the logistic regressions, party vote as expressed by survey respondents is the dichotomous dependent variable, and respondents' positions on the left-right scale from 1 to 10 are the only independent variable. The analysis is limited to some countries that had a combined Freedom House score of 10 or less in 1996. The analysis includes the three largest parties (according to the number of respondents who expressed a party preference in the survey) in each country.[13] For a country-level score, we started with the results of two simulations (not shown) based on the estimated logistic regression coefficients (Column 3). The first simulation estimated the predicted probability that voter A would choose party i rather than party j if A located herself at 3.25 on the left-right scale (3.25 is the exact median point between the exact center and the furthest left point). The second simulation estimated the predicted probability that voter A would choose party i rather than j if A located herself at 7.75 on the left-right scale (7.75 is the exact median point between the exact center and the furthest right point, 10.00). The column labeled 'First difference probabilities ...' shows how much the likelihood of voting for i rather than j changed with the change in the voter's position from 3.25 to 7.75. If a voter at 3.25 had a 0.25 predicted probability of voting for i and a voter at 7.75 had a 0.65 predicted probability of voting for i rather than j, then the first difference probability would be 0.40. The country level score is the mean for the three scores for the pairs of parties for that country.[14]

The cross-national differences in ideological voting are huge. As expected, the predictability of the vote on the basis of left-right position is higher in countries with lower electoral volatility. The correlation between a country's electoral volatility and the mean of the first difference probabilities in Table 18.2 is −.56 ($n = 32$, significant at $p < .001$). This strong correlation between ideological voting and the stability of interparty competition suggests that the three theoretical approaches discussed earlier were probably right that programmatic/ideological linkages are the main way to build an institutionalized party system. Nevertheless, in a few cases (the USA and Australia, for example), electoral stability is very high despite moderate ideological structuring of the vote, whereas a few post-communist cases (the Czech Republic and Bulgaria) exhibit moderate to high electoral volatility despite high ideological structuring. The huge variance in ideological voting strongly supports our argument that social scientists cannot assume that party competition is programmatic or ideological. This assumption is misleading in most fluid party systems.

We expected that where programmatic/ideological anchoring of parties in society is weaker, party supporters would have more scattered distributions along the left-right scale because strong programmatic/ideological linkages to parties rest on programmatic/ideological consistency among parties' loyal voters. To test this hypothesis, Table 18.3

provides a measure of the extent to which a country's parties were cohesive along the left-right dimension. We constructed the country score by beginning with the standard deviation of each party's supporters along the left-right dimension, then weighted the parties by their number of supporters.[15] The correlation between a country's ideological anchoring in Table 18.2 and its weighted standard deviation in Table 18.3 is −.50, significant at $p < .01$ ($n = 30$). This correlation supports the hypothesis that ideological/programmatic consistency within parties facilitates ideological structuring of party competition.

Although programmatic or ideological linkages between voters and parties are not the only ways to create party system stability, they are an important means by which voters become attached to parties and hence an important means by which parties become rooted in society. Where ideological linkages to parties are strong, electoral volatility tends to be lower, precisely as Lipset and Rokkan (1967) and spatial theorists postulate.[16] Where there is a weak linkage between voters' ideological and programmatic position and their preferred party, voters are more likely to drift from one party to the next – that is, they are more likely to be floating voters.

This evidence suggests a need to rethink theories about voters, voting, and party competition in less institutionalized party systems. The programmatic and ideological linkages between voters and parties are weaker in these systems than most of the theoretical literature assumes. Spatial models and other theoretical approaches that assume ideological voting are not wrong, but there is considerable variance in how accurately they portray party competition in different countries – a fact that spatial models have not acknowledged. Ideological voting is a powerful aspect of party competition in most of the advanced industrial democracies; it is much weaker in most post-1978 competitive regimes. By implication, some of the theoretical tools and assumptions that have been central in understanding party competition in the advanced industrial democracies are less useful, indeed sometimes problematic, in analyzing less institutionalized party systems. For example, the assumption that most voters' electoral decision is programmatic or ideological is unwarranted and misleading in many post-1978 competitive regimes.

The modest correlation between ideological structuring of party competition and electoral stability suggests one other key point. All three theories discussed in this section overlook or

Table 18.2   *Ideological voting in 33 countries*
Dependent variable for columns 2 to 5: respondents' expressed party vote
Independent variable: respondents' left-right position on a 1 to 10 scale

Country	Pair of parties (Dependent variable)	Significance of left-right logistic coefficient	Nagelkerke R^2	First Difference Probabilities between values 3.25 and 7.75 of left-right position on a 1 to 10 scale	Mean of First Difference Probabilities
Italy	Forza Italia v. PDS	0.000	0.85	.93	.72
	Forza Italia v. AN	0.000	0.13	.25	
	PDS v. AN	0.000	0.91	.98	
Sweden	Moderata Samligspartiet v. Social Democrats	0.000	0.82	.93	.69
	Moderata Samligspartiet v. Vansterpartiet	0.000	0.94	.91	
	Social Democrats v. Vansterpartiet	0.000	0.23	.24	
Portugal	PSD v. PS	0.000	0.50	.88	.64
	PSD v. CDU	0.000	0.82	.80	
	CDU v. PS	0.000	0.47	.25	
Czech Rep.	ODS v. CSSD	0.000	0.62	.82	.62
	ODS v. KCSM	0.000	0.89	.82	
	CSSD v. KCSM	0.000	0.52	.22	
Netherlands	PvdA v. CDA	0.000	0.47	.75	.60
	PvdA v. D'66	0.000	0.11	.40	
	CDA v. D'66	0.000	0.28	.65	
Chile	Socialists (PS+PPD) v. PDC	0.000	0.12	.40	.56
	Conservatives (UDI+RN) v. PDC	0.000	0.33	.54	
	Conservatives (UDI+RN) v. Socialists (PS+PPD)	0.000	0.53	.73	
Uruguay	Colorado v. Nacional	0.066	0.01	.13	.56
	Colorado v. Frente Amplio	0.000	0.62	.77	
	Nacional v. Frente Amplio	0.000	0.58	.79	
Spain	PP v. PSOE	0.000	0.63	.80	.55
	PP v. Izquierda Unida	0.000	0.62	.85	
	PSOE v. IU	Not significant	0.00	–	
France	Socialist v. RPR	0.000	0.76	.92	.54
	Socialist v. National Front	0.000	0.59	.71	
	RPR v. National Front	Not significant	0.01	–	
Poland	Solidarność v. PSL	0.000	0.18	.39	.52
	Solidarność v. SLD	0.000	0.53	.66	
	PSL v. SLD	0.000	0.24	.50	
UK	Conservative v. Labour	0.000	0.43	.73	.52
	Conservative v. Liberal Democrats	0.000	0.21	.52	
	Labour v. Liberal Democrats	0.000	0.07	.32	

Table 18.2   *(Continued)*

Country	Pair of parties (Dependent variable)	Significance of left-right logistic coefficient	Nagelkerke R^2	*First Difference Probabilities between values 3.25 and 7.75 of left-right position on a 1 to 10 scale*	Mean of First Difference Probabilities
West Germany	SPD v. CDU/CSU	0.000	0.35	.71	.51
	SPD v. Greens	0.010	0.03	.13	
	CDU/CSU v. Greens	0.000	0.47	.69	
Denmark	Socialdemokr. v. Konservative	0.000	0.52	.77	.50
	Socialdemokr v. Venstre	0.000	0.52	.74	
	Konservative v. Venstre	Not significant	0.00	–	
Greece	PASOK v. Nea Demokratia	0.000	0.70	.82	.50
	PASOK v. Politiki Anixi	0.000	0.18	.28	
	Nea Demokratia v. Pol.Anixi	0.000	0.17	.40	
Switzerland	Radical Démocratique v. Socialist	0.000	0.40	.70	.48
	Radical Démocratique v. Christian Democrats	Not significant	0.01	–	
	Socialist v. Christian Democrats	0.055	0.46	.73	
Bulgaria	Union of Democratic Forces v. Socialist Party	0.000	0.63	.67	.45
	Union of Democratic Forces v. Agrarian Party	0.000	0.28	.47	
	Socialist Party v. Agrarian Party	0.000	0.22	.20	
Norway	Labour v. Progressive	0.000	0.10	.28	.43
	Labour v. Conservative	0.000	0.38	.59	
	Progressive v. Conservative	0.000	0.10	.42	
US	Republicans v. Democrats	0.000	0.15	.42	.42
Japan	Liberal Democratic Party v. New Frontier party	0.000	0.11	.25	.38
	Liberal Democratic Party v. Socialist Party	0.000	0.30	.53	
	New Frontier party v. Socialist Party	0.009	0.08	.35	
Belgium	CD&V v. PS	0.000	0.49	.34	.36
	CD&V v. VLD	Not significant	0.01	–	
	PS v. VLD	0.000	0.48	.73	
Slovenia	Liberal Democracy v. People's Party	0.002	0.06	.31	.36
	Liberal Democracy v. Christian Democrats	0.000	0.20	.55	
	People's Party v. Christian Democrats	0.032	0.04	.21	

(Continued)

Table 18.2   (Continued)

Country	Pair of parties (Dependent variable)	Significance of left-right logistic coefficient	Nagelkerke R²	First Difference Probabilities between values 3.25 and 7.75 of left-right position on a 1 to 10 scale	Mean of First Difference Probabilities
Hungary	MSZP v. FIDESZ	0.000	0.32	.57	.31
	MSZP v. FKGP	0.010	0.04	.12	
	FIDESZ v. FKGP	0.000	0.14	.23	
Australia	Australian Labor v. Liberal Party	0.000	0.16	.45	.30
	Australian Labor v. Green Party	0.006	0.01	.05	
	Liberal Party v. Green Party	0.000	0.17	.39	
Argentina	PJ v. UCR	0.000	0.05	.22	.26
	PJ v. Frepaso	0.000	0.13	.37	
	UCR v. Frepaso	0.034	0.03	.18	
Taiwan	Nationalist Party v. Democratic Progressive Party	0.000	0.13	.41	.25
	Nationalist Party v. New Party	0.005	0.02	.13	
	Democratic Progressive Party v. New Party	0.002	0.05	.22	
Mexico	PRI v. PRD	0.000	0.13	.28	.20
	PAN v. PRD	0.000	0.04	.18	
	PRI v. PAN	0.000	0.03	.13	
Venezuela	AD v. COPEI	Not significant	0.00	–	.19
	AD v. Causa R	0.000	0.22	.28	
	COPEI v. Causa R	0.000	0.21	.29	
Brazil	PMDB v. PT	0.000	0.08	.22	.18
	PMDB v. PSDB	0.064	0.02	.12	
	PT v. PSDB	0.000	0.15	.19	
Ukraine	Democratic Party Ukr. v. Communist Party Ukr.	Not significant	0.02	–	.15
	Democratic Party Ukr. v. Popular Movement Ukr.	0.000	0.13	.30	
	Communist Party Ukr. v. Popular Movement Ukr.	0.007	0.04	.16	
Russia	Communist Party v. Our Home Russia	0.000	0.10	.28	.12
	Communist Party v. Lib-Dem. Party	0.040	0.03	.08	
	Our Home Russia v. Lib-Dem. Party	Not significant	0.01	–	
Peru	Cambio 90 v. UPP	Not significant	0.00	–	.06
	Cambio 90 v. APRA	Not significant	0.00	–	
	UPP v. APRA	0.015	0.03	.18	
Romania	CDR v. PDSR	0.001	0.03	.18	.06
	CDR v. PD	Not significant	0.01	–	
	PDSR v. PD	Not significant	0.01	–	

(Continued)

Table 18.2   (Continued)

Country	Pair of parties (Dependent variable)	Significance of left-right logistic coefficient	Nagelkerke R^2	First Difference Probabilities between values 3.25 and 7.75 of left-right position on a 1 to 10 scale	Mean of First Difference Probabilities
India	Indian National Congress v. BJP	0.023	0.02	.08	.05
	Indian National Congress v. Janata Dal (People's Party)	Not significant	0.01	–	
	BJP v. Janata Dal (People's Party)	0.024	0.02	.08	

Column 6 is the mean of the 3 scores in Column 5, counting coefficients not significant at p<.10 (Column 3) as equal to 0 in Column 5.

Sources: European Election Study 1994 (Belgium, Denmark, France, Greece, Italy, Netherlands, Portugal, UK, West Germany), Comparative Study of Electoral Systems 1996–2000 (Czech Republic, Hungary, Romania), World Values Survey 1997, (all the remaining countries).

Table 18.3   Standard deviations of party supporters' left–right positions

Country	Country score*	Country	Country score*
Sweden	1.35	Ukraine	1.77
West Germany	1.46	Japan	1.83
Spain	1.46	USA	1.83
Portugal	1.48	Argentina	1.85
Italy	1.49	Russia	1.86
Netherlands	1.49	Bulgaria	1.87
France (94)	1.50	Uruguay	1.88
Norway	1.51	Hungary	1.90
Denmark	1.55	Belgium	1.93
Greece	1.56	Poland	1.98
UK (excl. Northern Ireland)	1.64	Peru	2.10
Slovenia	1.65	Mexico	2.45
Switzerland	1.65	India	2.52
Czech Republic	1.67	Romania	2.59
Taiwan	1.67	Brazil	2.84
Australia	1.68	Venezuela	3.00
Chile	1.68		

Note: The weighted country mean is the mean standard deviation for all parties with at least two party supporters, weighted by the number of party supporters. The weighting means that all individuals who expressed a party preference are weighted equally, provided that their party had at least one other supporter among survey respondents. The reason for excluding parties with only one supporter is that the standard deviation must be zero if $N=1$.

Sources: as Table 18.2

understate three non-programmatic and non-ideological linkages that might orient voters (Kitschelt, 2000), though only two of the three could create stable bonds between voters and parties and thereby foster strong party roots in society. These non-programmatic rationales deserve close attention in less institutionalized party systems. First, voters might choose more on the basis of clientelistic goods than ideological position. In this case, a voter might cast a ballot for a politician or party even though a competitor is ideologically closer to her preferred position. By securing clientelistic goods, voters can advance their material interests in a way that would not be possible through public goods.[17] Second, all three theories overlook that voting might be personalistic, without a strong link to ideological preferences or to sociological location (Silveira, 1998). A voter may cast her ballot not on the basis of an ideological preference but rather because of sympathy for the personality traits of a candidate. Under these conditions, the ideological bond between individuals and parties is weak, and there may be no other bond that creates an enduring allegiance to a given party. Third, voters might become attached to parties on the basis of traditional/affective ties, somewhat independent of clientelism and programmatic predilections. In contemporary competitive regimes in which television has a strong impact in politics, however, traditional/affective linkages are almost certain to erode.

PARTY ROOTS IN SOCIETY AND PERSONALISTIC VOTING

In this section, we examine a different aspect of party roots in society. Widespread voting based on the personality characteristics of candidates, devoid of programmatic or ideological content, is a telling sign of weak party roots in society. With strong bonds between voters and parties, whether constructed through programmatic/ ideological, clientelistic, or traditional/affective linkages, voters remain faithful to their party, and candidates' personalities are of secondary importance.

Leaders and personalization have become increasingly important in elections outcomes, even in countries with parliamentary systems of government. This phenomenon has been called the 'presidentialization of modern election campaigns' (Crewe and King, 1994; Kaase, 1994). In the advanced industrial democracies, citizen evaluations of leaders contain programmatic, ideological, or party identification components. In fluid party systems, personalism devoid of programmatic and ideological components usually plays a much greater role in voting (Silveira, 1998).[18] In more institutionalized systems, voters are more likely to identify with a party, and parties dominate patterns of political recruitment and deliberation. In fluid systems, many voters choose according to personality more than party; anti-party politicians

are more able to win office. Populism and anti-politics are more common. Personalities more than party organizations dominate the political scene.

Personalistic voting is an important and partly measurable political phenomenon (King, 2002a, 2002b), yet it has been neglected in most of the theoretical literature on voting, including spatial models and works based on the left–right scheme. In fluid systems, individual personalities, independent of party and programmatic preferences, have a sizable impact in electoral campaigns. Many citizens vote to a significant degree on the basis of the personal characteristics of candidates. Personalistic voting is common, and political independents can successfully seek high-level office. Space for populists is greater, especially in presidential systems since candidates appeal directly to voters without needing to be elected head of a party in order to become head of state. Candidates can capture high executive office such as the presidency and governorships without being rooted in an established party.

One way to assess the importance of personalism in electoral campaigns is data on outsider presidential candidates. Electorally competitive independent presidential candidates and candidates from new parties reflect a high degree of personalism and voters' openness to candidates from outside the established parties. For operational purposes, we define outsider presidential candidates as independents (with no party affiliation) or candidates from a party that won less than 5% of the lower chamber vote in the previous election and did not have presidential candidates in any election prior to the previous one.

Table 18.4 presents data on the share of the vote won by outsider presidential candidates in six Latin American countries and (for comparative purposes) the USA.[19] Outsiders won the presidential election in Peru in 1990, Venezuela in 1993 and 1998, and Colombia and Ecuador in 2002.[20] This extraordinary political occurrence manifests weak institutionalization of the existing party system. Another outsider (Evo Morales) made it to the runoff round in the presidential election in Bolivia in 2002. In Colombia, Venezuela, Ecuador, and Bolivia, outsiders won at least 50% of the valid vote in one of the last two (as of 2005) presidential elections.

Brazilian President Fernando Collor de Mello (1990–92) created a party in order to run for president in 1989, and he defeated the candidates of the established parties. Seven months after his inauguration, his party won

Table 18.4   *Average share of vote won by outsider presidential candidates in five most recent presidential elections, select countries*

Country	Elections included	% of vote won by outsider candidates, most recent election	Average % of vote won by outsider candidates, last five elections
United States	1984–2000	0.3	6.0
Brazil[a]	1989–2002	0.0	13.4
Ecuador	1988–2002	58.9	17.5
Bolivia	1985–2002	51.3	22.1
Venezuela	1983–2000	40.2	26.5
Colombia	1986–2002	66.5	28.5
Peru	1985–2001	27.9	32.7

[a] Data for Brazil include four elections only because there have been only four popular presidential elections since the transition to democracy in 1985.

only 40 of 503 lower chamber seats in the October 1990 congressional elections. Clearly, his appeal was personalistic and not party-based. His party disappeared in the months following his 1992 resignation from office in order to avoid his impeachment. Peruvian President Alberto Fujimori (1990–2000) also created a party in order to run for the presidency; he, too, campaigned against parties and subsequently eschewed efforts to build a party. In Peru, political independents dominated the 1995 municipal elections. Having seen from Fujimori that anti-party appeals could win popular support, a new cohort of anti-party politicians emerged. Fujimori used focus groups and surveys to determine who ran on the ballot of his highly personalized party. Fujimori himself, rather than the party, controlled congressional nominations (Conaghan, 2000). This personalistic control of candidate selection is the antithesis of what is found in an institutionalized system. Moreover, as remains true in Russia, candidates could gain ballot access without a party and could win election as independents. Former coup leader Hugo Chávez created a new party in his successful bid for the presidency of Venezuela in 1998. In a similar vein, in Ecuador in 2002, former coup leader Lucio Gutiérrez created a new party in his successful campaign for president.

Personalism and anti-party politicians are also common in some post-communist cases. Former Russian President Boris Yeltsin was not a member of a party and undermined parties. Alexander Lebed, who finished third in the 1996 Russian presidential election, ran as an independent. Non-partisan candidates have fared well in the plurality races for both chambers of the Russian parliament. In the 1993 elections, well over half of the single-member

district candidates for the lower chamber were independents without partisan affiliation, and only 83 of the 218 deputies elected belonged to a party (Moser, 1995: 98). In 1995, more than 1000 of the 2700 candidates for the single-member district seats were independents. Independents won 78 of the 225 single-member seats; the largest single party could muster only 58 seats (White *et al.*, 1997: 203, 224). Former King Simeon II of Bulgaria also created an electorally successful personalistic political vehicle.

Why is personalistic voting widespread in some party systems even after considerable time under democratic rule? We cannot fully address this question here, but some brief speculations are in order. First, historical sequences in party building are important. In the old, well-established democracies, parties became deeply rooted in society before the emergence of the modern mass media, especially television. In Western Europe, working-class parties integrated workers into the political system and provided fundamental sources of identity (Chalmers, 1964; Pizzorno, 1981). A similar phenomenon occurred with Christian Democratic parties (Kalyvas, 1996). In contrast, in most weakly institutionalized systems, television became a mass phenomenon before parties were deeply entrenched in society. Candidates for executive office can get their messages across on television without the need to rely on well-developed party organizations (Sartori, 1989), allowing the emergence of highly personalistic parties (Gunther and Diamond, 2003: 187). Second, the poor regime performance of many post-1978 competitive regimes has discredited governing parties (Remmer, 1991; Roberts and Wibbels, 1999; Tavits, 2005) and, even more broadly, has discredited parties as vehicles of representation. The discrediting of parties has opened the doors to personalistic anti-party crusaders. Third, in many post-1978 competitive regimes, parties are programmatically diffuse (Kitschelt *et al.*, 1999: 164–90; Ostiguy, 1998), making it difficult for voters to determine which party is closest to their own positions, or they may be ideologically unreliable, undertaking radical shifts in positions (Stokes, 2001). In such circumstances, voters are volatile and more likely to flock to personalistic candidates, who often campaign against parties. Fourth, personalistic voting is likely to be stronger in presidential systems than in parliamentary systems and most of the advanced industrial democracies have parliamentary systems, and many post-1978 competitive regimes have presidential systems.

The prevalence of personalism is related to the second and fourth dimensions of party system institutionalization. Personalistic linkages between voters and candidates tend to be stronger where party roots in society are weaker. They also tend to be stronger with weak party organizations and weakly institutionalized parties. In weakly institutionalized party systems, parties have precarious resources and are weakly professionalized. Many parties are personalistic vehicles (Conaghan, 2000).

Voting based on the rational evaluation of leaders could in principle be a sign of political sophistication and greater electoral accountability. King (2002a) calls such reasoned evaluations, which have programmatic/ideological content, the indirect effects of candidate evaluations. In many fluid party systems, however, the relationship between individuals' ideological position and their evaluation of political leaders is weak. Their evaluation of leaders is not based on programmatic and ideological principles.

Table 18.5 shows the product moment correlation of individuals' evaluation of political leaders and their position on the left–right scale. The relationship between leadership evaluation and ideology is high for the advanced industrial democracies, but lower in countries with weakly institutionalized party systems. In a few countries (Mexico, Peru, and Taiwan), the relationship between citizen evaluation of leaders and their left–right position was almost zero. The correlation between countries' mean Pearson correlation in Table 18.5 and their electoral volatility (Table 18.1) is 0.41 ($p < 0.10$, $n = 19$), demonstrating a somewhat stronger linkage between ideological position

and leadership evaluation in institutionalized party systems.

Leadership evaluation might in principle be a reasonable means to promote representation and electoral accountability, but where leadership evaluation is not well connected to ideological or programmatic issues, it indicates non-programmatic personalism. According to many views (Barnes, 1977; Converse and Pierce, 1986), representation devoid of programmatic content is meaningless; representation exists only because of a programmatic/ideological match between the views of representatives and citizens (see also Luna and Zechmeister, 2005). Such representation occurs only by accident if at all when there is no relationship between citizens' ideological positions and their assessment of political leaders. In many post-1978 competitive regimes, the connection between citizens' ideological position and their preferred political leaders is weak.

The importance of personalistic voting devoid of much ideological content in less institutionalized party systems suggests again the need for caution in applying theoretical models predicated on the assumption that voters' electoral choice is programmatic or ideological. This is often not the case in fluid party systems.

CONCLUSION

Awareness of the importance of party system institutionalization has grown in the past decade, but social scientists who work on fluid party systems need to continue rethinking the way we theorize about and compare party systems. Some theories that have been presented as universalistic, for example, spatial theories of voting and party competition, in fact are more useful for analyzing the advanced industrial democracies than fluid party systems. It is essential to be aware of these differences between fluid and more institutionalized systems and to avoid assuming that purportedly universalistic theories constructed implicitly on the basis of the advanced industrial democracies will equally apply to fluid party systems. Analyzing less institutionalized party systems sheds light on important issues that do not surface in examining the advanced industrial democracies.[21]

Party systems vary markedly in levels of institutionalization, and institutionalization varies independently of the number of parties and the level of polarization. Whereas analysts

Table 18.5   *Ideological anchoring of leaders' evaluation in 19 countries included in the CSES study (Pearson correlation coefficients)*

Czech	Vaclav Klaus	0.60**
Republic	Milos Zeman	−0.42**
(1996)	M. Grebenicek	−0.63**
Average		0.54
Sweden	Goran Persson	−0.39**
(1998)	Carl Bildt	0.58**
	Gudrun Schyman	−0.48**
Average		0.48
Spain	Jose Maria Aznar	0.57**
	Joaquin Almunia	−0.32**
	F. Frutos	−0.29
Average		0.39
Australia	Paul Keating	−0.33**
	John Howard	0.43**
	Tim Fischer	0.39**
Average		0.38
Denmark	P. Nyrup Rasmussen	−0.36**
(1998)	U. Ellemann-Jensen	0.52**
	P. Stig Møller	0.26**
Average		0.38
Portugal	J. Barroso	0.55**
(1997)	A. Guterres	−0.24**
	P. Portas	0.35**
Average		0.38
Hungary	Gyula Horn	−0.39**
(1998)	Viktor Orban	0.34**
	Jozsef Torgyan	0.36**
Average		0.36
Norway	Thorbjorn Jagland	−0.17**
(1997)	Carl Ivar Hagen	0.45**
	Jan Petersen	0.40**
Average		0.34
Switzerland	Christoph Blocher	0.50**
(1999)	Ruth Dreifuss	−0.34**
	Franz Steinegger	0.18**
Average		0.34
United Kingdom	Tony Blair	−0.30**
(1997)	John Major	0.40**
	Paddy Ashdown	−0.16**
Average		0.29
United States	Bill Clinton	−0.27**
	Bob Dole	0.31**
Average		0.29
Russia	Zyuganov	−0.51**
(1999)	Kiriyenko	0.18**
	Luzhkov	−0.12**
Average		0.27

(Continued)

Table 18.5   *(Continued)*

Germany	Schroeder	−0.21**
(1998)	Kohl	0.26**
	Waigel	0.28**
Average		0.25
Netherlands	Wim Kok	−0.10**
(1998)	Frits Bolkesetein	0.34**
	J. De Hoop	0.21**
Average		0.22
Slovenia	Janez Drnovsek	−0.19**
	Marjan Podobnik	0.12**
	Janez Jansa	0.36**
Average		0.22
Romania	Emil Constantinescu	0.19**
	Ion Iliescu	−0.17**
Average		0.18
Taiwan	Lee Tung-Hui	0.10*
	Peng Ming Min	−0.02
	Lin Yang-Gang	0.19**
Average		0.10
Mexico	E. Zedillo	0.12**
(2000)	D. Fernández de Cevallos	0.11**
	Cardenas Solorzano	−0.05
Average		0.08
Peru	A. Toledo	−0.05
	A. García	0.03
	L. Flores	0.13**
Average		0.04

Entries are Pearson correlation scores between respondents' left–right ideological self-placement and their evaluation of specified leaders. The country average is an unweighted average of the absolute values of the three individual correlations for the country. Non-significant correlations do not differ statistically from 0 at the 90% confidence level, and hence we treated them as a correlation of 0 in calculating the country average.

*Significant at 0.10 level.

**Significant at 0.05 level.

who compare party systems on the basis of the number of parties would lump together multiparty cases regardless of the level of institutionalization, the weakly institutionalized cases differ markedly from solidly entrenched ones. Treating all multiparty systems as an undifferentiated category when there are vast differences in institutionalization is misleading. Ecuador, Norway, Peru, Russia, and Sweden have multiparty systems, but the systems in Norway and Sweden are much more institutionalized than those in Ecuador, Peru, and Russia. Lumping together these cases of multipartyism conceals profound differences in the nature of the systems.

Institutionalization also varies significantly relative to ideological distance in the party system. Some polarized systems (e.g., France from the 1960s to the 1980s, Italy from the 1940s to the 1980s) were well institutionalized. Other polarized systems (e.g., Brazil in the mid- to late 1980s, Venezuela since 1998) are less institutionalized and function in a different manner. A key issue in the comparative study of party systems, as much as the number of parties and the ideological distance among them, is their level of institutionalization.

Our focus in this chapter has been on the crucial differences in party system institutionalization and ways in which these differences dictate a need to rethink party system theory. Spatial constraints prohibit an extended discussion of the consequences of weak party system institutionalization. Mainwaring and Scully (1995),

Mainwaring (1999: 323–36), Moser (1999, 2001), Payne *et al.* (2002), and Stoner Weiss (2001) have written about some such consequences. Our intuition is that institutionalization has important consequences for democratic politics. Otherwise, it would not be a paramount issue in studying party systems. We therefore close with two observations about consequences of weak system institutionalization.

First, weak institutionalization introduces more uncertainty regarding electoral outcomes and can weaken democratic regimes. The turnover from one party to others is higher, the entry barriers to new parties are lower, and the likelihood that a personalistic anti-system politician can become the head of government is much higher. Such uncertainty proved inimical to democracy until the 1980s, when the end of the Cold War reduced the stakes of political conflict and facilitated the post-1989 expansion of democracy and semi-democracy in the world. Even in the post-Cold War context, the much higher level of personalism in weakly institutionalized party systems can pave the way toward authoritarianism – e.g., President Alberto Fujimori in Peru in 1992 or toward the erosion of democratic or semi-democratic regimes – e.g., President Hugo Chávez in Venezuela since 1998 (Mayorga, forthcoming; Tanaka, forthcoming).

Second, weak institutionalization is inimical to electoral accountability. In most democracies, parties are the primary mechanism of electoral accountability. For electoral accountability to work well, voters must be able to identify – in broad terms – what the main parties are and what they stand for (Hinich and Munger, 1994). In contexts where parties frequently appear and disappear, where the competition among them is ideologically and programmatically diffuse, and where personalities often overshadow parties as routes to executive power, the prospects for effective electoral accountability suffer.[22]

For electoral accountability and political representation to function well, the political environment must provide citizens with effective information cues that enable them to vote in reasoned ways without spending an inordinate time reaching these reasoned decisions. In institutionalized systems, parties provide an ideological reference that gives some anchoring to voters. Voters can reduce information costs using the shortcuts at their disposal, thus increasing the levels of electoral accountability. The limited stability of less institutionalized party systems and the weak programmatic/ideological

content that party labels provide in these contexts reduce the information cues that these systems offer voters. The weaker information cues hamper the bounded rationality of voters, undercutting the potential for electoral accountability based on a rational evaluation of policies, governments, and leaders. Where electoral accountability suffers, the promise that representative democracy holds, that elected politicians will serve as agents of the voters to advance some common good or to advance interests of specific constituencies, may break down (Luna and Zechmeister, 2005).

In one of the most famous quotes in the history of the analysis of political parties, Schattschneider (1942: 1) wrote that 'Political parties created modern democracy and modern democracy is unthinkable save in terms of the parties'. If the history of modern democracy is built on political parties, then we can expect democracy to have some deficiencies where parties are less stable mechanisms of representation, accountability, and structuring than they have been in the advanced industrial democracies.

NOTES

* We are grateful to Michael Coppedge, Marta Fraile, Anna Grzymala-Bussa, Frances Hagopian, Kevin Krause, Iganacio Lago, Carol Mershon, José Ramón Montero, Richard Rose, and Edurne Zoco for comments. Edurne Zoco, Angel Alvárez, Lorenzo Brusattin, and Terence Merritt provided research assistance. Peter Baker, Eugene Bartkus, Viva Bartkus, Pradeep Chhibber, Dwight Dyer, Kevin Krause, Bong-jun Ko, Mark Jubulis, Vello Pettai, Marina Popescu, Gabor Toka, Edward Rakhimkulov, and Edurne Zoco helped us identify party splits, mergers, and changes of name.
1. We follow the definitions of democracy and semi-democracy in Mainwaring *et al.* (2001). Competitive political regimes include both democracies and semi-democracies.
2. Our focus is on party *systems*. Other scholars have looked at the institutionalization of *parties* (Dix, 1992; Gunther and Hopkin, 2002; Huntington, 1968: 12–28; Janda, 1980; Levitsky, 2003; Mény, 1990; Panebianco, 1988; Randall and Svåsand, 2002). Party institutionalization in democracies is positively and strongly correlated to party system institutionalization, but the relationship is not linear, as Mainwaring and Scully (1995: 20–1), Randall and Svåsand (2002), Stockton (2001), and Wallis (2003) have noted.

3. Because Huntington's discussion of institutionalization is well known, it is worth noting that our concept differs from his. We focus on party *systems*; he focused on parties. More important, he viewed parties as more institutionalized when they were more autonomous with respect to social groups. We believe contrariwise that strong links between parties and social groups manifest deeper party roots in society and higher institutionalization.

4. When a party split into two or more parties from election T1 to T2, we compared its T2 total with the largest split-off. We then treated the smaller new splinter party as if it had no votes in election T1. When two or more parties merged and created a new organization, we calculated volatility using the original party with the highest percentage. If two or more parties merged for election T2, but competed in election T1 as separate parties, we assumed that the one(s) with fewer votes disappeared in election T2. We gave a zero value to this party in T2 and counted its share of the vote in T1 as its percentage of change. When a party changed its name but had an obvious continuity with a previous party, we counted them as being the same organization. We usually treated independents as a category because we lacked the data needed for comparing individuals' results from one election to the next.

5. Freedom House publishes an annual report on the state of civil liberties and political rights in most countries. Scores ranges from 1 (best) to 7 (worst). We combined the two scores, creating an index from 2 (most democratic) to 14 (most authoritarian).

6. We did not include Bangladesh and the Philippines because of incomplete electoral results. For Ecuador, we used results for deputies selected in a country-wide district, not the separate results for federal deputies elected in province-wide districts.

7. For Belgium, France, Italy, the Netherlands, the UK, and West Germany, we used the European Election Study 1994.

8. Janda (1980) also argued that party institutionalization is a question of age. Tavits (2005) argues that in post-Communist Europe, volatility first increased only to later diminish.

9. We disagree that the left–right dimension necessarily refers exclusively or even primarily to an economic dimension. Rather, it incorporates historically changing issues, of which economic issues were salient in most advanced industrial democracies. In many advanced industrial democracies, religion has been a better predictor of left–right position than class. Increasingly in the past two decades, post-materialism has become an important predictor of left–right position (Inglehart, 1984, 1990; Kitschelt, 1994).

10. Iversen (1994b) and Merrill and Grofman (1999) integrate the proximity and directional spatial models. Iversen (1994a) integrates spatial theory with an understanding that parties influence voters. Hibbing and Theiss-Morse (2002) criticize spatial theory; they argue that ideological voting is less important than spatial models claim.

11. One important contrasting approach to ideological voting is voting based on government performance. For example, Fiorina's (1981) seminal work assumes voting on the basis of retrospective assessments about policy benefits. Theories about economic voting (Kiewet and Kinder, 1979) are also predicated upon the assumption that voters make their electoral choices as a function of government performance. See Sánchez-Cuenca (2003) for a synthesis of ideological and performance-based approaches to voting.

12. The left-right scale is a good summary of ideology in most countries (Alcántara, 1995; Dalton, 1985; Inglehart, 1984; Sani and Sartori, 1983). In many Latin American countries, large numbers of voters do not have a good grasp of the left-right scale, but, in a similar vein, they do not have a sophisticated grasp of programmatic issues. In a personal communication, Kevin Krause noted that in some countries with significant ethnic divides (e.g., Slovakia), left-right position is not a good summary of ideology.

13. For the USA, we used only two parties because the third party was electorally insignificant.

14. We calculated coefficients that were not significant at $p \leq .10$ as equal to 0 because they are statistically distinguishable from 0 at that level.

15. See Inglehart and Klingemann (1976, Table 13.3) for comparable data on standard deviations of party supporters in Western Europe in 1973. Ireland was an outlier, with a tenuous relationship between left–right self-location and party preference.

16. With weak ideological voting yet very stable electoral patterns, the USA is a notable exception to this generalization. US exceptionalism shows that programmatic/ideological linkages are not the only route to a stable party system. High entry barriers to new parties help explain the US anomaly. They help enable the Republicans and Democrats to dominate the electoral market despite modest ideological structuring.

17. We do not have data that would allow us to compare the extent of clientelistic voting across different countries. Considerable evidence – although it is not systematic – indicates that clientelism is more widespread in most third- and fourth-wave democracies than in the advanced industrialized democracies. See Ames (2001), Guevara Mann (2001), Hagopian (1996), Hartlyn (1988: 170–83), Legg and

Lemarchand (1972), Mainwaring (1999: 175–218), O'Donnell (1996), Scott (1972), and Stokes (forthcoming).

18. Silveira (1998) is an excellent study of personalistic voting in Brazil. He emphasizes the non-programmatic, non-ideological aspects of poor Brazilian voters. This theme has echoes in some literature on the USA (Converse, 1964; Hibbing and Theiss-Morse, 2002), but it cuts against most of the recent work on the advanced industrial democracies. The literature on populism is relevant to the analysis of personalistic voting. Populist leaders establish a direct, personalistic relationship to the masses. See Roberts (1995), Weffort (1978) and Weyland (1999).

19. The following gives additional details of how we coded whether candidates were outsiders or not:

1. Our intention was to count only those parties that are really new. Therefore, if a party changed its name from election t to election $t+1$, we did not count it as a new party at $t+1$.
2. For the same reason, we did not count an alliance (coalition) of previously existing parties as a new party.
3. We did not count a merger of two previously existing parties as a new party.
4. In cases of a party schism, neither of the resulting parties is counted as new.
5. We count as independents candidates who did not have a party affiliation.

20. There are two types of outsiders: those who had never been national politicians and ran against the establishment – such as Alberto Fujimori, Hugo Chávez, and Lucio Gutiérrez – and those outside the party system – such as Rafael Caldera and Álvaro Uribe Vélez. The former have no prior national political experience and the latter are dissidents from traditional parties. Our analysis includes both kinds of politician.

21. Along similar lines, Mainwaring (2003) argues that parties in less institutionalized democracies (most post-1978 cases) have different objectives than parties in the advanced industrial democracies. Parties in less institutionalized democracies are concerned about objectives involving the political regime (preserving or undermining it) in addition to electoral and policy objectives.

22. Electoral accountability also suffers where parties undertake radical policy shifts, as occurred in many Latin American countries in the 1980s and 1990s (Stokes, 2001). In some fluid systems, large numbers of legislators switch parties during their terms (Heller and Mershon, 2005). This practice also weakens electoral accountability.

REFERENCES

Alcántara, Manuel (1995) 'La elite parlamentaria latinoamericana y el continuo izquierda-derecha', in Wilhelm Hofmeister and Josef Thesing (eds), *Transformación de los sistemas politicos en América Latina*. Buenos Aires: Konrad Adenauer/CIEDLA, pp. 385–410.

Ames, Barry (2001) *The Deadlock of Democracy in Brazil*. Ann Arbor: University of Michigan Press.

Barnes, Samuel H. (1977) *Representation In Italy: Institutionalized Tradition and Electoral Choice*. Chicago: University of Chicago Press.

Bartolini, Stefano and Mair, Peter (1990) *Identity, Competition and Electoral Availability: The Stabilisation of European Electorates, 1885–1985*. Cambridge: Cambridge University Press.

Bendel, Petra (1993) 'Partidos políticos y sistemas de partidos en Centromérica', in Dieter Nohlen (ed.), *Elecciones y sistemas de partidos en América Latina*. San José: Instituto Interamericano de Derechos Humanos/CAPEL, pp. 315–53.

Bielasiak, Jack (2002) 'The institutionalization of electoral and party systems in postcommunist states', *Comparative Politics*, 34(2): 189–210.

Budge, Ian (1994) 'A new spatial theory of party competition: Uncertainty, ideology and policy equilibria viewed comparatively and temporally', *British Journal of Political Science*, 24: 443–67.

Chalmers, Douglas (1964) *The Social Democratic Party of Germany: From Working Class Movement to Modern Political Party*. New Haven, CT: Yale University Press.

Conaghan, Catherine M. (2000) 'The irrelevant right: Alberto Fujimori and the new politics of pragmatic Peru', in Kevin J. Middlebrook (ed.), *Conservative Parties, the Right, and Democracy in Latin America*. Baltimore, MD: Johns Hopkins University Press, pp. 255–84.

Converse, Philip E. (1964) 'The nature of belief systems in mass publics', in David Apter (ed.), *Ideology and Discontent*. New York: Free Press, pp. 206–61.

Converse, Philip E. (1969) 'Of time and stability', *Comparative Political Studies*, 2(2): 139–71.

Converse, Philip E. and Pierce, Roy (1986) *Political Representation in France*. Cambridge, MA: Harvard University Press.

Coppedge, Michael (1998) 'The dynamic diversity of Latin American party systems', *Party Politics*, 4: 547–68.

Cox, Gary (1990) 'Centripetal and centrifugal incentives in electoral systems', *American Journal of Political Science*, 34: 903–35.

Crewe, Ivor and King, Anthony (1994) 'Are British elections becoming more "presidential"?', in M. Kent Jennings and Thomas E. Mann (eds), *Elections at Home and Abroad: Essays in Honor of Warren E. Miller*. Ann Arbor: University of Michigan Press.

Dalton, Robert J. (1985) 'Political parties and political representation: Party supporters and party elites in nine nations', *Comparative Political Studies*, 18: 276–99.

Dalton, Robert J., McAllister, Ian and Wattenberg, Martin (2000) 'The consequences of partisan dealignment', in Robert J. Dalton and Martin Wattenberg (eds), *Parties without Partisans: Political Change in Advanced Industrial Democracies*. Oxford: Oxford University Press, pp. 37–63.

Dix, Robert (1992) 'Democratization and the institutionalization of Latin American political parties', *Comparative Political Studies*, 24: 488–96.

Downs, Anthony (1957) *An Economic Theory of Democracy*. New York: Harper & Row.

Enelow, James and Hinich, Melvin (1984) *The Spatial Theory of Voting: An Introduction*. Cambridge: Cambridge University Press.

Fiorina, Morris (1981) *Retrospective Voting in America National Elections*. New Haven, CT: Yale University Press.

Fleury, Christopher J. and Lewis-Beck, Michael S. (1993) 'Anchoring the French voter: Ideology versus party', *Journal of Politics*, 55: 1100–9.

Fuchs, Dieter and Klingemann, Hans Dieter (1990) 'The left-right schema', in M. Kent Jennings, Jan W. van Deth, *et al.*, *Continuities in Political Action: A Longitudinal Study of Political Orientations in Three Western Democracies*. Berlin: Walter de Gruyter, pp. 203–43.

Grzymala-Busse, Anna (2002) 'The effects of Communist party transformation on the institutionalization of party systems', in András Bozéki and John Ishiyama (eds), *The Communist Successor Parties of Central and Eastern Europe*. Armonk, NY: M.E. Sharpe, pp. 323–40.

Guevara Mann, Carlos (2001) 'Forsaken virtue: An analysis of the political behavior of Panamanian legislators, 1984–1999', Ph.D. University of Notre Dame.

Gunther, Richard P. and Diamond, Larry (2003) 'Species of political parties. A new typology', *Party Politics*, 9: 167–99.

Gunther, Richard P. and Hopkin, Jonathan (2002) 'A crisis of Institutionalization: The collapse of the UCD in Spain', in Richard P. Gunther, Juan Ramón Montero, and Juan J. Linz (eds), *Political Parties: Old Concepts and New Challenges*. Oxford: Oxford University Press, pp. 191–230.

Hagopian, Francis (1996) *Traditional Politics and Regime Change in Brazil*. New York and Cambridge: Cambridge University Press.

Hartlyn, Jonathan (1988) *The Politics of Coalition Rule in Colombia*. Cambridge: Cambridge University Press.

Heller, William B. and Mershon, Carol (2005) 'Party switching in the Italian Chamber of Deputies', *Journal of Politics* 67: 536–59.

Hibbing, John and Theiss-Morse, Elizabeth (2002) *Stealth Democracy: Americans' Beliefs about How Government Should Work*. Cambridge: Cambridge University Press.

Hinich, Melvin and Munger, Michael (1994) *Ideology and the Theory of Political Choice*. Ann Arbor: University of Michigan Press.

Huntington, Samuel (1968) *Political Order in Changing Societies*. New Haven, CT: Yale University Press.

Huntington, Samuel (1991) *The Third Wave: Democratization in the Late Twentieth Century*. Norman: University of Oklahoma Press.

Inglehart, Ronald (1979) 'The impact of values, cognitive level and social background', in Samuel H. Barnes, Max Kaase, *et al.* (eds), *Political Action*. Beverly Hills, CA: Sage, pp. 343–80.

Inglehart, Ronald (1984) 'The changing structure of political cleavages in Western society', in Russell J. Dalton, Scott Flanagan, and Paul Beck (eds), *Electoral Change in Advanced Industrial Democracies: Realignment or Dealignment?* Princeton, NJ: Princeton University Press, pp. 24–69.

Inglehart, Ronald (1990) *Culture Shift in Advanced Industrial Democracy*. Princeton, NJ: Princeton University Press.

Inglehart, Ronald and Klingemann, Hans-Dieter (1976) 'Party identification, ideological preference and the left–right dimension among Western mass publics', in Ian Budge, Ivor Crewe and Dennis Farlie (eds), *Party Identification and Beyond: Representations of Voting and Party Competition*. London: Wiley, pp. 243–73.

Iversen, Torben (1994a) 'The logics of electoral politics: Spatial, directional, and mobilizational effects', *Comparative Political Studies*, 27: 155–89.

Iversen, Torben (1994b) 'Political leadership and representation in West European democracies: A test of three models of voting', *American Journal of Political Science*, 38: 45–74.

Janda, Kenneth (1980) *Political Parties: A Cross National Survey*. New York: Free Press.

Johnson, Elaine Paige (2002) 'Streams of least resistance: The institutionalization of political parties and democracy in Indonesia', Ph.D. dissertation, University of Virginia.

Kaase, Max (1994) 'Is there personalization in politics? Candidates and voting behavior in Germany', *International Political Science Review*, 15: 211–30.

Kalyvas, Stathis N. (1996) *The Rise of Christian Democracy in Western Europe*. Ithaca, NY: Cornell University Press.

Kiewet, Roderick D. and Kinder, Donald (1979) Economic discontent and political behavior: The role of personal grievances and collective economic judgments in congressional voting', *American Journal of Political Science*, 23: 495–527.

King, Anthony (2002a) 'Do leaders' personalities really matter?', in Anthony King (ed.), *Leaders' Personalities and the Outcomes of Democratic Elections.* Oxford: Oxford University Press, pp. 1–43.

King, Anthony (2002b) 'Conclusions and implications', in Anthony King (ed.), *Leaders' Personalities and the Outcomes of Democratic Elections.* Oxford: Oxford University Press, pp. 210–22.

Kitschelt, Herbert (1994) *The Transformation of European Social Democracy.* Cambridge: Cambridge University Press.

Kitschelt, Herbert (2000) 'Linkages between citizens and politicians in democratic politics', *Comparative Political Studies*, 33: 845–79.

Kitschelt, Herbert (2003) 'Party competition in Latin America and post-communist Eastern Europe: Divergence of patterns, similarity of explanatory variables'. Paper prepared for delivery at the 100th Annual Meeting of the American Political Science Association, Philadelphia, August 27–31.

Kitschelt, Herbert *et al.* (1999) *Post-communist Party Systems: Competition, Representation, and Inter-Party Competition.* Cambridge: Cambridge University Press.

Klingemann, Hans-Dieter (1979) 'Measuring ideological conceptualization', in Samuel H. Barnes, Max Kaase, *et al.* (eds), *Political Action.* Beverly Hills, CA: Sage, pp. 279–303.

Knutsen, Oddbjørn (1997) 'The partisan and value-based component of the left-right self-placement: Comparative study', *International Political Science Review*, 18: 191–225.

Kuenzi, Michelle and Lambright, Gina (2001) 'Party system institutionalization in 30 African countries', *Party Politics*, 7: 437–68.

Laponce, Jean A. (1981) *Left and Right: The Topography of Political Perceptions.* Toronto: University of Toronto Press.

Legg, Keith and Lemarchand, Rene (1972) 'Political clientelism and development: A preliminary analysis', *Comparative Politics*, 4: 149–78.

Levitsky, Steven (2003) *Transforming Labor-Based Parties in Latin America: Argentine Peronism in Comparative Perspective.* Cambridge: Cambridge Unversity Press.

Lipset, Seymour Martin and Rokkan, Stein (1967) 'Cleavage structures, party systems, and voter alignments: An introduction', in Seymour Martin Lipset and Stein Rokkan (eds), *Party Systems and Voter Alignments: Cross-National Perspectives.* New York: Free Press, pp. 1–64.

Luna, Juan P. and Zechmeister, Elizabeth J. (2005) 'Political representation in Latin America. A study of elite-mass congruence in nine countries', *Comparative Political Studies*, 38: 388–416.

Mainwaring, Scott P. (1999) *Rethinking Party Systems in the Third Wave of Democratization: The*

Case of Brazil. Stanford, CA: Stanford University Press.

Mainwaring, Scott P. (2003) 'Party objectives in context of authoritarianism or fragile democracy: A dual game', in Scott Mainwaring and Timothy R. Scully (eds), *Christian Democracy in Latin America: Electoral Competition and Regime Conflicts.* Stanford, CA: Stanford University Press, pp. 3–33.

Mainwaring, Scott and Scully, Timothy R. (1995) 'Party systems in Latin America', in Scott Mainwaring and Timothy R. Scully (eds), *Building Democratic Institutions: Party Systems in Latin America.* Stanford, CA: Stanford University Press, pp. 1–34.

Mainwaring, Scott, Brinks, Daniel and Pérez-Liñan, Aníbal (2001) 'Classifying political regimes in Latin America, 1945–1999', *Studies in Comparative International Development*, 36(1): 37–65.

Mair, Peter (1997) *Party System Change: Approaches and Interpretations.* Oxford: Clarendon Press.

Markowski, Radek (2000) 'Party system institutionalization and democratic consolidation: On the idiosyncracies of the Polish case', in Janina Frentzel-Zagorska and Jacek Wasilewski (eds), *The Second Generation of Democratic Elites in Central and Eastern Europe.* Warsaw: Institute of Political Studies, Polish Academy of Sciences, pp. 65–89.

Mayorga, René Antonio (forthcoming) 'Outsiders and neo-populism: The road to plebiscitary democracy', in Scott Mainwaring, Ana María Bejarano, and Eduardo Pizarro (eds), *When Representation Fails: The Crisis of Democratic Representation in the Andes.* Stanford, CA: Stanford University Press.

Mény, Yves (1990) *Government and Politics in Western Europe.* Oxford: Oxford University Press.

Merrill III, Samuel and Grofman, Bernard (1999) *A Unified Theory of Voting: Directional and Proximity Spatial Models.* Cambridge: Cambridge University Press.

Molina, José and Pérez, Carmen (2004) 'Radical change at the ballot box: Causes and consequences of electoral behavior in Venezuela's 2000 elections', *Latin American Politics and Society*, 46(1): 103–34.

Moser, Robert (1995) 'The emergence of political parties in post-Soviet Russia', Ph.D. dissertation, University of Wisconsin.

Moser, Robert (1999) 'Electoral systems and the number of parties in post-Communist states', *World Politics*, 51: 359–84.

Moser, Robert (2001) *Unexpected Outcomes: Electoral Systems, Political Parties, and Representation in Russia.* Pittsburgh: University of Pittsburgh Press.

O'Donnell, Guillermo (1996) 'Illusions about consolidation', *Journal of Democracy* 7(2): 34–51.

Ostiguy, Pierre (1998) 'Peronism and anti-Peronism: Class-cultural cleavages and political identity in

Argentina', Ph.D. dissertation, University of California, Berkeley.

Panebianco, Angelo (1988) *Political Parties: Organization and Power*. Cambridge: Cambridge University Press.

Payne, Mark, Zovatto, Daniel, Carillo Flórez, Fernando and Allamand Zavala, Andrés (2002) *Democracies in Development: Politics and Reform in Latin America*. Washington, DC: Inter-American Development Bank and the International Institute for Democracy and Electoral Assistance.

Pedersen, Mogens N. (1983) 'Changing patterns of electoral volatility in European party systems: Explorations in explanation', in Hans Daalder and Peter Mair (eds), *Western European Party Systems: Continuity and Change*. Beverly Hills, CA and London: Sage, pp. 29–66.

Pizzorno, Alessandro (1981) 'Interests and parties in pluralism', in Suzanne Berger (ed.), *Organizing Interests in Western Europe: Pluralism, Corporatism, and the Transformation of Politics*. New York: Cambridge University Press, pp. 247–84.

Przeworski, Adam (1975) 'Institutionalization of voting patterns, or is mobilization the source of decay?', *American Political Science Review*, 69: 49–67.

Rabinowitz, George and MacDonald, Stuart Elaine (1989) 'A directional theory of issue voting', *American Political Science Review*, 83: 93–121.

Rabinowitz, George, MacDonald, Stuart Elaine and Listhaug, Ola (1991) 'Old players in an old game: Party strategy in multiparty systems', *Comparative Political Studies*, 24: 147–85.

Randall, Vicky and Svåsand, Lars (2002) 'Party institutionalization in new democracies', *Party Politics*, 8: 5–29.

Remmer, Karen (1991) 'The political impact of economic crisis in Latin America in the 1980s', *American Political Science Review*, 85: 777–800.

Roberts, Kenneth M. (1995) 'Neoliberalism and the transformation of populism in Latin America: The Peruvian case', *World Politics*, 48(1): 82–116.

Roberts, Kenneth M. and Wibbels, Erik (1999) 'Party systems and electoral volatility in Latin America: A test of economic, institutional, and structural explanations', *American Political Science Review*, 93: 575–90.

Rose, Richard, and Munro, Neil (2003) *Elections and Parties in New European Democracies*. Washington, DC: CQ Press.

Sánchez-Cuenca, Ignacio (2003) 'How can governments be accountable if voters vote ideologically' Working Paper 191, Center for Advanced Study in the Social Sciences, Instituto Juan March.

Sani, Giacomo, and Sartori, Giovanni (1983) 'Polarization, fragmentation, and competition in Western democracies', in Hans Daalder and Peter Mair (eds), *Western European Party Systems*. Beverly Hills, CA: Sage, pp. 307–40.

Sartori, Giovanni (1976) *Parties and Party Systems: A Framework for Analysis*. New York and Cambridge: Cambridge University Press.

Sartori, Giovanni (1989) 'Video-power', *Government and Opposition*, 24(1): 39–53.

Schattschneider, Elmer Eric (1942) *Party Government*. New York: Farrar and Rinehart.

Schedler, Andreas (1995) 'Under- and overinstitutionalization: Some ideal typical propositions concerning old and new party systems'. Working Paper 213, Kellogg Institute for International Studies, University of Notre Dame.

Scott, James (1972) 'Patron-client politics and political change in Southeast Asia', *American Political Science Review*, 66: 91–113.

Scully, Timothy R. (1992) *Rethinking the Center: Cleavages, Critical Junctures, and Party Evolution in Chile*. Stanford, CA: Stanford University Press.

Silveira, Flavio (1998) *A Decisão do voto no Brasil*. Porto Alegre: Edipucrs.

Stockton, Hans (2001) 'Political parties, party systems, and democracy in East Asia: Lessons from Latin America', *Comparative Political Studies*, 34(1): 94–119.

Stokes, Susan (2001) *Mandates and Democracy: Neoliberalism by Surprise in Latin America*. Cambridge: Cambridge University Press.

Stokes, Susan (forthcoming) 'Perverse accountability: A formal model of machine politics with evidence from Argentina', *American Political Science Review*.

Stoner Weiss, Kathryn (2001) 'The limited reach of Russia's party system: Underinstitutionalization in dual transitions', *Politics and Society*, 29: 385–414.

Tanaka, Martín (forthcoming) 'From cisis to collapse of the party systems and dilemmas of democratic representation: Peru and Venezuela', in Scott Mainwaring, Ana María Bejarano, and Eduardo Pizarro (eds), *When Representation Fails: The Crisis of Democratic Representation in the Andes*. Stanford, CA: Stanford University Press.

Tavits, Margit (2005) 'The development of stable party support: Electoral dynamics in post-Communist Europe', *American Journal of Political Science*, 49: 283–98.

Tóka, Gábor (1997) 'Political parties and democratic consolidation in East Central Europe', in Larry Diamond, Marc F. Plattner, Yun-han Chu, and Hung-mao Tien (eds), *Consolidating the Third Wave Democracies: Themes and Perspectives*. Baltimore, MD: Johns Hopkins University Press, pp. 93–134.

Torcal, Mariano, Gunther, Richard P. and Montero, José Ramón (2002) 'Anti-party sentiments in southern Europe', in Richard P. Gunther, José Ramón Montero and Juan J. Linz (eds), *Political Parties: Old Concepts and New Challenges*. Oxford: Oxford University Press, pp. 257–90.

United Nations Development Programme (2003) *Human Development Report*. New York: Oxford University Press.

Valenzuela, J. Samuel (1997) 'The origins and transformations of the Chilean party system', in Fernando J. Devoto and Torcuato S. Di Tella (eds), *Political Culture, Social Movements and Democratic Transitions in South America in the XXth Century*. Milan: Feltrinelli, pp. 47–99.

Van Cott, Donna Lee (2000) 'Party systems development and indigenous populations in Latin America: The Bolivian case', *Party Politics*, 6: 155–74.

Wallis, Darren (2003) 'Democratizing a hegemonic regime: From institutionalized party to institutionalized party system in Mexico?', *Democratization*, 10(3): 15–38.

Weffort, Francisco (1978) *O Populismo na Política Brasileira*. Rio de Janeiro: Paz e Terra.

Westholm, Anders (1997) 'Distance versus direction: The illusory defeat of the proximity theory of electoral choice', *American Political Science Review*, 91: 865–83.

Weyland, Kurt (1999) 'Neoliberal populism in Latin America and Eastern Europe', *Comparative Politics*, 31: 379–401.

White, Stephen, Rose, Richard and McAllister, Ian (1997) *How Russia Votes*. Chatham, NJ: Chatham House.

19

PARTY POLITICS IN POST-COMMUNIST TRANSITION

Zsolt Enyedi

Party politics in post-communist countries typically is analyzed from the vantage points of democratization and consolidation despite the fact that the most recent developments in these party systems are often unrelated to the transition process or to communism *per se*. The collapse of the one-party totalitarian regime has presented party politics with a unique challenge. As a result, party behavior is substantially different from both the established liberal democracies and other third-wave democracies. The fact that the inclusion of citizens into the political body preceded the phase of contestation sets the region apart from Western Europe, where a competitive oligarchic system democratized, and Southern Europe, where both mobilization and contestation were at a low level under authoritarianism (van Biezen, 2003: 26). When democratization reached Eastern Europe, its citizens were already mobilized and politicized (Mair, 1997: 180). Endowed with the skills of 'cognitive mobilization', they can rely on their own education-based knowledge and on the information provided by the mass media.

Scholarship has moved away from emphasizing the underlying commonalities (Kitschelt, 1992), to accentuating the subregional specificities within the post-communist world (Ágh, 1998b; Evans and Whitefield, 1993; Kitschelt, 1995). However, heterogeneity makes post-communist party politics even more popular as the target of research. The similar immediate past and the diverging outcomes hold out to researchers the unique promise of tracing the effect of various institutional and cultural factors. There is one major obstacle that hinders the establishment of quasi-experimental research designs: it is difficult to disentangle the consequences of the political transition from the regional peculiarities. The Central Asian cases are yet to be incorporated into party research, the status of African socialist systems is contested, while Cuba, China or Vietnam are not (yet) in the post-communist box. That is, post-communist studies are predominantly Eastern European studies; the conceptual and the area studies approaches are intimately interwoven.

THE RELEVANCE OF PARTIES IN DEMOCRATIC CONSOLIDATION

The post-communist transformation is regarded as unique in its comprehensive character. A new economic system, a new political system, new constitutional regimes and, sometimes, new states were to be built simultaneously (Offe, 1991; Bunce, 1995). Parties had to face the legacy of weak or non-existent democratic experience and complete concentration of power under communism. Observers claim that both the difficulty and the necessity of building strong parties follow from the extent of these changes. Kitschelt (1996: 2), for example, states: 'In post-communist regimes, the early formation of powerful parties may be an even more important ingredient of democratic consolidation than elsewhere'. This expectation is built on the venerable tradition in political science that assigns crucial functions to parties in the stabilization of democratic regimes

(Huntington, 1968; Diamond, 1997; Mainwaring and Scully, 1995).

The actual role that parties fulfill in the region is hotly debated, however. Some authors include parties among the chief agents of the transition and consolidation (e.g., Ágh, 1998a; Elster *et al.*, 1998) while others consider them marginal and inconsequential (Tóka, 1997). Typically, the international environment and the deteriorating economic situation are regarded as the principal background factors of the transition, and communist *nomenklaturas*, the counter-elites and various civic initiatives ('fora', 'movements', or 'national fronts') are regarded as the principal local actors. Markowski (2001) argues that the development of diffuse political support may precede and not follow the institutionalization of the party system. The general ambiguity surrounding the role of parties is well illustrated by the comments of Lewis. On the one hand, he claims that parties were marginal in democratic transition, particularly in its early stages (Lewis, 2000: 20). On the other hand, he asserts: 'Competitive parties have been one of the primary organized agencies of political change and the main vehicle for the institutional development of post-communist democracy' (Lewis, 2000: xi).

The reach of the party system varies significantly across the region. Party competition is still under severe constraints in the regimes of Central Asia. Authoritarian regimes also developed in Belarus and Azerbaijan, and the pluralist political system has not yet been institutionalized in Georgia and Armenia. In these countries the struggle for power between elite factions unfolds on non-electoral fields, while elections only register the victory retrospectively (Segert, 1996: 232). Economies that depend on specific natural resources and that are organized according to informal rules provide a particularly hostile environment for regular alternation in power. The wars and civil wars that followed the collapse of communism in Yugoslavia, Moldova, and Georgia also hindered the stabilization and differentiation of parties. The two major Eastern European countries, Russia and Ukraine, possess a higher degree of pluralism, but both the relevance and the equality of their political parties are questionable. In Russia parties have little influence on the composition of the government. The military and security apparatuses, economic interest groups, regional governors, and the executive are the major players. Referring to government-sponsored parties, Sakwa (2001: 84) claims, 'Rather than parties forming the government, in Russia it was the executive branch that tended to take the initiative in party formations'.

As Freedom House scores attest, most other former communist countries can be considered formally democratic. But in many of them there were periods when the state developed particularly close ties with a party or a group of parties. Analysts often claimed to detect the reemergence of pre-war hegemonic parties and predominant party systems (Ágh, 1996: 255). Finally, however, only Central Asia, the Caucasus and Belarus produced the respective pattern. In other areas, frequent turnovers in government are more typical. Instead of authoritarianism, rather extreme competition endangers the stabilization of democracy (Mair, 1991). Elections end with government alternation more often than was the case after the democratic transition in the West partly because in Eastern Europe the representatives of the *ancien régime* could return to power (Beyme, 2003).

Structured competition, strong and stable links between parties and citizens, and stable party organization – in other words, party system institutionalization – has encountered considerable obstacles all over the post-communist world. Scholars most often point to the following hostile factors: weakness and instability of sociopolitical differentiation (meaning, in its moderate version, the lack of cleavages or, in its more radical formulation, the complete atomization of the society), alienation from the political system, elite-driven political transition, the particularly large influence of electronic media, anti-party sentiments, weak civil society, international constraints on government activities, and the shortness of democratic experience (Evans and Whitefield, 1993; Katz, 1996; Mair, 1997; Hanley, 2001).

High electoral volatility, low popularity of parties, relatively low turnout, small party membership, weak partisan identities, weak grounding of parties in civil society, their financial dependence on state, and low level of organizational loyalty among politicians are the most glaring signs of weak institutionalization. The lack of members and loyal supporters makes it difficult for parties to articulate and aggregate preferences. High volatility and shifting loyalties in the party elite weaken the accountability and responsiveness of officeholders (Tóka, 1997: 170).

Based on these observations, a major group of scholars emphasized the fluidity and immaturity of post-communist party politics. Another group of researchers, however, are ready to point out the emergence of relatively stable structures and the predominant role of parties, particularly in East-Central Europe. The difference between these two approaches is discussed below at systemic, sociological, organizational, and institutional levels.

The institutionalization perspective directs attention to the difference between the power of parties and personalities (Mainwaring, 1998). A contrast between individual political entrepreneurs and political parties indicates the dominance of the latter in Central Europe, and the prominence of the former in the former Soviet Union, with the exception of the Baltic countries. However, as the defeat of many famous individuals proves, personal popularity is nowhere a powerful enough electoral asset. Party leaders often have unquestioned authority within their parties, and their charismatic appeal may explain a considerable portion of the vote. But charismatic leadership does not always hurt party government. When leaders such as Klaus and Orbán emerge from within a party, maintain party loyalty, and invest considerable energy in working out an ideological framework, their role may even strengthen the crystallization of the party system. These leaders proved to be more effective politicians than their more famous colleagues (e.g., Wałęsa and Havel) exactly due to their firm party backing. Outsiders, such as the 1990 Polish presidential candidate Tyminski, achieve impressive results from time to time, but without a party behind them they cannot consolidate their achievements. The new political class was by and large created by the parties in these countries (Ágh, 1996: 260).

Independents have unprecedented influence, however, in the eastern part of the postcommunist world. In 2000 in Belarus 74% of legislators did not belong to parties. In Ukraine in 1994 two-thirds, and in 2002 21%, of the MPs were independent (Lewis, 2003: 154–5). The weakness of parties is most obvious at the level of local politics. Typically less than half of local councilors are party members.

Observers agree that political parties are rather weak in performing the functions of integration, mobilization, and mediation (Lewis, 2001: 486). However, in East-Central Europe their weakness in the representative functions is counterbalanced by their strength in procedural functions: organization of parliament and government, recruitment, etc. Through the privatization process they are able to create new owners and even new social strata. The dominant weight of parties in governing the society and in selecting the political elite may justify the concept of 'overparticization'. In Ágh's (1996: 251) view, parties may even endanger democracy by leaving no space for other organizations. Few institutions can challenge the influence of parties in these countries. The *esprit de corps* of the bureaucracy, the military, the judicial system, etc., was broken during the transition. The main exception to this rule is the mass media.

Goal definition and policy formulation are in the hands of presidents and lobby groups in the Eastern part of the region, while in Central Europe the political agenda is determined by parties and the principal decisions are made by party officials or by those who are under their control. Scholars are critical of the ability of parties to articulate preferences, but one must remember that alternative organizations such as trade unions, social movements, and civic initiatives also lack mobilizational potential and popularity.

Well-entrenched party systems are no guarantee for democratic consolidation if they compete according to clientelistic and not programmatic principles. Kitschelt (1995, 1996: 21, 2001) claims that this is particularly true when the electorates are relatively sophisticated, which is the case in most post-communist countries. Empirical analyses indicate that the ideological structuration of Eastern European party systems is comparable to the Western ones and is above the Latin American average (Kitschelt, 2003), but the intra-regional variation is considerable.

In Kitschelt's model, the chances of programmatic competition are related to the level of sociocultural development of the society, the sophistication of the electorate, the nature of the communist and pre-communist regimes, the type of transition, and the newly built institutional frameworks. All these factors are interconnected and bundled into various trajectories. In societies that were agrarian before the communist regimes, that lacked working-class movements and democratic experience, communism developed a nepotistic face. The regime faced no serious opposition, and, therefore, the elite could initiate preemptive reforms and stabilize its power through clientelistic linkages. The continued dominance of the old elite does evoke opposition in the society, but the emotionally loaded tensions between the communist and anti-communist social networks merely reinforce personalism and clientelism. On the other extreme, a high level of socioeconomic development (industrialization, urbanization, modern bureaucracy) and full-fledged party politics prior to communism, coupled with a replacement type of transition, present ideal conditions for programmatic competition.

As indicated by this logic, the success of the democratization process is often linked to the failure of the *ancien régime* forces to maintain a strong bargaining position. One way for the communist elite to preserve its grip on power is exactly to promote rules (majoritarian electoral system, presidentialism, etc.) that weaken the partisan logic and strengthen the role of personalities. Clientelism, patronage, and rent-seeking are also claimed to be closely related to the former communist parties' ability to maintain continuity (Kitschelt, 1996).

The negative impact of *ancien régime* elites on the consolidation of party systems is far from obvious, however. On average, the politicians of the successor parties were more loyal, professional and efficient than their opponents, who, in the first years at least, were amateurs, lacking organizational skills, party loyalty, and commitment to politics (Kopecký, 2003: 142–3). Many scholars work with a definition of a 'political party' that excludes the leading organizations of one-party states, since they are more like state organs than like voluntary organizations. The success of the communist organizations in the democratic era indicates, however, that there was more 'partyness' in these institutions than typically perceived.

DIMENSIONS OF PARTY SYSTEMS

Those scholars who describe post-communist party systems as open and inchoate attribute the high level of fluidity to such structural factors as the lack of stable party affiliations and the large stakes of competition (Mair, 1997). Given the high electoral volatility and the weakness of partisan traditions, politicians have no particular reason to be loyal to losing parties. Even joining non-parliamentary parties may be rational: parties that did not exist during the previous election captured a significant share, sometimes even the majority, of the votes in Russia (1999), Poland (2001), Slovakia (1998, 2001), Bulgaria (2001) and Latvia (1998, 2002). As a result, the loyalty of politicians does not always exceed that of voters. In Russia almost one-third of the seats changed hands between the election and the first Duma session in 1999. In Estonia, among those candidates who ran at successive elections, only 41% stuck to their party (Kreuzer and Pettai, 2003: 85).

Party system stability is not uniformly low in the region. In the Czech Republic and Hungary only one new parliamentary party emerged during the last decade, and they were both splinter groups of existing parties. In the Czech parliament, only two deputies quit their party between 1998 and 2002 (Williams, 2003: 53). Where a stable pattern of conflict develops, it seems to have a stabilizing effect on the attitudes and behavior of the voters. The relatively low electoral volatility of the Czech party system and the decrease in the Hungarian volatility, for example, are attributable to the consolidated structure of party competition (Toole, 2000).

The predictability of party systems increases if certain parties are unwilling to cooperate with each other. In this regard considerable structure characterizes post-communist party systems.[1] There are strong attempts on behalf of parties to isolate each other. The antagonism between 'arch-enemies' (e.g., Solidarity and the Social Democrats in Poland, the Social Democrats and the Civic Party in the Czech Republic, Meciar's Movement and the Christian Democrats in Slovakia, the Democrats and the Socialists in Albania or the Socialists and Fidesz in Hungary) helped the development of a bipolar structure.

The fact that the range of potential governing parties is restricted also contributes to the closure of the party systems. Orthodox communists are not seen as acceptable coalition partners in East-Central Europe, and the extreme right is also typically excluded (short-lived exceptions come from Slovakia and Yugoslavia). The West appears as a major constraining force in this regard. The victorious parties in Yugoslavia, Hungary and Romania, for example, received serious warnings not to rely on the support of respectively the Radicals, the MIÉP and the Greater Romania Party. In the Czech Republic, two parties have been permanently excluded from coalition alternatives. By stigmatizing the Republican party (SPR-RSC) and the Communist party (KSCM), the major parties have pushed one-fifth of the parliament out of the game. In this regard not so much openness but rather overdetermination seems to characterize coalition building.

Post-communist party systems are fragmented (Bielasiak, 2002), but the difference between Western and Eastern Europe is not dramatic (Birch, 2001). But note that, due to the various forms of cooperation between parties it is rather difficult to enumerate them. The Polish AWS, for example, was composed of more than 30 parties and other organizations (Szczerbiak, 2001). The widespread cooperation of parties in the region makes particularly obvious how weak the political science literature is on cooperation and fusion, as opposed to competition.

Institutional tinkering, together with the growing experience of voters, led to a decrease in the number of parties in East-Central Europe (Bielasiak, 2002: 204). The introduction of PR electoral rules in some countries seems to point in the opposite direction, but high fragmentation typically preceded, rather than followed this institutional change (Jasiewicz, 2003: 182).

The experience of small Western European countries taught political science that fragmentation does not necessarily undermine stability. The recent history of post-communist countries has a parallel message concerning polarization. Kitschelt (1996) highlights that programmatic polarization has both beneficial and pernicious effects: it may destabilize the system through frequent changes in policies and through stalemate, but it may also help by structuring programmatic divisions and increasing the level of representation. The empirical evidence indicates that high polarization typically goes together with more thorough consolidation in the region.

Polarization is not yet able, however, to stabilize electoral behavior. The classical dilemma of electoral behavior research was how to explain the stability of voting despite the general lack of political information, knowledge and stable attitudes towards political issues. In Eastern Europe the situation is one of instability in party affiliations despite the strong attempts of parties to create mental barriers and to offer the sense of deep divisions in society.

PATTERNS OF CONFLICT

As far as the emerging shape of the party systems is concerned, Western parties and party federations provide one of the most important stimuli, socializing the Eastern parties into their programmatic and coalitional preferences (Pridham, 2001). Pre-communist traditions also influence the landscape of parties. Cultural debates that were dormant for a long time reemerged, and considerable continuity with pre-war geographic voting patterns can be observed in some of these countries (Wittenberg, 1998), although the reestablished historical parties proved to be surprisingly weak.

While Western party families do have their local representatives, there are still relatively many parties that have no links to European party alliances and cannot be easily fitted into Western (or any) categories. Unreformed communist parties, populist but not extreme right groups (e.g., the Movement for Democratic Slovakia, People's Movement Rukh, Slovenian People's Party, the National Movement of Simeon II), the 'parties of power' (i.e., presidential parties), and electoral alliances formed around charismatic leaders (e.g., the Party for Civic Understanding (SOP) and Direction (SMER) in Slovakia) encountered difficulties finding allies in the West.

Center-right parties exist both in their Christian democratic and conservative variants, but some of them are probably better labelled as right authoritarian (Segert, 1996). They are often characterized by statist, anti-individualist and, therefore, anti-capitalist rhetoric. The left is typically dominated by the communist successor parties, some of them adopting a nationalistic rhetoric, others modernizing themselves into social democrats (Segert, 1996; Bozóki and Ishiyama, 2002). The extreme right, led by charismatic leaders, is present in most countries. These parties typically differ from their Western siblings in focusing not on immigration but on nationalism.

Party competition is most frequently projected into a two-dimensional space. According to Kitschelt's (1992) deductive reasoning, the rules specifying who is a legitimate player (inclusive or exclusive citizenship), and the nature of the rules the players are expected to follow (hierarchical or participatory mode of decision-making) form the first, libertarian–authoritarian or cosmopolitan–particularist dimension. Attitudes concerning the assets players are endowed with (market or non-market logic of distribution of resources) form the second axis. Where a free market is the status quo, libertarians are expected to have negative views on it and to search for alternatives. In state dominated economies anti-market views, however, must go together with an authoritarian orientation.[2]

In 'patrimonial regimes', which were characterized in the pre-communist era by a low level of bureaucratic institutionalization, intra-elite contestation, and interest articulation (e.g., Bulgaria and Romania), Kitschelt finds the political space is divided into communist and anti-communist authoritarians, the economic, political, and cultural divisions reinforce each other, and there is little room left for libertarians. In 'bureaucratic socialism' (the Czech part of Czechoslovakia, East Germany), early industrialization, secularization, and the strong working-class movement marginalized social division over morality and left distributive issues as the only source of division.

The dimension of authoritarianism–libertarianism is really consequential for party competition only in 'national-accommodative' regimes (Hungary, Poland, perhaps Croatia, Slovakia, Slovenia). In these countries the early reforms lessened the sharp economic differences. Parties looking for ways of differentiating themselves turn therefore to moral-cultural appeals involving issues such as nationalism, traditionalism, clericalism, anti-Westernism. Early industrialization and secularization did not crowd these issues off the agenda, and the fast collapse of state socialist political structure made the exclusive focus on anti-communism less plausible (Kitschelt, 2001: 312).

While it is difficult to prove the causal elements of the theory (e.g., that the relevance of a cultural issue is a function of the lack of differentiation on economic issues), the central role of cultural tensions is indeed a remarkable feature of the respective countries. Ideological competition typically produces three poles: the populist and libertarian socialists (post-communists) are pitted against pro-market libertarians and traditionalist Christian nationalists who are inclined to limit the market.

Most scholars (Berglund *et al.*, 2004: 605; Kitschelt *et al.*, 1999; Kitschelt, 2001: 312) regard the regime divide (anti-communism) as transitory, particularly in the national-accommodative countries. The logic behind this expectation is compelling, and yet a number of cases (e.g., Poland, Hungary, Bulgaria) seem to contradict it. In these countries anti-communism is one of the most important markers of right-wing identity and this issue has resurfaced in each electoral campaign since 1990.

Given the different trajectories, different patterns of competition can be found within close geographic proximity. In the Czech Republic, for example, one finds a unidimensional opposition between left and right, where the two poles are defined in economic terms. In Slovakia left–right terminology is much less useful in interpreting the alliance structure. Meciar's opposition includes Christian democrats, liberals, and social democrats, while among Meciar's supporters one finds nationalists and radical leftists alike. Authoritarianism seems to be a better label for the major divide (Krause, 2000). Until the 2004 European Parliament election Poland had been characterized by a well-entrenched logic of left–right alternation but a fluid right spectrum. In the party systems that belong to the Polish pattern, the real stake in party system formation is who dominates the right (Sitter, 2002: 447). A major source of instability in countries such as Romania, Poland, and Lithuania is that the repeated attempts at coordinating the right have failed. The decline in

Hungarian volatility, on the other hand, is largely due to the consolidation of Fidesz's reign over the right.

In those countries where a bipolar structure is discernible, the two poles are formed by socialist, social democratic and Christian conservative parties, similarly to the West. However, the bipolar pattern does not seem to be more resistant to change than other configurations. In Bulgaria, for example, a centrist movement could break through in spite of the earlier bipolar structure.

PARTY AND SOCIETY

The scope of support for the party systems is reflected in the level of turnout, strength of party identification, stability of voting patterns, level of party membership, and the attitudes of the citizens toward the party system. As indicated above, post-communist politics has a poor record on these dimensions, and this is from where the supporters of the immaturity thesis take most of their examples.

The distrust of parties is particularly high (Rose, 1995; Wyman *et al.*, 1995), and it goes together with a generally high level of dissatisfaction with democracy. Disappointment, rather than distrust, is indicated by the extraordinarily high electoral volatility figures (Tóka, 1998; Bielasiak, 2002). In Russia, around half of the electorate identifies with none of the parties, and consequently aggregate volatility was 51.4% in 1995 and 54.4% in 1999 (White, 2004). In some districts the option 'against all' is chosen by more people than any of the parties (Rose *et al.*, 2001). In Latvia, electoral volatility reached 74.2% by the third election (Kreuzer and Pettai, 2003: 84).

Turnout is typically low and somewhat declining, although cross-national differences are more remarkable than common trends. In some countries, parties clearly lost their mobilizational power as the party system crystallized,[3] while in others, they never had this power.[4] In a third group of countries, electoral participation seems to be a function of the degree of polarization.[5]

Most scholars suspect that behind the generally low level of popularity of party politics stand the weak linkages between parties and social groups. Post-communist politics is not based on cleavages in the way Western European politics was during the 20th century. This state of affairs is attributed to the nature of parties that emerged from elite debates concerning the institutional reforms and to the nature of societies that lack well-crystallized group structures. The novelty of market-based institutions may also hinder the development of economy-based group identifications. A large part of the literature regards the direct links between social structures and party systems as the key ingredient for the stabilization of the latter. The anchorage of parties in pre-existing social categories could speed up party system formation, and even compensate for a well-developed civil society (Evans and Whitefield, 1996).

Dissenters acknowledge that stable voting patterns are beneficial but claim that such patterns can occur in many ways, and not only through a strong correlation between social structure and vote. Tóka (1998) has demonstrated that pure value voting is stronger in cementing party loyalties in East-Central Europe than cleavage voting. There is little reason, in fact, to treat the social determination of party politics as a sign of democratic consolidation and party system maturity. In the era of media politics, secularization and individualization, tight group–party relations are unlikely to develop.

Despite the relative absence of well-crystallized social cleavages,[6] sociodemographic factors do shape electoral behavior. In particular, gender, age, education, region, level of religiosity, income and ethnicity have a strong influence on party preferences (Miller et al., 2000; Tóka, 1996, 1998). Ethnicity provides the most clear-cut cleavage line in the region, particularly when coupled with geographic concentration. Despite widespread views to the contrary, ethnic parties play a stabilizing role across the region.

Although observers regularly predict the future ascendance of the class cleavage (Mateju et al., 1999), up to now there have been few signs of class becoming a decisive factor. Successor parties typically attract lower-class voters but they cannot be regarded as class parties. The fear of the unknown on behalf of older voters with non-convertible skills explains the voter profile of these parties better than any kind of working-class movement.

PARTY ORGANIZATION

Post-communist parties are typically dominated by their leadership; the role of the members is secondary. Scattered information on the topic indicates that the trend towards centralization continues. The level of party membership is low, and membership fees contribute a small fragment of the parties' overall budget. Kopecký

(1995) attributes the neglect of members to the following reasons: the finances of the parties are based on other sources (mainly state transfers); the leaders see members as challengers; and the lack of preexisting party loyalties and the high level of depoliticization make it difficult to attract new members. Observers agree that post-communist transition did not produce mass parties. The labels applied vary, but the bottom line is that most parties in the region are known to have a shallow organizational structure (see also Mair, 1997; Katz, 1996: 122; Kopecký, 1995). Lewis (1996: 12) claims, 'The problem here is that the democratic post-communist parties not only lack anything like mass membership, they are also devoid of any developed organization or structure.' Some of the successor parties are recognized as exceptions: they rely more heavily on fees and have typically a more intensive internal life.

Researchers are likely to detect a higher level of organizational development if they focus less on members and more on organizational complexity. In terms of the degree of division of labor, the party's autonomy vis-à-vis its environment, the existence of branch offices around the country, elaborate party hierarchy and permanent and professional staff, the parties of the region score relatively well. They typically have a structure that is modeled after mass parties: they have registered members, national congresses, branches, local offices, constitutions, full-time staff, etc. (Katz, 1996: 122; van Biezen, 2003). Decision-making is centralized and bureaucratized, the parties' representatives are under the control of the parties' elected leadership, and the established parties can rely on a regular flow of contributions.

Given that the parties are often internally created and are particularly sensitive to electoral results, the party in public office was expected to dominate the extra-parliamentary arm of parties. But, as van Biezen (2003) showed recently, the party in central office in fact has the upper hand in East-Central Europe.[7] Most parties constrain the freedom of their parliamentary faction, the members of parliament regard the extra-parliamentary leadership as more influential and the central office receives significantly more money than the parliamentary faction.

THE INSTITUTIONAL ENVIRONMENT OF PARTIES

Institutions deserve attention as indicators of the weight of parties within the political system, showing their success in establishing an environment favorable to themselves. The analysis of institutions seems to strengthen the position of those who attribute a central role to parties in post-communist politics.

When it came to a choice between large versus small district magnitude, parliamentarianism versus presidentialism, and unicameralism versus bicameralism, the majority of the post-communist states opted for the former alternatives. These institutions allow for programmatic cohesion and provide a party-friendly environment. The central role of parliaments in democratization has contributed to the dominance of parties over interest groups. The recent shift of power to the executive branch and the 'fast-track legislative procedure' due to the EU accession weakened the parliaments in East-Central Europe, but the leverage of the parties *vis-à-vis* individual legislators was increased by the growing practice of detailed coalition agreements (Kopecký, 2003: 138, 148).

The dynamic analysis of the institutional reforms provides further evidence for the success of the established parties. Throughout the region, rules have been introduced to erect barriers against newcomers, halting the proliferation of parties. The thresholds for registration and for the entry into the electoral arena were raised, sometimes drastically. These new rules are aimed at preventing organizations other than nationally organized parties from accessing the parliament. Another group of recently introduced rules punishes the splitting of parliamentary groups by making it more difficult for the members of parliament to change group membership and by increasing the threshold for the establishment of parliamentary groups.

The rules of party finance are interpreted by most political scientists as further signs of the power of the established parties. Most post-communist states finance – in one way or another – their parties. The share of state money in a party's budget can be very high, reaching 70–80%. Scholars have been eager to point out that state finance endangers the links of parties to civil society, produces rent-seeking, and disadvantages parties that are too small to receive it. Probably the most frequently made criticism is that public money removes a key incentive for building party–society linkages (van Biezen, 2003: 41). Much less is written on the classical benefits of this institution, such as fair competition and relative transparency.

State finance, together with a number of other factors such as the relatively high electoral thresholds, the decisive role of parties in governing, their focus on the state instead of members, and the weakness of other social actors seem to make the 'cartel party' model applicable in the post-communist context (Ágh, 1998b: 109; Katz, 1996: 122; Sikk, 2003; Klima, 1998: 85). Critics of this thesis typically point at the lack of a 'fixed menu' of parties (Lewis, 1996: 12–14; Szczerbiak, 2001). But the concept of cartel is probably misleading even in those countries where new parties rarely manage to enter the parliament, since post-communist party systems are polarized, the stakes are high and coalition-making is constrained.[8]

Even if one would concentrate on the most often analyzed indicator of cartel party, that is, state finance, it must be acknowledged that state support may increase the parties' autonomy. By being granted a fixed portion of the state budget, parties can more freely shape their policies than if they were dependent on wealthy businessmen, corporations, or lobby groups. As van Biezen and Kopecký (2001) noted, actual state dependence may be exactly a result of illicit private financing, since that requires the parties to pay their sponsors with governmental spoils. A related concern, that state finance privileges large parties and freezes the party system, is equally exaggerated. In Estonia, for example, the increased reliance on public money was followed by the astonishing success of a new party and by increased volatility. The threshold for finance is typically somewhat lower than the electoral threshold, and in this sense it helps minor parties to stay competitive, although the principle of linking state finance to electoral results benefits, of course, the established parties.

The picture of state-dependent parties (Szczerbiak, 2001; Lewis, 2001; Katz, 1996; van Biezen, 2003) is heavily based on the examples of the Czech Republic and Hungary. The picture requires considerable qualification if one looks at the whole universe of Eastern European or post-communist party systems. Ukraine, Belarus, Latvia, and Moldova do not provide state support; Russia and Romania give only small amounts (Ikstens *et al.*, 2001). In Russia only 1.5% of the election-related income of the parties came from the state in 1999, not counting, of course, the privileged access of certain parties to national mass media and to the so-called administrative resources such as transport, offices, and publications (White, 2004). In other countries (e.g., Lithuania and Estonia) direct state finance was introduced only recently.

CONCLUSIONS

Post-communist party politics served political science with a number of lessons. Instead of summarizing the overview given above, let me provide in conclusion a short and subjective list of some of these suggestions:

1. Political scientists should pay more attention to the forms of cooperation between parties.
2. The non-structural party politics recently observed in developed democracies is not a parochial phenomenon; it is the dominant form of 21st-century politics.
3. Concepts such as that of the cartel party should be applied in their entire complexity in comparative research and not narrowed down to some of their easily measurable indicators like state finance.
4. More work is necessary on both East and West that uses a 'double-blind' approach, because at the moment stereotypes about the regions bias the interpretation of the data. It is hardly acceptable, for example, to regard individualistic party choice as a mature form of electoral behavior when it is observed in the West, but as a sign of immaturity if it comes from the East.
5. The research agenda of the coming years should include the systematic documentation of organizational developments, and theory-building should be based more directly on cross-national data sets.

Perhaps the most general conclusion that one can draw from the post-communist experience hitherto is that democratic politics by and large equals party politics. Whether this is an optimistic or pessimistic conclusion is left to the reader.

NOTES

1 Estonia stands out as the most obvious exception.
2 Kitschelt predicted that the parties far from the main dominant competitive dimension would not be able to attract many voters. The success of social democratic parties (some of them reformed successor parties) contradicted this early prediction, as did the appearance of economically right-wing and relatively nationalist authoritarian parties.
3 In the Czech Republic (Jasiewicz, 2003: 197) turnout was 98% in 1990, but only 58% in 2002.
4 In Poland turnout at the parliamentary elections varied between 43% and 52% (Markowski and Tucker, 2003).
5 In Hungary the second round of 2002 elections produced the most direct confrontation and the largest turnout (73%) thus far.
6 Körösényi (1999: 63) proposed that integration into the *ancien régime's* political class should be treated as a structural factor. Given that in a number of countries the vote of the communist *nomenklatura* is concentrated on one party, this innovation would show the level of social determinance to be significantly higher.
7 Note that the high degree of fusion between the two 'faces' creates serious problems for this type of analysis.
8 The fact that parties are so much focused on their electoral activity (van Biezen, 2003; Lewis, 2001; van Biezen and Kopecký, 2001) should probably also be interpreted as an indicator of their competitiveness and vulnerability, and not of their remoteness from civil society.

REFERENCES

Ágh, Attila (1996) 'The development of East Central European party systems: From "movements" to "cartels"' in Máté Szabó (ed.), *The Challenge of Europeanization in the Region: East Central Europe.* Budapest: Hungarian Political Science Association, pp. 247–64.
Ágh, Attila (1998a) *Emerging Democracies in East Central Europe and the Balkans.* Cheltenham: Edward Elgar.
Ágh, Attila (1998b) *The Politics of Central Europe.* London: Sage.
Berglund, Sten, Ekman, Joakim and Aarebrot, Frank (2004) 'Concluding remarks', in Sten Berglund, Joakim Ekman and Frank Aarebrot (eds), *Handbook of Political Change in Eastern Europe*, 2nd edn. Cheltenham: Edward Elgar, pp. 593–608.
Beyme, Klaus von (2003) 'Constitutional engineering in Central and Eastern Europe', in Stephen White, Judy Batt and Paul G. Lewis (eds), *Developments in Central and East European Politics 3.* Durham, NC: Duke University Press, pp. 190–210.
Bielasiak, Jack (2002) 'The institutionalization of electoral and party systems in postcommunist states', *Comparative Politics*, 34: 189–210.
Birch, Sarah (2001) 'Electoral systems and party systems in Europe East and West', *Perspectives on European Politics and Society*, 2: 355–77.
Bozóki, András and Ishiyama, John T. (2002) 'Introduction and theoretical framework', in András Bozóki and John Ishiyama (eds), *The Communist Successor Parties of Central and Eastern Europe.* Armonk, NY: M. E. Sharpe, pp. 3–13.

Bunce, Valerie (1995) 'Should transitologists be grounded?', *Slavic Review*, 54(1): 111–27.

Diamond, Larry (1997) 'Introduction: In search of consolidation', in Larry Diamond, Marc F. Plattner, Yun-han Chu and Hung-mao Tien (eds), *Consolidating the Third Wave Democracies: Themes and Perspectives*. Baltimore, MD: Johns Hopkins University Press, pp. xiii–xlvii.

Elster, Jon, Offe, Claus and Preuss, Ulrich Klaus (1998) *Institutional Design in Post-communist Societies: Rebuilding the Ship at Sea. Theories of Institutional Design*. Cambridge: Cambridge University Press.

Evans, Geoffrey and Whitefield, Stephen (1993) 'Identifying the bases of party competition in Eastern Europe', *British Journal of Political Science*, 23: 521–48.

Evans, Geoffrey and Whitefield, Stephen (1996) 'Cleavage formation in transitional societies: Russia, Ukraine, and Estonia 1993‒1995'. Presented at the annual meeting of the American Political Science Association, San Francisco.

Hanley, Sean (2001) 'Are the exceptions really the rule? Questioning the application of "electoral-professional" type models of party organisation in East Central Europe', *Perspectives on European Politics and Society*, 2: 453–79.

Huntington, Samuel P. (1968) *Political Order in Changing Societies*. New Haven, CT: Yale University Press.

Ikstens, Janis, Smilov, Daniel and Walecki, Marcin (2001) 'Party and campaign funding in Eastern Europe: A study of 18 member countries of the ACEEEO'. Paper presented at the ACEEEO annual conference, October 13–17.

Jasiewicz, Kryszlof (2003) 'Elections and voting behaviour', in Stephen White, Judy Batt and Paul G. Lewis (eds), *Developments in Central and East European Politics 3*. Durham, NC: Duke University Press, pp. 173–89.

Katz, Richard (1996) 'Party organizations and finance', in Lawrence LeDuc, Richard G. Niemi and Pippa Norris (eds), *Elections and Voting in Global Perspective*. London: Sage, pp. 107–33.

Kitschelt, Herbert (1992) 'The formation of party systems in East Central Europe', *Politics and Society*, 20(1): 7–50.

Kitschelt, Herbert (1995) 'The formation of party cleavages in post-communist democracies', *Party Politics*, 1: 447–72.

Kitschelt, Herbert (1996) 'Post-communist democracies: Do party systems help or hinder democratic consolidation?' Paper prepared for presentation at the Conference on Democracy, Markets, and Civil Societies in Post-1989 East Central Europe, May 17–19.

Kitschelt, Herbert (2001) 'Divergent paths of post-communist democracies', in Richard Gunther, Larry Diamond and Marc F. Plattner (eds), *Political Parties and Democracy*. Baltimore, MD: Johns Hopkins University Press, pp. 299–323.

Kitschelt, Herbert (2003) 'Party competition in Latin America and Post-communist Eastern Europe. Divergence of patterns, similarity of explanatory variables'. Paper prepared for the 100th annual meeting of the American Political Science Association, Philadelphia, August 27–31.

Kitschelt, Herbert, Mansfeldova, Zdenka, Markowski, Radoslaw and Tóka, Gábor (1999) *Post-communist Party Systems: Competition, Representation, and Inter-Party Cooperation*. Cambridge: Cambridge University Press.

Klima, Michal (1998) 'Consolidation and stabilization of the party system in the Czech Republic', *Political Studies*, 46: 492–510.

Kopecký, Petr (1995) 'Developing party organizations in East-Central Europe: What type of party is likely to emerge?', *Party Politics*, 1: 515–34.

Kopecký, Petr (2003) 'Structures of representation: new parliaments of Central and Eastern Europe', in Stephen White, Judy Batt and Paul G. Lewis (eds), *Developments in Central and East European Politics*. Basingstoke: Palgrave.

Körösényi, András (1999) *Government and Politics in Hungary*. Budapest: CEU Press-Osiris, pp. 62–77.

Krause, Kevin D. (2000) 'Public opinion and party choice in Slovakia and the Czech Republic', *Party Politics*, 6: 23–46.

Kreuzer, Marcus and Pettai, Vello (2003) 'Patterns of political instability: Affiliation patterns of politicians in post-communist Estonia, Latvia, and Lithuania', *Studies in Comparative International Development*, 38(2): 76–98.

Lewis, Paul G. (1996) 'Introduction and theoretical overview', in Paul Lewis (ed.), *Party Structure and Organization in East-Central Europe*. Cheltenham: Edward Elgar, 1–19.

Lewis, Paul G. (2000) *Political Parties in Post-communist Eastern Europe*. London: Routledge.

Lewis, Paul G. (2001) 'European parties East and West: Comparative perspectives', *Perspectives on European Politics and Society*, 2: 481–94.

Lewis, Paul G. (2003) 'Political parties', in Stephen White, Judy Batt and Paul G. Lewis (eds), *Developments in Central and East European Politics 3*. Durham, NC: Duke University Press, pp. 153–72.

Mainwaring, Scott (1998) 'Party systems in the third wave', *Journal of Democracy*, 9(3): 67–81.

Mainwaring, Scott and Scully, Timothy R. (1995) 'Introduction: Party systems in Latin America', in Scott Mainwaring and Timothy R. Scully (eds), *Building Democratic Institutions: Party Systems in Latin America*. Stanford, CA: Stanford University Press, pp. 1–34.

Mair, Peter (1991) 'Electoral markets and stable states', in Michael Moran and Maurice Wright (eds), *The*

Market and the State: Studies in Interdependence. Basingstoke: Macmillan, pp. 119–37.

Mair, Peter (1997) 'What is different about post-communist party systems?', in Peter Mair, *Party System Change. Approaches and Interpretations,* Oxford: Clarendon Press, pp. 175–98.

Markowski, Radoslaw (2001) 'Party system institutionalization in new democracies: Poland – a trend-setter with no followers', in Paul G. Lewis (ed.), *Party Development and Democratic Change in Post-communist Europe: The First Decade.* London: Frank Cass, pp. 55–77.

Markowski, Radoslaw and Tucker, Joshua A. (2003) 'Pocketbooks, politics, and parties: The 2003 Polish referendum on EU membership'. Working paper, Center for the Study of Democratic Politics, Princeton University.

Mateju, Petr, Rehakova, Blanka and Evans, Geoffrey (1999) 'The politics of interest and class realignment in the Czech Republic 1992–1996', in Geoffrey Evans (ed.), *The End of Politics? Class Voting in Comparative Context.* Oxford: Oxford University Press, pp. 231–253.

Miller, Arthur H., Erb, Gwyn, Reisinger, William and Hesli, Vicki L. (2000) 'Emerging party systems in post-Soviet societies: fact or fiction', *Journal of Politics,* 62: 455–90.

Offe, Klaus (1991) 'Capitalism and democracy by design? Democratic theory facing the triple transition in East Central Europe', *Social Research,* 59: 865–92.

Pridham, Geoffrey (2001) 'Patterns of Europeanization and transnational party co-operation: Party development in Central and Eastern Europe', in Paul G. Lewis (ed.), *Party Development and Democratic Change in Post-communist Europe: The First Decade.* London: Frank Cass, pp. 179–98.

Rose, Richard (1995) 'Mobilizing demobilized voters in post-communist societies', *Party Politics,* 1: 549–63.

Rose, Richard, Munro, Neil and White, Stephen (2001) 'Voting in a floating party system: the 1999 Duma elections', *Europe-Asia Studies,* 53: 419–43.

Sakwa, Richard (2001) 'Parties and organised interests', in Stephen White, Alex Pravda and Zvi Gitelman (eds), *Developments in Russian Politics 5.* Durham, NC: Duke University Press, pp. 84–107.

Segert, Dieter (1996) 'Party politics in the process of Europeanization – is there a special way for party development in Central Eastern Europe?', in Máté Szabó (ed.), *The Challenge of Europeanization in the Region: East Central Europe.* Budapest: Hungarian Political Science Association and the Institute for Political Sciences of the Hungarian Academy of Science, pp. 221–64.

Sikk, Allan (2003) 'Cartel party system in a post-communist country? The case of Estonia'. Paper presented at the ECPR Conference, Marburg, September 18–21.

Sitter, Nick (2002) 'Cleavages, party strategy and party system change in Europe, East and West', *Perspectives on European Politics and Society,* 3: 425–51.

Szczerbiak, Aleks (2001) 'Cartelisation in post-communist politics? State party funding in post-1989 Poland', *Perspectives on European Politics and Society,* 2: 431–51.

Tóka, Gábor (1996) 'Parties and electoral choices in East Central Europe', in Paul G. Lewis and Geoffrey Pridham (eds), *Stabilizing Fragile Democracies.* London: Routledge, pp. 100–25.

Tóka, Gábor (1997) 'Political parties in East Central Europe', in Larry Diamond, Marc F. Plattner, Yun-han Chu, and Hung-mao Tien (eds), *Consolidating the Third Wave Democracies: Themes and Perspectives.* Baltimore, MD: Johns Hopkins University Press, pp. 93–134.

Tóka, Gábor (1998) 'Party appeals and voter loyalty in new democracies', *Political Studies,* 46: 589–610.

Toole, James (2000) 'Government formation and party system stabilization in East Central Europe', *Party Politics,* 6: 441–61.

van Biezen, Ingrid (2003) *Political Parties in New Democracies: Party Organization in Southern and East-Central Europe.* Basingstoke: Palgrave Macmillan.

van Biezen, Ingrid and Kopecký, Petr (2001) 'On the predominance of state money: Reassessing party financing in the new democracies of Southern and Eastern Europe', *Perspectives on European Politics and Society,* 2: 401–29.

White, Stephen (2004) 'Russia's client party system', in Stephen White, David Stansfield, and Paul Webb (eds), *Political Parties in Transitional Democracies.* Oxford: Oxford University Press.

Williams, Kieran (2003) 'The Czech Republic and Slovakia', in Stephen White, Judy Batt and Paul G. Lewis (eds), *Developments in Central and East European Politics 3.* Durham, NC: Duke University Press, pp. 41–56.

Wittenberg, Jason (1998) 'The 1994 Hungarian election in historical perspective', in Gábor Tóka and Zsolt Enyedi (eds), *The 1994 Elections to the Hungarian National Assembly.* Berlin: Sigma, pp. 139–67.

Wyman, Matthew, White, Stephen, Miller, Bill and Heywood, Paul (1995) 'The Place of "Party" in post-communist Europe', *Party Politics,* 1: 535–548.

20

PARTY, ETHNICITY AND DEMOCRATIZATION IN AFRICA*

Shaheen Mozaffar

As they do with all sources of social cleavages, political actors activate ethnicity strategically for group organization, interest definition, and collective action to advance political goals. In democratic elections, ethnicity serves as an important source of strategic coordination over votes and seats (Mozaffar *et al.*, 2003). Political parties rely on ethnicity for mobilizing electoral support, especially when they are organizationally and programmatically weak, as they are in many African countries (van de Walle, 2003; van de Walle and Butler, 1999). But the strategic relationship of party and ethnicity is contingent on variations in the politicization of ethnicity and in the resulting morphology and associated demography of emergent ethnopolitical groups (politicized ethnic groups) reflected in two dimensions of ethnopolitical cleavages, fragmentation and concentration.

The central argument of this chapter is that the relationship between party and ethnicity is a strategic and contingent relationship. The chapter elaborates this argument by (a) contrasting its central premises with the flawed central premises of conventional accounts of the party–ethnicity relationship, (b) clarifying how ethnicity and ethnopolitical groups and cleavages defined by it serve as sources of strategic coordination over political outcomes, (c) describing a new data set on African ethnopolitical groups and cleavages, and (d) examining the contingent relationship between two dimensions of ethnopolitical cleavages – fragmentation and concentration – and the number of parties winning votes and seats in national legislative elections and the

number of parties competing in presidential elections in Africa's emerging democracies.

THE CONVENTIONAL ACCOUNT OF THE PARTY–ETHNICITY RELATIONSHIP

Conventional accounts, whether based on rational choice (Rabushka and Shepsle, 1972) or social-psychological (Horowitz, 1985) assumptions,[1] view the party–ethnicity relationship as a reflexive isomorphic relationship in which each ethnic group represents a cleavage, is totally separate from others, is unified by the homogeneous preferences of its members, and is also sufficiently large enough to support a party by itself. Thus, *ceteris paribus*, large numbers of ethnic groups and cleavages exemplifying high social fragmentation increase, and small numbers of groups and cleavages exemplifying low social fragmentation reduce, the number of parties competing for votes and winning seats in democratic elections. Conventional accounts also view ethnicity as preempting other bases of interest definition and group organization and thus as the only dimension along which political parties can mobilize in democratic elections. And since conventional accounts view ethnic interests as intrinsically antagonistic, elections become a zero-sum game, engendering a spiral of ethnic outbidding that seriously threatens democratic stability.

Conventional accounts, however, differ on the degree of threat posed by ethnic pluralism and ethnic parties to democratic stability. One view is that ethnic pluralism is inherently incompatible with democracy (Rabushka and Shepsle, 1972). The other view focuses on a variety of institutional mechanisms (e.g. consociationalism, power-sharing, proportional representation, affirmative action, federalism) to mitigate, if not entirely eliminate, the threat (Horowitz, 1985, 1991, 1993; Lijphart, 1977; Reilly, 2001). All accounts, however, proceed from three primordialist premises: (1) that the objective presence of ethnic markers (language, religion, tribe, caste, etc.) is prima-facie evidence of their political salience; (2) that these markers endow individuals and groups defined by them with single, immutable ethnic identities; and (3) that ethnic groups are corporate units with unproblematic solidarity as the source of cohesive voting in democratic elections.

All three premises are fundamentally flawed. The first two are invalidated by the accumulated findings of over three decades of comparative scholarship that attest to the multiplicity of ascribed identities, to the situational and instrumental malleability of ethnic identities, and to their construction and redefinition in the course of social, economic and especially political interactions (Chandra, 2001; Laitin, 1998).[2] The third denies the presence of both inter-group and intra-group cleavages, which leads to the incorrect conflation of deeply divided societies comprised of two internally cohesive and implacably antagonistic groups with multiethnic societies comprised of large numbers of often internally divided groups, none with sufficient numerical advantage for exclusive political domination (Mozaffar, 2001).[3] This assumption is especially problematic because it treats ethnic cleavages as *sui generis*, engendering a simplistic emphasis on reflexive ethnic outbidding as the dominant electoral strategy, which, if feasible at all, is most likely when group morphology results in a deeply divided society. The juxtaposition of inter-group and intra-group cleavages increases the cost of forging and maintaining group cohesion and of sustained electoral mobilization, but precisely because of this increased cost it also facilitates the formation of strategic intra-group and inter-group coalitions.

In sharp contrast to the primordialist premises of conventional accounts, the analysis presented in this chapter is premised on a constructivist conception of ethnicity that permits the treatment of ethnicity and ethnic identities defined by it as strategic resources that are contingently activated in politics, and helps to account for the strategic and contingent nature of the party–ethnicity relationship.

A constructivist conception of ethnicity, in other words, enables an analytically nuanced explication and politically mediated understanding of how ethnicity and party are related in modern democracies.

ETHNICITY, PARTY AND STRATEGIC COORDINATION[4]

In Africa's emerging democracies, the inherent uncertainty of electoral competition and the institutional legacies of colonial and postcolonial governance combine to underscore the salience of ethnicity as a source of strategic coordination over political outcomes and the heavy reliance of organizationally and programmatically weak political parties on it as a cost-effective instrument of electoral mobilization. The inherent uncertainty of electoral competition is heightened in emerging democracies because political actors possess incomplete information about the incentives and outcomes of new electoral institutions.[5] Ethnopolitical groups and cleavages help to overcome this information deficit. Ethnopolitical groups do so because the ascriptive ethnic markers that define their identities, and distinguish them from other similarly constituted groups, embody information that is strategically (not reflexively) activated to define group interests and reduce the cost of collective political action in response to the institutional incentives that structure the competition for power and resources. In Africa, colonial institutions established the initial institutional incentives for constructing and politicizing ethnic groups and identities, while varied postcolonial regimes reinforced the incentives for sustaining and occasionally redefining these groups and identities.

How ethnopolitical groups facilitate, and political parties organize, strategic coordination among voters and candidates over votes and seats depends largely on patterns of ethnopolitical fragmentation and concentration. However, the nature of constructed ethnopolitical groups and the resulting cleavages in Africa reveal a complex group morphology that seriously militates against the reflexive isomorphic relationship between ethnopolitical cleavages and political parties described in conventional accounts. Specifically, African ethnopolitical demography features politically salient differences within as well as among groups. The resulting high ethnopolitical fragmentation, *ceteris paribus*, either produces such a high degree of vote dispersion among large numbers of small parties that most are unlikely to secure enough votes to win seats, or produces small numbers of large multiethnic parties by encouraging them to campaign for votes across both inter-group and intra-group cleavages. Either way, high ethnopolitical fragmentation is likely to reduce the number of parties, especially the number of parties winning seats.

African ethnopolitical groups, however, also exhibit the highest levels of geographic concentration in the world (Gurr, 1993) Such concentrations, especially when they exist 'in above-plurality proportions in particular constituencies and geographical pockets' (Sartori, 1994: 40), help to counteract the reductive effect of ethnopolitical fragmentation on the number of parties. Geographic concentration also helps to solve the collective action problem associated with the dispersion of ethnopolitical groups. Geographic concentration by itself, however, is unlikely to overcome the reductive effect of high fragmentation due to the presence of large numbers of small ethnopolitical groups. Countries with low fragmentation, moreover, feature a small number of large ethnopolitical groups that are also likely to have dispersed populations and, therefore, do not need concentrated voters to sustain a small number of parties. These variations in the configurations of ethnopolitical cleavages suggest the likelihood of an interactive effect of ethnopolitical fragmentation and concentration on the number of parties able to win votes and seats, and especially on the number of parties that are competitive in presidential elections.

The relationship between party and ethnicity takes on heightened significance in presidential elections in Africa, where all new democracies, except Lesotho and South Africa, have adopted presidential systems. Presidential elections in African countries are important for three reasons. First, because the presidency is the top prize in the political game, presidential elections attract a large number of candidates, few of whom have any realistic chance of winning. Characteristic problems of post-authoritarian democracies, such as limited experience with competitive elections, information deficit about the extent of electoral support, plus personal ambition, prevent opposition candidates from coordinating on a single candidate to oppose incumbents armed with the standard advantages of incumbency. Second, an important strategic reason for the entry of large numbers of contenders in presidential elections is that African presidents possess substantial resources for patronage. Presidential contenders with weak winning potential often expect to demonstrate sufficient electoral support to bargain entry into post-election coalitions and secure state resources for their constituencies in return for political support for the winners. Third, for leading presidential candidates the electoral base and bargaining resources possessed by weaker candidates are also strategically important because of the salience of ethnopolitical groups for electoral support. Just as it constrains political parties in legislative elections, the combination of ethnopolitical fragmentation and concentration may also constrain leading presidential candidates from securing outright electoral majorities. And since the weaker candidates often control small but cohesive blocks of votes, leading presidential contenders have strong incentives to form minimum winning coalitions with them to ensure an electoral victory and a governing majority. As in legislative elections, the extent to which strong and weak presidential contenders are able to negotiate minimum winning coalitions will depend, among other things, on patterns of ethnopolitical fragmentation and concentration.

SPECIFYING CONSTRUCTED ETHNOPOLITICAL GROUPS AND CLEAVAGES

The data analysis presented in the next section draws on a new data set premised on constructivist logic, that is, it classifies only ethnopolitical groups (politically constructed ethnic groups) and measures two dimensions of cleavages among them – fragmentation and concentration. It also resolves the problem of endogeneity inherent in analyzing the relationship between party and ethnopolitical groups, because parties may be the source of politicization of ethnic groups. Due to space limitations, the following discussion is very brief.[6]

Constructivist logic turns on the notion that individuals have multiple ethnic identities that are constructed in the course of social, economic, and political interactions. Intrinsic to this logic are three specific processes that motivate the criteria for specifying ethnopolitical groups and cleavages: construction, politicization, and particization. An ethnic group is constructed when individuals in culturally plural societies self-consciously choose one or more objective ethnic markers to distinguish in-groups from out-groups. In Africa, as elsewhere, the individuals' choice of ethnic markers and the consequent size of constructed ethnic groups are constrained by the variety, complexity, and prior use of such markers, the associated cost of forming new groups and sustaining group solidarity, and colonial and post-colonial institutions of governance. Because of this process of constrained construction, African countries feature a distinctive ethnic group morphology with three defining features that are reflected in the structure of constructed ethnopolitical groups and that shape the pattern of their political interactions: (1) marked differences in group size, such that virtually no major ethnopolitical group comprises an outright majority in a country, although some comprise a large plurality; (2) considerable variety and complexity in ethnic markers, such that, even as they produce politically salient inter-ethnic differences, they also produce politically salient intra-group heterogeneity but limited cultural differences among large agglomerations of such groups; and (3) the territorial concentration of some ethnic groups that facilitates their construction as large and cohesive units for collective political action. These three features combine with the accommodation by post-colonial regimes of instrumental ('pork barrel') ethnopolitical demands to foster *communal contention* as the typical pattern of political interactions in which ethnopolitical groups serve as a cost-effective strategic resource for organizing political competition for power and resources. Communal contention, however, underscores the high start-up cost of new group formation and the high maintenance cost of group solidarity, thus discouraging political entrepreneurs from exaggerating cultural differences among groups and encouraging them instead to maintain strong group identities, including some coexisting subgroup identities, that are strategically sustained by their ability to access the state and secure valued goods and services for their followers (Laitin, 1986; Mozaffar and Scarritt, 1999: 239–42; Mozaffar et al., 2003; Posner, 2003; Rothchild, 1997; Vail, 1991).

Like all social cleavages, however, not all constructed ethnic cleavages become politicized, and even fewer become '*particized*, that is, made into important lines of partisan division' (Cox, 1997: 26; original emphasis). This crucial distinction between particization and other forms of politicization of ethnic cleavages helps to solve the problem of endogeneity in analyzing the relationship between political parties and constructed ethnopolitical groups and cleavages. The constructivist processes sketched above motivate five criteria for specifying ethnopolitical groups and cleavages.

The first, which derives from the distinction among the construction, politicization, and particization of ethnic groups and helps to avoid the endogeneity problem noted above, involves specifying only those groups that have demonstrated their actual political relevance or high potential political relevance based on past relevance, apart from or prior to particization. The decision rule established the incidence of at least one of the following several forms of long-standing politicization other than particization as a necessary and sufficient indicator of the construction of ethnopolitical groups: (a) organized group mobilization unrelated to party formation (primarily in ethnic associations or cliques of leaders within the same party, the bureaucracy, or the military); (b) articulation of grievances by leaders claiming to speak for a group rather than a party; (c) participation in collective action or (violent or non-violent) conflict with other groups or the state and being subjected to state violence; (d) encapsulation within or domination of an officially designated administrative unit; (e) occupying a disproportionate number of high positions in the bureaucracy or the military; and (f) controlling disproportionate socioeconomic resources.

The second criterion involved specifying all ethnopolitical groups, even at the risk of being overly inclusive. Thus the decision rule deliberately defined forms of non-party politicization broadly. Furthermore, the extensive secondary Africanist literature in history, anthropology, sociology, and political science was used to assess the demonstrated and potential political relevance of a wide range of ethnic groups to arrive at the list of ethnopolitical groups included in the data set.

The third criterion involved specifying ethnopolitical groups at three levels of inclusiveness in order to capture all cleavages that could influence the electoral mobilization efforts of political parties, including national dichotomous cleavages between top-level groups (which are found in 12 countries), as well as a variety of more complex multiethnic ones usually involving both middle-level groups (within or independent of top-level groups) and lower-level groups within them.

The fourth criterion involved specifying the geographic concentration of ethnopolitical groups and subgroups. As noted above, territorial concentration facilitates ethnopolitical group construction by furnishing a critical mass of individuals with similar interests based on common location, thus reducing the

Table 20.1   *Average effective numbers of electoral and legislative parties, and average relative reduction of parties, classified by ethnopolitical fragmentation and ethnopolitical concentration*

Ethnopolitical cleavage patterns	High concentration	Low concentration
High fragmentation	ENEP = 4.67 ENLP = 3.29 R = 0.22 N = 16(7)	ENEP = 2.17 ENLP = 1.80 R = 0.16 N = 13(5)
Low fragmentation	ENEP = 2.62 ENLP = 2.09 R = 0.21 N = 21(10)	ENEP = 2.72 ENLP = 1.79 R = 0.32 N = 10 (6)

Note: ENEP = effective number of electoral parties, ENLP = effective number of legislative parties. R = relative reduction of parties. N = number of elections (number of countries in parenthesis).

start-up cost of group formation and the maintenance cost of group solidarity.

The final criterion concerned establishing the time frame for specifying the cleavages. Thus, to be included in the data set, ethnic groups at all levels of inclusiveness must have been politicized at least 10 years prior to the first election analyzed in each country, which helped to avoid the problem of endogeneity, and the most recent evidence of their politicization must be no more than 20 years prior to this election, which helped to establish their continued, and potential for future, politicization.

DATA ANALYSIS

This section presents two sets of data analysis.[7] The first examines the relationship between ethnopolitical cleavages and the number of parties in legislative elections by focusing on the effects of ethnopolitical fragmentation and concentration on the average effective number of electoral parties (ENEP), the average number of legislative parties (ENLP), and average relative reduction of parties between votes and seats (R)[8]. This analysis is based on the results of 60 elections to the lower chamber of national legislatures in 28 countries that made the transition to democracy from 1980. Table 20.1 reports the results.

The combination of high ethnopolitical fragmentation and high concentration produces the expected increase in the number of parties that are able to win votes and seats, as the results in the top left-hand quadrant of Table 20.1 reflect (ENEP = 4.67, ENLP = 3.29). The results in the bottom right-hand quadrant reflect the expected reductive effect of low fragmentation combined with low concentration

(ENEP = 2.72, ENLP = 1.79). In these low fragmentation–low concentration countries, a large number of parties, usually associated with factional conflicts among ethnopolitical elites, enter the race, dispersing the small pool of votes among them. Thus the low ENLP value is reinforced by the high value of R = 0.32. The results (ENEP = 2.62, ENLP = 2.09) in the bottom left-hand quadrant show that, in countries with low ethnopolitical fragmentation, territorial concentration tends to reinforce the support base of the small number of ethnopolitical groups, which typically do not feature politically salient intra-group cleavages, as in Mozambique and the Republic of Congo. Where such cleavages do exist, territorial concentration helps to overcome them and mobilize support for a small number of political parties, as in Ghana and Sierra Leone.

Finally, the results in the top right-hand quadrant show that high ethnopolitical fragmentation in the absence of concentration produces the expected reductive effect on the number of parties able to win votes and seats (ENEP = 2.17, ENLP = 1.80). Here, the key mechanism that links fragmented groups to political parties is not only the combination of inter-group and intra-group coalitions but also the availability of multiple ethnic markers for mobilizing electoral support. South Africa is the notable example. There, ethnopolitical groups are highly fragmented due to substantial divisions among the nine groups that comprise the majority African population as well as among the English-speakers and the Afrikaners that comprise the white population. They are also spatially dispersed. However, the continued strategic importance of race as a cost-effective basis of electoral mobilization diminishes the political significance of intra-group cleavages among African voters, while white

Table 20.2 *Effective number of presidential parties, and winner's vote percentage, classified by ethnopolitical fragmentation and ethnopolitical concentration*

Ethnopolitical cleavage patterns	High concentration	Low concentration
High fragmentation	ENPP = 3.00 Winner's vote = 51.52% N = 16(7)	ENPP = 2.36 Winner's vote = 66.51% N = 11(5)
Low fragmentation	ENPP = 2.34 Winner's vote = 59.95% N = 18(9)	ENPP = 2.30 Winner's vote = 65.57% N = 17(9)

Note: ENPP = effective number of presidential parties. N = number of elections (number of countries in parenthesis).

voters typically tend to divide their votes among several smaller parties. As a result, the average ENEP and ENLP values in South Africa over two elections are 2.2 and 2.2, respectively.[9]

A notable aspect of the results in Table 20.1 is the high values of R, which measures the relative reduction of parties that obtains after votes are converted into seats. Characteristic information deficit about electoral support and associated problems of strategic coordination in competitive elections do not limit the entry of large numbers of political parties in early elections in new democracies. Sources of uncertainty become sources of strategic opportunity in new democracies. But since few of these parties have any reasonable chance of winning even the minimum number of votes to win one seat, most end up garnering a miniscule percentage of votes, leading to the high R values. The slightly lower value of R (0.16) for elections in countries with high fragmentation and low concentration reflects the effects of the combination of inter-group and intra-group coalitions that help to reduce the number of parties able to win votes and seats to a minimum.

The second set of data analysis focuses on the relationship between ethnopolitical cleavages and the number of political parties running candidates in presidential elections.[10] Table 20.2 reports the results, which show the values for the effective number of presidential parties (ENPP) and the winning candidate's margin of victory.[11] The analysis is based on the results of 62 elections in 30 countries, and utilizes the final results in plurality systems and first-round results in two-round majority runoff systems.

As with legislative elections, the combination of high ethnopolitical fragmentation and concentration increases the average effective number of presidential parties (ENPP = 3.00). This combination of ethnopolitical cleavages also tends to produce the most competitive presidential elections, as reflected in the

winning candidates' average vote margin of 51.52%. All other combinations of ethnopolitical cleavages reduce both the average effective number of presidential parties and the level of competition. However, while the average effective number of presidential parties remains virtually the same across all these three combinations, the combination of high ethnopolitical concentration and low ethnopolitical fragmentation produces slightly more competitive presidential elections, indicating, again, the favorable effect of territorial concentration on mitigating the effects of fragmentation.

In both legislative and presidential elections, then, the spatial concentration of ethnopolitical groups helps to offset the reductive effect of ethnopolitical fragmentation on the number of political parties. It also helps to offset the reductive effect of low district magnitude. For example, in Kenya, which has the third highest fragmentation score in the data set utilized here, even a moderate level of ethnopolitical concentration offsets the constraining effect of the plurality formula in single-member districts and increases the values for both ENEP (4.0) and ENLP (3.0). And in Malawi, which also uses the plurality formula in single-member districts, high ethnopolitical concentration combines with a moderate degree of fragmentation to produce virtually identical ENEP (2.8) and ENLP (2.7) values.

As argued above, ethnopolitical fragmentation associated with the complex group morphology of African ethnopolitical groups increases the transaction cost of electoral mobilization due to the combined presence of inter-ethnic and intra-ethnic cleavages, especially if such groups are also spatially dispersed. Spatial concentration helps to reduce the transaction costs of electoral mobilization as well as the transaction costs of forging and sustaining group solidarity. But what are the social and theoretical mechanisms by which spatial concentration helps to reduce these transaction costs? The scholarship on social movements

(Tarrow, 1994) offers some insights. This scholarship shows that unmediated communication of ideas, strategies, and resources is crucial for reducing the collective action costs of group cohesion. The effectiveness of such communication derives from the face-to-face interaction in small groups that typically constitutes the larger social movements as loosely linked 'congeries of social networks' (Tarrow, 1994: 22). African ethnopolitical groups are not social movements, but their morphologies are conceptually similar. The combinations of cleavages among and within groups that typically characterize African ethnopolitical groups diminish the effectiveness of strategic face-to-face interaction in forging groups that are sufficiently large and cohesive to sustain political parties of their own. Group concentration, however, helps to overcome this constraint. The physical proximity engendered by group concentration facilitates the strategic face-to-face interaction of small groups, which helps to solidify the otherwise loose links among the subgroups. The associated affinity of place that helps to define the common interests of the emergent, spatially anchored larger group in competitive elections thus facilitates the strategic and contingent relationship of ethnopolitical cleavages to political parties in legislative and presidential elections in Africa's emerging democracies.

CONCLUSION

In sharp contrast to the fundamentally flawed primordialist premises and the reflexive one-dimensional understanding of the party–ethnicity relationship derived from them in conventional accounts, this chapter has argued for a conception that is grounded in constructivist premises and stresses the strategic and contingent nature of that relationship. This conception avoids the widely-held pessimistic view of an intrinsic antipathy between ethnic diversity and democracy and enables a theoretically nuanced analysis and politically mediated assessment of the conditions under which the strategic and contingent relationship between ethnopolitical cleavages and political parties might or might not sustain viable democracies. Extended analyses presented elsewhere (Mozaffar, 2004; Mozaffar *et al.*, 2003) reinforce this conclusion as well as the brief analysis presented in this chapter. These extended analyses suggest that the strategic and contingent effects of ethnopolitical fragmentation and concentration, independently and interactively with each other and with

electoral institutions, lead to a remarkable degree of stability in the number of political parties that compete in legislative and presidential elections in Africa's emerging democracies. This stability, which obtains even in the face of a high degree of electoral volatility, offers reasons for cautious optimism about the prospects of democratic stability in the ethnically plural countries of Africa (Mozaffar and Scarritt, 2005).

NOTES

*   I thank the National Science Foundation for financial support of the larger project from which materials for this chapter are drawn, and the Boston University African Studies Center for continued research support. The chapter was written when I was a Visiting Research Associate at the Democracy in Africa Research Unit (DARU) of the Center for Social Science Research (CSSR) at the University of Cape Town. I wish to thank DARU Director Robert Mattes and the CSSR for providing me with a hospitable working environment and generous support. I am responsible for the chapter.

1. Rational choice assumptions stress the instrumentality of ethnicity in defining and pursuing group political goals. Psychological assumptions stress the psychic gratification – self-esteem and belonging – individuals derive from ethnic group membership.

2. Lijphart (2001) has recently reassessed his initial primordialist assumptions in light of constructivist interpretations of ethnicity and politics.

3. The use of the terms 'deeply divided' and 'fragmented' to refer to all ethnically diverse societies manifests this widespread conflation in the comparative literature. Reilly (2001) is a recent example. The term 'multiethnic' is used in this chapter as a convenient designation for fragmented societies.

4. Portions of this section draw on Mozaffar *et al.* (2003).

5. This information deficit diminishes, of course, after several election cycles as political actors learn to adjust to the mechanical and unintended consequences of electoral institutions, often leading to electoral system reform, as in Burkina Faso, Lesotho and Senegal (Elklit, 2002; Mozaffar, 2004; Mozaffar and Vengroff, 2001; Santiso and Loada, 2003). But administrative and especially political costs often militate against such reforms, as in the rejection by South Africa's ruling African National Congress of the recommendations of the electoral reform commission to move from the current pure proportional representation to a mixed-member proportional system.

6. The logic, method, and decision rules for constructing the data set are spelled out in greater detail in Mozaffar and Scarritt (2002), Mozaffar *et al.* (2003: 382–3), and Scarritt and Mozaffar (1999).

7. Cape Verde, Lesotho, São Tomé and Princípe, and Seychelles, each of which has one ethnopolitical group, and Burundi and Comoros, both of which have two undivided ethnopolitical groups and are therefore deeply divided societies, are excluded from both analyses.

8. ENEP and ENLP are the widely used Laakso–Taagepera indices that, respectively, measure the number of parties winning votes and the number of parties winning seats. See Laakso and Taagepera (1979), which provides the formula for calculating the two indices. R is an index that measures the reduction in the number of political parties that results from the translation of votes into seats, and was developed by Taagepera and Shugart (1989), which provides the formula for calculating the index.

9. These figures are especially significant because South Africa has an average district magnitude of 40 seats and the highly proportional Droop quota as the electoral formula, both of which should substantially increase the ENEP and ENLP values.

10. Independents are thus excluded from the analysis. Since not too many independents run in presidential elections, including them in the analysis does not change the results.

11. The formula for ENPP is the same as ENEP and ENLP, but using vote percentages of presidential candidates.

REFERENCES

Chandra, Kachan (2001) 'Cumulative findings in the study of ethnic politics', *APSA-CP*, 12(1): 7–11.

Cox, Gary W. (1997) *Making Votes Count: Strategic Corrdination in the World's Electoral Systems.* Cambridge: Cambridge University Press.

Elklit, Jørgen (2002) 'Lesotho 2002: Africa's first MMP elections', *Journal of African Elections*, 1(2): 1–10.

Gurr, Ted Robert (1993) *Minorities at Risk.* Washington, DC: US Institute of Peace Press.

Horowitz, Donald L. (1985) *Ethnic Groups in Conflict.* Berkeley: University of California Press.

Horowitz, Donald L. (1991) *A Democratic South Africa: Constitutional Engineering in a Divided Society.* Berkeley: University of California Press.

Horowitz, Donald L. (1993) 'Democracy in divided societies', *Journal of Democracy*, 4(4): 18–38.

Laakso, Markku and Taagepera, Rein (1979) '"Effective" number of parties: a measure with

application to Western Europe', *Comparative Political Studies*, 123–27.

Laitin, David D. (1986) *Hegemony and Culture: Politics and Religious Change among the Yoruba.* Chicago: University of Chicago Press.

Laitin, David D. (1998) *Identity in Formation: The Russian-Speaking Populations in the Near Abroad.* Ithaca, NY: Cornell University Press.

Lijphart, Arend (1977) *Democracy in Plural Societies: A Comparative Exploration.* New Haven, CT: Yale University Press.

Lijphart, Arend (2001) 'Constructivism and consociational theory', *APSA-CP*, 12(1): 11–13.

Mozaffar, Shaheen (2001) 'Are multiethnic and deeply divided societies different?' Paper presented at the annual meeting of the American Political Science Association, San Francisco.

Mozaffar, Shaheen (2004) 'Africa: Electoral systems in emerging democracies', in Joseph M. Colomer (ed.), *The Handbook of Electoral Systems.* New York: Palgrave.

Mozaffar, Shaheen and Scarritt, James (1999) 'Why territorial autonomy is not a viable option for managing ethnic conflicts in African plural societies', *Nationalism and Ethnic Politics*, 5: 230–53.

Mozaffar, Shaheen and Scarritt, James (2002) 'Constructivism, rationalism and the construction of a data set on ethnopolitical groups and cleavage patterns in Africa'. Paper presented at the annual meeting of the American Political Science Association, Boston.

Mozaffar, Shaheen and Scarritt, James R. (2005) 'The puzzle of African party systems', *Party Politics*, 11: 399–421.

Mozaffar, Shaheen, and Vengroff, Richard (2001). 'A "Whole system" approach to the choice of electoral rules in democratizing countries: Senegal in comparative perspective', *Electoral Studies*, 21: 601–16.

Mozaffar, Shaheen, Scarritt, James and Galaich, Glen (2003) 'Electoral institutions, ethnopolitical cleavages, and party systems in Africa's emerging democracies', *American Political Science Review*, 97: 379–90.

Posner, Daniel N. (2003) 'The colonial origins of ethnic cleavages', *Comparative Politics*, 35: 127–47.

Rabushka, Alvin and Shepsle, Kenneth A. (1972) *Politics in Plural Societies: A Theory of Democratic Stability.* Columbus, OH: Merrill.

Reilly, Benjamin (2001) *Democracy in Divided Societies: Electoral Engineering for Conflict Management.* Cambridge: Cambridge University Press.

Rothchild, Donald (1997) *Managing Ethnic Conflict in Africa: Pressures and Incentives for Cooperation.* Washington, DC: Brookings Institution Press.

Santiso, Carlos, and Loada, Augustine (2003) 'Explaining the unexpected: Electoral reform and democratic governance in Burkina Faso', *Journal of Modern African Studies*, 41: 395–419.

Sartori, Giovanni (1994) *Comparative Constitutional Engineering: An Inquiry into Structures, Incentives, and Outcomes*. New York: Columbia University Press.

Scarritt, James and Mozaffar, Shaheen (1999) 'The specification of ethnic cleavages and ethnopolitical groups for the analysis of democratic competition in contemporary Africa', *Nationalism and Ethnic Politics*, 5(1): 82–117.

Taagepera, Rein and Shugart, Matthew (1989) *Seats and Votes: The Effects and Determinants of Electoral Systems*. New Haven, CT: Yale University Press.

Tarrow, Sidney (1994) *Power in Movements: Social Movements, Collective Action, and Politics*. New York: Cambridge University Press.

Vail, Leroy (ed.) (1991) *The Creation of Tribalism in Southern Africa*. Berkeley: University of California Press.

van de Walle, Nicolas (2003) 'Presidentialism and clientism in Africa's emerging party systems', *Journal of Modern African Studies*, 41: 297–321.

van de Walle, Nicolas and Butler, Kimberly Smiddy (1999) 'Political parties and party systems in Africa's illiberal democracies', *Cambridge Review of International Affairs*, 13(1).

PART III

PARTY ORGANIZATION

21

PARTY MODELS

André Krouwel

INTRODUCTION

More than a century of scholarly attention to political parties has resulted in a substantial number of party models. Yet, so far all these party typologies have not accumulated into a more general theory on the genesis, development and transformation of political parties. This is caused primarily by the fact that most of the party models are seriously biased. First, most party models were developed in the context of western Europe and the United States of America, resulting in a limited 'travelling capacity' of these conceptualizations (Sartori, 1984) even across the Atlantic (see Ware, this volume). Secondly, most party models are very uni-dimensional in their approach, oftentimes focusing heavily or even exclusively on organizational aspects. Duverger (1954: xv) even argued that 'present-day parties are distinguished far less by their programme or the class of their members than by the nature of their organization. A party is a community with a particular structure. Modern parties are characterized primarily by their anatomy'. An anatomist, however, does his work by dissecting corpses, while party observers usually analyse political parties that are alive and kicking or are even still in their infancy. The fact that numerous scholars observed the same political parties yet only focused on a specific element at a particular stage in its development has proliferated the number of party models dramatically. Moreover, analysing parties merely by their bodily structures neglects one of the first observations, namely that a party is 'a body of men united, for promoting by their joint endeavours the national interest, upon some particular principle in which they are all agreed' (Burke, 1975: 113). Apparently not only organizational structures guide the behaviour of party members, but also some principle, some common goal, perspective or ideology. In addition, political parties perform many functions: they form the link between the state and civil society as they recruit and select the elite, nominate candidates for public office, form the executive or the (parliamentary) opposition to the incumbent power-holders and mobilize the people through political campaigns. Clearly, all these aspects also have to be included in party models and theories if we want to understand what a political party is, what it does and to what extent parties have transformed over time.

It is problematic that, when multiple dimensions have been used in modelling parties, often the organizational dimension is privileged over others and that additional aspects included in these typologies of parties generally refer to widely varying and inconsistent features (Gunther and Diamond, 2003). Another consequence of the large number of party models is the very low level of conceptual and terminological clarity and precision. In addition, proposed typologies are often neither mutually exclusive nor totally exhaustive. Furthermore, most of the proposed models of party do not include clear empirical indicators that would allow us to determine which parties actually do fall into each of the categories or when they have transformed into a different type (see Krouwel, 1999, 2003). Thus, we lack an effective way to classify different types of parties and consensus over indicators to determine what types of party we are observing.

CLASSIFYING AND LINKING PARTY MODELS

In the literature of political science basically three methods of party classification have been proposed and used. The first method is to simply list the party types and enumerate the major characteristics of each of the different models. Katz and Mair (1995: 18), for example, distinguish four party models (elite, mass, catch-all and cartel party) and then list 13 aspects on which these types of party differ. As a second method, some scholars identify 'genera' of party types and subsequently chart all the party types that have developed from each genus. An example of this method is Seiler (1984a, 1984b, 1993), who departs from Duverger's distinction between the internal and external origin of parties and from these two genera groups eight party types into their respective lineages. Gunther and Diamond (2003), to take another example, develop five genera on the basis of which they classify 15 species of party. A third method of classification is based on more abstract dimensions along which parties differ. Wolinetz (2002: 161), for instance, uses the dimensions of vote-seeking, policy-seeking and office-seeking to position six party types in a triangular space on the basis of their primary goal. Pomper (1992) positions eight party types on three dimensions (breadth of focus, goal orientation and functional mode).

Although there is undoubtedly a certain path-dependency in the development of political parties, the genera method is too deterministic. Moreover, it is almost impossible to develop indisputable and consistent genera and there is no generally accepted method to determine in what lineage the different party models should be grouped. The deductive method of positioning parties along abstract dimensions is also problematic as no generally accepted indicators for each of the dimensions are currently available, so the position of each

party type along the various dimensions becomes quite arbitrary.

Therefore I opt for the most parsimonious and straightforward method of differentiating parties on the basis of several crucial distinguishing characteristics. Not all party models that have been proposed are totally unique. Among the proposed models there is substantial similarity and overlap, and numerous party types that have been suggested are merely reformulations of an already existing model. On the basis of their similarities in focus and crucial features I have clustered the numerous party types into five basic species (see Table 21.1).

Many authors writing about the first modern parties that emerged in the late 19th century before the introduction of mass suffrage use various concepts basically to refer to the same phenomenon: loosely structured elite-centred cadre parties led by prominent individuals, organized in closed and local caucuses which have minimal organization outside parliament. Because of the significant overlap in characteristics I have grouped all models that refer to these first modern parties into the first cluster.

The second cluster comprises all models of mass parties. Wolinetz (2002: 146) argues that Panebianco's mass bureacratic party is basically equivalent to Duverger's mass party and Neumann's party of mass integration (see also Gunther and Diamond, 2003: 179). The defining elements of this type to which numerous authors refer are: the extra-parliamentary mass mobilization of politically excluded social groups on the basis of well-articulated organizational structures and ideologies.

The third species of party is the electoralist, catch-all party type. Panebianco's professional-electoral party is basically a respecification of Kirchheimer's catch-all model (see Wolinetz, 2002: 146; Katz, 1996: 118; Gunther and Diamond, 2003: 185), while the rational-efficient party model proposed by Wright (1971) basically describes the same phenomenon (Katz, 1996: 118). Catch-all parties originate from mass parties that have professionalized their party organization and downgraded their ideological profile in order to appeal to a wider electorate than their original class or religious social base.

A fourth species is the cartel party. The formation of a so-called 'state–party cartel' was described by Kirchheimer (1954b), long before Lehmbruch (1974: 97), Lijphart (1968, 1974: 76), or Katz and Mair (1995) proposed their later versions of cartel democracy (see Krouwel, 2003). Basically this party type is characterized

Table 21.1 Clusters of party models

Elite, caucus and cadre parties	Mass-parties	Catch-all, electoralist parties	Cartel parties	Business-firm parties
Patronage and charismatic parties (Weber), parties of personage (Neumann), caucus (Ostrogorski), parties of parliamentary origin (Duverger), parties of individual representation (Neumann, Kirchheimer), party of notables (Weber, Neumann, Seiler), elite parties (Beyme), clientelistic parties (Rueschemeyer et al.), modern cadre party (Koole), local cadre party (Epstein); governing caucus (Pomper)	Mass party (Michels, Duverger, Beer), class-mass and denominational mass parties (Kirchheimer), Weltanschauung and Glaubens party (Weber), parties of external origin, branch-based mass parties, cell-based devotee parties (Duverger), parties of democratic or total integration, party of principle (Neumann), amateur and party democracy model (Wright), militants party (Seiler), mass-bureaucratic party (Panebianco), programmatic party (Neumann, Wolinetz), fundamentalist parties (Gunther and Diamond); cause advocate party (Pomper)	Catch-all parties (Kirchheimer), professional-electoral parties (Panebianco), stratarchy (Eldersveld), rational-efficient, professional machine model (Wright, Schumpeter, Downs, Pomper), party machine (Seiler), multi-policy party (Downs, Mintzel)	Party-cartel (Kirchheimer), cartel-party (Katz and Mair)	Business-firm (Hopkin and Paolucci), franchise organizations (Carty), parties of professional politicians (Beyme), entrepreneurial parties (Krouwel)

by a fusion of the party in public office with several interest groups that form a political cartel, which is mainly oriented towards the maintenance of executive power. It is a professional organization that is largely dependent on the state for its survival and has slowly retreated from civil society, reducing its function mainly to governing.

The final cluster of party types that can be distinguished is of quite recent origin. Business firm types of party originate from the private initiative of a political entrepreneur and have, by and large, the structures of a commercial company. The image of the party leader, combined with some popular issues, is marketed by a professional organization to an ever more volatile electoral market. Table 21.1 provides an overview of many of the party types suggested in the literature, clustered into five generic models of party.

As a second step, in an attempt at cumulative theory-building, I will sequentially link the five generic party models. The main reason for this is that these five clusters of party models are not isolated and unconnected species. As Lipset and Rokkan (1967: 50) argued, most of the party organizations are far older than the majority of the electorates they represent. This means that, at least in part, observers from different times have been observing and describing the same political parties in subsequent stages of their development. Since most of the models are derived from these empirical observations of the same phenomena in different periods, linking them chronologically also provides an historical overview of major party characteristics culminating in a general theory of party transformation over the last century.

Mass parties emerged as a result of the political exclusion of large proportions of citizens by the dominant elite and their cadre parties of the proto-democracies of the late 19th and early 20th centuries. Kirchheimer (1954b, 1966) departed from Neumann's concept of the mass integration party and argued that, after the political integration of their followers had been successfully completed, these mass parties were transforming into catch-all parties in the late 1950s and early 1960s. Mass parties slowly professionalized their organizations, moderated their demands for social and political transformation and began to appeal to voters outside their original core electorate. As their party programmes became increasingly interchangeable and cooperation between former political enemies became the norm, rather than the exception, a political cartel was formed that

became increasingly impenetrable for new political actors and groups. Cartel parties slowly monopolize the resources of the state and create a legal environment that favours the incumbent parties and discriminates against new competitors. As a reaction to this exclusion, political entrepreneurs who have no access to the resources of the state use the resources and strategies of the private sector, particularly the commercial mass media, to gain access to the electoral arena and executive power. As this brief chronology shows, the five models in sequence provide a tool to assess party transformation over time.

In a similar vein, Katz and Mair (1995: 6) framed the development of political parties as a *dialectical* process, in which each new party type generates a reaction that will lead to a new party model and a further chain of reactions. They identified different party models within distinctive time periods on the basis of the relationship between political parties, civil society and the state (Katz and Mair, 1995: 12–18). Clearly, party transformation is an ongoing evolutionary process in which parties adapt to their particular social and political context. This is also why the models of party are sequentially interconnected: observers build on existing models or reformulate an earlier model when they perceive that these models are no longer applicable to current political parties. The main concern for a comprehensive theory of party transformation then becomes to identify the specific characteristics that make the models of parties mutually exclusive. Below I propose a number of indicators that can be used to differentiate the party models from one another.

THE ORGANIZATIONAL, ELECTORAL AND IDEOLOGICAL DIMENSIONS OF PARTY MODELS

Since existing typologies and models of political parties usually have been developed in a specific political and social context on the basis of a limited number of observations, the models vary substantially in their focus and level of sophistication. As argued above, most models focus on *organizational aspects*; often the level of centralization or federalization is taken as the basic feature (Lenin, 1961; Michels, 1962; Eldersveld, 1964, 1982; Kitschelt, 1994), along with territorial penetration and diffusion (Eliassen and Svåsand, 1975). Organizational forms such as the caucus (Ostrogorski, 1902), branch, cell, militia (Duverger, 1964), nucleus (Schlesinger, 1965, 1984) or cadre (Duverger, 1954; Koole, 1996) are also used to distinguish between party types. Others have proposed to define parties on the basis of the level of professionalization, bureaucratization, institutionalization and rational efficiency of the party organization (Wright, 1971; Downs, 1957; Panebianco, 1988) or their collusion with the state (Kirchheimer, 1954b; Katz and Mair, 1993, 1995). Party models also refer to the main functions of the party organization, for example the selection of candidates (Bryce, 1929; Schumpeter, 1942) or their representational and integrational functions. An example of the latter is the distinction between 'parties of individual representation', 'parties of democratic integration' and 'parties of total integration' (Neumann, 1956). Duverger's famous distinction between the internal and external origin of parties also needs to be included in this enumeration of possible organizational classification schemes.

Some models include *sociological or electoral characteristics* such as the representation of social groups in terms of class, religion or ethnicity (Duverger, 1954; Kirchheimer, 1954b). Party models such as mass parties, elite parties and amateur parties (Wright, 1971) are classified by the class nature of their membership, the most active or dominant social group within the party, the level of rank-and-file participation or the type of leadership (Weber, 1925; Neumann, 1956; Kirchheimer, 1954a, 1966; Wildavsky, 1959). Other party models, such as catch-all parties or ethnic parties, are typified by the width of their electoral appeal (Kirchheimer, 1966).

Concerning party classifications on the basis of *ideology*, Weber's typology of *Weltanschauungs-* or *Glaubensparteien* is often cited (Weber, 1925), while political scientists also frequently use ideological labels for parties such as right-wing, left-wing, extremist, protest, populist or fundamentalist. In grouping parties cross nationally into party families, generally ideological labels such as conservative, liberal, Christian democratic, social democratic, socialist, communist, Green or environmental are used. Combining ideology with sociological aspects has resulted in party typologies such as 'radical mass parties' and 'clientelistic parties' (Rueschemeyer *et al.*, 1992).

Party models should not be too reductionist, by emphasizing only a single dimension of political parties. Instead, parties should be regarded as complex phenomena with multiple attributes or properties that constitute one 'bounded whole', and jointly constitute a pure or ideal type from which real political parties

will deviate to varying degrees (Sartori, 1987: 182–5). Since there is no consensus as to which attribute or dimension should be privileged over others, I have opted for a broad range of analysis that is better able to capture the existing variation among different types of parties. This broad analysis includes first of all the *genetic origin* as a basic criterion guiding the classification of the different party types. The origin of parties determines to a large extent their initial format and their subsequent transformation is path-dependent on these foundational elements (Panebianco, 1988). In addition, I include three other dimensions to which earlier models refer: electoral, ideological and organizational. On the electoral dimension, the five party models can be distinguished on the basis of their *electoral appeal and social support* as well as the *social origin of the elite* they recruit. The ideological dimension comprises both the *basis for party competition* and the *extent of inter-party competition*. On the organizational dimension, the generic types are differentiated by examining the *importance and status of the membership organization* and the *position of the parliamentary party and party in public office*. The relative power balance between these three 'faces of a political party' is different within each of the five models. In addition, parties can be differentiated on the basis of two other organizational features: the *structure of the resources* that are available to the party and the *type of political campaigning* in which they engage. In this section I will discuss each of these nine characteristic features for each of the five party models.

The elite party model

One of the first scholars to describe a political party was Edmund Burke, who, writing in 1770, defined a party as a group of parliamentary representatives who agreed to cooperate upon a certain principle (Burke, 1975). These first political parties emerged in proto-democratic systems with suffrage limited to a small privileged class of the more propertied male population. An extra-parliamentary party organization was practically non-existent and the coordination between its members, a small elite from the middle and upper classes, was loosely structured. Wolinetz (2002: 140) describes this type of party as *closed caucuses* of prominent individuals. Distinguishing between internally and externally created parties, Duverger (1954) characterized these first parties by their emanation from groups of parliamentary representatives (see also Kirchheimer, 1954b). According to

Duverger, these internally created parties are commonly led by a small *cadre* of individuals with high socioeconomic status, who have only weak links with their electorate. Clearly, the defining sociological characteristic of elite parties is the high status of their members, who already had obtained politically powerful positions before the advent of an extra-parliamentary party organization. The emergence of these 'modern' extra-parliamentary parties, under the influence of the extension of the suffrage, was analysed by Mosei Ostrogorski (1902). He compared these organizations in Britain and the United States and, with the latter having a more extended electorate, concluded that power became increasingly concentrated in local party 'machines' that aimed at winning elections through an extensive system of patronage and clientelism.

At the organizational level, elite parties have basically two layers: in the constituencies and in parliament (Ostrogorski, 1902: VIII–IX; Katz and Mair, 2002: 114). The extra-parliamentary party is weakly articulated or even absent, and each constituency is able to provide its own resources so that central authority and control are weak. Katz and Mair (2002: 115) argue that the elite party is basically an agglomeration of local parties consisting of 'a small core of individuals with independent and personal access to resources able to place either one of their number or their surrogate in Parliament as their representative' (see also Ostrogorski, 1902: i). Such a picture of the elite party is also sketched by Duverger (1954: 1–2, 62–7) who characterized the caucus party by its local and embryonic organizational structures that were exclusively aimed at recruiting candidates and campaigning for them during the election period. In a similar vein, Neumann (1956) identified the earliest political parties as *parties of individual representation*, which are characteristic of a society with a restricted political domain and only a limited degree of participation. They articulate the demands of specific social groups and their 'membership activity is, for all practical purposes, limited to balloting, and the party organization (if existent at all) is dormant between election periods. Its main function is the selection of representatives, who, once chosen, are possessed of an absolute "free mandate" and are in every respect responsible only to their own consciences' (Neumann, 1956: 404).

Not much is said by the various authors on the ideological character of elite parties. What can be assessed is that, although the different groups of parliamentarians may have held 'widely diverging views' of what the national interest was (Katz, 1996: 116), competition between parties was relatively limited. Since all parties consisted of members of the higher echelons of society and only represented a limited section of the population, political conflict centred on the extent of unification and centralization of the state, the level of local autonomy and the level of state intervention in the economic process (primarily taxes and tariffs).

The mass party model

Whereas political power preceded the formation of the elite party, the mass party is the mirror image of the latter in that the formation of the party organization precedes the acquisition of power. Typically, mass parties are externally created and mobilize broad segments of the electorate previously excluded from the political process (Duverger, 1954; Kirchheimer, 1966). These parties have been typified by Neumann (1956) as parties of social integration, as they seek to integrate these excluded social groups into the body politic. Since they aim at a radical redistribution of social, economic and political power, these parties demand a strong commitment from their members, encapsulating them into an extensive party organization that provides a wide range of services via a dense network of ancillary organizations. In the words of Neumann (1956: 404):

> Modern parties have steadily enlarged their scope and power within the political community and have consequently changed their own functions and character. In place of a *party of individual representation*, our contemporary society increasingly shows a *party of social integration*. … It demands not only permanent dues-paying membership (which may be found to a smaller extent within the loose party of representation too) but, above all, an increasing influence over all the spheres of the individual's daily life.

The extra-parliamentary origin, in addition to the fact that mass parties represent and mobilize a particular and clearly defined social, religious or ethnic segment of society, influences their ideological and organizational character. In order to organize a politically excluded group, the mass party needs a coherent vision of a better and different world that has to be communicated in a compelling manner. As Panebianco (1988: 264) pointed out, the stress is on ideology, and 'believers' play a central role within the organization. Paradoxically, these 'parties of the excluded' attempt to integrate their followers by insulating them from possible counter-pressures (Katz, 1996: 118). This insulation is achieved by a distinct ideology that is ingrained in the minds of the members through propaganda, the party press and party-organized activities in all spheres of life (Neumann, 1956: 405). Ancillary organizations were created in the field of education, labour, housing, sports, banking, insurance and so on, so that all social, economic and cultural activities were consistent with the ideology. The ideological vision of a better world becomes visible and materializes within this social niche. Needless to say, the ideologies of these mass parties differ from the already powerful groups, but they also differ from various ideologies of other mass parties. The result is fierce and principled competition among parties. Among mass parties themselves there is substantial variance in ideology and (consequently) in organization.

Duverger (1954: 63–71) distinguishes between branch-based mass parties and cell-based devotee parties, the latter being more totalitarian in ideology and organization. This distinction is also found in Neumann, who separates the party of social integration from the party of total integration. A party of total integration is 'all inclusive' and 'demands the citizen's total surrender. It denies not only the relative freedom of choice among the voters and followers but also any possibility of coalition and compromise among parties. It can perceive nothing but total seizure and exercise of power, undisputed acceptance of the party line, and monolithic rule' (Neumann, 1956: 405). Lenin (1961: 464–5) describes such a party as a small and cohesive party of professional and totally committed revolutionaries that lead huge masses of uncritical followers.

The mass party can also be found in a religious variant, the denominational mass party (Kirchheimer, 1957a: 437, 1966), which Kirchheimer differentiated from the totalitarian party and the democratic mass party (Kirchheimer, 1954b). Both the denominational and the democratic mass party try to appeal to a maximum of voters to take over the administration and carry into effect a definite programme (Kirchheimer, 1954b). They are, however, still limited in their appeal and only aim to mobilize a specific social class or religious group. According to Gunther and Diamond (2003: 180–3), the mass party can also be found in nationalistic and fundamentalist variants, which are more proto-hegemonic in their ideology and tend towards the militia type of organization.

In terms of organization, all mass parties share the characteristic of extensive and centralized bureaucracy at the national level. The democratic variants of the mass parties are characterized by an elected and representative collegial leadership, often combined with formal powers for a national congress with representatives of the membership (Wolinetz, 2002: 146). Formally, mass parties are democratic organizations, but the ideological rigidity and the internal processes of training and recruiting members of the elite (through extensive socialization in the local branches and the internal educational system) make real competitive intra-party elections unlikely. Observing one of the first mass parties, Michels (1962) noted the bureaucratic rationalization within mass parties in which a small and unrepresentative elite gains control over the resources and means of communication. Michels thought that in any large organization power-concentration into the hands of an oligarchy is inevitable.

> It is organization which gives birth to the dominion of the elected over the electors, of the mandataries over the mandators, of the delegates over the delegators. Who says organization, says oligarchy. (Michels, 1962: 365)

Inevitable or not, mass parties are hierarchical in their structure as all activities of the ancillary organizations and the local party branches are coordinated by the extra-parliamentary leadership. In contrast to the elite parties where local caucuses voluntarily form a national organization, the central office of the mass party has a top-down approach. Local branches and cells are founded in order to increase the level of penetration of the party. Characteristic of mass party development is the establishment of an extra-parliamentary office that precedes the formation of a party in public office. As a consequence, the party in public office is controlled, disciplined and supervised by the extra-parliamentary leadership as all representatives are considered to have the same mandate (Katz, 1996: 118). The party in public office is simply instrumental to the implementation of the party's ideology (Katz and Mair, 2002: 118). These strong vertical organizational ties (Panebianco, 1988: 264) are needed to amass and pool resources at the central level of the extra-parliamentary party (Katz and Mair, 2002: 117). The mass party derives its name from the mass of members that form the core of the organization. Membership levels and the extent of involvement and participation of members in inner-party activities and electoral campaigning are part of the defining characteristics of mass parties (see Ware, 1985, 1987, 1996). Beyond the

voluntary work members are expected to do
for the party, they are also the main source of
income. Membership fees are used to finance
the central bureaucracy and the campaigning
activities of the mass party. Other sources of
income for mass parties derive from the activities of the ancillary organizations and their
own party press.

Electoralist catch-all parties

Mass parties in Europe have been very successful in integrating their followers in the body
politic and in replacing their ancillary organizations with full-blown welfare states at the
national level. Coupled with high levels of economic growth, the maturation of welfare states
resulted in the emergence of a substantial new
middle class made up of skilled manual workers, white-collar workers and civil servants.
Their interests converged and became indistinguishable from those of the old middle classes.
According to Kirchheimer, this diminished
social polarization went hand in hand with
diminished political polarization as the doc-
trines of mass parties slowly became interchangeable. Mass parties gradually transformed
into ideologically bland catch-all parties, and
this process culminated in a waning of principled opposition and a reduction of politics to the
mere management of the state (for a comprehensive version of Kirchheimer's theory of party
transformation, see Krouwel, 2003). Kirchheimer
distinguished the catch-all party from the
Weltanschauungs-party and argued that the
modern catch-all party was now forced to think
more in terms of profit and loss of electoral
support and policy (Wolinetz, 2002: 145–6). He
asserted that political parties had been reduced
'to a rationally conceived vehicle of interest
representation' (Kirchheimer, 1957b: 314–15).
Although catch-all parties still functioned as
intermediaries between elements of formerly
united groups, the working class accepted these
parties only because they promised to give priority to their material claims, not because of their
social vision. Catch-all parties were reluctant to
perform the role of opposition, as this would
seriously diminish their success in realizing
group claims. This transition from the ideologically orientated mass party to the interest-group-
oriented catch-all party is indicative of the
erosion of principled opposition.

Kirchheimer's development of the catch-all
thesis is a good example of how erratic theory-
generating processes are concerning party transformation. Kirchheimer formulated his catch-all

thesis on the basis of only a limited number of
observations, in particular the Italian Democrazia
Cristiana, the German Sozialdemokratische
Partei Deutschlands, the British Labour Party,
the French Union pour la Nouvelle République
and the German Christlich-Demokratische
Union (Kirchheimer, 1966). He hypothesized
that the catch-all development witnessed in
these cases was likely to be prevalent in many
countries in Western Europe and led to a more or
less generalized transformation of party systems. Kirchheimer was also fairly categorical in
identifying the properties of this new party –
including its ideological, organizational and
electoral dimensions – which is why there still
remains substantial confusion in the contemporary literature regarding precisely what a catch-
all party is and precisely which parties can
genuinely be regarded as catch-all (see Dittrich,
1983; Wolinetz, 1979, 1991, 2002; Schmidt, 1985,
1989; Smith, 1989; Krouwel, 1999).

As early as 1954, in an analysis of the West
German political system, Kirchheimer (1954a:
317–18) first introduced the concept of the
catch-all party. Over a period of at least 12 years
the somewhat loosely specified notion of the
catch-all party was continuously altered
(Kirchheimer, 1957a: 437, 1957b: 314, 1959: 270,
274; 1961: 256; 1966: 185). In none of his essays
does Kirchheimer develop an exact definition of
this new type of political party and at no time
did he ever provide a clear and coherent set of
indicators as to what precisely constituted a
catch-all party. Confusingly, the catch-all party
is sometimes referred to as the 'catch-all
people's party' (Kirchheimer, 1966: 190), at other
times as the 'catch-all mass party' (Kirchheimer,
1954a: 250, 1966: 191), the 'conservative catch-all
party' (Kirchheimer, 1954a: 250), the 'Christian
type of catch-all people's parties' (Kirchheimer,
1959: 270) and, in still another version, as the
'personal loyalty variant of the catch-all party'
(Kirchheimer, 1966: 187, n. 12). Indeed, 12 years
after its first introduction, Kirchheimer (1966:
190) had still only formulated a very cursory
definition of the catch-all transformation, a
process which he then conceived as involving
five related elements:

a) drastic reduction of the party's ideological bag-
gage. … b) Further strengthening of top leadership
groups, whose actions and omissions are now
judged from the viewpoint of their contribution
to the efficiency of the entire social system rather
than identification with the goals of their particular
organisation. c) Downgrading of the role of the
individual party member, a role considered a historical relic which may obscure the newly built-up

catch-all party image. d) De-emphasis of the class-gardée, specific social-class or denominational clientele, in favour of recruiting voters among the population at large. e) Securing access to a variety of interest groups for financial and electoral reasons.

Yet earlier versions list different characteristics as the key features of catch-all development (1964b; 1965). Kirchheimer (1964a: 16) included a feature dealing with the extra-parliamentary party, and argued that the change towards catch-allism involves: 'Further development of a party bureaucratic apparatus committed to organizational success without regard to ideological consistency'. In later versions, this element is formulated more generally, now referring to the relative power of the entire party leadership while dropping the idea that catch-all parties will develop more elaborate bureaucratic apparatuses (Kirchheimer, 1966: 190). Over the years, substantive alterations were also made in Kirchheimer's argumentation as to what factors influence the catch-all development in different European countries. At various stages Kirchheimer added arguments about the particular social structures that determine the success of a catch-all strategy, as well as an explanation as to why only major parties in the larger European countries could hope to appeal to wider electoral clienteles. Kirchheimer also reformulated his thesis with respect to the expressive and the aggregative function. First, he argued that the expressive function migrated from parties to other political institutions, while this claim is later reformulated in that catch-all parties continue to function as expressive institutions but are limited by widely felt popular concerns. Another late addition to his theory is that the loose-fitting structure of the catch-all party and its disconnection from society will considerably limit its scope for political action.

On the basis of Kirchheimer's entire *oeuvre*, his personal archive of unpublished papers, his lecture notes as well as the references he cites with the various elements of the catch-all thesis, it is possible to reconstruct Kirchheimer's original ideas (Krouwel, 1999; 2003). Thus, for example, concerning party transformation at the organizational level, Kirchheimer (1966: 190) cites Lohmar (1963: 35–47, 117–24), Pizzorno (1964: 199, 217) and Lipset (1964: 276). These references suggest that Kirchheimer regarded the downgrading of the role of party members as a multifaceted process, including a stagnation in the size of party memberships, a loss of attendance at party meetings and of readership of party newspapers, a transformation

towards a more balanced social profile, and a reduced importance of membership fees in overall party revenue. Additionally, the role of active party members with regard to the selection of the party leadership is also in decline, which erodes the members' function as mediators between the electorate and the political leadership. Party leaders are co-opted into the leadership group on the basis of their technical and managerial qualities rather than because of their ideological orientation or class origin. Moreover, with reference to Duverger, Kirchheimer (1966: 178, 182, 193, 199; 1954b: 246, 259) also argues that citizens are increasingly excluded from political participation, in that catch-all parties offer less and less opportunity for membership activity, particularly as they disconnect themselves from formerly affiliated organizations. Catch-all party organizations become increasingly professional and capital-intensive, and depend increasingly on state subsidies and interest-group contributions for their income, and on the commercial mass media for their communication needs (see also Panebianco, 1988: 264–6). This political professionalization, in which experts and managers with specialized tasks replace the old party bureaucracy, is also emphasized in Panebianco's (1988: 222–35) model of the electoral-professional party. Catch-all parties also use their connection with interest groups as a source of policy ideas (in the absence of a coherent and independent policy platform) and implement policy proposals originating from organized interests in exchange for financial resources and electoral support.

On the ideology of catch-all parties, Kirchheimer (1962: 3, 1966: 195) assumed that catch-all parties will adopt similar policy positions in the centre of the political spectrum and that they will emphasize similar issues. Concerning this centripetal political competition, Kirchheimer refers to Lipset (1964) and Duverger (1964), who argue that most major parties make a trans-class appeal, with programmes spearheaded by a commitment to collective bargaining and moderate political and socioeconomic changes. Parties on both the left and the right had amicably resolved the class conflict in an acceptance of social democratic ideology, since rightist parties had accepted the welfare state and economic planning and leftist parties had moderated their ideas for revision of capitalism. Alternation in cabinet composition no longer leads to a change in government policies. All political parties and their leaders co-operate closely with one another, thus leaving little room for political opposition. With reference to the Downsian 'multi-policy party', essentially equivalent to Kirchheimer's catch-all concept, it is suggested that catch-all parties sacrificed their former ideological position and the interests of their core electorate in order to maximize their electoral appeal (see also Mintzel, 1984: 66). Parties, however, are limited by the fact that voters will not vote if all parties stress totally identical programmes and will therefore compete with candidates and remnants of traditional loyalties, reducing politics to individual personalities. This pre-eminence of the public representatives of the party, personalized leadership and candidate-centred campaigns are also crucial characteristics of the electoral-professional party of Panebianco (1988: 266).

On the third and crucial electoral dimension, which gives the catch-all party its name, Kirchheimer argued that catch-all parties attempt to bridge the (already declining) socioeconomic and cultural cleavages among the electorate in order to attract a broader 'audience' (Kirchheimer, 1966: 184). This wider electoral 'catchment' of parties transformed the European mass parties into American-style catch-all parties that appeal to all social classes (Kirchheimer, n.d.: 27). Denominational mass parties were transforming into interdenominational catch-all parties, appealing to all voters except convinced anti-clericals, and social democratic parties were attracting voters far beyond the core working-class supporters. In sum, a catch-all party is characterized by an indistinct ideological profile, a wide electoral appeal aimed at vote maximization, a loose connection with the electorate, a power balance in favour of the party elite *vis-à-vis* the party members and a professional and capital-intensive organization (Krouwel, 1999: 59).

In the United States, Eldersveld (1964, 1982) and Schlesinger (1965, 1984) had also pointed towards parties that became primarily oriented towards the recruitment and selection of candidates for public office and organizing election campaigns. The representation and mobilization of specific social groups in the United States is also organized through professional interest organizations that contribute, financially or otherwise, to the election campaigns of individual politicians. Eldersveld (1964) sketches a picture of local candidate organizations that function almost autonomously without substantive coordination or support from a national party organization. He called it the stratarchy party model: parties with limited levels of formal organization and high autonomy. Parties

have a 'porous nature' and easily absorb anyone willing to work for them, run as a candidate or support them with a donation or vote. The party is merely an alliance of coalitions at the various levels (substructures) with little or no hierarchy. Similarly, Schlesinger (1965, 1984) describes parties basically as local candidate organizations: a nucleus mainly devoted to capturing public office. All party activities are specifically linked to an individual candidate and the different nuclei of the same party can even be in competition with each other for resources and votes. Nuclei have no members, only contributors of all sorts – in financial terms, in time spent on campaigning or by voting for a candidate. All these models stress the autonomy of political actors, but in Europe observers see an opposite development towards more state-dependent parties.

Partisan states: the cartel party model

Analysing the functional transformation of parties, Kirchheimer (1954b, 1957b) identified several types of political collusion. The first is an inter-party cartel of centrist catch-all parties that try to maintain their power position in public office. As a result of the disappearance of a goal-oriented opposition, combined with consensus on most important policy issues, genuine political competition is almost completely eliminated. The combination of vanishing political opposition with a shift of power from parliament to the executive resulted in a firm inter-party cartel, from which political competitors, particularly more radical parties, were increasingly excluded. A second type of collusion is the formation of a state–party cartel, where parties disconnect themselves from their social foundations and become amalgamated with the state, reducing politics to mere 'state management' by professional politicians (Kirchheimer, 1954b, 1957b). This extensive collusion of political parties with the state and the severing of the societal links of party organizations evidence a power shift from parliament to political parties. Kirchheimer alleged that the parliamentary party and the central party organization became highly interwoven at the personal level, resulting in an ever growing discipline of the parliamentary party. A third type of collusion, closely related to the catch-all development, is the tripartite power cartel consisting of political parties, the state and powerful interest groups. According to Kirchheimer, political parties try to 'close the electoral market' by seeking the loyalty of large groups of voters not on the basis of their ideology, but through their interest organizations. Parties are increasingly subsidized by interest groups, which are also their main channels of communication with the electorate. At the same time, the party on the ground is neglected and parties display an increasing aloofness towards civil society. Finally, Kirchheimer predicted further collusion between the executive, the leadership of the major political parties and the judicial powers (the courts), indicating an ongoing process of diffusion of state powers.

These distinctions by Kirchheimer are useful when we look at later versions of the cartel thesis. The most widely cited is Katz and Mair's (1995) cartel party thesis, in which the cartel is defined in terms of a state–party cartel: 'colluding parties [that] become agents of the state and employ the resources of the state [the party state] to ensure their own collective survival' (Katz and Mair, 1995: 5). To ensure this collective organizational survival, parties allocate substantial state support to themselves and regulate the activities of parties through the state. This state–party collusion is a reciprocal process in which, on the one hand, parties increasingly extract state resources and 'colonize' the institutions of the state and, on the other, the state increasingly regulates party political organizations and activities through law (Katz, 1996; Krouwel, 2003). Colonization of the state is evidenced by the fact that political parties become increasingly dependent on the state, allocating state resources to their organizations while disengaging from their former resources within civil society. Within this oligopolistic cartel, a vast portion of the state's resources and institutional assets is accrued in the hands of the elites of the major parties. Politicians make increasing use of public institutions such as ministerial bureaucracies (to which they appoint spokesmen, media and policy advisors) and other state agencies and public utilities or quasi non-governmental organizations (quangos) and the state-owned media for party-political purposes and electoral campaigning. What seems to be occurring is a symbiosis between political parties and the state, a weakening of the democratically crucial institutional differentiation of civil associations and formal state institutions. The state becomes 'partisan' as political elites weld party organizations and state institutions together to such an extent that citizens can no longer distinguish between them. While party organizations are formally considered as part of civil society in most constitutions, in reality

parties are 'colonizing' the state through extensive processes of patronage and overlapping functional linkages. More evidence of this development can be found in the fact that politicians often simultaneously perform formal functions within political parties as well as formal roles in the state (civil servant or minister). This symbiosis of a supposedly 'neutral' state bureaucracy and a professional political class is advanced as in most European countries political recruitment has to a large extent been narrowed to the state-employed civil servants. As Puhle (2002) has pointed out, this structural proximity and overlapping of state institutions and party organizations leads to serious democratic problems, as political parties cease to be 'intermediary' and 'representative', and also can lead to more patronage, clientelism and corruption.

Through increased formal regulation of party activities, established political parties seek to monopolize the route to executive office. In order to ensure these privileges, party elites obviously prefer to have them enshrined in law. Although political competition cannot be totally eliminated, cartel parties attempt to block competition from political 'outsiders' by using legal means to their political advantage. Both processes of state dependency and 'self-regulation' increase and intensify the reciprocal linkages between political parties and institutions of the state, colluding into a 'partisan state' (Krouwel, 2004).

Later specifications of the cartel thesis by Katz and Mair also include an argument concerning inter-party collusion. Cartel parties are seen to limit and carefully manage the level of inter-party competition through informal agreements and by sharing office. The cartel is largely implicit and entails the gradual inclusion of all significant parties in government. The range of acceptable coalitions is widened and the politics of opposition is abandoned (Katz, 1996: 119–21; Mair, 1997: 137–9; Katz and Mair, 2002: 124). This common goal has transformed apparent incentives to compete into a positive motivation *not to compete* (Katz and Mair, 1995: 19–20). Outside challengers are not formally excluded from electoral competition by the allocation of disproportionate state resources to the incumbent parties, they are simply excluded from executive office as long as possible and can only enter the cartel through absorption and adaptation (Katz and Mair, 1996: 531). Inter-party collusion creates its own opposition. Exclusion from executive power offers challengers ammunition to mobilize against the cartel parties (Katz

and Mair, 1995: 24). Favourable conditions for
the development of party cartels are a tradition
of strong state–party relations, patronage and a
political culture of inter-party cooperation.

In sum, what distinguishes cartel parties is
that,

> in contrast to more entrepreneurially oriented
> catch-all parties, cartel parties appeal to an even
> broader or more diffuse electorate, engage primar-
> ily in capital-intensive campaigns, emphasise their
> managerial skills and efficiency, are loosely organ-
> ised, and remote from their members. Even more
> important, rather than competing in order to win
> and bidding for support wherever it can be found,
> cartel parties are content to ensure their access to
> the state by sharing powers with others. (Wolinetz,
> 2002: 148)

At the organizational level the relation of the
cartel party to the state is central as the state
provides the institutional environment and the
resources by which cartel parties can retreat
from society. Long periods in government
transform the internal structure and power balance within parties as they enhance the status
of the party in public office (Katz and Mair,
2002: 124). State resources are progressively
accumulated by the parliamentary party and
the party in public office becomes increasingly
independent from the membership party on the
ground and its central office (Katz and Mair,
2002: 123). The organization of the cartel party
becomes characterized by a stratarchical relation between the various levels of the party:
both the local office-holders and the central
party are to a certain extent autonomous (Katz
and Mair, 1995: 21).

A second feature is increasing professionalization, accumulation of financial and human
resources in terms of staff at the parliamentary
face of the party, eventually leading to a domination of the party in public office (Katz and
Mair, 2002: 123). This domination is visible in
an increasing presence of representatives of
the party in public office appointed to the
party central office (Katz and Mair, 1993).
Concerning ideology, competition focuses
increasingly on the managerial skills, competence and efficiency of the party in public office
(Wolinetz, 2002: 148). In response to criticism
by Koole (1996: 517) that it was not clear what
this 'toning down of competition' exactly
entails, Katz and Mair argued that this has
to be seen as convergence of parties on the
left–right scale, an expansion of coalition combinations and the increasingly circumscribed
scope of policy innovation. Cartel parties display high levels of 'symbolic competition'

(Katz and Mair, 1996: 530). Not much is said
about the width of the electoral appeal, but
cartel parties seem to campaign for the support
of diffuse groups of voters that have weak
links – or none at all – to the party.

Politics incorporated: the business-firm party model

The fifth species, the business-firm party, is a
recent phenomenon in Europe but not on the
American continent (see Carty, 2001). Basically
there are two types: one is based on an already
existing commercial company, whose structures are used for a political project, while the
other type is a new and separate organization
specially constructed for a political endeavour.
Hopkin and Paolucci (1999: 320) describe
Berlusconi's Forza Italia as an example of the
first type: 'In Forza Italia the distinctions
between analogy and reality are blurred: the
"political entrepreneur" in question is in fact a
businessman, and the organisation of the party
is largely conditioned by the prior existence of
a business firm.' Hopkin and Paolucci (1999:
307) argue that business-firm parties will
emerge when a new party system is created.

In terms of organization, the business-firm
party generates its resources from the private
sector, which differentiates it from the cartel
parties that use state resources for their activities. Although business-firm parties may have
(financial) support from interest groups, such
groups are not their main source of income or
electoral support, or their main channel of
communication. This means that the extra-
parliamentary party is practically useless and
will not be developed on any meaningful
scale. What might be developed is a mechanism for mobilizing sympathizers to appear at
party conferences to cheer on the party leadership. In the words of Hopkin and Paolucci
(1999: 315), business-firm parties will have
only 'a lightweight organisation with the sole
basic function of mobilising short-term support at election time'. The party on the ground
will be limited to a minimum so it does not
hamper the leadership in its attempt to break
the mould of the party cartel. As the dues-
paying membership will be small and most of
the resources will be needed for campaigning
purposes, most of the activities will not be
assigned to party bureaucrats. 'Party bureaucracies are kept to a bare minimum, with technical tasks often "contracted out" to external
experts with no ties to the party' (Hopkin and
Paolucci, 1999: 333). This seems to be the

essence of the business-firm party: all party activities and tasks are brought under formal (commercial) contract in terms of labour, services and goods to be delivered to the 'party'. This means that the only individuals that have a more permanent stake in the party are the ones that occupy the party in public office. 'Grassroots membership is also limited, with a high proportion of party members being officeholders who see the party as a vehicle for acquiring political positions, rather than an end in itself' (Hopkin and Paolucci, 1999: 333). As the party and its ideology are no longer goals in themselves, the business-firm party, 'instead of being a voluntary organisation with essentially social objectives, becomes a kind of "business firm", in which the public goods produced are incidental to the real objectives of those leading it; in Olson's terminology, policy is a "byproduct"' (Hopkin and Paolucci, 1999: 311). Business-firm parties will have a flexible ideological orientation and an eagerness to attract superficial support from broad sectors of society (Hopkin and Paolucci, 1999: 315), but, unlike the catch-all party, they are not oriented towards interest groups for their policy ideas. Policy positions will be developed as products within firms: demand-oriented on the basis of 'market research' with focus groups, survey research and local trials to test their feasibility and popularity. These 'policy products' need to be wrapped in the most attractive package and will be aggressively put into the market. This explains why what seems to characterize business-firm parties more than their predecessors is their almost total orientation to the creation of 'free publicity' or even direct control of the media. The best wrapping for these popular policies is an attractive candidate (or even a single leader) so that the marketing of the policies can be reduced to the promotion of individuals. Not surprisingly, those best trained for this mediatized political arena are individuals working in the entertainment sectors, which explains why an increasing number of people from this sector are now finding employment in politics. As Hopkin and Paolucci (1999: 322–3) argue: 'characteristic of the leadership of the business firm party: personal popularity, organizational advantages, and crucially, access to unlimited professional expertise in mass communication'. Needless to say, this extreme emphasis on the individual personality leads to vulnerability of business-firm parties as well as a high degree of centralization of power around the party leader (Hopkin and Paolucci, 1999: 323).

A RUDIMENTARY THEORY OF PARTY TRANSFORMATION

In sequence, these five clusters of party models, which were derived from a mixture of empirical observation and theoretical speculation, provide a comprehensive theory of party transformation consisting of ten developmental factors (see Table 21.2). In an effort to boil down the multi-dimensional complexity which characterizes the transformation of parties in modern European democracies, and to try to make sense of what is a multi-faceted phenomenon, this final section will draw on this multi-dimensionality and sequentiality of the various party models to suggest that the ten factors can be combined into four key dimensions through which the character of parties may best be understood. The first of these is associated with the *genetic origin of parties*, the second dimension relates to the *electoral appeal and elite recruitment of parties*, the third dimension is ideological and refers to the *basis and extent of party competition*, while the fourth is concerned with the *organizational character of parties* (the balance of power between the three 'faces' of the party, their resource structure and type of campaigning). These four offer a more readily grasped summary of the complexity that was revealed in the description of the party models.

Changes in the genesis of political parties

The basic distinguishing feature of the five party types is their genetic origin. The party models suggest two axes along which the origin of parties can be positioned: first, their proximity to state institutions or origin from civil society; and, second, the agent that initiates the party foundation, that is, an individual enterprise versus a collective initiative (see Figure 21.1).

Elite or cadre parties originated from the initiative of individual parliamentary representatives of local constituencies who felt the need for more coordination of their parliamentary work and, with the emergence of the mass party, for their campaign efforts. In contradistinction, the mass party originated directly from civil society, usually emerging from a collective effort to mobilize politically excluded social groups. This extra-parliamentary origin meant that the 'party' was first a social movement, often in the form of workers' unions or religious

Table 21.2 Models of political party

Characteristics	Elite caucus or cadre party	Mass party	Catch-all, electoralist party	Cartel party	Business-firm
Period	1860–1920	1880–1950	1950–present	1950–present	1990–present
Genetic dimension					
Origin	Parliamentary origin	Extra-parliamentary origin	Originates from mass parties, linking or merging themselves with interest groups	Fusion of parliamentary parties and the state apparatus (and interest groups)	Originates from the private-initiative of political entrepreneurs
Electoral dimension					
Electoral appeal and social support	Limited electorate of upper social strata via personal contacts	Appeal to specific social, religious or ethnic group on the basis of social cleavages such as class and religion	Appeal to broad middle class, beyond core group of support	'regular clientele' that provides support in exchange for favourable policies	'electoral market' with a high level of volatility. Voters as consumers.
Social basis and type of elite recruitment	Self-recruitment, private initiative. Candidates from mainly upper-class origin	Class or religious based internal recruitment on the basis of ideological and organizational commitment and via inner-party educational system	External recruitment from various interest groups	Recruitment mainly from within the state structures (civil servants)	Self recruitment, private initiative
Ideological dimension					
Basis for party competition	Traditional status of individual candidates	Ideology and representation of a social group	The quality of management of the public sectors	Maintenance of accrued power by sharing executive office	Issues and personalities (as a political product)
Extent of party competition	Very limited on the basis of personal status and wealth	Polarized and ideological competition (centrifugal competition)	Centripetal competition on technicalities	Diffusion of political disagreement. 'Conflicts' become symbolic: artificial competition on issues.	Permanent struggle for media-attention

Table 21.2 (Continued)

Characteristics	Elite caucus or cadre party	Mass party	Catch-all, electoralist party	Cartel party	Business-firm
Period	1860–1920	1880–1950	1950–present	1950–present	1990–present
Organizational dimension					
Importance of membership organization (party on the ground)	Non-existent cr minimal	Voluntary membership organization is the core of the party	Marginalization of members	Members as a pool for recruitment of political personnel	Minimal and irrelevant
Position of party in central office	Minimal, party in central office subordinate to party in public office	Symbiosis between party in central office and party on the ground	Subordinate to party in public office	Symbiosis between party in central office and party in public office	Minimal and irrelevant
Position of the party in public office	Core of the party organization	Subject to the extra-parliamentary leadership	Concentration of power and resources at the parliamentary party group	Concentration of power at the parliamentary party leadership and government (party in public office)	High level of autonomy for individual political entrepreneurs in the party to 'promote' themselves
Resource structure	Personal wealth	Membership contributions, ancillary organizations and party press	Interest groups and state subsidies	State subsidies	Corporate and social interests and commercial activities
Type of political campaigning	Personal contracts	Labour-intensive mass mobilization	Professionalization and more capital intensive organization	Professional permanent organization	Ad-hoc and non-permanent use of experts: 'contracting-out'. More use of marketing techniques

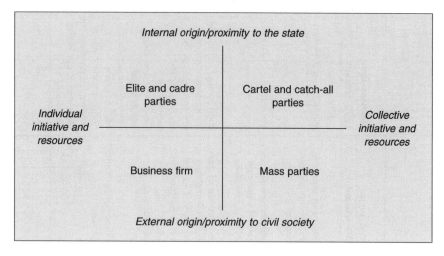

Figure 21.1   Origin of political parties

organizations relatively distant from or even hostile to the state. Their primary goal was to change political institutions, achieve universal suffrage and other political rights such as freedom of organization and expression, as well as a more inclusive electoral system.

Mass parties were very successful in their attempts at democratization and as a result they gradually transformed into catch-all parties, as their party in public office increased its linkages with interest groups and abandoned its own attempts at mass mobilization outside election time. Thus, catch-all parties result from the merger of the party in public office of the former mass party with an interest-group organization, while simultaneously disconnecting itself from the party on the ground and civil society. A next stage in party development occurs when the party in public office dissociates itself more and more from interest groups and becomes amalgamated with state structures. The party in public office of these cartel parties comes to dominate the entire party structure because it taps into the resources of the state while societal resources (from the party on the ground and the interest groups) become irrelevant to its activities and survival. As a reaction to this colonization and monopolization of state resources, new competitors emanate from the individual initiative of political entrepreneurs that use private resources for their political project. These entrepreneurs use the organizational format of business companies to structure their organization as they go about the manufacturing of politics in a

similar fashion to any other production process.

The transformed electoral appeal of parties

In terms of electoral appeal and support, the party models basically suggest a negative relationship between the social heterogeneity of party support and the strength of the party–voter link. Parties can opt for a broad electoral appeal, but this will coincide with weaker party–voter links, while parties with a narrower or class-distinctive social base will have supporters that are more strongly connected with 'their' party. The various models also refer to the sociological character of elite recruitment. At the elite level the models distinguish between parties that have an open system of elite recruitment, while in other parties the route to the top is centrally controlled and limited to 'party apparatchiks'. Variations on these two axes are summarized in Figure 21.2.

Elite parties had a very limited electoral appeal as the suffrage was extended only to the upper classes. With the extension of the suffrage, under pressure from the mass parties, elite parties had to widen their electoral appeal in order to compete with the mobilization of the class mass and religious mass parties. Initially, elite parties recruited their representatives from a small social niche of the upper social strata. While mass parties only appealed to their core electorate, they advocated and adopted

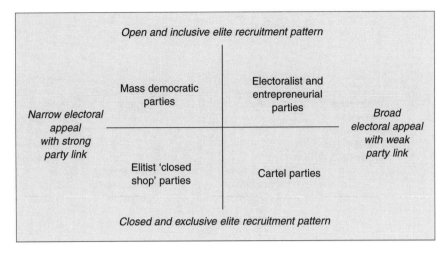

Figure 21.2   Electoral dimensions of party models

a more open structure for elite recruitment, encompassing the middle classes, and even some members of the lower classes entered the political elite through the internal educational structures of the mass party. Electoralist catch-all parties have a broad appeal on both axes, broadening their appeal beyond that of the former mass parties, and also recruit their elite from a wide social spectrum, especially representatives from various interest groups. Similar broad patterns of elite access are found within entrepreneurial party types where each individual with a significant mobilizing potential is qualified to run on the party ticket and voters from all walks of life are welcomed. The cartel party, on the other hand, displays the most closed type of elite recruitment as incumbent parties seek to maintain their control of public office by narrowing the scope of elite recruitment. Control by the cartel over elite recruitment outside their own party organizations is attempted through legal and financial hurdles for potential competitors.

Fading ideologies and different types of party competition

At the ideological level, the various party models differentiate between polarized and more moderate, pragmatic competition. Parties either compete on the basis of a coherent and principled political programme (as with the mass parties) or adopt a more flexible and strategic use of policies. The second axis

differentiates parties oriented towards the representation of interests from parties oriented towards office control based on the promise of good governance by competent managers of the state. Figure 21.3 provides a schematic overview of the various strategies that can be extracted from the models.

Elite parties competed on the basis of the traditional status of their candidates, without too much emphasis on their ideological differences. Similarly, cartel parties cater to a fixed clientele that provides them with electoral support in exchange for favourable policies. Both the elites of the cadre parties and the cartel parties are primarily office-oriented almost regardless of the policies to be implemented, and present themselves as the 'natural' managers of the affairs of the state. Mass parties, on the other hand, were initially oriented towards the mobilization of a core electorate that they sought to represent in the state structures. The fact that mass parties each represented different social groups and competed against an incumbent elite augmented their emphasis on diverging and fundamental ideological visions of a better world. After the relative success of their mass mobilization, these parties transformed into more pragmatic and ideologically more flexible or even ideologically bland catch-all parties. Less focused on a coherent ideology and eventually also abandoning the representation of specific social groups, party competition was narrowed down to the managerial qualities of the leadership of the party in public office (moving parties to the right-hand

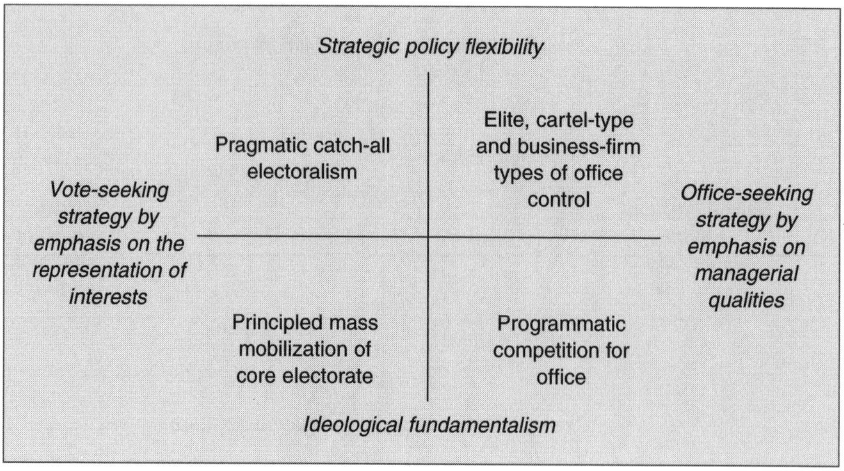

Figure 21.3   Ideological dimensions of party models

side of Figure 21.3). Control of office has now become the main driving force of political actors and the incumbent cartel parties try to fend off political entrepreneurs who seek to replace the elites in office by campaigning on specific popular issues (not a coherent programme) and the attractiveness and competencies of the individual leaders of these business-firm parties.

Changing power structures and organization of political parties

Since most emphasis is placed on the organization of parties in each of the models, the most complex array of changes can be seen at the organizational level. Most of the party models focus on the relative importance of the membership party, the party on the ground, in relation to the party in public and central office. Other aspects that the models highlight are the income structure and the type of electoral campaigns that parties conduct. Nevertheless, this complex series of changes, described above, can be summarized in a two-dimensional model of the organizational transformation of political parties. First, the party models all refer to the internal power balance in terms of centralization of decision-making, whereby in some parties the leadership hierarchically controls and coordinates all party activities, while in other parties more horizontal, open and democratic structures dominate. Secondly, the models emphasize the difference between professional and

capital-intensive party organizations and their more amateuristic predecessors that had a more voluntary character. These two aspects are presented graphically in Figure 21.4.

Over time, the party models show that political parties transformed from the amateuristic and temporary structures of the elite party, to a more permanent bureaucracy and an extensive extra-parliamentary membership organization in which volunteers performed a large number of tasks. The transformation into electoralist catch-all parties and cartel parties entailed a further process of professionalization and more capital-intensive organizational structures. Eventually the membership organization becomes almost redundant and is only seen as a pool for the recruitment of candidates. The party in central office, practically absent within the elite parties, becomes the core of the mass party from which all activities are initiated and coordinated. As mass parties come to occupy the executive more frequently and for long periods of time, power gradually shifts towards the party in public office. Slowly the party in public office comes to dominate the extra-parliamentary party, and this process is invigorated by the allocation of resources from the state that mainly accumulate in the parliamentary party. At the final stage, the party in central office is completely absorbed by the leaders of the party in public office. Within business-firm parties, capital and expertise are centralized with the party leadership to such an extent that a separate organization that could be considered a party central office

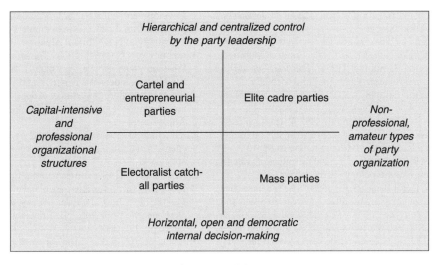

Figure 21.4   Organizational dimensions of party models

cannot be detected. The resources of the elite party were basically the private wealth of each of the individual candidates, which gave them high levels of autonomy. Mass parties, on the contrary, had to accumulate their financial and human resources from the large number of followers and volunteers within the party organization. As the catch-all party tapped into the vast resources of interest groups and later, as cartel parties, the resources of the state, more professionalization and centralization in decision-making became feasible. Political entrepreneurs and their business-firm types of party seem to resemble the old elite parties with respect to their resource structure. Again private capital is used for a political project, although the capital may not be directly in the hands of the party leadership, but provided by commercial companies and media empires. In terms of political campaigning, the models show an enormous transformation of political parties. While the representatives of the elite parties could easily attempt to meet each and every voter personally, the extension of the electorate made this impossible for the mass party. A labour-intensive campaign had to be organized to convince and mobilize all of the voters from the core social group to vote for the party at election time. With substantial financial resources from interest groups (catch-all parties) or the state (cartel parties), political campaigns became more professional. Increasingly outside expertise is hired, first on a permanent basis but later in a more *ad hoc*, non-permanent fashion when election time approaches.

CONCLUSION

This overview of party models has shown that parties are complex multi-faceted creatures, and their patterns of transformation are neither unidirectional nor linear. What we observe is a multiplicity of features, some of which, indeed, appear to work in opposite directions to one another. Moreover, even with the broad electoral, organizational and ideological elements of parties, change, when it occurs, tends to both ebb and flow, and sometimes, even concurrently, to run in contradictory directions. This attempt to bring all these elements into a more comprehensive theory of party transformation should be seen as a first step to try to make sense of the character and function of what is still one of the most crucial organizations in modern democracies.

REFERENCES

Bryce, L. (1929) *Modern Democracies*, London: Macmillan.

Burke, E. (1975) *Edmund Burke on Government, Politics and Society*, selected and edited by B.W. Hill. Hassocks: Harvester Press.

Carty, R.K. (2001) 'Political parties as franchise organizations', paper for the ECPR conference at the University of Kent in Canterbury, 6–8 September.

Dittrich, K. (1983) 'Testing the catch-all thesis: Some difficulties and problems', in H. Daalder and P. Mair (eds), *Western European Party Systems, Continuity and Change*. London and Beverly Hills, CA: Sage Publications, pp. 257–66.

Downs, A. (1957) *An Economic Theory of Democracy*. New York: Harper.

Duverger, M. (1954) *Political Parties: Their Organization and Activity in the Modern State*. London: Methuen.

Eldersveld, Samuel J. (1964) *Political Parties: A Behavioral Analysis*. Chicago: Rand McNally.

Eldersveld, Samuel J. (1982) *Political Parties in American Society*. New York: Basic Books.

Eliassen, K.A. and Svåsand, L. (1975) 'The formation of mass political organizations: An analytical framework', *Scandinavian Political Studies*, 10: 95–121.

Gunther, R. and Diamond, L. (2003) 'Species of political parties: A new typology', *Party Politics*, 9: 167–99.

Hopkin, J. and Paolucci, C. (1999) 'The business firm model of party organisation: Cases from Spain and Italy', *European Journal of Political Research*, 35: 307–39.

Katz, R.S. (1996) 'Party organizations and finance', in L. LeDuc, R. Niemi, and P. Norris (eds), *Comparing Democracies. Elections and Voting in Global Perspective*. Thousand Oaks, CA: Sage Publications, pp. 107–33.

Katz, R.S. and Mair, P. (1993) 'The evolution of party organizations in Europe: The three faces of party organization', W. Crotty (ed.), 'Political parties in a changing age', *American Review of Politics*, 14: 539–617.

Katz, R.S. and Mair, P. (1995) 'Changing models of party organization and party democracy: The emergence of the cartel party', *Party Politics*, 1: 5–28.

Katz, R.S. and Mair, P. (1996) 'Cadre, catch-all or cartel? A rejoinder', *Party Politics*, 2(4): 525–34.

Katz, R.S. and Mair, P. (2002) 'The ascendancy of the party in public office: Party organizational change in twentieth-century democracies', in R. Gunther, J. Montero, and J. Linz (eds), *Political Parties. Old Concepts and New Challenges*. Oxford: Oxford University Press, pp. 113–35.

Kirchheimer, O. (1954a) 'Notes on the political scene in Western Germany', *World Politics*, 6: 306–21.

Kirchheimer, O. (1954b) 'Party structure and mass democracy in Europe', reprinted in F.S. Burin and K.L. Shell (eds) (1969) *Politics, Law and Social Change: Selected Essays of Otto Kirchheimer*. New York: Columbia University Press, pp. 245–268.

Kirchheimer, O. (1957a) 'The political scene in West Germany', *World Politics*, 9: 433–45.

Kirchheimer, O. (1957b) 'The waning of opposition in parliamentary regimes', *Social Research*, 24: 127–56.

Kirchheimer, O. (1959) 'Majorities and minorities in Western European governments', *Western Political Quarterly*, XII: 492–510.

Kirchheimer, O. (1961) 'German democracy in the 1950's', *World Politics*, 13: 254–66.

Kirchheimer, O. (1962) Lecture notes entitled 'Political Parties, April 17, 1962', and 'Elections, May 1, 1962', pp. 1–13, box 2, 83.1, Kirchheimer Papers, State University of New York at Albany.

Kirchheimer, O. (1964a) 'The transformation of European party systems', paper prepared for the Conference on Political Parties and Political Development, Villa Falconieri, Frascati, Italy, 6–9 January, Box 2, 83.1, Kirchheimer Papers, State University of New York at Albany.

Kirchheimer, O. (1964b) 'Die Transformation des Westeuropäischen Parteisystems', box 2, 83.1, Kirchheimer's personal papers, German Intellectual Emigré Collection, Department of Special Collections and Archives, State University of New York at Albany, pp. 1–6.

Kirchheimer, O. (1965) 'Der Wandel des westeuropäischen Parteisystems', *Politische Vierteljahresschrift*, 6(1): 20–41.

Kirchheimer, O. (1966) The transformation of Western European party systems', in J. LaPalombara and M. Weiner (eds), *Political Parties and Political Development*. Princeton, NJ: Princeton University Press, pp. 177–200.

Kirchheimer, O. (n.d.) 'Parties, interest groups, elections', lecture notes, pp. 26–43, box 2, 83.1, Kirchheimer Papers, State University of New York at Albany.

Kitschelt, Herbert (1994) *The Transformation of European Social Democracy*. Cambridge: Cambridge University Press.

Koole, R. (1996) 'Cadre, catch-all or cartel? A comment on the notion of the cartel party', *Party Politics*, 2: 507–24.

Krouwel, A. (1999) *The catch-all party in Western Europe 1945–1990. A study in arrested development*. Doctoral dissertation, Vrije Universiteit Amsterdam.

Krouwel, A. (2003) 'Otto Kirchheimer and the catch-all party', *West European Politics*, 26(2): 23–40.

Lehmbruch, G. (1974) 'A non-competitive pattern of conflict management in liberal democracies: the case of Switzerland, Austria and Lebanon', in K. McRae (ed.), *Consociational Democracy. Political Accommodation in Segmented Societies*. Toronto: McClelland and Stewart, pp. 90–7.

Lenin, V.I. (1961) 'What is to be done? Burning questions of our movement', in V.I. Lenin, *Collected Works*, Vol. 5. Moscow: Foreign Languages Publishing House, pp. 347–530.

Lijphart, A. (1968) *The Politics of Accommodation. Pluralism and Democracy in the Netherlands*, Berkeley: University of California Press.

Lijphart, A. (1974) 'The Netherlands: The rules of the game', in K. McRae (ed.), *Consociational Democracy. Political Accommodation in Segmented Societies*. Toronto: McClelland and Stewart.

Lipset, S.M. (1964) The changing class structure and contemporary European politics', in *Daedalus*, 93(1): 271–303.

Lipset, S.M. and Rokkan, S. (eds) (1967) *Party Systems and Voter Alignments: Cross-national Perspectives*. New York: Free Press.

Lohmar, Ulrich (1963) *Innerparteiliche Demokratie, Eine Untersuchung der Verfassungswirklichkeit politischer Parteien in der Bundesrepublik Deutschland*. Stuttgart: Ferdinand Enke.

Mair, P. (1997) *Party System Change. Approaches and Interpretations*. Oxford: Clarendon Press.

Michels, R. (1962) *Political Parties: A Sociological Study of the Oligarchical Tendencies of Modern Democracy*. New York: Free Press.

Mintzel, Alf (1984) *Die Volkspartei: Typus und Wirklichkeit*. Opladen: Westdeutscher Verlag.

Neumann, S. (ed.) (1956) *Modern Political Parties. Approaches to Comparative Politics*. Chicago: University of Chicago Press.

Ostrogorski, Mosei (1902) *Democracy and the Organization of Political Parties*. London: Macmillan and Company.

Panebianco, A. (1988) *Political Parties: Organization and Power*. Cambridge: Cambridge University Press.

Pizzorno, A. (1964) 'The individualistic mobilization of Europe', *Daedalus*, 93(1): 199–224.

Pomper, Gerald M. (1992) 'Concepts of political parties', *Journal of Theoretical Politics*, 4(2): 143–59.

Puhle, H.-J. (2002) 'Still the age of catch-allism? Volksparteien and Parteienstaat in crisis and re-equilibration', in R. Gunther, J. Montero and J. Linz (eds), *Political Parties. Old Concepts and New Challenges*. Oxford, Oxford University Press, pp. 58–83.

Rueschemeyer D., Stephens, E.H. and Stephens J.D. (1992) *Capitalist Development and Democracy*. Cambridge: Polity Press.

Sartori, G. (ed.) (1984) *Social Science Concepts. A Systemic Analysis*. Beverly Hills, CA: Sage Publications.

Sartori, G. (1987) *The Theory of Democracy Revisited*, Part One. Chatham, NJ: Chatham House.

Schlesinger, Joseph A. (1965) 'The nucleus of party organization', in James G. March, *Handbook of Organizations*. Chicago: Rand McNally, pp. 775–86.

Schlesinger, Joseph A. (1984) 'On the theory of party organization', *Journal of Politics*, 46: 369–400.

Schmidt, M.G. (1985) 'Allerweltsparteien in Westeuropa', *Leviathan*, 13: 329–54.

Schmidt, M.G. (1989) '"Allerweltsparteien" und "Verfall der Opposition" – Ein Beitrag zu Kirchheimers Analysen westeuropäischer Parteien-systeme', in W. Luthardt, and A. Söllner, *Verfassungsstaat, Souveränität, Pluralismus: Otto Kirchheimer zum Gedächtnis*. Opladen: Westdeutscher Verlag, pp. 173–82.

Schumpeter, Joseph A. (1942) *Capitalism, Socialism and Democracy*. New York: Harper & Row.

Seiler, D.-L. (1984a) 'De la classification des partis politiques', *Res Publica*, XXVII: 59–86.

Seiler, D.-L. (1984b) 'Une généalogie des organisations des partis', *Res Publica*, XXVI: 119–41.

Seiler, D.-L. (1993) *Les Partis Politiques*. Paris: Armand Colin.

Smith, G. (1989) 'Core persistence, system change and the "peoples party"', *West European Politics*, 12(4): 157–68.

Ware, A. (1985) *The Breakdown of Democratic Party Organization*. Oxford: Clarendon Press.

Ware, A. (ed.) (1987) *Political Parties: Electoral Change and Structural Response*. Oxford: Basil Blackwell.

Ware, A. (1996) *Political Parties and Party Systems*. Oxford: Oxford University Press.

Weber, M. (1925) *Grundriss der Sozialökonomik, III. Abteilung Wirtschaft und Gesellschaft*. Tübingen: Mohr Verlag.

Wildavsky, Aaron B. (1959) 'A methodological critique of Duverger's political parties', *Journal of Politics*, 21: 313–18.

Wolinetz, Steven B. (1979) 'The transformation of Western European party systems revisited', *West European Politics*, 2(1): 4–28.

Wolinetz, Steven B. (1991) 'Party system change: The catch-all thesis revisited', *West European Politics*, 14(1): 113–28.

Wolinetz, Steven B. (2002) 'Beyond the catch-all party: Approaches to the study of parties and party organization in contemporary democracies', in R. Gunther, J. Montero and J. Linz (eds), *Political Parties. Old Concepts and New Challenges*. Oxford: Oxford University Press, pp. 136–65.

Wright, William E. (ed.) (1971) *A Comparative Study of Party Organization*. Columbus, OH: Merrill.

22

AMERICAN EXCEPTIONALISM

Alan Ware

One of the problematic aspects of the study of party organizations has been how to account for the undoubted differences between American parties and many of the European parties. Of course, taking account of unusual and distinctive institutions is something with which comparative political analysis must deal all the time, but the search for suitable analytic frameworks for party organizations that embrace those in the United States has been hampered by three quite specific factors.

First, there is the impact of what might be termed the ideology of 'American exceptionalism' on the American political science community. The Tocquevillian idea that American society was different from other societies, and that consequently its politics was also unique, was a powerful one. Too often the assumption that those exceptional values had a direct effect on organizational forms the parties developed has been held uncritically. Rossiter's (1960: 37) unsubstantiated claim was typical of a way of thinking; having identified a number of what he claimed were unique aspects of American politics (including local bossism), he noted 'Nowhere in the world ... is there a pattern of politics anything like ours'.

Secondly, among European political scientists there has been much misunderstanding as to how American parties operate. Duverger, for example, understood American parties to be the counterpart of the early cadre parties in Europe – that is, a grouping of notabilities (or elites) who come together to prepare for elections. There are similarities that are evident in many respects, but with one important exception. In Europe the attitude of the notabilities to those they recruited to perform campaigning tasks was that they were not in any real

sense *participants* in the party; in the parties that developed in the United States in the Jacksonian era widespread popular participation in parties was understood as the very cornerstone of democracy.

Thirdly, until the 1980s (and possibly later) relatively little was known about party organizations outside the United States and the larger countries in Western Europe. Although there were a few interesting attempts to broaden the range of parties incorporated into comparative analysis – such as that by Epstein (1964) in the case of Canada – until recently most studies focused on a much restricted range of party organizations in liberal democracies. The result was analytic frameworks that tended to juxtapose the electoral campaign-oriented American organizations with the supposedly policy-oriented, internally democratic, parties of which the European socialist parties were the most outstanding example (Wright, 1971). This reinforced the idea that American parties were, in some sense, different from most parties elsewhere, especially in that 'the ideological or policy clarification and goal definition function is rejected' (Wright, 1971: 33). Thus, American parties have often been treated as a type of party that is non-ideological, although Gerring's (1998) research has demonstrated there has been a pronounced ideological component to American national election campaigns since the 1830s.

Among them, these three factors have contributed to a misunderstanding of the relationship between the American parties and many European parties. Moreover, some political scientists have simply given up on the attempt to incorporate the former into a comparative framework; Panebianco (1988: xv) famously excluded American parties from his analysis by asserting that the factors affecting their emergence and development were different, but without discussing what the difference actually was. This chapter seeks to outline the main differences in party organizational structure in the USA, to consider the various explanations that might be given for those differences, and to explore the problems of incorporating American parties into some of the more popular analytic frameworks.

THE MAIN DIFFERENCES BETWEEN AMERICAN PARTY ORGANIZATIONS AND THOSE OF OTHER PARTIES

Many of the supposedly distinctive features of American parties are evident elsewhere. The 'exceptional' nature of American parties tends to lie in the extent to which some of these features have been developed and also in the particular combination of features prominent in the American parties. Four main differences are especially important in the contemporary United States.

Extensive legal control of parties

From the advent of mass-based parties in the 1830s until the late 1880s there was virtually no legal control. Parties issued their own ballot papers at elections, they controlled their own nomination procedures, they determined the structure of their own organizations, and so on. Beginning with the adoption of the official ballot (known in America as the 'Australian ballot') by most states at the end of the 1880s, extensive legal control of party activities commenced. From early in the 20th century most states required major parties to use the direct primary election as the system for nominating candidates for public office, and these parties were also required to have a particular kind of organizational structure, in which the lowest echelons of the party were also directly elected in publicly administered elections.

From a largely unregulated party system, the United States had moved rapidly to one that had the most extensive legal regulation of all liberal democracies. Some political scientists have seen this as being one of the most distinctive aspects of American parties; Epstein (1986: Chapter 6) has argued that parties are conceived in the United States as a kind of public utility, rather than a wholly private form of organization. However, it is important to recognize that the difference is partly a matter of

degree; a number of other countries require their parties to operate within a particular legal framework. (In Germany, for instance, a party must be democratic – although the courts rarely venture into the potential minefield as to what counts as democratic.) Moreover, some party-related activities that are not controlled by statute in the United States – an example being the forms of electioneering that are permissible – are regulated elsewhere, with particular practices being banned.

The absence of a dues-paying membership

In many countries the link between the would-be participant in a party and that party became primarily one of formal membership. That is, the party formally enrolled its activists, often after a trial period in which they were associated with the party; on joining the party, the member would be liable to pay dues annually to the party, and he or she could be removed from the party as a result of activities held to be incompatible with membership. Members had rights to be involved in certain procedures – such as the nomination of candidates – that non-members did not. The original exemplar of the membership model had been the German Social Democratic party, though the general model was adopted by most socialist parties. In turn, and as Duverger (1959) had observed, other parties in Europe started to make use of the device of the fee-paying member, even though they did not always grant extensive formal powers to their members.

By contrast, in the United States, neither major party developed this kind of structure. Before the introduction of legal regulation, the question of who could become involved in a party's activities was not a matter that was policed rigorously, although those known to have supported the opposing party recently might be excluded from the relevant meetings – by force, if necessary. After the introduction of devices like the direct primary, it became difficult to identify party 'traitors' and hence exclude them from activities such as candidate selection – even in states that opted for so-called 'closed primaries'. In practice, therefore, today the American parties have 'members' who differ from the dues-paying members of most parties, in that they are entirely self-selected. However, as with legal regulation, the absence of a dues-paying membership is not unique to American parties; for example, the two largest Canadian parties, the Liberals and the Progressive Conservatives, for most of the 20th century did not enrol members in this way.

Highly decentralized party structures

Even when they started out as decentralized structures, as in France, with power residing among locally based leaders, over time most parties centralized a number of key activities. National parties might still leave control over certain functions to local units – for example, the selection of parliamentary candidates in the case of the British Conservatives – but many functions came to be controlled at the centre. In the United States, there was no such centralization. Not only did the power of nomination continue to rest at the local level, but those who were elected to public office could remain largely independent of their fellow party representatives, providing they retained the loyalty of their local voters. Furthermore, over time power within the nomination process has become even more decentralized. In the 19th century it was the county-wide party organizations that were normally the most important actors in that process. With the advent of television campaigning, individual candidates could assume that role; after the 1960s increasingly at all levels of office candidates' own organizations became the main structures deployed both in nomination contests and in general elections.

While this feature does mark a difference with many other parties, it is important not to exaggerate that difference. First, there are some significant centralizing tendencies in American parties. For example, the ability of major politicians to raise large sums of money that they can then disperse to likely challengers from their party creates informal links of obligation that tie otherwise independent political actors to each other. Consequently, crude versions of the 'business firm' model of parties tend to overemphasize the autonomy American politicians have in office. Not only must they keep the local interests in their own electoral coalition content, they also operate in an environment where major opponents in their party might be able to help resource a primary challenge to them; for instance, the behaviour of Republican moderates in the House over the Clinton impeachment becomes inexplicable unless this factor is recognized. (For a version of the model that does not make this kind of mistake, see Schlesinger, 1985.) Secondly, not all the other democracies displayed an early tendency towards centralization in their party structures. France, for example, did not; it was not until the incentives provided by the switch to a semi-presidential system in the Fifth Republic that the essentially local nature of French parties was transformed. Thirdly, personal campaign organizations are not unique to American parties. They are also found in those electoral systems that tend to pit different members of a party against each other – for example, the single transferable vote (as used in Ireland) and the single non-transferable vote (as used in Japan before the mid-1990s).

The non-programmatic nature of party competition

American parties do not develop policy programmes within their organizations, nor do they campaign on the basis of such a programme at elections. The policy platforms that are published before an election are general in nature, do not constitute a kind of promise to the electorate, and the party's candidates are not bound to support it. Consequently, these platforms receive little attention in the campaign. Because they do not develop policy, the parties lack the kinds of research units within their organizations that might develop policy programmes.

However, this different approach to campaigning does not mean that American parties are non-ideological – a charge frequently raised against them. Gerring's (1998) systematic analysis of presidential election campaigns shows that, once mass-oriented parties emerged, there have been clear differences between the two main parties in the ideological appeals they make to voters. Those appeals have changed over time, but ever since the 1830s there has been electoral competition based on ideology between the parties. Moreover, the non-programmatic style is one that is not unique to the United States; it is common in those presidential elections where, at some point in the electoral process, the winning candidate has got to secure the votes of more than half of those voting. This requirement tends to discourage policy programmes – partly because, at least formally, legislation is not the responsibility of the elected chief executive, and partly because the size of coalition needed to win a presidential election may be so great that it becomes difficult to construct detailed *winning* programmes.

WHAT ARE THE CAUSES OF THE DIFFERENCES?

While most commentators agree on the differences between American party organizations and organizations elsewhere, there is considerable disagreement as to what the causes of those differences are. That disagreement includes the question of whether there is one main cause of 'exceptionalism', or several unrelated causes of that apparent phenomenon.

Anti-party political values

Many American political scientists subscribe to the Tocquevillian view that the origins of the distinctive party structures lie in unique political values, though few now articulate the more general argument associated with an earlier generation that it was a whole set of exceptional political values and practices that the United States acquired (Rossiter, 1960). Rather it is a particular argument that is now often invoked to account for most of the observed differences – namely that in the United States there has always been at least an ambivalence, and at worst outright hostility, to political parties. It is argued that anti-partyism can account directly for the introduction of a compulsory legal framework imposed upon the major parties; that in turn meant that membership-based parties were neither possible nor necessary, and they were under less pressure to become programmatic. Even the decentralized state of the parties might be understood as a response to the unpopularity of parties – keeping them decentralized (and hence more low-profile) made it less likely that they would stir up yet more antagonism among mass publics.

In the last two decades, when survey evidence indicates that parties certainly did become less popular than they had been, the argument from anti-partyism has been much used in accounting for the distinctiveness of party organizations (see, for example, Katz and Kolodny, 1994: 26–7; Pomper, 1992: 132–4; Wattenberg, 1991: 32–4). The argument has an obvious appeal but there are three main objections to it that suggest it is of limited utility.

First, in spite of frequent assertions that anti-partyism is stronger in American politics (or, perhaps, permeates politics there more deeply), there is no available cross-national survey data of either political elites or mass publics to demonstrate that this is true. There are also plenty of examples of periods in European countries when anti-partyism was strong, so that it is an explanation that is far from self-evident. Secondly, even if it could be demonstrated that, for much of the 20th century, anti-party sentiments were more prevalent in America than elsewhere, it remains the case that American party structures became established

in the 1830s, and that for more than 60 years parties were at the centre of social and political life (McCormick, 1986; Silbey, 1991). Arguments that somehow earlier deep-rooted anti-partyism (of a kind usually associated with Madison) somehow just got submerged in this period, only to resurface later, are unconvincing – unless a firm link can be established between different periods of anti-partyism, and so far it has not been. Thirdly, although it is often argued that anti-partyism was responsible for the legal regulation of party nominating procedures, and the subsequent adoption of the direct primary, the evidence actually points in a different direction. As with the earlier adoption of the Australian ballot, it was party politicians, rather than anti-party reformers, who were at the forefront of moves for legislation. Their motivation was usually the desire to modernize practices that no longer worked well, and such reforms could not be effected through party rules, with the law being the only way of doing so (Ware, 2002).

The decentralization of the American state

Party organizations tend to develop structures that reflect the structure of governmental institutions they are attempting to control. As Finegold (1995: 29) observed of the impact of American local government reform at the end of the 19th century: 'The structure of local party organization reflected the structure of local government. Governmental consolidation encouraged party consolidation, and governmental fragmentation encouraged party fragmentation.' More generally, the point could be made that in a state that had the separation of powers, federalism, and, after the Jacksonian era, a very large number of directly elected public offices, a decentralized party structure was inevitable. However, by itself, this kind of argument is insufficient – it cannot account for the absence of a phenomenon evident in some Canadian provinces. There, one of the effects of the pressures of federalism has been the formal separation of the federal and the provincial parties, and, in some cases, also the successful formation of parties that compete at the provincial level but not at the federal level. With only a few minor exceptions, in the United States the same parties have engaged in competition for all levels of office.

Consequently, an argument from the impact of governmental fragmentation has to be used in conjunction with an argument from the development of a national political career structure in America (Watts, 1987). Two features of this are relevant in this context. Unlike Canadian provincial politicians, state politicians often run for federal office (and, less frequently, the opposite career move also occurs). However, while at all levels of office individual politicians have their own base of electoral support, the US Congress and most state legislatures organize their business around parties; it is parties that make committee assignments, for example. Although some political careers have been sustained by politicians who chose not to align themselves with either of the major parties, there are strong incentives not to do this. The result is a near-monopoly enjoyed by the two parties at all levels of partisan contest.

The development of mass political organizations before urbanization

This is an argument about the effect of changes of scale in the polity – changes that could account for the pressure to adopt an extensive legal framework for the parties. That in turn would account for the failure of membership-based parties to emerge. American parties began mobilizing mass electorates (almost exclusively white and male) in the 1830s in a country that consisted mainly of small towns and rural areas. In such a society formal rules of participation were often unnecessary, and the proceedings of parties at all levels were largely informal – relying on tradition and convention to resolve disputes. This was a face-to-face society in which order could be maintained in the party without recourse to formal rules, and many state parties did not have written rules. With population growth electoral districts became larger, and with mass immigration it was no longer the case that this was mainly a polity in which participants in a party knew each other. Consequently, abuses of political procedures increased, so that many party elites had an incentive to attempt to reform their parties. The classic example of this is the party ballot. Intra-party disputes about nominations could lead to rival candidates for local offices being run at general elections, with alternative ballots being issued to voters. This produced relatively high levels of ticket splitting, a practice that party elites within a county usually wished to minimize. With the introduction of the Australian ballot at the end of the 1880s, a reform supported by many of those elites, ticket splitting was reduced in the following decade (Reynolds and McCormick, 1986).

This third argument holds that one key difference between the United States and other liberal democracies is that mass party structures elsewhere had to deal with problems associated with larger scale at their inception. Thus one of the consequences of democratization preceding urbanization in America was that large parties, mobilizing mass electorates, could develop without formal internal rules and procedures. In conjunction with the decentralized form of the state, these parties could operate effectively for a while without the kind of structures that parties in other countries would need later when they started mass electoral mobilization. The American parties had to address the problems associated with scale eventually, but by that time there were already structures containing political actors who had a stake in maintaining certain aspects of the status quo. That restricted the form that organizational change could then take – a point that is compatible with Panebianco's (1988) most general argument about the constraints on long-term change in party organizations.

The impact of presidential government

A recent, and important, explanation for the failure of American parties to develop a policy-making role is that it was the result of how the presidency developed under Franklin Roosevelt. This is an argument most closely associated with Milkis (1993: 5), who argued that:

> Roosevelt aimed at building a more progressive form of government within the presidency, rather than through a more permanent link between the executive and legislature. This required extending the personal and nonpartisan responsibility of the president to the detriment of collective and partisan responsibility.

The expansion of federal government activity in the 1930s could have been done in a way compatible with a more programmatic role for parties, but it was not. Not all political scientists agree with Milkis that Roosevelt actually intended to weaken parties. Coleman, for example, argues that Roosevelt had a desire for 'more cohesive parties and for institutional entrenchment of the New Deal, not simply a system of presidential aggrandizement'. However, he too accepts that the effect of the presidency developing in the way that it did was to prevent the development of a policy formation role for parties: 'Institutionalizing

New Deal reforms in the state would not build a "party state" but would lead instead to a diminished stature for party over time'. (Coleman 1996: 59).

The main query to be raised about this kind of argument is whether a de-basing of the role of party in policy-making is something that is always likely to happen in a presidential system. Not only do presidential contests typically turn less on battles of rival programmes than do parliamentary elections, because of the need to construct a large electoral coalition, but once in office presidents often have the resources to develop policy semi-independently of party colleagues in the legislature. Thus, the differences that might be being explained by this factor are more differences between the role of parties in presidential and parliamentary systems, rather than differences that are peculiar to the United States.

The impact of competition from other forms of party structure

An argument developed by Duverger (1959) was that superior forms of party organization would drive out inferior ones – the latter being those that were less successful at mobilizing mass electorates. Thus, according to him, mass parties relying on formally enrolled members had tended to replace cadre parties organized around a small caucus – an argument rejected by Epstein (1967), on the grounds that looser forms of party organization were more flexible, and more appropriate to new forms of election campaigning. But can the absence of competition from membership-based parties account for the failure of the major American parties to develop this, or other forms, of party structure?

The answer is probably 'no'. The alleged efficacy of membership-based parties lay in their ability both to reach a large number of potential voters, and to acquire resources to enable themselves to carry out the activities associated with that. However, the American parties had devised means of doing this in the 1830s without formal membership. On the one hand, elections were held frequently, and the parties turned the activities associated with this regular vote mobilization into a form of participatory recreation. This style of campaigning started to decline towards the end of the 19th century (see McGerr, 1986), but in the meantime it had contributed to a massive vote mobilization for several decades. On other hand, the use of the spoils system gave parties access to resources through control of public office; they simply did not need the income that membership dues would have provided.

HOW DO AMERICAN PARTIES FIT INTO SOME MODELS OF PARTY STRUCTURES?

One of the consequences of the influence of the three factors identified in the opening section of this essay is that frameworks for analysing party structures have often been devised into which the American parties do not easily fit. Certainly, this is true of three of the most famous frameworks.

Cadre and mass parties

In their original form in the mid-19th century, American parties could be said to exhibit features of both cadre and mass parties. As Scarrow (1996: 19) observes, 'For Duverger a true mass party is identified by its aspirations to enrol a wide segment of supporters, and to offer them year round opportunities for participation'. However, this is precisely what American parties did. The ethos of the political system then was that political participation was desirable in a polity, and that it should be transmitted through the parties. Because so many offices became elected during the 1830s, and because terms of office were usually short, most communities had at least one set of elections each year. In that era American parties were engaged in mass activity much of the time. In that sense they were not elitist institutions. However, they were elitist in a different sense – in that there were few formal decision-making procedures by which organizational leaders were selected. Leaders emerged from the set of interpersonal relations within the party, and for that reason it was appropriate for Duverger to understand American parties as a kind of cadre party. However, Duverger also believed that mass parties were distinguished by their 'formal enrolment procedures', and most definitely the American parties lacked such procedures.

After the 1890s the major American parties tended to lose some of their 'mass' characteristics. Participatory activities during election campaigns were replaced by ones in which party supporters were more akin to spectators (McGerr, 1986). During the Progressive era the enthusiasm for as extensive a system of elective office as possible waned, and over the next century tenure of office also tended to increase. The result was that activity in the parties became much more intermittent than it had been in the 19th century. Moreover, with the move towards more candidate-centred styles of campaigning, it became possible to see the parties as being a kind of cadre party in which the main political elites were the candidates themselves (Ware, 1985: 14–15). Yet, with respect to their origins, they do not fit easily into either the cadre or the mass category.

Mass parties and catch-all parties

Yet another feature of Duverger's concept of the mass party poses difficulties when examining American parties. The mass party was the 'representative of pre-defined sectors of society' (Katz and Mair, 1995: 7). Yet this was precisely the role of American parties in the 19th century – they mobilized specific social groups. What Thelen (1986: 23) says of Missouri was true of most other states: 'Parties became the political arm of ethnic, religious and sectional cultures. Each new group from Europe joined the party opposite to the one that had attracted its most bitter enemy from their homeland'. However, there were three differences between the social bases of parties in the United States and those found in much of Europe. First, class was not a source of party mobilization in the two major parties, and there were no large class-based mass parties. Secondly, the decentralized nature of the American parties meant that the same social group might be mobilized by one party in one city and by the other party in a different city, so that nationally the parties' social bases resembled much more a mosaic than clear lines of division. Thirdly, one of the effects of presidentialism had been to provide a disincentive for the formation of more than two major parties, so that social groups tended to combine with other groups in a given party, rather than having a party of their own to promote their interest.

During the 20th century the connections between specific social groups and particular parties became weaker, thereby furthering the popular impression that American parties sought votes from wherever they could obtain them. Thus, when Kirchheimer (1966) introduced the idea of the 'catch-all' party that was replacing the mass party in Europe, it was misleadingly seen as an aspect of the 'Americanization of European politics' (Katz and Mair, 1995: 8). What was correct about this view was that since the end of the 19th century American parties had had to pursue more of a catch-all strategy as social group links started to weaken. What was misleading was that the American experience had actually been remarkably similar to the European – except that the change to a more 'catch-all' approach to election campaigning had occurred about six decades earlier. Until the 1890s American parties had largely won elections by mobilizing the party faithful, rather than by engaging in 'catch-all' strategies.

Catch-all and cartel parties

One of the most recent models of parties, the cartel party, sees parties as becoming part of the state. The 'parties still compete, but they do so in the knowledge that they share with their competitors a mutual interest in collective organizational survival and, in some cases, even the limited incentive to compete has actually been replaced by a positive incentive not to compete' (Katz and Mair, 1995: 19–20). Such parties draw many of the resources they need from the state directly (in the case of financial subventions) or indirectly (in the case of access to publicly controlled television channels). However, if this is a new form of party model, dating perhaps from 1970, then it must be admitted that in the case of the United States some of the features of the cartel party were more evident in the 19th century than they are now. Certainly, the parties then used control of government to generate the contracts and jobs that were the lifeblood of the party. Although they competed fiercely against each other for spoils, when their mutual interests were threatened they worked together to keep out other parties. For example, following the introduction of the Australian ballot one of the most persistent problems facing third parties was actually to get on to the official ballot; in many states rules were designed to make it difficult for these parties to mount a challenge. Moreover, legislatures were usually organized in such a way as to disadvantage representatives of other parties.

This is not to say that the cartel party is not a useful concept, nor to deny that in many respects there is growing evidence of recent co-option of the state by parties – even by parties in the United States. However, there is a case for arguing that some aspects of cartelization were to be found in America in an earlier era, and this exposes further the need for party models to be more sensitive to the particular development of American parties. That development resembles many aspects of party development elsewhere, but there are also important differences – and those differences are not always the ones to which commentators draw attention.

REFERENCES

Coleman, John J. (1996) *Party Decline in America: Policy, Politics and the Fiscal State*. Princeton, NJ: Princeton University Press.

Duverger, Maurice (1959) *Political Parties*, second English edition. London: Methuen.

Epstein, Leon D. (1964) 'A comparative study of Canadian parties', *American Political Science Review*, 58: 46–59.

Epstein, Leon D. (1967) *Political Parties in Western Democracies*. London: Pall Mall.

Epstein, Leon D. (1986) *Political Parties in the American Mold*. Madison: University of Wisconsin Press.

Finegold, Kenneth (1995) *Experts and Politicians: Reform Challenges to Machine Politics in New York, Cleveland and Chicago*. Princeton, NJ: Princeton University Press, 1995.

Gerring, John (1998) *Party Ideologies in America, 1828–1996*. Cambridge: Cambridge University Press.

Katz, Richard S. and Kolodny, Robin (1994) 'Party organization as an empty vessel: Parties in American politics', in Richard S. Katz and Peter Mair (eds), *How Parties Organize: Change and Adaptation in Party Organizations in Western Democracies*. London, Sage, pp. 23–50.

Katz, Richard and Mair, Peter (1995) 'Changing models of party organization and party democracy: The emergence of the cartel party', *Party Politics*, 1: 5–28.

Kirchheimer, Otto (1966) 'The transformation of West European party systems', in Joseph LaPalombara and Myron Weiner (eds), *Political Parties and Political Development*. Princeton, NJ: Princeton University Press, pp. 177–200.

McCormick, Richard L. (1986) *The Party Period and Public Policy: American Politics from the Age of Jackson to the Progressive Era*. New York: Oxford University Press.

McGerr, Michael E. (1986) *The Decline of Popular Politics: The American North, 1865–1928*. New York: Oxford University Press.

Milkis, Sidney M. (1993) *The President and the Parties*. New York: Oxford University Press.

Panebianco, Angelo (1988) *Political Parties: Organization and Power*. Cambridge: Cambridge University Press.

Pomper, Gerald (1992) *Passions and Interest: Political Party Concepts of American Democracy*. Lawrence: University of Kansas Press.

Reynolds, John F. and McCormick, Richard L. (1986) 'Outlawing "treachery": Split tickets and ballot laws in New York and New Jersey, 1880–1910', *Journal of American History*, 72: 835–58.

Rossiter, Clinton (1960) *Parties and Politics in America*. Ithaca, NY: Cornell University Press.

Scarrow, Susan E. (1996) *Parties and their Members: Organizing for Victory in Britain and Germany*. Oxford: Oxford University Press.

Schlesinger, Joseph A. (1985) 'The new American political party', *American Political Science Review*, 79: 1152–69.

Silbey, Joel H. (1991) *The American Political Nation, 1838–1893*. Stanford, CA: Stanford University Press.

Thelen, David (1986) *Paths of Resistance: Tradition and Disunity in Industrializing Missouri*. New York, Oxford University Press.

Ware, Alan (1985) *The Breakdown of Democratic Party Organization, 1940–1980*. Oxford: Oxford University Press.

Ware, Alan (2002) *The American Direct Primary: Party Institutionalization and Transformation in the North*. Cambridge: Cambridge University Press.

Wattenberg, Martin (1991) *The Rise of Candidate-Centred Politics*. Cambridge, MA: Harvard University Press.

Watts, Ronald L. (1987) 'The American Constitution in comparative perspective: A comparison of federalism in the United States and Canada', *Journal of American History*, 74: 769–91.

Wright, William E. (1971) 'Comparative party models: Rational efficient and party democracy', in William E. Wright (ed.), *A Comparative Study of Party Organization*. Columbus, OH: Charles E. Merrill, pp. 17–54.

23

MOVEMENT PARTIES

Herbert Kitschelt

INTRODUCTION

Movements, interest groups, and parties are the main vehicles of political interest articulation and intermediation. Students of political parties do not commonly employ the notion of 'movement party' as a formal concept with a specific terminological content. To supply such content is the first task of this chapter. In a nutshell, I characterize the transition from movement to party as one in which political entrepreneurs change the institutional setting in which they operate *and* make investments in an organizational infrastructure of collective action as well as procedures of social choice that create collective preference schedules ('party programs'). Political entrepreneurs in movement parties shift to the institutional site of partisan electoral competition without making requisite investments in overcoming challenges of collective action and social choice that party politicians encounter in electoral and legislative arenas. I then sketch theoretical arguments accounting for the conditions under which political entrepreneurs switch from extra-institutional movements to movement parties as their primary vehicle to bring societal interests to bear on policy-making. Next, I turn to the circumstances that induce politicians to convert movement parties into political parties pure and simple or to stick to the movement party hybrid. The remaining two sections illustrate the general theoretical considerations with two applications. The first of these discusses the trajectory of ecological parties, one variant of a broader party family I have called 'left-libertarian' parties. Many of such parties originate in social movements

and, at least initially, choose organizational forms that embody principles of 'movement parties'. The second application is concerned with what can very broadly be termed the far right in the party systems of advanced postindustrial democracies. Although such parties do not typically originate in social protest movements, right-wing political entrepreneurs have a tendency to adopt organizational models and tactics consistent with the analytical type of movement party. But like ecology parties, they then face challenges that compel them to reconsider their organizational forms and programmatic appeals or face electoral demise.

MOVEMENTS, PARTIES, AND MOVEMENT PARTIES

It is a well-known problem that the boundaries between different modes of collective political interest articulation figuring under the rubrics of movements, interest groups, and parties are empirically fuzzy (cf. Burstein, 1998). Nevertheless, we can identify conceptual types that are more or less approximated by empirical manifestations. At least two dimensions of properties allow us to differentiate modes of interest articulation in democratic polities: institutional and functional criteria.

First, actors advance collective interests in three different institutional arenas through distinct types of practices. If they participate in institutions of territorial democratic representation through competitive multi-candidate elections to legislatures, teams of candidates for electoral office and their supporters form political parties. If they band together to influence and bargain with politicians in legislative and executive institutions through the provision of information, persuasion, financial contributions to parties within the bounds of legality, or the credible threat of withdrawing electoral support from electoral office-holders, they constitute interest groups. Finally, if they resort to 'street politics' of protest and disruption in pursuit of a collective purpose outside or against the institutionalized channels of political communication and politicians inserted in them – whether in a non-violent or a violent fashion – they participate in political movements (cf. Della Porta and Diani, 1999: 13–16). Empirical organized vehicles of collective interest mobilization may practice all three strategies, but each with a characteristically different profile of emphasis on protest, influence through institutional channels, or electoral contestation.

Second, borrowing from Aldrich (1995), we may distinguish vehicles of political interest mobilization not according to institutional, but functional criteria by the extent to which such vehicles invest in solutions to *problems of collective action* and *problems of social choice*. The coordination of collective action in time and space requires resources such as human labor and capital equipment that organize social communication, induce participation, and effect cooperation among members of a large constituency of potential contributors. Organizations exert power by conferring the capacity to mobilize people in disruptive action, lobbying, or voting on a constituency and its leaders. But the extent to which entrepreneurs mobilize resources for political organization varies across practices of collective interest articulation.

Social movements geared to disruptive protest build little organizational structure to solve problems of collective action. They therefore have a limited spatio-temporal reach and can bring together large numbers of participants only for short periods of time. Interest groups and political parties, in contrast, embody greater investments in organizational structure that extend their spatio-temporal reach. They define membership roles, predictable contributions to the organizational effort (member fees, fund drives), an organizational structure with a division of labor among political professionals, and a chain of command, whether its members are recruited by election or appointment.

In functional terms,[1] political entrepreneurs make investments in enhancing collective action capabilities only if such efforts and resource expenditures are warranted in order to reach collective objectives.[2] This is the case where entrepreneurs anticipate that the salient objectives of collective mobilization amount not to a single-shot collective decision – e.g. abolish child labor, enfranchise women, prevent the stationing of nuclear armed missiles – but a temporally sustained and spatially extensive mobilization of constituencies whose pursuit requires continuous refinement and updating of specific objectives. The issue of child labor turns into that of industrial relations more generally, that of nuclear arms into the issue of defense policy, and so forth.

Political entrepreneurs overcome problems of social choice if they construct a single collective preference schedule over jointly pursued objectives in a collective mobilizational effort, even though each individual participant may subscribe to a somewhat divergent individual preference schedule over salient collective goals. Just as the solution of collective action problems, the production of a collective preference schedule requires labor and capital resources assembled in organizational structures to coerce or bribe members' compliance with collective objectives, or to sustain a participatory process of interest aggregation that commands the voluntary compliance of all constituency members involved. The collective preference schedule, manifested in organizational ideologies and policy programs, is the result of hard organizational labor and deep resource investments distributed over an often protracted collective process of learning.

Again in functional terms, entrepreneurs invest in the construction of a complex collective preference schedule over manifold objectives that overcomes the problem of individual preference heterogeneity only if salient collective objectives cannot be decomposed into separable modules and 'contracted out' to independent vehicles of interest mobilization. In other words, entrepreneurs incur the transaction costs of organizing compliance around a complex set of collective objectives only if *each* salient collective objective is interdependent with *every other* salient collective objective. Analytically, social movements and interest groups simplify problems of social choice and thus reduce organizational transaction costs by isolating decomposable collective objectives. They lower the cost of organizational compliance building by focusing on relatively simple objectives: environmental protection, but not population control; wage bargaining, but not abortion rights. By contrast, if entrepreneurs mobilize around complex, intrinsically interdependent collective objectives, they form political parties.

Table 23.1 *Functional challenges and modes of collective mobilization*

		Investments in solving problems of collective action	
		Generous (when spatio-temporal extension of collective stakes)	Meager (when spatio-temporally discrete stakes)
Investments in solving problems of social choice	Generous (when interdependent stakes)	Political parties	Clubs of public intellectuals
	Meager (separable stakes)	Interest groups	Social movements

So far, I have developed only (1) a semantic convention of how to name efforts of collective mobilization with different investments in solving problems of social choice and collective action, and (2) a task structure based logic that gives rational political entrepreneurs incentives to choose a particular mode of mobilization from the available menu (Table 23.1). Interestingly, the resulting fourfold table leaves a cell that is rarely discussed in theories of political mobilization, but may sometimes play an important role. Where individuals invest resources in the refinement of collective objectives, such as the development of political programs and ideologies, but then do not organize collective action in operational terms, they constitute the 'organic intellectuals' (Antonio Gramsci) of a societal constituency that may orient collective action, once other leaders step in and organize interest groups and parties.[3]

The interesting theoretical problem that leads us to the issue of 'movement parties' now consists in examining the interface between *functional*, i.e. task structure related, and *institutional* incentives for choosing different collective mobilizational vehicles. Functional incentives may direct political entrepreneurs toward one mode of mobilization (say, movements), but empirically they choose another (say, political parties). Why would such discrepancies occur? And what happens empirically when political entrepreneurs choose an organizational form that expresses a mismatch between institutional arena and functional profile of movement demands? For example, what happens if social movement entrepreneurs who address spatio-temporally discrete and substantively separable stakes therefore invest little in solving problems of collective action and social choice, but nevertheless enter the field of party competition?

Before addressing these questions in the next two sections, let me introduce another set of linguistic conventions that label all the logically feasible configurations with a mismatch between functional incentives of a task structure to invest in an organizational infrastructure of collective social choice on the one hand, and institutional incentives to coordinate around a particular mode of collective mobilization, on the other (Table 23.2). The 'congruent' modes of mobilization run diagonally from the top left (disruptive causes making few investments in solving problems of collective action and social choice) to the bottom right (causes that seek electoral representation and invest both in solving problems of collective action and social choice). The object of this chapter, however, 'movement parties', constitute an incongruent option located in the top right of the table.

Movement parties are coalitions of political activists who emanate from social movements and try to apply the organizational and strategic practices of social movements in the arena of party competition. This entails several things. First of all, they make little investment in a formal organizational party structure. Movement parties may have no formal definition of the membership role. Anyone who comes to a meeting or activity of the party is considered a 'member' in the sense of entitlement to participation (and voting on motions, where it is called for). Movement parties also lack extensive and intensive formal organizational coverage. They lack a staff of paid professionals and a physical infrastructure of communication (offices, vehicles, etc.).

Second, social movement parties invest little in the process of solving problems of social choice. They lack an institutionalized system of aggregating interests through designated organs and officers with authority to formulate binding decisions and commitments on behalf of the party. The way movement parties diverge from the institutionalized type, however, varies widely. At one extreme, movement parties may be led by a *charismatic leader* with a patrimonial staff and personal following

Table 23.2 *Interfacing functional and institutional conditions in the choice of modes of collective mobilization*

| | | Institutional arenas of collective action | | |
		Extra-institutional disruption	Influence politics	Electoral representation
Extent of investment	CA: Low SC: Low	Social movements	Reform movements	Movement parties; charismatic politicians
in solving problems of Collective	CA: High SC: Low	Militant interest groups	Interest groups	Special interest parties; clientelistic parties
Action (CA) or Social	CA: Low SC: High	Militant intellectual clubs	Lobbying clubs	Legislative clubs ('cadre parties')
Choice (SC)	CA: High SC: High	Revolutionary organizations	Syndicalist and corporatist groups	Programmatic legislative parties

over which s/he exercises unconditional and unquestioned control. At the other extreme, movement parties may attempt to realize a grassroots democratic, participatory coordination among activists. Here all relevant decisions are taken in assemblies of activists and implemented by delegates elected to very short non-renewable tenure in representative political offices, whether they are intra-party or legislative. Both charismatic patrimonialism and grassroots democracy lead to a capricious, volatile and incomplete collective preference schedule. Attention is devoted to a small set of issues, while many others are neglected. The pursuit of these salient objectives may be inconsistent and contradictory.

Third, in terms of external political practice, movement parties attempt a dual track by combining activities within the arenas of formal democratic competition with extra-institutional mobilization. One day, legislators of such parties may debate bills in parliamentary committees, but the next day, they participate in disruptive demonstrations or the non-violent occupation of government sites.

The transition from movement party to any other form of party then involves investments in either organizational structure or modes of interest aggregation. Whether or not political activists are ready to make these investments, however, depends on circumstances discussed below. Furthermore, exactly what it means that politicians invest in organizational structure and modes of preference aggregation depends on exogenous factors such as technology (modes of communication, transportation) and human capital (e.g. level of education in an electorate). The conventional model of the mass membership party that was embodied by socialist workers' parties and Christian confessional parties in Europe from the late 19th to the last

third of the 20th century in this perspective constitutes a specific expression of investments wedded to an age with weak electronic mass media and a comparatively uneducated population by standards of the early 21st century.

FROM MOVEMENT TO 'MOVEMENT PARTY'

There is no a priori guarantee that politicians choose the 'correct' institutional arena, given their objectives and their ability to make investments in solving problems of collective action and social choice. Why, then, would social movements sometimes constitute movement parties? At least four theories, outlined below, have attempted answers to this question. The last two are theoretically and empirically the most relevant for democratic polities.

First, the evolution of political forms may be a matter of *political learning through trial and error.* Social movement activists may realize that their stakes really entail a comprehensive reorganization of society rather than singular measures of policy reform. As they develop broad-ranging ideologies and programs, they clash with established political parties on a wide variety of political issues. Movement entrepreneurs at that point may decide to enter the competitive electoral arena with a new party.

Second, the transition from movement to movement party may be a special case of a *game with incomplete and asymmetrical information* (Hug, 2001). Movement entrepreneurs have 'private information' about the size of the constituency that would support them, were they to enter the arena of party competition with the movement's political appeals. Politicians in established parties may discount the threat emanating from the entry of movement entrepreneurs into the electoral arena and not embrace the objectives sought by such entrepreneurs because they do not properly assess the magnitude of defection from their own party in case of continued intransigence. But the premise of the game-theoretical model, namely the informational advantage of external challengers, may be misleading. If anything, conventional parties have much better knowledge of the electoral landscape than their potential challengers because they have the resources to collect information, e.g. through opinion polls.

Third, whether or not movement entrepreneurs enter electoral politics depends on the interplay between the intensity and salience of their constituents in pursuit of the movement interest and the *barriers to entry created by electoral laws and other formal or informal thresholds that restrict the growth of a new challenger* (e.g. party finance, access to electronic mass media). A movement entrepreneur will enter the arena of party competition with some prospect of success only if barriers to entry are sufficiently low so that the expected electoral support level provides a reasonable prospect of winning an electoral quorum entitling the new party to legislative representation. The entire literature on electoral laws and party system format bears on this question (cf. Taagepera and Shugart, 1989; Lijphart, 1994; Cox, 1997). Systems of proportional representation with low thresholds of representation are more forgiving and should stimulate a greater proliferation of movement parties with, at least initially, narrow issue appeals than polities with high barriers to electoral representation.

While the literature on party entry finds evidence confirming this general hypothesis, the amount of statistical variance explained by electoral laws is often quite mediocre. The number of parties and new party entry varies substantially across similar electoral systems. Furthermore, hardly anywhere does the number of relevant political parties approach Cox's formula of $m+1$, the number of candidates elected in a district plus one.

This is where, fourth, spatial theory of party competition, drawing on social and political mobilization of conflicts of interest in society ('cleavages') comes in. Only where an intensely felt, salient political interest harbored by a quantitatively significant constituency lacks representation in the existing party system are movement entrepreneurs likely to enter the electoral arena. But in contrast to signaling models in game theory, it is not ignorance

that prevents existing electoral parties from competing for the newly mobilized constituency, but a rational calculation of voter trade-offs. Existing parties may refrain from trying to win (or hold) voters motivated by hitherto unrepresented, but salient, issue positions simply because they figure that such appeals would alienate significant other elements of their electoral constituency whose loss would equal or outweigh the support of the newly mobilized constituency.[4]

Social movement entrepreneurs may enter electoral politics not necessarily with the ex ante expectation to establish permanent parties. It suffices that they think of their effort as creating 'blackmail parties' (Sartori, 1976) that force established parties to take the electoral trade-offs of alternative programmatic appeals and constituency representation seriously. Movement parties are there to mix up the legislative agenda and to get issues discussed and decided that otherwise might be swept under the carpet by established parties for fear of dividing their own electorates.

Party formation then results from the *interplay between the formal and informal barriers to entry* into the game of electoral competition movement entrepreneurs encounter and the *intensity of hitherto unrepresented political interests* in the existing spectrum of political parties. Social movement parties are most likely to appear where (1) collective interests are intensely held by a large constituency willing to articulate their demands through disruptive, extrainstitutional activities, (2) established parties make no effort to embrace such interests for fear of dividing their own electoral constituency and (3) the formal and informal thresholds of political representation are moderate to low.

PRESERVING OR ABANDONING THE MODE OF MOVEMENT PARTY

When parties invest in organizational structure and an extensive and intensive refinement of their programmatic reach, they abandon the mode of movement party in favor of one of the remaining types listed in Table 23.2. What makes the continued existence of movement parties feasible or compels them to change by penalty of extinction in case of resistance? Three theoretical answers to this question have inspired the literature.

The first is a principal–agent model and goes as far back as 1911 (Michels, 1962), but also underlies more recent treatments such as Panebianco (1988). According to this model, the exigencies of electoral competition sooner or later induce the entrepreneurs of the movement party to abandon the interests of their constituencies by choosing organizational forms and strategies that are geared to the pursuit of votes and legislative office more than constituency service and by toning down disruptive, extra-institutional protest in favor of legislative politics of bargaining and electioneering. A party leadership, supported by a professional staff of functionaries, makes its peace with the societal status quo, abandons or at least waters down the unique organization and objectives of the movement party and creates a wide hiatus to political preferences and aspirations of the rank-and-file activists and constituencies. The main problem of this popular theoretical argument is that it does not take seriously multi-party electoral competition, generating an exit option for voters and party activists if they are dissatisfied with a leadership. In a democracy, unaccountable agents will find the ranks of their principals thinning out. Increased gaps of representation result in voter defection to other existing parties or the entry of new challenging parties, contingent upon institutional entry conditions. Because incumbent politicians anticipate this reaction, they stay sufficiently close to the heartbeat of their constituencies so that radical dissenters who exit usually can only take small elements of an established party's following with them.

A second theoretical strand makes a more plausible argument why politicians invest in addressing problems of collective action and social choice. It builds on learning from institutional incentives.[5] Legislatures are organs of territorial representation that are not functionally constrained in their policy agenda. In a system of territorial rather than functional representation, anything and everything can become a salient subject of the legislative agenda. Passing the annual government budget highlights the thematic diversification of legislative politics and compels territorial representatives to take a stance on a wide range of issues. Parties and politicians therefore cannot easily refuse to develop positions on large areas of the legislative schedule that are salient to at least some other politicians and their constituencies and instead confine themselves to a single or a small number of issues on which they have an articulate position. Social movement parties often experience chaos of internal coordination when they are compelled to articulate positions on issues outside their primary purview. This appearance of disarray and lack of internal coordination may prompt voter defection from the party and ultimately the movement party's demise. After winning a first round of elections on an issue-specific 'movement partisan' appeal, in preparation for subsequent rounds of competition it therefore often becomes imperative for party politicians to generalize the party's appeal in programmatic-ideological terms. For those critical minorities of rational voters who are information misers, but respond to the programmatic cues set by parties and therewith may often at the margin decide the difference between victory and defeat of parties in elections, a moderately coherent party program simplifies the act of electoral choice. Knowing a party's position in highly general left–right/ liberal–conservative terms and/or a few issue positions enables such voters to predict the parties' positions on many other issues without having to incur high search and information costs. For rational information misers, it is more attractive to vote for a predictable, coordinated party than an unpredictable movement party.

The institutional theory, like the principal–agent theory, however, has the problem of underpredicting the tenacity of movement parties. While, in general, it may be true that institutional cues may spell the demise of single-issue or narrowly focused parties competing over multiple rounds of electoral politics, there are counter-examples that illustrate the occasional viability and resurgence of movement parties. One way to fix this problem is to bring in more institutional arguments, for example about the ballot format and the candidate nomination procedures in electoral politics (cf. Carey and Shugart, 1995; Morgenstern, 2003), in order to account for greater or lesser incentives for politicians to produce coherent programmatic parties. But, as Morgenstern (2003) shows, it may be necessary to bring in the cleavage structure of a polity to account for the diversity of party strategies in identical institutional settings.

A third theory, therefore, builds on a spatial-programmatic interpretation of party competition as a configuration of party alternatives aligned in a very low-dimensional space of programmatic party alternatives that capture relevant salient issues (cf. Hinich and Munger, 1994). In direct contrast to the Michelsian principal–agent model, it is the principals themselves who indirectly compel the agents to adjust their programmatic positions. They are rewarded or punished based on their political

284

HANDBOOK OF PARTY POLITICS

achievements. In other words, the strategic conduct of a movement party and its competitors influences the preference distribution among electorates. Voter preferences, in turn, feed back into a party's strategies by rewarding or punishing it in elections.

The support of militant organizational forms and narrow, salient objectives that defy the institutional incentives, practices, and ideological justification depends on the strategic configuration in which a movement party is placed. Following Gamson (1990), let us distinguish the impact of movement politics according to procedural and substantive gains, the former indicating the inclusion of the movement party in procedures of policy-making (such as cabinet membership), the latter indicating the change of policies salient to movement parties in line with their objectives. Perversely, the more a movement party achieves in terms of procedural gains and/or substantive policy change, the more it may change its voters' preferences or salient interests such that the party experiences growing pressure to abandon its existing profile of organization and policy appeal.

Social movement parties are most tenacious and durable where governments and established parties make neither procedural nor substantive concessions. As long as the issues at the heart of a movement party mobilization remain salient, the party is likely to thrive. Where substantive, but no procedural concessions are forthcoming, the movement party may feel pressure to hedge its bets by expanding its thematic purview and generalizing its message so that it remains attractive, even if the constituency for whom the movement party's core issues are decisive were to shrink. Next, where movement parties achieve procedural inclusion and substantive concessions on policies relating to their core objectives, they demonstrate competence to their constituencies that gives them a lease on life. At the same time, procedural inclusion in policy formation entangles a party in many decisions on issues that are far removed from its original core objectives. Particularly as a party's original core issues may become less salient due to policy reform, it becomes critical for the party to diversify its appeal while simultaneously showing consistency in its pursuit of objectives based on a programmatic-ideological framework.

The worst situation for a movement party undoubtedly occurs when it achieves procedural concessions, such as cabinet participation, but gains little in terms of substantive concessions. The urgency of thematic generalization is

here very intense, as the party's rationale for existence can no longer be credibly defended with its original substantive policy objectives. In fact, social movements supporting such objectives may abandon the party so that it has to find entirely new electoral support groups. In most instances, therefore, inclusion without policy concessions should lead to the demise of a movement party and its displacement by existing parties or a new entrant renewing the struggle of the deceased party.

A special case of the configuration with procedural inclusion but substantive exclusion exists where a bipolar configuration of competition among established parties may enable a new party that has hitherto been in the opposition to tip the balance of forces toward victory or defeat of one partisan camp. In that instance, movement parties will be hard pressed to declare which side of the bipolar opposition they are willing to support. Even voters who emphasize a movement party's core issues may attribute a great deal of weight to which side wins government control and how victory affects the overall complexion of salient public policies. To become a credible and calculable player in this game, voters will want the movement party to generalize its issue appeals.

MATCHING PARTISAN COMPETITION, ORGANIZATIONAL FORM AND STRATEGIC APPEAL: THE EXPERIENCE OF ECOLOGICAL MOVEMENT PARTIES

Movement parties confined to the opposition benches with few opportunities to influence government policy or little leverage to change the make-up of governments have the easiest time to preserve a fluid movement party structure, configured around grassroots democratic principles or charismatic authority. Examples abound, however, that the strategic salience of a new movement party for government formation makes a thematically narrow interpretation of the parties' policy objectives around the core concerns of social movements highly unattractive even for voters sympathetic on the parties' core issues. New parties running under the labels of ecology, environmentalism, and Green politics in the 1970s and 1980s provide evidence for these propositions.[6]

Ecological movements generated their own electorally successful parties only where such movements were (1) strongly mobilized, where simultaneously (2) no existing party already represented the issue position and where there was (3) a history of center-left governments and corporatist interest intermediation. In Scandinavia and the Netherlands, environmentalism and corporatism were strong, but left-socialist parties adopted ecology and feminism in the 1970s and 1980s and thus left little room for a successful new ecology party.[7] Furthermore, even under the most favorable structural circumstances, tactical conditions facilitated or impeded the successful emergence of ecological movement parties. They grew most successfully at times when their appearance was unlikely to upset the chances of the center-left to govern. Thus, the German and Austrian Greens began to grow strongly only when the social democrats had already lost office or been forced into a coalition government. In Belgium and Switzerland, conditions of government formation made ecology parties strategically irrelevant for the bargaining power of social democracy throughout the 1980s. It is no accident that in all cases of electoral success, Green or ecology movement parties soon began to generalize their ideological appeal in order to create a closer match between the imperatives of territorial representation and electoral accountability, on the one hand, and the legislative appeals and activities of the new parties, on the other.

Ecological movements failed to form successful movement parties where the competitive balance between government and opposition would have impaired the chance of the moderate left to govern. This applies to Britain and France in the 1970s and 1980s and to Sweden in the late 1980s and early 1990s. What is more important, although partially endogenous to the strategic configuration among conventional parties, the ecology parties in all three countries refrained from generalizing their programmatic claims beyond the domains broadly related to energy and the domestic or global environment. Because all three countries already had radical left-socialist parties (France, Sweden) or party factions (Britain) on the left of conventional social democratic or socialist parties, ecologists initially found it unattractive to adopt a left-leaning general programmatic profile. But in all three cases, their strategy to situate themselves outside the generalized left–right programmatic-ideological spectrum and insist on a narrow core issue driven movement party appeal produced electoral failure. Voters caring about ecology were not prepared to support parties that ultimately might hurt the chances of the

conventional center-left to govern a country. In France and Sweden ecology parties eventually gained substantial electoral support when they became partners of conventional social democratic parties.

Placed in a very different structural and strategic situation than their British and French counterparts, the German Greens embarked on a programmatic generalization almost from their inception and developed complex party manifestoes by the mid-1980s. Here also, their electoral stability and performance have been wedded over the past twenty years to the party's willingness to make a credible commitment to center-left government coalitions, whenever such arrangements appear feasible in legislatures.[8] With some delay, the same center-left alignments paid off for the Austrian and the Belgian Greens. In all instances, government participation intensified the urgency of programmatic generalization, as ecology parties had to take stances on and bargain with government partners on issues covering a wide variety of policy areas.

The development of general political programs did not come easy in ecological and other left-libertarian parties. Even the core demands concerning environmental protection, feminism, and peace or security policy have a somewhat disjointed character (cf. Talshir, 2002). Matters are further complicated by questions of economic distribution. The linkage among different elements of Green or left-libertarian ideology does not result from logical necessity or normative theoretical stringency, but from the coalitional structure of economic and cultural interests configured around left-libertarian parties, especially those of the young, well-educated, disproportionately female professionals mostly with jobs in the non-profit and public personal service sector (Kitschelt, 1994: Chapter 1).

The organizational structure of the ecology parties was initially molded in the image of a grassroots democratic movement party with member assemblies making most decisions and holding elected office-holders in rotating appointments on a short leash. But both the framework of legislative institutions as well as the exigencies of bargaining and governance when ecology parties had strategic leverage over government formation and ultimately ministerial portfolios compelled Green activists and politicians to undergo an organizational learning process in which critical elements of the original governance structure were abandoned. Rather than being punished for a process of internal reform that amounted to 'selling out to the system', however, voters rewarded the parties for their strategic flexibility and programmatic generalization and punished them for strategic intransigence in external bargaining and for organizational chaos in internal processes of interest aggregation. Such changes in the organization of ecology parties include a longer tenure and stability of office-holders in the party apparatus or in electoral office as well as greater reliance on principles of formal delegation and representation (cf. Burchell, 2002; Müller-Rommel and Poguntke, 2002).

All this is not to say that the process is unilinear and irreversible, nor that ecology parties are asymptotically approximating the organizational structures of conventional parties in postindustrial democracies. They still stand out as 'framework' or 'cadre' parties with very low member/voter ratios. Furthermore, political decision-making in ecology and other left-libertarian parties tends to be more participatory and less predictable than in other parties because of substantial internal diversity of political opinions and factionalism. Furthermore, ecology parties at times have responded to incentives promoting a return to organizational patterns and strategic appeals common to the movement party. This is the case where disruptive ecological protest movements intensify and/or where ecology parties lose their strategic significance for government formation because conventional center-left parties are too weak or coalesce with parties of the center right. Instead of following Michels (1962) and postulating an 'iron law' of organization, amounting in this case to an irreversible transition of ecology parties from the type of 'movement party' to that of a conventional center-left 'programmatic party' supplementing social democracies in forming governing coalitions, it is more plausible that the parties follow contingent structural and strategic incentives that make a return to the pattern of movement party possible, if circumstances are conducive. Where the incentives lead away from movement parties toward organizational investments in party structure and ideological investments in programmatic generalization, ecology parties that stick to the profile of movement party are destined to fail in elections.

MOVEMENT PARTY APPEAL WITHOUT MOVEMENT SUPPORT? THE NEW RADICAL OR EXTREME RIGHT

Setting left-libertarian parties aside, there is one other cohort of new parties that has made electoral inroads in many postindustrial democratic polities. These parties are variously called radical right, extreme right, right-wing populist, right-authoritarian, or new radical right.[9] There are family resemblances and overlaps among all parties nominated as members of this cohort. But these parties also vary in how they emphasize and combine positions on at least five programmatic elements: (1) aspects of political governance (democracy/authoritarianism; modes of interest intermediation through popular participation, the 'political class', corruption etc.), (2) social exclusion (multiculturalism; immigration and immigrant culture); (3) nationalism (also integration of the European Union); (4) moral traditionalism (family, women, reproductive rights); and (5) economic distribution and governance (scope and redistributive thrust of social policies and taxation, regulation of market participants). Rather than disputations over the 'correct' general definition of the current extreme right, it is probably more productive to account for different expressions of rightist forces in different polities, identified by the positions they articulate on these five dimensions.

The concern of this article is not with the growth and profile of these parties more generally, but only with the extent to which they articulate practices and strategies of 'movement parties'. As in the case of left-libertarian parties, the electoral rise of radical rightist parties presupposed the presence of salient issue positions that remained unrepresented by existing conventional political parties and thereby made possible the entry of ambitious political entrepreneurs into the arena of party competition. Unlike ecology parties, the growth of new rightist parties does not coincide with strong, disruptive movement activities. It would therefore be wrong to claim that such parties grow out of movements. On the one hand, they may constitute substitutes for movements. Extreme rightist violence against immigrants and cultural minorities may be empirically lower where rightist parties are stronger (Koopmans, 1996). Rightist parties preempt or contain rightist violence. On the other hand, the rightist parties themselves have served as initiators of disruptive protest events against immigration, European integration, high taxes, and so forth. With regard to their strategy and tactics of expressing interests and grievances, extreme rightist parties are thus 'movement parties' only in the sense that they create or displace social movement practices.

Relatively little systematic comparative research exists concerning the organizational structure of rightist parties in postindustrial democracies. They tend to exhibit, however, certain traits common to movement parties, namely a lack of investment in solving problems of collective action and social choice. They have generally small formal memberships, as measured by member/voter ratios. Their organizational structure is quite fluid and often characterized by feuding cabals of rival activists, resulting in considerable instability of collective decision-making and political representation in legislatures and party executives. At the same time, the informality and fluidity of many right-wing extremist parties does not primarily derive from bottom-up participatory politics promoted by rank-and-file activists, but from the dominance of a single or of a handful of rival charismatic political leaders who govern the party in a despotic, patrimonial fashion. Fissures, splits, and succession crises at the level of national and regional leaders are therefore common to right-extremist parties.[10] Organizational stability of extreme rightist parties is predicated on the undisputed control of a party by a single charismatic individual.[11]

In terms of the programmatic generalization of the rightist parties' strategic appeals, the evidence is mixed and controversial in the scholarly community. Let us distinguish here the level of party leaders' external appeals and of voters' policy preferences. In terms of the leaders' pronouncements, it is clear that rightist parties have highlighted single-issue positions, such as opposition to immigration, to European integration, to high taxation, to clientelistic practices among politicians belonging to 'cartel parties' (Katz and Mair, 1995), to women's reproductive rights, or to environmental regulation. In a way theoretically characterized by Hinich and Munger (1994), however, these may be salient issues of the day that politicians 'map' on underlying broad ideological dimensions that are indirectly communicated to voters. While rightist politicians emphasize currently salient single issues, they take care to formulate them against an ideological background dimension that makes them compatible with a host of other potentially consistent policy positions.

The electoral and organizational development of various extreme rightist parties illustrates the importance of combining intense single-issue appeal with a broader programmatic coherence of philosophy and political values. The Danish and Norwegian Progress parties started out in 1972/73 as protest affairs against high progressive income taxation. Once in parliament, they discovered, however,

that there is a great deal more to the politics of taxation than a simple change of tax rates. The resulting legislative disarray of the parties translated into their electoral decline in subsequent elections. They made a comeback only in the 1980s when they could combine a renewed and diversified single-issue appeal, now including anti-immigration platforms, with a more comprehensive programmatic grasp that signaled to voters where they stood on issues that separate left and right in their respective party systems. Incipient right-wing radical parties have not always succeeded in bringing about an electorally winning issue and programmatic appeal. Examples of a failure to achieve this combination include the Swedish New Democrats in the early 1990s, as well as the German Republicans. The most spectacular instance of failure is probably Pim Fortuyn's list before and after the 2002 Dutch parliamentary election. Out of nowhere the culturally divisive, ethnocentrist appeal of this new party in an environment characterized by the post-9/11 shock, economic decline, and the centripetal convergence of the existing major parties made it the second strongest party in the Dutch parliament. But lacking a broad programmatic collective preference schedule and stripped of its charismatic leader who fell victim to an assassin days before the election, it took only a few months until the party broke apart as a result of conflicts over numerous policy issues and was virtually wiped out in new legislative elections.

Also at the level of right-wing party voters, there is little support for the idea that a single-issue could carry the day for a party. Right-wing voters tend not to be protest or single-issue voters (see van der Brug et al., 2000). While they attribute great importance to the issues made salient by the charismatic leadership of right-wing parties, they express a broader configuration or profile of beliefs and preferences that is distinctly different from left and left-libertarian voters and partly different from voters of the conventional center-right parties. While there have been disputes about the extent to which extreme right party voters also support market-liberalizing economic policies, even manual working-class voters supporting the extreme right do not endorse social democratic and left-libertarian redistributive economic policies.

Both at the level of elite programmatic appeals and popular preference profiles among electoral supporters of the extreme right, we need not assume that the right wing's 'winning formulas' are perfectly static and uniform in time and space. The Italian Lega Nord under Umberto Bossi certainly provides a vivid example of how quickly parties controlled by a single individual can recast their appeal and electoral coalition, contingent upon the changing strategic configuration of partisan politics (Ignazi, 2003: 53–62). What is relevant for the analytical concern with 'movement parties', however, is that in the overwhelming number of cases right-wing extremists articulate broader programmatic concerns that set them apart from the pure model of movement party, even though their leaders' appeals often focus on individual issues and even though such leaders may initiate movement activities, such as marches and demonstrations, to promote the popular salience of their parties' core issues.

As in the case of left-libertarian parties, organizational and strategic elements consistent with the type of movement party become particularly controversial when extreme rightist parties exercise decisive influence over the political complexion of governments and sometimes join government coalitions (cf. Minkenberg, 2001). Being compelled to take responsibility for a wide variety of policies and to bargain with coalition partners whose issue and ideological positions differ from those of their own party, extreme rightist parties often exhibit intense internal strain that may translate into the demise or the reorganization of the parties.

CONCLUSION

Movement parties are transitional phenomena, but not in the linear sense the tradition from Michels (1962) to Panebianco (1988) has suggested. The main problem is not a systematic tendency of ambitious, self-interested party leaders, as agents, to abandon the interests of their principals, whether they are party activists or electorates. Effective inter-party competition domesticates the rent-seeking propensities of political leaders, where liberal democracies with full civil and political rights prevail.

Movement parties are unstable, because a variety of incentives nudge politicians and their constituencies towards accepting organizational structures and strategic appeals inconsistent with those of movement parties. The institutional premises of territorial representation in legislatures make programmatic generalization of issue appeals at the expense of the emphasis on single issues attractive to both voters and party politicians. Whereas institutional incentives operate permanently, other incentives for politicians in movement parties to change their practices and appeals may exist only intermittently. At least three such conditions may induce politicians to move away from the profile of movement party: a declining salience of the core movement issue that originally inspired the mobilization; a policy reform consistent with movement demands; and the incorporation of the movement party in government executives that are forced to take responsibility for a wide variety of salient political issues. All these conditions do not imply that movement parties are impossible. But they lead to the prediction that movement parties, in the analytical characterization provided in this chapter, are comparatively rare phenomena.

NOTES

1   To avoid misunderstandings, my use of the term 'functional' has nothing to do with 'explanatory functionalism' in the social sciences. It is shorthand for actions based on attributes of the task structure, i.e. the nature of the collective goals pursued by political mobilization.

2   For simplicity's sake, I define political entrepreneurs here as actors who derive personal rewards from the successful pursuit of collective constituency objectives. I thus abstract for now from principal–agent problems.

3   An example may be the intellectual fermentation taking place in private clubs and homes in eighteenth-century France in the run-up to the great revolution, discussed in Bendix (1978).

4   For a spatial conceptualization of party strategies in terms of constituency trade-offs, see Przeworski and Sprague (1986) and Kitschelt (1994).

5   My account builds loosely on Aldrich's (1995) analysis of the emergence of Congressional structure out of the chaos of cycling majorities in the first hundred years of American independence.

6   As contributions to the literature on ecology and Green parties, or left-libertarian parties more generally, see especially Burchell (2002), Dalton and Kuechler (1995), Kitschelt (1989), Kitschelt and Hellemans (1990), Müller-Rommel (1989, 1993), Müller-Rommel and Poguntke (2002), Poguntke (1993) and Richardson and Rootes (1995).

7   While both left-socialist Scandinavian or Dutch parties and ecology parties belong to the cohort of left-libertarian parties, they appeared at different times, although both groups of parties end up with similar general ideological orientations in the 1980s.

8   On this point, see my analysis of the German and Belgian Green's participation in governments covering the 1980s (Kitschelt, 1989: Chapter 9).

9   The most important literature on this broad party family includes Betz (1994), Hainsworth (1992, 2000), Ignazi (2003), Kitschelt (1995), Merkl and Weisberg (1993, 1997), Minkenberg (1998), Mudde (2000), Perrineau (2001), and Schain *et al.* (2002).

10   Examples in the 1990s include the splits of the Danish and the French extreme right-wing parties. Intense internal struggles triggered by charismatic leaders have also taken place on the Austrian, German, and Italian extreme right.

11   Between 1990 and 2003, this condition of comparative organizational calm appears to have characterized the Flemish, Norwegian and Swiss right.

REFERENCES

Aldrich, John (1995) *Why Parties?* Chicago: University of Chicago Press.

Bendix, Reinhard (1978) *Kings or People?* Berkeley, CA: University of California Press.

Betz, Hans-Georg (1994) *Radical Right-Wing Populism in Western Europe*. New York: St. Martin's Press.

Burchell, Jon (2002) *The Evolution of Green Politics. Development and Change Within the European Green Parties*. London: Earthscan Publishers.

Burstein, Paul (1998) 'Interest organizations, political parties, and the study of democratic politics,' in Anne N. Costain and Andrew S. McFarland (eds), *Social Movements and American Political Institutions*. Lanham, MD: Rowman and Littlefield, pp. 39–56.

Carey, John M. and Shugart, Matthew Soberg (1995) 'Incentives to cultivate a personal vote: a rank ordering of electoral formulas,' *Electoral Studies*, 14: 417–39.

Cox, Gary (1997) *Making Votes Count*. Cambridge: Cambridge University Press

Dalton, Russell J. and Kuechler, Manfred (eds) (1995) *Challenging the Political Order*. New York: Oxford University Press.

Della Porta, Donatella, and Diani, Mario (1999) *Social Movements. An Introduction*. Oxford: Blackwell.

Gamson, William (1990) *The Strategy of Social Protest*. Belmont, CA: Wadsworth.

Hainsworth, Paul (ed.) (1992) *The Extreme Right in Europe and the United States*. New York: St. Martin's Press.

Hainsworth, Paul (ed.) (2000) *The Politics of the Extreme Right*. London: Pinter.

Hinich, Melvin J. and Munger, Michael C. (1994) *Ideology and the Theory of Political Choice*. Ann Arbor: University of Michigan Press.

Hug, Simon (2001) *Altering Party Systems*. Ann Arbor: University of Michigan Press.

Ignazi, Paolo (2003) *Extreme Right Parties in Western Europe*. Oxford: Oxford University Press.

Katz, Richard S. and Mair, Peter (1995) 'Changing models of party organization and party democracy. The emergence of the cartel party', *Party Politics*, 1: 5–28.

Kitschelt, Herbert (1989) *The Logics of Party Formations*. Ithaca, NY: Cornell University Press.

Kitschelt, Herbert (1994) *The Transformation of European Social Democracy*. Cambridge: Cambridge University Press.

Kitschelt, Herbert (1995) *The Radical Right in Western Europe. A Comparative Analysis*. (in collaboration with Anthony J. McGann). Ann Arbor: University of Michigan Press.

Kitschelt, Herbert and Hellemans, Staf (1990) *Beyond the European Left*. Durham, NC: Duke University Press.

Koopmans, Ruud (1996) 'Explaining the rise of racist and extreme right violence in Western Europe: Grievances or opportunities?' *European Journal of Political Research*, 30: 185–213.

Lijphart, Arend (1994) *Electoral Systems and Party Systems: A Study of Twenty-Seven Democracies, 1945–1990*. Oxford: Oxford University Press.

Merkl, Peter H. and Weisberg, Leonard (eds) (1993) *Encounters with the Contemporary Radical Right*. Boulder, CO: Westview.

Merkl, Peter H. and Weisberg, Leonard (eds) (1997) *The Revival of Right-Wing Extremism in the Nineties*. London: Frank Cass.

Michels, Robert (1962) *Political Parties*. London: Collier-Macmillan.

Minkenberg, Michael (1998) *Die neue radikale Rechte im Vergleich. USA, Frankreich, Deutschland*. Opladen: Westdeutscher Verlag.

Minkenberg, Michael (2001) 'The radical right in public office: Agenda setting and policy effects,' *West European Politics*, 24(1): 1–21.

Morgenstern, Scott (2003) *Patterns of Legislative Politics*. Cambridge: Cambridge University Press.

Mudde, Cas (2000) *The Ideology of the Extreme Right*. Manchester: Manchester University Press.

Müller-Rommel, Ferdinand (1989) *New Politics in Western Europe. The Rise and Success of Green Parties and Alternative Lists*. Boulder, CO: Westview Press.

Müller-Rommel, Ferdinand (1993) *Grüne Parteien in Westeuropa*. Opladen: Westdeutscher Verlag.

Müller-Rommel, Ferdinand, and Poguntke, Thomas (2002) *Green Parties in National Government*. London: Cass.

Panebianco, Angelo (1988) *Political Parties: Organization and Power*. Cambridge: Cambridge University Press.

Perrineau, Pascal (2001) 'Die Faktoren der Wahldynamik des Front National,' in Dietmar

Loch and Wilhelm Heitmeyer, *Schattenseiten der Globalisierung*. Frankfurt/Main: Suhrkamp, pp. 186–205.

Poguntke, Thomas (1993) *Alternative Politics. The German Green Party*. Edinburgh: Edinburgh University Press.

Przeworski, Adam and Sprague, John (1986) *Paper Stones. A History of Electoral Socialism*. Chicago: University of Chicago Press.

Richardson, Dick and Rootes, Chris (1995) *The Green Challenge. The Development of Green Parties in Europe*. London/New York: Routledge.

Sartori, Giovanni (1976) *Parties and Party Systems*. Cambridge: Cambridge University Press.

Schain, Martin, Zolberg, Aristide and Hossay, Patrick (eds) (2002) *Shadows over Europe: The Development and Impact of the Extreme Right in Western Europe*. Basingstoke: Palgrave Macmillan.

Taagepera, Rein and Shugart, Matthew Soberg (1989) *Seats and Votes. The Effects and Determinants of Electoral Systems*. New Haven, CT: Yale University Press.

Talshir, Gayil (2002) *The Political Ideology of Green Parties. From the Politics of Nature to Redefining the Nature of Politics*. New York: Palgrave Macmillan.

Van der Brug, Wouter, Fennema, Meindert and Tillie, Jean (2000) 'Anti-immigrant parties in Europe: Ideological or protest vote?' *European Journal of Political Research*, 37: 77–102.

24

POLITICAL PARTIES AS MULTI-LEVEL ORGANIZATIONS

Kris Deschouwer

THE OBVIOUS NATIONAL CONTEXT

One of the major assumptions of much of the analysis of party politics is that it is situated in the context of national states. The national state is therefore normally seen as the primary institutional context shaping party politics. The direct and evident association between parties and the state is the result of the historical coincidence of state formation and the development of mass politics. The formation of parties organizing and shaping public opinion occurred within the territorial limits of the national states and often even along cleavage lines that were at the heart of the state formation process itself, like the tensions between church and state and between center and periphery (Lipset and Rokkan, 1967; Flora et al., 1999). Crucial notions such as citizenship, and its concrete derivatives such as voting rights and democratic representation, were defined in this same environment of the national state.

Scholars of political parties have analysed these origins and further developments of political parties, and have therefore taken the national parties as their most obvious unit of analysis. And if a system of parties was being studied, this referred to the interactions of the party units inside one single statewide political system. Of course not all modern states are unitary states, and parties have developed and been analysed in federal states as well. This has, however, mainly been done by looking at them state by state. The comparative literature

on political parties in federal states is rather scarce (Chandler, 1987; Scharpf, 1995). One of the reasons is probably that federal states are indeed different from unitary states, but do not all function in the same way. And these internal differences might be crucial for the understanding of the political parties. Furthermore, when parties have been analysed in federal settings, the assumptions still were that the central state was the most important center of decision-making and that the central organization of the political parties was the core of the parties, the reference point for analysing their internal organizations. Regional parties have received attention in the very specific literature on regionalism (De Winter and Türsan, 1998), but this has also paid little attention to the specificities of the institutional context in which they function.

To assume that parties function either in a unitary or in a fairly centralized and hierarchical federal state context is no longer tenable. Many states have been going through rapid and sometimes spectacular processes of devolution and decentralization: Spain, Belgium, Italy, the UK, France. This has led to increased attention for the functioning of party politics in these new settings (Jeffery and Hough, 2003) and to the search for a proper comparative language to deal with them (Deschouwer, 2000b, 2003; Hopkin, 2003; Thorlakson, 2001). The gradual integration of the European Union and the direct election of the European Parliament have also created interest in the dynamics of party competition in complex and multi-level

Table 24.1   *A typology of parties in multi-level systems*

		Participating in elections		
		Regional level only	National level only	Regional and national level
Territorial	One region	1	4	7
pervasiveness	Some regions	2	5	8
	All regions	3	6	9

systems (Reif and Schmitt, 1980; Reif, 1984; Andeweg, 1995). The very peculiar polity that is the (temporary) result of European integration and the very varying and mostly asymmetric state institutions that have recently been put into place, have also made clear that the notion of 'federalism' has become either too limited to encompass the meaning of the new political institutions, or – if all the new variants are included – too broad for good analysis. The conclusion is that we need to question and problematize the institutional context in which political parties function. This context must be one of the crucial variables – because it varies indeed – related to the strategic and organizational choices of political parties.

In this chapter we will focus on political parties in multi-level systems. In the first place we will develop a classification of parties that allows us to identify specific characteristics of parties in multi-level systems. Then we will explicitly bring in the institutional context, to show how it directly affects the position of parties in the system and therefore their functioning. We will decompose the broad notion of federalism or multi-level system into three dimensions: formal institutions, electoral rules and cycles, and societal heterogeneity.

A TYPOLOGY OF MULTI-LEVEL PARTY ORGANIZATIONS

Parties in multi-level systems face particular problems that are the direct consequence of the organization of the political system. In order to analyse properly the functioning of these parties, we need in the very first place to identify their specificity. We need to identify variations between parties that are typical of a multi-level system. Attempts to do so have been very much inspired by the Canadian party system, with its separation between federal and provincial parties and party systems (Dyck, 1991; Smiley, 1987; Thorlakson, 2001). Two dimensions of variation have been identified, but have to be kept separate because they are to a large degree independent of each other.

The first dimension is the *presence* of a party at the different levels of the political system. The second refers to its *territorial pervasiveness*. That is a different dimension indeed, because the presence of more than one level on the same territory is exactly the typical feature of a multi-level system. Both dimensions can be combined into a typology with nine logical positions, as presented in Table 24.1. For the sake of clarity and of parsimony we reason within the logic of a political system with two autonomous levels of decision-making. We use the term 'regional' to refer to the lower level and 'national' to refer to the higher level. Most of the examples will be drawn from federal or decentralized states, but we will refer once in a while also to the European Union.

Parties in multi-level systems are confronted with the choice of participating in elections at only one or at both levels of the system. That leads logically to three types of parties. The first is a party that participates at the regional level only. It is thus typically specific to one single region in the multi-level system. The Parti Québecois in Canada is a good example of this. Another example is the Partei Rechtsstaatlicher Offensive in the German *Land* of Hamburg. One might say that this type of party does not require special theoretical attention. It is indeed only competing in one single, and single-level, system, and can therefore be understood with the same theoretical tools as those used for the analysis of national political parties in their national party system. This is, however, only true to a limited extent. Indeed, the fact that this party functions in a multi-level system can have quite important consequences for the way in which it behaves, for its political opponents will be engaged in the more complex competition at more than one level.

The second type is the party that participates at the federal level only. This is a rather exceptional situation in federal systems, but the category is certainly not empty. The Canadian Bloc Québecois, for instance, participates only in federal elections. If we look at the European Union as a multi-level system, more examples can be found. Parties that participate in

European elections only, and not in national elections, can be found in several countries. The specific meaning of the European elections, and the opportunity they offer to voice Eurosceptic attitudes, make this level the ideal one for these parties to operate at (Taggart, 1998). They could of course also defend this Eurosceptic view in national elections, but there are a few good reasons not to do so. One of these is the 'division of labour' between national and European elections, where the European dimension is avoided in national elections (Mair, 2000). Another reason for not running at the national level can also be the electoral system. If in France the Rassemblement pour la France of Charles Pasqua engages only at the European level, it can do so because the electoral system is proportional at that level and because the bipolar structure of the French national political competition – kept in place by the majoritarian electoral system – is very weak in European elections.

The third type groups the parties that participate both in regional and in national elections. This category is much more populated than the previous ones. Many parties in multi-level systems do indeed participate at both levels. Most of the regionalist parties in the autonomous communities in Spain for instance, are present in the regional elections (where some of them try to win office) and in the elections for the Cortes in Madrid. The major political parties in most multi-level systems also compete in both elections.

The second dimension is the territorial pervasiveness of the parties. This is actually a continuum, varying between parties being active in only one of the regions to parties covering the whole territory. In Table 24.1 we have divided this continuum into three broad categories. The first – parties covering only one region – are regional parties or parties that are typical of one single region in the system. The Partei Rechtsstaatlicher Offensive only covers Hamburg. The Catalan Convergencia i Unio and all the other regionalist parties of Spain only cover their own region. The same goes for the Scottish Nationalist Party, Plaid Cymru, etc. The German CSU or the Parti Québecois and the Bloc Québecois are other examples. All the Belgian political parties also limit their activities to one of the two main language communities of the country. This illustrates also that the territorial pervasiveness differs from presence at one or two levels. Parties covering only one region can indeed choose to participate only at the regional level, only at the federal level, or in both levels.

The second category consists of parties that cover more than one region, but not the complete territory of the multi-level system. Some parties cover a few regions, such as the Lega Nord in Italy or the PDS in Germany. Both also participate in elections both in their regions and at the federal level. Germany and Spain offer interesting examples of parties that are almost complete, but are absent in just one region. That is the case for the German CDU, leaving Bavaria to the CSU. It is also the case for the Spanish PSOE, leaving Catalonia to the Catalan PSC.

Finally there are the pervasive or complete parties that cover all regions. This category is populated with the American parties, the major Swiss parties, the Spanish Partido Popular, the German SPD, the Austrian parties, the Australian parties, etc.

As we already said, not all categories are empirically very densely populated. Most parties have to be placed in the right-hand column of parties being present at both levels, with territorial pervasiveness as a meaningful further classification. Categories 1 and 4 are less populated but contain some cases, mainly from Canada and from member state party systems in the European Union. The relative emptiness of categories 5 and 6 (parties present only in federal elections but in more than one region) actually illustrates a problem of definition. If we want to classify parties, we need to identify the unit of analysis that will be so called. Especially in multi-level systems, the identification of the unit party can be very tricky. The Canadian parties – always difficult to place – are a nice illustration of this. Dyck (1991) has labelled them 'truncated parties' (see also Wolinetz and Carty, 2006) because the provincial organization and the federal organization are so separated from each other, with separate membership and separate finance, that they can hardly be considered to be one single organization. Still doing so reflects the implicit assumption that there is a single organization party of which the provincial units are a part. If the separation goes as far as in the Canadian case, one might as well choose to define the parties as two different units: for instance, a Liberal Party participating at the national level only, and provincial parties participating at the provincial level only. For both we can then add the distinction between presence at only one or at both levels. What used to be studied as internal relations of one party organization then becomes the analysis of relations – both horizontal and vertical – between parties of the same ideological family within a multi-level political system (Deschouwer, 2003).

The two dimensions of variation presented in Table 24.1 are both relevant for the party organization, but in different ways. The major issue is that of vertical integration. It occurs when a party is present at more than one level. Parties present at only one level have only one organization and a single strategy to develop. That is the case for parties of type 1 and 4 in Table 24.1. Adding a second level introduces a potential tension in the organization. There must be some place in the organization where the two levels can be coordinated. The degree to which the party allows internal division and eventually formal organizational divisions to function at both levels is a major research question for this type of party.

If a party is not territorially limited to one region, the problem of vertical integration is (potentially) of a different nature. Not only is there the need to coordinate between the two levels, but also the need to coordinate and control for horizontal variation across the regions. In other words, the party needs to organize in a way that allows it to deal with the territorially varying problems of vertical integration. It is clear that the type of society in which the party functions (the territorial heterogeneity) is one of the major causes of potential difficulties in integrating the varying demands.

If vertical integration is high, the different levels and the varying territories have a limited degree of autonomy. In that case the hierarchical lines in the party are clearly going from the national to the regional level. If integration is low, the regional organizations of the party have some freedom to make their own decisions. This freedom does not need to be uniform. In pervasive parties the regional levels can be very different and therefore enjoy a different level of autonomy.

The degree of autonomy of regional-level organizations is not a one-dimensional phenomenon. Several indicators can reveal varying forms and degrees of autonomy. A first set of indicators refers to the party organization and thus to the autonomy of the regional branch. The membership structure, for instance, can be very revealing. In the German and Austrian parties, the members join at the regional level, and this membership automatically implies membership of the national party. In the Swiss parties, the cantonal level is clearly the most important in this respect. Members join at the cantonal level, and this is the only membership possible. The membership of the national parties is indirect: the cantonal parties join, not the individual members. In Canada, some of the parties (such as the Liberal Party and the Progressive Conservative

Party) are so loosely coupled that they have actually two different membership organizations at the regional level: one for the national party and one for the regional party (Thorlakson, 2001).

The recruitment of political personnel is another indicator of regional autonomy and also often the stakes of conflicts between the levels. The British Labour Party has been trying to control leadership and candidate selection at the regional level in Scotland, Wales and Greater London, but has not been able to keep the same degree of control of these areas as for the rest of the country (Hopkin, 2003). Strong regional leaders can – in systems with real regional political autonomy – build their legitimacy on strong regional electoral results and put pressure on the national leadership. Political recruitment in multi-level parties is often a bottom-up affair, where strong regional leaders (eventually leading the regional government) make their way up to the national leadership.

Membership, recruitment of leadership and of candidates for elections, but also, for instance, financial autonomy and control over the lower levels of the party organization (the local sections) are all indicators that allow one to see the extent to which the two levels are separated and whether the hierarchical lines go from top to bottom or vice versa. A guaranteed presence of the regional sections in national party decision-making is another useful indicator.

Another set of indicators focus on party strategies. Parties in multi-level systems operate in varying political conditions and can need very distinctive strategies for each of these. These strategies include the decision to participate in elections, campaign strategy, formulation of policy proposals and coalition strategy. For the latter, the developments in the German SPD are interesting. Reunification and the presence of the PDS in the five new *Länder* have created tensions. Traditionally the national party organization kept a fairly high control over the coalition strategies of the regional units, but it has been confronted with the demands of the Eastern regional units to decide more freely on the choice of the coalition partners, including the PDS (Jesse, 1997).

A good deal of variation can be seen here, both within and between multi-level systems. The Australian Labor Party has gradually become more and more integrated, and has strong control over the activities of the regional branches. It can even expel a regional branch from the party. The Australian National Party, on the other hand, remains much more decentralized and has a more confederal type of national organization (Thorlakson, 2001). The

Swiss parties are again an example of a high degree of regional autonomy, although – as in Australia – the Socialist Party is much more integrated. Cantonal parties regularly defend positions different than the national party on referendum issues (Sciarini and Hug, 1999). When members of the Swiss federal government are to be elected, both the national party organization and some cantonal organizations often propose and defend different candidates. The American political parties are another example of very loosely coupled parties (Katz and Kolodny, 1994).

EXPLAINING THE VARIATION: THE INSTITUTIONAL CONTEXT

The degree of vertical integration of a party or the autonomy of its regional branches can vary widely. This variation can occur both *between* countries and *within* countries. It is in the first place related to a party's position in the system, i.e. to its place in the classification presented above. This position, however, is the result of developments and eventually deliberate choices of the parties operating in a very specific institutional environment. Both its position in the system and the way in which it deals with vertical integration and horizontal variation are related to that environment. That is why a proper analysis of parties in multi-level systems needs to bring in explicitly the characteristics of the institutional environment. It can be divided into three dimensions: formal institutions, electoral systems and cycles, and societal heterogeneity.

The formal institutions

Analysing parties in federal settings has seldom been done in a comparative way. The main reason is that federalism is too broad a concept. It needs to be broken down into concrete characteristics that can be linked to party politics. Actually, only one feature has been put forward and identified as crucial for party politics: the distinction between dual and cooperative federalism (Chandler, 1987; Scharpf, 1995). It is indeed important. If the federal (or multi-level) system displays a neat division of competencies between the levels, the relations between the two levels of policy-making are limited. That allows and pushes the parties to have fairly autonomous regional branches. Regional autonomy allows the most suitable strategies for that level to be chosen without interfering with the activities of the party at the national level (see also Thorlakson, 2001; Deschouwer; 2000b, 2003).

If the levels of policy-making are interconnected, the relations between the regional and the national branches of the parties take on a different nature. This interconnectedness can be due to the fact that the allocation of competencies explicitly allows for mixed areas, in which both levels need to move together. That is the case in Germany. It can also be the consequence of a *functional* logic of the multi-level system (as opposed to a *jurisdictional* logic), in which the higher level produces general framework laws that need to be implemented by the lower level. That is, for instance, very much the case for the European Union. A third source of strong linkage between the levels is the formal presence of the regional level in national decision-making. The German Bundesrat organizes this presence, while in Canada and in Australia it is formalized in conferences of the prime ministers (and in the EU in the Council of Ministers). The consequences for the functioning of parties are evident: they become very deeply involved in intergovernmental relationships. Intergovernmental politics becomes party politics and vice versa (Lehmbruch, 1976; Rydon, 1988; Jeffery, 1999; Hadley *et al.*, 1989). The regional branches then cannot be too autonomous. Regional policy-making and regional elections become relevant for federal policy-making and will be framed in these terms.

Another dimension of the formal institutions of multi-level systems that is closely connected to the previous one is the degree of autonomy of the regions. Indeed, if the degree of autonomy is low, the logic of the distribution of the competencies is not likely to play a significant role. It does, however, if (some of) the regions have the real control over a number of important policy domains. This is of course a matter of degree, for which it is not easy to define a clear cut-off point. In unitary states, there can certainly be some degree of decentralization, but since it does not go very far and does not give the lower level a sufficient degree of autonomy, the analysis of party politics does not need to bring in explicitly the institutional environment as a variable shaping party organizations and strategies. The need for a multi-level game and for the parties to incorporate it into their organization only emerges in a system where the regional level has at least some degree of sovereignty.

The other extreme of regional autonomy can have far-reaching effects on the political parties. If the autonomy of the lower level goes very far, as in Switzerland, the USA or Belgium, the regional branches of the parties become the core of the party, and the higher level – for parties crossing the levels – becomes a loose association of the regional branches. The lines of command in the party – if we accept that the higher level is still considered to be a party – then go from bottom to top. In such a situation, it is not unlikely that the parties organize separately for regional and national matters, as in Canada, or simply fall apart into separate regional parties, as in Belgium (Deschouwer, 1994).

The degree of autonomy and the type of distribution of competence are two variables broad enough but still relevant to be used in comparative analysis of party organizations in multi-level systems. They can and must also be used for comparative analysis *within* multi-level systems, when these systems are asymmetric. In the examples that we have given so far, we generally referred to the parties of one or more countries to illustrate how the institutional context affects party life. But party life itself becomes asymmetric when the system allows for varying degrees of autonomy between regions and varying logics of the way in which competencies are distributed between national and regional level. The British system after devolution and the Spanish system are good cases for looking at the way in which parties adapt to this institutional variation. Degrees of vertical integration and regional branch autonomy vary then between regions.

Electoral systems and cycles

If assemblies and eventually also executives have to be elected at different levels, the techniques used to do so can differ. This might again also be the case in unitary systems, where lower tiers (provinces, local municipalities) have elected bodies. But in systems where the different levels have real powers, variations in the way in which elections are organized can have quite far-reaching consequences. The number of seats available per region is normally higher in regional than in national elections. In majoritarian systems this does not affect party strategies, but it clearly does in proportional systems. The higher number of seats at the regional level leads in general to lower thresholds of representation, and this can influence a party's decision to participate at the level with the lower threshold, and its decision to go alone or in association with another party (Lutz, 1998; Lancaster, 1999).

This effect is very visible in European elections, where in 1999 all countries adopted a proportional system. For some parties in France

and in the UK, the European level suddenly offered better possibilities for representation than the national elections. We have already mentioned the Rassemblement pour la France. In the UK, the Green Party and the UK Independence Party were able to gain European seats, while they have no chance at all of gaining representation at the national level. Within the UK, the additional vote system for Scottish Parliament and Welsh Assembly elections also offers a different environment at the regional level.

Much more important than the electoral systems and formulae is the timing of elections. The idea that elections at one level are in one way or another linked to the elections at the other level has been developed mainly in the German context (Dinkel, 1977), with its relatively high number of regions organizing elections at different times. The direct election of the European Parliament from 1979 on and its analysis by Reif and Schmitt (1980) has led to the notion of 'second-order elections'. The idea is that this election of the members of the European Parliament by country cannot be seen as a European election. It is a series of national elections with the national parties competing, but with less at stake. The European election is framed in national terms but the outcome has no impact on it, as a first-order election would have. Reif (1984) has refined the analysis of the interaction between levels by drawing attention to the position of the European elections in the national electoral cycle. European elections are not necessarily 'mid-term' elections, but can be earlier or later in the electoral cycle, and therefore have some real effects on the politics in the specific country. The notion of second-order elections has – parallel with the processes of devolution and decentralization – been used to analyse the relationship between regional and national elections in multi-level systems in general (Heath et al., 1999; Abedi and Siaroff, 1999; Jeffery and Hough, 2003; Pallarés and Keating, 2003; Detterbeck and Renzsch, 2003).

In fact, there are two different dimensions of electoral timing that need to be taken into account: vertical and horizontal simultaneity. Vertical simultaneity is the coincidence of elections at two levels: a regional election taking place on the same day as the national election. This vertical simultaneity reduces the autonomy of the regional level. The statewide electoral stakes overshadow the regional stakes. For the regional branches of the parties also participating in the national election, the selection of candidates and of campaign strategies and themes will need to be done in close cooperation with the national party level (Versmessen, 1995; Deschouwer, 2000a). That is, however, only valid if the national level of the party is the core level, i.e. if the national party is a vertically integrated party and not a loose association of the regional branches. That latter is the case in European elections, and therefore the simultaneity of parliamentary elections in a member state and elections of representatives in the European Parliament leads to the devaluation of the European elections. Here the national parties are the core level, and not the European party federations that hardly interfere in strategic choices of the national parties.

If the elections at two levels are not organized on the same day, the relation between the two electoral *cycles* is the crucial contextual condition for the functioning of the parties. Obviously the temporal disconnection offers more opportunities for the regional branches to engage freely in the regional political competition. A regional election organized close to a national election, however, again reduces regional autonomy. A regional election immediately after a national election can easily be read as a confirmation of the national election. Depending on the results of the latter, a regional party branch might try to surf on the winning wave and refer explicitly to the dynamics at the national level, or on the contrary try to make clear that the regional issues are different. In both cases, the connection is explicitly made, and the national party organization will be inclined to monitor the regional elections closely.

If the regional election comes very late in the national cycle and is organized just before the next national election, the chances of being 'pulled up' to the higher level are even greater. It is then difficult to avoid seeing the regional election as the final test, and national parties competing in the upcoming national election will make sure that the regional election is organized according to the needs of the national party. A very nice illustration of this mechanism was the election in Lower Saxony in 1998, bringing Gerhard Schröder to the position of prime minister of the region, but in the very first place confirming that he would lead the SPD in the national elections.

If the electoral cycles are disconnected, the position of the regional election in the national cycle is not necessarily fixed. This means that the regional specificity of the election and thus the potential autonomy of the regional branch can vary over time. Party politics in multi-level systems is definitely not a static affair.

The second dimension of electoral timing is horizontal simultaneity: the organization of multiple (or all) regional elections on the same day. Here again simultaneity reduces autonomy. The mechanism is obvious: the results of regional elections on the complete territory of the multi-level polity can be aggregated and thus read within the national frame of competition. In May 2000 most of the Italian regions went to the polls to elect regional parliaments and regional prime ministers. The national opposition leader, Silvio Berlusconi, framed the election as a test of the popularity of the opposition. The results were disappointing for the governing Ulivo coalition, and the national prime minister, Massimo D'Alema, resigned.

Regional elections in Australia, Canada, Austria, Germany or Switzerland are all held on different days. In this condition the regional party branches – depending also on vertical simultaneity and on the type of distribution of competencies and degree of regional autonomy – can be and must be fairly autonomous, and the national party needs to be able to manage the high degree of territorial diversity. In the USA, elections are organized simultaneously, but the other elements of the institutional context do not force the regional parties to stick to a common national strategy and framing of the elections. The different aspects of the institutional environment clearly interact with each other, and that is why one cannot simply refer to a general notion such as federalism or decentralization to grasp the way in which the institutional context shapes parties in a multi-level system.

As with the degree of autonomy of the regions, the logic of electoral timing can differ between regions of the same country. In Italy, regions with a special statute do not have regional elections on the same day as other regions. In Spain, a number of 'historical' regions have an electoral timing of their own, while all the others organize their regional elections on the same day. The granting of a different timing to the historical regions illustrates a willingness to give these regions a special and more autonomous statute.

Societal heterogeneity

Asymmetry has already been raised several times as an element increasing the complexity of a political system and the analysis of the functioning of its political parties, because it is a crucial element that needs to be taken explicitly into account. Asymmetry in multi-level systems has a double meaning (Watts, 1999). It can refer to the asymmetric division of competencies to the regions, i.e. to the fact that regions of the same national system are not institutionally equal. That is what we have taken into account so far. However, we have also implicitly referred to the second one: the territorial variation and heterogeneity of the society. Many of the more recent processes of devolution giving birth to multi-level systems, such as Spain's autonomous communities, Belgium's language communities or the UK's countries, have been attempts to take into account the variations in territorial identity within national states. In these recent examples, societal heterogeneity has been translated into asymmetric institutions. Yet in multi-level systems with symmetric formal institutions the societal heterogeneity can also be a crucial factor shaping the regional dynamics of party politics and thus both the vertical and horizontal relations between party branches. The main reason is the dissimilarity of the party landscape amongst regions and between regions and the federal level.

An 'index of dissimilarity' has been developed (originally with reference to Canada) to measure the differences between the regional and national party landscapes (Johnston, 1980; Abedi and Siaroff, 1999). The index compares the results of the national elections in a region with the results of the nearest regional election. The index thus measures the proportion of the voters who voted differently in the two elections. In some cases it can be extremely low – for example, 3% in Baden-Württemburg in 1972 or 4% in Extramadura in 1989. But it can also reach very high levels – 26% in Catalonia in 1982 or even 64% in British Columbia in 1974 (Jeffery and Hough, 2003: 208).

There are, however, two organizational challenges for parties in multi-level systems. There is indeed the difference between the national and the regional competition, but the variation among regions needs to be managed as well. If all regions have a high index of dissimilarity or if the index varies strongly among regions, the more pervasive parties have to accommodate to this territorial diversity. Territorial diversity means the existence of different party systems in the different regions and thus varying structures of party competition calling for different strategies and thus for more autonomy for the regional level of the parties (or for the regional branch of the party in the region that displays a deviant structure of competition). Different party systems and structures of competition also ask for more autonomy in the coalition behaviour of the regional branches. We have in this respect already referred to the varying relations between the SPD and the former communist PDS in the five new regions of the German federation.

CONCLUSION

Political parties in multi-level systems deserve special attention. The institutional context in which they function has to be brought explicitly into the analytic models, because they face very peculiar challenges. Figure 24.1 summarizes this specific analytic logic for the study of parties in multi-level systems. In the first place

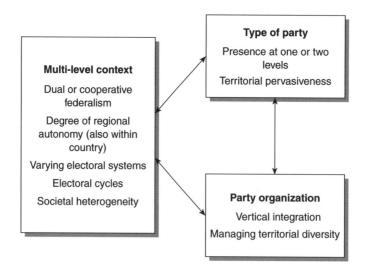

Figure 24.1   Framework for the analysis of parties in multi-level systems

we need a classification of parties that takes the position of the party in the system into account. The presence at only one or at both levels is the first dimension of this typology, its presence across regions or its territorial pervasiveness is the second dimension.

As far as the party organization is concerned, a party in a multi-level system is confronted with two specific organizational problems. The first is vertical integration, the linking of the activities and strategies at two different levels. The second – related to it in a way that depends on the party's position in the system – is the managing of territorial variation between the regions in which the party participates in regional politics, national politics or both levels at the same time.

In the third place, the analysis of parties in multi-level systems must explicitly problematize the type of system in which the party functions. Classic notions distinguishing between unitary and federal states cannot suffice in a world where the variation between systems has become impressive. Five crucial variables of a multi-level system have been identified. The first is the distinction between dual federalism (neatly separated competencies between the levels) and cooperative federalism (both levels obliged to coordinate their actions). The second is the degree of regional autonomy, which can vary between states but also and increasingly within states. The third is the variation between electoral systems used at the national and the regional level. The fourth is the interconnection of the electoral cycles at the regional and national level. And the fifth is the degree of territorial heterogeneity of the society in which (especially more pervasive) parties have to function.

The life of parties in a multi-level system is not a static affair and is not easy to capture in a few straightforward and unambiguous categories and propositions. Parties in multi-level systems live in, adapt to and sometimes try to adapt the complex institutional context in which they function. Giving a straightforward answer to the question how parties organize in multi-level systems is therefore not easy. It depends.

REFERENCES

Abedi, A. and Siaroff, A. (1999) 'The mirror has broken: increasing divergence between national and Land elections in Austria', *German Politics*, 8(1): 207–27.

Andeweg, R. (1995) 'The reshaping of national party systems', *West European Politics*, 18: 58–78.

Chandler, W.M. (1987) 'Federalism and political parties', in W.M. Chandler and H. Bakvis (eds), *Federalism and the Role of the State*. Toronto: University of Toronto Press, pp. 149–70.

De Winter, L. and Türsan, H. (1998) *Regionalist Parties in Western Europe*. London: Routledge.

Deschouwer, K. (1994) 'The decline of consociationalism and the reluctant modernization of the Belgian mass parties,' in R.S. Katz and P. Mair (eds), *How Parties Organize: Adaptation and Change in Party Organizations in Western Democracies*. London: Sage, pp. 80–108.

Deschouwer, K. (2000a) 'Belgium's quasi-regional elections of June 1999', *Regional and Federal Studies*, 10(1): 125–32.

Deschouwer, K. (2000b) 'The European multi-level party systems: towards a framework for analysis'. Robert Schuman Centre Working Paper, European University Institute, Florence.

Deschouwer, K. (2003) Political parties in multilayered systems', *European Urban and Regional Studies*, 10: 213–26.

Detterbeck, K. and Renzsch, W. (2003) 'Multi-level electoral competition: the German case', *European Urban and Regional Studies*, 10: 257–70.

Dinkel, R. (1977) 'Der Zusammenhang zwischen Bundes- und Landeswahlergebnissen', *Politische Vierteljahresschrift*, 18: 348–60.

Dyck, R. (1991) 'Links between federal and provincial parties and party systems', in H. Bakvis (ed.), *Representation, Integration and Political Parties in Canada*. Toronto: Dundern Press, pp. 129–77.

Flora, P., Kuhnle, S. and Urwin D.W. (eds) (1999). *State Formation, Nation-Building and Mass Politics in Europe. The Theory of Stein Rokkan*. Oxford: Oxford University Press.

Hadley, C., Morass, M. and Nick, R. (1989) 'Federalism and party interaction in West Germany, Switzerland, and Austria', *Publius*, 19(4): 81–97.

Heath, A., McLean, I., Taylor, B. and Curtice, C. (1999) 'Between first and second order: a comparison of voting behaviour in European and local elections in Britain', *European Journal of Political Research*, 35: 389–414.

Hopkin, J. (2003) 'Political decentralization, electoral change and party organizational adaptation: a framework for analysis', *European Urban and Regional Studies*, 10: 227–38.

Jeffery, C. (1999) 'Party politics and territorial representation in the Federal Republic of Germany', in J. Brzinski, T. Lancaster *et al.* (eds), *Compounded Representation in Western European Federations*. London: Frank Cass, pp. 130–66.

Jeffery, C. and Hough, D. (2003) 'Regional elections in multi-level systems', *European Urban and Regional Studies*, 10: 199–212.

Jesse, E. (1997) 'SPD and PDS relationships', *German Politics*, 6: 89–102.

Johnston, R. (1980) 'Federal and provincial voting: contemporary patterns and historical evolution, in. D.J. Elkins and R. Simeon (eds), *Small Worlds: Provinces and Parties in Canadian Political Life.* Toronto: Methuen, pp. 106–30.

Katz, R.S. and Kolodny, R. (1994) 'Party organization as an empty vessel: parties in American politics', in R.S. Katz and P. Mair (eds), *How Parties Organize. Change and Adaptation in Party Organizations in Western Democracies.* London: Sage, pp. 23–50.

Lancaster, T.D. (1999) 'Complex self-identification and compounded representation in federal systems', in J. Brzinski, T. Lancaster *et al.* (eds), *Compounded Representation in Western European Federations.* London: Frank Cass, pp. 59–89.

Lehmbruch, G. (1976) *Parteienwettbewerb im Bundesstaat.* Stuttgart: Kohlhammer.

Lipset, S.M. and Rokkan, S. (eds) (1967) *Party Systems and Voter Alignments.* New York: Free Press.

Lutz, G. (1998) 'The interaction of national and regional electoral systems and their influence on representation in Switzerland'. Paper presented at the ECPR Joint Sessions of Warwick.

Mair, P. (2000) 'The limited impact of Europe on national party systems', *West European Politics,* 23(4): 27–51.

Pallarés, F. and Keating, M. (2003) 'Multi-level electoral competition: regional elections and party systems in Spain', *European Urban and Regional Studies,* 10: 239–56.

Reif, K.-H. (1984) 'National electoral cycles and European elections', *Electoral Studies,* 3(3): 244–55.

Reif, K.-H. and Schmitt, H. (1980) 'Nine second order national elections. A conceptual framework for the analysis of European election results', *European Journal of Political Research,* 8: 3–44.

Rydon, J. (1988) 'The federal structure of Australian political parties', *Publius,* 18(1): 159–71.

Scharpf, F. (1995) 'Federal arrangements and multi-party systems', *Australian Journal of Political Science,* 30: 27–39.

Sciarini, P. and Hug, S. (1999) 'The odd fellow: parties and consociationalism in Switzerland', in K.R. Luther and K. Deschouwer, *Party Elites in Divided Societies. Political Parties in Consociational Democracy.* London: Routledge, pp. 134–62.

Smiley, D. (1987) *The Federal Condition in Canada.* Toronto: McGraw-Hill Ryerson.

Taggart, P. (1998) 'A touchstone of dissent: Euroscepticism in contemporary Western European party systems', *European Journal of Political Research,* 33: 363–88.

Thorlakson, L. (2001) 'One party or several? Party organization in federations'. Paper presented at the conference 'Multi-level Electoral Competition: Devolution in Comparative Context', Institute of German Studies, University of Birmingham, September.

Versmessen, E. (1995) 'In the kingdom of paradoxes: the Belgian regional and national elections of May 1995', *Regional and Federal Studies,* 5(2): 239–46.

Watts, R. (1999) *Comparing Federal Systems.* Montreal: McGill-Queens University Press.

Wolinetz, S. and Carty, K. (2006) 'Disconnected competition in Canada' in D. Hough and C. Jeffery (eds), *Devolution and Electroral Politics* Manchester: Manchester University Press.

25

PARTY MEMBERSHIP AND PARTICIPATION*

Knut Heidar

WHAT IS PARTY MEMBERSHIP?

Party membership is defined in this chapter as 'an organizational affiliation by an individual to a political party, assigning obligations and privileges to that individual'. The role of party member is a formal role, to be distinguished from the behaviorally defined role of party activist. How parties organize themselves and administer membership varies widely. Parties usually keep a register of their members, and issue membership cards. Members are generally obliged to pay annual membership fees (dues) and to pledge not to be members of other parties simultaneously. Socialist parties may expect their members to also be members of trade unions; Christian parties may expect party officers to be practicing Christians. The trend is to lower the threshold for party membership by limiting obligations and reducing dues. Membership privileges include participating in party activities: electing party officials, nominating candidates for public office, debating policies, and participating in decision-making and in social events. Sometimes the affiliation is *collective*, as when a non-party organization, such as a trade union, signs up parts of its membership as a bloc. But in this case identifying the individual party member would be difficult.

Both parties with formal membership and those with informal membership have party activists. Having formal membership, however, is not a criterion for an organization to meet the definition of 'party'. US political parties do not have formal memberships, but do have party activists (see Eldersveld, 1986; Stone *et al.*, 2004). In Africa there are parties without formal

membership (Carbone, 2003) and parties whose members belong to several parties simultaneously (Erdmann, 2004: 65).

Party membership means different things depending on the situation. In states with one-party systems it is often difficult to distinguish between party members and public officials (Giliomee and Simkins, 1999). The definition of 'party member' is more varied and culturally contingent than what is signified by the terms 'citizen' and 'voter' – which are defined by public law and election behavior, respectively. Party membership is usually a more demanding form of participation than voting. Duverger (1964: 61) mentions a series of 'concentric circles ... of ... ever-increasing party solidarity' – suggesting terms such as 'supporters', 'adherents', 'militants', and 'propagandists' as useful descriptions of party attachment. These circles are described behaviorally, and are, according to Duverger, closer to the 'real nature of participation' than is formal membership. Accordingly, the levels of party attachment 'define the content of the sociological bond which unites the members of the community to which we give the name "party"'. Party membership bonds may also be described organizationally, according to the nature of obligations imposed and privileges bestowed on members (Scarrow, 1996: 16–18).

Varieties of membership

The significance of party membership springs from the character of these bonds, and to some extent also defines the type of party organization. In top-heavy 'catch-all' parties, party members are assigned less importance than in 'mass' parties. In 'mass' parties the members generally have strong links to the party organization. Likewise, in 'caucus' parties, where the parliamentary party wing has a tradition of autonomy, the extra-parliamentary party is left to fill the role of fan club, helping to mobilize voters.

In the early 20th century, debates in US political parties regarding their nomination rules for primaries (local, state, and national) illustrate the point that member linkage affects the way the party works. The custom was that the party had the discretion to decide which party members qualified to participate in the nomination of the party's electoral candidates. Abuses led to public regulations (Merriam, 1907). In some states a voter who wanted to influence the party's nomination was required to declare his or her intention to support the party's candidates in the election. In other states there were 'tests', including a declaration that one sympathized with the party's goals, or a declaration that one believed in most of the principles of the party. Or one was simply asked: 'Are you a Republican or a Democrat?' This public regulation of the nomination process left the US parties without party members in the formal sense defined above. When the Libertarian Party of California in 2004 advertised for 'members' on the web, the 'sociological bond' reflected the US 'no-member' tradition (www.ca.lp.org). One can either register to vote as a Libertarian or sign up with the party as a 'dues-paying member'. As a dues-paying member one is eligible to vote on central committee business, and to be a delegate to the annual state convention. However, it is also necessary to declare that one does not 'believe in or advocate the initiation of force as a means of achieving social or political goals'.

In the 20th century socialist parties had tough membership requirements, reflecting a strong member–party bond. To join Argentina's Socialist Party during the 1930s one needed to declare in writing acceptance of party statutes, principles, methods, and programs. The applicant also needed sponsorship by two people who had been party members for at least six months. Moreover, one had to wait one year to be eligible to vote for party officials and six months to vote on all other questions (Wellhofer, 1972). This high threshold was more 'socialist' than 'Argentine' in its origin. The Peronist populist party of the 1950s had no formal membership policy. It accepted 'opportunists from all sectors' and exercised 'overt and tacit coercion' to make public employees join the party (Little, 1973: 658).

Party membership in one-party dictatorships illustrates another membership bond. According to Leninist party theory only one party can be allowed to control the state. Under the Soviet regime, prospective party members were carefully screened. For a time they were 'candidate members' before being trusted to practice 'democratic centralism' (Ware, 1987). Party membership in one-party states gave access to privileges: jobs, information and education. For these reasons the 'party' label and consequently the institution of party membership may be suspect in new democracies recently evolved from one-party to multi-party systems (Bratton, 1999).

The nature of party membership depends on social context. At one extreme membership is an expression of belonging – a simple reflection of religious, class or ethnic identity. Entering the party is a natural occurrence within one's social milieu – parties and party membership are expressions of 'segmented' or 'encampment' societies. One grows up in a Catholic family, a Catholic neighborhood, goes to Catholic schools, reads the Catholic press and belongs to Catholic organizations – including the Catholic Party (Beyme, 1985: 192). Most famous were the Austrian cradle-to-grave parties where one lived within the class 'laager' of society, where most individual needs had organizational outlets. The Austrian social democrats, to counter the omnipresence of the Catholic Church, developed in the early interwar period an extensive organizational flora, including the Workers' Stamp Collecting Association. Party membership was only one of many expressions of living in a strong, closed class community.

Forms and entitlements

There are basically three forms of party membership: individual, auxiliary, and collective. *Individual* membership is established when an individual signs up with the party – generally at the branch level, but increasingly at the national level by signing up through the mail or over the Internet. One is expected to agree with basic party goals and to be of a certain age. Parties often require that members have citizenship. The Irish Fianna Fáil used to ask only for 'a connection to Ireland through birth, residence or Irish parentage', while its adversary Fine Gael was only open to Irish citizens (Beyme, 1985: 168). Most Canadian parties do not require members to be Canadian citizens, but in fact almost all members are (Cross and Young, 2004: 435). With implementation of transnational elections for the European

Parliament and new (local) voting rights for immigrants, citizenship may not be as widely required for membership in European parties.

Often parties have *auxiliary organizations* for youths, women, and pensioners. These organizations are internal subdivisions of the party organization. Youths' organizations generally have both minimum and maximum age requirements; however, being of voting age is not necessary. Dual memberships are often possible – in both a party branch and the youths' or women's organization – which makes an accurate count of party members difficult.

Finally, *collective* ('corporate') membership is found when an organization that is not formally of the party enlists all or some of its members in the party. Obviously these organizations are close to the party, for example trade unions or farmers' associations. In the early European labor movement, the relationship between party and trade unions was described as 'one body, two arms'. A local, industrial trade union branch might be a subunit of both its national trade union and a particular party, dealing with the business of both at its meetings. As trade unions grew less partisan, particularly after the schism following the Russian Revolution in 1917, individual trade union members sometimes had the option of stating formally their reservations against being registered as party members. Collective membership was – and to some extent still is – particularly important to many European social democratic parties. Sometimes collective membership was arranged locally, as in Scandinavian countries. Sometimes it was arranged nationally, as in Britain. National trade unions generally enlisted their members in a party for financial and/or power reasons. The individual trade unionist might not realize he was also a party member. Such corporate arrangements make it hard to define 'membership' as an individual attachment, although the transaction is registered as membership in party statistics. This is sometimes labeled 'affiliated membership' in the literature (Katz and Mair, 1992). Generally, collective membership within social democratic parties has been replaced by other ways to maintain close relationships with friendly external organizations.

Counting party members

Accuracy in establishing membership totals is difficult; parties' membership claims must be treated with caution. Because the character of party membership can vary according to time and place, establishing uniformity in counting (and eventually comparing) is difficult. In fascist militia groups, communist cadres, and 'catch-all' party branches – all of which have unique membership bonds – membership numbers would signify very different organizational capabilities in each case. Nevertheless, it would be useful to know when and where such parties gained or lost members.

Basically there are two ways to estimate party membership levels: probing party registers and studying party membership claims made in surveys. *Party registers* are often based on varied and changing operative principles, and are seldom up-to-date. Membership files, donor registers and mailing lists might be combined indiscriminately by the party to arrive at a membership total. Ambitious activists may register half-hearted individuals as members, taking a 'perhaps' for a 'yes', and disregarding whether individuals pay dues. To look good or to qualify for more delegates at national conferences, or for increased public subventions, party branches might falsify membership totals. Keeping up-to-date files to reflect members who are deceased, are not paying dues, or have terminated membership is difficult. For example, should secretariats count, for a certain time, members who stop paying dues? The introduction of computerized files in the 1980s and 1990s, and greater professionalism among party administrators, have reduced the impact of such problems.

Using the *survey* method could be problematical. Apart from chance uncertainties, people may not know or remember that they are members, or may even falsely claim membership out of embarrassment at not being a member.

Although party membership claims should be handled with care, there is usually an interesting story behind the figures. Critical evaluations of membership figures may give important insights into a party's evolution and party trends. Changes in party membership numbers have, for example, been discussed in the 'decline of parties' debate, although most authors stress that membership decline is only one factor among many in evaluating party strength. Empirical works interpreting changes in party membership are generally focused on Western European countries (Katz and Mair, 1992), and most studies register a decline in recent decades (Scarrow, 2000; Mair and van Biezen, 2001). Many new democracies in Southern Europe (since the 1970s) and in Central Europe (in the 1990s), however, experienced increases in party membership. Earlier, relatively high party membership levels in the 1950s and 1960s may reflect a boom in participation following World War II, and not a 'golden age' of party vitality as during the advent of democracy in the early 20th century. Due to a lack of reliable data, however, these long-term tendencies are not much studied (but see Bartolini, 2000). Despite the recent overall decline in membership – often interpreted as a decline in the segmented social structure of post-industrial societies (known as 'individualization') – there are large differences between levels of party membership across Europe. Austria still has a high level of member density (party members as share of party vote), despite having declining party membership. Likewise, parties within the same country show persistent, wide differences in their ability and/or willingness to recruit members.

WHY PARTIES WANT MEMBERS AND WHY PEOPLE WANT TO JOIN

Why do parties recruit members and why do people join parties? Parties may want members to help in campaigning, to provide electoral legitimacy, to run and finance the organization, to recruit new candidates for public office, to anchor the party in civil society, to sound out grassroots opinion and to develop new policies (Katz, 1990; Scarrow, 1994: 28; Ware, 1996: 63–84). No doubt party leadership will welcome differently the contributions of members in each of the above areas. If the intention originally was to recruit members to run successful electoral campaigns, leadership may find members wanting, even demanding, to influence party policies. New, alternative sources of income – such as public subvention – may change the calculus on the benefits of membership, reducing the incentive to generate party income from membership dues.

The 19th-century parliamentary party factions – the 'caucus' or 'cadre' parties – had mostly local supporters. These parties emerged from parliamentary politics without a formal organization linking supporters to the parliamentary party through a nation-wide extra-parliamentary structure. Many liberal and conservative parties in Europe long resisted the challenge of the socialist mass-membership parties, and fought elections with the aid of informal networks. In the early 20th century the US campaign-based parties showed that parties could operate without a membership organization, even in a mass democracy, if forced to do so by public regulations. Still, most parties today organize a membership, even though the distinction between members and supporters is often vague, as in the French Gaullist party in the 1960s or in Berlusconi's Forza Italia since the mid-1990s.

Motivations

Why do individuals want to become party members? The question applies only if membership requires an active choice. In the British labor movement a great difference has been found between members exercising an active choice and simply being signed up. When the rules for collective trade union membership of the Labour Party were changed from 'opting in' (declaring that membership is wanted) to 'opting out' (declaring membership unwanted) after 1945, the percentage of trade union members also affiliated to the Labour Party rose from 49% to 91% (Beyme, 1985: 175).

The calculus on the benefits of party membership depends on party type as well as on political and social setting. People join to gain influence, material favors, information, social benefits or mental satisfaction. Among the things members may lose are money, time and alternative opportunities. What is known about people's motivations for joining a party is scattered; there is no generally acknowledged typology for it. Most studies build, however, on the Clark and Wilson (1961) distinction between material, social and purposive incentives for organizational commitment. Member surveys in the UK, Ireland, and Scandinavia show that people mostly express political (purposive) motives for joining – from ideological convictions to fighting for or against particular policies/politicians (Seyd and Whiteley, 1992; Gallagher and Marsh, 2002; Heidar and Saglie, 2003). Paul Sabatier (1992) has developed a 'commitment theory', according to which individuals join and become active in a political organization because of their strong ideological sympathies with the organization's political goals. Purposive motives appear to be especially prominent in newly formed parties (Clarke et al., 2000). Some members also report social reasons, such as family tradition and social norms. A study of the Italian Socialist Party in the 1960s found that about one-third listed influence of family and friends as the reason for membership (Barnes, 1967). With movement networks declining, however, and with a weaker social element in party organization, social motivations for party membership may well have weakened (Ware, 1987). Studies of US party activism show that ideological motivation is more frequently present in affluent counties (Conway and Feigert, 1968). In patronage parties, such as early US local party organizations ('party machines'), material incentives – for example, public employment or preferential treatment – were dominant. As late as 1990 the *New York Times* reported that to get a civil service job in Illinois, applicants had both to pass an examination *and* to get approval from a precinct captain and the county party chairman (quoted in Beck and Sorauf, 1992: 117). Today, European member surveys show that very few members express career benefits or material rewards as their motives for joining. However, these motives are less socially acceptable and therefore probably underreported. Motivational research is in any case difficult as motives may be vague, complex and volatile (McCulloch, 1990).

Who are the members?

Who will become party members? The answer is – as for political participation in general – that the most resourceful individuals sign up for party membership. Within the specific social, cultural or geographical segments mobilized by the party, people with relatively high scores on education, income, and socioeconomic status (SES) are disproportionately filling membership ranks (Widfeldt, 1995). But membership is not only pursued on an individual basis, creating the usual 'high-SES' biases. Parties are mobilizing agents, often organizing recruitment campaigns among special groups. European social democratic parties around 1900 often had significant numbers of leaders from the middle or upper classes, but still worked especially hard to enlist working-class members. They targeted the trade unions, the industrial plants, and the poorer neighborhoods. Ideology obviously was important, as the goal of the early socialists was to liberate the working class. Youths and women have always been groups targeted by many parties, as evidenced by the special party organizations often created for them. Some parties based their politics on promoting agrarian, religious, and ethnic interests, and sought to enlist members from these groups. Recruitment drives served two purposes besides increasing membership in general. First, parties sought to increase *internal legitimacy* by recruiting among the people on whose behalf they fought. Second, they sought to increase *electoral legitimacy* by giving voters a sense of social representation through party membership. When a party pursues a people's party strategy its targeting of particular groups probably declines.

Another factor impacting membership profiles is competition from alternative organizational networks for a party's recruitment base. In countries with strong organizations mobilizing low-SES citizens – for example, like an established network of organizations mobilizing broad segments among farmers, religions denominations, or ethnic groups – party recruitment (and party voting) may be enhanced among the lower-SES groups (Rokkan and Campbell, 1960). On the other hand, alternative organizations may be detrimental to general party recruitment by being more attractive, as when single-issue political action committees appear more attractive to people who 'want things done', or when environmentalist groups are more attractive to young activists than the 'generalist' parties (Lawson and Merkl, 1988).

Women in the party

In the latter decades of the 20th century, integration of women was a major goal of many parties. Some parties, such as the Icelandic Women's Alliance established in the 1980s, were open only to women. But women's parties are rare and usually small. Most parties have had predominantly male memberships. However, in many countries male membership is declining, particularly in Scandinavia. In Denmark and Norway, female membership rose from roughly one-third to roughly one-half the total membership from the early 1970s to 1990 (Sundberg, 1995). Several parties today have a majority female membership. At the other extreme, women in Tanzania (Tenga and Peter, 1996) and Malaysia (Rogers, 1986) struggle to be included in political parties at all. However, reports show rising levels of female involvement at lower party levels in those countries.

Causes of change in party membership

An obvious starting point in explaining membership trends is the party's general political support. Strong support among the people creates the potential for a large membership. Still, organizational factors enter the process: parties may increasingly/decreasingly be willing or able to recruit supporters. An example is the change by center-right parties from caucus into membership parties in order to contain the influence of socialist mass parties – what Duverger called the 'contagion' from the left. Changing organizational structures and the status of members may be a deliberate strategy of established party elites to pursue their interests (Panebianco, 1988: 191). Also contextual political, social and economic factors enter the process. Public regulations changing rules for collective membership – requiring individuals to opt in or opt out – have (as discussed above) huge effects on membership size. Public party finance may also have consequences for the number of members when subvention is based on membership. Indeed, membership numbers were falsified in Danish and Norwegian youths' parties in the 1980s and 1990s in order to obtain public funds. Parties winning office or taking over the state, as in communist countries after a revolution, may offer security and career prospects that make them attractive to prospective members. Social forces may enhance membership, as when parties reach a 'critical mass' in a community, making it appear easy (or even necessary) to join the party – cf. Tingsten's (1937) 'law of social gravity'. Finally, economic fluctuations may influence membership trends, although not always in clear-cut ways (Beyme, 1985: 175–88). Indirectly, the economic slump between the First and Second World Wars led to increased membership in fascist parties. Recessions after World War II did not. Two factors explaining declines in party membership in many Western European parties since the 1970s are the rise of affluence and the political consumerist attitudes prevalent in post-industrial societies.

PARTY MEMBER ACTIVITIES

What do party members do? Members' activities vary substantially according to the nature of the party and also to how much time members have, their interests, and the opportunities available to them. The following concerns studies of parties in advanced industrial societies, primarily Western Europe and Canada. First, these studies find that many members join their party primarily as an expression of support, and that after joining they are inactive and have no intention of becoming active. In the German CDU in the 1970s roughly one-third of members attended

at most one party function annually (Falke, 1982: 73). In Britain, up to 50% of Labour Party members, and 75% of Conservative Party members, reported being inactive during an average month. Most, however, took part in at least one activity during the five years preceding surveys (Whiteley and Seyd, 2002: 95–7). Surveys (1991 and 2000) of Norwegian party members showed that more than 50% did not take part in any party activities whatsoever during the preceding year, and that about 20% stated they had no intention of being active (Heidar and Saglie, 2003: 770).

Second, studies indicate that the proportion of members participating in party activities on a regular basis varies from 10% to 45% (Scarrow, 2000: 95). What constitutes 'on a regular basis' can be debated. For example, at the turn of the last century 7–8% of members in Danish liberal and Christian parties were classified as 'active' although they reported spending only slightly more than 5 hours monthly on party activities. Using the same criterion, 25% of Socialist People's Party and Red-Green Alliance members could be considered 'active' (Pedersen *et al.*, 2004: 375). In the 1990s, studies of British parties showed that, by the same criterion, 10–20% of party members could be considered 'active' (Whiteley and Seyd, 2002: 95). The criteria for being an 'active' party member, however, will vary according to both the particular party cultures and the methods of measurement used in the research. The way activism is operationalized will naturally reflect the analytical focus of the particular research, making cross-country comparative summaries difficult.

Third, members' activities occur both inside and outside the party. Inside the party they attend meetings, engage in debates, and organize party affairs. Outside the party they take part in electoral campaigns, argue the party's case at work, write articles and run for public office. Bringing out the vote was the main task of members in the early caucus parties and remains important – despite centralized media campaigns (Scarrow, 1996; Carty and Eagles, 2003). Offers of extra financial support to the party are often counted as activity, although one could argue that these are merely expressions of party support, much like when one joins the party without intending to be an active member. There are no clear 'activity thresholds' which allow for a simple, unambiguous definition of 'party activity'. Membership activity profiles come in all shapes and sizes. On the one hand, about 80% of Canadian party members attended branch meetings during the last year and more than 70% volunteered in election campaigns (Cross and Young, 2004: 440). On the other, about 25% attended a leadership convention and 6% sought a federal nomination.

Recent changes in information technology have made new activities available to party members (Römmele, 2003). The Internet has opened new communication channels and debate arenas. Members, however, appear slow to adapt to these new opportunities. In 2000 only about 10% of party members in Norway – which early on had, as a nation, a relatively high level of access to the Internet – visited their party's home page at least once a month, and even fewer used e-mail in party affairs (Heidar and Saglie, 2003). However, among office-holders, and particularly among younger office-holders, the Internet was more widely used. Forty percent of office-holders aged under 40 used e-mail at least once monthly to keep in contact with fellow party members.

Fourth, there are different types of activists. Party activists may differ both in their type (internal–external) and in their level of activity (high–low). The 'party builder' would be high in intensity and focused on internal activities, while the 'party supporter' would occasionally argue the party's case among friends, neighbors or workmates. Very little is known about different types of activists. In the old days, when people belonged to communist 'cadre' parties, the fascist militia or liberal 'caucus' parties, one assumed the differences in activist types to follow the party type. In contemporary advanced industrial societies, differences in levels of activism between parties are not that marked. Levels of activism vary just as much *within* a party as *between* parties. An extensive study on 'high-intensity' party members in Britain in the early 1990s found that, in the Labour Party, about 10% of members reported working for the party more than 10 hours monthly, while the figure was 5% in the Conservative Party (Whiteley and Seyd, 2002). In the research literature on specific parties or countries, levels of activism have been found to be in decline during the 1990s (Zielonka-Goei, 1992: 102). Whether this is a general trend, however, is hard to know. Systematic, comparative data are not readily available (Selle and Svåsand, 1991). Due to declining membership, parties may require more activity from remaining members to keep up their organization (Scarrow, 1993). In Norway, however, levels of party member activism were fairly stable from 1991 to 2000 – although party membership declined

significantly, suggesting that other contextual variables had an impact (Heidar and Saglie, 2003).

Why differences in party activism?

One's decision to join a party as a member (see above) and one's decision to engage in various party activities may involve parts of the same calculus, but the two decisions need not be taken for the same reason(s). Both decisions are dependent on both supply and demand factors. Duverger (1964: 116) distinguished between *totalitarian* and *restricted* parties, that is, parties that demanded virtually total commitment and parties that demanded very little from their members. Party ideology plays a central part when party members are expected to act as the vanguard of historical necessities. The Leninist (totalitarian) party model demanded total involvement by members. This requirement made for an absurd situation when a new 'party activity' was introduced by the Soviet Communist Party in 1926: members were asked to repent their views. Stalin's 'organic theory' of the party was put into practice when the Central Committee decided that a party task should be 'to try to make the opposition bloc admit that its views are wrong' (van Ree, 1993: 43).

A party generally wants its members to be active, although the reasons will vary both from party to party and over time according to the party's required/needed level of activism. The 'contagion from the right' argument of Leon Epstein (1967: 260) asserted, with reference to Duverger, that modern media would cause the displacement of existing membership functions by new campaign techniques. This development, it was asserted by Epstein, would make European mass parties more similar to American campaign parties. By the same token, one could also argue that the advent of the Internet will change the character of future party activism (*Party Politics*, 2003). Finally, as discussed above, an organization's size may affect member activism, as when a smaller membership must perform tasks previously performed by a larger membership.

Party members give different reasons for engaging in party activities. There are efforts to map their motivations (see above) and also to explain them. A standard explanatory approach is to analyze sociodemographic and socioeconomic motivations. In a study of British Labour Party members, Seyd and Whiteley (1992) compared active and inactive party members, and found a tendency for socioeconomic variables to be correlated with party activism.

A member's activism may also be explained by his or her preferences for particular policies. In the terminology of rational choice theory, a party's favored policies take on the character of a 'collective good' when implemented (Whiteley and Seyd, 1996: 218). Policy preferences interacting with an actor's objective ability to make a decisive contribution towards a goal may explain activism. Rational choice theory predicts a positive correlation between party members' ideological convictions and their levels of participation. A study of Danish party members, however, found only weak correlations between ideological radicalism and party member activism (Hansen, 2002: 191). Also, central to research on party activism is the notion that social norms induce party activism. The 'expectations–values–norms' theory sees actors as 'embedded in networks of social norms and beliefs, which provide internal and external motivations to behave in certain ways' (Whiteley and Seyd, 2002: 45). Hence, party members surrounded by family and peers are likely to be more active than party members who are not part of such networks. Party identification is another factor to consider, because it has proved to be a strong predictor of members' activism levels. The basic notion is that party activism is not the result of party members' cognitive (cost–benefit) evaluations, but rather of members' loyalty and affection for a group or party (Whiteley and Seyd, 2002: 55). Finally, it is likely that some party activists are driven by political ambition, either to improve their own welfare or to improve the welfare of others. 'The relevance of political ambition for party organization should be obvious' (Schlesinger, 1991: 33). The argument assumes that the individual's behavior is explicitly goal-directed. As a theoretical explanation for party activism, political ambitions can be seen as the antithesis of a theoretical explanation stressing 'expressive incentives'.

With the exception of socioeconomic variables, the explanatory factors described above have been merged into one overarching 'general incentives model', and Whiteley and Seyd have on several occasions applied this model to explain party activism in British parties (Seyd and Whiteley, 1992; Whiteley et al., 1994; Whiteley and Seyd, 2002). Based on member surveys, their conclusion is that the general incentives model tends to outperform its rivals. They also found support for their general incentives model in their study of Irish

Fine Gael members (Gallagher et al., 2002). They concluded that the 'SES model adds nothing to what can be explained by the general incentives model' (p. 111). A test of the general incentives model based on survey data of Danish party members found that it fits the facts better than did other models (Hansen, 2002: 251–59).

Other models fare no better or worse than the general incentives model. Empirical studies suggest that a number of factors – even theoretically antithetical ones – are relevant in explaining party activism. A supplementary explanatory approach that, so far, has received surprisingly little attention in empirical research focuses on the party variable. Since the work of Duverger, it has been generally accepted that different party types, or ideological party 'families', have distinctive participatory cultures, for example totalitarian versus restrictive parties. Bringing back 'party' or 'party family' as an explanatory variable will introduce a version of the 'expectations–values-norms' theory. Different parties are expected to attract different kinds of people, and to shape them through different party cultures. The German Greens attracted high-intensity members in the 1980s (Poguntke, 1992). Research on Norwegian party members has shown that party is strongly correlated with levels of party member activism, even when controls are made for SES variables (Heidar, 1994: 76).

Are party members special? May's law of curvilinear disparity

May (1973) argued that 'sub-leaders' in parties hold more extreme views than both party voters (non-leaders) and the party leadership. His position differed from the standard one, which assumed that party leaders held more 'ideological' or 'party correct' views than their followers (McClosky et al., 1960). May predicted, and claimed to find, hierarchical contrasts between the sub-leaders and others in opinions on policy alternatives. Party sub-leaders would, according to his theory, be devoted activists. Their recruitment and socialization would make them more 'ideological' than rank-and-file supporters. On the other hand, top leaders must moderate (or appear to moderate) their views for two reasons: compromises are necessary in public office; and competition for moderate voters. One could reasonably expect to find, according to May's law, empirical differences in political views at different hierarchical levels in parties. The expectation that one would find 'militants', 'ideologues' or 'true believers' among party activists is commonplace among political commentators. But does empirical research confirm such expectations?

Studies within both the formal context of European party organizations and the informal context of US party organizations suggest that the answer is 'no' (Norris, 1995: 33; Herrera and Taylor, 1994). Norris studied the British Conservative and Labour parties, focusing on party candidates for the 1992 election, members attending selection meetings for candidates, and party voters. She found that members of both parties tended to hold views located between the moderate voters and the more radical leaders, and that the relationship between the different layers in the party was more complex than suggested by May. First, the motives of the party sub-leaders and senior leaders were more varied (than suggested by May's law) – as were the forces shaping political opinions at different levels. Norris found that high ideological commitment was among the major factors inducing party leaders to stand for election. On the other hand, one might expect that the sub-leadership faced moderating forces when fighting local elections. Observers also easily overrate how representative the extremist sub-leaders and their factions are within parties: they are usually very vocal in order to put pressure on the leadership, but do not necessarily speak for the average party member. Norris explains the negative test of May's law with the argument that mixed ideological and electoral incentives shape the opinions of both party leaders and their members. A study of Irish Fine Gael shows that the members were far from being extremists (Gallagher and Marsh, 2004). Instead they held 'impeccably middle-of-the-road opinions' (p. 418). A study of several Norwegian parties of political views at different levels on a number of issues found a curvilinear pattern in one-third of the cases, but failed to find a clear pattern – which left the authors wondering why curvilinearity occurred in some cases but not in others (Narud and Skare, 1999).

There is no final verdict on how special the political opinions of party members (or sub-leaders) are within parties. Even if the literature has failed to produce a consensus on May's law (Scarrow et al., 2000: 131), the law of curvilinear disparity, with its 'grain of truth' and clear predictions, continues to generate empirical research on opinion formation

processes within political parties. Perhaps one need to be reminded that May presented more than one hypothesis on how opinion formation takes place within parties.

Michels' law of oligarchy

The research inspired by Robert Michels' 'law of oligarchy' is both older and more voluminous than the research inspired by May's law. While May basically held an optimistic view on the impact of members – it matters what sub-leaders/members think and do – Michels was essentially pessimistic, arguing that neither leadership's rules nor members' opinions matter. In its original version, Michels' law stated: 'to say organization is to say a tendency to oligarchy' (Michels, 1925: 25; quoted in Beyme, 1985: 232). In the English book based on a translation of the Italian edition of Michels' work, the 'fundamental sociological law of political parties' is formulated in the following terms: 'It is organization which gives birth to the domination of the elected over the electors, of the mandataries over the mandators, of the delegates over the delegators. Who say organization, say oligarchy' (Michels, 1962: 365). In this spiced-up version, the moderating 'tendency to' has been left out, which makes a substantial difference. But as with May, it is the forceful hypothesis embedded in Michels' law, the argument that democratic parties do not and cannot exist, that has made his law of oligarchy so widely researched and hotly contested.

Michels analyzed the 'new politics' of the early 20th century that emerged with the advent of mass suffrage and extra-parliamentary parties. While Ostrogorsky (1902) had discussed how permanent party organizations outside parliament would pervert the reasoned debate among elites, Michels questioned whether the new mass parties really mattered politically, since the oligarchs ruled anyway. He argued – using the institutional approach of his mentor Max Weber – that the party leadership governed the party organization by necessity. Creating an organization would in itself create the basis for an oligarchy. The leaders would control the decision-making process and the channels of information, and they could manipulate the support of the uninformed and unprofessional membership, making empty rituals of formal democratic policy-making processes.

To prove his case, Michels selected for his empirical research the German Social Democratic Party, a party with a strong claim to being internally democratic. If oligarchy still prevailed in that party, he argued, then his law would also apply to parties with less or even no intention of letting their members influence policies. To some, his law has appeared self-evident and applicable to all parties. E.E. Schattschneider found it hard to imagine what a democratization of the US parties actually would entail, let alone 'whether democratization, if it were possible, would be appropriate to the legitimate functions of the parties in a modern political system' (1942: 58). If true, if internal party democracy were impossible, there would be no point in studying party members in order to understand party decision-making. What happens inside the party would not impact the policies pursued by the party leaders. The study of members would, of course, still be interesting for other reasons, such as seeking to understand the basis for and dynamics of grassroots activism, the recruitment processes, the potential for the mobilization of voters, etc.

Michels' law has been the starting point for numerous studies. As with May's law, however, this is not because the studies generally confirm that members are unimportant, but because the 'grain of truth' – or the 'tendency to' – gives a useful analytical reference point for empirical studies. Most empirical research, in fact, concludes that even in parties dominated from the top, the party leadership cannot afford to overlook completely the political opinions of its members, regardless of the formal structures of the party organization (McKenzie, 1955). Michels did, however, also provide an extensive list of (researchable) factors that may limit the members' opportunities to influence party decisions, such as members' background and resources (Barnes, 1967), organization size (Tan, 1998), level of institutionalization (Panebianco, 1988), leadership types (Weber, 1964), etc. A study of the party organizations in a number of mature democracies summed it all up: 'There are now many instances around the democratic world where party leaders operate a coalition of power in which grass-roots members are significant junior partners' (Scarrow et al., 2000: 149). The impact of members varies, of course. Research indicates that, in the new Eastern European democracies, member input is fairly limited (van Biezen, 2000). In parties with weak or no membership, the discussions focus on relationships between leaders and activists or followers (Eldersveld, 1964). Changes in the party environment also impact the degree of member influence. State financing of parties may reduce the need to accommodate members, but little evidence for this is offered (Pierre et al.,

2000). The Internet may be used both to enhance member influence and to strengthen leadership control (Party Politics, 2003). The Internet could make direct democracy within parties more workable, but any evidence of this is far from conclusive (Party Politics, 1999). It would also be difficult for members to influence, for example, candidate selection in the media-driven electoral campaigns of early 21st-century politics (Party Politics, 2001).

There are several ways to do empirical research on members' participation in decision-making processes within political parties. The traditional approach is to study particular political issues to determine how the process evolved and who influenced the final outcome. Michels' book is full of such cases. Another approach (also adopted by Michels) is to study organizational rules (Katz and Mair, 1992). Researchers can also interview or survey party leadership and/or members to get their evaluation of how the organization works (Party Politics, 2004). Finally, one may rely on 'expert opinions' to compare degrees of centralization of power in parties (Janda, 1980). One should note, however, that members' influence may differ in different aspects of party work. In a study of party rules in about 18 democracies, members' influence patterns turned out to be different for candidate selection, leadership selection, and policy-making (Scarrow et al., 2000).

CONSEQUENCES OF PARTY MEMBERSHIP

Party membership has an impact on party processes, the leadership, and the members themselves. The German Greens were in the 1980s very much occupied with building an organization that sustained members' influence and hampered the 'oligarchic tendencies' of a party organization. Consequently they instituted collective leadership, rotation, and direct democracy, placing severe restrictions on their leadership, which they suspected of being unreliable (Poguntke, 1994). The effects of party members on internal party political decision-making have been discussed above; in this section I will look at the effects of party membership on the individual member and on the political system/society.

Effects on the individual member

As noted, some party members are unaware of their membership, and consequently it does not affect them as individuals. At the other extreme (if one is aware of one's party membership) such awareness can have dramatic effects. In illiberal regimes it may lead to persecution, imprisonment, even execution/ assassination. Tsarist Russia jailed and exiled communist agitators in the early 20th century, just as the Soviet Communists jailed, hospitalized, and exiled their dissenters. In liberal regimes the consequences of membership are generally less drastic, although Communist party members in Western countries could lose their (non-party) jobs during the most intense periods of the Cold War.

The goals motivating one to become a party member (rectifying injustice, working with others on important matters, personal gain) may actually be realized by one's membership in the party. Studies of Chicago machine politics during its heyday in the 1920s and 1930s showed that over half the precinct captains held public sector jobs (Gosnell, 1937; Epstein, 1967; Crotty, 1986). Keeping those jobs depended on their ability to bring out the Democrat vote. The spoils from winning power generally go to a small number of top party politicians (locally and nationally) who enter public office, but electoral success may also bring spoils to a (varying) number of political-administrative personnel. Mostly these are party leaders, but at the lower levels party membership may be the qualification that in the end decides who gets the job.

The mechanisms through which party membership may benefit the rank-and-file members are as manifold as human imagination and corrupt practices allow. Access and friendships within the inner circle of top financial elites under the socialist governments in France under Mitterrand (1988–95) depended on social prestige, residence, and party membership – although most importantly on graduation from the school the École Nationale d'Administration for top bureaucrats, (Kadushin, 1995). In communist regimes, one's job and career opportunities depended on membership in the party. After the Bolsheviks won power in Russia, they founded the Institute of Red Professors in 1921 to educate the new socialist intelligentsia of the Soviet Union (Fox, 1993). In Communist China, party membership influences recruitment into administrative and managerial positions (Bian, 1995). Evidence points, however, to a dual career pattern in China, whereby membership is always a prerequisite for administrative positions, but does not necessarily enhance professional careers (Walder *et al.*, 2000).

On polity and society

The sum of micro membership experiences has macro consequences for the political system. Party membership may educate members or make them more cynical. Either development will affect the nature of political debate. Membership may give members a stake in the system – creating positive feedback on participation and legitimacy. Engaged members will take part in local-level electoral campaigns, bringing out the vote beyond what can be achieved by sophisticated national campaigns focusing on branding and personalities (Carty and Eagles, 2003). At the aggregate level, however, it is difficult to find clear relationships between party membership size and electoral strength (Scarrow, 2000). Party experiences might also frustrate members, causing them to go to the sidelines of politics for a while (Hirschman, 1982), or causing them to switch parties. If such switches occur in large enough numbers, it would ultimately result in the demise of old and the rise of new parties.

According to the participatory democracy school of thought, party member participation and debate in internal party affairs will provide a link between civil society and politics that supplements the link provided by competitive debate at the party system level (Teorell, 1999). The organizational encapsulation, by labor organizations, of the newly enfranchised, largely apolitical and underprivileged masses, helped to stabilize the new mass politics. These organizations contribute to making cross-national allegiances less important; shift the locus of conflict from the economy to the political arena; increase participation; and consequently strengthen the legitimacy of liberal democracy (Rokkan, 1962; Wellhofer, 1981). The argument that parties induce system stability and legitimacy has also been made, citing cases as diverse as the Rural African Party in Tanzania during the 1960s (Miller, 1970) and clientelist politics in the Philippines (Nowak and Snyder, 1974). The party organization in these cases and others provided services to its members and supporters while at the same time creating mobilization, control, and stability at the level of the political system.

Party membership may have more general implications for the individual and the society at large. To maintain its control over the Soviet Army, the Russian Communist Party filled its officer corps with loyal party members, and then constantly educated them in communism (Brzezinski, 1952). More commonplace is the 'partyfication' of public administration. In the

USA, urban political machines were once heavily
staffed with party members; incoming presidential administrations gave government and
other jobs to loyal party supporters. Similar
practices occurred in several European countries, including Austria and Belgium, where
national ministries and public service apparatus also were once filled with party supporters
(Daalder, 1987). These practices, however, are
in decline due to civil service reforms.

Finally, one may ask whether democracy
requires or needs party members. How 'democracy' is defined will play a big role in determining the answer to this question, but the standard
answer would be 'no'. For example, for elections to be free and fair under political systems
with universal suffrage, it is not *necessary* that
competing parties have party members (or that
competing candidates be party representatives,
for that matter). However, the *quality* of democratic processes *might* be improved were more
citizens to be party members, but that would
depend, naturally, on the quality of party
democracy case by case.

PARTY MEMBER RESEARCH
IN THE FUTURE

Research on party membership is part of
a broad effort to understand parties, citizen
participation, and democratic processes.
Sustained empirical research is required to
improve our understanding of the individual
party member and the institution of party
membership and the effects it has on political
processes. Most research on political parties
has a European bias (Diamond and Gunther,
2001). The same bias applies to most research
on party members. Therefore, more studies of
party members and party membership in
countries besides the advanced industrial
countries of Europe, with their established liberal democracies, are called for. Such studies
will call into question the accepted understanding of what the phenomenon of 'party
membership' is, and will demand a more
empirically applicable typology of membership than the variable geometry employed by
Duverger.

Beyond extending the studies of membership in space and – to the extent possible – in
time, the research would probably be most
fruitful for general political science if it were
pursued along two main lines: studying party
membership as 'political participation' and
party members as 'political agents'. Studying

membership as participation would mean
approaching this in the same way as other
researchers approach voting. The relevant
questions would be: Who are the members?
How much do they participate? Why do they
take part in varying degrees? One recent example of this line of research is the study of 'high-
intensity' members' participation by Whiteley
and Seyd (2002). Studying members as political agents, on the other hand, would raise
questions about the impact of member activity.
The original questions were posed by Robert
Michels: How is decision-making conducted in
political parties? And to what extent do
members influence decision-making? Answers
to these questions will be difficult to find
because searching for them places the same
demands on researchers of political parties as
those which have always been placed on
researchers of power in general. They must
answer the question: Who governs? In this
field there is an obvious need for more empirical studies of the decision-making processes in
political parties.

NOTE

*   Parts of this text are based on work done jointly
    with Jo Saglie, Institute for Social Research, Oslo,
    and with Berhard Hansen, Århus. I also have
    benefited from comments by Jo Saglie and Lars
    Svåsand on an earlier draft.

REFERENCES

Barnes, Samuel H. (1967) *Party Democracy. Politics in
an Italian Socialist Federation*. New Haven, CT: Yale
University Press.
Bartolini, Stefano (2000) *The Political Mobilization of
the European Left, 1860–1980. The Class Cleavage*.
Cambridge: Cambridge University Press.
Beck, Paul Allan and Sorauf, Frank J. (1992) *Party Politics
in America*, 7th edn. New York: HarperCollins.
Beyme, Klaus von (1985) *Political Parties in Western
Democracies*. Aldershot: Gower.
Bian, Yanjie (1995) 'Communist Party membership
and regime dynamics in China', *Social Forces*,
79: 805–41.
Bratton, Michael (1999) 'Political participation in a
new democracy', *Comparative Political Studies*,
35: 549–88.
Brzezinski, Zbigniew (1952) 'Party controls in the
Soviet Army', *Journal of Politics*, 14: 565–91.
Carbone, Giovanni M. (2003) 'Political parties in a
"no-party democracy": Hegemony and opposition

under "movement democracy" in Uganda', *Party Politics*, 9: 485–502.

Carty, Kenneth R. and Eagles, D. Munroe (2003) 'Preface: Party organization and campaigning at the grass roots', *Party Politics*, 9: 539.

Clark, Peter and Wilson, James Q. (1961) 'Incentive systems: A theory of organizations', *Administrative Science Quarterly*, 6: 219–66.

Clarke, Harold D., Kornberg, Allan, Ellis, Faron and Rapkin, Jon (2000) 'Not for fame or fortune. A note on membership and activity in the Canadian Reform Party', *Party Politics*, 6: 75–93.

Conway, M. Margaret and Feigert, Frank B. (1968) 'Motivation, incentive systems, and the political party organization', *American Political Science Review*, 62: 1159–173.

Cross, William and Young, Lisa (2004) 'The contours of political party membership in Canada', *Party Politics*, 10: 427–44.

Crotty, William (1986) 'Local parties in Chicago: The machine in transition', in William Crotty (ed.), *Political Parties in Local Areas*. Knoxville: University of Tennessee Press.

Daalder, Hans (ed.) (1987) *Party Systems in Denmark, Austria, Switzerland, the Netherlands, and Belgium*. London: Frances Pinter.

Diamond, Larry and Gunther, Richard (eds) (2001) *Political Parties and Democracy*. Baltimore, MD: Johns Hopkins University Press.

Duverger, Maurice (1964) *Political Parties. Their Organization and Activity in the Modern State*, 3rd edn. London: Methuen.

Eldersveld, Samuel J. (1964) *Political Parties: A Behavioral Analysis*. Chicago: Rand McNally.

Eldersveld, Samuel J. (1986) 'The party activist in Detroit and Los Angeles: A longtudinal view, 1956–1980', in William Crotty (ed.), *Political Parties in Local Areas*. Knoxville: University of Tennessee Press.

Epstein, Leon (1967) *Political Parties in Western Democracies*. London: Pall Mall.

Erdmann, Gero (2004) 'Party research: Western European bias and the "African labyrinth"', *Democratization*, 11: 63–87

Falke, Wolfgang (1982) *Die Mitglieder der CDU: Eine empirische Studie zum Verhältnis von Mitglieder- und Organisationsstruktur der CDU 1971–1977*. Berlin: Duncker & Humblot.

Fox, Michael S. (1993) 'Political culture, purges, and proletarization at the Institute of Red Professors, 1921–1929', *Russian Review*, 52: 20–42.

Gallagher, Michael and Marsh, Michael (2002) *Days of Blue Loyalty. The Politics of Membership of the Fine Gael Party*. Dublin: PSAI Press.

Gallagher, Michael and Marsh, Michael (2004) 'Party membership in Ireland: The members of Fine Gael', *Party Politics*, 10: 407–26.

Gallagher, Michael, Liston, Vanessa, Marsh, Michael and Weeks, Liam (2002) 'Explaining activism levels

amongst Fine Gail members: A test of Seyd and Whiteley's general incentives model', *Irish Political Studies*, 17: 97–113.

Giliomee, Hermann and Simkins, Charles (1999) *The Awkward Embrace: One-Party Domination and Democracy*. Cape Town : Tafelberg.

Gosnell, Harold F. (1937) *Machine Politics: Chicago Model*. Chicago: University of Chicago Press. Reprinted 1968.

Hansen, Bernhard (2002) *Party Activism in Denmark – A Micro Level Approach to a Cross-Sectional Analysis of the Correlates of Party Activism*. Århus: Politica.

Heidar, Knut (1994) 'The polymorphic nature of party membership', *European Journal of Political Research*, 25: 61–86.

Heidar, Knut and Saglie, Jo (2003) 'A decline of linkage? Intra-party participation in Norway 1991–2000'. *European Journal of Political Research*, 42: 761–86.

Herrera, Richard and Taylor, Melanie K. (1994) 'The structure of opinion in American political parties', *Political Studies*, 42: 676–89.

Hirschman, Albert O. (1982) *Shifting Involvements: Private Interests and Public Action*. Oxford: Martin Robertson.

Janda, Kenneth (1980) *Political Parties. A Cross-National Survey*. New York: Free Press.

Kadushin, Charles (1995) 'Friendship among the French financial elite', *American Sociological Review*, 60: 202–21.

Katz, Richard S. (1990) 'Party as linkage: A vestigial function?', *European Journal of Political Research*, 18: 143–61.

Katz, Richard S. and Mair, Peter (eds) (1992) *Party Organizations: A Data Handbook on Party Organizations in Western Democracies*. London: Sage.

Lawson, Kay and Merkl, Peter (eds) (1988) *When Parties Fail. Emerging Alternative Organizations*. Princeton, NJ: Princeton University Press.

Little, Walter (1973) 'Party and state in Peronist Argentina, 1945–1955', *Hispanic American Historical Review*, 53: 644–62.

Mair, Peter and van Biezen, Ingrid (2001) 'Party membership in twenty European democracies, 1980–2000', *Party Politics*, 1: 5–21.

May, John D. (1973) 'Opinion structure of political parties: The special law of curvilinear disparity', *Political Studies*, 21: 135–51.

McClosky, Herbert, Hoffmann, Paul J. and O'Hara, Rosemary (1960) 'Issue conflict and consensus among party leaders and followers', *American Political Science Review*, 54: 406–27.

McCulloch, Alistair (1990) 'Joining a political party: A reassessment of the economic approach to membership', *British Journal of Sociology*, 41: 497–516.

McKenzie, Robert T. (1955) *British Political Parties*. London: Heinemann.

Merriam, Charles Edward (1907) 'Some disputed points in primary election legislation', *Proceedings of the American Political Science Association*, 4: 179–88.

Michels, Robert (1925) *Soziologie des Parteiwesens*. Stuttgart: Kröner. (Originally published in 1911.)

Michels, Robert (1962) *Political Parties*. New York: Free Press.

Miller, Norman N. (1970) 'The Rural African Party: Political participation in Tanzania', *American Political Science Review*, 64: 548–71.

Narud, Hanne Marthe and Skare, Audun (1999) 'Are party activists the party extremists? The structure of opinion in political parties', *Scandinavian Political Studies*, 22: 45–65.

Norris, Pippa (1995) 'May's law of curvilinear disparity revisited', *Party Politics*, 1: 29–47.

Nowak, Thomas C. and Snyder, Kay A. (1974) 'Clientelist politics in the Phiippines: Integration or instability?', *American Political Science Review*, 68: 1147–70.

Ostrogorsky, Moisei I. (1902) *Democracy and the Organization of Political Parties*. London: Macmillan.

Panebianco, Angelo (1988) *Political Parties: Organization and Power*. Cambridge: Cambridge University Press.

Party Politics (1999) 'Special issue: Party democracy and direct democracy'.

Party Politics (2001) 'Special issue: Democratizing candidate selection: Causes and consequences'.

Party Politics (2003) 'Special issue: Party politics on the net'.

Party Politics (2004) 'Special issue: Party members and activists'.

Pedersen, Karina, Bille, Lars, Buch, Roger, Elklit, Jørgen, Hansen, Bernhard and Nielsen, Hans Jørgen (2004) 'Sleeping or active partners? Danish party members at the turn of the millenium', *Party Politics*, 10: 367–84.

Pierre, Jon, Svåsand, Lars and Widfeldt, Anders (2000) 'State subsidies to political parties: Confronting rhetoric with reality', *West Europeran Politics*, 23: 1–24.

Poguntke, Thomas (1992) 'Unconventional participation in party politics. The experience of the German Greens', *Political Studies*, 40: 239–54.

Poguntke,Thomas (1994) 'Basisdemokratie and political realities: The German Green Party', in Kay Lawson (ed.), *How Political Parties Work*. Westport, CT: Praeger.

Rogers, Marvin L. (1986) 'Changing patterns of political involvement among Malay village women', *Asian Survey*, 26: 322–44.

Rokkan, Stein (1962) 'The comparative study of political participation. Notes toward a perspective on current research', in A. Ranney (ed.), *Essays on the Behavioral Study of Politics*. Urbana: University of Illinois Press.

Rokkan, Stein and Campbell, Angus (1960) 'Citizen participation in political life: Norway and the United States of America', *International Social Science Journal*, 12: 69–99.

Römmele, Andrea (2003) 'Political parties, party communication and new information and communication technologies', *Party Politics*, 9: 7–20.

Sabatier, Paul A. (1992) 'Interest group membership and organization: Multiple theories', in Mark P. Petrecca (ed.), *The Politics of Interests. Interest Groups Transformed*. Boulder, CO: Westview Press.

Scarrow, Susan E. (1993) 'Does local party organization make a difference? Political parties and local government elections in Germany', *German Politics*, 2: 377–92.

Scarrow, Susan E. (1994) 'The "paradox of enrollment": Assessing the costs and benefits of party membership', *European Journal of Political Research*, 25: 41–60.

Scarrow, Susan E. (1996) *Parties and Their Members*. Oxford: Oxford University Press.

Scarrow, Susan E. (2000) 'Parties without members?', in Russell Dalton and Martin Wattenberg (eds), *Parties without Partisans*. Oxford: Oxford University Press.

Scarrow, Susan E., Webb, Paul and Farrell, David M. (2000) 'From social integration to electoral contestation: The changing distribution of power within political parties', in Russell Dalton and Martin Wattenberg (eds), *Parties without Partisans*. Oxford: Oxford University Press.

Schattschneider, E.E. (1942) *Party Government*. New York: Rinehart.

Schlesinger, Joseph A. (1991) *Political Parties and the Winning of Office*. Ann Arbor: University of Michigan Press.

Selle, Per and Svåsand, Lars (1991) 'Membership in party organizations and the problem of decline of parties', *Comparative Political Studies*, 23: 459–77.

Seyd, Patrick and Whiteley, Paul (1992) *Labour's Grassroots – The Politics of Party Membership*. Oxford: Clarendon Press.

Stone, Walter J., Rapoport, Ronald B. and Schneider, Monique B. (2004) 'Party members in a three-party election: Major party and reform activism in the 1996 American Presidential election', *Party Politics*, 10: 445–69.

Sundberg, Jan (1995) 'Women in Scandinavian party organization', in Lauri Karvonen and Per Selle (eds), *Women in Nordic Politics. Closing the Gap*. Aldershot: Dartmouth.

Tan, Alexander C. (1998) 'The impact of party membership size: A cross-national analysis', *Journal of Politics*, 60: 188–98.

Tingsten, Herbert (1937) *Political Behaviour*. London: King.

Tenga, Nakazael and Peter, Chris Maina (1996) 'The right to organize as mother of all rights: The experience of women in Tanzania', *Journal of Modern African Studies*, 34: 143–62.

Teorell, Jan (1999) 'A deliberative defence of intra-party democracy', *Party Politics*, 5: 363–82.

van Biezen, Ingrid (2000) 'On the internal balance of party power: Party organizations in new democracies', *Party Politics*, 6: 395–418.

van Ree, Erik (1993) 'Stalin's organic theory of the party', *Russian Review*, 52: 43–57.

Walder, Andrew G., Li, Bobai and Treiman, Donald J. (2000) 'Politics and life chances in a state socialist regime: Dual career paths into the urban Chinese elite, 1949 to 1996', *American Sociological Review*, 65: 191–209.

Ware, Alan (1987) *Citizens, Parties and the State*. Cambridge: Polity Press.

Ware Alan (1996) *Political Parties and Party Systems*. Oxford: Oxford University Press.

Weber, Max (1964) *Max Weber: The Theory of Social and Economical Organization*. Toronto: Collier-Macmillan.

Wellhofer, Spencer (1972) 'Dimensions of party development: A study in organizational dynamics', *Journal of Politics*, 34: 153–82.

Wellhofer, Spencer (1981) 'The political incorporation of the newly enfranchised voter: Organizational encapsulation and Socialist Labor Party development', *Western Political Quarterly*, 34: 399–414.

Whiteley, Paul and Seyd, Patrick (1996) 'Rationality and party activism: Encompassing tests of alternative models of political participation', *European Journal of Political Research*, 29: 215–34.

Whiteley, Paul and Seyd, Patrick (2002) *High-Intensity Participation – The Dynamics of Party Activism in Britain*. Ann Arbor: University of Michigan Press.

Whiteley, Paul, Seyd, Patrick and Richardson, Jeremy (1994) *True Blues – The Politics of Conservative Party Membership*. Oxford: Clarendon Press.

Widfeldt, Anders (1995) 'Party membership and party representativeness', in Hans-Dieter Klingemann and D. Fuchs (eds), *Citizens and the State*. Oxford: Oxford University Press.

Zielonka-Goei, Mei Lan (1992) 'Members marginalising themselves? Intra-party participation in the Netherlands', *West European Politics*, 15: 93–106.

26

ELECTORAL MOBILIZATION IN THE UNITED STATES

James W. Endersby, John R. Petrocik and Daron R. Shaw

Simply put, Americans are not politically active. Thirty-five percent reported an attempt to persuade someone to vote a particular way in 2000; about 11 percent displayed a campaign button or sticker on their person, lawn, or car; 11 percent reported a contribution to a candidate, party, or some group that worked on behalf of a candidate or party; 5 percent remember attending a political rally or meeting; only 3 percent did any work on behalf of a party or candidate. Each activity requires energy, spare time, disposable income, or a level of interpersonal aggressiveness that many people simply do not have.

Voting is much less demanding and civic norms encourage Americans to vote, but even this activity is not that attractive to many Americans. In the 1996 American National Election Study (ANES) survey, 50 percent agreed that it is acceptable to stay home if one doesn't care how an election comes out. Only 41 percent thought that a person had an obligation to vote even if the person didn't care who won. This expressed indifference is corroborated by turnout rates. Just over 17.5 percent took part in the primaries that selected the candidates who ran in the 2000 general election. The low participation rate of Democrats (less than 14.7 million) might be explained by the virtually uncontested nomination of Vice-President Gore, but only 20.7 million Republicans turned out – and no one should describe George Bush's nomination as uncontested. Americans did better in the general election where turnout exceeded 51 percent, about 15 points above the turnout rate for the 1998 congressional elections.[1] But 'better' still

leaves the United States well below the norm for almost any comparable country. The turnout rate for our presidential elections has averaged about 55 percent of the voter-age population (VAP) since 1980; a figure which is about 25 points below the average of other Anglo-American democracies, and about 30 points below the average turnout rate for the nations of Western Europe, with whom we share a substantially common political culture. As Figure 26.1 indicates, only the Swiss have been less likely to participate.

Interestingly, American turnout is not lower because Americans have unusually low interest in public affairs or weak partisanship. On average, Americans display interest levels and party attachments that are similar to those of citizens of countries with much higher turnout rates. Since both interest in politics and partisanship have some natural ceiling, a program to increase interest or party attachments is not likely to do much to increase turnout levels from their current 55–60 percent or more in presidential elections (Powell, 1982; Teixeira, 1992; McDonald and Popkin, 2001).

The differential is likely to be found among institutional variables – registration requirements, voter canvassing and election day mobilization, and fewer elections – not in American citizenship norms (which are not so terrible in comparative perspective). This chapter reviews the role of voter canvassing and election day mobilization in promoting turnout. The working hypothesis that drives this chapter is that a significant contributor to low turnout is the style of campaigning in America.

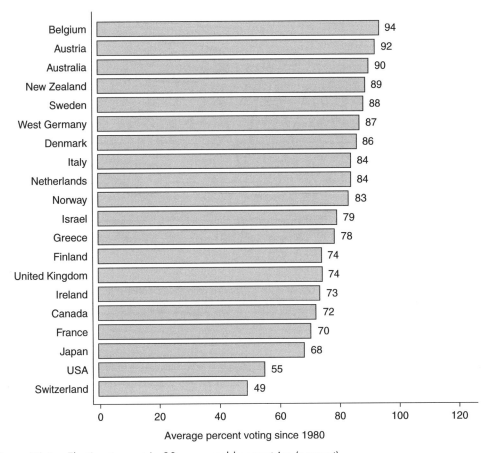

Figure 26.1   Election turnout in 20 comparable countries (percent)

THE PARTISAN CONSEQUENCES OF ELECTORAL MOBILIZATION

American campaigns do relatively little to shape turnout. They spend the bulk of their resources on attempting to shape the direction of the vote, effectively assuming that turnout will reach a level 'typical' of turnout of the type of election at hand and that the best way to win an election is to 'improve' the vote share among the expected voters. Political science has encouraged this by demonstrating repeatedly that non-voters typically share the preferences of voters. The argument that turnout tends to have an inconsistent partisan bias is, however, not uncontested.

Lijphart's prominent (1997) essay arguing that a bias exists reflects a substantial literature linking turnout and electoral mobilization to partisan outcomes. Campbell's early (1966) study of shifts in party fortunes between higher-turnout presidential and lower-turnout congressional elections

provided a basis in survey data for the biased turnout hypothesis. Subsequent analyses of election results provided additional empirical support (recent examples include Tucker and Vedlitz, 1986; Nagel, 1988; Avery, 1989; Radcliff, 1994; Pacek and Radcliff, 1995; and – more tentatively – Nagel and McNulty, 1996). Sporadic popular political commentary often reported circumstances that reinforced the notion that turnout has a direct effect on election outcomes (Duncan, 1991; Freedman, 1996). Commentaries that attributed the success of the GOP, especially in presidential elections, to a decline in turnout since the 1960s (Edsall, 1984; Burnham, 1987, Piven and Cloward, 1988) created a chorus of support for schemes that might increase turnout – same-day registration, 'motor voter' bills, and so forth.

The literature on party system change provided important ancillary support for the biased turnout thesis. It identified a similar turnout/mobilization process as a critical ingredient in party realignments, arguing that

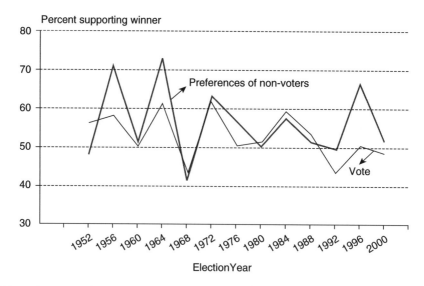

The 1980, 1992, and 1996 preferences of non-voters are calculated only for those interviewed during October in order to account for a clear shift in preferences in the last half of the September–October campaign period.

Figure 26.2   The presidential preferences of voters and non-voters

any party system with a low rate of participation is vulnerable to substantial change because the segments of the society who are involved are virtually never a representative sample of those who do not participate. When these peripherals are mobilized they typically transform the party balance because the newly mobilized rarely find attractive choices among the parties of the limited electorate (some examples of this literature include Lubell, 1952; Eldersveld, 1949; Key, 1955; Burnham, 1970; Przeworski, 1975; Andersen, 1979; Petrocik, 1981a; Petrocik and Brown, 1999).

Despite its intuitive appeal and fragmentary supportive evidence, the turnout bias thesis is not well supported by direct evidence. Kernell (1977) was among the first to demonstrate that the on-year/off-year oscillation in party fortunes (described by Campbell, 1966) was less a function of turnout differences than it was a retrospective reaction to the incumbent president and, perhaps, the loss of coattails in the off-year contest. Wolfinger and his colleagues (Rosenstone and Wolfinger, 1978; Wolfinger and Rosenstone, 1980; Highton and Wolfinger, 2001), Crewe (1981), Erikson (1995a, 1995b), DeNardo (1980), Petrocik (1981b, 1987), Petrocik and Shaw (1991), Petrocik and Perkins (2003), Teixeira (1987, 1992), Calvert and Gilchrist (1991), Gant and Lyons (1993), and a host of textbook authors who included a chapter on turnout (e.g., Beck

and Hershey, 2001) have found little or no support for the bias thesis. Recent research by Citrin *et al.* (2003) which reports a partisan bias to turnout in Senate elections in the 1990s, nonetheless finds it to be inconsistent, varying in size and party beneficiary according to election-specific factors that may include incumbency, campaign resources, etc. Notably, the bias, even when it was observed, would almost never be large enough to change the outcome of the elections even if 100 percent of the non-voters were persuaded to turn up at the polls.

RECENT PATTERNS: VOTERS AND NON-VOTERS IN NATIONAL ELECTIONS

Figure 26.2 summarizes how closely non-voter preferences match those of voters. It plots two lines: the reported vote for the winner in presidential elections from 1952 through 2000 and the expressed preferences of those who reported not voting in the ANES surveys of those years. The preferences of non-voters were expressed prior to the election (eliminating some of the bandwagon effect that is observed when candidate preference is obtained after the election); their voter status is determined by their post-election report. The pattern is

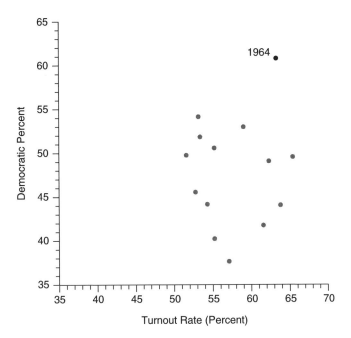

Figure 26.3   Turnout and the presidential vote, 1948–2000

clear. Whether the election is lopsided or close, a two-party struggle, or one with a significant third candidate, non-voters expressed the same candidate preferences as did voters – and sometimes a bit more so. The pattern is not perfect. Non-voters preferred Stevenson in 1952 and seem to have preferred Carter in 1980 (but see Petrocik, 1987). Overall, however, whether the election is lopsided or close, a two-party struggle, or one with a significant third candidate, non-voters express the same candidate preferences as do voters – and sometimes a bit more so (see below for more on surge effects). A 100 percent turnout rate would have produced the same winner, at either the same or a slightly greater margin.

Of course the similarity of the preferences of voters and non-voters that is observed in survey data appears in aggregate election results. Figure 26.3 plots the Democratic presidential vote against turnout; Figure 26.4 presents plots of the Democratic vote for Congress against turnout for presidential election years (the points) and for mid-term elections (the untilled diamonds).

The data are clear. Democrats won and lost with high turnout among the 14 presidential elections (Figure 26.3). House elections in the on years and the off years show the same pattern (Figure 26.4). In off years the Democratic share of the congressional vote was actually slightly higher (by about 1 percent), although the typical turnout rate for off-year elections from 1950 through 1998 averaged approximately 15 points *below* the turnout typical of presidential elections. The pro-GOP tides of some presidential elections were absent, so there was a less depressing effect on the Democratic vote in the off years. Petrocik and Perkins' (2003) analysis of turnout effects on election outcomes in congressional elections by district through time confirms this pattern. Non-voters tend to echo the preferences of voters, and perhaps even exaggerate them, depending on the magnitude of the forces influencing the vote. A close contest among voters and the more involved produces a roughly similar division among the less involved peripherals. Short-term forces sufficient to boost turnout are likely also to favor a candidate. They tilt the candidate preference of the core electorate and have an even greater influence on the peripheral electorate. Consequently, not only are lopsided elections unlikely to be undone by higher turnout, they are likely to become even more lopsided as turnout increases beyond a normal level since the entering voters create an electorate with a larger than normal proportion of peripheral voters.

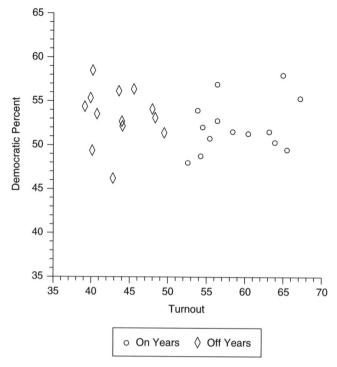

Figure 26.4   Turnout and the congressional vote, 1948–2000

THE BASICS OF TURNOUT

The most defensible estimates of turnout, based on the fraction who vote as a proportion of the VAP that is not legally disqualified, are that about 55 percent vote in presidential elections (53 percent in 1996 and 51 percent in 2000) and about 40 percent show up in off-year national elections (40 percent in 1998 and 39 percent in 2002). But these figures are only estimates. We know (with considerable accuracy) how many votes are cast, but we are unsure about how many might be cast if all those who are eligible actually turned up at the polls. The most commonly reported turnout rate is calculated as a proportion of the VAP. It has the virtue of making easy comparisons among jurisdictions within the United States, and between the United States and any given country. But these strengths are dominated by a weakness: it significantly deflates the turnout rate by including many ineligibles – resident aliens, the criminal population, and various other institutionalized individuals (Burnham, 1987; McDonald and Popkin, 2001). What is the 'correct' turnout rate? Including aliens and

others who are legally barred from voting in a count of the eligible electorate is unreasonable since by custom and law we specifically bar their participation. Similarly, a turnout rate that is calculated as a proportion of the registered electorate misses many millions who could have voted had they satisfied the technical requirement of officially registering an intention to vote. Put differently, the unregistered eligibles have, by intention or inadvertence, indicated they will not be voting *before* the polls open – when we find out how many of the rest will abstain.

WHO VOTES: THE SOCIAL AND DEMOGRAPHIC BASIS OF THE VOTE

Turnout rates vary by (in rough order of importance) race, age, education, income (and similar SES markers), marital status, and geographic region (the data are in Table 26.1).[2] Type of employment matters: government employees, especially those in states with a tradition of patronage, turn out at higher rates than comparable citizens. Unionization also

Table 26.1   *US election turnout by demographics, 1988 and 2000*

	Percent of population in 2000	Reported turnout in 2000 (n=1807)	1988 validated turnout (n=2040)		
			Voted	Reg'd, didn't vote	Unreg'd
Total	100%	75%	58%	11%	32%
Gender					
Male	48	75	59	11	30
Female	52	71	56	11	33
Race					
White	76	74	62	10	29
Black	12	73	40	18	42
Hispanic	6	56	49	10	41
Other	3	67	41	17	42
Age					
18–24	13	51	31	11	58
25–39	29	69	51	13	36
40–54	29	77	66	8	26
55–64	13	84	67	7	26
65+	17	81	68	12	20
Income					
Low	39	62	43	14	44
Middle	30	70	59	10	31
High	32	86	71	9	20
Education					
Less than high school	15	46	40	11	49
High school	33	66	51	12	37
Some college	28	77	64	10	26
College degree	16	92	79	10	11
Post-graduate	8	94	84	9	8
Marital status					
Married	60	79	66	9	26
Formerly married	17	67	51	12	37
Never married	24	61	46	14	40
Religion					
Protestant	54	72	57	12	31
Catholic	27	79	62	9	29
Jewish	2	89	66	6	28
Other	10	64	45	11	44
Agnostic/Atheist/None	14	60	42	21	37
Born again					
Yes	40	73	56	12	33
No	60	76	61	10	29
Church attendance					
Every week	37	83	71	9	20
Almost every week	16	83	63	11	26
Once or twice a month	23	75	59	8	33
A few times a year	24	73	54	12	34
Never	1	80	43	12	45
Length at residence					
0–11 months	12	51	45	13	42
12 months–2 years	18	63	51	9	40
3–5 years	17	71	52	12	36
6–10 years	17	80	58	10	32
11–25 years	22	83	66	9	25
25+ years	14	81	76	10	15

(Continued)

Table 26.1   (Continued)

	Percent of population in 2000	Reported turnout in 2000 (n=1807)	1988 validated turnout (n=2040)		
			Voted	Reg'd, didn't vote	Unreg'd
Occupation					
Executive, management	13	87	69	8	22
Professional	18	85	79	7	14
Craftsman, skilled worker	11	66	48	15	37
Sales	12	72	60	9	31
Administrative worker	16	75	63	12	25
Service	11	58	50	13	37
Machine operator	5	66	38	12	50
Transportation	4	72	48	15	38
Agriculture	2	69	–	–	–
Working status					
Employed	64	74	59	10	31
Temporarily laid-off	1	65	44	16	41
Unemployed	4	55	28	14	58
Retired	17	82	69	9	22
Homemaker	8	66	55	13	33
Student	3	62	50	11	39
Union household					
Yes	15	77	62	9	29
No	85	72	56	11	32
Region					
New England	7	82	72	10	18
Mid-Atlantic	16	80	53	9	38
East North-Central	21	77	67	8	26
West North Central	9	81	73	7	20
Deep South	26	67	43	16	41
Border South	6	75	46	11	42
Mountain	5	61	55	6	39
Pacific	11	62	68	10	22
Population Size					
Major city	10	80	57	15	28
Minor city	14	75	54	13	33
Major suburb	8	79	63	10	26
Other suburb	21	71	58	9	33
Adjacent area	28	72	57	11	32
Rural	19	68	55	9	36

Notes: Data are taken from the American National Election Studies, of 1988 and 2000. Validation of the self-reported vote was not undertaken in the 2000 ANES. Explanations of the region and population size variables can be found in the technical appendices of the ANES codebooks.

matters. The difference in the voting rates of union versus non-union households in 1988 is quite striking, given the slightly more down-scale status of union households. The direct mobilization efforts of unions (more on that below) probably deserve credit for this difference. Employment, *per se*, is also associated with turnout. The unemployed do not vote at rates comparable to those who are employed, retired, homemakers, or students.[3]

Catholics and Jews vote at slightly higher rates than do Protestants, but most of this religious difference is a proxy for region and race-ethnicity. Turnout differences by religion are trivial or non-existent among northern whites. Lower overall turnout among Protestants reflects the Protestant traditions of African-Americans and southern whites. Catholic turnout is partially suppressed by the concentration of Hispanics among Catholics. Religiosity, however, is correlated with turnout: 59 percent of those with a religious identification voted in 1988, while only 43 percent of atheists, agnostics, and those with no religious preference cast ballots. Among believers, church attendance is also related to turnout. The turnout in 1988 was 71 percent of those attending church weekly, compared to 43 percent for those who never attend services. Living circumstances, from length of residence in a given community to the part of the country in which that community is located, also correlate with turnout. Among these factors, the length of residence is the most significant. Newcomers (those who have been at their current residence 6 months or less) exhibited a 41 percent turnout rate in 1988, compared to a 76 percent rate for those who had been at their residence for over 25 years. This 35 point effect is obviously related to structural factors, such as registration, as well as to other demographics, such as age and marital status.

There are also slight turnout differences according to the size of the community and its regional location. Americans living in the suburbs of major cities turned out more than those living in smaller cities or rural areas. Distances may also matter. Gimpel *et al.* (2004b) have found that turnout rates are higher for those living within a mile of the polling place than for those who live farther away. New Englanders (at 72 percent) and those living on the Pacific coast (68 percent) are the most likely voters, while southerners turn out at the lowest rates (44 percent).

WHO VOTES: THE ATTITUDES AND BELIEFS OF VOTERS AND NON-VOTERS

Although demography can sometimes be plausibly *and directly* related to turnout (consider ethnicity: in the past African-Americans were systematically denied the right to vote), demographic differences matter because they produce circumstances that shape attitudes that are the direct influence on individual turnout. For example, Americans who are interested in politics vote; those who are not, do not. A closely related attitude is whether one cares about the election outcome: 67 percent of those who cared 'a great deal' voted, compared with 43 percent of those who 'do not much care' (Table 26.2). Voters who think that an election is close are more likely to vote (at 61 percent) than those who foresee a lopsided result (53 percent). Popular commentary and recent research have

focused on declining confidence in government as a factor in low turnout (Hetherington, 1999). The evidence here is contradictory and mixed, and findings depend on fine distinctions between the electorate's trust in government and their sense that government is effective. On average, however, there is evidence that those who regard government as ineffective and confusing have low turnout rates.

Strong partisans (Republicans and Democrats) are much more likely to vote than are weak partisans and independents (although Republicans have a higher turnout rate than Democrats at any given level of partisan intensity). But issue orientation, in general, does not seem to matter. The relationship between ideology and turnout is complicated, and while there is a small correlation, it is only small. Self-described conservatives have slightly higher turnout rates, but conservative preferences on specific issues are not necessarily associated with high turnout. Republicans have slightly higher turnout rates than Democrats; and there will be a turnout difference between conservatives and liberals if the issue is closely tied to party identification.

THE INFLUENCE OF POLITICAL INSTITUTIONS AND SYSTEMIC PROCESSES ON TURNOUT

No one is required to pay a fee in order to vote, but it is not completely costless. Trooping to the polls requires time that could be spent doing something – watching television, going shopping, painting a bedroom, or reading a book – that is personally rewarding, and at least represents another use of one's time. A person who will be out of town might decide to vote absentee, a choice which might require even more energy: the registrar of voters must be asked for an absentee ballot application, the application must be completed and mailed, and the ballot must be completed and mailed. Deciding whom to support can be costly if only for the time it takes to become informed. The huge number of offices, many non-partisan, or propositions for which we must often vote can stymie even the conscientious and informed since they might require just that much more commitment to the vote than a person feels, causing them to abstain.

This 'cost' feature of voting is represented by political institutions that structure campaigns, the way parties mobilize, voting requirements, and so forth. The United States has many such institutions and practices. They affect the turnout of individuals and groups in any given

Table 26.2   *US election turnout by attitudes, 1984–88 ANES*

			1984–88 validated turnout		
				Did not vote Registered?	
	% of Pop.	% of VAP.	Voted	Yes	No
Party identification					
Strong Republican	14	18	74	7	19
Weak Republican	14	15	61	10	29
Lean Republican	14	13	54	12	34
Independent	11	7	39	9	52
Lean Democratic	12	11	53	13	34
Weak Democratic	18	16	54	13	33
Strong Democratic	17	20	67	11	23
Ideology					
Conservative	60	65	64	10	26
Moderate	10	8	55	10	35
Liberal	30	27	55	13	33
Efficacy and trust attitudes					
Trust government just about always*	4	3	61	11	29
Trust government most of the time*	41	42	72	9	19
Trust government only some of the time*	54	54	70	9	21
Government too powerful	63	62	67	8	24
Government not too powerful	36	37	69	10	22
Government wastes a lot*	66	70	74	8	15
Government wastes some*	3	28	65	10	25
Government wastes hardly anything*	4	3	48	10	42
External efficacy					
Government cares what I think*	57	64	68	10	22
Government doesn't care*	43	36	53	12	35
Internal efficacy					
Government not too complicated*	71	78	71	9	20
Government too complicated*	29	22	57	11	32
People like me have a say*	68	76	69	10	21
People like me have no say*	32	24	46	14	40

Notes: Asterisks indicate data come from 1984 ANES; all other data are from the 1988 survey. Turnout estimates are higher for the 1984 results because turnout was higher and the questions were only asked of post-election survey participants.

election, they play a role in holding down turnout levels in the United States compared to similar countries.

VOLUNTARY PRE-ELECTION REGISTRATION

The Federal Election Commission reports a registration percentage (based on the VAP) of 76 percent for 2000 (up about 2 points from 1996). If the VAP is reduced to eliminate ineligibles, the Commission's estimated registration rate is over 80 percent, a figure that is surely too high and may only reflect a failure to purge deadwood from the rolls (a possible result of state attempts to meet the spirit as well as the letter of the 1994 'motor voter law'). Like turnout, therefore, the exact registration rate is unknown, but a reasonable estimate would be in the low seventies.

Registration is important because those who are registered have a high turnout rate (Kelly *et al.*, 1967; Erikson, 1981; Highton, 1997). A plausible (and not too conservative) estimate of the turnout rate among the registered (based on the voter validation portion of the 1988 ANES) is about 85 percent. If everyone was registered does

Table 26.3 *Registration and turnout in 1988 (validated data)*

	Turnout	Registered	Turnout of registered
Years of education			
Less than high school	40	50	80
High school	51	62	82
College	79	87	91
Post-graduate degree	84	90	93
Age			
18–24	31	42	74
25–39	51	63	81
40–64	67	72	93
65 and above	68	78	87
Time at current address			
Less than 1 year	41	53	77
1 year	48	59	81
2 or more years	61	70	87
Interest in politics			
Very little	34	45	76
Some	58	68	85
A great deal	78	85	92

that imply a turnout rate of about 85 percent – and a participation rate that would put us in the middle of the pack of comparison countries (see Figure 26.1)? Probably not, although research has concluded that liberalized registration rules would have a large effect on participation rates.

The largest estimate of the effect of registration is that American turnout is 14–15 percentage points below where it would be with election day registration. The most conservative estimate, based on turnout changes that occurred when Minnesota and Wisconsin introduced election day registration, pegged the increase in turnout at 1–2 points. A more systematic study that examined turnout and registration data for the period from 1960 through 1986 concluded that election day registration would increase turnout by about 4 percentage points. Still other studies have estimated that election day registration would increase turnout by 7–9 percentage points. This last estimate seems to be the most likely consequence of eliminating prior registration requirements. The methodology used to derive this estimate is the most defensible, and at least three separate studies have produced registration effects in the range of 7–9 percentage points (see Teixeira, 1992).

WHO IS AFFECTED BY REGISTRATION?

Registration depresses the turnout of those who are less interested in politics or must exert noticeable effort to become registered: the less

educated, younger, or the geographically mobile. The less educated tend to be less involved in public and community affairs and less likely to think of the need to register in the absence of considerable stimulation; younger citizens are much more likely to change their address frequently, and every change of address imposes a requirement to reregister. These conditions – mobility, education, etc. – often occur together (see Rosenstone and Wolfinger, 1978; Wolfinger and Rosenstone, 1980; Nagler, 1991). Further, registration deadlines are often earlier than the arousal of interest in the election for many Americans. Only the drum beat of the election campaign will stir many to consider voting, but an interest in the election is likely to be peaked only when the campaign is at full tide – and that is often too late for many to recognize that they are unregistered, discover how to become registered, and actually do it.

Table 26.3 summarizes the effects of registration the registration on voters who are unlikely to solve the registration puzzle. The first column reports the difference in the turnout rates between those who are the least and best educated, the younger and the older, those who have no interest in politics and those who pay at least some attention, and those who recently changed their place of residence and those who have had the same address for at least 2 years. On average, those who have some college education, are 40 years of age or above, and have some interest in public affairs are about 30 percentage points more likely to vote than their counterparts who, respectively, never completed high school, are under 24 years or age, or have no interest in public affairs. Among those who are registered (the second column) the differences between these educational, age, interest levels, and mobility levels are substantially reduced (and age differences completely disappear).

Registration does not affect all groups uniformly. The largest effects (of about 10 percentage points) are found among the younger and less educated, minorities, and southerners. Better educated and older voters, white voters, and those who live in areas where participation is already reasonably high (the Midwest, for example) are the least affected (Wolfinger and Rosenstone, 1980).

Registration reform in the past 30 years has had limited effects on turnout. The estimated 7–9 point turnout reduction imposed by prior registration requirements translates into a projected 61–62 percent turnout – 20 points below the turnout rates of the currently registered – if election day registration had been the law of the land in recent elections. The shortfall is a reminder that registration is only part of the story. Registration is a burden for those who have enough intrinsic interest in public affairs to vote only when the effort to vote is minimal. 'Enough intrinsic interest' is key, and it is lacking among many, perhaps most, of the unregistered.

A useful illustration of the importance of individual motivation is given in Cain and McCue's (1985) study, which compared the turnout rate of individuals who registered on their own initiative with the turnout rate of those who were registered as a result of an organized effort by voter mobilization groups. Fifty-six percent of the former turned out, only 41 percent of the latter voted. Democratic identifiers registered by Democratic-organized groups were the least likely to vote after they were registered. Only a follow-up with organized get-out-the-vote (GOTV) efforts yielded high turnout among the group-registered. The difference between group-registered and self-registered is that the self-registered wanted to vote and, when they were eligible, did vote. The group-registrants were less interested in voting. They registered only when external pressure was applied; they voted only when external pressure was applied. Voting simply was not a habit for them (Gerber *et al.*, 2003; Green and Shachar, 2000; Plutzer, 2002).

THE SYSTEM OF REPRESENTATION

In proportional representation systems, which attempt to ensure that parties win offices in proportion to the number of votes they receive, each party has a strong incentive to get every potential

supporter to the polls. When the electoral system is less committed to proportionality the incentive to mobilize every prospective voter is less compelling. Single-member/simple plurality representation systems (typical throughout the United States where we elect one office-holder from each district) are likely to generate high turnout only when the election is competitive. A district (for a school board, city council, county supervisor, state legislature, or the House of Representatives) that regularly supports one party by a wide margin (the typical condition for America's artfully gerrymandered districts) is not likely to be subject to vigorous registration or GOTV drives. The loser is usually pleased just to 'show the flag' and the winner, facing no challenge, rarely feels a need to mobilize voters since those who turn out for their own reasons can be relied upon to elect the candidate of the district's majority party. Presidential elections, which aggregate votes by state, have a similar operational dynamic.

OFF-YEAR ELECTIONS

The drop-off in turnout from presidential to congressional elections runs to about 12–17 percentage points, and turnout for municipal elections commonly runs as low as 20–25 percent (and even lower turnout rates are not unusual). Americans see a considerable difference in the importance of these different types of elections, and the money, effort, and media attention they draw reflect this assessment. Those with a lower sense of civic duty and less interest in public affairs are much less stimulated to vote by the mild attention off-year elections receive compared to the presidential year benchmark which attracts the most attention. Lower turnout is the result.

LONG BALLOTS

Long ballots with candidates for justice of the peace, road inspector, and so forth depress turnout by encouraging 'roll-off' – the tendency of voters to stop voting as the choice gets farther down ballot. The longer the ballot, the greater the roll-off will be because it occurs with even relatively short ballots.

MULTIPLE ELECTIONS

Although it cannot be proven, and the magnitude of the effect is unknown, there is a predisposition to believe that the frequency of our elections tends to depress turnout. The idea is that a consolidated ballot would probably produce a greater overall level of participation because elections would be less common and, thereby, more intrinsically interesting to voters and commentators of all stripes. The evidence for this is indirect, but more than impressionistic.

In one study of multiple election effects, the citizens of Middlefield, Connecticut, had the opportunity during a 4-year period to vote in three general elections (1974, 1976, and 1978), two town elections (1975 and 1977), and a referendum in 1976 that was scheduled apart from the presidential election (Boyd, 1981). Turnout varied from a high of just under 80 percent for the 1976 election to a low of 41.3 percent for the referendum. Excepting the referendum, turnout was 69 percent or greater in every election. The interesting fact, for getting a sense for who votes, is that only 11 percent did not vote at any time in this period. Put differently, almost 90 percent voted in at least one of these elections. The core rate of non-participation was only 11 percent. Sixty-two percent voted at least five times; a third voted in all six elections.

A similar study across multiple elections in Kentucky produced results that are probably more similar to the national pattern. Sigelman et al. (1985) looked at ten elections, including primaries, state contests, a presidential race, and two congressional elections between 1978 and 1982. While the highest turnout recorded during the period was 50 percent for the 1980 presidential election, that fraction undercounted the share that participated at least once in the period. In Kentucky, very few were high-propensity voters: only 13 percent turned out for seven or more of the ten elections for which they could have voted. One the other hand, only 29 percent were unregistered and another 10 percent were registered but never voted. In other words, upwards of 60 percent voted at least once during the 4 years. This seems like only a modest improvement until one realizes that, as Middlefield had unusually high turnout rates, the people of Kentucky participate less than the national average. If the difference between national turnout and the turnout rate in Kentucky is adjusted, the result suggests that consistent non-voters may be as few as 30 percent – and the proportion of Americans who vote at least occasionally may be as high as 70 percent.

A plausible conclusion: core turnout in national elections may be about 35–40 percent, while another 30–35 percent may move in and out of the electorate depending upon the appeal of the election, canvassing efforts by parties or candidates, and institutional and personal restraints.

A caveat is in order: these data do not prove that turnout would be higher if Americans were called upon to vote less frequently. That acknowledged, it seems possible that the frequency with which Americans are called upon to vote may allow those with a weaker sense of civic duty or interest in politics to abstain in an election without feeling that they have been remiss in their duty as a citizen – producing, in any given election, a lower turnout rate than might be observed if elections were less common.

POSTAL, ABSENTEE, AND HOLIDAY VOTING

Sixteen states have conducted voting by mail since 1977. Four states – Alaska, Minnesota, Utah, and Washington – have expanded the practice to include partisan elections. Oregon is the only state to have used it for significant statewide special and partisan elections. In principle, postal voting should reduce the cost of voting to a near minimum and thereby increase participation. Oregon's much publicized mail ballot to elect a senator had a very high participation rate for a special election: 57.9 percent for the December 1995 primary election and 66.3 percent in the January 1996 general. Similarly, Oregon turnout for the 2000 presidential election was 67 percent. These 'by mail' elections have been too varied by type and have occurred over too long a period to provide a good data-set for reliably estimating the impact of mail balloting on turnout. That granted, there is some reason to believe that mail ballots may increase participation in elections. Among two recent odd-year special elections conducted by mail the participation rate was 41.4 percent, compared to 39.7 percent for three equally recent odd-year special elections conducted at polls in the conventional manner. Whether that effect would generalize to other states, or produce higher than normal turnout in high-stimulus general elections, is unknowable.

Absentee ballot requirements have been sufficiently liberalized in most states and communities that the impact of absentee voting on participation rates has been dwarfed by the sheer numbers who frequently choose it as an alternative to in-person voting, not as a substitute for abstention. In some states (California is a good example), absentee voting is approaching 40 percent of the total vote cast in general

Table 26.4 *An illustration of party alignment*

Groups	Christian	Labor	Liberal	Farmer	Total
High-alignment party system					
Religiously observant	80	5	5	10	100%
Working class	10	85	5	0	100%
Middle class	40	20	40	0	100%
Rural	5	5	5	85	100%
Language minority	10	60	20	10	100%
Low-alignment party system					
Religiously observant	55	40	5	0	100%
Working class	30	55	15	0	100%
Middle class	35	25	40	0	100%
Rural	45	45	10	0	100%
Language minority	20	60	20	0	100%

Note: Table entries are hypothetical only, illustrating patterns common to highly aligned Western European party systems. No country or party system in particular is represented.

elections. It is so common that absentee voters are almost representative of the electorate – or at least less distinctive than when absentee voting began to grow in the 1980s. Its probable effect on overall turnout at this time is modest to the point of insignificance. Early and 'no-fault' absentee voting in states such as Texas, Nevada, and New Mexico, for example, had no discernible effect on turnout in the data examined thus far.

In several countries where turnout is substantially higher than it is in the USA, voting is done on weekends, or election day is a national holiday, and some have suggested that a similar arrangement in the USA would increase turnout. The effect seems unlikely. Countries with election holidays are different from the United States in so many other ways related to turnout (the registration of voters) that it is unlikely that American turnout is depressed by our practice of holding elections on weekdays.

THE PARTY SYSTEM

This has several dimensions. Most are fairly trivial, and some (the number of parties) are strongly related to the feature which does have an impact on voter turnout: the alignment between social groups and parties. Alignment refers to the degree to which (1) a party draws heavy support from particular groups and (2) supporters of a given party are homogeneous in their religion, class, ethnicity, or place of residence. An example of a party system with the maximum degree of alignment would be one in which the supporters of each party were drawn from a single religion, and all members of a given religion supported the same party. The parties in an unaligned party system draw supporters from every religion equally, and each religion is represented in each party in proportion to their occurrence in the society. Table 26.4 presents a hypothetical example.

High-alignment party systems have higher turnout rates because highly aligned parties stimulate social as well as political identities, and elections are occasions to support parties which exist as a political expression of a salient social distinction – being Catholic, French-speaking, working class – with which people identify. Disputes around social identities – and they will exist as parties coincide with social groups – draw people to the polls more easily than simple political identities such as being a conservative, a Republican, or a supporter of limited government (Powell, 1986; Lijphart, 1984; Teixeira, 1992). The American electorate has an even lower turnout rate than one would have expected from the weak alignment of groups with the parties, an 'underperformance' which reflects the multiple turnout depressing institutions and practices characteristic of the United States.

CAMPAIGN STYLES

While civic leaders of every stripe encourage Americans to vote, candidates and political strategists occasionally make decisions which depress participation. In some cases the pressure to hold turnout down is intentional. For example, a special election is scheduled for

Table 26.5   *Campaign styles and turnout in Senate elections, 1992*

Campaign Style	Study	
	1	2
Predominantly Negative	49.7%	51.8%
Mixed	52.4%	50.3%
Predominantly Positive	57.0%	58.9%

Notes: Table entries are percentage of the VAP turning out for the election. The data for study 1 are from Ansolabehere and Iyengar (1996). Study 2 is from Martin Wattenberg (1996).

mid-March because strategists have decided that the small number who are the most likely to turn out at such an odd time are more likely to support the issue or candidate than the electorate which will participate in a higher-turnout election. The long-term consequence for turnout rates of a history of such calculations is probably quite small, but it may help to depress turnout rates on average by making non-voting a more common experience.

Potentially much more consequential is the attack style of campaigning that has become standard in American elections. Two recent studies show a difference in the turnout rates of aggressive attacking compared to 'positive' campaigns for the US Senate. However, as Table 26.5 indicates, the studies do not agree on the nature of the effect. Using 'mixed campaign style' states as a benchmark, one study shows lower turnout when the campaign style of the candidates is 'negative' and higher turnout when the campaign style is 'positive'. The second study did not show an unusual decline in turnout associated with negative campaigning, but it did show higher than average turnout when the campaign was predominantly positive. Further, the studies disagree about the robustness of the findings. It is possible that the differences are trivial or even completely absent when other features of these campaigns are considered for their impact on turnout. In brief, the effect of campaign styles remains unclear, but there are data indicating an effect. What we know about the predisposition of voters toward political debate makes it at least plausible that attacking negative campaigns can create enough disaffection to depress participation.

THE MEDIA

The media became more critical of government, politics, and politicians after the mid-1960s than it had been in previous decades.

Today, its tendency is to be more critical of incumbents than challengers, more critical of stronger candidates than it is of weaker candidates, and more critical of candidates who try to limit opportunities for reporters to watch them carefully.

We have only limited data on the effect of this media style on turnout, and no solid evidence that the critical tone of media coverage depresses turnout or that it has played a part in depressing turnout in recent years (although the decline in turnout and the rise of a critical media do correlate in the aggregate). However, we do have data demonstrating that higher media users are more likely to be critical of public officials and less likely to have a positive evaluation of the candidates of their party. Positive feelings toward candidates play a role in the vote choice; media-induced ambivalence toward the candidates (both – or all – candidates) in an election may influence the decision about whether they vote at all.

OFFICE-HOLDING, THE SEPARATION OF POWERS, AND DIVIDED GOVERNMENT

The separation of legislative and executive elections in the United States (both nationally and in the states) is also believed to suppress turnout. Legislative candidates tend to their own election, usually assured because of incumbent-protecting district lines, and often do not consider driving turnout in their district to its maximum in order to provide more votes for a statewide candidate. The result, some speculate, is turnout levels which reflect the individual citizen's enthusiasm for voting, a result which will always be lower than turnout which results from individual willingness to vote that is boosted by coordinated GOTV efforts by candidates.

When the separation of powers yields divided government, there is some evidence

Table 26.6   *Party canvassing and turnout, 1988 (percent)*

	Percentage of:		Validated turnout and registration		
Contacted by	Sample	Voters	Voted	Registered but did not vote	Not registered
A party or candidate	24	31	78	8	13
Not contacted	76	69	54	11	35

Source: 1988 ANES.

that the division may further depress turnout between 2–6 percentage points, depending upon how long the government has been divided between the parties. Only a few studies have been done on this feature of American politics, and the processes are not well understood, but it seems likely that separated offices reduces turnout-enhancing coordination between executive and legislative candidates. A period of divided outcomes may encourage legislative and executive candidates to separate their campaigns even further and, thereby, reduce the ability of mobilization efforts to identify and turn out potential supporters.

MOBILIZING VOTERS

This relative lack of coordinated mobilization of potential supporters seems particularly important, given evidence that voter mobilization has a substantial impact on turnout (evidence of this can be found in research from the 1960s, but for recent examples, see Huckfeldt and Sprague, 1992; Gerber and Green, 2000, 2001; Green *et al.*, 2003). Of the three dimensions of campaigns – creating candidate awareness, creating candidate positivity, getting voters to the polls – most contemporary campaigns place the least emphasis on getting voters to the polls whether measured by the amount of money or workforce effort expended on it. For instance, in the state legislative election study described below, on average, less than 10 percent of campaign expenditures are invested in GOTV but over one-fourth pays for mass media advertising. The best recent data on turnout (found in the 1988 ANES) show that only about 24 percent of voters remember any contact with a campaign worker (Table 26.6), while almost all remember some exposure to a campaign message.

But contact by campaign workers increases turnout. Among those who remember no contact, 54 percent voted – a figure that was virtually identical to an a priori estimate of who was the most likely to turn out (the turnout estimator

as in Petrocik, 1991). By contrast, turnout was about 10 percentage points *higher* than expected (according to the prediction of the turnout model) among those who were contacted by some campaign. Other studies, specifically designed to estimate the effect of canvassing voters, found total turnout effects of as much as 6 percentage points from in-person canvassing and about 4 points from telephone canvassing.

In any given election, therefore, turnout will be a product of three factors: the aggregated individual equilibrium-level interest in voting, the enthusiasm for the race generated by the attention it receives, and tailored efforts to mobilize voters who are not sufficiently motivated to participate by (1) the excitement of the election and (2) their intrinsic interest in voting.

Competitiveness will not (by itself) increase turnout. Rather, competitiveness creates conditions – more candidate events, advertising, party and candidate contacting, and GOTV efforts – which increase the likelihood that people will be exposed to and drawn into the election (Cox and Munger, 1989; Gimpel *et al.*, 2004a). Voters are analogous to sports fans: there are some diehards, but many only follow the game casually and these casual fans are much more apt to watch the games that generate the most publicity (i.e., the Super Bowl). If this game is supposed to be competitive, it will generate additional media coverage and social attention, which, in turn, create attention and interest among the public.

A CASE STUDY: MISSOURI LEGISLATIVE ELECTIONS

A sample of Missouri legislative elections offers an opportunity to further examine the effects of mobilization efforts on voter participation by assessing the effects of expenditures principally intended to get out the vote on turnout compared to the effects of campaign expenditures that are more intended to persuade. The data in Table 26.7 are drawn

Table 26.7   *Summary statistics for the Missouri case study (two major parties only)*

Variable	Mean	Std.dev.	Minimum	Maximum
Individual Campaigns (n=193)				
Turnout for candidate (%)	20.746	6.853	6.386	49.907
Expenditures per capita ($)	0.468	0.422	0.000	03.970
Canvassing (%)	9.442	15.711	0.000	100.000
Direct mail (%)	34.703	23.856	0.000	89.137
Advertising (%)	25.508	24.055	0.000	93.087
Signs and appearances (%)	11.475	13.403	0.000	70.033
Campaign support (%)	15.065	15.990	0.000	94.565
Miscellaneous (%)	2.252	6.758	0.000	49.481
Off year Election (0,1)	0.492	0.501	0.000	1.000
Two party Elections (n=104)				
Turnout for election (%)	38.501	8.982	15.576	59.579
Expenditures per capita ($)	0.868	0.685	0.001	4.414
Canvassing (%)	10.255	15.527	0.000	100.000
Direct mail (%)	35.113	20.478	0.000	81.893
Advertising (%)	25.147	21.689	0.000	80.968
Signs and appearances (%)	10.522	10.646	0.000	69.185
Campaign support (%)	16.468	16.960	0.000	94.565
Miscellaneous (%)	2.495	6.822	0.000	49.481
Off-year election (0,1)	0.500	0.502	0.000	1.000

from the periodic reports of campaign receipts and expenditures filed by candidate committees.[4] All campaign expenses over $100 must be itemized. Many House campaigns also identify the purpose of expenditures below this limit. Expenditure items were coded into one of six categories according to whether they were mobilization efforts, attempts to enhance name recognition, or attempts to control the campaign agenda and persuade partisans and independents to support one candidate over another (Endersby and Petrocik, 2001).

The category of campaign expenditures designed specifically to mobilize voters is *canvassing*. This includes expenses for traditional GOTV activities. Activities coded as canvassing include phone banks and door-to-door visits – interactions between the candidate or campaign staff and potential voters. Relevant costs include those for voter registration lists, door hangers, transportation expenses identified for GOTV, phone banks and charges, campaign staff to man them. Canvassing efforts are those intended to identify potential voters and encourage their participation.

Other campaign expenditures are less clearly identified as mobilization. *Direct mail* efforts to reach voters are less personal. Candidates may attempt to encourage partisans to vote; but they may also use direct mail to distinguish their records from those of their opponents. The literature on the effects of direct mail is not clear as to whether direct mail

should influence turnout. *Advertising* includes expenditures for newspaper and radio advertising, as well as cable or other mass media. Messages intended for the general populace, however, typically boast of the relative merits of one candidate over another and usually cannot be directed to partisan supporters exclusively. *Signs and appearances* are more passive forms of communication. Yard signs, bumper stickers, and billboards can be used to enhance name recognition, but these are unlikely to either mobilize inactive supporters or control the public agenda. *Campaign support* includes any other identifiable expenditures to mount an election campaign. Most of these expenses pertain to maintaining a campaign office. Any remaining expenditures that cannot be identified fall into the *miscellaneous* category. Small costs, which are not itemized, are included as well as other unusual expenses, which do not fit into any other category.

A measure of a campaign canvassing effort can be calculated as the percentage of canvassing expenses to total expenditures (excluding transfers and cash on hand after the election). The percentage is a proxy for the type of campaign mounted by a House candidate. For instance, campaigns that try to mobilize voters should spend a higher percentage of funds on canvassing than those emphasizing name recognition or persuasion of independent voters.[5]

The analysis is limited to major party candidates from 26 districts for the House of

Table 26.8   *Turnout for candidate as a function of campaign expenditures, all Democratic and Republican state House candidates*

	All races (0–100% margin)	Contested races (70–30% margins)	Close races (60–40% margins)
Canvassing effort	0.115***	0.075***	0.083***
(% of expenditures)	(0.028)	(0.023)	(0.024)
Total expenditures	0.344	1.623**	0.904
(dollars per capita)	(1.044)	(0.792)	(0.707)
Off-year election	−5.967***	−6.023***	−5.761***
(1 = Yes, 0 = No)	(0.877)	(0.678)	(0.644)
Constant	22.436***	21.272***	21.466***
	(0.761)	(0.590)	(0.560)
R^2	0.245	0.360	0.432
(Adjusted)	(0.233)	(0.348)	(0.418)
S.E.	6.00	4.23	3.54
F	20.42***	29.82***	31.70***
n	193	163	129

***Significant at the 0.01 level

**Significant at the 0.05 level

*Significant at the 0.10 level

Representatives for four election cycles: 1992, 1994, 1996, and 1998 (two presidential and two off-year elections). The total sample of all elections, then, regardless of competition, is 104. The sample was created to be representative of House districts and reflected regional divisions of the state. A total of 193 Democratic and Republican candidates appeared on general election ballots in the sampled districts. Although many minor party candidates appeared on the ballot, these candidates have little likelihood of winning a House seat in Missouri and attract relatively small amounts of campaign contributions. Turnout and party competition vary significantly by House district.

THE INFLUENCE OF EXPENDITURES ON TURNOUT

There are several theoretically viable ways to measure an effort to mobilize the number of supporters in an election. The best compare the number of partisans to some measure of a normal vote. However, for state legislative elections, with low levels of partisan competition, no measure of a normal vote is at hand. Turnout, however, can still be evaluated. First, if the campaign's mobilization efforts are successful, the number of voters casting ballots for the candidate should be higher. So one measure of campaign effects is the number of votes cast for a candidate divided by the population (eligible voters). Second, campaign efforts mounted by one or both campaigns may influence

turnout on behalf of both candidates. Another measure, then, is the variation in turnout for both parties in the election. Below, the effects of one campaign's expenditures are considered first on the ratio of votes cast for a candidate. Next, the percentage of campaign expenditures within each category for both campaigns is compared to two-party turnout.

Tables 26.8 and 26.9 report the results from multiple regression models predicting voter participation as a function of canvassing effort, considering the overall size of the campaign – total expenditures per capita. Table 26.8 shows results for individual campaigns; Table 26.9 does the same for the two-party election. These models are considered in three different contexts that may influence mobilization, recognition, or agenda-setting effects.

The first includes all campaigns, including uncontested elections. The second narrows the number of campaigns to 'contested' races; that is, weakly competitive elections where the candidate receives between 30 and 70 percent of total votes. The third reduces the range to 'close' elections, here defined as those in which a candidate receives between 40 and 60 percent of the vote.

Table 26.8 reveals that mobilization is significantly and positively related to greater numbers of partisan voters, controlling for the influence of per capita expenditures – which has a mild effect. This strong result holds across all classes of election environments – from all races to close races. If expenditures on canvassing increase a mere 10 percent, candidates should expect around a 1 percent growth in the number of supporters casting ballots at the polls. Although

Table 26.9   *Turnout in election as a function of campaign expenditures, all state House elections (two-party candidates)*

	All races (0–100% margin)	Contested races (70–30% margins)	Close races (60–40% margins)
Canvassing effort	0.125***	0.125**	0.162**
(% of expenditures)	(0.041)	(0.052)	(0.070)
Total expenditures	1.821*	0.349	−0.465
(dollars per capita)	(0.939)	(0.999)	(1.447)
Off-year election	−12.468***	−11.660***	−10.739***
(1 = Yes, 0 = No)	(1.282)	(1.336)	(1.617)
Constant	41.869***	43.777***	43.828***
	(1.189)	(1.289)	(1.641)
R^2	0.502	0.519	0.487
(Adjusted)	(0.487)	(0.500)	(0.462)
S.E.	6.43	5.84	6.08
F	33.61***	28.04***	19.01***
n	104	82	64

***Significant at the 0.01 level

**Significant at the 0.05 level

*Significant at the 0.10 level

the level of significance falls slightly as elections become closer, the explanatory power of this simple model grows, accounting for less than a quarter to over 40 percent of the variance.

Table 26.9 provides similar models for two-party elections. The canvassing coefficient remains positive and significant. The absolute magnitude of the effect grows, although the level of significance is lower than for corresponding models for individual campaigns. For general elections, an overall increase in canvassing efforts equal to 1 percent of total expenditures generates 0.125 percent more turnout. This seems particularly influential, given the multitude of variables affecting voter participation in general elections. Per capita campaign expenditures in the aggregate, however, do not appear to lead to higher turnout. The off-year indicator and canvassing explain approximately half of the variance in turnout in state legislative contests. In short, despite numerous difficulties with measurement error, we find strong evidence supporting the theory that mobilization efforts give rise to higher turnout.

CONCLUSION

Political science research typically shows that while both attitudes and institutions matter for turnout, institutions – such as election laws and organized efforts to mobilize voters – are more often causal. High turnout rates throughout the 19th century were maintained by election schedules, which coincided with the schedules of county courts and local fairs. Public balloting, in which voters verbally declared their preference before local registrars, also pressured those who were eligible to discharge their public duty and (often) satisfy promises and obligations to candidates and important figures in the local community who organized for the parties and the candidates. Most of this institutional facilitation of turnout came to an end with the Progressive era reforms of the 1890s, which, we generally believe, eroded the ability of the parties to mobilize voters.

The shift from 'retail' to 'wholesale' campaigning – coincident with the rise of 'personal' campaigns, television, and the reputed decline of the American political parties – has also mattered. Media campaigns broadcast to the masses shape perceptions of candidates but their contribution to getting out the vote on election day is modest.

Perhaps surprisingly, given the amount of scholarly interest in and attention to turnout, there is much that remains controversial or vague. Given numerous problems with measurement of the variables – difficulties with classifying campaign expenditures, measuring turnout and changes in levels of voter participation, and the lack of controls for party (and interest group) campaign efforts – significant results are difficult to attain.

The finding that campaigns that emphasize canvassing efforts, regardless of total expenditures, produce higher levels of turnout is discernible through the cacophony of white noise.

The empirical evidence for the notion that mobilization efforts, at least canvassing efforts, can identify partisans and encourage them to show their support at the polls is strong.

This research into mobilization effects also suggests that the direction in which many contemporary campaigns have been oriented – that is, to greater expenditures on advertising and name recognition – may have exhausted its potential. Traditional means of increasing the number of votes by identifying and encouraging supporters to turn out may be resurgent. Parties have discovered that they may significantly increase their vote (regardless of whether the opposing party responds and there is no concomitant change in vote share). Also, more participation by voters satisfies a growing concern about civic responsibility and the legitimacy of election results.

These practical and normative concerns were noticed at the highest levels of Democratic and Republican campaign planners in 2004. Both the Democratic National Committee (with its '5104' plan) and the Republican National Committee (with its '72 Hour' plan) invested substantial resources in GOTV, canvassing, and grassroots programs for 2004, partly reflecting recent research of Gerber and Green (2001) and Huckfeldt and Sprague (1992), as well as by the success of Democratic group outreach programs in the 1998 and 2000 elections. The ultimate impact of these efforts, and the possibility that they will be institutionalized as we proceed into the 21st century, remain an open question.

NOTES

1 Turnout figures are from the Federal Election Commission, utilizing Census Bureau estimates of the voting-age population. Turnout for 2000 is based on the Census Bureau's projections for the voting-age population.
2 The 1988 ANES is used to describe individual turnout differences because that is the last year for which the ANES collected validated turnout data. Although validated turnout data are not error-free, their accuracy is superior to self-reports.
3 In fact, the gap between these groups apparent from the 1988 data is a whopping 23 points.
4 Initial responsibility for receiving campaign disclosure rested with the Office of the Secretary of State. An independent agency, the Missouri Ethics Commission, now serves this function.
5 Of course, not only candidates engage in mobilization and other campaign efforts. Political parties may be more effective at encouraging

supporters to cast ballots, and party efforts are not included in the data discussed above. Political parties also attempt to encourage partisans to support all their candidates in a general election, not just for the state House. In addition, interest groups such as labor unions may devote considerable resources to mobilization and other independent expenditures. Other than legal restrictions to file reports for contributions and expenditures, businesses, unions, and other associations are unregulated in Missouri elections (Casey *et al.*, 1995). The efforts of parties and groups, of course, are not included in the empirical tests of the influence of campaigns on turnout. So any detectable effects should be underestimated.

REFERENCES

Andersen, Kristi (1979) *The Creation of a Democratic Majority, 1928–1936*. Chicago: University of Chicago Press.

Ansolabehere, Stephen and Iyengar, Shanto (1996) *Going Negative*. New York: Free Press.

Avery, M. (1989) *The Demobilization of American Voters*. New York: Greenwood.

Beck, Paul Allen and Hershey, Marjorie Randon (2001) *Party Politics in America*. New York: Addison Wesley Longman.

Boyd, Richard W. (1981) 'Decline of U.S. voter turnout: structural explanations', *American Politics Quarterly*, 9: 133–59.

Burnham, Walter Dean (1970) *Critical Elections and the Mainsprings of American Politics*. New York: Norton.

Burnham, Walter Dean (1987) 'The turnout problem', in A. James Reichley (ed.), *Elections American Style*. Washington, DC: Brookings.

Cain, Bruce and McCue, Ken (1985) 'The efficacy of registration drives', *Journal of Politics*, 47: 1221–30.

Calvert, J. and Gilchrist, J. (1991) 'The social and issue dimensions of voting and nonvoting in the United States'. Paper presented at the 1991 Annual Meeting of the American Political Science Association, Washington, DC.

Campbell, Angus (1966) 'Surge and decline', in Angus Campbell, Phillip E. Converse, Warren E. Miller and Donald E. Stokes, *Elections and the Political Order*. New York: John Wiley.

Casey, Greg, Endersby, James W. and King, James D. (1995) 'Interest groups in Missouri', in Richard J. Hardy, Richard R. Dohm and David A. Leuthold, *Missouri Government and Politics*, rev. ed. Columbia: University of Missouri Press.

Citrin, Jack, Shickler, Eric and Sides, John (2003) 'What if everyone voted? Simulating the impact of increased turnout in Senate elections', *American Journal of Political Science*, 47: 75–90.

Cox, Gary W. and Munger, Michael C. (1989) 'Closeness, expenditures, and turnout in the 1982 U.S. House elections', *American Political Science Review*, 83: 217–31.

Crewe, Ivor (1981) 'Electoral participation', in David Butler, Howard R. Penniman and Austin Ranney (eds), *Democracy at the Polls: A Comparative Study of Competitive National Elections*. Washington, DC: American Enterprise Institute.

DeNardo, James (1980) 'Turnout and the vote: The joke's on the Democrats', *American Political Science Review*, 74: 406–20.

Duncan, Dayton (1991) *Grass Roots: One Year in the Life of the New Hampshire Presidential Primary*. New York: Penguin.

Edsall, Thomas Byrne (1984) *The New Politics of Inequality*. New York: Norton.

Eldersveld, Samuel J. (1949) 'Influence of metropolitan party pluralities on presidential elections'. *American Political Science Review*, 49: 1189–1206.

Endersby, James W. and Petrocik, John R. (2001) 'Campaign spending influences on turnout: mobilization versus agenda-setting'. Prepared for presentation at annual meetings of the Southwestern Social Science Association, Fort Worth, TX, March 16–18.

Erikson, Robert S. (1981) 'Why do people vote? Because they are registered', *American Politics Quarterly*, 9: 259–76.

Erikson, Robert S. (1995a) 'State turnout and presidential voting: a closer look', *American Politics Quarterly*, 23: 387–96.

Erikson, Robert S. (1995b) 'Pooling and statistical control: a rejoinder to Radcliff', *American Politics Quarterly*, 23: 404–8.

Freedman, Samuel G. (1996) *The Inheritance: How Three Families and America Moved from Roosevelt to Reagan and Beyond*. New York: Simon and Schuster.

Gant, M. and Lyons, W. (1993) 'Democratic theory, nonvoting, and public policy: the 1972–1988 presidential elections', *American Politics Quarterly*, 21: 185–204.

Gerber, Alan S. and Green, Donald P. (2000) 'The effects of canvassing, telephone calls and direct mail on voter turnout: a field experiment', *American Political Science Review*, 94: 653–4.

Gerber, Alan S. and Green, Donald P. (2001) 'Do phone calls increase voter turnout?', *Public Opinion Quarterly*, 65: 75–86.

Gerber, Alan S., Green, Donald P. and Shachar, Ron (2003) 'Voting may be habit-forming: evidence from a randomized field experiment', *American Journal of Political Science*, 473: 540–55.

Gimpel, James G., Dyck, Joshua J. and Shaw, Daron R. (2004a) 'Better late than never: voter registration timing and its effects on turnout'. Paper prepared for delivery at the annual meeting of the Midwest Political Science Association, Chicago, April 15–18.

Gimpel, James G., Leonitti, Ann Marie, Dyck, Joshua J. and Shaw, Daron R. (2004b) 'Location, knowledge, and time pressures in the spacial structure of convenience voting'. Paper prepared for delivery at the annual meeting of the Midwest Political Science Association, Chicago, April 15–18.

Green, Donald P. and Shachar, Roni (2000) 'Habit-formation and political behavior: evidence of consuetude in voter turnout', *British Journal of Political Science*, 30: 561–73.

Green, Donald P., Gerber, Alan S. and Nickerson, David W. (2003) 'Getting out the vote in local elections: results from six door-to-door canvassing experiments', *Journal of Politics*, 65: 1083–97.

Hetherington, Marc J. (1999) 'The effect of political trust on the presidential vote, 1968–1996', *American Political Science Review*, 93: 311–26.

Highton, Benjamin (1997) 'Easy registration and voter turnout', *Journal of Politics*, 59: 565–75.

Highton, Benjamin and Wolfinger, Raymond E. (2001) 'The political implications of high turnout', *British Journal of Political Science*, 31: 179–92.

Huckfeldt, Robert and Sprague, John (1992) 'Political parties and electoral mobilization: political structure, social structure, and the party canvass', *American Political Science Review*, 81: 70–86.

Kelley, Stanley, Jr., Ayres, Richard J. and Bowen, William G. (1967) 'Registration and voting: Putting first things first', *American Political Science Review*, 61: 359–79.

Kernell, Samuel (1977) 'Presidential popularity and negative voting: an alternative explanation of the midterm congressional decline of the President's party', *American Political Science Review*, 71: 44–66.

Key, V.O., Jr. (1955) 'A theory of critical elections', *Journal of Politics*, 17: 3–18.

Lijphart, Arend (1984) *Democracies: Patterns of Majoritarian and Consensus Government in Twenty-One Countries*. New Haven, CT: Yale University Press.

Lijphart, Arend (1997) 'Unequal participation: democracy's unresolved dilemma', *American Political Science Review*, 91: 1–14.

Lubell, Sam (1952) *The Future of American Politics*. New York: Harper.

McDonald, Michael P. and Popkin, Samuel (2001) 'The myth of the vanishing voter', *American Political Science Review*, 95: 963–74.

Nagel, Jack H. (1988) 'Voter turnout in New Zealand general elections, 1928–1987', *Political Science*, 40 (December): 16–38.

Nagel, Jack H. and McNulty, John E. (1996) 'Partisan effects of voter turnout in senatorial and gubernatorial elections', *American Political Science Review*, 90: 780–93.

Nagler, Jonathan (1991) 'The effect of registration laws and education on U.S. voter turnout', *American Political Science Review*, 85: 1393–1405.

Pacek, Alexander and Radcliff, Benjamin (1995) 'Turnout and the vote for left-of-centre parties: a cross-national analysis', *British Journal of Political Science*, 25 (January): 137–43.

Petrocik, John R. (1981a) *Party Coalitions*. Chicago: University of Chicago Press.

Petrocik, John R. (1981b) 'Voter turnout and electoral preference: the anomalous Reagan elections', in K.L. Schlozman (ed.), *Elections in America*. New York: Allen & Unwin.

Petrocik, John R. (1991) 'An algorithm for estimating turnout as a guide to predicting elections', *Public Opinion Quarterly*, 55: 643–7.

Petrocik, John R. and Brown, Thad A. (1999) 'Party system structure and electorial realignments', in Birol Yesilada (ed.), *Comparative Political Parties and Party Elites: Essays in Honor of Samuel J. Eldersveld*. Ann Arbor, MI: University of Michigan Press.

Petrocik, John R. and Perkins, William (2003) 'Short-term forces and the partisan bias of turnout: House elections, 1972–2000'. Paper prepared for delivery at the 2003 Annual Meeting of the American Political Science Association, Philadelphia, August 27–31.

Petrocik, John R. and Shaw, Daron (1991) 'Nonvoting in America: attitudes in context', in William Crotty (ed.), *Political Participation and American Democracy*. New York: Greenwood Press.

Piven, Francis Fox and Cloward, Richard A. (1988) *Why Americans Don't Vote*. New York: Pantheon.

Plutzer, Eric (2002) 'Becoming a habitual voter: inertia, resources, and growth in young adulthood', *American Political Science Review*, 96: 41–56.

Powell, G. Bingham (1982) *Contemporary Democracies: Participation, Stability, and Violence*. Cambridge, MA: Harvard University Press.

Powell, G. Bingham (1986) 'American voter turnout in comparative perspective', *American Political Science Review*, 80: 17–44.

Przeworski, Adam (1975) 'Institutionalization of voting patterns, or is mobilization the source of decay', *American Political Science Review*, 69: 49–67.

Radcliff, Benjamin (1994) 'Turnout and the Democratic vote', *American Politics Quarterly*, 22: 259–76.

Rosenstone, Steven and Wolfinger, Raymond (1978) 'The effect of registration laws on voter turnout', *American Political Science Review*, 72: 22–45.

Sigelman, Lee, Roeder, Philip W., Jewell, Malcolm E. and Baer, Michael A. (1985) 'Voting and nonvoting: a multi-election perspective', *American Journal of Political Science*, 29: 749–65.

Teixeira, Ruy A. (1987) *Why Americans Don't Vote: Turnout Decline in the United States, 1960–1984*. New York: Greenwood.

Teixeira, Ruy A. (1992) *The Disappearing American Voter*. Washington, DC: Brookings.

Tucker, Harvey J. and Vedlitz, Arnold (1986) 'Does heavy turnout help democrats in presidential elections?', *American Political Science Review*, 80: 1291–8.

Wattenberg, Martin (1996) 'Negative campaign advertising: mobilizer or demobilizer'. Prepared for presentation at the Annual Meeting of the American Political Science Association. San Francisco.

Wolfinger, Raymond and Rosenstone, Steven (1980) *Who Votes?* New Haven, CT: Yale University Press.

27

PROFESSIONAL STAFF IN POLITICAL PARTIES

Paul Webb and Robin Kolodny

INTRODUCTION

One of the most under-researched fields in the study of political parties is that of party employees. This is curious given how much we now know about most other significant aspects of party life, including developments in party ideology and policy; the role, powers and social background of party members and leaders; the recruitment and sociology of legislators and candidates; and the marketing of parties. By contrast, relatively little is known of the men and women on the organizational payroll who run the day-to-day operations of parties up and down the countries in which they operate. This is a significant oversight, which leaves us with a deficient understanding of an important aspect of party organizational development.

While it surely goes without saying that party staff have always been of general importance to the operation and functioning of party organizations, it seems likely that their importance is greater now than ever before. In part this is because it is clear that the modern age of election campaigning and political marketing makes certain types of professional expertise all the more pertinent. Indeed, even in the context of parliamentary democracies, where politics is generally less candidate-centred than under presidentialism, there is nothing particularly novel in the argument that election campaigning in the televisual era relies far more on centralized professional resourcing than on local party activism (see, for instance, McKenzie, 1955: 591; Butler and Rose, 1960). In addition (and relatedly), it is likely that parties have come to rely increasingly on paid professionals in the context of the now ample evidence of party membership decline and 'de-energization' around the democratic world (Katz *et al.*, 1992; Mair and van Biezen, 2001; Seyd and Whiteley, 1992; Whiteley *et al.*, 1994). As the voluntary wings of party organizations have gone into decline, so the resources available through paid professionals have increased. Here, we explore the implications of these changes for political parties. First, we define our subject by exploring the scope and range of party political work, identifying in particular the professional elements within it. Next, we offer a detailed definition of 'professionalism' in this context, before proceeding to a review of the literature on party work at the levels of central and subnational organizations, political consultancy and governmental bodies. Finally, we reflect on the implications for future research.

UNDERSTANDING PARTY PROFESSIONALS: THE RANGE AND SCOPE OF THEIR WORK

In essence, we are engaged in an examination of scholarship on those who work for political parties. What do we mean by 'work' in this context? Perhaps the main function of major political parties across the contemporary democracies is to run election campaigns. While this function might once have been restricted to relatively short periods of time during and immediately before an election, today it is clear that election campaigns are run continuously. Whether a polity has fixed elections or not, the political party must constantly monitor public opinion and modify either its issue positions or presentation of such positions accordingly. In addition, office-holders understand that the positions they take or actions they engage in today may have enormous effects at the next election. Therefore, they appreciate the need for continuous campaigning by the parties and the professional staff employed to assist in forming and articulating partisan positions.

In effect, then, for all such parties, the work of their employees will often be bound up with the electoral imperative. The tasks connected with this function include the following:

- the recruitment and nomination of candidates for election;
- research into policy issues and opponents;
- the development of policy;
- the raising of funds to fight elections;
- the publicizing and marketing of party policies and issue positions;
- the gauging of public opinion;
- the mobilization of voter support.

In addition to staff employed in connection with electoral functions, we should note that parties employ staff to perform a variety of tasks associated with the day-to-day running of the organization – accountants and financial staff, human resources and personnel, press officers, membership officers, organizers and agents. Overall, those who conduct this range of duties and functions can be broken down into:

- amateurs (volunteers and party members);
- professional staff on the regular party pay-roll;
- professional consultants on limited-term contracts or fees.

While there has been a resurgence of interest in the numbers and roles of 'amateur' activists in recent years (Seyd and Whiteley, 1992; Whiteley et al., 1994; Scarrow, 1996; Widfelt, 1999; Carty and Blake, 2001; Mair and van Biezen, 2001), our horizons in this chapter are limited to the contribution of the latter two categories, the paid professionals of party politics.

For our purposes, professionals work in the political process full-time (as their primary employment) and are paid for their work. They can be divided into two categories: staff and consultants. Staff are obviously on the payroll of the political parties. However, as Katz and Mair (1992) have argued, the state frequently employs individuals who perform important work for political parties. For example, the full-time staff of members of legislative bodies and political offices of executives can often be considered as being in support of the political party of that member. Monroe (2001) makes this case for the staff working in the constituency offices of partisan electoral officials as well. Therefore, both party organizations and states pay the salaries of professional staff members. Consultants, on the other hand, are independent contractors for the party. They work primarily in the political realm (see Farrell et al., 2001, for a typology), but are not technically employees of the parties. Recent work by Kolodny and Dulio (2003) suggests that when political party organizations make conscious decisions to hire professional consultants in lieu of hiring and training professional staff, then the consultants ought to be viewed as the equivalent of employees. Therefore, our review of the literature on party workers (below) will explore three categories in turn: professional staff on the party payrolls; professional political consultants; and professional staff paid by the state but engaged in essentially party political work. Before reviewing this literature, however, it is important first to develop a clearer understanding of precisely what 'professionalism' might mean in the context of party political work.

DEFINING PROFESSIONALISM IN PARTY WORK

Political scientists tend to use the term 'professional' in the context of party politics without giving much consideration to its proper definition. There is no need for this since there is a well-developed sociological literature on the concept. This literature recognizes 'a continuum of professionalization on which groups can be located according to the number of professional characteristics which they exhibit' (Romzek and Utter, 1997). A review of some of the key items in this literature (Wilensky, 1959; Brante, 1990; Raelin, 1991) suggests that the characteristics most usually emphasized include the following:

Expertise. At the heart of the notion of professionalism lies the notion of some special competence which sets the professional apart from other workers. This will most probably reflect a particular education and perhaps formal vocational training or qualification. In the USA, certificate and degree programmes in campaign management are proliferating rapidly, training today's corps of party officials, campaign managers, and political consultants. These programmes are emerging in response to a need for more specially trained individuals to handle the technical tasks required by contemporary campaigning (Jalonick, 2002/03).

Autonomy. In view of the professional's expertise, s/he tends to be entrusted with an unusual degree of job autonomy; though answerable to the 'client', the professional's specialist knowledge means that s/he cannot be dictated to by line managers. To some extent this distinguishes a professional from a mere 'bureaucrat', who is a general functionary under the supervision of a manager.

Mobility. Angelo Panebianco (1988: 227) points out that, by virtue of their expertise and autonomy, professionals are usually in a good position to sell their labour on the external job market if they so choose. Traditional party bureaucrats, however, will typically be engaged in work such that it would be difficult for them to find an equivalent job in the external market; this relative non-transferability of their skills helps explain the bureaucrat's subordination to line managers and political leaders. An illustration of the growing potential for mobility across sectors is provided by the USA, where the boundaries between party employment, full-time consultancy and governmental staff positions are becoming blurred (Thurber and Nelson, 2000; Johnson, 2001). Whether this development is part of a gathering cross-national trend can only be revealed by new empirical research.

Self-regulation. Given his or her specialist knowledge, only the professional is in a position to protect clients against entry into the job market of charlatans or incompetents. Hence, a profession will typically have the right to establish and police its own code of vocational ethics. For instance, the political consultancy industry in the USA has begun to make such an effort in this direction by establishing the American Association of Political Consultants. An entire volume dedicated to ethics in campaigns highlights the development of ethical standards and the almost complete inability to police them due to the permeability of the profession (Nelson *et al.*, 2002).

Commitment. Although an archetypal professional may enjoy a considerable degree of job autonomy, s/he will be expected to display a special level of devotion to the tasks undertaken.

These key characteristics provide us with an ideal-type of professionalism. In previous work, one of the authors defined a professional as 'a member of the workforce with a relatively high status and strong position in the labour market flowing from a special degree of expertise, commitment, autonomy and capacity for self-regulation, which in turn reflects a particular education and formal training' (Webb and Fisher, 2003). By implication, 'professionalization' refers to an institutional process by which professionals become more central to an organization (in our case, a political party organization). By contrast, traditional party bureaucrats will have less status, expertise, job autonomy or capacity to regulate their own activities, and are less likely to have been through a special formal education. Given that their status and rewards will usually be lower, moreover, they are less likely to be expected to demonstrate a special devotion to duty. This calls to mind work conducted more than three decades ago by Kornberg and colleagues on party workers in North America, where they described the prevalence of an amateur ethos, lack of career prospects, low prestige and pay, poor commitment and a lack of any professional reference group among party workers; this syndrome would seem poles apart from our notion of a political professional (Kornberg *et al.*, 1970).

Notwithstanding the foregoing discussion, it is notable how often people use terms such as 'professionalism' and 'professionalization' in a rather less rigorous sense than we have adumbrated here. More colloquial usage seems to imply that professionalization can consist simply of an enhanced degree of workplace effectiveness flowing from a greater sense of commitment or devotion to work-related duties among employees. This may well go hand in hand with the introduction of new working procedures designed to facilitate greater effectiveness. This 'soft' notion of professionalization contains some elements from our pure ideal-type (commitment and effectiveness), but lacks the classic elements of specialist training, expertise, autonomy and self-regulation. A rare study of professionalism among staff in a contemporary central party office reveals that, while professionalization in the classic ideal-typical sense has partial relevance, professionalization in the soft sense seems to have become far more diffuse throughout the party apparatus (Webb and Fisher, 2003).

It should be noted that, in respect of most parliamentary democracies, there are obvious limits to the professionalization of party employees in terms of the specialist ideal-type. There is a major institutional and systemic constraint at work which helps explain why there are likely to be far fewer autonomous, self-regulating professionals working for parties in these countries than in the USA. In America, the candidate-centred nature of politics is such that an extensive profession of political consultancy has emerged which conforms closely to the ideal-type; in most parliamentary democracies political life remains more party-centred, notwithstanding the encroachment of personality politics, and there is unlikely to be the same scope for such a large autonomous body of political professionals. Thus, although congressional candidates in the USA are assisted by their parties, they are largely free to direct their own election campaigns; in doing so, they hire professional consultants. By contrast, there is far less sense of separate personal campaigns being fought in each constituency in most parliamentary systems, as the major parties coordinate national electioneering efforts to a greater extent. That is, campaigns are more genuinely *party* campaigns. Such an approach requires the professional services of relatively few consultants at the centre, and this limited demand cannot sustain a large professional corpus of independent, self-certifying and self-regulating political consultants.

This is not to say that there is no scope for professionals, however, and indeed, we have seen them becoming far more important in certain spheres of party work for some years now, most obviously in respect of opinion pollsters, advertising consultants and related fields of political marketing and media presentation, but also in newer fields such as fundraising (Webb and Fisher, 2003). Even so, only a minority of party employees could be deemed 'professional', unless we accept a less demanding definition of the term. A more flexible yet still meaningful definition of 'professionalism' might suggest that, in a party context, a professional is someone who has been educated to degree level, and/or has a formal vocational qualification, and who has achieved relevant specialization through on-the-job experience and training. This places primary emphasis on the elements of expertise, though it says little directly of factors such as autonomy, commitment and mobility (though these things are likely to be frequent corollaries of expertise). This approach would certainly result in the impression of far more widespread professionalization of parties.

Note, too, that professionalization is a process which can be directly facilitated by the party

itself to some extent. That is, an organization intent on developing a professional body of personnel can take responsibility for effecting this by engaging with programmes of staff development and training. Such activities might include paying for staff to take courses and qualifications provided externally (for instance, in accountancy) or the direct in-house provision of training in relevant skills; for example, parties might provide training for local organizers or agents, on activities such as canvassing, getting out the vote, call-handling, dealing with local party finances, and so on. Indeed, there is a lengthy tradition of this kind of specialist professional recruitment and development in some parties (Frasure and Kornberg, 1975; Braggins, 1999; Webb and Fisher, 2003).

In summary, we may surmise that detailed comparative empirical study of party employees is unlikely to find that professionalization now suffuses every aspect of most parties' working practices: not all employees will display each of the core characteristics of the ideal-type professional – expertise, job autonomy, commitment, vocational identification, a code of professional ethics and membership of a professional body which regulates its members. Nevertheless, it is plausible to suppose that a more flexibly defined notion of professionalism applies widely. That is, where training, expertise and commitment are manifest, we might reasonably suppose that we have identified 'professionals in pursuit of political outcomes' (Romzek and Utter, 1997: 1263).

If so, then the dominant perception of contemporary political science in this respect – that 'professionalization' is a relatively narrowly defined process which flows from the growing reliance on external communications and marketing professionals – will have to be revised in favour of the view that professionalization is somewhat more diffuse than this, embracing many within parties' regular bureaucracies. This then raises questions as to how far such a development has been deliberately engineered by party managers, and what factors might have motivated such a development. To what extent would it reflect deliberate strategic choice, and to what extent would it flow inevitably from broader trends in education and employment in advanced industrial societies? Moreover, what are the implications for political parties? To be 'more professional' may be positive from the point of bureaucratic rationality, but does it carry any implications for the purposive or ideological complexion of the party? Typically, professionalism is associated with the recruitment of people with special skills on a 'meritocratic' basis. But are such individuals driven more by self-interested career goals than by ideological commitment? Farrell *et al*. (2001: 22) have recently described the growing prevalence within Western European party organizations of a 'revolving door philosophy' toward their staff: 'specialists are employed for particular services, and once the task is complete the employee is (and should be) dispensable'. Given the mobility of professionals and the possibility that electoralist party organizations adopt a highly instrumental attitude towards some of them, it would hardly be surprising to discover that they were motivated less by ideological conviction than by personal professional goals. Little research has been done on this to date, though there have been some rare exceptions over the years (Wright, 1967; Fisher and Webb, 2003).

THE LITERATURE ON PARTY EMPLOYEES

Party employees and the mass party

Now that we have established a clear sense of what 'professionalism' consists of in the context of party politics, we are in a position to survey the literature, such as it is. The role of paid party officials first received attention in the literature on political parties in the era in which European political systems were democratized (the late 19th and early 20th centuries). Perhaps the best-known example is provided by Robert Michels' celebrated study of the 'oligarchical tendencies' of mass parties. His frequently rehearsed argument proposed that salaried party officials constituted 'expert leaders' with specialist technical training in the business of running and organizing a political party. 'It is by very necessity that a simple employee becomes a "leader", acquiring a freedom of action that he ought not to possess. The chief then becomes accustomed to dispatch important business on his own responsibility, and to decide various questions relating to the life of the party without making any attempt to consult the rank and file. It is obvious that democratic control thus undergoes a progressive diminution, and is ultimately reduced to an infinitesimal minimum' (Michels, 2001: 27). Through a comparative study of various socialist parties (especially the German Social Democrats), he demonstrated his argument that these party professionals held a place of great importance within the organization.

An innovatory feature of the mass party, when it first emerged, was that it constituted an authentically national organization. That is, while the classic cadre party was essentially a loose alliance of parliamentarians, each with his own power base in a particular locale, the mass party consisted of a multiplicity of local branches of an integrated national structure. This 'socialist invention' (Duverger, 1954) spawned imitators on the political right, which had to adapt by developing new forms of local and national organization. It is not surprising, therefore, to find that party scholars during this period sometimes adopted a local focus, studying the development of local branches and of the role that paid officials played within them.

Studies of the early stages of national and local party organization in the era of democratization are as likely to be the work of historians as of political scientists. Certainly this is true in respect of work on the role of famous 19th-century local party officials in Britain such as F.R. Bonham of the Conservatives or Joseph Parks of the Liberals (Gash, 1953; Jennings, 1961). The structure and life of local party organizations, and the role of officials within them, were subsequently described and analysed in a number of studies (McKenzie, 1955; Rose, 1963, 1974; Bealey *et al*., 1965; Leonard, 1965; Butler and Pinto-Duschinsky, 1970; Pinto-Duschinsky, 1972; Wilson, 1973; Frasure and Kornberg, 1974, 1975). The core questions addressed by these studies concerned the social background, functions, training and effectiveness of party officials. In North America, equivalent research, in structurally quite different organizational settings, focused on similar themes, including the recruitment patterns, socialization, training and participation of party officials (Bowman and Boynton, 1966a, 1966b; Ippolito and Bowman, 1969; Kornberg *et al*., 1969, 1970, 1973, 1979). Essentially the same questions, plus the ideological orientations of officials, feature in studies of continental European parties (Wright, 1967; Sani, 1972). It also should be noted that the apparatchiks of Europe's (former) communist parties have often attracted analysis (Marijinen, 1996; Harasymiw, 1996).

Party personnel and the party of electoral contestation

We have remarked how Duverger referred to the mass party as a 'socialist invention'. Social democratic and labour parties were founded primarily as agents of social integration and group representation for the newly enfranchised masses during the era in which Western European politics was democratized. During this time they devised and pursued ideological programmes which were driven by social group interests, and they sought to capture the loyal political support of these groups, perhaps even to 'encapsulate' them in a network of interconnected social, economic and political organizations (Wellhofer, 1979). But for 40 years now, commentators have been describing the transformation of Western political parties away from the classic mass party model into something inherently less concerned with the functions of mass integration or the articulation of specific social group interests. Since Otto Kirchheimer (1966) major parties have generally been regarded as motivated primarily by vote-winning and office-seeking goals, a change which requires, *inter alia*, the downgrading of narrow group ties and softening of class ideologies in favour of broadly aggregative programmatic appeals. This conception of party change lies at the heart of Kirchheimer's own model of the 'catch-all' party, but is equally central to later conceptions which have added further layers of analysis, such as Angelo Panebianco's 'electoral-professional' party (1988), and Katz and Mair's 'cartel party' (1995). As a form of shorthand, we refer to all of these ideal-types under the banner of 'parties of electoral contestation', or simply 'electoralist parties'.

The single most notable feature of the literature on the paid personnel of such parties is that it has focused overwhelmingly on the role of professional consultants with specialist technical expertise. Primarily, this expertise lies in the field of political marketing and communication – opinion polling, public relations, advertising, journalism and film-making. The closest heuristic ideal-type is the 'electoral-professional party' – an organization primarily motivated by electoral rather than ideological or expressive imperatives and characterized, *inter alia*, by the pre-eminence of the leadership and the centrality of professionals within the party organization (Panebianco, 1988: 264).

However, while the importance of certain kinds of professional consultants such as pollsters, advertisers and marketing experts has often been empirically demonstrated (Hughes and Wintour, 1990; Bowler and Farrell, 1992; Webb, 1992; Scammell, 1995; Kavanagh, 1995; Swanson and Mancini, 1996; Farrell and Webb, 2000; Medvic, 2001; Herrnson, 2000; Farrell *et al.*, 2001; Lees-Marshment, 2001), the notion of 'professionalization' has rarely if ever been considered to extend beyond this in the context of

contemporary party politics. This points us to an issue which has been overlooked in the literature on party employees. While there is an emerging literature on professionals and consultants who parties hire to help them in the business of marketing, campaigning and communication (see Dulio, Chapter 28, this volume), there is a need for wider research on other kinds of party staff. Specifically, political scientists need to engage with questions such as: how 'professional' are party employees, and in what senses are they professional? Are professionals different from other types of party staff in terms of their social and political profiles and motivations? If so, what does this imply for political parties? What roles do the professionals play within parties? What issues of accountability and regulation do they give rise to? These issues should be added to the pre-existing concerns of political scientists working in the area (on the recruitment, socialization, training and activities of paid employees), all of which retain their intellectual validity in the contemporary context.

Having established a sense of the broad historical development of research on party professionals, it is useful to reflect on the literature in terms of more thematic analysis. Specifically, what are the features of the work which has been conducted on the three categories of party political professional whom we earlier identified?

Payroll professionals within party organizations

Perhaps the most prominent theme of research on payroll party professionals has been its quantitative focus. Thus, Farrell and Webb (2000: 117) have reviewed data on trends in paid staffing across nine Western European countries to show that the majority experienced increasing numbers of paid staff between 1960 and 1990, especially in their central offices and parliamentary organizations. However, at the subnational level things were rather different; only a minority of parties showed net growth across time, and some (notably the main British parties) experienced quite dramatic local staff wastage. Staffing trends in the US context are considerably more erratic, especially at the national level (Cotter and Bibby, 1980; Herrnson, 1988; Goldman, 1990; Kolodny, 1998). With fixed election times, staffing levels tend to be high during election years and low during 'off' years. However, there is some evidence of a trend at the subnational level: levels of staffing in both election years and 'off' years are on the rise, though admittedly there have been few systematic studies of state party staffing and none in recent years (Gibson *et al.*, 1983). As we will show below, American parties have increased their reliance on paid professionals, but they have done this more by hiring former employees as independent contractors than by employing permanent employees.

The growing reliance of modern parties on paid professional staff is well demonstrated by the example of the British Labour Party (Webb and Fisher, 2003). In 1964 there was one Labour Party employee for every 2786 individual members, whereas by 1998 there was one employee for every 1231 members, a net change of 56 per cent in the staff–membership ratio. The change in this ratio is even more pronounced if we narrow the focus to the real locus of staff growth, the central (extra-parliamentary) party organization; in 1964 there was one central party employee for every 16,602 individual members, but by 1998 there was one for every 2263 members, a change of 86 per cent. Even allowing for the vagaries of measuring party membership accurately, there is no doubt that there has been a substitution over time of paid for voluntary labour. We can be confident, given the overall trends in party resourcing across advanced industrial democracies, that the British Labour Party is not atypical in this respect.

This, then, seems to point to the growing centrality of paid professional staff members within party organizations across Western Europe. Moreover, although the data are less comprehensive, there is growing evidence to suggest that parties in post-communist Eastern Europe are much the same. That is, few – outside the communist successor parties themselves – have large memberships, but many have quickly developed their professional staff establishments to run the central party organizations, especially in respect of the management of election campaigns, and often on the back of state funding (Kitschelt, 1992; Kopecký, 1995; Lewis, 1994; Lewis and Gortat, 1995; Perkins, 1996; Mair, 1997; Szczerbiak, 1999, 2001, 2003; van Biezen, 2000; Olson, 1998; van Biezen and Kopecký, 2003). Essentially the same point could be made in respect of some of the parties in the recently emerging democracies of Latin America (Angell *et al.*, 1992).

Professional political consultants

The discussion of political marketers or consultants has recently become quite rich. Some studies seek to identify these individuals (Farrell *et al.*, 2001; Johnson, 2001; Thurber and Nelson, 2000) while others seek to put their role in the electoral process in context (Kolodny and Logan, 1998; Dulio, 2004). Significant surveys of the consulting industry were conducted in 1999 and 2003 by the Center for Congressional and Presidential Studies at American University under the direction of James A. Thurber and Candice J. Nelson. These surveys found that consultants tended to have been party employees at an earlier point in their career, believed their party experience to be important in the conduct of their professional activities, and saw their role as complementary to the parties (Thurber, 2000; Kolodny and Logan, 1998). Kolodny (2000) likewise found, in a survey of political party executive directors at the state level, that party officials considered many consultants to be employees in another form – that is, rather than work on the payroll, consultants could be retained as needed for defined projects, which was preferable to retaining large numbers of less trained staff. This body of research clearly points in the direction of regarding professional consultants as a category of party employee – their retention substitutes for hiring additional staff in party central office, while previous party employment is a significant factor in the likelihood of their being awarded the party work. However, others working in this area see the hiring of paid professionals as being done at the expense of party infrastructure (Sabato, 1981; Blumenthal, 1982; Shea, 1996; Nimmo, 2001; Plasser, 2001). Most of these studies rely on anecdote rather than on (admittedly difficult to obtain) systematic data sets. Indeed, as the profession is still poorly institutionalized, there are no professional organizations or official channels to identify the core of professionals doing party work under this rubric. While collecting data in the US case is difficult, internationally it is virtually impossible (though note the exceptional effort of Farrell and Bowler, 2000).

'Party' professionals on the public payroll

Beginning in the 1970s, political scientists began to look closely at the work being carried out by individuals paid by the government in support positions for elected officials. In the US context, Salisbury and Shepsle (1981) declared that a congressional office was an 'enterprise' devoted to the manufacture and maintenance of an important commodity: a positive image of the elected official. While the staff were not engaged in explicitly partisan work (and due to legal restrictions in place for 60 years, must never engage in political work as part of their regular job duties), their dutiful reminders of the goodwill of their bosses when interacting with their constituents meet an implied partisan need. Likewise, Monroe's (2001) study of staff in the constituency offices of elected officials finds that these individuals continually interact with the district staff of other elected officials sharing the same geographic constituency (in the US case, that means a member of the US Congress, a state legislature, or a local county or city municipality) on official government matters. This interaction creates close networks that in many ways resemble old-style political machines in that they consist of an elite which is knowledgeable about a wide variety of issues, individuals and political opportunities.

In similar vein, the executive offices contain a number of paid staff who should be considered party staff members. In the US example, there are many offices within the executive branch whose employees perform communications functions that must be seen as party-supporting. These include the White House Press Office, the Office of Communications, speech writers, media relations specialists, and a host of other positions whose occupants are expected to 'spin' the day's events in a favourable light for the president (Grossman and Kumar, 1981; Maltese, 1994). Kathryn Dunn Tenpas (2000) explains how political consultants were hired by incumbent presidents to provide advice not only on electoral strategy but also on policy formulation.

In a European context, it is common for some jobs which are, in effect, partisan to be at the expense of the public purse. This has been most obviously so in countries with pronounced traditions of clientelism or patronage, notably the 'partitocratic' cases of Italy and Belgium (Bardi, 2002; Deschouwer, 2002). But almost everywhere some jobs are funded in this way. In the UK, for instance, the governing party is able to rely on a growing number of 'special advisers' appointed at the taxpayer's expense to help ministers. While most Cabinet members are able to appoint up to two such advisers, there is no limit on the number that the prime minister can appoint to assist in the work of the Downing Street machine. Tony Blair has exploited this possibility in an historically remarkable way. When his predecessor John Major left Downing Street in June 1997, he enjoyed the support of just eight special advisers; by 1998/9, Blair had increased this to 25, a level which has remained broadly constant since then. By 2003, some 27 advisers out of 81 who worked across all central government ministries in Whitehall were located in the Prime Minister's Office (Heffernan and Webb, 2005). This development has become increasingly controversial, raising various issues about the autonomy, role and accountability of such advisers. As a result, the independent Committee on Standards in Public Life (2003) issued a report in which it recommended clear legal definitions of the precise roles and lines of accountability concerning special advisers, a move later backed by the Public Administration Select Committee (2004) of the House of Commons. At the time of writing, however, it seems that the present incumbent of 10 Downing Street is unwilling to embrace all of the strictures proposed by these bodies. In any case, it is clear from our perspective that professionals such as these, though notionally 'civil servants', are in effect party servants.

CONCLUSIONS

This brief review demonstrates that the work of party professionals has long been of interest to political scientists. The most typical academic approach has in effect been from the perspective of political sociology. Thus, interest in the social profile, recruitment, socialization, training and activity of employees has been the core motivation of scholarship. These issues remain pertinent today – perhaps ever more so in these times of political consultancy, state-funded party politics, and electoral professionalism. The professional staff of party politics lie at, or close to, the nexus of political power across the democratic world. In view of this, there would seem to be a strong case for more wide-ranging, systematic comparative research into their backgrounds and roles. But the key questions, while embracing the concerns of political sociology, could and should go further: Who are the professionals of party politics? What do they do? What implications do they carry for party theory and democratic theory? In what ways, if at all, can and should they be held accountable? Is there any need to establish a regulatory framework within which they should operate?

We would argue that questions such as these provide a significant agenda for research, though we are under no illusions as to the ease with which it can be conducted. Quite apart from the usual issues of research in general (funding!) and comparative politics in particular (concept stretching and measurement), there is a further potential obstacle in this case: this research depends fundamentally on the willingness of the parties themselves to cooperate in granting access to data and employees. On previous limited experience, this is not a problem to be taken lightly, especially in so far as gathering survey data on party employees is concerned (Webb and Fisher, 2003). On the other hand, individual party employees are often willing to grant interviews and to discuss matters with a striking degree of candour, which suggests that qualitative methods may hold the key to unlocking this particular research programme.

REFERENCES

Angell, A., d'Alva Kinzo, M. and Urbaneja, D. (1992) 'Latin America', in D. Butler and A. Ranney (eds), *Electioneering*. Oxford: Clarendon Press.

Bardi, L. (2002) 'Italian parties: Change and functionality', in P.D. Webb, D.M. Farrell and I. Holliday (eds), *Political Parties in Advanced Industrial Democracies*. Oxford: Oxford University Press.

Bealey, F., Blondel, J. and McCann, W.P. (1965) *Constituency Politics: A Study of Newcastle under Lyme*. London: Faber.

Biezen, I. van (2000) 'On the internal balance of party power: Party organizations in new democracies', *Party Politics*, 6: 395–417.

Biezen, I. van and Kopecký, P. (2003) 'On the predominance of state money: Reassessing state financing in the new democracies of southern and eastern Europe', in P. Lewis and P. Webb (eds), *Pan-European Perspectives on Party Politics*. Leiden: Brill, pp. 97–126.

Blumenthal, S. (1982) *The Permanent Campaign*. New York: Simon and Shuster.

Bowler, S. and Farrell, D.M. (1992) *Electoral Strategies and Political Marketing*. Basingstoke: Macmillan.

Bowman, L. and Boynton, G.R. (1966a) 'Activities and role definitions of grass roots party officials', *Journal of Politics*, 28: 121–43.

Bowman, L. and Boynton, G.R. (1966b) 'Recruitment patterns among local party officials: A model and some preliminary findings in selected locales', *American Political Science Review*, 60: 667–76.

Braggins, J. (1999) 'They're organizers Jim, but not as we knew them …', *Labour Organiser*. London: Labour Party.

Brante, T. (1990) 'Professional types as a strategy of analysis', in M. Burrange and R. Torstendahl (eds), *Professionals in Theory and History: Rethinking the Study of the Professions*. Newbury Park, CA, and London: Sage Publications.

Butler, D. and Pinto-Duschinsky, M. (1970) *The British General Election of 1970*. London: Macmillan.

Butler, D. and Rose, R. (1960) *The British General Election of 1959*. London: Macmillan.

Carty, R. Kenneth and Blake, Donald E. (1999) 'The adoption of membership votes for choosing party leaders: The experience of Canadian parties', *Party Politics*, 5: 211–24.

Committee on Standards in Public Life (2003) *Defining the Boundaries within the Executive: Ministers, Special Advisers and the Permanent Civil Service, Ninth Report*, Cm. 5775 London: The Stationery Office.

Cotter, C.P. and Bibby, J.F. (1980) 'Institutional development and the thesis of party decline', *Political Science Quarterly*, 95: 1–27.

Deschouwer, K. (2002) 'The colour purple: The end of predictable politics in the Low Countries', in P.D. Webb, D.M. Farrell and I. Holliday (eds), *Political Parties in Advanced Industrial Democracies*. Oxford: Oxford University Press.

Dulio, D.A. (2004) *For Better or Worse? How Political Consultants are Changing Elections in the United States*. Albany: State University of New York Press.

Duverger, M. (1954) *Political Parties: Their Organisation and Activity in the Modern State*. London: Methuen.

Farrell, D.M. and Bowler, S. (2000) 'The internationalization of campaign consultancy', in J.A. Thurber and C.J. Nelson (eds), *Campaign Warriors: Political Consultants in Elections*. Washington, DC: Brookings Institution Press, pp. 153–74.

Farrell, D.M. and Webb, P. (2000) 'Political parties as campaign organizations' in R.J. Dalton and M.P. Wattenberg (eds), *Parties without Partisans: Political Change in Advanced Industrial Democracies*. Oxford: Oxford Univerity Press, pp. 102–28.

Farrell, D.M., Kolodny, R. and Medvic, S. (2001) 'Parties and campaign professionals in the digital age: Political consultants in the US and their counterparts overseas', *Harvard International Journal of Press/Politics*, 6: 11–30.

Fisher, J.T. and Webb, P.D. (2003) 'Political participation: The vocational motivations of Labour Party employees', *British Journal of Politics and International Relations*, 5: 166–87.

Frasure, R. and Kornberg, A. (1974) 'A note on constituency agents and conflict in Labour Parties', *Political Quarterly*, XLV: 489–92.

Frasure, R. and Kornberg, A. (1975) 'Constituency agents and British party politics', *British Journal of Political Science*, 5: 459–76.

Gash, N. (1953) *Politics in the Age of Peel*. London: Longman.

Gibson, J.L., Cotter, C.P., Bibby, J.F. and Huckshorn, R.J. (1983) 'Assessing party organizational strength', *American Journal of Political Science*, 27: 193–222.

Goldman, R.M. (1990) *The National Party Chairmen and Committees: Factionalism at the Top.* Armonk, NY: M.E. Sharpe.

Grossman, M.B. and Kumar, M.J. (1981) *Portraying the President: The White House and the News Media.* Baltimore, MD: Johns Hopkins University Press.

Harasymiw, B. (1996) *Soviet Communist Party Officials: A Study in Organizational Roles and Change.* Commack, NY: Nova Science Publishers.

Heffernan, R. and Webb, P.D. (2005) 'Prime ministerial presidentialization in the UK' in T. Poguntke and P.D. Webb (eds), *The Presidentialization of Democracy in Advanced Industrial Societies: A Study in Comparative Politics.* Oxford: Oxford University Press.

Herrnson, P.S. (1988) *Party Campaigning in the 1980s.* Cambridge, MA: Harvard University Press.

Herrnson, P.S. (2000) 'Hired guns and house races: campaign professionals in house races', in J.A. Thurber and C.A. Nelson (eds), *Campaign Warriors: Political Consultants in Elections.* Washington, DC: Brookings Institution Press.

Hughes, C. and Wintour, P. (1990) *Labour Rebuilt: The New Model Party.* London: Fourth Estate.

Ippolito, D.S. and Bowman, L. (1969) 'Goals and activities of party officials in a suburban community', *Western Political Quarterly*, 22: 572–80.

Jalonick, M.C. (2002/03) 'Preparing for a career in politics, public affairs,' *Campaigns and Elections*, December/January: 79–82.

Jennings, I. (1961) *Party Politics: The Growth of Parties.* Cambridge: Cambridge University Press.

Johnson, D.W. (2001) *No Place for Amateurs: How Political Consultants are Reshaping American Democracy.* London: Routledge.

Katz, R.S. and Mair, P. (1992) *Party Organizations: A Data Handbook on Party Organizations in Western Democracies, 1969–90.* London: Sage Publications.

Katz, R.S. and Mair, P. (1995) 'Changing models of party organization and party democracy: The emergence of the cartel party', *Party Politics*, 1: 5–28.

Katz, R.S., Mair, P. *et al.* (1992) 'The membership of parties in European democracies, 1960–1990' *European Journal of Political Research*, 22: 329–45.

Kavanagh, D. (1995) *Election Campaigning: The New Marketing of Politics.* Oxford: Basil Blackwell.

Kirchheimer, O. (1966) 'The transformation of West European party systems', in J. LaPalombara and M. Weiner (eds), *Political Parties and Political Development.* Princeton, NJ: Princeton University Press, pp. 177–200.

Kitschelt, H. (1992) 'The formation of party systems in East-Central Europe', *Politics and Society*, 20: 7–50.

Kolodny, R. (1998) *Pursuing Majorities: Congressional Campaign Committees in American Politics.* Norman: University of Oklahoma Press.

Kolodny, R. (2000) 'Electoral partnerships: political consultants and political parties', in J.A. Thurber and C.A. Nelson (eds), *Campaign Warriors: Political Consultants in Elections.* Washington, DC: Brookings Institution Press.

Kolodny, R. and Dulio, D. (2002) 'Political party adaptation in US congressional campaigns: Why political parties use coordinated expenditures to hire political consultants', *Party Politics*, 9: 729–46.

Kolodny R. and Logan, A. (1998) 'Political consultants and the extension of party goals', *PS: Political Science and Politics*, 31: 155–9.

Kopecký, P. (1995) 'Developing party organizations in East-Central Europe: What type of party is likely to emerge?', *Party Politics*, 1: 515–34.

Kornberg, A., Smith, J. and Bromley, D. (1969) 'Some differences in the political socialization patterns of Canadian and American party officials: A preliminary report', *Canadian Journal of Political Science*, 2: 64–88.

Kornberg, A., Smith, J. and Clarke, H.D. (1970) *Semicareers in Political Work: The Dilemma of Party Organizations.* Thousand Oaks, CA: Sage.

Kornberg, A., Smith, J. and Clarke, H.D. (1979) *Citizen Politicians – Canada: Party Officials in a Democratic Society.* Durham, NC: Carolina Academic Press.

Kornberg, A., Smith, J., Clarke, M.-J. and Clarke, H.D. (1973) 'Participation in local party organizations in the US and Canada', *American Journal of Political Science*, 17: 23–47.

Lees-Marshment, J. (2001) *Political Marketing and British Political Parties: The Party's Just Begun.* Manchester: Manchester University Press.

Leonard, R.L. (1965) 'Who are Labour's agents?' *New Society* (15 July).

Lewis, P.G. (1994) 'Political institutionalisation and party development in post-communist Poland', *Europe-Asia Studies*, 46: 779–800.

Lewis, P.G. and Gortat, R. (1995) 'Models of party development and questions of state dependence in Poland', *Party Politics*, 1: 599–608.

Mair, P. (1997) *Party System Change.* Oxford: Oxford University Press.

Mair, P. and van Biezen, I. (2001) 'Party membership in twenty European democracies, 1980–2000', *Party Politics*, 7: 5–22.

Maltese, J.A. (1994) *Spin Control: The White House Office of Communications and the Management of Presidential News.* Chapel Hill: University of North Carolina Press.

Marijinen, A. (1996) 'Entrée en politique et professionalisation d'appareil: Les écoles centrales de cadres du parti communiste Italien, 1945–50', *Politix*, 35: 89–108.

McKenzie, R.T. (1955) *Political Parties.* London: Heinemann.

Medvic, S. (2001) *Political Consultants in U.S. Congressional Elections.* Columbus: Ohio State University Press.

Michels, R. (2001) *Political Parties: A Sociological Study of the Oligarchical Tendencies of Modern Democracy.*

Kitchener, Ontario: Batoche Books. First published in 1915.

Monroe, J.P. (2001) *The Political Party Matrix: The Persistence of Organization*. Albany: State University of New York Press.

Nelson, C.J., Dulio, D.A. and Medvic, S.K. (2002) *Shades of Gray: Perspectives on Campaign Ethics*. Washington, DC: Brookings Institution Press.

Nimmo, D. (2001) *The Political Persuaders: The Techniques of Modern Election Campaigns*, 2nd edn. New Brunswick, NJ: Transaction Publishers.

Olson, D. (1998) 'Party formation and party system consolidation in new democracies in Central Europe', *Political Studies*, 46: 432–65.

Panebianco, A. (1988) *Political Parties: Organisation and Power*. Cambridge: Cambridge University Press.

Perkins, D. (1996) 'Structure and choice: The role of organizations, patronage and the media in party formation', *Party Politics*, 2: 355–75.

Pinto-Duschinsky, M. (1972) 'Central Office and "power" in the Conservative Party', *Political Studies*, XX: 1–16.

Plasser, F. (2001) 'Parties' diminishing relevance for campaign professionals', *Harvard International Journal of Press/Politics*, 6: 44–59.

Public Administration Select Committee (2004) *Draft Civil Service Bill*. London: The Stationery Office.

Raelin, J.A. (1991) *The Clash of Cultures: Managers Managing Professionals*. Cambridge, MA: Harvard Business School Press.

Romzek, B.S. and Utter, J.A. (1997) 'Congressional legislative staff: Political professionals or clerks?', *American Journal of Political Science*, 41: 1251–79.

Rose, R. (1963) 'The professionals of politics', *New Society*, XLV: 10–12.

Rose, R. (1974) *The Problem of Party Government*. London: Macmillan Press.

Sabato, L.J. (1981) *The Rise of Political Consultants: New Ways of Winning Elections*. New York: Basic Books.

Salisbury, R. and Shepsle, K. (1981) 'US Congressman as enterprise', *Legislative Studies Quarterly*, 6: 559–76.

Sani, G. (1972) 'La professionalizzazione dei dirigenti di partiti Italiani', *Rivista Italiana di Scienza Politica*, 2: 303–33.

Scammell, M. (1995) *Designer Politics: How Elections Are Won*. Basingstoke: Macmillan.

Scarrow, S.E. (1996) *Parties and Their Members*. Oxford: Oxford University Press.

Seyd, P. and Whiteley, P. (1992) *Labour's Grassroots: The Politics of Party Membership*. Oxford: Clarendon Press.

Shea, D. (1996) *Campaign Craft: The Strategies, Tactics, and Art of Political Campaign Management*. Westport, CT: Praeger.

Swanson, D. and Mancini, P. (1996) *Politics, Media, and Modern Democracy*. Westport, CT: Praeger.

Szczerbiak, A. (1999) 'Testing party models in East-Central Europe: Local party organization in post-communist Poland', *Party Politics*, 5: 525–37.

Szczerbiak, A. (2001) *Poles Together? The Emergence and Development of Political Parties in post-Communist Poland*. Budapest: Central European University Press.

Szczerbiak, A. (2003) 'Cartelisation in post-communist politics: State party funding in post-1989 Poland', in P. Lewis and P.Webb (eds), *Pan-European Perspectives on Party Politics*. Leiden: Brill, pp. 127–50.

Tenpas, Kathryn Dunn (2000) 'The American presidency: surviving and thriving amidst the permanent campaign', in Norman Ornstein and Thomas Mann (eds), *The Permanent Campaign and its Future*. Washington, DC: Brookings Institution Press, pp. 108–33.

Thurber, J.A. (2000) *Battle for Congress: Consultants, Candidates and Voters*. Washington, DC: Congressional Quarterly Press.

Thurber, J.A. and Nelson, C. (eds) (2000) *Campaign Warriors: The Role of Political Consultants in Elections*. Washington, DC: Congressional Quarterly Press.

Webb, P.D. (1992) 'Election campaigning, organisational transformation and the professionalisation of the British Labour Party', *European Journal of Political Research*, 21: 267–88.

Webb, P.D. and Fisher, J. (2003) 'Professionalism and the Millbank tendency: The political sociology of New Labour's employees', *Politics*, 23: 10–20.

Wellhofer, E.S. (1979) 'Strategies for party organization and voter mobilization: Britain, Norway and Argentina', *Comparative Political Studies*, 12: 169–204.

Whiteley, P., Seyd P. and Richardson, J. (1994) *True Blues: The Politics of Conservative Party Membership*. Oxford: Clarendon Press.

Widfeldt, A. (1999) *Linking Parties with People? Party Membership in Sweden 1960–1997*. Aldershot: Ashgate.

Wilensky, H.L. (1959) *Intellectuals in Labor Unions*. New York: Free Press.

Wilson, D.J. (1973) 'Constituency party autonomy and central party control', *Party Studies*, XXI: 167–74.

Wright, W.E. (1967) 'Ideological-pragmatic orientations of West Berlin local party officials', *Midwest Journal of Political Science*, 11: 381–402.

28

PARTY CRASHERS? THE RELATIONSHIP BETWEEN POLITICAL CONSULTANTS AND POLITICAL PARTIES

David A. Dulio

The role that professional political consultants play in US elections today has become a puzzle that academics and journalists alike have recently started to piece together. 'Hitmen' ('Political Advertising's Hitmen', 1980), 'image merchants' (Hiebert *et al.*, 1971), and 'issue choosers' (O'Shaughnessey, 1990) are among the litany of disparaging labels that have been used to describe political consultants. The conventional wisdom holds consultants responsible for many of the problems that seem to plague modern elections in the United States, including the high cost of elections, the negative nature of campaigns, and the lack of issue-based debates between candidates.[1]

Arguably the most important indictment levied against professional consultants is that they are partially, if not fully, responsible for the decline of the parties' role in electioneering. What these characterizations gloss over, however, is that political consultants have important ties to political parties that relate to how parties conduct elections and strive to meet their goals. To some extent both consultants and parties serve the same master – they are responsible for helping to elect candidates to office.

How these two important electoral actors relate to each other in the current state of elections is the focus of this chapter. First, the development of professional consultants in elections is briefly considered *vis-à-vis* political parties. Next, two competing interpretations of the consultant–party relationship are outlined – are consultants and parties allies or adversaries?

The consequences of this relationship are also briefly considered in the following context: Is this relationship beneficial to modern political parties or does it hinder their progress to their main goal (i.e., gaining and holding seats in government)? The close and important relationship that professional political consultants have with parties does not stop on election day, however. To that end, I illustrate how consultants and parties are linked during the non-campaign season – when elected officials are supposed to be tending to the 'people's business'. The chapter concludes with a look into the future of this relationship, with a special focus on how recent campaign reforms may affect both actors.

THE SIMULTANEOUS DEVELOPMENT OF CONSULTANTS AND PARTIES

The question of how professional consultants relate to political parties today can only be fully answered by looking back at how each has changed through the history of electioneering. Indeed, the two actors have an interrelated past.

The fact that political parties once dominated campaigning in the United States has been well documented (Sorauf, 1980; Crotty, 1984; Ware, 1985; Herrnson, 1988, 2000, 2004; Aldrich, 1995; Maisel and Buckley, 2005). The 'party-centered' electoral system was one in which parties controlled just about every aspect of campaigning from candidate recruitment and voter contact to message development and get-out-the-vote operations (Sorauf, 1980; Herrnson, 1988; Keefe, 1998; Ware, 1985). However, after their 'golden age' parties lost much of this electioneering prowess. Many critics of campaign consultants lay a good deal of the blame for this loss of power at the feet of political professionals. These sentiments are nicely summarized by Larry Sabato (1981: 286) who argues that consultants 'along with their electoral wares, have played a moderate part in ... the continuing decline of party organization ... [and have] abetted the slide, sometimes with malice aforethought. ... The services provided by consultants, their new campaign technologies, have undoubtedly supplanted party activities and influence'.

Political consultants, however, are not to blame for the decline in electoral power political parties have suffered. Other factors surrounding, and changes to, the electioneering landscape weakened parties before consultants ever appeared on the scene. Consider, for instance, the Robert La Follette-led Progressive Movement of the early 1900s. The reforms instituted by the Progressives, such as the introduction of the direct primary, the elimination of patronage (with the Pendleton Act), and registration and ballot reforms, all served to weaken parties. These reforms (and others like them) meant that the party no longer controlled candidate recruitment, it was easier for voters to split their tickets, and rather than the party being the monopolizing force behind campaigns, candidates were now encouraged 'to develop their own campaign organization[s]' (Herrnson, 1988: 26).

In addition, the electorate to which candidates and parties were making their electoral pitches was undergoing drastic changes. In the early 1930s roughly 75 million people were eligible to vote in presidential elections; by the late 1960s that number had risen to over 120 million. 'Party organizations, designed for campaigning to a limited electorate on a personal basis, were not an efficient means for reaching [the] ... growing pool of voters' (Salmore and Salmore, 1989: 41). This meant that candidates had to find another way to communicate with potential voters. At the same time, the United States was in the middle of a push toward a media-dominated society; that candidates looked to television as a communication tool was inevitable.

As a result of these changes, the shift from a style of campaigning that was party-based and focused on personal contact to one that was more candidate-centered and mass-communication-based began to appear. In other words, campaigns moved away from being labor-intensive – stressing 'canvassing and public meetings' – to being capital-intensive – characterized by a high 'degree of campaign professionalism' (Farrell, 1996: 168–9). It soon became clear that candidates and parties could no longer campaign in the way that they once had. Candidates needed help; they demanded assistance with the electioneering tools of the day. With this, candidates turned to those with the requisite skills – professional political consultants.

That said, however, professional political consultants did not become major players in federal elections until the mid-1900s.[2] It was not until this time that there was broad use of consultants by candidates in congressional and presidential elections. One estimate of consultant activity during the 1950s found only 41 public relations firms offering complete campaign management services; by 1972 that number had only risen to 100 (Rosenbloom, 1973). Further, as of the 1978 campaign, only 9 percent of all candidates for the US House of Representatives were found to have hired a campaign manager, while only 39 percent hired a media consultant (Goldenberg and Traugott, 1984). Indeed, '[f]rom its start ... , the campaign management industry grew rather slowly. A few companies went in and out of business shortly after World War II, and some public relations and advertising firms started accepting political clients in the late 1940s. [It was not until] the 1950s [that] there was a slow but steady expansion' (Rosenbloom, 1973: 50).

Therefore, the ascendance of professional political consultants was a reaction to rather than a cause of political party decline. Political consultants stepped in to fill a void that was left when parties were weakened and when they could not help all their candidates as effectively as they once did (Dulio, 2004).

Parties have continually modified their behavior according to the electoral context of the day. Both parties saw their electoral power wane in the wake of the reforms and changes of the late 1800s and early 1900s to a point where they were described as being 'peripheral' to the campaign (Herrnson, 1988). After a period of weakness parties underwent what some have called a resurgence (Kayden and Mahe, 1985) or a revitalization (Aldrich, 1995) when they began to regain some of their influence in elections by offering technologically sophisticated services to their candidates (e.g., help with fundraising and television production) and by re-dedicating themselves to raising money. Parties were now the 'intermediary' (Herrnson, 1988) through which campaigns were waged and were 'in service' to their candidates (Aldrich, 1995). The ascendance of political consultants to an important role in US elections is simply another adjustment both major parties have made over time.

Further evidence of this can be seen in more recent adaptations of political parties in the United States – the Democratic National Committee (DNC), and the Republican National Committee (RNC), as well as their campaign committees, the Democratic Congressional Campaign Committee (DCCC), the Democratic Senatorial Campaign Committee (DSCC), the National Republican Congressional Committee (NRCC), and the National Republican Senatorial Committee (NRSC). Through these arms of their headquarters, parties actually began to work with political consultants and seek out their help.

For instance, during the 1970s and 1980s both parties saw their fundraising coffers swell to their highest levels ever (Herrnson, 1988; White and Shea, 2004); however, they could not have accomplished this without the help of private political consultants who were not formally connected to the party. From their newly built headquarters on Capitol Hill, and at the direction of their chairmen, both the Republicans and Democrats launched direct-mail fundraising campaigns. However, they each looked to professional consultants for help; RNC Chair William Brock looked to consultant Richard Viguerie, and DNC Chair Charles Mannatt hired the firm of Carver, Matthews, Smith, and Company. Additionally, Republicans hired pollsters such as Robert Teeter, Richard Wirthlin, and Stanley Finkelstein to conduct survey research for the party and their candidates; Democrats looked to survey research consultants such as Peter Hart and Matt Reese for similar help (Herrnson, 1988). What is more, even at the time that parties were said to be 'in service' to their candidates and providing the services that were in great demand by candidates of the day – such as help with the production of television commercials – political consultants were not far removed from the process. Both parties constructed state-of-the-art television production facilities in their headquarters and offered their candidates assistance in making television ads for their campaigns. However, while in their use of the Harriman media center Democratic candidates looking for help could use the sophisticated facilities at hand and take advantage of the technical expertise of the staff (e.g., lighting and editing), the candidates had to 'provide their own ideas and copy … [and]

hire their own advertising experts and script writers' (Herrnson, 1988: 62). Even when parties were in control of the services that were going to candidates, consultants played a major role in the provision of those services (Dulio, 2004).

FRIENDS OR FOES?

There are different interpretations of the historical relationship between political consultants and political parties. Some claim consultants pounced on parties when they were weak so as to make a quick buck, see the development of consultants as a threat to parties, and claim that consultants have pushed parties further into decline (Sabato, 1981). Others, however, see the relationship between consultants and parties as more benign, where parties can even reap benefits from a partnership with consultants (Kolodny and Logan, 1998; Kolodny and Dulio, 2003; Dulio and Thurber, 2003; Dulio, 2004; Dulio and Nelson, 2005).

The question of whether consultants and parties are friends or foes is an important one for a number of reasons, the most compelling of which may be that, in one view, American elections, and politics in general, are critically in need of political parties (Schattschneider, 1942) – if parties are not healthy, neither is democracy. The relationship between the two actors, however, is difficult to get at. The role of professional consultants in American politics has not been as deeply studied as other questions in political science.[3] There are at least two explanations for the lack of information on consultants in the academic literature. First, there is a genuine lack of data about consultants generally and what it is they do during a campaign. And second, political science has tended to focus on behavioral questions (e.g., why voters vote the way they do) which means that 'our attention has moved away from the electoral institutions in which consultants now play such a commanding role … [and that] we play less attention to the dynamics of electoral institutions and the processes of campaigning' (Petracca, 1989: 11). Many of those studies that have been done on consultants, however, contain little or no systematic exploration of consultants' place in campaigns. Most of these accounts are descriptive in nature and their conclusions are based mainly on speculation and assertion from anecdotal evidence.

For similar reasons, explorations of the consultant–party relationship are even less numerous. However, as noted above, those who have examined the connection between consultants and parties fall into two general camps – they see them as either allies or adversaries. The allies versus adversaries hypothesis was first put forth by Robin Kolodny and Angela Logan (1998). 'According to the adversarial view, consultants do not compliment parties and act as little more than advertising agencies' (Kolodny and Logan, 1998: 155). However, under the allied view, 'consultants do for candidates what parties simply cannot', and 'consultants value party goals' and 'are not anathemic to a party's mission, i.e., to elect like-minded candidates who will promote a certain agenda through the implementation of public policy' (Kolodny and Logan, 1998: 155).

The claims of those who subscribe to the consultants-and-parties-as-adversaries view interpret the development of the two actors over time as one of competition in a zero-sum game (i.e., if one actor's power increases the other's must decrease) and conclude that because parties are weaker than they were before, the rise of the consultants must be the cause. The specific criticisms of those in this camp include that consultants have wrestled control of campaigns away from candidates (Petracca, 1989), homogenized American politics, increased the costs of campaigns, and narrowed the focus of elections (Sabato, 1981). In their view, consultants control every aspect of a campaign from the issues that the candidate will run on to how the candidate will communicate with the public. In other words, consultants now do what the party machines of yesteryear once did.

Those who see consultants and parties as adversaries also interpret the ascendance of consultants and modern electioneering techniques as a displacement of parties in their role as the main players in elections. In other words, consultants appeared and pushed parties to the side of the campaigning process (Sabato, 1981). Consultants' use of mass-media communications techniques and other technically sophisticated tactics to communicate with voters was perceived as 'creating a campaign climate where individual candidates [took] the voting public's focus away from party platforms' (Kolodny and Logan, 1998: 155).

The clearest, and arguably the most convincing, argument made by those who see consultants as detrimental to parties is that consultants, rather than parties, are the individuals candidates now turn to for campaign advice and the necessary help during their campaigns (Sabato, 1981). As noted above, political parties once

monopolized electioneering. Even when the first blows to strict party control of a candidate's campaign were felt – when individual campaign managers headed campaigns – the party was not too far removed – these first 'managers' were closely tied to the party (Medvic, 1997; Ware, 1985). However, once the use of consultants took hold as an acceptable electioneering practice, candidates had less need for the operatives who worked at the local, state, or national party headquarters. Specifically, when candidates needed help in defining their campaign theme and message (i.e., the rationale for their campaign and the reason(s) why someone should vote for them), a strategy for communicating that message, and the delivery vehicles to carry that message (e.g., radio and television commercials, and direct mailings) they turned not to the party but to consultants who, for example, knew how to conduct survey research with scientific samples, and how to produce television ads. Sabato (1981: 286) sums this up nicely when he argues that 'The services provided by consultants, their new campaign technologies, have undoubtedly supplanted party activities and influences'. It should also be noted that Sabato does not rely on any systematic analysis of consultant or party behavior or conduct; rather, his arguments, and those of most others who subscribe to the adversarial view, are based on assertion and conjecture.

Those who take the opposite view and see consultants and parties as allies interpret the adaptation of both actors over time in a different manner. To them, the ascent of consultants is not a detriment to parties; instead, they argue, consultants stepped in to fill an electioneering void that was created by changes in the context of campaigning (i.e., the increased numbers of eligible voters and the reforms instituted in the late 1800s and early 1900s). For instance, as Paul S. Herrnson (1988: 26) notes, after the reforms initiated by the Progressives were put in place, instead of the party headquarters being the place candidates went for advice, candidates were encouraged 'to develop their own campaign organization[s]' which included more of a dependence on non-party funding and other politicos to help raise the requisite funds. Moreover, when candidates began to turn to more technologically advanced ways of communicating with voters, '[p]olitical parties could not offer the specific information and persuasion techniques these candidates believed were vital to their chances for victory' (Kolodny, 2000a: 111). The party operatives of that time simply did not have the technical skills that were needed to conduct survey research or produce a television spot (Dulio, 2004). In other words, 'consultants do for candidates what the political parties simply cannot: they offer targeted technical assistance and personalized advice' (Kolodny and Logan, 1998: 155).

The consultants-and-parties-as-allies perspective is also bolstered by evidence which shows the close working relationship the two actors have had over time. Consultants would be nowhere without clients – without them they would have no revenue. Aside from the obvious avenues consultants have for acquiring clients – they apply for campaign jobs with candidates they would like to work for, or candidates seek out the consultant – consultants may be put in touch with a potential client by the party itself (Sabato, 1981). Both parties have a long-standing practice of recommending consultants to their candidates (Herrnson, 1988). Moreover, political parties have looked to consultants for help when they have needed it over the years. For instance, as noted above, when the parties were in the midst of their 'revitalization', political consultants were not too far removed from some of the major activities – consultants helped the parties build their donor bases in their fundraising initiatives of the 1970s and consultants were brought in to assist in the provision of services such as survey research and television production to candidates.

Further, recent evidence shows that parties themselves hire consultants to provide certain services that they either no longer provide or are not as well equipped to provide as consultants. In a recent survey, professional political consultants were asked about their relationship with the national party organizations.[4] Part of the battery of questions included an assessment of who was better suited to provide certain services during a campaign. The consultants who were part of the survey (505 from across the USA) were clear in indicating that certain services were better supplied by the individuals in their industry than by those at the party headquarters. However, they also said that there were some services that were better handled by the party as opposed to outside consultants, indicating a partnership in electioneering services. The division of labor that appears from the survey responses is basically between tasks that are technically sophisticated and require a good deal of personal candidate attention and those that require large amounts of staff and time (Dulio, 2004). In general, consultants reported that they are

better at providing the services that are centered on message creation and delivery – supplying strategic advice, producing television ads and direct mail pieces, and conducting public opinion polling – while the parties are a better source for services such as fundraising, opposition research, and get-out-the-vote operations (Dulio, 2004). The consultants in the survey also replied that they welcomed these same services from the party when they were working on a competitive campaign, further illustrating that consultants see parties as a partner in their efforts.

Interestingly, operatives at the parties' headquarters agree with the consultants' assessment and add further evidence to the allied view. In a separate study and survey, senior state party operatives and national party officials were asked the same battery of questions. Political party staffers agreed that professional consultants have supplanted parties in providing campaign services that are focused on message creation and delivery (Dulio and Thurber, 2003; Dulio and Nelson, 2005; see also Kolodny, 2000a). Furthermore, 70 percent of these staffers said that consultants provide services that political parties are incapable of providing. In other words, 'consultants are viewed by the parties as being complements to the parties' overall strategy, not competitors to it' (Kolodny, 2000a: 129). Moreover, those currently in charge at the state parties' headquarters across the USA reported that they would continue the long-standing practice of recommending consultants to candidates running in their state in the 2002 election cycle; 60 and 73 percent of those interviewed at the national party headquarters reported that they would recommend consultants to candidates running for House and Senate, respectively.[5]

The proponents of the allied view also cite evidence of political party behavior to illustrate that they work in concert with consultants today. For instance, the same study of party officials referenced above found that nearly 90 percent of party organizations planned to hire a pollster during the 2002 election cycle; over 80 percent reported they would hire a direct mail specialist and nearly 70 percent said they would hire a media consultant.[6] Additionally, while both parties looked to consultants for help in providing services to candidates during their 'rejuvenation' of the late 1970s and 1980s, modern parties look almost exclusively to consultants to produce the services they help provide to their candidates. One manifestation of this phenomenon is in how political parties spend their resources.

One study of a certain type of spending available to parties – coordinated expenditures[7] – helps illustrate this point. During the 1998 and 2000 election cycles, both major US parties spent roughly $30 and $25 million dollars respectively in coordinated funds for services to help their candidates. These dollars 'typically are for campaign services that a Hill committee or some other party organization gives to a candidate or purchases from a political consultant on the candidate's behalf' (Herrnson, 2000: 93). In 1998 over 90 percent of all coordinated money was paid to outside political consultants and in 2000 nearly 94 percent of these dollars went to consultants for services such as television ad production (as well as the air time for those ads), direct mail campaigns, and public opinion polls (Kolodny and Dulio, 2003).

The importance of these figures, say those who argue consultants and parties are allies, is found mainly in what they purchase. As noted above, both national parties used to offer assistance with technical campaign services such as television production to their candidates from their headquarters in Washington, DC. The new arrangement parties have with consultants does not include producing or providing these same services. Rather, they pay political consultants to provide them. Parties have moved from being a 'party in service' (Aldrich, 1995) to a new era of party service: the party-as-billpayer (Dulio, 2004). Evidence is found in decisions the parties have made about how best to get their candidates the services they need. Take the production of television ads, for example. Before 1986, 'About 25 to 30 candidates [got] the full treatment' from the NRCC in terms of help with their media campaign, which included meetings with the campaign pollster, the party field director, and one of the party's writers (Herrnson, 1988: 63). However, in the late 1990s the Republicans stopped using their media center and began to farm out to professional consultants the production of those television ads they were going to have a hand in. According to one former party staffer, this decision was an easy one to make: 'in order to retool [the media center], almost every election cycle, maybe two at the most, you are going to have to raise anywhere from $3 million to $5 million to $10 million to redo that and it is not worth it … For $10 million you can fund a lot of candidates' (quoted in Dulio, 2004). Democrats have also almost completely done away with using their media center to help candidates and instead look to consultants to provide the same services they once

offered (Kolodny and Dulio, 2003). Parties have continued to adapt, realizing that it is simply more efficient to pay consultants to do the same work (Dulio, 2004).

Finally, the consultants-and-parties-as-allies view is buttressed by data illustrating that political party headquarters have been a major training ground for today's political consultants. In three different studies roughly half of the consultants operating today were found to have an employment history with the party organization at one level or another (Kolodny and Logan, 1998; Thurber et al., 2000; Dulio, 2004). What is more, those consultants who have a history of working for the party often return to work for the party in their capacity as outside consultants. Over three-quarters of consultants who had once worked for a party organization had a party organization as a client after they had left the party to go into business for themselves; this is in comparison to only 44 percent of those with no past party experience (Kolodny and Logan, 1998). This has led some to argue that consultants who once worked for the party never really leave the party and remain part of a 'party network', or an extended party organization (Kolodny, 2000b; Schwartz, 1990).

This brings us to the question of whether the appearance and subsequent expansion of consultant influence in US elections has been beneficial or detrimental to political parties. The allies versus adversaries question gives us a brief look at the answer to this question. Obviously, those who are in the consultants-and-parties-as-adversaries camp argue that consultants' presence has hindered parties at a significant cost (i.e., parties have been taken out of the electoral game), and those who argue the allied view is correct see the relationship in more optimistic terms.

Many of those approaching the relationship from the adversarial perspective focus on aspects of the party organization that are not as strong as they once used to be for evidence that consultants are detrimental to the parties' existence. One piece of evidence of this kind would be that parties no longer control campaigns from top to bottom; parties no longer select the candidates to run in an election and they no longer help direct the campaign in terms of the issues (i.e., the message) on which the candidate will run. Those in the allied camp argue that the loss of party power in this area had already occurred and that the consultants' role helps parties achieve their goals.

Those who approach the relationship from the allied perspective cite the fact that consultants, and the services they offer, allow parties to focus on their main goal – winning and holding seats in government (Kolodny, 1998). In addition, those in this camp point to a more efficient party organization in existence today. Modern party organizations that 'subcontract' work to political consultants can supply more services to more candidates under this model than if they tried to provide all the services to their candidates (Kolodny, 2000b; Dulio, 2004). As one state party executive director put it, 'Consultants help us in areas that we either lack the professional experience or the hardware to accomplish our goals' (quoted in Kolodny, 2000a: 127). This is beneficial in that parties are able to focus on the aspects of electioneering that they perform best so as to help more of their candidates win elections – raising money, for example. By focusing on raising the funds that are required for campaigning in the modern context and looking to various consultants to produce the services that candidates demand, parties are serving more candidates in a better manner than they would be if they tried to produce every election service in house. The parties have realized this, and one example is found in their use of their media centers. When the party tried to provide media services to their candidates, they could only provide a 'full blown media campaign' to 25–30 candidates (Herrnson, 1988: 63). Many more candidates got help in the 1998 and 2000 election cycles when the parties paid consultants with coordinated dollars. Moreover, this way the candidates get a more complete service in that it is more personalized and deals specifically with their campaign in their district or state.

The answer to the question of whether political parties and political consultants are friends or foes is a lengthy one that is broader than the scope of this chapter. Would parties like to be more involved in they way their candidates run their races? Undoubtedly. However, the current context of elections is not conducive to that kind of party–candidate relationship. As the electoral landscape has changed so have electoral actors (parties, candidates, voters, etc.). Indeed, the relationship between consultants and parties is simply another reaction to the changing electoral context. Parties have continually adapted over time; from monopolizing electoral politics (Sorauf, 1980) and campaigning to being 'peripheral' actors in campaigns (Herrnson, 1988) to being 'intermediaries' and 'in service' to their candidates (Herrnson, 1988; Aldrich, 1995). 'Rather than seeing the proliferation of consultants as a sign

of party decline', argues Robin Kolodny (2000b: 20) 'their presence is actually a next step in party evolution'. The use of, and reliance on, consultants is simply another adaptation that parties have made so they can remain focused on their main goals. Indeed, 'consultant use by parties and candidates is a rational response' to the changing electoral environment (Kolodny, 2000b: 20).

BEYOND ELECTION DAY

While professional political consultants obviously have close ties with candidates and political parties during campaign season, the two are also linked well beyond election day. The term 'permanent campaign', first coined by the then journalist Sidney Blumenthal (1982), elicits images of candidates in constant campaign mode between elections. This is not an inaccurate picture, and as Anthony King (1997) describes, candidates are often 'running scared'. Because candidates run for office so frequently in the United States (the best example are members of the House of Representatives who are elected every two years, but may face a primary challenge less than 18 months after being sworn into office) they need to continually engage in the activities that they would if they were in the middle of a campaign. While some candidates retain the services of political consultants between campaigns (pollsters and fundraisers are the ones most likely to be active between campaigns), parties and consultants also work together between campaigns to shape policy alternatives and to work toward the passage of government initiatives.

Another aspect of the 'permanent campaign' that has received less attention than the image of candidates constantly campaigning is the continual quest for public support around ideas for public policy solutions. To this end, elected officials in Congress and the White House look to outside political consultants for help. As president, Bill Clinton took the idea of the permanent campaign to new heights. He was criticized for being 'poll-driven' and relying on public sentiment to govern. Who was it that provided Clinton with the poll data that he supposedly looked to? The same individuals who would have provided the data if he were campaigning – professional political consultants. While presidents have supplemented their advisory network with political consultants since the Nixon administration, it was the Clinton White House that raised the bar in terms of looking to outside consultants for advice (Tenpas, 2000). At different times during his presidency, Clinton sought advice from campaign consultants including Dick Morris, Paul Begala, James Carville, Mandy Grunwald, Stan Greenberg, Bob Squire, Hank Sheinkopf, Marcus Penczer and Mark Penn (Tenpas, 2000).

The relevant piece of the puzzle here is that when presidents have looked to political consultants for advice, they have *not* been on the official White House payroll. Instead, their paychecks have been signed by someone at the national party headquarters.[8] With regard to exactly how much the DNC or the RNC has spent on consultants who served as advisors to presidents, Tenpas (2000) provides some startling estimates. For instance, by combing through reports filed with the Federal Election Commission, Tenpas (2000: 115) estimates that the RNC spent roughly $2 million annually on polling for President Reagan, and that the DNC spent $1 million and $2.5 million on pollsters for presidents Carter and Clinton, respectively. Moreover, Tenpas (2000: 114) shows that '[i]n 1995 the salaries for President Clinton's fifteen most senior White House staff members totaled $1.8 million' but that '[d]uring that same year, the DNC spent over $2.9 million' on seven consulting firms that conducted polling and helped design media campaigns for the White House. Parties in Congress also look to pollsters and other consultants for assistance, whether it be to provide reelection advice or to help shape and sell policy solutions (Jacobs and Shapiro, 2000; Lipinski, 2001; Dulio and Medvic, 2003).

Whether President Clinton was 'poll-driven' when he made decisions about the policy direction his administration would take is beyond the scope of this chapter. What is important here is that elected public officials and political parties have begun to use techniques and tactics in their governing strategies that are normally associated with campaigning. Polling has obviously been used by both parties in the White House and in Congress, but it goes beyond this one service to earned media (i.e., press relations) and paid media (i.e., television advertisements) strategies. For instance, the Clinton administration broke new ground in this respect when it ran television ads during the budget battle of 1996 to try to build public support for the President's plan. And it is the professional political consultant who provides these services. After all, as Dick Morris (1999: 75) has said, 'Each day is election day in modern America'.

THE FUTURE OF THE PARTY–CONSULTANT RELATIONSHIP

Political consultants and political parties currently have a strong and close relationship, as indicated by the fact that parties have hired consultants in the past to provide services for their own purposes and for those services demanded by their clients, and that parties recommend consultants to their candidates looking for a specific kind of campaign assistance. For a number of reasons, this relationship is only likely to get stronger in the future. First, consultants are here to stay as a means of providing technically sophisticated electioneering services. Given the candidate-centered nature of campaigns in the United States, candidates will continue to build their own campaign organizations that will be dominated by outside professionals. More importantly, however, the consultant–party relationship will very likely be affected in the future by the rules and regulations concerning how campaigns are run, and specifically the rules about how money can be raised and spent in campaigns.

The regulations pertaining to how money can be raised and spent in campaigns have impacted consultants' influence in elections in the past. The Federal Election Campaign Act (FECA) and its amendments in the early 1970s helped lay the groundwork for consultant influence at that time. 'These reforms set the stage for [political action committees] to become the major organized financiers of election campaigns and drove candidates to rely upon professional campaign consultants to design direct mail fund-raising operations' rather than look to the party for fundraising help (Herrnson, 1988: 28). The party–consultants relationship will also likely be affected by more recent reforms relating to how money is raised and spent in elections.

The Bipartisan Campaign Reform Act of 2002 (BCRA) will dictate how candidates and parties raise money in campaigns well into the future.[9] The most important aspect of the law for the purposes of this discussion is that which makes raising and spending of so-called soft money by the national political parties illegal. These were dollars that could be raised and spent in an unlimited manner and did not fall under the disclosure requirements of the previous regulations. The relevant point here is that the BCRA takes away a major financing avenue that both major parties used very effectively in the election cycles of the late 1990s and early 2000s. In short, political parties have one less avenue for providing funds to their candidates.

In light of this, the consultant–party relationship may get even closer in election cycles to come.[10] The BCRA may have created another void in party power that consultants can step in to fill. While the BCRA makes it illegal for national parties to raise and spend soft money, the law says nothing about non-profit or 'issue groups' doing the same. As some observers have already noticed, these groups 'could not be run by party committees or candidates, but could be run by their former employees' (Dart, 2002: 14A). And as outlined above, large numbers of current political consultants are former party employees. Furthermore, the rules written by the Federal Election Commission interpret the law to apply to the 'agents' of parties and candidates as well as the parties and candidates themselves. However, political consultants are not included in the regulations as being agents of parties or candidates. This may create a scenario where political consultants establish new fundraising entities that can raise and spend the dollars that political parties now may not. Incidents of this kind of behavior are already evident. During the 2004 election cycle, the first to be governed by the new BCRA rules, several new funding and electioneering entities were launched to make up for the loss of soft money at the national party headquarters. These new groups were typically established as so-called 527 groups – groups that, because of their tax status, do not have to register or report to the Federal Election Commission, and are able to raise and spend money in unlimited and unregulated amounts. Many of the most prominent 527 groups in 2004, such as America Coming Together, The Media Fund, and Progress for America, had political consultants, former party operatives, or campaign advisors leading them. Thus, the same kind of changing environment that brought consultants and parties close together in the past may be appearing in the current electoral context and may mean an even more intimate relationship between these two important electoral actors.

In short, the relationship that political parties have with political consultants is an important one that can be beneficial to both actors. Political consultants can cultivate and maintain a business relationship and political parties are assisted in working toward their main goal of capturing and holding seats in government. This relationship is one that has been driven not by consultants trying to push parties to the side of the campaigning process, but by changes in the electioneering landscape that created a demand for the services they provide. In turn, consultants filled a void that was left by parties (Dulio, 2004). 'If candidates and issue groups believed that their electoral needs could be entirely served by political parties, then there would be no market for a bevy of outside … political consultants' (Kolodny, 2000a: 110).

Today, consultants and parties both see a division of labor in terms of the electioneering services that are best performed by each actor. They both describe outside consultants as being better equipped to provide the services geared toward message creation and delivery (e.g., television ad production, direct mail creation, and polling) and parties as better equipped to provide services that require more staff time and resources (e.g., get-out-the-vote, opposition research, and fundraising). There is also evidence of a 'party network' in that party headquarters are a major training ground for private consultants, and that parties look to these consultants for help more than those who have no prior history with the party organization.

The party–consultant connection does not end on election day, however. Consultants are looked to for campaign advice between campaigns as part of the obvious aspect of the 'permanent campaign', but they are also turned to by the White House and the parties in Congress for advice in battles over policy alternatives, as evidenced by the presence of numerous campaign consultants in the Clinton White House. President George W. Bush has only continued this trend. This important relationship is only likely to get stronger in the wake of recent campaign reforms that may create a changing electoral environment that once again produces a void that consultants will step in to fill. No matter what the future campaign landscape brings, however, political consultants will inevitably be part of the picture, working alongside parties to help them win elections.

NOTES

1. For examples of these types of criticisms, see Sabato (1981), Petracca (1989), and O'Shaughnessey (1990); for a less pessimistic perspective on consultants' role see, for instance, Dulio (2004) or Nelson *et al.* (2002).
2. There is debate as to who the first true political consultants were in the United States. Many cite two individuals from California, Clem Whitaker and Leone Baxter, who started the firm Campaigns Inc. in 1933, as the first consultants.

However, a better characterization of this duo is as precursors to the modern consultants who wage campaigns with technological sophistication and are specialists in certain areas of electioneering. See Dulio (2004) and Medvic (1997) for more on this point.

3. The topic of consultants was not dealt with specifically until 1981 and Larry Sabato's important work in *The Rise of Political Consultants*. There were exceptions, of course, including Kelly (1956), Nimmo (1970), Agranoff (1972), and Rosenbloom (1973), but it was Sabato's work that took on the question of consultants' role head-on. Recently, however, there has been more attention paid to consultants in the academic literature (for a review of this literature, see Dulio, 2004).

4. This particular survey was conducted as part of the 'Improving Campaign Conduct' project at American University's Center for Congressional and Presidential Studies which was funded by The Pew Charitable Trusts. See Dulio (2004: Appendices 1 and 2) for a detailed description of the survey.

5. These data are taken from a survey of party staffers also conducted for the 'Improving Campaign Conduct' project. See the full survey report, entitled 'The role of political consultants: 2002 election cycle' at www.american.edu/ccps, see also Dulio and Nelson (2005). A copy of the survey can be obtained from the author. See Kolodny (2000a) for data from another survey of party elites that confirms this evidence.

6. Again, see Kolodny (2000a) for further evidence of this phenomenon.

7. Coordinated expenditures are monies that political parties may spend on behalf of their candidates in coordination with those candidates' campaigns. These dollars are different from both soft money – unlimited and unregulated dollars that parties could spend for 'party building' purposes (raising and spending these dollars at the federal level was made illegal by the Bipartisan Campaign Reform Act of 2002) – and independent expenditures – also unlimited and unregulated funds parties can spend in a race but without coordination with the candidate's campaign. See Kolodny (1998) for a detailed account of coordinated expenditures and their role in party strategy.

8. President George W. Bush did not follow his predecessors in this regard. He hired long-time direct mail consultant Karl Rove to be his chief political advisor in the White House and put him on the government payroll.

9. A full account of the BCRA and what its likely effects on electioneering will be is beyond the scope of this chapter. For a more complete discussion, see Malbin (2003).

10. See Dulio (2004) for a more detailed discussion on this point.

REFERENCES

Agranoff, Robert (1972) *The New Style in Election Campaigns*. Boston: Holbrook Press.

Aldrich, John A. (1995) *Why Parties: The Origin and Transformation of Political Parties in America*. Chicago: University of Chicago Press.

Blumenthal, Sidney (1982) *The Permanent Campaign*, revised edn. New York: Simon and Schuster.

Crotty, William J. (1984) *American Parties in Decline*. Boston: Little, Brown.

Dart, Bob. (2002) 'Campaign finance limits not a cure-all', *Atlanta Journal and Constitution*, February 15: 1A, 14A.

Dulio, David A. (2004) *For Better or Worse? How Professional Political Consultants Are Changing Elections in the United States*. Albany: State University of New York Press.

Dulio, David A. and Medvic, Stephen K. (2003) 'The permanent campaign in Congress: Understanding congressional communication tactics'. Paper presented at the Annual Meeting of the Midwest Political Science Association, Chicago, April 3–6.

Dulio, David A. and Nelson, Candice J. (2005) *Vital Signs: Perspectives on the Health of American Campaigning*. Washington, DC: Brookings Institution Press.

Dulio, David A. and Thurber, James A. (2003) 'The symbiotic relationship between political parties and political consultants: Partners past, present and future', in John C. Green and Rick Farmer (eds), *The State of the Parties: The Changing Role of Contemporary American Parties*, 4th edn. Lanham, MD: Rowman and Littlefield.

Farrell, David M. (1996) 'Campaign strategies and tactics', in Lawrence LeDuc, Richard G. Niemi and Pippa Norris (eds), *Comparing Democracies: Elections and Voting in Global Perspective*. Thousand Oaks, CA: Sage Publications.

Goldenberg, Edie N. and Traugott, Michael W. (1984) *Campaigning for Congress*. Washington, DC: CQ Press.

Herrnson, Paul S. (1988) *Party Campaigning in the 1980s*. Cambridge, MA: Harvard University Press.

Herrnson, Paul S. (1992) 'Campaign professionalism and fundraising in congressional elections', *Journal of Politics*, 53: 859–70.

Herrnson, Paul S. (2000) *Congressional Elections: Campaigning at Home and in Washington*, 3rd edn. Washington, DC: CQ Press.

Herrnson, Paul S. (2004) *Congressional Elections: Campaigning at Home and in Washington*, 4th edn. Washington, DC: CQ Press.

Hiebert, Ray, Jones, Robert, Lotito, Ernest and Lorenz, John (eds) (1971) *The Political Image Merchants: Strategies in the New Politics*. Washington, DC: Acropolis Books.

Jacobs, Lawrence R. and Shapiro, Robert Y. (2000) *Politicians Don't Pander: Political Manipulation and the Loss of Democratic Responsiveness.* Chicago: University of Chicago Press.

Kayden, Xandra, and Mahe, Eddie, Jr. (1985) *The Party Goes On: The Persistence of the Two-Party System in the United States.* New York: Basic Books.

Keefe, William J. (1998) *Parties, Politics and Public Policy in America,* 8th edn. Washington, DC: CQ Press.

Kelley, Stanley (1956) *Professional Public Relations and Political Power.* Baltimore, MD: Johns Hopkins University Press.

King, Anthony (1997) *Running Scared: Why America's Politicians Campaign Too Much and Govern Too Little.* New York: Free Press.

Kolodny, Robin (1998) *Pursuing Majorities: Congressional Campaign Committees and American Politics.* Norman: University of Oklahoma Press.

Kolodny, Robin (2000a) 'Electoral partnerships: Political consultants and political parties', in James A. Thurber and Candice J. Nelson (eds), *Campaign Warriors: Political Consultants in Elections.* Washington, DC: Brookings Institution Press.

Kolodny, Robin (2000b) 'Towards a theory of political party institutional capacity, or why parties need political consultants to remain viable in the C20th'. Paper presented at the Elections Public Opinion and Parties working group of the Political Studies Association, Edinburgh, September 8–10.

Kolodny, Robin, and Dulio, David A. (2003) 'Political party adaptation in US congressional campaigns: Why political parties use coordinated expenditures to hire political consultants', *Party Politics,* 9: 729–46.

Kolodny, Robin, and Logan, Angela (1998) 'Political consultants and the extension of party goals', *PS: Political Science and Politics,* 31: 155–9.

Lipinski, Daniel (2001) 'The outside game: Congressional communication and party strategy', in Roderick P. Hart and Daron R. Shaw (eds), *Communication in U.S. Elections: New Agendas.* Lanham, MD: Rowman and Littlefield.

Maisel, L. Sandy and Buckley, Kara Z. (2005) *Parties and Elections in America: The Electoral Process,* 4th edn. Latham, MD: Rowman Littlefield.

Malbin, Michael (ed.) (2003) *Life after Reform: When the Bipartisan Campaign Reform Act Meets Politics.* Lanham, MD: Rowman Littlefield.

Medvic, Stephen K. (1997) 'Is there a spin doctor in the house? The impact of political consultants in congressional campaigns'. Ph.D. dissertation, Purdue University.

Morris, Dick (1999) *The New Prince: Machiavelli Updated for the Twenty-First Century.* Los Angeles: Renaissance Books.

Nelson, Candice J., Medvic, Stephen K. and Dulio, David A. (2002) 'Political consultants: hired guns or gatekeepers of democracy', in Candice J. Nelson, David A. Dulio and Stephen K. Medvic (eds), *Shades of Gray: Perspectives on Campaign Ethics.* Washington, DC: Brookings Institution Press.

O'Shaughnessey, Nicholas J. (1990) *The Phenomenon of Political Marketing.* New York: St. Martin's Press.

Petracca, Mark P. (1989) 'Political consultants and democratic governance', *PS: Political Science and Politics,* 22: 11–14.

'Political Advertising's Hitmen' (1980) *Marketing & Media Directions,* 15: 59–61, 180–2.

Rosenbloom, David L. (1973) *The Election Men: Professional Campaign Managers and American Democracy.* New York: Quadrangle Books.

Sabato, Larry J. (1981) *The Rise of Political Consultants: New Ways of Winning Elections.* New York: Basic Books.

Salmore, Stephen A., and Salmore, Barbara G. (1985) *Candidates, Parties, and Campaigns: Electoral Politics in America.* Washington, DC: CQ Press.

Schattschneider, E.E. (1942) *Party Government.* New York: Farrar and Rinehart.

Schwartz, Mildred (1990) *The Party Network: The Robust Organization of Illinois Republicans.* Madison: University of Wisconsin Press.

Shea, Dan M. (1996) *Campaign Craft: The Strategies, Tactics, and Art of Political Campaign Management.* Westport, CT: Praeger.

Sorauf, Frank J. (1980) 'Political parties and political action committees: Two life cycles', *Arizona Law Review,* 22: 445–64.

Tenpas, Kathryn Dunn (2000) 'The American presidency: Surviving and thriving amidst the permanent campaign', in Norman Ornstein and Thomas Mann (eds), *The Permanent Campaign and Its Future.* Washington, DC: American Enterprise Institute/ Brookings Institution Press.

Thurber, James A., Nelson, Candice J. and Dulio, David A. (2000) 'Portrait of campaign consultants', in James A. Thurber and Candice J. Nelson (eds), *Campaign Warriors: Political Consultants in Elections.* Washington, DC: Brookings Institution Press.

Ware, Alan (1985) *The Breakdown of Democratic Party Organization, 1940–1980.* New York: Oxford University Press.

White, John Kenneth and Shea, Daniel M. (2004) *New Party Politics: From Jefferson and Hamilton to the Information Age,* 2nd edn. Belmont, CA: Wadsworth.

PART IV

PARTY AND SOCIETY

29

PARTY AND SOCIAL STRUCTURE

Peter M. Siavelis

INTRODUCTION: POLITICAL PARTIES AND SOCIETY

Political parties provide the primary links between society and the state in most contemporary democracies. However, until the turn of the last century political parties were painted in a very negative light, with most analysts portraying them as self-interested factions that interfered with potentially 'purer' forms of representative democracy (Daalder, 1983: 3; Sartori, 1976: 3–12). It was not until after World War II that parties approached near-universal acceptance as necessary, functional, and legitimate democratic actors. However, as democracy becomes the rule rather than the exception world-wide, trust in political parties has eroded. What is more, citizen attachments to parties are on the decline both in advanced industrial democracies and in the developing world. Scholars have pointed to the diminishing importance of parties, suggesting that the citizen–party nexus has been cut (Dalton *et al.*, 1984; Lawson, 1988; Dalton, 1999: 65–6). The cleavages that defined political parties for most of the post-war period are much less relevant. Further, cross-national survey data show decreasing confidence in political parties. While this is part of a more general decline in confidence in political institutions, the low esteem in which parties are held is of special concern given their traditional roles as the main interlocutors between the governed and

those who govern. Has our conception of parties come full circle? Once again, are parties to be considered the oligarchic expressions of self-interested elites that get in the way of governing, or is this new attitude towards parties simply a result of underlying social change, which has transformed the qualitative, yet still essential, roles that parties play?

This chapter asks where the study of society–party connections has been, and where it is going. Underlying this question is the deeper issue of whether parties still perform (or can reassume) the varied functions traditionally ascribed to them in modern democracies, or whether a new interlocutor between citizens and the state outside the traditional party model might be on the horizon. The chapter begins with an analysis of the earliest literature dealing with society–party relations. It analyzes the evolution in our understanding of cleavages, from the generative cleavages that emerged during the foundation of national societies to those rooted in post-industrial value change. In light of the deep changes wrought by the fall of communist systems and the birth of the 'third way', the essay then analyzes work which asks whether there is 'a left left', and, assuming there is, how the left is likely to look in the future. It then explores the literature on so-called new parties, and closes with a discussion of potentially fruitful avenues for future research on society–party connections. The chapter concludes that while parties may be in decline (at least in terms of their traditional roles), the richness of the literature on parties is not, and indeed, there has been a convergence in theoretical work on society–party relations in recent years.

FORMALISM IN THE STUDY OF PARTIES

At the turn of the twentieth century, the study of politics was virtually indistinguishable from that of history. Political science (if it could be described as such) was prescriptive, descriptive and normative. Yet it is no coincidence that it was in the study of parties that political science initiated its long and contentious divorce from history. The work of Michels and Ostrogorski on political parties can arguably be considered some of the first that are distinguishable from the descriptive, historical tradition (see Michels, 1959; Ostrogorski, 1964). Nonetheless, neither hid their disdain for political parties, which were viewed as overt and negative manifestations of social conflict. What is more, even when parties become an object of study, theorists focused principally on party structures and formal organizations (Michels, 1959; Duverger, 1954; Neuman, 1956). While the role of society was implicit in terms of speaking of the functions that political parties performed, or the reality that 'oligargarchies' tended towards the domination of citizens, few early studies explicitly addressed the connection between society and political parties.

Despite the dearth of explicit discussions of the society–party connection in early political science literature, the seeds of the focus and methods used today were planted by important precursors to modern theorists. First, in empirical terms, Daalder traces the roots of the study of the social bases of politics to Hume and his distinction between 'parties of interest vs. parties of principle'. He also notes that, decades before the development of the modern cleavage literature, traditional analyses spoke of party conflict in terms of 'town vs. country, church vs. anticlericals, one estate against another; and later of classes which were thought to be inevitably in conflict with one another' (1983: 16).

SOCIAL CLEAVAGES AND PARTY POLITICS

The modern study of the social origins of parties is rooted in the notion that rather than simple associations of interest, parties emerge organically from deep-seated divisions within society. An important normative shift also set the stage for the more serious study of the social bases of political parties. The late 19th and early 20th century saw an evolution towards a conception of parties as natural and legitimate, especially with movements toward mass suffrage expansion. Transformations in the substantive and methodological bases of political science also underwrote changes in the study of parties. The two world wars, the crisis of democracy in Europe, and particularly the fruits of the Weimar Republic, drove home the reality that the formalistic, institutionally based and normative focus of the discipline failed to capture the essence of politics. Throughout the 1950s deeper questions about the social basis of politics grew out of the behavioral revolution. The advent of survey research provided the tools to better understand complex society–party relations, and to more effectively advance and test arguments connecting parties to social divisions.

While Lipset's early work points out that 'lower income groups vote mainly for the parties of the Left, while the higher income groups vote for parties of the Right' (1960: 223–4) and that '[i]n every democracy conflict among different groups is expressed through political parties which basically represent a democratic translation of class struggle' (1960: 221), it is really later work by Lipset and Rokkan that provides the classic and most complete elaboration of the connection between social cleavages and political parties (Lipset and Rokkan, 1967; Rokkan, 1970, 1975). Based on a comparative study of Western European countries, these scholars argued that processes of early national development and the industrial revolution divided societies, and that the resulting social cleavages became politicized in the form of political parties with the advent of modern democracy. In particular, they point to two successive revolutions during Western Europe's long march to democracy: the national revolution and the industrial revolution. These revolutions prompted four primary lines of cleavage that shaped the development of European party systems: center–periphery, state–church, land–industry, and owner–worker. What is more, they maintained that party manifestations of these cleavages remain relevant after the initial impetus for their formation has disappeared, leading them to their now famous assertion that 'the party systems of the 1960's reflect with few but significant exceptions the cleavage structures of the

1920's' (Lipset and Rokkan, 1967: 50). Early research in large part confirmed Lipset and Rokkan's findings. Rose and Urwin (1969, 1970) found remarkably consistent levels of electoral support for parties born from the cleavages explored by Lipset and Rokkan from the end of World War II to the 1970s.

While the notion that cleavages can be frozen remained an undercurrent in the literature on society–party connections, scholars allowed for variation among party systems based on the particular constellation of cleavages within different countries (including language, ethnicity, race) and whether or not these cleavages were cross-cutting (that is to say, non-reinforcing) or coincident (see Lipset, 1983). In general, cross-cutting cleavages were said to tend toward the formation of parties with more heterogeneous bases, because differences among groups are dampened by multiple loyalties and other social characteristics that individuals share. Dahl (1966: 378) cautioned against a simple application of this theory, arguing that the strength of the cleavage also determines the type of party system that ultimately emerges as cleavages become politicized.

While the literature on crisis and cleavages developed primarily out of the Western European and US experience, these ideas have also been applied to the study of party development in other places. Many early theories of party system development (such as Duverger, 1954) had little application in the developing world. However, Lipset and Rokkan's general contentions regarding the relationship of crisis to party development were quite relevant. LaPalombara and Weiner (1966) underscored that crises of legitimacy, integration, and participation and how they were handled by emerging democracies were determinative in defining the party systems of developing countries. They continued by arguing that these crises are often telescoped, and that their timing and sequencing were central to defining the nature of emerging party systems. While replete with normative preferences for two-party systems and biases tied to notions of 'modernity', this work is one of the first that systematically applies theories developed out of the Western European experience to non-European areas.

Nonetheless, cleavage analysis was not without its critics. Some suggested that the cleavage literature tended toward sociological reductionism by ignoring the multidimensionality of the determinants of citizen–party identification. Others pointed to problems with the definition and measurement of concepts such

as social class and religiosity (Urwin, 1973). Shamir's (1984) time series analysis underscored that Lipset and Rokkan were mistaken to contend that party systems had been frozen in the first place, pointing to volatility during the years on which their study was based. In addition, Mair (1983) convincingly summarized the many studies which showed a good deal of electoral volatility beginning in the 1970s. Others noted that the treatment of political parties as dependent variables in the cleavage literature created two sets of problems. In normative terms, traditional cleavage analysis removed the influence of the voter, by suggesting that the determinants of party support rested solely with voters' characteristics, and underplaying voter agency in electoral choice. In empirical terms, the early cleavage literature overlooked parties as independent variables, whose activities also shaped society (Urwin, 1973: 195). Finally, the cleavage literature, and particularly that which underscored freezing in partisan structures, left theorists with little capacity to explain change. It was precisely party system change that prompted a shift in the study of society–party relations, bringing into question widely held notions about the solidity of well-developed party systems.

Despite these criticisms and problems, cleavage analysis remains at the core of work on party–society relations. Contrary to what its most strident critics would suggest, this literature became quite nuanced as it developed, and has been applied successfully to case studies in new, transitional, and consolidated democracies. Also, the substantial contribution of cleavage analysis is evinced in how its concepts and terminology continue to be used in contemporary studies of democracy. For example, cleavages remain at the heart of Inglehart's (1997) analysis of the materialist and post-materialist dimensions of politics and at the core of Kitschelt's (1994, 1995) work on new parties and party change. Indeed, cleavage analysis is inherently useful because politics in modern societies is fundamentally a struggle between different groups seeking to obtain resources and to promote their values and visions for society. These differences spur conflict, and parties have historically been best equipped to structure debate on these conflicts and to negotiate the terms of debate that lead to public policy decisions.

The language of cleavages has also seeped into other areas of political inquiry beyond the study of party development. Cleavage analysis is central to Arend Lijphart's (1977, 1980) work on consociational government, where cleavages such as religion, class, and language take center-stage. Finally, the tools of cleavage analysis are used in work on democratic transition and consolidation, where scholars have analyzed the salience of democratic/authoritarian and communist/post-communist cleavages (although not in as satisfying detail as they might, as noted below).

Notwithstanding the continued usefulness of the terminology and tools of cleavage analysis, by the mid-1960s it was clear that the widespread assumptions about Western political parties that grew out of it were experiencing fundamental change. First, in the United States, a dramatic increase in the number of independents in the 1960s and 1970s, and the later party realignment of the South, raised questions concerning the durability of the New Deal party system and the cleavages that spawned it. Theorists questioned whether these changes signaled the simple realignment and dealignment of the US party system, or were harbingers of its decomposition. Voters were increasingly independent, faction politics seemed to dominate, and voters lacked the clear identification with the issues that social cleavage analysis would predict (Burnham, 1970, 1975).

Second, from the 1960s Western European party systems were increasing volatile, with the appearance of new parties. Most almost immediately disappeared, but a substantial number survived. However, the diversity of party change across the continent made it difficult for theorists to systematically account for it, suggesting that the core assumptions underlying cleavage analysis and party system freezing were no longer valid. Once again, some noted that the age of the party had perhaps ended, and other modes of interest representation would prevail in post-industrial societies (Lawson and Merkl, 1988b: 3).

Third, growing affluence in the post-war period led theorists to predict an era of consensus politics and an end to ideology. However, the protest movements of the 1960s and 1970s shook up politics, and were accompanied by resurgence in ethnic and regional conflicts that confounded predictions of partisan stability in post-war politics.

Finally, the 1970s and 1980s unexpectedly ushered in a period where survey data and voting behavior showed that traditional assumptions about the connection between social class and party identification had been turned on their heads. The so-called 'new right' emerged as a conservative counterattack against the economic policies of traditional welfare states, but also, and perhaps more importantly, against the 'new left' which had grown out of the social movements of the 1960s. The 'new left' was new in its adoption of an increasingly 'non-economic' social agenda during the 1960s and 1970s in addition to its traditional orientation concerning social class and the preferred role of the state. Abortion, gender equality, gay rights, civil rights and environmentalism increasingly emerged as divisive issues that were more important than the traditional economic and social class cleavages that previously defined party politics. However, not only the salience of these issues, but also the kinds of party alignments they produced within mass electorates, were novel. Middle classes and highly educated professionals were more sympathetic to the social agenda of the new left, while it was blue-collar and lower-class voters who increasingly identified with the counterattack of the new right. As a result of these changes it became increasingly difficult to predict voter choice based on traditional social divisions. Franklin et al. (1992) found strong evidence that the analysis of social cleavages was less and less a useful tool to predict voter choice.

DEMOGRAPHIC SHIFTS, VALUE CHANGE, AND POLITICAL PARTIES

During the 1980s these deep transformations prompted scholars to reassess the connection between social divisions and their party manifestations. While the language of cleavages remained an implicit tool of analysis, a consensus began to develop that the traditional connection between cleavages and parties (and primarily between social class and partisan identification) needed to be reassessed. Scholars began to analyze the sources of partisan change, and the consequences of partisan change in terms of the overall role that parties play in society.

With respect to the sources of change, scholars advanced two major streams of analysis. One viewed changes in partisan identification as a result of post-war demographic shifts (and primarily those produced by post-industrialism), while the other interpreted party transformation as a result of value change. While there is an analytical distinction between these arguments, they are certainly complementary and often overlap in their core assumptions and modes of analysis. Indeed, many tie value change to underlying demographic shifts.

The principal proponents of arguments based on demographic change pointed to widespread affluence and dramatic shifts in the occupational and social structures of advanced industrialized societies to account for change in the Western European and American party systems. They noted that previous analysts (Lipset and Rokkan, 1967; Campbell *et al.*, 1960; Converse, 1976) were correct in underscoring long-term and stable party alignments among the electorate in the first decades following World War II. However, Dalton *et al.* (1984: 8) note that with the growth of affluence '[p]artisan change – rather than partisan stability' became the 'common pattern' in advanced industrial democracies. The result of these changes was a trend toward the decomposition of electoral alignments and the fragmentation of the 'socio-psychological bonds between voters and parties'. As advanced industrialism eroded traditional relationships and community identification, interpersonal connections and institutional attachments became more fluid, with increased competition among competing social networks that divided citizen loyalties. These processes played out in the decomposition of electoral alignments in Western countries, which Dalton *et al.* argue is evinced in the fractionalization and volatility of party systems in the 1960s and 1970s.

Dalton *et al.* point to two principal potential avenues of change for these 'decomposed' party systems. The first is realignment, where there is a shift in the social bases underlying particular parties and/or party coalitions. With realignment, groups previously unaffiliated with a partisan option choose one, or those who have abandoned one party decide to associate themselves with another. Such realignments have been well accounted for in the American literature, but they are also a fundamental feature of European politics (Key, 1959; Butler and Stokes, 1974; Rose, 1974). The other pattern for party systems in transition is one of dealignment, which occurs when a significant portion of the electorate dissociates itself from traditional parties. Dealignment is a process or an end stage, signifying either the fist stage in an electoral realignment, or the decline of political parties as the basic organizational units of politics (Inglehart and Hochstein, 1972).

A related strain of the literature on party transformation also recognizes post-industrial demographic and social changes, but focuses more on values and how value change results in shifts in partisan alignments (Inglehart, 1977, 1997). Inglehart, the most influential analyst of value change, argues that generational and concomitant value change account for the

transformed social bases of parties. In particular, he argues that those who came to age during the post-war period did not experience the deprivation, depressions and the economic scarcity of their parents. This, along with enhanced educational opportunities, has transformed the fault lines of European societies. Among younger generations, who Inglehart contends have 'post-materialist' values, there is less concern with ideology and the economic role of the state, and much more concern with non-economic social issues such as abortion rights, equality, participation, the environment, and personal morality. These issues have displaced the typical 'old politics' that was important to the war generations, who had a 'materialist' orientation, and were much more concerned with economic stability and growth, domestic order, and military and social security. In essence, Inglehart argued that class-based political polarization had been replaced by value-based political polarization. Inglehart's formula helps account for the new popularity of the 'right' among contemporary working classes, where the materialist message resonates more, better reflecting their value orientations.

Inglehart has built a large edifice of theory on the materialist–post-materialist distinction, with extensive analysis of cross-national survey data, which has now been undertaken in over 40 societies. Inglehart's surveys, and particularly those that apply to major European countries, have consistently demonstrated a trend towards post-materialism.

Flanagan underscores a different kind of value change, though one could reasonably consider it a subdimension of the larger issues with which Inglehart deals (Inglehart, 1997: 122). In particular, he argues that along with sociocultural and economic transformation has come a decline in respect for authority, religion, and the work ethic as they have traditionally been understood (Flanagan, 1982). Traditional values have in large part been replaced by values more related to self-actualization – quality of life, leisure activities, a tolerance for distinct lifestyles, openness to new ideas, and non-conformity. Also, Flanagan builds on this work to more squarely criticize Inglehart's argument and elaborate a new theory of value-driven politics. Flanagan suggests that while he generally shares many of the assumptions and findings of Inglehart's work, a reliance solely on an analysis of the materialist–post-materialist distinction is insufficient. Flanagan introduces another libertarian–authoritarian axis that differentiates the new right from the old right, arguing for what amounts to three sets of value orientations. His category 'libertarian' is essentially the same as the one identified by Inglehart as 'post-materialist'. However, while some of the 'old right' is simply materialist, Flanagan contends that we must differentiate a new and distinct cluster of values that differentiates the old right – with its concern for strictly material values – from the new right – concerned with 'security and order ... respect for authority, discipline and dutifulness, patriotism' and characterized by 'intolerance for minorities, conformity to customs, and support for traditional religious and moral values' (Inglehart and Flanagan, 1987: 1304).

Inglehart's arguments and other analyses of realignment and dealignment were not without their critics. Clark and Dutt (1991) argued that rising levels of unemployment actually contributed to post-materialist values, a contention at odds with Inglehart's arguments. Others took issue with the essence of Inglehart's work, challenging his interpretation of the phenomena that led to an exploration of value change in the first place. Several scholars questioned whether dealignment has occurred in particular cases, or, more seriously, whether dealignment is even a real trend in broader terms. Keith *et al.* (1992) contended that the rise of independent voting in the United States was grossly overstated by proponents of the dealignment argument, and that most voters who identified themselves as independents actually leaned strongly towards one of the two established parties. Other scholars similarly challenged claims about partisan change in Europe (Mair, 1993; Bartolini and Mair, 1990).

Irrespective of differing in interpretations of their source, what do these changes mean for the future role of parties in Western democracies, and indeed, in new and developing democracies? Scholars answer this question in different ways, but three sets of responses tend to predominate. First, parties have ceased to be the dominant or most effective instruments of interest representation. Second, the role of ideology has been transformed, with consequences for the nature of the connection between societies and parties. Third, new sets of parties, both in traditional democracies and in new democracies, either play an increasing role or have the potential to displace traditional parties.

Parties, society and representation

Transformations in the connections between society and parties have led some scholars to surmise that parties, given advancing technology, changing loyalties, and social change, may have become less than optimal agents of representation. Lawson and Merkl (1988b: 3) sum it up most directly by arguing that 'it may be that the institution of party is gradually disappearing, slowly being replaced by new political structures more suitable for the economic and technological realities of twenty-first century politics'. Scholars then suggest that neo-pluralist or neo-corporatist forms of representation may be the wave of the future. Indeed, for some, the predominance of the individual, and citizen capacity, trumps group representation altogether. For example, Bartolini and Mair (2001: 333) find that 'citizens have an apparent capacity for direct action and no longer seem reliant on political mediation'. Schmitter (2001) argues that parties have lost or abandoned their role in interest representation and aggregation. While parties continue to structure campaigns and elections and maintain some symbolic importance, they are much less imbedded in the overall governing process and in interest representation than they were in the past. This is particularly the case in new democracies where parties cannot rely on the habit of performing traditional roles, and the legitimacy that comes with time and success. Therefore, parties in new and reconstituted democracies must perform all of the standard functions assumed by political parties and face the simultaneous task of institutionalizing their own organizations (Montero and Gunther, 2002: 3).

While parties' social bases are less identifiable, their functions transformed, and a good deal of party volatility exists, those who sound the death knell of parties overstate their case. Parties and other social organizations and forms of interest representation can coexist. Parties can take on varied and new functions, not necessarily competing with other social organizations. In addition, party organizations and party elites have the capacity to respond and adapt to social change, belying the image of parties as inflexible dinosaurs sometimes suggested in the literature. Indeed, scholarly consensus is emerging that the literature on party decline and disappearance was alarmist and inaccurate. In no democracies have parties been displaced as the major agents of interest representation. Several studies also suggest that parties have actually done a pretty good job of adapting to change, assuming new roles that allow them to function and often prosper (Tarrow, 1990; Aldrich, 1995). Despite voter cynicism, dealignment, fractionalization, and instability in their ranks, parties continue to be central representative actors, and will remain so.

Ideology, parties and society: Is there a left left?

The fall of the Berlin Wall and the purported triumph of market capitalism profoundly transformed the left. Indeed, many scholars argued that ideology itself had ceased to be significant to the social bases of politics, a reality that would eventually be reflected in party systems. Across Europe, leftist parties have become less ideological, more pluralistic, and have accepted competitive markets as the key to growth. Statism is on the decline and the patterns of trade unionism and industrial production that provided the social bases for left-wing parties have been transformed. Lipset and Rokkan long ago established the left–right cleavage as the most important for understanding party systems in Western democracies. With the transformation of leftist politics around the world, and with class no longer the primary cleavage differentiating parties, the obvious question is whether there is a left left.

While macro-political processes and the fall of the Soviet Union certainly contributed to the left's transformed role, deeper social and economic changes were also at play. Post-industrialism, increasing affluence, and the growth of the service and information economy eroded the left's underlying social bases. Indeed, Debray (1990: 26) notes that the '[l]eft lost its coherent social base when it could no longer define itself as the mouthpiece of the "working masses"'. Therefore, the question of whether there is a left left is intimately tied to the debate on the significance of social class.

Clark and Lipset (1991) argue that social class stratification has indeed weakened, resulting in a shift in how politics is organized. In large part echoing the arguments of Inglehart, they find that other value-based issues have become increasingly important. However, they also add individualism, technological shifts, and changes in the family and other sociocultural factors as additional elements that have led to decline in the importance of social class. They outline how new forms of stratification have replaced social class, and argue that indices of class voting have decreased in all of the countries they analyze.

Hout et al. (2001) disagree. They explore the multiple declarations of an end to class politics that have been advanced during the past thirty years by post-materialist, functionalist, and new social movements theorists. They argue that while class structures have changed in the post-industrial era, class stratification is an enduring reality and new forms of inequality will not simply replace or erase previous ones. They specifically challenge Clark and Lipset who, they contend, confound class and social hierarchies. The simple reality that social hierarchies are less salient does not translate into the disappearance of class. Further, Hout et al. argue that Clark and Lipset's distinction between manual and non-manual labor may no longer be a valid way to conceptualize social classes, and that they confuse debates over class issues with the question of whether class continues to be a determinant of voting behavior. Hout et al. conclude that class continues to have an important impact on party politics, but that this influence varies across contexts and over time. Indeed, they argue that in some cases social class has actually become more important. Weakliem (2001) adds to these criticisms, contending that collapsing parties into the categories of 'left' and 'right' (as is usually done for convenience in studies of class voting) ignores the significant ideological differences that can exist between parties lumped into the same categories.

In light of these realities, where do the parties of the left stand in terms of their social bases and electoral possibilities, irrespective of the source of change? Eley (2002: 483) notes that defeats and disappointments at the hands of capitalism have led socialists to accept the status quo and settle for the 'more modest aims of civilizing capitalism, stressing democracy, social citizenship and rights at work'. Democracy and the defense of civil rights, human rights and the welfare state have become central concerns for the left. In addition, though initially overlooking the demands of new social movements, socialist and social democratic parties eventually reached out to them, and provided an environment in which they could thrive. Sasoon (1997) notes how the fall from favor of the Keynesian and Marxist ideals that underwrote the left's success have forced it into a defensive position. Debray agrees, though he maintains that the redefined left is best poised to step in and defend the old left's victories, and by doing so, serve as an antidote to the incivility and ethnic and religious strife that capitalism in its current form has spawned. To do so, however, it must abandon its utopian pretensions, and develop socialism as a 'moral sense and a civil method' (1990: 28).

Lipset argues that rather than disappearing, European leftist parties are moving or have moved towards the development of a more US-style, non-socialist model. According to him, European economic and class structures have come to 'resemble those of the United States' (1997: 76). The advent of post-industrial societies and concomitant decline in the size and power of European labor movements have undermined the class bases of politics. Lipset analyzes changes in the social bases of politics and their party consequences using an 'apolitical' Marxist lens. Fundamentally, he accepts that social class and the structure of production indeed determine 'political superstructures', including political parties. While he recognizes variations based on differences among cases, he contends that we should view the European left as becoming increasingly American. In country after country, parties on the left have accepted capitalism, and debates revolve around distribution of resources and 'post-materialist' political issues rather than the essential structure of the economy. 'New social democrats' and 'third-wayers', for Lipset, are the quintessential symbols of this transformation.

However, the extent of this Americanization is questionable, and probably overstated. While there are cross-regional commonalities that respond to deep social changes across the developed world, the European and American left differ profoundly in nature and character. First, the American left has been less class-based, much more centrist, and much less of a dominant historical force than its European counterparts. Second, the American left is shaded by the deep individualistic and libertarian character of American society, which contrasts sharply with the egalitarian and communitarian European left. Finally, in terms of concrete expression of a new left agenda, European parliamentary, and usually multiparty, systems still have more of an inherent capacity to allow for the expression of a multidimensional left than the hypermajoritarian US presidential system. In short, elements of the traditional leftist tradition are likely to remain significant to Western European party systems, and to counteract their Americanization.

Rather than the left disappearing or simply morphing into a more American-style left, Sassoon (1997) points to a convergence between traditional communist and socialist parties and the social democratic left. This convergence has also been accompanied by a more general convergence between the left and the right in terms of their core guiding principles, making for more 'centrist' party systems. He traces this convergence not just to value change, but also to the universalizing forces of globalization, the increasing homogeneity of electorates,

rapid communication, and the necessity to present succinct and more universally acceptable political messages in an era of sound-bite politics.

Despite continuing ruminations, consensus has emerged that there is, indeed, a 'left left', but that its definition and its role have changed. Nowhere in the major countries of Western Europe is the left unelectable, and in the late 1990s and early 2000s there has been resurgence in the popularity of parties of the left, with socialist or social democratic parties assuming power in the UK, Sweden, Spain, and Germany. What is more, while the utopian ideals of eliminating capitalism and fundamentally transforming the social order have been abandoned, leftist parties retain a central commitment to defend past achievements, to promote an agenda of social reform, and to protect human and civil rights. Indeed, one could argue that the left has successfully adapted to change by pirating the agenda of the so-called 'new' post-materialist parties and, in essence, derailing the challenge they were presumed to pose.

Society and new parties

The term 'new parties' is used in two principal ways in the contemporary literature on party systems, referring to both parties that emerged after an authoritarian or totalitarian regime, and those that emerged in long-established democracies with the aim of displacing existing parties or breaking into the party system. However, as other chapters in this volume cover the emergence of political parties in the wake of non-democratic regimes more explicitly, this chapter will focus primarily on new parties in existing democracies. 'New' parties are characterized as such for chronological reasons, but also because their social bases do not correspond to the traditional left–right dimension of politics. Lane and Ersson (1991) distinguish between 'structurally' based parties which emerge out of traditional cleavage dimensions and give rise to class-based, religious, regional or ethnic parties, and those that emerge from 'non-structural' issues. There is also an implicit and sometimes explicit assumption that new parties emerge when other parties fail to assimilate emerging popular movements. Indeed, Lawson and Merkl's edited volume dealing with new parties is entitled *When Parties Fail* (1988a). Parties based on non-structural issue dimensions usually are centered around one or a few national policies. The environmentally oriented European Green parties represent a quintessentially 'new' party movement, as do feminist parties and anti-nuclear, anti-EU and anti-NATO parties. Though the majority of new parties have emerged on the left (either in its 'new' post-materialist or 'old' materialist form), fascist and extreme right-wing parties also fall under the rubric of 'new' parties, as they address issues that for some voters traditional parties have ignored.

Theorists have advanced a number of explanations for the emergence of new parties. Smith (1989: 360) argues that partisan dealignment and a marked decrease in party attachments provide 'windows of opportunity' for new parties to enter closed party systems. Harmel and Robertson (1985) contend that explanations for the emergence of new parties take one of three forms: explanations based on social factors (new cleavages or issues), political factors (ideology, party behavior, the availability of leaders, or the salience of new issues), or structural factors (type of electoral system, the freedom to organize, the extent of government centralization, or whether the system is presidential or parliamentary). They go on to test a multiplicity of variables advanced by scholars and find that the propensity to form new parties is related strongly to sociocultural diversity. They find that while there is little relationship between structural variables and the propensity to form new parties, the eventual success of new parties is related to the permissiveness of the electoral system.

While most analyses of 'new' parties have focused on the left, and particularly the post-materialist left, new rightist parties have also emerged across Western Europe. Kitschelt (1995) employs a framework that mirrors his previous treatment of the transformation of social democratic parties (1994) to explain the emergence of these 'new' extreme right parties, rejecting the notion that they simply represent the re-emergence of parties of the traditional right. In explaining their emergence Kitschelt argues that there has been a shift in the competitive space of Western European party systems. While the well-worn left–right cleavage dimension persists, superimposed upon it is a 'libertarian–authoritarian' divide. Competition has shifted away from the purely economic cleavage as the main axis of competition toward the libertarian–authoritarian axis, providing space for the emergence of new right-wing parties. He does not argue that the class cleavage is insignificant or has been completely displaced. Rather, it has been combined with a new emerging cleavage that has transformed the competitive space for political parties and the nature of

what have been traditionally understood as 'left' and 'right' politics.

Despite the quantity of literature devoted to studying the emergence of new parties, scholars question the existence and significance of the phenomena as a symptom of fundamental change. First, many point to the dearth of durable new parties, underscoring the obstacles to their emergence and subsistence even in the face of dealignment and the decomposition of established parties (Rose and Mackie, 1988; Harmel and Robertson, 1985). Even parties that overcome these obstacles are usually ephemeral and have difficulty in entering the realm of 'relevant' parties.

Second, Mair (1991: 63) finds that while the growth of 'new parties' has been a significant and measurable trend in Western Europe, it has probably been overstated. If anything, Mair argues that 'new' small parties probably have simply replaced 'old' small parties, making for limited substantive effect on the overall competitive dynamic of post-war European party systems.

Finally, despite the widespread emergence of new parties and predictions of profound electoral realignment, the political expression of underlying cleavage structures, though not identical, remains strikingly similar to the past. While social change, value change, and declining partisan attachments certainly have affected party competition in Western democracies, voters frequently continue to identify with the same 'political family' of parties. For these scholars, the oft-predicted 'unfreezing' of partisan alignments has yet to occur (Bartolini and Mair, 1990).

CONCLUSIONS: MULTIPLE AND EXAGGERATED REPORTS OF DEATH

The relationship between society and parties is characterized as much by change as continuity. In terms of change, collective identities are waning, and political preferences are more individualized. The social bases of party support are more complex, and less predictably aligned along the class cleavage. The meaning of right and left has been transformed, with important consequences for party competition. However, the overall electoral balance between parties of the 'left' and 'right' (however defined) in Western democracies has not changed much, and there has been little vote redistribution between the two major blocs. Major parties have proven relatively resilient (with the exception of Christian democratic parties) and have often absorbed the post-materialist agendas of their new party competitors. What is more, there is evidence that new parties often simply inherit the supporters of old parties that have disappeared.

While there remains disagreement in the literature with respect to the nature of society–party connections, over the last ten years there has also been a good deal of scholarly convergence. Debates in the literature customarily began with a death report of one kind or another. Parties were declared irrelevant, social class pronounced dead, cleavages said to have ceased to be significant, or the left to have breathed its last. Nonetheless, recent literature has been less inclined toward strident death declarations, and has better recognized the complex interaction of the old with the new. There is a consensus in the literature that social and economic changes have transformed parties. However, scholars also agree that parties continue to be the central and most widely recognized agents of representation. Similarly, while cleavages and their party manifestations are in flux, most scholars now recognize that neither social class nor class cleavages have ceased to be central organizing concepts for understanding party systems. While the meaning of the left may have been transformed, leftist politics (perhaps defined differently) is alive and well.

This convergence is certainly a positive development. However, there are lacunae in the literature. First, the literature on the relationship between society and parties is least developed for new and transitional democracies. Scholars must untangle whether and how the assumptions and theoretical conclusions developed for the USA and Western Europe apply in the developing world. Inglehart (1997: 7) argues with respect to value change, and particularly post-materialist values, that 'across many societies, once given processes are set in motion, certain important changes are likely to happen'. This statement smacks of the teleologies that characterized developmentalist literature in the 1950s and 1960s and seems to assume that social and economic changes will automatically lead to value change, and similar partisan effects in the developing world. Is this the case? Also, even without deep changes in social class or levels of industrialization, we see post-materialist values taking hold in the developing world. Is this a result of social change, or have post-materialist values taken hold as the result of a contagion effect?

In addition to this theoretical concern, we also lack cross-national empirical studies of society–party relations in the developing world. It is no surprise that most of this chapter deals with European party systems, which have been the primary object of theorizing. There are a number of case studies that underscore the transformation of society–party relations in particular or a few cases, and a smattering of articles that assume that transformations similar to those underway in the USA and Western Europe are also taking place in the developing world. However, with few exceptions (see Mainwaring and Scully, 1995), we still lack systematic cross-national and cross-regional studies of these phenomena. The literature is similarly underdeveloped when it comes to the role of political parties in democratic transitions. There is certainly more written on the development of parties in post-communist systems, including analyses of the multidimensional interaction of pre- and post-communist cleavages. However, while the centrality of parties is always seen as important in transitions from non-communist authoritarian regimes, there is little comparative theorizing on the precise role that parties play in structuring social relations in processes of democratic transition, democratic consolidation, or how and whether authoritarian/democratic cleavages assume significance following transitions – Moreno (1999) is an exception. We must analyze the longer-term effect of the new pro- and anti-authoritarian cleavages that often emerge in democratizing societies.

Second, theorists have dealt insufficiently with parties as autonomous actors. Most of the literature treats parties as dependent variables that react to structural changes in economies and social relations. While analysis of political parties as dependent variables is certainly a valid enterprise, parties are also independent agents that frame issues and elaborate party platforms, affecting how cleavages translate into values, beliefs, and political behavior. This is increasingly important with the advent of mass, centralized, and professionally orchestrated campaigning. On a related note, we need better accounts of the differences between deep value change and how short-term issues cycle through the electorate with the help of party advertising and publicity. For example, in the United States to what extent does the promotion of issues such as gay marriage, the role of religion in society, and anti-immigration rhetoric by the parties and candidates themselves help to set the political agenda that shapes how political values develop, with which party citizens identify, and how political beliefs are expressed?

Finally, the literature on the society–party nexus should do more to analyze internal party processes. The most analyzed point of contact between citizens and parties is in the voting booth. We have extensive studies of voting behavior, but little on the other potential connections between parties and citizens. Neither individual connections nor those mediated through other groups or the media are well accounted for in the literature. Citizens interact with party organizations, finance campaigns, are influenced by party publicity, and potentially play a role in the recruitment and selection of candidates. To understand these complex interactions, more serious study of internal party processes is essential in order to uncover the nuts and bolts of society–party relations beyond simply measuring voting as the determinative indicator of citizens' ties to parties.

REFERENCES

Aldrich, John (1995) *Why Parties? The Origin and Transformation of Political Parties in America.* Chicago: University of Chicago Press.

Bartolini, Stefano and Mair, Peter (1990) *Identity, Competition and Electoral Availability: The Stabilisation of European Electorates 1885–1985.* Cambridge: Cambridge University Press.

Bartolini, Stefano and Mair, Peter (2001) 'Challenges to contemporary political parties', in Larry Diamond and Richard Gunther (eds), *Political Parties and Democracy.* Baltimore, MD: Johns Hopkins University Press.

Burnham, Walter Dean (1970) *Critical Elections and the Mainsprings of American Politics.* New York: Norton.

Burnham, Walter Dean (1975) 'American politics in the 1970's: Beyond party', in Louis Maisel and Paul M. Sacks (eds), *The Future of Political Parties.* Beverly Hills, CA: Sage Publications, pp. 238–77.

Butler, David and Stokes, Donald (1974) *Political Change in Britain.* New York: St. Martin's Press.

Campbell, Angus, Converse, Philip, Miller, Warren and Stokes, Donald (1960) *The American Voter.* New York: Wiley.

Clark, Harold D. and Dutt, Nitish (1991) 'Measuring value change in Western industrial societies: The impact of unemployment', *American Political Science Review,* 85: 905–20.

Clark, Terry and Lipset, Seymour Martin (1991) 'Are social classes dying?', *International Sociology,* 6: 397–410.

Converse, Philip E. (1976) *The Dynamics of Party Support.* Beverly Hills, CA: Sage Publications.

Daalder, Hans (1983) 'The comparative study of European parties and party systems: An overview', in Hans Daalder and Peter Mair (eds), *Western European Party Systems: Continuity and Change.* London: Sage.

Dahl, Robert (1966) *Political Oppositions in Western Democracies.* New Haven, CT: Yale University Press.

Dalton, Russell (1999) 'Political support in advanced industrial democracies', in Pippa Norris (ed.), *Critical Citizens: Global Support for Democratic Governance.* Oxford: Oxford University Press.

Dalton, Russell, Beck, Paul Allen and Flanagan, Scott (1984) 'Electoral change in advanced industrial democracies', in Russell Dalton, Scott Flanagan and Paul Beck (eds), *Electoral Change in Advanced Industrial Democracies: Realignment or Dealignment.* Princeton, NJ: Princeton University Press.

Debray, Régis (1990) 'What's left of the left?', *New Perspectives Quarterly,* 7: 26–8.

Duverger, Maurice (1954) *Political Parties: Their Organization and Activity in the Modern State.* London: Methuen.

Eley, Geoff (2002) *Forging Democracy: The History of the Left in Europe, 1850–2000.* Oxford: Oxford University Press.

Flanagan, Scott (1982) 'Changing values in advanced industrial societies', *Comparative Political Studies,* 14: 403–44.

Franklin, Mark, Mackie, Tom and Valen, Henry (eds) (1992) *Electoral Change.* New York: Cambridge University Press.

Harmel, Robert and Robertson, John D. (1985) 'On the study of new parties', *International Political Science Review,* 4: 403–18.

Hout, Mike, Brooks, Clem and Manza, Jeff (2001) 'The persistence of classes in post-industrial societies', in Terry Clark and Seymour Martin Lipset (eds), *The Breakdown of Class Politics.* Baltimore, MD: Johns Hopkins University Press.

Inglehart, Ronald (1977) *The Silent Revolution: Changing Values and Political Styles among Western Publics.* Princeton, NJ: Princeton University Press.

Inglehart, Ronald (1997) *Modernization and Postmodernization: Cultural, Economic and Political Change in 43 Societies.* Princeton, NJ: Princeton University Press.

Inglehart, Ronald and Flanagan, Scott (1987) 'Value change in industrial societies', *American Political Science Review,* 81: 1289–1319.

Inglehart, Ronald and Hochstein, Avram (1972) 'Alignment and dealignment of the electorate in France and the United States', *Comparative Political Studies,* 5: 343–72.

Keith, Bruce E., Magleby, David B. and Nelson, Candice J. (1992) *The Myth of the Independent Voter.* Berkeley: University of California Press.

Key, V.O., Jr. (1959) 'Secular realignment and the party system', *Journal of Politics,* 21: 198–210.

Kitschelt, Herbert (1994) *The Transformation of European Social Democracy.* Cambridge: Cambridge University Press.

Kitschelt, Herbert (1995) *The Radical Right in Western Europe.* Ann Arbor: University of Michigan Press.

Lane, Jan-Erik and Ersson, Svante O. (1991) *Politics and Society in Western Europe.* London: Sage Publications.

LaPalombara, Joseph and Weiner, Martin (1966) *Political Parties and Political Development*. Princeton, NJ: Princeton University Press.

Lawson, Kay (1988) 'When linkage fails', in Kay Lawson and Peter Merkl (eds), *When Parties Fail: Emerging Alternative Organizations*. Princeton, NJ: Princeton University Press.

Lawson, Kay and Merkl, Peter (eds) (1988a) *When Parties Fail: Emerging Alternative Organizations*. Princeton, NJ: Princeton University Press.

Lawson, Kay and Merkl, Peter (1988b) 'Alternative organizations: Environmental, supplementary, communitarian, and authoritarian', in Kay Lawson and Peter Merkl (eds), *When Parties Fail: Emerging Alternative Organizations*. Princeton, NJ: Princeton University Press, pp. 3–12.

Lijphart, Arend (1977) *Democracy in Plural Societies*. New Haven, CT: Yale University Press.

Lijphart, Arend (1980) 'Language, religion, class and party choice: Belgium, Canada, Switzerland and South Africa compared', in Richard Rose (ed.), *Electoral Participation: A Comparative Analysis*. London: Sage.

Lipset, Seymour Martin (1960) *Political Man*. New York: Doubleday.

Lipset, Seymour Martin (1983) 'Radicalism or reformism: The sources of working class politics', *American Political Science Review*, 77: 1–18.

Lipset, Seymour Martin (1997) 'The Americanization of the European left', *Journal of Democracy*, 12: 74–87.

Lipset, Seymour Martin and Rokkan, Stein (1967) 'Cleavage structures, party systems and voter alignment: An introduction', in Seymour Martin Lipset and Stein Rokkan (eds), *Party Systems and Voter Alignments*. New York: Free Press.

Mainwaring, Scott and Scully, Timothy (1995) *Building Democratic Institutions: Party Systems in Latin America*. Stanford, CA: Stanford University Press.

Mair, Peter (1983) 'Adaptation and control: Towards an understanding of party and party system change', in Hans Daalder and Peter Mair (eds), *Western European Party Systems: Continuity and Change*. Beverly Hills, CA: Sage Publications.

Mair, Peter (1991) 'The electoral universe of small parties in postwar Western Europe', in Ferdinand Müller-Rommel and Geoffrey Pridham (eds), *Small Parties in Western Europe: Comparative and National Perspectives*. London: Sage Publications.

Mair, Peter (1993) 'Myths of electoral change and the survival of traditional parties', *European Journal of Political Research*, 24: 121–33.

Michels, Robert (1959) *Political Parties*. New York: Dover Publications.

Montero, José Ramón and Gunther, Richard (2002) 'Introduction: Reviewing and reassessing parties', in Richard Gunther, José Ramón Montero and Juan Linz (eds), *Political Parties: Old Concepts and New Challenges*. Oxford: Oxford University Press.

Moreno, Alejandro (1999) *Political Cleavages: Issues, Parties, and the Consolidation of Democracy*. Boulder, CO: Westview Press.

Neuman, Sigmund (1956) *Modern Political Parties*. Chicago: University of Chicago Press.

Ostrogorski, Moisei (1964) *Democracy and the Organization of Political Parties*. Garden City, NY: Anchor Books.

Rokkan, Stein (1970) *Citizens, Elections, Parties*. Oslo: Universitetsforlaget.

Rokkan, Stein (1975) 'Dimensions of state formation and nation building: A possible paradigm for research on variations within Europe', in Charles Tilly (ed.), *The Formation of National States in Western Europe*. Princeton, NJ: Princeton University Press.

Rose, Richard (ed.) (1974) *Comparative Electoral Behavior*. New York: Free Press.

Rose, Richard and Mackie, Thomas (1988) 'Do parties persist or fail: The big tradeoff facing organizations', in Kay Lawson and Peter Merkl (eds), *When Parties Fail: Emerging Alternative Organizations*. Princeton, NJ: Princeton University Press.

Rose, Richard and Urwin, Derek (1969) 'Social cohesion, political parties, and strains in regimes', *Comparative Political Studies*, 2: 7–67.

Rose, Richard and Urwin, Derek (1970) 'Persistence and change in Western party systems since 1945', *Political Studies*, 18: 287–319.

Sartori, Giovanni (1976) *Parties and Party Systems: A Framework for Analysis*. Cambridge: Cambridge University Press.

Sassoon, Donald (1997) 'Introduction', in Donald Sassoon (ed.), *Looking Left: Socialism in Europe After the Cold War*. London: New Press.

Schmitter, Philippe C. (2001) 'Parties are not what they once were', in Larry Diamond and Richard Gunther (eds), *Political Parties and Democracy*. Baltimore, MD: Johns Hopkins University Press.

Shamir, Michel (1984) 'Are Western European party systems "frozen"?', *Comparative Political Studies*, 17(1): 35–79.

Smith, Gordon (1989) 'A system perspective on party system change', *Journal of Theoretical Politics*, 13: 34–63.

Tarrow, Sidney (1990) 'The Phantom of the Opera: Political parties and social movements of the 1960s and 1970s in Italy', in R. Dalton and M. Kuechler (eds), *Challenging the Political Order: New Social and Political Movements in Western Democracies*. Oxford: Oxford University Press.

Urwin, Derek W. (1973) 'Political parties, societies, and regimes in Europe: Some reflections on the literature', *European Journal of Political Research*, 1: 179–204.

Weakliem, David (2001) 'Social class and class voting: The case against decline', in Terry Clark and Seymour Martin Lipset (eds), *The Breakdown of Class Politics*. Baltimore, MD: Johns Hopkins University Press.

30

CLEAVAGES

Peter Mair

Almost 50 years ago, in what has since become one of the classic texts in political sociology, S.M. Lipset (1960: 220) observed that 'in every modern democracy conflict among different groups is expressed through political parties which basically represent a "democratic translation of the class struggle." … On a world scale, the principal generalization which can be made is that parties are primarily based on either the lower classes or the middle and upper classes.' The notion of the class struggle being democratically translated into politics is compelling, and thanks to Lipset, it has since remained part of the terms of reference of the discipline.[1] But of course this was not the only social struggle that was being translated. As Lipset went on to indicate in *Political Man* (1960: 221), and as he later extensively elaborated in his path-breaking work with Stein Rokkan on European political development (Lipset and Rokkan, 1967), religious, cultural and regional struggles were also translated into political divides, albeit less evenly and less frequently than the struggle between classes. Moreover, while class conflict proved the most pervasive of the various social conflicts carried through into the political realm, it was not universal, even among the established democracies, and it was translated with differing levels of meaning and intensity. It scarcely figured at the party political level in the Irish Republic, for example, where, despite sometimes pronounced class identities, the various attempts to politicize class opposition were usually drowned out by the overwhelming attention that was paid to nationalist issues (Mair, 1992). In the crucially formative election of 1918 in Ireland, the Labour Party had stood aside to allow the newly expanded electorate a clear

run in expressing support for the nationalist movement, and thereafter the party had never proved capable of moving away from the margins of the system. Nor did it translate into the party political realm in the United States, despite various social biases in the distribution of partisan support between Democrats and Republicans. Working-class support may have proved crucial to building and maintaining the postwar Democratic coalition (Hout *et al.*, 1999), but, in contrast to the majority of European states, it never led to the mobilization of a major socialist or social democratic party (Lipset and Marks, 2000). In countries such as the Netherlands and Switzerland, where class conflict was successfully translated into party political alternatives, it never succeeded in developing into the overriding polarity, and was always vulnerable to the challenge posed by the translation of other divides. In France and Italy, by contrast, class conflict not only proved one of the most dominant sources of political opposition, but also one of the most radicalized and intense, with communist parties quickly gaining the upper hand in the contest to represent the interests of the organized working class.

In practice, then, what might be seen as a fairly simple and straightforward process – the translation of social conflict into political and party alternatives – turns out to be quite fraught and complex. There is nothing automatic at work here, and while conflicts are sometimes translated into partisan divides, at other times and in other places they are not, or only partially so. Class divides are usually translated into politics, but, as we have seen, this is not always the case, and not always in the same way. Religious divides are also sometimes translated, but not in all circumstances, and not always with the same intensity. Gender divides, however important at the level of society, have scarcely been translated at all.

What accounts for this variation? To a large degree, as Sartori (1990) has emphasized in an assessment of Lipset and Rokkan's approach to voter alignments, it depends on the actual translator, or, as he then put it, on 'the persuader'. In other words, the social conditions that are eventually translated into party politics should be seen as the necessary facilitating conditions, while the primary agency that is at work is the party – or other organization – that intervenes to politicize those conditions. 'To put it bluntly', argues Sartori (1990: 169), 'it is not the objective class (class conditions) that creates the party, but the party that creates the "subjective" class (class consciousness) … [W]henever parties reflect social classes, this signifies more about the party end than about the class end of the interaction'. In part, then, it is supply that makes for demand. Of course the same is also true for other divisions. It was the churches and their affiliated organizations that helped to translate religious divisions into electoral alignments, for example, even though the political parties that grew to prominence during this mobilization process soon developed their own momentum and outpaced the intentions of their original founders. As Kalyvas (1996: 257) has concluded: 'Confessional parties were not the historically predetermined and automatic reflection of preexisting identities and conflicts, nor were they the emanation of structural, economic, or political modernization. They were instead a contingent outcome of the struggle among various organizations facing a multitude of challenges under tight constraints.' In short, the shift from society to politics is determined at least in part by the active intervention of political forces in the society.[2]

Much of the writing on cleavages – whether they are seen as social, political, or cultural – has tended to neglect this dynamic perspective. In some cases, cleavages are treated as if they were the more or less natural outgrowth of social stratification. If there are divides in the society, it is these which are seen to explain the presence of parties and politics; and if these divides then change, such that old lines of stratification fade away, and new ones emerge to take their place, this inevitably leads to the eclipse of one set of parties and to the emergence and growth of others. Political change in this sense is to be explained by social change, and in this way we acquire what Sartori (1990) refers to as a deterministic 'sociology of politics'. In other and more recent approaches,

cleavages are assumed to be about belief systems, with traditional social structural divides such as classs or religion being seen to erode, only to be replaced by something that is built almost exclusively on preferences, mind-sets, or 'values' (see especially Flanagan, 1987; Inglehart, 1990; Kriesi, 1998), and that has few if any relevant social correlates. In the one approach, norms and beliefs are not seen to be important; in the other, social structure counts for little.

It is evident that neither of these two alternatives is wholly satisfactory. The notion of value-free religious mobilization, for example, is clearly a contradiction in terms. The notion of a value-free class conflict is also difficult to conceive. Even the most dyed-in-the-wool workers' movements that mobilized in the early years of mass politics could hardly be seen in this way. Indeed, whether its demands were couched within a frame that emphasized the rights of workers and the need for social justice, or whether they were seen to prefigure the inauguration of a classless society, the politics of this particular social structural divide was inevitably held together by a strong sense of collective solidarity and by a firm commitment to a more or less shared ideology. On the other side, it is also difficult to think of a cleavage being built exclusively on values. Even if we were to regard the materialist–postmaterialist divide as a real cleavage, for example, we could hardly avoid recognizing that the values on the latter side of that divide have been most commonly espoused by younger, better-educated, and reasonably prosperous citizens: Green parties attract fewer votes in underclass ghettos.

In reality, both social structure and values play a role in all cleavages, even if in one case it is the values which carry the greater weight, and in another the social structure. This is also the conclusion that is reached by Knutsen and Scarbrough (1995: 519) in their authoritative review of both the evidence and the literature: 'The structural basis of political conflict, rather than being eroded, appears quite resilient … At the same time, we should note that the impact of structural variables is less significant, and the independent impact of value orientations more significant, than is implied by the cleavage model.' This also depends, of course, on how the different elements are measured, and with what degree of accuracy. Knutsen and Scarbrough (1995: 519) also note, for example, that 'the significance of value orientations has grown over the period 1973–90' – but, lacking the necessary instruments, neither they nor any one else can measure the real weight of value orientations when mass politics was first mobilized at the beginning of the twentieth century, or even when it became consolidated in the 1950s and 1960s. The fact that it is only social structure that can be measured in earlier periods does not mean that it is only social structure which then mattered.

But however important social structure and values may be for our understanding of cleavages, there is also something extra involved, and that is organization. Divisions may exist within the society, and these, in turn, may be associated with particular values or identities, but this does not necessarily mean that they will all become politically relevant. This is the key point which Sartori (1990) underlines in his reference to the importance of translation and persuasion, and it is also the point which Schattschneider (1983: 69) makes when he speaks of some issues – and we might well add some identities or some values – being organized into politics while others are organized out. In other words, the shift from society to politics occurs when a particular social divide becomes associated with a particular set of values or identities, and when this is then brought into the political world, and made politically relevant, by means of an organized party or group. But although these three elements can easily be distinguished from one another at the analytic level, in practice they are heavily interdependent. It is the shared social experiences that allow for the emergence of a collective sense of identity and a common value system; and it is the effect of organizational intervention, or persuasion, that helps to consolidate that identity and make it relevant to politics. In some cases, a formal political organization is scarcely required, since the social group is already very cohesive, and is bound together by a network of other, non-political organizations; in other cases, the identity is scarcely expressed until prompted by a group of entrepreneurial political leaders.[3]

In other words, and as was first outlined in an earlier analysis of the stabilization of European electorates (see Bartolini and Mair, 1990: 212–49; see also Bartolini, 2000: 15–24, and Gallagher *et al.*, 2005: 264–72), cleavages have three distinct characteristics. In the first place, a cleavage involves a social division that distinguishes between groups of people on the basis of key social-structural characteristics such as status, religion, or ethnicity. A cleavage is therefore grounded in a distinct social reality. Second, there must be a clear sense of collective identity involved, in the sense that the groups on which the cleavage is grounded must be aware of their shared identity and interest as farmers, workers, Catholics, or whatever. Among women, for example, it was the long-term absence of such a collective identity that constituted one of the major obstacles to the successful political mobilization of a gender cleavage. Third, a cleavage must find organizational expression, whether through a political party, a trade union, a church, or some other body. Each of these elements is an essential part of a cleavage, and it is here that the approach developed by Bartolini and Mair (1990: 211–20) differs from much of the other traditional work in this field. In many treatments, for example, the notion of cleavage is qualified, such that reference is made to 'political cleavages', to 'social cleavages' or to 'value cleavages', and so on, in a way that suggests that the different components can be separated out from one another and used to define different types of cleavage. In fact, such efforts at disaggregation simply lead to conceptual confusion, for there is almost nothing in a so-called political cleavage, for example, that is different from a political conflict or divide, and hence nothing that demands the use of the term 'cleavage'. It is equally impossible to distinguish the notion of a so-called 'social cleavage' from the notion of 'social stratification', and hence here too there is no real added value in the term 'cleavage'. By contrast, when the concept of cleavage is restricted to those phenomena in which social reality, identity and organization combine and interact with one another, we then bring it back to a consideration of those fundamental divides that have shaped the parties and the party systems of contemporary Europe, and that have been so ably theorized by Lipset and Rokkan (1967; see also Rokkan, 1970, 1999).

This also serves to emphasize one additional property of cleavages: they are deep structural divides that persist through time and through generations. They persist for a variety of reasons. In the first place, they persist because the interests that are involved remain relevant, and the groups that are involved retain their sense of collective identity. Second, they persist because alternative political identities are only likely to be mobilized when large numbers of new votes become incorporated into the political system, and this process came to an end with universal suffrage. Third, the rules of the game – the form of electoral system, the structure of the parliamentary system, the institutional set-up more generally – tend to favour the persistence of the parties that devised the rules in the first place, and hence also favour the persistence of the cleavages on which these parties have been built. Finally, they persist because they continue to be organized into politics by parties that seek to survive by controlling the terms of reference of political conflict and by narrowing down their electoral markets; as Schattschneider (1983: 66) once noted, 'the definition of the alternatives is the supreme instrument of power'.

In this context it is also revealing to recall that in Lipset and Rokkan's comparative analysis of four centuries of political developments in Europe they note the existence of just four core cleavages – the Church–State cleavage, the center–periphery cleavage, the primary–secondary economy cleavage, and the owner–worker cleavage. To be sure, this long period was also marked by innumerable other divides between political actors and parties; but it was not marked by innumerable cleavages. On the contrary, as Flora (1999: 7) notes in his evaluation of Rokkan's general theory, these are 'fundamental oppositions … which stand out from the multiplicity of [other] conflicts rooted in social structure'. When talking about cleavages, therefore, we are talking about the elementary building blocks of modern democratic development, and there are plenty of different terms that can then be used for the many other more tangential, peripheral, or short-term divides that play a role in contemporary politics.

Even building blocks can decay, however, and precisely because a cleavage is constituted by three components, it can come under stress for a variety of different reasons. In one case, social change can result in the gradual erosion of the social reality underpinning the cleavage, such as when modernization and urbanization ate away at the traditional social base of the Scandinavian agrarian parties, forcing them to become more catch-all centre parties in an effort to maintain their positions within their respective party systems. In another case, the cleavage can decay when the sense of collective identity begins to fragment, and when interests are no longer seen to be shared. In yet other cases, the cleavage can decay because the organizations which shape it develop an ambition for more expansive political strategies, and no longer foster a reliance on traditional heartlands. What rarely seems to happen in contemporary politics, however, is the wholesale substitution of a cleavage, such that one fading alignment is replaced by another emerging divide. At most, the evidence seems to point towards dealignment, in which weakening cleavages give way to non-structured electorates, and in which the powerful and stabilizing combination of social stratification, collective identity and organized expression yields to the emergence of more volatile individualized or particularized sets of preferences. Alternatively, where a new politics does

where it does

look like it is gaining ground, as might be seen to be the case with the mobilization of Green parties, on the one hand, or right-wing populist parties, on the other, the effect seems often short-lived and the challenge seems capable of adaptation. Finally, it is also striking to note how new issues and new concerns can sometimes breathe life into what had been an otherwise dormant cleavage, as was the case, for example, when the European issue seemed to reinvigorate the once highly salient centre–periphery cleavage in Norway.

When cleavages do decay, this is usually manifest in increasing levels of aggregate electoral instability – voters become more inclined to shift between parties and to cross cleavage boundaries, and their behaviour may therefore become less predictable and more random. As has been argued elsewhere, however (Bartolini and Mair, 1990; Mair, 2001), electoral volatility as such does not necessarily indicate cleavage decline. Rather, it is important to note the type of volatility that is involved, and its location within the party system. Shifts of votes between friends, or between cleavage allies, are in this sense less important than shifts of votes between enemies, for while both may indicate a weakening of the hold of individual party organizations, it is shifts between enemies which are more likely to indicate a weakening of the hold of cleavages. Shifts in aggregate electoral support from social democratic parties to communist parties in the early years of the twentieth century, or from communist parties back to social democratic parties at the century's close are clearly of relevance to our understanding of party systems and how they change, but they tell us little about the degree of cleavage closure. Similarly, shifts from one Protestant party to another in the Netherlands, or from one bourgeois party to another in France, may impact little on the overall cleavage structure, but they may well have a major impact on how the parties compete with one another. For this reason it is important to distinguish between overall levels of instability or volatility in the system, on the one hand, and levels of inter-area or inter-block volatility as given by the different cleavages structures, on the other (Mair, 1983: 408–14; Bartolini and Mair, 1990: 41–6). As more than a century of mass politics has shown, voters are much more willing to cross the boundaries separating individual political parties than they are to cross the lines of cleavage. Hence, while parties have come and gone, cleavages have tended to persist. This is also why cleavages are important.

NOTES

1. As Lipset (1960: 220, n.1) acknowledged, the term was actually adapted from the title of a book by Dewey Anderson and Percy Davidson, *Ballots and the Democratic Class Struggle* (1943), described by Lipset as being among 'the first American classics of the political-behavior field'.
2. This emphasis on the role of agency is also characteristic of the more recent literature on democratization (Kitschelt, 1992; Doorenspleet, 2005: 2–8), a field in which there has also been an attempt to move beyond the social-structural determinants that were originally emphasized by Lipset (1959).
3. See, for example, the interesting contrast in patterns of nationalist political mobilization in Northern Ireland and Scotland that is noted by McAllister (1981).

REFERENCES

Anderson, Dewey and Davidson, Percy E. (1943) *Ballots and the Democratic Class Struggle: A Study in the Background of Political Education.* Stanford, CA: Stanford University Press.

Bartolini, Stefano (2000) *The Political Mobilization of the European Left, 1860–1980: The Class Cleavage.* Cambridge: Cambridge University Press.

Bartolini, Stefano and Mair, Peter (1990) *Identity, Competition and Electoral Availability: The Stabilisation of European Electorates, 1885–1985.* Cambridge: Cambridge University Press.

Doorenspleet, Renske (2005) *Democratic Transitions: Exploring the Structural Sources of the Fourth Wave.* Boulder, CO: Lynne Rienner.

Flanagan, Scott C. (1987) 'Changing values in industrial societies revisited: Towards a resolution of the values debate', *American Political Science Review*, 81: 1303–19.

Flora, Peter (1999) 'Introduction and interpretation', in Stein Rokkan, *State Formation, Nation-Building, and Mass Politics in Europe: The Theory of Stein Rokkan* (edited by Peter Flora, Stein Kuhnle and Derek Urwin). Oxford: Oxford University Press, pp. 1–91.

Gallagher, Michael, Laver, Michael and Mair, Peter (2005) *Representative Government in Modern Europe*, 4th edn. New York: McGraw-Hill.

Hout, Michael, Manza, Jeff and Brooks, Clem (1999) 'Classes, unions, and the realignment of US presidential voting', in Geoff Evans (ed.), *The End of Class Politics? Class Voting in Comparative Perspective.* Oxford: Oxford University Press, pp. 83–96.

Inglehart, Ronald (1990) *Culture Shift in Advanced Industrial Society.* Princeton, NJ: Princeton University Press.

Kalyvas, Stathis N. (1996) *The Rise of Christian Democracy in Europe.* Ithaca, NY: Cornell University Press.

Kitschelt, Herbert (1992) 'Political regime change: structure and process-driven explanations', *American Political Science Review*, 86: 1028–34.

Knutsen, Oddbjørn and Scarbrough, Elinor (1995) 'Cleavage politics', in Jan W. van Deth and Elinor Scarbrough (eds), *The Impact of Values.* Oxford: Oxford University Press, pp. 492–523.

Kriesi, Hanspeter (1998) 'The transformation of cleavage politics: The 1997 Stein Rokkan lecture', *European Journal of Political Research*, 33: 165–85.

Lipset, S.M. (1959) 'Some social requisites of democracy: Economic development and political legitimacy', *American Political Science Review*, 53: 69–105.

Lipset, S.M. (1960) *Political Man.* London: Heinemann.

Lipset, S.M. and Marks, Gary (2000) *It Didn't Happen Here: Why Socialism Failed in the United States.* New York: W.W. Norton.

Lipset, S.M. and Rokkan, Stein (1967) 'Cleavage structures, party systems and voter alignments: an introduction', in S.M. Lipset and Stein Rokkan (eds), *Party Systems and Voter Alignments.* New York: Free Press, pp. 1–64.

McAllister, Ian (1981) 'Party organization and minority nationalism: A comparative study in the United Kingdom', *European Journal of Political Research*, 9: 237–56.

Mair, Peter (1983) 'Adaptation and control: towards an understanding of party and party system change', in Hans Daalder and Peter Mair (eds), *Western European Party Systems: Continuity and Change.* London: Sage, pp. 405–29.

Mair, Peter (1992) 'Explaining the absence of class politics in Ireland', in John H. Goldthorpe and Christopher T. Whelan (eds), *The Development of Industrial Society in Ireland.* Oxford: Oxford University Press, pp. 383–410.

Mair, Peter (2001) 'The freezing hypothesis: An evaluation', in Lauri Karvonen and Stein Kuhnle (eds), *Party Systems and Voter Alignments Revisited.* London: Routledge, pp. 27–44.

Rokkan, Stein (1970) *Citizens, Elections, Parties.* Oslo: Universitetsforlaget.

Rokkan, Stein (1999) *State Formation, Nation-Building, and Mass Politics in Europe: The Theory of Stein Rokkan* (edited by Peter Flora, Stein Kuhnle and Derek Urwin). Oxford: Oxford University Press.

Sartori, Giovanni (1990) 'The sociology of parties: A critical review', in Peter Mair (ed.), *The West European Party System.* Oxford: Oxford University Press, pp. 150–82. Originally published in 1969.

Schattschneider, E.E. (1983) *The Semisovereign People: A Realist's View of Democracy in America.* Fort Worth, TX: Holt, Rinehart and Winston. Originally published in 1960.

31

POLITICAL PARTIES *AND* SOCIAL CAPITAL, POLITICAL PARTIES *OR* SOCIAL CAPITAL*

Eric M. Uslaner

Social capital and political parties seem like natural compatriots. Both involve gathering people together for a common purpose. Parties organize people to win elections. Social capital is all about bringing people together for any number of purposes. Surely forging campaigns and winning elections falls under this general rubric.

Putnam (1993: 171) argues that social capital reflects 'norms of reciprocity and networks of civic engagement'. Participation in political party activity, like social capital more generally, has been in decline over the past four decades (Putnam, 2000: 37–45; Seyd and Whiteley, 2002: 88). The linkage seems straightforward, but the notion of social capital proves to be a catch-all for all types of norms, values, and social connections. We need to unpack the concept to see whether parties really represent social capital. Despite the initial impression that political parties are one form of social capital – and the links forged in some of the literature between the two (Putnam, 2000: 37–45; Andersen and Young, 2000; Weinstein, 1999) – there is reason to be skeptical of the connection.

Social capital matters, Putnam and others argue, because it brings people together to solve common problems. Many forms of civic engagement, from joining choral societies and bowling leagues to informal social ties such as picnics, bring people together for reasons unrelated to civic life. People do not join bowling leagues to become better citizens. However, Putnam (1993, 2000) argues that membership in voluntary associations and informal social connections can lead people to trust each other, to discuss issues of community concern, and

to band together for collective action. In this sense, some forms of social interaction – bridging 'social capital', which links us to people who are different from ourselves (Putnam, 2000: 22) – are 'best'. Bridging social capital creates bonds across ethnic and class lines and 'can generate broader identities and reciprocity, whereas bonding social capital [connecting us to people like ourselves] bolsters our narrower selves' (Putnam, 2000: 23). For Putnam, however, almost *all* forms of social interaction help people get together to take collective action. The decline in social capital – in membership in voluntary associations, in informal socializing, in trust in other people, and (of course) in participation in political parties – is worrisome. Americans no longer connect to each other, they trust each other less, and our social and political life has become more contentious.

The linkage of parties and social capital, I argue, is misplaced. To show this, I must first unpack the notion of social capital. Briefly, my argument is threefold. First, the social connections part of social capital presumes that people interact with each other in voluntary organizations and that these ties bring people together. Yet, the evidence we have on members of major political parties – parties primarily concerned with winning office – suggests that: most members do very little for the party and may largely be 'checkbook' members; and when members do attend party meetings, they rarely socialize with each other. Across nations, there is little connection between joining voluntary associations and membership in political parties. In the American states, there is little connection between the strength of party organizations and membership in voluntary organizations. Political parties are essentially elite institutions devoted to winning elections and governing. They do have members, but widespread participation in party governance would effectively destroy the ability of parties to win elections and formulate policy. Michels (1963) recognized this over a century ago and Schattschneider (1941) reiterated the argument six decades ago.

Second, the nostalgia for an era of widespread participation in parties may be misplaced. There may be less participation in party organizations now than in the past, but conjuring up a picture of a bygone era when hordes of citizens were involved in party work is an exercise in fantasy. Perhaps 40 years ago – or a century ago – more people participated in voluntary organizations (at least in the United States). Yet, even then, the share of people who worked for parties was tiny. And there is little evidence that participation was widespread elsewhere. Yes, some parties have extensive member participation. But these tend to be minor parties more focused on elaborating policy goals than on winning offices (Strøm, 1990). When a party such as the Greens in Germany (and other European countries) decides to enter a government as a coalition partner, it must shift its focus away from widespread citizen participation toward more centralized control and moderate positions on issues.

Finally, and perhaps most critically, the idea that people would get together in voluntary associations and develop trust in their fellow citizens is questionable. The notion that people might get together in *political parties* and develop faith in people of different backgrounds is not tenable. As there are different types of social capital more generally, so there are different types of trust (Uslaner, 2002: Chapter 2). Here I only need distinguish between *generalized* and *particularized* trust. The former is faith in strangers, in people who *may be different from yourself*. It is *not* based upon adult experiences, such as joining voluntary associations (much less political parties). Rather, you learn it early in life from your family.

Generalized trust reflects an optimistic world-view. Even if you could learn it as an adult from various forms of civic engagement, there are two key obstacles to doing so: First, most people spend little time in any voluntary organization, at best a few hours a week. This will hardly suffice to make people more (or less) trusting in their fellow citizens (Newton, 1997: 579). Second, we are simply unlikely to meet people who are different from ourselves in our civic life. Now, choral societies and bird-watching groups – two of the groups that Putnam (1993) found so central to civic life in Italy – will hardly *destroy* trust. And there is nothing wrong with such narrow groups. They bring lots of joy to their members and don't harm anybody. But they are poor candidates for creating generalized trust (Rosenblum, 1998). Political party activity is not as benign as membership in bird-watching societies. The whole purpose of joining a political party is to interact with people who share your values. So party membership is likely to enhance particularized (in-group) trust at the expense of out-group trust.

PARTIES AND GROUP MEMBERSHIP

Putnam (2000: 37–45) treats political parties like any other voluntary organization. Weinstein (1999) and Andersen and Young (2000) make a more explicit linkage between political parties and social capital. Both posit an *indirect* rather than direct linkage. Neither claims that parties themselves are traditional voluntary associations that bring people together. Weinstein argues that party mobilization leads to greater political participation, a thesis in political behavior that long pre-dates the concern about social capital. He demonstrates that aggregated levels of party contact in the American states strongly affect participation rates. He also shows that party mobilization has a powerful effect on a combined measure of community organizational life (group membership, serving as an officer in a club, attending club meetings) and informal socializing (visiting friends and entertaining people at home). The connection between party mobilization and turnout is not at all surprising. We have long known that party mobilization and the face-to-face contact it brings can have a powerful effect on turnout (Gosnell, 1927; Gerber and Green, 2000; Rosenstone and Hansen, 2003: 89–90). The link with organizational life is new (see below) and is worthy of further concern. So is the connection with informal socializing. This relationship is curious: Why should contact with a party worker make me more likely to hold a dinner party or visit a friend's house?

The Andersen–Young argument links political party organizations to voluntary associations in the United States. Andersen and Young argue that parties have built their organizations by mobilizing existing groups, such as ethnic, labor, church, teachers, business, and farm associations as well as volunteer fire

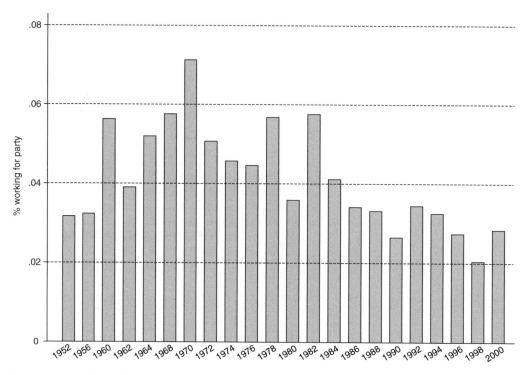

Figure 31.1   Share of Americans working for party, 1952–2000

Source: American National Election Study cumulative file (1948–2000)
Regression with time: $1.714 - 0.001^*$ Year ($r^2 = 0.587$)

companies. Wheat farmers played a key role in establishing political parties in Canada and the United States, the Saskatchewan branch of the Canadian Cooperative Foundation and North Dakota's Non-Partisan League (Lipset, 1968: 259–61). Andersen and Young (2000: 8–10) also summarize surveys of party leaders in American communities and delegates to party conventions; they find that most were also active in civic organizations.

The modern party has retained its ties to other voluntary organizations. Political parties sponsor sports clubs and professional teams, as well as other social groups. In Israel, most of the major banks were initially established by unions or religious organizations affiliated with political parties. Today there are far fewer face-to-face ties between the party and the citizen than in the past. Parties now develop ties with advocacy organizations that place little emphasis on direct contact with citizens and are more concerned with raising funds for campaigns. Putnam (2000: 40) argues: 'While membership in a political club was cut in half between 1967 and 1987, the fraction of the public that contributed to a political campaign

nearly doubled.' Party contact with voters has fallen dramatically over time (see Figure 31.1 for the trend in the American National Election Study, showing a powerful downward trend with a strong fit, $r^2 = 0.587$). Rosenstone and Hansen link this decline to falling turnout. And Putnam (2000: 45) points to a 42 % decline in the share of Americans who report working for a political party from 1973 to 1994. Most European parties lost members from the 1980s to the 1990s (Ware, 1996: 73). There were much sharper declines over a longer time frame in Denmark (Bille, 1994: 137) and the Netherlands (Koole, 1994: 287); and in a shorter period (1990 to 1999) for the British Labour Party (Seyd and Whiteley, 2002: 88).

The portrait drawn by Putnam and by Andersen and Young is one of dedicated party workers serving their communities and mobilizing voters. It is a sign of social capital at work. Yet, it is an exaggeration of the role of party members in politics. Seyd and Whiteley (2002: 88, 118–19) found that for most Labour Party members in Great Britain the party was little more than a 'checkbook' organization, or what Putnam (2000: 32) called a 'tertiary' organization. Members contributed money (64% of Labour members did in 1999) and displayed campaign posters (90%), but fewer than half of the members delivered party leaflets or even reminded others to vote. And fewer than a quarter of members helped with mailings, canvassed door-to-door, raised money from others, or drove voters to the polls. Only 10 percent participated in phone banks, ran street stalls, or attended vote counting. By the late 1990s, 65 percent of Labour Party members devoted no time at all to party activities and 75 percent said that they were not at all active or not very active. The story is similar in Italy, where 'ordinary members [have] little contact with the party's organization and scarcely participat[e] in any of its activities' (Bardi and Morlino, 1994: 255).

The modern party member gets involved in politics much in the same way that people who belong to groups such as Common Cause or many environmental organizations (from the National Wildlife Federation to Greenpeace). They come for the program (or for Labour, the programme), not for the social interaction (Seyd and Whiteley, 1992: 212–17; Rothenberg, 1992). Even among the more highly committed German Greens, only 20 percent of party members in Frankfurt attended meetings in the early 1980s (Kitschelt, 1989: 152).

Perhaps, as Putnam (1993: 115) argues, people join the party for ideological reasons, but develop social ties and a cooperative spirit as a 'by-product' of their membership. Party organizations once offered opportunities for social interactions in the United States and Europe. British, American, and German local party organizations in the early 20th century were often more social clubs than ideological forums; people gathered together to play snooker, drink beer, and collect stamps, rather than discuss the issues of the day. These clubs were not very effective in getting people to perform real party work. The 'recreational' activities led to 'an apolitical culture within the organization' (Ware, 1992: 83). By the mid-20th century, young people deserted party organizations for singles bars for their social lives. The people who continued to congregate in party organizations often had little time for or interest in socializing (Ware, 1992: 81–5; Scarrow, 1996: 190–1). In his study of political reform clubs in New York, Chicago, and Los Angeles in the 1950s and early 1960s, James Q. Wilson (1962: 167–8) recounted what one Los Angeles leader told him: 'The club movement is not basically a social movement ... My social friends are not in the clubs. I don't go to the homes of the people I know in the clubs and they don't come

to mine.' Club meetings, Wilson (1962: 168) argued, were 'long and often dull in the extreme, with a seemingly endless agenda and interminable speakers'.

Seyd and Whiteley (2002: 98) found that a bare majority of Labour Party members who were not at all active (40 percent of the sample) thought membership was a good way to meet 'interesting people'; 75 percent of active and 84 percent of very active party members agreed that party membership helps establish social ties, but active members constitute just 25 percent of party members. Meetings of strongly ideological parties in Europe often degenerated into hostile debates between the in-group clique and new members who might not be as strongly committed, driving out all but the most dedicated (Ware, 1992: 82; Kitschelt, 1989: 126–7).

It is hardly surprising to find that the most active party members find friends in the organization. It also makes sense that these strong activists take an active role in other organizations. They are, after all, the most dedicated partisans. Are party members more likely to be civic activists more generally? The 1996 American National Election Study asked about membership in parties, labor unions, and other groups (business, veterans, church, other religious, elderly, women's, political, civic, ideological, children, hobby, community, fraternal, service, educational, cultural, and self-help). There was a moderate correlation ($r = 0.198$) between membership in parties and political groups, and modest correlations with service and cultural groups (0.13 each). All of the other groups had correlations of 0.10 or less (seven had correlations less than 0.05, including ideological groups). The 'civic activists' who belonged to both parties and either service or cultural groups comprised just 1.56 percent of the total sample. Overall, then, joining a party in the United States does not lead to greater civic activism, except among a small handful of people.

Nor is there evidence that strong party organizations lead to a more civic environment. Mayhew (1986) classified the American states according to the strength of their political party organizations, ranging from the very powerful 'traditional party organizations' (high 'TPO' scores) in the industrial states to the much weaker parties (especially in the West). Do states with stronger party organizations also have a more vibrant civic life? Figures 31.2 and 31.3 suggest not. There is a weak *negative* correlation between party organization strength and Putnam's state-level measure of social capital ($r = -0.293$) from *Bowling Alone* (Putnam, 2000) and his more specific measure of civic group membership in the states ($r = -0.158$).

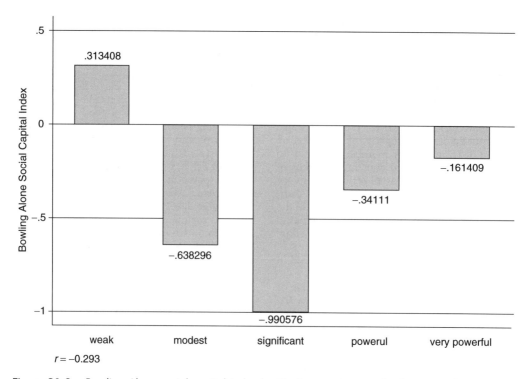

Figure 31.2   *Bowling Alone* social capital index by Mayhew party organization strength

States with strong party organizations have lower social capital.

The United States is hardly typical, so I turn to the World Values Surveys. Here we see much stronger correlations between party membership and participation in other voluntary organizations (ranging from $r = 0.248$ for church membership to 0.427 for environmental organizations, with unions, and charitable, sports, arts, professional groups in between). These are much more powerful correlations (especially since they are based on more than 150,000 cases). They warrant further analysis, so I aggregated the membership scores by country. I excluded Nigeria and the United States because both had inexplicably high memberships in parties (almost 40 percent in Nigeria and 26 percent in the United States). The aggregate picture still suggests a significant link between membership in parties and in professional associations (the civic group with the highest simple correlation), $r^2 = 0.368$ (see Figure 31.4). However, this result stems almost entirely from the low rates of membership across all organizations in the former communist nations (see Howard, 2003). When I eliminate these countries, the r^2 falls to 0.152 (see Figure 31.5). Overall, then, the relationship between

parties and civic life is modest at best. A handful of people participate in both forms of organization, but membership in parties is not common (averaging around 8 percent in the World Values Surveys) and *active participation* is the preserve of a small share of activists (4 percent in the World Values Survey say that they are active members).

Is this low rate of participation a contemporary phenomenon? Katz and Mair (1995) argue that modern political parties have become like cartels. Modern parties are like businesses, controlled from above and forsaking ideological purity. As party membership has fallen, control of the party apparatus has shifted to the parliamentary parties, which have sought greater autonomy from constituency groups.

Parties are more centralized at the turn of the 21st century. Yet, we cannot look back to halcyon days where large numbers of citizens took an active role in party affairs. Major parties in most democracies did have more members 50 to 100 years ago. However, membership figures give a distorted view of how active members are. Ware (1992: 82) argued that the machine parties of the early 20th century were 'highly inefficient in recruiting labour to perform party

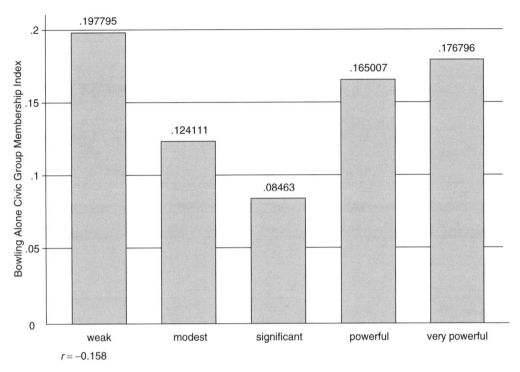

Figure 31.3   *Bowling Alone* civic group membership index by Mayhew party organization strength

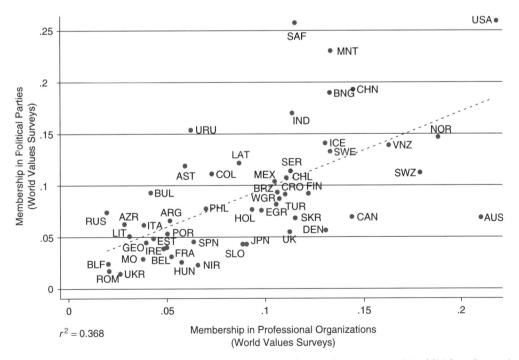

Figure 31.4   Membership in party organizations and professional associations (World Values Surveys)

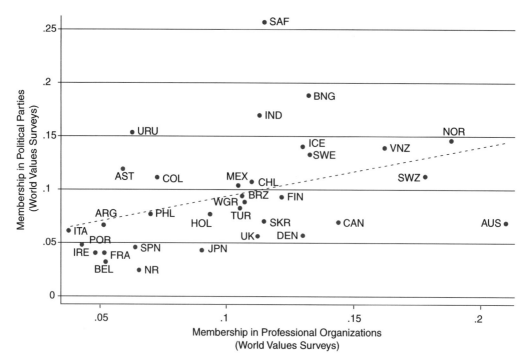

Figure 31.5 Membership in party organizations and professional associations
(World Values Surveys)

$r^2 = 0.152$, excluding former Communist nations and USA.

tasks'. Lipset (1968: 259–66) noted that large shares of the populations of Saskatchewan and North Dakota were members of populist parties in the 1940s. However, he cautioned (Lipset, 1968: 265) that '[t]he Saskatchewan pattern ... provides no panacea for those who would plan society so as to create the basis for popular community activity'. The rural political setting (where neighbors regularly interacted with each other) and the poverty of the farm economy provided a recipe for a highly mobilized protest politics that is unlikely to be met in most political settings, even in the 19th century.

While Putnam (2000: 45) bemoans the sharp drop in citizens working for a political party in the United States, the 1973 starting point was just 6.3 percent of the American population, down to 2.8 percent by 1994 (Uslaner with Brown, 2004).[1] There are fewer party contacts with voters in the United States (Rosenstone and Hansen, 2003) and in Britain (Scarrow, 1996: 188). In both countries, however, the share of people who worked for political parties at any time in the past half century was minuscule, perhaps not even as high as 5 percent. The decline in party work, Scarrow (1996: 190) argues, is 'small, rather than ... dramatic'.

Parties and other voluntary organizations have an uneasy relationship. Parties have often depended upon outside organizations for support. In many instances, such as labor parties especially in Western Europe, parties are legal extensions of other organizations. These groups provide both activists and funding for the parties. Yet, they also constrain the parties. Outside groups will set the party programs, limiting the maneuverability of parties in elections. In more than a handful of cases, this will produce strains between a party seeking to win a national election and an outside group committed to a particular platform. Labour in Britain struggled with the trade union movement in the 1990s, finally declaring its independence and campaigning (successfully) as 'New Labour'. Christian democratic parties throughout Europe are associated with the Catholic Church; they have struggled to maintain moderate positions on controversial social issues such as abortion and gay rights, even in defiance of Church doctrine.

Parties seeking to win elections have an incentive to limit participatory democracy. Party leaders need to maintain control of their own platforms. Civic groups care less about

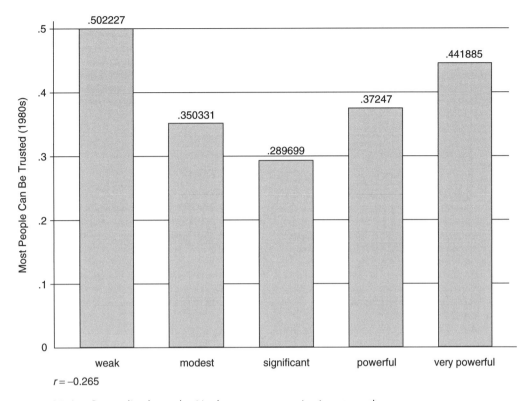

Figure 31.6   Generalized trust by Mayhew party organization strength

winning elections than about pursuing a cause. Too much social capital can mean weak parties that cannot contest elections. Party activists are much more ideological than the rank-and-file members, party supporters in the electorate, and especially the much heralded median voter (Aldrich, 1995; Flanagan, 1995; Seyd and Whiteley, 1992: 212–17). Parties need ideologies – to govern, to attract activists, and indeed even to win elections (Hinich and Munger, 1994). Yet they must not become too extreme, lest they pay an electoral price. And, if they had their way, the most dedicated activists would push the parties past the point of electoral safety (Strøm, 1990: 577; Uslaner, 1999: Chapter 5).

It is hardly surprising that the parties with the largest shares of activists represent radical policies, where militants disdain the goal of winning elections. For many of these radical parties, such as environmental parties in Belgium, the most militant members care more about community activism than about national electoral strategies (Kitschelt and Hellemans, 1990: 136–8). These policy-oriented parties can 'afford' widespread participation and even 'infiltration' by other interests. Office-seeking parties must try to constrain

their members' participation. Party leaders need activists to help run the campaigns, but want to limit participation. So they may offer party workers the 'selective benefit' of greater opportunities to run for office in the future (Strøm, 1990: 576–8). Since barely a handful of members ever run for office,[2] such a pay-off restricts the influence of party members.

PARTIES AND TRUST

If generalized trust is a key component of social capital, we should not look to political parties – or indeed political life – to foster it. Much of political life is not about bringing people together for cooperation. Politics thrives on mistrust (Barber, 1983; Warren, 1996). Elections are inherently polarizing events and the further apart parties are from each other on an ideological spectrum, the less likely they are to bring about trust in people who are different from oneself.

In Figure 31.6, I show levels of generalized trust in the American states by Mayhew's

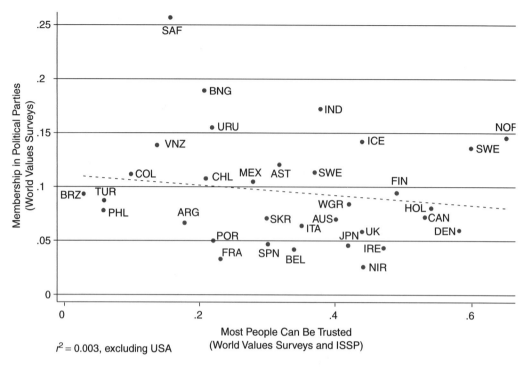

Figure 31.7   Membership in party organizations and generalized trust

traditional party organization index. And there is at least modest evidence ($r = -0.265$) that strong parties lead to less trust. States with the strongest party organizations have *less trusting citizenries*. Cross-nationally, there is less support for this linkage. When I plot generalized trust against party membership across the countries in the World Values Survey (Figure 31.7), there is no relationship at all between party membership and trust ($r^2 = 0.003$). There is stronger support for the negative relationship in roll call voting in the United States. As generalized trust has fallen in the United States, party polarization in legislative voting has increased (Uslaner, 2000).

Party activity is all about building *particularized trust* (in-group trust) rather than generalized trust. Strongly ideological activists are likely to see cooperating with the opposition as illegitimate. Seventy percent of Americans who are strong ideologues believe that 'compromise is just selling out', compared with 53 percent of moderates. Three-quarters of people who are both strong ideologues and who are politically active view compromise with suspicion (compared to 43 percent of the inactive non-ideologues).[3]

When activists play a stronger role in shaping the party's agenda, the party shifts more strongly toward ideological extremes (Aldrich, 1995). Where the parties are tightly controlled by a small elite, electoral considerations dominate over ideological purity. New York State Senator George Washington Plunkitt, head of the Tammany Hall Democratic machine in New York City in the early 20th century, had little time for the great issues of the day. He was a political boss and his two primary concerns were winning elections and dispensing patronage. To ensure his continued power base, he maintained cordial relations with the opposition Republicans (Riordon, 1948: 51–2): 'When Tammany's on top I do good turns for the Republicans. When they're on top they don't forget me. ... Me and the Republicans are enemies just one day in the year – election day. Then we fight tooth and nail. The rest of the time it's live and let live with us.'

REPRISE

Major political parties are elite institutions focused on winning elections and formulating public policies to govern the nation. In each case, social capital may prove to be more of a hindrance than a help to a party's mission. Too much participation can push a party to an ideological extreme and make it more difficult for the party to win an election. The Labour Party in Great Britain reasserted itself, and became dominant, in the 1990s by denying its membership base the power to set party policies. The Greens in several European countries have fought internal battles over what strategy to follow. The 'Realo' (realist) faction in the German party prevailed in a fierce intra-party battle, leading the Greens to join the Social Democrats in a governing coalition. The Greens' leader, Joschka Fischer, a former radical, became German foreign minister and a supporter of a largely activist foreign policy vehemently opposed by the 'Fundi' wing of the party.

Parties cannot afford too much participation. Not only do they abjure the ideological drift of the activists, but governing coalitions cannot tolerate constant meddling from constituents on the details of public policy. Parties don't need, and their leaders don't want, the camaraderie of a choral society or a bowling league. Parties need to mobilize voters *on election day*. At other times, the party leaders prefer that voters go their own way.

Parties also don't depend upon trust. A trusting environment helps parties reach agreement across the aisle on controversial policy issues (Uslaner, 2002: Chapter 7). Parties may find the commitment to seek compromises to be anathema to their goal of getting elected. If the party promises compromise too early, it has no message and voters may have little reason to choose it over the opposition. No wonder, then, that among the chorus of civic leaders bemoaning the loss of trust and civic engagement, party leaders have been consciously absent.

NOTES

* The assistance of Mitchell Brown and Paul Sum is greatly appreciated. I am also grateful to the Russell Sage Foundation and the Carnegie Foundation for a grant under the Russell Sage program on The Social Dimensions of Inequality (see http://www.russellsage.org/programs/proj_reviews/social-inequality.htm) and to the General Research Board of the Graduate School of the University of Maryland – College Park. Some of the data reported here come from the Inter-University Consortium for Political and Social Research (ICPSR), which is not responsible for any interpretations.

1. The figures from the American National Election Study are very similar: 5.7 percent in 1968 and 2.7 percent in 1996.
2. In the Roper Political and Social Trends data cited above, in 1994, 2.8 percent of respondents worked for a political party, while just 0.7 percent ever claimed to run for office; 23 percent of people who worked for a party had at least once engaged in a sit-in or protest, compared to 16 percent who ran for office.
3. These data come from Hibbing and Thiess-Morse (1995). I am grateful to John Hibbing and Beth Thiess-Morse for providing them to me.

REFERENCES

Aldrich, John H. (1995) *Why Parties? The Origin and Transformation of Party Politics in America*. Chicago: University of Chicago Press.

Andersen, Kristi and Young, McGee (2000) 'How political parties and voluntary associations interact in shaping civil society'. Presented at the Annual Meeting of the American Political Science Association, Washington DC, August/September.

Barber, Bernard (1983) *The Logic and Limits of Trust*. New Brunswick, NJ: Rutgers University Press.

Bardi, Luciano and Morlino, Leonardo (1994) 'Italy: Tracing the roots of the great transformation', in Richard S. Katz and Peter Mair (eds), *How Parties Organize*. London: Sage.

Bille, Lars (1994) 'Denmark: The decline of the membership party?', in Richard S. Katz and Peter Mair (eds), *How Parties Organize*. London: Sage.

Flanagan, Tom (1995) *Waiting for the Wave: The Reform Party and Preston Manning*. Toronto: Stoddart.

Gerber, Alan S. and Green, Donald P. (2000) 'The effects of personal canvassing, telephone calls, and direct mail on voter turnout: A field experiment', *American Political Science Review*, 94: 653–63.

Gosnell, Harold F. (1927) *Getting out the Vote: An Experiment in the Stimulation of Voting*. Chicago: University of Chicago Press.

Hibbing, John and Thiess-Morse, Elizabeth (1995) *Congress as Public Enemy*. New York: Cambridge University Press.

Hinich, Melvin J. and Munger, Michael C. (1994) *Ideology and the Theory of Political Choice*. Ann Arbor: University of Michigan Press.

Howard, Mark Morje (2003) *The Weakness of Civil Society in Post-Communist Europe*. New York: Cambridge University Press.

Katz, Richard S. and Mair, Peter (1995) 'Changing models of party organization and party democracy: The emergence of the cartel party', *Party Politics*, 1: 5–28.

Kitschelt, Herbert (1989) *The Logics of Party Formation*. Ithaca, NY: Cornell University Press.

Kitschelt, Herbert and Hellemans, Staf (1990) *Beyond the European Left: Ideology and Political Action in the Belgian Ecology Parties*. Durham, NC: Duke University Press.

Koole, Ruud A. (1994) 'The vulnerability of the modern cadre party in the Netherlands', in Richard S. Katz and Peter Mair (eds), *How Parties Organize*. London: Sage.

Lipset, Seymour Martin (1968) *Agrarian Socialism*, updated edition. New York: Anchor.

Mayhew, David R. (1986) *Placing Parties in American Politics*. Princeton, NJ: Princeton University Press.

Michels, Robert (1963) *Political Parties: A Sociological Study of the Oligarchical Tendencies of Modern Democracy*. New York: Free Press.

Newton, Kenneth (1997) 'Social capital and democracy', *American Behavioral Scientist*, 40: 575–86.

Putnam, Robert D. (1993) *Making Democracy Work: Civic Traditions in Modern Italy*. Princeton, NJ: Princeton University Press.

Putnam, Robert D. (2000) *Bowling Alone: The Collapse and Revival of American Community*. New York: Simon and Schuster.

Riordon, William (1948) *Plunkitt of Tammany Hall*. New York: Alfred A. Knopf.

Rosenblum, Nancy L. (1998) *Membership and Morals*. Princeton, NJ: Princeton University Press.

Rosenstone, Steven J. and Hansen, John Mark (2003) *Mobilization, Participation, and Democracy in America*. New York: Macmillan.

Rothenberg, Lawrence S. (1992) *Linking Citizens to Government*. New York: Cambridge University Press.

Scarrow, Susan E. (1996) *Parties and Their Members*. Oxford: Oxford University Press.

Schattschneider, E.E. (1941) *Party Government*. New York: Rinehart and Winston.

Seyd, Patrick and Whiteley, Paul (1992) *Labour's Grassroots: The Politics of Party Membership*. Oxford: Clarendon.

Seyd, Patrick and Whiteley, Paul (2002) *New Labour's Grassroots: The Transformation of the Labour Party Membership*. London: Palgrave Macmillan.

Strøm, Kaare (1990) 'A behavioral theory of competitive parties', *American Journal of Political Science*, 34: 565–98.

Uslaner, Eric M. (1999) *The Movers and the Shirkers: Representatives and Ideologues in the Senate*. Ann Arbor: University of Michigan Press.

Uslaner, Eric M. (2000) 'Is the Senate more civil than the House?', in Burdett Loomis (ed.), *Esteemed Colleagues: Civility and Deliberation in the Senate*. Washington, DC: Brookings Institution.

Uslaner, Eric M. (2002) *The Moral Foundations of Trust*. New York: Cambridge University Press.

Uslaner, Eric M. with Brown, M. Mitchell (2004) 'Inequality, trust, and civic engagement', unpublished manuscript, University of Maryland, College Park.

Ware, Alan (1992) 'Activist–leader relations and the structure of political parties: "Exchange" models and vote-seeking behaviour in parties', *British Journal of Political Science*, 22: 71–92.

Ware, Alan (1996) *Political Parties and Party Systems*. Oxford: Oxford University Press.

Warren, Mark E. (1996) 'Deliberative democracy and authority', *American Political Science Review*, 90: 46–60.

Weinstein, Jeremy M. (1999) 'Abandoning the polity: Political parties and social capital in American politics'. Presented at the Annual Meeting of the American Political Science Association, Atlanta, September.

Wilson, James Q. (1962) *The Amateur Democrat: Club Politics in Three Cities*. Chicago: University of Chicago Press.

32

POLITICAL PARTIES AND SOCIAL STRUCTURE IN THE DEVELOPING WORLD

Vicky Randall

INTRODUCTION

The relationship between political parties and their putative social base raises complex questions, even in the context of developed democracies and abundant information. Outside this context, while losing none of its importance, the relationship becomes even more difficult to pin down. This chapter attempts to capture themes and implications of the existing literature while suggesting some of the analytical difficulties entailed and stressing that much relevant research is at an early stage.

First a couple of words are necessary about the parameters of this discussion. The chapter is concerned with the non-Western or developing world, which is conventionally understood to include Africa, Asia, the Caribbean, Latin America and the Middle East. The coherence of such a huge category, even in the heyday of Third World-ism, was always in doubt. These days, as the shared colonial legacy recedes and economic differentiation between and within its regions increases, the diversity of the developing world – and of its political systems and societies – becomes ever more apparent, making generalization increasingly problematic.

In addition, it is concerned with 'social structure', a term which has been understood in many different ways, ranging from a Marxist-inspired focus on economically based social classes to the social institutions of functional sociology. Here it will be interpreted quite broadly to include social classes, categories, groups, and even, where appropriate, institutions and associations.

The chapter proceeds as follows. The next section comments on political parties in the developing world, both what we know about them and how they have been studied. The different possible ways in which one could think about the relationship between parties and their social base are then suggested and provide the framework for the subsequent discussion, looking at parties and social cleavages, parties and electoral behaviour, appeals by party leaders and links between parties and particular social organizations, descriptive and substantive representation and parties themselves helping to create cleavages.

POLITICAL PARTIES IN THE DEVELOPING WORLD

Whilst doubtless queries could be raised about how political parties are to be defined and recognized in a developing world context, these are not the most pressing problems facing the present discussion, which are more to do with the availability of data and scholarly analysis. On the one hand there has long been a relative shortage of such information, and it has been very uneven in terms of geographical coverage. Whilst in some countries, notably India, research into political parties has been solid and continuous, elsewhere, following a number of important pioneering studies, with the onset of authoritarian systems of government in the

1970s there was a sharp decline in scholarly interest. (Re)democratization and the particular emphasis on the contribution political parties can make to democratic consolidation has only relatively recently rekindled interest in this subject. Now there is a great deal of research, with an ever widening range of countries included. Much of this focuses primarily on analysing elections and their results, but other research has taken up themes in the wider democratization literature about parties' contribution to democracy, institutionalization of parties and party systems, and so on, though there is still little direct discussion of the relationship between parties and their social bases. So a more recent problem is simply keeping up to speed with this proliferating literature, and the present discussion makes no claim to comprehensive coverage.

Second, and at the risk of stating the blindingly obvious, the great number of political parties and party systems in the developing world are hugely diverse. Some, like Congress in India, have existed a very long time, others only appeared with the most recent wave of democratization; some, like Congress and the Bharatiya Janata Party (BJP) in India, the Kuomintang (KMT) in Taiwan, the Institutionalized Party of the Revolution (PRI) in Mexico and the African National Congress (ANC) in South Africa, are agreed to be highly 'institutionalized' and/or organized, whilst others scarcely exist beyond their name, and so forth. There have been few systematic attempts to categorize them, although Gunther and Diamond (2003) have made a valuable start in this direction.

Having said that, and always bearing in mind the important exceptions, to which we return below, certain features are regularly observed, no less in recent years than in the earlier phase of scholarly interest in such parties, features also apparent in some Western parties but to a lesser extent. Thus parties in the developing world are regularly observed to be weakly institutionalized, a confused concept (Randall and Svåsand, 2002) but often understood to include 'rootedness' in society. Parties have frequently been constructed simply as ephemeral vehicles for their leaders' personal ambition, and where links with social sectors do exist these are often of a clientelistic nature. Parties generally lack a distinct membership or clearly defined membership criteria, which might give some practical and/or symbolic linkage with society or a section of it. Again typically they do not seek to differentiate themselves by developing coherent programmes or policy debates through which distinct social interests could be identified and promoted. All these features seem likely to reduce the possibility of strong, meaningful links with society.

One reason why parties are often weakly institutionalized is that long periods of authoritarian rule have meant that party development was repeatedly interrupted. Furthermore, there has often been a close association between political parties and the state. Development and democratization could be expected to increase the possibility of party autonomy from the state and, through improved communications, of party leaders strengthening links with their 'grassroots'. Paradoxically, however, it is argued that in countries like Chile (Munck and Bosworth, 1998) or Brazil, as in the West, party leaders place increasing reliance on television to reach the electorate which limits the development of the party as an organization and thus the possibility of group representation within and through it.

CONCEPTUALIZING THE RELATIONSHIP BETWEEN PARTIES AND SOCIAL STRUCTURE,

Panebianco (1988: 3–4) has famously warned against the 'sociological prejudice ... that the activities of parties are the product of the "demands" of social groups, and that, more generally, parties themselves are nothing more than manifestations of social divisions in the political arena'. Nonetheless the literature on political parties is surprisingly vague about the sense(s) in which and the mechanisms through which a party can be said to be linked to or based on a social sector. This is, however, true of the literature as a whole, not just that concerned with parties in the developing world. To discuss the relationship between parties and social structure(s) we need first to distinguish different possible forms or aspects of that relationship, around which the analysis can be organized.

Much analysis of the relationship between parties and social structure in the Western world takes as its point of departure the Lipset and Rokkan (1967) model discussed in Chapters 29 and 30 of this *Handbook*. How relevant or helpful is that model for understanding party–society relations in the developing world? More simply, we can ask about patterns of electoral support for parties on the one hand, and the ways in which party leaders seek to project particular party identities on the other. We can also consider links between parties and particular social institutions and organizations. But this is still not quite the same question as whom the party actually does stand for. This requires us to explore the thorny issue of representation, especially in its descriptive and more substantive forms.

PARTIES AND CLEAVAGES

The Lipset–Rokkan model was not devised to explain the emergence of parties in the developing world, but reflected a particular western European history. We can nonetheless ask how far either its categorization of cleavages or its thesis both about the sequence and the manner in which parties were originally formed is of relevance in a developing world context. The model identified a series of potential cleavage lines – between church and state, centre and periphery, urban and rural sectors and labour and capital – which do indeed have relevance for the developing countries, but only up to a point. In the first place, the church–state opposition needs to be extended to include competing confessional parties and the centre–periphery opposition needs to include conflict based on ethnic/regional rivalry as well as opposition to the centre. Second, even then these categories may not adequately convey distinctive qualities of social structures, for instance the depth of attachment to ethnic or religious identity, or the scale of social inequality.

They also omit a cleavage or basis of identification that has been very important in the formation of political parties in the developing world, that of the (oppressed) nation versus the (neo-)imperial power. So many of the biggest, most powerful parties have grown out of the movement for national liberation – Congress, the PRI, a succession of parties in sub-Saharan Africa such as KANU (Kenya), the TANU-Chama Cha Mapinduzi (Tanzania), the ANC (South Africa), FRELIMO (Mozambique), and SWAPO (Namibia). It is possible to argue, as Sinnott (1984) has claimed for the Republic of Ireland, that such parties fall into the center–periphery cleavage category because at the time of their formation they represented the oppressed periphery of a metropolitan centre – but really, given its prominence, this cleavage deserves a category of its own (for a fuller discussion see Randall, 2001).

The Lipset–Rokkan model implies that, with economic development and national integration, increasingly the class-based cleavages will come to the fore. In terms both of predominant cleavages and of the direction of change, Latin America is the developing region that comes closest to this pattern. There, with the possible exception of the PRI in Mexico, parties have not arisen out of a national versus (neo-)colonial cleavage, and to varying degrees by the mid-20th century it was possible to place parties on a left–right axis, reflecting the prominence of social class divisions. Chile in particular, according to Scully (1995), is almost a classic case of party system evolution on Lipset–Rokkan lines. Originating in the 19th century from conflict between clerical and secular forces, by the early 20th century the system incorporated parties reflecting urban class divisions and later a new centre party based on the peasantry.

Elsewhere the model is less helpful and has been less frequently used in explaining either the main underlying social cleavages or the direction of change. However, it may still shed light on the process through which parties were originally formed. Lipset and Rokkan observed that, in Western Europe, party systems formed in the critical period on the eve of mass suffrage reflected or embodied the most salient political cleavages at that time, which then acquired a degree of institutional fixity, making it difficult for parties representing new bases of cleavage to form and break in. This has arguably also been true in many developing countries. Moreover, and anticipating what will be said later about parties creating their own cleavages, some parties or party systems have managed to survive in this way, even when forced underground during periods of authoritarian rule – the party tradition going back to Danquah and Busia and which has resurfaced in the recently victorious NPP in Ghana (Nugent, 2001) is an example.

This leads, finally, and as indeed recognized by Lipset and Rokkan (1967: 3), to the possibility that parties can themselves 'produce their own alignments' independent of pre-existing geographical, social or cultural differences. The political institution – the party – could to some degree act back on social structure creating, for instance, a family of new quasi-social institutions that play a part in socializing their participants and institutionalizing the party. An example would be the succession of parties in the Peronist tradition, of which the latest manifestation is the Justicialist Party (JP) in Argentina.

PARTIES AND ELECTORAL BEHAVIOUR

The Lipset–Rokkan model, whilst positing a historical link between the origin of party systems and politicized cleavages, does not greatly reflect on the nature of the link between party leaders and their perceived social base. In practice those following in this tradition of analysis have largely relied for evidence of relationship on patterns of voting behaviour, including estimates of their volatility or continuity, supplemented perhaps by independent measures of party identification. This is true more generally of attempts to answer the question of which social group(s) a party stands for. Patterns of electoral support are inferred either through aggregate ecological analysis, exit polls or voting intention surveys. This kind of analysis, at its most sophisticated in India perhaps, has been applied increasingly to elections throughout the developing world. The discussion that follows can only highlight emerging themes and makes no claim to be exhaustive with regard to this proliferating literature.

As already implied, social structures and thus the range of potential social constituencies for parties vary greatly between and even within regions of the developing world. Social class differences are paramount in Latin America. This is partly a reflection of relatively advanced levels of industrialization and urbanization. It is also a consequence of its colonial history. This bequeathed a hegemonic Roman Catholic church strongly identified with the state. It also virtually eliminated the native population in many parts of Latin America, and elsewhere generally resulted in a system where ethnic groupings were 'ranked' in Horowitz's term, or aligned with rather than cross-cutting lines of social stratification (Horowitz, 1985). Ethnicity, then, has been largely absent as an independent basis of party support, although Donna Van Cott has recently produced interesting work on the difference that having large Indian communities can make to party formation, with particular reference to the case of the Movimiento Nacionalista Revolucionario (MNR) in Bolivia (Van Cott, 2000). Despite the relative salience of class divisions sociologically speaking, however, these do not necessarily determine

patterns of party support. A decade ago Dix (1989) argued that the alignment of class divisions with voting patterns apparent in many Latin American countries in the 1960s had weakened everywhere but in Chile and Argentina. The trend, in the era of redemocratization was for what he chose to call 'catch-all' parties, deliberately seeking to maximize their cross-sectional appeal. Myers (1998) provides an example of this in Venezuela where in the 1950s his own ecological analysis suggested that the two main parties, Acción Democrática and COPEI, had relatively differentiated bases of social support but by 1978 public opinion research found that demographic variables had little bearing on voting intentions. The reasons for this regional trend are doubtless complex and locally varied but include, as in the West, the restricted programmatic options for historically left parties.

In stark contrast with Latin America, in Africa, by common agreement, 'ethnicity', whatever exactly is understood by this term, has much greater social salience than social class (except perhaps in South Africa) or, hitherto, than religion. And it is widely assumed to underpin both party formation and party strategy: Ottaway (1999: 311), for instance, refers to the 'overt or covert ethnic character of the majority of the emerging political parties'. This is true despite legislation or constitutional provisions, in a number of countries such as Tanzania, Cameroon and Ghana, designed to prevent the formation of parties or electioneering on this or other particularistic bases. The role of ethnicity in shaping patterns of electoral support is confirmed, for instance, in Nugent's (2001) analysis of the simultaneous presidential and parliamentary elections in Ghana in 2000. In analysing patterns of electoral support, it is admittedly sometimes difficult to differentiate between ethnicity and regionalism, given the tendency for ethnic groups to be geographically concentrated, an issue explored in Kaspin's (1995) excellent analysis of the 1994 presidential and parliamentary elections in Malawi. There is also some debate as to how far tropical Africa's parties actually are ethnic, in the sense of based on a single ethnic group, as opposed to multi-ethnic (Scarritt and Mozaffar, 2002). Certainly in most national contexts, and depending on the nature of ethnic cleavages, both traditional ruling parties and emerging opposition parties with any realistic chance of winning power or even becoming significant players, need to draw support from more than one such community.

In much of Asia, and to a lesser extent the Middle East, social structure is more complex, with significant fracturing on ethnic, religious and class/caste lines. Asia of course covers a very diverse range of countries. In South Korea the picture is simplified: given that it is largely homogeneous in ethnic terms and that there have been severe ideological and constitutional constraints on trade union involvement in party politics, the primary determinant of electoral support for parties, since democratization got under way in 1987, has been region (Kim, 1998). India, however, epitomizes Asian complexity, which is compounded by its federal system of government. Given that competitive party politics has prevailed since independence in 1947, systematic study of voting behaviour goes back a long way (for a valuable discussion of the methods, strengths and findings of ecological analysis in the 1960s and 1970s, see Brass, 1985). One distinctive feature of Indian social structure is the caste system, whose character has of course profoundly changed, partly as a consequence of its encounter with democratic forms of politics, but which is still recognized to be of major relevance to voting behaviour. The Congress Party, originally based on the movement for national independence, remained electorally dominant at the national level into the 1990s. It drew support from all sectors of society, although especially from both the upper castes and least privileged sectors (the Untouchables or 'Dalits', tribals or 'adivasis', and Muslims). However, Chhibber and Petrocik (1990) found that when analysed at individual state level, its electoral support was much more homogeneous, and based on particular, if locally varying, caste and other groupings, a view more recently echoed by Heath and Yadav (2002). The 1990s saw the rise of a number of state-based parties that draw disproportionately on the electoral support of particular caste blocs, such as the Bahujan Samaj Party (BSP) based in Uttar Pradesh which draws a large share of the Dalit vote. At the same time at the national level Congress has been successfully challenged – until the 2004 general election – by the BJP, widely perceived as a Hindu chauvinist party. Electoral support for the BJP obviously comes primarily from Hindus; however, they constitute around 83% of India's population, and interest has focused rather on the disproportionate rates of support from upper castes, especially in the north-western 'Hindi heartland'. The success of the BJP has involved widening its social bases of support to include lower castes and

regions further south as well as allying with parties with contrasting electoral bases (Heath, 1999).

Given the chequered history of competitive party politics in the Middle East, the scope for analysing patterns of electoral support for parties has inevitably been limited. Of particular potential interest, however, are the increasingly numerous Islamist parties. These obviously differ in many respects one from another and several may coexist in a single country. Some are conservative and closely linked with the prevailing regime. But others are more oppositional in character, have often developed out of a wider movement, and have relatively strong social 'roots'. Again obviously their electoral supporters have in common a Muslim religious identity which they may perceive to be threatened, even in such overwhelmingly Muslim countries, by secularizing policies of government. Nonetheless, whilst hard psephological analysis is hard to come by, it appears that support comes disproportionately from particular social sectors and for different reasons. The role of the professional middle class and students in supporting more radical Islamic movements is often noted. In his study of support for Turkey's Welfare (Refah) Party, Gülalp (2001) also underlines the importance of the small-scale, provincial business sector which suffered under state-centred Import Substitution Industrialization (ISI) type development policies in the 1960s and 1970s but has expanded in the era of economic globalization. But purely in terms of numbers most significant has been support amongst the rapidly growing urban poor due in no small measure to the extensive welfare work undertaken by such parties and associated organizations. It was in the poorest neighbourhoods, where the Turkish Welfare Party 'spoke the language of socio-economic justice and equality' (Gülalp, 2001: 442) that its vote grew most rapidly in the 1990s. Likewise, in Algeria, the welfare network of the Islamist movement provided the Front Islamique du Salut (FIS) 'with a significant and loyal pool of potential voters' in 1992 (Willis, 2002: 10).

ALTERNATIVE WAYS TO IDENTIFY A PARTY'S SOCIAL BASE

In addition to looking at patterns of electoral support to identify a party's social base, one could focus on what the party leadership does to attract support in terms of the manipulation of symbols, public statements, targeted campaigning, programmes, manifestos (where these are available) and so forth. To which group(s) do they appear to be appealing? A useful resource would be something like the Manifesto Research Group (Budge, 1994) to collect and analyse such material. In a developing world context, little systematic work of this kind has yet been undertaken and further difficulties arise from the fact that in many cases parties either do not produce programmes or they barely differ from one another. Thus according to Wanjohi (2003: 251), 'nearly all party manifestos in Kenya look alike, often using the same phraseology, and even identical paragraphs'.

Alternatively, a clue to the social character of a party may lie in the nature of the social institutions or organizations into which it is historically and/or actually linked. For instance, parties like the PT in Brazil and successive Peronist parties in Argentina, or the MMD in Zambia and the ANC in South Africa, have had close links with trade unions. India's BJP is closely linked to Rashtriya Sevak Sangh (RSS), a highly disciplined militant Hindu organization, and its 'family' of voluntary associations.

PARTIES AND THE REPRESENTATION OF SOCIAL GROUPS

But none of these indicators of a party's social base necessarily tells us who the party really stands for. This raises the wider issue of representation, which is of course as relevant to Western political parties as to those of the developing world. Which social groups do parties represent, and in what sense? From the perspective of normative political theory, almost nothing seems to have been written about the role parties ideally should play in representation of social groups (a partial exception is Birch, 1972), perhaps because this is actually a very difficult question to answer (Randall, forthcoming).

Pitkin (1967) and others, writing about representation more generally, have distinguished different forms. Most relevant for us is the distinction between descriptive and substantive representation. In the former case, in a party context, specific attributes of the social group in question are reflected, say, in the composition of party membership, its key decision-making bodies or its candidates for the legislature. In the latter, the perspectives and interests of that group are voiced and carried forward in internal debate and/or party policy. A problem of which post-structural arguments have made us more aware here is of course how such interests come to be identified and articulated – if they are not 'objectively' to be read off, what part does the party itself play in constructing them?

Liberal theorists of representation have questioned the value of descriptive representation, arguing that there is no guarantee delegates selected on this basis will promote the interests of the group whose characteristics they share. However, more recently, feminist theorists in particular have suggested that measures to increase descriptive representation – or 'the politics of presence' – may be valuable symbolically, to correct past injustices, and membership of a group may be necessary to understand and articulate its distinctive experience and concerns (Phillips, 1995). Whether or not this is so, descriptive representation is often a very real concern, explicitly or implicitly, for parties in developing countries. It is an intrinsic feature of ethnically based political parties in sub-Saharan Africa that their leaders, parliamentary candidates and suchlike should themselves be members of the ethnic group they claim to stand for. In India, all parties, including communist parties, have had to take descriptive representation, in terms particularly of caste, into account when selecting candidates for local, state and national elections.

Especially following the 1995 UN Women's Congress in Beijing, the issue of women's representation, and specifically of gender quotas, has come to the fore. The trend has gone furthest in Latin America, where between 1991 and 2000 twelve countries passed laws requiring that 20–40% of candidates for national elections should be women. Such provisions in practice have had mixed success in terms of actually increasing the number of women candidates, one important factor being the good-faith compliance of parties themselves. Several major parties also use gender quotas for internal party positions, including El Salvador's FMLN and Nicaragua's FSLN (Htun and Jones, 2002). In sub-Saharan Africa a number of parties, including three based on movements of national liberation – the ANC in South Africa, FRELIMO in Mozambique and SWAPO in Namibia – have adopted gender quotas (Yoon, 2001). While adoption of quotas in a number of cases reflects the lobbying of women activists themselves, it has also often coincided with the party's desire, in a (re)democratizing era, to establish its pluralist, democratic credentials. As to whether gender quotas enhance women's substantive representation in and through the party, this varies from case to case, and feminist commentators further disagree amongst themselves. For instance, Goetz and Hassim (2001) see gender quotas in the ANC as indirectly helping to bring about three 'path-breaking' pieces of legislation for women – the 1996 Termination of Pregnancy Act and, in 1998, the Domestic Violence Act and the Maintenance Act, but Vincent (2002) is less sanguine. Htun and Jones conclude that gender quotas have not necessarily directly affected policy but have helped to transform collective gender awareness by stimulating debate, a view confirmed in Sacchet's (2003) recent study of gender quotas in Brazil's PT.

SUBSTANTIVE REPRESENTATION

The question of how far political parties further the substantive representation of particular social groups could take us into political and philosophical terrain well beyond the implicit brief of this chapter. What is intended here is the more limited but necessary discussion of some of the factors tending to constrain such representation. Many parties in the developing world are primarily vehicles for individual politicians hastily scrambled together for electoral purposes with the vaguest of social bases and minimal attempt to elicit the views of their potential supporters. But even where parties make more efforts to cultivate such a base, the extent of communications with supporters may be constrained by, for instance, geographical distance and the town–rural divide (it is regularly noted that in tropical Africa opposition parties have difficulty extending their organizations beyond the main urban centres) and by social distance. Van Cott (2000) describes how from the late 1950s Bolivia's MNR appealed to highland Indians, helping them to recover their communal lands. But thereafter, Van Cott suggests the Indians did not seek representation in conventional political terms, wanting rather to be left alone; in return their vote provided the party with its 'conservative anchor'. Of course it could be said that in this case the Indians got what they wanted – until the economic situation deteriorated.

Clientelism is a pervasive feature of parties in the developing world; accounts so far suggest that neither democratization nor measures to constrain the public sector and public expenditure in keeping with neo-liberal prescriptions have significantly eroded it. A relatively underexplored question is the implication of clientelism for representation: certainly, as Piattoni (2001), writing in a European context, has noted, in clientelism the level of discourse is never lifted up from the particular. Some accounts imply that it is incompatible with and indeed inimical to representation as commonly understood. Alternatively, it might be possible to see clientelism, as some Africanists do, as a distinct form of representation. According to van de Walle and Butler (1999: 26), 'In Africa today. ... parties do not really serve to aggregate interests; rather they serve a representation function in a context of clientelistic politics' (see also Chabal and Daloz, 1999). That still leaves open the question of whether and in what sense (short or long term) this clientelistic exchange of their votes for favours is in the voters' interests.

An alternative, though not necessarily incompatible, model would be of some form of corporatist representation of different social groups – women, youth, peasants, unions and so forth – within a party, or through affiliated organizations. A well-known historical example would be Mexico's PRI. In contrast to clientelism, this model does give formal recognition to groups; however, it often goes with a very centralized system of party decision-making. Fears, for instance, have been expressed that South Africa's ANC is moving in this direction.

CONCLUSION

Analysis of the relationship between political parties and social structure in the developing world is flawed by the same conceptual evasions and confusions as in the West. In addition, while research on parties has burgeoned in the era of (re)democratization, there is much less research directly focused on this question. There are also particular fields where more basic information would be valuable, such as the social bases of Islamic parties, and also of the small but growing number of Green parties in the developing world. Cleavage theory has something to offer for the analysis of society–party relationships, especially in Latin America. But much more work needs to be done in investigating and conceptualizing the representation of social groups, including the implications of clientelism.

BIBLIOGRAPHY

Birch, A.H. (1972) *Representation*. Basingstoke: Macmillan.

Brass, Paul (1985) 'Indian election studies', in Paul Brass, *Caste, Faction and Party in Indian Politics. Vol. 2: Election Studies*. Delhi: Chanakya Publications.

Budge, Ian (1994) 'A new spatial theory of party competition', *British Journal of Political Science*, 24: 443–67.

Chabal, Patrick and Daloz, Jean-Pascal (1999) *Africa Works*. London: James Currey.

Chhibber, P.K. and Petrocik, J.R. (1990) 'Social cleavages, elections and the Indian party system', in R. Sisson and R. Roy (eds), *Diversity and Dominance in Indian Politics. Vol. 1: Changing Bases of Congress Support*. New Delhi and London: Sage.

Dix, Robert H. (1989) 'Cleavage structures and party systems in Latin America', *Comparative Politics*, 22: 23–37.

Goetz, Anne-Marie and Hassim, Shireen (2001) 'In and against the party: Women's representation and constituency – building in Uganda and South Africa'. UNRISD Programme Paper.

Gülalp, Haldun (2001) 'Globalization and political Islam: The social bases of Turkey's Welfare Party', *International Journal of Middle East Studies*, 33: 433–48.

Gunther, Richard and Diamond, Larry (2003) 'Species of political parties: A new typology', *Party Politics* 9: 167–99.

Heath, Anthony and Yadav, Yogendra (2002) 'The United Colours of Congress: Social profile of Congress voters, 1996 and 1998' in Zoya Hasan (ed.), *Parties and Party Politics in India* Oxford: Oxford University Press. Paper written in 1999.

Heath, Oliver (1999), 'Anatomy of the BJP's rise to power', *Economic and Political Weekly*, Aug. 21–28, 2511–17.

Horowitz, Donald (1985) *Ethnic Groups in Conflict*. Berkeley and Los Angeles: University of California Press.

Htun, Mala N. and Jones, Mark P. (2002) 'Engendering the right to participate in decision-making: Electoral quotas and women's leadership in Latin America', in N. Craske and M. Molyneux (eds), *Gender and the Politics of Rights and Democracy in Latin America*. Basingstoke: Palgrave.

Kaspin, Deborah (1995) 'The politics of ethnicity in Malawi's democratic transition', *Journal of Modern African Studies*, 33: 595–620.

Kim, Yong-Ho (1998) 'Korea', in Wolfgang Sachsenroder and Ulrike E. Frings (eds), *Political Party Systems and Democratic Development in East and Southeast Asia. Volume II. East Asia*. Aldershot: Ashgate.

Lipset, S.M. and Rokkan, S. (1967) 'Cleavage structures, party systems and voter alignments: An introduction', in Seymour Martin Lipset and Stein Rokkan (eds), *Party Systems and Voter Alignments. Cross-National Perspectives*. New York: Free Press.

Munck, Gerardo and Bosworth, Jeffrey A. (1998) 'Patterns of representation and competition: Parties and democracy in post-Pinochet Chile', *Party Politics*, 4: 471–93.

Myers, David J. (1998) 'Venezuela's political party system: Defining events, reactions and the diluting of structural cleavages', *Party Politics*, 4: 495–521.

Nugent, Paul (2001) 'Winners, losers and also rans: Money, moral authority and voting patterns in the Ghana 2000 elections', *African Affairs*, 100: 405–28.

Ottaway, Marina (1999) 'Ethnic politics in Africa: Change and continuity' in R. Joseph (ed.), *State, Conflict and Democracy in Africa*. Boulder, CO: Lynne Rienner.

Panebianco, Angelo (1988) *Political Parties: Organizations and Power*. Cambridge: Cambridge University Press.

Phillips, Anne (1995) *The Politics of Presence*. Oxford: Oxford University Press.

Piattoni, Simona (2001) 'Clientelism, interests and democratic representation', in Simona Pattioni (ed.), *Clientelism, Interests and Democratic Representation: The European Experience in Historical and Comparative Perspective*. Cambridge: Cambridge University Press.

Pitkin, Hannah (1967) *The Concept of Representation*. Berkeley: University of California Press.

Randall, Vicky (2001) 'Party systems and voter alignments in the new democracies of the Third World', in Lauri Karvonen and Stein Kuhnle (eds), *Party Systems and Voter Alignments Revisited*. London and New York: Routledge.

Randall, Vicky (forthcoming), 'Political parties in Africa and the representation of social groups', in Matthias Basedau, Gero Erdmann and Andreas Mehler (eds), *Elections and Political Parties in Contemporary Sub-Saharan Africa. Conceptual Problems, Empirical Findings and the Road Ahead*. Uppsala: Nordic Africa Institute.

Randall, Vicky and Svåsand, Lars (2002) 'Party institutionalization in new democracies', *Party Politics*, 8: 5–29.

Sacchet, Teresinha (2003) 'Making women count: Campaigns for gender quotas in Brazil'. Unpublished PhD thesis, University of Essex.

Scarritt, James R. and Mozaffar, Shaheen (2002) 'Why do multiethnic parties predominate in Africa and ethnic parties do not? A theory illustrated by the case of Zambia'. Unpublished paper.

Scully, Timothy (1995) 'Reconstituting party politics in Chile', in S. Mainwaring and T. Scully (eds), *Building Democratic Institutions: Party Systems in Latin America*. Stanford, CA: Stanford University Press.

Sinnott, Richard (1984) 'Interpretations of the Irish party system', *European Journal of Political Research*, 12: 289–307.

Van Cott, Donna Lee (2000) 'Party system development and indigenous populations in Latin America: The Bolivian case', *Party Politics*, 6: 155–74.

Van de Walle, Nicolas and Butler, Kimberley Smiddy (1999) 'Political parties and party systems in Africa's illiberal democracies', *Cambridge Review of International Affairs*, 13(Autumn–Winter): 14–28.

Vincent, Louise (2002) 'Beyond the numbers: Do quotas for women count?' Unpublished paper presented to UKPSA Women and Politics Group Conference, London: February.

Wanjohi, Nick G. (2003) 'Sustainability of political parties in Kenya', in M.A. Mohamed Salih (ed.), *African Political Parties*. London: Pluto.

Willis, Michael J. (2002)'Political parties in the Maghrib: ideology and identification. A suggested typology', *Journal of North African Studies*, 7(Autumn): 1–28.

Yoon, Mi Yung (2001) 'Democratization and women's legislative representation in sub-Saharan Africa', *Democratization*, 8: 169–90.

33

POLITICAL PARTIES AND OTHER ORGANIZATIONS

Thomas Poguntke

FUNCTIONS

The analysis of patterns of relationships between parties and their organizational environment is key to understanding parties' survival, organizational stability and electoral success (Panebianco, 1988: 12; Streeck, 1987: 488). Essentially, parties 'use' other relevant organizations that constitute their environment to create linkages to diverse groups of potential voters (Lawson, 1980; Poguntke, 2000, 2005). While such organizations vary widely as regards their own organizational format, their focus and, above all, their specific kinds of relationships to one or more political parties, they share one characteristic: they articulate and aggregate interests *vis-à-vis* parties and are, as such, important intermediaries between parties and society at large. The essence of these relationships is that votes are exchanged for policies or, more realistically, policy pledges. This exchange is based on more or less permanent and formalized negotiations between party elites and organizational elites (see below) by which policy concessions (by the party) are traded for the mobilization of organizational support (by the organization) (Poguntke, 2000: 23–31). From the perspective of political parties, they serve as 'collateral organizations' reaching out to specific societal interests, which may not be directly accessible for political parties which need to serve, by definition, a wider and more contradictory range of interests. Hence, those concerned with one specific interest may find it more attractive to join a relevant interest organization rather than a party. By creating ties to such collateral organizations, political parties are capable of extending their anchorage in society beyond their core constituency (Duverger, 1964: 107; Beyme, 1980: 196ff.), thereby stabilizing their electorate (Webb, 1992: 1–7; Lane and Ersson, 1987: 121).

Historically, the relevance of collateral organizations reached its peak during the heyday of the mass party of integration in Europe (Neumann, 1956), when dense networks of collateral organizations created almost impermeable subcultures which enclosed individuals literally 'from the cradle to the grave' and which almost stifled communication across subcultural boundaries (Bartolini and Mair, 1990: 216; Steininger, 1984: 146). These networks of collateral organizations were an essential factor in the process of stabilizing the cleavage structures underlying (Western) European party systems in the 1920s (Lepsius, 1973; Lipset and Rokkan, 1967; Bartolini and Mair, 1990: 235–43).

In some deeply segmented societies the potential conflict between these subcultures could only be contained through elite accommodation based on power sharing and mutual veto. This model of consociational democracy reached perfection in the Netherlands and Austria but elements of it were applied elsewhere (Daalder, 1987; Lijphart, 1968, Gerlich, 1987; Luther and Deschouwer, 1999). Party political elites were the chief negotiators for 'their' socioeconomic subculture (pillar), which was characterized by a dense network of interest organizations tied formally or informally to one or several parties representing a specific subculture. Elsewhere, there was less segmentation but all Western European party systems were, until the 1960s, dominated by mass parties representing the major socioeconomic cleavages

Table 33.1   *Types of collateral organizations*

Type of organization	Independent collateral organization	Corporately linked collateral organization	Affiliated organization	Ancillary organization
Type of party membership	individual membership optional	collective membership (individual optional)	individual membership	individual membership
Overlap of membership	partial	partial	partial	total
Membership rights	individual	collective (individual)	individual	individual
Type of organizational tie	informal	formal	formal	formal
Control by party	low	low	high	very high
Influence of collateral organization	variable	high to very high	variable	variable
Most frequent type of interest	external		internal	

Source: Poguntke, 2000: 38.

and attempting to maintain exclusive formal or informal ties to interest organizations belonging to their own political camp. During the heyday of the mass party of integration, election campaigns were primarily aimed at mobilizing a party's constituency, not at winning over votes from other political camps.

When, from the 1960s onwards, the combined forces of post-war economic growth, the development of the welfare state and general socioeconomic modernization began to erode these sharp social boundaries, and hence the secure electoral basis of the mass party of integration, the organizational and strategic answer of many large parties in Western Europe was the catch-all model (Kirchheimer, 1966). This involved de-emphasizing ideological competition in favour of the managerial qualities of the senior candidates for public office and, above all, the pluralization of parties' social ties. Now the aim was to reach out to as many relevant social forces as possible rather than stabilizing the core support, and the ties between parties and the major social interests became less exclusive. This did not change significantly as parties continued to lose secure social anchorage and began to move ever closer to the state, a trend that gave rise to the proposition that we were seeing the emergence of a new type of party, the cartel party, at the end of the last millennium (Katz and Mair, 1995).

As the patterns of interaction between parties and major interest organizations became more pluralistic in Western Europe, they began to resemble the dominant North American pattern, where exclusive ties between parties and organized interests have been largely unknown. This trend towards pluralistic party–interest-group relations was accelerated through the emergence of a significant number of new parties, particularly from the late 1960s onwards, which either did not forge any close ties with social interests (like most parties of the different variants of the extreme/populist right) or with new social actors (like Green parties) (Betz and Immerfall, 1998; Ignazi, 2003; Kitschelt, 1989; Poguntke, 1987). In any case, even parties that have not sought to link up to 'external interests' (see below), or have not succeeded in doing so, have created their own, party-dependent collateral organizations.

TYPES OF COLLATERAL ORGANIZATIONS

The exact nature of the relationship between party and collateral organization varies from full independence to close organizational integration (Table 33.1). In its most independent incarnation, collateral organizations have *no formal ties* to political parties. Their exclusive relationship with a specific political party (or a political camp) rests on a mutual understanding concerning a broad commonality of interests. While there is no guaranteed access for the collateral organization to party decision-making bodies, this model of organizational interaction leaves the interest organization with maximum autonomy. Party and organization enter into negotiations about policies knowing that support by the collateral can be withdrawn at any time without involving any formal organizational changes. Strong societal interests such as employers' federations or churches have, by and large, preferred to maintain an arm's-length relationship with political parties generally sympathetic to their cause. Good examples are the Catholic lay organizations in Italy, which have never had formal ties to the Christian Democrats (Bardi and Morlino, 1994: 250). Similarly, the Economic Council of the German CDU has never entered into a formal relationship with the German Christian Democrats (Haungs, 1983: 135–7).

Interest organizations that are tied to parties through *corporate membership* are the potentially most powerful variant of collateral organizations. This involves collective membership of organizational members in a party and can lead to extensive control of the party by the elites of collateral organizations. The classic example for this constellation is the British Labour Party prior to far-reaching reforms in the 1990s. While the case of the British Labour Party has gained widespread attention in scholarly and public debate, the so-called Labour Party, model based on corporate membership links between a left-wing party and the trade union movement, has remained the exception rather than the rule. In any case, it was phased out by the early 1990s in Norway and Sweden, while it was substantially reformed in the UK (Svåsand, 1992: 763, 1994b: 305; Pierre and Widfeldt, 1992: 813, 1994: 337; Alderman and Carter, 1994, 1995: 444; Richards, 1997: 30ff.; Webb, 1992: 35, 1994: 115).

Affiliated and *ancillary organizations* are the classic variants of party-created suborganizations. As such, they represent a conscious organizational strategy by parties attempting to diversify their appeal by creating target-group-specific suborganizations catering for the needs and interests of specific socio-economic groups (e.g. the young, women, religious or ethnic minorities). *Affiliated* organizations are technically largely independent organizations that are linked to their party on the elite level through *ex officio* seats of the affiliated organization's leadership on party executive bodies.

Also, partial membership overlap is typical, which indicates that collateral organizations are indeed capable of reaching beyond their party's natural constituency. Their degree of autonomy varies but a minimum is guaranteed through the affiliated organization's independent organizational structure. *Ancillary* organizations, on the other hand, are fully integrated in the main party structure and have no independent membership. They are therefore least suitable for broadening a party's appeal but can be subjected to tight party discipline.

Throughout, we have implicitly referred to two types of political interests that are organized in collateral organizations. So-called *external interests* exist independently and, in most cases, prior to a political party. Many are related to the classic socioeconomic cleavages, others to the agenda of the new politics (Lipset and Rokkan, 1967; Dalton *et al.*, 1990; Hildebrandt and Dalton, 1978). This includes working-class interests organized in trade unions, agrarian interests, religious interests, economic interests and ecological interests. Frequently, the foundation of political parties has been initiated by such external interest organizations, which have provided parties with an external legitimation (Duverger, 1964: xxx–xxxvii; Panebianco, 1988: 50–3). This pattern is not imperative. A party may create an affiliated organization in order to organize party members and sympathizers who are trade unionists, or it may decide to launch an environmental organization in order to connect to the environmental movement.

Internal interests, on the other hand, are created through organizational activity by the party. Strictly speaking, there is no pre-existing social group like Christian democratic women or social democratic teachers. Parties create satellite organizations with a view to getting a hold on sizeable segments of the electorate with specific socioeconomic interests and fairly homogeneous political preferences. This kind of 'target group' organizational strategy attempts to create an organizational forum for such potential interests.

TYPES OF RELATIONSHIPS

The preceding discussion of different kinds of collateral organizations has shown that they need not have formal organizational ties with a party. As long as both collective actors share an understanding that they belong to the same political camp, a more or less permanent negotiation relationship can be maintained which allows the exchange of policy pledges for support. The principal mechanism here is *reaction* to pressure (Lawson, 1988: 15), that is, party elites need to be convinced that the collateral organization in question actually is capable of either mobilizing or withholding electoral support based on whether or not preferred policy concessions are made. The relative power of both partners varies according to political context.

To be sure, formal ties between organizations may also involve reaction to pressure but they are primarily based on organizational *penetration*, that is, the guaranteed access of (mainly) organizational elites to party decision-making bodies (or vice versa). In relatively few cases, there is also a proportional representation of organizational membership in one or several of the party's rule-making bodies. This makes exchange relationships more predictable (not least as a result of shared information) and more durable, because there are high thresholds against terminating such connections. Not only would this require a formal rule change, which usually involves specific procedural hurdles such as a qualified majority, it would also represent an explicit political statement regarding the relationship under question. This is only likely to come about either if both partners agree that the continuation of an exclusive relationship is detrimental, or if one partner decides that the other is no longer needed. In any case, it is a highly visible political move, which means that formalized ties between organizations will normally survive phases of strained relationships. Clearly, linkage based on formal organizational ties is more durable, stable and effective than linkage through informal ties, and this is what makes it particularly valuable for party political elites. There is however, a disadvantage: strong organizational ties to powerful collateral organizations may limit party elites' freedom for manoeuvre, as the example of the British Labour Party demonstrates (Seyd and Whiteley, 2004).

NEW SOCIAL MOVEMENTS

Given the advantages of permanent organizational ties, parties that depend primarily on support from the new social movement sector are at a structural disadvantage. New social movements are characterized by a predominant lack of formal organization, which makes formal ties to party organizations very difficult. They can be understood as networks of networks (Neidhart, 1985: 197) based on a high degree of symbolic integration and low levels of role differentiation (Neidhart and Rucht, 1993: 315–17; Rucht, 1994: 79, 154). Particularly in phases of high mobilisation, they tend to generate steering committees which can be regarded, to a limited degree, as functional equivalents of decision-making bodies of traditional organizations (Schmitt, 1989; Rochon, 1988: 77–82). While the capacity of such movements to act collectively depends to a considerable degree on movement elites active in such coordination bodies (Kaase, 1990: 90), their political mandate typically remains precarious. In fact, their elevated position within the movement rests to a considerable degree on external ascription (mainly by the mass media or other political actors), while their legitimation through the movement itself remains weak. After all, new social movements simply lack the degree of internal formalization that is the essential precondition for elite selection, because individual movement organizations tend to guard their autonomy. The absence of movement elites with a reliable mandate makes new social movements therefore unlikely candidates for formal organizational ties with political parties.

While political parties can at best expect to forge informal ties to new social movements, even those are of limited value for party elites seeking to stabilize their electorate. The reason is that new social movements are weak interest aggregators, which limits the effects of linkage. They tend to be based on the smallest common denominator, endorse a plurality of ideological and strategic orientations and frequently limit inherent centrifugal tendencies by calling for maximal solutions (Neidhart and Rucht, 1993: 318; Rucht, 1993: 265). Hence, political parties that depend primarily on linkage through new social movements (e.g. Green parties) have to live with a structurally weak social anchorage, which can provide them with comparatively little electoral stability. While good relations with new social movements may be a significant (though highly contingent) electoral asset in phases of high protest mobilization, they are of little value in quiet times.

There are, however, highly formalized and professionalized elements within new social movements which would, in principle, meet all the organizational requirements to be stable and reliable partners for party elites. Organizations such as Greenpeace, Amnesty International and other kinds of non-governmental organization could permanently liaise with a political

Table 33.2   *Collateral organizations of Western European parties (1960–89)**

Type of organization	N	%
Youth	1287	24.1
Women	1036	19.4
Trade unions	656	12.3
Other	512	9.6
Leisure	491	9.2
Education	472	8.8
Self Help	281	5.3
Media	244	4.6
Middle Class Interests	147	2.8
Religion	144	2.7
Agrarian	69	1.3
Total	5339	100

*counts of collateral organizations per year over a 30-year period.
Source: Poguntke, 2000: 135

party. However, these movement organizations are particularly concerned with maintaining their non-partisan image, which is, after all, also a precondition for their substantial fundraising capacity (Dalton, 1994). Furthermore, the very fact that they are primarily based on 'cheque book participation' means that they are poor mobilizers of mass support and hence of limited value for political parties seeking to stabilize their electorates.

FINDINGS

Parties and collateral organizations

Given the evident problems of data collection, it is hardly surprising that systematic comparative data on the development of informal ties between political parties and interest organizations are non-existent. Yet, a wealth of literature on party and party system change, particularly in the wake of the debate about Kirchheimer's catch-all thesis, has shown that the relationships between parties and independent collateral organizations have become more tenuous.

When it comes to information concerning collateral organizations that are formally tied to political parties, we are empirically on fairly safe ground as these links are normally documented in party statutes. In most cases, this involves different variants of *ex officio* seats for members of collateral organizations in the party's decision-making bodies. To a lesser degree, it also takes the form of proportional representation of the collateral organization's

membership on the party's main rule-making body, usually the party congress (Poguntke, 2005: 51–53). A detailed analysis of the data collected by the Party Organization Project (Katz and Mair, 1992) has shown that youth and women's organizations dominate the organizational periphery of Western Europe's parties' (Table 33.2). They are followed by collateral organizations concerned with trade union interests. This does not necessarily involve a direct organizational tie between a party and a trade union, as this category also includes party-created ancillary or affiliated organizations that target trade union members.

It is noticeable that those categories that directly relate to the classic socioeconomic cleavages amount to a mere 19.2 per cent of all collateral organizations that existed over the 30-year-period under investigation (i.e. middle-class interests, trade unions, agrarian sector, religion). The conspicuously low number of collateral organizations with a specifically denominational mission indicates that some of the most powerful cleavage-forming interests have preferred an independent arm's-length relationship with political parties. The most eye-catching finding is, however, that the entire new social movement sector in all its variable incarnations has not connected at all to Western European party systems. In other words, the entire spectrum of the protest movements from the 1970s onwards, ranging from the anti-nuclear and ecological movements to the peace movements and anti-globalization activists, have not connected formally with political parties.

While many New Politics parties had consolidated their presence in Western European party systems by the late 1980s, they still lacked organizational connectedness to important elements of their core constituency. To be sure, this can be explained to a large extent by the specific organizational nature of the new social movements and the behavioural dispositions of their activists, who tend to be sceptical about party politics (Dalton, 1994: 227; Poguntke, 1992: 244–54). Furthermore, it is also a reflection of the organizational philosophy of New Politics parties, which regarded themselves as the natural party political ally of the movements and hence tended to regard it as superfluous to create ancillary or affiliated organizations in order to connect to the new social movements. Still, the failure of this new party family to create its own organizational periphery left it electorally exposed to the mobilization cycles of the new social movement sector.

New Politics parties are not unique in their lack of organizational roots. All parties that originated after World War II and that have no clear pre-war organizational ancestor are united in their almost complete lack of formal ties to collateral organizations. While it is not entirely surprising that these latecomers could not connect to the major cleavage-forming interests since they emerged long after the 'full mobilization of electoral markets' (Lipset and Rokkan, 1967), it is nevertheless remarkable that they also invested very little energy in creating some of the standard collateral organizations such as youth or women's organizations. To be sure, this would have been superfluous in some cases; Green parties have such a strong commitment to the women's movement that a separate ancillary or affiliated organization would have appeared meaningless – just as some agrarian parties never developed formal links to agrarian organizations. And as Greens are increasingly turning 'grey' (and into more conventional parties), we are seeing the first Green youth organizations. By and large, however, the findings show that new parties, quite independent of their ideological orientation, have tended to follow an organizational strategy which distinguishes them from traditional parties: they concentrate on the core political organization of the party and invest little energy in creating the organizational periphery which is typical of parties that lived through the heyday of the mass party (Poguntke, 2000: 131–61; 2005).

Parties and new social movements

The organizational limits to formal ties between political parties and new social movements have already been addressed. Yet, the social movements of the 1970s and ‸‸‸ played a crucial role in changing Western party systems. As mentioned above, the emergence of a new family of New Politics parties (now mainly referred to as Green parties) is intimately related to a very high level of protest mobilization in most Western democracies. Sustained by underlying shifts towards postmaterialist values and fuelled by the resistance to the so-called old politics agenda of economic growth and military strength (Hildebrandt and Dalton, 1978; Baker et al., 1997), an alliance of different movements sharing a broad and fairly unspecific vision of what the world should look like first mobilized against the growth of nuclear power generation and then expanded into a general ecology movement (Rucht, 1994; Dalton and Kuechler, 1990; Kriesi et al., 1995). When NATO decided in 1979 to deploy a new generation of intermediate-range nuclear missiles in Western Europe, the movements found a new focal point and protest mobilization reached unprecedented levels in many Western European countries. By and large, established parties found it difficult to address the issues raised by the movements, which eventually led to a growing preparedness among many movement activists to engage in party politics themselves. In other words, the structural inability of established parties to reconcile their traditional political goals with the new agenda resulted in the emergence of a new party family, and the new social movements were to a very substantial degree the driving force behind this (Kitschelt, 1988; Müller-Rommel, 1985, 1989; Poguntke, 1987).

A closer look at the first generation of Green party elites shows that they had almost invariably gained their initial political experience as activists in the new social movements. Since Green parties grew out of the movements, their initial party programmes were little more than a reflection of the central concerns of the various new social movements. In return, large parts of the new social movements regarded the newly founded Green parties as their natural ally in the realm of party politics and provided them with electoral support. In a nutshell, the Green parties surfed into many Western European parliaments on a wave of high new social movement mobilization. Initial electoral success tended to upstage some of the inherent problems of this 'symbiotic' party–movement relationship. New social movements are, by definition, weak interest aggregators, which tend to integrate and mobilize support by advertising maximal solutions, such as the immediate closure of all nuclear power stations – a demand that became the hallmark of all Green parties emerging in the late 1970s and early 1980s. As Green parties were increasingly drawn into the normal party political game of negotiation and compromise, new social movements tended to find it difficult to accept that their primary goal was now only one among several important political objectives the Green party wanted to pursue. Inevitably, friction occurred and movement support for the Greens became less reliable. As a consequence, Green parties and new social movements began to move apart, reasserting their separate identities, not least when Green parties began to assume executive responsibilities, first at local and regional levels and then, finally, in national governments (Müller-Rommel and Poguntke, 2002). Partially a result of this, but also because they had succeeded in establishing themselves as credible political actors in many countries, the electoral performance of Green parties was only moderately affected when movement mobilization declined noticeably in the late 1980s and 1990s (Müller-Rommel, 2002).

COLLATERAL ORGANIZATIONS AND SOCIAL CHANGE

When the catch-all strategy was beginning to generate electoral benefits in the 1960s, more and more large parties began to reach beyond their core constituencies and establish contacts with relevant interest organizations. The very essence of this strategy, that is, the attempt to move out of clearly defined social subcultures and establish contacts with as many relevant social interests as possible, required that such contacts should remain non-exclusive and hence non-formalized. At the same time, however, all Western European parties maintained existing formal ties to different kinds of collateral organizations. Consequently, longitudinal analysis shows that there has been virtually no change in the number of collateral organizations formally linked to parties in Western Europe between 1960 and 1990 (Poguntke, 2000: 155). A more detailed analysis using a standardized measure of the strength of these organizational linkages yields similar results: while there has been a modest decline in linkage through collateral organizations connecting parties to external interests, linkage through internal collateral organizations has compensated for this modest erosion. Overall,

the picture is one of great stability (Poguntke, 2000: 168–9). The data show little difference between parties that originated as cadre and mass parties, which is a powerful indication of the adaptive pressures generated by the mass party model. Clearly, there was a contagion from the left (Duverger, 1964: xxvii).

The more refined measure shows again that new parties are virtually without formal organizational linkages, which makes these parties more vulnerable to electoral fluctuation. Empirical analyses have shown that parties with strong organizational linkages to society have more stable electorates. This is also true for linkage through a party's own membership organization: large memberships are positively associated with stable electoral results, and a growing membership tends to go together with electoral gains (Poguntke, 2005: 56–8). Party elites can reach out to their electorate through their own membership organization as individual members act as disseminators of the party's message within their own social context. Members of collateral organizations can fulfil similar functions, advertising the party's views in their community and, to a degree, communicating grievances back to their organizational elites who will then formulate appropriate demands *vis-à-vis* party elites. Clearly, this is a simplified depiction of complex processes of interest articulation and aggregation but it describes the basic mechanism that was mentioned in the introduction to this chapter: policy pledges are exchanged for organizational support in stabilizing and/or mobilizing voters for a given party.

There is a price to be paid for support by collateral organizations: strong ties to strong collateral organizations limit the freedom of manoeuvre of party elites. This applies not only to the few but conspicuous examples of strong ties between parties and trade unions or the Catholic Church. It is generally true for all kinds of collateral organizations. Even ancillary organizations, that is, organizations that are fully integrated in the main party structure, will provide an organizational arena for dissenting views and a potential power base for rebellious counter elites. A more differentiated organizational structure and more representation of ancillary or affiliated organizations in a party's main decision-making bodies will increase the likelihood of programmatic or strategic moves being blocked by alliances of veto players.

Essentially, this means that party elites of new parties have, by and large, more strategic flexibility than their colleagues in traditional parties when it comes to repositioning their party. Furthermore, their electoral disadvantage is declining as the substantive strength of organizational linkages is declining across the board. Clearly, the enormous stability of formal ties between party organizations and various types of collateral organizations reflects the continuing relevance of such linkages for traditional parties. As societies have become socially more diverse (van Deth, 1995), however, these organizations have found it increasingly difficult to maintain their attractiveness. On the one hand, ever fewer people fall into neat social categories such as the classic manual worker, who has nothing to lose but his chains, or the archetypal church-going Catholic farmer in Southern Europe (Streeck, 1987. 474–82; Wessels, 1991: 457; Rucht, 1993: 271ff.; Katz, 1990: 145). And even those who still belong to these groups may have far more independent views than in the past, not least because, with the advent of the mass media, information is no longer controlled by social elites (Poguntke, 2000: 56ff.). Whereas these organizations are still important mobilizers and aggregators, their overall role has clearly declined. Many have suffered membership decline, while others have become internally more pluralistic. To be sure, the apparent stability of linkage via collateral organizations conceals, to a degree, their diminishing substantial importance. Still, they have in most cases remained important allies for party elites, which explains that organizationally mediated linkage has remained so staggeringly stable. After all, as long as mutual benefits outweigh the problems caused by increasing heterogeneity, both party and organizational elites have no reason to terminate exclusive relationships. The few conspicuous cases where close links between parties of the left and the trade unions have been severed indicate, however, that a point can be reached where a formerly beneficial symbiosis turns into a liability (Alderman and Carter, 1995; Richards, 1997: 30ff.; Svåsand, 1994a: 315; Webb, 1992: 35; 1994: 115; Widfeldt, 1997: 91).

Overall, then, the organizational anchorage of Western European party systems has clearly declined over the past decades. First, the growing vote share of new parties without significant ties to collateral organizations means that the aggregate anchorage of party systems has been reduced. Second, traditional parties have managed to maintain most of their ties to different types of collateral organizations but their capacity to 'deliver' votes and interest aggregation has suffered due to ongoing processes of social differentiation. Finally, there is every indication that democratic latecomers in Southern and East-Central Europe have developed party systems which, by and large, lack the social foundations which gradually eroded in traditional Western European party systems. The result is an increasingly pluralistic system of interaction between organized interests and party politics, a system that increasingly resembles the pattern familiar from the United States.

REFERENCES

Alderman, Keith and Carter, Neil (1994) 'The Labour Party and the trade unions: Loosening ties', *Parliamentary Affairs*, 47: 321–37.

Alderman, Keith and Carter, Neil (1995) 'The Labour Party leadership and deputy leadership elections of 1994', *Parliamentary Affairs*, 48: 438–55.

Baker, Susan, Kousis, Maina, Richardson, Dick and Young, Stephen (eds) (1997) *The Politics of Sustainable Development*. London: Routledge.

Bardi, Luciano and Morlino, Leonardo (1994) 'Italy: Tracing the roots of the great transformation' in Richard S. Katz and Peter Mair (eds), *How Parties Organize. Change and Adaptation in Party Organizations in Western Democracies*. London: Sage, pp. 242–77.

Bartolini, Stefano and Mair, Peter (1990) *Identity, Competition, and Electoral Availability. The Stabilisation of European Electorates 1885–1985*. Cambridge: Cambridge University Press.

Betz, Hans-Georg and Immerfall, Stefan (1998) *The New Politics of the Right: Neo-Populist Parties and Movements in Established Democracies*. New York: St. Martin's Press.

Beyme, Klaus von (1980) *Interessengruppen in der Demokratie*. Munich: Piper.

Daalder, Hans (1987) 'The Dutch party system: From segmentation to polarization – and then?', in Hans Daalder (ed.), *Party Systems in Denmark, Austria, Switzerland, the Netherlands, and Belgium*. London: Frances Pinter, pp. 193–284.

Dalton, Russell J. (1994) *The Green Rainbow. Environmental Groups in Western Europe*. New Haven, CT: Yale University Press.

Dalton, Russell J. and Kuechler, Manfred (eds) (1990) *Challenging the Political Order: New Social and Political Movements in Western Democracies*. New York: Oxford University Press.

Dalton, Russell J., Kuechler, Manfred and Bürklin, Wilhelm (1990) 'The challenge of new movements', in Russell J. Dalton and Manfred Kuechler (eds), *Challenging the Political Order: New Social and Political Movements in Western Democracies*. New York: Oxford University Press, pp. 3–22.

Duverger, Maurice (1964) *Political Parties*. London: Methuen.

Gerlich, Peter (1987) 'Consociationalism to competition. The Austrian party system since 1945', in Hans Daalder (ed.), *Party Systems in Denmark, Austria, Switzerland, the Netherlands, and Belgium*. London: Frances Pinter, pp. 61–106.

Haungs, Peter (1983) 'Die Christlich Demokratische Union Deutschlands (CDU) und die Christlich Soziale Union in Bayern (CSU)', in Hans-Joachim Veen (ed.), *Christlich-demokratische und konservative Parteien in Westeuropa*. Paderborn: Schöningh, pp. 9–194.

Hildebrandt, Kai and Dalton, Russell J. (1978) 'Political change or sunshine politics?', in Max Kaase and Klaus von Beyme (eds), *Elections and Parties. German Political Studies, Vol. 3*. London: Sage, pp. 69–96.

Ignazi, Piero (2003) *Extreme Right Parties in Western Europe*. Oxford: Oxford University Press.

Kaase, Max (1990) 'Social movements and political innovation', in Russell J. Dalton and Manfred Kuechler (eds), *Challenging the Political Order. New Social and Political Movements in Western Democracies*. New York: Oxford University Press, pp. 84–101.

Katz, Richard S. (1990) 'Party as linkage: A vestigial function?', *European Journal of Political Research*, 18: 143–61.

Katz, Richard S. and Mair, Peter (eds) (1992) *Party Organizations. A Data Handbook on Party Organizations in Western Democracies, 1960–90*. London: Sage.

Katz, Richard S. and Mair, Peter (1995) 'Changing models of party organization and party democracy: The emergence of the cartel party', *Party Politics*, 1: 5–28.

Kirchheimer, Otto (1966) 'The transformation of the Western European party system', in Joseph LaPalombara and Myron Weiner (eds), *Political Parties and Political Development*. Princeton, NJ: Princeton University Press, pp. 177–200.

Kitschelt, Herbert (1988) 'Left-libertarian parties. Explaining innovation in competitive party systems', *World Politics*, 15: 194–234.

Kitschelt, Herbert (1989) *The Logics of Party Formation. Ecological Politics in Belgium and West Germany*. Ithaca, NY: Cornell University Press.

Kriesi, H., Koopmans, Ruud, Duyvendak, Jan Willhem and Guigni, Marco (1995) *New Social Movements in Western Europe. A Comparative Analysis*. Minneapolis: University of Minnesota Press.

Lane, Jan-Erik and Ersson, Svante O. (1987) *Politics and Society in Western Europe*. London: Sage.

Lawson, Kay (1980) 'Political parties and linkage', in Kay Lawson (ed.), *Political Parties and Linkage. A Comparative Perspective*. New Haven, CT: Yale University Press, pp. 3–24.

Lawson, Kay (1988) 'When linkage fails', in Kay Lawson and Peter H. Merkl (eds), *When Parties Fail. Emerging Alternative Organizations*. Princeton, NJ: Princeton University Press, pp. 13–38.

Lepsius, M. Rainer (1973) 'Parteiensystem und Sozialstruktur: zum Problem der Demokratisierung der deutschen Gesellschaft', in Gerhard A. Ritter (ed.), *Deutsche Parteien vor 1918*. Köln: Kiepenheuer und Witsch, pp. 56–80.

Lijphart, Arend (1968) *The Politics of Accommodation: Pluralism and Democracy in the Netherlands*. Berkeley: University of California Press.

Lipset, Seymour M. and Rokkan, Stein (1967) 'Cleavage structures, party systems, and voter alignments: An introduction', in Seymour M. Lipset and Stein Rokkan (eds), *Party Systems and Voter Alignments: Cross-National Perspectives*. New York: Free Press, pp. 1–64.

Luther, Kurt Richard and Deschouwer, Kris (eds) (1999) *Party Elites in Divided Societies. Political Parties in Consociational Democracy*. London and New York: Routledge.

Müller-Rommel, Ferdinand (1985) 'Social movements and the Greens', *European Journal of Political Research*, 13: 53–67.

Müller-Rommel, Ferdinand (ed.) (1989) *New Politics in Western Europe. The Rise and Success of Green Parties and Alternative Lists*. Boulder, CO: Westview Press.

Müller-Rommel, Ferdinand (2002) 'The lifespan and the political performance of Green parties in Western Europe', in Ferdinand Müller-Rommel and Thomas Poguntke (ed.), *Green Parties in National Governments*. London: Frank Cass, pp. 1–16.

Müller-Rommel, Ferdinand and Poguntke, Thomas (eds) (2002) *Green Parties in National Governments*. London: Frank Cass.

Neidhart, Friedhelm (1985) 'Einige Ideen zu einer allgemeinen Theorie sozialer Bewegungen', in Stefan Hradil (ed.), *Sozialstruktur im Umbruch*. Opladen: Leske + Budrich, pp. 193–204.

Neidhart, Friedhelm and Rucht, Dieter (1993) 'Auf dem Weg in die "Bewegungsgesellschaft"? Über die Stabilisierbarkeit sozialer Bewegungen', *Soziale Welt*, 44: 305–26.

Neumann, Sigmund (1956) 'Towards a comparative study of political parties', in Sigmund Neumann (ed.), *Modern Political Parties. Approaches to Comparative Politics*. Chicago: University of Chicago Press, pp. 395–421.

Panebianco, Angelo (1988) *Political Parties: Organization and Power*. Cambridge: Cambridge University Press.

Pierre, Jon and Widfeldt, Anders (1992) 'Sweden; Political Data Yearbook 1992', *European Journal of Political Research*, 22: 519–26.

Pierre, Jon and Widfeldt, Anders (1994) 'Party organizations in Sweden: Colossuses with feet of clay or flexible Pillars of Government?', in Richard S. Katz and Peter Mair (eds), *How Parties Organize*.

Change and Adaptation in Party Organizations in Western Democracies. London: Sage, pp. 332–56.

Poguntke, Thomas (1987) 'New politics and party systems: The emergence of a new type of party?', *West European Politics*, 10: 76–88.

Poguntke, Thomas (1992) 'Unconventional participation in party politics. The experience of the German Greens', *Political Studies*, 40: 239–54.

Poguntke, Thomas (2000) *Parteiorganisation im Wandel. Gesellschaftliche Verankerung und organisatorische Anpassung im europäischen Vergleich*. Wiesbaden: Westdeutscher Verlag.

Poguntke, Thomas (2005) 'Parties without firm social roots? Party organisational linkage', in Kurt Richard Luther and Ferdinand Müller-Rommel (eds), *Political Parties in the New Europe: Political and Analytical Challenges*. Oxford: Oxford University Press, pp. 43–62.

Richards, Andrew (1997) *The Life and Soul of the Party: Causes and Consequences of Organizational Change in the British Labour Party, 1979–1997*. Working Paper 1997/95. Madrid: Instituto Juan March de Estudios e Investigaciones.

Rochon, Thomas R. (1988) *Mobilizing for Peace. The Antinuclear Movements in Western Europe*. Princeton, NJ: Princeton University Press.

Rucht, Dieter (1993) 'Parteien, Verbände und Bewegungen als Systeme politischer Interessenvermittlung', in Oskar Niedermayer and Richard Stöss (eds), *Stand und Perspektiven der Parteienforschung in Deutschland*. Opladen: Westdeutscher Verlag, pp. 251–75.

Rucht, Dieter (1994) *Modernisierung und neue soziale Bewegung*. Frankfurt am Main: Campus.

Schmitt, Rüdiger (1989) 'Organizational interlocks between new social movements and traditional elites: The case of the West German peace movement', *European Journal of Political Research*, 17: 583–98.

Seyd, Patrick and Whiteley, Paul (2004) 'From disaster to landslide: The case of the British Labour Party', in Kay Lawson and Thomas Poguntke (eds), *How Political Parties Respond. Interest Aggregation Revisited*. London and New York: Routledge, pp. 41–60.

Steininger, Rudolf (1984) *Soziologische Theorie der politischen Parteien*. Frankfurt am Main: Campus.

Streeck, Wolfgang (1987) 'Vielfalt und Interdependenz. Überlegungen zur Rolle von intermediären Organisationen in sich ändernden Umwelten', *Kölner Zeitschrift für Soziologie und Sozialpsychologie*, 39: 471–95.

Svåsand, Lars (1992) 'Norway', in Richard S. Katz and Peter Mair (eds), *Party Organizations. A Data Handbook on Party Organizations in Western Democracies, 1960–90*. London: Sage, pp. 732–80.

Svåsand, Lars (1994a) 'Change and adaptation in Norwegian party organizations', in Richard S. Katz and Peter Mair (eds), *How Parties Organize. Change and Adaptation in Party Organizations in Western Democracies*. London: Sage, pp. 304–31.

Svåsand, Lars (1994b) 'Die Konservative Volkspartei und die Christliche Volkspartei Norwegens: Unbequeme Nachbarn im bürgerlichen Lager', in Hans-Joachim Veen (ed.), *Christlich-demokratische und konservative Parteien in Westeuropa 4. Schweden-Norwegen-Finnland-Dänemark*. Paderborn: Schöningh.

van Deth, Jan W. (1995) 'A macro setting for micro politics', in Jan W. van Deth and Elinor Scarbrough (eds), *The Impact of Values*. Oxford: Oxford University Press, pp. 76–119.

Webb, Paul D. (1992) *Trade Unions and the British Electorate*. Aldershot: Dartmouth.

Webb, Paul D. (1994) 'Party organizational change in Britain: The iron law of centralization', in Richard S. Katz and Peter Mair (eds), *How Parties Organize. Change and Adaptation in Party Organizations in Western Democracies*. London: Sage, pp. 109–33.

Wessels, Bernhard (1991) 'Vielfalt oder strukturierte Komplexität? Zur Institutionalisierung politischer Spannungslinien im Verbände- und Parteiensystem der Bundesrepublik', *Kölner Zeitschrift für Soziologie und Sozialpsychologie*, 43: 454–75.

Widfeldt, Anders (1997) *Linking Parties with People? Party Membership in Sweden 1960–1994*. Göteborg: Göteborg University.

34

CLIENTELISM AND PARTY POLITICS

Jonathan Hopkin

INTRODUCTION

Clientelism is a term which describes the distribution of selective benefits to individuals or clearly defined groups in exchange for political support (although as we shall see below, there are a range of more precise definitions). Clientelism occupies a curious position in the scholarship on party politics, and there is a degree of confusion over its relationship to the electoral process. On the one hand, it appears to be associated with pre-modern social contexts and is therefore connotated with cultural and economic 'backwardness'. On the other hand, clientelistic dynamics can frequently be found in the most apparently advanced socio-economic contexts, as attested by the abundant scholarly literature on 'pork-barrel' political exchange in the contemporary United States. Moreover, the confusion is exacerbated by the wide and diverse range of political exchanges which can be accommodated by the concept of clientelism.

The first objective of this analysis is therefore to present a more precise conceptualization of clientelism. It will then proceed to examine the origins and modalities of political clientelism, and assess its implications for party democracy.

CONCEPTUALIZING CLIENTELISM

Stripped down to the essentials, clientelism is a form of personal, dyadic exchange usually characterized by a sense of obligation, and often also by an unequal balance of power between those involved (see Eisenstadt and Roniger, 1984: 48–9; Piattoni, 2004). This definition reflects the origins of the concept as a descriptor of hierarchical patron–client relationships in traditional rural societies (Piattoni, 2001a: 9). These relationships involve 'the patron providing clients with access to the basic means of subsistence and the clients reciprocating with a combination of economic goods and services (such as rent, labor, portions of their crops) and social acts of deference and loyalty' (Mason, 1986: 489). In other words, clientelism is a way of describing the pattern of unequal, hierarchical exchange characteristic of feudal society, in which patrons and clients were tied to durable relationships by a powerful sense of obligation and duty.

This kind of 'notables' clientelism (Tarrow, 1967) – which is also referred to as 'old clientelism' (Weingrod, 1968) – survived into the modern democratic age in many parts of the world, and therefore became enmeshed in the dynamics of electoral politics. In clientelistic contexts patrons, or their agents, stand for election and their clients vote for them, sometimes out of a general sense of obligation and attachment, sometimes as part of a specific exchange for services rendered or promised. Either way, voting behaviour is a function of a personalized and instrumental view of political participation: voters simply use their vote to sustain their patrons, thus earning the patrons' protection and help. Voters neglect the broader political consequences of their electoral choices, and representatives elected through clientelistic mechanisms cannot credibly claim a mandate to pursue a broad programme of public policies. Moreover, the rigid and unchanging nature of traditional clientelism undermines the 'feedback' function of electoral politics, making alternation in political power an artefact of elite decisions (as, for example, in the *turno pacífico* of late nineteenth- and early twentieth-century Spain, or the *trasformismo* of Italy in the same period).

In some cases, clientelism has evolved into something quite different from this kind of traditional social exchange. Studies of postwar Italy in particular have suggested the emergence of a 'new clientelism' (Tarrow, 1967; Weingrod, 1968; Caciagli and Belloni, 1981), in which political behaviour is still characterized by patterns of exchange, but of a new kind. Socioeconomic modernization brought greater geographical mobility and urbanization, higher levels of education, the replacement of agrarian by industrial employment, and the decline of traditional rural elites. These developments weakened traditional patron–client ties, which made way for new forms of exchange. Organized political parties, with relatively bureaucratized structures, replaced landlords and local notables as patrons. Clients, enjoying higher living standards and less instinctively deferential, demanded more immediate material benefits in exchange for their votes. In this new, 'mass party' clientelism, patrons have to 'buy' votes by distributing concrete excludable benefits and favours to individual voters or groups of voters. In the Italian context this is referred to as the 'vote of exchange' (Parisi and Pasquino, 1979; Katz, 1986).

This new clientelism shares some of the features of the old. The relationship is still instrumental, and the benefits provided to clients are still largely private and excludable. But there are also important differences. First, the relationship is less hierarchical, more 'democratic'. There remains an imbalance of power, in that the patron has control over resources that the client needs, but there is less of a sense of deference and dependency on the part of the client, who feels increasingly free to use her vote as a commodity to be exchanged for whatever maximizes her utility. Second, as a result of this less hierarchical and personalized context, the new clientelism is more conducive to fluidity and change in electoral behaviour, opening up possibilities of greater competition and elite turnover.

The differences between these two types of clientelism are significant enough to undermine the precision of the concept. The client who votes automatically for her patron out of a sense of deference, and the implicit and imprecise promise of protection and aid, is a very different social actor from the client who shops around for the patron who offers the best deal, and may even switch patrons if the flow of benefits dries up (see Allum, 1997). The old clientelism is very much a form of social and political exchange, in that it 'involves the principle that one person does another a favor, and while there is a general expectation of some future return, its exact nature is definitely *not* stipulated in advance' (Blau, 1964: 93). The new clientelism instead resembles 'economic' or 'market' exchange, in which the client seeks to maximize utility irrespective of any sense of obligation towards or identification with another actor. Gellner (1977: 5–6) draws the distinction with striking clarity:

> Economic benefits are, at least ideally, calculable, noncommittal and single-shot: hence an economic operation is isolable, and does not need to give rise to any permanent relationship. ... By contrast, the long-term imponderables which are being 'exchanged' in a political relationship, ipso facto give a much deeper colouring to the links between the parties to the transaction.

Although clientelism will rarely be exclusively of one kind or another, the extent to which 'economic' dynamics prevail has major implications for party democracy. If the only reason for supporting the party is a direct economic exchange which excludes feelings of loyalty or ideological affinity, there is little to anchor the clientele to the party if benefits are not forthcoming. This opens up the possibility of political instability and upheaval, rather than the continuity or even stagnation more often associated with clientelistic political systems.

WHY CLIENTELISM?

It is difficult to measure the role of clientelism in party politics in a given political system accurately (Wantchekon, 2003). Some statistical analyses, particularly for the United States, have studied budgetary allocations across territory in order to estimate the flow of selective, excludable benefits to particular localities (for example, Stein and Bickers, 1995; Frisch, 1998). However, such analyses focus on benefits to groups of varying size, and can rarely detect the kind of personalized, one-to-one exchange that is characteristic of much clientelistic politics. Most of our knowledge and understanding of clientelism in its most personalized form therefore comes from case studies which have used an ethnographic approach to identify the presence of clientelistic dynamics (for collections of such work, see Gellner, 1977; Eisenstadt and Lemarchand, 1981; Eisenstadt and Roniger, 1984;

Piattoni, 2001b). Such case studies, naturally enough, select on the dependent variable, leaving us with little basis on which to assert that some political systems are more clientelistic than others. However, it is broadly held that advanced Western democracies are less clientelistic than developing countries, and that amongst the advanced democracies, those in Northern Europe and in the English-speaking world are the least clientelistic, although there is little in the way of hard comparative evidence to back up these claims.

A variety of explanations have been advanced to account for this apparent variation in clientelism across nations (for extensive reviews see Piattoni, 2001a, 2004). Structural explanations identify long-standing institutions and patterns of behaviour which prevent political systems from breaking out of practices of clientelistic exchange. Most famously, Putnam's (1993) account of the varying performance of regional governments in Italy explained corrupt and clientelistic party politics in terms of the presence or absence of reserves of social capital. In some regions (in the Centre and North), traditions of 'civicness', originating in early experiences of representative political institutions in the medieval period, established a pattern of associationalism and collective action which formed the basis for public interest-oriented behaviour by voters once electoral democracy took root. In these areas, citizen participation in the political process is motivated by a sense of responsibility towards the community, and the electoral process revolves around competing packages of collective goods. In the ill-governed South of Italy, in contrast, no such civic tradition has been established, and citizens find it hard to overcome collective action problems. As a result, voters do not trust political parties to provide collective goods, and tend instead to seek selective, private benefits in exchange for political support (see Banfield, 1958, for a classic description). For Putnam, the absence of a tradition of 'civicness' is the prime cause of clientelism: without such a normative compass, citizens will tend to see the democratic process as an opportunity to win excludable benefits for themselves, and political parties will see it as their job to allocate such benefits in exchange for votes. Similar normative assumptions underpin the classic interpretations of 'machine politics' in American cities, where clientelism was directed at 'working class people, especially immigrants unfamiliar with American ways and institutions' (Banfield and Wilson, 1963: 118).

This view has been roundly criticized for its determinism, as well as its alleged empirical inaccuracy (Levi, 1996; Sabetti, 1996). Putnam's interpretation of Italian history fails to account for a number of inconsistencies, and also fails to consider the role of socioeconomic marginality (Pizzorno, 1971) in depressing civic endeavour in the geographically isolated South. Putnam's broad-brush, structuralist approach is countered by other scholars who have placed greater emphasis on historical contingency and strategic interaction. Martin Shefter (1994) has argued that the extent of clientelistic mobilization by political parties is a function of the sequencing of the process of democratization: in countries where political parties and competitive elections emerged before the creation of an autonomous bureaucracy, politicians could exploit the resources available in the state administration for partisan ends, allocating public jobs on political grounds (to party activists and loyal voters). Filippo Sabetti's (2000) analysis of the emergence of the Italian state shows that the process of institutional design and development is complex and multidimensional, and that the failure to decisively implant 'good government' in Italy was a contingent outcome rather than the inevitable result of its historical legacy. Simona Piattoni (2004) has countered deterministic views of clientelism and its origins by employing game theory to explain how the process of clientelistic political exchange can lead to a variety of outcomes, including the (more or less) optimal provision of public goods by government.

Given the difficulties involved in identifying and measuring clientelism, it is unlikely this debate can easily be resolved. Both the structuralist and the strategic interpretations of clientelism run into serious theoretical and empirical problems. Reductive determinism, especially analyses such as Putnam's which see political systems as 'doomed' (Sabetti, 2000) to clientelism by distant events such as medieval conquests, lacks an adequate account of the mechanisms through which structures are reproduced and maintained. Strategic explanations, in contrast, neglect the role of structure in defining the 'games' within which actors develop their strategies. Empirically, structuralist theories need to account for the persistence of clientelism in supposedly virtuous England until well into the nineteenth century (O'Gorman, 2001), and for the extensive evidence of apparently vibrant 'civic' behaviour in the Italian South at various times since the medieval period (Sabetti, 2000). Strategic analyses need to show that the abundant evidence of clientelistic dynamics in postwar Italian parties, and the lack of such evidence for the Swedish parties, for example (Papakostas, 2001), can indeed be explained in terms of the peculiarities of strategic choice, rather than the very different socioeconomic conditions in which democracy developed in the two countries. Up to now there has not been enough systematic comparative-historical research to resolve these uncertainties.

VARIETIES OF CLIENTELISM: PATTERNS OF EXCHANGE IN ELECTORAL POLITICS

On a practical level, clientelism manifests itself in a variety of ways, depending on the kinds of resources available to patrons, and the kinds of citizen demands that have to be met. In the most traditional contexts, clientelism could draw on age-old reserves of loyalty and deference, so that patrons could obtain political support from their clients without providing too many concrete benefits. Banfield's famous study of the Southern Italian village of 'Montegrano' in the 1950s found that 'just before elections the Christian Democratic party distributes small packages of pasta, sugar, and clothing to the voters' (1958: 26). In situations of dire poverty, such gifts may be enough to buy votes, particularly if there is a pre-existing foundation of deference towards the patron. The patron–client relationship in the rural context is not strictly reliant on the distribution of specific material benefits, however: for Tarrow (1967: 68), the patron is 'a support in time of famine, his advice will be formally sought before marriages and land purchases, and he is asked for recommendation in the peasant's frequent encounters with the bureaucracy'. Where this type of 'old' clientelism is well entrenched, the establishment of democratic politics will be conditioned by the local notables' mediating role between voters and the state. Patrons become proprietors of 'packages' of votes, and are able to trade these votes with the leaderships of the political parties, linking themselves with a larger network of clientelistic relationships. This kind of party organization compromises the cohesiveness and durability of the political party: factionalism and weak leadership authority are likely to result.

The 'new' clientelism, characteristic of more economically advanced settings, is subtly different in its impact on party politics. Whilst the local notables of the 'old' clientelism are sources of political legitimacy in and of themselves, the local party bosses in the 'new' clientelism have far less autonomy. Notables can conceivably change their political affiliation without compromising their relationship with their clientele, since what matters for voters is their continued willingness to provide protection and assistance. Local party leaders in the 'new' clientelism are far more dependent on their party affiliation to maintain their clienteles, and are therefore less inclined to change parties. The 'machine politics' of the American cities in the nineteenth and twentieth centuries illustrates this point. Banfield and Wilson's (1963: 118–19) description of the big city machines in the 1950s shows how the party representatives are embedded in a formal organization with its own hierarchy and career structure:

> the job of the precinct captain is to get out the vote for his party's slate ... [he] is chosen by and works under the direction of a ward leader, usually an alderman or elected party official ... . It is up to him to ... dispense the larger items of patronage, favors, and protection to those who have earned them. ... Captains are often 'payrollers', that is, they have appointive public jobs that they could not get or keep if it were not for the party ... . The hope that the party will in due course run them for alderman keeps these captains at work.

In the new clientelism, the patron is the party organization, rather than any individual within it. Clientelistic favours are distributed by members of the party organization, who in turn receive authorization for this activity from the upper tiers of the party hierarchy. Clientelism therefore becomes bureaucratized, and less personalized, although the personal contact between party representatives and individual voters remains important for maintaining the relationship. In this respect, mass party clientelism is a significant departure from notables' clientelism.

The new clientelism is consistent with internal party cohesion and formalized chains of command. Indeed, the case of the Italian Christian Democrats in the 1950s and 1960s shows that clientelism can be a key tool of party institutionalization. DC leader Fanfani used clientelism to overcome the party's dependence on external interest groups and bureaucratize its organization, establishing systematic patterns of resource distribution through the party structures. Since the party controlled the key spending ministries in Rome, local party bosses on the ground needed to cement close ties with national leaders in order to gain access to the clientelistic benefits they distributed to their voters. This system, over time, became quite sophisticated, and similar techniques were also adopted by the Italian Socialists after they became a mainstay of government coalitions in the early 1960s.

The new clientelism is closely associated with the expansion of the economic and social role of the state. In traditional contexts, the state often has a more limited role, particularly in regard to its expenditure. Notables are often deployed by their clients to help with the bureaucratic requirements of the state, such as conscription, rather than to access material benefits. As the state's role has expanded in much of the world to involve a detailed regulation of economic activity and the provision of a wide range of financial benefits (welfare and pensions, industrial and agricultural subsidies, public housing) and public services (education, health), the parties governing the state have had a greater ability to manipulate and channel these resources in exchange for political support. Often, the parties seek to make the criteria for the access to resources deliberately opaque, in order to enhance the discretionary nature of the distribution and extract greater political returns (Tanzi, 2000; Golden, 2003). Once again, the Italian case is one of the best-documented: standard practices ranged from strictly partisan allocation of jobs in the state-run postal service or railways, to the selective distribution of bogus sickness pensions and a variety of subsidies and development projects of questionable utility. Similarly, in Spain, the Socialist party established a rural employment subsidy (the PER – Plan for Rural Employment) which was directed at its own electoral strongholds in the South, and which gave local mayors a large degree of discretion over the allocation of the money (Hopkin, 2001: 128).

The growth in the role of the state has also led to a vast expansion in state personnel, which in many cases has been exploited by political parties to give jobs to their activists and supporters – what Lyrintzis (1984), in his analysis of the Greek case, calls 'bureaucratic clientelism'. A high profile example of this is the case of Jacques Chirac's tenure as mayor of Paris, during which his party allegedly gave 'no show' council jobs to a number of activists who actually continued to work full-time on party business. In Austria, jobs in the state bureaucracy have been routinely allocated on the basis of party affiliation (Mueller, 1989). The Spanish Socialist Party, which won power in 1982 at a very early stage in its organizational development, by 1987 had appointed around

25,000 new state functionaries, bypassing the public administration's normal recruitment procedures; many of these jobs went to party supporters (Hopkin, 2001: 126). Although patronage in the allocation of state jobs can be extensive, it cannot alone underpin a clientelistic electoral strategy, and, in the European case at least, it seems to have been deployed most often to shore up party organizations by providing salaries for committed party workers and facilitating party control of policy implementation. To this extent, clientelism may play an important role in bolstering the institutions of party democracy.

CLIENTELISM AND PARTY DEMOCRACY

Most scholars have stressed the negative implications of clientelism for party democracy. Positive interpretations, noting clientelism's ability to link political representatives to citizens, and to provide a mechanism for ensuring 'constituency service' (Cain et al., 1987) and party response to immediate citizen needs, have been far less common. The main reason is that the use of the vote as a currency to buy material benefits subverts the obstensible purpose of the electoral process in a representative democracy. Many populist conceptions of democracy envisage that citizens cast their votes in terms of their own understanding of the 'public interest', and that the most widely shared view of this public interest will inform political decision-making through the workings of the representative institutions. In fact, this idealized view is conceptually problematic, as the social choice literature has shown: according to Kenneth Arrow's 'impossibility theorem', there is no adequate decision rule for aggregating individual preferences, and therefore no way of establishing what the 'public interest' actually is (Arrow, 1951; see also Schumpeter, 1994). This problem strengthens the case of liberal theorists who dismiss notions of collective interest and instead stress the sovereignty of individual choice in electoral politics (for the liberal–populist distinction in democratic theory, see Riker, 1982).

From a populist position, clientelism is criticized because it gives primacy to the distribution of individual, selective benefits to citizens, to the detriment of the provision of collective goods. Most populist theories emphasize equality of access to the political process, and the very unequal distribution of benefits in clientelism violates this principle. To take one example, the expansion of the welfare state in clientelistic polities has led to a wide range of inefficiencies and injustices, with some individuals and groups benefiting disproportionately at the expense of others, for the sole reason that their votes were deployed in clientelistic exchange. Moreover, if votes are cast purely in terms of the benefits received, then this leaves governing parties free to disregard popular opinion in all policy decisions which do not relate to the direct allocation of resources in exchange for votes. For this reason clientelism has often been associated with authoritarianism. Liberal theorists are less concerned with the inequality of outcome characteristic of clientelistic resource distribution. However, liberal theory does tend to stress equal citizen rights, and therefore liberals can object to clientelism on the grounds of the differential access to the political process that results from clientelistic exchanges. A further liberal objection is that clientelism has often involved the extensive deployment of government resources to satisfy clienteles, which implies heavy government intervention in private property rights in order to raise the necessary revenues. In short, clientelism is generally an unwelcome phenomenon from the point of view of mainstream normative democratic theory.

The picture is more ambiguous from the point of view of the practical implications of clientelism for democratic politics. Clientelism has been associated with both excessive continuity and violent change in party systems. The examples of Italy and Austria provide a neat illustration of this ambiguity: until the 1990s both countries were widely perceived as being locked into an immovable party system cartel by the mechanisms of patronage, clientelism and interparty collusion (Mair, 1997). But in the 1990s, both party systems underwent turbulent changes (spectacularly so in the case of Italy), changes which were widely interpreted as the result of voter protest against the clientelistic party cartels. However, periods of stifling continuity followed by abrupt change have also been noted in apparently far less clientelistic party systems (for instance, the UK). There is little strong comparative evidence to blame clientelism for the difficulties facing party democracy in advanced industrial democracies.

Clientelism is essentially a variant of 'special interest politics' – a mechanism through which political parties and their representatives can obtain political support in exchange for selectively allocating benefits through state institutions. In many ways, it gives less cause for concern than the opaque money-raising practices of many contemporary parties which are willing to tailor public policies to corporate interests and various other lobbies in exchange for money. Corrupt party financing subverts citizen equality by allowing the wealthy to buy political favours which redistribute further advantage to them. Clientelism instead often allocates benefits to the least privileged, and since these clients often have little more than their vote to trade, the redistributive consequences of any specific clientelistic exchange will tend to be less significant. However, mass party clientelism on a large scale is ultimately both inegalitarian (because it does not respond to universalistic criteria) and economically unsustainable (because it feeds a continuing demand for redistribution). The case against clientelism as a form of linkage in party democracy therefore remains strong.

REFERENCES

Allum, P. (1997) '"From two into one". The faces of the Italian Christian Democratic Party', *Party Politics*, 3: 23–52.

Arrow, Kenneth (1951) *Social Choice and Individual Values*. London: Chapman and Hall.

Banfield, Edward (1958) *The Moral Basis of a Backward Society*. New York: Free Press.

Banfield, Edward and Wilson, James Q. (1963) *City Politics*. New York: Vintage.

Blau, P. (1964) *Exchange and Power in Social Life*. New York: Wiley.

Caciagli, Mario and Belloni, Frank (1981) 'The "new" clientelism in Southern Italy: The Christian Democratic Party in Catania', in Shmuel Eisenstadt and René Lemarchand (eds), *Political Clientelism, Patronage and Development*. London: Sage, pp. 35–56.

Cain, Bruce, Ferejohn, John and Fiorina, Morris (1987) *The Personal Vote. Constituency Service and Electoral Independence*. Cambridge, MA: Harvard University Press.

Eisenstadt, Shmuel and Lemarchand, René (eds) (1981) *Political Clientelism, Patronage and Development*. London: Sage.

Eisenstadt, Shmuel and Roniger, Luis (1984) *Patrons, Clients and Friends. Interpersonal Relations and the Structure of Trust in Society*. Cambridge: Cambridge University Press.

Frisch, Scott (1998) *The Politics of Pork: A Study of Congressional Appropriation Earmarks*. New York: Garland.

Gellner, Ernest (1977) 'Patrons and clients', in Ernest, Gellner and John Waterbury (eds), *Patrons and Clients in Mediterranean Societies*. London: Duckworth, pp. 1–6.

Golden, Miriam (2003) 'Electoral connections: The effects of the personal vote on political patronage, bureaucracy and legislation in postwar Italy', *British Journal of Political Science*, 33(2): 189–212.

Hopkin, Jonathan (2001) 'A "southern model" of electoral mobilization? Clientelism and electoral politics in post-Franco Spain', *West European Politics*, 24(1): 115–36.

Katz, Richard S. (1986) 'Preference voting in Italy: Votes of opinion, belonging or exchange', *Comparative Political Studies*, 18: 229–49.

Levi, Margaret (1996) 'Social and unsocial capital: A review essay of Robert Putnam's *Making Democracy Work*', *Politics and Society*, 24: 45–55.

Lyrintzis, Christos (1984) 'Political parties in post-Junta Greece: A case of "bureaucratic clientelism"?', *West European Politics*, 7: 99–118.

Mair, Peter (1997) *Party System Change*. Oxford: Oxford University Press.

Mason, T. David (1986) 'The breakdown of clientelism in El Salvador', *Comparative Political Studies*, 18: 487–518.

Mueller, Wolfgang (1989) 'Party patronage in Austria: Theoretical considerations and empirical findings', in Anton Pelinka and Fritz Plasser (eds), *The Austrian Party System*. Boulder, CO: Westview, pp. 327–56.

O'Gorman, Frank (2001) 'Patronage and the reform of the state in England 1700–1860', in Simona Piattoni (ed.), *Clientelism, Interests, and Democratic Representation*. Cambridge: Cambridge University Press, pp. 54–76.

Papakostas, Apostolis (2001) 'Why is there no clientelism in Scandinavia? A comparison of the Swedish and Greek sequences of development', in Simona Piattoni (ed.), *Clientelism, Interests, and Democratic Representation*. Cambridge: Cambridge University Press, pp. 31–53.

Parisi, Arturo and Pasquino, Gianfranco (1979) 'Changes in Italian electoral behaviour: The relationships between parties and voters', in Peter Lange and Sidney Tarrow (eds), *Italy in Transition*. London: Frank Cass, pp. 6–30.

Piattoni, Simona (2001a) 'Clientelism in historical and comparative perspective', in Simona Piattoni (ed.), *Clientelism, Interests, and Democratic Representation*. Cambridge: Cambridge University Press, pp. 1–30.

Piattoni, Simona (ed.) (2001b) *Clientelism, Interests, and Democratic Representation*. Cambridge: Cambridge University Press.

Piattoni, Simona (2004) 'Clientelismo. Scambio, sistema, strategia'. Unpublished manuscript, University of Trento.

Pizzorno, Alessandro (1971) 'Amoral familism and historical marginality', in Mattei Dogan and Richard Rose (eds), *European Politics: A Reader*. Boston: Little Brown, pp. 87–98.

Putnam, Robert (1993) *Making Democracy Work: Civic Traditions in Modern Italy*. Princeton, NJ: Princeton University Press.

Riker, William (1982) *Liberalism against Populism*. San Francisco: Freeman.

Sabetti, Filippo (1996) 'Path dependency and civic culture: Some lessons from Italy about interpreting social experiments', *Politics and Society*, 24: 19–44.

Sabetti, Filippo (2000) *The Search for Good Government. Understanding the Paradox of Italian Democracy*. Montreal: McGill-Queen's University Press.

Schumpeter, Joseph (1994) *Capitalism, Socialism and Democracy*. London: Routledge.

Shefter, Martin (1994) *Political Parties and the State. The American Historical Experience*. Princeton, NJ: Princeton University Press.

Stein, Robert and Bickers, Kenneth (1995) *Perpetuating the Pork Barrel: Policy Subsystem and American Democracy*. Cambridge: Cambridge University Press.

Tanzi, Vito (2000) *Policies, Institutions and the Dark Side of Economics*. Cheltenham: Edward Elgar.

Tarrow, Sidney (1967) *Peasant Communism in Southern Italy*. New Haven, CT: Yale University Press.

Wantchekon, Leonard (2003) 'Clientelism and voting behaviour: Evidence from a field experiment in Benin', *World Politics*, 55: 399–422.

Weingrod, Alex (1968) 'Patrons, patronage and political parties', *Comparative Studies in Society and History*, 10: 377–400.

35

PARTY AS A CARRIER OF IDEAS

Francesca Vassallo and Clyde Wilcox

INTRODUCTION

In the USA the Republican Party gained unified control of national government in 2002. Soon thereafter, party leaders began to push for policies that would promote private competition with government programs – school vouchers that would enhance the growth of private schools, a health care plan that would help private insurance companies compete with Medicare, federal aid to faith-based charities that might enable them to compete with national welfare programs, and a plan that might enable private mutual fund companies to compete with the national pensions system. Republicans claimed that these were vigorous new ideas that would improve the quality of services, while Democrats charged that they were recycled attempts to dismantle the welfare state.

Regardless of whether these ideas were new, they were expedient for electoral politics. School vouchers appealed to African-Americans and Latinos trapped in poor inner-city schools and to traditional Catholics, all of whom were traditional Democratic constituencies. The Republicans' health care plan would expand coverage for prescription drugs for the elderly, another traditional Democratic bloc. Not only did each of these programs appeal to Democratic voters – they were also centered in a policy domain that the Democrats had long been perceived to dominate.

School vouchers were not only politically expedient in dividing the Democratic coalition, but also consistent with long-time Republican preferences for small government and

competition. In contrast, the prescription drug benefit plan was consistent with the party's long-standing commitment to competition, but inconsistent with the party's opposition to entitlement programs of the welfare state. Many Republican legislators complained that their party had sold its ideology for the votes of the elderly.

Political parties package and promote ideas for the political system. Their platforms serve as repositories for ideologies. There is considerable continuity in party ideologies and programs from one election to another, although party positions are not frozen. Moreover, many types of political parties advocate similar ideas in different countries: Christian Democratic parties, Socialist parties, and Green parties, for example, frequently share platform elements and may cooperate across country lines. In some cases, political parties provide aid to similar parties in developing countries, including help with manifestoes and policy proposals.

PARTY IDEOLOGIES AND IDEAS

The earliest accounts of political parties often described individuals bound together by common ideas. Edmund Burke defined the party as a body of men 'united, for promoting for their joint endeavours the national interest, upon some particular principle in which they are all agreed' (Burke, 1889). Most textbooks argue that parties form to advocate policy ideas. Kernell and Jacobson (2003), writing of the American case, argue that the first parties were created as temporary expedients to allow like-minded citizens to promote their shared vision of the common good.

Under this conception, policies and ideologies are the reason why parties exist. Many scholars have described ideologies as central to parties. A party's ideology is seen as a 'characterization of a belief system that goes to the heart of a party's identity' (Mair and Mudde, 1998: 220). Carver (2004: 9) suggests that ideologies are 'an agenda of things to discuss, questions to ask, hypotheses to make'. Political ideologies portray the true essence of parties, as in 'what they are', as Mair and Mudde (1998: 220) put it, not in what they do. A political party without an ideology would have no base for existence, and could not perform any task in the political context since 'ideologies in this sense represent the core identities of parties and provide blueprints of alternative solutions for current problems of societies' (Volkens and Klingemann, 2002: 144).

Yet other scholars argue that parties are merely coalitions of individuals seeking to control government (Downs, 1957). Under this conception, political ideologies are 'means of obtaining votes', and parties choose ideas and ideologies to maximize their share of the popular vote, or to perhaps create a minimum winning coalition of parties. Downs' seminal analysis sought to predict optimal party ideologies based on the electoral system and the distribution of the voters' preferences.

Yet even if parties adopt ideologies only to gain votes, they may still have an incentive to maintain a relatively constant set of issues across elections. Downs suggests that parties may adopt consistent platforms in order to convince voters of their reliability (Budge, 2003). Volkens and Klingemann (2002) suggest that parties may lose supporters if they dramatically change their manifesto, and that an ideology provides parties with a fundamental force for continuity. Moreover, ideologies are tools that parties can use not only to attract votes but also to motivate activists and to form bridges with non-party organizations. Ideologies provide a conceptual map to politics for party leaders, activists, and voters to interpret campaigns and issues. They reduce the information costs associated with sorting out party positions on many concrete issues (Budge, 1994).

For all of these reasons, most political parties can be identified with at least some ideological elements, and often with a general ideology. These ideologies vary in their specificity, and they may evolve over time, but parties do not usually greatly change their positions on the left–right dimension (Budge, 2003). Thus the durable dimensions of ideological differences between parties have been the focus of most research (Lijphart, 1990).

Parties may be seen as the repository of ideologies, but they are also the short-term carrier of ideas. The specific policy ideas debated by parties will vary across countries and in between election cycles. In the USA and Europe, political parties today debate methods to combat terrorism, an issue far less salient on national agendas just 5 years earlier. As most Western nations face the eventual retirement of a significant segment of its working population, debates over the best way to finance these retirements have arisen in some but not all countries. Party issue positions must change as societies face new problems.

The specific ideas that parties choose to implement their ideologies and attract voters come from many sources. Social movements and interest groups may develop policy proposals and insert them into the political dialogue. Research institutes, think tanks, and academics may recommend policies. Many political parties have their own research arms to help them more thoroughly develop their agendas (the Konrad Adenauer Foundation for the Christian Democrats in Germany, for instance).

In recent years, political consultants have played a role in selecting specific policy ideas for the political parties. In 1994, the Republican party in the USA offered a 'Contract with America' that included ten specific policy pledges, some (but not all) of which were implemented when the party gained control of Congress. The specific items were chosen from a list through focus groups and careful polling. Consultants helped the British Labour Party develop its agenda in the 1990s, and are working in new democracies to form agendas for parties and candidates.

However policy ideas originate, they are linked to the political agenda by political parties in elections. When countries face difficult decisions, political parties can articulate and debate alternative solutions, and elections can then lead to a societal decision. Political parties typically carry these ideas across several election cycles, although it is not unusual for parties to coopt specific ideas offered by other parties in order to eliminate the issue in the campaign.

CLEAVAGES IN PARTY SYSTEMS

The sources of party ideologies are generally thought to lie in socially ordered cleavages.

Political parties often represent groups that actively contest with others over the distribution of material goods or values. These cleavages vary across societies, although scholars have sought to identify the most common ones. Seymour Martin Lipset and Stein Rokkan (1967) produced one of the earliest and most influential typologies. The authors identified four main cleavages around which groups and parties mobilize: center–periphery, state–church, land–industry, and owner–worker. They argue that these cleavages reflect in part a solidification of conflicts that date from 40 years earlier. The cleavages were 'frozen' into the party system, and thus survived despite social change. Later research has repeatedly confirmed the continuity of these cleavages: Knutsen (1988: 349) concludes that 'the old structural cleavages in the Lipset–Rokkan model still have the strongest impact in most Western democracies'.

Other scholars have proposed differing lists for the major ideological dimensions of party systems (Taylor and Laver, 1973; Dodd, 1976; Harmel and Janda, 1976). Lijphart (1990) identified eight dimensions within party systems, including socioeconomic, religious, cultural–ethnic, urban–rural, regime support, foreign policy, and postmaterialism. These dimensions were generally identified by non-quantitative analysis, based primarily on Western European party systems.

However frozen these cleavages may have been, social change in the decades subsequent to Lipset's and Rokkan's analyses has thawed the cleavage structure, created new cleavages, and elevated the importance of some cleavages while reducing that of others. In Western Europe, religious cleavages have declined in importance, as societies became more secular. The platforms of Christian democratic parties have changed to accommodate this secularization. Yet religion remains an important source of division, for Knutsen shows that in Norway in the 1980s religion remained the second largest factor in predicting party identification. In Canada, although religion remained a significant source of voting in 1980, it was not a significant predictor of fidelity in voting over time (Irvine and Gold, 1980). Yet in the USA, many observers have described the emergence of a new cleavage based on religiosity that emerged in the 1990s (see Wilcox and Larson, 2004, for a discussion).

Throughout the 1980s and 1990s class cleavages appear to have become less salient in Western Europe and the USA, and cultural cleavages more important. The materialist–postmaterialist dimension identified by Inglehart (1977, 1990) has emerged in most Western democracies. Inglehart argued that as voters came to take material well-being for granted, politics would come to hinge on conflicts over expressive values. Klingemann et al. (1994) modify the original Lipset–Rokkan typology to add this new cleavage. Postmaterialist values are reflected best by the emergence of left-libertarian and Green parties, and in the discussion of issues of gender, sexual identity, civil liberties, and the environment by many existing parties. In many cases postmaterialism has not spawned new parties but instead transformed the platform of existing parties, as the Democratic Party in the USA has moved from an emphasis on labor issues to one that stresses the environment, women's equality, and libertarian positions on abortion and gay rights.

Of course, not all cleavages in a society are translated into political parties, and thus some issues are depoliticized rather than incorporated into party ideologies. Electoral systems may help to limit the number of political parties that can compete effectively, thereby limiting in turn the number of cleavages that can be represented by the parties. Zielinski (2002) has argued that in the new democracies of Eastern Europe, the parties that survive the early elections help to determine which cleavages are politicized. He argues that class conflict may be precluded in some cases by the constellation of parties that solidify after the initial shakeout. Cleavages may become politicized as new parties emerge or depoliticized as older parties disappear. Other types of organizations besides parties may press issues into the party system (Lawson and Merkl, 1988).

PARTY MANIFESTOES AND IDEOLOGIES

For most political parties, ideologies and ideas are embodied in party platforms, manifestoes, and programs. These official party statements contain some mix of ideological statements, abstract principles, broad goals, and specific policy proposals. Party manifestoes provide scholars with an indication of both abstract party ideologies, and narrower, concrete policy proposals to implement that ideology. Manifestoes may remain unchanged for several years, although they are routinely revised and published before or during election campaigns. Manifestoes generally stress the importance of various policy areas, and sometimes also contain promises to potential voters about policies that the party will pursue if granted the reins of power. The promises are concrete representations of the broader ideological principles that the parties have staked out. (A notable exception is the USA, where platforms bind no one. In 1996, after the Republican platform committee rejected a tolerance plank on abortion, party nominee Bob Dole announced that he had not read the platform, and did not intend to.)

It is also important to note that there are often important ideological cleavages within parties, so that manifestoes often represent compromises between contending party elements. This is especially likely in catch-all parties that may seek a broad appeal across several social groups. Although not all party factions are ideologically based, many truly are.

Most party manifestoes retain the same general ideological principles for significant periods of time, even when parties change their names and organizational structures. In the aftermath of the fall of the Soviet Union, Western European communist parties adopted new names but made few changes in their general ideological stance (Mair and Mudde, 1998: 221).

At the same time, rational vote-seeking parties will adjust their positions to respond to shifts in the voters' preferences and in response to the positions of other parties. Moreover, as circumstances change, new issues are thrust to the fore of politics. The war on terrorism sparked by the September 11, 2001 attacks on the USA presented political parties in Britain, Spain, Poland, Germany, and elsewhere with a new issue that did not fit neatly into previous pronouncements.

Sometimes these new issues fit very poorly into previous ideological cleavages. In the USA, the 2004 ruling of the Massachusetts Supreme Court that the state must permit gays and lesbians to marry confronted the Republican Party with a choice between its abstract ideological commitment to states' rights, and its more recent abstract commitment to conservative Christian social policy. The similar issue of civil unions (PACS) in France cut across party lines to unite Gaullist President Chirac with the Socialist Prime Minister Jospin.

Over longer stretches, even the general principles of parties change. In the USA, the Republican Party accepted the welfare state in the 1950s, but by the 1980s had launched an assault on its key programs (Shafer, 2003). At times, parties abandon their general principles in pursuit of more centrist policies, resulting in 'catch-all parties' (Kirchheimer, 1966). In Europe,

this is most commonly ascribed to former socialist parties that seek to keep some ties to workers while appealing more broadly to middle-class voters. The British Labour Party is a case in point, finally returning to power after it modified its platform to appeal to more middle-class concerns, while retaining vestiges of its working-class roots. It is often argued that most Latin American party systems center around large, catch-all parties (Dix, 1989; but see Coppedge, 1998).

In other cases, parties may undergo profound changes, dropping key ideological elements or more from their manifestoes. After the collapse of the Soviet Union many Eastern European communist parties faced severe pressures, yet most did not disappear as many had predicted. In the Czech Republic the party made few changes in its ideology or policy proposals, and has dwindled to a small, marginalized entity. In Slovakia, the SDL restructured and adopted a shifting ideological stance that left it open to charges of inconsistency. In Poland, the party reemerged as the Social Democracy of Poland, which supported continued economic reforms but promised more competent administration. Finally, the Hungarian Socialist Party reemerged as the defender of the social safety net (Grzymala-Busse, 2002).

In some federal countries such as the USA and Canada, the same political party may take very different positions in different states or provinces (for a somewhat different example, see Chhibber and Petrocik, 1990). In the USA, some state party platforms include planks that are quite extreme, and even bizarre. In 1988 the Washington State Republican platform called for the end to 'mind altering techniques' in the public schools, and opposition to 'New Age Movement philosophy, including reincarnation, mystical powers, Satan worship, etc. as introduced in the textbooks of our education system' (Hertzke, 1993: 167–8). In Virginia, the 1994 platform embraced the state's 'colonial, Confederate, and American heritage' and stated that 'to ensure that military firearms suitable for militia be readily available to twentieth-century militia in Virginia … semiautomatic rifles are twentieth-century milita firearms' (Rozell and Wilcox, 1996).

The written manifestoes of Western European political parties have been systematically analyzed by the Manifesto Research Group. Their analysis coded the statements in the programs into one of 54 separate policy domains, and then calculated the percentage of all statements that focused on this policy. Their analysis resulted in some 20 policy dimensions, making it difficult for even the most imaginative scholar to visualize party locations (Budge *et al.*, 1987).

Yet ultimately Budge (2001) chose to project this complexity onto a single left–right dimension. A variety of different methodologies confirm that the left–right dimension is a satisfactory representation of the space in which parties compete, and that it is understood by party elites and to a lesser extent by voters (for a summary, see Budge, this volume).

Moreover, different methodologies seem to come to similar conclusions about the placement of parties on this single, underlying dimension (Gabel and Huber, 2000). Thus Huber and Inglehart (1995) collapse ten specific concepts to create the left–right dimension.[1] They overlap but are not identical to the ten concepts that Thomas (1980)[2] had employed.

There is little doubt that this single dimension simplifies reality – most modern democracies have both economics and values conflicts that are not perfectly correlated with one another. As Huber and Inglehart (1995: 90) note: 'it is an amorphous vessel whose meaning varies in systematic ways with the underlying political and economic conditions in a given society'. Dalton (1996) reports that left–right self placement by voters in Western democracies is correlated with different sets of issues in different countries. In many countries, including Sweden, the Netherlands, Norway, Finland, and France, it is highly correlated with economic issues. In Spain, West Germany, the Netherlands, and the USA abortion attitudes are also strong predictors. In most nations post materialist values are also sources of left–right self-placement.

In the case of Latin America, Coppedge (1998) argues for the need to include both a left–right and a religious–secular dimension to sort out the various parties. But most scholars see the analytic payoff of a single dimension as outweighing that disadvantage. In addition to simplifying many statistical problems, the single left–right dimension makes visualizing party space far simpler.

It is important to note that not all parties are focused on ideology. In Latin America and Africa, many parties center on individual leaders (personalized parties), and others are clientelistic. Personalism and clientelism are not incompatible with ideology, and indeed some parties that are vehicles for strong leaders are quite ideological. Yet in Latin America, some countries appear to have largely ideological parties, and others have largely non-ideological, personalistic, and clientelistic parties (Coppedge, 1998).

POLITICAL PARTY FAMILIES

Political parties are often categorized into ideological families (Seiler, 1980; Beyme, 1985), although this is not always a straightforward procedure (Mair and Mudde, 1998; Volkens and Klingemann, 2002: 158; Beyme, 1985). Most typologies have emerged from historical analyses of European party systems (Mair and Mudde, 1998), but some attempts have also been made to include parties from other political systems (Seiler, 1980; Ware, 1996; Alexander, 1973). Parties can also be grouped based upon their membership in international federations according to the federation's requirements and updating of lists. However, some parties may belong to more than one federation, when sharing more than one exclusive ideological position.

Typologies based on party families do not precisely translate into ideological classification, because even within ideological families there is a range of issue emphases and even issue positions. Within families, different parties have drifted in different directions (Volkens and Klingemann, 2002). The list below identifies major families of parties that are commonly identified.

Communist parties

Occupying the far left of the ideological spectrum, communist parties have generally sought to expand state control of the means of production and increased benefits for workers. These parties trace their ideological roots to Karl Marx's *Communist Manifesto* of 1848, and in the early 20th century many sought to destroy the capitalist system. They advocated revolutionary overthrow of governments and the establishment of a dictatorship of the proletariat.

Early in the 20th century many communist parties in different countries allied themselves with the Soviet Union, but over time many began to criticize Soviet foreign policy, and in some cases the domestic policy of Stalin. In response, many communist parties moved to accept the rules of liberal democracy and sought instead to influence public policy. When included in governing coalitions, communist parties tried to increase government ownership of key sectors of the economy, and to expand the social welfare state, including education and health care. They also generally advocated peace and disarmament, claiming that capitalism was the source of most wars.

Today the ideas portrayed by parties belonging to the communist family deal mainly with social, political and economic equality in society: the ultimate goal, as Vincent (1995: 86) states, is 'to regulate human consumption in an egalitarian manner'. As the standard of living has increased for workers throughout Europe and elsewhere, communist parties have changed their names, and in many cases reconstituted themselves. They have faced competition on the left from Greens and socialists, and have faced dwindling support in much of the world.

Socialist parties

Socialist parties have generally comprised the largest leftist parties in most democracies. Socialism shares common ideological roots with communism, but many socialist parties have explicitly distanced themselves from communist parties. Socialist parties have been more willing to accept democracy and elements of a market economy. The typical manifestoes of socialist parties have 'incorporated demands for the extension of democratic suffrage, trade union rights, parliamentary reform and social justice for working people' (Vincent, 1995: 89).

Socialist programs have focused on expanding state intervention in the economy, on the social welfare state, progressive taxation, and peace and disarmament (Beyme, 1985). In many European countries – France, Spain, Italy, Greece, and some Scandinavian countries – socialist parties have altered their ideological profiles sufficiently to be labeled 'new left' by some observers. Recently, in Britain (under Tony Blair) and Germany (under Gerhard Schröder), socialist parties have moved sharply to the center, resembling in some ways the US Democratic Party more than perhaps their socialist counterparts in other countries.

Left-libertarian parties

Left-libertarian parties take a postmaterialist stance on economic and social issues. They oppose the emphasis of right and left parties on economic growth at the expense of other values such as the environment. They support more egalitarian policies but are critical of the bureaucratic welfare state, which is thought to stifle participation and autonomy. They reject the consumerist values of the market economy, focusing instead on values stemming from communities, civil society, etc. (Kitschelt, 1988).

Left-libertarian support comes from younger, better-educated voters from the middle class with leftist values. Supporters and sympathizers also tend to support peace movements, environmental movements, feminist movements, and gay and lesbian rights movements. It is the issues promoted by these movements more than the traditional economic issues that motivate supporters of left-libertarian parties.

Lacking a coherent economic agenda, left-libertarian parties are vulnerable when existing parties (especially socialist parties) incorporate some of their postmaterialist policy goals into their manifestoes. Left-libertarian parties have also struggled to define their role in relation to the official party system, for they have characteristics of social movements that are especially attractive to their members. Nonetheless, as parties they still seek to win seats in elections.

Green parties

Green parties are perhaps a subset of left-libertarian parties, but their focused environmentalist goals might mark them as a distinctive family in their own right. Green parties frequently articulate not a coherent ideology, but rather a network of values derived from leftist and postmaterialist positions. Green movements and parties have arisen in reaction to environmental destruction and threats. In particular, Green supporters promote issues that deal with health and the environment, as indicated by their emphasis on the relationship between the individual and his or her surroundings.

Green parties began with a narrow focus on environmental policies, hoping that respect for the environment or the peaceful cohabitation with endangered species would soon become new political issues for the political arena. To broaden their appeal, they needed to develop 'people-oriented issues' (Beyme, 1985: 131). Eventually Green parties sought to reject key assumptions of the economic system that were considered to be the cause of environmental degradation. In many countries they also came to reject affluence, unequal distribution of power, and social status as the basis of inequality (Kitschelt, 1988: 225).

Green movements experienced difficulties in transforming from political movements into political parties. Some activists supported the transition, arguing that political parties were essential to gain influence over political decisions, but others argued that political parties were inherently corrupt and that they embodied elements of social structure that were incompatible with Green ideals. While Green movements remained outside the party system they could offer critiques of that system, but once they joined the ranks of political parties such critiques were problematic (see the disagreement between Realos and Fundis in the German Green Party).

In other cases, the decline of Green ideas in the early 1990s, about two decades after their emergence, was simply the final result of a 'convergence of generational change and political economic decline' (Kitschelt, 1988: 226). The conditions that allowed the development and successful expansion of the movement gradually receded, undermining the context in which the green ideals had proliferated. Still present in the party systems of many European countries, the Green parties are nowadays fragmented and divided regarding a possible conciliation between their ideals and the economic reality: another obstacle to their electoral reemergence in the future.

In the USA, the nascent Green Party suffered a setback in 2000, when nominee Ralph Nader won tens of thousands of votes in Florida to help elect Republican candidate George W. Bush. Bush was clearly far less 'green' than Democratic nominee Al Gore, whose book *Earth in the Balance* articulated a strong environmental stance. The winner-take-all electoral system in the USA resulted in an interesting anomaly, as major Green interest groups such as the Sierra Club and Friends of the Earth spent millions encouraging their members to vote against the Green Party and for the Democratic nominee.

Liberal parties

Liberal parties are usually positioned slightly right of the center in the left–right spectrum, and can move in either direction to attract votes. This potential advantage has inherent risks, since parties from the left and right frequently accuse liberal parties of lacking core principles, and of changing their manifestoes solely to win votes. Although in the USA 'liberalism' is associated with bigger government and more economic regulation, the family of European liberal parties promotes smaller government, less state regulation of the economy, and a free market economy.

Today, the main features of traditional liberal parties are 'religious tolerance, free inquiry,

self-government, and the market economy' (Kirchner, 1988: 3). The relative importance of these elements depends upon the specific country the scholar considers. At the core of liberal ideology is the belief that individuals have rights and needs that are distinct from those of society at large, but worthy of respect. This leads to support for limited government, including a smaller welfare state. In their support for progress, tolerance, and the free market (Vincent, 1995), liberal parties have struggled with the issue of equality. This has been a particularly complicated issue for German liberals in their coalition decisions.

Christian democratic parties

Christian democratic parties are typically the largest right-of-center parties, formed in the late 19th and early 20th centuries in Europe in part as a reaction to secularization and liberalism (Beyme, 1985). Initially, all Christian democratic parties had ties to established churches, providing a useful infrastructure. In many countries, Christian democratic parties draw from both Catholic and Protestant voters, although at times competing parties have appealed for the votes of these two religious constituencies.

Christian democratic parties have traditionally supported the capitalist economic system but also regulation and taxation of business. Their religious basis has led to support for a strong welfare state to protect the poor. They have stressed law and order programs in times of social unrest, and have emphasized the importance of moral traditionalism and a respect for the institutions of the state. Petrocik (1998) has argued that the US Republican Party has attained some of the characteristics of a Christian democratic party, minus the support for social welfare and business regulation.

New right parties

At the far right of the spectrum are new right parties. Although new right parties often are historically linked to fascist and Nazi parties, most have disavowed this heritage. New right parties continue to stress nationalism and a national identity that is often starkly contrasted to the values of new immigrants. The new right appears to do best in societies that are deeply divided on values and have a polarized party system (Volkens and Klingemann, 2002: 153), where there are many conservative citizens who have low levels of interpersonal trust (Wilcox et al., 2003).

New right parties have sought to expand their issue agenda, and their programs now include support for economic liberalism and a free market economy. Many oppose key elements of the social welfare state. Although in the past rightist parties called for state centralization, they now call for a reduction in state control of the economy.

Supporters of new right parties are usually well-educated citizens who are disappointed with the conservative parties in their countries (Kitschelt and Gann, 1995: 14). New right parties also endorse religious values, and draw support from religious citizens. As Europe faces ongoing waves of immigration, new right parties continue to find support, through the 'use of diffuse public sentiments of anxiety' (Betz, 1994: 4) *vis-à-vis* possible instability.

CONCLUSIONS

Political parties serve as repositories for ideologies and ideological fragments, maintaining similar tendencies and manifesto elements across many election cycles. Party manifestoes vary on many dimensions, but these differences can usually be projected on to the left–right dimension in ways that permit meaningful comparison. Although parties do change ideologically between elections, they usually retain a general ideological tendency.

Parties also serve as carriers for narrower policy ideas. As societies face new problems, parties propose solutions and adopt solutions proposed by others, and debate these solutions in electoral campaigns. In this way elections can serve to choose among ideas. Parties often carry ideas for several years, but they are more easily changed than ideologies.

Entire families of parties may share a common set of ideological elements and policy proposals. This is true both because parties communicate across national boundaries, and because similar types of cleavages arise in many societies, allowing for the creation of similar parties. The similarity of political ideas that parties represent in different political systems ultimately confirms the validity of a possible idea-based typology, beyond country-specific electoral systems.

NOTES

1   Economic or class conflict, centralization of power, authoritarianism vs. democracy, isolation vs. internationalism, traditional vs. new culture, xenophobia, conservatism vs. change, property rights, constitutional reform, and national defense (Huber and Inglehart, 1995: 78, Table 1).

2   Nationalization and control of means of production, government role in economic planning, distribution of wealth, providing for social welfare, secularization of society, extension of the franchise, electoral system, party government, governmental centralization, and reform vs. revolution (Thomas, 1980: 350–3).

REFERENCES

Alexander, Robert (1973) *Latin American Political Parties*. New York: Praeger.

Betz, Hans-Georg (1994) *Radical Right-Wing Populism in Western Europe*. New York: St. Martin's Press.

Beyme, Klaus von (1985) *Political Parties in Western Democracies*. New York: St. Martin's Press.

Budge, Ian (1994) 'A new spatial theory of party competition: Uncertainty, ideology, and policy equilibria viewed comparatively and temporally', *British Journal of Political Science*, 24: 443–67.

Budge, Ian (2001) 'Theory and measurement of party policy positions', in Ian Budge, Hans-Dieter Klingemann, Andrea Volkens, Judith Bara and Eric Tanenbaum, *Mapping Policy Preferences*. Oxford: Oxford University Press.

Budge, Ian (2003) 'Anthony Downs: Master di molti modelli', *Rivista Italiana di Scienza Politica*, XXXIII (3): 375–408.

Budge, Ian, Robertson, David and Hearl, Derek (1987) *Ideology, Strategy and Party Change: Spatial Analyses of Post-War Election Programmes in 19 Democracies*. Cambridge: Cambridge University Press.

Burke, Edmund (1889) *A Philosophical Inquiry into the Origin of Our Ideas of the Sublime and Beautiful*. London: George Bell.

Carver, Terrell (2004). 'Ideology: The career of a concept', in Terence Ball and Richard Dagger (eds), *Ideals and Ideologies*. New York: Longman.

Chhibber, Pradeep K. and Petrocik, John J. (1990) 'Social cleavages, elections and the Indian party system', in Richard Sisson and Ramashray Roy (eds), *Diversity and Dominance in Indian Politics*, *Volume 1*. New Delhi: Sage Publications.

Coppedge, Michael (1998) 'The dynamic diversity of Latin American party systems', *Party Politics*, 4: 547–68.

Dalton, Russell (1996) 'Party cleavages, issues, and electoral change', in Lawrence LeDuc, Richard G. Niemi and Pippa Norris (eds), *Comparing Democracies: Elections and Voting in Global Perspective*. Thousand Oaks, CA: Sage.

Dix, Robert H. (1989) 'Cleavage structures and party systems in Latin America', *Comparative Politics*, 22: 23–37.

Dodd, Laurence (1976) *Coalitions in Parliamentary Government*. Princeton, NJ: Princeton University Press.

Downs, Anthony (1957) *An Economic Theory of Democracy*. New York: Harper.

Gabel, Matthew J. and Huber, John D. (2000) 'Putting parties in their place: inferring party left-right ideological positions from party manifestoes data', *American Journal of Political Science*, 44 (1): 94–103.

Grzymala-Busse, Anna (2002) *Redeeming the Communist Past*. New York: Cambridge University Press.

Harmel, R. and Janda, Kenneth (1976) *Comparing Political Parties*. Washington, DC: American Political Science Association.

Hertzke, Allen (1993) *Echoes of Discontent: Jesse Jackson, Pat Robertson, and the Resurgence of Populism*. Washington, DC: CQ Press.

Huber, John and Inglehart, Ronald (1995) 'Expert interpretations of party space and party locations in 42 societies', *Party Politics*, 1: 73–111.

Inglehart, Ronald (1977) *The Silent Revolution*. Princeton, NJ: Princeton University Press.

Inglehart, Ronald (1990) 'The nature of value change', in Peter Mair (ed.), *The West European Party System*. Oxford: Oxford University Press.

Irvine, William P. and Gold, H. (1980) 'Do frozen cleavages ever go stale? The bases of the Canadian and Australian party systems', *British Journal of Political Science*, 10: 187–218.

Kernell, Samuel and Jacobson, Gary (2003) *The Logic of American Politics*. Washington D.C.: CQ Press.

Kirchheimer, Otto (1966) 'The transformation of Western European party systems', in J. LaPalombara and M. Weiner (eds), *Political Parties and Political Development*. Princeton, NJ: Princeton University Press.

Kirchner, Emil (1988) *Liberal Parties in Western Europe*. Cambridge: Cambridge University Press.

Kitschelt, Herbert (1988) 'Left-libertarian parties: Explaining innovation in competitive party systems', *World Politics*, 40: 194–234.

Kitschelt, Herbert and Gann, Anthony (1995) *The Radical Right in Western Europe*. Ann Arbor: University of Michigan Press.

Klingemann, Hans-Dieter, Hofferbert, Richard I. and Budge, Ian (1994) *Parties, Policies and Democracy*. Boulder, CO: Westview Press.

Knutsen, Oddbjørn (1988) 'The impact of structural and ideological party cleavages in West European democracies: A comparative empirical analysis', *British Journal of Political Science*, 18: 323–52.

Lawson, Kay, and Merkl, Peter M. (1988) *When Parties Fail: Emerging Alternative Organizations*. Princeton, NJ: Princeton University Press.

Lijphart, Arend (1990) 'Dimensions of ideology in European party systems', in Peter Mair (ed.), *The West European Party System*. Oxford: Oxford University Press.

Lipset, Seymour Martin and Rokkan, Stein (eds) (1967) *Party Systems and Voter Alignments: Cross-National Perpectives*. New York: Free Press.

Mair, Peter and Mudde, Cas (1998) 'The party family and its study,' *Annual Review of Political Science*, 1: 211–29.

Petrocik, John (1998) 'Reformulating the party coalitions: The "Christian Democratic" Republicans'. Presented at the annual meeting of the American Political Science Association, Boston.

Rozell, Mark J. and Wilcox, Clyde (1996) *Second Coming: The Christian Right in Virginia Politics*. Baltimore, MD: Johns Hopkins University Press.

Seiler, Daniel Louis (1980) *Parties et familles politiques*. Paris: Presses Universitaires de France.

Shafer, Byron (2003) *The Two Majorities and the Puzzle of Modern American Politics*. Lawrence, KS: University Press of Kansas.

Taylor, M. and Laver, M. (1973) 'Government coalitions in Western Europe', *European Journal of Political Research*, 1: 237–48.

Thomas, John Clayton (1980) 'Ideological trends in Western political parties', in Peter H. Merkl (ed.), *Western European Party Systems*. New York: Free Press.

Vincent, Andrew (1995) *Modern Political Ideologies*. Oxford: Blackwell.

Volkens, Andrea and Klingemann, Hans-Dieter (2002) 'Parties, ideologies, and issues', in Kurt Richard Luther and Ferdinand Müller-Rommel (eds), *Political Parties in the New Europe*. New York: Oxford University Press.

Ware, Alan (1996) *Political Parties and Party Systems*. Oxford: Oxford University Press.

Wilcox, Allen, Weinberg, Leonard and Eubank, William (2003) 'Explaining national variations in support for far right political parties in Western Europe, 1990–2000', in Peter Merkl and Leonard Weinberg (eds), *Right Wing Extremism in the 21st Century*. London: Frank Cass.

Wilcox, Clyde and Brocker, Manfred (2005) 'The Christian Right and the Presidential Election of 2004', in Torsten Oppelland (ed.), *Die USA in Wahljar 2004*. Trier: Wissenschattliche Verlag, Atlantische Texte.

Zielinski, Jakub (2002) 'Translating social cleavage into party systems: The significance of new democracies', *World Politics*, 54: 184–211.

36

IDENTIFYING DIMENSIONS AND LOCATING PARTIES: METHODOLOGICAL AND CONCEPTUAL PROBLEMS

Ian Budge

INTRODUCTION: BASIC QUESTIONS

Parties not only carry ideas but focus them into a specific programme for the medium-term development of society. These programmes have ideological roots in Marxist and socialist writings, Judeo-Christian doctrine, market-based neo-liberalism, nationalism or traditional conservatism. Parties apply these ideologies to the issues of the day in order to generate preferred solutions, which they advocate in election campaigns as one way of attracting or consolidating their vote.

Ideologies serve not only to suggest solutions to issues but also, and perhaps even more importantly to filter out those that parties emphasize and those they ignore. The number of potential issues which might be taken up in a given society is vast – notionally the number of individuals living in it multiplied by the number of their concerns. Of course, individual concerns overlap, and many are dealt with by other means than politics – markets or churches for example. Nevertheless the potential over-spill into politics is enormous. A prime purpose of party ideology therefore is to indicate what topics deserve attention and which do not – given that constraints of time and attention, as well as the simplifications involved in appealing to a mass audience, severely limit the number that can be discussed.

Not only can a class-based ideology, for example, serve to identify the 'important' class-related issues which should be dealt with, it also gives a guarantee that these will appeal to habitual and potential supporters of the party who will have been originally mobilized by a class-based appeal. The same can be said of all the party families discussed above. All base their appeal on clusters of ideologically related issues which then define the choice situation faced by voters in the election. Parties and their ideologies thus serve an important function for electors as well as governments: they structure the public choices electors make, rendering them manageably simple – and of course, on the reverse side, strongly restricting choice, sometimes to the extent of being accused of ignoring the 'real' issues of the time.

If parties compete only on a limited number of super-issues to which specific issues of the campaign are ideologically related and squeezed down, the question then arises of how these super-issues themselves relate to each other. Some parties (e.g. socialists and Christians) may advocate more government intervention to solve social problems such as homelessness, while others (e.g. neo-liberals and conservatives) oppose this in the name of market and social freedoms. It is easy to see this confrontation as arising from one fundamental disagreement, about the scope of government intervention in society, on which different parties can be placed at different positions. Not only is the idea of reducing passing issues to this fundamental disagreement helpful in simplifying choices and letting us decide where we are in relation to the parties. It also permits us to develop a simple one-dimensional

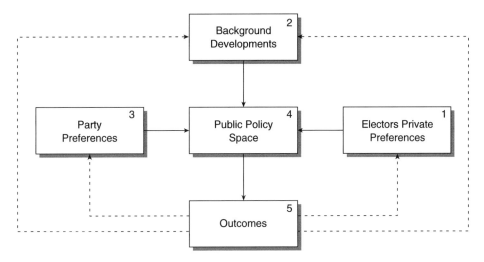

Figure 36.1 Inputs to public policy space

spatial 'map' of politics (cf. Figure 36.2) which specialists can then use to measure changes in party positions during and between elections – indeed, not only changes in party positions but also changes in electoral preferences.

Such a simplification is clearly an immensely useful tool for political scientists, not least in allowing for straightforward measurement of ideological and policy positions. Strong substantive doubts remain, however, as to whether all the complexities and nuances of party politics – or even all the important ones – can be captured so simply. Indeed, for many outside the field, the reduction of all politics to one dimension of difference is not so much useful simplification as simple-mindedness. Objections have taken two major forms: policy space is not one- but many-dimensional, or – more radically   political complexities cannot be mapped spatially at all.

Most of this chapter is taken up with discussing these points in the context of available theory and evidence about parties, electors and their interactions. Before going on to review the history of this debate it is as well to note one fundamental question about the *purpose* of our spatial and dimensional analyses. Is it to uncover the 'real' dimensions or super-issues underlying contemporary debate, as used and perceived by all the participants in it? Or is it to devise a useful analytic tool, which may not exactly mirror the 'real' political situation but gives plausible and useful results nonetheless? Answers to these questions are interrelated but

it is useful to keep the two apart and be sure about which we are addressing in the often tangled debate about dimensionality.

Figure 36.1 summarizes many of the points made above. It shows how both parties and electors face problems in translating their private preferences into the public space defined by party policies as relayed above all by the media. The elector has to decide how her private preferences for a quiet and orderly neighbourhood, personal prosperity, good health and better schools for her grandchildren can be expressed by a choice between Liberal, New Labour, Christians and Greens. This is a hard translation. It is important to realize that it is a translation and that electors do not think instinctively in terms of the public choices available.

Parties, too, have to make a translation – how to define their private desires (e.g. for office or a theocratic state) into an acceptable public position that will not repel votes. Other thresholds are involved in policy-making. 'Objective' or 'background' developments help define current issues of concern but may not be reflected directly in the public space: for example, an increase in unemployment may stimulate demands for greater government efficiency and hence job-cutting. Public policies, especially those which seem to have won elections, affect the government policies which are implemented but perhaps not in a one-to-one way given problems of implementation or the absence of information about cause and effect.

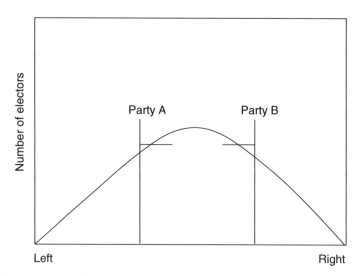

Figure 36.2   Downs' model of two-party competition: vote-seeking parties converge on the median elector's position under certainty about policy positions

In what follows we will be concerned mainly with the ways in which the public policy space itself is conceived and measured. But both of course are inevitably influenced by its dependencies on the other spaces shown in Figure 36.1, even if its internal structures are to some extent autonomous.

HISTORICAL DEBATES

Public policy has been a key focus of political science since the Greeks. The idea that it could be represented and measured spatially was, however, popularized mostly by Anthony Downs (1957), drawing on earlier suggestions by Hotelling (1929) and Smithies (1941). Though Downs' *Economic Theory* can for the most part be expressed non-spatially (Budge and Farlie, 1977: 102–30) its most memorable representation is the one shown in Figure 36.2. Where preferences and policies for more or less government intervention are arrayed along a single dimension of electoral preferences peaking in the middle there would only be scope for two parties to compete. To get a majority and hence form a government, office-seeking parties will converge in policy terms during the election campaign on the preference of the median elector. The winning party will be the one closest to the electoral median and has an incentive to translate that preference into public policy in order to maintain a credible

position at the next election. Figure 36.2 provides the basis for a spatial version of government mandate theory, the main contemporary justification for representative democracy. It thus became the focus for much mathematical modelling in the rational choice tradition over the last 40 years (see Enelow and Hinich, 1984; Coughlin, 1992).

The representation also covers the type of policy parties will adopt in elections which will affect their subsequent behaviour in government. In this connection Downs proposed a contrasting spatial representation of a multi-party system (Figure 36.3) where parties did not converge but held on to their existing votes and policy position. Consequently no party got a majority to form a single-party government and electors were deprived of the ability in influence government policy, not knowing which coalition government would form – a critique often subsequently applied to multi-party systems based on proportional representation (cf. Powell, 2000).

Downs' spatial representations were developed analytically and supported with anecdotal evidence. The vast expansion in election surveys of the 1960s and 1970s prompted many researchers to investigate empirically how electors pictured policy space and located themselves in it. Computer developments aided this: general-purpose scaling programs – both factor-analytic and non-metric – became widely available and could be applied to questions about the closeness of electors to parties

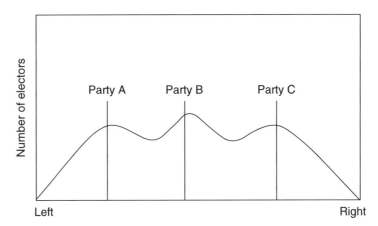

Figure 36.3   Downs' model of multi-party competition: immobility of parties at each mode of the distribution of preferences under certainty about policy positions

(for a review, see Budge and Farlie, 1978). In general such analyses produced two-dimensional policy spaces, the main dimension being indeed a class-based left–right one, but with another religious–moral dimension cross-cutting it. This result seemed to correspond more to the enduring cleavages identified by Lipset and Rokkan (1967) at the base of European party systems (class, religious, centre–periphery) rather than the one-dimensional space assumed by Downs (1957).

The 'real' dimensionality of public policy space assumed wider theoretical importance because of the rediscovery by Arrow (1951) of Condorcet's problem of cylical voting majorities (Table 36.1); see Condorcet (1975). Under democratic voting rules unstable majorities like those shown in the table are always possible. Stable majorities can be guaranteed, however, if there is a one-dimensional distribution of preferences. Indeed, a driving motive behind Downs' choice of a one-dimensional representation for his argument was precisely the need to guarantee a stable majority (Downs, 1957: 67–8: see also Black, 1958). Conversely, McKelvey (1979) and Schofield (1985) demonstrated that there was no guarantee of stable majorities emerging in any n-dimensional space for $n \geq 2$.

Though Niemi (1969, 1983) showed that the actual probability of cycles emerging in multidimensional spaces was low, debate focused on the need to avoid them altogether. This, together with the methodological criticisms that could be made of survey-derived spaces (see below), fuelled renewed interest in one-dimensional solutions. These had first, however, to meet the influential objection made by

Stokes (1966), that Downs' space cannot give a comprehensive or even a useful representation of election politics because it misses out the major issues which are generally 'valence' in nature rather than 'positional'. By positional Stokes means ones where parties take up graduated 'pro' and 'con' positions (e.g. for and against government intervention). The more important issues, he argued, are 'valence ones' where there is only one position available – corruption, for example, where you must, electorally, be against it. Who also could fail to support peace?

This objection was met by Robertson (1976). His *Theory of Party Competition* innovated in two ways. First it used written texts (British party manifestos) rather than surveys to derive a policy space. Secondly, it dealt with the valence objection – in a way which was supported by the handling of issues by the parties themselves in their manifestos – by suggesting that *all* issues were 'valence issues' in the sense of having only one generally approved position associated with them. On tax, for example, it is theoretically possible to be for or against. To advocate higher taxes is such a potentially suicidal position however that parties will in general only talk about cutting them. Some parties (market liberals, for example) have better credibility on tax cutting than, for example socialists, and hence will emphasize the importance of 'their' tax issue in an election while others downplay it – seeking instead to convince electors of the importance of (increasing) welfare. By counting emphases (sentences or words) of a manifesto on opposing issue categories such as 'tax' and 'welfare' it is thus

Table 36.1 *The paradox of voting: Electors' individually consistent preference orderings give rise to cyclical and unstable majority choices*

Preference orderings over policy alternatives or candidates	Classic case of the paradox (% of electors)	Less extreme case of the paradox (% of electors)
A → B → C	33.3	22.2
A → C → B	0	11.1
B → C → A	33.3	22.2
B → A → C	0	11.1
C → A → B	33.3	22.2
C → B → A	0	11.1
% voting to choose A over B	66.6	55.5
% voting to choose B over C	66.6	55.5
% voting to choose C over A	66.6	55.5

A, B and C represent three policy alternatives or candidates. The arrow → represents preferences as between alternatives. Thus A → B → C stands for 'A is preferred to B and B is preferred to C'.

possible to characterize parties' policies quite precisely and construct theoretically based left–right spaces in which to put them and to measure their movements over time (cf. Figure 36.4 for the US parties, 1948–2000). A whole series of studies based on post-war manifestos and platforms in around 50 post-war democracies were carried out by the Manifesto Research Group (Budge *et al.*, 1987, 2001, 2006; Laver and Budge, 1992; Klingemann *et al.*, 1994). These used policy spaces both in particular domains and at a general left–right level to examine not only party movements but also their relationship to electoral preferences, government functioning and policy outputs – usually measured within the same spaces. Attempts have been made to computerize these procedures. This would enable spatial analysis to be applied to a much wider range of documents (including legislation), but they remain at an experimental stage for now (Bara, 2001; Kleinnijenhuis and Pennings, 2001; Laver and Garry, 2001; Laver *et al.*, 2003).

MAJOR EMPIRICAL FINDINGS OF SPATIAL AND DIMENSIONAL ANALYSES

It is clear that discussions about space and dimensionality have been driven by a mixture of theoretical, conceptual, measurement and substantive concerns, powered by developments in computer technology. This has been very fruitful in developing the field and perhaps serves as a model for cumulative research in other areas of political science. What have been the major substantive findings to come out from the research? What are their implications

for our conception of party politics, for our understanding of dimensionality and for our future use of spatial analyses themselves? Taking these questions in order we can say the following:

1) Spatial analyses have shown most spatial theories of party behaviour proposed during the 1960s and 1970s not to be upheld by their evidence. This applies above all to minimum winning and policy proximity theories of government coalition formation (Budge and Laver, 1992: 416–17). The major positive finding about governments has been that the median parliamentary party participates in 80% of them (van Roozendahl, 1990, 1992; Budge and Laver, 1992: 415–20; Müller and Strøm, 2000: 563–9). This has given rise to alternative theories of median party dominance in policy-making (van Rozendahl, 1990, 1992; Laver and Shepsle, 1996; McDonald *et al.*, 2004).

2) In general, winning party policy positions have been shown to influence government ones (McDonald *et al.*, 1999) and to match changes in final policy outputs. Given the inertia of the latter, the exact nature of the relationship remains to be explored. Mandate theories of representative democracy do, however, appear to be upheld by comparative spatial research (McDonald *et al.*, 2004).

3) At election level, spatial analyses have shown parties not to converge (Budge, 1994; Adams, 2001) but to maintain the same relative position over time even in pure two-party systems (cf. Figure 36.4). Downs' (1957) static model of party positioning in Figure 36.3 thus seems a more accurate representation of their behaviour than his better-known convergence model (Figure 36.2).

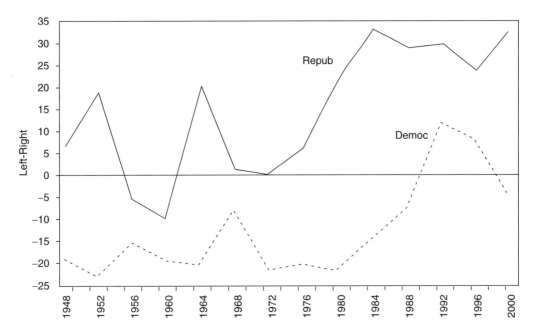

Figure 36.4   US parties' ideological movements on a left–right scale, 1948–2000

4) Party positions do not seem particularly responsive to electoral preferences within specific issue domains (McDonald *et al.*, 2004). But they do seem responsive within a general left–right dimension (Adams *et al.*, 2004; McDonald *et al.*, 2004).

5) This finding has reinforced the growing consensus that a unidimensional left–right space is probably the best representation of party-electoral space. As Roy Pierce (1999: 30), summing up 50 years of survey research, puts it: 'The issue to which they [voters] … give high priority … is the ideological super-issue … the Left–Right dimension on the European continent or the liberal-conservative dimension in the United States. Voter–party congruence on more specific issues, even those that are traditionally linked to the ideological dimension, is much more limited' (see also Inglehart and Klingemann, 1976: Klingemann, 1995). Survey evidence on this point is reinforced by analyses of party texts. Most of the research cited above carried out parallel analyses in multi-dimensional and unidimensional left–right space (see in particular Budge *et al.*, 1987; Laver and Budge, 1992), reaching the same broad conclusions in both, but more clearly in left–right space.

Highly inductive comparative factor analyses also reached the conclusion that a left–right dimension dominated the policy space (Budge *et al.*, 1987: 293; Gabel and Huber, 2000). In analyses of or around elections, a unidimensional left–right space thus seems the right one to use, in terms of both analytic convenience and of the way in which parties and electors see the political world at that time (though perhaps not at other times: see Figure 36.6).

6) This conclusion has far more than analytical consequences, for it takes us back to the initial question of the whole debate over dimensionality: is it possible to find an equilibrium point round which a stable democratic majority can emerge (cf. Table 36.1)? The median position guaranteed in a one-dimensional policy space is such a point. Perhaps, therefore, the structuring of the space in left–right terms accounts for another major finding from the empirical research that has been done: few or no voting cycles have been discovered. This confirms Niemi's (1969) point – not being able to guarantee that a voting cycle will *not* appear is not equivalent to expecting that it will appear *frequently*. Generally cycles seem precluded by the structuring of political debate.

Figure 36.5   The dominant position of the median actor, C, in a one-dimensional policy space

EMERGENCE OF THE MEDIAN

The growing confidence in the existence of a median position has led to a growing exploitation of its uses in spatial theory. Party convergence on the median in a Downsian sense (Figure 36.2) may not be present. But this is not to imply that the median position may not dominate in policy terms. To see why, we need only consider Figure 36.5, which sets the standard power of the median argument in the kind of left–right space which has now emerged as empirically appropriate for democratic electors and parties. When distributed along this kind of continuum, the relevant actors prefer any policy closer to their own position to any further away. This puts C, at the median, in the most powerful position. Actors both to Left and Right need C to form a majority. C can thus bargain for a public policy close to its own position, by threatening to join the alternative majority if C does not get its own way. Compared to the policy position of its rivals on one wing, C's position will be preferred by partners on the other wing whatever coalition it joins. Thus C's position will constitute the point towards which majority-backed policy always tends.

It is important to realize that this standard 'power of the median argument' applies both to electors and policy-oriented parties. It is the reason why the median is so often used as an indicator of popular majority preferences (Powell, 2000: 163–7: McDonald et al., 2004). Without the median voter a knowable and coherent majority cannot be formed, by definition. The same logic must apply to parties if their internal discipline is tight enough for them to be regarded as unitary actors. Even if C is very small compared to other parties, these still need C's support to form a majority. Just as in the electorate, party C can bring policy close to its position by threatening to defect to the opposing wing. Under majority voting rules in a legislature, C is policy king.

The growing confidence in the applicability of left–right space and therefore in the existence of a median actor in parliaments as well

as electorates has helped shift the focus in policy-making theories from governments to median parties (van Roozendahl, 1990, 1992; Laver and Shepsle, 1996; McDonald et al., 2004). An extension of this is to see representative democracy as based on a median rather than a government mandate, leading to an evaluation of electoral systems in terms of whether or not they bring median elector and median legislative party into line (McDonald and Budge, 2005). This may improve the democratic credentials of 'consensus democracy' (Lijphart, 1999) and unify our ways of looking at different 'visions' of democracy (Powell, 2000).

MEASURING LEFT–RIGHT SPACE

These theoretical advances stem from the ability of empirical investigations to shed light on the nature of the left–right public space shared by parties and electors. To a major extent this is created by the way parties choose to present themselves to electors. Under representative democracy electors have no choice outside the alternatives offered by the parties. If these choose to array themselves in left–right terms, as they seem to do, electors have to evaluate policies in these terms and vote for the party positions offered to them. Election left–right space is thus a party dominated space if not entirely a party-defined one (see below). It is not just projected or scaled down from electors' policy spaces (Figure 36.1). Rather it is projected from the *party* space at the right-hand side of the figure into which electors have to insert themselves. The primarily party-based nature of public space is what justifies basing measurements, even of electors' preferences, primarily on the parties' definition of the situation (Kim and Fording, 1998).

The growing realization that election space is basically unidimensional left–right spurred efforts in the 1970s to get electors to rate both themselves and the parties on a 10- or 20-point pictorial 'ladder' between these positions (cf. Inglehart and Klingemann, 1976). The additional realization that parties were responsible for creating the space and presenting it to electors led to the transfer of this technique to surveys of party experts, who were asked to place parties along such scales (Castles and Mair, 1984; Huber and Inglehart, 1995). Though widely used, such placements had limitations (Budge, 2000). In particular, they were entirely static (McDonald and Mendes, 2001), being

Table 36.2   *Grouping theoretically left and right topics to form a text-based scale*

Right emphases: sum of %s for sentences mentioning:		Left emphases: sum of %s for sentences mentioning:
Military: positive		Decolonization
Freedom, human rights		Military: negative
Constitutionalism: positive		Peace
Effective authority		Internationalism: positive
Free enterprise		Democracy
Economic incentives		Regulate capitalism
Protectionism: negative	minus	Economic planning
Economic orthodoxy		Protectionism: positive
Social Services limitation		Controlled economy
National way of life: positive		Nationalization
Traditional morality: positive		Social Services: expansion
Law and order		Education: expansion
Social harmony		Labour groups: positive

simply a quantification of the traditional classification of political parties into Communist, socialist, centre, liberal and conservative families. This rendered them irrelevant for studying party movements *between* elections, as shown in Figure 36.4, for example.

One extension of expert judgements (Laver and Hunt, 1992) was to create a multidimensional party space on the grounds that only this would be complex enough to represent party policy differences properly. However, the placements made in this expert survey along the specific policy dimensions all relate strongly to an underlying left–right continuum (McDonald and Mendes, 2001: 141) – suggesting once again that the latter is an adequate representation of the space. (For a study of congruence between party and electoral positions within such a space, see Klingemann, 1995.)

In so far as they can be compared, the different attempts to 'put parties in their place' (Gabel and Huber, 2000) along the left–right dimension, whether based on texts or on expert judgements, concur substantially in their positioning. This result not only validates the various scales as such but also the general idea of a left–right representation of election space (Gabel and Huber, 2000; Budge *et al.*, 2001).

The content of left–right differences

The derivation of scales from party election programmes has produced a specification of the themes associated with left and right positions, respectively (Budge and Klingemann, 2001: 21–2). These are listed in Table 36.2. While based on ideological writings, the listings group themes which are focused on by

parties themselves in their programmes, over some 50 post-war democracies. These fall into three broad groupings on each side. Right-wing emphases are broadly on freedom (with a particular application to the economy), an ordered society, and strong defence. The left wants an extended sphere for government, welfare and protection of labour, and peaceful internationalism. These broadly opposing positions are not linked with each other in terms of strict logic, and in fact Christian parties put together themes from both left and right, landing up in a 'centrist' position as a result. The themes are linked because ideological writings and party policy documents on both sides *do* put them together, seeing, for example, worker's interests being best served by the creation of appropriate government structures both at home and abroad.

Possible variations in dimensionality over time

Once we get away from the idea that there is a real issue space out there, on an analogy with physical space, it is possible to see the constituent issues involved in left–right differences coming together at certain points notably around elections – and being separated out at other times, notably during the governmental and parliamentary phases of representative democracy. As has been emphasized elsewhere in this volume, parties are unique linking institutions as they operate at different levels – both among electors, in legislatures and in governments. However, they may not focus on all these levels at the same time. Around elections their dialogue may be primarily with the mass

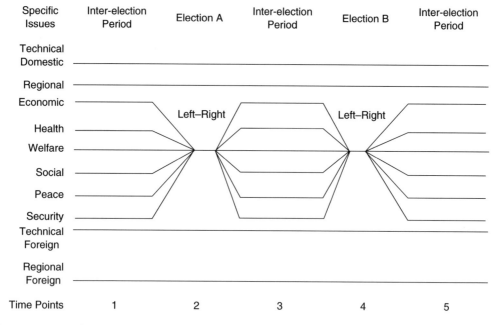

Figure 36.6   Public policy space: the dynamics of dimensionality

public, rendering it necessary to compress current issues into one unidimensional left–right space, as Pierce (1999) has noted.

During the inter-election period, however, parties focus their attention on the legislative and governmental arenas. The mechanics of debate there are different, shaped by the institutional division of policy areas between ministries and the structuring of parliamentary procedures around these. Foreign policy is thus not normally discussed in relation to internal social regulation, nor education in close relation to health and welfare. Discussion of each of these areas takes place within different contexts and at different times (cf. Shepsle and Weingast, 1981). The result is a likely splitting of the unified left–right dimension into separate dimensions for each policy. As the next election draws closer and debate broadens out again to the mass public, these different threads are again drawn together into a unified left–right continuum. The resulting expanding and contracting effect is illustrated in Figure 36.6. (Less central issues, shown by lines at the edges of the figure may just get totally ignored in the election.)

It must be emphasized that this process is conjectural and hypothetical, if plausible, at this point. Whether the public space varies in its dimensionality over time is, however, an interesting research question which to our knowledge has not yet been raised. Answering it could get us away from sterile debates about whether the 'real' public space is unidimensional or multidimensional: it may be both, at different times.

Even so, however, the suggestion here is that the multi-dimensional space is not the Euclidean one which gives rise to voting cycles. Its essence, given by the ministerial structuring of debate, is that dimensions are separable and indeed separate. Each is discussed on its own, as a single policy dimension, so there is always a median around which a majority can cohere (Ordeshook, 1986: 250).

This could raise another problem, however, very relevant for mandate theories. If elections designate the parliamentary median party in terms of a general left–right context, but this then splits between elections into separate policy dimensions with different medians (which may also differ from the overall left–right one) how could one guarantee that the popularly chosen party dominated? This may be difficult though a comparative study of 16 democracies indicates that it does dominate, with some 'slippage' in specific policy areas (McDonald and Budge, 2005).

CLASSIFYING SPATIAL REPRESENTATIONS OF PARTIES AND ELECTORS

The points made above can be put in context by listing the various types of spatial representations of political parties which have been made over the last 50 years and commenting on their salient features (Budge and Farlie, 1977: 31–101, 176–81; 1978):

1 *Pure a priori policy space.* This is based on theoretical grounds (such as ideological writings), and is represented *par excellence* by the Downsian spaces illustrated in Figures 36.2 and 36.3. Direct operationalizations of such a space would fall under this category. This type of space is driven by the way electors are seen to organize their public preferences because of information economizing (Downs, 1957: 98–100). Parties then locate themselves in it. A practical example is given by the Inglehart and Klingemann (1976) left–right 'ladder' used with electors, where electors also placed the parties.

2 *Party-dominated pure policy space.* On the other hand most operationalizations of policy space discussed here concentrate on locating the policy alternatives offered by parties, to which electors under representative democracy have no choice but to adapt. The scales on which parties are placed are theoretically derived in terms of party ideology. One such is the Manifesto Research Group left–right scale illustrated in Figure 36.4 and Table 36.2, with other Manifesto Research Group policy scales (Budge *et al.*, 2001).

In so far as expert placements of parties are made on theoretical criteria (cf. Huber and Inglehart, 1995) or are based on the ideological classification of parties into families (Beyme, 1985: 29–136), they would also fit this category. These placements usually result in a one-dimensional left–right scale. But both expert judgements (Laver and Hunt, 1992) and manifestoes (Laver and Budge, 1992) are capable of generating multi-dimensional spaces with the separable dimensions discussed above.

3 *Inductive policy spaces.* These are typically associated with factor analyses of policy texts or issue questions. If unconstrained they will usually end up with four or five dimensions, which are by convention represented orthogonally to each other.[1] However, factor analyses can be constrained to produce only one dimension which generally turns out to be left–right (Gabel and Huber, 2000). Being an inductive technique, factor analyses will reflect co-variation within all of the existing data set. This has two undesirable consequences: First, if the data set is expanding (new elections being added, for example) new factor analyses may well produce different results than the old ones. So the policy space and conclusions based on it may change. Second, in comparative analyses the locations of very different parties at different periods are made interdependent, for example, the position of Swedish Social Democrats in 2001 depends on that of Italian neo-fascists in 1948.

4 *Inductive policy-background spaces.* The nature of factor-analytic spaces depends on what is put in. If social characteristics of party candidates or electors are added to issues and policy the result is a mixed space rather than a pure policy space. One should be conscious of this when making inferences from the representation about, for example, party movement.

5 *Party defined spaces.* The spaces listed above are bounded by policy points, such as (pure) left, (pure) right. Spaces can, however, be bounded by pure party positions, in which case locations within the space are defined by their distance from these. A well-known example of such a space is the distribution of party identifiers, bounded by strong Republicans to one side and strong Democrats to the other. Budge and Farlie's (1977) comparative analyses of parties and electors created a 'likelihood ratio space' whose ends were defined by pure party positions – in a two-party system, a line: in a three-party system, a triangle, etc. Electors were distributed over the space in terms of characteristics and opinions which defined their proximity to the party. Recently Laver and Garry (2001) have proposed a pure policy version of this idea, in which words differentially associated with the parties are used to measure the distance between them.

6 *Party inferred spaces.* The non-metric scaling techniques applied to electors' feelings of proximity to parties, used extensively in the 1970s, typically gave rise to two-dimensional spaces in which the nature of the dimensions was inferred from the positions of all parties on them. Thus a dimension on which socialists opposed conservatives was interpreted as a left–right one, while one

where Christians opposed liberals was taken as a religious (clerical versus lay) dimension. The limitation here is that the space offers no opportunity of tracing party movement over time, since that changes the meaning of the dimensions and makes spaces non-comparable.

The most important research lesson to be drawn from this listing is that the operationalization of a space should meet the theoretical purposes which investigators have in mind. Because of the very close interconnections between theory, measurement and substantive research in this field, it is likely that pure policy representations will be most used in the future, as they have been for the last 20 years.

NOTE

1. The convention of producing orthogonal dimensions for presentational purposes has generally led analysts to forget that dimensions are usually correlated. Adams and Adams (2000) have shown that spaces with correlated dimensions very much reduce the risk of voting cycles and unstable majorities.

REFERENCES

Adams, James F. (2001) 'A theory of spatial competition with biased voters', *British Journal of Political Science*, 31: 121–58.

Adams, James F., Clark, Michael, Ezrow, Laurence and Glasgow, Garrett (2004) 'Understanding change and stability in party ideologies: Do parties respond to public opinion or to past election results?', *British Journal of Political Science*, 34: 589–610.

Arrow, Kenneth J. (1951) *Social Choice and Individual Values*. New York: Wiley.

Bara, Judith, L. (2001) 'Using manifesto estimates to validate computerized analyses', in Ian Budge, Hans-Dieter Klingemann, Andrea Volkens, Judith Bara and Eric Tanenbaum, *Mapping Policy Preferences: Estimates for Parties, Voters and Governments 1945–1998*. Oxford: Oxford University Press.

Black, Duncan, (1958) *The Theory of Committees and Elections*. Cambridge: Cambridge University Press.

Beyme, Klaus von (1985) *Political Parties in Western Democracies*. Aldershot: Gower.

Budge, Ian (1994) 'A new spatial theory of party competition: uncertainty, ideology and policy equilibria viewed comparatively and spatially', *British Journal of Political Science*, 24: 443–64.

Budge, Ian (2000) 'Expert judgements of party policy positions: uses and limitations', *European Journal of Political Research*, 37: 103–15.

Budge, Ian and Farlie, Dennis J. (1977) *Voting and Party Competition*. London: Wiley.

Budge, Ian and Farlie, Dennis (1978) 'The potentiality of dimensional analyses for explaining voting and party competition', *European Journal of Political Research*, 6: 203–31.

Budge Ian and Klingemann, Hans-Dieter (2001) 'Finally! Comparative over-time mapping of party policy movement', in Ian Budge, Hans-Dieter, Klingemann, Andrea Valkens, Judith Bara and Eric Tanenbaum, *Mapping Policy Preferences: Estimates for Parties, Voters and Government 1945–1998*. Oxford: Oxford University Press.

Budge, Ian and Laver, Michael (1992) 'The relationship between party and coalition policy in Europe', in Michael Laver and Ian Budge (eds), *Party Policy and Government Coalitions*. London: Macmillan.

Budge, Ian, Klingemann, Hans-Dieter, Volkens, Andrea, Bara, Judith, and Tanenbaum, Eric (2001) *Mapping Policy Preferences: Estimates for Parties, Voters and Governments 1945–1998*. Oxford: Oxford University Press.

Budge Ian, Klingemann, Hans-Dieter, Volkens, Andrea and Bara, Judith (2006) *Mapping Policy Preferences, 1984–2004: Eastern Europe and the OECD*. Oxford: Oxford University Press.

Budge, Ian, Robertson, David and Hearl, D.J. (eds) (1987) *Ideology, Strategy and Party Change: Spatial Analyses of Party Programs*. Cambridge: Cambridge University Press.

Castles, Francis G. and Mair, Peter (1984) 'Left–right political scales: Some expert judgements', *European Journal of Political Research*, 12: 73–88.

Condorcet, Marquis de (1975) *Essai sur L'Application de l'Analyse à la Probabilité des Decisions Rendues à la Pluralité des Voix*. Paris: Imprimerie Royale. First published in 1785.

Coughlin, Peter J. (1992) *Probabilistic Voting Theory*. Cambridge: Cambridge University Press.

Downs, Anthony (1957) *An Economic Theory of Democracy*. New York: Harper.

Enelow, J.M. and Hinich, Melvin J. (1984) *The Spatial Theory of Voting*. Cambridge: Cambridge University Press.

Gabel, Matthew and Huber, John (2000) 'Putting parties in their place', *American Journal of Political Science*, 44: 94–103.

Hotelling, Harold (1929) 'Stability in competition', *Economic Journal*, 39: 41–57.

Huber, John and Inglehart, Ronald (1995) 'Expert interpretations of party space and party location in societies', *Party Politics*, 1: 73–111.

Inglehart, Ronald and Klingemann, Hans-Dieter (1976) 'Party identification, ideological preference and the left–right dimension among Western mass publics', in Ian Budge, Ivor Crewe and Dennis Farlie (eds), *Party Identification and Beyond: Representations of Voting and Party Competition*. London: Wiley, pp. 243–73.

Kim, Hee-Min and Fording, Richard (1998) 'Voter ideology in Western democracies', *European Journal of Political Research*, 33: 73–97.

Kleinnijenhuis, Jan and Pennings, Paul (2001) 'Measurement of party positions on the basis of party programmes, media coverage and voter perceptions', in M. Laver (ed.), *Estimating the Policy Position of Political Actors*. London: Routledge, pp. 162–82.

Klingemann, Han-Dieter (1995) 'Party Positions and Voter Orientations', Chapter 6 of H-D Klingemann and Dieter Fuchs, *Citizens and the State*, (Oxford, OUP, 1995).

Klingemann, Han-Dieter, Hofferbert, Richard I. and Budge, Ian (1994) *Parties, Policies, and Democracy*. Boulder, CO: Westview.

Laver, Michael and Budge, Ian (eds) (1992) *Party Policy and Government Coalitions*. London: MacMillan.

Laver, Michael and Garry, John (2001) 'Estimating policy positions from political texts', *American Journal of Political Science*, 43: 619–34.

Laver, Michael and Hunt, Ben W. (1992) *Policy and Party Competition*. London: Routledge.

Laver, Michael and Shepsle, Kenneth (1996) *Making and Breaking Governments*. New York: Cambridge University Press.

Laver, Michael, Benoit, J. and Garry, John (2003) 'Estimating policy preferences using words as data', *American Political Science Review*, 97: 351–79.

Lijphart, Arend (1999) *Patterns of Democracy: Government Forms and Performance in 36 Countries*. New Haven, CT: Yale University Press.

Lipset, Seymour Martin and Rokkan, Stein (1967) 'Cleavage structures, party systems and voter alignments', in Seymour Martin Lipset and Stein Rokkan (eds), *Party Systems and Voter Alignments*. New York: Free Press.

McDonald, Michael and Budge, Ian (2005) *Parties, Electors, Democracy: Bestowing the Median Mandate*. Oxford: Oxford University Press.

McDonald, Michael D. and Mendes, Silvia M. (2001) 'The policy space of party manifestoes', in Michael Laver (ed.), *Estimating the Policy Position of Political Actors*. London: Routledge.

McDonald, Michael D., Budge, Ian and Hofferbert, Richard I. (1999) 'Party mandate theory and time series analysis: A theoretical and methodological response', *Electoral Studies*, 18: 587–96.

McDonald, Michael, Budge, Ian and Pennings, Paul (2004) 'Choice versus sensitivity: a party reponsiveness to issues', *European Journal of Political Research*, 43: 845–68.

McDonald, Michael, Mendes, Silvia and Budge, Ian (2004) 'What are elections for? The median mandate', *British Journal of Political Science*, 34: 1–32.

McKelvey, R.D. (1979) 'General conditions for global intransitives in formal voting models', *Econometrica*, 47: 1085–1111.

Müller, Wolfgang C. and Strøm, Kaare (eds) (2000) *Coalition Governments in Western Europe*. Oxford: Oxford University Press.

Niemi, Richard (1969) 'Majority decision making with partial dimensionality', *American Political Science Review*, 63: 688–97.

Niemi, Richard (1983) 'Why so much stability? Another opinion', *Public Choice*, 41: 261–70.

Ordeshook, Peter (1986) *Mathematical Political Theory*. Cambridge: Cambridge University Press.

Pierce, Roy (1999) 'Mass–elite linkages and the responsible party model of representation', in Warren Miller, Roy Pierce, J. Thomassen, R. Herrera, S. Holmberg, P. Essiasson and Bernhard Wessels, *Policy Representation in Western Democracies*. Oxford: Oxford University Press, pp. 29–58.

Powell, G. Bingham (2000) *Elections as Instruments of Democracy: Majoritarian and Proportional Visions*. New Haven, CT: Yale University Press.

Robertson, David (1976) *A Theory of Party Competition*. London and New York: Wiley.

Schofield, Norman (1985) *Social Choice and Democracy*. Berlin: Springer-Verlag.

Shepsle, Kenneth A. and Weingast, Barry (1981) 'Structure-induced equilibrium and legislative choice', *Public Choice*, 37: 503.

Smithies, Arthur (1941) 'Optimum location in spatial competition', *Journal of Political Economy*, 49: 423–39.

Stokes Donald (1966) 'Spatial models of party competition', in Angus Campbell, Phillip Converse, Warren E. Miller and Donald E. Stokes (eds), *Elections and the Political Order*. New York: Wiley, pp. 161–77.

Van Roozendahl, Peter (1990) 'Centre parties and coalition formation: A game-theoretic approach', *European Journal of Political Research*, 18: 325–48.

Van Roozendahl, Peter (1992) 'The effect of dominant and central parties on cabinet composition and duration', *Legislative Studies Quarterly*, 14: 5–36.

PART V

PARTIES AND THE STATE

37

PARTY LAW

Wolfgang C. Müller and Ulrich Sieberer

WHAT IS PARTY LAW?

Party law can be understood as legislation
specifically designed to regulate the life of
party organizations. Alternatively, party law
can be defined as the total body of law that
affects political parties. In the former case
party law is a clearly defined body of law that
may exist or not in specific countries. In the
latter case some parts of the legal order, such as
family law, are likely to be irrelevant to the
organization and activities of political parties
(except, of course, policy-making), but a vast
territory remains. In this contribution we try to
steer a middle way between these two extremes.
In the theoretical sections of this chapter we
address issues of party law in a more general
sense. In the empirical sections we focus on the
legal regulation of extra-parliamentary party
organizations, parties as electoral organizations,
and parliamentary parties.

Party law can be derived from the main constitutional texts and other constitutional law
(where such a category exists), special party
laws, those laws and regulations that govern
elections (electoral laws, campaign regulation),
parliamentary organization, political finance,
other political activities (e.g. organizing demonstrations), and/or laws that regulate the activities of voluntary organizations in a more general
sense. Party law also can be found beyond the
confines of the nation state. European Union

treaties have already explicitly recognized the
important role of political parties. More detailed
legislation (Regulation (EC) No. 2004/2003) was
enacted in 2003 (with the generous rules on
party finance coming into force only after the
2004 European elections).

However defined, party law is the domain of
academic lawyers. Political scientists, while
interested in the substance of party regulation
in some selected fields, in particular with
regard to elections and party finance, have not
devoted much attention to party law as such.
Geographically, Germany is the heartland of
party law. As we show in the empirical
sections of this chapter, there is no democratic
country in which political parties are subjected
to more detailed explicit regulation. This fact
has triggered a wealth of academic publications, many of which originate from a research
institute for the study of party law (now
located at the University of Düsseldorf). While
most of these publications are 'hard core' law
studies and delve into details of German party
law, an increasing part is devoted to comparative themes, mostly with a focus on Western
Europe. Likewise, this chapter mainly relates
to party law in European countries (for the
United States, see the chapter by Lowenstein).
It aims to map the universe of types of party
regulation rather than provide full coverage of
individual cases.

In this chapter we are mainly concerned
with the formal and *de facto* recognition of

political parties through the legal order. A *formal recognition* – or 'authorization' (Pedersen, 1982) – means that a political party assumes a legally defined role in the political system and is formally recognized by the state. It is relevant to the extent that only a party (in the formal sense) enjoys specific freedoms and/or can perform specific functions and/or have access to resources of some kind. A *de facto recognition* provides the same benefits as official recognition but without requiring the party to go through an authorization process. However, the party will have to fulfil specific criteria in order to win the benefits that result from *de facto* party status.

WHY PARTY LAW?

Why would the state privilege political parties? One answer is based on power. Political parties have established themselves as the engines of the political process in the 20th century. It is parties that breathe life into the formal institutions of government and hence make the rules for themselves. In a democracy, however, parties need to legitimize their claim to a privileged position in the political process. Historically, the prominent role played by parties in operating the institutions of democratic government was heavily contested (Daalder, 2002). Yet, beginning with Hans Kelsen (1929), political parties have increasingly been considered as playing a necessary and valuable role in the democratic process (Schattschneider, 1942; Ware, 1987). Specifically, parties are trusted to provide democracy through inter-party competition and by being vehicles for political participation via intra-party democracy between elections.

Party law can take it for granted that political parties fulfil these functions (hence no specific regulation is required to arrive at these ends). Alternatively, party law can contain regulations that are designed to make the parties actually live up to these democratic claims. Finally, any regulation can be perverted. Rather than promoting democracy, party law can serve the partisan needs of incumbents.

The mainstream of democratic theory puts a premium on inter-party competition as a means of democracy. Yet, competition is an ambiguous concept, involving potentially conflicting dimensions (Demsetz, 1982; Strøm, 1989; Bartolini, 2002). It relates to the behaviour of parties, voters, and the institutional environment in which parties interact with each other and with the voters. In short, parties compete with each other if there is conflict of interest, that is, the gains of one party are the losses of another. This relates to vote shares, offices and policies (Dahl, 1966). Not all of party behaviour aims at winning at the expense of other parties. However, if *no* party behaviour falls into that category we have perfect collusion and no competition. With regard to voters, competition requires availability, that is, flexibility in demand. Hence voters react to party behaviour (past record, future promises). Finally, competition requires contestability, that is, an open electoral market, so that new parties can enter the race. While political institutions in general have the greatest impact on the ease of entry and conflict of interest dimensions of party competition, party law specifically impacts mainly on the former.

Entry takes specific forms over the various stages in the life cycle of a party. According to Pedersen (1982), this cycle begins with some individuals declaring their willingness to start a new party. Clearly, the political and legal order in the most fundamental sense is essential for parties crossing the threshold of declaration. Without the basic political freedoms (freedom of expression, access to alternative information, associational autonomy, etc.) that are necessary conditions for democracy (Dahl, 1989: 222), party declaration requires heroes and all too often fails. Party law, as defined in this chapter, is critical for the next step, the threshold of authorization – becoming a party in the legal sense. According to one standard definition, a party is an organization that fields candidates in elections. Typically, electoral activities are preceded by organizational efforts that, in turn, are likely to require legal recognition either as a political party, provided the respective legal order has a *sui generis* type for that, or as a political or voluntary organization. Crossing the threshold of representation requires the winning of parliamentary seats. Here the electoral law is critical. Contesting elections typically requires some form of authorization. Moreover, the electoral law provides *institutional* incentives (such as legal thresholds and complex districting arrangements) for pre-electoral coordination and the building of national parties. In a structured party system such rules tend to benefit the existing parties *vis-à-vis* new entrants. The last of Pedersen's thresholds is that of relevance. This can be defined in a variety of different ways and is clearly a behavioural one that depends on the political power distribution. Hence, party law as defined in this chapter is most relevant in the second and third phases of the party life cycle, although electoral law remains important throughout the entire lifetime of parties.

The ease of entry is one crucial aspect of party competition. Can we conclude that the easier the entry, the more competitive the party system? And does greater competitiveness mean more democracy and hence a better state of affairs? As Sartori (1976: 327) has put it, 'ever more "competitiveness" is not an unmixed blessing'. The atomization of a party system – approaching perfect economic decentralization, the predominant definition of competition in economics (Demsetz, 1982) – undermines one of the essential functions of political parties: the structuring of electoral choices. This is exemplified by Poland in its first truly democratic elections in 1991 when 111 parties fielded candidates and 29 entered parliament, with the strongest party winning a mere 12.3% of the votes and only one other party more than 10%. Excessive party system fragmentation was corrected by holding the next elections under a nationwide 5% threshold, leading to 35 parties contesting the election and only eight winning seats.

But would it not be better to leave the structuring of the party system, that is, the reduction of alternatives, entirely to market forces? The claim for some state intervention in the political market rests on two arguments. First, an atomized party system is bad for the country, as it is likely to result in government instability and insufficient political problem-solving capacity, and thereby may also have detrimental effects for democracy. Second, given the infrequency of elections, citizens can acquire only a limited experience of voting during their lifetime (Demsetz, 1982: 81–2). Indeed, assuming a four-year term and 50 years of voting experience, the average voter will have the chance to cast his or her vote in no more than 12 or 13 elections. Hence, eliminating 'loony' parties or candidates and forcing the others to demonstrate some level of support before they are allowed to contest elections is legitimate and beneficial to voters. While party law cannot guarantee an 'optimal' number of parties, it can cut back excessive supply.

Accepting that democracy is served by some restrictions on entry, the question remains at which stage in the life cycle of political parties entry should be restricted and what the criteria should be on which entry is denied. As the empirical sections below show, nations have given different answers to these questions. And these questions are linked to other aspects of party regulation, in particular to public funding and access to other scarce resources such as time in public mass media.

While too many choices may hamper the effectiveness of inter-party competition, the seizure of power by an undemocratic party is a more direct threat to democracy. Hence, party law may aim to protect democracy by outlawing such parties. Yet, the problem is that those undemocratic parties that employ democratic means in order to win political power in the first place as a rule do not openly declare their goal of doing away with democracy once they have succeeded. Also, undemocratic attitudes may only develop once parties have assumed office. Under such circumstances there is always the danger that the power to outlaw political parties will be abused. Rather than ensuring competition, it may serve the purpose of eliminating competitors that appear particularly threatening to incumbents but not to the democratic system. Therefore, in a democracy the right to outlaw political parties should be severely restricted. Incumbents should not be involved in that process and all guarantees of the rule of law should fully apply (Morlok, 2003).

While the number and character of parties are highly relevant for achieving the benefits of political competition, there is at least one other condition that must be met in order to make elections meaningful: they must be consequential. In making their bid for the voters, political parties claim that they can control the remainder of the democratic chain of delegation and hence can keep their implicit contracts with the voters (Müller, 2000). This requires that political parties be cohesive, that is, keep on board those elected under their respective brand names and ensure that these politicians observe the party line. If parties disintegrate after elections, voters may still be able to hold individual members of parliament (MPs) accountable (depending on their ambitions for re-election and the electoral system), but are unlikely to see the parties' electoral pledges realized.

The most important incentives to ensure party cohesion are the attractiveness of the party's brand name (provided MPs aim to be re-elected) and the fact that all but pivotal MPs are likely to have less policy influence outside their party. Party law can provide additional incentives that tie those elected under a party label to that party. The most drastic means to do so is to enforce automatic resignation of defectors from parliament – as is the case in India, provided that it is not a party split in which the party is abandoned by a minimum of one-third of its MPs (Sartori, 1997: 192). Even harsher rules were applied in Czechoslovakia in the inter-war period, where the electoral commission tended to expel MPs who changed their party affiliation (Pfeifer, 1958). Less drastic rules may restrict the ability of defecting MPs to form new parliamentary parties, get a share of parliamentary resources, and make use of parliamentary instruments.

Finally, what is the potential role of party law in making political parties live up to their second democratic predicament, to provide intra-party democracy? Democratic theory generally considers this goal second to inter-party democracy, and according to McKenzie (1982: 195) 'intra-party democracy, strictly interpreted, is incompatible with democratic government'. Consequently, McKenzie (1982: 195) has advocated 'oligarchical control by the party leaders of the party organization' as being 'indispensable for the well-being of a democratic polity'. McKenzie's dictum rests on the potentially conflicting signals party officials in public office receive from their voters and party members and the assumption of high barriers to entry to the electoral market. While these conditions are not always given, the fact remains that intra- and inter-party democracy may conflict. Hence, from a normative perspective, the limits to intra-party democracy are clearly drawn when it comes to exercising influence on public officials who are accountable to the general electorate.

Party law can require intra-party democracy from political parties and it can aim at setting some standards against which real parties can be measured. Given the variety of party organizational forms that have evolved over time, however, such standards need to be very abstract. Also, the danger of abusing such clauses that refer to intra-party democracy is probably greater than those that refer to the behaviour of parties in inter-party competition.

PARTIES IN THE CONSTITUTIONAL AND LEGAL FRAMEWORK

The degree to which parties are formally incorporated into the legal order varies considerably in Western democracies. Some countries, such as Germany, France, Italy, Spain, Portugal and Greece, formally acknowledge parties in their constitutions. According to a recent review (Avnon, 1995), nine countries had legislated specific party laws by the early 1990s, most notably among them Germany where the

most detailed party law was passed in 1967. Other established democracies with party laws are Finland, Israel, Spain, Portugal (not mentioned by Avnon) and Austria. More recently, party laws have been introduced in Poland and the Czech Republic. In most other Western democracies parties are only indirectly incorporated into the legal framework, usually via party finance laws and the electoral law. Some countries, such as the UK and Ireland, only acknowledge parties in their parliamentary rules (Schefold *et al.*, 1990: 777).

Formal recognition of parties mainly occurs in constitutions written after periods of one-party dictatorship (Avnon, 1995). Therefore, it is not surprising that many new constitutions in Eastern Europe, such as Poland, the Czech Republic and Bulgaria, acknowledge the role of political parties and that the first two countries have also passed special party laws. In contrast, systems with a long democratic tradition have seen little need to formally acknowledge the important role of political parties in a comprehensive form and mention them only as need occurs in electoral and party finance laws.

As noted above, Germany is the heartland of party law and much attention has focused on Article 21 of the Basic Law. It was one of the earliest and at the time (1949) most comprehensive constitutional rules on parties. Article 21 regulates the freedom to create parties, their role in the formation of the political will, intra-party democracy, the duty of parties to account for their assets, and the procedures for outlawing parties as unconstitutional. (A less comprehensive article on parties had previously appeared in the Italian constitution of 1947 (see Schefold, 2002: 134).) The German Law on Political Parties of 1967, the first comprehensive party law in Western Europe, seems to have influenced the form of such laws in Spain and Portugal (Schefold *et al.*, 1990: 767, 784). In particular, its definition of political parties in § 2(1) has been much discussed. It reads:

Parties are associations of citizens which exert influence permanently or for longer periods of time on the formation of the political will at federal or *Land* level and participate in the representation of the people in the German Bundestag or state parliaments (*Landtag*) provided that they offer sufficient guarantee of the sincerity of their aims in the general character of their circumstances and attendant conditions, particularly with regard to the size and strength of their organization, their memberships and their conduct in public.

Overall, the position of political parties in German constitutional law is so strong that they have been recognized as 'institutions of constitutional law' (*verfassungsrechtliche Institutionen*) by the Federal Constitutional Court.

Political parties are also formally recognized at the EU level. Article 138a of the Maastricht Treaty mentions that parties are 'important as a factor for integration within the Union'. Accordingly, they 'contribute to forming a European awareness and to expressing the political will of the Union'. This formulation is paraphrased in the Treaty Establishing a Constitution for Europe (signed in October 2004). Article 46(4) reads: 'Political parties at European level contribute to forming European political awareness and to expressing the will of citizens of the Union.'

Most commonly, parties are organized in the form of private associations. Some of them have a legal personality of their own (*Rechtsfähigkeit*) but this seems to make little difference in practice. Some parties in Germany and France are *rechtsfähig* while others are not, but this does not affect party competition in these countries (Schefold *et al.* in Tsatsos *et al.*, 1990: 782–3). Acquiring legal personality is not necessarily linked to crucial legal rights of parties, as the German case indicates. Here, parties, while not always legal persons in their own right, have been granted legal standing of their own by the Federal Constitutional Court when their constitutional rights are at stake, for example in connection with elections, party financing, tax privileges for donations, and in their relations with the government.

EXTRA-PARLIAMENTARY PARTY ORGANIZATION

Most systems do not require any special registration of parties other than fulfilling the requirements for founding private associations (a certain number of members, a written statute, etc.) and (where applicable) special provisions of party law (for example, the requirements of § 2(1) of the German Party Law).[1] Some countries, such as Greece and Austria, require a formal registration (in Greece with the Supreme Court, in Austria with the Ministry of the Interior) without rendering the registration difficult. Other countries pose more extensive requirements that actually make the foundation of new parties cumbersome. In Portugal, 5000 supporting signatures and a draft party statute are required for registration as a party with the

constitutional court. Along with financial disadvantages, this requirement raises considerable hurdles for establishing a new party (de Sousa, 1990: 606–7, de Sousa, 1993: 314–15). These hurdles are even higher in Spain. According to the law of associations, parties need to register with the Ministry of Internal Affairs, and the relevant procedure is demanding. As one country expert states, it gives the government a certain influence on the foundation of new parties. This is particularly true in the run-up to an election, where delay in formal recognition can be crucial (Puente-Egido, 1990: 656–9, 677–9).

The names of established parties are often protected by party law. The German Party Law provides detailed prescriptions on the name a new party may choose. § 4 requires the names and acronyms of new parties to be clearly distinguishable from existing ones (Morlok, 2003: 439). Similar rules exist in Denmark (Vesterdorf, 1990: 91), Portugal (de Sousa, 1990: 607) and Spain – the latter providing a clear example of the relevance of party law for party 'brand names'. Several legal disputes emerged over that issue during the formation of the post-authoritarian party system. Specifically, those political activists who had stayed in the country during the dictatorship and those who had spent the time in exile presented conflicting claims on specific party names. The courts decided these cases by applying the rules of patent law (Puente-Egido, 1990: 658, 677–8). In contrast, Britain does not legally protect party names at all (Smith, 1990: 316).

In line with the premium democracy places on the free foundation of parties, restrictions on anti-democratic parties are rare. The main example is Germany, where the Constitutional Court can declare unconstitutional and dissolve parties that, 'by reason of their aims or the behaviour of their adherents, seek to undermine or abolish the free democratic basic order or to endanger the existence of the Federal Republic of Germany' (Art. 21(2), Basic Law). This procedure was used twice in the early years of the Federal Republic, with a neo-Nazi party (the Sozialistische Reichspartei, SRP) and the German Communist Party (KPD) declared unconstitutional. More recently, some extreme right groups were declared unconstitutional in the early 1990s, although the most publicized attempt to ban the right-wing National Democratic Party (NPD) failed in 2003. This failure points to the potential risks of outlawing extremist parties, as they can use failed attempts as propaganda. Indeed, the

NPD crossed the threshold of representation in the *Land* of Saxony in 2004. Spain and Portugal also have specific procedures for forbidding parties according to party laws. In 2003, the Basque nationalist party Herri Batasuna was banned by the Spanish Constitutional Court because it was considered a standing supporter of the terrorist ETA. More recently, special procedures for outlawing parties can be found in the Polish constitution and the party law of the Czech Republic (see country chapters in Tsatsos, 2002).

Other countries only have procedures for outlawing private associations in general, which are also applicable to political parties. Such provisions can be contained in the Constitution (as in Art. 78(2) of the Danish Constitution), in the general law of associations (as in the Netherlands), or in laws for protecting the state (such as the act on combat groups and private militias of 1936 in France, the Prevention of Terrorism Act 1974 in the UK, or the Irish Offences against the State Act 1939). While the French law has been used repeatedly (see Fromont, 1990: 243), both Ireland and the UK have been very reluctant to make use of their provisions against political parties. Sinn Féin has not been outlawed in either country, even though the IRA is considered an 'unlawful organization' in both. Belgium offers a recent example of outlawing a political party, in this case the far-right Vlaams Block, which was considered a racist organization and therefore outlawed by the Belgian High Court in 2004 (Erk, 2005). The Court's verdict was based on the Belgian Anti-Racism Act of 1981.While the constitutions of some countries (e.g., France, Greece, Italy and Portugal) demand that parties observe democratic principles (generally interpreted as inter-party democracy), only the German (Art. 21(1)) and the Spanish (Art. 6(3)) constitutions commit the parties explicitly to intra-party democracy. These requirements are spelled out in more detail at the level of party law in Germany, Spain, Portugal and Finland. Most other countries do not have specific legal rules on intra-party democracy. Here, only the general principles regulating private associations are applicable, which in some cases (e.g. Denmark and the Netherlands) contain certain minimal standards of democracy such as equality of the members or the making of decisions by the majority principle. In general, the detailed prescription of intra-party decision-making processes is left to the individual party statutes (Schefold *et al.*, 1990: 809–11). Ironically, under the now abandoned rule that the party leader is elected by the parliamentary party, the major British parties would not pass the test of intra-party democracy as established by the German Party Law and its interpretation by the Constitutional Court, which demand the participation of party members in the selection of party leaders.

PARTIES AS ELECTORAL ORGANIZATIONS

In order to live up to the standard political science definition, political parties need to run in elections. Here, the relevant legal rules are most frequently contained in the electoral laws. Campaign finance regulations are a second major source of laws which have drawn considerable attention in the last decades (on campaign finance and party finance more generally, see the chapter by Nassmacher in this volume).

The first complex with regard to parties as electoral organizations refers to how parties get ballot access (Bowler *et al.*, 2003; Hug, 2001: 178–81). Here, we focus on the national level; for subnational elections other rules may apply. First, there are countries in which the parties, while important in practice, do not play a legally recognized role in the electoral process. For example, in France and the UK, both countries with single-member districts, only individuals get access to the ballot. Candidates in France may even change their stated party affiliation between the first election and the run-off (Fromont, 1990: 238). But even some countries with a list electoral system do not grant parties a formal role. In Luxembourg, for example, lists are formally accepted on the ballot when supported by 25 registered voters in the respective district. In practice, though, parties dominate the nomination process in all these countries. Nevertheless, as the British example shows, individual candidates, either for themselves or for a newly founded party, may get easy access to the ballot without the support of an established party, especially if the number of signatures needed to get on the ballot is low and the deposit to be paid is not excessive (10 signatures and £500 in the British case).

Other countries formally recognize the important role played by parties in the electoral process by allowing only party lists on the ballot. Usually, a certain number of signatures are needed and at times a financial deposit has to be paid. The hurdles for ballot access differ considerably: while only 10 voters' signatures are needed in the Netherlands, the Danish electoral law requires as many as 1/175 of the number of valid votes in the last elections, which means approximately 20,000 signatures (Bowler *et al.*, 2003). According to the German Federal Electoral Law (§§ 18(2), 20(2), 27(1)), parties have to present 200 signatures of citizens living in the relevant single-member constituency to place a candidate on the ballot paper and 0.1% of the eligible voters (or at most 2000 signatures) in order to submit a candidate list at the state level (*Landesliste*). While independent candidates can run in the single-member constituencies, only parties fulfilling the requirements of party law (see the definition in § 2 of the Party Law) are allowed to submit lists for the PR part of the elections (Morlok, 2003: 434–7). In addition to a certain number of signatures, financial deposits are required in many countries. Amounts currently vary considerably (see Bowler *et al.*, 2003). While Dutch parties have to pay a deposit of €11,250 (approx. US$ 13,641, exchange rates as of August 2005) to place a list on the ballot, party lists in New Zealand only pay NZ$1000 (US$682). In countries with single-member constituencies, amounts between NZ$300 (US$205) in New Zealand and ¥3 million (US$26,671) in Japan have to be paid per constituency. These deposits are generally non-refundable in Austria (and hence are called contributions to the costs of elections) but refunded in most other countries if the candidate or the party wins a certain number of votes. These thresholds also vary but are usually around 5% of the vote for constituency candidates. In list systems the hurdle is usually lower, amounting to only 0.5% of all party votes in New Zealand and three-quarters of the electoral quotient (which is the total of all valid votes divided by 150) in the Netherlands.

In many countries parties that already enjoy parliamentary representation are exempt from the above-mentioned requirements. Thus, they do not have to collect signatures and pay the deposit in the Netherlands, and they are exempt from the collection of signatures in Denmark and Italy (Bowler *et al.*, 2003: Table 5.A1). In Germany, the requirements do not apply to parties that are represented in the Bundestag or a state parliament (*Landtag*) with at least 5 MPs due to their own electoral success in the preceding elections. 'Internally created' parties, however, are excluded from this privilege. Similarly, new parties founded by incumbent MPs no longer get automatic ballot access in Denmark since a change in the electoral law in 1965.

Comparing the rules governing ballot access in the 1960s and the late 1990s, Bowler *et al.* (2003: 90–1) observe a development towards stricter access rules in six countries, while four made access easier. Increased requirements can be observed in the Netherlands (higher deposit), Austria, Norway, Finland, Switzerland, and New Zealand (higher number of signatures). Contrary to this trend, access has become easier in Britain, France, Australia, and Canada where lower deposits (in real, if not necessarily in nominal, terms) are required today and the thresholds for reimbursement have been lowered.

The electoral law can also contain elements that provide a *de facto* recognition of political parties (i.e. individual candidates would be severely disadvantaged *vis-à-vis* parties). These include legal thresholds in large districts or the entire nation and complex districting arrangements. Even if 'party' is never mentioned in the electoral laws, such arrangements require political coordination in large geographical areas and hence constitute *de facto* recognitions of parties. Some countries (e.g. Greece and Turkey) make this explicit by penalizing *ad hoc* cooperations relative to political parties (particularly by demanding higher thresholds).

Formal legal rules with regard to the process by which parties nominate candidates for elections are rare. Such rules are contained in the party law in Greece and Germany but only in very general terms. § 17 of the German Party Law requires secret votes on party candidates and refers to the electoral law (containing more detailed instructions) and party statutes for the exact procedures. Similarly, the Greek Party Law demands candidate nomination by the appropriate party organs in accordance with the party statutes. Some legal rules on candidate selection also exist in Norway (since 1921), and Finland (since 1970) (Scarrow *et al.*, 2000: 138). In the absence of legal rules candidate nomination is only governed by party statutes and practice (Schefold *et al.*, in Tsatsos *et al.*, 1990: 820). In particular, the introduction of member votes for nominating candidates has been much discussed and introduced by some parties as a way of improving the democratic performance of parties and to counter anti-party sentiments (Bille, 2001).

With regard to the conduct of electoral campaigns, access to the media, especially TV, has been intensively researched (see Bowler *et al.*, 2003). In most countries, parties are given free public broadcasting time prior to elections. As Bergman *et al.* (2003: Table 4.7) show, this time is either granted equally to all parliamentary parties (e.g. in Denmark, Iceland, and the Netherlands) or in proportion to their size (e.g. in Germany, Austria, France, the UK, Ireland, and Italy (since 1993)). Proportional access is also the rule in Australia, New Zealand, and Japan. A second distinction can be made according to the question of whether parties not currently represented in parliament get free broadcasting time equal to parliamentary parties. In Western Europe, only Austria does not grant parties outside parliament any free TV access. Most other countries provide those parties with a minimum amount of TV time. Only Denmark and the UK treat parties not represented in parliament on an equal footing with parliamentary parties. In addition to free public broadcasting, some countries, such as Iceland, the Netherlands and Greece, allow parties to buy additional TV time for campaign spots. The other Western European countries either ban or restrict this form of campaigning. Finally, Finland does not grant parties free broadcasting time and does not restrict private commercial advertising and thus leaves electoral advertising completely to market forces. Bowler *et al.* (2003: 91–2) find a slight trend towards easier access for new parties in countries such as Australia, Canada, Ireland, Italy and New Zealand, while access has become somewhat more restricted in France and the Netherlands.

Campaign finance is perhaps the most intensely discussed and researched problem with regard to parties as electoral organizations. The survey by Bergman *et al.* shows that public party finance is nowadays a universal feature of Western European democracies. One important question with regard to competition and the entry of new parties is whether parties without parliamentary representation receive public funding as well. This is true in about half the Western European countries (Austria, Denmark, France, Germany, Greece, Norway, and Sweden). No public funding is available to parties not represented in parliament in Belgium, Finland, Iceland, Ireland, Italy, Luxembourg, the Netherlands, Portugal, Spain and the UK. Nevertheless party systems in which new parties are not barred from public finance do not appear to be more prone to change than systems in which parliamentary parties are in a privileged position (Bergman *et al.*, 2003: 142–5).

Bowler *et al.* (2003) find a relaxation in the requirements for receiving public campaign finance in more than two-thirds of the countries in their sample of Western democracies which make access for new parties easier. Yet, these changes have often been accompanied by additional funds for larger parties or parliamentary party groups. This may well strengthen the competitive advantages of established parties (Bowler *et al.*, 2003: 92–3). The 2003 EU regulation on political parties offers a striking example of preferential treatment of established parties as opposed to potential newcomers with regard to obtaining public funding.

The total amounts of public funding received by political parties have risen considerably in some European countries. Farrell and Webb (2000) show that subsidies to the national parties have risen by 369% in Austria (1975–90), 88% in Ireland (1977–89) and 43% in the Netherlands (in a similar period). Other countries, such as Sweden (−32%, 1976–88), Finland (−13%, 1975–87) and Germany (−6%, 1972–87), have witnessed some reductions. In most countries in the sample, the relative importance of public subsidies as compared to other forms of party income has increased. The sharpest rises occurred in Norway (from 57.1% to 83.6%) and Germany (from 58.4% to 70.3%). Sweden (from 62.9% to 52.1%) is the only example of decreasing reliance on public funding, while its relative importance has remained basically unchanged in Finland, Ireland and the Netherlands, albeit at very different levels.

PARTIES IN PARLIAMENT

Once parties have crossed the threshold of representation they can form parliamentary party groups (PPGs). While PPGs are acknowledged in the constitution or in statutory law in some countries, the detailed legal rules governing their rights and conduct in parliament can for the most part be found in the parliamentary standing orders. To the extent that PPGs receive public subsidies, often other regulations (such as laws on campaign finance and/or subsidies to the extra-parliamentary party organization) prove relevant.

First, we may differentiate several ways in which PPGs are recognized. Germany, Italy, Sweden and (indirectly) Austria recognize PPGs in their constitutions. In other countries, such as Denmark and France, PPGs are formally recognized in the standing orders of parliament. Finally, some countries, most notably the UK, do not formally recognize PPGs at all (Heidar and Koole, 2000c: 252).

Next, the rules differ on the number of MPs needed to form a PPG. While the Scandinavian countries and the Netherlands have no formal numerical requirement (implying that the rights of a PPG can be claimed by any individual MP), several parliaments require PPGs to consist of a minimum number of parliamentarians. Italy and France require PPGs to consist of approximately 3% of all MPs, and Germany has set the minimum at 5% (Heidar and Koole, 2000b: 7). Besides the numerical requirement, PPGs must usually consist of MPs elected under the same party label or, as in the case of the CDU/CSU in Germany, at least represent parties that do not compete with each other in the electoral arena. Exceptions are the so-called technical party groups that are founded by MPs elected under different party labels mainly in order to enjoy the benefits connected with PPG status. Examples include the Technical Group of Co-ordination and Defence of Independent MEPs (1979–84) and the Rainbow Group (1984–94) in the European Parliament (Raunio, 2000: 241). In the Spanish parliament, members who do not join a voluntarily founded PPG are automatically included in the mixed group which could thus be considered a technical PPG. Usually PPGs only consist of a group of MPs of one chamber, the exception being Austria where PPGs contain members of both chambers of parliament as well as of the European Parliament (Müller and Steininger, 2000).

The importance of the rules on obtaining the status of a PPG party depends on the prerogatives these enjoy in parliamentary business. Shaun Bowler (2000: 162) presents data according to which about half of the Western democracies in his sample do not privilege PPG members compared to unattached MPs. Examples of such countries are Australia, Belgium, Denmark, Finland, the Netherlands, New Zealand, and the UK. Other countries, such as Austria, Canada, France, Germany, Luxembourg, Norway and Sweden, grant particular privileges to PPGs. In addition, committee appointments are made almost everywhere on the basis of party groups. The only exceptions in Europe are Belgium and Sweden. Finally, PPGs enjoy certain advantages with regard to legislation (provided that bills cannot be introduced by any MP). Germany, Austria, Spain, and Italy are examples of countries where a certain number of MPs (usually the minimum size of a PPG) is needed in order to introduce bills (Wiberg, 1995). According to the Standing Orders of the German Bundestag (§§ 75, 76), bills may also be initiated by a PPG itself, that is, the PPG leadership. This rule not only makes for a less cumbersome process than gathering individual signatures, but also

strengthens the autonomy of party leadership within a legislature (see Schüttemeyer, 1994).

Besides the rules for parliamentary business, public financing of PPGs is a second important topic. The country chapters in Heidar and Koole's (2000a) volume on PPGs in Europe indicate that public subsidies to PPGs are the rule, while the amounts paid differ considerably. PPG status also can generate the public provision of staff resources not available to individual MPs. While, for example, the French PPGs only have a claim for some secretarial staff and have to borrow parliamentary assistants from their MPs, and the British PPGs' staff consists of only a few persons, PPGs in Germany employed a total of 727 persons (between 0.8 and 3.5 staff members per PPG member) in 1994 (not counting the personal staff of individual MPs). Somewhat lower levels are observed in Belgium, with 1 staff person for each PPG member (1996), Austria (total 148, averages 0.55–2.11 per PPG member, 1996), and the Netherlands (averages 0.36–1.83, 1991). Still lower is the staffing of the PPGs in Denmark (total 73, average 0.42, 1995) and Finland (total 43, average 0.22, 1995).

CONCLUSION

Party law, as defined in this chapter, is the legal regulation of extra-parliamentary party organizations, parties as electoral organizations, and parliamentary parties. In a synthetic perspective, lumping together various national patterns, it addresses issues of party–state relations (the parties' legal existence, their access to public resources), inter-party relations (issues of competition such as name protection and campaign behaviour), the 'ownership rights' of both party members and party voters, and important aspects of the relations between parties and party-nominated holders of public office. In democracies, to which this chapter has confined itself, the limits of what party law can and should achieve are narrowly drawn. Yet, in various forms and with relevant differences between countries, party law has great impact on the early stages in party life.

NOTE

1 Newly founded parties in Germany are indirectly required to present a certain number of supporters' signatures in order to retain the status of a

political party: § 2(2) of the Party Law states that parties lose their party status if they have not participated in any election at the federal or state level for 6 years. In order to participate in these elections, parties not presently represented in the Bundestag or a state parliament have to present a certain number of signatures according to electoral law; the numerical requirements for Bundestag elections are discussed later in this chapter.

REFERENCES

Avnon, Dan (1995) 'Parties' laws in democratic systems of government', *Journal of Legislative Studies*, 1(2): 283–300.

Bartolini, Stefano (2002) 'Electoral and party competition: Analytical dimensions and empirical problems', in Richard Gunther, José Ramón Montero and Juan J. Linz (eds), *Political Parties*. Oxford: Oxford University Press, pp. 84–110.

Bergman, Torbjörn, Müller, Wolfgang C., Strøm, Kaare and Blomgren, Magnus (2003) 'Democratic delegation and accountability. Cross-national patterns', in Kaare Strøm, Wolfgang C. Müller and Torbjörn Bergman (eds), *Delegation and Accountability in Parliamentary Democracies*. Oxford: Oxford University Press, pp. 109–220.

Bille, Lars (2001) 'Democratizing a democratic procedure: Myth or reality? Candidate selection in Western European parties, 1960–1990', *Party Politics*, 7(3): 363–80.

Bowler, Shaun (2000) 'Parties in legislatures. Two competing explanations', in Russell J. Dalton and Martin P. Wattenberg (eds), *Parties without Partisans. Political Change in Advanced Industrial Democracies*. Oxford: Oxford University Press, pp. 157–79.

Bowler, Shaun, Carter, Elisabeth and Farrell, David M. (2003) 'Changing party access to elections', in Bruce E. Cain, Russell J. Dalton and Susan E. Scarrow (eds), *Democracy Transformed? Expanding Political Opportunities in Advanced Industrial Democracies*. Oxford: Oxford University Press, pp. 81–111.

Daalder, Hans (2002) 'Parties: Denied, dismissed, or redundant? A critique', in Richard Gunther, José Ramón Montero and Juan J. Linz (eds), *Political Parties*. Oxford: Oxford University Press, pp. 41–57.

Dahl, Robert A. (ed.) (1966) *Political Oppositions in Western Democracies*. New Haven, CT: Yale University Press.

Dahl, Robert A. (1989) *Democracy and Its Critics*. New Haven, CT: Yale University Press.

De Sousa, Marcelo Rebelo (1990) 'Die institution der politischen Partei in Portugal', in Dimitris Th. Tsatsos, Dian Schefold and Hans-Peter Schneider (eds), *Parteienrecht im europäischen Vergleich*. Baden-Baden: Nomos, pp. 591–634.

De Sousa, Marcelo Rebelo (1993) 'Die politischen Parteien und das Recht der Opposition in Portugal', *Jahrbuch des Öffentlichen Rechts*, N.F., 41: 309–17.

Demsetz, Harold (1982) *Economic, Legal, and Political Dimensions of Competition*. Amsterdam: North-Holland.

Erk, Jan (2005) 'From Vlaams Blok to Flaams Belang: the Belgian far-right renames itself', *West European Politics*, 28(3): 493–502.

Farrell, David M. and Webb, Paul (2000) 'Political parties as campaign organizations', in Russell J. Dalton and Martin P. Wattenberg (eds), *Parties without Partisans. Political Change in Advanced Industrial Democracies*. Oxford: Oxford University Press, pp. 102–28.

Fromont, Michael (1990) 'Die Institution der politischen partei in Frankreich', in Dimitris Th. Tsatsos, Dian Schefold and Hans-Peter Schneider (eds), *Parteienrecht im europäischen Vergleich*. Baden-Baden: Nomos, pp. 219–59.

Heidar, Knut and Koole, Ruud (eds) (2000a) *Parliamentary Party Groups in European Democracies. Political Parties behind Closed Doors*. London: Routledge.

Heidar, Knut and Koole, Ruud (2000b) 'Approaches to the study of parliamentary party groups', in Knut Heidar and Ruud Koole (eds), *Parliamentary Party Groups in European Democracies. Political Parties behind Closed Doors*. London: Routledge, pp. 4–22.

Heidar, Knut and Ruud Koole (2000c) 'Parliamentary party groups compared', in Knut Heidar and Ruud Koole (eds), *Parliamentary Party Groups in European Democracies. Political Parties behind Closed Doors*. London: Routledge, pp. 248–70.

Hug, Simon (2001) *Altering Party Systems*. Ann Arbor: University of Michigan Press.

Kelsen, Hans (1929) *Vom Wesen und Wert der Demokratie* (2nd edn). Tübingen: Mohr.

McKenzie, Robert T. (1982) 'Power in the Labour Party: The issue of intra-party democracy', in Dennis Kavanagh (ed.), *The Politics of the Labour Party*. London: Macmillan, pp. 191–201.

Morlok, Martin (2003) 'Parteienrecht als Wettbewerbsrecht', in Peter Häberle, Martin Morlok and Vassilios Skouris (eds), *Festschrift für Dimitris Th. Tsatsos*. Baden-Baden: Nomos, pp. 408–47.

Müller, Wolfgang C. (2000) 'Political parties in parliamentary democracies: Making delegation and accountability work', *European Journal of Political Research*, 37(3): 309–33.

Müller, Wolfgang C. and Steininger, Barbara (2000) 'Not yet the locus of power. Parliamentary party groups in Austria', in Knut Heidar and Ruud Koole (eds), *Parliamentary Party Groups in European Democracies. Political Parties behind Closed Doors*. London: Routledge, pp. 71–88.

Pedersen, Mogens N. (1982) 'Towards a new typology of party lifespans and minor parties', *Scandinavian Political Studies*, 5(1): 1–16.

Pfeifer, Helfried (1958) 'Gewissensfreiheit der Abgeordneten und der Parteienstaat', *Juristische Blätter*, 80: 373–8, 436–43, 462–5.

Puente-Edigo, José (1990) 'Die Institution der politischen Partei in Spanien', in Dimitris Th. Tsatsos, Dian Schefold and Hans-Peter Schneider (eds), *Parteienrecht im europäischen Vergleich*. Baden-Baden: Nomos, pp. 635–94.

Raunio, Tapio (2000) 'Second-rate parties? Towards a better understanding of the European Parliament's party groups', in Knut Heidar and Ruud Koole (eds), *Parliamentary Party Groups in European Democracies. Political Parties behind Closed Doors*. London: Routledge, pp. 231–47.

Sartori, Giovanni (1976) *Parties and Party Systems*. Cambridge: Cambridge University Press.

Sartori, Giovanni (1997) *Comparative Constitutional Engineering*. Basingstoke: Macmillan.

Scarrow, Susan E., Webb, Paul and Farrell, David M. (2000) 'From social integration to electoral contestation. The changing distribution of power within political parties', in Russell J. Dalton and Martin P. Wattenberg (eds), *Parties without Partisans. Political Change in Advanced Industrial Democracies*. Oxford: Oxford University Press, pp. 129–53.

Schattschneider, E.E. (1942) *Party Government*. New York: Rinehart & Co.

Schefold, Dian (2002) 'Die Parteiinstitution in Italien', in Dimitris Th. Tsatsos (ed.), *30 Jahre Parteiengesetz in Deutschland. Die Parteiinstitution im Internationalen Vergleich*. Baden-Baden: Nomos, pp. 133–42.

Schüttemeyer, Suzanne S. (1994) 'Hierarchy and efficiency in the Bundestag: The German answer to institutionalizing parliament', in Gary W. Copeland and Samuel C. Patterson (eds), *Parliaments in the Modern World. Changing Institutions*. Ann Arbor: University of Michigan Press, pp. 29–58.

Smith, Gordon (1990) 'Die Institution der politischen Partei in Gropbritannien', in Dimitris Th. Tsatsos, Dian Schefold and Hans-Peter Schneider (eds), *Parteienrecht im europäischen Vergleich*. Baden-Baden: Nomos, pp. 301–36.

Strøm, Kaare (1989) 'Inter-party competition in advanced democracies', *Journal of Theoretical Politics*, 1(3): 277–300.

Tsatsos, Dimitris Th. (ed.) (2002) *30 Jahre Parteiengesetz in Deutschland. Die Parteiinstitution im internationalen Vergleich*. Baden-Baden: Nomos.

Tsatsos, Dimitris Th., Schefold, Dian and Schneider, Hans-Peter (eds) (1990) *Parteienrecht im europäischen Vergleich. Die Parteien in den demokratischen Ordnungen der Staaten der Europäischen Gemeinschaft*. Baden-Baden: Nomos.

Vesterdorf, Peter L. (1990) 'Die Institution der politischen Partei in Dänemark', in Dimitris Th. Tsatsos, Dian Schefold and Hans-Peter Schneider (eds), *Parteienrecht im europäischen Vergleich*. Baden-Baden: Nomos, pp. 73–150.

Ware, Alan (1987) *Citizens, Parties and the State*. Cambridge: Polity Press.

Wiberg, Matti (1995) 'Private members' initiatives and amendments', in Herbert Döring (ed.), *Parliaments and Majority Rule in Western Europe*. Frankfurt am Main: Campus, pp. 448–87.

38

REGULATION OF PARTY FINANCE

Karl-Heinz Nassmacher

If a scandal makes political finance an issue that engages the interest of a broader public, democracies that hitherto have been reluctant to introduce stricter legislation on the financing of parties and candidates will start to regulate these matters more tightly. Thus countries with established traditions of democracy can offer useful experience to nations in transition to democracy.

RULES ON PARTY EXPENDITURE

Traditionally campaign spending in the Anglo-Saxon orbit is subject to legal constraints. A close relationship with first-past-the-post electoral systems which create manufactured majorities seems obvious. Restrictions, however, 'have proved a constitutional minefield' as supreme courts have had to decide 'whether particular laws adhere to the frequently contradictory principles of fairness and of freedom of expression,' (Pinto-Duschinsky, 2002: 52).

Bans

As far as expenditure is concerned, this instrument is rarely used. Only in Britain (and its dominions) has campaign expenditure by a non-candidate been banned since 1883. The current issue is independent expenditures, referred to as 'third-party advertising'.

A ban on paid media advertising is more frequent. Before the 1980s, only the allotment of time was a major issue in most European countries. As commercial channels became available, the opportunity to buy additional time had to be considered as well. Because expenditures

rose, parties tried to handle the problem in different ways: by providing more free media time (see the discussion on indirect subsidies below), by relying upon an informal agreement among the media which offered some paid advertising time on local or regional radio and television (Sweden), by regulating access to paid media time (by setting conditions for TV spots) or by prohibiting the purchase of media time altogether (e.g. Britain, France and Spain). In 1992, a rule of the latter type was struck down by the High Court in Australia, because it interfered excessively with the freedom of speech necessary for free elections (Chaples, 1994: 34). In the Netherlands, paid political advertising was never banned, but until 1998 it was precluded by a code of conduct among advertising agencies. Most countries control the allocation of broadcasting time (see below).

Spending limits

In Britain, campaign spending at the constituency level has been limited since 1883. Such limits were introduced to prevent wealthy candidates from buying votes. Meanwhile campaigns have become much more nationalized. A new law, effective since 2001, limits the campaign expenditures of national party organizations as well. The maximum amount varies by type of election. The British tradition of establishing spending limits for constituency candidates also spread to the dominions.

In 1974, Canada was first in limiting spending during a campaign period by registered political parties as well as by constituency candidates. Canadian parties have coped strategically with national campaign ceilings: whereas the NDP tried to boost campaign spending (because of the national reimbursement), the PC increased pre-campaign publicity in order to stay within the nationwide campaign spending limit. In 2004, Canada introduced spending limits for constituency nomination contestants. In Australia the mechanism of expenditure limitation has been abolished after decades, because it was regarded as useless in the context of modern party democracy (Amr and Lisowski, 2001: 66).

In France, Italy, Spain and Portugal, expenditure limits for both candidates and parties are on the statute book. French limits depend on the type of election and the number of voters involved. Spanish law establishes the legal maximum to be spent by a party as a fixed amount per electoral district plus an additional sum depending on the number of inhabitants of the constituency. Parties in Portugal are allowed to spend up to a percentage of the monthly minimum wage for each candidate on their list. In Italy, election expenditure per candidate is restricted. An additional limit applies for parties that field candidates in all constituencies. In Israel, a fixed amount per seat held in parliament is the basis for all calculations on spending limits, with some leeway for small parties.

Most cases show that it is rather difficult to draw a line between current expenses and campaign spending, or between the expenditures of candidates and those of the parties supporting them. The stricter the rules for campaign expenses are, the more likely media advertising by 'independent' groups ('Citizens for …' or 'Citizens against …' will spring up (Mendilow, 1989: 140)). Because LDP candidates in Japan during the 1980s and early 1990s exceeded the legal limit somewhere between 6 and 13 times, expenditure limits were abolished in 1994.

In Germany, Austria, Switzerland, the Netherlands and Sweden, there are no legal limits on party or candidate expenditure, either by total amount or by specific item, either for campaign expenses or for routine spending. In Austria, a voluntary agreement among the major parties was tried, but it has been discontinued (Sickinger, 1997: 335).

RULES ON PARTY INCOME

Due to the important role of parties in democratic systems, various rules have been adopted which either restrict or favour specific types of political income. Incentives to stimulate specific fundraising activities by political parties are still rare among these rules (Austin and Tjernström, 2003: 220–3).

Bans

In most countries, anonymous contributions (see the next section) are *banned*. Parties in France, Spain, Portugal and Israel may not accept money from foreign governments or institutions (except the European Parliament). However, virtually all parties received ample financial support from abroad, especially during the transition years. In order to prevent disguised contributions, in Israel loans can be negotiated from banks only (Mendilow, 1996: 348).

Since 1995, candidates and parties in France have been forbidden to receive funds from private corporations and public sector companies. In Italy, Spain, Portugal and Japan, donations from public or semi-public entities are banned. Moreover, labour unions and other organizations in Japan may no longer donate to individual politicians. Do such bans work? Until 1993 it was illegal for Portuguese parties to receive financial contributions for routine activities or election campaigns from national companies or foreign individuals and companies. However, this prohibition did not prevent *de facto* financing by private business, usually through individuals as intermediaries.

Although Germany and Austria do not apply such bans there are practical *restrictions*. In Austria, political donations by organized interests are subject to an income tax surcharge to be paid by the recipient party; in Germany, the Constitutional Court has banned tax benefits for corporate donors. In the Netherlands, parties are restrained from soliciting corporate donations simply by traditional ethics (Koole, 1994: 126).

Contribution limits

Portugal stipulates *ceilings* for all kinds of donations. Spanish law *limits* donations, and the limits have tended to become stricter over time (van Biezen and Nassmacher, 2001: 148). In Japan, different contribution limits have been set for annual totals of donations given by individuals to parties and their fundraising bodies, to financial support groups of politicians and to other political organizations (e.g. habatsu or koenkai). Since 1994, individual politicians have been limited to one personal fundraising committee. In 1994, Israel reduced the ceiling for contributions to parties. Separate limits are stipulated for contributions to internal party primaries for the nomination of candidates on the party list. By a rule introduced in 2004, individuals in Canada may contribute no more than C$5000 per year to a party, to a leadership contestant or to a non-party candidate for the federal parliament. For corporations and trade unions the rule is much stricter.

In many countries (Britain, Australia, Germany, Austria, Switzerland, the Netherlands and Sweden) there is no statutory limit on the total amount of political contributions which a person or corporation may give to a party or a candidate.

Direct subsidies

Meanwhile nearly all liberal democracies have introduced direct public funding of political parties. Only Switzerland – with the exception of two cantons (Drysch, 1998: 121) – remains aloof. Everywhere public money makes the work of parliamentary groups more professional. In Britain, the 'Short money', given to the opposition in Parliament, was a first step towards public subsidies; recently the UK has introduced public funding for policy research. In general, public subsidies were meant to reduce the influence of big donors and to avoid corruption or to cover rising expenses for electronic media and the party. Public funding is given to parties, to candidates or to both. Party subsidies are available for routine operations and/or for campaigns. The total amount available for public funding can be distributed in different ways. Frequently parties receive an amount of money for every vote polled or for each member of parliament (MP).

There are various thresholds to qualify for a subsidy. The German threshold (0.5 per cent of the national vote or 1.0 per cent in a minimum of three state elections) is lower than any other. Portugal, with about 0.6 per cent, and Austria, with 1.0 per cent of the national vote, are next in line. Canada requires a party to win 2 per cent of the national vote in those constituencies in which it has endorsed a candidate, in order to receive a subsidy; Japanese law requires 5 seats or 2 per cent of the vote. Political parties in Sweden receive a general party subsidy at the national level which depends on the average number of parliamentary seats held by a party after the two most recent elections. This is complemented by an office assistance subsidy which consists of a fixed base amount and an additional sum that depends on the number of MPs. For parties without seats in the Riksdag, thresholds of 2.5 per cent and 4.0 per cent of the vote, respectively, are applied. The amount of additional funding for parties at the regional and local level is decided upon by the respective assemblies and given per seat as well as according to votes. In Austria, an annual subsidy for party organizations is supplemented by campaign subsidies for federal and European elections. On top of federal subsidies, each of the nine Austrian states grants funding to political parties as well. Quite similar to Sweden, most of the public money given to parties in Austria is provided at the subnational level.

The Netherlands has now turned to very modest direct subsidies (at the national level only). Before 1999, only indirect support via affiliated foundations was available for specific purposes (research, training and youth). Party subsidies continue to be goal-oriented, but the list of purposes now includes contacts with foreign parties and information for party members. Campaign spending is explicitly excluded. Funds for youth organizations and research institutes are earmarked (Gidlund and Koole, 2001: 121).

The Italian, Spanish and Portuguese systems of direct funding of political parties, although different from each other in detail, include annual subsidies for routine activity and subsidies for campaign expenses (van Biezen, 2000: 331, 336). Israel provides party subsidies for campaigning as well as operating expenses. Traditionally, the 'financing unit', a fixed amount per seat held in parliament, is the basis for all calculations. Any new party is entitled to a retroactive campaign subsidy based on its representation in the newly elected parliament. In addition, each party participating successfully in local elections is entitled to a municipal subsidy.

Due to a reform in 1994, Japan provides government subsidies for political parties. During the late 1990s, almost half of the total subsidy was collected by the dominant party of many decades (LDP, Jiminto), while three to five other parties (regularly in opposition) shared between them roughly the other half.

This review of national rules indicates that there is no incentive against cost explosion. Quite to the contrary, Israel, Japan, Italy and Austria have the highest level of party expenditure. Specific rules seem to be more appropriate to address this problem. Ceilings for public funding are inherent in reimbursement rules, which provide only a percentage of total expenditure (for candidates, as in France, or for parties and candidates, as in Canada), in matching rules (as applied to US presidential primaries) or in the legal stipulation that only a given percentage of party income can be provided by the public purse (e.g. the 'relative maximum' rule in Germany).

In France, parties which have presented themselves for the legislative elections in at least 50 single-member districts receive public funding in proportion to the number of votes won in the first round and the number of seats held. New parties not receiving this subsidy may collect a public matching grant, provided that they are able to solicit a given amount of money from a given number of people. A campaign reimbursement of up to 50 per cent of the legal spending limit is paid to individual candidates who win at least 5 per cent of the vote in their constituency in the first round. Candidates for the presidency may claim one-third of their legal campaign spending (Koole, 2001: 82).

In Canada, every eligible party is entitled to a quarterly allowance per valid vote plus 50 per cent of its declared election expenses. Constituency candidates are reimbursed for up to 60 per cent of the applicable spending limit, if the candidate obtained at least 10 per cent of the valid votes cast. About half of all candidates and roughly two-thirds of the major party candidates qualify for reimbursements.

In Germany, subsidies are limited by two ceilings. First, no party may receive its public entitlement unless it has collected an equal amount from membership fees, individual or corporate donations. Second, public subsidies to all parties may not exceed a total of €133 million, in due course to be adjusted for cost inflation. About 40 per cent of this subsidy is distributed according to the number of votes polled. The other 60 per cent of the subsidy matches small donations by individuals and membership fees at a rate of 2:1 (Gunlicks, 1995: 101 21). The six parties represented federally regularly receive more than 95 per cent of the total allocation, while the rest is distributed among five to ten minor parties. No such subsidies are available for local party organizations or individual party candidates.

Among parties, there is an increasing dependence on public subsidies. However, this differs by country (due to the overall financial regimes) and by party (due to their political legacies). Workers' parties are less dependent on public financing (mainly because of income from dues and unions), while bourgeois parties (in France and Sweden) and Green parties (in all European countries) receive more

than 80 per cent of their income from state funds. Conservative parties, which in former times depended on large donations, now have problems getting along without public subsidies because their traditional source of funds is questioned publicly. In third-wave democracies (e.g. Spain) up to 90 per cent of the total annual income of parties is transferred from the public purse (van Biezen, 2000: 335).

Tax benefits

In order to encourage (preferably small) contributions to candidates and parties, a tax exemption can be granted. The benefit of paying less tax (especially income tax) is available for different amounts and different donors (individuals and/or corporations), for example, in Australia, Austria, the Netherlands and Portugal. In Italy, donations of € 190 to € 19,000 to parties are tax-deductible for individuals or corporations which may claim a 22 per cent income tax benefit (Melchionda, 1997: 206). In 1994, Japan introduced tax benefits for contributions to a political party or a fundraising or support group (*koenkai*), but not to a candidate. In order to qualify for the tax benefit the contribution has to be made by an individual and the total amount per year has to exceed ¥ 10,000 (= US$89). The taxpayer may choose between a tax deduction (not exceeding 25 per cent of his or her total income) or a tax credit of 30 per cent (Levush, 1997: 142).

Since 1974, individuals and corporations in Canada have been able to claim a tax credit against income tax. The tax credit system (federally and, meanwhile, in all provinces) has stimulated individual giving by the middle class and family businesses, both of which provide large amounts of money in small donations. This public bonus for political donations from private sources has reduced the parties' dependency on corporate donations. Agents of all candidates as well as registered parties may issue (official) tax receipts. In the 1980s, more than two-thirds of the government's total contribution to parties and candidates took the form of tax credits (Stanbury, 1993: 95). The high level of economic development and the general well-being of Canadian citizens were essential prerequisites for the success of this public incentive. The tax credit tends to favour parties organized along mass party lines and those able to reach great numbers of people via direct mail drives (Paltiel, 1989: 72).

Today the tax benefit in Germany, which equally applies to donations by an individual and to dues paid by a party member, is limited to individual contributions. The maximum contribution eligible for tax benefits is fixed at about €3000. For half of the maximum, each individual taxpayer may claim a 50 per cent tax credit; the other half can be deducted from taxable income. No tax benefits are available for corporate donations. Large donations have been almost completely replaced by public subsidies.

Many countries do not provide tax benefits for private donors – Sweden, Spain, Israel, Switzerland and the UK among them. In Switzerland only 9 of the 23 cantons, but not the federation, offer a tax deduction to political donors (Drysch, 1998: 83). The UK has distanced itself from tax relief because this form of state aid to political parties is considered to be too expensive.

Indirect subsidies

Voter registration is taken care of by the state in European countries. Local governments pay for election officers, polling station facilities and delivery of election materials. In Israel, the state is responsible for the transportation of voters to and from distant polling booths (Mendilow, 1989: 133).

Media access is most important among the indirect subsidies. In countries with state-owned radio and TV stations, airtime traditionally has been provided for policy statements and party advertising. Sometimes private media offer the same service because this is required by law. Free airtime is allocated either according to party strength (number of seats and/or extent of popular vote) or on equal terms. In Israel, a compromise between both methods governs the allocation of broadcasting time (Levush, 1997: 116). In Australia, no party may receive more than half of the total time (Chaples, 1994: 32–5). In Japan, there are free spots on public television and radio as well as free newspaper advertisements. The number of all these advertisements is governed by the number of candidates. The most restrictive conditions apply in Switzerland, where parties are not allowed to present their own advertising material in the electronic media.

In some countries, such as Britain, candidates are entitled to a free mailing to every elector within the constituency or to reduced postage for mass mailings. Spain provides quite large sums of public money for the costs of direct election mailings.

Free use of halls in public buildings (e.g. schools) for rallies or meetings (Britain, Japan, Spain) and reduced rates for office space (Italy) are other options. Free space for posters on billboards may also be provided (Spain, the Netherlands, Israel and Germany).

For Germany, Austria and the Netherlands, public subsidies for party-affiliated foundations have to be mentioned. However, only part of their work is relevant party competition: the training of party workers, candidates and municipal councillors, and political (not necessarily policy) research for the parties.

If one portion of a subsidy to parliamentary groups is earmarked for advertising (as it is in Austria) there is strong indication that party organizations will save for extra spending. Furthermore, incumbent politicians may 'abuse' their offices and assistants, paid for by a flat grant, or specified allowances for free travel, postage, telephone and computer facilities.

RULES ON TRANSPARENCY

Time and again scandals have unleashed demand for more transparency in political funding. The major aim of legal action is to make political money an issue of public policy, in which the public keeps a lasting interest. Although perfect transparency may not be achieved, the desire for proper financial conduct is legitimate in any democracy. Limitations of action will result from principle as well as from practicality.

Disclosure of donors' identity

People have a right to know who are the backers of a party. Nevertheless disclosure of donors' identity is riddled with contradictions. The very idea of the secret ballot suggests that a donor's privacy should be protected. Considerable influence by 'fat cats', however, undermines democratic equality ('one person, one vote'). The practical solution will distinguish between donors (individual, corporation, organization) and look for cut-off points. The legislative task at hand is to find an enduring and reliable separation between contributing money (as a means of political participation) and buying access to decision-makers or a specific decision (as incidents of influence peddling).

While Swedish law still upholds the traditional view that the privacy of each donor has to be respected (Gidlund, 1994: 108), Austria has found the 'half-way' solution of gathering information (for later inspection by the federal audit office in the event of a scandal) but not disclosing any donor's identity to the public (Sickinger, 1997: 134). Most democracies now have disclosure rules that separate individual from corporate donors and define a threshold for amounts that have to be disclosed. In this respect Germany, Britain and the Netherlands are at the high end (between US$5000–10,000), while the USA, Canada, France and Japan represent the low end (with disclosure thresholds ranging between US$ 100 and US$ 400). In Australia, the threshold for disclosure is A$1500. In Portugal, donations by individuals which exceed 10 times the monthly minimum wage have to be disclosed.

Furthermore, any disclosure regulation has to identify the legal procedure, a person or institution who is responsible and the kind of information which has to be disclosed. The latter can be very different. Alongside the amount donated, name (as in Canada and the UK) and address (as in Australia) can be required. Stricter rules may also stipulate the disclosure of ID number (e.g. in Spain), the employer or occupation of the donor, and the date of the donation (e.g. in France). For a policy to be effective, the information disclosed should be accurate, timely, accessible and comprehensible to potential users.

Some countries have instituted additional provisions. In Britain, donations must be reported quarterly between elections, and within 7 days during a campaign period. In Japan, disclosure also applies to individuals and corporations buying tickets for fundraising events. In Portugal, any donation by a legal entity has to be accompanied by a written confirmation. In Italy, a corporate donation must be approved by the board of directors and (according to statute law, but rarely in practice) has to be disclosed twice – in the donor company's annual report and in the recipient party's balance sheet. Full disclosure always places an administrative burden on the parties, occasionally even without really improving their openness and accountability (Young, 1991: 20).

Reporting of party funds

In nearly all countries, parties and candidates either are required by statute law to give a report or do so on a voluntary basis. Information given in such reports is often rather incomplete. This especially concerns the elements of a party which provide reports and the categories which are to be reported. Reports usually include various sources of party income

and items of expenditure – staff and offices, advertisements in print media, radio and TV, campaign material, direct mailing, and opinion polling. The major problem of reports in many countries is that data for the regional and local party organizations are not included. The reports (most of them have to be submitted annually and additionally after elections) must be presented to a specific branch of public administration, parliament or a special agency (see below). Usually the reports have to be published.

Among the Anglo-Saxon countries, Canadian reporting rules are the most rigorous. The chief agents of registered parties have to report each year; after an election the parties as well as the official agent of each candidate must file a return on the election expenses incurred. Recently constituency associations, leadership campaigns and nomination contestants have been added to those who file financial reports. Although Britain, where legislation has concentrated on candidates for more than a century, and Australia have some experience in political finance rules, the reporting regime in both countries is less developed.

Sweden and the Netherlands have a legal tradition of not reporting party funds because their parties are considered to be part of civil society. Both countries, however, provide for some transparency, although financial reports cover the national party organization only and do not follow a common format (Gidlund, 1991: 20; Koole 1990: 50, 62). In other European countries, reporting is stipulated by law, although to different degrees. Party reports in Austria have to prove that public subsidies have been spent in accordance with the law: several *Länder* demand reports, albeit less strict than federal law. Thus the data published by Austrian parties are by no means comprehensive (Sickinger, 1997: 236) and the level of transparency is much less than for their German counterparts.

Annual reports in Germany include income and expenditure, debts and assets of the entire party organization at all levels (local, state and federal). This comprehensive accountability has been in effect since 1984 and is safeguarded by a detailed clause in the constitution (Article 21). The only major problem of previous years has been solved by recent regulation: a separate category for 'assessments' (contributed to party coffers by federal, state and European legislators as well as municipal councillors) has been restored to the reporting schedule.

Regulations in France, Italy, Portugal and Spain look almost perfect as laid down in the statute book. However, each country offers specific loopholes, among them support committees in campaigns, local party branches, and a strict separation between annual and campaign reports. In Japan, parties, candidates and their support groups have to give detailed statements of their income and expenditure. Israeli parties have to include affiliated bodies, such as newspapers, in their reports. Nevertheless the funding situation in these countries is far from transparent. Moreover, enforcement is a serious problem.

RULES ON ENFORCEMENT

Many different authorities and agencies are responsible for monitoring, control and enforcement. Nevertheless, public opinion informed by watchful eyes in the media will be more important. Public agencies cannot have much impact without public interest in their activities.

Monitoring and control

Problems with monitoring and control of party and campaign funding have led to changes in regulation and increased transparency in many countries. As there is no regulation on party funding, no control is required in Switzerland. Despite considerable public funding, Swedish law does not touch upon the autonomy of parties either. Austria and the Netherlands restrict public scrutiny to auditing the spending of public subsidies. For this purpose, both countries rely on the professional expertise of a chartered accountant selected by the recipient party (Koole, 1990: 50; Sickinger, 1997: 132–5).

With the exception of just a few countries, financial reports by parties and candidates are published in an official document (Spain, Portugal, France, Italy, Germany) and/or in newspapers (Austria and Italy). In some countries, the financing of political life is dealt with by different administrative bodies (e.g. in France, Italy, Spain), by just one public authority (as in Austria, Germany, Japan, the Netherlands) or by a special agency (e.g. in Australia, Britain, Canada and the USA). The latter agency is responsible for the auditing of reports and will act on behalf of the general public.

Case studies of several countries show that highly sophisticated rules and over-regulation of the subject do not lead to best practice (Austin and Tjernström, 2003: 141–5). Much depends on the set of instruments available and the political will to use them. In Australia, tougher legislation, combined with efficient operation of an agency (see below), has effectively limited abuse. In Britain, the statutory limits for campaign spending in constituencies were generally accepted, but rarely checked (Pinto-Duschinsky, 1981: 249). Especially in by-elections, limits were often exceeded without anyone complaining.

In France, the very complex and sometimes contradictory nature of legal stipulations leaves transparency of party funds still lacking. In other countries, reporting procedures look perfect at first glance, but there is still room for grave doubts concerning efficiency and impact. In Italy, for example, it was an open secret for many years that expenses reported in published accounts exceeded declared income. Spanish and Portuguese parties have proven reluctant to introduce tight obligations and timely reporting. State auditors have limited authority to go beyond the information which is offered by the parties (van Biezen, 2000: 332; del Castillo, 1994: 100).

In Israel, the state controller found that most parties had laundered money and illegally transferred foreign funds during the 1999 campaign. Before that scandal broke two major loopholes had already been identified: the establishment of non-profit organizations and the raising of large contributions ahead of the nine-months reporting period (Hofnung, 1996: 144). In Japan, national and local election agencies administer the process of reporting and disclosure. However, they are not allowed to verify financial statements. Frequent scandals show that bans are not monitored effectively.

In Germany, the parliamentary administration under supervision of the speaker of the federal parliament has to check parties' financial reports, to publish them and to comment on them in a parliamentary paper. Over the course of decades, reporting has gradually improved to impressive quality. However, time and again some find loopholes in the regulation, generally in its less developed disclosure part. It all started with a massive influx of donations assigned to the name of a party's bagman or termed 'anonymous', and money from corporate sources (laundered to ensure a tax-exempt status). Occasionally corporate donations are split among subsidiaries of big companies (which is perfectly legal, but incurs the wrath of the media). More recently, scandals have involved (clandestine) funds of a party leader, (unreported) surplus funds held in a foreign bank account and donations by a businessman interested in a specific policy decision although they were disclosed properly. A watchful administration and an active public will do more to stop such practices than stricter regulation.

Sanctions and enforcement

Because Sweden has no rules on the statute book, no sanctions are necessary for enforcement. The Netherlands operates disclosure rules but they have no specific sanctions in the event of non-cooperation. Everywhere else fines and imprisonment are rare. Under the legal regime for constituency campaigns in Britain, it is up to a defeated candidate to file a legal case against the winner. The year 1999 saw the first major post-war case against a sitting MP and her election agent (*Crown vs. Jones and Whicher*). Although both were initially found guilty of spending twice the constituency limit, the decision was later reversed on appeal.

If parties in Austria or Germany do not meet reporting requirements, public subsidies will be withheld. When it was revealed that a major party in Germany had not reported considerable assets held in foreign bank accounts by one of its state branches, the speaker of the federal parliament refused to grant the full amount of the public subsidy to the federal party. In addition, a severe cash penalty was imposed for not disclosing the identity of various donors who had contributed to the former party leader's secret fund. In passing, it should be noted that a scandal similar to the one which struck Germany in early 2000 could not have occurred in the Netherlands, Sweden, Canada, Britain, Austria or Switzerland – simply because no legislation of an equally demanding character was in place in these countries at the time.

In Italy, infringement of the law seems to be generally accepted by candidates, parties and donors as well as in wider sections of civil society. Thus the practical value of various sanctions (fines, prison sentences of up to 4 years, or suspension of subsidy allocations) is reduced. In the event of a suspected violation of the law in France, the attorney general can take up the matter, but administrative and penal sanctions are very modest. If irregularities with candidates' campaign reports occur, an electoral judge can apply electoral sanctions (e.g. declare a candidate ineligible).

The prerogatives of Spanish authorities are even more restricted. Election officials may report breaches of the law to the public prosecutor, but they cannot impose any sanction

(van Biezen and Nassmacher, 2001: 151). The audit office may recommend that the public subsidies for a party not complying with the rules be reduced. Authority to impose sanctions ultimately rests with the Spanish parliament. Sometimes parties actually prefer to pay a relatively small fine, rather than to comply with all legal provisions. In Portugal, in 1996 three of the four parliamentary parties were fined a total of US$10,000 for infringements of the law.

In Israel, the Knesset Finance Committee frequently has retroactively increased the financing unit, that is, the amount of the public subsidy as well as the spending limit. If inspection by the state controller reveals any suspicion of a criminal act, he must refer the matter to the attorney general. Traditionally enforcement of rules has been less strict than the letter of the law prescribes. If accounting rules or deadlines for reporting and disclosure are violated in Japan, the person responsible can be fined or imprisoned. Implementation, however, has been rather lenient: up to 1992 no MP had been prosecuted (Blechinger, 1998: 240, 342–3). Since 1994 the number of cases in which politicians have been sentenced for violation of the political funds control law has increased.

Experience in Italy, Israel and elsewhere, not least the USA, has shown that detailed regulation sometimes achieves the opposite of what was intended either because it opens up the search for legal loopholes or because political actors change the rules to suit their purposes. If rules are applicable, much depends on their enforcement (Austin and Tjernström, 2003: 145–53).

Enforcement agencies

Although Paltiel (1976: 108) considered an independent agency in charge of enforcing party financing rules as a necessary element of any reform legislation, such bodies operate in no more than five democracies: Australia, Britain, Canada, France and the USA. (For the US Federal Election Commission see Chapter 39 in this Handbook.) In Canada, the chief electoral officer is charged with additional duties: to look into alleged violations of funding rules and to impose sanctions if necessary. As the Canada Elections Act can only be enforced through the criminal courts, most offences are resolved with punitive measures. Outright violations of the law are rare due to financial regulations that work effectively for candidates and parties.

The Australian Election Commission (AEC) is composed of a (former) federal judge as chair, the Electoral Commissioner as chief executive and another part-time, non-judicial member, hitherto the Australian Statistician. The AEC is empowered to probe into party accounts. For continuous monitoring of political funds, it has developed a three-year audit cycle to cover all state branches of the registered parties. Personnel resources constitute a major limitation.

French presidential elections fall under the jurisdiction of the Conseil Constitutionnel, which has only limited powers to apply sanctions. A special authority, the CCFP, is comprised of nine members, appointed for 5 years, and has 30–40 staff. It approves, rejects or changes the reports which candidates submit regarding their campaign spending, as well as the annual reports by political parties (Doublet, 1997: 43–6). Nevertheless, the powers of the CCFP are rather limited.

Recently in Britain, an independent Electoral Commission of five commissioners has been installed. It oversees compliance with new requirements (especially monitoring of donations, their disclosure and submission of proper party accounts). The commission may recommend to the Director of Public Prosecutions that he ask a court to apply criminal sanctions (fines, imprisonment) against those responsible within the parties.

After reform legislation, political parties in most Western democracies are officially recognized, their nationwide campaigns under purview of a law, their financial operations subject to statutory transparency. One can probably say that 'compulsory reporting and disclosure of … income and cost had a sanitising effect' on parties and elections (Paltiel, 1989: 73).

REFERENCES

Amr, D. and Lisowski, R. (2001) 'Political finance in old dominions: Australia and Canada', in K.H. Nassmacher (ed.), Foundations of Democracy. Approaches to Comparative Political Finance. Baden-Baden: Nomos Verlag, pp. 53–72.

Austin, R. and Tjernström, M. (eds) (2003) Funding of Political Parties and Election Campaigns. Stockholm: International IDEA.

Blechinger, V. (1998) Politische Korruption in Japan. Ursachen, Hintergründe und Reformversuche. Hamburg: Institut für Asienkunde.

Chaples, E.A. (1994) 'Developments in Australian election finance', in H.E. Alexander and R. Shiratori (eds), Comparative Political Finance Among the Democracies. Boulder, CO: Westview Press, pp. 29–40.

del Castillo, P. (1994) 'Problems in Spanish party financing', in H.E. Alexander and R. Shiratori (eds), Comparative Political Finance Among the Democracies. Boulder, CO: Westview Press, pp. 97–104.

Doublet, Y.M. (1997) L'Argent et la politique en France. Paris: Economica.

Drysch, T. (1998) Parteienfinanzierung. Österreich, Schweiz, Bundesrepublik Deutschland. Opladen: Leske + Budrich.

Gidlund, G.M. (1991) 'Public investments in Swedish democracy', in M. Wiberg (ed.) The Public Purse and Political Parties. Public Financing of Political Parties in Nordic Countries. Jyväskylä, Finland: Gummerus Printing, pp. 13–54.

Gidlund, G.M. (1994) 'Regulation of party finance in Sweden', in H.E. Alexander and R. Shiratori (eds), Comparative Political Finance Among the Democracies. Boulder, CO: Westview Press, pp. 105–114.

Gidlund, G. and Koole, R.A. (2001) 'Political finance in the north of Europe: The Netherlands and Sweden', in K.H. Nassmacher (ed.), Foundations for Democracy. Approaches to Comparative Political Finance. Baden-Baden: Nomos Verlag, pp. 112–130.

Gunlicks, A.B. (1995) 'The new German party finance law', German Politics, 4(1): 101–121.

Hofnung, M. (1996) 'The public purse and the private campaign: political finance in Israel', Journal of Law and Society, 23(1): 132–148.

Koole, R.A. (1990) 'Political parties going Dutch: party finance in the Netherlands', Acta Politica, 25(1) 1: 37–62.

Koole, R.A. (1994) 'Dutch political parties: money and the message', in H.E. Alexander and R. Shiratori (eds), Comparative Political Finance Among the Democracies. Boulder, CO: Westview Press, pp. 115–132.

Koole, R.A. (2001) 'Political finance in Western Europe: Britain and France', in K.H. Nassmacher (ed.), Foundations of Democracy. Approaches to Comparative Political Finance. Baden-Baden: Nomos Verlag, pp. 73–91.

Levush, R. (ed.) (1997) Campaign Financing of National Elections in Foreign Countries. Washington, DC: Law Library of Congress.

Melchionda, E. (1997) Il finanziamento della politica. Rome: Riuniti.

Mendilow, J. (1989) 'Party financing in Israel: experience and experimentation, 1968–85', in H.E. Alexander (ed.), Comparative Political Finance in the 1980s. Cambridge: Cambridge University Press, pp. 124–152.

Mendilow, J. (1992) 'Public party funding and party transformation in multi-party systems', Comparative Political Studies, 25(1): 90–117.

Mendilow, J. (1996) 'Public party funding and the schemes of mice and men: the 1992 elections in Israel', Party Politics, 2(3): 329–354.

Paltiel, K.Z. (1976) Party, Candidate and Election Finance. A Background Report. Royal Commission on Corporate Concentration, Study No. 22. Ottawa: Queens Printer.

Paltiel, K.Z. (1989) 'Canadian election expense legislation 1963–1985: a critical appraisal or was the effort worth it?' in H.E. Alexander (ed.), *Comparative Political Finance in the 1980s*. Cambridge: Cambridge University Press, pp. 51–75.

Pinto-Duschinsky, M. (1981) *British Political Finance, 1830–1980*. Washington, DC: American Enterprise Institute.

Pinto-Duschinsky, M. (2002) 'Handbook on financing of parties and election campaigns', in International Conference *Political Finance: Regulation and Practice*. Kiev, Ukraine: Foundation Europe XXI (www.europexxi.kiev.ua), pp. 48–63.

Sickinger, H. (1997) *Politikfinanzierung in Österreich. Ein Handbuch*. Thaur, Austria: Druckhaus Thaur.

Stanbury, W.T. (1993) 'Financing federal politics in Canada in an era of reform', in A.B. Gunlicks (ed.), *Campaign and Party Finance in North America and Western Europe*. Boulder, CO: Westview Press, pp. 68–120.

van Biezen, I. (2000) 'Party financing in new democracies. Portugal and Spain', *Party Politics*, 6(3): 329–342.

van Biezen, I. and Nassmacher, K.H. (2001) 'Political finance in southern Europe: Italy, Portugal, Spain', in K.H. Nassmacher (ed.), *Foundations of Democracy. Approaches to Comparative Political Finance*. Baden-Baden: Nomos Verlag, pp. 131–154.

Young, Lisa (1991) 'Toward transparency: an evaluation of disclosure arrangements in Canadian political finance', in L.F. Seidle (ed.), *Comparative Issues in Party and Election Finance*. Toronto: Dundurn Press, pp. 3–44.

39

LEGAL REGULATION AND PROTECTION OF AMERICAN PARTIES

Daniel H. Lowenstein

Tocqueville famously observed that in America, most political questions of the moment become the subject of litigation sooner or later (2000: 257). In the case of questions relating to political parties, it was later. Indeed, until the final decades of the nineteenth century, American parties had little to do with any sort of law. When legal regulation finally came, it was imposed by state legislatures. It was not until well into the twentieth century that the courts entered the fray independently of legislatures. When they did, it was initially to add new legal restraints on parties, primarily as part of the effort to extend voting rights to African-Americans in southern states. Since the 1970s, the courts have more frequently employed the Constitution to protect the parties against regulation imposed by legislatures.

This chapter briefly describes the regulation of parties by legislatures and later by the courts and then describes and analyzes in greater detail the more recent constitutional protection of parties against legislative control, especially in connection with the nomination of candidates. Attention is given to the efforts of minor parties and independent candidates to obtain judicial protection. Finally, some other areas of law affecting parties are briefly canvassed.

REGULATION

National political parties at first functioned as caucuses formed by leaders in Congress and later became mass organizations that served not only the goals of ambitious politicians but also mobilized political efforts on the great dividing controversies – especially over the scope of the federal government's powers and functions and over slavery (Aldrich, 1995; Silbey, 2002). By and large, the formation and operation of the parties occurred with neither protection nor regulation by the law. In the period beginning in the 1880s and continuing for about three decades, state legislatures imposed numerous far-reaching regulations on parties. One of the first and most important was the adoption of the secret or 'Australian' ballot.[1] Although this change did not operate directly on the parties, it affected them greatly because it entailed a state-provided ballot, thus ending the usual practice of casting ballots provided to voters by parties. Other important legislation included regulation of party membership and governance and the requirement that parties nominate candidates in direct primary elections. As a corollary to the adoption of the state-provided ballot and the direct primary, legislatures determined other important questions such as the requirements for candidates and parties to appear on the ballot.

State courts almost invariably upheld these and other regulations against claims that they violated state constitutional guarantees of free elections and freedom of speech and association. The state courts regarded the new laws as intended to protect the rights of voters, in part because judges shared with Mugwumps and Progressives the view that party leaders and elected officials were often corrupt. Because of the parties' central role in elections, the courts were willing to regard them as quasi-state agencies subject to legal control (Winkler, 2000).

The parties' relation to the state gained new importance in the mid-twentieth century when African-Americans challenged their exclusion from Democratic Party primaries in the South. The Fifteenth Amendment prohibits denial of the vote on racial grounds and the Fourteenth Amendment guarantees equal protection of the laws. When the Supreme Court enforces these and other constitutional rights it invokes the 'state action' doctrine, which assumes that a given action is attributable either to the state or to a private person. When the state acts, it is subject to the Fourteenth and Fifteenth Amendments and other constitutional provisions guaranteeing individual rights. When private persons act, they are protected by the constitutional restraints on the government.

The white primary cases were a series of decisions by the Supreme Court prompted by persistent efforts of the Texas legislature and the Texas Democratic Party to use the state action doctrine to shield their exclusion of blacks from primaries. In the decisive case of *Smith v. Allright*, 321 US 649 (1944), the Court decided that the primary and general elections were 'fused ... into a single instrumentality'. Texas's detailed regulation of and involvement in the primaries turned the nomination process into a state function, despite its being conducted by the ostensibly private Democratic Party. *Smith v. Allright* did not itself end the disfranchisement of blacks in the South – it took the Voting Rights Act of 1965 to accomplish that – but it helped (Lawson, 1999). The white primary cases are generally regarded as one of the bright spots in the history of the Supreme Court.

However, in the 1970s, when parties sought and the courts intimated they might be ready to offer a measure of protection against state regulation, some scholars began rethinking the Court's treatment of party nominations as state action. Controversy focused on the last and the most difficult of the white primary cases. The case arose in Fort Bend County, Texas. In that county, the Jaybird Democratic Association, a group founded in 1889, held a straw vote every year several months before the official Democratic primary. The Jaybird vote was open to any white voter. The winner of the Jaybird vote had no special official status under state law and had to compete on an equal basis with every other candidate in the primary. In practice, however, losers in the Jaybird primary seldom ran in the primary and the Jaybird victor always won the primary and general elections. In *Terry v. Adams*, 345 US 461 (1953), a majority split between three separate opinions held that the Jaybirds' exclusion of blacks from the straw

vote violated the Fifteenth Amendment. *Terry* continues to trouble and divide scholars (Kester, 1974; Rotunda, 1975; Katz, 2004).

What prompted continued interest in the white primary cases was the obstacle they were thought to pose to extension of constitutional protection to parties. The difficulty is, if the conduct of the party primary is regarded as state action, does that mean the state can determine how the primaries are conducted free of any constitutional protection for the parties whose nominations are at stake?

As we trace the Supreme Court's movement from regulation to protection we shall see that the Court's eminently wise solution to the state action problem has been to ignore it (Persily, 2001b: 758). The first important stirrings in the direction of protection for parties came in a series of controversies in the 1970s over the selection and seating of delegates at national Democratic conventions. *Brown v. O'Brien*, 409 US 1 (1972), went to the Supreme Court on the eve of the 1972 Democratic National Convention. The credentials committee, whose rulings would be subject to review by the convention delegates, had upheld challenges to the California and Illinois delegations. The California challenge was based on the fact that California had conducted a winner-take-all primary. George McGovern, who had won the primary, was assured the nomination for president if he received all the California delegates, whereas the nomination might be up for grabs if the California delegation were divided among the candidates in proportion to their vote percentages. The Illinois delegation, which was controlled by Chicago Mayor Richard Daley, was challenged for underrepresenting women, minorities, and young people.

A federal appellate court overruled the credentials committee by restoring the full McGovern delegation from California, but left standing the rejection of the Daley delegates from Illinois. The Supreme Court undid the appellate court's intervention because of the lack of time for adequate consideration and the availability of the convention as a forum to reconsider the credentials committee's decisions.[2] But the Court also expressed 'grave doubts' about the appellate court's decision to intervene and noted '[h]ighly important questions' concerning justiciability, whether the actions of the credentials committee were state actions, and the involvement of 'vital rights of association'.

Another case involving the Illinois delegate controversy arose later, when an Illinois state judge held the anti-Daley delegates in contempt of court for accepting delegate seats at the convention, in violation of an injunction the judge had issued previously. In *Cousins v. Wigoda*, 419 US 477 (1975), the Supreme Court ruled that the state judge had no power to control the actions of the national convention.

The most interesting of the cases involving the national conventions was *Democratic Party of the United States v. Wisconsin ex rel. La Follette*, 450 US 107 (1981), prompted by the Democratic National Committee's call for the 1980 convention, which required that participation in the selection of delegates be limited to Democrats only. Wisconsin had employed an 'open' primary since 1903, when it became the first state to adopt the direct primary system for nominating candidates (Wekkin, 1984). An open primary is one in which each voter may vote in the primary of whichever party he chooses on election day, without regard to party membership or affiliation.[3] Wisconsin Democrats defied the national party by conducting an open primary in 1980. A Wisconsin state court ordered the national party to seat Wisconsin's delegates at the convention, despite the violation of the national party rules. The Supreme Court reversed the state court's order.

Speaking for the Court, Justice Stewart emphasized that he was not ruling that the national Democrats could prevent Wisconsin from conducting an open primary. Wisconsin had an interest in conducting its elections as it chose and the national Democrats had an interest in how the delegates to their convention were selected. These interests were not incompatible:

> The National Party rules do not forbid Wisconsin to conduct an open primary. But if Wisconsin does open its primary, it cannot require that Wisconsin delegates to the National Party Convention vote there in accordance with the primary results, if to do so would violate Party rules.

At first blush this seems silly and one is inclined to agree with Justice Powell, who made the point in dissent that the purpose of holding a primary is to determine how much support the competing presidential candidates will receive from the state's delegation to the national convention. What good does it do to tell the state that it is perfectly free to run its primary any way it chooses, but that the primary will count only if it is run the way the national party orders? However, subsequent events showed that Stewart was right and Powell wrong. *La Follette* left both the Wisconsin party and the national party with considerable leverage. Despite the Supreme Court's ruling and

the violation of the national party's rules, the Democratic convention seated the Wisconsin delegation. In 1984, the Wisconsin Democrats yielded by selecting delegates at caucuses, but by 1988 the national Democrats had given in, revising the national rules to permit Wisconsin to use an open primary.

The law of *Cousins* and *La Follette* is that although the states may select delegates pretty much as they choose within their own borders, the national party at its convention is free to accept or reject the delegates sent by the state and may choose to replace these delegates with substitutes selected using any method it cares to honor. This *seems* to be a victory for the national party, because it has the last word. But the last word that the national party actually will utter is determined politically. In the political process, the states carry weight. Despite the diminished glory of contemporary conventions, they still receive public attention – attention that a national party will not lightly direct toward an arcane flap over delegate selection (Lowenstein, 1993: 1771–7).

O'Brien, *Cousins*, and *La Follette* each contained suggestions that the Court would protect the parties from undue state regulation, but none did so unequivocally. Because they were disputes between the national party and state law (with the state party lining up on the side of state law in *La Follette*), questions of federalism loomed large in each case. Confusion could result if there were no single arbiter of the rules for seating at the convention and there was no alternative to the convention itself serving as the arbiter (Peltason, 1999: 14). Furthermore, the three cases could also be read as exercises in judicial restraint, as the Court sought to ensure that both state and federal judges played as small a role as possible in party affairs.[4] Because the recognition of parties' rights was equivocal, the need to reconcile the cases with the state action rulings in the white primary cases was abated.

PROTECTION

The watershed case in which the entitlement of parties to the protection of the First Amendment was firmly established was *Tashjian v. Republican Party of Connecticut*, 479 US 208 (1986). Connecticut had a closed primary system and an unusually large number of voters not registered in either party. Republican Senator Lowell Weicker was known as a maverick and figured he could get an extra measure of protection against a primary challenge from a more conservative or 'regular' Republican if independents could vote in the Republican primary. Republican state legislators, however, had no desire to change the system under which they had been elected. The Republicans agreed on a compromise allowing independents to vote in the Republican primary for the top offices on the ticket, but retaining the closed primary for lower offices, including state legislators.

Democrats, who controlled the state legislature, refused to change the existing law, which closed all primaries to everyone but party members. Later the Republicans took control of the legislature and passed a bill embodying their compromise, but a Democratic governor vetoed it. The Republicans then went to court, claiming that the state's refusal to allow them to include independents in a portion of their primary was a denial of the party's freedom of association.[5] In *Tashjian*, the Supreme Court agreed with the Republicans and struck down the closed primary law, not because the closed primary itself was unconstitutional but because it was up to the party, not the state legislature, to decide who could vote in the party's primary.[6]

The Court emphasized that the nomination of candidates is the 'basic function' of a political party. It soon became clear, however, that the party's constitutionally protected right of association extended beyond the nomination process. In *Eu v. San Francisco County Democratic Central Committee*, 489 US 214 (1989), the Court freed parties from laws dictating their governance on a host of matters such as the term of office for party chairs. *Eu* also extended the party's constitutionally protected control over its nominations by preventing California from enforcing a statute that prohibited parties or their official committees from endorsing candidates in primaries.[7] The political significance of the latter ruling is questionable. Party endorsements in primary races have had declining electoral value and may now be worth little (Maisel and Bibby, 2002: 75).

The Supreme Court gave no explanation in *Tashjian* and *Eu* of where parties stood under the state action doctrine or how these decisions could be reconciled with the white primary cases. Perhaps for this reason, commentators tend to assume that the legal and constitutional questions related to parties reduce to the question of the conceptual relation of parties to the state (Peltason, 1999; Persily and Cain, 2000; Maisel and Bibby, 2002).[8] But despite the lack of an articulated rationale from the Supreme Court, there is little or no doubt on

this question at present. Parties are *both* state actors subject to constitutional and statutory limits on their ability to deprive individuals of constitutional rights *and* private actors whose own constitutional rights merit protection.

For a long time, a number of leading constitutional law scholars have contended that the state action doctrine should be regarded as a matter of degree rather than as an either/or proposition. As these scholars would have it, when an action or practice is challenged, the degree of state involvement and the extent to which personal privacy and autonomy are at stake are elements that should be part of the substantive constitutional determination, in contrast to the state action doctrine, which posits an either/or question as a threshold bar to substantive consideration of a constitutional claim (Horowitz, 1957; Van Alstyne and Karst, 1961; Glennon and Nowak, 1976; Tushnet, 1988).[9] The Supreme Court has shown no sign of accepting this view in general but has followed it silently in the case of political parties (Rush, 1993). Occasional cases continue to be brought to stop claimed party infringement of individual rights. For example, in *Morse v. Republican Party of Virginia*, 517 US 186 (1996), a divided Court interpreted the preclearance requirement of Section 5 of the Voting Rights Act to extend to a party's decision to nominate its candidates at a convention (Petterson, 2002). However, current-day litigation occurs far more often because a party seeks protection of its speech and associational rights against legal control. The preponderance of this form of litigation has two causes. Disputes comparable to the white primary cases seldom arise because of the politically motivated tendency of parties toward inclusion rather than exclusion. On the other hand, cases in which parties seek judicial protection are encouraged by the courts' recognition of the parties' unique position as mediators between the government and the electorate and as organizing forces in elections (Lowenstein, 1993; Persily, 2001b).

Currently, a far more difficult and practically significant conceptual issue than state action is the question of just whom the Court is protecting when it upholds the associational rights of parties. Political science has long understood parties to be loose organizations whose major activities are conducted outside their formal structures. The most common classification recognizes three aspects of a party: the party in the electorate, the party organization, and the party in or running for office (Key, 1964; Hershey and Beck, 2003). Even that classification simplifies the complex and loose structure of political parties. As several legal scholars have pointed out, the 'party' asserting a violation of associational rights in litigation is often one element of the party seeking to nullify a political victory achieved by other elements of the same party (Lowenstein, 1993, 1998; Persily, 2001a, 2001b; Garrett, 2002; Kang, 2006). That was not much of a problem in *Tashjian*, in which the Republicans stood united behind the compromise they had reached. Their conflict plainly was with the Democrats. But it was very much a problem in *Eu*, in which the plaintiffs were '[v]arious county central committees of the Democratic and Republican Parties, the state central committee of the Libertarian Party, members of various state and county central committees, and other groups and individuals active in partisan politics in California'.[10] Setting aside the Libertarians, why should this ragtag group of plaintiffs be assumed to speak for the major parties more than the Democratic and Republican legislators who had adopted the laws in question?[11] In *Eu*, dissident Democrats and Republicans invoked the 'party's' associational rights in order to persuade the courts to overturn the wishes of more politically influential elements within the parties.

The problem of who should be recognized as speaking for the party can be particularly acute when someone who plausibly claims to represent the party wishes to prevent a candidate from running in the party's primaries. In such cases, the would-be candidates and any voters who support them have rights – or interests, at least – that must be considered, and the conflict will involve the would-be candidate, conflicting groups within the party, and, often, state laws. The most important cases to date have involved efforts to exclude David Duke from the Republican presidential primary in Florida and Georgia in 1992 and to exclude Steve Forbes in 1996 and John McCain in 2000 from the Republican presidential primary ballot in New York.

Georgia's statutes ordered the Secretary of State to create a preliminary list of persons recognized by the news media throughout the country as presidential candidates. A committee composed of the party leaders in the two houses of the legislature and the state party leader was authorized to remove candidates from this list. The Secretary of State included Duke on the list and, as you probably have guessed, the three-member Republican committee removed him. A federal appellate court went back and forth but in the end upheld the removal of Duke from the ballot.[12]

In New York, a statutory scheme made it difficult for even a strong candidate to satisfy the signature requirements to qualify for the presidential primary ballot in all parts of the state, especially a candidate without the support of the state party organization. The courts generally ruled favorably to Forbes and McCain.

Nathaniel Persily (2001a: 2212–13), at the conclusion of a thorough study of these cases, suggests that for party leaders to control access to the primary ballot they should be required 'to develop [their] criteria well before the primary campaign begins'. His suggestion would have worked well in New York, where the legislature had enacted *ad hoc* rules shortly before the primary campaign, when the lineup of candidates was known. However, his proposal would not work well for parties confronted with would-be candidates like David Duke. It was reasonable for Republican leaders to decide Duke's candidacy would be detrimental to their party, on the basis not of objective criteria but of a judgment that Duke's background would associate the party with ideas repugnant to the overwhelming majority of its adherents. An improvement on Persily's proposal would be to permit the party to bar candidacies *either* on the basis of objective criteria adopted well in advance as he suggests, *or* on the basis of openly discretionary judgments. It is unlikely that responsible Republicans would have openly ruled that Forbes or McCain should have been excluded from the ballot. If they had done so, they would have faced severe criticism. Instead, they attempted to avoid an open discretionary judgment by hiding behind onerous and discriminatory petition requirements.

None of the controversies involving candidate access to the primary ballot have reached the Supreme Court. The next case in the *Tashjian–Eu* line to do so was *California Democratic Party v. Jones*, 530 US 567 (2000), which like Tashjian involved party control over who could vote in primaries. *Jones* arose when a group of ideologically moderate Republicans circulated initiative petitions to switch California from closed to 'blanket' primaries. Blanket primaries are even more open than 'open' primaries.[13] In an open primary, a voter can obtain a primary ballot for any party without regard to party membership or affiliation. In a blanket primary, there is only one ballot, listing all the candidates for nomination in all parties. The voter can vote for one candidate for each office, but only the candidates in each party are running against each other for that party's nomination. A voter can vote in the Democratic primary for one office, the Republican primary in a second, the Libertarian primary in a third, and so on. The supporters thought this system would make it easier for them to win Republican primaries in California.

The initiative, known as Proposition 198, was approved by the voters in 1996 by a 60–40 margin. Both major parties and some minor parties preferred the closed primary and challenged Proposition 198 on the authority of *Tashjian*. *Jones* resembled *Tashjian* in that the political parties who challenged the blanket primary were unified. It is no doubt true, as some scholars have argued, that a majority of registered Democrats and registered Republicans who voted did so in favor of Proposition 198 (Garrett, 2002: 128). However, they were voting as citizens, not as Democrats or Republicans, and the question no doubt framed itself for most of them as giving themselves more options. A Democratic voter, say, would win the opportunity to vote for a Republican rather than a Democrat when the Republican choice seemed more consequential or interesting. It is not at all clear that a majority in either party would vote in a party election simply to open their own primary to non-members, thus diluting their own votes in favor of others who would be unlikely to hold congenial opinions.

What is remarkable about the *Jones* decision is not that the Supreme Court decided in favor of the parties but that it has been a relatively controversial decision. Two members of the Court – Justices Stevens and Ginsburg – dissented, and the four federal judges in the lower courts had ruled for the state. Political scientists, who tend to be friendly to strong parties, have defended the decision (Cain, 2001),[14] but legal scholars have criticized it (Ortiz, 2000; Hasen, 2001; Issacharoff, 2001; Magarian, 2003). The hostility among legal scholars to the result in *Jones* is reflective of a shift in the past decade or so, during which many of them have expressed varying degrees of discomfort with the two-party system. Previously, legal scholars usually ignored parties but when they gave them any attention at all, they tended to take a favorable or at least neutral view of the major parties (Gottlieb, 1982; Geyh, 1983; Fitts, 1988).

What all the commentators have failed to do – and indeed, what the Supreme Court majority barely did – was to consider how clearly *Jones* was controlled by the precedent of *Tashjian*. One scholar (Pildes, 2001: 151) dismissed the question with a vague reference to 'open precedents', perhaps in the postmodern belief that all precedents are 'open'. At least Pildes, unlike most other commentators, referred to the question of precedent. Neither he nor anyone else has attempted to explain why *Tashjian* was not

controlling. The dissenting justices in *Jones* asserted that although *Tashjian* 'extended First Amendment protection to a party's right to invite independents to participate in its primaries', doing so did not suggest that parties had a 'right not to associate' that would nullify a state's effort to open primaries to non-party voters. These justices and, presumably, the scholars who criticize *Jones* read *Tashjian* as expressing a constitutional preference for open primaries over closed. Under that view, a closed primary would require the assent of *both* state law and the party. *Either* state law or the party could impose an open primary. But that view is flatly contradicted by Justice Marshall's opinion for the Court in *Tashjian*. Justice Marshall was as explicit as he could be that the Court was *not* addressing the relative merits of different types of primaries but simply holding that it was for the party and not the state legislature to decide:

> The relative merits of closed and open primaries have been the subject of substantial debate since the beginning of this century, and no consensus has as yet emerged. [The state] invokes a long and distinguished line of political scientists and public officials who have been supporters of the closed primary. But our role is not to decide whether the state legislature was acting wisely in enacting the closed primary system in 1955, or whether the Republican Party makes a mistake in seeking to depart from the practice of the past 30 years.

Of course, the Court could have overruled *Tashjian* in *Jones*. It did not do so and no commentator has said it should have. It follows that the Court's role in *Jones* was 'not to decide whether [initiative voters were] acting wisely in enacting' the blanket primary, but to order the state to permit the parties to run their primaries as they choose.[15]

Tashjian and *Jones* do not remove all control over candidate selection from the state. For one thing, the majority in *Jones* stated explicitly that although the state cannot generally control who may vote in primaries, it can require that party nominations be by primaries rather than by conventions or other methods.[16] The Court left open whether a party on its own could open its primary to members of other parties. It will be recalled that in *Tashjian*, the Republican plaintiffs wanted to conduct what is known as a 'semi-closed' primary, in which independent voters but not those affiliated with other parties might participate. If the Republicans had proposed to conduct a fully open primary, they would have affected the association between the Democratic Party and its members. Accordingly, the Court in *Jones* left open whether a party can switch to a fully open primary unilaterally.

On May 23, 2005, as this book was going to press, a divided Supreme Court resolved this question in *Clingman v. Beaver*, 125 S.Ct. 2029, a case that might be read as undermining *Tashjian* and thereby greatly diminishing the parties' constitutional right of association. Oklahoma employs a 'semi-closed' primary, in which independents may, at a party's option, vote in the party's primaries. In *Clingman*, the Court rejected the Libertarian Party's claim that it was constitutionally entitled to allow voters to participate in the Libertarian primaries despite being registered as Republicans or Democrats or as members of other parties. The members of the majority disagreed on how much this restriction imposed on the Libertarians' freedom of association, but all of them agreed that the imposition was insufficiently serious to require 'strict scrutiny', which had been applied in *Tashjian*. If the Court had upheld the Oklahoma system on the ground that the state has an interest in protecting the association between other parties and their members that was not present in *Tashjian*, the conclusion might have been debatable, but it would not have cast doubt on *Tashjian* itself. By ruling that the strict standard of review used in *Tashjian* is not applicable, the decision may have far-reaching implications. The majority distinguished *Tashjian* on the ground that in Connecticut but not in Oklahoma, voters had to register as a member of the party in order to vote in its primary. That is true, but some will see it as of little significance when, in both cases, the main point is that the state is preventing a willing party from allowing willing voters to participate in its nominating process. It remains to be seen whether *Clingman* becomes a step toward the overruling of *Tashjian* and, presumably, *Jones*.

Even if *Tashjian* and *Jones* stand, a state can structure its elections as Louisiana has done, without any party nominations at all. Louisiana holds a two-stage election. In the first stage, all candidates of all parties run against each other. If any candidate gets a majority of votes he is elected. If no candidate wins a majority, the two with the most votes run against each other in the second stage. Typically, they would consist of one Republican and one Democrat, but in a strong one-party area they might be two Republicans or two Democrats. Although candidates are identified as members of a party, they appear on the second-stage ballot not as party nominees but by virtue of their finishing among the top two in the

first stage. The state is not unconstitutionally interfering in a party's nomination process because there are no party nominations. Few state legislatures are likely to be attracted by the Louisiana system and California voters rejected a variant when it was proposed as an initiative in 2004, though a similar measure was approved in Washington.[17] Persily (2001b: 811–15) argues that the state's option to adopt the Louisiana system is a sufficient political check in the unlikely event that either of the major parties should incline to closing its primaries to an excessive degree.

MINOR PARTIES

Most scholars believe that structural features of American government have been responsible for the two-party system that has characterized our politics for most of our history. The most often mentioned of these features is the single-member district system of electing legislators. The inability of a party that wins less than a plurality in a given district to get any representation is such a well-known deterrent to support of third parties that political science has given it a name, Duverger's law (Duverger, 1959: 216–28; Riker, 1982). Duverger's law can explain why there tend to be two major parties in any given area, but it does not explain why a country as large and geographically diverse as the United States does not have regional parties as has sometimes been the case, for example, in Canada. Elmer Schattschneider (1942: 81–3) argued that the electoral college was the most likely cause for our two-party system being national. However, even these two features do not explain why the same two parties have predominated for the last century-and-a-half, after an initial period in which the identity of the two major parties changed every generation or so. The most likely explanation is that the introduction of direct primaries ensured that the major parties would remain flexible and responsive to changing public needs and viewpoints (Lowenstein and Hasen, 2004: 535–6). Voters usually gravitate to third parties only when the major parties get seriously out of touch with them (Rosenstone *et al.*, 1996: 162). Primaries make it unlikely that such situations will persist.

These features of the American system may have prevented third parties from succeeding, but they have not prevented them from trying. Minor parties do not have the representation in the legislature that would permit them to ensure that the state's laws meet their needs. It is therefore not surprising that they have resorted more often than the major parties to the courts for relief. The most common occasion for such litigation is a third party's (or independent candidate's) desire for a place on the ballot. As we have seen, the adoption of the secret ballot in the late nineteenth century made it necessary for the first time for the state to provide a ballot. It followed that the state had to decide which parties and candidates would be listed on the ballot.

The state of Ohio can be credited with assuring third parties and independent candidates seeking ballot access a degree of constitutional protection. Ohio's rules for third parties to reach the ballot in presidential elections were so restrictive that in 1968 George Wallace, running under the banner of the American Independent Party, was unable to satisfy them. The Ohio requirements for independent presidential candidates were beyond the reach of John Anderson in 1980. The Supreme Court required Ohio to let Wallace and the American Independents on the ballot in *Williams v. Rhodes*, 393 US 23 (1968), and did the same for Anderson in *Anderson v. Celebrezze*, 460 US 780 (1983). These cases are founded not on the right of the party or the candidate, but on the voting rights of their supporters.

Despite the Wallace and Anderson legal victories in Ohio, the Court has permitted states to set up barriers that will exclude parties and candidates unable to show at least a reasonably impressive degree of support. Thus, in *Jenness v. Fortson*, 403 US 431 (1971), the Court upheld Georgia requirements that had kept all or nearly all third-party and independent candidates off the ballot since their adoption nearly three decades earlier. *Jenness* and similar decisions have been sharply criticized by legal scholars, who tend to favor greater liberality toward third parties (Smith, 1991; Winger, 1996, 2002). The ballot access cases have also been criticized for failing to set a clear standard for determining what requirements are valid, primarily because the 'standard of review' that the Court uses has been shifting and sometimes unclear (Tribe, 1988; Latz, 1991). However, if we consider the results of the cases that have reached the Supreme Court rather than the Court's verbal formulae, the standards do not seem especially unclear. With the assistance of the Court, Wallace and Anderson were able to appear on every state's ballot in 1968 and 1980. In 1992 and 1996, Ross Perot was able to accomplish the same without the necessity for Supreme Court intervention.[18]

States cannot enforce requirements whose effect is to bar from the ballot candidates or parties with enough support to have a substantial impact on the election. Others can be excluded.

Although the latter result is not to the liking of some scholars, there is good reason for it. One point commonly made against third-party and independent candidates is that with only slight support they may prevent a major party winner from obtaining a majority or swing the result from one major party to the other by taking more votes from one party than from the other.[19] The major parties have been known, by various covert means, to encourage and even subsidize minor candidacies for just this reason. Another reason for not allowing ballot access to candidates without impressive support is that their presence clutters the ballot and makes voting more difficult. This is a lesson that ought to have been learned from Florida in 2000. Ten presidential candidates (and their running mates) appeared on the ballot, although only five were known to more than a handful of voters.[20] If Florida law had barred the remaining five candidates from the ballot, there would have been neither a butterfly ballot in Palm Beach County nor two pages of presidential candidates in Duval County.

One important reason for the difference between the Court and its critics among the scholars is that the Court permits states to regard elections as occasions for selecting the officials who will operate the government rather than as occasions for public expression. What underlies much of the scholarship seeking greater constitutional protection for minor parties is the belief that voting should be protected not only as an instrumental but as an expressive activity (Karst, 1975: 52–65; Winkler, 1993). In *Burdick v. Takushi*, 504 US 428 (1992), the Court said that '[a]ttributing to elections a more generalized expressive function would undermine the ability of States to operate elections fairly and efficiently'.[21]

Given the Court's outlook, it is not surprising that in cases in which third parties or independent candidates have sought benefits other than ballot access, the results, though mixed, have tended to go against them (Lowenstein and Hasen, 2004: 548–79). Thus, in *Buckley v. Valeo*, 424 US 1, 85–109 (1976), the Court upheld public financing of presidential election campaigns that pose formidable obstacles to third-party eligibility,[22] though in *Brown v. Socialist Workers '74 Campaign Committee*, 459 US 87 (1982), the Court also required that third parties be excused from campaign disclosure requirements if they can show that disclosure may expose them to official or private retribution. *Arkansas Educational Television Commission v. Forbes*, 523 US 666 (1998), held that an independent candidate has no constitutional right to participate in a debate between the major party candidates organized and broadcast by a public television station.[23] And in the most widely despised case involving parties in recent years, *Timmons v. Twin Cities Area New Party*, 520 US 351 (1997), the Court upheld an anti-fusion law.

Fusion candidacies arise when an individual appears on the ballot as the candidate of two or more parties. Only a few states allow fusion candidacies and only in New York are they a significant part of the electoral system (Epstein, 1999: 65). In *Timmons* the New Party sought to nominate a state legislative candidate who was already the candidate of the Democratic-Farmer-Labor (DFL) party.[24] The Supreme Court, in a 6–3 decision, upheld the anti-fusion law that prevented the joint nomination.

The scholarly opposition to *Timmons* was led by Richard Hasen (1997), who read the case as permitting infringement of First Amendment rights in furtherance of the state's interest in preserving the two-party system. He based his interpretation primarily on the Court's statement that 'the Constitution permits the Minnesota Legislature to decide that political stability is best served through a healthy two-party system'.[25] Other scholars accepted Hasen's interpretation (Peltason, 1999: 20; Amy, 2002; Thompson, 2002: 70–80).

Hasen's reading is a possible one, but it is not the most plausible reading and certainly not the friendliest. He emphasizes the term 'two-party' in the final phrase of the quoted passage. The phrase takes on a different meaning if instead we emphasize 'healthy'. So read, the Court's statement does not suggest that *preservation* of the two-party system is a state interest that can justify constitutional infringements, but rather that *given* the existence of a two-party system, the state has an interest in keeping it healthy. We have seen that certain features of the American system create incentives and disincentives likely to result in a two-party system. Proponents of proportional systems may be unhappy about that consequence, but single-member districts, the electoral college and primaries do not restrict speech or associational rights of parties, candidates, or anyone else. The state cannot restrict such rights to promote the two-party system, but neither does the First Amendment require the state to adopt an institutional structure that will encourage multiple parties. Given the two-party system that the state has the right to promote and that does in fact exist, *Timmons* says, unremarkably, that the state *does* have an interest in keeping that system healthy.[26]

Opinions will often differ over what makes a healthy system, but the case against the fusion system is strong. Although scholars have criticized anti-fusion laws as 'entrenching' the two major parties (Issacharoff and Pildes, 1998: 683–7), the history of fusion in New York casts severe doubt on that claim. Fusion has been much less a device for minor parties to compete against the major parties than a means of putting pressure on candidates. Indeed, the leading student of the subject concludes that the minor parties in New York are better described as pressure groups than as parties (Scarrow, 1983: 63–4). Those parties 'nominate' major party candidates much more often than they field their own candidates (1983: 56) and when they do run candidates of their own it is usually punishment of the major-party candidate for not being sufficiently compliant. Thus, the proposal for the creation of the Conservative Party in 1962 stated that its function would be to 'exercise leverage' on the major parties (1983: 61). The purpose of the Right to Life Party, according to a spokesman, is 'not to have our own people elected to office. We leave politics to the politicians. We would prefer to endorse rather than run our own people' (1981: 61). Howard Scarrow reports that although the Liberal Party 'began as a group of dedicated idealists, ... few today doubt that its dedication to principle has given way to obsession with patronage. Similarly for the Conservatives' (1983: 73).

There is nothing obviously wrong about providing minor parties with a mechanism for putting pressure on major-party candidates; nor does the fact that fusion can be and is abused differentiate it from most other features of the political system. But if there is nothing obviously wrong about fusion, neither is there anything obviously right about it. Though minor parties find it convenient to be given the tactical tool of fusion, that does not make it a First Amendment requirement. It may seem that a restriction on a party's ability to nominate the candidate of its choice strikes at the heart of the party's associational rights, as *Tashjian* and *Jones* demonstrate (Fitts, 2002: 103–104). But as the Right to Life spokesman quoted by Scarrow accurately stated, what minor parties do in a fusion system is more akin to endorsing than to nominating. Under parliamentary procedures familiar to all, a candidate is nominated once, though he may be seconded or endorsed many times. The imposition on the New Party in *Timmons* is not a distortion of its ability to put a candidate before the public, but rather prevention of the party's desire to use the ballot for expressive purposes – a desire that the Court had said in *Burdick* the state did not have to accommodate.

OTHER ISSUES AFFECTING PARTIES

We have canvassed the central constitutional issues defining the legal status of political parties. There are other issues that affect the parties in significant ways. Space permits a bare mention of three of these: campaign finance, redistricting, and patronage.

We have already seen that in *Buckley v. Valeo* the Supreme Court upheld a system of public financing that ordinarily excludes minor parties. Two cases affecting the major parties were decided in the past decade. Both arose out of some expenditures made by the Colorado Republican Party to purchase advertising critical of the Democratic candidate for the United States Senate. Because the expenditures occurred before the Republican candidate had been nominated in the primary, the party could plausibly claim that it had acted independently of the candidate.

In *Colorado Republican Federal Campaign Committee v. Federal Election Commission (Colorado Republican I)*, 518 US 604 (1996), the Court held that the party had the same right as other entities – a right established in *Buckley v. Valeo* – to spend independently of candidates without limitation. In *Federal Election Commission v. Colorado Republican Federal Campaign Committee*, 533 US 431 (2001), the Court upheld limits on party spending that is coordinated with a candidate. Two justices, Ginsburg and Stevens, would have upheld limits in both situations. Four justices, Kennedy, Rehnquist, Scalia, and Thomas, would have struck them down in both situations. The position of the centrist justices, Breyer, O'Connor, and Souter, was entirely consistent with the Court's campaign finance doctrine if it is assumed that for purposes of campaign finance regulation parties should be treated the same as other private entities. But in practice, the decisions in combination are perverse. Either of the 'extreme' positions would have been better. The two decisions encourage a party to separate its campaigning from its candidates, an incentive that serves no discernible purpose.[27]

The Supreme Court's most recent campaign finance decision, *McConnell v. Federal Election Commission*, 540 US 93 (2003), upheld almost all the provisions of the Bipartisan Campaign Reform Act. These included harsh limitations on the financial activities of both national and state parties (Symposium, 2004).

Of all political activity in the United States, perhaps none is as intensely partisan as redistricting. The Supreme Court has decided a great number of districting cases since it determined in *Baker v. Carr*, 369 US 186 (1962), that such controversies are justiciable. Only two were direct challenges to districting plans on the ground that they were unconstitutional partisan gerrymanders. In the first, *Davis v. Bandemer*, 478 US 109 (1986), the Court held that partisan gerrymandering claims were justiciable but rejected the particular challenge to the plan for the Indiana legislature. The lead opinion, by Justice White, was obscure, but seemed to indicate that a major party could rarely, if ever, win a partisan gerrymandering claim against its rival (Lowenstein, 1990). Recently, in *Vieth v. Jubelirer*, 541 US 267 (2004), the Supreme Court unsettled the question thoroughly. Four justices, unable to make sense of *Davis v. Bandemer*, asserted there are no judicially manageable standards for deciding partisan gerrymandering claims and therefore would have declared such claims non-justiciable. Four dissenting judges believed manageable standards existed, but were unable to agree on what the standard should be, putting forth three competing proposals. The deciding vote was cast by Justice Kennedy who, in an unusually irresponsible move even for a member of the Supreme Court, said there might be a manageable standard but he did not know of any. Therefore he dismissed the case before the Court, but refused to say that partisan gerrymandering claims are non-justiciable. This left lower court judges who must hear future partisan gerrymandering claims in a quandary.[28]

The practice of partisan patronage was already in an advanced state of decline when the Supreme Court, in *Elrod v. Burns*, 427 US 347 (1976), declared it a violation of the First Amendment for most government employees to be fired for partisan reasons. The Court applied the same rule to government hiring in *Rutan v. Republican Party of Illinois*, 497 US 62 (1990). More ambitiously, the Court most recently has attempted to bar overly partisan criteria in the award of government contracts, in *Board of County Commissioners, Wabaunsee County v. Umbehr*, 518 US 668 (1996), and *O'Hare Truck Service v. City of Northlake*, 518 US 712 (1996). Whether these latest rulings will have much of an effect is perhaps questionable.[29]

CONCLUSION

For nearly a century, political parties enjoyed minimal contact with the law. When regulation came, it came from the state legislatures and it was far-reaching. The courts did not take much of an affirmative role until well into the twentieth century, when they subjected parties to constitutional restraints, primarily in the cause of extending voting rights to African-Americans in the South. Constitutional regulation is still potentially available, though it is infrequently needed. State legislatures, which of course are constituted by Democrats and Republicans, continue to regulate the parties, though when they regulate the major parties to a large extent they are regulating themselves. Nevertheless, beginning in the 1970s and more clearly in the 1980s, the Supreme Court has extended constitutional protection to the parties. Whether the justices are aware of it or not, in some of the cases they appear to be supporting one side of an intraparty dispute. Minor parties do not constitute state legislatures and therefore are more commonly dissatisfied with the regulations applicable to them. The Supreme Court has assured a place on the ballot for third parties who can demonstrate they are likely to be reasonably competitive. On other issues, minor parties have usually been less successful.

Academics being academics, they tend to be preoccupied with theories. Some believe they can discern a consistent theoretical approach in the Court's decisions on parties and on election issues more generally (Maveety, 1991). Others believe the Court lacks a theory but believe it should find one (Rush, 1993). Some would like to thrust a theory upon the Court (Issacharoff and Pildes, 1998; Pildes, 1999). Curmudgeons find the prospect of a political theory sanctioned and imposed by the judiciary somewhere between preposterous and pernicious (Lowenstein, 2002).

NOTES

1 An Australian election law specialist commented recently that his countrymen are puzzled by the American use of this term, rather as the French are puzzled by French fries and New Yorkers by New York steaks.

2 As it happened, the Convention reached the same conclusions as the federal appellate court. That is, the rejection of the Daley delegates was sustained, but the entire McGovern delegation was seated, thus assuring McGovern the nomination.

Of course, the convention acted for political, not legal, reasons. Then again, many would say that in this and many other election cases, the courts also acted for political, not legal, reasons.

3 Austin Ranney (1975: 167) observed that 'the so-called "closed" primaries are just a hair more closed than the so-called "open" primaries'. But Gary Wekkin (1984: 180–90) argues that the difference between closed and open primaries is important.

4 Another case from the 1970s, *Marchioro v. Chaney*, 442 US 191 (1979), supports this interpretation. There the Court stretched to avoid deciding a state party's claim of associational rights in a challenge to a state statute.

5 There is no explicit guarantee of freedom of association in the Constitution. However, the Supreme Court found such a guarantee implicit in the First Amendment in *NAACP v. Alabama*, 357 US 449 (1958).

6 It is therefore not inconsistent with the letter or spirit of *Tashjian* that after the state enacted legislation allowing parties to open their primaries to non-members in order to comply with the Court's dictate, both major parties eventually adopted a closed primary (Garrett, 2002: 120).

7 California law also prohibits parties and their committees from endorsing candidates in non-partisan elections, which in California include all judicial and local elections. That prohibition is more clearly unconstitutional than the ban struck down in *Eu*. Although the ban on endorsements in primaries is plainly a denial of freedom of speech when applied to the party committees speaking in their own names, it is hard to see why the committees or the state conventions have a constitutional right to endorse in the name of the party itself. The purpose of the primary, after all, is to find out who the party's choice is to be. In a non-partisan election, unless the party committees can endorse in the name of the party, there is no way for the party to speak at all. The question of party endorsements in non-partisan elections went to the Supreme Court in *Renne v. Geary*, 501 US 312 (1991), but the Court disposed of the case on procedural grounds without reaching the merits.

8 One scholar criticizes recent party decisions on the ground that they 'try to take their guidance from' the white primary cases (Pildes, 1999: 1620–1). No one who reads *Tashjian*, *Eu*, and *Jones* (discussed below) is likely to agree with this premise.

9 For a thoughtful opposing view, see Schwarzschild (1988).

10 489 US 219.

11 Unlike *Tashjian*, there was nothing in *Eu* suggesting that either major party was imposing

rules on the other party over its objection. To the contrary, the governance rules for Democrats and Republicans were contained in separate portions of the Elections Code and there was a tradition of comity that permitted either party's legislators to amend its own provisions without interference by the other party.

12 *Duke v. Cleland*, 954 F.2d 1526 (11th Cir. 1992); *Duke v. Cleland*, 5 F.3d 1399 (11th Cir. 1993); *Duke v. Massey*, 87 F.3d 1226 (11th Cir. 1996). In Florida, the committee that excluded Duke consisted of equal numbers of Republicans and Democrats. The court ruled in favor of Duke. That made sense, because a bipartisan panel could hardly speak for the Republican Party, unless there was an understanding that the Republican members of the panel would make the decisions for the Republicans and the Democratic members for the Democrats. The 11th Circuit opinion does not indicate any such practice or understanding, *Duke v. Smith*, 13 F.3d 388 (11th Cir. 1994).

13 Bass (1998) refers to blanket primaries as 'wide open primaries'. Although his locution is more descriptive, I use 'blanket primaries' because it is the term in general use.

14 Empirical studies of the blanket primary by political scientists are contained in Cain and Gerber (2002).

15 479 US 222–3. It is not surprising that the popular press sometimes misunderstood the Court's holding in *Jones* and described it as holding the blanket primary unconstitutional. It is disappointing to see distinguished scholars making the same error (e.g. Pildes, 2001: 148–9; Maisel and Bibby, 2002: 75).

16 For an early exploration of this question, see Gottlieb (1982).

17 In Washington, parties have claimed that the identification of a candidate on the ballot as, say, a 'Republican' or a 'Libertarian' without the party's authorization is a violation of the party's constitutional rights. That issue is currently being litigated.

18 Green Party candidate Ralph Nader appeared on the ballot in all but seven states in 2000.

19 Persily and Cain (2000: 807) favor access for a party that has potential to swing the election result, even when the expected vote for the minor party is minute, and therefore the only reason for its possible decisiveness is the expected extreme closeness of the major-party race. This seems to me precisely the situation in which it is best for the minor party or candidate not to appear on the ballot.

20 These were Bush, Gore, Nader, Buchanan, and the Libertarian candidate.

21 Elizabeth Garrett (2002: 124) criticizes *Timmons*, discussed below, for not understanding the expressive purposes of minor parties. The quoted language from *Burdick* suggests that the Court is guilty of no failure to understand the purposes of minor parties. Rather, it holds that the state has no obligation to divert elections from *their* purpose, which is instrumental. One can agree with the quoted language from *Burdick* without agreeing with its holding that it is constitutional for a state to refuse to allow write-in votes.

22 For criticism, see Nicholson (1977).

23 For criticism, see Raskin (1999). For criticism of the criticism, see Lowenstein (1999).

24 The DFL is the outgrowth of a merger of the Democrats and the Farmer-Labor party and for all practical purposes is the Minnesota branch of the Democratic Party.

25 520 US 367.

26 There is nothing new about this idea. For example, when the Court upheld a 'sore loser' statute that prevented losing candidates in party primaries from running as independents in the general election, *Storer v. Brown*, 415 US 724 (1974), it was allowing a modest infringement on the voting rights of the candidate's supporters in furtherance of healthier two-party competition.

27 For commentary, see Ryden (2002). For thorough coverage of constitutional issues related to campaign finance regulation, see Lowenstein and Hasen (2004, 717–1024).

28 For a more detailed commentary on Vieth, see Berman (2005); Carvin and Fisher (2005); Cox (2004); Gerken (2004); Issacharoff and Karlan (2004); Lowenstein (forthcoming). For suggestions on how to emerge from the quandary created by Vieth, see Gardner (2004) and Hasen (2004). See, generally, Lowenstein and Hasen (2004, 326–60).

29 For commentary, see Bowman (1991, 2002); and Hasen (1993). See, generally, Lowenstein and Hasen (2004: 505–31).

REFERENCES

Aldrich, John (1995) *Why Parties? The Origin and Transformation of Party Politics in America*. Chicago: University of Chicago Press.

Amy, Douglas J. (2002) 'Entrenching the two-party system: The Supreme Court's fusion decision', in David K. Ryden (ed.), *The U.S. Supreme Court and the Electoral Process* (2nd edn). Washington, DC: Georgetown University Press.

Bass, Harold F., Jr. (1998) 'Partisan rules, 1946–1996', in Byron E. Shafer (ed.), *Partisan Approaches to Postwar American Politics*. New York: Chatham House.

Berman, Mitchell N. (2005) 'Managing gerrymandering', *Texas Law Review*, 83: 854.

Bowman, Cynthia Grant (1991) '"We don't want anybody anybody sent": The death of patronage hiring in Chicago', *Northwestern University Law Review*, 86: 57–95.

Bowman, Cynthia Grant (2002) 'The Supreme Court's patronage decisions and the theory and practice of politics', in David K. Ryden (ed.), *The U.S. Supreme Court and the Electoral Process* (2nd edn). Washington, DC: Georgetown University Press.

Cain, Bruce E. (2001) 'Party autonomy and two-party electoral competition', *University of Pennsylvania Law Review*, 149: 793.

Cain, Bruce E. and Gerber, Elisabeth R. (eds) (2002) *Voting at the Political Fault Line: California's Experiment with the Blanket Primary*. Berkeley: University of California Press.

Carvin, Michael A. and Fisher, Louis K. (2005) 'A legislative task: Why four types of redistricting challenges are not, or should not be recognized by courts', *Election Law Journal*, 4: 2.

Cox, Adam B. (2004) 'Partisan gerrymandering and disaggregated redistricting', *Supreme Court Review*, 2004: 409.

Duverger, Maurice (1959) *Political Parties: Their Organization and Activity in the Modern State* (2nd English edn). London: Methuen.

Epstein, Leon D. (1999) 'The American party primary', in Nelson W. Polsby and Raymond E. Wolfinger (eds), *On Parties: Essays Honoring Austin Ranney*. Berkeley: University of California Press.

Fitts, Michael A. (1988) 'The vices of virtue: A political party perspective on civic virtue reforms of the legislative process', *University of Pennsylvania Law Review*, 136: 1567.

Fitts, Michael A. (2002) 'Back to the future: The enduring dilemmas revealed in the Supreme Court's treatment of political parties', in David K. Ryden (ed.), *The U.S. Supreme Court and the Electoral Process* (2nd edn). Washington, DC: Georgetown University Press.

Gardner, James A. (2004) 'A post-*Vieth* strategy for litigating partisan gerrymandering claims', *Election Law Journal*, 3: 643.

Garrett, Elizabeth (2002) 'Is the party over? Courts and the political process', *Supreme Court Review*, 2002: 95.

Gerken, Heather K. (2004) 'Lost in the political thicket: The court, election law and the doctrinal interregnum', *University of Pennsylvania Law Review*, 153: 503.

Geyh, Charles G. (1983) '"It's my party and I'll cry if I want to": State intrusions upon the associational freedoms of parties – *Democratic Party of the United States v. Wisconsin ex rel. La Follette*', *Wisconsin Law Review*, 1983: 211.

Glennon, Robert J., Jr. and Nowak, John E. (1976) 'A functional analysis of the Fourteenth Amendment "state action" requirement', *Supreme Court Review*, 1976: 221.

Gottlieb, Stephen E. (1982) 'Rebuilding the right of association: The right to hold a convention as a test case', *Hofstra Law Review*, 11: 191.

Hasen, Richard L. (1993) 'An enriched economic model of political patronage and campaign contributions: Reformulating Supreme Court jurisprudence', *Cardozo Law Review*, 14: 1311.

Hasen, Richard L. (1997) 'Entrenching the duopoly: Why the Supreme Court should not allow the states to protect the Democrats and Republicans from political competition', *Supreme Court Review*, 1997: 331.

Hasen, Richard L. (2001) 'Do the parties or the people own the electoral process?', *University of Pennsylvania Law Review*, 149: 815.

Hasen, Richard L. (2004) 'Looking for standards (in all the wrong places): Partisan gerrymandering claims after *Vieth*', *Election Law Journal*, 3: 626.

Hershey, Marjorie Randon and Beck, Paul A. (2003) *Party Politics in America* (10th edn). New York: Longman.

Horowitz, Harold W. (1957) 'The misleading search for "state action" under the Fourteenth Amendment', *Southern California Law Review*, 30: 208.

Issacharoff, Samuel (2001) 'Political parties with public purposes: Political parties, associational freedoms, and partisan competition', *Columbia Law Review*, 101: 274.

Issacharoff, Samuel and Karlan, Pamela S. (2004) 'Where to draw the line? Judicial review of partisan gerrymanders', *University of Pennsylvania Law Review*, 153: 541.

Issacharoff, Samuel and Pildes, Richard H. (1998) 'Politics as markets: Partisan lockups of the democratic process', *Stanford Law Review*, 50: 643.

Kang, Michael S. (forthcoming, 2006) 'The hydraulics and politics of party regulation: a supralegal theory of political parties', *Iowa Law Review*, 91.

Karst, Kenneth L. (1975) 'Equality as a central principle in the First Amendment', *University of Chicago Law Review*, 43: 20

Katz, Ellen (2004) 'Resurrecting the white primary', *University of Pennsylvania Law Review*, 153: 325.

Kester, John G. (1974) 'Constitutional restrictions on political parties', *Virginia Law Review*, 60: 735.

Key, V.O., Jr. (1964) *Politics, Parties, and Pressure Groups* (5th edn). New York: Crowell.

Latz, Martin E. (1991) 'The constitutionality of state-passed congressional term limits', *Akron Law Review*, 25: 155.

Lawson, Steven F. (1999) *Black Ballots: Voting Rights in the South*. Lanham, MD: Lexington Books.

Lowenstein, Daniel H. (1990) 'Bandemer's gap: Gerrymandering and equal protection', in Bernard

Grofman (ed.), *Political Gerrymandering and the Courts*. New York: Agathon Press.

Lowenstein, Daniel H. (1993) 'Associational rights of major political parties: A skeptical inquiry', *Texas Law Review*, 71: 1741.

Lowenstein, Daniel H. (1998) 'Political parties and the Constitution', in Mark E. Rush (ed.), *Voting Rights and Redistricting in the United States*. Westport, CT: Greenwood Press.

Lowenstein, Daniel H. (1999) 'Election law miscellany: Enforcement, access to debates, qualification of initiatives', *Texas Law Review*, 77: 2001.

Lowenstein, Daniel H. (2002) 'The Supreme Court has no theory of politics – and be thankful for small favors', in David K. Ryden (ed.), *The U.S. Supreme Court and the Electoral Process* (2nd edn). Washington, DC: Georgetown University Press.

Lowenstein, Daniel H. (forthcoming, 2005) 'Vieth's gap: Has the Supreme Court gone from bad to worse on partisan gerrymandering?', *Cornell Journal of Law and Public Policy*, 14.

Lowenstein, Daniel H. and Hasen, Richard L. (2004) *Election Law* (3rd edn). Durham, NC: Carolina Academic Press.

Magarian, Gregory P. (2003) 'Regulating political parties under a "Public rights" First Amendment', *William & Mary Law Review*, 44: 1939.

Maisel, L. Sandy and Bibby, John F. (2002) 'Election laws, court rulings, party rules and practices: Steps toward and away from a stronger party role', in John C. Green and Paul S. Herrnson, *Responsible Partisanship? The Evolution of American Political Parties Since 1950*. Lawrence: University Press of Kansas.

Maveety, Nancy (1991) *Representation Rights and the Burger Years*. Ann Arbor: University of Michigan Press.

Nicholson, Marlene Arnold (1977) '*Buckley v. Valeo*: The constitutionality of the Federal Election Campaign Act amendments of 1974', *Wisconsin Law Review*, 1977: 323.

Ortiz, Daniel R. (2000) 'Duopoly versus autonomy: How the two-party system harms the major parties', *Columbia Law Review*, 100: 753–74.

Peltason, Jack W. (1999) 'Competing for attention and votes: The role of state parties in setting presidential nomination rules', in Nelson W. Polsby and Raymond E. Wolfinger (eds), *On Parties: Essays Honoring Austin Ranney*. Berkeley: University of California Press.

Persily, Nathaniel (2001a) 'Candidates v. parties: The constitutional constraints on primary ballot access laws', *Georgetown Law Journal*, 89: 2181.

Persily, Nathaniel (2001b) 'Toward a functional defense of political party autonomy', *New York University Law Review*, 76: 750.

Persily, Nathaniel and Cain, Bruce E. (2000) 'The legal status of political parties: A reassessment of competing paradigms', *Columbia Law Review*, 100: 775.

Petterson, Paul R. (2002) 'Partisan autonomy or state regulatory authority? The Court as mediator', in David K. Ryden (ed.), *The U.S. Supreme Court and the Electoral Process* (2nd edn). Washington, DC: Georgetown University Press.

Pildes, Richard H. (1999) 'The theory of political competition', *Virginia Law Review*, 85: 1605.

Pildes, Richard H. (2001) 'Democracy and disorder', in Cass R. Sunstein and Richard A. Epstein (eds), *The Vote: Bush, Gore, and the Supreme Court*. Chicago: University of Chicago Press.

Ranney, Austin (1975) *Curing the Mischiefs of Faction*. Berkeley: University of California Press.

Raskin, Jamin B. (1999) 'The debate gerrymander', *Texas Law Review*, 77: 1943.

Riker, William H. (1982) 'The two-party system and Duverger's law: An essay on the history of political science', *American Political Science Review*, 76: 753.

Rosenstone, Steven J., Behr, Roy L. and Lazarus, Edward H. (1996) *Third Parties in America* (2nd edn). Princeton, NJ: Princeton University Press.

Rotunda, Ronald D. (1975) 'Constitutional and statutory restrictions on political parties in the wake of *Cousins v. Wigoda*', *Texas Law Review*, 53: 935.

Rush, Mark E. (1993) 'Voters' rights and the legal status of American political parties', *Journal of Law & Politics*, 9: 487.

Ryden, David K. (2002) 'To curb parties or to court them? Seeking a constitutional framework for campaign finance reform', in David K. Ryden (ed.), *The U.S. Supreme Court and the Electoral Process* (2nd edn). Washington, D.C.: Georgetown University Press.

Scarrow, Howard A. (1983) *Parties, Elections, and Representation in the State of New York*. New York: New York University Press.

Schattschneider, E.E. (1942) *Party Government*. New York: Holt, Rinehart and Winston.

Schwarzschild, Maimon (1988) 'Value pluralism and the constitution: In defense of the state action doctrine', *Supreme Court Review*, 1988: 129.

Silbey, Joel H. (2002) 'From "essential to the existence of our institutions" to "rapacious enemies of honest and responsible government": The rise and fall of American political parties, 1790–2000', in L. Sandy Maisel (ed.), *The Parties Respond* (4th edn). Boulder: Westview Press.

Smith, Bradley A. (1991) 'Judicial protection of ballot-access rights: Third parties need not apply', *Harvard Journal on Legislation*, 28: 167.

Symposium (2004) '*McConnell v. Federal Election Commission*', *Election Law Journal* 3: 115.

Thompson, Dennis F. (2002) *Just Elections: Creating a Fair Electoral Process in the United States*. Chicago: University of Chicago Press.

Tocqueville, Alexis de (2000) *Democracy in America*, Harvey C. Mansfield and Delba Winthrop (eds). Chicago: University of Chicago Press.

Tribe, Laurence H. (1988) *American Constitutional Law* (2nd edn). Mineola, NY: Foundation Press.

Tushnet, Mark (1988) 'Shelley v. Kraemer and theories of equality', *New York Law School Law Review*, 33: 383.

Van Alstyne, William W. and Karst, Kenneth L. (1961) 'State action', *Stanford Law Review*, 14: 3.

Wekkin, Gary D. (1984) *Democrat versus Democrat: The National Party's Campaign to Close the Wisconsin Primary*. Columbia: University of Missouri Press.

Winger, Richard (1996) 'How ballot access laws affect the U.S. party system', *American Review of Politics*, 16: 321.

Winger, Richard (2002) 'The Supreme Court and the burial of ballot access: A critical review of *Jenness v. Fortson*', *Election Law Journal*, 1: 235.

Winkler, Adam (1993) 'Expressive voting', *New York University Law Review*, 68: 330.

Winkler, Adam (2000) 'Voters' rights and parties' wrongs: Early political party regulation in the state courts, 1886–1915', *Columbia Law Review*, 100: 873.

40

PARTY STATES AND STATE PARTIES

Paul G. Lewis

IDEA AND HISTORY OF
THE PARTY STATE

The idea of party states – that is, of one-party regimes or of states with a single party – has always been a controversial one. It has long raised doubts of a conceptual nature amongst those concerned with the study of political parties, and in some views has represented a challenge to the very meaning of the term 'party'. This is because the idea of party implies an absence of political wholeness, some element of pluralism and a necessary association with other organizations taking part in the political process, which thus also form part of the overall political regime. Analysis of the 'single party', or the one-party regime, has nevertheless occupied a central place in the field of study of modern parties and appeared as a prominent feature in discussion and interpretation of the key political developments of the 20th century. The single party was long recognized to be the central component of the Soviet system, as well as of the broader spectrum of communist and totalitarian regimes that played such an important role in the politics of the last century. In the early years of this century, it remains a wholly necessary part of the study of contemporary Chinese politics and is still relevant to the other surviving communist regimes (North Korea, Cuba, Vietnam and Laos) and one-party states. As such, it continues to deserve serious attention in any study of contemporary political parties.

On the face of it there certainly seems to be something strange about focusing attention on 'the party without counterpart' (Sartori, 1976:

42). Why not, after all, just talk of a no-party system in situations where the governing body and main structures of rule do not tolerate opposition or organized manifestations of dissent? The paradox associated with the idea of the one-party regime diminishes, however, when the existence and operation of such an arrangement is seen in terms of its relation to the development of the state and the form taken by regimes at specific historical conjunctures as modern societies became politicized. The single party did not emerge in an historical vacuum, but was formed and rose to power in contexts strongly marked by the recent extension of the suffrage and under conditions in which early party pluralism was thought to have failed or had so far developed little support. Such were the conditions in the Russia of 1917, where the Kerensky regime was faced with the impossible task of maintaining the country's war effort on the basis of a barely established party pluralism and in the face of effective local power exercised by workers' *soviets* (or councils); in Italy during 1922, where a newly unified nation was devastated by wartime losses for which it received little reward or recompense; or in the Germany of 1933, where the Weimar Republic crumbled under the burden of economic depression and unemployment. The seizure of power by Lenin, Mussolini and Hitler – albeit, in the latter case, with considerable support at the polls – thus gave birth to a novel kind of political institution in a new situation, one where 'The one party in power kills the other parties but remains a party-like organizational weapon' (Sartori, 1976: 40–2, 43). The single party – either Soviet communist, Italian fascist or German Nazi – is one that has taken power after it has defeated competing parties and eliminated them from the political arena, invariably by violent means, as well as annihilating or neutralizing all other major forms of social resistance.

The idea of the party state involves specific conceptions both of party and state. The state in which the single party has emerged has typically been one weakened by war or at an early stage of development, and one often struggling too with a devastated economy. These were the conditions that prevailed in Russia, Italy and Germany after World War I, as well as in China after 1945. They provided the single party with particular opportunities for leadership, control and purposive action and placed special responsibilities on it as an agency of political coordination and guidance. In this context the single party becomes a prime means of social integration. The early single parties that took this classic form were dynamic organizations and to a large extent institutions of mobilization intended to perform combined functions of political, social and economic construction. It is therefore important to pay due recognition to both sides of the equation – that we are essentially concerned here with strong *parties* in weak *states*. It is not difficult here to detect the contrast that emerges with countries like the United States and Great Britain at equivalent stages of party development – strong states that provided quite different conditions for the birth and steady growth of parties with more limited functions of political representation as agencies of democratic participation.

The single party is, therefore, a particular kind of political organization that arose in a specific historic context, one whose origins and early classic forms were confined to Europe during World War I and the following years. The single-party model was also adopted there during the inter-war period by Portugal (under Salazar) and Spain (under Franco), although it had considerable influence elsewhere during the years preceding World War II. After 1945 its influence spread globally. Between 1962 and 1968 thirty-three states, most of them communist, held elections that gave all seats in the legislature to one and the same party (Sartori, 1976: 221). One-party rule clearly had considerable political success and appeal (for rulers if not always their subjects), and seemed to satisfy a range of political demands. One thing it could not do, of course, was form the basis for an electoral democracy or a party system – for the simple reason that its actions left no other party for it to develop systematic relations with. If the idea of a polity in which party

politics is restricted to one organization already raises doubts for a number of analysts, the suggestion of a 'one-party system' can indeed be rejected as a contradiction in terms.

The appropriate conceptualization here is that of the party–state system, where the single party broadly appears as a duplicate of the state. The single party invariably has official status as the supreme political organization in a monolithic state. All opposition parties were dissolved in Italy in 1926 and the right to form new ones removed. Independent parties in Nazi Germany were dissolved or proscribed in May 1933 and in December a law was passed to secure the unity of Party and *Reich*, thus establishing an official state party. In the Soviet Union, on the other hand, it was not until the Stalin Constitution of 1936 appeared that the role of the Communist party was formally recognized and described there as the 'leading core of all organizations of the working people, both public and state'.

But in any concrete manifestation of the model, the correspondence between party and state is never complete. Party and state necessarily remain different kinds of institutions so long as they do not completely merge their identities in a distinctive new form of organization. There is scope for differentiation between party and state in different ways: the proportion of those holding public office who are party members may be subject to considerable variation; party career systems can differ from those of the bureaucratic career system typical of state structures; there may well be conflict between the interests of party representatives and leaders and those of the technical intelligentsia concerned with state affairs; the different hierarchies that make up the state structure (including police forces and the army) can find it difficult to integrate with the apparatus of the party itself (Sartori, 1976: 45). There is also the strong likelihood of tension and conflict emerging between the two structures, or of one dominating the other. In view of the strong tendencies to centralization that permeate the party state, there is also the distinct possibility that a dominant leader may rise above both party and state and exercise a general dictatorship over both. Despite an apparently solid and monolithic character, the party state carries major elements of instability.

DIMENSIONS OF SINGLE-PARTY RULE

While, not surprisingly, party–state relations are an important dimension of single-party operations and direct attention to features of the way in which one-party regimes operate, they also have other distinctive characteristics. Many, but not all, single parties have adopted and placed great emphasis on promulgating a particular ideology. This has been particularly true of totalitarian regimes and the classic cases of one-party rule that developed in the Soviet Union, Italy and Germany before World War II. Sartori (1976: 222–4) indeed suggests that distinctions can be drawn between one-party totalitarian patterns, one-party authoritarianism and one-party pragmatic regimes. The latter, by definition, are less concerned with the ideological objectives and constraints of political rule and preoccupied with the politics of expediency. Examples offered here – from the early 1970s – were Portugal (under National Political Action), Liberia (dominated by the True Whigs), Tunisia (ruled by the Neo-Destour Party) and Spain during the latter years of Franco's rule. It should be noted, however, that these are quite isolated and somewhat marginal examples of one-party rule.

By the time this observation was made in 1976 – and indeed until the late 1980s – communist regimes provided by far the largest subcategory of one-party rule and embodied the most durable variant of the totalitarian model that emerged between the world wars. To an even greater extent than the Nazi or fascist regimes, it can be argued, communist regimes were driven by ideology and shaped by a distinctive vision of state development and socioeconomic growth. The prominence of communist ideology was linked with the greater scope and intensity of party input into the state under communist regimes, as well as a correspondingly stronger influence on state policy and its political output (Ware, 1996: 131). It was a characteristic that was associated with the greater staying power of communist regimes in contrast to those of a fascist nature, and to the continuing appeal of the communist single-party model in many parts of the world after 1945.

Single parties have also invariably been mass parties, firstly because party-state leaders are eager to maximize membership to reflect what can then be construed as popular support for the regime in a situation where elections (if they are held at all) are won unopposed and offer only a spurious political victory. It gives the party further chances to spread its message and promulgate the ideology, as well as providing a means for diffuse social and political control. From the point of view of actual and potential members, possession of a party card is attractive because it opens the way to appointment to public office within the state administration, career advancement within parallel or closely entwined party-state hierarchies and, yet more practically, various ways of improving an individual's social and economic position. Under a one-party regime, membership is closely equivalent to joining a trade union within a closed shop, and anything up to a third of the working population might become party members on this basis. Such large memberships produce their own problems, however, and the material incentives for membership carry a strong likelihood of corruption and rapidly declining commitment to the party's ideological goals. Not surprisingly, too, party organization is quite distinctive within a one-party regime. The wide-ranging tasks carried out by the single party and its large membership mean that the organization is highly developed and correspondingly complex. The concentration of power within a party–state system also leads to a high degree of centralization, a feature for which communist parties have been particularly well known.

Discussion of single parties and the analysis of one-party regimes are often linked with the concept of totalitarianism. The most influential elaboration of the concept relates it to six key factors, generally referred to as the 'totalitarian syndrome' (Friedrich and Brzezinski, 1965: 21–2). These include some of the characteristics already discussed, like that of the single mass party typically led by one man and closely linked with the state bureaucracy as well as the existence of an official ideology providing some vision of an ideal future society. Further characteristics making up the syndrome are a party–state monopoly both of weapons of combat and of the means of mass communication, combined with a system of terroristic police control. A slightly later addition to the original set of factors was the central control and direction of the economy, a feature more closely modelled on Soviet experience than on that of Nazism or fascist states. The concept of totalitarianism was clearly intended to be a distillation of the distinctive traits of Nazi, fascist and Soviet rule and was for this – as well as other reasons – roundly condemned by Soviet writers as well as being treated with reserve by considerable numbers of political scientists. It nevertheless had the merit of placing the theory and practice of Soviet rule, and of the other communist regimes established after 1945, in some kind of comparative context.

Whether all single parties fit the totalitarian model is a question about which there has been some disagreement. Sartori has not been the only one to differentiate between one-party regimes. Duverger (1964: 276–7) was also eager to argue the case that not all single parties are totalitarian either in ideas or in organization. He refers, in particular, to the People's Republican Party (PRP) that ruled in Turkey from 1923 to 1946 and is defined as pragmatic and even democratic in orientation. In 1930, for example, Turkish leader Kemal Atatürk encouraged the formation of a Liberal Party to facilitate a transition to modern pluralism – but this was soon dissolved as it 'became the rallying ground for all opponents of the regime'. In 1935, on the other hand, the election of a number of independents to parliament was organized to form an opposition in a move that similarly failed to impress many independent observers. These measures in fact did little to establish the democratic credentials of the PRP and tended to confirm the drive of the single party to maximize the centralization of power and impel it in an authoritarian direction. Similar tendencies have been seen elsewhere, sometimes going so far as to undermine the apparent dominance of the single party and subject it to the pervasive processes of personalized totalitarian dictatorship.

The role of the single party within the totalitarian model is indeed particularly open to question with respect to the position of the supreme leader, whose dominance is often associated both with the practice of one-party rule and the establishment of a totalitarian system. The classic cases of one-party rule have all produced notoriously brutal dictatorships. In each of these three cases of totalitarian one-party rule there was a common sequence of developments as revolutionary movements took power while their leaders then moved to entrench the dominance of the single party and also to consolidate their own position. Lenin and Mussolini both ruled within nominal coalitions for a period of time (although only for six months in Lenin's case) before the influence of alternative organizations and potential competitors was eliminated. But, from certain points of view, the leader's rise to uncontested dominance represented not so much a victory achieved *through* the single party as a victory *over* it. Thus Mussolini's triumph was that of state leader rather than one of party chief, while the party that helped him gain power was increasingly assigned to a relatively low-level executive role. With the consolidation of fascist power, the job of the party was just 'to conform, applaud and obey' (Mack Smith, 1993: 149). Hitler's Nazi party retained greater power but saw it divided between competing bureaucratic empires headed by figures such as Göring, Goebbels and Himmler. Party–state relations were an area of considerable juridical confusion and the party as an institution was never in a position to dominate the state apparatus, which it took over wholesale and (unlike the analogous Soviet experience) largely intact from the Weimar regime (Bracher, 1973: 297).

PARTY LEADERSHIP IN COMMUNIST SYSTEMS

These observations raise several questions about the nature of the party state and the role of the single party, particularly as it existed in some of the major historical cases of the phenomenon:

- To what extent can the existence of one-party rule and the establishment of party states be associated with the development of totalitarian systems?
- How far is there a role for the single party within a totalitarian system; or should totalitarianism be seen rather as a form of no-party system?
- Does totalitarianism destroy the single party or can it reflect a stage in a sequence of political developments that change the nature of the single party but do not necessarily destroy it?

One problem in confronting such questions is that many one-party regimes have had a quite limited time-span. The extremism of the ideology that imbued the totalitarian party state and the political behaviour of its leaders – that was not just highly dynamic on the international stage but often downright aggressive – soon led to war and eventual defeat for Germany and Italy in hostilities they had themselves provoked. In the case of Spain and some other countries, on the other hand, one-party rule did not survive the death of its founder and sole leader. In all these variants the fate of the single party was inextricably – and fatally – bound up with that of its leader.

Soviet experience was somewhat different, as the communist party retained at least a semblance of institutional life under Lenin and only became fully subjugated to the leader some time later when Stalin had succeeded after the party founder's death. The Soviet case was also a particularly important one as party–state relations and both the theory and practice of the leading role of the communist party were the subject of extensive debate and contrasting views throughout the life of the communist polity. The problematic role of the single party surfaced at various stages of party–state development. It was recognized at an early stage that its 'leading role' in organizing and spearheading a revolution in the name of and, indeed, with the participation of the working class was a very different thing from overseeing and exercising overall leadership of an extensive state administration. In the early years of the regime experienced party activists naturally moved to organize and direct the executive committees of the soviets (i.e. the new state administration). In one of his last pieces, written in 1923, Lenin (1967: 782) raised the question of whether a party institution could be amalgamated with a soviet institution and stated: 'I see no obstacles to this. What is more, I think that such an amalgamation is the only guarantee of success in our work.'

Nevertheless in subsequent years, after the leader's early death in 1924, a central component of the Leninist myth was that the party should lead but not substitute for the activities of the state administration. As virtually the whole of Soviet public life – political, social and economic – was rigorously controlled and managed by a totalitarian central leadership, the extent of this activity was indeed enormous, and yet more costly and wasteful if state administration was duplicated by that of the party hierarchy. But in practice the problem was largely side-stepped with the consolidation of Stalin's personal power following the purges of 1936–8 which also saw the destruction of the party as an institution and the undermining of its monopolistic position (Schapiro, 1970: 621). No party congress was held between 1939 and 1952, and the Central Committee did not meet for years at a time (indeed, in 1937 around 70 percent of its existing members were physically eliminated). The conclusion of Schapiro (1972: 63) was the general one that 'descriptions of Germany under Hitler and of Russia under Stalin as "one-party states" are completely misleading … the seeming "monopoly" of the party's power is in fact nothing of the kind'. But a clear problem of party–state relations re-emerged under Khrushchev who eventually – after extensive intra-elite conflict – became party-state leader after Stalin's death in 1953.

Under the post-Stalin leadership, the mass purges of Soviet society and regular elimination of large numbers of party members were brought to an end. During the period of Khrushchev's dominance in particular, the institutional framework of the party was restored, a reinvigoration of party organs

occurred and there was a resumption of party activities on a regular basis. Schapiro (1970: 624–5), on the other hand, points out that Khrushchev as party leader retained full control over the party apparatus and activities and that party officials had no autonomy in the conduct of their organizational duties. In effect Khrushchev retained a large measure of arbitrary power over party activities and the party-state regime as a whole, leaving the single party no real opportunity to act or develop as a 'monopolistic' party in its own right. Schapiro thus argues that Khrushchev's ascendancy remained totalitarian in character and had no place for single-party activity in any autonomous sense even under a form of autocratic rule that was distinctively less arbitrary and considerably more institutionally circumscribed than that of Stalin.

But it is surely significant in this context that Khrushchev's eventual removal in 1964 was engineered by leading party-state officials resolutely opposed to attempts at further institutional reform. This alone suggests that the party as an institution – or at least influential sectors within it – retained some capacity for autonomous activity and that the party had been not so much destroyed under Stalin as eclipsed and left with some capacity for revival. The puzzle of what party leadership really meant nevertheless remained and in the late 1980s party leader Mikhail Gorbachev (1988: 281) – with increasing desperation – was still calling for the clear delineation of the functions of party and government bodies in line with the 'Leninist concept'.

The system of one-party rule effectively established by Lenin in 1921 clearly had considerable staying power, surviving its institutional eclipse under Stalin, the Hitlerite invasion of 1941, and roughly 40 years of cold war. Unlike other one-party regimes, neither dictatorial leadership nor a millenarian ideology led it into self-destructive wars, and it also weathered the political crisis that followed the death of a wholly dominant leader. In this sense the communist system proved to be capable of self-reproduction, unlike other forms of one-party or totalitarian regime. It was, partly on this basis, replicated in Soviet-controlled Eastern Europe after 1945, followed by Chinese leaders in their revolutionary success of 1949, and emulated in other countries of Asia, Africa and Latin America. What should be recognized as an authentic Marxist-Leninist regime soon became a matter of uncertainty, and it was clear that the simple declaration by some Third World, anti-Western leader of his communist credentials was by no means the same thing as the replication of the Soviet-style one-party regime. The general Soviet view in the early 1980s was that the 'socialist community' (i.e., that composed of countries whose credentials it accepted) contained, apart from the USSR itself: Bulgaria, Cuba, Czechoslovakia, the German Democratic Republic, Hungary, Laos, Mongolia, Poland, Romania and Vietnam. Less friendly with the USSR but still regarded as having an authentic 'socialist orientation' were Albania, China, North Korea, Yugoslavia and (with some reservation) Cambodia.

All were regarded as party states run on Soviet lines with authentic ruling communist parties. A number of these countries also had subsidiary, satellite parties which did not in any sense exercise power or challenge communist authority but which were retained, generally as left-overs from independent parties of the former regime, as political supports or transmission belts for the ruling single party. Following some Polish political scientists, this situation has led several analysts to write of 'hegemonic parties', even though the countries that had them did not differ from the other communist party states in any politically significant way (Sartori, 1976: 23; Ware, 1996: 249). While Poland is often cited as the prime (and implicitly unique) communist example here, such quasi-parties also existed in China, Bulgaria, Czechoslovakia, East Germany, North Korea and Vietnam without significantly qualifying the character of one-party rule.

Single parties in Africa

Single parties – by no means all based on the communist model – also dominated much of Africa following the decolonization of the 1950s and 1960s. The reason is not very difficult to identify. Just as the single party emerged in Europe after World War I in response to the problems of critically weakened and devastated societies, so it promised an equivalent solution to the further disintegration of already fragile communities under the pressure of the twin processes of modernization and colonial withdrawal: channels of communication were thus 'opened up between otherwise hostile or non-communicating groups, bringing them into sets of relationships out of which the state is built. This, more than any other factor, is the basis of the success of the single-party state' (Apter, 1967: 188–9).

As in Europe and other parts of the world, though, the one-party regimes in Africa were quite diverse. Emerson (1966: 274–87) clearly distinguished, for example, between single-party authoritarian regimes and those of a more pluralist character. Ghana, Guinea and Mali were notable left-wing examples of the former variety. The first two were led by eminent and highly articulate socialist politicians, Kwame Nkrumah and Sékou Touré, who departed in various ways from major features of the communist model. Touré, for example, stressed the importance of national unity and proclaimed the classlessness of African society. In a somewhat more confusing manner, he also accepted the need for dictatorial methods but also emphasized their democratic character in that they were designed to safeguard and develop the rights of the people. Houphouet in the Ivory Coast, however, established a monopolistic Democratic Party with a bourgeois tendency that aimed to maintain close post-colonial links with France. Yet another single-party variant was seen in Tanganyika, where Nyere's TANU placed particular emphasis on African nation building (Emerson, 1966: 284). But signs of a less stable path of African development could already be seen in a tribally divided and already violent Congo which, unusually at that time, lacked both a strong party and a charismatic leader. Doubts were already being raised about the social rifts that were opening up in the new African nations and the likelihood that it was only military force that would be able to secure national integration.

The single-party phase of post-independence African states was in fact quite short. In 1964 some two-thirds of African states had established one-party states and some, such as Algeria, Ghana and Tanzania, had written the single party into their constitutions. But soon after independence, the primacy of the single party rapidly declined, its leaders and main activists increasingly concerned with the work of government. More prosaically, party leaders had less reason to mobilize popular support in both political and material terms once independence was achieved and control of the state apparatus secured. It did not take long, argued Wallerstein (1966: 214), for the one-party state to become the no-party state. Many African states soon degenerated into various forms of personal dictatorship or outright despotism, often with a heavy reliance on military force. These were often linked with another form of party-state regime, that of Afro-Communism. By 1975 the People's Republics of the Congo and Benin (formerly Dahomey), as well as a socialist Somali state, had been formed. They were followed by Ethiopia, Madagascar,

Upper Volta (now Burkina Faso), and the small Portuguese ex-colonies (Hughes, 1992). During the 1980s around a fifth of African states turned to some form of Marxism. This, however, was not always equivalent to one-party rule as power and effective control over the governing apparatus were often in the hands of the military.

As in the Soviet Union and other parts of the communist world, the relationship between party and state was an uncertain one. In many African states acceptance of the communist world did not go much further than the public pronouncements of a small group of power-holders. Former one-party regimes also moved towards another form of party government – that of dominant parties which placed the ruling organization in a more pluralist political framework that had the characteristics of a party *system*. In Senegal, President Senghor thus formally replaced one-party rule by a multi-party system but did not interrupt or endanger the governing party's tenure of power. Reasonably fair elections were also held in Botswana and The Gambia after independence in 1966 and 1965 respectively, without challenging the position of the ruling party. In Zimbabwe, too, Mugabe did not carry out his early intention to install a one-party regime and continued to rule, as he had since independence, through the dominant ZANU organization (Clapham, 1993: 429).

DOMINANT PARTIES AND PREDOMINANT-PARTY SYSTEMS

In distinction to a one-party regime rooted in a party–state system, it is also necessary to take some account of parties that are indeed dominant but maintain their position in the face of electoral competition from other parties. Despite superficial resemblances, the concept and political practice of such a dominant party is quite different from that of the single party located in a party–state system. Under the conditions of political fluidity seen in weak states or newly independent nations like those in Africa, though, the distinction between the two kinds of party is less clear and it is easier to change from one ill-defined form of regime to another. They clearly belong to different categories of political organization, however. In contrast to single parties which are not vulnerable to such competition and relate primarily to the state, dominant parties are situated within a broader universe of parties and form

part of a predominant-party system (Sartori, 1976: 192–4). This is quite different from the single party that is the central component of a one-party regime (and whose unique position may well be enshrined in the constitution). To the extent that the dominance of such a party is achieved through some process of effective electoral competition, a certain adherence to democratic norms and the observation of basic political rights are necessary. Almond (1960: 41) thus speaks in this context of 'dominant non-authoritarian party systems' and relates them directly to states in which nationalist movements became dominant after securing independence.

Dominant parties may of course, and in practice do, exist in many parts of the world. The main problem lies in deciding whether the dominance of a party is indeed an electoral one or is achieved through political repression and the denial of civic rights to actual or potential competitors. Sartori (1976: 193) thus lists 21 dominant parties from the 1970s but casts doubt on the rectitude of electoral practices in some countries and disregards the dominance of the major party in six countries as being unlikely to have been secured by democratic means. Authentic dominant parties have indeed been a mixed bunch and range from India (under the Congress Party) to South Korea and Japan in Asia, Chile and Uruguay in Latin America, and from Israel to the Scandinavian social democracies of Norway, Sweden, Denmark and Iceland. Most such parties have more recently succumbed to the pressures of electoral competition and have now lost their dominant status. There are of course many other parties that appear to dominate as autonomous institutions but are in fact a front for various kinds of dictatorship or autocratic rule, as indeed many have argued was also the case with the totalitarian party. Both are nevertheless distinct from the dominant party that emerges in an electorally competitive predominant-party system and from the single party that retains institutional autonomy and operates within a functioning party–state system.

COMMUNIST PARTY STATES AND POLITICAL CHANGE

Despite their relative longevity and the capacity of the Marxist-Leninist party to survive its eclipse under Stalinist totalitarianism, the communist party state also showed its eventual vulnerability to pressures for political change.

Pre-war fascist regimes, by virtue of their innate aggression and bellicosity, soon found themselves fighting wars from which they failed to emerge victorious and were thus destroyed. Communist party states on the other hand, despite their undoubted problems, were able to survive longer and in some cases have persisted into the 21st century. From 1978 (with the beginning of radical reform and the encouragement of free-market activities in China), nevertheless, it was possible to describe the communist world as being in a state of increasing turmoil – and passing after 1989 into open crisis (Ferdinand, 1991: ix). In some ways it was the sheer breadth of responsibility that helped bring about the collapse of the communist party state. In the early stages of regime development, the penetration of the single party into extensive areas of the state, society and economy was a source of strength and a prime means of amassing power. But these sectors soon began to produce different forms of negative feedback. The party found it impossible to run all parts of the state administration, and the demands of professionalism and specialist autonomy became a direct challenge to both practice and theory of party leadership.

If it was initially the state that began to take its revenge on the single party, though, it soon became the economy that threatened the party, state and entire system of centralized control, administration and planning (Ferdinand, 1991: 300). The Chinese leadership had begun to take pre-emptive measures in this area during 1978. During the 1980s demands in this area also grew in the Soviet Union and fed the growing pressure there for economic and political change. The Soviet party state was directly confronted with a range of problems connected with market-oriented reforms – or rather the general lack of them. One problem that flowed directly from the party's assumption of a general, leading role and its increasingly administrative character was that the party as a political institution was unable to escape the consequences of failure within the administrative realm. This weakened one of the major bases of the party's legitimacy and contributed significantly to the progressive erosion of its political authority (Gill, 1994: 11–12). Leaders since Khrushchev had resolutely turned their back on these problems and it fell to Gorbachev to confront them more squarely. Gorbachev, it seemed, had a genuine belief in the possibility of effective *party* rule and appeared to think that the Communist Party had a real capacity to mobilize the energies and support of the Soviet population while turning its back on direct administration. By abolishing the party's monopoly, opening the way to a multi-party system and (in March 1990) removing references to the party's leading role from the Soviet constitution he demonstrated his faith in the capacity of the party to achieve these tasks in the face of direct political competition.

But if no longer a single party (at least in formal terms), it soon became equally clear that the Soviet party's aspiration to be a dominant one was also threatened. After a failed coup in August 1991 mounted by those aiming to preserve the traditional foundations of Soviet rule, the extent of the party's failure was reflected in Gorbachev's call for the Central Committee to dissolve itself and his personal resignation as General Secretary. In a matter of days communist party activity was banned throughout the Russian Republic, and four months later the Soviet Union was itself dissolved. Attempted reform, then, soon led to total failure and collapse of both components of the party state built up since 1917. Administrative supervision had indeed become the party's prime task, and the reforms initiated by Gorbachev meant that it soon found itself without any role that fitted the organizational structures it had evolved over the decades. It had failed to take on board the demands of a wholly new culture and the new national – and indeed – global conditions under which it had to operate. The party was unable to effect such a transformation and it was, in particular, the 'move from bureaucratic politics to the politics of the streets that outflanked the party' (Gill, 1994: 178). The transformation from party-state leviathan to political party in any normal sense was, not surprisingly, a task the communist organization was just not equipped to accomplish.

The issue of party leadership was, as we have seen, hardly a new one and had its roots in the early years of the Soviet regime – as the continuing references to Lenin in this context clearly showed. As the Soviet regime – and communist regimes in general – 'matured' and increasingly lost their dynamic force it became a central issue in the diagnosis of the problems that increasingly afflicted the communist system and the reform initiatives undertaken to correct them. The pressures for change were widespread and certainly not restricted to the Soviet Union. Such problems came to the fore with particular force in more developed countries such as Hungary and Poland – and had particular prominence there because of the weak roots of communism and the political instability this had caused on more than one occasion. Reform initiatives were thus undertaken there well before they came on to the Soviet agenda. In Poland during the 1970s, for example, party leader Edward Gierek launched wide-ranging policy and institutional changes under the slogan – dangerously devoid of content as it soon turned out – 'the party leads and the government governs'. In fact it led to much confusion among party cadres and growing political passivity at local level (Lewis, 1989: 63–6). Such projects could in fact be regarded as attempts to rationalize the irrational. They demonstrated not just the problems the communist party state faced in bringing about change but also showed, it was argued by Hungarian analysts, that the Leninist regimes represented an archaic political form and were rooted in pre-modern conceptions of rule that were just not susceptible to adaptation to contemporary conditions (Horváth and Szakolczai, 1992: 209).

CONTEMPORARY PARTY STATES

With the transformation of many communist regimes and the dissolution of the Soviet Union at the end of 1991, the single party as a distinctive form within the international family of political parties and the party state as a particular kind of contemporary political regime have become increasingly rare. It is difficult to be precise about how many one-party regimes there actually are or have been at any one time. Conceptual issues, as noted above, contribute to this uncertainty. Whether totalitarian regimes and personal dictatorships left much room for any kind of party as an effective political institution has been the subject of extensive debate. The status of the one-party regimes that sprang up in post-colonial countries during the early independence period also raises doubts, this time more on empirical grounds in terms of how far the political space was institutionalized at all with respect to any kind of party development. For the 1960s Sartori was able to point to 33 states that had single parties. The number of one-party regimes is unlikely to have declined in the decades that immediately followed. As a rough guide we may note that the series of volumes devoted to Marxist regimes published in the 1980s by Frances Pinter (in the UK) and Lynne Rienner (in the USA) listed 32 states with such regimes: ten of these were located in Africa, nine in Europe and six in Asia. This is considerably more than would have been identified as authentic members of the 'socialist community'

by Soviet authorities, but it provides some indication of the number of regimes with such an idea of their political identity and of the number of single parties then in existence. These totals together suggest a fairly stable constellation of one-party regimes from the 1960s to the 1980s.

Despite the beginnings of the third wave of democratization in the 1970s, then, the single-party category appeared for a time to be quite resilient, supported by the survival and spread of the communist regime in the Third World. This picture underwent rapid and extensive change, beginning with the transformation of the regimes in Hungary and Poland in 1989. Communist one-party regimes quickly began to go the way of their fascist predecessors. A global survey of regimes in 2000 showed eight single parties to be still in existence, most of them communist (Freedom House, 2001). The latter were: Cuba, North Korea, Vietnam, Laos and China. They are a diverse group. Cuba, wholly dominated by Castro since the 1959 revolution, is as much personal dictatorship as one-party state, and the party as such never played quite the role there as it did in the communist model developed in the core European countries. The North Korean regime is yet more autocratic in nature, seeming to take the unusual form of a hereditary dictatorship set in a communist framework. Vietnam has liberalized its political system to a significant extent but remains dominated by a single party. Laos remains a relatively traditional communist state, although its party is split between pro-China and pro-Vietnam factions.

By far the largest and most significant member of this residual category, though, is the People's Republic of China, which has interpreted and reformulated the principle of the leading role of the party in ways quite different from those seen in Eastern Europe and the Soviet Union. The other single parties identified in 2000 were a mixed bunch. One was Eritrea, whose leaders had abandoned Marxism before the country achieved independence in 1993 and whose regime continued to have significant military underpinnings. With a socialist, rather than communist, background there was only Iraq – a country subject to decisive and externally engendered regime change in 2003. Finally, Libya has remained strongly dominated by Colonel Qadhafi who has ruled as much with the aid of a complex structure of revolutionary and people's committees as through any single party.

The major remaining party state on a global scale and great exception, therefore, in terms of single-party survival is China – which took the alternative path to that followed by the Soviet Union by progressing cautiously with political change and pressing ahead with radical economic reform. It could be argued that China took the more orthodox Marxist route by concentrating on the economic basis while the Soviets retained a Leninist focus by leading the way with political change. When one-party rule in the Soviet Union was formally abandoned in 1990 (with dire consequences for the integrity of the state as a whole in 1991), China took care to maintain conditions that permitted the survival of the single party. Following a tradition that can be traced back several millennia, the approach of the Chinese leadership to political change has been cautious and carefully formulated in terms of the prevailing ideology. The primary change enunciated at the 16th National Congress of the Chinese Communist Party in 2002 was to affirm the importance of private entrepreneurs and those active in China's rapidly growing free market – but within the existing party–state system.

Party cadres themselves had begun to 'jump into the sea' of business around 1993, and links between party membership and entrepreneurial activity had been increasingly close since then. The 16th Congress, however, moved forward to adapt the party charter in line with former general secretary Jiang Zemin's advocacy of the 'three represents', which portray the communist party not just as the vanguard of the Chinese working class but also as that of the Chinese people and of all the nationalities of China – that is, as something like a catch-all party capable of representing all sectors of a rapidly modernizing society (Fewsmith, 2003: 4, 13). One central feature of the communist regime that was not abandoned was the principle of the single party. Nevertheless, if Jiang's commitment to quadrupling China's GNP in 20 years is indeed achieved on the basis of capitalist development it is not at all clear what function a monopolistic communist party will actually be performing. Some indication of the path developments might take is given by the prevalent opinion that the political model that seems to underlie the path of change envisaged is that of Singapore.

If – with the signal exception of China – the party state has largely disappeared as a major political category, it is equally difficult to detect many dominant parties in the sense of those acting within a predominant party-system based on contested and reasonably free elections. The Freedom House (2001: 662–3) list of 120 electoral democracies – nearly two-thirds

of the world's regimes – thus only includes Djibouti as such a regime having any kind of dominant party. Former major examples of dominant parties have yielded to established processes of party alternation. This has been the case with India's Congress Party, Japan's Liberal Democrats and Italy's Christian Democrats. Parties identified by Freedom House as playing a dominant role under less democratic regimes have been considerably more numerous, including 26 of those with the lowest democratic ranking (scoring 4 or more on the Freedom House political rights and civil liberties ranking). Seventeen of these were to be found in Africa, reflecting yet further instability in that continent following the earlier prominence of one-party and broadly communist regimes. Both single and dominant parties have thus become considerably less numerous than they were for much of the second half of the 20th century.

One obvious reason for the decline in the number of single parties has been the growing proportion of the world's regimes classified as having some reasonably convincing form of democratic rule, a consequence of the high tide of such regimes associated with the third wave of democracy that began in 1974. There continue to exist, of course, various forms of standard dictatorship (presidential, monarchical, military, etc.) in which one or more official parties may play some public role, but the existence and nature of such façade parties have not been the focus of attention in this chapter. Contemporary dictatorships, it must be concluded, do not tend to be linked with the party-state form. There are likely to be different reasons for this. As noted at the beginning, the emergence and operation of the single party is closely linked with the nature of the state in which it is located. Fascist parties, for example, characteristically emerged in Europe between the world wars in weak or newly formed states devastated by war and economic depression at a time when strong parties and strong states were seen as the primary solution to collective problems. Some of these features could also be seen in revolutionary Russia, but the Communist Party and the party–state regime it created also developed distinctive strategies of economic growth and state-led socioeconomic development. This one-party model had considerable success and developed enormous appeal both in Europe and elsewhere, and was replicated in various parts of the world after 1945.

One major point to note, then, is that state–economy relations and the ways in which political parties can influence patterns of socioeconomic development have all changed greatly over recent decades. Since the 1970s, in particular, free-market capitalist processes have become increasingly dominant in patterns of socioeconomic development and the single party, like many other institutions, has been critically affected and to a large extent undermined by the complex of forces gathered under the conceptual umbrella of 'globalization'. These are likely to be the major factors underlying both the rise and fall of the single party, although links can also be drawn with arguments relating to the overall decline of the party in sustaining a modern political order and the prevailing weakness of ideological alternatives to liberal democracy associated with influential views concerning the 'end of history'. Such lines of inquiry cannot be elaborated on here. But in any case all such views should be judged in the light of ongoing Chinese developments.

REFERENCES

Almond, G.A. (1960) 'Introduction: A functional approach to comparative politics', in G.A. Almond and J.S. Coleman (eds), *The Politics of the Developing Areas*. Princeton, NJ: Princeton University Press, pp. 3–64.

Apter, D.E. (1967) *The Politics of Modernization*. Chicago: University of Chicago Press.

Bracher, K.D. (1973) *The German Dictatorship*. Harmondsworth: Penguin.

Clapham, C. (1993) 'Democratisation in Africa: Obstacles and prospects', *Third World Quarterly*, 14(3): 423–38.

Duverger, M. (1964) *Political Parties*. London: Methuen.

Emerson, R. (1966) 'Parties and national integration in Africa', in J. LaPalombara and M. Weiner (eds),

Political Parties and Political Development. Princeton, NJ: Princeton University Press, pp. 267–301.

Ferdinand, P. (1991) *Communist Regimes in Comparative Perspective*. Hemel Hempstead: Harvester Wheatsheaf.

Fewsmith, J. (2003) 'The Sixteenth National Party Congress: The succession that didn't happen', *China Quarterly*, 173: 1–16.

Freedom House (2001) *Freedom in the World: The Annual Survey of Political Rights and Civil Liberties*. Piscataway, NY: Transaction.

Friedrich, C.J. and Brzezinski, Z.K (1965) *Totalitarian Dictatorship and Autocracy* (2nd edn). New York: Praeger.

Gill, G. (1994) *The Collapse of a Single-Party System*. Cambridge: Cambridge University Press.

Gorbachev, M. (1988) *Perestroika: New Thinking for Our Country and the World*. London: Fontana/Collins.

Horváth, A. and Szakolczai, Á. (1992) *The Dissolution of Communist Power: The Case of Hungary*. London: Routledge.

Hughes, A. (1992) 'The appeal of Marxism to Africans', *Journal of Communist Studies*, 8(2): 4–20.

Lenin, V.I. (1967) 'Better fewer, but better', in *Selected Works, Vol. 3*. Moscow: Progress, pp. 774–86.

Lewis, P.G. (1989) *Political Authority and Party Secretaries in Poland*. Cambridge: Cambridge University Press.

Mack Smith, D. (1993) *Mussolini*. London: Weidenfeld.

Sartori, G. (1976) *Parties and Party Systems: A framework of Analysis*. Cambridge: Cambridge University Press.

Schapiro, L. (1970) *The Communist Party of the Soviet Union*. London: Methuen.

Schapiro, L. (1972) *Totalitarianism*. London: Macmillan.

Wallerstein, I. (1966) 'The decline of the party in single-party African states', in J. LaPalombara and M. Weiner (eds), *Political Parties and Political Development*. Princeton, NJ: Princeton University, Press, pp. 201–14.

Ware, A. (1996) *Political Parties and Party Systems*. Oxford: Oxford University Press.

PART VI

PARTIES IN THE FUTURE

41

THE INTERNATIONAL ROLE OF POLITICAL PARTIES

Kay Lawson

What role do political parties play in the arena of world politics? Do national parties have access to that arena, and if so, how? How strong are the few transnational parties that exist? Whether national or international, do parties work openly and democratically in international politics or is their influence indirect, difficult to ascertain, and sometimes undemocratically carried out?

To seek to answer these questions, as well as to place the discussion of the international role of political parties in a meaningful context, it is necessary to begin with a few words about how the traditional role of parties as agencies of linkage has changed. As we will see, these changes strongly influence what parties can and will do at levels above the nation state.

Although political parties still claim to serve as agencies of democratic linkage between citizen and state, this claim, always subject to question, is now more difficult to substantiate. In nation after nation, citizen trust is low, abstention is high, and increasing dependence on funding by large donors (directly or illegally) means that after electoral victory the parties' programs are sometimes set aside for policies rewarding those who have contributed the most. Major parties are accused of entering into cartel-like collusion, seemingly better linked to each other than to those whom they are expected to serve (Katz and Mair, 1995). Participatory linkage (giving rank-and-file supporters a serious role to play in

internal party decision-making) has all but disappeared in many nations, and responsive linkage (paying serious attention to supporters' policy preferences) is also harder to find once the campaign dust has settled and the real work begins (Lawson, 1980; Lawson *et al.*, 1998).

Linkage by reward continues, but is more selective (and thus less democratic) and, some have argued, more difficult to maintain in modern political systems, as the inexorable process of globalization steadily shifts key decisions away from the state and forces compliance with conditions established by the interaction of the world market and international or regional treaties and rules. Internal redistribution of resources, for fair purposes or foul, is no longer so easily arranged: even corruption has been globalized (Ignazi *et al.*, 2005).

Do national parties therefore risk becoming interesting anachronisms, full of sound and fury, empty of consequence, entirely controlled by others? Are they incapable of serving intranational goals outside national perimeters? Are they hopelessly outperformed at the international level by TNCs, NGOs, INGOs and TSMOs, organizations that serve limited clienteles for limited purposes and that normally make no pretense of democratic linkage to others?[1]

Inasmuch as democracy itself posits connection with – indeed, rule by – the *demos*, these questions are not trivial. Although arguments that the state remains a powerful entity are persuasive (Reis, 2004), if the trend is nonetheless in the direction of increasing regionalization and/or internationalization, and if no other agency is seriously filling the *multiple* democratic deficits emerging in the process of globalization, then it is indeed time to investigate the role parties play now and are likely to play in the future at levels of governance above the state.

The purpose of this chapter is to consider how far that investigation has proceeded, with an emphasis on the questions of linkage raised above. We may say from the outset that the investigation is far from complete, a condition that will permit us to raise a number of questions at the end that others may find interesting to pursue in future work. First, however, we will examine some of the information we have regarding how *national* parties take part in international governance. This will give us the background we need for a second section, exploring the frequent claim or assumption that at the international level it is NGOs in one form or another that now do the work of parties, and do it better. Then we will consider transnational parties: where they exist, how they are organized and perform. A final section will consider the present and probable future role of parties at the international level from a somewhat different perspective, one more tightly linked to the forces of globalization than to international governance.[2]

NATIONAL PARTIES IN INTERNATIONAL GOVERNANCE

Although parties have been seriously weakened as agencies of democratic linkage, and are often controlled by a non-democratic few, this does not mean that they are weak as instruments of power. National political parties are and always have been among the most powerful participants in the international arena. International agencies do not spring full grown from the weary shoulders of Atlas – the decision to form them is made by partisan politicians within nation states. When these partisans win national elections they win control of appointments to such bodies, and they normally appoint their own partisan supporters to represent the government they now control. Any others who win such appointments on the sole grounds of their expertise must always be very careful not to act contrary to their appointers' partisan plans. Most of the appointments made do not require legislative approval and national parties' successful

campaigners (i.e. elected officials) are thus able to send whom they wish into the international arena, except as they may be constrained by the need to reward their most generous supporters.

Moreover, the capacity of national party leaders to fashion international policies and agreements does not depend merely on such appointments, nor is it exercised only at the time and place such decisions are made. Parties bring their power to bear on international policy-making both long before and far away, within the nation states. Laura Macdonald and Mildred A. Schwartz (2002) have examined the role of national parties in Mexico, the United States and Canada in developing the North American Free Trade Agreement (NAFTA), showing in detail how parties in all three nations took pro- and anti-NAFTA stances in election campaigns in the years leading up to the treaty. Particularly interesting were the efforts of the parties out of power: in Canada such parties offered 'loud and strong opposition' in the Canadian parliament, while in Mexico the Partido de Acción Nacional (PAN) demanded (in vain) a referendum on the question of ratification, and in the United States the Democratic Party was forced to engage in a long process of intraparty negotiation as its small business supporters rallied to populist appeals for greater trade barriers while its allies in high-technology industries lobbied hard for freer trade. The impact of these stabs at opposition was, however, quite limited. In Canada, even the leftist parties, when in power, 'appeared powerless to resist the global and domestic pressures toward removing trade barriers' (Macdonald and Schwartz, 2002); the PAN has not repudiated the treaty now that it has come to power; and of course the Clinton Democrats came out strongly in its favor. Macdonald and Schwartz (2002: 145) interpret this to mean that 'the leaders of all three governments approached their tasks as though the national political systems in which they operated – including their own parties – would not be an impediment to their goals.' This interpretation, however, implies a largely non-existent difference between governmental and party leaders in the cartelized party world of today and it is probably more reasonable to assume that, having taken the appropriate and possibly useful electoral stances of opposition and gained power, party representatives in government are often more complicit than supine – free to support the very policies it was tactically wise to oppose prior to victory.

On the other hand, some national parties that are normally not in power (or are very much in the minority within ruling coalitions) have had an undeniable impact on the formation of international policy. The Greens are of course the preeminent example of powerful opposition that does not falter (or at least not much) after election scores are in. Since the late 1970s Green parties in Western Europe have played a major role in bringing environmental dangers to the attention of their own and other nations' governments, working hard and often successfully to force national governments not only to adopt ecologically sounder policies at home but also to send their representatives to international meetings armed with demands for stronger action at that level – the only level where such global environmental problems as desertification, climate change, and ozone layer depletion *can* be solved (Richardson and Rootes, 1995).

What constitutes success is, however, relative – and arguable. According to Hein-Anton van der Heijden (2002), the cartelization of major political parties, in particular their tendency to become merely helpful parts of the state, seriously impedes the power of the Greens to achieve the passage of sufficiently strong pro-environment policies, be it at the national or international level. Yet what van der Heijden calls party failure at the international level, focusing as he does on the Greens, anti-environmentalists and leaders of non-Green parties might well term party success: blocking the passage of international treaties and regulations that national governments find unacceptable because harmful to favored domestic economic interests and/or invasive of sovereign power of the state is something that partisan representatives *can* and often do accomplish at the international level.

In any case, we clearly must be very careful not to exaggerate what parties can achieve – or will even try to achieve via national governments in order to foster international democratization (never the same thing as winning the adoption or blockage of particular policies). In the first place, most of the world's governments are not themselves based on free and fully competitive elections. Secondly, candidates for office, with or without meaningful competition, do not normally make the policies they expect to pursue (in person or via appointments) in international bodies a key part of their campaigns. Partisan appointees to international bodies who have been appointed by and/or won office without attention to an international agenda will be highly unlikely to feel themselves strongly guided by public opinion at home.

Or are things changing? The US invasion of Iraq in 2003 against the collective will of the United Nations and the expressed views of many of her traditional allies provoked an altogether unusual measure of public concern and attention regarding US participation in international bodies during the 2004 presidential election season, and helped set the political agenda in Britain as well. Whether this situation has set a new precedent – one that could conceivably contribute to the democratization of international decisions via national parties – or is simply a passing phenomenon remains to be seen.

Another way parties may sometimes work at home to influence the direction of international governance is to focus on *implementation*. Green parties, for example, often play a strong role in calling attention to violations of international environmental agreements. Parties whose support base is mostly industrial working class or agricultural small farmers may do the same. But here, too, the sword of democratization is two-edged. The same kinds of parties, plus parties serving business interests, may find it more 'democratic' to seek to block the application of specific international statutes within their home states than to work to ensure their implementation, thereby weakening rather than strengthening linkages with the international decision-making body.

DO NGOs DO IT BETTER?

If parties are so limited in their willingness and ability to use the power they have via national governments to serve as agencies of international democratization, are NGOs any better? A brief detour in their direction seems worthwhile.

To begin with, it must be said that NGOs themselves are not particularly democratic; even the least responsive of political parties will have statutes requiring consultation with its membership and give them at least *pro forma* attention, but NGOs are under no such obligation. 'Membership' usually requires nothing more than sending money once; consultations are almost always advisory only and designed to elicit funds rather than to seek genuine guidance. Green movements are unusual in sometimes calling for nominations to leadership positions, but the list of those allowed to nominate is typically quite restricted. For example, as of 1998 Greenpeace USA had 400,000 members but distinguished between normal members and voting members. 'The former can if they wish join the activist network [and] take part in mail protests or demonstrations, but only 190 members are voting members; to be such a member you must have at least six years' commitment to Greenpeace and the decision to grant such status is made by the five member Board of Directors' (Lawson, 1998).

Even the most enthusiastic defenders of NGOs as agents of positive globalization seldom claim they are or even should be instruments of international democratization.[3] They focus instead on how the web of interactions NGO activists have created among themselves is steadily building a global civil society (Iriye, 1999; Ronit and Schneider, 2000). Although the amazing proliferation of NGOs in the past twenty years and their massive presence in or 'parallel' to regional or international meetings on key global topics lend considerable credibility to this claim, it is also true that 'practically all major NGOs with the financial means to attend regional and global intergovernmental meetings are from the world's "North"' (Borgese, 1999: 987). Building the global civil society may be the first step to building representative linkages to international governing institutions, but there is obviously a long way to go to complete that step and little sign that doing so is a high priority for most existent NGOs.

Studies of NGOs often focus on the work they do outside governments and outside conferences: raising international consciousness of the problems of particular groups and populations and gathering funds that permit them to take direct action themselves (such as the work of the Grameen Bank in Bangladesh and of Acción International in Latin America). Such studies often make it clear that when NGOs do become more intrinsically connected to the work of governance, be it via specific national governments or international agencies, any linkage established is at the present time very likely to be from the top down. Michael Edwards and David Hulme (1995), for example, discuss how international aid agencies sometimes funnel their assistance through NGOs they deem especially good at reaching the poorest and neediest. Mark Leonard (2002) urges national governments (especially the US government) to find ways to work with NGOs that have 'credibility, expertise, and appropriate networks' such as Human Rights Watch or Oxfam. Such state sponsorship sometimes seriously compromises NGO credibility with local populations and diminishes their potential for serving as meaningful agencies of democratic linkage. The US invasion of Iraq has provided some particularly pointed examples. On the American side, the US Agency for International Development gave out 'humanitarian contracts' to NGOs with the stipulation that they agreed not to speak to the media and to recognize that they are 'an arm of the [US] government' (Klein, 2003). On the Iraqi rebel side, NGO workers were kidnapped and menaced with execution. We may, of course, say that NGOs represent a new kind of democracy, with representation achieved not via elections or binding consultations, but via participation (even merely monetary) in organized groups that represent their members' most cherished interests, be they humanitarian or selfishly economic, and that in turn bring pressure to bear successfully on international bodies involved in making decisions that affect those interests. Such a truncated and, finally, *uncivil* definition of democracy, abandoning hope for a wider citizenship in which represented individuals take a measure of responsibility for all the decisions made by a polity, may well be all that can be hoped for at the international level, at least for now.

However, even this rudimentary democratization via the NGO is difficult to find in the work of international bodies. Although NGOs are much more openly present than parties and indeed sometimes quite vociferous at international meetings, their actual impact therein appears to be much less than often imagined. Most of the world's NGOs are weakly financed and inadequately supported by public opinion. They have no assured place in the halls of global power; they must constantly renew their assault on the consciences or pocketbooks of those who do have the power to decide. They can fail. They can disappear.

Furthermore, even stronger NGOs serving on impressive international advisory boards appear to have little or no real power. Eva Etzioni-Halevy (2002: 207) points out, for example, that although the International Monetary Fund (IMF) maintains contact with a wide range of NGOs, including labor unions, religious and women's groups, such groups are seen by the IMF 'first and foremost as targets for communication from the IMF and the dissemination of information about the IMF ... a means of engaging and bringing the IMF's views to a wide range of interlocutors'. The IMF (1998) itself claims only that such groups 'provide opportunities for the IMF to listen'.

Similarly, Clark *et al.* (1998) find that although NGOs 'are an integral part of UN thematic conferences', they are commonly 'shut out of the most crucial stage of conference planning ... and are given subordinate roles in conference documents'. Such limitations have been demanded by specific government delegations and agreed to by the UN (whose customary practices in any case include a taboo against overt criticisms of member governments at UN-sponsored events). Significantly, Clark *et al.* (1998: 35) conclude, 'State sovereignty sets the limits of global civil society'.

Nor do even the wealthiest TNCs always prevail via or above the nation state. Leslie Sklair (2002) has argued that a new Transnational Capitalist Class (TCC) is able to work through national governments for effective control of international policy, and demonstrates the process with case studies including the global tobacco business. However, Aynsley Kellow (2002), noting the success of other NGOs in fighting international seed companies using new techniques of genetic modification, argues that in fact well-organized NGOs working in global coalitions can and often do hold transnational business interests very much in check.

In sum, although NGOs are in certain respects strong and impressive actors in the international arena and do seek to serve a wide range of interests, they are nonetheless not working as agencies of democratic linkage, and we should not be misled by the glowing encomiums they receive, and often deserve, into imagining otherwise. Unlike parties, their successes are often more visible than their failures or limitations. We often cannot see exactly what the national parties are up to internationally, and they often work anything but democratically, but they nonetheless clearly control the work of international governance much more powerfully than do the NGOs. All the more reason for scholars to hold the mirror of democratic linkage up to them and see what is going on – and what is not.

TRANSNATIONAL PARTIES AND PARTY NETWORKS

'Transnational' is, say Harlan Cleveland and Walter Truett Anderson (1999: 879), 'a word whose time has come'. Although so far we have stressed the power national parties have via partisan representatives sent to international bodies, we are not forgetting the more obvious form of party activity at the international level: international and regional parties and party networks.

There are four major international networks: socialist, liberal, Christian democratic, and conservative. Of these, the oldest, best known, and strongest is the Socialist International. This transnational party network traces its roots back to the International Association of the Working Man (founded in 1864) and the Second International (founded in 1889) and was recreated after World War II in its present form, rapidly building up to 125 member organizations from 105 countries. Strongest in Western Europe, it has gained strength in Latin America and Eastern Europe as well (Wells, 1998).

The three other transnational party networks are younger, smaller, and weaker. The Liberal International was founded in 1947 and has members 'and observers' from 69 countries. The Christian Democratic International was also founded in 1947 and has 67 member parties. The very conservative International Democratic Union was founded in 1983 and has 70 member parties from 56 countries (Wells, 1998).

All four organizations work to spread the political ideologies to which they are committed by holding meetings, attending the meetings of other parties and groups, publishing books and pamphlets, and so forth. But their best-known and most effective initiative has been within the Parliament of the European Union (Gaffney, 1996; Hix and Lord, 1997). There, the first three of these four party families have become the Party of European Socialists (PES), the European Liberal, Democratic and Reformist Group (ELDR), and The European People's Party – European Democrats (EPP/ED). Conservative transnational party activity in the EU is represented by the Union for a Europe of Nations (UEN), which is characterized as 'Eurosceptic', and the Europe of Democracies and Diversities (EDD), 'highly critical of the EU and further European integration'. (Day, 2000: 238). Other EU party groupings are the far left European Unitary Left/Nordin Green Left (EUL/NGL) and the Greens, organized as the European Federation of Green Parties/European Free Alliance (GR/EFA). The 732 seats filled in the 2004 European elections were divided as follows, in order of ideology (left to right): EUL/NGL 36; PES 200; GR/EFA 41; EDD 17; ELDR 66; EPP-ED 275; UEN 27; NA 70, unaffiliated 70 (*International Herald Tribune*, 2004a).

The EU parties are examined in far greater detail in a subsequent chapter in this book by Robert Ladrech, as well as by other authors (Hix, 2002; Hix and Lord, 1997; Bardi, 2002; Ladrech, 1997). Here, however, it is appropriate to examine briefly whether or not these party groups are in fact fostering democratic linkage at a supranational level.

Once again the answer is complex. In the first place, the institutional design of the EU poses special problems for representative democracy. The European Parliament, added to the European Economic Community in 1967, was a non-elected body with no legislative functions for the first 12 years of its existence. Member nations appointed representatives to it, and the Parliament's only function was to oversee the work of the Executive Commission (it had the right to approve commissioners and to force the resignation of the entire Commission at any time by a two-thirds vote, as well as the right to approve or reject the annual budget with respect to non-obligatory expenses, i.e. those not demanded by the terms of the founding treaty). Not until 1979 were direct elections held; the electoral system to be used was (and remains) for the individual states to decide. In 1987, the Single European Act (SEA) gave the Parliament the right to accept, reject or amend policies proposed by the Council of Ministers relating to member states' internal markets, although the Council may, if unanimous, overrule a rejection. Otherwise, the principal decision-making bodies of the EU remained the European Commission, which meets once a week and proposes rules and regulations, and the Council of Ministers, which is the true legislative and executive organ of the EU; the members of both bodies are appointed by the member states.

The limited reforms enacted over the past several decades were not seen as sufficient, and it became more and more common to speak of the EU's 'democratic deficit' and to recommend greater powers for the Parliament as the cure. Finally, in 2003–4 a new European constitution was written that takes much more serious steps in the direction of democratization. If this draft constitution is ratified by the member states, it will mean that no proposition of the Commission can be adopted without the approval of the Parliament as well as the Council of Ministers (Article 33). The draft constitution also calls for the Parliament to be given the right to elect the President of the Commission, the Union's single most powerful leader, presently chosen by the European Council (the biannual meeting of Europe's heads of states and foreign ministers) and merely 'approved' by the Parliament (Ferenczi, 2004a).

Although these are definite moves toward further empowering the one organ of the EU that is linked to voting citizens, the changes should not be exaggerated. The clause giving the Parliament 'codecision' powers over laws is limited to projects that do not concern fiscality, social questions or police cooperation. The nomination of the President would still be made by the European Council – the difference is that instead of being expected to *approve*, the Parliament would have a true right to *elect*, backed up by the power to refuse: if the candidate did not receive a majority in Parliament a new candidate would have to be proposed within a month.

The constitution also calls for a change in what constitutes a majority within the Council of Ministers. A new 'qualified majority' would be required, consisting of at least 55% of the member states representing at least 15 different states and at least 65% of the EU population. (Ferenczi, 2004b). Although praised by the two most powerful EU leaders, Gerhard Schröder of Germany and Jacques Chirac of France, as constituting an important measure of democratization, this must be taken with a grain of salt: as noted, the Council of Ministers is not itself linked to voting citizens; Schröder and Chirac are national party leaders. The relationship between the national parties and the supranational parties in the EU is complex, the division of power between them uncertain, and the capacity of the new constitution to effect significant change in that regard is far from clear (Deschouwer, 2000).

In deciding whether the cup of EU democratization is now approaching half full or still more than half empty, several considerations are in order. First, as noted, the constitution has yet to be ratified. Second, there is certainly good reason to doubt that, if it is, the Members of the European Parliament (MEPs) will begin to exercise their new powers more in accord with the votes their party groups helped gain for them than with their home governments. Hix (2002) has shown that up until now national party policies have been the strongest predictors of how members will vote, regardless of which supranational party group they belong to. Furthermore, many MEPs are responsive to particularized group interests, and take an active part in what are known as 'intergroups' dedicated to such matters as language and culture, minorities, consumer rights, animal rights, etc. Although such groups have no formal status, the deputies belonging to them do seek to influence EU decision-making on their behalf (Lequesne and Labastida, 2004).

Another reason to be cautious in predicting greater democratization in a more powerful European Parliament is that, despite the protestations of scholars, European voters themselves have so far shown remarkably little understanding of or concern for the policies candidates for election propose to adopt if elected to serve in Strasbourg. The record low turnout in the 2004 European elections and the very poor showing of candidates ideologically linked to presently ruling national parties were unanimously interpreted, no doubt correctly, as a 'vote-sanction' against the policies of those parties at home and 'dissatisfaction with politics in general' rather than as the rejection of particular EU laws and regulations or disgust with that body's lack of true democratization. (Service France, 2004; *International Herald Tribune*, 2004b). The candidates themselves were accused (again no doubt correctly) of having lacked 'a sufficient consciousness of the importance of the institutions of the Union' and of having failed to find a way to bring the issues at stake into play (Ferenczi, 2004c). One author says flatly, 'the citizen is singularly absent from the democratic process' of the EU (Delperée, 2004). His answer is to call for a change in the political culture of the organization, but it seems reasonable to amend that recommendation to include a call for a change in the political culture of the candidates and their electorates as well.

Overall then, we must conclude that even the best-developed of transnational parties, those active in the EU, do not yet play a stronger role in supranational politics than their national counterparts, nor a more democratic one. However, interesting changes have been made and others are proposed, changes which do have a potential for shifting power to the parties and for permitting their electorates, when they finally awaken to the issues at stake, to insist on more democratic links to them.

FOR FURTHER STUDY: DENATIONALIZATION WITHOUT INTERNATIONALIZATION

Globalization is an international process, but its advance does not always mean the internationalization of governance. We have seen that national parties, while not necessarily following democratic norms, are nevertheless strong agencies, perhaps the strongest, in determining the course of affairs in international decision-making bodies, playing this role via their appointed representatives of national governments. Given the difficulty some still have in accepting the cartel model for contemporary parties (despite ample evidence that it is in fact operative even at the international level, as successful parties work in collusion with national governments on behalf of the goals

they jointly set), it is tempting to stop here: recent scholarship goes against the dream of parties as agencies of democratic linkage between citizens and states, and these are hard truths to accept.

However, it is precisely at the international level that we begin to see the glimmerings of yet another disturbing change in the role parties play. National parties may be in collusion with national governments, but to whom do those governments belong and, if they have new owners, what do their new proprietors seek? Can we still be confident that elected leaders in charge of democratic governments always rule on behalf of the popular majorities who elected them?

National parties are formed – or re-formed – in new contexts now and carry out new functions. Their successful representatives sometimes take on a role that is, in a certain sense, *against the state*, and even against governance altogether. Such partisan leaders do not act against the holders of power, but against the very principles of the democratic state. They do so by subordinating national domestic goals to the imperatives of economic globalization, either because they believe that this will in fact make the nation collectively more prosperous, or simply in order to serve their own interests and those of their most important supporters.

Few would doubt that this is what has in fact been taking place in post-communist Russia, where studies have amply demonstrated that the new parties are at the service of powerful private interests with whom the national government negotiates to maintain its power (Pshizova, 2004; Golosov, 2003). Many perceive the 2003 invasion of Iraq by the United States as an activity undertaken on behalf of powerful oil interests, and some have gone so far as to see the events of September 11, 2001 as themselves the work of such interests. The determination of British and Italian elected leaders to send members of their own military to join that enterprise, against popular majorities of well over 80% opposing such initiatives, has been difficult to understand within the confines of the standard democratic paradigm. No doubt the phenomenon, if phenomenon there be, is not as widespread as some alarmists would imagine. Leaders are, after all, normally accorded flexibility of response in amazing and frightening times, in democracies as in other forms of government, and are not expected to follow the polls on a daily basis. Furthermore, it has never been the case that democratic governments in nation states give unreserved allegiance to the idea or practice of international governance, even in domains where they know themselves to be incapable of effective action. International acceptance of the idea of sovereignty militates strongly against internationalization of governance. Nonetheless, if parties are now more and more often working hand in hand with governments that are fundamentally anti-democratic, privileging the business contract over the social one on which the modern state is supposedly based, and if such parties' representatives are carrying this perspective into the international arena, then the consequences may be far greater than yet imagined. Indeed, the perils of sporadic acts of terrorism, however dreadful to witness, may prove to have considerably less long-range significance for the human condition than will this ruthless rejection of democratic norms.

It is, of course, hard to believe that political parties, so long considered the key mechanism for turning democratic dreams into something approximating democratic practice, could become dangerous instruments for achieving so opposite a goal. As Leon Epstein (1983) pointed out, those who study parties tend to be strongly committed to 'a long established conception of the special importance of parties in a democratic society ... essential intermediaries for effective representation of a large and diverse electorate'. He confesses that he himself has never really departed 'from the intellectual context of [this] continuing commitment'. Yet he dares to suggest that 'the context along with the commitment may not be immutable'. Now, more than two decades later, we certainly no longer believe parties are always effective agencies of democratic linkage between citizens and the state. The context has changed indeed, and the commitment has been shaken. We must consider the possibility that some parties are not only ever less capable of providing such linkage but are not really interested in doing so at all: they have different plans for the use of power.

NOTES

1   NGOs = non-governmental organizations; INGOs = international non-governmental organizations; TNCs = transnational corporations; TSMOs = transnational social movement organizations. Although not mutually exclusive, all these terms are used in the literature.
2   A fourth related topic, how some national parties seek to influence the creation and programs of parties in other nations, is another way parties play an important role internationally, one that space does not permit us to cover here. For an interesting study of the relationship between Western parties and the new parties of post-communist Europe, see Pridham (2000).
3   For a remarkable exception, see the discussion by Jacques Attali (2004). But although Attali praises NGOs' actions on behalf of democratic values and calls for them to be given a far greater and more institutionalized role within the United Nations, he says nothing about their having or being required to have democratic links to their memberships.

REFERENCES

Attali, Jacques (2004) 'Les ONG, rempart contre l'apocalypse', Le Monde (September 11): 1, 20.
Bardi, Luciano (2002) 'Parties and party systems in the European Union: National and supranational dimensions', in Kurt Richard Luther and Ferdinand Müller-Rommel (eds), Political Parties in the New Europe: Political and Analytical Challenges. Oxford: Oxford University Press.
Borgese, Elisabeth Mann (1999) 'Global civil society: Lessons from ocean governance', Futures, 31: 983–91.
Clark, Ann Marie, Friedman, Elisabeth J. and Hochstetler, Kathryn (1998) 'The sovereign limits of global civil society: A comparison of NGO participation in UN world conferences on the environment, human rights, and women', World Politics, 51 (October): 1–35.
Cleveland, Harlan and Anderson, Walter Truett (1999) 'Introduction. Transnational: A word whose time has come', Futures, 31: 879–85.
Day, Alan J. (2000) Directory of European Union Political Parties. London: John Harper Publishing.
Delpérée, Francis (2004) 'La Citoyenneté de l'Union', in Louis Dubouis (ed.), L'Union européenne. Paris: La Documentation Française.
Deschouwer, Kris (2000) 'The European multi-level party systems: Towards a framework for analysis'. Robert Schuman Centre Working Paper 2000/47, European University Institute, Badia Fiesolana, Italy.
Edwards, Michael and Hulme, David (1995) 'NGO performance and accountability in the post-cold war world', Journal of International Development, 7: 849–56.
Epstein, Leon (1983) 'The scholarly commitment to parties', in Ada Finifter (ed.), Political Science: The State of the Discipline. Washington, DC: American Political Science Association.
Etzioni-Halevy, Eva (2002) 'Linkage deficits in transnational politics', International Political Science Review, 23(2): 203–22.

Ferenczi, Thomas (2004a) 'Le projet de Constitution renforce sensiblement les pouvoirs du Parlement', *Le Monde* (June 14): 4.

Ferenczi, Thomas (2004b) 'L'Europe élargie s'est dotée d'une Constitution âprement négociéé', *Le Monde* (June 21): 2.

Ferenczi, Thomas (2004c) 'Pourquoi l'influence française s'est affaiblie à Bruxelles', *Le Monde* (August 18): 5.

Gaffney, John (ed.) (1996) *Political Parties and the European Union*. New York: Routledge.

Golosov, Grigorii (2003) 'The vicious circle of party underdevelopment in Russia: The regional connection', *International Political Science Review*, 24: 427–43.

Griffin, David Ray (2004) *A New Pearl Harbor*. Northampton, MA: Olive Branch Press.

Hix, Simon (2002) 'Parliamentary behavior with two principals: Preferences, parties and voting in the European Parliament', *American Journal of Political Science*, 46: 688–98.

Hix, Simon and Lord, Christopher (1997) *Political Parties in the European Union*. London: Macmillan.

Ignazi, Piero, Farrell, David M. and Römmele, Andrea (2005) 'The prevalence of "linkage-by-reward" in contemporary parties', in Andrea Römmele, David M. Farrell and Piero Ignazi, *Political Parties and Political Systems: The Concept of Linkage Revisited*. Westport, CT: Praeger.

International Herald Tribune (2004a) 'Europe elects a Parliament', *International Herald Tribune* (June 15): 3.

International Herald Tribune (2004b) 'Low EU vote tied to apathy', *International Herald Tribune* (July 29): 3.

International Monetary Fund (1998) *International Monetary Fund Annual Report and Summary of Proceedings 1998*. Washington, DC: IMF.

Iriye, Akira (1999) 'A century of NGO's', *Diplomatic History*, 23: 421–35.

Katz, Richard S. and Mair, Peter (1995) 'Changing models of party organization and party democracy: The emergence of the cartel party', *Party Politics*, 1: 5–28.

Kellow, Aynsley (2002) 'Comparing business and public interest associability at the international level', *International Political Science Review*, 23: 175–86.

Klein, Naomi (2003) 'Now Bush wants to buy the complicity of aid workers', *Canadian Globe* (June 23).

Ladrech, Robert (1997) 'Partisanship and party formation in European Union politics', *Comparative Politics*, 29: 167–85.

Lawson, Kay (1980) 'Political parties and linkage', in Kay Lawson (eds), *Political Parties and Linkage: A Comparative Perspective*. New Haven, CT: Yale University Press.

Lawson, Kay (1998) 'How parties are failing to adapt to domestic and global change'. Unpublished paper presented at European University Institute, March 16, p. 27.

Lawson, Kay, Römmele, Andrea and Karasimeonov, Georgi (1998) *Cleavages, Parties and Voters: Studies from Bulgaria, the Czech Republic, Hungary, Poland and Romania*. Westport, CT: Praeger.

Leonard, Mark (2002) 'Diplomacy by other means', *Foreign Policy*, 132(Sept/Oct): 48–53.

Lequesne, Christian and Labastida, Alejandro Ribo (2004) 'Institutions et jeux institutionnels', in Louis Dubouis (ed.), *L'Union européenne*. Paris: La Documentation Française.

Macdonald, Laura and Schwartz, Mildred A. (2002) 'Political parties and NGOs in the creation of new trading blocs in the Americas', *International Political Science Review*, 23: 135–58.

Pridham, Geoffrey (2000) 'External influences on party development and transnational party cooperation: The case of post-communist Europe'. Paper presented to meetings of Political Studies Association-UK, London, April 10–13.

Pshizova, Susanna (2004) 'Representative rule or the rule of representations: The case of Russian political parties', in Kay Lawson and Thomas Poguntke (eds), *How Political Parties Respond: Interest Aggregation Revisited*. London and New York: Routledge.

Reis, Elisa (2004) 'The lasting marriage between nation and state despite globalization', *International Political Science Review*, 25: 251–7.

Richardson, D. and Rootes, C. (eds) (1995) *The Green Challenge: The Development of Green Parties in Europe*. London: Routledge.

Ronit, Karsten and Schneider, Volker (2000) *Private Organizations and their Contribution to Problem Solving in the Global Arena*. London: Routledge.

Service France (2004) 'Entre abstention et vote-sanction, des enjeux trés nationaux', *Le Monde* (June 14): 8.

Sklair, Leslie (2002) 'The transnational capitalist class and global politics: Deconstructing the corporate state connection', *International Political Science Review*, 23: 159–74.

van der Heijden, H.A.B. (2002) 'Political parties and NGOs in global environmental politics', *International Political Science Review*, 23: 187–202.

Wells, David (1998) 'Acting globally: Transnational NGOs and political networks', *The Workbook* (Fall/Winter).

42

THE EUROPEAN UNION AND POLITICAL PARTIES

Robert Ladrech

INTRODUCTION

Political party activity in the European Union (EU) is represented in three interconnected dimensions. First, and foremost, is the national dimension in which national political parties are active. As regards the EU, it is the national party that selects candidates to stand in elections to the European Parliament (EP), and also exerts varying degrees of influence over its national delegation, for instance in the election of its leader. Second, there is the European Parliament itself. Its work is organized by parliamentary party groups, which, among other functions, select offices such as committee chairs, rapporteurs, etc. Apart from the four main party groups – social democrats, Christian democrats and conservatives, liberals, and greens – the formation of new party groups involves the input of national parties. Thirdly, there is the transnational dimension, the linking of national parties across the EU by party family in transnational party federations. As with the EP party groups, four transnational party federations exist, all having a level of organization that has evolved over the past 20 years or so. They are the European People's Party (EPP), the Party of European Socialists (PES), the European Liberal, Democrat and Radical Party (ELDR), and the European Green Party. In 2004, many of the parties making up the far left EP party group – which includes most of the remaining communist parties in Western Europe – announced the formation of their own transnational party federation, the European Party of the Left. These transnational party federations will be explored below in greater depth, but it should be clear at the outset that among the three dimensions of party activity mentioned, the transnational dimension is the least developed of the three in terms of direct impact on EU policy-making and perceived relevance by ordinary national party members. Yet one of the key functions of these transnational party federations is to link and deepen the relationship between the EP party groups and national parties: in other words, to link the national and supranational dimensions.

The development of the EU over time has had consequences for party activity. The European integration process, in particular the enhancement in the powers of the EP, has directly influenced EP party groups and transnational party federations. For EP party groups, direct elections, beginning in 1979, initiated a slow process of change in candidate selection, as well as having a varying impact on national politics. For the transnational party federations, their creation in the mid- to late 1970s was predicated upon the belief that a more partisan politics at the European level would emerge due to direct EP elections, and some level of organization among similar parties was needed in preparation for this eventuality. Between 1979 and the present, transnational party federations have experienced some modest organizational development, and this has roughly paralleled major increases in the policy competence of the EU, especially in the realm of monetary union (the creation of a single currency). In July 2004, a Party Statute concerning European transnational party federations came into force, and represents a significant change in the relationship between the federations and the EP party groups and national parties. These changes affecting the party federations, as well as their role in EU politics will be explored in more detail. First we turn to the background and description of the major party federations.

THE TRANSNATIONAL PARTY FEDERATIONS

In anticipation of direct elections to the EP, three party-family-linked transnational party federations were established: the Christian democratic EPP, the social democratic Confederation of Socialist Parties of the European Community (CSPEC), and the liberal ELDR. Initially small secretariats, they eventually became closely linked with their respective party groups in the EP, to the extent that personnel working in their secretariats and funding derived from the party groups. Beginning in the early 1990s, the EPP and CSPEC began a review and eventual organizational enhancement of their respective party federations. Ostensibly, the catalyst for this attention was the 1992 Maastricht Treaty on Economic and Monetary Union, the EU initiative to establish a single currency by the end of the decade. For many in national party leaderships, this leap in the European integration process represented a very material challenge to domestic policy-making and politics. The notion of better coordination across national boundaries seemed much less of an abstract idea. The party federation already represented, in an embryonic state, an organizational mechanism whereby this cooperation and coordination, at least initially on an ideational level, could quickly commence. Indeed, Johansson (2002) argues that the EPP was a factor in the ability of Christian democrat prime ministers/party leaders to bring British Prime Minister Margaret Thatcher on board to support such an historic integrationist initiative as monetary union. Additionally, the Maastricht Treaty contained the first reference to the existence and role of transnational, or European, parties (Article 138a). It reads: 'Political parties at the European level are important as a factor for integration within the Union. They contribute to forming a European awareness and to expressing the political will of the citizens of the Union.'

The rest of the 1990s witnessed an increase in activities of both of these main party federations in terms of bringing party leaders and others into contact and collaboration on EU directed policy ideas (the CSPEC, as part of its organizational evolution, changed its name to

the Party of European Socialists in 1992). The EPP, PES and ELDR developed affiliated organizations, each of them having a youth wing. Before proceeding further, a brief sketch of the four current party federations is presented. Following this, an analysis of their role in the EU and relationship with their constituent national parties and party groups is detailed.

The European People's Party

The EPP was established in 1976. This party federation was primarily composed of Christian democratic parties, from large countries such as Germany and Italy, and smaller ones such as Belgium and the Netherlands. These parties were already members of a larger pan-European organization, the European Union of Christian Democrats (EUCD). As for their position regarding European integration, these parties have a long tradition of supporting not only the integration process launched in the 1950s, with its primary focus on economic integration, but also political integration, even endorsing the creation of a federal European union. This stance is consistent with their founding beliefs in supranational authority, as witnessed by their acceptance of religious authority, and for the specifically Catholic parties, the authority of Rome. Thus ideological differences over the finality of European integration were not a divisive issue among the founding parties of the EPP.

Along with the PES, Liberals and Greens, the EPP drew financial support from its EP party group. Although, unlike the others, it did not have its offices in the same building as the group, it was nevertheless intimately tied to EP dynamics. For instance, some of its presidents had also held the same office in the group (e.g. Martens). Despite this link with the EP, the EPP, as with the other transnational party federations, is a tool of the party leaders. Consequently, in order to understand the strategy of the EPP over the course of the past thirty years, one must look to the dominance of its constituent parties and their preferences. In the case of the EPP, the German Christian Democratic Union (CDU), under the leadership of Chancellor Helmut Kohl, played a critical role in its evolution. The EPP could be said to have been an additional field of action for Kohl's German foreign or European economic policy. Beginning to break out of the traditional formats of Christian social market economics in the 1980s, Kohl employed the meeting of EPP party leaders to support a more neo-liberal thrust in EU economic and then monetary policy. The export of this revision to traditional Christian democracy was also aimed at the new parties arising in the former Soviet-dominated countries of Eastern Europe after 1989. In this respect, the expansion of the EPP to take in conservative and liberal parties was a product of the attempt to influence and coordinate broad policy orientations among as large a pool of parties as possible. This same strategy was also shared by the EPP group in the EP. The fruit of this expansion could be seen in the EP with the plurality gained in both the 1999 and 2004 elections to the EP.

Although EPP member parties range from Christian democratic to ones such as Forza Italia and the French neo-Gaullist UMP, the linkage between the modest secretariat of the EPP and its national constituent parties remains one of support for elite interaction. Despite having the option of individual membership, the EPP is not a concern of internal national party politics. As such, beyond the interests of national party leaders, the EPP, along with its EP group, is remote from national politics and exists primarily within the confines of EU-level political dynamics.

The Party of European Socialists

The transnational party federation of the EU's social democratic parties, founded in 1974, was the Confederation of Socialist Parties of the European Community. The only one of the transnational party federations to have member parties in all EU member states, along with the EPP, CSPEC represented, at least in theory, the major alternative orientation towards a neo-liberal EU. However, unlike the EPP, ideological differences among left-of-center parties prevented the same degree of cohesiveness on matters of major European integration initiatives as was the case with the EPP. Until the mid- to late 1980s, the British Labour Party and the Danish Social Democratic Party opposed most integration proposals. Their eventual embrace – however conditional – of further European integration by the 1990s allowed a reexamination of the role of the CSPEC. In November 1992 the CSPEC transformed itself into the PES, and in so doing was charged by its national party leaders to assist in the development of better coordination of social democratic initiatives at the EU level, but also in programmatic development. Unlike the EPP, social democracy had been inextricably linked with national state action, and the reluctance to

'give up' control to a supranational authority was a cause of divisiveness among PES member party leaderships (although the degree of difference declined over the 1990s).

Links between the PES and its EP party group were characterized as one of dependence. Office space as well as financial support was the norm until the coming into force of the EU Statute on European Parties in 2004 (see below). Unlike the EPP, however, the presidency of the PES was kept very separate from the EP group leadership, none of its presidents ever having served as group president: Claes (Belgium) and Cook (UK), both foreign ministers, Scharping (Germany), defense minister, and Rasmussen (Denmark), a former prime minister.

The PES has for most of its existence opposed individual membership (though this is due more to the objections of a few member parties than a widely shared belief). Its links with its member parties beyond the party leadership are superficial. Most national party representatives to the PES are appointed rather than elected, and the fact that its manifesto for EP elections has served at times as the official document for national campaigns is widely unknown within parties. In its 2004 Congress, though, the PES elected a new president in its very first competitive election, between Rasmussen and Amato (Italy). Both men pledged to make the PES more relevant to national party members and raise the profile of the PES in general. It remains to be seen whether or not this attempt will succeed. Like the EPP, the PES has also established memberships in Eastern and Central Europe, some being completely new parties established after 1989, a few reformed former communist parties.

European Liberal, Democratic and Reform Party

The ELDR, formerly the Federation of Liberal and Democrat Parties, was founded in 1976. From the beginning, the ELDR experienced a much more heterogeneous ideological composition than the EPP or the PES. There is a noticeable variation along left–right issues as well as on the pro-integration/anti-integration axis. In addition to ideological variation, the ELDR is made up of relatively small national parties, reflected in the size of the ELDR group in the EP as well as in transnational coordination, where liberal parties in government are scarce. Along with the EPP and PES, the ELDR was established in anticipation of direct elections to the EP, and the possibility of a European party system developing. Also like the two other transnational party federations, organizational changes in the ELDR (leading to, among other things, the name change), occurred in the wake of the Maastricht Treaty, here the catalyst being more specifically Article 138a.

In addition to financial support from its EP group, the relations between the party and group have developed only to a modest degree. This is partly explained by the ideological variance within both group and party, and also the unbalanced relationship between the ELDR's national party members and their strength in the EP. In particular, until 1999 when proportional representation was introduced for EP elections in the United Kingdom, the British Liberal Democrats were underrepresented in the EP, but were one of the largest delegations in the ELDR party (Sandström, 2002).

After the 2004 EP elections, a new centrist group in the EP was formed. This was composed of the existing ELDR group along with a breakaway French party from the EPP-ED group, the UDF, plus a handful of members of the European Parliament (MEPs) from minor parties in Italy. In the autumn of 2004, plans were announced for a new transnational party, jointly presented by the UDF party leader Bayrou, Italian Margharita party leader Rutelli and former president of the European Commission Prodi. How this party related to the ELDR is unclear, although it certainly occupies a portion of the ideological space of the ELDR.

European Green Party/European Federation of Green Parties

Of the four transnational party federations, the European Greens were not present in the first directly elected European Parliament. An early form of transnational cooperation including more than just Green Parties, the 'Coordination of Green and Radical Parties in Europe', was created in 1980. In anticipation of more financial and organizational support from the EP, a new transnational organization comprising only Green parties was founded in 1983, the European Green Coordination (EGC). It was not, however, until after the Green parties' breakthrough in the EP elections of 1989 that serious thought of a transnational party federation approaching the organizational development of either the EPP, PES or ELDR was undertaken. Thus in 1993, the European Federation of Green Parties (EFGP) was established. A basic difference between the EFGP and the other transnational party federations is that non-EU European parties were allowed

full membership; associate status was the norm for the other party federations.

Relations between the EFGP and the Green group in the EP have also diverged from those of the other three transnational party federations. No linkage between the EGC and the Green members of the EP (known as GRAEL – Green Alternative European Link) existed before 1989. Until 1992, better relations between the two components hardly resulted in more than exchange of information and seminar and conference interaction (Dietz, 2002). Closer cooperation since the EP election in 1994 has resulted in minor organizational changes wherein the Green group is more integrated in the party. Yet, compared to the other party federations, the Green group operates in a much more autonomous fashion, and although the number of parties in the Group has expanded due to EU enlargement, and thus the balance between parties in the Group and in the EP is more even, the ideological antipathy towards supranationalism on the part of some national Green parties precludes any substantial organizational progress towards the model of either the EPP or PES.

In the spring of 2004, the EFGP transformed itself into the European Green Party (although owing to the aforementioned ideological hostility, the name European Federation of Green Parties is retained). One substantial difference between the European Green Party and its predecessor was the creation of a common platform for the 2004 elections to the EP, used in all national Green party campaigns. It remains to be seen if a further adjustment in terms of closer relations between the group and party will take place.

FUNCTIONS OF TRANSNATIONAL PARTY FEDERATIONS

Party–group relations

From the brief sketch above, it is clear that transnational party federations have evolved since their establishment in the mid-1970s. All four European parties have experienced organizational changes in terms of internal decision-making as well as relations with their respective EP party groups. Article 138a draws attention in the first instance to the role of European level parties 'as a factor for integration within the Union'. By attempting to join national party orientations with the party groups in the EP, a general notion of direction in terms of policy was ultimately hoped for. Organizational enhancements over the 1990s, for example employing qualified majority voting instead of unanimity on certain issues, were expected to make the transnational parties more effective in communicating their preferences to their respective EP groups. Problems have been encountered along the way, however. For the EPP, the relationship with the group was complicated by its tactical alliance with the British Conservative delegation. Not a member of the EPP party, they have consistently been at odds with one of the basic and founding features of the EPP, support for a stronger supranational dimension in the form of federal union. In fact, the EPP group was renamed the EPP-ED, with ED standing for European Democrats. Tension between the British Conservatives and more traditionally minded Christian democratic national delegations has been therefore a problematic feature of party–group relations.

The PES party–group relationship is the most unproblematic of all the main actors. In contrast to the others, ideological differences among the national member parties diminished over time, leading some commentators to note actual convergence. The British Labour Party and the PASOK of Greece are but two examples of this change. In terms of how this impacted matters at the European level, it is a contributing factor to explain the rise in voting discipline in the group. It also led to the ability to find a common ground in terms of policy pronouncements, supported by the group, as for instance was the case for an Employment Chapter in the 1997 Amsterdam Treaty. By and large, though, the party has not evolved into a dominant position *vis-à-vis* the group. As with all the transnational parties, in reality steps to strengthen their organizational profiles have been opposed by one or more member national parties (to be discussed further below).

Although improved from the first decade of existence, the improvement of relations between the ELDR party and its group has been modest. This is explained by the continuing left-liberal vs. right-liberal split in party and group. Although in the second half of the 1999–2004 EP session the ELDR group president held the EP presidency in alliance with the EPP-ED, the skill with which he wielded influence helped the image of the Parliament more than it helped matters between the party and group.

Finally, the Greens, although also improving their party–group relations in recent years, are far from the level of integration, however modest, seen in the EPP and PES. Continued

attachment to national sovereignty, a position energetically and explicitly held by some of the national member parties, prohibits increased organizational change that results in national group delegations' autonomy becoming prescribed by others.

The situation, then, after 30 years of historic change in European integration, broadly speaking, is the continued centrality of national parties in the development and evolution of party activity at the European level. In the three-way relationship, national parties remain the 'gatekeepers' on transnational party activity, and continue to have a role, though in preliminary stages, in EP party group activity.

Elections and campaigns

Article 138a also mentions the importance of 'forming European awareness and a political will'. Bearing in mind that the first three transnational party federations were established with direct elections to the EP in mind, it is not surprising then that one of their primary tasks was to help coordinate European Parliament election campaigns. Producing a common election manifesto was seen by promoters as a vital task in order to demonstrate a European perspective. Unfortunately, this proved much more difficult than was expected. Although the four party federations have had a common manifesto since 1979 (1989 for the Greens), they quite often had opt-outs by various parties, and, even more importantly, were usually ignored in the actual campaigns of the national member parties. Elections to the EP have been described as 'second-order', and in most instances the competitive dynamics in each national arena has more to do with government–opposition politics than with issues of a European nature. In some countries, additional parties spring up solely to contest these elections, and at times breakaway political formations appear (this has been the case particularly for France). Time and effort are expended by the party federations in this activity (specifically their secretariats and manifesto working parties), yet at the end of the day national parties continue to jealously guard 'their' domestic political systems from European or transnational 'intrusion'.

Party leader summits

Most of the activity of party federations, especially with the original three, involves national party elites. No one activity better illustrates this than the party leader summits. Party leaders, in many cases including prime ministers (other than the Greens), have met under the auspices of their respective party federations. Members of their party family in the European Commission also attend. Beginning in the early 1990s, these meetings became formalized, with meetings every 6 months on the eve of EU summits. Hix (1996) has argued that these party leader meetings are important instances of coordination by senior political figures, and contribute towards the actual negotiations in the EU summit itself. The impact of these meetings, which are dependent upon various media for their dissemination, is probably greater for the party federations in terms of strengthening the networks of party leaders and their assistants and advisors. Nevertheless, they do represent a public expression of party family solidarity, and at least on a symbolic level are useful. Party leader summits have, of course, more meaning for the EPP and PES, since they are the party federations that include most prime ministers, decreasing in importance for the ELDR, and non-existent for the Greens.

Coordination activities: The Convention on the Future of Europe

In the spring and summer of 2002, a Convention on the Future of Europe was convened. The primary task of this Convention was to draft a constitution for the EU, essentially to consolidate the various treaties, streamline them, and make the whole more understandable for Europe's citizens. The Convention was made up of MEPs, national parliamentarians, representatives from member state governments, and an assortment of representatives from the European Commission and various interest groups and non-governmental organizations. As a group, MEPs undoubtedly had more expertise in the relevant issues than did their national counterparts, and indeed, sitting in party group formation they contributed in a critical manner to the work of the Convention. Costa (2004) notes, though, that the party federations played a key role in structuring the positions of the groups. In the case of the EPP, the party had already approved a constitutional document, and the PES, although without such a specific contribution, presented a 'Priorities for Europe' document that assisted in the coordination process.

Statute on European Parties

Article 138a, and its successor in the Amsterdam Treaty, Article 191, did little more than state a

general desire for European-level parties to have a role in the European integration process. The efforts of the party federation presidents to give a more concrete and legal foundation to their organizations met with some success when the European Council summit in Nice 2000 approved a Statute on European Parties that achieved many of their aims. This statute came into effect in July 2004, and has significant implications for the linkage role of party federations, in the short term and in the longer term. In the short term, the financial, administrative, and (in all cases except the EPP) office space dependence of the party federations on their respective party group comes to an end. The PES, ELDR and European Green Party have relocated their offices out of the EP. Furthermore, direct subsidy from the group to the party has ended. Party federations now draw funding from a pool of money granted by the European Commission, as well as attracting a percentage of 'own' finance, stipulated to be at least 20% of their operating budget. The cost of office space and the relative decline in financing has meant that the range of activities by the party federations has been curtailed. Increased contributions by national member parties are unlikely, as they are themselves in continual search for funds. Thus one dimension in the linkage between party federations and party groups has changed substantially, in the short term to the detriment of the party federations.

In the longer term, the new circumstances in which the party federations find themselves promote a more independent position than they have experienced to date. The president of the PES, elected in 2004, suggested that one possible solution to the funding requirement would be to ask national party members – that is, individuals – to contribute. Admittedly, this would only work if the PES had a higher profile within the national parties, and to this end Rasmussen pledged himself ready to engage. The Statute on European Parties has plunged the party federations into a new and more uncertain environment, and it remains to be seen how they will adapt.

CONCLUSION

European transnational party federations were created in the anticipation that the European integration process, with the advent of direct elections to the European Parliament, may evolve toward a form of parliamentary government. Accordingly, political parties would have their place, in the work of the EP itself and perhaps, depending on the direction of the integration process, in the promotion of candidates in competitive elections to the presidency of the European Commission. After thirty years of existence, the party federations have experienced only modest organizational growth, and their linkage function between the supranational and national dimensions remains extremely modest. On the other hand, the EU's development during the same period, although significant, and in terms of monetary union historic, has not been such to resemble a parliamentary system, no matter how much increased influence the EP has itself achieved. Coupled with national party/government hesitancy – if not explicit rejection – to cede real influence to organizations that may at some point in the future work against themselves, party federations are in a weak position forcefully to implement the aspirations in Article 138a. They remain important sites for the cooperation and occasional coordination of national political elites, a way of reducing their transaction costs when attempting to act on a European level. The implementation of the European Constitution, and the evolution in the manner in which European Commission presidents are chosen, are medium-term events that may have consequences for party federations as they continue to find a role for themselves.

REFERENCES

Costa, Olivier (2004) 'La contribution de la composante "Parliament européen" aux négociations de la Convention', *Politique Européenne*, no. 13 (Spring): 21–41.

Dietz, Thomas (2002) 'European Federation of Green Parties', in Karl Magnus Johansson and Peter Zervakis (eds), *European Political Parties between Cooperation and Integration*. Baden-Baden: Nomos.

Hix, Simon (1996) 'The transnational party federations', in John Gaffney (ed.), *Political Parties and the European Union*. London: Routledge.

Johansson, Karl Magnus (2002) 'Another road to Maastricht: The christian Democrat coalition and the quest for European Union', *Journal of Common Market Studies*, 40: 871–94.

Sandström, Camilla (2002) 'European Liberal, Democrat and Reform Party', in Karl Magnus Johansson and Peter Zervakis (eds), *European Political Parties between Cooperation and Integration*. Baden-Baden: Nomos.

43

PARTY TRANSFORMATIONS: THE UNITED STATES AND WESTERN EUROPE

William Crotty

The function of political parties is both to adapt to social transformations and to enable the society to manage its divisions in a peaceful manner. It is the role of the parties to identify the demographic and other cleavages found in the population; to offer policy programs providing competing resolutions to the paramount problems of the time (and, not incidentally, reflecting the core interests of their base); and to mobilize support for their positions sufficient to elect their candidates and to realize their issue agendas. Parties' responsibilities include: forming coalitions, establishing policy commitments, selecting candidates, and mobilizing voters. In the process of such critical democratic linkage functions, they coalesce electoral support among relatively like-minded groups, respond to their needs, and attempt (through government action) to address those needs once in office. It can be viewed as a continuing cycle of identification and resolution, one vital in keeping a democracy viable and responsive to the concerns of its citizens.

As John H. Aldrich (1995) writes, at any one period in time parties can be identified and contrasted both in terms of their social mission and the manner in which they choose to approach it. A party is structured

in a particular context – in terms of problems it is constructed to address ... . The party is created to address a central, defining problem and institutionalized to resolve it over the long term. ... that problem changes over time and with it the form of party that political elites create to seek to resolve matters in their favor. ... The historical context yields different concerns ... and these well may

have ... a consequence that particular sets of institutional arrangements within these very broad constraints are better choices for politicians seeking to resolve those differing problems on favorable terms.

The demands of society change, and the parties change to meet them. In this sense, parties are derivative institutions, reflecting the nature and concerns of the society that develops them.

The following posits the fundamental functions parties address and examines the conceptual and empirical explanations given for the parties' systemic evolution. The focus is on Western Europe and the United States, beginning with the latter. In the conclusion, some thoughts are offered as to the consequences of the transformations under way. The most basic objective in such an analysis is to assess the qualitative aspects of change as they relate to implementing a liberal (in the classic sense), representative, and democratic governing order.

PARTY FUNCTIONS IN A DEMOCRATIC SOCIETY

Parties are of core importance to the conduct of fully representative democratic politics. Although they are seldom broadly perceived in such a positive light, a democracy cannot operate without a vital, competitive, and responsive party system (Schattschneider, 1960, 1942; Dalton, 2002; Hofstadter, 1969; Aldrich, 1995; Coleman, 1996; Crotty, 2001a, 2001b).

Table 43.1 *Functions served by the parties*

Parties-in-the-Electorate
Simplifying choices for voters
Educating citizens
Generating symbols of identification and loyalty
Mobilizing people to participate

Parties-as-Organizations
Recruiting political leadership and seeking
   governmental office
Training political elites
Articulating political interests
Aggregating political interests

Parties-in-Government
Creating majorities in government
Organizing the government
Implementing policy objectives
Organizing dissent and opposition
Ensuring responsibility for government actions
Controlling government administration
Fostering stability in government

Source: Dalton and Wattenberg, 2000: 5.

V.O. Key, Jr. (1964), the most influential of American social scientists in laying the foundation for the study of political parties, distinguished three levels of party activity: the party-in-the-electorate; the party as organization; and the party-in-government. Building on this tripartite classification, Russell J. Dalton and Martin P. Wattenberg (2000) subclassify the functions served by a party in a democratic society. These are listed in Table 43.1. In abbreviated form, they can be summarized as follows:

- mobilizing voters and organizing electoral choice;
- including a mass electorate in political decision-making;
- recruiting a nation's political leadership through its policy-making and administration of public affairs in regard to the most pressing social concerns, while remaining accountable to the needs of its base-level supporters.

The basic questions given this agenda, then, are: How well do the contemporary political parties perform the functions critical to a democratic society? How and with what degree of success do parties adapt to societal pressures? What drives party transformations? How can such change and its broader consequences be accounted for and evaluated?

FOUNDATIONS OF PARTY CHANGE

Social change leads to party transformations. One of the basic elements in this process is the nature and consolidation of the parties in the social fabric of a nation, measured in this case by levels of party support and the impact of party affiliations on voter decision-making. Another, is the question of the parties' ability to mobilize voters to the extent that the mass electorate, at a minimum, participate in elections. Thirdly, there is the question of accountability, in the sense of how representative the parties are in reflecting and responding to the views of their electors and being held responsible for their actions and policies through the medium of elections.

We begin by looking at the American system in detail, and then suggest that it may be indicative of the movements affecting party systems throughout the Western world.

THE PARTIES' ROOTS IN THE ELECTORATE

It has been fashionable in recent decades to speak of the political parties' weakening hold on the electorate (Burnham, 1970; Wattenberg, 1991, 1998; Crotty, 1986; Dalton, 2002; Dalton and Wattenberg, 2000; Lawson and Merkl, 1988). Much of the debate has focused on what has come to be referred to as 'party decline'. Basically the argument is that parties fulfill their electoral function less satisfactorily, and that non-party groups, individuals, and for-hire consultants have become increasingly important in financing candidates and winning campaigns. The parties have become further separated both from their base in the electorate and, with the party reform movement of the late 1960s and early 1970s, even lose control of the choice of the candidates who run under their label.

Possibly the most damaging aspect of the 'decline' literature has been the emphasis on the increasingly distant relationship between the parties and their supporters or identifiers and, as a consequence, the declining impact of the parties on electoral decision-making. To fully appreciate the argument, it is necessary to go back to the earliest of the national, survey-based, empirical studies of mass party affiliation and its prominence in determining election outcomes. These initial studies had shown party identification to be the principal factor influencing voter choice (Campbell *et al.*, 1960, 1966;

Miller and Shanks, 1996). A series of later studies questioned the primacy of the parties' influence, emphasizing instead the increasing importance of issue positions in electoral decision-making, reflecting the changing nature of the times, of policy importance in a campaign, and of a candidate's appeal (Pomper, 1972; Pomper and Lederman, 1980; Nie et al., 1976).

In broad terms, and looking at the electoral system as a whole (as against the forces influencing individual choice), the shift appears to have begun in the mid- to late 1960s. Walter Dean Burnham (1970) spoke of what he called 'party decomposition' and 'long-term electoral disaggregation'. Burnham and others have developed this argument by focusing on the 'dealignment' of the electorate from the parties, that is, the increasing independence of voters in deciding on candidates and being influenced by issue positions in a campaign. These emphases have led to a decreasing impact of party affiliation on the electoral decision. Burnham contends that the election of 1968 ushered in a new era in American politics, one in which 'the parties were decisively replaced at the margins by the impact of the "permanent campaign"' (Burnham, 1970; see also Paulson, 2000).

Others have taken up the cry. A number of studies have demonstrated a substantial decline in party identification over the four to five decades (or more) since the party identification measure was introduced. The early years which provided the baseline for subsequent studies and in which much of the theorizing was built came to be called the 'stable-party period'. More recent decades have seen volatility and unpredictability in voting outcome that have undermined the stability produced by the decisive influence of party loyalty in determining the vote.

As party ties have weakened, there has been a concurrent rise in the number of Independents. Three characteristics stand out about the increase in the independence of the electorate. First is the reconfiguration of the composition of the Independent bloc. It was once considered the most apathetic, most ill-informed, and least politically involved of all party-related voting categories. In more recent times, the move towards the Independent group in the electorate has shown quite the opposite trend: those with high levels of formal education, the better-off economically and more professional occupations with greater political sophistication and more issue sensitivity in deciding their vote are coming to dominate the Independent bloc. Those groups closest to the political extremes, the least knowledgeable and the least well-off in society, and the least active as well as the most

knowledgeable and better-off (and considerably more politically active), combine in the Independent category. The influx into this category of those who traditionally would have been considered the most atypical of Independent voters has been taken as a sign of disillusionment with, and potential rejection of, the contemporary parties.

As a consequence, the Independent vote has increased in importance in deciding election outcomes. The images associated with the parties are less positive and less compelling for such voters (Crotty, 2001a, 2001b; Owen et al., 2001; Wattenberg, 1991, 1998; Dalton and Wattenberg, 2000). The shifts in voter alignments have also resulted in a major decline in party-line voting (i.e., the correlation between voting for the same party at different levels of the electoral system, roughly 0.80 in the first decades of the twentieth century, has come down to levels of 0.4 and 0.3 in more recent elections). Split-ticket voting has become a staple of contemporary elections and what has come to be called the 'candidate-centered campaign' dominates the current political scene. The changes in party relevance are directly correlated with demographic factors such as income, formal education, lifestyles, occupation, and age (the oldest voters in the electorate are the most partisan, the youngest – and those entering politics during the height of the Vietnam era – the least partisan). Dealignment tendencies increase as one systematically moves towards younger voter groups.

Within a restructured political environment, what then is the role of the parties? The parties do not disappear, but their ability to shape voting decisions within the electorate and to attract mass support has been threatened. Martin P. Wattenberg writes: 'most voters now view parties as a convenience rather than as a necessity'. He goes on to reassert the historic importance of parties by posing the question that brings into relief the transitions under way: 'regardless of whether the public recognizes it or not, parties are necessities for structuring the vote. Political scientists have long recognized the indispensable functions performed by parties, and dealignment has only reinforced this view. ... the key question then is not whether political parties can survive in an atmosphere of dealignment, but whether they still perform many of their key functions' (Wattenberg, 1991: 32).

Not everybody accepts this critique. Warren E. Miller argued for the continued importance of party identification as a principal force in structuring voter decision-making (Miller, 1990, 1998, 2002; Miller and Stokes, 1996). Miller contends that the events associated with the

late 1960s and the early 1970s – the war in
Southeast Asia, Watergate, political assassina-
tions, widespread disorder and violence, the
civil rights revolution, counter-culture demonstrations against authority – did significantly
affect young adults during this time period and
thus have had a lasting impact on the quality
and intensity of this age group's ties to the parties. The impact of these events was less pronounced in influencing the party loyalties of
older generations. As Miller (1998: 115) put it:

> the larger impact of the anti-politics debate seems to
> have been a generational effect: The young reacted
> to the events of the period more sharply and possi-
> bly even more permanently than did the older
> cohorts. It was the refusal and delay of the young in
> accepting partisan ties, not the lasting rejection of
> the loyalties once held by their elders, that produced
> the indicators of dealignment in the mid-1970s.

Given this, future partisan identifications
might have been expected to continue to fall
off, but:

> the post-1976 evidence points to an increase in the
> incidence of party attachments among the young
> and strengthening of their partisan sentiments.
> … where the strength of partisan sentiments is
> concerned, a pervasive upturn since the 1970s has
> been led by the same young cohorts whose original
> entry into the electorate was dominated by non-
> partisans. Each of the younger cohorts who con-
> tributed so much to the apparent national
> dealignment has experienced a dramatic increase in
> both the incidence and the intensity of partisan sen-
> timents in each of the elections of the 1980s as the
> political climate normalized. Their level of attach-
> ment … remained much below the norm that we
> associate with their generational counterparts in the
> 1950s, but primarily because they started from such
> an abnormally low point when they first entered
> the electorate. They have in fact made a large con-
> tribution to the national indications of renewed
> partisanship. (Miller and Shanks, 1996: 109)

Miller contends that party identification, while
showing changes in intensity and in the comprehensiveness of affiliation, remains a powerful
influence on and predictor of the vote (Miller,
1990, 1996, and with Goldstein and Jones, 2002).

In many respects, the contending sides may
not be as far apart as they appear. Partisan identification has declined (and other factors have
increased in importance accordingly) but it is
still significant for those who vote. The parties
do not reach out as systematically or as effectively as they might to organize or draw into the
electorate the less politically sophisticated non-
voters or members of minority groups. Failure to

mobilize non-voters is a fundamental weakness
of the modern party system (Conway, 2001a).

While substantial disagreement exists as to
the extent of partisan dealignment and its consequences, it pales in significance compared to
efforts to explain the future directions of parties.
A realignment of the New Deal party system,
one that would reinvigorate it and position it as
a force of primary relevance in contemporary
politics, has long been anticipated. Miller claims
a realignment did occur in the 1960s and in the
Reagan era, and Burnham and Paulson (among
others) also view 1968 as a critical realigning
election or period. None of these candidates to
be called realigning elections, however, reached
significant groups in the apolitical strata of the
electorate or fundamentally changed the cleavage system supporting the major parties. On the
other hand, Wattenberg and others would argue
that Americans perceive the conventional party
system as irrelevant to the resolution of the
major issues of the day and that because the
political parties are seen as less relevant, or irrelevant, a realignment is non-functional and
unlikely (Wattenberg, 1991, 1998; Dalton and
Wattenberg, 2000).

The issues may appear technical and remote
from everyday concerns. In truth, the argument is over the importance of the political
party in determining election outcomes and in
structuring choices for the mass electorate. The
future of the parties' role in all of these scenar-
ios at best is unclear and at worst assumes a
weak and diminishing significance. Given
Burnham's (and others') contention that parties are the most effective agencies ever created
to organize and represent mass electorates, and
since there are no obvious contenders to fill
this role, these are not encouraging signs.

Several conclusions can be asserted with
some degree of certainty: the current parties are
less significant than they were at the height of
the 'stable-party period' in the 1950s; their
impact on voter decision-making is more in
question today than in earlier times; political
candidates run now on their own initiative; the
parties' contribution, beyond supplying links to
fundraisers, consultants and pollsters, is minimal; and the future of the political parties in
these regards is speculative and uncertain.

PARTIES AND DEMOCRATIC
MASS MOBILIZATION

A chronic problem, and one of the most extraordinary failures of the political parties and the

political system more generally, is voter turnout. The United States has consistently had one of the lowest voter turnouts among industrialized nations. It is not a welcome situation for those who believe democracy means the participation of all, or as many as possible, in deciding a nation's direction.

E.E. Schattschneider has called the rate of participation in elections 'the *sickness* of democracy'. He raised the question as to what is 'the limit of tolerance of passive abstention' within the American system. As Schattschneider (1960: 104) notes, the problem is severe and 'it points out a profound contradiction between theory and practice in American democracy':

> Every regime lives on a body of dogma, self-justification, glorification, and propaganda about itself. In the United States this body of dogma and tradition centers about democracy. The hero of the system is the voter who is commonly described as the ultimate source of all authority. The fact that something like 40 million [in the 1950s] adult Americans are so unresponsive to [the] regime that they do not trouble to vote is the single-most truly remarkable fact about it.

More recently, the overall level of participation in elections has hovered at around one-half of the eligible voters in presidential contests (49.1% in 1996, 50.7% in the 2000, and 57% in 2004) and one-third to 40 percent in mid-term congressional races.

Schattschneider goes on to make the point that the major way of stimulating significant change in public policy is through an expansion of the political community and that extensions of the electorate have been a by-product of party conflict. Political parties are the principal agents for creating a more inclusive electorate and for expanding the frontiers of democratic decision-making (Keyssar, 2000). The evidence is that they are not doing an acceptable job in these regards. The consequences could be grave: 'If we have lost the capacity to involve an expanding public in the political system, it is obvious that American democracy has arrived at a turning point' (Schattschneider, 1960: 98).

There is a distinct pattern dividing participants and non-participants. Those less likely to vote include those with the least formal education, those of lower socioeconomic status, minorities, the less well-off economically, younger people, and those not affiliated with a political party or having a low level of interest in campaigns or election outcomes.

It could be contended that America has a class-driven electorate: those of higher socioeconomic status participate in politics, while those of lower socioeconomic standing do not. This pattern of a class-divided turnout and a low rate of participation is not found to the same extent in democratic nations with more encompassing and active party systems (Dalton, 2002).

One argument has been that those who choose not to vote participate in other ways. Such is not the case. M. Margaret Conway writes:

> Citizens of higher socioeconomic status are more likely to engage in several kinds of political activities, including organizational and campaign activities and contacting public officials as well as voting in elections [than those of lower socioeconomic status]. They also perform each of these activities more frequently. This pattern of more frequent performance of several types of political activity by persons of higher socioeconomic status does not occur in all developed democracies. In some countries, social and political organizations mobilize individuals of lower socioeconomic status and bring them to levels of political activity similar to those attained by the middle class. (Conway, 1991: 21)

The advantages of professional and economic status are magnified, not lowered, when other forms of political participation are examined (Verba et al., 1995).

Registration barriers to the vote have lessened substantially in recent decades, although the American system of personal registration presents more of an obstacle than that experienced in other countries. Yet as registration barriers have weakened since the 1960s, the participation levels have not increased (Flanigan and Zingale, 1994: 46). No one has a clear answer as to why, or what can be done to increase overall participation in the long run. An estimated two-thirds to 70% of registered voters participate in elections, a turnout comparable to most advanced industrial nations.

A general disillusionment with politics and detachment from the political system appear to play a significant role in explaining low turnout. Two general sets of factors can be identified as important. One can be labelled 'social connectedness', or the extent to which individuals are integrated into the community, and the other 'political connectedness', the extent to which they believe a political presence important and politicians and parties relate to their concerns and can address their problems (Teixeira, 1980; see also Wolfinger and Rosenstone, 1980; Rosenstone and Hansen, 1993). The designations get at the basic idea of a disconnection from the political system that appears to affect millions of Americans.

Voter mobilization and the extension of the bounds of participation in the political system are functions of the individual parties and the party system more generally. The evidence is they are doing a poor job. In terms of expanding the voting pool to include the interests of the less well-off and those without other political resources, they have been lacking. This can contribute to the picture of a party system more unified and cohesive at elite levels and designed to service such elites in election campaigns and in office, but one deficient at the mass level.

Some class and economic interests fare better than others. They do so because they participate in politics. The parties and candidates confine their campaign appeals to the known or most likely voters in the established voting universe, preferring not to venture into uncertain waters through expensive and unpredictable efforts to mobilize those with weaker political attachments. The result, in effect, is a middle-class electorate. Its interests are the ones both parties choose to address in campaigns. Unfortunately, it is one that excludes around one-half of those potentially eligible to vote.

A constantly underrepresented electorate limits the possibilities for structural change. The same voters repeatedly participating in elections have fashioned a middle- and upper middle-class electorate, one to which both parties have adapted. Representation for the groups identified as participation-oriented places policy and strategic boundaries on the parties seeking to win office, ones that confine the issues publicly debated and the parties' sensitivity to these. Agenda redirection or expansions of the voting pool would likely occur only under the most extraordinary of electoral circumstances.

EXPLAINING PARTY CHANGE: SECULAR AND CRITICAL REALIGNMENTS

The most basic of questions in parties' research is how to approach and understand party developments over time in a meaningful manner. It is to this concern we now turn.

In broad terms, there are two prevalent approaches to identifying and explaining party change. One is to look at party votes and operations in an individual election or for a specified period and compare them to previous research on the parties' appeals and approaches. This is a fundamentally incremental form of analysis.

Somewhat similar is the concept of 'secular realignments' as developed by V.O. Key, Jr. Key identified and suggested the foundation for two realigning developments. A secular realignment involves gradual but identifiable party transformation or change in individual group coalitional affiliations over a significant period of time. 'Critical elections' or 'critical realigning periods', by contrast, are intense, short-term transformative patterns that rearrange the party and political landscape on a permanent basis. While secular realignments are always on-going to some extent, critical realignments are rare.

A few cautionary notes: First, the conceptual and taxonomic approach identified is based on the American experience. Secondly, 'any … gross characterization of elections presents difficulties in application. The actual election rarely presents in pure form a case fitting completely any particular concept.' Still, and despite the variety and diversity of forces acting on the electorate, the political parties, and the society, he argues that 'a dominant characteristic often makes itself apparent' (Key, 1955: 17). Finally, this is still very much a body of work in progress.

SECULAR REALIGNMENTS

Considerably less spectacular than critical realignments, but also considerably more frequent (to an extent, they occur in all elections) are secular realignments. They are often difficult to discern and to analyze meaningfully in any given election. Such a conceptual approach:

> supposes the existence of processes of long-run, or secular, shifts in party attachment among the voters … [E]lection returns merely record periodic readings of the relative magnitudes of streams of attitudes that are undergoing steady expansion or contraction … [T]he rise and fall of parties may … be the consequence of trends … that … persist over decades and elections may mark only steps in a more or less continuous creation of new loyalties and [the] decay of old. The slow rate at which that process may occur suggests the potency of the frictions to change built into the electorate by its attachment to old symbols, old leaders, [and] old parties. (Key, 1959: 198; emphasis added)

Such elections, with their gradual – at times virtually imperceptible – changing alignments, are the norm in party politics.

Such a secular reconstitution of support patterns is subtle in any one categorical group in a particular election. It is usually not readily apparent as a contribution to a long-term redefinition of the parties' coalitions. Different patterns of voting for individual parties are likely to swing in one direction or the other, depending on the candidates and electoral circumstances, before flattening out in a cumulative and permanent repositioning. In many cases, a cause for confusion is the occurrence of a given group of voters shifting their proportion of the vote in favor of their party or the opposition, but remaining predominantly loyal to their original party choice.

The changes can be difficult to detect and are not usually obvious in any one election, but require a series of election outcomes to become apparent. Differences in party votes by demographic groups from one election to another, usually small though occasionally substantial, can be driven by an issue or a candidate attractive to or more representative of the interests of a particular voting bloc.

This approach is the most prevalent form of party analysis, and can be done exceedingly well. The series of books (since 1980) by Paul R. Abramson, John H. Aldrich, and David W. Rhode on *Continuity and Change ...* focusing on successive elections and the party, demographic attitudinal, candidate, and issue/ideological factors that drive the vote and affect the parties' coalitional support (as well as its impact on the outcome) illustrates the explanatory power of the perspective (see Abramson *et al.*, 2002, as an example). Each election and its party voting configurations are critiqued independently and within a longitudinal and comparable conceptual framework that stretches back to the original *The American Voter* (Campbell *et al.*, 1960), whose approaches have dominated the field since. The research by Abramson, Aldrich, and Rhode and its refined application in subsequent elections provides the most in-depth, intensive, and comprehensive understanding of the parties' shifting group alignments and their impact on election results.

Another series of edited quadrennial studies of presidential elections, appearing immediately after the final vote count, critiques the parties, their appeals, and the consistency of their voting blocs; the issues dominant in the campaigns; the appeal of the candidates; the resource base (financial, organizational, extra-party group involvement) of the parties and their candidates; the primary processes; the campaign strategies of the contenders; and the significance of the election results for policy priorities in the new administration. These include a number of studies edited by Gerald M. Pomper, Michael J. Nelson, and William Crotty, among others (see, for example, Pomper, 2001; Nelson, 2001; and Crotty, 2001a).

These studies are valuable for appreciating the parties' role within the context and dynamics of a given election. They are less helpful in fathoming and developing the evolutionary process under way in the parties' membership, group loyalties, and their long-run repositioning within the electorate.

CRITICAL REALIGNMENTS

'Critical realignments', with their defining symbol of a specific 'critical election', are far more dramatic and much rarer. They are seen as pivotal to the fundamental recasting of a nation's politics and party coalitions. These are elections in which 'voters are ... unusually deeply concerned, in which the extent of electoral involvement is relatively quite high, and ... the decisive results of the voting reveal a sharp alteration of the pre-existing cleavage within the electorate. Moreover, and perhaps this is the truly differentiating characteristic ... the realignment ... seems to persist for several succeeding elections' (Key, 1955: 4). In such elections, the extent of voter participation is great, 'profound readjustments occur in the relations of power within the community', and 'new and durable electoral groupings are formed' (Key, 1955: 17). Such critical elections are milestones in the adjustment of parties to the social needs of the period and measuring points in the evolution of a nation's democratic representation.

These elections permanently reshape the terrain the opposing parties must contend with, restructure their coalitions, and reorient the policy agendas and political environments, setting the stage for a new generation of party battles. Normally one party or the other moves from minority to long-term majority status, substantially broadens its appeal, attracts new adherents, and measurably increases its dominance and political power in relation to its opposition. They are, of course, fundamentally important to an appreciation of the parties' role in the society and its relevance to political representation.

Such realigning elections (or electoral eras) are infrequent. Those indicated (and broadly accepted as such) include the outcomes of 1800, 1828, 1860, 1896, and 1932. The 'system of 1896', as it has been called, was significantly different from the others. There was no shift in party control. However, the Republican party, in a contest with the Democratic–Populist coalition, moved from a competitive but generally successful position, to one that dominated politics up to the New Deal. There was also arguably a realignment in 1968 (Burnham, 1970; Paulson, 2000; Miller and Shanks, 1996), although this is not universally accepted. The post-World War II period has seen the decline of the New Deal party system (Petrocik, 1981), but the dynamics of the forces at work in the generations that followed have appeared more complex and less clearly developed than those leading up to previous realignments.

DEVELOPING THE REALIGNMENT THESIS

There has been a rich and extensive use of realignment concepts to explain processes of party change. The most influential of these has been the contribution of Burnham. Setting out to provide Key's original ideas with 'qualitative depth and meaning' (Burnham, 1970: 1), he describes a critical election, or realigning set of elections, as

> marked by short, sharp reorganizations of the mass coalitional bases of the major parties which occur at periodic intervals on the national level; are often preceded by major third-party revolts which reveal the incapacity of 'politics as usual' to integrate, much less aggregate, emergent political demand; are closely associated with abnormal stress in the socioeconomic system; are marked by ideological polarizations and issue-distances between the major parties which are exceptionally large by normal standards; and have durable consequences as constituent acts which determine the outer boundaries of policy in general, though not necessarily of policies in detail. (Burnham, 1970: 10)

Further, realignments are not random, rather 'there has been a remarkable uniform periodicity in their appearance'. Such realignments 'emerge directly from the dynamics of … constituent-function supremacy in American politics in ways and with implications … [that] involve constitutional readjustments … [and] are ultimately associated with and followed by transformations in large clusters of policy' (Burnham, 1970: 9).

The importance of realignments cannot be underestimated. They are adaptive devices for the parties in representing the popular will; they link people to political elites in a manner meaningful to contemporary societal conditions; and they allow for the peaceful adjustment and evolution of party institutions to the social/economic restructuring that occurs in society:

> critical realignment emerges as decisively important in the study of the dynamics of American politics … But even more importantly, critical realignment may well be defined as the chief tension-management device available to so peculiar a political system. Historically, it has been the chief means through which an underdeveloped political system can be recurrently brought once again into some balanced relationship with the changing socioeconomic system, permitting a restabilization of our politics and a redefinition of the dominant Lockian political formula in terms which gain overwhelming support from the current generation. (Burnham, 1970: 181–2)

The concept is the most powerful analytic tool in parties research and one that connects the party, voting, social restructuring, and the constitution of the state into a meaningful, comprehensible, and analytically applicable tool for understanding party and social change and adaptation with the attendant policy consequences and shifts in representational pressures.

There is a general acceptance of realignments in the years specified up to 1932 (or the period 1928–36) (Andersen, 1979). There is, as noted, considerably more debate over realignments, or their need or value, in the modern era's party system. A number of candidates have been put forward in addition to the election of 1968 (or the 1968–72 electoral period). These include 1980–84 and 2000–04. To the extent that there is a degree of consensus, it focuses on the 1968 results.

In a well-documented and analytically strong assessment, Arthur Paulson (2000) makes the case. It is his (and others') contention that the 1960s witnessed 'the most compelling realignment in American history' (Paulson, 2000, xxiv). His argument is that: the realignment evolved from factional struggles in both parties and was decided in favor of the ideological wings of each; ideological politics (along with the advantages of incumbency) explains the increased prevalence of split-ticket voting and frequent periods of divided government; beginning in the 1970s with the Nixon administration and carrying through the Reagan and two Bush presidencies, and as a consequence of the realignment, a new conservative agenda replaced that of the New Deal and Lyndon Johnson's Great Society; by the 1990s the top-down new alignment had spread to each party's relationship to its base. The overall outcome was two ideologically charged, highly polarized parties bounded only by the necessities of the American electoral system (Paulson, 2000: xxiv–xxvi).

As this analysis would indicate, critical elections (or electoral eras) are transformative periods in the life of the parties, ones that align the parties with changing cleavage structures and newly dominant political forces in the society. The results have fundamentally important consequences for the representative institutions, direction for the government, and for the policy agenda that prevails.

THE CRITICS OF REALIGNMENT THEORY

Not everyone accepts those assumptions. Some challenge the elections chosen to be highlighted and the historical circumstances surrounding them. Others reject the entire conception of elections with realignment potential.

The critiques have been numerous. The most thoroughly developed opposition to the realignment conception has been put forward by David R. Mayhew (2002). He acknowledges that 'the study of American electoral realignments … has been one of the most creative, engaging, and influential intellectual enterprises by American political scientists'. But he goes on to ask: 'How good is the realignment genre as a guide to the last two centuries of American electoral, party, and policy history?' His assessment is: 'not very good at all … Worst yet, I believe … the genre has evolved from a source of vibrant ideas into an impediment to understanding' (Mayhew, 2002: 1, 5).

Mayhew ranks the realignment theorists in terms of boldness and inclusiveness roughly from Key at one end, with a narrowed conception and limited claims, through to Burnham and his more ambitious explanatory agenda. He then combs through the proponents for 15 propositions that can be tested, or at least examined in detail, emphasizing a review of historical data and events. After analyzing the forces surrounding key elections and party and policy transformations, Mayhew (2002: 165) is clear in his conclusion: 'The realignments way of thinking adds little or no illumination, but it does exact opportunity costs. Other lines of investigation might be more promising'.

This points to one of the implicit negatives of realignment theorizing emphasized by its critics: it ties economic and social restructuring to party and political representation. It harbors a certain ideological perspective, or even bias, toward the representative function of party in political decision-making and the focus is on class issues and mass-level voter concerns. Nevertheless, it remains as the most useful and forceful of explanatory models for making sense of party transformations. Minimally, it has proven a force for stimulating debates of the periods in question, the nature of party transformations, how these can be most effectively analyzed, and, in the long run, what their broader consequences entail. The challenge for its critics is to develop alternative conceptual schemes with explanatory power comparable to, or refinements and reapplications of, the realignment thesis.

THE EUROPEAN EXPERIENCE

The European system includes a wide variety of electoral forms and a broader range of party and policy alternatives (Lijphart, 1994; Katz and Mair, 1994). Most Western European countries employ some form of proportional representation, in which every vote has meaning. In the United States, voters in non-competitive, Republican- or Democratic-dominated areas play little role in campaigns and have less impact on policy agenda that those in the most competitive areas. Losing voter coalitions in districts won by the opposing party (even if 51% to 49%) are not represented in legislative seat distributions under the single-member, first-past-the-post electoral system (Duverger, 1954; Lijphart, 1994).

The electoral systems adopted have consequences for party operations. In comparing the parties in Europe and the United States, Russell J. Dalton writes:

> Parties are the primary institutions of representative democracy, especially in Europe … Parties define the choices available to voters. Candidates in most European nations are selected by the parties and elected as party representatives, not as individuals. Open primaries and independent legislators (including the Germans) vote directly for party lists rather than individual candidates. Political parties also shape the content of election campaigns. Party programs help define the issues that are discussed during the campaign. … In many European nations, the parties, not individual candidates, control advertising during the campaign. Political parties and party leaders thus exercise a primary role in articulating the public's concerns.

And, in terms of enactment of policy programs and campaign commitments:

> Once in government, parties control the policymaking process. Control of the executive branch and the organization of the legislative branch are decided on the basis of party majorities. The parties' control is often absolute, as in the parliamentary systems of Europe, where representatives from the same party vote as a bloc ... American parties are less united and less decisive, but even here parties actively structure the legislative process. Because of the centrality of political parties to the democratic process, political scientists describe many European political systems as a system of 'responsible party government' (Dalton, 2002: 125–6).

These processes provide different levels of access and magnify the influence of political participation and party mobilization rewards (at least in comparison with the United States).

In the words of Arend Lijphart (1994: 139), 'the degree of electoral disproportionality or proportionality [in skewing the outcome relative to the voter cast in elections for a party or candidate] responds very sensitively to the rule of the electoral system'. There is a closer and more direct alignment in European systems between the party vote and parliamentary representation than in the United States. The European party systems also perform many key functions – representing public opinion, offering policy alternatives, mobilizing an electorate, and having the discipline to enact their party programs when in office – more effectively than American parties.

There is, then, a contrast of significance with political parties in America. Nonetheless, trends found in the United States may be endemic to democratic parties in advanced industrial societies such as those found in Western Europe. The European parties thus experience, if less intensely, the same problems as do the American parties. These include:

- declines in partisanship and party identification;
- party dealignment;
- decreases in party mobilization;
- a changing electoral environment;
- a fall-off in the formal affiliation with party organizations;
- a more limited organizational role in campaigns;
- a greater emphasis on the candidate heading the tickets;
- a greater personalization (and less institutionalized approach) in party and electoral politics;

- a more fragmented party constituency;
- a greater reliance on for-hire public relations strategists, campaign consultants, and skilled media personnel in getting their message across to voters; and
- a continuingly strong, yet less distinctive (in comparison with previous times) party presence in policy formation and implementation in government (Dalton and Wattenberg, 2000).

This last point is particularly disturbing given the primacy of the European parties in establishing policy objectives in campaigns and acting on these once in office.

Richard S. Katz and Peter Mair (1995) have argued that a new type of party may be emerging in European politics, the 'cartel party'. In this form of party system, parties and state 'interpenetrate' and 'collude'. Kaare Strøm (2002: 202) refers to this as 'opportunistic institutional engineering' (see also Gunther and Diamond, 2003).

Distinctive programs and party appeals are deemphasized, leaving electors and more generally the representative system with a blurring of policy strands and less directly accountable party operations. Miki L. Caul and Mark M. Gray (2000: 236–7) write:

> If voters are unable to 'feel' and 'see' much difference in the programmatic outputs and economic performance of different party governments it becomes more likely that they may no longer see much relevance in going to the polls or even paying attention to politics. In systems where parties look and act more alike the differentiation may increasingly come down to the style and personality characteristics of party leaders and candidates ... The trivialization of party politics may ensue. Although party command over policy and economic outcomes may be constrained by global and social forces beyond their control, it is unlikely that the average voter has been aware of such changes. The focus of public policy will remain on parties – voters and the media expect them to have an impact. However, if the patterns found in ... fifty years of data continue, parties will more than likely persist with a limited capacity to affect aggregate policy outcomes and are likely to continue to struggle to significantly differentiate themselves on policy matters.

It may be that as European parties in a broad outline move further toward the American model the era of 'responsible party government' long associated with these party systems will be increasingly compromised. If so, there are significant impacts on democratic governance:

Table 43.2   *Lipset and Rokkan's four cleavages*

Cleavage	Critical Juncture	Issues
Center–periphery	Reformation–Counter-Reformation: 16th–17th Centuries	National vs. supranational religion; national language vs. Latin
State–church	National Revolution: 1789 and after	Secular vs. religious control of mass education
Land–industry	Industrial Revolution: 19th Century	Tariff levels for agricultural products; control vs. freedom for industrial enterprise
Owner–worker	The Russian Revolution: 1917 and after	Integration into national polity vs. commitment to international revolutionary movement

Source: Lipset and Rokkan, 1967: 47.

When parties make fewer and fewer efforts to mobilize citizens they worsen inequality of participation. Parties that centralize and professionalize their office in lieu of citizens active as party members might contribute to the demobilization of the public and the diminished understanding and trust in the democratic process. Parties that develop public funding sources in order to insulate themselves from the ebbs and flows of public support will inevitably distance themselves from those they represent. Running elections and governing by marketing principles may be successful in the short term for parties, but this strategy may well undermine the democratic process in the long term. (Dalton and Watterberg, 2000: 284)

There are consequences, potentially profound, for the changes in process. The ultimate impact on the current party system and the more significant consequences for the democratic order look to be less appealing than the system presently in operation.

ASSESSING CHANGE IN EUROPEAN PARTY SYSTEMS

There are a number of ways to approach the evaluation of political party systems. In this section we discuss five such ways.

Party electoral analyses

This approach is broadly similar to those employed in research in the United States. These examine the electoral connection to the vote, the continuing patterns of support for the parties, and the dominating effect of identifiable factors such as policy issues, party loyalties, and candidate appeal on the election outcome. The conceptual and analytic approach borrows heavily from comparable American research (Campbell *et al.*, 1960). A study by David Butler and Donald E. Stokes, *Political Change in Britain* (1971) represents an example of what can be accomplished. The most influential contemporary analyst applying this approach may well be Russell J. Dalton (as an example, see Dalton, 2002) although others have applied related perspectives.

Social cleavage analysis

This approach focuses on the divisions within a society that give rise on the macro level to the founding and evolution of competitive party systems. The group and related issue concerns that explain different individual party developments are given priority treatment. The early work of S.M. Lipset and Stein Rokkan, as illustrated in their collaborative work *Party Systems and Voter Alignments: Cross-National Perspectives* (1967), provided a foundation for such analytic approaches. Conceiving of the formation of party systems in broadly historical terms and from a national developmental point of departure, Lipset and Rokkan identify four decisive cleavages that resulted from critical junctures in a nation's political development and provided the orientation for its particular party system (Table 43.2).

Organizational analysis

This perspective has been relied on to a greater extent in assessments of Western European parties, and has proven of greater explanatory power, than in studies of American parties. The reasons for the differences in application are clear: the European parties are far better structured and their organizations more important in aligning voters, developing and implementing policy programs, and providing social and other benefits on a year-round basis. A seminal contributor to this approach was Duverger (1954), with his emphasis on electoral forms and contrasting of organizational structures and their roles within national party systems.

Many have used variations on the organizational conception before and since, among them Michels (1959), Joseph La Palombara and Myron Weiner (1966), M. Ostrogorski (1902), Giovanni Sartori (1976), Hans Daadler and Peter Mair (1983), Alan Ware (1987, 1988), Kenneth Janda (1980), Peter Merkl (1980), and Kay Lawson and Peter Merkl (1988).

The more recent evidence indicates that the parties' organizational role is shifting. David M. Farrell and Paul Webb (2000: 123, 125) write:

> Political parties have invested heavily in election campaigning, making full use of new technologies, adapting their organizations and employing specialist agencies and consultants. As a result, the party of today and the way it operates in the context of electioneering, is a significantly different creature from what it was twenty years ago. ... [F]irst, parties have tended to become more centralized and professionalized; second, they have become more cognizant of citizen opinion and demands; and third, party and (especially) leader image has come to assume a prominent thematic role in campaigning. ... [P]arties and their organizations have shown many signs of change as they have sought to adapt to the altered political, social, and technological environments in which they find themselves, and they undoubtedly will have further adaptations to negotiate in the future. They remain stubbornly persistent entities with important roles to play at the heart of the contemporary democratic process.

In all of this, including also, and most pointedly, American parties, it is clear that party members and voters more generally are having an increased impact on organizational decision-making. However, in Europe, unlike the United States, the cohesiveness of the party operations and the role of the party leadership in deliberations remain important. In assessing the move towards what they refer to as 'electoralist party organization', Scarrow et al. (2000: 149) conclude:

> [G]rass-roots party members (and even non-member supporters sometimes) commonly play a significant role in selecting legislative candidates and in legitimizing election programmes, though party elites generally retain vetoes over candidate selection and enjoy considerable autonomy in shaping party policy. ... [P]arty members are gaining significant rights to elect their leaders. Intra-party decision-making has thus become more inclusive, but not necessarily in a way that restricts

the strategic initiatives of leaders. ... [T]here are now many instances around the democratic world where party leaders operate a coalition of power in which grass-roots members are significant junior partners.

Party organizations and their leadership remain important, although they are adapting to a changing social and political environment in which the parties' base is exercising greater influence.

Realignment/dealignment theorizing

This conceptual approach has been less evident in research on European party change. Dalton et al. (1984: 7–8) argued that the electoral, and consequently party, map of European (and American) democracies was being fundamentally challenged:

> [T]he prevailing theme in comparative party research was the persistence of democratic party systems. In addition to Lipset and Rokkan's treatise on the freezing of cleavage alignments ... studies ... concluded that the major question facing researchers was to explain the observed stability in democratic systems. ... [S]omething has changed dramatically ... [T]he parties are being presented with new demands and new challenges. Partisan change – rather than partisan stability – is a common pattern in virtually all ... nations.

Their argument exemplifies the radical shift in analytic perspectives of party stability, from an emphasis on explaining stability and a traditional continuity in approaches, policy appeals, and electoral support to one forced to deal with the dynamics inherent in change.

In a later work Dalton (2002) advances this line of thought. He acknowledges that realignments have marked past behavioral patterns of change in European (and American) party history. The changes evidenced in the contemporary party dynamics also fuel speculation as to new realignments along different issue lines, reactive to developing societal cleavages. But he warns that the political cleavages of what he refers to as 'the New Politics' (see below) bear little relationship, and may well be far more transitory, than those that sustained former realignments and went on to serve as the foundation for the party systems that emerged:

> The process of partisan realignment is normally based on clearly defined and highly cohesive social groups that can develop institutional ties to

the parties and provide clear voting cues to their members. A firm group base provides a framework for parties to develop institutional ties to the groups and for groups to socialize and mobilize their members.

There are few social groupings comparable to labor unions or churches that might establish the basis of a New Politics realignment. ... generational differences in support for New Politics parties might indicate an emerging New Politics cleavage, but age groups provide a very transitory basis for mobilizing voters. Other potential group bases of voting cues, such as education or alternative class categorizations, so far remain speculative, without firm evidence of realigning effects. (Dalton, 2002: 168–9)

Realignment theory remains a useful approach to establishing criteria for party change and the durability of the coalitions being reshaped. It may not fully explain the more subtle shifts in social and partisan cleavages taking place in electorates, and may need either refinement or a reconfiguration of analytic approaches. It has been relevant in the understanding of previous shifts in party behavior. In an age of 'dealignment', its precise role as an explanatory tool needs clarification.

Postmaterialism and party change

Party systems in contemporary democracies give every appearance of moving away (more incrementally than radically) from the class polarization and economic divisions that formed their base to a new focus on lifestyle issues (self-actualization, gender concerns, social inequalities, consumerism, environmental safeguards, limitations on nuclear energy and weapons, human rights priorities) that, as Dalton (2002: 168) indicates, 'may provide the basis for a new partisan alignment'.

It is possible that these postmaterialist values are becoming of greater importance in patterns of party support and in the appeals candidates and parties adopt in campaigns. Ronald Inglehart (1977, 1990, 1997) has done the most to develop this line of inquiry. Postmodern political and value structures are built on post-economic developments and party bases:

Postmodern values would be difficult to sustain without a thriving industrial and technological infrastructure. Even in terms of postmodern

values, the rejection of modernity would be unattractive if it meant going back to a life expectancy of 35 years, coupled with the need for sexual abstinence before marriage and for women to spend their entire adult lives in childbearing and childrearing. Postmodernity must necessarily coexist with modernity. (Inglehart, 1997: 339)

The value structure projects an assault (in varying degrees) on established and traditional institutions of authority and rising levels of citizen participation, that might well significantly redefine political, and party, agendas and operations. The impact of such changes has broad significance for democratic systems built on a vital and competitive party system. What is less clear is the rate of the transformation and its stability in creating durable partisan alignments and a degree of predictability in explaining party behavior.

These are among the major variations in the main forms of inquiry into European party systems. Each has its appeal. What stands out is the general agreement on the party changes under way, rather more so than on their long-term significance and impact.

CONCLUSION

Parties and politics are in transition. This much all agree on. How the escalation in the changes under way will affect the parties and their representative role in a society is speculative. One argument is that party 'decline' or 'decomposition' or 'fragmentation' or 'dealignment', whatever it may be called, evidences a serious threat to the ability of parties to conduct their business and erodes the crucial tie between the parties and a democratic state. Others, while accepting that change is in progress, see it more as the natural process of party evolution in response to social, economic, and, in the more contemporary era, global forces. While redirecting party energies, the assumption is that it should not severely affect the functional dependence of a democratic state on the party system.

Richard Gunther and Larry Diamond, after surveying party developments worldwide, conclude:

Political parties are not what they used to be. ... they lack the depth of involvement and emotional and ideological attachment that they commanded a century, even two or three decades, ago. ... there is growing evidence that membership in political parties is declining, that parties' ties with allied secondary associations are loosening or breaking, that their representation of specific social groups is less consistent, and that public opinion toward parties is waning in commitment and trust. Does this mean ... that parties as institutions are declining, that they are ceasing to play a crucial role in modern democracies, and that their former functions may be performed as well or better by other kinds of organizations – social movements or interest groups? ... Are political parties in modern democracies losing their importance, even their relevance, as vehicles for the articulation and aggregation of interests and the waging of election campaigns? Or have we entered an era, more keenly felt in the advanced democracies but increasingly apparent in the less developed ones as well, where technological and social change is transforming the nature of the political party without diminishing its importance for the health and vigor of democracy? (Diamond and Gunther, 2001: 3)

It is their belief that a shift, while not linear in development nor simultaneous in societies, is taking place, but this is marked by the type of parties that dominate in a democratic state. The European party model may not be (and does not appear to be) relevant for all parties. What we may be experiencing is 'the progressive displacement of mass-based parties by organizations that are structured in different ways, pursuing different objectives, or pursuing the same objectives through different means' (Diamond and Gunther, 2001: 4). Such a continual evolution would retain the primacy, and mass representative functions, of parties in a democracy.

The parties in Europe and the United States are adjusting to communications and technological advancements, a less and less party-dependent electorate, a globalized world community with a macro focus, and international pressures that parties historically have found difficult to deal with. The social and technological changes under way have not been kind to the party systems. The basic concern is the degree to which they can maintain their electoral integrity and continue as representative institutions that link voter, government, and policy outputs in a meaningful and accountable form. The shape of the political universe is changing; the hope is that as party systems adjust to the needs of a democratic society, the functional importance of the parties will not be compromised.

REFERENCES

Abramson, Paul, Aldrich, John and Rohde, David (2002) *Change and Continuity in the 2000 Elections.* Washington, DC: CQ Press.

Aldrich, John H. (1995) *Why Parties? The Origin and Transformation of Political Parties in America.* Chicago: University of Chicago Press.

Andersen, Kristi (1979) *The Creation of a Democratic Majority.* Chicago, IL: University of Chicago Press.

Burnham, Walter Dean (1970) *Critical Elections and the Mainsprings of American Politics.* New York: W.W. Norton.

Butler, David and Stokes, Donald (1969) *Political Change in Britain.* New York: St. Martin's Press.

Campbell, Angus, Converse, Philip E., Miller, Warren E. and Stokes, Donald E. (1960) *The American Voter.* New York: Wiley.

Campbell, Angus, Converse, Philip E. Miller, Warren E. and Stokes, Donald E. (1966) *Elections and the Political Order.* New York: Wiley.

Caul, M.L. and Gray, Mark (2000) 'From platform declarations to policy outcomes: Changing profiles and partisan influence over policy', in Russell Dalton and Martin Wattenberg (eds), *Parties without Partisans: Political Change in Advanced Industrial Democracies.* New York: Oxford University Press, pp. 208–38.

Coleman, John J. (1996) *Party Decline in America: Policy, Politics, and the Fiscal States.* Princeton, NJ: Princeton University Press.

Conway, M. Margaret (1999) *Political Participation in the United States,* 2nd edn. Washington, DC: CQ Press.

Conway, M. Margaret (2001a) 'Political mobilization in America', in William J. Crotty (ed.), *The State of Democracy in America.* Washington, DC: Georgetown University Press, pp. 31–47.

Conway, M. Margaret (2001b) 'Political participation in American elections: Who decides what?', in William J. Crotty (ed.), *America's Choice 2000: Entering a New Millennium.* Boulder, CO: Westview Press, pp. 79–95.

Crotty, William (1986) *Political Parties in Local Areas.* Knoxville: University of Tennessee Press.

Crotty, William (ed.) (2001a) *America's Choice 2000: Entering a New Millennium.* Boulder, CO: Westview Press.

Crotty, William (ed.) (2001b) *The State of Democracy in America.* Washington, DC: Georgetown University Press.

Daadler, Hans (2001) *Political Parties and Democracy.* Baltimore, MD: The John Hopkins University Press.

Daalder, Hans and Mair, Peter (1983) *Western European Party Systems: Continuity and Change.* Beverly Hills, CA: Sage Publications.

Dalton, Russell J. (2002) *Citizen Politics: Public Opinion and Political Parties in Advanced Industrial Democracies*, 3rd edn. Chatham, NJ: Chatham House/Seven Bridges.

Dalton, Russell and Wattenberg, Martin (2000) *Parties without Partisans*. New York: Oxford University Press.

Dalton, Russell, Flanagan, Scott, Beck, Paul Allen, and Alt, James E. (1984) *Electoral Change in Advanced Industrial Democracies: Realignment or Dealignment?* Princeton, NJ: Princeton University Press.

Diamond, Larry and Gunther, Richard (eds) (2001) *Political Parties and Democracy*. Baltimore, MD: Johns Hopkins University Press.

Duverger, Maurice (1954) *Political Parties*. New York: Wiley.

Farrell, David and Webb, Paul (2000) 'Political parties as campaign organizations', in Russell Dalton and Martin Wattenberg (eds), *Parties without Partisans: Political Change in Advanced Industrial Democracies*. New York: Oxford University Press, pp. 102–29.

Flanigan, William and Zingale, Nancy (1994) *Political Behavior of the American Electorate*. Washington, DC: CQ Press.

Flanigan, William H. and Zingale, Nancy (2003) *Political Behavior of the American Electorate*. Washington, DC: CQ Press.

Gunther, Richard and Diamond, Larry (2003) 'Species of political parties: a new typology', *Party Politics*, 9: 167–99.

Hofstadter, Richard (1969) *The Idea of a Party System: The Rise of Legitimate Opposition in the United States, 1780–1840*. Berkley: University of California Press.

Inglehart, Ronald (1977) *The Silent Revolution: Changing Values and Political Styles*. Princeton, NJ: Princeton University Press.

Inglehart, Ronald (1990) *Culture Shift in Advanced Industrial Society*. Princeton, NJ: Princeton University Press.

Inglehart, Ronald (1997) *Modernization and Postmodernization: Cultural, Economic, and Political Change in 43 Societies*. Princeton, NJ: Princeton University Press.

Janda, Kenneth (1980) *Political Parties: A Cross-National Survey*. New York: Free Press.

Katz, Richard S. and Mair, Peter (1992) *Party Organizations: A Data Handbook on Party Organizations in Western Democracies*. London: Sage Publications.

Katz, Richard S. and Mair, Peter (eds) (1994) *How Parties Organize: Change and Adaptation in Party Organizations in Western Democracies*. London: Sage Publications.

Katz, Richard S. and Mair, Peter (1995) 'Changing models of party organization and party democracy: The emergence of the cartel party', *Party Politics*, 1: 5–28.

Key, V.O., Jr. (1955) 'A theory of critical elections', *Journal of Politics*, 17: 3–18.

Key, V.O., Jr. (1959) 'Secular realignment and the party system', *Journal of Politics*, 23: 198–210.

Key, V.O., Jr. (1964) *Politics, Parties, and Pressure Groups*, 5th edn. New York: Thomas Crowell.

Keyssar, Alexander (2000) *The Right to Vote: The Contested History of Democracy in the United States*. New York: Basic Books.

Lawson, Kay and Merkl, Peter (1988) *When Parties Fail: Emerging Alternative Organizations*. Princeton, NJ: Princeton University Press.

LaPalombara, J. and Weiner, Myron (1966) *Political Parties and Political Development*. Princeton, NJ: Princeton University Press.

Lipset, Seymour Martin and Rokkan, Stein (1967) *Party Systems and Voter Alignments*. New York: Free Press.

Ljiphart, Arend (1994) *Electoral Systems and Party Systems: A Study of Twenty-Seven Democracies 1945–1990*. New York: Oxford University Press.

Mayhew, David R. (2002) *Electoral Re-alignment: A Critique of an American Genre*. New Haven, CT: Yale University Press.

Merkl, Peter H. (1980) *Western European Party Systems: Trends and Prospects*. New York: Free Press.

Michels, Robert (1959) *Political Parties: A Sociological Study of the Oligarchical Tendencies of Modern Democracy*. New York: Dover Publications.

Miller, Warren E. (1990) 'The electorate's view of the parties', in *The Parties Respond: Changes in American Parties and Campaigns*. Boulder, CO: Westview Press, pp. 97–115.

Miller, Warren E. (1998) 'Party identification and the electorate of the 1990's', in *The Parties Respond: Changes in American Parties and Campaigns*, 3rd edn. Boulder, CO: Westview Press, pp. 109–27.

Miller, Warren. E., updated by Kenneth Goldstein and Mark Jones (2002) 'Party identification and the electorate at the start of the twenty-first century', in *The Parties Respond: Changes in American Parties and Campaigns*, 4th edn. Boulder, CO: Westview Press, pp. 79–98.

Miller, Warren E. and Shanks, J. Merrill (1996) *The New American Voter*. Cambridge, MA: Harvard University Press.

Nelson, Michael (2001) *The Elections of 2000*. Washington, DC: CQ Press.

Nie, Norman H., Verba, Sidney and Petrocik, John R. (1976) *The Changing American Voter*. Cambridge, MA: Harvard University Press.

Ostrogorski, Mosei (1902) *Democracy and the Organization of Political Parties*. New York: Macmillan.

Owen, Diane, Dennis, Jack and Klofstad, Casey A. (2001) 'Party relevance over time', in William Crotty (ed.), *The State of Democracy in America*. Washington, DC: Georgetown University Press.

Paulson, Arthur (2000) *Realignment and Party Revival: Understanding American Electoral Politics at the Turn of the Twenty-First Century*. Westport, CT: Praeger.

Petrocik, John R. (1981) *Party Coalitions: Realignments and the Decline of the New Deal Party System*. Chicago, IL: The University of Chicago Press.

Pomper, Gerald M. (1972) *The Performance of American Government: Checks and Minuses*. New York: Free Press.

Pomper, Gerald M. (2001) *The Election of 2000: Reports and Interpretations*. New York: Chatham House Publishers

Pomper, Gerald M. with Lederman, Susan S. (1980) *Elections in America: Control and Influence in Democratic Politics*, 2nd edn. New York: Longman.

Rosenstone, Steven J. and Hansen, John M. (1993) *Mobilization, Participation and Democracy in America*. New York: Macmillan.

Sartori, Giovanni (1976) *Parties and Party Systems: A Framework for Analysis*. Cambridge: Cambridge University Press.

Sartori, Giovanni (2001) *Political Parties and Democracy*. Baltimore, MD: The John Hopkins University Press.

Scarrow, Susan (2000) 'Parties without members? Party organization in a changing electoral environment', in Russell Dalton and Martin Wattenberg (eds), *Parties without Partisans: Political Change in Advanced Industrial Democracies*. New York: Oxford University Press, pp. 79–102.

Scarrow, Susan, Webb, Paul and Farrell, David M. (2000) 'From social integration to electoral contestation: The changing distribution of power within political parties', in Russell Dalton and Martin Wattenberg (eds), *Parties without Partisans: Political Change in Advanced Industrial Democracies*. New York: Oxford University Press, pp. 127–57.

Schattschneider, E.E. (1942) *Party Government*. New York: Holt, Rinehart, and Winston.

Schattschneider, E.E. (1960) *The Semisovereign People: A Realist's View of Democracy in America*. New York: Holt, Rinehart, and Winston.

Strøm, Kaare (2000) 'Parties at the core of government', in Russell Dalton and Martin Wattenberg (eds), *Parties without Partisans: Political Change in Advanced Industrial Democracies*. New York: Oxford University Press.

Teixeira, Ruy (1992) *The Disappearing American Voter*. Washington, DC: The Brookings Institute.

Teixeira, Ruy (1980) *Who Votes?* New Haven, CT: Yale University Press.

Verba, Sidney, Schlozman, Kay Lehman and Brady, Henry (1995) *Voice and Equality: Civic Volunteerism in American Politics*. Cambridge, MA: Harvard University Press.

Ware, Alan (1988) *Political Parties: Electoral Change and Structural Response*. Oxford: Blackwell.

Wattenberg, Martin (1991) *The Rise of Candidate-Centered Politics: Presidential Elections of the 1980s*. Cambridge, MA: Harvard University Press.

Wattenberg, Martin (1998) *The Decline of American Political Parties: 1952–1996*. Cambridge, MA: Harvard University Press.

Wolfinger, Raymond and Rosenstone, Steven J. (1980) *Who Votes?* New Haven, CT: Yale University Press.

44

PARTIES IN THE MEDIA AGE

Holli A. Semetko

The transformation of political parties over the course of the 20th century has coincided with the growth of the media in countries around the world. The media provide an ever-changing context in which political parties operate and an array of opportunities for parties, candidates, and elected politicians to connect with, or disconnect from, citizens. The Internet also provides unique opportunities for new (and old) political personalities and social movements to gain attention and garner support. And rapid developments in telecommunications technology and their uses suggest that cell phones and handheld devices are being used by younger citizens in political ways, unimaginable to older generations who rely on the press and television for news and information. The evolving media landscape presents both opportunities and threats to political parties, at a time when parties in general can be said to suffer from a serious image problem.

THE IMAGE PROBLEM FOR POLITICAL PARTIES

At a time when political parties appear to be the least trusted of institutions, the media and new communications technologies provide an opportunity to enhance the image and reputations of political parties. This opportunity exists in part because media are among the most highly trusted institutions in many countries around the world. One of the most striking comparisons that holds across the 25 member states of the European Union, as well as Latin America, is that the proportion of publics who express trust in media institutions is considerably higher than those who express trust in government or parliament. And political parties even fall behind government and parliament on the trust measures.

Figure 44.1 shows the percentage of publics in Europe who responded positively to the question 'I would like to ask you a question about how much trust you have in certain institutions. For each of the following institutions, please tell me if you tend to trust it or tend not to trust it?' And Figure 44.1 displays the corresponding percentages of Latin Americans who responded 'a lot of confidence' and 'confidence' to the question 'How much confidence do you have in each of the following groups, institutions or persons mentioned on the list?'. The mean for confidence in political parties in Latin America is 11% in 2003, down from 28% in 1997, and the mean for Europe using the forced choice trust or not trust form of the question, compares at 20% in the EU-15 and 13% in the new EU-10 member states in 2003. In Europe and Latin America, political parties appear at the bottom of the trusted list, while media such as radio, television and the press appear at the top.

The lack of trust or confidence in political parties, coupled with the fact that in most modern societies television and even the printed press nowadays have become more personalized and celebrity or personality-driven, means a serious image problem for political parties. As organizations or institutions, political parties remain distant unless presented by a familiar or friendly face. The average party spokesperson probably would not be a good choice to put forward as a communicator unless s/he was already a known quantity

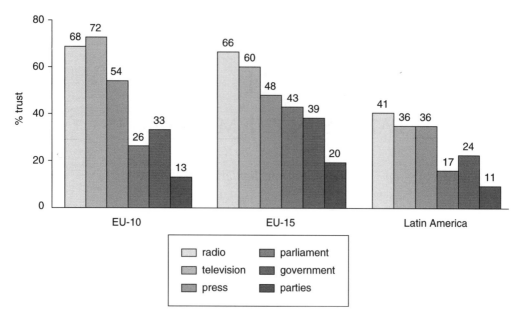

Figure 44.1   Trust in institutions by new and old E.U. member states and Latin America (2003)

Source: Eurobarometer 60, 2003; Eurobarometer 2003.4; Latinobarometro 2003. All figures rounded to the nearest integer. For Latinobarometro 2003 the question was: 'Please look at this card and tell me how much confidence you have in each of the following groups/institutions. Would you say you have a lot, some, a little or no confidence?' The reported figures are the sum of respondents who expressed 'a lot of confidence' and 'some confidence'.

or had some celebrity status. An important finding from the 1970s and 1980s in the USA was that local media are 'softer' on local members of Congress and 'harder' on Congress as an institution, a reference to the fact that individual members of Congress tended to receive favorable coverage in their own districts while Congress itself tended to be reported in more negative terms as a faceless institution (Robinson, 1983). Political parties are like Congress unless personalized by the personalities, positions, and records of their leaders and top candidates. And even the softer (more docile) side of the local press has changed as the appetite for scandals, personalities, and conflict has become greater in all outlets over the past few decades (Tumber and Waisbord, 2004).

As the Internet, local cable TV, and talk-radio have expanded opportunities for individuals interested in politics to tune in and get involved, political parties have gained ground by being able to utilize these channels, assuming they can do so effectively (Esser *et al.*, 2001). They have also lost ground, however, in

no longer being able to control the campaigning activities of their candidates who might call in directly or place themselves on the screen to further their own candidacies, at times to the dismay of party strategists. This is particularly relevant to and annoying for political parties in multi-party parliamentary systems with electoral lists, whose candidates are attributed importance by their numeric position on the list; for most parties those positions have been largely decided by the leader of the party. Some of the most liberal of European political parties have become Stalinist in their attempts to control their candidates' webpages, to ensure that each individual's webpage would be equally dull or that none would be unusually interesting, aiming to guarantee that the leader and the few at the top of the list maintain the highest media profiles. But candidates often exercise their own consciences, and the Internet provides each with an opportunity to host his or her own webpage and weblog under different names to get around party rules. And when political parties in list systems attempt to introduce internal democracy in the selection of candidates, by opening up the list-making process so that party members may vote for party candidates and thus influence the numeric position of candidates on the party's electoral list, an internal party election can quickly become externally driven by candidates vying for publicity in the national news media and shaping their own publicity with their own direct (e)mail and weblogs.[1] In general terms, then, in the context of political parties and the media in multiparty list systems, the new media provide opportunities to enhance the authority of individuals and candidates, and one consequence may be to diminish the authority of the party or its leaders (Newell, 2001).

Against this backdrop of opportunities for and threats to political parties, in this chapter I discuss the communications contexts in which political parties operate, with examples from different national and international contexts. I argue that political parties, and for that matter political scientists and political communications researchers, face three major challenges. The first challenge is simply keeping up with the changes in the media industry and the ongoing developments in the national communications landscapes, and the implications of these changes for making connections with audiences and potential voters (see Entman, 1989). The second challenge, related to the first, is how to measure the impacts of these changes on political attitudes, political participation, and election and referendum outcomes. And the third challenge for political parties seeking to influence the ways in which issues are framed in the news and in public opinion is external and stems from globalization and transnational forms of communication. We also need more in the way of theory to assess the impact of the changing media environment on the development of political parties.

CHALLENGE NO. 1. THE MEDIA INDUSTRY AND THE CHANGING COMMUNICATIONS LANDSCAPE

The growth of the media industry over the past century has not been identical across sectors. The increasing numbers of radio and television outlets over the past few decades, and the growth in the numbers of magazines and specialist journals, for example, have not been entirely characteristic of the newspaper industry which has faced declining sales in many countries. One reason for declining newspaper sales is economic. The rise of local free sheets financed by advertising has impacted traditional newspaper sales in many countries. And in many societies in transition, the cost of newsprint alone makes it difficult for traditional newspapers that rely on sales and advertising for their operations.

Competition from other media as sources for information and entertainment is yet another reason for declining newspaper sales. The Radio Advertising Bureau in the US put it this way:

> Declining ad revenue, decreasing circulation – it's a one-two punch that one would expect to knock newspaper out. However, the position most newspapers enjoy in their local markets won't disappear tomorrow. Many advertisers still swear by this medium – even if it's from sheer habit … Americans spend 151 hours per year (2.9 hours per week) reading the newspaper, 15 hours less than in 1995 – and that number is projected to drop another 7 hours per year by 2005. Moreover, only slightly more than half of all newspaper readers look at 'Section I' of their paper (the front page section), and that's far and away the most heavily read part of the paper. Younger readers don't depend on the print media the way their grandparents did. Readers under age 35 are spending less time than ever with their local paper. In most markets, circulation is flat or declining, while paper costs and other factors continue to drive production costs up. (Media Facts, 2000, Newspapers, www.rab.com)

And these declines continued in spite of the many ways in which the content of newspapers has changed in recent decades – we have witnessed a greater emphasis on 'soft' as opposed to 'hard' news, the costly addition of colorful photos and graphics, and the increasing emphasis on compelling visuals, as well as the launch of entire sections devoted to news about non-news subjects such as cooking and lifestyles, travel and entertainment, and reviews of consumer products and technology. Stories emphasize the more sensational elements that attract and hold readers' attention, and in the coverage of politics this often means more attention to conflict than to a facts-based explanation of the issues.

The party press has declined as political parties are rarely owners of newspapers nowadays (Seymour-Ure, 1974, and 1991), but the influence and political sympathies of proprietors continues to be potentially great (Evans, 1983). And despite the generally 'softer' contents, newspaper reporting can be laden with judgments (often negative in tone) in election campaigns and this can and does influence voters some of the time (Curtice and Semetko, 1994; Dalton *et al.*, 1998).

Television network news in the US has watched its audience decline over the past decade, losing viewers to competing cable news programs as well as entertainment programming. The consequence for national political parties is that any 'free' coverage they might have received on national news programs reaches a smaller audience. For parties at the local level the opportunity to reach potential supporters through coverage on local television news still exists, but the content of local news is very dependent on the local market. Local television news is 'soft' in avoiding policy issues other than specific ones of immediate importance to the local community, and contents appear to be focused on crimes, accidents, and the weather (Graber, 2000; McLeod *et al.*, 1999).

That said, 'soft' news and entertainment talk show programs, such as Oprah Winfrey, are apparently a real opportunity for audiences to learn something about political issues and form opinions on such topics as foreign affairs (Baum, 2002, 2003). For political parties, this requires having the ability to deliver a message in the form of a personality or celebrity who is important enough to influence the producer's calendar. It means a different type of strategy, a kind of two-step flow model, in which the celebrities who are likely to be hosted on such programs are also the ones the party has befriended and primed to discuss issues on air in a way that fits with the party's perspective on the issue.

The characteristics of the US media market are more apparent now than ever before in many countries around the world: declining trends in newspaper readership, many new broadcasting channels, and audiences characterized by greater fragmentation. What does this mean for political parties outside the USA, where multi-party parliamentary systems are the norm? In the long-established democracies, in many countries in Western Europe for example, the opportunities and challenges for established parties are similar to those described above for the main parties in the USA (Mair, 2004), with the advantage in Europe that levels of political knowledge and political identification appear to be higher than in the USA. That said, in Italy, that Silvio Berlusconi's social and economic position as a major media industrialist put him on an ideal path to electoral office is seen by many as evidence of the (too) close relations between media, campaigning, and

governance (Mazzoleni, 1995), and Berlusconi's parallel influence over public and commercial broadcasting in Italy has led many to think about the varied forms of media systems and the meaning of 'free press' in contemporary democracy (Hallin and Mancini, 2004).

In the ten most recent additions to the EU, most of which were part of the Soviet system until the late 1980s, there is even less trust in political parties. Parties face the more difficult task of gaining recognition and earning trust among electorates with very low levels of party identification, though there is some evidence that party systems in the from of voter loyalty are beginning to take shape (Miller *et al.*, 2000). In neighboring countries such as Russia and the Ukraine, political parties in parliament appear to be losers if they are not among the handful of 'parties of power' blessed by the support of the president (Semetko and Krasnoboka, 2003; Oates, 2003; Oates and Roselle, 2000). New parties outside parliament and dissident journalists and activists have had some success at influencing public opinion by contesting the framing of issues in the mainstream media by putting alternative perspectives on the Internet; these challenges to the state may diminish, however, as those in power clamp down on regulating the Internet.

While most parents of teenagers have observed the importance of SMS text messages sent by cell phone to their children, this relatively new phenomenon has more recently been described as able to influence political opinions and behaviors as well. While there is a growing literature on the role of the media and Internet in the development of new social movements and challenges to the state, mobile phones and hand-held computers are also presenting opportunities for groups to organize in more spontaneous ways that may, or may not, coincide with the interests of (some or none of the) established political parties (Castells, 2003, 2004). This presents an obvious challenge to social researchers – how do we measure the political contents and uses of cell phones?

CHALLENGE NO: 2. ASSESSING IMPACTS ON ATTITUDES, POLITICAL PARTICIPATION, AND ELECTIONS AND REFERENDUMS

Many studies drawing on data collected in the United States find negative effects of the media on political attitudes. In the mid-1970s and early 1980s, the news media, and television news in particular, were linked with growing political malaise, not least because of the emphasis on negative news such as political corruption (Robinson, 1983). The US experience with cable in the 1980s has shown that more (outlets) can actually mean less (exposure) in terms of the numbers of citizens who actually tune into political news (Entman, 1989). Research on US presidential election campaigns over three decades identified trends that are no more heartening: campaign news has become more negative, more interpretative rather than descriptive, and more game-oriented than policy-oriented since 1960 (Patterson, 1980, 1993, 2000). In one analysis the 2000 presidential election campaign coverage was summed up as 'a plague on both parties' (Lichter, 2001). US television news is blamed for the ever shrinking soundbite (Hallin, 1997), for providing 'episodic' reporting on political issues without making sense of them in a larger thematic historical context (Iyengar, 1994), for reporting complex political issues in simple and strategic terms (Capella and Jamieson, 1997), and, ultimately, for the decline of civic engagement and social capital (Putnam, 1995, 2000).

Other studies, however, have focused on the positive correlation between media use and various measures of civic engagement and political cognition. Increases in political interest, discussion, and ideological sophistication over the past few decades in a number of countries have been linked to the rise of the media and the educative role of television in particular (Dalton, 1996; Inglehart, 1990). Television news viewing in the USA and UK, and a number of other countries, has been associated with higher levels of political knowledge, participation, and personal efficacy (Brehm and Rahn, 1997; Norris et al., 1996; Norris, 2000). The 1997 British election study, for example, revealed a positive association between attention to news and higher levels of political knowledge and civic engagement, and an experiment designed to test the effects of television news in the general election campaign found that exposure to positive news about a party had stronger effects on vote choice than exposure to negative news (Norris et al., 1999).

Research examining the effects of the news media on political attitudes has, in sum, put forth broadly conflicting explanations. From one perspective, media use diminishes involvement and contributes to political cynicism and declining turnout; from another, media use contributes to political involvement, trust, efficacy, and mobilization. Aarts and Semetko (2003) address these explanations with detailed measures of media use drawing on data from the 1998 Dutch National Election Study (DNES). The Dutch case is representative of what can be found in many countries outside the USA: a multiparty parliamentary system, a national press, and what was once a public service broadcasting system and is now a fully competitive system. The 1998 DNES is unusually rich because of the many questions regarding the specific news and entertainment programs citizens use regularly, which provide a more realistic and comprehensive picture of media use in comparison with the standard set of exposure measures used in most national election studies. The authors concluded:

> Our study establishes that although media use can be clearly linked to some aspects of political involvement, the relationship is more complex than is often assumed in the literature. To take the example of television, watching public television news regularly has a positive influence on a number of political involvement measures including knowledge, internal efficacy, and turning out to vote, whereas regularly watching commercial television news has a negative impact on these aspects of political involvement. This pattern supports a dual effects hypothesis. All of these relationships remain significant when controlled for political interest, age, level of education, and other types of media exposure. We also address a problem that is central to media effects research, the problem of endogeneity. Lacking panel data, we use two-stage least squares to address these concerns. We believe this is appropriate and that it strengthens our conclusions because it largely rules out self-selection. (Aarts and Semetko, 2003: 775–6)

The study finds a lack of relationship between the respondents' media use and trust in institutions, in contrast to previous research. Norris (2000: 243, 289), for example, argues on the basis of 1996 Eurobarometer data and 1998 American National Election Study data that media use is a consistently significant predictor of 'positive institutional confidence'. And in another study, Moy and Pfau (2000) found that media use, as measured by exposure to US network news, has a negative effect on trust in US government institutions.

The study concludes with broader implications for developments in the new larger Europe that encompasses 25 countries and more than 450 million people:

> Our analysis of media use and its effects on political involvement gives us the opportunity to reflect

upon what may be the beginning of a more serious development in Dutch democracy, one that may also threaten other European countries that have experienced increasing competition in their broadcasting systems in recent years. We refer to a democracy divided between the involved and the uninvolved because of media choices. Viewing behavior separates the more knowledgeable, the efficacious, and the politically involved from those who are not, revealing what might be described as a 'virtuous circle' for some and a 'spiral of cynicism' for others. Our findings suggest that the virtuous circle described by Norris (2000) may only exist in a European context for those who rely largely on public television for their news, and this number has diminished as competition for audiences increases. At the same time, commercial news viewing in the Netherlands and probably in a number of other European countries, if not ultimately contributing to what Capella and Jamieson (1997) have dubbed a spiral of cynicism, then at least is contributing to diminishing political involvement.

The relatively recent competitive developments in the broadcasting systems of western Europe are for the most part anchored in more than four decades of press freedom and free elections with established party systems and comparatively strong political parties. In eastern Europe and the former Soviet Union, however, similar competitive developments in the broadcasting systems occur when citizens have little experience with free elections, the political parties are very weak, and party systems are in their infancy. In Russia and the former Soviet republics, since most people can hardly afford a daily newspaper, television is arguably an even more important source of information and entertainment than in the West. In these societies in transition, as well as in Latin America, research suggests there is a positive relationship between media use and satisfaction with democracy, trust in institutions, and other measures of political attitudes. But given the limited range of questions about media use in the surveys that establish this correlation, such a general conclusion may mask a more complex set of relationships. (Aarts and Semetko, 2003: 777–8)

The role of television in politics in these countries today is under conditions quite apart from those under which research on this subject first began (Swanson and Mancini, 1996). Contrast, for example, the study by Jay Blumler and Denis McQuail (1968) on Britain with the work of Ellen Mickiewicz (1999) on Russia.

Political advertising

How have parties responded to the added complexity of the field of competition in election campaigns given the more fragmented media market? In the USA, money has been funneled into the most profitable (as measured by number of vote switchers or new voters) media markets in election campaigns. We know that money is specifically targeted to battleground states in presidential elections, and within these states to specific segments of the potential voting public. Where one lives in large part determines the type of presidential election campaign one experiences. We know more about this in the USA than in other countries because of the new technology available to capture the contents and measure the reach of political advertising in major metropolitan markets in the 2000 election (Goldstein and Freedman, 2002). Several lessons for those who seek to measure the impact of political advertising are put forward by a study of close to 1 million televised political ads aired during the 2000 election. The authors argued:

> First, we illustrate the importance of looking at spots actually *broadcast* rather than examining the individual ads *produced*, in order to gain an accurate picture of the campaign environment. Second, we show that for an accurate portrayal of a campaign – particularly of candidates' relative advantages in a given race – it is necessary to look at ads broadcast not just by the campaigns themselves but by parties and interest groups as well. Third, we demonstrate the importance of paying attention to advertising in races below the presidential level. Looking at races for House and Senate seats can provide a different – sometimes a dramatically different – picture of the kinds of persuasive messages citizens have been exposed to. Fourth, the targeting data allow us to examine the relationship between competitiveness and campaign tone. We show that more competitive Senate and House races are characterized by substantially higher levels of negativity … (Goldstein and Freedman, 2002: 6)

The ability to capture the contents of the ads broadcast in competitive markets takes us to the next level in media effects research. Until now, the studies that have been based on experimental data or aggregate-level data provide mixed findings on important issues such as the effect of negative advertising and negative campaigning on voter turnout (Ansolabere et al., 1999; Wattenberg and Brians, 1999; Kahn and Kenny, 1999).

Outside the USA political parties are not as free to utilize their financial resources to target potential voters with emotionally compelling images on television. Put differently, outside of the USA political parties are on a more equal footing when presenting themselves in broadcast political advertising because of democratic rules and traditions that make possible the allocation of free time and put restrictions on the purchase of time, so that a range of competing political voices can be heard at election time (see, for example, Semetko, 1996, 2003; Scammell and Semetko, 1995; Kaid, 1999a, 1999b, 2004; Kaid and Dimitrova, 2004; Kaid and Holtz-Baeha, 1995; Kaid and Johnson, 2001).

Because of these rules and traditions, political parties in Britain, for example, recognize that their party election broadcasts (PEBs) aired during election campaigns, and party political broadcasts (PPBs) aired outside of election campaigns during routine periods, actually have a more limited reach than in previous decades when the small number of TV channels aired the 5- to 10-minute PEBs simultaneously so viewers had nowhere to turn to escape them, unless they turned away entirely from the screen. Nowadays, with a great many more channels available, and with PEBs no longer required to be even 2 minutes long, parties may have a greater opportunity to craft compelling ads of 10–30 seconds, but they cannot control when they are aired. Germany has permitted parties to purchase air time on commercial channels in recent elections, as have a number of European countries. During the 2004 European parliamentary elections, restrictions on length and format of free-time ads were reduced, allowing for shorter and more spot ads.

In many countries with the free-time tradition, parties may benefit from two to ten spots per party in a campaign (Plasser, 2002, 2001). In the USA in 2000, by contrast, presidential candidates spent approximately $240 million for more than 100 spot ads (Devlin, 2001). Costs are much lower elsewhere, though they have been rising. To take just one example, in Britain between 1983 and 1997 Labour's general election campaign expenditure went up from £2.2 to £26.0 million and the Conservatives' jumped from £3.6 to £28.3 million, and this was for the entire campaign operation, not only advertising (Norris *et al.*, 1999: 39).

Preliminary findings from a cross-national comparative analysis of key characteristics of political advertisements in general elections in 19 countries, including the USA, Korea, and several Western European countries, as well as Bulgaria, Romania, and Poland, reveal that the US emphasis on negative advertising is the exception as the vast majority of ads elsewhere were positive (Kaid and Dimitrova, 2004). This may be largely due to the fact that in multiparty systems, parties need to form coalitions after the campaign, so it does not pay to focus on negatives when a party might have to work closely with another party in government or opposition just after the election.

Referendums, parties and the media

Citizen initiatives and referendums have become an important means of enacting or preventing legislation in countries around the world. These represent challenges to the authority of elected representatives in the long run, and in the short run they can make campaigning an even more complicated affair for political parties. Although the 'yes' or 'no' nature of the proposition appears to be rather simple, referendum issues are often complex and multi-faceted. Party campaigning and political rhetoric are more difficult than in a routine election campaign, because citizens are not voting for a party or candidate but for one or another position on an issue. Referendum issues may split parties in two, as has been the case in Britain on both the question of membership of the European Economic Community and joining the euro. Referendum campaigns may also result in a transformation of the party system, with parties on the extreme ends of the left–right continuum finding themselves on the same side of the referendum fence; in other words, parties that normally oppose one another in general elections may suddenly be on the same side of the issue, as in the 1994 Nordic referendums on EU membership (Jenssen *et al.*, 1998). Referendums are also opportunities for new parties or movements to come into existence specifically to take a stand on the issue, as was the case in Denmark's referendum on the euro in 2000 (DeVreese and Semetko, 2002a, 2002b, 2004a, 2004b). Cues to voters in referendums are therefore often more ambiguous than in a routine election campaign, and parties are more likely to never have control over their message as in an election (Neijens *et al.*, 1998).

Referendums put parties in a difficult position because parties are usually unaccustomed to cooperating amongst themselves on campaign strategies, and this can be especially problematic when the other parties are those of a distinctly different political persuasion. The ways in which the political parties on one side of the issue choose to discuss or frame the various aspects of the topic can be crucial to the success of getting their agenda across in the news and, eventually, to their camp's success or failure in the referendum itself (DeVreese and Semetko, 2004b). But a party's attempts to control the framing of the issue in a referendum are open to being foiled by the interest of the news media in the statements by a political personality or the latest developments in a conflict. Unlike a routine election, in a referendum campaign conflict is more likely to be within camps than between camps. With no candidates or parties on the ballot, citizens must decide among alternatives that may be unfamiliar. A number of volumes dedicated to the study of referendums (see Farrell and Schmitt-Beck, 2002; Hug, 2003; Mendehlson and Parkin, 2001; and LeDuc, 2003) only mention the media in rather descriptive and peripheral terms.

Keeping in mind the need to know more about how political parties and candidates campaign and how journalists report on referendums, and the consequences of this for public opinion and the vote, DeVreese and Semetko (2004a) investigate campaign effects in a European referendum, drawing on panel survey data, media content data, focus groups, and interviews with journalists and campaign managers; the authors show how media and political elites sought to frame the referendum issue in the news and how the public came to understand the issue. They find that news about the referendum not only influenced public perceptions of the campaign, the referendum issue and the party leaders in a close race, but also shaped the voting decision and the political future of the incumbent governing party in the country. The media present an increasingly important challenge to the authority of elected political parties simply by using the 'media logic' or journalistic norms so common to conventional political reporting in the coverage of referendum campaigns (Mazzoleni, 1995).

The Internet

Doris Graber (2001) shows that because of the way in which the brain processes information, visual media such as television and the Internet are and can be even more important in the future for political learning. Despite the fact that the Internet can strengthen existing divisions in society and create even bigger gaps between those with and without access (Davis, 1999; Margolis and Resnick, 1997; Norris, 2001), the Internet offers an array of opportunities for citizens to learn and become involved (Margolis and Resnick, 1999; Bimber, 1999).

There is a common profile to the demographic characteristics of users in a number of established democracies. Internet users tend to be better educated and better off financially than non-users (Norris, 2001). The problem is that citizens still make comparatively little use of the Internet for political information in election campaigns in societies in which it is most widely available: only 2 percent with Internet access in the 2001 UK election and 7 percent in the 2000 US election claim to have visited party websites during the 2001 and 2000 elections, respectively (Coleman, 1998; Stromer-Galley, et al., 2001). Research comparing the characteristics of parties campaigning on the web in the 2001 UK and 2000 US elections concluded that the parties themselves are slow to offer innovative approaches to interacting online with supporters and potential new voters (Gibson and Ward, 2003; Gibson and Rommele, 2001). Howard Dean's 2004 presidential campaign initially fueled the perception that the Internet could drive grassroots support and dramatically improve fundraising capabilities during the primary season, but this phenomenon petered out in a matter of months and led to one of the earliest conclusions to a primary season. There will undoubtedly be numerous studies on the Internet's role in the 2004 US election campaign, and the findings are far from predictable.

Research on the political role of the Internet has been limited to societies in which there has already been rapid growth in its use among the general public. Two views exist on the impact of the Internet on the political structures: one view is that it reinforces the current political structure by giving visibility to the most powerful parties (Margolis and Resnick, 1997, 1999), and another is that the Internet gives more visibility to smaller or new parties thus challenging the current political order (Gibson and Ward, 1998; see also Gibson and Ward, 2003).

Research conducted at election time in the USA and the UK has shown that the websites of traditional news organizations are a more popular destination for Internet users than party or candidate websites (Research Center for the People and the Press, 2000). And although some traditional news media outlets in these two countries are perceived to be politically biased by some citizens, it is generally accepted that the news media operate independently of state control or government pressure. In this respect, then, the information to be obtained from traditional news media websites in established democracies may be perceived to be more objective or credible than the information on party or candidate websites.

In societies in transition, however, traditional news media are often under pressure from the government of the day to toe the party line, so to speak. The Assembly of the Council of Europe documented the many ways that states or governments pressure and threaten news organizations and journalists in many societies in transition. In these countries, therefore, traditional news media may not readily be perceived as any more independent or objective as a source of political information than partisan information sources. A comparison of Russia and Ukraine, two countries with similarly low levels of Internet use in households, provides an interesting contrast to previous research conducted in established democracies.

Geographically the largest countries in Europe, Russia, with 147 million people, and the Ukraine, with 50 million, also rank high in terms of national populations. Both countries are members of the Assembly of the Council of Europe and have therefore adopted legislation on the freedom of the press and media, but in practice and often during election campaigns news has heavily favored the incumbent and the parties in power (Brants and Krasnoboka, 2001; Fossato and Kachkaeva, 2000; McFaul *et al.*, 2000; Mickiewicz, 1999; Oates and Roselle, 2000). In the January 2001 meetings of the Assembly of the Council of Europe, both countries were severely criticized for inhibiting freedom of expression via censorship, legal pressures and physical aggression against journalists. Ukraine in particular was singled out for human rights abuses. One study comparing party and news websites in the two countries concludes:

> Our research shows very clearly that assumptions based on the political role of the Internet in established democracies do not always hold for societies in transition, where even the term 'political party' has a different connotation. At the same time, however, some of our results are similar to those found in developed democracies ... Our study also shows that 'new' political parties in these two countries sometimes have an even greater prominence online and better quality websites than 'old' parties. New parties in Russia and Ukraine, defined as those created after the previous parliamentary elections, are better equipped to compete with 'old' parties because of the Internet ... It is also worth noting that in many cases when both a party and the party leader have websites, the personal websites of the leaders are much more popular than the political party websites. This illustrates that the Web may also help to personalize politics in a way reminiscent of what Mickiewicz (1999) says of television in Russia. Parties are often created around leaders, rather than the other way around, and people tend to vote for leaders rather than for parties. Based on the numbers of visits to online sites, the Internet reinforces this trend. The new type of 'authoritarian democracy' and the dominance of the ruling elite on the political scene and in traditional media pushes many parties in Ukraine and Russia to use the only free, cheap and accessible medium, namely the Internet, for their communication with citizens. For those who are opposed to or critical of governing authorities, it is under these most threatening of circumstances that the Internet provides an opportunity for communication and for obtaining information that would not otherwise be found in traditional media outlets ... Online-only media ... appear to have more credibility as a source of information for Internet users in these societies in transition than offline media online. This is in contrast to established democracies, such as the USA or the UK, for example, where hits on websites of online versions of offline media are far more common than hits on online-only media. This difference is a reflection of the political constraints under which journalists in these societies are working. Whereas journalists in established democracies have considerable freedom to criticize the government of the day, in Russia and Ukraine and many societies in transition, this kind of behavior can result in a variety of forms of pressure being brought to bear on the individual journalist and/or news organization. (Semetko and Krasnoboka, 2003)

Both Russia and Ukraine have, since this study was conducted in 2001–2, attempted to further regulate and control the Internet because of its presumed anti-government biases, whereas many journalists and those in opposition in those countries believed it to be a source of uncensored and objective information.

CHALLENGE NO. 3. GLOBALIZATION AND TRANSNATIONAL FORMS OF COMMUNICATION: DEVELOPING THEORETICAL PERSPECTIVES ON POLITICAL PARTIES AND THE MEDIA

For national political parties, the field of competition for influencing perceptions has widened as transnational news media may encourage citizens to challenge the interpretations of national political parties on issues that are global or have international relevance. Take, for example, the debate on the veil in France in early 2004, when some French politicians in Jacques Chirac's party (UNP/RPR) called for Al-Jazeera to be banned in France because of the channel's alleged ability to harm French national interests (Cherribi, 2005). Transnational media such as Al-Jazeera provide opportunities for those interested to follow news from a different region of the world. For many political parties in many countries, this translates into less opportunity to influence citizens via the mainstream national news outlets, and more opportunity for audiences of foreign media to consider alternative viewpoints and agendas. And as local or national issues become part of a larger global exchange of views via the media, individual prime ministers and presidents become the focus of international media attention with less room for party debate.

Bilingual second- and third-generation citizens may also turn to foreign news outlets to follow news in their parents' and grandparents' homeland and to get another perspective on world events from what is offered in their national news media. And increasingly in the USA, Spanish-language news media are speaking to growing populations of Spanish speaking Americans.

All of these developments point up the need to further develop theory for understanding party competition and party systems in an era of electoral dealignment (Mair *et al.*, 2004), in this increasingly complex field of local, national, and international communications systems. Anthony Giddens (2003) and Manuel Castells (2004) offer contemporary social theory perspectives on the communications field. There is also a well-developed literature on party systems and electoral competition (Lijphart, 1995; Kitschelt *et al.*, 1999). And research on protest voting and populism (Mazzoleni *et al.*, 2003) or 'telepopulism' (Peri, 2004) also contributes to our thinking about the challenges political parties face in today's complex media environment. Political communications research also provides evidence on the processes by which political parties and candidates aim to shape the media and hence the public agenda, and use the media to get their messages across, particularly during election campaigns (Semetko *et al.*, 1991; Scammell, 1995; de Vreese and Semetko, 2004a and b).

CONCLUSIONS

There is no doubt that the explosion of outlets around the world made possible through the liberalization of the airwaves since the 1970s, the development of cable and satellite technologies in the 1980s, and the growth of the Internet and wireless telephony since the 1990s, has made life more complicated for political parties in established democracies. Political parties also find themselves facing a more complex and changing citizenry, one that is increasingly demographically diverse in terms of ethnicity, language, interests, and income and education levels. These multicultural populations make voting behavior less predictable. In election campaigns, political parties rely more heavily on consultants and market research to customize messages for tailored and targeted audiences (Plasser, 2002), though not all parties have made the leap to professional campaigning (Gibson and Römmele, 2001).

NOTE

1. In the Netherlands, for example, in the run-up to the June 2004 European Parliament election, one liberal (VVD) party candidate moved from number 19 to number 10 on the party's list after running a successful 'internal' campaign for the votes of party members to finalize the numeric order of the party list, a campaign that involved direct (e)mail, weblogs, and coverage in the national news media.

REFERENCES

Aarts, K. and Semetko, H.A. (2003) 'The divided electorate: Effects of media use on political involvement', *Journal of Politics*, 65(3): 759–84.

Ansolabehere, S., Iyengar, S. and Simon, A. (1999) 'Replicating experiments using aggregate and survey data: The case of negative advertising and turnout', *The American Political Science Review*, 93(4): 901–09.

Baum, M. (2002) 'Sex, lies and war: How soft news brings foreign policy to the inattentive public', *The American Political Science Review*, 96(1): 91–109.

Baum, M. (2003) *Soft News Goes to War: Public Opinion and American Foreign Policy in the New Media Age.* Princeton, NJ: Princeton University Press.

Bimber, B. (1999) 'The Internet and citizen communication with government: Does the medium matter?', *Political Communication*, 16: 409–28.

Blumler, J.G. and McQuail, D. (1968) *Television in Politics: Its Uses and Influences.* London: Faber.

Brants, K. and Krasnoboka, N. (2001) 'Between soundbites and bullets. The challenges and frustrations of comparing old and new democracies', in Y. Zassoursky and E. Vartanova (eds), *Media for the Open Society: West-East and North-South Interface.* Moscow: Faculty of Journalism/IKAR Publisher, pp. 281–305.

Brehm, J. and Rahn, W. (1997) 'Individual-level evidence for the causes and consequences of social capital', *American Journal of Political Science*, 41(3): 999–1023.

Capella, J.N., and Jamieson, K.H. (1997) *Spiral of Cynicism: The Press and the Public Good*. New York: Oxford University Press.

Castells, M. (2003) *The Power of Identity*. London: Blackwell.

Castells, M. (2004) *The Internet Galaxy*. London: Oxford University Press.

Cherribi, S. (2005) 'From Baghdad to Europe: Al-Jazeera's reporting on the Iraq war, the veil in France and recent developments in Europe'. Paper presented at the annual meeting of the American Political Science Association.

Coleman, S. (1998) 'Interactive media and the 1997 UK general election', *Media, Culture & Society*, 20(4): 687–94.

Curtice, J. and Semetko, H.A. (1994) 'Does it matter what the papers say?', in A. Heath, R. Jowell and J. Curtice (eds), *Labour's Last Chance: The 1992 Election and Beyond*. Aldershot: Dartmouth, pp. 43–64.

Dalton, R. (1996) 'Comparative politics: Micro-behavioral perspectives', in R. Goodin, and H.-S. Klingemann (eds), *A New Handbook of Political Science*. Oxford: Oxford University Press, pp. 336–52.

Dalton, R.J., Beck, P.A. and Huckfeldt, R. (1998) 'Partisan cues and the media: Information flows in the 1992 presidential election', *The American Political Science Review*, 92(1): 111–26.

Davis, R. (1999) *The Web of Politics: The Internet's Impact on the American Political System*. New York and Oxford: Oxford University Press.

Davis, R. and Owen, D. (1998) *New Media and American Politics*. New York: Oxford University Press.

Entman, R. (1989) *Democracy without Citizens: Media and the Decay of American Politics*. Oxford: Oxford University Press.

Esser, F., Reinemann, C. and Fan, D. (2001) 'Spin doctors in the United States, Great Britain, and Germany: Metacommunication about media manipulation', *Harvard International Journal of Press/Politics*, 6(1): 16–45.

Evans, H. (1983) *Good Times, bad Times*. London: Weidenfeld and Nicolson.

Farrell, D.M. and Schmitt-Beck, R. (eds) (2002) *Do Political Campaigns Matter? Campaign Effects in Elections and Referendums*. London and New York: Routledge.

Fossato, F. and Kachkaeva, A. (2000) Russian media empires VI. *Radio Free Europe/Radio Liberty*, http://www.rferl.org/nca/special/rumedia6/index.html

Gibson, R. and Römmele, A. (2001) 'Party-centered theory of professionalized campaigning', *Harvard International Journal of Press/Politics*, 6(4): 31–43.

Gibson, R. and Ward, S.J. (1998) 'UK political parties and the Internet', *Harvard International Journal of Press/Politics*, 3(3): 14–38.

Gibson, R. and Ward, S.J. (2003) 'Online and on message? Candidates websites in the 2001 general election', *British Journal of Politics and International Relations*, 5(2): 188–205.

Gibson, R., Nixon, P. and Ward, S. (eds) (2003) *Political Parties and the Internet: Net Gain?* New York: Routledge.

Giddens, A. (2003) *Runaway World: How Globalization is Reshaping our Lives*. London: Routledge.

Goldstein, K. and Freedman, P. (2002) 'Lessons learned: Campaign advertising in the 2000 elections', *Political Communication*, 19(1): 5–28.

Graber, D.A. (2000) *Mass Media and American Politics*. Washington, D.C.: Congressional Quarterly Press.

Graber, D.A. (2001) *Processing Politics: Learning from Television in the Internet Age*. Chicago: University of Chicago Press.

Hallin, D. (1997) 'Soundbite news: Television coverage of elections, 1968–88', *Journal of Communication*, 42, 3.

Hallin, D. and Mancini, P. (2004) *Comparing Media Systems: Three Models of Media and Politics*. Cambridge: Cambridge University Press.

Hodess, R., Tedesco, J.C. and Kaid, L.L. (2000) 'British party election broadcasts: A comparison of 1992 and 1997', *Harvard Journal of International Press/Politics*, 5(4): 55–70.

Hug, S. (2003) *Voices of Europe: Citizens, Referendums and European Integration*. Oxford: Rowman and Littlefield.

Inglehart, R. (1990) *Culture Shift in Advanced Industrial Society*. Princeton: Princeton University Press.

Iyengar, S. (1994) *Is Anyone Responsible? How Television Frames Political Issues*. Chicago: University of Chicago Press.

Jenssen, A.T., Pesonen, P. and Gilljam, M. (eds) (1998) *To Join or not to Join? Three Nordic Referendums on Membership in the European Union*. Oslo: Scandinavian University Press.

Kahn, K.F. and Kenney, P.J. (1999) 'Do negative campaigns mobilize or suppress turnout? Clarifying the relationship between negativity and participation', *American Political Science Review*, 93(4): 877–89.

Kaid, L.L. (1999a) 'Comparing and contrasting the styles and effects of political advertising in European democracies', in L.L. Kaid (ed.), *Television and Politics in Evolving European democracies*. Commack, NY: Nova Science Publishers.

Kaid, L.L. (1999b) 'Political advertising: A summary of research findings', in B. Newman (ed.), *The Handbook of Political Marketing*. Thousand Oaks, CA: Sage Publications, pp. 423–38.

Kaid, L.L. (2004) 'Political advertising', in L.L. Kaid (ed.), *The Handbook of Political Communication Research*. Mahwah, NJ: Lawrence Erlbaum Associates, pp. 155–202.

Kaid, L.L. and Dimitrova, D. (2004) 'Political Advertising in Established and Evolving Democracies'. Paper presented at the annual meeting of the American Political Science Association.

Kaid, L.L. and Holtz-Bacha, C. (1995) *Political Advertising in Western Democracies: Candidates and Parties on Television*. Thousand Oaks, CA: Sage Publications.

Kaid, L.L. and Johnston, A. (2001) *Videostyle in Presidential Campaigns: Style and Content of Political Television Advertising*. Westport, CT: Praeger.

Kitschelt, H., Mansfeldova, Z., Markowski, R. and Toka, G. (1999) *Post Communist Party Systems*. Cambridge: Cambridge University Press.

LeDuc, L. (2003) *The Politics of Direct Democracy: Referendums in Global Perspective*. Peterborough, ON: Broadview Press.

Lichter, S.R. (2001) 'A plague on both parties: Substance and fairness in TV election news', *Harvard International Journal of Press/Politics*, 6(3): 8–30.

Lijphart, A. (1995) *Electoral Systems and Party Systems: A Study of Twenty-seven Democracies 1945–1990*. New York: Oxford University Press.

Mair, P. (2004) *Political Parties and Electoral Change: Party Responses to Electoral Markets*. London: Sage.

Margolis, M. and Resnick, D. (1997) 'Campaigning on the Internet: Parties and candidates on the World Wide Web in the 1996 primary season', *Harvard International Journal of Press/Politics*, 2(1): 59–78.

Margolis, M. and Resnick, D. (1999) 'Party competition on the Internet in the United States and Britain', *Harvard International Journal of Press/Politics*, 4(4): 24–47.

Mazzoleni, G. (1995) 'Towards a 'videocracy'? Italian political communication at a turning point', *European Journal of Communication*, 10(3): 291–XXXX.

Mazzoleni, G., Stewart, J. and Horsfeld, B. (2003) *The Media and Neo-populism: A Contemporary Comparative Analysis*. New York: Praeger.

McFaul, M., Petrov, N. and Ryabov, A. (2000) 'Russia in the course of 1999–2000 elections cycle', *Moscow Carnegie Centre*, http://pubs.carnegie.ru/books/2000/09np.

McLeod, J.M., Scheufele, D.A. and Moy, P. (1999) 'Community, communication, and participation: The role of mass media and interpersonal discussion in local political participation', *Political Communication*, 16(3): 315–36.

Mendelsohn, M. and Parkin, A. (eds) (2001) *Referendum Democracy: Citizens, Elites, and Deliberation in Referendums Campaigns*. New York, Palgrave.

Mickiewicz, E. (1988) *Split Signals: Television and Politics in the Soviet Union*. New York and Oxford: Oxford University Press.

Mickiewicz, E. (1999) *Changing Channels: Television and the Struggle for Power in Russia*. New York and Oxford: Oxford University Press.

Miller, A., Erb, G., Reisinger, W. and Hesli, V.L. (2000) 'Emerging party systems in post-Soviet societies: Fact or fiction?', *The Journal of Politics*, 62: 455–90.

Moy, P. and Pfau, M. (2000) *With Malice Toward All? The Media and Public Confidence in Democratic Institutions*. Westport, CT: Praeger.

Neijens, P., Minkman, M. and Slot, J. (1998) 'Opinion formation in referendum campaigns', *Acta Politica: International Journal of Political Science*, 33: 300–16.

Newell, J.L. (2001) 'Italian political parties on the web', *Harvard International Journal of Press/Politics*, 6(4): 60–87.

Norris, P. (2000) *A Virtuous circle? Political communications in Post-industrial Democracies*. Cambridge: Cambridge University Press.

Norris, P. (2001) *Digital Divide? Civic engagement, information poverty and the Internet in democratic societies*. New York: Cambridge University Press.

Norris, P., Curtice, J., Sanders, D., Scammell, M. and Semetko, H.A. (1999) *On Message: Communicating the Campaign*. London: Sage.

Norris, P., LeDuc, L. and Niemi, R. (1996) *Comparing Democracies: Elections and Voting in Global Perspective*. London: Sage.

Oates, S. (2003) 'Television, voters and the development of the "broadcast party"', in V. Hesli and B. Reisinger (eds), *The 1999–2000 Elections in Russia: Their Impact and Legacy*. Cambridge and New York: Cambridge University Press.

Oates, S. and Roselle, L. (2000) 'Russian elections and TV news: Comparison of campaign news on state-controlled and commercial television channels', *Harvard International Journal of Press/Politics*, 5: 30–51.

Patterson, T.E. (1980) *The Mass Media Election: How Americans Choose their President*. New York: Praeger.

Patterson, T.E. (1993) *Out of Order*. New York: Vintage.

Patterson, T.E. (2000) *Doing well and doing good: How soft news and critical journalism are shrinking the news audience and weakening democracy – And what news outlets can do about it*. Faculty Research Working Paper Series, RWP01-001. Cambridge, MA: John F. Kennedy School of Government, Harvard University.

Peri, Y. (2004) *Telepopulism: Media and Politics in Israel*. Palo Alto, CA: Stanford University Press.

Plasser, F. (2001) 'Parties' diminishing relevance for campaign professionals', *Harvard International Journal of Press/Politics*, 6(4): 44–59.

Plasser, F., with Plasser, G. (2002) *Global Political Campaigning: A Worldwide Analysis of Campaign Professionals and their Practices*. Westport, CT: Praeger.

Putnam, R. (1995) 'Bowling Alone', *Journal of Democracy*, 6(1): 65–78.

Putnam, R. (2000) *Bowling Alone: The Collapse and Revival of American Community*. New York: Simon and Schuster.

Robinson, M.J. (1983) *Over the Wire and on TV: CBS and UPI in Campaign '80*. New York: Russell Sage Foundation Publications.

Scammell, M. (1995) *Designer Politics: How Elections are Won*. Houndmills/Basingstoke: St. Martin's Press.

Scammell, M. and Semetko, H.A. (1995) 'Political advertising on television: The British experience', in L.L. Kaid and C. Holtz-Bacha (eds), *Political Advertising and Western Democracies*. London: Sage.

Semetko, H.A. (1996) 'Political balance on television: Campaigns in the US, Britain and Germany', *Harvard International Journal of Press/Politics*, 1: 51–71.

Semetko, H.A. (2003) 'The UK media system', in D.H. Johnston (ed.), *Encyclopaedia of International Media and Communications*. New York: Academic Press.

Semetko, H.A., and Krasnoboka, N. (2003) 'The political role of the Internet in societies in transition – Russia and Ukraine compared', *Party Politics*, 9(1): 77–104.

Semetko, H.A., Blumler, J.G., Gurevitch, M. and Weaver, D.H. (1991) *The Formation of Campaign Agendas*. Creskill, NJ: Lawrence Erlbaum.

Seymour-Ure, C. (1974) *The Political Impact of Mass Media*. London: Constable.

Seymour-Ure, C. (1991) *The British Press and Broadcasting since 1945*. Oxford: Blackwell.

Stromer-Galley, J., Foot, K.A., Schneider, S.M. and Larsen, E. (2001) 'How citizens used the internet in election 2000', in S. Coleman (ed.), *Elections in the Age of the Internet: Lessons from the United States*. London: Hansard Society, pp. 21–6.

Swanson, D.L. and Mancini, P. (1996) *Politics, Media and Modern Democracy: An International Study of Innovations in Electoral Campaigning and their Consequences*. Westport: Praeger.

Tumber, H. and Waisbord, S. (eds) (2004) *Political Scandals and Media Across Democracies*, Volumes I and II. American Behavioral Scientist.

Vreese, C.H. de and Semetko, H.A. (2002a) 'Public perception of polls and support for restrictions on the publication of polls: Denmark's 2000 euro referendum', *International Journal of Public Opinion Research*, 14(4): 367–90.

Vreese, C.H. de and Semetko, H.A. (2002b) 'Cynical and engaged – Strategic campaign coverage, public opinion, and mobilization in a referendum', *Communication Research*, 29(6): 615–41.

Vreese, C.H. de and Semetko, H.A. (2004a) *Political Campaigning in Referendums: Framing the Referendum Issue*. London: Routledge.

Vreese, C.H. de and Semetko, H.A. (2004b) 'News matters: Influences on the vote in a referendum campaign', *European Journal of Political Research*, 43: 699–722.

Wattenberg, M.P. and Brians, C.L. (1999) 'Negative campaign advertising: Demobilizer or mobilizer?', *American Political Science Review*, 93(4): 891–99.

45

CYBER PARTIES

Helen Margetts

What difference does increasing use of the Internet make to party politics? Trends in party development discussed in this volume have already pointed to the end of the era of the 'mass' party characterized by widespread and formal membership, and the rise of 'cartel', 'electoral-professional', 'post-materialist' or 'new politics' parties. This chapter points to the emergence of another 'ideal type' of political party – the 'cyber' party. The development of the cyber party is fuelled by increasing use of information and communication technologies (ICTs) by both citizens and organizations and the increasing potential of the Internet as the ideal forum for political activity.

Other chapters have discussed changing patterns of political participation which put pressure on parties to change, particularly declining membership, fluctuating party allegiance and the rise of single-issue political activity. This chapter first explores the pressure on political parties to develop an Internet presence in response to widespread use of the Internet. It then puts forward the development of the ´cyber party´ as a potential organizational response, through Internet-mediated party competition, relationships with members, supporters and voters and internal organization. Finally, the chapter considers some of the consequences of the emergence of the cyber party – both in terms of threats that cyber parties might pose to a democracy and the dangers for parties which do not innovate. Widespread societal use of the Internet is a recent phenomenon, levels of penetration even in some developed countries (particularly Southern Europe) are still low and evidence suggests that 'the strongest and most significant indicator of the presence of all parties

online is technological diffusion, measured by the proportion of the population online' (Norris, 2001b: 9). Therefore this chapter is necessarily speculative, drawing on evidence where available but also extrapolating from current trends in political activity to give a potential – but by no means inevitable – view.

INTERNET-MEDIATED POLITICAL PARTICIPATION

Use of the Internet throughout society has risen rapidly across the world since the mid-1990s. Estimates of Internet penetration vary considerably across even developed countries and across methodologies of calculation. In 2002, the relatively cautious International Telecommunications Union comparative ranking suggested that 55 per cent (ITU, 2003) of US citizens used the Internet, 51 per cent of Canadians and 48 per cent of Australians. Across Europe, figures vary considerably but are in general higher in northern Europe (42 per cent in the UK, 41 per cent in Germany, 51 per cent in the Netherlands, 57 per cent in Sweden, although only 31 per cent in France) and lower in the South (35 per cent in Italy and 16 per cent in Spain). Other rankings show higher figures, putting the US between 67 per cent (Accenture, 2003) and 75 per cent (Nielsen NetRatings, 2004). Percentages of Internet penetration are radically higher for some groups; for example, in the UK around 40 per cent for 18–25-year-olds even by 1999. The Internet is still a rare privilege in the least developed countries, where just two in every thousand members of the population have Internet access (ITU, 2003). But figures in most countries are rising quickly, for example by 40 per cent a year in Russia according to some estimates (*Moscow Times*, 16 March 2004). Web surfers are estimated to be more politically active than the general population; for example, 86 per cent of Internet users are registered voters in the USA, compared with 70 per cent of the general population (Nielsen NetRatings, 20 March 2004).

The Internet has rapidly proved itself an ideal forum for political activity, and since the 1990s, interest group activity has rapidly shifted to web-based venues. Demonstrations such as the June 1999 and April 2000 Reclaim the Streets marches in London and anti-war demonstrations across the world in 2003 were largely organized on the Internet. The Internet is also facilitating new forms of political participation and protest, fuelled by what Tim Jordan (1999, 2000) has labelled 'hacktivisim' – a technology-driven form of mobilization, which allows assorted ideologies to find a common place. For example, in November 1999, the organization Euro-Hippies jammed the World Trade Organization's web server with repeated e-mail questions in a virtual joining of protests. A representative claimed that the environmental movement had been revolutionized by the Internet, as 450,000 activists from different countries who had never met protested together in virtual fora over five days. More traditional forms of political participation are also turning to the Internet. In 2000 the general secretary of the Trades Union Congress launched a new electronic database for trade unionists, stating that 'the future of organised labour lies with the Internet' (*Guardian*, 10 February 2000). The union database will include a bulletin board detailing disputes across the world, a databank on the 50 per cent of workplaces in Britain with no union representation and the dissemination of information on the use of cyber-picketing.

As usage of the Internet rises across society there is growing pressure on organizations of all kinds to respond. Nodality, denoting the property of being in the middle of information or social networks (Hood, 1983), is a key tool of organizations, which the Internet offers great potential to increase. Government agencies are in a unique position both to demand information from citizens and to dispense information to them, which is why Christopher Hood defines nodality as one of the four 'tools' of government policy. But other organizations too strive to increase their nodality, particularly political parties which must compete with a wide range of other organizations for citizens' attention and leisure time. The Internet and web-based technologies offer great potential for organizations to increase their nodality (Margetts, 1998, 1999). The Hutton inquiry in the UK, the investigation into the death of the government scientist Dr David Kelly, is a good contemporary example; all evidence, hearings and rulings were available for citizens on the inquiry's website, making the details of the inquiry far more accessible than previous such investigations. While the staff of the inquiry was tiny, the website received between 10,000 and 30,000 unique visitors on many days of evidence-giving and once the material was so readily available, media organizations quick to take advantage of an easy story disseminated it all over the international news networks. However, as society in general moves on-line, established organizations that lag behind in developing an Internet presence can find themselves with a net loss of nodality.

Competition has spurred many private organizations to move beyond exchanging information with their customers to providing services on-line, such as Internet banking. Companies like Prudential (Egg), the Financial Times (FT.com) and EasyJet (Easy Everything.com) have developed new business arms with new branding that exist solely for Internet customers. Organizations such as the auctionsite eBay and the electronic bookshop Amazon have a customer presence only on-line. Private companies at the forefront of web development invest a great deal of time and resources tracking and analysing the behaviour of their website users and devising new options to expand usage and retain users, capitalizing on the 'build-and-learn' nature of web-based technologies. For public sector organizations, pressure has come from modernizing politicians who see the Internet in particular, and technological development more generally, as a magic wand to increase public sector efficiency (Margetts, 1999). In general, public sector organizations have lagged behind those in the private sector in web development, but the potential benefits are clearly transformative (Dunleavy and Margetts, 1999, 2002). Managers in the more innovative public sector organizations, such as the Australian Tax Office (ATO), anticipate a future where their organization becomes entirely 'digital': as one Australian official put it, eventually 'ATO will become its web site' (Dunleavy and Margetts, 1999).

PARTY RESPONSES:
THE CYBER PARTY?

This section puts forward the cyber party as a possible response to these trends in political participation, a new 'ideal type' of political party, with its origins in developments in media technology ICTs and, particularly the Internet, combined with new trends in political participation. Some of the characteristics of cartel parties are true of cyber parties also (the blurring of the distinction between members and supporters, for example) and some new causal factors play a role: the low start-up costs for minor parties to develop an Internet presence, for example, which can lead to more lively party competition.

Relationships between cyber parties: Party competition

As so much social interaction moves on-line, there is pressure for political parties to do the same, particularly given that their key competitors for citizens' attention and participation are interest groups and social movements, which have been particularly innovative in using the Internet. There appears to be a differential response among parties. In spite of early predictions that Internet usage would 'reinforce the dominance of the larger, better resourced parties' (Ward and Gibson, 1998) some larger political parties have lagged behind: 'critics charge that most parties have been slow to adapt, conservative in approach, and unimaginative in design' (Norris, 2001a), even while pressure groups are recruiting e-activists to participate in campaigns 'from the comfort of one's own armchair' (www.oxfam.org.uk). For example, in the UK London elections in 2000, a Conservative Party spokesman admitted that while 'most people in London use e-mail its importance to campaigning is deeply underestimated by many in the party's hierarchy' (*Guardian*, 2 December 1999).

Meanwhile, newer and smaller parties have shown themselves to be more innovative – their incentives are greater, as an Internet presence can give them a forum in which to compete for nodality on a more equal footing with more established parties. The formation of new parties is benefited by the low start-up costs of websites compared with other types of technology and the low marginal costs of additional users (see Dunleavy and Margetts, 1999,

2002). Norris (2003: 43) found that 'party websites have strengthened communicative pluralism in Europe by widening information about minor and fringe parties', facilitating 'bottom-up as well as top-down communication'. In London in 2000, where Ken Livingstone stood and won as an independent, his website, superior to those of the other mayoral candidates, was a vital tool in supplementing his skeletal campaign team. Traditional methods of participation are made much easier for smaller parties by electronic linkages: the Green party provides a 'webkit' on its national website, to facilitate local Green groups to start up their own websites and campaign machinery. In addition, Internet presence is not – and cannot be – regulated in the same way as television presence, so new parties have far more opportunity to compete against well-established parties in cyberspace than they do on television. In addition, moving from an interest group or social movement to a political party has become easier, due to the potential of the web to link formerly disaggregated interests, particularly across geographic, ethnic and linguistic divisions. In March 2000 the 'digital hit squad' of a grassroots Internet community for connecting black people (Dogonvillage.com) targeted black voters in the Democratic primary elections held on the Internet in Arizona, USA and claimed to increase turnout by more than 1000 per cent (*Guardian*, 27 April 2000). Recent improvements in ICTs have made communication across linguistic divisions easier; even the free Microsoft hotmail will translate e-mails into different languages. The written text – read at one's own pace – provides the option for better comprehension and communication than a physical meeting, while Internet radio provides new possibilities for websites to overcome literacy barriers to political activity.

Thus the Internet environment provides the potential for new patterns of party competition, and there is preliminary evidence from the 21st century from a number of countries. In Japan, Tkach-Kawasaki (2003) found that the Internet has had a significant impact on the fortunes of smaller parties which were much more sophisticated than the Liberal Democratic Party in incorporating the Internet into their media and fundraising strategies, opening up cross-party competition in what has long been a dominant-party system. Semetko and Krasnoboka (2003: 91) found that new parties in Russia and the Ukraine are better equipped than old parties because of the Internet. In the UK, the BNP, UKIP and the Greens rival the three largest parties in terms of resource generation (Gibson *et al.*, 2003). In South Korea, a world leader in broadband access, the 2002 presidential election was dubbed the 'Internet election' as Roh Moo-hyun emerged victorious from relative obscurity against a member of the country's ruling elite via a campaign waged principally on the Internet. The electoral landscape was changed by unprecedented turnout among younger voters, with 59 per cent of people in their twenties and thirties (versus 38 per cent those in their fifties and sixties) voting for Roh (*Financial Times*, 22 December 2002).

The cyber party's relationship with members, supporters and voters

So what might be the defining characteristics of a cyber party? The key defining feature is that cyber parties use web-based technologies to strengthen the relationship between voters and party, rather than traditional notions of membership: such technologies are fuelling the trend towards lower levels of membership, rather than being used to ameliorate it. In the UK in 2000, Smith (2000: 81) found that, in general,

> Research suggests that ICTs are not being used within parties … to reinvent or rejuvenate a mass party organisation. Instead, significant emergent relationships around parties facilitated by ICTs are those which are based upon … improving and developing forms of campaigning which make very little recourse to the role and initiative of mass membership.

In fact, the use of ICTs within party organizations can make membership involvement more problematic rather than easier. For example, Smith also points out that the British Labour Party's fears about the technical competence of constituency parties led to the use of their 'Elpack' system (used to process canvass returns and produce constituency profiles and mailing lists) being suspended for the actual polling day on 1 May 1997, and traditional paper-based systems being used instead.

In place of members, cyber parties offer voters the opportunity to develop closer linkages with the party and more of the benefits traditionally ascribed to members. In a cross-country study of recent elections across Europe, party websites were found to be 'inspired by the search for new communication channels between politicians and the electorate' (Tops *et al.*, 2000a: 178). In the USA parties are increasingly sophisticated at appealing to voters'

special interests: Republican candidates use data-sifting techniques to target specific groups of voters on the Internet with banner advertising, and at a controversial point in his campaign for Republican nomination in 2000, McCain's campaign team fired off 43,000 explanatory e-mails to supporters (*Guardian*, 18 January 2000). In Britain, the Labour Party uses a combination of ICTs to focus on Conservative-held marginal constituencies, using the telephone to identify and influence 'floating voters' and electoral database software linked to desktop publishing packages which allow candidates to 'personally' keep in touch with potential supporters and invite them to public meetings.

By 2004, many political parties were using their websites to offer services on open access to supporters as well as to members with password access. The UK Liberal Democrats' site, for example, allows all users of its website to access folders containing policy documents and draft manifestoes and to sign up for customized content. Many party websites invite users to adopt an intermediary status between member and voter. The UK Labour Party offers visitors to its site at http://www.labour.org.uk who do not wish to become members five 'Additional Ways to Get Involved', including 'Helping to make policy' and pledging support to future election campaigns as well as making donations and signing up for 'enews'. The Conservative party site at http://www.conservatives.com offers a similar range of options and under William Hague's leadership offered membership of the Conservative Network – 'a new active style of politics for people in the 25–45 age range with career/family pressures and an itinerant lifestyle', including free registration on the Network's database and a range of regional events and seminars. Discussion groups run by political parties are often open (for example, the Dutch Green party during the 1988 election; Al Gore's on-line questioning by gay and lesbian voters on the Gay.com website in 2000; all the facilities of the 'Virtual Party Headquarters' of the German CDU, SPD and FDP (Bieber, 2000: 71)).

A key way in which voters and supporters become involved in the cyber party is through leadership recruitment. Mair (1997) has already identified the cross-national trend for ordinary members in many parties across Europe (as opposed to middle-level elites or activists) to be empowered via postal ballots and one-member, one-vote procedures rather than party conferences. Such procedures are

considered less of a threat to party organization
as ordinary and spatially dispersed members
are less likely to mount a serious challenge
against leadership positions. By the same argument, voters and supporters of a party are even
less likely to mount a challenge. As the Internet
makes such involvement more feasible, there
may be an increase in the number of parties
introducing primary elections as a means of
candidate selection, as in the US presidential
elections. In the USA, state laws specify how
candidates may gain access to the primary
ballot and who is to count as being a party
'supporter' or 'member', but 'In fact, the absence
of formal membership in American parties
means that, in practice, voting in primaries
has been extended to a wide range of people
whose connection to the party is merely that
they want to vote in that party's primary election' (Ware, 1995: 260). Some kind of electronic
registration, with publicly provided terminals,
could qualify people to vote in primaries.
Democratic primary elections held on the
Internet in Arizona in March 2000 increased
turnout by 622 per cent (*Guardian*, 27 April
2000).

The cyber party: internal organization

The Internet also offers the potential for new
forms of internal organization, for political
parties as for any other organization. There is
no doubt that the capability of well-designed
websites to present a coherent front-end to
fragmented organizations aids the ability
of parties to provide a point of reference.
Websites can be used to link up local or
sectoral units of decentralized parties and could
be used to good effect in making coalition
arrangements intelligible to the electorate. Web
presence also provides parties with the opportunity to use the style of their site to present
their image to voters. In the Netherlands, for
example, commentators observed how during
the 1998 election campaign, the sites of Dutch
political parties reflected the image each party
had of itself:

> Because of its design and the way in which the
> party site appears on the Internet, the PvdA pre-
> sents itself as a modern people's party which is
> determined to 'conquer' the electorate by using
> every technological means possible. The VVD is
> shown as a light-hearted party aiming to entertain.
> And the SP as an activist party trying to convince
> the electorate to take up arms against injustice
> and abuse. The groenLinks site, with its different

> discussion platforms, reflects the grass-roots
> character of the party. While the CDA with its ordi-
> nary and scarcely interactive site affirms its posi-
> tion towards traditional values and standards.
> (Tops *et al.*, 2000b: 93–4)

Most political parties will dedicate part of their
website to detailing their philosophy and
values during election campaigns. Technological
innovations can also be used to tailor the presentation of a party to individual voter preferences, particularly useful in a multi-party
system. In the Netherlands, a voter compass
has been used via which visitors to the site
could determine which party coincided best
with their political views, acting as 'a new
instrument which fills the vertical relationship
between politicians and voters'. The IPP's
compass was visited 12,500 times; another created by a consultancy organization (Bolesian)
was visited 28,000 times. Similar compasses
were available during the 2000 London mayoral elections (for example, www.fantasy-
mayor.com), although it is not known if the
many Livingstone supporters who were told to
vote Green on the basis of their expressed preferences let the compass deter them from their
original intention.

The extent to which political parties can centralize and direct existing administrative organization is enhanced by the use of web-based
technologies, particularly intranets. British
political parties have invested extensively in
decision support systems geared exclusively to
political communications (Perri 6, 2001) and all
now enjoy facilities to transmit information via
dedicated communications networks, using
e-mail and bulletin board systems both to
exchange information in forums for supporters
and through restricted channels used by party
leaderships to issue campaigning information
(Smith, 1998: 79). The Labour Party's Excalibur
system, which holds the records of the political
views of millions of voters and also the political
histories and speeches of opponent politicians
in order to discover and capitalize upon inconsistencies and hypocrisy (Smith, 1998) was
used to great effect during the 1997 general
election, and by 1998 the Conservative Party
was using similar technology. The UK Labour
Party in government from 1997 used ICTs
extensively for communication within the parliamentary party, keeping MPs 'on-message'
through extensive use of bleeps and mobile
telephones. In 2000, they introduced a new
electronic government information and rebut-
tal system (the Knowledge Network Project) to
'help Whitehall stay on message and respond

to critical attacks by MPs, the press and the public' and to 'explain the government's core message' to citizens without the 'distorting prism of media reporting'. The system included a database of policy issues with the government's line to take, use of which would feed every department with 'lines to take on every key issue' (*Guardian*, 18 January 2000). Opposition critics complained bitterly that the new system would politicize the civil service and might be used for Labour Party purposes during forthcoming election campaigns.

Party financing is evidently an important issue in the continuing existence and shape of political parties, and membership dues have traditionally been a regular and uncontroversial source of income for political parties. Some analysts argue that grassroots members are vital to elections, with the intensity of campaigning having a crucial impact on electoral performance, and lack of paid-up foot-soldiers will cause serious financial problems for older parties (Whiteley in the *Guardian*, 18 February 2000; Denver *et al.*, 2002), for example making it necessary to use paid staff (for example, although not a party, Greenpeace already use contract staff for campaigning). How can cyber parties overcome this problem, if they have even lower levels of membership than other types of party?

First, Internet technologies (unlike the large-scale, high-risk information technology projects that preceded them) have already demonstrated enormous cost savings on previously expensive administrative tasks such as telephone calls and postage, as already demonstrated in more technologically advanced governments: in Singapore, for example, electronic tax filing is estimated to have saved £7 per head of population. Second, the Internet and e-mail can be used to raise money and create networks of supporters who play a role in election campaigning, circumventing the roles ascribed to members in many countries. The USA, where Internet penetration is high and politicians have a longer experience of on-line campaigning, provides an illustration of what is possible. In 2000, Bill Bradley, the challenger to Al Gore for the Democratic nomination, raised $1.3 million on-line. It is estimated that presidential candidates raised a total of $30 million by the time of the US election in November 2000; Al Gore raised 20 per cent of his campaign income on-line (*Guardian*, 18 January 2000). In the 2004 Democratic primaries, the early front-runner, Howard Dean, became famous for the proportion of his campaign finance raised on-line ($41 million in 2003 alone, with unprecedented numbers of small donations), including a record-breaking $800,000 during a 24-hour period. The Internet 'drove Dean's rise from outsider to front-runner', and his website amassed a list of e-mail addresses of 600,000 supporters. Dean's use of the web was notable for its interactive style, with a personal web log (Blog) and various devices for putting supporters in touch with each other (Meetup). His rival John Kerry was quick to follow his lead in introducing such innovations and on 'super Tuesday' in 2004 when Kerry emerged victorious as the Democrat candidate, his first plea to his Democrat audience was 'Go to JohnKerry.com' to pledge financial support (the on-line donation form was just one click from the front page). The next day alone he raised $1.2 million (beating Dean's record) and 1500 new campaign volunteers signed up on-line (*United Press International*, 3 March 2004).

THE FUTURE FOR THE CYBER PARTY

The 'cyber party' is an ideal type: widespread Internet penetration is too new, its potential too unrealized for there to be substantive empirical evidence of its existence. Technological development will not inevitably lead to the formation of cyber parties, nor will cyber parties exist entirely in cyberspace – but much of what cyber parties do could take place via the Internet. It would, after all, have been inconceivable 20 years ago that there should be a bookshop such as Amazon where customers have no physical interaction with either books or a shop before they buy. As Oscar Wilde once said, 'the problem with Socialism is that it cuts so dreadfully into the evenings'. Web-based political participation can make political participation virtually cost-free and overcome the problem of attending those meetings that Wilde was referring to, making political activity possible at home and at any time.

There is a resistance to such a view within many political cultures where the assumption is that political participation should involve suffering. Consider this comment from the UK member of parliament, Dr Tony Wright, in response to the suggestion that party supporters might use the Internet at home late in the evening to participate in party business:

> If you describe it in that casual incidental way that gives a picture of people in a sense of having nothing better to do than to press buttons, not because they have anything particular to contribute

but because it is dead easy to do it. (Public Administration Committee, 2000)

There is an association of political activity with pleasure in some technologically aided movements that works against the 'political participation as pain' principle: protests that celebrate environmental activism, animal rights and anti-capitalism and that integrate pleasure into popular protest, particularly derived from dance-floors, clubs and rave venues (Jordan, 1999; McKay, 1998). Such movements suggest that pleasure might be something that political parties could add to the other more pedestrian selective benefits (such as Visa cards and party filofaxes) they already offer. A political environment where voters become involved in policy decisions and candidate selection at the painless click of a button, coming together only to express the strongest of their feelings in a demonstration or protest, may be more vibrant than one where a dwindling number of disillusioned members force themselves to tramp the streets at election time.

There are threats to the future of cyber parties that will need to be confronted if the trend continues. Key threats include strategic penetration: if voters are able to influence party policy and candidate selection in the ways suggested above, what is to prevent strategic penetration of citizens who claim to have voted for a party at the last election, or say that they will do so at the next election? The USA provides examples of how non-Democrat or non-Republican voters have registered for the party they did not vote for and endeavoured to influence decisions, usually at local level where small 'selectorates' and low turnout mean a small number of strategic voters are more likely to influence the result. However, many building societies during the 1990s suffered from 'carpet-baggers' who tried to force UK building societies into forming banks rather than retaining mutuality and have found a variety of ways around the problem (*Guardian*, 5 November 1999). Strategic penetration of political parties is more complex and there are many cross- pressures on voters which may disincentivize such strategies. A non-Tory interloper in the Conservative leadership selection, voting for an extremist candidate (Margaret Thatcher, for example, in the 1970s) in order to reduce the party's chances of victory at the election, may find themselves with a Conservative party leader and a prime minister that they did not want.[1]

Like any organizational development occasioned by technological change, there is nothing inevitable about the development of the cyber party. The failure of Dean's presidential campaign in the Democratic primary elections of 2004 illustrates a potential pitfall. Some supporters blamed their own habitat for his eventual collapse, describing an 'echo chamber of Web diaries and Internet message boards that lulled activists into thinking they were winning votes for Dean merely by typing messages to one another' (*Los Angeles Times*, 7 February 2004). Others likened his implosion as the leading candidate to the dot-com crash in how much money the campaign raised and squandered. But most commentators agreed that Dean's campaign was a harbinger of a more interactive political future, labelling Dean 'the Wright brothers' first airplane' – 'You wouldn't want to put passengers on it. But that doesn't mean it isn't important' (*Los Angeles Times*, 7 February 2004).

Parties experience increasing competition for citizens' attention, especially with the increase of single-issue protests and a 'DIY culture' of political activity. Parties that continue to rely on the notion of membership for their 'legitimizing myth' rather than working on their digital presence may find themselves suffering a loss of comparative nodality and having to turn to alternative resources to retain influence. The incremental 'build-and-learn' characteristics of web-based technologies mean that parties, like all organizations, have to start interacting with supporters in order to develop the relationship. An Internet presence is not something that can be set up overnight. With organizations of all kinds responding to pressure to invest time and resources in web-based technologies to develop their relationship with their customers, political parties which do not follow suit may find themselves increasingly cut off from their supporters.

NOTE

1. These points were made by Patrick Dunleavy during discussion of this paper at the Democratic Audit's specialist group on political parties on 29 July 2000.

REFERENCES

Accenture (2003) 'e-government Leadership: engaging the customer', The Government Executive Series, April 2003.

Bieber, C. (2000) 'Revitalizing the party system or Zeitgeist-on-line? Virtual party headquarters and virtual party branches in Germany', *Democratization*, 7: 59–75.

Denver, D., Hands, G., Fisher, J. and McAllister, I. (2002) 'The impact of constituency campaigning in the 2001 general election', in *British Parties and Election Review*, Vol. 12: London: Frank Cass, pp. 80–94.

Dunleavy, P. and Margetts, H. (1999) *Government on the Web*. London: National Audit Office.

Dunleavy, P. and Margetts, H. (2002) *Government on the Web 2*. London: National Audit Office.

Gibson, R., Margolis, M., Resnick, D. and Ward, S. (2003) 'Election campaigning on the WWW in the USA and UK: A comparative analysis', *Party Politics*, 9: 47–75.

Hood, C. (1983) *The Tools of Government*. London: Macmillan.

ITU (International Telecommunications Union) (2003) *World Telecommunication Development Report: Access Indicators for the Information Society*. Geneva: ITU.

Jordan, T. (1999) *Cyberpower: The Culture and Politics of Cyberspace and the Internet*. London: Routledge.

Jordan, T. (2000) 'Hacktivism: Direct action on the electronic flows of information societies'. Paper presented to PSA2000, the conference of the Political Studies Association, 10–13 April.

Mair, P. (1997) *Party System Change: Approaches and Interpretations*. Oxford: Clarendon Press.

Margetts, H. (1998) 'Computerising the tools of government', in I. Snellen and W. van de Donk (eds), *Public Administration in an Information Age*. Amsterdam: IOS Press.

Margetts, H. (1999) *Information Technology in Government: Britain and America*. London: Routledge.

McKay, G. (ed.) (1998) *DIY Culture: Party and Protest in Nineties Britain*. London: Verso.

Nielson (2004) Nielson NetRatings, 18 and 19, March 2004. nielsen-netratings.com.

Norris, P. (2001a) 'Digital parties: Civic engagement and online democracy'. Paper presented to the workshop on Internet participation, ECPR Joint Sessions, Grenoble, April.

Norris, P. (2001b) 'A virtuous circle? The impact of political communications in post-industrial democracies'

in K. Dowding, J. Hughes and H. Margetts, *Challenges to Democracy*. London: Macmillan.

Norris, P. (2003) 'Preaching to the converted? Pluralism, participation and party websites', *Party Politics*, 9: 21–45.

Perri 6 (2001) 'E-governance: Weber's revenge?', in K. Dowding, J. Hughes and H. Margetts (eds), *Challenges to Democracy*. London: Macmillan.

Public Administration Committee (2000) Minutes of Evidence for Tuesday 11 January 2000. *Innovations in Citizen Participation in Government*, 17 May 2000, HC 79–v.

Semetko, H. and Krasnoboka, N. (2003) 'The political role of the Internet in societies in transition: Russia and Ukraine compared', *Party Politics*, 9: 77–104.

Smith, C. (1998) 'Political parties in the information age', in I. Snellen and W. van de Donk (eds), *Public Administration in an Information Age*. Amsterdam: IOS Press.

Smith, C. (2000) 'British political parties: continuity and change in an information age' in J. Hoff, I. Horrocks and P. Tops (eds), *Democratic Governance and New Technology*. London: Routledge, pp. 71–86.

Tkach-Kawasaki, L. (2003) 'Politics@Japan: Party competition on the Internet in Japan', *Party Politics*, 9: 105–23.

Tops, P., Horrocks, I. and Hoff, J. (2000a) 'New technology and democratic renewal: The evidence assessed', in J. Hoff, I. Horrocks and P. Tops (eds), *Democratic Governance and New Technology*. London: Routledge.

Tops, P., Voerman, G. and Boogers, M. (2000b). 'Political websites during the 1998 parliamentary elections in the Netherlands', in J. Hoff, I. Horrocks and P. Tops (eds), *Democratic Governance and New Technology*. London: Routledge.

Ward, S. and Gibson, R. (1998) 'The first Internet election? UK political parties and campaigning in cyberspace', in I. Crewe, B. Gosschalk and J. Bartle (eds), *Why Labour Won the General Election of 1997*. London: Frank Cass.

Ware, A. (1995) *Political Parties and Party Systems*. Oxford: Oxford University Press.

INDEX